CAMBRID(

E

MW01169665

Printing and publishing history

The interface between authors and their readers is a fascinating subject in its own right, revealing a great deal about social attitudes, technological progress, aesthetic values, fashionable interests, political positions, economic constraints, and individual personalities. This part of the Cambridge Library Collection reissues classic studies in the area of printing and publishing history that shed light on developments in typography and book design, printing and binding, the rise and fall of publishing houses and periodicals, and the roles of authors and illustrators. It documents the ebb and flow of the book trade supplying a wide range of customers with products from almanacs to novels, bibles to erotica, and poetry to statistics.

Early English Printed Books in the University Library, Cambridge

An erudite and popular librarian, Charles Edward Sayle (1864–1924) devoted his career to cataloguing and editing rare books in the University of Cambridge. His obituary praised him as 'a fine example of the type of man who likes to catalogue things in the right order.' This catalogue of incunabula and early printed books in the University Library was his most important project, taking over a decade to complete. Commissioned by the Library Syndicate in 1894, the catalogue was published in four volumes between 1900 and 1907. Even upon completion, Sayle's list was not final, as the rare book collections at the Library were undergoing a period of great expansion, having grown by a third during his cataloguing work, both through purchases and by donations or bequests. This final volume indexes the books by author, printer, engraver, and place of printing, and provides a list of notable titles of particular artistic, musical or bibliographical interest.

Cambridge University Press has long been a pioneer in the reissuing of out-of-print titles from its own backlist, producing digital reprints of books that are still sought after by scholars and students but could not be reprinted economically using traditional technology. The Cambridge Library Collection extends this activity to a wider range of books which are still of importance to researchers and professionals, either for the source material they contain, or as landmarks in the history of their academic discipline.

Drawing from the world-renowned collections in the Cambridge University Library, and guided by the advice of experts in each subject area, Cambridge University Press is using state-of-the-art scanning machines in its own Printing House to capture the content of each book selected for inclusion. The files are processed to give a consistently clear, crisp image, and the books finished to the high quality standard for which the Press is recognised around the world. The latest print-on-demand technology ensures that the books will remain available indefinitely, and that orders for single or multiple copies can quickly be supplied.

The Cambridge Library Collection will bring back to life books of enduring scholarly value (including out-of-copyright works originally issued by other publishers) across a wide range of disciplines in the humanities and social sciences and in science and technology.

Early English Printed Books in the University Library, Cambridge

1475 to 1640

Volume 4: Indexes

C.E. Sayle

Cambridge
University Press

CAMBRIDGE UNIVERSITY PRESS

Cambridge, New York, Melbourne, Madrid, Cape Town, Singapore,
São Paolo, Delhi, Dubai, Tokyo

Published in the United States of America by Cambridge University Press, New York

www.cambridge.org
Information on this title: www.cambridge.org/9781108007801

This edition first published 1907
This digitally printed version 2009

ISBN 978-1-108-00780-1 Paperback

EARLY
ENGLISH PRINTED BOOKS

1475 TO 1640

INDEXES

Cambridge:
PRINTED BY JOHN CLAY, M.A.
AT THE UNIVERSITY PRESS.

EARLY ENGLISH PRINTED BOOKS

IN THE UNIVERSITY LIBRARY CAMBRIDGE

(1475 TO 1640)

VOL. IV

INDEXES

CAMBRIDGE:
AT THE UNIVERSITY PRESS
1907

CAMBRIDGE UNIVERSITY PRESS WAREHOUSE,
C. F. CLAY, MANAGER.
London: FETTER LANE, E.C.
Glasgow: 50, WELLINGTON STREET.

Leipzig: F. A. BROCKHAUS.
New York: G. P. PUTNAM'S SONS.
Bombay and Calcutta: MACMILLAN AND CO., LTD.

NOTE BY THE LIBRARIAN.

THE history of the work which this index volume completes goes back to 1892. In that year Mr Sayle circulated privately proposals for a 'Hand-list of Early English Books in the University of Cambridge to A.D. 1640,' in the preparation and publication of which the colleges and libraries concerned were to be asked to cooperate. This more comprehensive scheme came to nothing. But in May, 1894, the Library Syndicate, after much careful consideration of alternative methods, invited Mr Sayle to proceed with the preparation of a catalogue of the Early English Books contained in the University Library.

Three years was mentioned as the time which would be occupied in making such a catalogue. If the three years have grown to twelve[1], those who have watched the progress of the work are satisfied that the time has not been wasted. No one who has not tried to catalogue early books has any conception of the difficulties that constantly stop the explorer's progress.

The work had hardly begun when the death of Mr Samuel Sandars deprived the Library of a liberal and judicious benefactor. The stream of donations which had flowed since 1870 ceased; but he bequeathed to the University his library, which included more than 400 of the books with which this Catalogue is concerned, together with a sum of £500 to be spent on similar books. He had already contributed largely to this class, nos. 18*b*, 26, 47, 49, 55, 86, 100, 112, 141, 148, 995*b*, 997 being among those for which the Library is indebted to him. The books which formed part of his own collection are distinguished in the present work by the mark 'Sandars Collection'; and it will be observed that the only Shakespeares we possess come from this source.

[1] The third volume appeared in November, 1903. For the subsequent retardation of the index volume I am almost entirely responsible.

About 200 books have since been given by various donors, and about 1560 have been bought. Thus the collection is larger by about a third than it was when Mr Sayle began the preparation of his Catalogue.

I am sorry that it was not found possible to note, as the work went on, the source from which each book came to the Library. In many cases it would have been easy, but in others it would have taken time; and the task was already complicated enough. Cuthbert Tunstall's *de arte supputandi* (no. 280) was given by the author in 1522. Archbishop Parker and the other Elizabethan benefactors were more concerned with precious manuscripts and with standard editions printed abroad: but Parker gave some, perhaps all, of the historical works in the publication of which he himself was concerned.

At the end of the sixteenth century the University printers probably sent their books direct to the Library[1], and some are still here marked 'Sum Academiae Cantabrigiensis.' King James I and Francis Bacon presented their works in 1620. (See nos. 2807 and 3497.) But it is not till the middle of the century that any considerable arrival of books has to be recorded. From 1646 to 1662 Archbishop Bancroft's library, brought from Lambeth when bishops were abolished, formed part of the University Library: but in the latter year it was restored to Lambeth. Fortunately Dr Holdsworth, Master of Emmanuel, who died in 1649, had foreseen this possibility; and had provided for it by a codicil added to his will. So by the loss of Bancroft's 12,000 volumes the University became entitled to Holdsworth's 10,000. This bequest was the subject of a dispute between the College and the University. The whole story will, I hope, be told by Mr J. W. Clark when he takes in hand the Annals of the Library: but one consequence of the dispute was the formation of an unusually precise catalogue of the whole collection. Most of the books, Fathers, Schoolmen, Councils, Aristotelian Commentators, etc., are of course foreign: but I have been able to pick out 876 English books printed before 1641: and of these no less than 606 appear to be still in the Library. I have accordingly made a table shewing under what numbers in the present catalogue books from the Holdsworth Collection are to be found.

[1] In 1622 a Grace was passed ordering the University Printer to send a copy of every book printed to the Library within a month.

The unique folio *Directorium sacerdotum* printed by Caxton is no longer here: stolen about 1778, it is now in the British Museum. But the *Mirror of the World*, the *Festial*, and the *Golden Legend* remain, as well as the Ales and Lattebury printed at Oxford (nos. 74 and 75).

The dispute over Dr Holdsworth's books was not terminated till December, 1664. In the meantime Henry Lucas died, leaving his valuable library[1] to the University. It contained upwards of 230 books of the class which is contained in this Catalogue. Lucas's volumes are almost always distinguished by his name or initials, in welcome contrast to Holdsworth's, which (except in the case of a presentation copy) contain no trace of his ownership.

Bishop Hacket's bequest in 1670 contained some 200 early English books (e.g. nos. 162, 439); but I know of no other event deserving of mention here until we come to the year 1715, when King George presented to the University the library of the late Bishop of Ely, John Moore. It is well known that to this gift are due most of the Caxtons, Wynkyn de Wordes, and other early 'black-letter' books which the University possesses: but it is equally certain that in the thirty-five years which elapsed before the collection could be properly housed, large numbers of books were stolen; how many we have no means of ascertaining.

From 1778 to 1797 Dr Farmer held the office of Proto-Bibliothecarius. Unfortunately his private collection never became part of the University Library, though its existence sometimes led bibliographers to describe books belonging to it as 'in the Public Library.'

More than the first half of the nineteenth century passed without any notable addition, so far as I know. Then books began to come in. In 1870, Henry Bradshaw gave his Irish collection, to which, on his death in 1886, his executors added a second Irish collection together with his breviaries and other liturgical books. Some of these are distinguished in the first two volumes of the present Catalogue by the mark 'Bradshaw Collection': in the third volume they have ordinary class-marks; but it may be mentioned that the Irish books, marked 'Hib,' were mostly his. The books themselves may in all cases be identified by a stamp or label.

[1] 4038 volumes and 29 bundles of pamphlets.

Dr Venn's large collection of works on Logic, presented in 1889, contained only nine English books before 1640: the library of Professor Adams, bequeathed in 1892, added 139; in both cases the class-mark preserves the donor's name. I have already spoken of the Sandars Collection. On the whole, more books have been given in the last forty years than in the hundred and fifty which preceded them. Lord Acton's vast collection, presented in 1902 by Mr John Morley, hardly concerns us now; for, incredible as it may appear, among the 60,000 or more volumes which composed it, less than 30 were English before 1640.

Mr Sayle asks me to record here his indebtedness to various friends and correspondents for help in preparing the fourth volume: Dr Salomone Morpurgo (no. 7934); Heer E. W. Moes (no. 7811); Mr W. Aldis Wright (nos. 964, 6081, 6322, and others); Mr Madan; Mr A. W. Pollard; Mr E. G. Duff (note on p. 425); Mr Alfred de Burgh (no. 7900); Mr C. Dodgson (6081); Mr A. M. Hind (8055); Mr H. F. Moule (7982); Mr R. Steele (7064, 7072); and Mr E. J. Worman (850).

FRANCIS JENKINSON.

March 7, 1907.

TABLE OF THE NUMBERS IN THIS CATALOGUE OF BOOKS FROM DR HOLDSWORTH'S LIBRARY.

15	702	1011	1473	2122	2594	3289	3928
23	705	1019	1480	2132	2612	3294	3949
41	720	*or*	1483	2145	2622	3298	3981
74	727	1020	?1527	2168	2637	3344	4066
75	737	1026	1561	2171	2647	3356	4106
80	748	1031	1619	2187	2687	3429	4175
105	749	1037	1623	2200	2696	3434	4186
124	751	1048	1626	2203	?2715	3437	4205
153	762	1065	1629	2223	2747	3451	4206
163	763	1075	1631	2258	2753	3455	4224
210	764	1084	1637	2266	2756	3458	4236
283	766	1089	1648	2272	2762	3459	4255
286	768	1095	1655	2285	2771	3463	4257
305	782	1100	1694	2288	2777	3470	4263
331	791	1120	1696	2293	2842	3476	4265
347	801	1155	1731	2297	2858	3477	4300
386	806	1168	1739	2326	2874	3478	4306
416	816	1191	1744	2334	2888	3479	4313
421	823	1192	1745	2343 B	2889	3482	4327
428	825	1196	1751	2349	2917	3486	4367
433	833	1199	1753	2354	2924	3487	4386
452	839	1201	1756	2356	2930	3490	4393
461	840	1202	1757	2357	2944	3492	4395
466	841	1203	1758	2360	2951	3496	4405
468	842	1206	1759	2363	2952	3515	4427
472	850	1241	1760	2364	2960	3527	4472
478	855	1246	1817	2366	2969	3533	4504
480	878	1254	1825	2372	2992	3537	4508
or	886	1255	1827	2404	2995	3573	4532
481	895	1282	1850	2416	3012	3579	4539
499	902	1300	1871	2423	3029	3580	4547
500	904	1304	1883	2426	3068	3590	4555
526	908	1325	1898	2429	3080	3597	4569
532	912	1356	1910	2432	3092	3603	4581
563	921	1368	1923	2439	3096	3639	4594
570	924	1369	1925	2448	3100	3645	4622
591	930	1375	1961	2453	3102	3672	4631
622	931	1389	1967	2456	3122	3682	4646
630	938	1398	1968	2467	3124	3742	4661
634	945	1400	1969	2468	3132	3759	4686
636	953	1408	1974	2480	3136	3761	4687
658	956	1413	2015	2486	3176	3768	4698
662	960	1414	2018	2493	3183	3805	4699
or	967	1425	2041	2510	3184	3853	4708
663	974	1428	2047	2534	3218	3863	4742
671	975	1435	2073	2551	3223	3868	4748
or	987	*or*	2077	2557	3230	3872	4752
672	990	1436	2096	2559	3241	3921	4777
682	992	1460	2099	2576	3271	3927	4785

4793	5295	5643	5950	6263	6394	6588	6848
4808	5309	5662	5954	6268	6411	6589	6851
4811	5310	5663	5955	6270	6412	6594	6853
4817	5317	5664	5966	6272	6413	6595	6855
4854	5364	5674	5967	6274	6414	6616	6863
4909	5368	5675	5998	6281	6416	6617	?6866
4935	5371	5699	6002	6284	6422	6621	6870
4945	5372	5704	6003	6286	6425	6624	6889
4955	5376	5705	6019	6288	6432	6638	6907
4973	5378	5706	6024	6291	6433	6639	6908
5002	5379	5718	6027	6300	6446	6679	6911
5027	5396	5732	6036	6302	6458	6695	6940
5037	5405	5734	6041	6306	6459	6712	6948
5054	5419	5790	6063	6308	6460	6715	6974
5056	5428	5791	6069	6319	6462	6725	6999
5064	5437	5801	6095	6325	6463	6726	7005
5071	5444	5806	6108	6331	6473	6728	7015
5075	5448	(*or*	6120	6332	6474	6731	7051
5078	5454	5843)	6122	6336	6505	6732	7058
5091	5459	5838	6126	6349	6505A	6740	7059
5096	5462	5848	6136	6357	6522	6742	7152
5106	5466	5859	6147	6362	6526	6746	7221
5133	5475	5871	6150	6372	6527	6754	7247
5178	5481	5887	6151	6373	6537	6760	7271
5193	5497	5888	6176	6375	6540	6761	7303
5217	5508	5900	6198	6380	6542	6762	7528
5233	5527	5903	6206	6381	6544	6775	7689
5235	5542	5919	6217	6382	6548	6777	7700
5242	5581	5920	6236	6383	6566	6795	8077
5246	5624	5927	6241	6385	6569	6819	
5273	5627	5930	6257	6386	6576	6821	
5278	5634	5940	6262	6388	6579	6846	

ABBREVIATIONS.

[SUPPLEMENTARY TO VOL. I. pp. vii—ix.]

Ath. Cantab. Athenae Cantabrigienses. By C. H. Cooper and T. Cooper. 2 vols. Cambridge, 1858–1861. 8°.

Baker MSS. Cambridge University Library. Catalogue of MSS. (Vol. v., pp. 193 *seq.*) Cambridge, 1867. 8°.

Baker-Mayor. T. Baker. History of the College of St John the Evangelist. Ed. by J. E. B. Mayor. 2 vols. Cambridge 1869. 8°.

Bibl. Soc. Bibliographical Society. Transactions. London, 1893 *seq.* 8°.

Bible Society. Historical Catalogue of the printed editions of the Holy Scripture in the Library of the British and Foreign Bible Society. By T. H. Darlow and H. F. Moule. Vol. 1. London, 1903. 8°.

Corrie. List of Books relating to the Family of Love, in the possession of the Rev. Dr G. E. Corrie. Cambridge, 1880. 8°.

Cotton. H. Cotton. Editions of the Bible. Ed. 2. 1852. 8°.

Crawford. Bibliotheca Lindesiana. Hand List of Proclamations. 3 vols. and Supplement. Aberdeen, 1893–1901. F°.

Dempster. T. Dempster. Historia Ecclesiastica Gentis Scotorum. Ed. alt. 2 tom. (Bannatyne Club.) Edinburgi, 1829. 4°.

Dexter. H. M. Dexter. The Congregationalism of the last three hundred years. New York, 1880. 8°.

Dibdin. T. F. Dibdin. Typographical Antiquities. 4 vols. London, 1810–1819. 4°.

Dix. E. R. McC. Dix. Books printed in Dublin in the 17th century. 4 Parts. Dublin, 1898–1906. 4°.

Dommer. A. v. Dommer. Die aeltesten Drucke aus Marburg in Hessen, 1527–1566. Marburg, 1892. 8°.

Dore. J. R. Dore. Old Bibles. Ed. 2. London, 1888. 8°.

Gray. G. J. Gray. General Index to Hazlitt's Handbook and his Bibliographical Collections. London, 1893. 8°.

Greg. W. W. Greg. A List of English Plays written before 1643 and printed before 1700. (Bibliographical Society.) London, 1900. 8°.

Grove. G. Grove. A Dictionary of Music and Musicians. 4 vols. and Appendix. London, 1879–1890. 8°.

Halkett and Laing. A Dictionary of the Anonymous and Pseudonymous Literature of Great Britain. By S. Halkett and J. Laing. 4 vols. Edinburgh, 1882–8. 8°.

Hartshorne. C. H. Hartshorne. The Book Rarities in the University of Cambridge. London, 1829. 8°.

Joecher. C. G. Joecher. Allgemeines Gelehrten-lexicon. 4 Bde. Leipzig, 1750. 4°.

Lee. J. Lee. Memorial of the Bible Societies of Scotland. Edinburgh, 1824. 8°.

W. R. Macdonald. J. Napier, Baron of Merchiston. The Construction of the Wonderful Canon of Logarithms. Trans. by W. R. Macdonald. Edinburgh, 1889. 8°.

Munk. W. Munk. Roll of the Royal College of Physicians of London. Ed. 2. 3 vols. London, 1878. 8°.

Reed. T. B. Reed. A History of the Old English Letter Foundries. London, 1887. 8°.

Schneeli und Heitz. G. Schneeli u. P. Heitz. Initialen von H. Holbein. Strassburg, 1900. 4°.

Soule. Harvard Law Review. Vol. XIV. pp. 557–587 (Year-Book Bibliography. By C. C. Soule).

G. W. Sprott. G. W. Sprott. The Book of Common Order of the Church of Scotland (Church Service Society). Edinburgh, 1901. 8°.

Type Facsimile Society. Publications, 1900 *seq.* London. 4°.

Vanderhaeghen. Marques typographiques des imprimeurs et libraires qui ont exercé dans les Pays-Bas, etc. By F. Vander Haeghen, R. Vanden Berghe and Th. J. I. Arnold. Gand, 1894. 8°.

Watt. R. Watt. Bibliotheca Britannica. 4 vols. Edinburgh, 1824. 4°.

Wodrow. History of the Kirk of Scotland. By John Row. (Wodrow Society.) Edinburgh, 1842. 8°.

LIST OF INDEXES.

		PAGES
I	Books	1–377
	*** See also Index VIII	
II	Printers, Stationers, etc. . .	381–404
III	Engravers, Painters, etc.	407–419
IV	Towns	423–426
V	Portraits.	429–436
VI	Music	439–440
VII	Bibliographica	443–447
VIII	Books (Supplement to Index I) .	451–454

INDEX I

INDEX OF BOOKS.

INDEX.

No.

ABC. *See* Mayer (J.). Mayers catechisme... 1623.
— Whitford (R.). A werke of preparation... 1531.
A. (Sir A.). *See* Catholick Judge (The). 1623.
A. (A.). Verses in Whitaker (W.). Praelectiones. 1599. . . 5598
A. (A.), *A. C.* Verses in Cambridge University Gratulatio. 1623. . 5695
A. (A.), *A. Cl.* Verses in Camb. Univ. Gratulatio. 1623. . . 5695
A. (C.), *C. S.* Verses in Camb. Univ. Gratulatio. 1623. . . . 5695
A. (C.) Monsig^r. fate voi. 1617. 4°. 6534
See Cotton (P.). The interiour occupation of the soule. 1618. 12°.
— Airay (C.). Fasciculus. 1633.
— Richeome (L.). Holy Pictures. 1619.
A. (E.). *See* France. An excellent discovrse...translated...by E. A[ggas?]. 1592.
— Henry IV. *of France.* The Order of Ceremonies. [Ab. 1594.] 4°.
— Pasquier (E.). The Jesuite displayed...trans....by E. A. [Edward Aggas?] 1594.
A. (E. G. S.) [=Grimstone (E.)]. *See* Baudier (M.). The history...of the Grand Seigneur... 1635.
A. (F.). Verses in Crashaw (W.). Falsificationum. 1606. . . 2262
A. (G.). Pallas armata. 1639. 8°. 5170
A. (G.). Verses in Neville (A.). Kettus. 1582. . . . 1317
A. (H.). Verses in Lok (H.). Ecclesiastes. 1597. 4°. . . . 2246
— Barlow (W.). Vita Cosin. 1598. 4°. . . . 1707
See Ainsworth (H.). Annotations...Exodvs. 1617.
— — Arrow against Idolatrie. 1624.
— Hawkins (H.). Partheneia Sacra. 1633.
A. (H.), *kinsman of R. Cosin.* Verses in Barlow (W.). Vita R. Cosin. 1598. 4°. 2246
A. (I.). Verses in Cowper (W.). Pathmos. 1619. 4°. . . . 4066
— Cowper (W.). The Workes. 1629. F°. 3810
— Gostwyke (R.). Deo &c. 1616. 4°. 5678
— Lynne (W.). The beginning. [1548?]. 4°. 769
See Beroaldus (M.). A Short view... 1590.
A. (I.), *A. C.* Camb. Univ. Gratulatio. 1623. 4°. . . . 5695
A. (J.). An historicall narration of the ivdgement of Some...English Bishops...concerning gods election. 1631. 4°. . 4196, 4197
See Ap Robert (J.). The Yovnger Brother... 1635(–4).
A. (J.). *See* Bruele (G.). Praxis medicinæ. Ed. 2. 1639. 4°.
A. (L.). *See* Mirror of Knighthood. Pt iii. Bk 2, 3. 1598–9.
A. (L. T.). *See* Masque of the League. 1592. 8°.
A. (Master H.). *See* S. (C.). The copie of a letter. 1603. 4°.
A. (M. I. L. P.). Verses in Forbes (P.). Funerals. 1635. . . 6007
A. (P.). *See* Forbes (P.). Eubulus. 1627. 4°.

No.
A. (R.). A briefe chronologie of the holie scriptures. 1600. 8°. . 1265
Verses in Whitaker (W.). Praelectiones. 1599. 4°. . . 5598
See Allot (R.). Englands Parnassus. 1600.
A. (R.), *Preacher in Somersetshire*. *See* B. (R.). Davids Musick. 1616. 4°.
A. (T.). *See* Dyer (Sir J.), *Lord Chief Justice*. La Table... 1588.
A. (T.) [=Ashe (T.)]. *See* Plowden (E.). Abridgement. 1607.
A. (W.). Verses in Stafford (A.). The femall glory. 1635. 8°. . 4018
See Rollock (R.). Lectvres vpon...Thessalonians. 1606.
A. (Sir W.), *knight*. *See* Stirling (William Alexander, earl of).
Aachen. *See* Aix.
Abbas (Georgius). *See* Abbot (G.), *abp*.
Abbey of the holy Ghost. [1496.] 4°. 56
Abbot (Edward). Verses *bis* in Comenius (J. A.). Porta linguarum. 1633. 7613
See Biddulph (W.). The travels. 1609, 1612.
Abbot (George). A briefe description of the whole worlde. 1605. 4°. 3202
— Ed. 5. 1620. 4°. 4131
— 1634. 12°. 4953
Exposition upon...Jonah. 1600. 4°. 2252
— 1613. 4°. 2271
Quæstiones sex. Oxoniæ. 1598. 4°. 5246
Reasons...for the upholding of papistry...unmasked. Pt I. 1604. 4°. 5264
Sermon...at the funerall...of...Thomas Earle of Dorset. 1608. 4°. 3369
Treatise of the perpetuall visibilitie and succession of the true church. 1624. 4°. 2545, 2546
See Bible (Engl. Royal Version). 1611.
— Bradwardine (T.)...De Cavsa Dei. 1618.
— Clare (J.). The Converted Iew. 1630.
— Foxe (J.). Acts. 1631. Vol. III., p. 98.
— Hart (Sir W.). The Examinations...of George Sprot. 1609.
Abbot (Rob.). Antichristi demonstratio. 1603. 4°. 2576
— 1608. 8°. 2610
Antilogia. 1613. 4°. 2272
De gratia et perseverantia. 1618. 4°. 3482
De suprema potestate regia. 1619. 4°. 3493
Defence of the reformed Catholicke. 1606. 4°. 1755
— Part 3. 1609. 4°. 1759
— 1611. 4°. 2404
Mirrour of Popish Svbtilties. 1594. 4°. 2716
True ancient Roman Catholike. Part I. 1611. 4°. . . 3074
— *See* Bishop (W.). A disproofe... 1614.
See Angelos (C.). Christopher Angell... 1618.
— — Ἐγκώμιον... 1619.
— Norris (S.). An antidote. 1622. 4°.
Abbot (Samuel), *M.D.* Verses in Hippocrates. 1633. 8°. . . 5812
Abel (Laurence), *B.A.* *See* Aretius (J.). Primvla Veris... 1613.
Aberdeen. *See* Wedderburn (D.). Abredonia. 1625.
Aberdeen, City of. Verses in Adamson (J.). Εἰσόδια. 1618. . . 5960
Aberdeen University. Generall Demands. 1638. 4°. . . 7636
See Scotland. *Covenant.* The answers of some Brethren. 1638.
Aberdeen Ministers and Professors of Divinity. *See* Generall Demands. 7636
Abergavenny (Lady Frances). *See* Bentley (T.). The monvment of Matrones. 1582.
Abergavenny (Henry Nevill, Lord). Verses in Coryat (T.). Coryat Crudities. 1611. 4°. 3076
Abernethie (Thomas). Abjuration of Poperie. Edinburgh. 1638. 4°. 5984
See Ramsay (A.). A warning. 1638. 4°.
Abernethy (John). A christian & heavenly treatise. Ed. 3. 1630. 4°. 4342

No.

Abernethy (John) *cont.* Verses in Person (D.). Varieties. 1635. 4°. 4365
Abingdon School. [*In usum.*] *See* Godwin (T.). Romanae historiae. 1614, 1625, *etc.*
Abraham Aben Hassan. *See* Ferdinand (P.). Hæc sunt verba. 1597.
Abraham Aben Kattani. *See* Abraham Aben Hassan.
Abraham (Ric.). Verses in Oxf. Univ. Magd. Coll. 1612. 4°. . . 5302
Absaloms funerall preached. 1610. *See* Harris (R.). . . 3208
Abstemius (Laurentius). *See* Æsop. Æsopi Phrygis Fabulæ... 1635.
Abstract of certaine acts. *See* Cosin (R.). An abstract... (1584.)
Academiarum quæ aliquando. 1590. *See* Windsor (M.).
Academies. England. *See* Cambridge. Oxford.
Academies. France. *See* Henry VIII. (*Marriage.*) Montpellier, 1631. Nîmes. Paris.
Academies. Germany. *See* Giessen. Jena. Koenigsberg, 1584. Strassburg. Wittenberg.
Academies. Italy. *See* Henry VIII. (*Marriage.*)
Academies. Portugal. *See* Coimbra.
Academies. Scotland. *See* Aberdeen. Adamson (J.). Τὰ τῶν μουσῶν εἰσόδια, 1618. St Andrews, 1629.
Accentuarius. *See* no. 333.
Acciajuoli (Donato). *See* Plutarchus. Parallel Lives... 1603 *etc.*
Accidence. *See* Stanbridge (J.). Accidentia. [1521?] *etc.*
Shorter Accidence. Londonij, J. Toye, Antverpiae, apud M. Caesarem, May 1534. 8°. 6089
Achelley (John). Verses in Gilbert (Sir H.). A true reporte. 1583. 4°. 1354
Achilles Tatius. De Clitophontis & Leucippes amorib. libri VIII. Cantabrigiae. [1589?] 8°. 5540
Ackland (A.). Verses in Oxf. Univ. Horti. 1640. 4°. . . . 5499
Acontius (Jacobus). Stratagematum Satanae libri octo. Oxonii, 1631. 8°. 5385
Acosta (Joseph). The naturall and morall historie of the East and West Indies. Trans. E. Grimstone. 1604. 4°. . . . 2855
Acton (John) *or* J. de Athone. Constitutiones. Legatine. 1504, 1506. F°. 6147; 6149
Acworth (G.). De visibili Rom'anarchia. 1573. 4°. . . . 834
See Parker (M.). De antiqvitate... 1572.
Adam, The Historie of. *See* Holland (Henry). 1606. 4°.
Adames (Jonas). The order of keeping a court leete and court baron. 1593. 4°. 2219
Adamides (Johannes). Verses in Buchanan (G.). Ecphrasis. 1620. 8°. 3595
Adamnan, *Saint.* [Life of S. Columba.] *See* B. (B.) *Franciscan Friar.* The life. 1625. 4°.
Adamo (Anthony de), *pseud.* *See* Mainardi (A.).
Adams (Richard), *Cath.* Verses in Camb. Univ. Συνῳδία. 1637. . 5790
Adams (Tho.). The blacke devill. 1615. 4°. 2782
The gallants burden. 1612. 4°. 2309
— 1616. 4°. 2317
The happines of the Church. 1618. 4°. 4063
Heaven and earth reconcil'd. 1613. 4°. 2312
The sovldiers honovr. 1617. 4°. 2449
The spirituall nauigator. 1615. 4°. 2783
Adamson (Alexander). Verses in Adamson (J.). Εισόδια. 1618. . 5960
Adamson (Henry). Verses in Adamson (J.). Εισόδια. 1618. . 5960
Adamson (John). Τὰ τῶν μουσῶν εἰσοδια. The Muses welcome. (Ἐξοδια.) Edinburgh. 1617–8. F°. 5960
Verses in Person (D.). Varieties. 1635. 4365
Adamson (Patrick). De sacro pastoris munere. Operâ T. Voluseni. 1619. 8°. 3590
Poëmata sacra. 1619(–18). 4°. 3492
Vita et Palinodia. *See* Melville (A.). Musae. 1620. 4°.
Aderb (F.). Verses in Camden (W.). Britannia. 1586. 8°. . 1324 *etc.*

No.
Adlington (William). *See* Apuleius. The XI. Bookes. 1639. 4°.
Admonition to all such as shall intend...matrimony...Set forth by...M. [Parker]. Single sheet. F°. 3675
Admonition to the Bishoppes of Winchester &c. 'M. Wood, Roane,' 1 Oct. 1553. 8°. 6238
Admonition to the Parliament. ['Wandsworth,' 1572.] 8°. . 5895
See Exhortation. An Exhortation to the Byshops... [1572.]
A second Admonition. 1572. *See* Cartwright (T.).
Adrey (Dan.). Verses in Barlow (W.). Vita R. Cosin. 1598. . 1707
Adrian V. (*formerly* Cardinal Ottobuoni). *See* Lyndwood (W.). Constitutiones. (Legatine.) 1504. 6147
— — 1505 *etc.* 6149
Adrichomius (C.). A briefe description of Hierusalem. 1595. 4°. . 2328
Advertisement from a French Gentleman. 1585. 8°. . . . 6781
Advertisements...for due order in...Common prayers. (1565) 1584. 4°. 1822
Advise of a Sonne...to his deare Mother. Oxford, 1616. 4°. . . 5325
Ægidius (Petrus). *See* Æsop. Æsopi Phrygis Fabulæ.... 1635.
Ælfric, *Abp.* *See* Testimony. A Testimonie of Antiquitie. [1566?] 8°.
See Lisle (W.). A saxon treatise. 1623. 4°.
— — Divers ancient monuments. 1638. 4°.
— T: (T.). Whetstone of reproofe. 1632. 8°. . . . 7817
Ælianus, *Tacticus*. The Tactiks. Trans. J. Bingham. 1616. F°. . 3379
Τάξις παλαιὰ καὶ ὀνομασίαι τῶν ἀρχόντων. *See* Crespin (J.). 1581. 1506
Æmilius Probus. The Lives of Epaminondas...and...other... *See* Plutarch. [Parallel Lives]... 1603 *etc.*
Æneas Sylvius. *See* Pius II., *Pope*.
Ængelrammus (J.). *See* Enghelram (J.).
Æpinus (J.). De Purgatorio. R. Grafton. 1549. 4°. 7095
De formandis sacris concionibus. *See* Reuchlin (J.). De arte concionandi. 1570. 8°.
Æquivoca. Multorum verborum &c. F. Baligault, Paris. [1494?] 4°. 136
— W. de Worde. 1505. 4°. 150
Æschines contra Ctesiphontem et Demosthenis pro corona (Græcé), a J. Sturmio illustratae. 1624. 8°. 3516
Æsop. Fabulae...ex collatione...variorum. (Lat.). Cantab. 1635. 8°. 5768
Fables in Englishe. Avian. Alfonce. Pogge. [156–]. 8°. . 7147
The Etymologist of Æsop's Fables. 1602. 8°. 2254
Africa. Congo. 1597. *See* Lopes (D.). A report.
Aga, Zarain. *See* Zarain Aga.
Agard (Arthur). *See* Powell (T.). The Repertorie of Records. 1631.
Agatharchides. Agatharcidis et Memnonis historicorum...omnia. (Gr. Lat.) Oxoniæ, 1597. 8°. 5243
Aggas (Edward). *See* A. (E.).
See La Noue (F. de). The politicke...discourses. 1587(–8). 4°.
— Pasquier (E.). The Jesuite displayed... 1594.
Aggeus (Augustinus), Haius. *See* Burgo (J. de). Pupilla oculi. 1510.
Aglionby (Ed.). Verses in Wilson (Sir T.). Vita. 1551. 4°. . 631
Aglionby (Geor.). Verses in Camdeni Insignia. 1624. . . 5346
Aglionby (John). *See* Bible. English (Royal.) 1611. . . 2635
Agnello (G. B.). Espositione...sopra...Apocalypsis spiritus secreti. 1566. 4°. 1175
Agricola (Rodolphus). *See* Aphthonius. Progymnasmata. 1631 *etc.* 8°.
Agriculture. *See* Fitzherbert (Sir A.). 1525.
De Benese (Sir R.). 154– .
Tusser (T.). 1586.
Platt (Sir H.). The Jewell House. 1594.
Estienne (C.). Maison Rustique. 1616. 2447
Mascal (L.). The Government. 1627.

No.

Agriculture *cont.* *See also* Forestry. Gardens. Husbandry.
Agrippa (H. C.). Of the vanitie and vncertaintie of artes and sciences. Trans. I. Sandford. 1575. 4°. 7265
Ahmed, Doctor. *See* Muhammad. Mohammedis Imposturæ. 1615.
Aidius (Andreas). Verses in Forbes (P.). An exquisite commentarie. 1613. 3218
'Αιλανδος ('Ενρικός). Verses in Cheke (Sir J.). De obitu M. Buceri. 1551. 734
Ailesbury (Thomas). *See* Aylesbury (Thomas).
Ailmer (Samuel), *M.D.* Verses in Hippocrates. 5812
Ainsworth (Henry). Animadversion to Mr R. Clifton's advertisement. Amsterdam. 1613. 4°. 6353
Annotations vpon the five bookes of Moses; the booke of Psalmes, and the song of Songs. 1627 (1626). F°. 4236
— 1639. F°. 4947
Annotations upon...Genesis. 1616. 4°. 6392
— Exodus. 1617. 4°. 6393
— Leviticus. 1618. 4°. 6396
— Numbers. 1619. 4°. 6397
— Deuteronomy. 1619. 4°. 6398
— Psalmes. Ed. 2. 1617(–8). 4°. 6395
Arrow against idolatrie. 1624. 8°. 6950
Communion of Saincts. 1628. 8°. 6976
Epistle sent unto two daughters of Warwick. G. Thorp, Amsterdam. 1608. 4°. 6352
Solomons Song of Songs in English metre. 1623. 4°. . . 6401
See Ainsworth (J.). The Trying ovt of the Trvth... 1615.
— Amsterdam, *English Church in.* An apologie or defence... 1604.
— Smyth (J.). Paralleles. 1609.
Ainsworth (John). The trying out of the truth. 1615. 4°. . 6900
Airay (Christopher). Fasciculus praeceptorum logicorum. Ed. alt. 1633. 8°. 5434
Aire, Poor Clares of. *See* Wadding (L.). The history of...S. Clare... 1635.
Aisgill (Joshua). Verses in Holyoake (F.). Dictionarium. 1640. . 3058
Aix, *Canons of S. Mary's.* *See* Polyander (J.). A disputation against the Adoration of the reliques. 1611.
Alabaster (William). Ecce sponsus venit. 1633. 4°. . . . 5056
Roxana. 1632. 8°. 5054
Spiraculum Tubarum. [1633?] F°. 5057
Verses in Cambridge. Acad. Cantab. Lachrymae. 1587. 4°. . 7356
See Racster (J.). A booke of the seven planets. 1598.
Alan (Alexander). *See* Alesius (A.).
Alarume Bell for London. 157–. *See* Carr (J.).
Alaygre (Antony). *See* Allègre.
Alba (Ferdinando Alvarez, duke of). *See* Libellvs svpplex... 1571.
Albert, Archduke of Austria. *See* Netherlands. II. Southern Provinces. 1603.
Albertus Magnus. Secreta mulierum et virorum. Machlinia. [1482.] 4°. 95
Secrets. [1549?] 8°. 1083
Quæstiones de modis significandi. J. Notary. [1496.] 4°. . 116
See Herbal. 1561.
Alberus (Erasmus). *See* Francis (St) of Assisi. The Alcoran... 1550.
— — 1603.
Albingenses. *See* Perrin (J. P.). The bloudy rage. 1624.
Albucasis. *See* Braunschweig (H.). The noble experyence. 1525.
Albumazar. 1615 *etc.* *See* Tomkis (T.).
Albyterio. *See* Estienne (C.). Maison Rustique. 1616. . . . 2447
Alcock (John). Desponsacio virginis xpristo. W. de Worde. [1496.] 4°. 57
Mons perfectionis. W. de Worde. 1497. 4°. 49

No.
Alcock (John) *cont.* W. de Worde. 1501. 4°. 144
Alcoran of the barefoot Friars. *See* Francis (St) of Assisi.
Alcuin. *See* Foliot (G.). Expositio in Canticum Canticorum. 1638.
Alday (John). *See* Boaistuau (P.). Theatrum Mundi.
Aldem (John). Verses in Camb. Univ. Epicedium. 1612. 4°. . 5665
Aldrich or Aldrisius (Robert). *See* Horman (W.). Antibossicon. 1521.
— Vulgaria. 1519. 4°. 267
Aldrich (Sy), *T.C.C.* Verses in Barlow (W.). Vita R. Cosin. 1598. 4°. 1707
Aldrisius (R.). *See* Aldrich.
Alehouses. *See* Articles of Direction. 1609.
Aleman (Matheo). The Rogue: or the life of Guzman de Alfarache. Part 1. 1623. F°. 4079
— Part 2. 1623. F°. 3599
— 2 Parts. Oxford, 1630. F°. 5427
Alemannus (Nicolaus). *See* Ryves (Sir T.). Imperatoris Ivstiniani. 1626.
Alen (Edmond). *See* Allen (E).
Alesius (Alexander). Of the auctorite of the word of god. [Ab. 1537.] 8°. 6674
See Alexander of Hales. Expositio. 1481.
Alessio Piemontese. The secretes. Trans. W. Warde. 1562. 4°. . 1298
— Pt. 1. 1580. 4°. 1184
— Pt. 2. [Ab. 1580.] 4°. 1518
— Pt. III. 1566. 4°. 1399
— Bk. IV. Trans. R. Androse. 1569. 4°. 1407
Alexander of Hales. Expositio super Aristotelis De anima. Oxford, 1481. F°. 74
Alexander Severus (Marcus Aurelius), *Emperor of Rome.* *See* Elyot (Sir Thomas). The Image of Governance.
Alexander VI, *Pope.* Proclamation. Ab. 1496. F°. . . 7064–5
[Drama.] *See* Barnes (B.). The divils charter. 1607.
Alexander (William), *earl of Stirling.* *See* Stirling (William Alexander, *first earl of*).
Alexander (Sir William), *Knight.* *See* Stirling (William Alexander, *first earl of*).
Alexis, of Piedmont. *See* Alessio Piemontese.
Aleyn (Charles), *Sid.* Verses in Camb. Univ. Epithalam. *bis* 1625. 5702
Alfarache (Guzman de). *See* Aleman (M.). The Rogve. 1623.
Alfonce (Petrus). *See* Alfunsi.
Alfred, *King.* [St Gregory's Pastoral.] *See* Vulcanius (B.). De Literis. 1597. 8°.
See Asser, *bp.* Ælfredi regis res gestæ. [1574.]
— Powell (R.). The life of Alfred. 1634.
Alfunsi (Petrus). Fables. *See* Æsop. Fables. 156– *etc.*
See Churl & the Bird.
Algiers. *See* Jacob, *ship.* A relation... 1622.
Ali Abençufian. Almansor...Published by R. Ashley. 1627. 4°. . 4338
'Alí ibn Rudwán. *See* Braunschweig (H.). The noble experyence. 1525.
— Herbal. 1561.
Aliggrode (Jacques de). *See* Miggrode (J. de).
Alington (Sir Giles). *See* Brant (S.). Stultifera Nauis. 1570. F°.
Alington (Robert). Consequentiae. *See* Libellus Sophistarum. 1510. 4°.
Alison (Ric.). Plaine confvtation of...Brownisme. 1590. 4°. . 2378
Allègre (Antoine). *See* Guevara (A. de). A dispraise. 1548.
Alleine (Richard). *See* B. (R.). Davids Musick. 1616. 4°.
Allen (Edmond). *See* Catechism. A catechisme... 1551.
— Erasmus (D). Paraphrase. 1548 *etc.*
Allen (Elias), *instrument maker.* *See* Gunter (E.). De sectore. 1623.
— Oughtred (W.). The circle. 1632.
— Delamain (Richard). The making...of a...horizontall Quadrant. W. Leake. 1637. 8°.
See Oughtred (W.). The circles of proportion. 1639. 4°.

No.

Allen (Isaac). Verses in Camb. Univ. Threno-thr. 1603. 4°. . 5616
Allen (John), *Instrument Maker*. *See* Delamain (R.). The making... of a...horizontall Quadrant. 1637. 8°.
Allen (John). The Younger Brother. *See it under* J. Ap-robert.
Allen (Robert). [A treatise of Christian beneficence. 1600?] 4°. . 6826
Allen (Thomas). *See* Chrysostom...opera... 1613.
— More (Sir T.). Epistola. 1633.
Allen (Thomas), *of Gloucester Hall, Oxford*. *See* Hakewill (G.). An apologie. 1630.
Allen (William), *Cardinal*. Apologie...of the two English Colleges. Mounts in Herault. 1581. 8°. 6432
Treatise made in defence of Priesthood. Louvain. 1567. 8°. . 6418
True sincere...defence of English Catholiques. 1584. 8°. . . 6775
See Bible, N.T. Rhemes, 1582. 4°.
— Bible, O.T. (Douai version). 1609–10 *etc.*
— Charke (W.). A treatise. 1586.
— D. (G.). A briefe discoverie of Doctor Allens...drifts... 1588.
— Fulke (W.). Two treatises... 1577.
— Parsons (R.). The conference. 1594.
— Rich (B.). A New Irish Prognostication... 1624.
Allenson (John). *See* Whitaker (W.). Praelectiones. 1599 *etc.*
— — Tractatus. 1600.
Allenson (William). Verses in Camb. Univ. Lacrymæ. 1619. 4°. . 5689
Allestre (Richard). A new Almanack and Prognostication. 1637. 8°. 4648
— 1640. 8°. 4672
Alley (Peter). Verses in Coryate (T.). Coryates crvdities. 1611. 4°. . 3076
Alley (W.). Πτωχομυσεῖον. The poore mans Librarie. 1565. F°. . 806
— 1571. F°. 820
See Bible. Eng. (Bishops'). 1568. F°.
Alliaco (Petrus de). *See* Clemangiis (N. de). Specvlvm... 1606.
Allibond (Peter). *See* L'Espine (J. de). Confutation of the Popish Transubstantiation. 1592.
Allibond (Peter). Verses in Oxf. Univ. Horti. 1640. 4°. . . 5499
See Renecher (H.). The golden chayne of salvation. 1604. 4°.
Alliston (Edward). *See* Ovid. Fasti. 1640.
Allot (R.). Englands Parnassus. 1600. 8°. 1990
Almada (Ruy Fernandez de). Verses in Aleman (M.). The Rogve. 1623. F°. 4079
Almanack. 1530. *See* Thibault (J.).
154–. J. Redman. 8°. 709
1554. *See* Lon (H.).
1561. — Mounslowe (A.). (Prognostication.)
1563. — Nicolson (J.). Prognostication.
1581. Single sheet. 6772
1582. *See* Brief Treatise. 8°.
1591. — Buckminster. (Prognostication.)
1591–2. — Dade (J.). Almanacke and Prognostication 1591. 8°. 1338
— — A triple almanack (A Prognostication). 4°. . 1339
1592. — — A new almanack. 8°. 1340
1593. — *See* Gray (W.). (Prognostication.)
1595. — Buckminster (T.).
1596. — Frende (G.). (Title of Prognostication only.)
1600. — Watson (R.). A doble Almanacke.
1604. — Dade (J.).
1617. — Keene (J.).
1618. — Bretnor (T.).
1619. — Drekin ( ).
1625. [ ] Cambridge, 1625. 8°. 5700
1629. *See* Pond (E.).
1629. — Rivers (P.).

No.

Almanack *cont.* 1633-6. — Ephemerides.
1636. — (Broad). Cambridge. F°. 7675
1637. — Allestree (R.).
See Perkins (S.).
1640. — Allestree (R.).
See also Prognostication.
Almansor (Jakub), *King. See* Ali Abençufian, *pseud.* Almansor the learned... 1627.
Almond for a Parrat, or Cutbert Curryknaues Almes. [Marprelate Press. 159-?] 4°. 1920
Alms. *See* Bucer (M.). A Treatise... [1557?]
Alphonsus (Petrus). *See* Alfunsi.
Alsop ( ), *B.A., C.C.C.* Verses in Camb. Univ. Carmen. 1635. 4°. 5770
Alsop (Bernard), *printer. See* More (Sir T.)... Vtopia. 1624 *etc.*
Alsop (John), *Christ's.* Verses in Cam. Univ. Anthologia. 1632. 4°. 5741
Hippocrates. 1633. 8°. 5812
Cam Univ. Fasciae. 1633. 4°. 5808
Cam. Univ. Rex redux. 1633. 4°. 5748
[License]. Hall (Jos.). Christian Moderation. 1640. . 4332
Alston (Edward), *M.D.* Verses in Hippocrates. 1633. 8°. . . 5812
Alting (Henry). A votiue oration for...Frederick V. Trans. W. Walker. 1615. 4°. 3900
Alum. *See* Proclamations. 1614. Oct. 10.
Alva (Ferdinando Alvarez, duke of). *See* Alba.
Alvaro Pelayo, *Bp. of Silves. See* Pelayo.
Alworth ( ). *See* Bastwick (J.). Πράξεις. 1636.
Alymes (R. de Lusing, Lord of). *See* Lucinge.
Amadis, de Gaule. *See* Lobeira (V.).
Amaltheo (Cornelio). Verses in Harvey (G.). Gratulationum. 1578. 4°. 1495
Amboyna. A true declaration. *See* East Indies. East India Company. A true relation. 1624.
— Wilkinson (R.). The Stripping of Joseph. 1625.
— East Indies. East India Company. A remonstrance... 1632.
Ambrosius. Christian offices crystall glasse. Trans. R. Humfrey. (Truths triumph.) 1637. 4°. 5163
America. 1611. [Lery (J. de).] *See* Boemus (J.). The manners. 1611. 4°.
America, Transportation to. *See* Proclamations. 1637 (April 30).
See New England.
Amerotius. De Græcorum notis Arithmeticis. *See* Crespin (J.). 1581.
Ames (William). Bellarminus enervatus. Oxoniae, 1629. 12°. . 5424
— Ed. nov. Tom. i. 'Ap. J. Humpfridum.' 1633. 12°. . 7014
— Tom. ii—iv. 'H. Robinson.' 1632. 12°. . . . 6402
Conscience. 1639. 4°. 7043
Coronis ad collationem Hagiensem. Ed. 6. 1632. 12°. . . 4711
English Puritanisme. *See* under Bradshaw (W.).
Fresh suit against human ceremonies. 1633. 4°. . . 7015
Reply to Dr Mortons generall defence. 1622. 4°. . . . 6929
See Baynes (P.). The Diocesans Tryall. 1621.
— Bradshaw (W.). The unreasonablenes of the Separation... 1640.
— Burgess (J.). An answer...to...a reply... 1631.
— — The lawfvlnes of Kneeling... 1631.
— Canne (J.). A necessitie of separation. 1634.
Amherst (Arth.), *S.J.O.* Verses in Oxf. Univ. Horti. 1640. 4°. 5499
— Snelling (T.). Thibaldus. 1640. 8°. 5502
Amirault (Moïse). *See* Copie of the letter. 1631. 4°. . . 3545
Amner (J.). Sacred Hymnes. 1615. 4°. 2030
Amsterdam, English Church. An apologie or defence of...Brownists. (Ed. H. Ainsworth.) 1604. 4°. 6376, 6377
See Ainsworth (H.). An animadversion... 1613.
— Clapham (H.). Theologicall Axioms... 1597.

No.

Amsterdam, English Church *cont.* *See* H. (I.). A description. 1610.
— Johnson (F.). A Christian Plea... 1617.
— Robinson (J.). Of Religious Communion... 1614.
Amsterdam, Ships from. *See* Neck (J. van). The Journal. 1601. 4°.
Amyot (Jacques), *Bp. of Auxerre.* *See* Plutarchus. [Parallel Lives]... 1603 *etc.*
Anabaptists. *See* Bullinger (H.). An holsome Antidotus. 1548.
— Calvin (J.). A short instruction. 1549.
— Description. A Discription of what God... 1620.
— H. (I.). A description of the Church. 1610.
— Jessop (E.). A discovery... 1623.
— Johnson (F.). A brief treatise. 1609.
— — A Christian Plea. 1617.
— Knox (J.). An answer. 1560.
— Turner (W.). A preseruatiue... 1551.
Anatomy. *See* Banister (J.). 1591. 7772
— Bartholinus (C.). 1633. 12°. 7661
— Geminus (T). 1559.
Anchoran (John). *See* Comenius (I. A.). Porta Lingvarvm... 1631 *etc.*
Anderson (A.). The shield of our Safetie. 1581. 4°. . . . 1853
Anderson (Adam). Verses in Adamson (J.). Εισόδια. 1618. . 5960
Anderson (Henry). Verses in Adamson (J.). Εισόδια. 1618. . . 5960
Anderson (Patrick). The ground of the catholike and roman religion. 1623. 4°. 6550
Anderton (James). The apologie of the romane church. 1604. 4°. . 6855
Liturgie of the Masse. By J. Brereley. Cologne, 1620. 4°. . 6336
Luthers life. S. Omers, 1624. 4°. 7692
The protestants apologie. By J. Brereley. 1608. 4°. . . 6516
See Augustine (St.). Saint Avstins religion... 1625.
— Book intitvled: the english Protestants Recantation. 1617. . 6908
— James I. Cygnea Cantio. 1629.
— Morton (T.). A Catholike appeale... 1610.
Anderton (Lawrence). One god, one fayth. 1625. 8°.. . . 6966
Progenie of catholicks. Widow Courant, Rouen, 1633. 4°. . 6264
See Book...the English Protestants Recantation. 1617. . . 6908
— Society of Twelve. 1626. 6576
Andrea (Richardus ab). *See* Andrews.
Andreæ (Antonius). Quaestiones. J. Lettou. 1480. F°. . . 88
Super Porphyrii Isagogen ad Categ. Aristotelis etc. St. Alban's. [1481.] 4°.. 84
Andreae (Richard). *See* Andrews.
Andreas Asulanus. *See* Torresanus (A.) of Asolo.
Andrewe (George). A quaternion of sermons... 1624. Dublin, 1625. 4°. 6028
Andrewe (Lawrence). *See* Braunschweig (H.). The vertuose boke Of Distyllacyon... 1527.
— Wonderful Shape. [1527?]
Andrewes (Lancelot). Concio. 5 Aug. 1606. 1610. 4°. . . 2621
Copie of a sermon...good Friday...8 April 1604. 1604. 4°. . 2580
— [1604.] 4°. 2581, 2582
xcvi. Sermons. 1629. F°. 4426
— Ed. 2. 1631. F°. 4344
— Ed. 3. 1635 (-4). F°. 4361
Opuscula quædam posthuma. 1629. 4°. 3038
Responsio ad apologiam Bellarmini. 1610. 4°. . . . 2622
Sermon of the pestilence. 1603. 1636. 4°. 4369
Sermon. 28 Sept. 1606. 1606. 4°. 2591
— [1606?] 4°. 2592
Sermon preached [on Gal. iv. 4, 5]...Christmas day...1609. *See below* Two Sermons... 1610.
Sermon. Christmas day 1609. [1610?] 4°. 2625

No.
Andrewes (Lancelot) *cont.* Sermon. Aug. 5. at Holdenbie. 1610. 4º. 2623
Sermon [on Luke ii. 10, 11] preached...Christmas day...1610. *See below* Two Sermons... 1610.
Sermon. Christmas day 1610. [1611?] 4º. 2634
Sermon...Easter day. (King's Accession.) 1611. 4º. . 2632, 2633
Sermon. Easter day 1614. 1614. 4º. 2650
Sermon. 5 Nov. 1617. 1618. 4º. 3483
Sermon. Easter day 1618. 1618. 4º. 3484
Sermon. Easter day, 16 April 1620. 1620. 4º. . . 2660
Tortura Torti. 1609. 4º. 2612
Two Sermons. Christmas day 1609, 1610. 1610. 4º. . 2626
See Blackwell (G.). A large examination... 1607.
— Bible. Eng. [Royal Version]. 1611.
— Burhill (R.). Contra M. Becani. 1613.
— — Pro Tortvra Torti... 1611.
— — De potestate regia. 1613.
— Collins (S.). Epphata. 1617.
— — Increpatio. 1612.
— Cosin (Richard). An apologie for svndrie proceedings... 1593.
— Fitzherbert (T.). An adioynder to the Supplement. 1613.
— — A supplement. 1613.
— — The Obmvtesce. 1621.
— Thomson (R.). Elenchvs Refvtationis Torturae Torti. 1611.
Andrewes (Roger). *See* Bible. Eng. (Royal Version). 1611.
Andrews (Richard), *M.D.* Verses in Seneca. Tragœdiæ. 1624. 8º. 3444
Camden (W.). Tomus alter. 1627. Fº. 3168
Hippocrates. 1633. 8º. 5812
Androse (Richard). *See* Alessio Piemontese. 1569.
Angel (Father) of Joyeuse. *See* Joyeuse.
Angel (J.). The agrement of the holye Fathers. [1555.] 8º. . 1239
Angelino (Pietro). *See* Agnello (G. B.). Espositione sopra Apocalypsis... 1566. 4º.
Angelos (Christopher). Πόνησις. Oxford, 1617. 4º. 5329
Christopher Angell...who tasted of many stripes. Oxford, 1618. 4º. 5332
Ἐγκώμιον. Cambridge, 1619. 4º. 5685
Ἐγχειρίδιον. Cantabrigiae, 1619. 4º. 5686
Πόνος...περὶ τῆς ἀποστασιας τῆς ἐκκλησιας. (Labor...de apostasia.) 1624. 4º. 3147
Anglerius (Peter Martyr). History of Trauayle in the West and East Indies. 1577. 4º. 970
Anianus. *See* Avianus.
Animalium quadrupedum, avium, florum, fructuum, muscarum et vermium...delineationes...A booke of beast. 'R. Danell'. [Ab. 1628.] 4º. 4917
Anjou (Henry, duke of). *See* Henry III., King of France.
Anne, St, *Charterhouse of. See* Coventry.
Anne, of Denmark, *Queen Consort of James I.* [Marriage.] *See* Damman (Sir Adrian). Schediasmata. 1590.
See Cambridge University. Lacrymæ... 1619.
[Funeral verses.] *See* Camden (W.). Remaines. 1623.
See Jonson (Ben). The characters. [1609.]
Anne, Princess, *daughter of Charles I.* (1637–). *See* Cambridge Univ. Συνῳδια. 1637. 5790
Annesley (Henry). *See* Hawkins (H.). Partheneia. 1633.
Anscell (Thomas). Verses in Hippocrates. 1633. 8º. . . . 5812
Anselm, *Saint. See* Volusianus. Epistolæ duæ... 1569.
Anstie (Stephen). Verses in King (E.). Jvsta. 1638. 4º. . 5829
Answere for the tyme, to the examination...to mayntayne the apparrell ...against...the mynisters of London. [Geneva?] 1566. 8º. 6327–9
Answere of a Mother. *See* W. (Ez.). 1627.

No.

Answere to a papystycall exhortacyon pretendynge to auoyde false doctryne. [Ab. 1548.] 8°. 6696
Answer to certaine objections &c. *See* Limbomastix. 1604.
Answere to certaine scandalous Papers. *See* Salisbury (Robert Cecil, earl of). 1606.
Answere to the Hollanders Declaration, concerning the Occurrents of the East-India. Part 1. 1622. 4°.. 3681
Anthologia Græca. *See* Stockwood (J.). Progymnasma. 1597.
Anthony (Francis). Apologia veritatis...pro auro potabili. 1616. 4°. 3759
Medicinae, chymicae, et veri potabilis auri assertio. Cantabrigiae, 1610. 4°. 5658
See Cotta (J.). Cotta contra Antonium. 1623.
— Rawlins (T.). Admonitio psevdo-chymicis. [1620?]
Antichrist. The byrth and lyfe of. W. de Worde. [Ab. 1520.] 4°. 209
[The description and confutation of mysticall Antichrist the Familist. 1606?] 4°. 6866
See Olde (J.). [1557?]
— Parker (R.). 1607.
Anti-coton. *See* Cotton (P.).
Antidotarius. R. Wyer. n. d. 8°. 543
Antiduello. *See* Espagne (J. d'). Antidvello. 1632.
Antimartinus. *See* L. (A.). Antimartinus. 1589.
Antinomus Anonymus. *See* Hinde (W.). The office...of the Morall Law... 1623.
Antiphoner (Sarum). Antiphonale. W. Hopyl, Paris, imp. F. Byrckman. 1519 (1520). 6155–6
Antiquodlibet or an advertisement to beware of secular Priests. R. Schilders, Middelburg. 1602. 8°. 6460
Antisanderus. Cantabrigiae, 1593. 4°. 5558–9
Antisixtus. *See* Hurault (M.). Antisixtvs. (Lat.). 1590. 4°.
— — (English). 1590. 4°.
Antoninus (Marcus Aurelius). Meditations. Trans. M. Casaubon. Ed. 2. 1635. 4°. 4283
— *See* Quin (W.). Corona virtutum. 1613.
Antoninus (Marcus Aurelius). *See* Guevara (A. de).
The golden boke. (Trans. Lord Berners.) 1546. 8°.; *id.* The Dial of Princes. 1557, etc.
Antoninus Pius. *See* Quin (W.). Corona virtutum. 1613.
Antoninus, *Saint, Abp. of Florence.* *See* Constantine I. A treatyse... [Ab. 1525.]
Antonius (Franciscus). *See* Anthony (F.).
Antony, *abp. of Florence.* *See* Antoninus.
Antwerp. 1520. *See* Laet (J.). Prenostication. 4°.
1530. *See* Thibault (J.). [Prognostication.]
An historicall discourse. 1586. 4°. 2116
Flemish Church in. *See* Corro (A. de). An epistle. 1570 (1569).
Anwykyll (John). Compendium totius grammatice. Oxford. [1483.] 4°. 76–7
— Deventer, 1489. 4°. 143
? Declension of nouns. *See* Grammar Lat. (Frag.). 15– . 4°. 221
Aphorismes...of the Iesuits. 1609. 4°. 7499
Aphthonius. Progymnasmata. Cum scholiis Lorichii. Cantabrigiæ, 1631. 8°. 5730
— 1635. 8°. 5769
Apocalypsis spiritus secreti. *See* Aguello (G. B.). Espositione... 1566.
Αποδημουντοφιλος. Verses in Coryate (T.). Coryats Crudities. 1611. 4°. 3076
Apollinarius. Μετάφρασις τοῦ ψάλτηρος. 1590. 8°. 1722
Apologeticon et...in Belgicogermania...narratio. [Ab. 1580?] 8°. . 6771
Apologia Ecclesiæ Anglicanæ. *See* Jewel (J.). 1562 *etc.*
Apologia pro christiano batavo. 1610. 8°. 6884
Apology. Apologie for svndrie proceedings... 1593. *See* Cosin (Richard).
Apologie of the reformed churches of France. 1628. 4°. . 7815

No.

Apology *cont.* Apologie or answere in defence of the Church of England. *See* Jewel (J.). 1562 *etc.*
Apology or defence for the Christians of Fraunce...by Sir J. Bowes. 1579. 8°. 855
Apostles' Creed. *See* Broughton (H.). An exposition... [1613 ?]
See Gill (A.). The sacred philosophie. 1635.
— Jackson (T.). The eternall truth. 1613.
— — The third booke. 1614.
Apparel of Ministers. *See* Bullinger (H.). Fiftie...sermons. 1587. 4°. 7820
See Answer for the tyme.
Appeal to the Parliament. *See* Leighton (A.). 1628.
Appelius (J.). A true relation of the...Earle Philippus Lodovicus...of Hanaw. Trans. S. R. 1612. 4°. 7523
Appleford ( ), *Regin.* Verses in Camb. Univ. Voces. 1640. 5836
Appletree (Thomas). *See* England. Elizabeth. A trve report... 1579.
Ap-Robert (J.). The Yonger Brother his apology. 1618. 4°. . . 6535
— Oxford, 1635–4. 4°. 5412
Apuleius (L.). The XI. bookes of the golden asse. Trans. W. Adlington. 1639. 4°. 7571
Ar. (A.). The practise of princes. 1630. 4°. 6997
Ar. (Mar.). *See* Fitz-Herbert (T.). A defence. 1602.
Arabic Language. *See* Wakefield (R.). Oratio. 1524. 4°.
— Rive (E.). An Heptaglottie. 1618.
— Greaves (T.). De linguæ &c. 1639.
Aragon. *See* Habington (W.). The Queen of Arragon. 1640.
Arboriculture. 1590. *See* Mascall (L.). A booke. 4°.
Arcæus (F.). A most excellent...method of curing woundes. 1588. 4°. 1592
Arcandam. The most excellent, profitable and pleasant booke...to fynd the fatal desteny. [1562 ?] 8°. 1284
Arceus (Franciscus). *See* Arcæus.
Archangel (Father). *See* Forbes (John).
Archbishops. *See* A very lively portrayture. 1640. . . 7579
Archbold (Ed.), *T.C.C.* Verses in Barlow (W.). Vita R. Cosin. 1598. 4°. 1707
Archbold (John). The beauty of holines. 1621. 4°. . . . 3135
Archdeacon (Daniel). *See* True Discourse. A true Discourse... 1588
Architecture. *See* Serlio (S.). The fourth Booke. F°. 1611.
— Wotton (Sir H.). 1624.
Archpriest controversy. *See* Blackwell (G.).
Ardern (Johannes). *See* Arcæus (F.). A...method of curing woundes...1588.
Areskinus (Gul.). *See* Erskine.
Aretino (Leonardo). *See* Bruni (L.), *Aretino.*
Aretius (Jacobus). Primula Veris...Carmen Seculare. 1613. 4°. . 3090
Arfeville (Nicolas Nicolay, *sieur d'*). *See* Nicolay. 1825
Argall (J.). De vera pœnitentia. 1604. 8°. 2258
Argall (Richard). *See* Legh (G.). The Accedens of Armory. 1562 *etc.*
Argent (John), *M.D.* Verses in Hippocrates. 1633. . . . 5812
— [License.] *See* London. College of Physicians. 1633.
Argentine (Richard). *See* Ochino (B.). Sermons. 1548.
— — Certayne Sermons. [Ab. 1550.]
— Zwingli (U.). Certeyne Preceptes. 1548.
Arias (Francisco). A treatise of patience. Trans. T. M. 1630. 12°. 6558
Arias Montanus (Benedictus). *See* Willet (A.). Hexapla in Genesin 1605
— — Exodvm. 1608
Ariosto (L.). Orlando Furioso. Trans. J. Harington. Ed. 1. 1591. F°. 2228
— — Ed. 3. With Epigrams. 1634. F°. 4448
[Gli Suppositi.] The Supposes. *See* Gascoigne (G.). A Hundreth sundrie Flowers. [1572.] 4°.
— *See* Gascoigne (G.). The Posies. 1575.
Aristeas. The auncient history of the Septuagint. English by I. Done. 1633. 8°. 3693

No.

Aristippus, or The Jouiall Philosopher. 1630. *See* Randolph (T.).
Aristotle. [De anima.] *See* Alexander of Hales. Expositio. 1481. F°.
De poetica. (Lat. a. Th. Goulston.) 1623. 4°. 3432
[De virtutibus (Gr. Lat.)] per S. Grynaeum. 1634. 8°. *See* no. 5717.
Textus Ethicorum. Oxoniae, 1479. 4°. 73
[Ethics.] *See* Brerewood (E.). Tractatus Ethici... 1640.
— Buridanus (J.). 1637.
See Dedicus (J.). Questiones moralissime... 1518.
— Epitome doctrine...per T. Golium &c. Cantabrigiae, 1634. 8°. 5717
— Heiland (S.). Aristotelis Ethicorum...libri per Quaestiones. 1581. 8°.
[Metaphysics.] *See* Andreæ (A.). Quaestiones. 1480. F°.
[Organon. Categoriæ.] *See* Andreæ (A.). [1480.] 4°.
Categories. *See post* Organon. Andreæ (A.).
[— De Interpretatione.] *See* Andreæ (A.). [1480.] 4°.
[Organon.—Posterior Analytics.] *See* Powell (G.). Analysis. 1594. 5239
— 1631. 8°. 5391
[— Appendix.] *See* Pacius (J.). Institutiones. 1597.
Physica. *See* John Canon. [148 .]
[— Epitome.] *See* Case (J.). Ancilla Philosophiæ... 1599.
[— Synopsis.] *See* Hauwenreuter (J. L.). 1594.
[Politics.] Politiqves (Eng.). 1598. F°. 2422
— *See* Buridanus (J.). 1640.
— — Case (J.). Sphæra Civitatis. 1588.
[Rhetoric Gr. Lat.] Ed. T. Goulston. 1619. 4°. . . . 3927
[Dialectic.] *See* Case (J.). Svmma. 1584 *etc.*
Secreta secretorum (Eng.). R. Copland. 1528. 4°. . . . 339
Armada, Spanish. A form of Prayer. 7294
Armele, *Saint.* Lyfe. Pynson [15—]. 4°. 292
Armen. *See* Arnemuyden.
Armigilus, *Saint.* *See* Armele.
Arminianism. *See* Du Moulin (P.). The anatomy of Arminianism. 1620 *etc.*
— Rous (F.). The Trvth of three Things... 1633.
Arminians, or Remonstrants. *See* Johnson (F.). A Christian Plea... 1617.
Arminius. *See* Carleton (D.). The speech... 1618. 4°.
— Yates (J.). Gods arraignment. 1615. 4°.
Armour (John). Verses in Forbes (P.). Funerals. 1635. . . . 6007
Armuijen. *See* Arnemuyden.
Arnaldus, *de Villa Nova.* *See* Regimen. [15—] *etc.*
Arnalt and Lucinda. *See* Desainliens (C.). The Italian Schoole-maister. 1597. 8°.
Arnauld (Antoine). The arrainement of the whole societie of Iesuites in Fraunce. (The resolution of the Vniversitie.) 1594. 4°. . 2864
Arnemuyden or Armuijen. *See* Middelburg. Middleborovv. [1574.]
Arnold (Richard). Chronicle. *See* London. In this boke. [1503? *etc.*]
Arnoux (Jean). *See* Du Moulin (P.). The bvckler of the faith. 1620. 4°.
Arondaeus (Justinus). Verses in Adamson (J.). Εισόδια. 1618. . 5960
Arquerius (J.). *See* Calendar of Scripture. 1575.
Arragon. *See* Aragon.
Arraignment. The arraignement of the whole creature. *See* H. (R.). 1631(-2).
Ars moriendi. The crafte to live & dye well. W. de Worde. 1505. F°. 148
— W. de Worde. 1506. 4°. 151
See also Art how to dye well. 1623.
Arsanes. Orations...agaynst Philip. [1560?] 8°. 868
Art how to dye well. (A true relation of...Bellarmine.) By C. E. 1623. 8°. 6551

No.

Arte of english poesie. *See* Puttenham (G.). 1589.
Art of Memory. *See* Ravennas (P.). The art. [154 .]
Art to live & die well. *See* Ars moriendi.
Art. *See* Artes.
Artemidorus Daldianus. The ivdgement or exposition of dreames. 1606. 8°. 2000
Artephius. The secret booke. *See* Flamel (N.). 1624.
Artes of Logike... *See* Fenner (D.)... 1584.
Arth (Henry). Provision for the poore. 1597. 4°. 2721
Arthington (Henry). The seduction of H. A. [1593.] 4°. . 2566
See Arth (Henry). Provision. 1597.
— Cosin (R.). Conspiracie for Pretended Reformation... 1592.
Arthur, *King*. *See* Fox (L.). North-west Fox... 1635.
— Leland (J.). Assertio. 1544.
— — A Learned and True Assertion. 1582. 4°.
— Malory (Sir T.). The story. 1557 *etc.*
Articles (England, Church of). Articles agreed on by the Bishoppes...at London 1552. June 1553. 4°. 628
— 1562. Jugge & Cawood. 1571. 4°. 966
— R. Jugge. [1573?] 4°. 971
— B. Norton & J. Bill. 1628. 4°. 2832
— — 1630. 4°. 2839
— Dublin, 1634. 4°. 6052
Articuli de quibus convenit...in synodo, Londini. 1562. J. Day. 1571. 4°. 819
— Item Liber...canonum. 1571. Oxoniae, 1636. 4°. . 5469
Articles (Visitation). 1559. Jugge & Cawood. 1559. 4°. . . 959
— C. Barker. [1583?] 4°. 1684
— J. Kingston for C. Barker. [1584?] 4°. 1189
— (Richard Bancroft.) 1601. 4°. 2410
Articles (Canterbury Province). R. Jugge. [1575?] 4°. . 972, 973
— W. Seres. 1576. 4°. 940
— Articuli. 1584. C. Barker. [1584.] 4°. 1685
Essex Archdeaconry. (E. Layfield.) 1635. 4°. . . . 4208
— — 1639. 4°. 4217
London. E. Bonner. 1554. *See* Bale (J.). Declaration.
— (W. Laud.) 1628. 4°. 3543
— Second triennial. 1631. 4°. 7542
— (W. Juxon.) 1637. 4°. 4380
— — 1640. 4°. 4399
Norwich. (R. Montagu.) E. Purslowe for H. Seile. 1638. 4°. 4121
— — Cambridge. 1638. 4°. 5793
York. 1590. 4°. 1728
Articles. *See* Certain articles... 1572. 5898
Articles (Ireland Church). Articles of Religion...Dublin. 1615. J. Frankton, Dublin. 1615. 4°. 6015
— T. Downes. 1629. 4°. 2558
— R. Y. for T. Downes. 1628. 4°. 4971
— 'Irish Stock.' 1629. 4°. 6990
Articles of direction touching Alehouses. 1609. 4°. . . . 2613
Articles of Peace, entercourse and Commerce. (James I...Philip III... Albertus and Isabella Clara Eugenia. 18 August 1604.) 1605. 4°. 2590
(Great Britain and France.) 1629. 4°. 3473
(Charles...and Philip the fourth of Spaine. 5 Nov. 1630.) 1630. 4°. 2669
Articuli ad narrationes nouas. Pynson. [1525?] 8°. 293
Berthelet. 1530. 8°. 417
[Ab. 1530.] 8°. 6669
R. Redman. 1539. 8°. 382
1561. 8°. *See* Narrationes. 7169

No.

Arts. *See* Artes.
Arundel and Surrey (Thomas Howard, second earl of), 1592—1646. *See* Official Publications. Charles I. 1639. Lawes.
— Selden (J.). Marmora Arundelliana. 1628. 4°.
— Crowne (W.). A true relation. 1637. 4°.
[Licence.] *See* Du Praissac. Art of Warre. 1639.
Arundell of Wardour (Thomas first baron). *See* Morton (T.). A discharge of five Imputations.
Arundell (F.). Verses in Cam. Univ. Rex redux. 1633. 4°. . 5748
Arusiensis episcopus. *See* Canutus.
Arviragus and Philicia. *See* Carlell (L.). 1639.
Ascham (Anthony). Verses in A. (G.). Pallas armata. 1639. 8°. . 5170
Ascham (Margaret). *See* Ascham (R.). The Scholemaster...
Ascham (R.) Apologia...contra Missam. 1577. 8°. . . 1623
Epistolarum libri tres. [1576?] 8°. 1654
— 1578. 8°. 1624
— 1590 (1589). 8°. 2063
Report...of the affaires...of Germany... [1570?] 4°. . . 869
Scholemaster. 1570. 4°. 813
— Ed. 2. 1571. 4°. 821
— 1589. 4°. 2104
Toxophilus. Ed. 2. 1571. 4°. 1220
— 1589. 4°. 2103
[Letters.] *See* Fleming (A.). A panoplie. 1576. 4°.
Verses in Blundeville (T.). Three morall treatises. 1580. 8°. . 1419
Ashaw (Sir Le). Verses in White (J.) of Eccles. The Way to the true Church. 1610 *etc.* 4°. . . . 3454 *etc.* (Works) 2296
Ashcombe (Robert). *See* Ayschecum.
— — Voces. 1640. 5836
Ashe (Thomas). Perfect table a touts les...Reportes de Sir E. Coke. 1606. 8°. 3224
See Coke (Sir E.). Fasciculus florum. 1618. 8°.
— Dyer (Sir J.). La Table... per T. A[she?]. 1588.
— Plowden (E.). Abridgement. 1607.
Asheton (Tho.). Verses in Camb. Univ. Genethl. 1631. . . 5731
Ashley (I.). Verses in Contarini (G.). The Commonwealth. 1599. 4°. 2153
Ashley (Robert). *See* Ali Abençufian, *pseud.* Almansor the learned. . 1627.
— Barri (C.). Cochin-China... 1633.
— Le Roy (L.). Of the interchangeable course. 1594. F°.
Ashton (Abdias). *See* Assheton.
Ashton (George). Verses in Camdeni Insignia. 1624. . . . 5346
Ashton (Gualther). The prisoners plaint. 25 August 1622. 1623. 4°. 4515
Ashton (Ro.), *M.A. Pemb.* Verses *ter* in Cam. Univ. Anthologia. 1632. 4°. 5741
— Fasciae. 1633. 4°. 5808
— Rex redux. 1633 *bis.* 4°. 5748
— Carmen. 1635. 5770
— *Συνωδία.* 1637. 5790
Ashwell (Gedeon), *KC.* Verses in Camb. Univ. *Συνωδία.* 1637. 4°. 5790
— Oxf. Univ. Horti. 1640. 4°. 5499
Ashwell (John). The letters whyche... *See* Joye (G.). [1527?] *etc.*
Askew (Anne). *See* Bale (J.). The first examinacyon... 1546-7.
— Bentley (T.). The monvment of Matrones. 1582.
— Crowley (R.). The confutation. 1548.
Askew (Egeon). Brotherly reconcilement. 1605. 4°. . . . 1753
Askham (Antony). *See* Ascham.
Aslachus (Cunradus). The Description of heaven...Engl. by R. Jennings. 1623. 8°. 4516
Assembly of Gods. *See* Lydgate (J.).
Asser. Ælfredi regis res gestæ. [1574.] F°. 870
Assertion for true and christian church-policie. 1604. 8°. . . 6463

No.

Asshaw (Le). *See* Ashaw.
Assheton (Abdias). *See* Whitaker (W.). Praelectiones. 1599.
Assize of Bread and ale. Berthelet. n.d. 8°. 508
Assize of Bread. R. Wyer. n.d. 4°. 544
1601. 4°. 2157
1632. 4°. 3186
1636. 4°. 5104
See Crompton (R.). L'avthoritie. 1594.
Assizes. Liber Assisarum &c. 1516? F°. 342
Le Liver des Assises. 1580. F°. 1140
Abridgement of the Boke of Assises. 1553. 8°. . . . 1106
See Brief Declaration. 1636.
Astley (John). *See* Ascham (R.). A report... [1570–1?]
Aston (Sir Arthur). [Letters Patent.] 1606. 4°. . . . 2595
Aston (Edward). *See* Boemus (J.). The manners. 1611. 4°.
Astræa. The History of Astræa. *See* Urfé (H. d'). 1620.
Astrology. *See* Indagine (J. ab). Briefe introductions. . . 790
Astrological Discourse. 1583. *See* Harvey (R.).
1598. *See* Dariot (C.).
1620. *See* Melton (J.). Astrologaster.
Astronomy. 1602. *See* Torporley (N.). Diclides. 4°.
1618. *See* Fleming (A.).
1619. *See* Bainbridge (J.). An astronom. description.
1638. *See* Wilkins (J.). The discovery.
Asulanus (Andreas). *See* Torresanus (A.) of Asolo.
Athanasius, *Saint*. *See* Volusianus. Epistolæ duæ. 1569.
Athanasius. *See* Pole (R.). The seditious...Oration of Cardinal Pole... [1560?]
Athon (Johannes de). *See* Acton. 6149
Atkins (Hugo). Verses in Fuller (T.). Holy warre. 1639. F°. . 5806
Atkins (William). Verses in Parkinson (J.). Paradisus terrestris. 1629. F°. 2561
Atkinson (William). *See* Imitatio Christi. [ab. 1503?]
Atkynson (William), *D.D.* *See* Atkinson.
Attersoll (William). A commentarie vpon...Philemon. Ed. 2. 1633. F°. 4623
The pathway to Canaan. 1609. 4°. 7440
Atye (Henry). Verses in Camb. Univ. Epicedium. 1612. 4°. . 5665
Auchmoty (John). [Letters Patent to Sir A. Aston &c.] 1606. 4°. . 2595
Audiguier (Vital d'). Lisander and Calista. 1635. F°. . . . 4983
Audoenus (Joannes). *See* Owen (J.).
Aufield (G.), *King's Coll.* Verses in Camb. Univ. Lacrymae. 1619. . 5689
Augsburg Confession. Confessyon of the faythe of the Garmaynes... the Apologie of Melancthon. Trans. R. Taverner. [1535.] 8°. 386
The Confessyon... [Pt. 2 only. Another edition.] *See* Melanchthon (P.). The Apologie. 1536.
See Zwingli (U.). The rekening. 1543. 6106
Augur (Nicholas). Verses in Comenius. Porta linguarum. 1631 *etc.* 4434 *etc.*
Augustinus. Confessions. Trans. W. Watts. 1631. 12°. . . . 4883
— Ed. 2. Paris, 1638. 12°. 6204
Certaine godly Meditations. (Prayers.) *See* Becon (T.). The Pomaunder of Prayer. [1553?] *etc.*
Certaine selecte prayers...Meditations (Manuell). J. Day. 1577. 8°. 845
A pretiovs booke of heavenlie meditations, called A priuate talke. 1581. 12°. 1423
Certaine select prayers...Meditations. (Manuell.) 1586. 8°. . 1938
A right christian treatise...praiers...by T. Rogers...Psalter. Yardley & Short. 1591. 12°. 7384
A precious booke of heavenly meditations, called A priuate talk of the soule with God. Trans. T. Rogers. (Prayers—Psalter—Manuall.) 1629. 12°. 3300, 7831

No.

Augustinus *cont.* Meditations, soliloquia, and manuall. Paris, 1631. 12°. 6202
[Manual.] *See supra*, Certaine Select Prayers.
[Meditations.] *See supra*, Certaine Select Prayers.
Of the Citie of God: with comm. J. L. Vives. Trans. J. H. 1610. F°. 3572
— 1620. F°. 3593
— (Selection.) *See* Gregorius I. The dialogues. 1608. 12°.
A worke of the predestination of saints (Of...perseuerance). Trans. N. Lesse. [1550.] 8°. 772
Two bookes..of the Predestination of saintes...of perseverance. Trans. J. Scory. [Ab. 1556.] 8°. 6728
[De hæresibus.] *See* Vicentius Lirinensis. Peregrini adversus prophanas hæreses. 1631.
[De reddendis decimis. (*Eng.*)] *See* Spelman (Sir H.). De non temerandis Ecclesiæ. 1613 *etc.*
Psalter. *See ante*, 'A Right Christian Treatise.' 1591. 12°.
Sermo de misericordia et de oracione pro defunctis. *See* Rolle (Ric.). Explanationes. [1483.]
Saint Austins religion...Summes; in answer to Mr John Breerely. (By W. Crompton.) 1625. 4°. 4085
[Of Faith and Works.] *See* Treatise of Iustification. 1569.
See Crompe (J.). Collections ovt of S. Augustine...upon the... Apostles' Creed. [1638–9.]
Augustinus of Abingdon. *See* Austin.
Augustus, or, an Essay. 1632. 12°. 4203
'Αυλωνόσιτος (Ιοαννης). Verses in Adamson (J.) Εισόδια. 1618. . 5960
Aunby (George). Verses in Camb. Univ. Lacrymæ. 1619. 4°. . 5689
Aungell (John). *See* Angel.
Aungervile (Ricardus d'), *bp. of Durham.* *See* Bury (Richard de).
Aurelio and Isabella. *See* Flores (J. de). Histoire. 1556 *etc.* 8°. 7803 *etc.*
Aurelius (Abrahamus). In nuptias...Friderici V. comitis Palatini. 1613. 4°. 3091
See Texeda (F. de). Texeda Retextus. 1623.
Aurelius Antoninus (Marcus). *See* Antoninus (Marcus Aurelius).
Aurifaber (Joannes). *See* Jonas (J.). The true hystorye. [1546?] 8°.
Ausonius. Selection (Trans.). *See* Beaumont (Sir J.). Bosworth field. 1629.
Austin (St), of Abingdon. *See* Edmond Rich.
Austin (Anne). *See* Austin (W.). Devotionis...flamma. 1635 *etc.*
Austin (William). Devotionis Augustinianae flamma. 1635. F°. . 4725
— Ed. 2. 1637. F°. 4734
Hæc homo. 1638. 12°. 5132
Verses in Coryate (T.). Coryates Crvdities. 1611. 4°. . 3076
— Ravenscroft (T.). A briefe discourse. 1614. 4°. . . 2029
Austine (Rob.), *K.C.C.* Verses *bis* in Camb. Univ. Lacrymæ. 1619. 4°. 5689
— Dolor. 1625. 5701
— — Epithalam. 1625. 5702
[License 1633.] *See* Preston (J.). Remaines. 1637.
Austria, *House of.* *See* Bohemica Jura defensa. 1620. . . 7515
Austria. Albertus (and Isabella Clara Eugenia), *Archduke and Archduchess.* *See* Articles... 1605. 2590
Austria. Ferdinand, archduke of. *See* Bohemica Jura defensa. 1620. 7515
Austria. Isabella Clara Eugenia, Infanta of Spain, *Archduchess.* *See* Boyscot (F., baron of). 1623.
Austria, *Wars in.* *See* W. (S.). The appollogie of the Earl of Mansfield. 1622. 4°. 6936
Avenar (J.). The Enimie of Securitie. 1580. 12°. 1417
— 1600(-3). 12°. 2336
Avianus. *See* Æsop. Æsopi Phrygis Fabulæ. 1635.
[Fables (Eng.).] *See* Æsop. The fables. [1560?] 8°.

No.

Avicenna. *See* Braunschweig (H.). The noble experyence. 1525.
See Herbal. 1561.
— Petrus *Hispanus*. The treasury. [1550.] 8°.
— Prognostication. 153–.
Avila (Juan de). The audi filia. Trans. L. T. 1620. 4°. . . 6539
Avila y Zuñiga (L. de). The comentaries of...the wars in Germany. 1555. 8°. 1108
Avity (P. d'). The estates, empires, and principallities of the world. 1615. F°. 2446
Awcon [*i.e.* Aachen]. *See* Aix.
Awdelay or Awdeley (John), *alias* Sampson (John) *or* Awdelay (Sampson). *See* Fulke (W.). A comfortable Sermon... [1574?]
Aylesbury (Thomas). The Passion Sermon at Pauls-crosse...7 Aprill 1626. 1626. 4°. 4413
Sermon 2 June 1622. 1623. 4°. 3600
Aylmer (J.). An harborowe for faithfull...agaynst the...Wemen. 'Strasborowe.' 1559. 4°. 7117
See Broughton (H.). Letters... [1591?]
— Collection of certaine sclavnderous Articles... 1590.
Aymon. The four sons of Aymon. Caxton. [1489?] F°. . . 32
— W. de Worde. 1504. F°. 146
— W. Copland, for T. Petit. 1554. F°. 1080
Ayschecum (Robert). qu. Ashcombe? *See* Lyndewood (W.). Constitutiones. 1504.
Ayscu (Edward). A historie contayning the warres...between England and Scotland. 1607. 4°. 3563
Ayton (Sir Robert). Verses in Fisher (A.). A defence. 1630. . 3176
Azores. *See* Terceira, *Island of.*
Azpilcueta (Martino de), *the 'casuist Navarre.'* *See* Hall (J.). The peace of Rome. 1609. 4°.
B. (A.). The life...of S. Thomas archbishope of Canterbury. Coloniae, 1639. 8°. 6337
Verses in Camb. Univ. Epicedium. 1612. 5665–6
— Holland (H.). Herωologia. 1620. 6642
See Bellarmino (R.). Of the seaven words. 1638. 12°.
— Camus (J. P.). The spiritvall director. 1633. 12°.
— [*i.e.* Bacon (A.).] *See* Jewel (J.). An apologie. 1564.
— Lessius (L.). Rawleigh his ghost. 1631. 8°.
— Musket (G.). The Bishop of London... 1623.
— Stoughton (J.). XIII. Sermons. 1640.
— — XV. Choice sermons. 1640.
— T. (W.). Vindiciæ... 1630.
— [=Lord Essex?] *See* Tacitus. The end of Nero. 1591 *etc.*
B. (A.), *A.P.* Verses in Camb. Univ. Gratulatio. 1623. 4°. . . 5695
B. (A.), *C.C.C.* Verses in Wadsworth (J.). Further Obss. 1630. 4°. 7788
B. (B.). The life of...S. Patricke...Bridgit...Columbe. St Omers. 1625. 4°. 6553
See Barnaby Barnes. 1598.
B. (A. D.). *See* James I. The court. 1619. 4°.
B. (C.). Verses in King (E.). Ivsta. 1638. 4°. 5829
— Overbury (Sir T.), His Wife. Ed. II. 1622. 8°. . . 3380
— Stubbes (P.). The anatomie of abuses. 1585. 8°. . . 1446
See Barksdale (C.). Monumenta litteraria... 1640.
— Turberville (G.). The Noble Arte. 1575.
B. (D.). [=Daniel Buck.] *See* Jacob (H.). A defence. 1599.
B. (E.). Sermon...at Pauls crosse on Trinity Sunday. 1571. 1576. 8°. 7232
See True Discourse. A true Discourse... 1588.
— Bolton (E.). The elements of armories. 1610.
— Burton (E.). 1623.
B. (E.), *C.T.* Verses *bis* in Camb. Univ. Gratulatio. 1623. 4°. . 5695

No.

B. (E. M.) [*i.e.* E. Bolton]. *See* Florus. The Roman Histories. [1618] *etc.*
B. (F.). Verses in Canini (A.). Ἑλληνισμος. 1624. 8°. . . 3150
See Imitatio Christi. 1620 *etc.*
— Shakspeare (W.). Poems. 1640. 8°.
B. (F.), *C.T.* Verses in Camb. Univ. Gratulatio. 1623. . . 5695
B. (G.). Verses in Adamson (J.). Εισόδια. 1618. . . . 5960
— Wadsworth (J.). Further Obss. 1630. 7788
See Buchanan (G.). Ane detectioun. [1572?] 8°.
B. (G.), *Cantabridg.* Verses in Du Bartas. Weekes. 1605–6 *etc.* 4°. 2476
— Greene (R.). Ciceronis Amor. 1605. 1792
B. (G.), *C. Regal.* Verses in Camb. Univ. Gratulatio. 1623. . 5695
B. (H.). A verie profitable sermon...before her majestie. 4°. . 7330
See Bull (H.). Christian Prayers. 1584.
[=Bullinger (H.).] *See* Treatise. A Treatise of the Cohabitacyon of the Faithfull. 1555.
[=Burton (H.).] *See* Butterfield (R.). Maschil. 1629.
[Qu. Billingsley?] *See* Martyr (P.). Most learned...Commentaries ...vpon...Romanes. 1568.
Verses in Davies (R.). A Funerall Sermon. 1577. 4°. . . 1416
— Spenser (E.). The faerie queen. 1590 *etc.* . . . 1960 *etc.*
— Chaucer (G.). The Workes. 1598 *etc.* F°. . . . 2423
— Whitaker (W.). Praelectiones. 1599. . . . 5598
— Camb. Univ. Thr-thr. 1603. 5616
— Allestree (R.). A new almanack. 1637. 8°. . . 4648
— Allestree (R.). Allestree. 1640. 8°. 4672
B. (H.), *Rector of S. Matthew's, Friday Street.* *See* Burton (H.). 1628.
B. (I.) [=Brinsley (J.)]. *See* Cicero. The first Book of Tullies Offices. 1616.
[=John Barnes?] *See* Du Moulin (P.). Father Cotton... 1615.
Verses in Gascoigne (G.). The Posies. 1575. 4°. . . 1482
— Camb. Univ. Thr-thr. 1603. 4°. 5616
— Breton (N.). Characters. 1615. 8°. 3902
See Du Moulin (P.). The waters of Siloe. 1612. 8°.
— Fortresse of Fathers... 1566.
— Hieron (S.). The Sermons. 1620 *etc.*
— — The workes. [1624–5.] F°.
B. (I.), *A.C.* *See* Sutcliffe (M.). De presbyterio. 1591.
B. (I.), *D.D.* A sermon...at the funerall of...Henrie earle of Kent. 1615. 4°. 3105
B. (I. de). Verses in Gascoigne (G.). The Posies. 1575. 4°. . 1482
B. (J.). Verses in Welby (H.). The Phœnix. 1637. 4°. . . 3713
— King (E.). Ivsta. 1638. 4°. 5829
[*i.e.* J. Bale? *or* J. Bradford?] *See* Brief. A Bryfe and faythfull declaration. 1547.
See Paris. Sorbonne. The copie of a late decree. 1610.
— Hieron (S.). The Spirituall Fishing. 1618.
B. (J.), *D.D., Chaplain to his Majesty.* A sermon preached at Mapple-Durham. 1616. 4°. 3414
B. (L.). The answere. *See* Coloma (C.). The Attestation. 1631. 8°.
A Pastorall Æglogue vpon...Sir Philip Sidney... *See* Spenser (E.). The faerie queen. 1611.
B. (M.). Verses in Comenius. Porta linguarum. 1631. 8°. . 4435
B. (Mist.). Newes. *See* Overbury (Sir T.). His Wife. 1638.
B. (N.). Verses in Warre (James). The tovch-stone. 1621 *etc.* 4503 *etc.*
B. (N.), *Gent.* *See* Breton (N.).
B. (O.). Verses in Barlow (W.). Vita R. Cosin. 1598. . . 1707
B. (P.). Verses in Gascoigne (G.). The Posies. 1575. 4°. . 1482
B. (P.), *of the Middle Temple.* Verses in Overbury (Sir T.). His Wife. Ed. II. 1622. 8°. 3380

No.

B. (P. D.) [=P. de Belligent]. *See* Camden (W.). Annales. 1625.
B. (R.). A Watchword for Wilfull Women. 1581. 8°. . . 1231
Verses in Breton (N.). Characters. 1615. 8°. 3902
— Bullein (W.). The Gouernment of Health. 1595. 8°. . 2841
— Camb. Univ. Thr-thr. 1603. 5616
— Camdeni Insignia. 1624. 5346
— Verstegan (R.). A restitution. 1605 *etc.* . . 6140 *etc.*
— Warre (James). The tovch-stone. 1630. . . . 4546
See Buenting (H.). Itinerarivm. 1619 *etc.* . . 7821 *etc.*
— Davies (R.). A Funerall Sermon... 1577.
See Gerhard (J.). The Soules Watch. 1621. 12°.
— Parsons (R.). The first part of the resolution of religion. 1603. 8°.
— Pettie (G.). A petite Pallace. [1576.] 4°.
B. (R.), *Esq.* The difference betwene the auncient Phisicke...and the latter Phisicke. 1585. 8°. 1859
[Qu. R. Brathwaite?] *See* France. An Epitome. 1639. . . 7754
B. (R.), *of Lincolnes Inne, Esq.* *See* Beling (R.).
B. (R.), *Pastor to Ashele, in Norfolk.* *See* James I. [Declaration.] A remonstrance... (Translated by R. B.) 1616 *etc.*
B. (R.), *Chaplain to Abp Laud.* *See* White (F.), *bp.* A replie. 1624.
B. (R.), *St John's, Taxor.* *See* Buckley (R.).
B. (R.), *Cantabrigiæ.* Verses in Mercator (G.). Historia. 1635. F°. 4637
B. (R.), *S. Hosp.* Verses in Mercator (G.). Historia. 1635. F°. . 4637
B. (R.), *S.S.M.* Verses in Mercator (G.). Historia. 1635. F°. . 4637
B. (R.) and R. A. Davids musick. 1616. 4°. 2994
B. (R. A.) [=R. Anthony Batt]. *See* Fisher (J.). A treatise of prayer. 1640.
B. (S.). *See* Bredwell (S.). The rasing of the fovndations... 1588.
— Dissertatio brevis. 1626. 6970
— An excellent and materiall discourse. 6971
B. (S. I. B.). Verses in Gray (T. de). The compleat horseman. 1639. F°. 4042
B. (T.). Verses in Gascoigne (G.). The Posies. 1575. 4°. . . 1482
See Broke (T.). Certeyn Meditations. 1548. 8°.
— Bedford (T.). A Treatise. 1580. 1630
— Camus (J. P.). Admirable events. 1639.
— Du Jon (F.), *the elder.* The Apocalyps... 1596.
— [=T. Ball.] *See* Preston (J.), *D.D.* Sermons. 1630 *etc.*
See Segar (Sir William). Honor Military... 1602.
B. (T.), *A.P.* Verses *bis* in Camb. Univ. Gratulatio. 1623. 4°. . 5695
B. (T.), *C.* [*Qu.* Bowes or Beard?] *See* La Primaudaye (P. de). The french academie. 1589.
B. (T.), *fellow of Magdalen College, Oxford.* *See* Brasbridge (T.). Abdias. 1574.
B. (T.), *Regal.* Verses in Camb. Univ. Gratulatio. 1623. . 5695
B. (W.). *See* Eight learned personages. 1601. 4°.
— Eunapius. The Lyves of Philosophers... 1579.
— Free Schoole of Warre. 1625.
— Michaelis (S.). The admirable historie... 1613.
— Ortelius (A.). Theatrum. 1606.
— Ussher (J.). An answer. 1624 *etc.* . . . . 6027 *etc.*
[=W. Bishop, bp of Chalcedon.] *See* Wotton (A.). A defence. 1606.
Verses in Dodonæus (R.). A niewe herball. 1578 *etc.* F°. . 6130
— Massinger (P.). The Bond-man. 1638. 5150
— — The dvke of Millaine. 1638. 5151
— Roberts (L.). The merchants mappe. 1638. . . . 5133
[=W. Basse.] *See* Shakspeare (W.). Poems. 1640. . . 4681
B. (W.), *Priest.* *See* Anderton (L.). One God, One Fayth. 1625. 8°.

No.

B. (W.), *Inner Temple*. Verses in Overbury (Sir T.). His Wife. Ed. II. 1622. 3380
Babington (Anthony). *See* Kempe (W.). A dvtifvll invective. 1587. 4°.
— Whetstone (G.). The censure. 1587.
Babington (Gervase). Works. 1637. F°. 4306
Briefe conference betwixt mans frailty and faith. 1602. 8°. . 7299
Profitable exposition of the Lords Prayer. 1588. 8°. . . 2199
See Certaine Considerations... 1605.
— Certaine demandes. 1605.
Babington (H.), *B.A.*, *T.C.C.* Verses in Camb. Univ. Voces. 1640. 5836
Babington (John). Pyrotechnia. 1635. F°. 4011
Bachcroft (Tho.). [Licence.] *See* Du Praissac. The art of warre. 1639.
Bacher (John). *See* Baker.
Bacon (Lady Anne). *See* Jewel (J.). An Apologie. 1564.
— Ochino (B.). Certayne Sermons. [1550?]
Bacon (Francis). Opera. Tom. I. (De ... augmentis scientiarum.) 1623. F°. 4769
Operum moralium et civilium tomus. Cura G. Rawley. 1638. F°. 5186
— Adj. libri duo instaurationis magnae. 1638. F°. . . . 5187
Certaine Miscellany Works. Ed. W. Rawley. 1629. 4°. . 4820
Apophthegmes new and old. 1625. 8°. 3741
Certaine considerations touching...the Church of England. [1604?] 4°. 3221
— 1640. 4°. 7578
— 1640. 4°. 7618
Charge...touching duells. 1614. 4°. 3581
Considerations touching a warre with Spaine. 1629. 4°. . 6989
[De dignitate & augmentis scientiarum.] *See above* Opera. 1623.
De sapientia veterum. 1609. 12°. 2614
— 1617. 12°. 3474
— Ed. 4. 1634. 12°. 3049
— Wisedome of the ancients. Trans. Sir A. Gorges. 1622. 12°. 3503
Declaration of the practices and treasons by Roberte late Earle of Essex. 1601. 4°. 2572–3
Elements of the common lawes of England. 2 Parts. 1636–5. 4°. 5079
— 1639. 4°. 5083
Essayes. (Meditationes sacrae.) J. Windet for H. Hooper. 1597. 8°. 2142
— J. Windet for H. Hooper. 1598. 12°. 2147
— [W. Jaggard] for J. Jaggard. 1606. 8°. 2763
— [W. Jaggard] for J. Jaggard. 1612. 8°. 2776
— J. Beale. 1612. 8°. 3778
— For J. Jaggard. 1613. 8°. 2760
— [W. Jaggard] for J. Jaggard. 1613. 8°. 2779
— A. Hart, Edinburgh. 1614. 8°. 5951
— J. Dawson for E. Jaggard. 1623. 8°. 3857
— J. Haviland for H. Barret. 1625. 4°. 4795
— J. Haviland for H. Barret and R. Whitaker. 1625. 4°. . 4796
— J. Haviland for R. Allot. 1629. 4°. 4821
— J. Haviland. 1632. 4°. 4843
— J. Beale. 1639. 4°. 3837
— Saggi morali...con vn' altro suo trattato Della sapienza degli antichi. J. Bill. 1618. 8°. 3485
Historia vitae & mortis... J. Haviland, imp. M. Lownes. 1623. 8°. 4770
Historie of life and death. J. Okes for H. Mosley. 1638. 12°. . 3716
— J. Haviland for W. Lee and H. Mosley. 1638. 12°. . 4864
Historie of the raigne of King Henry the Seventh. 1622. F°. . 3139
— 1629. F°. 4822
Instauratio magna. J. Bill. 1620. F°. 3497
Of the proficience and aduancement of Learning. 1605. 4°. . 3220
— 1629. 4°. 5071
— Oxford. 1633. 4°. 5397

No.

Bacon (Francis) *cont.* Interpr. G. Wats. Oxford. 1640. F°. . 5497
Sylva sylvarum. Ed. W. Rawley. (New Atlantis.) J. Haviland for W. Lee. 1627. F°. 4806
— Ed. 2. J. Haviland for W. Lee. 1629(–8). F°. . . 4819
— Ed. 3. J. Haviland for W. Lee. 1631. F°. . . . 4838
— Ed. 4. J. Haviland for W. Lee and J. Williams. 1635. F°. 4855
— Ed. 5. J. Haviland for W. Lee. 1639. F°. . . 4876
Sir Francis Bacon his apologie ... concerning the late Earle of Essex. 1604. 8°. 3315
The Vse of the Law. *See* Doddridge (Sir J.). The Lawyers Light...1629.
Bacon (Nic.). Verses in Camb. Univ. Carmen. 1635. 4°. . 5770
Bacon (Roger). De retardandis senectutis accidentibus. Oxonie. 1590. 8°. 5233
Baddeley (Richard). *See* Camerarius (P.). The Living Librarie. 1621 *etc.* *See also* Badley.
Bade (Josse), *Ascensius.* *See* Expositio hymnorum. 1510.
— Lyndwood (W.). Provinciale. 1501 *etc.*
— — Constitutiones. 1504 *etc.*
— Mantuanus (B.). Adolescentia. 1569 *etc.*
— Terentius. Comedie. 1504.
— Whittington (R.). Grammatica. 199
Baden (Giles), *C.C.C.* Verses in Camb. Univ. Lacrymae. 1619. 4°. 5689
— — Dolor. 1625. 5701
— — Epithalam. 1625. 5702
Badius (Jodocus), *Ascensius.* *See* Bade.
Badley (Richard). Verses in Coryate (T.). Coryates Crvdities. 1611. 4°. 3076
See also Baddeley.
Baffin (William). *See* Fox (L.). Northwest Fox. 1635.
Bagshaw (Christopher). *See* Ely (H.). Certaine briefe notes... [1603.]
— Featley (D.). Transubstantiation. 1638.
Bagshaw (Edward), *the elder.* *See* Bolton (R.). Mr Boltons last... Things... 1635.
— — A short...Discourse... 1637.
— — Two sermons. 1635.
Baibridge (J.). Verses in Holyoake (F.). Dictionarium. 1640. 4°. 3058
See also Bainbridge.
Bailey (Walter). A work...of the sight. *See* Guillemeau (J.). A worthy treatise. [159–.] 12°.
Briefe treatise concerning...Eye-sight. *See* Vaughan (Sir W.). Directions for health. Ed. 6. 1626 *etc.*
Bailey. *See* Bayly.
Bailius (T.). *Qu.* T. Bayly, *D.D.*? *See* Theophylactus. Comm. 1636. F°. 7649
Baillie (Alex.). A true information of the unhallowed offspring. Würzburg. 1628. 8°. 6658
Baillie (James). Spiritual marriage...sermon. 1 Jan. 1626. 1627. 4°. 4190
Baillie (Robert). Ladensium αὐτοκατάκρισις. 1640. 4°. . . 6373
Bainbridge (John), *M.D.* An astronomicall description of the late Comet. 1619. 4°. 3930
See Hakewill (G.). An apologie. 1630.
— Parkinson (J.). Theatrum. 1640. F°.
— Proclus. Σφαῖρα. 1620.
Verses in Camdeni Insignia. 1624. 5346
— Hippocrates. 1633. 5812
See also Baibridge.
Bainbrigg (Ch.). Verses in King (E.). Ivsta. 1638. 4°. . . 5829
Bainbrigg (Thomas). *See* Hippocrates. 1633.
[Imprimatur.] Davenant (J.). Determinationes. 1639.
Baines (Thomas), *Christ's.* Verses in Camb. Univ. Voces. 1640. . 5836
Baites (I.). Verses in Cambridge Lachrymae. 1587. . . 7356
Baker (G.). The Composition or making of...Oil... [1574.] 8°. . 1286
The nature...of Quicksilver. *See* Clowes (W.). A profitable...booke. 1637.

No.

Baker (G.) *cont.* *See* Cauliaco (G. de). Guydos Questions. 1579.
— Gerard (J.). The herball. 1597. F°.
— Gesner (C.). The newe Iewell of Health. 1576.
— Vigo (J. de). The whole worke. 1586.
Baker (Humphry). The wel spring of sciences. Ed. 4. 1591. 8°. . 1377
— 1631. 8°. 4147
Baker (Sir J.). Verses in Cheke (Sir J.). De obitu M. Buceri. 1551. 734
Baker (John). Lectures vpon the twelue Articles of our Christian Faith. 1613. 8°. 3646
Baker (Sir Ric.). Meditations & disquisitions upon Ps. i. 1638. 4°. 5188
— — 1640. 4°. 5207
— — Ps. li. 1638. 4°. 5189
— — Seven consolatorie psalmes. 1640. 4°. 5179
— — Penitentiall Psalmes. 1640. 4°. 5180
— — Lords Prayer. Ed. 4. 1640. 4°. 5096
See Balzac. New Epistles. 1638. 8°.
— Cato (D.). Cato variegatus. 1636. 4°.
Baker (Rob.). Verses in Camb. Univ. Carmen. 1635. . . . 5770
Baker (Sa.). [Licenses.] *See* Mason (H.). Hearing. 1635.
— — Sparrow (Ant.). A sermon. 1637.
Baker (Tho.), *King's*. Verses in Camb. Univ. Epicedium. 1612. . 5665
Baker (Tho.), *John's*. Notes in A. Maunsell. . . . 7843–4
Baker (William). Verses in Coryate (T.). Coryates Crvdities. 1611. 3076
— Selden (J.). Jani. 1610. 3389
Baker (William), *notary public*. *See* King (H.). Sermon. 1621.
Balbani (N.). The Italian convert...life of G. Caracciolus. Eng. by W. C. 1635. 4°. 3953
Newes from italy...life of G. Caracciolus... Trans. from Beza by W. Crashaw. 1608. 4°. 7463
Balbus (J.). Catholicon. *See* no. 195 and p. 1729.
Balcanquall (Robert). Verses in Adamson (J.). Εἰσόδια. 1618. . 5960
Balcanquall (S.). Verses in Camb. Univ. Genethl. 1631. 4°. . 5731
— Fasciæ. 1633. 5808
— Carmen. 1635. 5770
— Συνῳδία. 1637. 5790
Balcanquall (W.), *Pemb. Coll. Camb.* Verses in Camb. Univ. Epicedium. 1612. 5665
Balcanquhall (Walter), *Dean of Durham*. The honour of christian churches. 1633. 4°. 4443
See Carleton (G.). An examination... 1626.
— Charles I. A large declaration. 1639. F°.
— Dort Synod. A ioynt attestation. 1626. 4°.
— — Suffragium. 1626 *etc.*
Balduck [*i.e.* Bois-le-duc]. *See* Hertogenbosch, 's.
Balduinus, *Archbishop of Canterbury*. De uenerabili...altaris sacramento. Cantabrigiae. 1521. 4°. 5503
Itinerarivm Cambriæ. *See* Ponticus (L.), libri sex. 1585.
Baldwin (Justinian). Verses in Rogers (T.). A philosophicall discourse. 1576. 8°. 1348
Baldwin (William). Treatise of Morall Phylosophye. 1 Feb. 1550. 8°. 667
— T. Palfreyman. Ed. 3. R. Tottill. 1 July 1567. 8°. . 7182
— 'Ed. 3.' R. Tottell. 1575. 8°. 1129
— [Ab. 1580.] 8°. 6766
— R. Robinson. 1587. 8°. 2184
— Ed. 4. 1591. 8°. 1599
— 'Ed. 4.' T. East. 1596. 8°. 1605
— Ed. 6. T. Snodham. [Ab. 1620.] 8°. 7527
— *See* Eunapius, no. 1444 (appendix). p. 1733.
— Higgins (J.). A mirrour. 1610.
Bale (J.). The Actes of Englyshe votaryes. 'Wesel.' 1546. 8°. 947

No.
Bale (J.) *cont.* The Actes...T. Raynalde. 1548. 8°. . . . 694
— A. Veale. 1551. 8°. 1068
— J. Tysdale. 1560. 8°. 1255
Brefe Chronycle concerning...Sir J. Oldecastell... [1548?] 8°. . 1038
Declaration of E. Bonners articles. 1561. 8°. . . . 1258
Epistle exhortatorye of an Englyshe Christyane...Henry Stalbrydge. [Ab. 154–.] 8°. 6694
Epistel Exhortatorye of an Inglyshe Chrystian...by H. Stalbrydge. [1548.] 8°. 1039
Expostulation...agaynste...a franticke papyst of Hamshyre. 8°. . 7134
First examinacyon of...Anne Askewe. 'Marpurg, Novembre, 1546.' 8°. 6331
Illustrium maioris Britanniæ. 'Per T. Plateanum: Gippeswici, J. Overton,' 1548. 4°. 6314, 6315
Image of both Churches. R. Jugge. [1548?] 8°. . . . 974
— Day and Seres. [1549?] 8°. 910
— J. Wyer. 1550. 4°. 1101
— Vol. I. only. [Ab. 1550?] 16°. 7137
— T. East. [1570?] 8°. 1567
Lattre examinacyon of Anne Askewe. 'Marpurg, 16 Jan. 1547.' 8°. 6332
Mysterye of inyquyte...of Ponce Pantolabus. 'Geneva M. Wood.' 1545. 8°. 6693
Pageant of Popes. 1574. 4°. 1223
Vocacyon of J. Bale. 'Rome. S. Angell.' 1553. 8°. . . 1049
Yet a course at the Romyshe foxe. 'O. Jacobson, Zurich,' 1543. 8°. 6304
See Admonition to the Bishoppes. 1553.
— Brief. A Bryfe and faythfull declaration. 1547.
— Jonas (J.). The true hystorye of...Luther. [1546?] 8°.
— Lambert (J.). A treatyse. [Ab. 1549?] 8°.
— Margaret of Angoulême. A Godly Medytacyon. 1548.
Bales (P.). The writing schoolemaster. 1590. 4°. 2205
Ball (John). A friendly triall. Cambridge. 1640. 4°. . . 5835
A short treatise...of Christian Religion. Ed. 9. 1633. 8°. . 3190
— Ed. 11. 1637. 8°. 5107
A treatise of faith. Ed. 3. 1637. 4°. 4992
Ball (Ro.). The mirror of pure devotion. 1635. 12°. . . 7623
Ball (Thomas). *See* Preston (J.). The doctrine of the saints infirmities. 1637. 12°.
— — The golden Scepter &c. 1638. 4°.
— — Life eternall. 1631 *etc.* 4°.
— — Sermons. 1630 *etc.*
Ballad. 1602. *See* Proper new Ballad.
Ballard (John). *See* Kempe (W.). A dvtifvll invective. 1587. 4°.
Ballendinus (Gualt.). Verses in Person (D.). Varieties. 1635. . 4365
See also Ballentinus, Bannatinus.
Ballentinus (Gualterus). Verses in Adamson (J.). Εἰσόδια. 1618. . 5960
See also Ballendinus, Bannatinus.
— Spence (R.). Illustrissimi ducis διαγραφή. 1628? 4°. . 6995
Balliolus (Jacobus). Verses in Barclay (W.). Iudicium. 1620. . 3594
Ballowe (Tho.). Verses in Camdeni Insignia. 1624. . . 5346
Balmford (James). *See* Gataker (T.). A ivst defence. 1623.
Balzac (Jean Louis Guez, Sieur de). Letters. Trans. W. Tirwhyt. 1634. 4°. 3694
New Epistles. Trans. Sir R. Baker. Vols. 2 & 3. 1638. 8°. 4658
Collection of some modern epistles. Vol. 4. Oxford. 1639. 8°. 5486
See Du Moulin (P.). A wittie encounter. 1636.
Bamberg, Bishop of. *See* Briefe relation. 1599. . . . 1979
Banastre (Laurence), *Clar.* Verses in Camb. Univ. Epithalam. 1625. 5702
Banckes (William). Verses in Camb. Univ. Lacrymae. 1619. . 5689
Bancroft (Richard). Davngerous positions and proceedings. 1593. 4°. 1967
— 1640. 4°. 5021

No.

Bancroft (Richard) *cont.* Sermon. 9 Feb. 1588. 1588. 8°. . 2099
— — 1636. 4°. 4901
— — *See* Informations... 1608.
Survay of the pretended holy discipline. 1593. 4°. . . 1968
See Blackwell (G.). A large examination... 1607.
— Briefe Discovery of the vntruthes... [1590?]
— Certaine demandes... 1605.
— Davidson (I.). D. Bancrofts rashnes... 1590.
— Articles. London Diocese. 1601.
— Rainolds (J.). Svmma colloqvii. 1610.
Bandello. [Fables.] *See* Gascoigne (G.). The Posies. 1575.
See Markham (G.). The dvmbe Knight. 1633.
Banister (John). The workes. 1633. 4°. 4000
A compendiovs chyrurgerie. 1585. 12°. 2113
A needefull...treatise of Chyrurgerie. 1575. 8°. 1224
[Printed label on casket. Ab. 1591.] 8°. . . . 7772
Verses in Baker (G.). The Composition of Oil. [1574.] . . 1286
Banister (Richard). *See* Guillemeau (Jacques). A treatise of...the Eyes. 1622. 12°.
Bankes (Tho.). A verie godly...sermon against...Malignitie. 1586. 8°. 1939
Bannatinus (Walter). Verses in Adamson (J.). Ἐισόδια. 1618. . 5960
See also Ballendinus, Ballentinus.
Banning (R.). Verses in Cambridge Lachrymae. 1587. . . . 7356
Banquet of Jests. Ed. 6. 1640. 12°. 5087
Baptista Mantuanus. *See* Mantuanus.
Barbar (Thomas). *See* Du Jon (F.). The Apocalyps. 1596.
Barbier (J.). Janua linguarum quadrilinguis. 1617. 4°. . . 2282
See Saul (A.). The famovs game of Chesse-play... 1640.
Barcham (John). *See* Guillim (J.). A display of Heraldrie... 1611 (1610).
Barchby (John). Grammatica Latina. R. Pynson. 1516. 4°. 7751. Cf. 221
Barckley (Sir Ric.). A discourse of the felicitie of man. 1598. 4°. . 2247
— 1603. 4°. 1868
— 1631. 4°. 4974
Barclay (Alex.). [Egloges. Ab. 153– .] 4°. 6675
See Brandt (S.). The Shyp of Fools. (Lat. and Eng.) 1509. F°. 257
— — 1570. F°. 999
— Durantinus (C. F.). The Conspiracie of Catiline... 1557.
— Gringore (P.). The castell of laboure. 1506.
— Pius II. [Ecloges i—iii.] [1548?]
— Sallustius. Iugurth. [1520?] *etc.*
Barclay (John). Poematum libri duo. 1615. 4°. 3901
— Oxonii. 1636. 12°. 7665
Argenis. (Lat.) Ed. 2. [Frankfurt?] 1622. 8°. 3286
— (Trans. K. Long.) 1625. F°. 4086
— — Ed. 2. 1636. 4°. 4117
— (Trans. Sir R. Le Grys.) 1628. 4°. 3034
— — 1629. 4°. 3039
— Euphormionis Lusinini...partes quinqȝ. Oxoniae. 1634. 12°. 5406
Mirrour of mindes. Trans. T. May. 1631. 12°. 4884
Barclay (William). De potestate papae. 1609. 8°. 6877
— Of the authoritie of the pope. 1611. 4°. 2090
— *See* Buckeridge (J.). De potestate. 1614.
— Sheldon (R.). Certain general reasons... 1611.
Iudicium de certamine G. Eglisemmii cum G. Buchanano... Psalmi CIIII. 1620. 8°. 3594
Bard (George). *See* Philips (E.). Certain...sermons. 1605. 4°.
Bard (Hen.), *K.C.* Verses in Cam. Univ. Rex redux. 1633. 4°. . 5748
— Συνωδία. 1637. 4°. 5790
Bardi (Girolamo). *See* Mexia (P.). The historie. 1604.

No.
Baret (John). Alvearie or triple dictionarie. [1573.] F°. . . . 7249
Alvearie or Quadruple Dictionarie. [1580.] F°. . . 1418
Barfeldus (L.). Verses in Holyoake (F.). Dictionarium. 1640. 4°. 3058
Bargrave (Isaac). A sermon against selfe policy. 1621. 1624. 4°. 3688
Sermon...before...the lower House of Parliament February the last, 1623. 1624. 4°. 3858
Sermon preached...March 27. 1627. 1627. 4°. 4703
Barkby (John). *See* Barchby.
Barker (Ant.), *T.C.* Verses in Camb. Univ. Voces. 1640. . . 5836
Barker (Christopher), *Regal.* Verses in Camb. Univ. Voces. 1640. . 5836
Barker (John). [Funeral.] *See* Gataker (T.). The decease of Lazarus. 1640. 4°.
Barker (L.). Verses in Cambridge Lachrymae. 1587. 4°. . . . 7356
Barker (T.). *See* D. (T.). The bloody banquet. 16– .
Barker (William). *See* Gelli (G. B.). The fearefull fansies. 1599.
— Xenophon. The VIII. bookes. 1567. 8°.
Verses in Hippocrates. 1633. 8°. 5812
— Chaucer (G.). Amorum. 1635. 4°. 5414
Barkham (Ed.), *K.C.C.* Verses in Cam. Univ. Epicedium. 1612. 5665
Barkham (George). Verses in Danes (J.). Paralipomena. 1638(–9). 4741–2
Barkham (John). *See* Crakanthorp (R.). Defensio. 1625.
Barkham (T.). Verses in Speed (J.). The theatre. 1611. F°. . 3215
Barklay (John). *See* Barchby.
Barksdale (Clement). Monumenta literaria...ex historiis J. A. Thuani. 1640. 4°. 4911
Barlandus (Adrianus). *See* Æsop. Æsopi Phrygis Fabulæ... 1635.
Barlement (Noel). Colloquia et dictionariolum octo linguarum. Middelburg. 1631. obl. 8°. 6482
Barlow (Barnabas). Verses in Camb. Univ. Dolor. 1625. . . . 5701
— — Epithalam. 1625. 5702
— Genethl. 1631. 4°. 5731
— Anthologia. 1632. 4°. 5741
— Fasciae. 1633. 4°. 5808
Hippocrates. 1633. 5812
Barlow (G.), *fellow of King's.* *See* W. Barlow.
Barlow (Jerome). *See* Roy (W.). The Boke Reade me frynde & be not wrothe. 1546.
Barlow (John). The good mans priviledge. 1618. 4°. . . . 7475
The good mans refuge in affliction. 1618. 4°. 2999
The true guide to glory. 1619. 4°. 3423
Barlow (Ralph). Verses in Hill (T.). The arte of vulgar arithmeticke. 1600. 4°. 2197
Barlow (William), *Bp of Chichester.* A dialoge...of these Lutheran faccions. 1553. 8°. 987
See Bible. Eng. (Bishops')[1]. 1568. F°. 963
Barlow (Will.), *Bp of Lincoln.* Vita...R. Cosin. 1598. 4°. 1707, 7852
An answer to a catholike Englishman. 1609. 4°. . . . 3617
A brand, Titio erepta. 1607. 4°. 7361
A defence of the articles of the protestants religion. 1601. 4°. 1988
A sermon at Paules crosse. 1 Martij 1600. With a discourse of the Late Earle of Essex. 1601. 8°. 2870
The sermon. 10 Nov. 1605. 1606. 4°. 2169
The first of the foure sermons at Hampton Court. 1607. 4°. . 2173
The summe & substance of the conference at Hampton Court. 1604. 4°. 2163, 2164
— 1625. 4°. 3523
— 1638. 4°. 4903
Verses in Horne (C.). In obitum G. Whitakeri. 1596. . . 7332
See Bible. Eng. (Royal Version). 1611.

[1] 'Esdras, Judith, Tobit and Wisdom' *DNB.*

No.

Barlow (Will.) *cont.* Fitzherbert (T.). A supplement. 1613.
— — An adioynder to the supplement. 1613.
— James I. An apologie... 1609.
— Parsons (R.). A discussion of the answere of Mr William Barlow... 1612.
Barlow (William), *Archdeacon.* Magneticall Advertisements. 1616. 4°. 3906
— Ed. 2. 1618. 8°. 3923
See Ridley (M.). Magneticall Animadversions... 1617.
Barlow (William), *translator.* *See* Bohemia. Two letters. 1620.
Barlow (William), *K.C.C.* Verses in Camb. Univ. Carmen. 1635. 4°. 5770
— — Συνωδία. 1637. 4°. 5790
Barnaud (Nicolas). *See* Eusebius Philadelphus: Dialogi. 1574. . 6760
Barnes (Barnaby). The divils charter. 1607. 4°. 3564
Foure bookes of offices. 1606. F°. 2435
See Florio (G.). A worlde of wordes. 1598 *etc.* 4°. . . 2069
Barnes (John). *See* Du Moulin (P.). A conference... 1615.
— — Father Cotton. 1615.
Barnes (Juliana). *See* Berners.
Barnes (Robert). [Works.] *See* Tindale (W.). The whole workes... 1573.
[Protestation.] *See* Standish (J.). A lytle treatise. 1540.
A supplicatyon. [Ab. 153–.] 8°. 6678
The supplication of doctour Barnes. H. Singleton. [1548?] 8°. 1058
See Coverdale (M.). A confutacion. [154–.] 8°.
— More (Sir T.). The cōfutacyon of Tyndales... 1532–3.
Barnes (Robert), *of Oxford.* A sermon...at Henly...27 Aprill, 1626. Oxford. 1626. 4°. 5359
Barnes (T.). The gales of grace. 1622. 8°. 2541
The wise mans forecast. 1624. 4°. 3859
See Isocrates. Archidamus. 1624.
Barnes (W.). Verses in Barlow (W.). Vita R. Cosin. 1598. 4°. . 1707
Barnevelt (John van Olden). *See* Oldenbarneveld.
Barnwell (Thomas), *alias* Fleming, *Abp.* *See* Fleming.
Baro (P.). De fide. 1580. 8°. 1882, 1883
De præstantia & dignitate diuinae legis. [1587?] 8°. . . 1655
In Jonam Prophetam Prælectiones 39. 1579(8). F°. . . 850
A speciall treatise of Gods providence. [1588?] 8°. . . . 1952
See H. (E.), *servus Domini Iesu Christi.* De fide... 1592.
Baron (Robert). Ad G. Turnebulli Tetragonismum...apodixis. Abredoniae. 1631. 8°. 6003
Disp. theologica. Abredoniae. 1633. 8°. 6005
Philosophia theologiae ancillans. Andreapoli. 1621. 8°. . . 5997
Theses in Adamson (J.). Εἰσόδια. 1618. 5960
Baron (Stephen). Sermones (De regimine principum). W. de Worde. [15– .] 8°. 210
Baronets. His Majesties Commission...touching...Baronets. 1611. 4°. 2638
Three Patents concerning...Baronets. 1617. 4°. . . 2657
Baronius (Cæsar). *See* Cooke (A.). Pope Joane. 1610 *etc.*
— Crakanthorp (R.). Jvstinian the Emperor. 1616.
— Lydiat (T.). Emendatio. 1609.
— Mornay (P. de). The mysterie of iniquitie. 1612. F°.
— Vignier (N.). Concerning the Excommunication. 1607.
Baronius (Robert). *See* Baron.
Barrell (Ro.). Verses in Oxf. Univ. Horti. 1640. 5499
Barret (John). *See* Baret (J.).
Barret (William). A copie of a recantation... The proceedings...of the University heads of Cambridge... *See* Prynne (W.). Anti-arminianisme... [1629?] *etc.*
Ivs regis. 'Basileiæ. Ap. H. Pistum.' 1612. 8°. . . . 3641
Barri (Christophoro). Cochin-China, by R. Ashley. 1633. 4°. . 3735

No.
Barrington (John). Verses in Cam. Univ. Fasciae. 1633. . . 5808
Barrough (Philip). The method of physick. Ed. 6. 1624. 4°. . 2295
— Ed. 7. 1634. 4°. 4449
— Ed. 8. 1639. 4°. 4472
Barrow (Henry). A brief discoverie of the False Church. 1590. 4°. 6795
Examinations of H. B., J. Grenewood, and J. Penrie. [After 1593.] 4°. 7699
[Letter.] *See* Amsterdam, *English Church in.* An apologie... 1604.
See Collection of certain Letters. 1590.
— Collection of certaine sclaunderous articles. 1590. 4°.
— Gifford (G.). A short reply. 1591.
— Some (R.). A godly treatise... 1589.
Barry (Gerald). Militarie discipline. Brussels. 1634. F°. . . 6638
See Hugo (H.). The seige of Breda. 1627 (1628).
Barry (James), baron Santry. The case of tenures. Dublin. 1637. F°. 7683
Bartæus (Richard). Verses in Wilson (Sir T.). Vita. 1551. 4°. . 631
Bartello. *See* Bandello.
Barthema (Lodovico). *See* Vertomannus.
Barthlet (J.). The Pedegrewe of Heretiques. 1566. 4°. . . 1400
Bartholinus (Caspar). Anatomicae institutiones corporis humani. Oxonii. 1633. 12°. 7661
Bartholomæus Anglicus. De proprietatibus rerum. W. de Worde. [1495?] F°. 58
— Berthelet. 1535. F°. 430, 431
Batman upon Bartholome. 1582. F°. 1584
See Governal of Health.
— Herbal. 1561.
Bartholomæus Picernus *or* Pincernus. *See* Pincernus (B.).
Bartholomæus, of Pisa. *See* Francis (St.) *of Assisi.* The Alcoran... 1550 *etc.*
Barthram, *Priest.* *See* Ratramnus, *Corbiensis.*
Bartlet (John), *stationer.* *See* Manifold wisedome. 1640.
Barton (F.), *T.C.C.* Verses in Cam. Univ. Rex redux. 1633. . 5748
— Camb. Univ. Συνωδία. 1637. 4°. 5790
Barton (William). Arithmeticke Abreviated. 1634. 8°. . . 3828
Bartox (Martine). The Recantation... *See* Haren (J.). The Repentance. 1610.
Basil, *Saint.* [Of Fasting.] *See* Treatise of Justification. 1569.
Basil (Mart.). Verses in Cam. Univ. Genethl. 1631. . . . 5731
Basille (Theodore). *See* Becon (T.).
Baskerville (Sir Simon). [Licence.] *See* Jorden (E.). A discourse. 1633.
Verses in Parkinson (J.). Theatrum. 1640. F°. . . 4680
Basse (William). Verses in Shakspeare (W.). Poems. 1640. 8°. . 4681
See A helpe to discourse. Ed. 12. 1636. 12°.
Basson (Thomas). Verses in Whetstone (G.). The honovrable repvtation. 1586. 4°. 6495
Bastard (Thomas). Verses in Coryate (T.). Coryates crvdities. 1611. 4°. 3076
— Holyoake (F.). Dictionarium. 1640. 4°. 3058
Bastingius (H.). *See* Heidelberg Catechism.
Bastwick (John). The answer...to...Sir J. Banks. 1637. 4°. . 7030
Briefe relation of...the Starre-Chamber. 1637. 4°. . . 7035
Elenchus religionis papisticae. 1627. 8°. 5031
Letany. 1637. 4°. 7031
The answer...Letany pt 2. 1637. 4°. 7032
The vanity and mischeife...Letany pt 3. 1637. 4°. . . . 7033
A more full answer...Letany pt 4. 1637. 4°. 7034
See The Beast is wounded... (1638). 6366
— Laud (W.). A speech... 1637.
Bate (John). The mysteries of nature & art... Ed. 2. 1635. 4°. 4012
Bate (Mat.). Verses in Oxf. Univ. Horti. 1640. 5499

No.

Bateman (Stephen). *See* Batman.
Baterel (Guillermus). *See* Buridanus (J.). I. Bvridani...in octo libros politicorum... 1640.
Bath. The bathes of Bathes Ayde. 1572. *See* Jones (J.). A briefe... discourse. 1574.
Thermæ Bathonicæ... *See* Johnson (T.), *M.D.* Mercurius Botanicus. 1634.
See Jorden (E.). A discourse. 1633.
— Venner (T.). Via recta. 1620 *etc.*
Bathe (W.). Songs and Psalmes. [1596?] 8°. 1604
Batman (Stephen). The doome. 1581. 4°. 1314
See Bartholomeus, *Anglicus.* Batman vppon Bartholome... 1582.
— Rogers (J.). The Displaying of an horrible secte. 1578 *etc.* 8°.
Batt (Anthony). *See* Fisher (J.). A treatise of prayer. 1640.
Battles. All the famous Battels. *See* Polemon (J.). 1585?–7.
Bauderon (Price). Pharmacopœa. 1639. F°. 5200
Baudier (Michael). The history of the...Grand Seigneurs (of the Serrail). Trans. E. Grimstone. (The history of...China.) 1635. 4°. 3197
Baudius (Dominicus). Verses in L'Obel (M. de)...in G. Rondelletii... officinam. 1605. F°. 7247
Bauhinus (Caspar). *See* Crooke (H.). Μικροκοσμολογία. 1631.
Bavande (William). *See* Ferrarius (J.). A woorke. 1559.
Bavaria, Duke of. 1579. *See* Casimir (J.).
Baxius (Nicasius). *See* Buchler (J.). Sacrarum...phrasium...Thesaurus. 16[3]. 12°.
Baxter (N.). *See* Downe (J.). A treatise. 1635.
Bayley (Tho.), *Magd. Coll. Oxford.* *See* Baylie.
Baylie (Richard). *See* Du Moulin (P.). The antibarbarian. 1630. 12°.
Baylie (Thomas), *Magd. Coll. Oxon., and at Manningford.* De merito mortis Christi. Oxoniae. 1626. 4°. 5360
Verses in Oxf. Univ. Magd. Coll. 1612. 5302
Bayly (John). Two sermons. Oxford. 1630. 4°. 5380
Bayly (Lewis). The practice of piety. 1637. 12°. . . . 5088
Bayly (T.), *artium Magister.* Verses in Salisbury (Sir T.). The history of Joseph. 1636. 4°. 4023
Bayly (Thomas). *See* Theophylactus. Comm. 1636. F°. . . . 7649
Bayly (Tho.), *K.C.C.* Verses in Camb. Univ. Dolor. 1625. . 5701
Bayne (Paul). *See* Baynes (P.).
Baynes (Paul). Christian Letters. 1628. 12°. 4914
Christians Garment. 1618. 4°. 4064
Commentarie vpon Colossians i & ii. 1633. 4°. . . . 4355
Diocesans tryall. 1621. 4°. . . . . 6924=7841, 6925
Helpe to true happinesse. Ed. 3. 1635. 12°. . . . 4984
Baynton (Andrew). *See* Palsgrave (J.). Lesclaircissement. 1530.
Beacon (Thomas). *See* Becon.
Beale (Francis). Verses in Jones (W.). A treatise. 1625. 4°. . 3351
Beale (Jerome). *See* Camb. Univ. Gratulatio. 1623.
— — True Copies. 1623.
— — Dolor. 1625. (Second state.) 5701A
— — Epithalamium. 1625. 5702
Beale (John), *printer.* *See* Hieron (S.). The Spirituall Fishing. 1618.
Beale (Will.). Verses in Cam. Univ. Anthologia. 1632. . . . 5741
— Rex redux. 1633. 5748
— Συνωδία. 1637. 5748
— Voces. 1640. 5836
— Isaacson (H.). Ephemerides. 1633. F°. 4206
Bear-baiting. *See* Field (J.). A godly exhortation. 1583.
Beard (Tho.). The theatre of gods judgements. Ed. 2. 1612. 4°. 2442
See La Primaudaye (P. de). The French Academie. 1618. F°.

No.
Beard (Tho.) *cont.* *See* Palatinate. A fvll declaration... 1614. . 2988
— Pedantius. 1631. [Wrongly attributed to him.] . . 3182
Béarn, Principality or Sovereignty. 1621. *See* Declaration made. 4°. 6927
— Rochelle, *Assembly in.* A letter. 1621.
Beast is wounded, or information from Scotland. Part I. [1638.] 4°. . 6366
Beatus. *See* Erasmus (D.). Two dyaloges. [Ab. 1550.] 8°.
Beauchamp (John). Verses in Cambridge Lachrymae. 1587. . 7356
Beauchamp (Lewis). *See* Melanchthon (P.). Very godly defense [1541?]
Beaumont (Francis). Verses in Jonson (B.). Catiline. 1611. 4°. . 2902
— *ter* in Workes. 1616. F°. 3115
See Chaucer (G.). The Workes. 1598 *etc.*
Beaumont (F.) and J. Fletcher. A king and no king. Ed. 4. 1639. 4°. 5201
The knight of the burning pestle. 1635. 4°. 3699
The maides tragedy. Ed. 4. 1638. 4°. 5190
The scornfull lady. Ed. 4. 1635. 4°. 4585
Beaumont (F.) and J. Fletcher *cont.* Ed. 5. 1639. 4°. . . 4948
Beaumont (Francis), *Jesuit.* Beaumont (Sir J.). Bosworth-field. 1629. 8°. 3040
Beaumont (John). Verses in Jewel (J.). Adv. T. Hardingum. 1578. 4°. 1535
Beaumont (Sir John), *Bart., the elder.* Bosworth-field. 1629. 8°. . 3040
Verses in Horatius. Odes. 1635 *etc.* . . . . 4857 *etc.*
Beaumont (Sir John), *Bart., the younger.* *See* Beaumont (Sir J.), *the elder.* Bosworth-field. 1629.
Beaumont (Joseph), *Pet.* Verses in Camb. Univ. Carmen. 1635. 5770
— Camb. Univ. *Συνωδία.* 1637. 4°. 5790
— King (E.). Ivsta. 1638 4°. 5829
— Hawkins (W.). Corolla. 1634. 5803
— Verses *bis* in Camb. Univ. Voces. 1640. 5836
Beautiful Baybush. [Ab. 1580?] 16°. 6767
Becanus (Martinus). Defence of the Roman Chvrch... *See* Lessius (L.). A consvltation... 1621.
De Dissidio Anglicano. *See* Harris (R.). Concordia. 1612.
Examen of the English Concord. *See* Harris (R.). The English Concord. 1614. 4°.
Supplicatio ad imperatorem. Summa. 1613. 4°. . . 2795, 7443
See Apologia pro Christiano Batavo... 1610.
— Burhill (R.). Contra M. Becani. 1613.
— — Pro Tortura Torti. 1611.
— Paris University. Summa actorum. [1613.]
— Reuter (A.). Libertatis Anglicanae... 1613.
— Thomson (Richard). Elenchvs Refutationis Torturae Torti. 1611.
— Tooker (W.). Dvellvm. 1611.
Beccarie de Pavie (Raimond de). *See* Fourquevaux.
Beccles. *See* Deloney (T.). A proper newe Sonet. 1586. F°.
Becke (Edmund). *See* Bible. Eng. (Matthew). 1549.
— — (Taverner). 1551.
— Erasmus (D.). Two dyaloges. [c. 1550.]
Becket (Thomas), *Saint.* [Life.] *See* B. (A.). The life...of S. Thomas... 1639.
Becon (Antony). Verses in Camb. Univ. Lacrymæ. 1619. 4°. . 5689
Becon (I.). Verses in Cambridge Lachrymae. 1587. . . . 7356
Becon (Richard). Solon his follie. Oxford. 1594. 4°. . . 5240
Becon (T.). Worckes. 1564. F°. 801
Castell of comforte. [1550?] 8°. 911
Christmas bankette. [1542?] 8°. 691
Confortable Epistle. 'Strasburgh.' 1554. 8°. . . . 1052
Davids Harpe. 1542. 8°. 679
Demaundes of holy scripture. 1577. 8°. 7125
Displaying of the Popish Masse. 1637. 12°. 3963

No.
Becon (T.) *cont.* Fortresse of the faythfull. 1550. 8°. . . . 905
Humble supplicacion vnto God. 'Strasburgh.' 1554. 8°. . 1053
Inuectyue ageinst...swearynge. 1543. 8°. 683
New Postil. 1566. 4°. 1216
New yeares gyfte. 1543. 8°. 684
Newes out of heauen. 1542. 8°. 680, 681
— N.D. 8°. 690
Pleasaunt newe Nosegaye. 1542. 8°. 682
Pomaunder of Prayer. [1553?] 8°. 871
— 1558. 8°. 789
— 1578. 16°. 851
Potacion or drinkynge for...Lent. 1543. 8°. 685
[Principles of christen religion. Ab. 1550?] 8°. . . . 7138
[Relikes of Rome. 1553?] 8°. 786
Reliques of Rome. 1563. 8°. 799
Right pathwaye vnto Prayer. 1543. 8°. 686
Sicke mans salve. 1570. 8°. 814
— 1577. 8°. 846
— 1594. 8°. 7385
True defence of Peace. (A deuout...prayer upon Ps. cxv...Deut. xxviii.) 1543. 8°. 687
Verses in Turner (W.). A preseruatiue. 1551. . . . 955
A humble peticyon ... of the ... famylye at Shene... *See* Wermueller (O.). A Spyrytuall...Pearle. 1550.
[Qu. Trans. of Psalms?] *See* Bible. English (Bishops'). 1568. F°. 964
See Homilies. 1547. . . . . 597, 653
Beda. History. Trans. T. Stapleton. Antwerp. 1565. 4°. . 6113
— St Omers. 1622. 8°. 7809
Beda (Noel), '*of Montagu College*,' *Paris*. *See* Bernardin (St). The Churche. 1511.
Bédé (Jean). The masse displayed. Oxford. 1619. 4°. . . 5334
The right, and prerogative of Kings. 1612. 8°. . . . 3642
Bedel (H.). A Sermon exhorting to pitie the poore...1571...called The Movth of the poore. 1573. 8°. 1276
Bedell (William). The copies of certaine letters. 1624. 4°. . . 3148
An examination of...recusancie. Cambridge. 1628. 8°. . 5720
Verses in Whitaker (W.). Praelectiones. 1599. . . . 5598
See Sarpi (P.). Interdicti Veneti historia. 1626.
— — Qvæstio qvodlibetica. 1630.
Bedford, Archdeaconry of. [Visitation.] *See* Adams (T.). Heaven & earth. 1613. 4°.
Bedford Level Commission. *See* Hond (H.). 1632.
Bedford (Francis Russell, second earl of). [Funeral.] *See* Sparke (T.) A sermon. 1585. 8°.
A glasse... *See* Raleigh (Sir W.). Instructions. 1636. 8°.
Bedford (T.), *Physician*. A treatise...of English Medicines. 1580. 4°. 1630
Bedford (Thomas), *Divine*. The sinne vnto death. 1621. 4°. . 3843
Bedingfield (Robert). Sermon...at Pauls crosse. 24 Oct. 1624. Oxford. 1625. 4°. 5347
Bedingfield (Thomas). *See* Corte (C.). The Art of Riding. 1584.
— Macchiavelli (N.). The Florentine Historie. 1595.
Bedle (Thomas). The princelie progresse of the chvrch militant. 1610. 8°. 3632
Bedrote (James). *See* Strasburg Preachers. A treatise. [154–.] 8°.
Bedwell (Thomas). *See* Schonerus (L.). De Numeris... 1614.
Bedwell (William). *See* Bible. English (Royal Version). 1611. . 2635
— Muhammad. Mohammedis Imposturæ. 1615.
— Ramus (P.). Via Regia Ad Geometriam... 1636.
— Schonerus (L.). De Numeris... 1614.
Bee, Bees. *See* Hill (T.). A pleasaunt instruction. 1568. 8°.

No.
Beedome (Thomas). Verses in Roberts (L.). The merchants mappe. 1638. 5133
Bee hive of the Romish Church. *See* Marnix (P. van).
Beesley (Joh.). Verses *bis*. in Oxf. Univ. Horti. 1640. . . 5499
Beeston (Christopher). *See* Heywood (T.). The hierarchie. 1635.
Beeston (William). *See* Heywood (T.). The hierarchie. 1635.
Beke (Robert). Verses in Warre (James). The tovch-stone. 1621. 4503
Bekinsau (J.). De supremo et absoluto regis imperio. 1546. 8°. . 486
Belcanquall. *See* Balcanquall.
Belcher or Belchier (William). Verses in Guillim (J.). A display. 1611 *etc*. 3211
Belgick Pismire. 1622. *See* Scott (T.). Vox populi. 1622-4.
Belgick Souldier. 1624. *See* Scott (T.).
Belling (Ric.). Verses in Shirley (J.). The royall master. 1638. . 4665
See Sidney (Sir P.). The Countesse of Pembrokes Arcadia. Ed. 7. 1629 *etc*. F°.
Bell (Adam), Clym of the Clough, and William of Cloudesle. 1536. 4°. 569
— [J. Roberts? 1605?] 4°. 1790
Bell (Edmund). Verses in Camb. Univ. Lacrymæ. 1619. . . 5689
Bell (James). *See* Foxe (J.). The Pope Confvted. 1580.
— — Sermon. 1578. 8°.
— Haddon (W.). Against Ierome Osorius. 1581.
— Luther (M.). [De Libertate Christiana.] A Treatise... 1579.
Bell (Thomas). The anatomie of popish tyrannie. 1603. 4°. . 1271
Hvnting of the Romish Foxe. 1598. 8°. 1993
Motives. Cambridge. 1593. 4°. 5560
— 1605. Cambridge. 4°. 5628
Popes funerall. 1605. 4°. 2736
— — [Pt 2.] *See below* The Regiment of the Church. 1606.
Regiment of the church. 1606. 4°. 2739
Survey of popery. 1596. 4°. 2845
Woefull crie of Rome...with T. Bels second challenge. 1605. 4°. 2737
See Bulkeley (E.). An apologie... 1608.
— C. (B.), *Student in Divinity* The dolefull knell. 1607. 8°.
— — The fore-rvnner. [1605?]
— Preston (J.). The Doctrine of the Saints Infirmities. 1636. 12°.
Bell (William), *alias* Bennet. Verses in Heywood (T.). The exemplary lives. 1640. 4675
Bellarmino (Roberto). An ample declaration of christian doctrine. Douai. 1604. 12°. 6568
Of the seven wordes spoken by Christ. Trans. A. B. 1638. 12°. 6559
[Disputationes.] *See* Vorst (C.). Enchiridion. 1606.
[Letter to Blackwell.] *See* Blackwell (G.). A large examination... 1607.
— — James I. Triplici nodo... 1607.
— — An apologie... 1609.
See Abbot (R.). De svprema potestate regia. 1619.
— — The Mirrour. 1594.
— Andrewes (L.). Responsio... 1610.
— — Tortvra Torti... 1609.
— Buckeridge (J.). De Potestate... 1614.
— Bunny (F.). A survey. 1595.
— Burhill (R.). Contra M. Becani. 1613.
— — Pro Tortura Torti. 1611.
— — De potestate. 1613.
— Collins (S.). Increpatio. 1612.
— Cooke (A.). Pope Joane. 1610 *etc*.
— Dillingham (F.). Disputatio brevis... 1602.
— — Disputatio de natura pœnitentiæ. 1606.
— — Tractatus brevis... 1603.
— Downham (G.). Treatise concerning Antichrist... 1603.

No.

Bellarmino (Roberto) *cont.* *See* Du Moulin (P.). The accomplishment. 1613.
— — De Monarchia Temporali Pontificis Romani... 1614.
— Fitzherbert (T.). A supplement. 1613.
— — An adioynder to the supplement. 1613.
— Gordon (J.). Antitortobellarminus. 1610.
— Guild (W.). Ignis Fatvvs. 1625.
— Hall (J.). The peace of Rome. 1609. 4°.
— Mornay (P. de). The mysterie of iniqvitie. 1612. F°.
— Rainolds (J.). De Romanæ ecclesiæ idolatria. 1596.
— — Defence of the ivdgment of the Reformed churches... adulterie... 1609 *etc.*
— Sarpi (P.). An apology. 1607.
— Sutcliffe (M.). De pontifice romano. 1599.
— — De Purgatorio. 1599.
— Thomson (R.). Elenchvs Refutationis Tortvrae Torti. 1611.
— Trelcatius (L.). A briefe institution. 1610.
— — Scholastica...Institutio. 1606.
— Whitaker (W.). Dispvtatio. 1588.
— — Praelectiones de Concilijs. 1600.
— Widdrington (R.). Apologia. 1611.
— — A cleare...confutation. 1616.
— — Last reioynder. 1619 *etc.* 4°.
— Yates (J.). Gods arraignment. 1615. 4°.
[Death] A true relation...by C. E. *See* The art how to dye well. [1623.] 8°.
Bellehachius (O.). Sacrosancta bucolica. 1583. 4°. . . . 1640
Bellenden (John). *See* Boece (H.). The hystory...of Scotland. [1542?]
See Holinshed (R.)....Chronicles... 1577 *etc.*
Bellew (Jas.). Verses in Oxf. Univ. Horti. 1640. . . . 5499
Belligent (P. de). *See* Camden (W.). Annales. 1625.
Belling (Ric.). *See* Beling.
Bellingham (James), *T.C.C.* Verses in Cam. Univ. Voces. 1640. . 5836
Bellonius. *See* Belon (P.).
Bellopoelius (Petrus). De pace. 1552. 4°. 1012
Verses in Cheke (Sir J.). De obitu M. Buceri. 1551. . 734
See Perussellus (F.). Svmma. 1551.
Belloy (Pierre de). *See* A Catholicke Apologie. 8°.
Bellum Grammaticale. *See* Guarna (A.).
Belon (Pierre). *See* Gesner (C.). Nomenclator. 1560. F°.
Bembo (Francesco). *See* Croce (G.). Mvsica. 1608. . . . 1617
— — 1611. 2507
Benedetti (Pietro). Verses in Veen (O.). Am. Emblemata. 1608. . 6138
Benedict de Canfield, *Capuchin.* *See* Canfield (B.).
Benedictus, *Saint.* [Rule of S. Benet.] *See* Horologium Sapientiae. [1490.]
Benedictines, English. [Letters of admission. Ab. 1625? *Douai?*] Broadside. 6612
Benedictus (S.), *Mesopotam. Moravus.* Verses in Dugres (G.). Compendium. 1636. 5781
Benedikt (Renatus), or Benoist, *Bp of Troyes.* *See* Ferguson (D.). Ane answer to ane Epistle...by Renat Benedict. 1563.
Benefield (Richard), *T.C.* Verses in Randolph (T.). The Jealous Lovers. 1640. 5852
Benefield (Sebastian). Commentary...vpon the first...of Amos. 1629. 4°. 4823
— Amos ii. 1620. 4°. 3938
— Amos iii. 1629. 4°. 4824
Doctrinæ christianae sex capita. Oxoniæ. 1610. 4°. . . 5293
Eight sermons. Oxford. 1614. 4°. 5318
Sermon...in Oxford, March xxiv. Oxford. 1611. 4°. . . 5296
Sinne against the holy ghost. Oxford, 1615. 4°. . . . 5322

No.
Benese (Richard). The maner of measurynge...Lande... [1536?] 8°. 542
Benet (H.). Verses in Oxf. Univ. Horti. 1640. 5499
Benett (Roger), *Cantabrigiensis*. *See* Jewel (J.). Adversus Thomam Haidingum. 1578.
Benevolus. *See* Benlowes (E.).
Benlowes (Ed.). Verses in Gerhard (J.). A golden chain. 1632. . 5744
Fletcher (P.). The purple island. 1633. 5752
Hippocrates. 1633. 5812
Quarles (F.). Hieroglyphikes. 1638. 4322
Sibbs (R.). The sovles Conflict. 1636 *etc.* . . 4304 *etc.*
Benlowes (W.). Verses in Fletcher (P.). The purple island. 1633. 4°. 5752
Bennet (Father). *See* Canfield.
Bennet (Sir John). *See* Blackwell (G.). A large examination... 1607.
Bennet (William). *See* Bell (William).
Bennett (Edward). A treatise...touching...Tobacco. [Ab. 1620.] 4°. 6922
Bennett (John), *R. Catholic*. The hope of peace. 'Franckford. Heires of D. Turner.' 1601. 4°. 6834
Benningius (Janus Bodecherus). Verses in Burgersdicius (F.)....Institutionum. 1637. 5789
Benoist (René). *See* Benedict.
Bense (Petrus). Analogo-diaphora...trium linguarum. Oxonii, 1637. 8°. 5454
Benson (John), *bookseller*. *See* Shakspeare (W.). Poems. 1640. 8°.
Benson (Th.). Verses in Oxf. Univ. Horti. 1640. 5499
Bentham (Joseph). The christian conflict. 1635. 4°. . . . 4453
The saints societie. 1636. 4°. 4459
The societie of the saints. [1636.] 4°. 4460
Bentham (Thomas), *bp.* *See* Bible. English (Bishops'). 1568. F°. . 963
Bentley (Edw.). Verses in Camdeni Insignia. 1624. . . . 5346
Bentley (T.). The monvment of Matrones. 1582. 4°. . . . 1425
The sixth (-seventh) Lampe of Virginitie. 1582. 4°. . . . 1816
Benton ( ). *See* Brabourne (T.). A Defence... 1632.
Bercke, *City of*. *See* Rheinberg.
Bercker (William). *See* Barker.
Berckhey. *See* Briefe relation. 1599.
Bercula (Thomas), *typographus*. [Qu. Berthelet?][1] *See* Whittington (R.). Vulgaria. 1520. 4°.
Bergen op Zoom. The besieging of Bergen...by the Prince of Parma. 1588. Middelburg, [1588]. F°. 7737
Berkeley (Maurice). Verses in Chaucer (G.). Amorum. 1635. . 5414
Berkeley (Sir William). The lost lady. 1638. F°. 3717
Bermudas. *See* Smith (J.). 3864
Bernard (John). Oratio pia...de vera animi tranqvillitate. 1568. 4°. 930
Bernard (Jos.). Verses in Bate (J.). The mysteries. 1635. 4°. . 4012
Bernard (Richard). The Bible-battells, or the sacred art military. 1629. 12°. 4408
Double catechisme. Cambridge, 1607. 8°. 5640
Faithfull shepheard. 1607. 4°. 2084
Gvide to grand-iury men. 1629. 12°. 3041
Isle of man. Ed. 7. 1630. 12°. 4409
— Ed. 8. 1632. 12°. 7598
— Ed. 10. 1635. 12°. 4856
Key of Knowledge for St Johns mysticall Revelation. 1617. 4°. 2998
Looke beyond Luther. 1623. 4°. 3023
Rhemes against Rome. 1626. 4°. 3030
Ruths recompence. 1628. 4°. 3035
Seaven golden candlestickes. 1621. 8°. 7490
See B. (R.). Davids musick. 1616. 4°.

[1] *See* The Bibliographer I. 13—15 (1881), for a letter by W. Blades.

No.

Bernard (Richard) *cont.* [Separatists Schisme.] *See* Robinson (J.). A ivstification of separation. 1610 *etc.*
See Smyth (J.). Paralleles. 1609.
— Terentius. Fabulae. 1598 *etc.*
— — Terence in English. 1607. 4°.
Bernard (Sam.). Verses in Oxf. Univ. Magd. Coll. 1612. . . . 5302
Camdeni Insignia. 1624. 5346
Bernard (Thomas). *See* Bernard (J.). Oratio... 1568.
Bernardinus of Siena. The chirche of the euyll men and women. W. de Worde. 1511. 4°. 164
Bernardus. A compendious...treatyse of well liuinge. Trans. T. Paynell. N.D. 8°. 583
Golden Epistle. (Reuelations of saynt Birgette.) T. Godfray. [1532?] 8°. 555
— — *See* Kempis (T. a). A boke. [Ab. 1535.] 8°.
— — Whitford (R.). A werke of preparation... 1531.
Meditations. W. de Worde. '1496.' [1499.] 4°. . . . 46
Medytacyons. W. de Worde. 19 Sept. 1525. 4°. . . . 189
— 1631. 12°. 2037
[Miracles.] *See* Gregorius I. The dialogues. 1608. 12°.
[Verses. (Lat. & Eng.).] *See* Daneau (L.). A Treatise. 1589.
See Betson (T.). A right profytable treatyse. [1500.] 4°. . 59
— Crashaw (W.). Qverela sive Dialogvs Animæ... 1632.
Bernardus, *Sylvester.* *See* Whitford (R.). A werke of preparation... 1531.
Berners (John Bourchier, second baron). *See* Froissart (J.). Chronicles. 1523 *etc.*
— Guevara (A. de). The golden boke. 1546 *etc.*
Berners (Juliana). The Book of St Albans, of Hawking etc. St Alban's. [1486.] F°. 87
The Gentlemans Academie. Or, The Booke of S. Albans. Reduced by G. M. 1595. 4°. 2840
— A Treatise of Hunting. W. de Worde. [Ab. 1530?] 4°. 211
Bernher (Augustine). *See* Latimer (H.). Certayne godly sermons. 1562. 4°.
— — Fruitfull Sermons. 1584 *etc.*
Beroaldus (M.). Short view of the Persian Monarchie. 1590. 4°. 2206
See Lively (E.). A true chronologie. 1597.
Berosus. *See* Lynche (R.). An historical treatise. 1601. 4°.
Berrier (Stephen). Verses in Camb. Univ. Lacrymae. 1619. . 5689
— Vaughan (W.). The golden fleece. 1626. 5029
Berryer (S.). *See* Berrier.
Bersman (Gregorius). *See* Ovid....Metamorphoseωn... 1631.
Bertaut (Jean). The parliament of Vertues Royal. *See* Sylvester (J.). The parliament. [1614.] 8°.
Berthelet (Thomas). Verses in Livius. The Hystory of Annibal & Scipio. 1590. 1770
See Bercula.
Bertie (Hon. Robert), *Sid. Coll. Camb.* Verses in Camb. Univ. *Συνῳδία.* 1637. 5790
Bertie (Roger). Verses in Cantabrigiensium dolor. 1625. . . 5701
— — Epithalamium. 1625. 5702
Best (Arthur). *See* *Λῶστος.*
Best (William). The churches plea. Amsterdam. 1635. 4°. . . 6359
See Paget (J.). An answer. 1635.
Betham (Peter). *See* Purlilia (James, earl of). 1544.
Bethune (Philippe de). The Counsellor of estate. Trans. E. Grimstone. 1634. 4°. 3695
Betson (Thomas). A ryght profytable treatyse. W. de Worde. [1500.] 4°. 59
Bettæus (Ric.). Verses in Parkhurst (J.). Ludicra. 1573. . . 838

No.

Betts (Richard), *rector of Achill.* *See* James I. [Declaration.] A remonstrance... 1616 *etc.*
Beuchame (Lewes). *See* Beauchamp.
Beurhusius (Fred.). De P. Rami dialecticae praecipuis capitibus disputationes. Ed. 2. 1582. 8°. 7268
See Ramus (P.). P. Rami...dialecticæ... 1589.
Beverwijk (J. van). Schat der Gesontheyt. Dordrecht. 1638. 8°. 7811
Bevis (Sir) of Hampton. W. de Worde. [1500.] 4°. 60
— W. de Worde. [15—.] 4°. 212
Bevys (Peter). Verses in Martyn (W.). Historie. 1615. . . 7489
Bewe (William). Verses in A. (G.). Pallas armata. 1639. . 5170
— Oxf. Univ. Horti. 1640. 5499
Bèze (Théodore de). Ad J. G. Stuckium Epistola et pastorum... responsio. Oxoniae, 1598. 8°. 5247
Discourse...life of...Calvin. Trans. I. S. 1564. 8°. . . 6749
Ecclesiastes. [1593?] 8°. 5546
Iob expounded. Cambridge. [Ab. 1593.] 8°. 5545
Jvdgement of a most reverend and learned man from beyond the seas. [1585?] 8°. 1910
Pro consolandis afflictis conscientiis. *See* Perkins (W.). Armilla aurea. 1590.
[The order...in comforting afflicted consciences.] *See* Perkins (W.). A golden chaine. Ed. 2. 1592. 8°.
— — Two treatises. 1595. 4° and 8°.
— — A golden chaine. 1600. 4°.
Popes canons. Trans. T. Stocker. 1585? 8°. 7363
Propositions and principles of divinitie...in the Vniversitie of Geneva...Faius. 1595. 8°. 5935
Quæstionum & responsionum christianarum libellus. 1571. 8°. . 1469
Tractatus...de vera excommunicatione. 1590. 8°. . . 1333
Treasure of trueth. Trans. J. Stockwood. [Ab. 1576?] 8°. . 7302
— 1581. 8°. 1839
Verses in Ursinus (Z.). Doctrinae. 1585. 5516
See Anderton (J.). Luthers Life. 1624. 4°.
— Balbani (N.). Newes from Italy. 1608. 4°.
— — Italian convert. 1635.
— Bible. English [Genevan. Tomson's Revision.] 1607 *etc.*
— — Job. [159-.]
— — Psalms. The Psalmes. 1581 *etc.*
— — Ecclesiastes. [159 .]
— Bible. (Lat.) 1585 *etc.*
— — Psalmorvm...libri quinque. 1580. 1539
— — N.T. 1574, *etc.*
— Bridges (J.), *bp.* A defence of the government... 1587.
— Confession of Fayth. [1568?]
— Dialogi. 1574. 6760
— England. Parliament. An admonition. 1572.
— Heywood (T.). Pleasant dialogues. 1637.
— Rollock (R.). Tractatus de vocatione. 1597. 8°.
— Saravia (H.). Defensio. 1594.
Bibeus (Sym), Lambhithensis. [Arms...of the Colleges of Oxford and Cambridge.] Tübingen (1602). Broadside. . . . 7695
Bible. Polyglot. Genesis. *See* Willet (A.). Hexapla. Ed. 3. 1632(3). F°.
Job. (Gr. Lat.) *See* Nicetas. Catena. 1637. . . 2696, 7849
Daniel. (Heb. Gk. Eng.) [By H. Broughton? Ab. 1595?] 4°. . 7773
Bible. Anglo-Saxon. *See* Psalterium Davidis. 1640. . . 4400
Gospels. 1571. 822

Bible. English—

CHRONOLOGICAL LIST.

						No.
1534	N.T.	Tindale	Antwerp	8°	Syn. 8 . 53 . 87	6090
1535		Coverdale	[Zurich & Southwark]	F°	Syn. 3 . 53 . 2	6279
		,,	,, ,,	F°	Syn. 3 . 53 . 3	6280
1535	N.T.	Tindale		8°	Syn. 8 . 53 . 91	6099
1536	N.T.	,,	[Berthelet]	F°	Sel. 3 . 215	433
1536	N.T.	,,	[Antwerp ?]	4°	Syn. 6 . 53 . 5	6079
1536	N.T.	,,	[Antwerp?]	4°	Syn. 6 . 53 . 18	6080
1537		Matthew's		F°	Sel. 2 . 42	6081
1538	N.T.	Coverdale	Antwerp, Crom.	8°	Syn. 8 . 53 . 92	6102
1538 Lent	N.T.	,,	Southwarke	4°	Sandars Coll.	5869
1538 July	N.T.	,,	,,	4°	Syn. 6 . 53 . 4	5870
1538	N.T.	Coverdale	[ ]	16°	Syn. 8 . 53 . 101, 102	6671
1539		Taverner	Byddell for Berthelet	F°	Sel. 3 . 213	570
1539	N.T.	,,	Petit	8°	Syn. 8 . 53 . 116	7704
1539		Cranmer	Paris	F°		6180
1539	N.T.	Coverdale	Antwerp, Crom.	8°	Syn. 8 . 53 . 93	6103
1540 April		Cranmer	Petyt & Redman for Berthelet	F°	Sel. 3 . 208	579
1540 April		,, Ed. 2	Grafton	F°	Sel. 1 . 6	587
1540 Nov.		,, Ed. 4	Whitchurch	F°	Sel. 1 . 8	648
1541 Nov.		,, Ed. 6	,,	F°	Sel. 1 . 7	649
1549 Aug. 17		Matthew's	Day	F°	Sel. 3 . 210[1]	902
1549 Oct. 31		,,	Raynalde & Hyll	F°	Sel. 3 . 211	698
1550		Coverdale	[Zurich & London]	4°	Syn. 5 . 55 . 1–6	6284–5
155?	N.T.	Cranmer	London	4°	1 . 19 . 16	632
1550	N.T.	Tindale	Day and Seres	8°	Sandars Coll.	906
1550	N.T.	J. C.	Gaultier	8°	Syn. 7. 55 . 14, 15 etc.	1095
1551		Matthew's	N. Hyll for J. Wyghte	F°	Sel. 3 . 212	1024
1551		Taverner		F°	Sel. 3 . 214	783
1552		Cranmer	N. Hyll	4°	1 . 19 . 22 (sel) etc.	1025
1552		Tindale	Jugge	4°	1 . 19 . 14 (sel) etc.	981
1553		Cranmer	E. Whitchurch	F°	Syn. 3 . 55 . 2	7100
1553		Coverdale	Jugge [Zurich ?]	4°	Syn. 5 . 55 . 5	956 6284–5
1553		Cranmer	Grafton	4°	1 . 36 . 13	629
[1553?]	N.T.	Tindale (Jugge's Revision)	Lond. R. Jugge	4°	Adams . 7 . 55 . 6	982
1560		Genevan	Geneva, R. Hall	4°	Sel. 3 . 21	6322
1566		Cranmer	Rouen	F°	1 . 15 . 3	6249
1568		Bishops'	Jugge	F°	1 . 15 . 4	964
1569		Genevan		4°	Syn. 6 . 56 etc.	6320
1569		Bishops'	Jugge	4°	1 . 19 . 16[2]	965
1571	Gospels	Parker	Daye	4°	1 . 24 . 9 etc.	822
1572		Bishops'	Jugge	F°	1 . 13 . 19 etc.	967
1575		,,	London	F°	Syn. 4 . 57 . 14	7774
1578		Genevan	C. Barker	F°	1 . 15 . 6	1663

Bible. English. Chronological List *cont.*

Bible. English.						No.
1578		Bishops'	Ass. of C. Barker	F°	1.15.19	1664
1582		Genevan	Barker	F°	Sandars Coll.	1672
1582	N.T.	Rhemes	J. Fogny	4°	Syn. 6.58.3	
1585		Bishops'		F°	Syn. 1.58	1678
[1593?]	N.T.	Genevan	Legate	32°	Syn. 9.59.1	5544
1595		Bishops'	Lond.	F°	1.15.7	1702
1599		Genevan (Tomson)	C. Barker	4°	Adams. 6.59.2^{1}	1708
1599		Genevan	'Barker,' Amsterdam	4°	Sandars Coll.	1708
		,,	,,	4°	Sandars Coll.	1709
1600	N.T.	Rhemes	Antwerp	4°	1.19.4	
1601	N.T.	Rhemes (Fulke)	Barker	F°	Syn. 3.60.4, 5	2571
1602		Bishops'	,,	F°	1.15.13	2574
1602	N.T.	Genevan	,,	8°	Syn. 8.60.116^{1}	7782
1607		Genevan (Tomson)	,,	F°	1.14.10^{2}	2601
1608	N.T.	Bishops'	,,	8°	Syn. 8.60.116^{2}	7783
1609	N.T.	Genevan	,,	16°	Sandars Coll.	2619
1609 (-10)	O.T.	Douai	L. Kellam	4°	Syn. 6.60.10, 11	6572
1611		Royal	Barker	F°	Syn. 2.61.1	2635
1611		,,	,,	F°	Syn. 1.61.2	2636
1611 (1617)		,,	,,	F°	Syn. 2.61.2	2655 (corr)
1611–2		Genevan (Tomson)	,,	F°	Sandars Coll.	2641
1613		Royal	,,	4°	Sandars Coll.	2645
1615		,,	,,	8°	Syn. 7.61.26^{1}	2651
1617 (1611)		,,	,,	F°	Syn. 2.61.2	2655
1617	N.T.	Rhemes (Fulke)	J. Bill	F°	1.14.1 (sel)	3478
1620		Royal	Barker and Bill	12°	Sandars Coll.	2661
1620 (-1)		,,	Norton and Bill	4°	Adams. 6.62.2^{3}	2809
1621	N.T.	Rhemes (Ed. 3)	Antwerp	12°	Syn. 8.62.85	6143
1628	N.T.	Royal	Edinburgh	8°	Syn. 8.62.88	5962
1628	N.T.	,,	Cambridge	24°	Syn. 8.62.43^{1}	5721
1628	N.T.	,,	,,	24°	Sandars Coll.	5722
1629		,,	Norton and Bill	F°	Syn. 4.62.26	7776
1629		,,	Cambridge	F°	1.14.12^{2}, etc.	5712
1630		,,	,,	4°	Sandars Coll.	5714
1631?		Genevan (Tomson)	Holland?	4°	A*.5.7 (D)	7007
1632 (1)		Royal	Barker & Ass. Bill	4°	Syn. 5.63.3	2676
1633 (2)		,,	,, ,,	F°	Syn. 3.63.1^{3}	2677
1633 (2)		,,	,, ,,	F°	Adams. 3.63.5^{3}	2678
1633		,,	,, ,,	4°	Adams. 5.63.1^{3}	2679
1633			Cambridge		Syn. 5.63.4	5716
1633	N.T.	Rhemes (Ed. 4)	Cousturier, Rouen	4°	Rel. c.63.1	6257
1633	N.T.	Rhemes	A. Mathewes	F°	Syn. 3.63.7	4570
1633	N.T.	Fulke	,,		1.14.2	4571
1634	N.T.	Royal	Barker and Ass. Bill	4°	Sandars Coll.	2686
1634		,,	,, ,,	8°	1.36.10^{1}	2687
1635		,,	Cambridge	4°	Rel. b.63.1	5815
1635	O.T.	Douay	Cousturier, Rouen	4°	Syn. 5.63.7, 8	6261
1637		Royal	Cambridge	4°	Adams. 6.63.1^{2}	5818
1637			,,		Syn. 5.63.5^{2}	5788
1637 (8)		,,	Cambridge	4°	Syn. 5.63.6	5822

Bible. English. Chronological List *cont.*

					No.
1638	Royal (Cambridge Revision)	Cambridge	F°	Rel. a. 63. 1	5821
1638	Royal	Barker & Ass. Bill	12°	1. 37. 5	2697
1638 (9)	,,	,, ,,	F°	Acton Library	7722
1639	,,	,, ,,	4°	Adams. 5. 63. 2	2704
1640 (39)	,,	,, ,,	8°	Syn. 7. 64. 88	2708
1640	,,	,, ,,	4°	Syn. 5. 63. 2	2707
1640	Genevan (Tomson)	Amsterdam	F°	Syn. 3. 64. 5	6364

ORDER OF VERSIONS:

i. Coverdale's (1535).
ii. Matthew's (1537).
iii. Taverner's (1539).
iv. Cranmer's (1540).
v. The Genevan Bible (1560).
vi. The Bishops' Bible (1568).
vii. Rhemes Version (1588 & 1609).
viii. Douai Version (1609).
ix. Royal Version (1611).

i.

Coverdale. Ed. 1. [C. Froschauer, Zurich.] 4 Oct. 1535. F°. . 6279
— — Ed. 2. [*id. ib.*] 4 Oct. 1535. F°. 6280
— N.T. Ed. 1. J. Nicolson, Southwark. 1538. 4°. . . 5869
— — 'Hollybushe.' Ed. 2. J. Nicolson, Southwark. 1538. 4°. 5870
— [Zurich] for A. Hester. 1550. 4°. 6284–5
— R. Jugge. 1553. 4°. 956

ii.

Matthew's. [S. de Cock, Antwerp.] 1537. F°. . . . 6081
— T. Raynalde and W. Hyll. 30 Oct. 1549. F°. . . . 698
— Ed. Becke. Day and Seres. 1549. F°. 902
— N. Hill for J. Wyghte. 1551. F°. 1024
— T. Petyt. 6 May, 1551. F°. 7148
— *See* Bible. Eng. [Taverner's]... 1551.

iii.

Taverner's. J. Byddell for T. Berthelet. 1539. F°. . . . 570
— J. Day. 1551. F°. 783

iv.

Cranmer. Ed. 1. F. Regnault, Paris, for Grafton and Whitchurch. April, 1539. F°. 646, 6180
— T. Petit and R. Redman, for T. Berthelet. April, 1540. F°. 579
— Ed. 2. R. Grafton. April, 1540. F°. 587, 647
— Ed. 4. Whitchurch. Nov. 1540. F°. 648
— Ed. 6. Whitchurch. Nov. 1541. F°. 649
— N. Hill (for A. Veale). 1552. 4°. 1025
— E. Whitchurch. 1553. F°. 7100
— Grafton. 1553. 4°. 629
— C. Hamillon, coste of R. Carmarden, Rouen. 1566. F°. . 6249
— Psalms. *See* Psalter. Canterbury. 1550. 4°.

v.

Genevan. R. Hall, Geneva. 1560. 4°. 6322
— J. Crispin, Geneva. 1570–1568. 4°. 6320
— C. Barker. 1578. F°. 1663
— C. Barker. 1582. F°. 1672
— J. Legate, Cambridge. 29 May, 1591. 8°. 7668
— Deputies of C. Barker. 1598–7. 4°. 7298

No.

Bible (Eng.), Genevan *cont.* (Tomson's Revision.) Deputies of C. Barker. 1599. 4°. 1708
— — [Amsterdam.] 1599. 4°. . . . 1709 and p. 1435
— R. Barker. 1607. F°. 2601
— R. Barker. 1608. 8°. 7418
— Edinburgh, Andro Hart. 1610. *See below* . . . 6364
— R. Barker. 1611(-12). F°. 2641
— [Amsterdam? Ab. 1631.] 4°. 7007
— T. Stafford, Amsterdam. 1640. F°. 6364

vi.

Bishops'. R. Jugge. 1568. F°. 964
— — [1569.] 4°. 965
— — 1572. F°. 967
— [R. Jugge?] 1575. F°. 7774
— Ass. of C. Barker. 1578. F°. 1664
— [C. Barker. 1585.] F°. 1678
— Deputies of C. Barker. 1595. F°. 1702
— R. Barker. 1602. F°. 2574

vii.

(Rheims version.) Appendix. *See* Bulkeley (E.). An answere...1588.
— Bernard (R.). Rhemes against Rome. 1626.

viii.

Douai. L. Kellam, Douai. 1609–10. 4°. 6572
— J. Cousturier, Rouen. 1635. 4°. 6261

ix.

Royal version. Ed. 1. First issue. R. Barker. 1611. F°. . 2635
— — Second issue. 1611. F°. 2636
— — 1611 (1617). F°. . . . . . . 2655 (corr)
— — 1613. 4°. 2645
— — 1615. 8°. 2651
— — 1617 (1611). F°. . . . . . . 2655 (corr)
— R. Barker and J. Bill. 1620. 12°. 2661
— B. Norton and J. Bill. 1620(-1). 4°. 2809
— — 1629. F°. 7776
— Cambridge. 1629. F°. 5712
— — 1630. 4°. 5714
— R. Barker and Ass. of J. Bill. 1632(-1). 4°. . . . 2676
— — 1633(-2). F°. 2677
— — 1633(-2). F°. 2678
— — 1633. 4°. 2679
— Cambridge. 1633. 4°. 5716
— R. Barker and ass. of J. Bill. 1634. 8°. 2687
— Cambridge. 1635. 4°. 5815
— 1637. 4°. 5788
— 1637. 4°. 5818
— 1637–8. 4°. 5822
— 1638. F°. 5821
— R. Barker and Ass. of J. Bill. 1638. 12°. . . . 2697
— — 1639 (1638). F°. 7722
— — 1639. 4°. 2704
— — 1640 (1639). 8°. 2708
— — 1640. 4°. 2707
The Third part of the bible. B. Norton and J. Bill. 1626. 12°. 2827
Abridgment. *See* Clapham (H.). A briefe. 1608. 12°.
Concordance. *See* Marbeck (John). 1550.
— Herrey (R. F.). 1587 *etc.*
— *See* Knight (W.). 1610.

No.

Bible (Eng.), Concordance *cont.* Way to true Happiness. 1610. 8°.
— Downham (J.). A briefe concordance. 1630. 8°.
Appendix. *See* Brief Sūme of the whole Byble... [154] etc. 1040 *etc.*
— Gerrard (P.). A Godly Inuectiue. 1547.
— Calendar of Scripture. 1575.
— Pagit (E.). The historie of the bible. [1602?] 12°.
— Way to true happines. 1615. 8°.
— Doctrine of the Bible. 1616.
— Buenting (H). Itinerarium. 1619. 4°. 7821
— Clapham (H.). A briefe of the bibles history. Ed. 4. 1639. 8°.
Herbal. *See* Lemnius (L.). 1587.
Illustrations. *See* Derendel (P.). True and lyuely portreatvres. 1553. 8°.
Preface. *See* Wyclif (J.). The true copye. 1550.

OLD TESTAMENT.

Selection. The pistles of the olde testament. *See* Bible. Eng. N.T. The newe Testament. 1534.
— Metrical. *See* Sandys (G.). A paraphrase. 1638.
Pentateuch (Exodus—Numbers). W. Tindale. [Marburg, 1530.] 8°. 6273
See Ainsworth (H.). Annotations... 1627 (1626)
— 1639.
Genesis. The first boke... Newly corrected and amended. [Marburg.] 1534. 8°. 6275
— Selection. *See* Broughton (H.). A treatise of Melchisedek.
See Ainsworth (H.). Annotations... 1616.
— Calvin (J.). A commentarie. 1578. 4°.
— Ross (A.). An exposition... 1626. 8°.
— Willet (A.). Hexapla. 1605 *etc.*
[ch. i—xv.] *See* Clapham (H.). Bibliotheca... 1597.
(Metrical.) *See* Hunnis (W.). A Hyve full of honey. 1578. 4°.
Exodus. *See* Ainsworth (H.). Annotations. 1617.
— — Willet (A.). Hexapla in Exodvm. 1608.
— [ch. xx.] *See* Knewstub (J.). The lectvres. 1577.
Leviticus. *See* Ainsworth (H.). Annotations. 1618.
— — Willet (A.). Hexapla. 1631.
— [ch. i.] *See* Clapham (H.). A manuell. 1606. 12°.
Numbers. *See* Ainsworth (H.). Annotations. 1619.
Deuteronomy (Selection). [ch. xxviii.] *See* Becon (T.). The true defēce of Peace... 1543.
— *See* Ainsworth (H.). Annotations... 1619.
Ruth. *See* Bernard (R.). Ruths Recompence. 1628. 4°.
I Samuel. *See* Willet (A.). An harmonie. 1607.
I & II Samuel. *See* Willet (A.). An harmonie. 1614.
Nehemiah. *See* Pilkington (J.). A godlie exposition. 1585. 4°.
Esther. *See* Brenz (J.). A Right Godly...discourse. 1584.
— — Cooper (T.). The Chvrches deliverance... 1609.
— [Verse.] *See* Quarles (F.). Hadassa. 1621.
Job. *See* Calvin (J.). Sermons... 1579 (1580).
— [ch. i & ii.] *See* Holland (H.). The christian exercise. 1596. 4°.
— [Metrical.] *See* Quarles (F.). Job militant. 1624. 4°.
— — Sandys (G.). A paraphrase. 1638.
Psalms (Prose). Psalter of David...after the texte of Felyne. T. Godfray. [1532?] 8°. 563
— David's Psalter, trans. G. Joye. M. Emperour, Antwerp. August, 1534. 16°. 6091
— The psalter or psalmes...after...the great Bible. 1550. 4°. . 7677
— [Ab. 1558?] 4°. 674
— Trans. A. Gilbie. H. Denham. 1581. 12°. 1424

No.

Bible (Eng.), Psalms (Prose) *cont.* R. Yardley and P. Short. 1590. 12°. 2322
— The Psalter. R. Barker. 1604. F°. 2587
— The Psalmes of David... Also with the Prose...1605. . 3223
— (The Great Bible). With Morning and Evening Prayer. Stationers. 1615. 4°. 2524
— — 1617. F°. 2656
— The book of prayses. By A. Top. Amsterdam. 1629. F°. . 6357
— Psalter. Edinburgh. 1636. F°. 7768
— — Dublin. 1637. 4°. 6060
— — Cambridge. 1638. 4°. 5792
— *See* Ainsworth (H.). Annotations... 1627 (1626) *etc.*
— — Calvin (J.). Psalms of David. 1571. 4°.
— — Martyr (P.). Most Godly Prayers. 1569. 8°.
— — Wilcox (T.). A right godly...Exposition. 1586.
— — — Workes. 1624.
— [Ps. 1–21.] *See* Strigelius (V.). Part. 1582. 4°.
— [— 22–35.] — A Proceeding. [1593?] 4°.
— [— 34–45.] — A second proceeding. 1593. 4°.
— [— 45–61.] — A third proceeding. 1595. 4°.
— [i–viii.] *See* Day (J.). Day's descant. 1620. 4°.
— [vii Penitential.] *See* Simson (A.). A sacred seplenarie. 1634. 4°.
— (Selection) [i–iii]. *See* B. (R.). Davids Musick. 1616. 4°.
— [i.] *See* Baker (Sir R.). 1638.
— [xv.] *See* Erasmus (D.). An exposicyon. 1537.
— [ii.] *See* Web (R.). Christs Kingdome. 1610.
— [xv.] *See* Turnbull (R.). An exposition. 1592 *etc.*
— [xxx.] *See* Primer. 1538. 4°. 6178
— [li.] *See* Savonarola (G.). An exposition. [153] *etc.*
— — Primer. 1538. 4°. 6178
— — Hieron (S). David's penitential. 1617. 4°.
— — Baker (Sir R.). 1638.
— [lxxx.] *See* Savonarola (G.). An other.
— [lxxxiii.] *See* Gostwyke (R.). Deo etc. 1616.
— [xci.] *See* Horne (R.). The shield. 1625. 4°.
— [cxv.] *See* Becon (T.). The true defēce of Peace... 1543.
— [cxx–cxxxiv.] *See* Luther (M.). A commentarie. 1637. 4°.
— [cxxii.] *See* Willet (A.). Ecclesia Trivmphans. 1614.
— [cxlv.] *See* Becon (T.). Dauid's Harpe... 1542.
— [Selection.] *See* Psalms. Deuout Psalmes. 1547 *etc.* . 655 *etc.*
— — Temple (W.). A logicall analysis. 1605. 4°. . 7469

Psalms (Metrical). STERNHOLD AND HOPKINS.

— Al such Psalmes...as Thomas Sterneholde didde in his life... Newly emprinted. E. Whitchurch. 24 Dec., 1549. 8°. . 664
— — E. Whitchurch. 1549? 8°. 665
— Kingston and Sutton. 1553. 8°. 1159
— One and fiftie psalmes...by Thomas Sterneholde: and...others. *See* Liturgies. Geneva. *English Church.* The forme. 1556. 8°. 6317
— The whole booke of psalms. J. Crespin, Geneva. 1569. 4°. . 6321
— J. Day. 1573. 4°. 7119
— [Ab. 1564–1577?] 8°. 6748
— J. Day. [Ab. 1573?] 4°. 7136
— [Ab. 1574?] 4°. 7120
— 1576. F°. 7123
— 1578. 4°. 7126
— 1578. 16°. 7127
— 1579. 4°. 856

No.

Bible (Eng.), Psalms (Metrical) *cont.* [Ab. 1579?] 8°. . . 7129
— 1580. 4°. 7130
— 1581. 4°. 7131
— 1583. 4°. 866
— 1583. 4°. 7132
— Ass. of R. Day. 1588. 4°. 7326
— [Ab. 158–?] 32°. 6792
— J. Wolfe for the ass. of R. Day. 1590. 4°. 7328
— 1591 (1587). 4°. 7329
— 1591. 4°. (Title.) 2130
— T. East. 1592. 8°. 1601
— J. Windet for ass. of R. Day. 1594. 4°. (Title.) . 2137, 2138
— 1595. 4°. (Title.) 2141
— 1597. 4°. (Title.) 2144
— 1598. 4°. 2148, 2149
— 1598. 8°. 2150
— 1599. F°. 2152
— The Booke of Psalmes. [R. Barker? 1599?] 4°. . . . 2568
— [1599?] 4°. 2569
— The whole booke. (Title.) J. Windet for the ass. of R. Day.
1600. 4°. 2156
— — 1601. 4°. 2158
— — 1602. 4°. 2159
— — 1603. 4°. 2161
— Stationers. 1604. F°. 2166
— J. Windet for the Stationers. 1604. 4°. (Title.) . . 2167
— Stationers. 1605. 4°. . (Title.) 2174
— The Psalmes of David...Also with the Prose. Stationers. 1605.
8°. 3223
— The whole booke. (Title.) Stationers. 1606. 4°. . . 2175
— — 1608. 4°. 3234
— 1609. F°. 2177
— 1609. 4°. (Title.) 2178
— Stationers. 1609. 8°. 3239
— — 1610. 4°. (Title.) . . . . . . 2181=7486
— — 1610. 8°. 7503
— — 1611. 4°. 7310
— — 1611. 8°. 3248
— — 1612. F°. 3250
— — 1612. 4°. (Title.) 2979
— — 1612. 4°. 2980
— — 1612. 16°. 3251
— — 1613. 8°. 3254
— — 1614. 4°. (Title.) 7311
— — 1614. 4°. 7505
— — 1615. F°. 3263
— — 1615. 4°. 7312
— — 1616. 4°. 7313
— — 1616. 8°. 3267
— — 1617. 4°. (Title.) 3419
— — 1617. 8° 3269
— — 1618. F°. 3270
— — 1618. F°. 3000
— — 1618. 4°. (Title.) 3001
— — 1619. 4°. 3007
— — 1619. 4°. 3274
— — 1620. 4°. 3281, 3282
— — 1622. 4°. (Title.) 3020
— — [1622?] 4°. 3021
— — 1622. 12°. 3287

No.
Bible (Eng.), Psalms (Metrical) *cont.* 1623. F°. (Title.) . . . 3290
— — 1623. 4°. 3291
— — 1623. 8°. 3292
— Cambridge. 1623. 8°. 5698
— Stationers. 1624. F°. 7480
— — 1626. 4°. (Title.) 3162
— — 1627. 8°. 3296
— The whole booxe. 1627. 32°. 7509
— — Stationers. 1628. 8°. 7784
— Cambridge. 1628. 8°. 5723
— — 1628. 8°. 5726
— — 1628. 12°. 7840
— — 1629. F°. 5713
— Stationers. 1629. F°. 3302
— — 1629. 8°. 3303
— G. Miller for the Stationers. 1629. 8°. 4429
— Stationers. 1629 (1630). F°. 7562
— — 1630. 4°. (Title.) 3178
— — 1630. 4°. 3304
— — 1630. 8°. 7511
— [Ab. 1630.] 32°. 7004
— Stationers. 1631. 8°. 3305
— — 1631. 32°. 3306
— [Abroad? Ab. 1631?] 4°. 7010
— R. Badger for the Stationers. 1632. F°. 4347
— G. Miller for the Stationers. 1632. 8°. 4440
— Stationers. 1632. 32°. 3307
— Cambridge. 1633. 4°. 5758
— W. Stansby for the Stationers. 1633. 8°. 3192
— 1634. 4°. (Title.) 3196
— Cambridge. 1634. 4°. 5765
— G. Miller for the Stationers. 1634. 8°. 4452
— Stationers. 1635. F°. 4457
— G. Miller for the Stationers. 1635. 8°. 4458
— Stationers. 1635. 32°. 3308
— The booke of psalmes...with apt notes. J. Legate for the Stationers. 1636. 4°. 4729
— The whole booke of Psalms. G. Miller for the Stationers. 1636. 12°. 4463
— — Stationers. 1636. 16°. 7512
— — A. Griffin for the Stationers. 1637, 4°. . . . 3968
— — Cambridge. 1637. 4°. 5820
— — [1637.] 4°. 7597
— — G. Miller for the Stationers. 1637. 12°. 4468
— — J. Haviland for the Stationers. 1638. F°. . . . 4872
— — E. Griffin and I. Raworth for the Stationers. 1638. F°. 7721
— — Cambridge. 1638. 4°. 5826
— — T. P. for the Stationers. 1638. 8°. 5090
— — G. Miller for the Stationers. 1638. 8°. . . . 4471
— — E. G. for the Stationers. 1639. 4°. 5206
— — G. Miller for the Stationers. 1639. 8°. . . . 4475
— — E. G. for the Stationers. 1640. F°. 7777
— — R. Bishop for the Stationers. 1640. 8°. . . . 5113

OTHER VERSIONS.

— (Metrical.) Trans. Abp. Parker. J. Day. [1567?] 4°. . 892
— — ...in the Kirk of Scotland. J. Canin (exp. H. Charteris and A. Hart), Dort. 1601. 8°. 6509
— — (Scots). The CL. psalmes. Edinburgh. 1632. 4°. 5963 (corrected)
— — Trans. King James I. Oxford. 1631. 12°. . . 5430

No.

Bible (Eng.), Psalms (Metrical) *cont.* — 1636. F°. 7769
— All the French Psalm tunes with English words...France and Germany. 1632. 12°. 3993
— The booke of psalmes. H. Tutill, Rotterdam. 1638. 12°. . 6661
— *See* Ainsworth (H.). Annotations... 1617–1618.
— — Book of Common Order. 1596. 8°.
— — — 1615. 5953
— — Hall (J.). Meditations and Vowes. 1621. 12°. . . 7793

APPENDIX.

— *See* Daman (W.). The psalmes. 1579. 8°.
— *See* Sandys (G.). A paraphrase. 1636.
— — 1638.
— [i–iv.] *See* Virgil [Æneis i–iv. Eng.]. 1583.
— (Selection.) [i, xii, xiii, xxiii, cxix, cxxv, cxxx, cxxxi, cxxxiii.] *See* Downe (J.). A Treatise.
— [xiv & cxxx.] *See* Bale (J.). An expostulation. [Ab. 1551.] 8°.
— [xiv.] Trans. by Elizabeth queen of England. *See* Margaret of Angoulême. A Godly Medytacyon. 1548.
— [xxi, lxv, cxlv.] *See* Hall (J.). Certayne Prouerbs. 1550.
— [xxiii, lxii, lxxiii, & lxxvii.] *See* Hooper (J.). Certaine... expositions. 1580.
— [xxxiv, liv, cxii, cxiv, cxv, cxlv?] *See* Hall (J.). Certayne Proverbs. 1549? etc.
— [xciv by W. Kethe.] *See* Knox (J.). The appellation. 1558. 8°.
— [ciii, cxii.] *See* Becon (T.). A comfortable Epistle. 1554.
— [civ, cxi, cxx–cxxii, cxxiv–cxxvi, cxxx.] *See* Dod (H.). Certaine Psalmes... 1603.
— [cx.] *See* Reynolds (E.). An explication. 1635.
— [7 Penitential Psalms.] *See* Wyat (Sir T.). Certayne psalmes... (1549.)
— — *See* Hunnis (W.). Seven sobs. 1589. 12°.
— *See* Baker (Sir R.). 1640.
— [Prose and Metre.] *See* Coote (E.). The English Schoolemaster... 1637.
— *See* Dod (H.). Certaine Psalmes... 1603.
— — Downe (J.). Certaine treatises. 1633.
— — Hall (J.). Certayn chapters... 1550.
— — Lok (H.). Ecclesiastes. 1597.
— — Segar (F.). Certayne Psalms... 1553.
— — Slatyer (W.). Psalmes... [1634.]
— — Tailor (R.). Sacred Hymns. 1615.

Proverbs, Ecclesiastes, Cantica Canticorum, Sapientia, Ecclesiasticus. (Story of Bel.). [Ab. 1549.] 8°. 6714
Proverbs. *See* Muffet (P.). A Commentarie. 1592.
— — Wilcox (T.). Workes. 1624.
— — Jermin (M.). Paraphrasticall Meditations. 1638.
— [ch. ix and x.] *See* Dod (J.) and Cleaver (R.). 1606.
— [ch. xv–xvii.] *See* Dod (J.) and Cleaver (R.). 1611.
— (Metrical.) *See* Hall (J.). The Prouerbes. 1549? etc.
— (Selection.) *See* Hall (J.). Certayn chapters... 1550.

Ecclesiastes. [1542.] *See* Proverbs.
— *See* Broughton (H.). A Comment... 1605.
— — Jermin (M.). A commentary. 1639.
— — Serres (J. de). A godlie...commentarie. 1585. 8°.
— — Pemble (W.). Salomons recantation. 1628.
— (Paraphrase.) *See* Lok (H.). Ecclesiastes. 1597.
— Metrical. *See* Sandys (G.). A paraphrase. 1638.
— — [ch. i–iii.] *See* Hall (J.). The Prouerbes. 1549? etc.

Song of Solomon. [1549.] *See* Proverbs.

No.

Bible (Eng.) *cont.* *See* Ainsworth (H.). Annotations... 1627 (1626).
— — 1639.
— Brucioli (A.). A commentary... 1598.
— Clapham (H.). The Song of Songs. Penned... 1602.
— Dove (J.). The Conversion of Solomon... 1613.
— Hall (Jos.). Salomons Diuine Arts. 1609.
— Wilcox (T.). Workes. 1624.
— (Metrical.) *See* Ainsworth (H.). Solomons Song of Songs. 1623.
— — *See* Fenner (D.). The song of songs. 1587, etc.
— — [ch. v, vi.] *See* Smith (Jude). A misticall deuise. 1575.
Isaiah. The Prophete Isaye translated into englysshe by G. Joye. 'B. Beckenth, Strassburg, 10 May 1531.' 8°. . . . 6094
Jeremiah. Jeremy the Prophete trans. G. Joye. [Antwerp?] May, 1534. 8°. 6098
— [xxiii.] *See* Luther (M.). A frutefull exposition. 1548. 8°. 7767
— (Metrical) 1566. *See* Horatius. Sermones. T. Drant. 1566. 4°.
Lamentations. 1587. 8°. 1944
— *See* Broughton (H.). The Lamentationes... 1606, 1608. . 6384
— — Jenkinson (A.). Meditations. 1609.
— — Udall (J.). A commentarie. 1593 etc. 4°. . . 7370 etc.
Ezekiel. [ch. ix.] *See* Brinsley (J.). The third part of the True-Watch. 1623. 4°.
Daniel. *See* Broughton (H.). Daniel... 1596, 1597, 1607.
— — Broughton (H.). An epistle. 1597. 4°.
— — Joye (G.). The exposicion... 1545 *etc.*
— — Willet (A.). Hexapla in Danielem. 1610.
— [ch. ix.] *See* Zwingli (U.). The accompt. 1555.

MINOR PROPHETS.

See Daneau (Lambert). A frvitfvll commentarie. 1594.
Hosea. [ch. xiv.] *See* Sibbes (R.). The returning backslider. 1639.
Joel. *See* Topsell (E.). Times Lamentation. 1599. 4°.
— [i.] *See* Udall (J.). The true remedie... [1587?]
Amos. [i, iii.] *See* Benefield (S.). A commentary. 1629. 4°.
— [ii.] *See* Benefield (S.). A commentarie. 1620. 4°.
Obadiah. *See* Brasbridge (T.).
— — Pilkington (Jas.). Aggeus and Abdias. 1562.
Jonah. *See* Hooper (J.). An ouersight. 1550.
— — King (J.). Lectures. 1597, 1618 etc.
— (Metrical.) *See* Quarles (F.). A feast for wormes. 1620. 4°.
Micah. *See* Gilby (A.). A commentarye... 1551.
Haggai. *See* Gryneus (J. J.). Haggeus. 1586.
— — Pilkington (J.). Aggeus. 1560 *etc.*
Zechariah. [i–ix.] *See* Pemble (W.). A short and sweete exposition. 1629.

APOCRYPHA.

Esdras Bk. IV. [xi.] *See* Prophesie. 1614.
Wisdom. [1549.] *See* Proverbs.
— (Metrical.) [ch. vi.] *See* Hall (J.). The Proverbs. 1549? etc.
— *See* Hall (J.). Certayn chapters. 1550.
Ecclesiasticus. [1549.] *See* Proverbs.
— (Metrical.) [ch. ix.] *See* Hall (J.). The Proverbes. 1549? etc.
— — [ch. li.] *See* Hunnis (W.). Certayne Psalmes... 1550.
Baruch. Selection. (Metrical.) [c. vi.] *See* Smith (Jude). A misticall deuise. 1575.
Song of the Three Children. (Metrical.) *See* Hunnis (W.). Certayne Psalmes. 1550.

No.

Bible (Eng.) *cont.* Story of Bel. [1549.] *See* Proverbs.
III Machabees. *See* Bible. Concordance. 8°.

NEW TESTAMENT.

N.T. (Polyglot.) Ed. E. Hutter. Noribergae. 1599. F°. . 6276
— Matthew. Ed. E. Hutter. Noribergae. 1599. 4°. . . 6277
— Mark. Ed. E. Hutter. Noribergae. 1600. 4°. . . 6278

— ENGLISH VERSIONS:

i. Tindale.	vi. Genevan.
ii. Coverdale.	vii. Bishops'.
iii. Taverner's.	viii. Rheims.
iv. Cranmer's.	ix. Royal.
v. I. C.	

i.

— Tindale. M. Emperour, Antwerp. 1534. 8°. . . 6090
— [Antwerp?] 1535. 8°. 6099
— Berthelet. 1536. F°. 433
— [S. de Cock, Antwerp.] 1536. 4°. . . . 6079, 6080
— M. Crom, Antwerp. 1538. 8°. 6102
— — 1539. 8°. 6103
— — Day and Seres. 1550. 8°. 906
— — R. Jugge. [1552.] 4°. 981
— — — [1553?] 4°. 982

ii.

— Coverdale. 1538. 16°. 6671

iii.

— Taverner. T. Petit for T. Berthelet. 1539. 8°. . . 7704

iv.

— Cranmer. The greate Bible... [Grafton?] 4°. . . 632

v.

— I. C. (Lat. & Eng.) T. Gaultier for I. C. 1550. 8°. . 1095

vi.

— Genevan. L. Tomson. C. Barker. 1583. 4°. . . 1675
— J. Legate... Cambridge. [1593?] 32°. 5544
— R. Barker. 1609. 16°. 2619

vii.

— Bishops'. 1601. *See below* Rhemes Version. 1601.

viii.

— Rhemes. J. Fogny, Rhemes. 1582. 4°. 6434
— — Ed. 2. D. Vervliet, Antwerp. 1600. 4°. . . 6139
— — Ed. 3. J. Seldenslach, Antwerp. 1621. 12°. . 6143
— — Ed. 4. J. Cousturier, Rouen. 1633. 4°. . . 6257
— — The text...with a confutation...by W. Fulke. R. Barker. 1601. F°. 2571
— — — J. Bill. 1617. F°. 3478
— — — 1633. F°. 4570–1
— — (Preface.) *See* Cartwright (T.). Σὺν θεῷ ἐν χριστῷ. 1602. 8°.
— — Appendix. *See* Bilson (T.). The true difference... 1585, 1586.

No.

Bible (Eng.). Rhemes *cont.* *See* Cartwright (T.). A Confvtation. 1618.
— — — Wither (G.). A view of the marginal notes. [1588?] 4°.

ix.

— Royal. B. Norton and J. Bill. 1625. 12°. 2826
— — Heires of A. Hart, Edinburgh. 1628. 8°. . . 5962
— — 'Revised.' Cambridge. 1628. 24°. . . . 5721
— — 'Revised by...command.' Cambridge. 1628. 24°. . 5722
— — *See* Rhemes Version. 1633.
— — R. Barker and ass. of J. Bill. 1634. 4°. . . . 2686
— R. Young, Edinburgh. 1636. 8°. 5978
— Paraphrase. (Matthew—Acts.) *See* Erasmus (D.). 1548 etc.
— Commentary. *See* Mayer (J.). A Commentarie. 1631.
— Epistles and Gospels. *See* Epistles and Gospels. 1538 etc.
— Gospels. *See* Hemmingsen (N.). A Postill. 1569.
— — Harmonies. *See* Calvin (J.). A harmonie. 1610. 4°.
— — — Garthwait (H.). *Μονοτεσσαρον*. 1634.
— — — Hind (J.). The storie. 1632.
— Matthew. *See* Ward (Ric.). Theologicall Questions. 1640.
— — Selection. [v—vii.] *See* Tindale (W.). Exposicion. [1530?] etc.
— Luke. Selection. (Benedictus-Metrical.) [i. 68–79.] *See* Hunnis (W.). Certayne Psalmes... 1550.
— John. *See* Traheron (B.). An exposition. 1557 etc.
— — [iv.] *See* Hildersam (A.). Lectures. 1629.
— — [xvii.] *See* Willet (A.). Ecclesia. 1614.
— Acts. *See* Calvin (J.). The commentaries. 1585. 4°.
— — *See* Gualther (R.). An hundred...homelyes. 1572. F°.
— — (Metrical.) *See* Tye (C.). The Actes... [1553?]
— Epistles. *See* Chytraeus (C.). A postil. 1570.
— Romans. *See* Calvin (J.). A Commentarie. 1583. 4°.
— — *See* Corro (A. à). A Theological Discourse. 1575.
— — *See* Martyr (Peter). Commentaries. 1568.
— — *See* Willet (A.). Hexapla. 1611 *etc.*
— — [i.] *See* Powel (G.). Prodromvs. 1602.
— — [i—iii.] *See* Sclater (W.). A key. 1611.
— — [vii.] *See* Elton (E.). The complaint. 1618.
— — [viii.] *See* Cowper (W.). Three heavenly treatises. 1609. 4°.
— — — Wilcocks (T.). Workes. 1624.
— — [xi.] *See* Sutton (T.). Lectures. 1632.
— — [xiii.] *See* Hooper (J.), *bp.* Godly...Annotations. 1551.
— I Cor. [vii.] *See* Erasmus. An exhortation. 1529.
— Galatians. *See* Luther (M.). A commentarie. 1575 *etc.*
— — *See* Prime (J.). An exposition. 1587.
— — (Selection.) *See* Perkins (W.). A commentarie. 1604.
— Ephesians. *See* Calvin (J.). The sermons. 1577. 4°.
— — *See* Chrysostom (St. John). An exposition. 1581.
— — *See* Hemmingsen (N.). The epistle. 1581 (1580). 4°.
— — *See* Ridley (L.). A commentary. 1540. 8°.
— Philippians. *See* Ridley (L.). An exposytion. [Ab. 1550.] 8°.
— Colossians. *See* Byfield (N.). An exposition. 1627.
— — — Calvin (J.). A Commentarie. [1581?] 4°.
— — — Dod (J.). Ten Sermons. 1610.
— — — Elton (E.). An exposition. 1620 *etc.*
— — — Rollock (R.). Lectures. 1603. 4°.
— Thessalonians. *See* Bullinger (H.). A commentary. 1538.
— — — Jewel (J.). An exposition. 1583.
— — — Rollock (R.). Lectvres. 1606.
— — — Sclater (W.). An exposition. 1627(–9). 4°.
— — [II] *See* Carlile (C.). A discourse. 1572.

No.

Bible (Eng.) *cont.* — *See* Squire (J.). A plaine exposition. 1630.
— — Selection. (Metrical.) *See* Hall (J.). Certayn chapters... 1550.
— Titus. *See* Taylor (T.). A commentarie. 1619. 4°.
— Philemon. *See* Attersoll (W.). A commentarie. 1633. F°.
— — — Jones (W.). 1635. F°.
— Hebrews. *See* Calvin (J.). A commentarie. 1605. 4°.
— — — Dickson (D.). A short explanation. 1635.
— — — Jones (W.). 1635. F°.
— — [i—vi.] *See* Dering (E.). XXVII. Lectures. 1576.
— Epistles Catholic. *See* Mayer (J.). Ecclesiastica Interpretatio. 1627. 4810
— James. *See* Hemmingsen (N.). A learned...Commentarie. 1577.
— — — Mayer (J.). Praxis Theologica. 1629.
— — — Turnbull (R.). An exposition. 1592 *etc.* . . 2133 etc.
— I Peter. [i—iii.] *See* Byfield (N.). A commentary. 1637.
— I John. *See* Calvin (J.). The Comentaries. [156–?]
— II & III John. *See* Jones (W.). 1635. F°.
— Jude. *See* Calvin (J.). The Comentaries. [156–?]
— — — Perkins (W.). A godlie...exposition. 1606. 4°.
— — — Ridley (L.). An exposition. [Ab. 1550.]
— — — Trigge (F.). A tovchstone. 1600.
— — — Turnbull (R.). An exposition. 1592 *etc.* . 2133 etc.
— — — Willet (A.). A catholikon. 1602. 8°.
— — — Willet (A.). Ecclesia. 1614.
— Revelation. *See* Bale (J.). The Image of both churches... [154–.] 8°.
— — — — 1550. 4°.
— — — Brightman (T.). A Revelation. 1615. 4°.
— — — — 1616. 8°.
— — — Du Jon (F.). The revelation. 1594. 4°.
— — — Du Jon (F.). The apocalyps... 1596.
— — — Bible (N.T.), Genevan. 1602. 8°. . . . 7782
— — — Forbes (P.). An exqvisite commentarie. 1613.
— — — Gifford (G.). Sermons. 1596 *etc.*
— — — Mayer (J.). Ecclesiastica Interpretatio. 1627.
— — — Napier (J.). A plaine discovery. 1593 etc.
— — — Plaine explanation. 162[3?] 4°. . . . 3434
— — — Symonds (W.). Pisgah evangelica. 1606.
— — [iv—vii.] *See* Cowper (W.). Pathmos. 1619.
— — [iv.] *See* Traheron (B.). An Exposition. 1573 etc.
— — [xi—xiii.] *See* L. (T.). An exposition... 1623.
— — [xvi.] *See* Burton (H.). The seven vials... 1628.
— — (Appendix.) *See* Bernard (R.). A Key of Knowledge. 1617.
— — — Broughton (H.). A revelation... 1610.
— — — Bullinger (H.). A hvndred Sermons. 1561.

GENERAL APPENDIX.

Chronology. *See* A. (R.). A briefe chronologie. 1600.
(A briefe and compendious Register... The Thyrde boke of The Machabees.) W. Lynne, 1550. 8°. 781
Concordance. (J. Downame.) Ass. of C. Cotton. 1632. 4°. . 5126
— Cotton (C.). A large concordance. Ed. 2. 1635. F°. . 3748
The doctrine of the Bible. 1630. 12°. 4144
See Sum.

GREEK VERSION.

Old Testament. Job. *See* Duport (J.). Θρηνοθρίαμβος. (Gr. Lat.) 1637. *Also* Nicetas. 1637. . . . . . 2696, 7849

No.

Bible (Greek) *cont.* Psalms. (Metrical.) *See* Apollinarius. Μεταφρασις. 1590.
— *See* Common Prayer. Greek. 1638.
New Testament. (Greek.) Ἡ καινη διαθηκη. T. Vautrollier, 1587. 16°. 1562
— Reg. Typog. 1592. 16°. 1692
— Cum notis R. Stephani, J. Scaligeri, & I. Casauboni. J. Bill, 1622. 8°. 3510
— Cantabrigiae. 1632. 8°. 5797–9
— Cum notis R. Stephani &c. 'R. Whitaker' [Elsevier, Leyden]. 1633. 8°. 6491
— Epistles of St Paul. (Gr. Lat.) *See* Theophylactus. 1636. F°.

IRISH VERSION.

New Testament. (Irish.) J. Frankton, Dublin, 1602. F°. . 6013

LATIN BIBLE.

Bible. H. Middleton, imp. C. Barker. 1580 (1579). 4°. . . 1629
H. Middleton, imp. W. Norton. 1581. 4°. 1635
— 1585. 4°. 1651
Imp. W. Norton. 1593(–2). F°. 1335
F. Junii. Ed. 3. G. Bishop, R. Newbery, & R. Barker, 1597. F°. 1737
Selections. Analysis. *See* Kis (S.). Tabulæ analyticæ. 1593. 4°. 7785
Pentateuch. App. *See* Ferdinand (P.). Haec sunt Verba dei. 1597. 5586
Deuteronomy. *See* Macalpine (J.). Enarratio. 1563.
Job. (Metrical.) *See* Adamson (P.)... Poëmata sacra. 1619–18.
See Duport (J.). Θρηνοθρίαμβος. (Gr. Lat.) 1637.
Psalmorum Davidis et aliorum... T. Beza auctore. T. Vautrollier impensis H. Francisci, 1580. 8°. 1539
Psalmi Davidis Tremellii et Junii. H. Denham for W. Seres, 1580. 16°. 1420
Psalterium Davidis carmine redditum per Heobanum Hessum. T. Vautrollier. 1581. 12°. 1543
Psalterium Davidis Latino-Saxonicum vetus, a J. Spelmanno. R. Badger, imp. P. Stephani & C. Meredith, 1640. 4°. . 4400
Psalterium Davidis. R. Young, 1640. 8°. 5012
Psalms. *See* Psalter.
— — Vicars (J.). Decapla. 1639.
— Liber psalmorum...a S. Munstero...versus. *See* Liber precum publicarum. 1594. 8°.
— (Paraphrase.) *See* Buchanan (G.). Ecphrasis... 1620.
— Selection. [i—l.] *See* Sampson (R.). Richardi... 1539.
— [li—c.] *See* Sampson (R.). Richardi... 1548.
— [i—xl.] *See* Perez (J. de). Expositiones. 1481.
— [vii Penitential.] *See* Fisher (J.). A treatise.
— [xxx—li. By Savonarola.] *See* Primer. 1538 *etc.* 4°.
— [civ.] *See* Barclay (W.)....Jvdicium. 1620.
— *See* Psalms. Psalmi seu Precationes. 1544. . . . 479
— *See* Fisher (J.). Psalmi. 1568. 16°.
— (Metrical.) *See* Buchanan (G.). Psalmorum Davidis. 1640. 12°.
— *See* Eobanus (H.). Psalterivm. 1581.
— Selection. *See* Gentili (S.). Paraphrasis. 1581.
— — In xxv Davidis Psalmos. 1584.
— *See* Johnston (A.). Paraphrasis. 1637.
Ecclesiastes. Salomonis concio ab. A. Corrano. 1579. 8°. . 1922
— *See* Cartwright (T.). In librvm... 1604.
— (Metrical.) *See* Eobanus (H.). Psalterium. 1581.
Song of Solomon. Thargum...paraphrasis in Canticum Canticorum. Ed. E. Rivio. 1614. 8°. 3653
— *See* Foliot (G.). Expositio. 1638.

No.

Bible (Lat.) *cont.* — *See* Tomson (W.). In Canticum Canticorum... 1583.
— — James (T.). Concordantiæ sanctorvm patrvm... 1607.
Jeremiah. *See* Lathbery (J.). Liber moralium. 1482.
Daniel. *See* Rollock (R.). In librvm... 1591.
Minor Prophets (Hosea—Jonah). *See* Lively (E.). Annotationes. 1587.
Jonah. *See* Baro (P.). Petri Baronis...in Jonam... 1579.
— (Lat. & Eng.) T. Gaultier, 1550. 8°. 1095
Novum Testamentum. J. Mayler, Feb. 1550. 4°. . . . 678
— T. Beza interpr. T. Vautrollier, 1574. 8°. 1526
— I. Tremellii. T. Vautrollier impensis C. Barker, 1580. 4°. 1540
— T. Beza interprete. T. Vautrollier. 1587. 8°. . . . 7272
— Matthew [v.] (Comm.). *See* James (T.). Index Generalis. 1624. 8°.
— Luke. *See* Piscator (J.). Analysis. 1596. 8°.
— John. *See* Piscator (J.). Analysis. 1595. 8°.
— Acts. *See* Piscator (J.). Analysis. 1597. 8°.
— Epistles of St Paul. (Harmonies.) *See* Piscator (J.). Analysis. Ed. 2. 1594. 8°.
— Romans. *See* Corro (A. à). Dialogvs. 1574.
— — — Rollock (R.). Analysis dialectica. 1594.
— — — Sampson (R.). In D. Pauli epistolam. 1546. 8°.
— I Corinthians. *See* Morton (T.). Prioris Corinthiacæ... 1596.
— — — Sampson (R.). In D. Pauli epistolam. 1546. 8°.
— Galatians. *See* Rollock (R.). Analysis logica. 1602.
— Titus. *See* Ascham (R.). Apologia... 1577.
— Philemon. *See* Ascham (R.). Apologia... 1577.
— Epistles General. (Harmony). Piscator (J.). Analysis. Ed. 2. 1597. 8°.
— James. [i, ii.] *See* Tuke (T.). Index. [1617.]
— Revelation. *See* Foxe (J.). Eicasmi. 1587.
— — — Fulke (W.). In sacram... 1573.
— — — Mede (J.). Clavis apocalyptica. 1627.
— — [i—xi.] *See* Trigge (F.). Noctes sacrae. 1590.
— — (Metrical.) *See* Adamson (P.).... Poëmata sacra. 1619-18.
— Epistles & Gospels. *See* Gulielmus Parisiensis. Postille. 1509.
— Selections. (Metrical.) *See* Smyth (W.). Gemma Fabri. 1598.
— Abridgment. (Metrical.) *See* Shaw (J.). Bibliorum svmmvla. 1623. 8°.
Analysis. *See* Pflacher (M.). Analysis typica. 1587. 4°.
Appendix. [Collation of Roman catholic versions 1589, 1592, etc. (Louvain).] *See* James (T.). Bellum papale. 1600.
— *See* Smyth (W.). Gemma Fabri.

SPANISH.

N.T. R. Field, 1596. 8°. 2240
— Romans. (Appendix.) *See* Valdes (J. de). The hundred and ten considerations. 1638.

SYRIAC.

N.T. *See* Bible. Lat. 1585.
— — — 1593(-2).

WELSH.

Bible. B. Norton & J. Bill, 1620. F°. 2808
N.T. H. Denham for H. Toy, 1567. 4°. 1402

No.
Bibliander (Theodorus). A godly consultation. 'R. Bonifante, Basill, Aug. 1542.' 8°. 6104
Bickley (Thomas). Verses in Elyot (Sir T.). Bibliotheca. 1552. . 502
— Humphrey (L.). I. Ivelli vita. 1573. 837
Biclæus (Thomas). *See* Bickley.
Bidding prayer. Fourme of bidding the common praiers. *See* England, Church of. Injunctions. 1547 etc.
1634. *See* Browne (T.). The copie. 1634. 4°. 5407
Biddulph (Peter). *See* Biddulph (W.). The travels.
Biddulph (William). The travels of certaine Englishmen. 1609. 4°. 3618
The travels of fovre Englishmen and a preacher into Africa. 1612. 4°. 2974
Bidillus (John). Verses in Wilson (Sir T.). Vita. 1551. . . 631
Bieston (R.). The bayte & snare of Fortune. Wayland [1554?]. F°. 639
Bifield. *See* Byfield.
Bill (Charles). Verses *bis* in Cambridge Lachrymae. 1587. . 7356
Bill (John), *printer*. *See* Bible. N.T. (Gr.). 1622.
— Dominis (M. A. de). Alter Ecebolius. 1624.
Bill (William), *Master Doctor*. Verses in Hutchinson (R.). The Image of God. 1560. 794
Billingsley (H.). *See* Euclid. The elements of geometrie. 1570.
— Martyr (P.). Commentaries. 1568. F°.
Bilson (Tho.). The effect of certaine sermons. 1599. 4°. . . 2334
The perpetval government of christes church. 1593. 4°. . 1695
— 1610. 4°. 2403
De perpetua ecclesiae christi gubernatione. 1611. 4°. . . 3455
Svrvey of Christs svfferings. 1604. F°. . . . 3356, 3357
True difference between...subjection and...rebellion. Oxford, 1585. 4°. 5223
— J. Jackson & E. Bollifant. 1586. 8°. 2097
See Broughton (H.). Declaration of generall corruption... 1604.
— — Replie vpon the R. R. F. Th. Winton... 1605.
— — Two little workes... 1604.
— Jacob (H.). A Defence. 1600.
— — An Attestation. 1613. 8°.
[Relief of Geneva.] *See* James I. Royal Letters. 1604. F°. . 7416
See Norris (S). An antidote. 1615 *etc.* 4°.
— — The Guide. 1621. 4°.
Bindlos (Robert), *T.C.C.* Verses in Cam. Univ. Voces. 1640. . 5836
Bing. *See* Byng.
Bingham (John), *Captain*. *See* Ælianus, *Tacticus*. The Tactiks of Ælian... 1616.
— Xenophon. The historie. 1623. F°.
Bingham (Richard), *Captain*. Verses in Gilbert (Sir H.). A true reporte. 1583. 1354
Binivs (Severinus). *See* Crashaw (W.). Ad Severinvm Binnivm... 1624.
Bion. [*Gr. Lat.*] *See* Poetæ minores. 1635.
Biondi (Giovanni Francesco). Donzella Desterrada, or the Banished Virgin. Trans. J. Hayward. 1635. F°. 4635
— Eromena. Trans. J. Hayward. 1632. F°. 7753
Birchensha (Ralph). Discourse upon...Tyrone and Odonnell...by Lord Mountjoy. 1602. 4°. 2872
Birckbek (Simon). The protestants evidence. 1634. 4°. . . 4581
— 1635. 4°. 5058
Bird (John). Grounds of grammar. Oxford, 1639. 8°. . . 5487
Bird (Richard). Verses in Jewel (J.). Adv. T. Hardingum. 1578. 1535
Bird (Samuel). Lectures...upon the 11. chapter of...Hebrewes...the 38. Psalme. Cambridge, 1598. 8°. 5591
Birkhed (Hen.). Verses in Oxf. Univ. Horti. 1640. . . . 5499

No.

Birstall (William), *fellow of King's Coll.* Verses in Ovid. Fasti. 1640. 5849
Birstall (William), *Regal.* Verses in Cam. Univ. Voces. 1640. . 5836
Bishop (J.). Beavtifvll Blossomes...of all kyndes. 1577. 4°. . . 1850
Courteous conference with the English Catholickes. 1598. 4°. 2344
See Beautiful Baybush. 6767
Bishop (William). A disproofe of D. Abbots Counter-proofe. Part 1. Paris, 1614. 8°. 6198
Reformation of a catholike deformed. Pt 2. 1607. 4°. . 6873
See Abbot (R.). A defence of...W. Perkins. 1606. 4°.
— — The trve ancient Roman Catholike... 1611.
— Copies of certaine discourses. 1601.
— Wotton (A.). A defence. 1606.
— — — The second part. 1607.
Bisse (James). Two Sermons. 1581. 8°. 1812
Bisterveld (Hadrian Damman à). *See* Damman.
Bizari (Pietro). Verses in Harvey (G.). Gratulationum. 1578. . 1495
Verses in Meteren (E. van). A trve discovrse. 1602. . . 2873
See Polemon (J.). All the famous Battels... [1557?]
Bizarri, Bizarrus (P.). *See* Bizari.
Blackwell (George). Declaratio motuum ac turbationum. 'Rhotomagi, ap. J. Molaeum,' 1601. 4°. 6835
Large examination of...Blakwell. 1607. 4°. 2602
In G. Blacvellum quaestio bipartita. 1609. 4°. . . 2365
[Letter to Card. Caietano.] *See* Philalethes (A.), *pseud.* An answere... 1602.
Relatio compendiosa. 'Rhotomagi, ap. J. Molaeum' [1601?]. 4°. 6836
See B. (I.). The Hope of Peace... 1601.
— Bell (T.). The anatomie of Popish tyrannie... 1603.
— Colleton (J.). A iust defence. 1602. 4°.
— Ely (H.). Certaine briefe notes... [1603.]
— James I. Triplici nodo... 1607.
— — An apologie... 1609.
— Sutcliffe (M.). A challenge. 1602.
— Watson (W.). A dialogve... 1601.
Blackwood (Adam). Martyre de la royne d'escosse. 'Edinbourg, J. Nafield,' 1587. 8°. 6786
— 1589. 12°. 6790
Blage (John). *See* Blague.
Blagrave (John). The art of dyalling. 1609. 4°. 3629
Baculum Familliare. 1590. 4°. 1854
Mathematical iewel. [1585.] F°. 1823
Very briefe...description of...Astrolabe...the Mathematicall Iewell. *See* Blundevile (T.). Exercises. 1622–1 *etc.*
Blague (Thomas). Sermon at the Charterhouse. 10 May 1603. 1603. 8°. 2880
Blair (James). Verses in Adamson (J.). Εἰσόδια. 1618. . . 5960
Blair (Robert). Verses in Adamson (J.). Εἰσόδια. 1618. . . 5960
Blake (William). Verses in Camdeni Insignia. 1624. . . 5346
Camb. Univ. Carmen. 1635. 5770
— Συνῳδία. 1637. 5790
Blancks (William), *Gonv.* Verses in Camb. Univ. Lacrymæ. 1619. . 5689
— Genethl. 1631. 5731
— Hippocrates. 1633. 5812
Blanford (Walt.). Verses in Oxf. Univ. Horti. 1640. . . 5499
Blanks (William). *See* Blancks.
Blarus, Blarius. *See* Blair.
Blastus (James), *a Cretan.* Verses in Hippocrates. 1633. . . 5812
Blaxton (Henry). Verses in Cambridge Acad. Cantab. Lachrymae. 1587. 7356
Blaxton (John). The English usurer. Ed. 2. 1634. 4°. . . 4895

No.
Blaxton (Josua). Verses in Camb. Univ. Epicedium. 1612. . . 5665
Blazing of Bawdrie. *See* C. (R.).
Blenerhasset (T.). Direction for the plantation in Vlster. 1610. 4°. 2024
See Higgins (J.). A mirrour. 1610.
Blickard (Stuck). Verses in Bodleiomnema. 1613. . . . 7756
Blomfield (S.). Verses in Dugres (G.). 1636. 5781
Blosius (Ludovicus). *See* Souls Desire. 1580.
Blount (Cecilia, Lady). A sermon...at the funeral of the Lady Blount, 6 Dec. 1619. 1620. 8°. 4162
Blount (Sir Christopher). *See* Bacon (F. Lord). A declaration... 1601.
Blount or Blunt (Edward). *See* Conestaggio (G.). Historie of... Portvgall. 1600.
— Dallington (Sir R.). A svrvey... 1605.
— Earle (J.). Microcosmographie. 1629.
— Horæ Subsecivæ. 1620.
— Juan *de Sancta Maria.* Christian policie. 1632. 4°.
— — Police unveiled. 1634. 4°.
Blount (Sir Henry). Voyage into the levant. 1636. 4°. . . 4730
— Ed. 3. 1638. 4°. 4737
Blount (Montjoy), Lord Montjoy. *See* Montjoy.
Blount (Sir Richard). *See* B. (J.), *D.D.*
Blower (Ralph). *See* W. (G.). A rich storehouse. 1630.
Blundeville (Thomas). Arte of logicke. 1619. 4°. . . 3126, 3127
The arte of ryding. [1575?] 8°. 942
Exercises. 1594. 4° 2136
— 1622–1. 4°. 3138
— Ed. 7. 1636. 4°. 5105
Foure chiefest offices belonging to Horsemanship. 1593. 4°. . 2323
— 1609. 4°. 2492
Three morall treatises. 1580. 8°. 1419
See Furio Ceriol (F.). A very briefe...Treatise... 1570.
Blunt (Edward). Verses in Oxf. Univ. Magd. Coll. 1612. . . 5302
Bo (Sir Jo.). Verses in Du Bartas. Weekes. 1605–6 *etc.* . 2476 *etc.*
Boaistuau (P.). Theatrum Mundi. [1566?] 8°. . . . 1438
See Chelidonius. A most excellent Hystorie. 1571. 4°.
Bocard (Andreas). *See* Lyndwood (W.). Prouinciale. 1501.
Boccaccio (Giovanni). [Decameron. Vol. I.] The modell of wit, mirth, eloquence, & conversation. 1625. F°. 3974
Decameron. Vol. II. 1620. F°. 3970
Fall of Princes. Pynson, 1494. F°. 106
Tragedies...of...Princes. Trans. J. Lydgate. Wayland [1554]. F°. 640
— R. Tottell. 1554. F°. 1105
See Lydgate (J.). Prouerbes of Lydgate (upon the fall of Princes).
Boccalini (Trajano). The new-found politicke. 1626. 4°. . . 5028
Boccus. History of kyng Boccus & Sydracke. T. Godfray [1532?]. . 556
See Sydrach. Certain reasons. 1528. 4°.
Bodenham (J.). Englands Helicon. 1600. 4°. 1780
Wits Theater of the little World. 1599. 8°. 1778
Bodenstein (Andreas). *See* Carolostadius.
Bodin (Jean). Commonweale. Trans. R. Knolles. 1606. F°. . 2436
See Bridges (J.). A defence... 1587.
— Malynes (G. de). Englands view. 1603.
Bodius. *See* Boyd.
Bodley (Laurence), *B.D.* [Funeral.] *See* Pecke (R.). Christs Watch-word. 1635. 4°.
Verses in Humphrey (L.). I. Ivelli vita. 1573. . . . 837
Bodley (Sir Thomas). Verses in Humphrey (L.). I. Ivelli vita. 1573. 837
[Death.] *See* Oxford University. Ivsta... 1613.
— — Merton College. Bodleiomnema. (Frag.) 1613. . 7756
Bodurda (Henry). Verses in Camb. Univ. Genethl. 1631. . . 5731

No.

Body of Policy. 1521. *See* Christine de Pisan.
Boece (Hector). Hystory and croniklis of Scotland. Trans. J. Bellenden. T. Davidson. Edinburgh. [1542?] F°. 5910
See Holinshed (R.)...Chronicles... 1577, 1587.
Boehme (Johann). *See* Boemus (Joannes), Aubanus.
Boemus (Joannes), *Aubanus*. The Fardle of facions. 1555. 8°. . 1164
— Manners Lawes and customes of all nations. Trans. E. Aston. 1611. 4°. 7534
Boethius (A. M. T.). De consolatione philosophie. Caxton [1477]. F°. 2
— J. Cawood. 1556. 4°. 995
— [Eng. only.] *See* Chaucer (G.). The Workes. 1598.
Of philosophicall comfort. 1609. 8°. 2176
[De divisionibus.] *See* Andreæ (A.). 1480. 4°. 84
Boethius (Hector). *See* Boece.
Bogislaus. *See* Boleslaus.
Bohemia. Articles of the league betweene Fredericke, and Gabriel prince of Hungaria. 1620. 4°. 6918
Bohemica Iura Defensa. The Bohemian Lawes...defended. Trans. I. H. 1620. 4°. 7515
Bohemiae regnum electiuum. A plaine and true relation. 1620. 4°. 6917
Two letters or embassies...conc. the troubles of Germany. Amsterdam, 1620. 4°. 6399
See Frederick I. A Declaration. 1620. 4°. 6485
— Prague. A true relation of the bloody execution. 1621. 4°. 6930
— W. (S.). The appollogie. 1622. 4°.
— Wittenberg University. 1620.
Bois (John). *See* Boys.
Bois-le-duc. *See* Hertogenbosch, s'.
Βοΐτων (Ἰλερμος). Verses in Cheke (Sir J.). De obitu M. Buceri. 1551. 734
Bolde Alexander. — — Epithalam. 1625. 5702
Boleslaus XIV, duke of Pomerania. *See* Sweden. Gustavus II Adolphus. 1631.
Boleyn (Thomas). *See* Wiltshire (Thomas Boleyn, earl of).
Bologna. *See* Rome, *Church of*. Consilium. 1613. 2313
Bolton (Edmund). The elements of armories. 1610. 4°. . . . 3573
Nero Cæsar. 1623. F°. 3433
— 1624. (1627.) F°. 3440
Verses in Jonson (B.). Workes. 1616. 3115
Camden (W.). Britannia. 1637. 3055–6
See Florus. The Roman Histories. [1618] *etc.*
— Philipot (J.). The City's Advocate. 1629. 4°. . . . 4691
Bolton (Sir Richard). A Justice of Peace for Ireland. Dublin. 1638. F°. 6062
See Ireland. Statutes. 1621.
Bolton (Robert). Workes. 1641. 4°. 7600
Discourse about...happinesse. Ed. 3. 1614. 4°. . . . 2985
— Ed. 5. 1625. 4°. 3028
— Ed. 6. 1636. 4°. 4731
— Ed. 7. 1638. 4°. 7624
Helpes to humiliation. Ed. 3. 1633. 4°. 4624
— Ed. 4. 1637. 4°. 3714
Instructions for...afflicted consciences. 1631. 4°. . . . 3044
— Ed. 2. 1635. 4°. 4013
— Ed. 3. 1640. 4°.
Foure last things &c. Ed. 3. 1635. 4°. 4454
— Ed. 4. 1639. 4°. 4473
Short and private discourse...concerning Usury. (E. Bagshawe.) 1637. 4°. 4465
Some general directions for...walking with God. Ed. 2. 1626. 4°. 3031
— Ed. 3. 1630. 4°. 3043
— Ed. 4. 1634. 4°. 4720

No.
Bolton (Robert) *cont.* Threefold treatise. 1634. 4°. 4107
Two sermons. 1635. 4°. 4455
[Life & Funeral Sermon.] *See* Estwick (N.). A learned...Sermon. 1633. 4°.
Bomelius (Henricus). Verses in Bale (J.). Illustrium sciptorum. 1548. 6314–5
Bonaventura. Speculum vitæ Christi. Ed. 1. Caxton [1485–6]. F°. 28
— Ed. 2. Caxton [1485–6]. F°. 29
— The mirrour of the blessed life of Christ. Pynson [1494]. F°. 111
[Life of Christ.] *See* Heigham (J.) The life. 1622. 12°.
See Whitford (R.). A werke of preparation... 1531.
Bond (John). *See* Horatius. Poemata. 1614.
— Persius (A.). Satyræ. 1614.
Bonde (William). *See* Pilgrimage of Perfection. 1526 *etc.*
Bonet (Honoré). *See* Pisan (C. de). The Fayt of Armes. [1489.]
Bonham (Edward). Verses in Gerhard (J.). Meditations. 1627 *etc.* . 5707, [5824 *etc.*
Bonham (John). Verses in Gerhard (J.). Meditations. 1627 *etc.* . 5707, [5824 *etc.*
Bonham (Thomas). The chyrurgeons closet...by E. Poeton. 1630. 4°. 4430
Verses in Clowes (W.). A right frvtefvll...Treatise. 1602. . 2013
— Gerhard (J.). The meditations. 1627 *etc.* . . 5735, 5824 *etc.*
— — Prayers. 1625 *etc.* . . . . . . 3321 *etc.*
See Parkinson (J.). Theatrum... 1640.
Bonham (Tho.), *K.C.C.* Verses in Cam. Univ. Epithalam. 1625. . 5702
Bonham (William). Verses in Camb. Univ. Lacrymæ. 1619. . 5689
Bonifacius, *pseud.* *See* Erasmus (D.). Two dyaloges. [Ab. 1550.] 8°.
Bonner (Edmund). Homelies sette forthe...diocesse of London. 1555. *See post* Profitable and necessarye doctrine. 4°.
Profitable and necessarye doctryne, with certayne homelies. J. Cawood. 1555. 4°. 991, 992
See Admonition to the bishoppes. 1553.
— Bale (J.). A declaration of Edmonde Bonners articles... 1561.
— — Yet a course at the Romyshe foxe... 1543.
— Bible. Eng. (Cranmer's). 1540 *etc.*
— Gardiner (S.). De vera obedientia... 1553.
— Homilies. 1547.
Booke intituled English Protestants Recantation. 1617. 8°. . . 6908
Book of Assises. *See* Assizes.
Book of Carving. W. de Worde. 1508. 4°. 156
Book of Children. *See* Phayre (T.). The regiment of Life. 1596.
Book of Comfort. W. de Worde. [15–.] 4°. 213
Book of Common Order. 1584. 16°. 6777, 6778
H. Charteris. Edinburgh. 1596. 8°. 5919
The CL. psalmes of David. A. Hart, Edinburgh, 1615. 8°. . 5953
— Heires of A. Hart. Edinburgh. 1632. 4°. 5963 (corrected p. 1743)
Book of Courtesy. Caxton. [1477–8.] 4°. 3
Lytell Johan. *See* Sulpitius (J.). Stans puer ad mēsā. W. de Worde. 4°.
Book of divers ghostly matters. [1490.] *See* Horologium Sapientie.
Book of Diversitees of Courtes. 1561. *See* Novae narrationes.
Book of Examples. *See* Right fruitful Book *etc.*
Book of Good Manners. 1487 *etc.* *See* Le Grand.
Book of Honor and Armes. [R. Jones, 1590.] 4°. . . . 1450
Book of Husbandry. *See* Fitzherbert (J.). 1525 *etc.*
See Henley (W. de). Boke. [15–.]
Book of Justices of peace. The Justice of peas. R. Copland. 1515. 4°. 338
Pynson, 1521. 4°. 278
R. Redman, n.d. 8°. 387
(5 parts.) T. Berthelet, 1544(–3). 8°. 471

No.
Book of Justices of peace (*cont*). [T. Berthelet, ab. 154- .] 8°. . 7085
Book of Medicines. 1575. *See* Treasure of Poor Men.
Book of Nobleness. Trans. John Larke. R. Wyer, n.d. 8°. . . 545
Book of Presidents. 1543. *See* Phaer (T.).
R. Tottell. 1584. 4°. 1146
Stationers. 1611. 8°. 3245
[Ab. 1620.] 8°. . . . . 7410+
Book of Principles. [Ab. 1640?] 12°. 7062
Book of Sports. 1633. 4°. 2682
Book of Sundry Instruments. (Headline.) [Ab. 1620?] 8°. Cf. no. 7410+
Book of Surveying. Pynson, 1526. 4°. 287
Surveyinge. Berthelet, 1539. 8°. 449
Booke of the forme of common prayers. R. Schilders, Middelburg, 1586. 8°. 6446
Ed. 4. R. Schilders, Middelburg, 1602. 8°. 6461
Book. The Boke. Reade me frynde and be not wrothe. 1546. *See* W. Roy.
Books. *See* Proclamations. 1623.
(Latin.) *See* Proclamations. 1625 (April 1).
Book-Collectors, Book-owners, Book-labels *etc.* *See* Bibliographical Index.
Booker (John). *See* Rastell (W.). A table. 1639. 8°.
Boorde or Borde (A.). The Breuiary of Healthe. W. Powell, 1557. 4°. 1015
— T. East, 1587. 4°. 1591
— T. East, 1598. 4°. 1608
Compēdyous Regyment or Dyetary of helth. R. Wyer, n.d. 8°. 546
— T. Colwell in the house of R. Wyer, 1562. 8°. . . 1328
— H. Jackson, 1576. 8°. 1851
Pryncyples of Astronomye. R. Copland ['1547'?]. 8°. . 340
Boordman (Andrew). Verses in Digby (E.). Theoria. 1579. . 1500–1
Booth (John). Verses in Camb. Univ. Genethl. 1631. . . 5731
— Anthologia. 1632. 5741
— Fasciae. 1633. 5808
— Rex redux *bis*. 1633. 5748
— Hippocrates. 1633. 5812
— Carmen. 1635. 5770
— *Συνῳδία*. 1637 *bis*. 5790
— Fuller (T.). Holy Warre. 1639 *etc.* 5806
— Cam. Univ. Voces. 1640. 5836
Booth (Robert). Verses in Digby (E.) Theoria. 1579. . 1500–1
Booth (William). Verses in Camb. Univ. Lacrymæ. 1619. . 5689
Borde (Andrew). *See* Boorde.
Bordeaux (John de). *See* John.
Boreman (R.), *T.C.C.* Verses in Cam. Univ. Anthologia. 1632. . 5741
— Rex redux *bis*. 1633. 5748
— *Συνῳδία*. 1637. 5790
Borgarucius (Julius). Verses in Castiglione (B.). De Curiali. 1571. 824
Borlase (Sir William). Verses in Horatius. Art of poetry. 1640. . 3728
Bossewell (John). Workes of Armorie. 1597. 4°. . . . 2895
Bostock (Richard). *See* B. (R.), *Eng.* The difference. 1585.
Boston Parish Church. Dispensation and privileges. Pynson [1505?]. Bds. 294
Boston (W.). Verses in Bellehachius (O.). Sacrosancta bucolica. 1583. 1640
Bosw. (G.), *Coll. Jes. Cantab.* *See* Boswell.
Boswell (Thomas), *Pemb.* Verses in Camb. Univ. Genethl. 1631. 5731
— Fasciae. 1633. 5808
— Hippocrates. 1633. 5812
See also Bouswell.
Boswell (William). *See* Texeda (F. de). Texeda Retextus. 1623.
Boswell (William). *See also* Bouswell. Verses in Dolor. 1625. 5701 *bis*.

No.
Boswell (William) *cont.* — Epithalamium. 1625. 5702
Boteler (George). Verses in Camb. Univ. Genethl. 1631. . . . 5731
— Anthologia. 1632. 5741
— Fasciae. 1633. 5808
— Rex redux. 1633. 5748
Boteler (Harrington). Verses in Camb. Univ. Lacrymae. 1619. . 5689
Boteler (Sir Philip). *See* Downham (G.). A fvnerall sermon... 1607.
Boteler (Sir Robert). [Funeral.] *See* H. (T.). A sermon. 1623. 4°.
Relations of the most famous kingdoms. 1608. 4°. . . 2764
Botero (G.). A treatise concerning the...greatness of Cities. Trans. R. Peterson. 1606. 4°. 1385
Cause of the Greatnesse of Cities. Trans. Sir T. H. 1635. 12°. 4112
Observations concerning the Sea. Trans. Sir T. H. *See ante* Cause of the Greatnesse of Cities. 1635. 12°. . . 4112
Boteler (G.), *Queens'*. Verses in Cam. Univ. Epithalam. 1625. . 5702
— 1616. 4°. 3664
— Inlarged. 1630. 4°. 4830
Bouaisteau (Pierre). *See* Boaistuau.
Boughen (Edw.). Sermon concerning decencie. 1638. 4°. . . . 5149
Sermon of confirmation...Visitation...Sept. 27. 1619. 1620. 4°. 4163
Two sermons. 1635. 4°. 4362
Bouillon (Henri de La Tour, duc de). *See* France. Louis XIII. . 1617
Bould (Alexander). Verses in Camb. Univ. Epicedium. 1612. . 5665
Bound (Nicholas). Verses in Baro (P.). In Jonam. 1579. . . 850
Bounty. A declaration of his maiesties royall pleasure...in matter of bountie. 1619. 4°. 2805
Bourbon (Charles de), *Cardinal*. *See* Charles de Bourbon.
Bourbon (Louis, duc de). *See* Cicero. De Senectute. 1481.
Bourchier (Anth.). Verses in Oxf. Univ. Magd. Coll. 1612. . 5302
Bourchier (Arthur). Verses in Whitney (G.). A choice. 1586. . 6496
Bourchier (John), second baron Berners. *See* Berners.
Bourchier (John). Jesus Nazarenus Rex Judaeorum. 1637. 12°. . 3709
Bourchier (John), *T.C.C.* Verses in Camb. Univ. Carmen. 1635. 5770
Bourdeaux, John de. *See* Governal of Health.
Bourman (Thomas). Verses in Cam. Univ. Rex redux. 1633. . 5748
Bourn (Reuben). Verses in Hodson (W.). The holy Sinner. 1639. . 5796
— Hodson (W.). The divine cosmographer. 1640. . . 5847
Bouswell (Tho.). *See also* Boswell. Camb. Univ. Epicedium. 1612. 5665
Bouswell (William), *Jesus Coll.* *See also* Boswell. Verses in Camb. Univ. Epicedium. 1612 *bis*. 5665
Robartes (F.). The Revenve. 1613. 5670
Bovington (Edward). Verses in Cheke (Sir J.). De obitu M. Buceri. 1551. 734
Bowdler (Tamberlayne). Verses in A. (G.). Pallas armata. 1639. . 5170
Bowes (Sir Jerome). *See* Apology or defence. 1579.
Bowes (Roger), *B.D.* *See* James I. [Declaration.] A remonstrance... 1616. 1619
Bowes (Thomas). *See* La Primaudaye (P. de). The French Academie. 1618. F°.
Bowge of Court. *See* Skelton (J.).
Bowle (Robert). *See* Bull (Robert).
Bowman (Francis), bookseller. *See* Balzac. A collection. 1639. 8°.
Bowman (John). Verses in Budden (J.). Gvl. Patteni vita. 1602. 5256
— Owen (J.). Epigrammatum. 1634. 4583
Bownd (Nic.). The doctrine of the sabbath. 1595. 4°. . . . 2222
Holy exercise of fasting. Cambridge, 1604. 8°. 5622
Medicines for the plague. 1604. 4°. 2433
Vnbeleefe of S. Thomas. Cambridge, 1608. 8°. 5651
See More (J.). A table. 1580.
Bowrchier (John). *See* Bourchier.

No.
Bowyer (Nicholas). Verses in Gascoigne (G.). The Steele Glas. 1576. 1486
Bowyer (Rob.). Verses in Oxf. Univ. Magd. Coll. 1612. . . 5302
Boyd (Alexander). Verses in Adamson (J.). Εἰσόδια. 1618. . 5960
Boyd (Robert). Speech in Adamson (J.). Εἰσόδια. 1618. . . 5960
Boyd (Zachary). Four letters of Comfort. Glasgow, 1640. 4°. *See* p. 1743.
Boyle (John). Verses in Cambridge Lachrymae. 1587. . . 7356
Boys (John). Works. 1622. F°. 4762
— 1630 (1629). F°. 7871
— 1638 (1629). F°. 4384
Exposition of the dominical epistles and gospels. Spring part. 1610. 4°. 2963
— Winter part. 1611. 4°. 2966
— Summer part. 1611. 4°. 2967
Exposition of all the principal scriptures used in our English Liturgie. 1610. 4°. 2962
Exposition of the last psalme. 1615. 4°. 2990
Verses in Horne (C.). In obitum Whitakeri. 1596. . . 7332
— Camb. Univ. Thr-thr. 1603. 5616
See Bible. Eng. (Royal Version). 1611.
— Chrysostom. Opera... 1613.
— Francklin (R.). ʼΟρθοτονία. 1630 *etc.*
Boyscot (Ferdinand, baron of). *See* Cambridge University. True Copies... 1623.
Boyse (John). *See* Boys.
Br. (H.). Verses in Davies (R.). A funerall sermon. 1577. 4°. . 1416
Br. (I.) [*i.e.* J. Br(erely), *pseud.*]. *See* Anderton (J.). Apologie. 1604.
Br. (R.). Verses in Davies (R.). A funerall sermon. 1577. . . 1416
Brabant. *See* Copy. Copie of a...letter. 1599.
Brabourne (Theophilus). A defence of...the Sabbath Day. 1632. 4°. 6403
Discourse upon the sabbath day. 1628. 8°. . . . 6977
See White (F.). A treatise of the sabbath-day... 1636.
Bracciolini (Poggio). *See under* Poggio.
Brackley (Sir T. Egerton, Visct). *See* Egerton (Sir T.), Visct. Brackley.
Bracton (H. de). De legibus & consuetudinibus Angliæ. 1569. F°. 1120
Bradford (John). Godlie meditations vpon the lordes prayer. R. Hall, 1562. 8°. 1300
— E. Allde, 1597. 16°. 2009
— E. Allde, 1604. 12°. 2015
Holy Meditations upon the Lords Prayer. Eliz. Allde, 1633. 12°. 2039
Hvrte of hering Masse. [1560?] 8°. 1084
Letters. *See* Coverdale (M.). Certain...letters. 1564.
Two godly letters. *See* Cotton (C.). The mirror of martyrs. 1615 *etc.* 12°.
See Brief. A Bryfe and faythfull declaration. 1547.
— Bull (H.). Christian Prayers. 1584. 8°.
— Melanchthon (P.). A Godlye Treatyse. [1550?] 8°.
Bradshaw (Francis). Verses in Oxford Univ. Magd. Coll. 1612. . 5302
Bradshaw (James). Verses in Oxf. Univ. Magd. Coll. 1612. . 5302
Bradshaw (Jo.). Verses in Brooke (R.). A discovery. 1622. . . 2793
Bradshaw (W.). English Puritanisme. 1605. 8°. . . . 6380
— 1640. 8°. 7045
Humble motives for association. 1601. 8°. . . . 6837
Mariage feast. A sermon... *See* Gataker (T.). Two marriage sermons... 1620. 4°.
Plaine and pithy exposition of...II Thessalonians. 1620. 4°. 3939
Preparation to...Christs Body and Bloud. Ed. 9. 1634. (The doctrine of communicating. Ed. 8. 1633.) 12°. . . 3827
Protestation of the Kings supremacie. 1605. 8°. . . 6381
Shorte treatise of the crosse in baptisme. Amsterdam, 1604. 8°. 6349
Twelve generall arguments. 1605. 8°. 6382

No.
Bradshaw (W.) *cont.* Unreasonablenes of the separation. 1640. 4°. 7046
See Ames (W.). English Pvritanisme. 1640.
— Canne (J.). A necessitie of separation. 1634.
Bradwardine (Thomas). De causa Dei. 1618. F°. 3486
Bradwell (Stephen). Verses in Heywood (T.). The exemplary lives. 1640. 4675
Brahmans. *See* Lord (H.). A display. 1630.
Braithwaite (Will.). His majesties gracious grant...for...printing... Musicke. 1636. 4°. 7029
Brandon, dukes of Suffolk. *See* Suffolk (Brandon, dukes of).
Brant (S.). The shyp of Fools (Eng. & Lat.). Pynson, 1509. F°. 257
Stultifera Nauis (Eng. Lat.). J. Cawood, 1570. F°. . . 999
Branthwaite (Robert). Verses in Taylor (J.). Workes. 1630. . 3812
Branthwaite (William). Verses in Cambridge Lachrymae. 1587. . 7356
— Taylor (J.). Workes. 1630. 3812
See Bible. Eng. Royal Version. 1611. 2635
Brasbridge (T.). Abdias the Prophet. 1574. 8°. 1477
Brassicanus (Johannes Alexander). *See* Salvianus. De gvbernatione Dei. 1633.
Brathwaite (G.). Verses in Camb. Univ. Genethl. 1631. . . . 5731
Brathwaite (R.). Verses in Smith (J.). The true travels. 1630. . 4836
Brathwaite (Ric.). Ar't asleepe Husband? 1640. 8°. 5114
English Gentleman. 1630. 4°. 4831
English Gentlewoman. 1631. 4°. 4198
Schollers Medley. 1614. 4°. 3652
Solemn Ioviall Disputation. 1617. 8°. . . . . . 7314_+
Survey of History. *See above* Schollers Medley. 1614.
— 1638. 4°. 3718
Verses in Brooke (R.). A discovery. 1622. 2793
Yorke (J.). The Union of Honour. 1640. 5216
See France. An epitome. 1639. 7754
— Silesio (M.). The Arcadian Princesse. 1635. 8°.
Braun (George) and F. Hohenberg. Civitates orbis terrarum. Lib. I–IV. Col. Agr. 1588. F°. 7732–5
Braunschweig (Hieronymus). The noble experience of...surgeri. Southwarke, 1525. F°. 5857
The vertuose boke of Distyllacyon. L. Andrewe, 1527. F°. . 412
A most excellent...apothecarye. Trans. J. Hollybush. Cologne, 1561. F°. 6333
Bray (William). [Licence.] *See* F. (I.). A Sermon. 1635.
Braybroke (Sir Gerard). *See* Holland (H.). Ecclesia Sancti Pavli. 1633.
Brazil. 1611. *See* Boemus (J.). The manners. 1611. 4°.
Brearley (William), *Christ's Coll.* Verses in Camb. Univ. Συνωδία. 1637. 5790
— King (E.). Ivsta. 1638. 5829
Breckman (Abraham). *See* Clapham (H.). Theologicall Axioms... 1597.
Breda, Siege of. *See* Lithgow (W.). 1637.
Bredwell (Stephen). Detection of E. Glouers hereticall confection. [1586?] 8°. 1943
The rasing of the fovndations of Brownisme. 1588. 4°. . 2124
See Gerard (J.). The herball. 1597. F°.
Bremen. *See* Martinius (M.). Græcæ linguæ fvndamenta. 1629. 8°.
Bremer (William). *See* Vicary (T.). The englishmans treasure. 1633. 4°.
Brencius (Joh.). *See* Brenz.
Brende (John). *See* Curtius (Q.). The historie. 1553 *etc.*
Brent (Sir Nathanael). *See* Mason (F.). Vindiciæ. 1625.
See Sarpi (P.). The historie. 1620 *etc.*
— Wall (G.). A Sermon. 1635.
Brentius (John). *See* Brenz.
Brenz (Johann). Homelye of the Resurrection. Translated T(homas) S(ampson). *See* Chrysostom. Sermō. 1550. 8°.

No.

Brenz (Johann) *cont.* A right godly and learned discourse. 1584. 8°. 1932
A very fruitful exposicion vpon vi. John. 1550. 8°. . . 907
Brerely (John), Priest, *pseud.* *See* Anderton (James).
Brerely (William). *See* Brearley.
Brerewood (Edward). De ponderibus et pretiis vett. nummorum. 1614. 4°. 3459
Enquiries touching the diversity of Languages. 1614. 4°. . 3099
— 1622. 4°. 3504
— 1635. 4°. 4899
Learned treatise of the Sabaoth, Oxford, 1630. 4°. . . 5381
— Ed. 2. Oxford, 1631. 4°. 5386
— Oxford, 1632. 4°. 5394
Tractatus ethici...per T. Sixesmith. Oxoniae, 1640. 4°. . 5462
Tractatus quidam logici. Oxoniae, 1628. 4°. . . . 5418
— Acc. duo Tractatus de Meteoris...de oculo. Oxoniae, 1631. 8°. 7796
See Byfield (R.). The doctrine of the sabbath. 1631.
Brerewood (Robert). *See* Brerewood (E.). De ponderibvs. 1614.
— — Enqviries... 1614 *etc.*
Bretnor. A new almanack and prognostication. 1618. 8°. . . 7508+
Bretnor (Thomas). *See* Sala (A.). Opiologia. 1618.
Breton (Sir Henry). *See* Charter Warren. A Treatise. 1617. 4°.
Breton (Nicholas). Characters vpon essaies morall and diuine. 1615. 8°. 3902
[Floorish upon Fancie...Toyes of an Idle Head. 1577 or 1582.] 4°. 1443 [(corrected)[1].
Good and the badde. 1616. 4°. 4053
Maries Exercise. 1597. 8°. 1607
Breton (Will.), *Emman.* Verses in Cam. Univ. Epithalam. 1625. . 5702
Brett (Richard). *See* Agatharcides. Agatharcidis et Memnonis historicorum...omnia. 1597.
— Bible. Eng. (Royal Version). 1611.
— Simeon *Metaphrastes.* Vitæ. 1597.
Brettargh (Katharine). Christian life and death. 1612. 4°. . . 2975
Bretton (Clement), *Sid. Coll. Camb.* Verses in Fuller (T.). Holy warre. 1639 *etc.* . . . . 5806 *etc.*
Breue. *See* Brief.
Brevia. *See* Natura Brevium. 115
See Registrum...breuium. 529, 530
— Returna brevium. 1532. 309
— Kitchin (J.). Le court...(Retorna Brevium).
Breviarium (Sarum).

	Cologne.	[1475.]	4°.	119
	Venice.	[1494.]	F°.	122
	P. Levet, Paris.	3 Id. Feb. 1494.	8°.	131
	R. Pynson.	[1508.]	4°.	7073
	Paris. For F. Byrckman.	1516.	F°.	6209+
P. H.	Portiforium. [Paris,	ab. 1518.]	8°.	6210+
P. E.	Paris.	12 Feb. 1518.	8°.	6211
	[N. Higman] imp. F. Regnault, & F. Byrckman. Paris.	7 Feb. 1519.	4°.	6159
	Widow of T. Kerver, for F. Byrckman.	1524.	8°.	6188+
P. E.	Widow of T. Kerver, Paris.	[Ab. 1525.]	16°.	6189
	C. Ruremund, Antwerpie, imp. F. Byrckman.	22 May, 1526.	4°.	6085
P. H.	J. Kerbriand s. Huguelin, Paris.	[Before 1528.]	16°.	6186
	Portiforium. J. Kaerbriand s. Huguelin, imp. J. Parvi.	23 April, 1528.	16°.	6187
P. H.	J. Petit, Paris.	1530.	8°.	6157

[1] Not Tarlton's book as there stated.

				No.
Breviarium (Sarum) *cont.*				
	Breviarium seu Horarium. C. Chevallon and F. Regnault.	1513.	F°.	6184
P. E.	F. Regnault, Paris.	[Before 1533.]	16°.	6172
P. H.	Portiforium. F. Regnault, Paris.	1533.	8°.	6171
P. E.	'F. Regnault, Paris.	1535.'	4°.	*See* 1197
	Portiforiū. [Cancel titles.] Whitchurch.	1541.	16°.	650
P. H.	R. Caly.	1555.	4°.	1196
P. E.	'F. Regnault, Paris. 1535.' [R. Caly.]	1555.	4°.	1197
P. H.	[Kingston and Sutton.]	7 March, 1555.	4°.	1163
	M. Boursette, vid. F. Regnault.	1555.	8°.	6181
	Portiforium. J. Amazeur, pro G. Merlin.	1556.	4°.	6195
	J. Le Blanc, pro G. Merlin, Paris.	1556.	8°.	6197
P. E.	Portiforium. R. and F. Valentine, Rouen.	1556.	16°.	6247
Breviarium (York).				
	Venice.	1 May, 1493.	8°.	121
	P. Violette, Rouen.	1507.	8°.	6232
P. E.	Temporale. F. Regnault for J. Gaschet, Paris.	15 Oct. 1526.	8°.	6163
		[Ab. 1555.]	8°.	6266+

Breviloquium. *See* Ortus vocabulorum. 1528. 4°. . 195, and p. 1729
Brevint, *de la Société de Jésus.* Verses in Oxf. Univ. Horti. 1640. 5499
Brewer (Richard). Verses in Cambridge Lachrymae. 1587. . . 7356
Brewer (Thomas). Verses in Helpe to discourse. 1635. . . 3833
— Heywood (T.). The exemplary lives. 1640. . . . 4675
— Taylor (J.). Workes. 1630. 3812
— Welby (H.). The Phoenix. 1637. 3713
Brewers. 1637. *See* Proclamations.
Brewster (William). *See* Ainsworth (H.). An animadversion... 1613.
Briant (Alexander). [An epistle towchinge the persecution of catholickes. Ab. 1582.] 8°. 6437
Brice (Sir Hugh). *See* Mirror of the World [1480?].
Brideoake (R.). Verses in Randolph (T.). Poems. 1640. . . 5852
Bridges (J.). A defence of the government established in the Church of England. 1587. 4°. 2122
See Defence of the ecclesiasticall Discipline. 1588. 4°.
— Dialogue. 1589.
— Fenner (D.). A defence of the godlie Ministers. 1587. 4°.
— Gualther (R.). An hundred...homelyes. 1572. F°.
— Marprelate (M.). Oh read ouer... [1588?] . 1915, 1916
Bridges (Stephen). Verses in Hippocrates. 1633. . . . 5812
Bridget, Saint. *See* Brigit.
Brief. Briefe and compendious Register. *See* Concordance. 1550. 8°.
Bryfe and faythfull declaration of ye true fayth of Chryst. 1547. 8°. 6703
Bryefe and playne declaracion of certayne sentences... *See* Brief. Bryfe and faythfull declaracion. 1547.
Briefe and plaine declaration... *See* Bridges (J.), *bp.* A defence of the government established... 1587.
Brief answer to a late Treatise. *See* Prynne (W.). The Lord's Day. 1635. 4°.
Briefe answere vnto certaine obiections. 1604. *See* Parkes (R.).
Briefe apologie or defence of Catholike Ecclesiastical Hierarchie. [1602?] *See* Parsons (R.).
Breue cronycle... *See* Gibson (T.). A breue Cronycle... [1548?]
Brefe declaration...conc. private dwelling Houses. 1636. 4°. . 5124

No.

Brief *cont.* Briefe declaration concerning private dwelling houses. 1639. 4°. 4666
Briefe description of the whole World. 1605. *See* Abbot (G.), *abp.*
Briefe discourse against the outward apparell... 1566 *etc.* *See* Crowley (R.).
Briefe discovrse concerning faith. *See* White (J.) of Eccles. The way to the true church. 1608 *etc.*
Brief discovrse concerning...Parliament. 1640. *See* Selden (J.).
Briefe discourse of the cruell dealings of the Spanyards, in Gulick and Cleve. 1599. 4°. 1978
Briefe discourse of the scriptures. 1614. 4°. 2314
Brieff discours off the troubles begonne at Franckford. [Zurich,] 1575. 4°. 6301
Briefe discovery of the untruthes and slanders...in a sermon. 8 Feb. 1588. 4°. . . . . 7323+
Briefe examination for the tyme...of certaine ministers in London. [1564.] 4°. 7143
Brief form of Confession. 16°. 6603
Briefe instructions for Churchwardens. [1637?] 4°. *See* Prynne (W.).
Briefe relation of what is hapned since...August 1598...the Dukedom of Cleue. J. Wolfe, 1599. 4°. 1977
Bryefe summe of the whole Byble. A. Scoloker [1548?]. 8°. . 1040
Bryefe summe of the whole Byble. R. Stoughton [1548?]. 8°. . 1065
Brief sum of the whole Bible. [Ab. 1548.] 8°. . . . . 7150+
Bryef sũme of the whole Byble. J. Walley [1551]. 8°. . 1026
Breef summary of Christian religion. 16°. 6602
Brief treatise conteyning many proper Tables. 1582. 8°. . 1007
Briefe treatise of Oathes. [Ab. 1590.] *See* Morice (J.).
Briefs. 1579. *See* Theloall (S.). Le digest. 1579.
Briggs (Henry). *See* Napier (J.). Arithmetica Logarithmica... 1624.
— — A description. 1618.
— — Logarithmaticall Arithmetike... 1631.
— — Mirifici Logarithmorum canonis descriptio. 1619.
Brigges (Samson). Verses in Cam. Univ. Anthologia. 1632. . . 5741
— Fasciae. 1633. 5808
— Rex redux. 1633. 5748
— Carmen. 1635. 5770
— Συνῳδία. 1637 *bis.* 5790
— King (E.). Ivsta. 1638. 5829
— A. (G.). Pallas armata. 1639. 5170
Bright (Tim.). Hygieina. [1581?] 8°. 1656
In physicam G. A. Scribonii...animadversiones. Cantabrigiae, 1584. 8°. 5506
Medicinae therapeuticae pars. 1583. 8°. 1641
Treatise of melancholy. 1586. 8°. 2117
— 1613. 8°. 3092
See Foxe (J.). An abridgement. 1589.
Brightman (T.). Revelation of the Revelation. Amsterdam, 1615. 4°. 6391
Revelation of S. John. Ed. 3. J. Claesson van Dorpe, Leyden, 1616. 8°. 6490
See Fowler (J.). A shield of defence. 1612.
Brightwell (Richard), *pseud.* *See* Frith (J.).
Brigit, *Saint.* [Orationes.] *See* Primer Sarum (Lat.). 1534.
[Revelations.] *See* Kempis (T. à). The following of Christ. [1520?]
— — Whitford (R.). A werke of preparation. 1531.
Certayne revelations. *See* Bernardus, *Saint.* [The golden Epistle. Ab. 1535.] 8°.
[Life.] *See* Capgrave (J.). The Kalendre. 1516.
See B. (B.), *Irish Franciscan.* The life. 1625. 4°.
— Villegas (A. de). The lives of saints. 1628.

No.
Brinkelow (H.). The cōplaint of Roderyck Mors. 'Geneve in Savoye by M. boys.' [1548?] 8°. 1044, 1045
The complaynt of Roderyck Mors. 'F. de Turona, Savoy.' 8°. 6306
Brinsley (J.). Lvdvs literarivs. 1612. 4°. 1890
— 1627. 4°. 3033
Posing of the parts. 1615. 4°. 1891
True watch, and rule of life. Ed. 5. 1611. 8°. . . . 3075
— Ed. 6. 1614. 8°. 3897
The true watch. Part 3. 1622. 4°. 4763
— — Ed. 2. 1623. 4°. 4771
See Cicero. The first Book of Tullies offices. 1616 *etc.*
— Cordier (M.). Corderius dialogues. 1625.
— Vergilius Eclogues. 1633 4°.
Brionaeus (M.). Verses in Bellehachius (O.). Sacrosancta bvcolica. 1583. 1640
Brisset (Georges). The apologie. 1610. 4°. 2411
Bristol (Map, 1575). *See* Braun (G.).
See Venner (T.). Via recta. 1638.
Bristol (Earl of). Third speech of the lord George Digby to the house of commons, concerning bishops and the citie petition. 9 Feb. 1640. 1640. 4°. 4486
Bristow (Richard). A briefe treatise...to finde out the truth. Antwerp, 1599. 8°. 6136
See Bible. Eng. O.T. [Douai version]. 1609–10, 1635.
— New Testament. Rhemes. 1582. 4°.
— To the Seminarye Priests... 1592.
Brittany. A true discourse concerning the deliuerie of Britaine. *See* France. An historicall collection. 1598.
Britton (J.). Briton. R. Redman, n.d. 8°. 388
— Ed. 2. By E. Wingate. 1640. 8°. 5009
Brixius (Germanus). *See* More (Sir T.). Epistola. 1520.
Broadsides. *See* Bibliographical Index. VII.
Brodus (William). Verses in Parkinson (J.). Paradisus terrestris. 1629. F°. 2561
Broeck (Maurice Van Hun, earl of Valkensteyn and). *See* Briefe relation. 1599. 1979
— Briefe discourse. 1599. 1978
Brograve (Jane). *See* Bulkeley (E.). An apologie... 1608.
Broke (Sir R.). La Graunde Abridgement. 1573. F°. . . . 1125
— 12 Oct. 1576. 4°. 7203
— 29 Sept. 1586. F°. 7210
[Abridgment.] *See* Plowden (E.). Les commentaires. 1599.
See Assizes. Le liver des Assises. 1580. F°.
— Year Books. Edward III. 1–10. 1596. F°.
— — Edward V—Henry VIII. 1597. F°.
— — Edward IV. 1599. F°.
— — Edward IV. Ann. 5. 1639. F°.
Broke or Brook (T.). Certeyn Meditacions...before...the Sacrament. 1548. 8°. 897, 898
See Common Prayer. Geneva. The forme of common praiers. 1550. 8°. 669
Broncar (Henricus). *See* Brouncker.
Brook (Ro.), *Suttonian*. Verses in J. A. Comenius. Porta linguarum. 1633. 7613
Brook (Thomas), *translator*. *See* Broke.
Brooke (Christopher). *See also* Brookes. [Eclogue.] *See* Browne (W.). The Shepheards Pipe. 1614. 8°.
[Eglogues.] *See* Wither (G.). The workes. 1620. 8°.
Verses in Coryat (T.). Coryats Crudities. 1611. 3076
Brooke (Fulke Greville, Lord). Certaine...workes. Written...with Sir P. Sidney. 1633. F°. 4102

No.

Brooke (John). *See* Viret (P.). A faithfull...exposition. 1582.
Brooke (Maurice, earle of). *See* Broeck.
Brooke (Ralph). A catalogue and succession. 1619. F°. . . . 2787
— 1622. F°. 3140
Discoverie of certaine errors. [1595?] 4°. 6812, 6813
— 1622. F°. 2793
See Camden (W.). Britannia... 1600.
Brooke (Sir Robert). *See* Broke.
Brooke (Robert). Verses in Comenius. Porta Linguarum. 1631. 8°. 4434–5
Brooke (Will.). Oxf. Univ. Magd. Coll. 1612. 5302
Brookes (Christopher). Verses in Cambridge Lachrymae. 1587. . 7356
See also Brooke.
Brosserius (Jo.), *Vindocinensis*. Verses in Humphrey (L.). I. Ivelli vita. 1573. 837
Broughton (Hugh). An advertisement of corruption. 1604. 4°. . 6464
— 1605. 4°. 6858
Apologie. 1592. 4°. 2347
Comment upon Coheleth. 1605. 4°. 6859
Concent of scripture. [Ab. 1585?] 4°. 2191, 2192
Daniel. D. Aubri, Hanau, 1607. 4°. 6634
Daniel his chaldaic visions. 1596. 4°. 2237
— 1597. 4°. 2195
Declaration of generall corruption. 1604. 4°. 6465
Defence of the holy genealogies. [1600?] 4°. 6827
Epistle to the learned nobilitie of England. (A request.) R. Schilders, Middelburg, 1597. 4°. 6452–3
Explication of...κατῆλθεν εἰς ᾅδῃ. Ed. 2. 1605. 4°. . . 6860
Exposition upon the Lords prayer. [After 1612.] 4°. . . 6891
Familie of David. Z. Heyns, Amsterdam, 1605. 8°. . . 6350
Lamentationes of Ieremy. 1606. 4°. 6865
— 1608. 4°. 6384
Letter to a friend. 1612. 4°. 2310
Letters about Sheol and Hades. 1599. 4°. 1980
[Letters to Q. Elizabeth, Whitgift &c. Ab. 1591.] 4°. . . 7236
Our lordes familie. Amsterdam, 1608. 4°. 6387
Principall Positions for groundes of the holy Bible. 1609. 4°. 6389, 6390
Replie vpon the R. R. F. Th. Winton. 1605. 8°. . . . 6861
Require of agreement. 1611. 4°. 6476
Revelation of the holy apocalypse. 1610. 4°. 6475
A Seder Olam. 1594. 4°. 6808
Textes of scripture. [Before 1623.] 4°. 2319
Treatise of Melchisedek. 1591. 4°. 2194, 7237
Two little workes defensive. 1604. 4°. 6466
Verses in Baro (P.). In Jonam. 1579. 850
See Beroaldus (M.). A Short View... 1590.
— Bible (Polyglot). Daniel. 1596.
Broughton (Ric.). The eccl. historie of great britaine. Tom. I. Douai, 1633. F°. 6595
Broughton (Robert). Verses in Hopton (A.). Concordancy. 1635. 3956
Broun (Tho.). [Licence. 2 July 1640.] Hayne (T.). Grammatices Latine compendium. 8°. 7819
Brouncker (Hen.). *See* S. (E.). De rebus gestis. [1570?]
Broune (Sir Anthony). *See* Leslie (J.), *bp*. A Treatise. 1571.
Brounus. *See* Brown.
Brousse (Jacques). *See* Joyeuse (H. de). The life. 1623. 8°.
Brown (Richard). Verses in Camb. Univ. Συνωδία. 1637. . . 5790
— King (E.). Ivsta. 1638. 5829
Brown (Thomas). 1551. *See* Browne.
Browne (John). Verses in Camb. Univ. Epicedium. 1612. . . 5665

No.

Browne (Robert). A booke...of all true Christians. R. Painter. Middelburg, 1582. 4°. 6443
Browne (Robert). *See* Bredwell (S.). Detection of Ed. Glouer. [1586.]
See also Brownists.
Browne (Thomas), *Preb. of Westminster*. Verses in Wilson (Sir T.). Vita. 1551. 631
— Llwyd (Humphrey). The Breuiary of Britayne. 1573. . 1440
— Price (Sir J.). Historia. 1573. 1473
Browne (Thomas), *D.D., Canon of Windsor*. The copie of a sermon. 24 Dec. 1633. Oxford, 1634. 4°. 5407
Verses in Camdeni Insignia. 1624. . . . . . 5346 *bis*.
See Camden (W.). Annales. Pt. IV. [Eng.] 1625–9.
Browne (William). Britannia's Pastoralls. 1625. 8°. 4797
The Shepherds Pipe. 1614. 8°. (fragment). 3654
Verses in Aleman (M.). The Rogve. 1623. 4079
Browning (John). Concerning publike-prayer. 1636. 4°. . . 4370
Brownists. *See* Alison (R.). A plain confvtation... 1590.
— Amsterdam, *English Church in*. An apologie or defence...1604.
— Gifford (G.). A short Reply. 1591.
— Jacob (H.). A Defence. 1599.
See also Browne (R.).
Brownrigge (Ralph). Verses in Camb. Univ. Carmen. 1635. . . 5770
[Licence.] Davenant (J.). Determinationes. 1639.
— Du Praissac. The art of warre. 1639.
Bruce (Andrew). Theses and Verses in Adamson (J.). Εἰσόδια. 1618. 5960
Bruce (Peter). Address and Theses in Adamson (J.). Εἰσόδια. 1618. 5960
Bruce (Robert). The way to true peace. 1617. 4°. . . . 2283
See Hume (A.). A didvction... 1602.
Bruch (Richard). The life of religion. 1615. 8°. 3786
See Gerhard (J.). The Conquest. 1623.
Brucioli (Ant.). Comm. upon the canticle of canticles. 1598. 8°. 2248
Bruele (Gualterus). Praxis medicinae. Ed. 2. 1639. 4°. . 4906
Bruni (Leonardo). The historie of L. Aretine. 1563. 8°. . . 1302
See Aristotle. [Ethics (Lat.).] 1479. 4°.
Brunius (Lancelotus). *See* Gerard (J.). The herball. 1597. F°.
Bruno (G.). Explicatio triginta sigillorum. (Ars reminiscendi.) [Ab. 1583?] 8°. 6774
Brunus, *Longoburgensis*. *See* Braunschweig (H.). The noble experyence. 1525. 5857
Brusius. *See* Bruce.
Bruto (Giovanni Michele). *See* Cicero. M. Tullii Ciceronis orationum volumen primum. 1601. 16°.
Brutus (Joannes Michael). *See* Bruto.
Bruyn (Ambrosius de). In originem,...bacchanaliorum, oratio. 1619. 4°. 4496
Bry (J. T. de). Caracters and diversitie of Letters. Frankfurt, 1628. 4°. 6632
Bryan (Sir Francis). *See* Guevara (A. de). A dispraise. 1548.
— The golden boke. 1546 *etc.*
Bryan (John). The vertvovs davghter...funerall of...Cicely Puckering. 1636. 4°. 4020
— 1640. 4°. 5208
Bryant (Sir Francis). *See* Bryan.
Brydges (Grey), 5th lord Chandos. *See* Chandos.
Buc or Bucke (Sir George). Verses in Camden (W.). Britannia. 1637. 3055–6
Yorke (J.). The Union of Honour. 1640. 5216
See Stow (J.). The Annales... 1615 *etc.*
Bucanus (Gulielmus). Institutions of christian religion. Trans. R. Hill. 1606. 4°. 3611
Bucer (Martin). The mynd and exposition...vppon...S. Matthew. Emden, 1566. 8°. 6411

No.

Bucer (Martin) *cont.* Treatise how...Almose ought to be distributed. [1557?] 8°. 6739
[Letter.] *See* A briefe examination. [1564.] 4°.
[Death.] *See* Cheke (Sir J.). De obitu. 1551.
See Anderton (J.). Luther's Life. 1624. 4°.
— Psalter of David... [153–?] 563
— Whether it be mortall sinne... [1571?]
Buchanan (G.). Ane detectioun of...Marie Quene of Scottes... [1572.] 8°. 872
Baptistes. 1578. 8°. 1534
De iure regni apud Scotos. [Edinburgh.] 1580. 4°. . . . 5917
— Ed. 3. 'Ad exemplar J. Rossei, Edinburgi.' 1581. 8°. . 6773
Ecphrasis paraphraseos...in psalmos Davidis: ab A. Julio elaborata. 1620. 8°. 3595
Psalmorum...Paraphrasis...studio N. Chytræi. 1640. 12°. . 5209
Rerum scoticarum historia. Edinburgh, 1582. F°. . . . 5920
Verses in Humphrey (L.). I. Ivelli vita. 1573. . . 837
— Harvey (G.). Gratulationum. 1578. 1495
See Barclay (W.). Ivdicium, De Certamine G. Eglisemmii cum G. Bvchanano, pro dignitate Paraphraseos Psalmi CIIII... 1620.
— Copy. The copie of a letter. [1572?]
— Heywood (T.). Pleasant dialogues. 1637.
— Mary, Queen of Scots. De Maria Scotorum Regina. [1572?]
— Polemon (J.). All the famous Battels... 1587.
Buchler (Joannes). Sacrarum profanarumque phrasium poeticarum thesaurus...auctus...a N. Baxio. Ed. 10. 16[ ]. . 4878
Bucholtzer (Abraham). *See* Beroaldus (M.). A short view... 1590.
Buck (Daniel). *See* Jacob (H.). A defence... 1599.
Buck (James). Treatise of the beatitudes. 1637. 4°. . . . 4213
Bucke. *See* Buc.
Buckenham (R.), *Pemb. Coll. Camb.* Verses in Whitaker (W.). Praelectiones. 1599. 5598
Buckeridge (John). De potestate papæ. 1614. 4°. 3460
Sermon. 23 Sept. 1606. [1606?] 4°. 2600
See Andrewes (L.). XCVI. Sermons... 1629 *etc.*
Buckhurst (Thomas Sackville, baron). *See* Dorset (Thomas Sackville, earl of) & baron Buckhurst.
Buckingham (Edward, duke of). *See* Elias, Knight of the swan. 1512. 4°.
Buckingham (George Villiers, Duke of). A manifestation or remonstrance. 1627. 4°. 4481, 7816
[Death.] *See* Spence (R.). Illustrissimi...ducis...διαγραφή. [1629?]
See Matthieu (P.). The powerfvll favorite. 1628.
Buckland (Thomas), *O.S.B.*, *D.D.* *See* Hill (Thomas), D.D. *alias* Buckland.
Buckley (Ric.), *St John's*, *Taxor.* *See also under* B. (R.). Verses in Camb. Univ. Συνωδία. 1637. 5790
Buckley (Will.). Verses in Cheke (Sir J.). De obitu M. Buceri. 1551. 734
— Wilson (Sir T.). Vita. 1551. 631
See Seton (J.). Dialectica. 1611 *etc.*
Buckminster (T.). Almanack and Prognostication. 1591. 16°. . 7238+
Almanack and Prognostication. 1595. 8°. 1342
Verses in Strigelius (V.). A third proceeding. 1595. . . 2844
Buckner (Th.). Verses in Oxf. Univ. Magd. Coll. 1612. . . 5302
Buclæus (Gulielmus). *See* Buckley.
Budden (John). Gul. Patteni...vita. Oxoniæ. 1602. 4°. . . 5256
Verses in Becon (Ric.). Solon. 1594. 5240
— Oxf. Univ. Magd. Coll. 1612. 5302
— Holyoake (F.). Dictionarium. 1640. 3058
See Smith (Sir T.). De republica. [1610?]
Buddle (George). A short and plaine discourse. 1609. 4°. . 3061

No.
Budge (John), *bookseller*. *See* Harington (Sir J.). The most elegant... epigrams. 1618.
Buenting (H.). Itinerarium. Trans. R. B. 1619. 4°. . . . 7821
— 1623. 4°. 2452
— 1629. 4°. 2456
Buessenmecher (Johann). *See* S. (E.). Historia Britannica 1640.
Bugenhagen (Johann), '*Pomeranus.*' [Sermon on the death of Luther.] *See* Jonas (J.). The true hystorye. [1546?] 8°.
Buildings. *See* Proclamation. 1615, 1618.
Bulkeley (E.). Answere to ten friuolous and foolish reasons. 1588. 4°. 1713
Apologie for the religion established in the Church of England. 1608. 4°. 3568
See Clemangiis (N. de). Specvlvm... 1606.
— Foxe (J.). Actes and Monvments. 1610 *etc.*
Bulkeley (Richard). Verses in Cam. Univ. Genethl. *bis.* 1631. . 5731
— — Anthologia. 1632. 5741
— — Fasciae. 1633. 5808
— — Rex redux. 1633. 5748
— Hippocrates. 1633. 5812
— Russell (J.). The two...battels. 1634. 5767
Camb. Univ. Carmen. 1635. 5770
Bull. *See* Holy Bull, &c. 1588. 4°. 1949
Bull (H.). Christian Prayers and holie Meditations. [1578.] 16°. . 1657
— 1584. 8°. 1645
See Hooper (J.). An apologye... 1562.
— Luther (M.). Commentarie upon the xv. psalmes. 1637. 4°.
Bull (Robert). *See* Dort. . . . . page 1465
Bullein (W.). Bulwarke of defēce. 1562. F°. 1170
— 1579. F°. 1230
Gouernment of health. 1595. 8°. 2841
Verses in Moore (P.). The hope of health. 1565. . . 1173
Bullinger (H.). Bullæ papisticæ...contra...Elizabetham...refutatio. 1571. 4°. 823
Christian state of Matrimony. 1575. 8°. 1278
Commentary upon...II Thessaloniās. Southwark, 1538. 8°. . 5871
Fiftie godlie and learned sermons. 1577. 4°. 1309
— 1584. 4°. 1321
— Whereunto...certaine epistles. 1587. 4°. 7820
Holsome Antidotus or counter-poyson, agaynst ... Anabaptistes. 1548. 8°. 1034
Hundred Sermons vpō the Apocalips. 1561. 4°. . . . 795
— 1573. 4°. 7118
Judgement...in certeyne matters of religion. 1566. 8°. . 6415
Most godly...Discourse of the...holy scripture. 1579. 8°. . 1798
Sermon made of the confessing of Christe... *See* Treatise. A Treatise of the Cohabitacyon of the faithfull. 1555.
Tragedies of Tyrantes. 1575. 8°. 1765
Treatise or Sermon...concernynge magistrates... 1549. 8°. . 777
Two Epystles. [Ab. 1549.] 8°. 6700
[Letters.] *See* Coverdale (M.). Certain...letters. 1564.
See Confession of Fayth. [1568?]
— Whether it be mortall sinne. [1570?]
— Wilkinson (W.). A Confutation. 1579.
Bullingham (Ed.). Verses in Yorke (J.). The Union of Honour. 1640. 5216
Bullingham (Nicholas), *Bp.* *See* Bible. Eng. (Bishops'). 1568. . 963
— Advertisements...for due order. 1584. 4°. 1822
Bullok (Tho.). Verses in Camb. Univ. Genethl. 1631. . . 5731
Bulwarde (Robert). *See* Fowler (J.). A shield of defence... 1612.
Bunny (E.). Briefe Answer, vnto...R. P. 1589. 8°. 1360
Of divorce. Oxford, 1610. 4°. 5294

No.

Bunny (E.) *cont.* — 1613. 4°. 5309
Of the head-corner-stone. 2 tom. 1611. F°. 2773
See Parsons (R.). A booke of christian Exercise. 1585 *etc.*
— — The Christian Directory... 1607.
— Resolution of Religion. The first part. 1603. 4°.
Bunny (F.). Comparison betweene the auncient fayth of the Romans and the new Romish Religion. 1595. 4°. 2187
Survey of the popes svpremacie. 1595. 4°. 2842
Bunting (Henry). *See* Buenting.
Bunyan (John), *Precursors of. See* Dent (A.). The plaine man's pathway. 1605. . . . . 1384 *etc.*
See The Soul's Desire. [1610?] 8°. 3073
Burby (Cuthbert), *printer. See* Mirror of Knighthood. Pt iii.
Burgersdijck (Franco). Idea philosophiae. Ed. 4. Oxonii, 1637. 12°. 5455
Institutionum Logicarum libri duo. Cantabrigiae, 1637. 8°. . 5789
Burges (Cornelius). Baptismall regeneration. Oxford, 1629. 4°. . 5376
New discovery of personal tithes. 1625. 12°. . . . 4701
Burges (John). *See* Burgess.
Burgess (John). Answer reioyned to...a reply to Dr Mortons Generall Defence of three nocent ceremonies. (The lawfulnes of kneeling.) 1631. 4°. 4547, 4548
[Apology.] *See* Covell (W.). A briefe answer. 1606.
See Ames (W.). A fresh suit... 1633.
— Clarke (T.) The Popes deadly Wound... 1621.
— Covell (W.). A briefe answer. 1606.
— Defence of the ministers reasons... 1607.
— Dispute. A dispute. 1608.
Burgh (Benet). *See* Cato (D.). [Parvus Cato—Magnus Cato.] 1477–8. 4°. 4
— — Cato cum Commento. 1483. F°. 20
Burghley (Will. Cecil, lord). Carmen gratulatorium aedium cecilianarum. 1571. Broadside. 6752
Execution of Justice in England. 1583. 4°. 7291
— Ed. 2. 1583. 4°. 7292
Ivstitia Britannica. 1584. 8°. 1556
Precepts, or directions. 1637. 8°. 7570
Verses in Wilson (Sir T.). Vita, 1551. 631
See Allen (W.). A trve sincere and modest defence...against...The execvtion of Ivstice in England. [1584.]
— Catharine [Parr], Queen. The lamentacion... 1547, 1548.
Burgo (J. de). Pupilla oculi. W. Hopyl. Paris, imp. W. Bretton, 1510. 4°. 6150
Burhill (Robert). Contra M. Becani...Controuersiam Anglicanam. 1613. 8° 3896
De potestate regia. Oxoniæ, 1613. 8°. 5310
Pro Tortura Torti...Responsio. 1611. 8°. 2637
In controversiam...tractatvs modestvs... *See* Howson (J.). Uxore dimissa. 1606.
Verses in Budden (J.). Gvl. Patteni...vita. 1602. . . . 5256
Buridanus (Johannes). Quæstiones in decem libros ethicorum Aristotelis. Oxoniæ, 1637. 4°. 5472
Quæstiones in octo libros politicorum Aristotelis. Oxoniæ, 1640. 4°. 5463
Burlase (Sir William). *See* Borlase.
Burleigh (Francis). *See* Bible. Eng. (Royal). 1611. 2635
Burley (Walter). Tractatus perbrevis. Oxonie, 1518. 4°. . . 5219
Burnaby. *See* Burneby.
Burne (Nicholas). The disputation conc. the controversit headdis of Religion...in...Scotland. Paris, 1581. 8°. 6216
Burneby (Thomas). Verses in Greene (R.). Ciceronis Amor. 1605. 1792
Burrant (Robert). *See* Cato. Preceptes. 1560. 16°.

No.
Burrell (John). Verses in Camb. Univ. Lacrymae. 1619. . . . 5689
Burrell (Percival). Sutton's Synagogue. 1629. 4°. . . . 4605
Burrell (Sam.), *K.C.C.* Verses in Cam. Univ. Epithalam. 1625. . 5702
Burroughes (Jeremiah). Excellency of a gracious spirit. 1638. 8°. 4315
Burton (Edward). Verses in Aleman (M.). The Rogve. 1623. . 4079
— Camden Insignia. 1624. 5346
Burton (Henry). An apology of an appeale. 1636. 4°. . . . 7021
Babel no Bethel. 1629. 4°. 4339
Baiting of the Popes Bull. 1627. 4°. 5032
Censure of simonie. 1624. 4°. 3149
For god and the king. 1636. 4°. 7022
Israels Fast. 1628. 4°. 7611
Law and the gospell. 1631. 4°. 4885
Plea to an appeale. 1626. 4°. 3352
Seven vials. 1628. 4°. 5036
See Bastwick (J.). A briefe relation. 1637. 4°.
— Butterfield (R.). Maschil. 1629.
— Cholmley (H.). The state of the now-Romane Chvrch. 1629.
— Dow (C.). Innovations Unjustly charged... 1637.
— Heylyn (Peter). A Briefe and Moderate answer... 1637.
— Laud (W.). A speech... 1637.
Burton (Richard). *See* Redman (J.) A reporte... 1551.
Burton (Robert). The anatomy of melancholy. Ed. 2. Oxford, 1624. F°. 5345
— Ed. 3. Oxford, 1628. F°. 5370
— Ed. 4. Oxford, 1632. F°. 5395
— Ed. 5. Oxford, 1638. F°. 5480
Verses in Camdeni Insignia. 1624. 5346
— Holyoake (F.). Dictionarium. 1640. 3058
See Beverwijk (J. van). Schat der Gesontheyt. 1638. 8°. . 7811
Burton (William). The Catalogue of Religious Houses... *See* Speed (J.). The theatre. 1611.
Description of Leicester Shire. [1622.] F°. 3971
Exposition of the Lords prayer. 1594. 8°. 2221
Verses in Camb. Univ. Thr-thr. 1603. 5616
— Lacrymae. 1619. 5689
Hodson (W.). The Divine Cosmographer. 1640 5847
Bury, St Edmunds, *Seal of.* Hawkins (W.). Corolla. 1634.
Bury (Richard de). Philobiblon. Ed. 2. Oxoniae, 1599. 4°. . 5250
Busbie (John), *printer. See* Southwell (R.). Mœoniæ. 1595.
Buscher (Heizo). Arithmetica. *See* Scheibler (C.). Philosophia. 1628.
Buscoducensis (Nicolaus). *See* Lucianus. Dialogi. 1531. 8°.
Bush (Edward). *See* B. (E.). A sermon. 1576. 8°.
Bush (Paul). The Extripacion of ignorancy. Pynson. [1526.] 4°. . 295
Busse, Siege of. *See* Hertzogenbush.
Busset (John and Richard). *See* Indulgence. Leo X. Pope. 1515.
Busshe (Paul). *See* Bush.
Bust (Hen.). Verses in Oxf. Univ. Magd. Coll. 1612. . . . 5302
Bust (John). Verses in Bernard (J.). Oratio. 1568. . . . 930
Bust (Matthew). Verses in Camb. Univ. Thr-thr. 1603. . . 5616
See John, *metropolitan of Euchaita.* Versus Iambici. 1610.
Butler (Charles). The english grammar. Oxford, 1633. 4°. . . 5435
Feminin' Monarchi'. Oxford, 1634. 4°. 5439
Oratoriae libri duo. Oxoniae, 1629. 4°. 5425
— *See post.* Rhetoricæ libri dvo... 1629.
Principles of musik. 1636. 4°. 4860
Rhetoricae libri duo. Oxoniae, 1600. 8°. 5252
— Acc. de oratoria. 1629. 4°. 7630
Συγγένεια. Oxoniae, 1625. 4°. 7657
Butler (Fra.). Verses in Shirley (J.). The royall master. 1638. 4°. 4665

No.

Butler (H.), *Pemb.* Verses in Cam. Univ. Epithalam. 1625. . 5702
Butler (John), *Captain.* Verses in Norton (R.). The Gunner. 1628. 4535
Butler (Samuel). *See* Habington (W.). The Queene of Arragon... 1640.
Butler (Thomas), tenth earl of Ormonde. *See* Ormonde.
Butler (William). Portrait. 1620. 8°. 4051
Butterfield (Robert). Maschil. 1629. 8°. 2560
See Burton (H.). Babel no Bethel... 1629.
— Spencer (T.). Maschil Vnmasked. [1629.]
Buttes (Henry). *See* Butts.
Button (Sir Thomas). *See* Fox (L.). Northwest Fox. 1635.
Butts (Henry). Dyets dry dinner. 1599. 8°. 2727
[Funerall discourse.] *See* C. (B.). Puritanisme. 1633.
Verses in Camb. Univ. Genethliacon. 1631. . . . 5731
Buxton. The Benefit of the auncient Bathes of Buckstones. 1572. *See* Jones (J.). A briefe discourse. 1574.
Byde (Pet.). Verses in Oxf. Univ. Magd. Coll. 1612. . . . 5302
Byfield (Adoniram). *See* Byfield (N.). The marrow... 1628.
— — The Rvle of Faith. 1626.
Byfield (Nicholas). A commentary upon 1 Peter i–iii. 1636 (1637). F°. 4305
Exposition vpon...Colossians. 1627. F°. 3166
Marrow of the oracles of god. Ed. 6. 1628. 12°. . . 4604
— Ed. 9. 1633. 12°. 4715
— Ed. 10. 1636. 12°. 4732
Principles or the patterne of wholesome Words. Ed. 3. 1627. 12°. 3167
— Ed. 6. 1637. 12°. 5164
Rule of faith. 1626. 4°. 4414
See Brerewood (E.). A learned treatise of the Sabbath... 1630 *etc.*
— Byfield (R.). The doctrine of the sabbath. 1631.
Byfield (Richard). The doctrine of the sabbath vindicated. 1631. 4°. 3045
Byllet (Arthur). *See* Dort. Page 1465.
Bylot (Robert). *See* Fox (L.). Northwest Fox. 1635.
Byng (Andrew). *See* Bible. Eng. (Royal). 1611. 2635
Byng (Henry). Verses in Camb. Univ. Genethl. 1631. . . 5731
— Anthologia. 1632. 5741
Byng (Humphrey). Verses in Cam. Univ. Anthologia. 1632. . 5741
— Rex redux. 1633. 5748
Byng (Jo.). Verses in Camb. Univ. Carmen. 1635. . . . 5770
— *Συνῳδία.* 1637. 5790
Byng (Thomas). Verses in Demosthenes. Thre Orations. 1570. . 1409
Castiglione (B.)....De Curiali. 1571. 824
Cambridge Lachrymae. 1587. 7356
— Thr-thr. *bis.* 1603. 5616
See Demosthenes... Olynthiacæ Orationes... 1571
Bynneman (Henry). Verses (qu. by him?) in Gascoigne (G.). The Posies. 1575. 1482
See Polemon (J.). All the famous Battels... [1577?]
Byrd (W.). Gradualia. Liber i. (Superius.) Ed. 2. 1610. 4°. 2503
— (Bassus). 1610. 4°. 2504
Gradualia. Liber ii. (Cantus primus.) 1610. 4°. . . . 2502
Gratification vnto M. Iohn Case. [1586?] F°. . . 1589
[Mass for four voices. 1588?] 4°. 1590
Psalmes, Sonets, and songs of sadnes. 1588. 4°. . . 1594
— [1588?] 4°. 1595
Sacrae Cantiones quinque vocum. Liber 1. 1589. 4°. . 1596
— Liber 2. 1591. 4°. 1600
Songs of sundrie natures. 1589. 4°. 1597
Byrde (Sir William). [Funeral.] *See* Price (S.). The two twins. 1624. 4°.
Bysshe (Paul). *See* Bush.

C. (Le S[r]). Verses in Puget de la Serre (J.). The mirrour. 1639. 4125

No.
C. (A.). An answer to a pamphlet... The Fisher catched... 1623. 4°. 6552
— *See* Featley (D.). The Romish Fisher. 1624.
True relations of sundry conferences. 1626. 4°. 6555
C. (A.) [=A. Cowley?]. Verses in Fletcher (P.). The Purple Island. 1633. 5752
C. (A.). *See* Colville (J.). The Palinode. 16– .
See Corro (A. de). Tableau. 1569.
— Laud (W.). A relation of the Conference. 1639.
C. (A.) [*i.e.* Copley (A.)]. An answere to a letter... 1601.
C. (A. B.). *See* Prynne (W.). The Vnbishoping of Timothy... 1636.
C. (A. S. F.). Verses in Skene (Sir J.). Regiam. 1613. . . 3458
C. (B.). Verses in Gascoigne (G.). The Posies. 1575. [Wanting in this copy.] 1482
C. (B.). The fore-runner of Bels Downefall. [Ab. 1605?] 8°. . 6471
C. (B.). Puritanisme the mother. 1633. 8°. 6562
C. (B.), *Bachelor of the Civil Law.* Decimarum et oblationum tabula. A tithing table. 1633. 4°. 4149
— 1635. 4°. 4151
C. (B.), *Student in Divinity.* The dolefull knell, of Thomas Bell. 'Roane.' 1607. 8°. 6267
C. (Barth.). Verses *bis* in Price (Sir J.). Historia. 1573. . 1473
C. (Bonh.), *Regal.* Verses in Camb. Univ. Gratulatio. 1623. . 5695
C. (C.). *See* Bolton (R.). A threefold treatise. 1634. 4°.
— Mornay (P. de). Three homilies. 1626.
C. (C.), *C.P.* Verses in Camb. Univ. Gratulatio. 1623. . . 5695
C. (C.), *Gent.* Verses in La Vardin (J. de). The historie. 1596. . 2239
C. (D.). *See* Playfere (T.). Nine Sermons. 1612 (1610) *etc.*
C. (D.), *C.T.* Verses in Camb. Univ. Gratulatio. 1623. . . 5695
C. (E.). Verses in Gascoigne (G.). The Posies. 1575. . . 1482
C. (E.). *See* Baynes (P.). A helpe to true happinesse. 1635.
C. (E.). [qu. E. Chaloner?] *See* Bédé (J.). The masse displayed. 1619. 4°.
— — Hieron (S.). The Spirituall Fishing. 1618.
C. (E.) [=E. Culverwell]. *See* Sibbes (R.). Divine meditations. 1638. 12°.
C. (E.), *Knight.* A little treatise... *See* Coke (Sir E.).
C. (E. D. L. I.). *See* Belloy (P. de).
C. (F.), *C.C.C.* Verses in Cam. Univ. Anthologia. 1632. . 5741
C. (G.). A Treatise of Mathematicall Phisicke. *See* Dariot (C.). A Briefe...Introduction. 1598. 4°.
Verses in Camden (W.). Britannia. 1586 *etc.* 1324
— Camdeni Insignia. 1624. 5346
— Hipolito. The true history. 1633. 8°. 7566
— Lemnius (L.). The touchstone. 1633. . . . 2040
See Du Moulin (P.). A learned treatise. 1632. 8°.
C. (G.) [*i.e.* Capelin (G.)]. *See* Familiar and Christian instrvction. 1582.
C. (G.), *C.C.* Verses in Camb. Univ. Genethl. 1631. . . 5731
C. (G.), *C.T.* Verses in Camb. Univ. Gratulatio. 1623. . . 5695
C. (H.). Verses in Camden (W.). Britannia. 1586 *etc.* . 1324 *etc.*
Greenham (R.). Workes. 1599 *etc.* . . . . . 2912 *etc.*
C. (H.) [=Charteris (H.)]. *See* Rollock (R.). Lectvres vpon...Thessalonians. 1606.
C. (H.) [=Connestable (H.), *pseud.*]. *See* Du Perron (J. D., cardinal). The Catholike Moderator. 1623.
C. (H.). *See* Whittington (R.). De octo partibus orationis. 6 April 1519. 4°.
C. (H.). *See* Greenham (R.). *Παραμύθιον.* 1598. 8°.
C. (H.), *M.A.* Verses in Hawkins (W.). Corolla. 1634. . . 5803
C. (I.). Verses in Camb. Univ. Thr.-thr. 1603. . . . 5616
— Harper (J.). The jewel of arithmetic. 1616–7. . . 2997

No.

C. (I.) *cont.* Smith (J.). The true travels. 1630. . . . 4836
— [*i.e.* J. Cleveland?] Horatius. De arte poetica. 1640. . 3728
C. (I.). Newes. *See* Overbury (Sir T.). His Wife. 1638.
C. (I.). *See* Bedford (T.). The sinne vnto death... 1621.
C. (I.) [=Sir J. Cheke?]. *See* Bible, Polyglot. N.T. (Lat. and Eng.). 1550.
C. (I.). *See* Cruso (J.). Militarie instructions. 1632.
C. (I.) [*qu.* Jeff. Chorlton?] *See* Garey (Samuel). Two Treatises. 1605.
C. (I.) [=Carter (J.)]. *See* Hildersam (A.). Lectures. 1629.
C. (I.). *See* Rodriguez (Alonso). A short and svre way. 1630.
C. (I.), *Ioan.* Verses in Oxf. Univ. Horti. 1640. . . . 5499
C. (I. B. A.). *See* Sutcliffe (M.). De presbyterio. 1591.
C. (J.). Verses in Fuller (T.). The historie of the holy warre. 1639. 5806
C. (J.). *See* Melanchthon (P.). The Epistle... 1547.
C. (J.), *Pemb.* Verses in Cam. Univ. Rex redux. 1633. . . 5748
C. (J. P. L.). *See* Pilkington (J.). Aggeus the Prophete. 1560.
C. (L.). *See* Widdrington (R.).
C. (M.). Verses in Gascoigne (G.). The Posies. 1575. . . 1482
Gostwyke (R.). Deo &c. 1616. 5678
C. (M.). *See* Cosworth (M.). 1597.
C. (M.), *Confessor to the English Nuns at Paris.* *See* Carre (T.). 1635.
C. (M.) [*i.e.* Parker (M.)]. *See* Jewel (J.). An apologie. 1564.
C. (M.) [=Coverdale (M.)]. *See* Wyclif (J.). Uvicklieffes Wicket. [1548?]
C. (N.). Verses in Barclay (J.). Argenis. 1625. . . . 4086
See Carpenter (N.). Achitophel. 1629. 4°.
— Fabricius (W.). Lithotomia. 1640.
C. (N.). *See* The Swedish Intelligencer Pt VIII. (The principall passages.) 1636. Feb. 6. 4°. 4644
C. (P.), *Chiriatros.* *See* Enchiridion Medicum. 16[12] *etc.*
C. (P.), *Praeli Corrector.* Verses in Camb. Univ. Lacrymae. 1619. 5689
C. (P.), *Regal.* Verses in Camb. Univ. Epicedium. 1612. . 5665
— Gratulatio. 1623. 5695
C. (P. D.). *See* Cotton (P.). Anti-coton. 1611.
C. (R.). The blasinge of Bawdrie. 1574. 8°. . . . 1441
C. (R.). The copie of a letter to...the Earle of Leycester. 1586. 4°. 1681
C. (R.). Verses in Butler (C.). Rhetorica. 1600. . . . 5252
Adamson (J.). Εἰσόδια. 1618. 5960
Camb. Univ. Gratulatio. 1623. 5695
Comenius. Porta linguarum. 1631 *etc.* 4434
King (E.). Jvsta. 1638. 5829
See Crashaw (R.). Epigrammatum. 1634. 8°.
— Estienne (H.). A world of wonders. 1607.
— Monginot (F. de). A resolvtion... 1618.
— Recorde (R.). The ground of arts. 1632. 8°.
Overbury (Sir T.), his Wife. 1638, *bis.* . . . 4870
C. (R.), *Esq.* [=Carew (Ric.)]. *See* Huarte (J.). Examen. 1594.
C. (R.), *Gent.* La Vardin (J. de). The historie. 1596. . . 2239
C. (R.), *Gentleman* [=R. Churche]. *See* Fumée (M.). The historie of...Hungarie. 1600.
C. (R.), *King's Coll.* Verses in Camb. Univ. Lacrymæ. 1619. . 5689
C. (*Mr* R.), *P. and Bachelor of Diuinitie.* *See* Chambers (R.).
C. (T.). An Hospitall for the diseased. 1579. 4°. . . . 1876
— 1598. 4°. 2010
C. (T.). The iust mans memoriall...to the...Earle of Pembroke. 1630 4°. 7346
C. (T.). A replye to an answere... [1574?] *See* Cartwright (T.).
C. (T.). A spirituall purgation...of Luthers Errour. H. Singleton, [1548?] 8°. 1059
C. (T.). Verses in Smith (H.). Ivrisprudentiæ &c. dialogus. 1592. 2413
H. (R.). The arraignement. 1631(–2). 4202
C. (T.). *See* Babington (G.). The Works... 1637.
C. (T.) [=T. Churchyard]. *See* Whetstone (G.). The Censure. 1587.

No.

C. (T.), *Coll. Jesu.* Verses in Cam. Univ. Anthologia. 1632. . 5741
C. (T.), *I.C., Cantab. Eborac.* Verses in Crashaw (W.). Falsificationum. 1606. 2262
C. (T.), *Joh.* Verses in Camb. Univ. Epicedium. 1612. . . 5665
C. (T.), *T.C.* Verses in Camb. Univ. Gratulatio. 1623. . . 5695
C. (T. B.) [=T. Bowes or T. Beard?]. *See* La Primaudaye (P. de). The French Academie. 1618. F°.
C. (Th.). Verses in Wither (G.). Abvses stript and whipt. 1614. . 3406
C. (Th. A. I.). *See* Eudes (M.).
C. (W.). The ambassador between Heauen and Earth. 1613. 12°. 3647
C. (W.). A boke of the propreties of Herbes. W. Copland [1549?]. 8°. 1085
C. (W.). [qu. Crashaw?] Fatall vesper...in the Black-Friers. 1623. 4°. 4772
C. (W.). Polimanteia. Cambridge, 1595. 4°. 5571
C. (W.). The widowes ioy. 1622. 4°. 3507
C. (W.). [Dialogue.] *See* Rogers (H.). An answer to Mr. Fisher... 1623.
C. (W.) [=Crashaw (W.)]. *See* Balbani (N.). The Italian convert. 1635.
C. (W.). *See* Crowley (R.). A briefe discourse. 1578. 8°.
— Hutton (M.). A sermon. 1579. 8°.
— Pasquale (C.). False complaints. 1605. 4°.
Ca. (R.). Verses in Overbury (Sir T.). His Wife. Ed. 11. 1622. . 3380
Ca. (Si.), *Gen.* Verses in Du Bartas. Weekes, 1621. . . 2535
Cabasilas (Nilus). *See* Nilus.
Cabot (Sebastian). *See* Fox (L.). Northwest Fox. 1635.
Cacot (Francis). *See* Perkins (W.). Works. Vol. 2. (A christian and plain treatise of...predestination). 1617. F°. . 3760
Caddell (Peter). *See* Cadell.
Cade (Anthony). A justification of the Church of England. 1630. 4°. 4097
Saint pavles agonie. 1618. 4°. 4154
Sermon necessary for these times. Cambridge, 1636. 4°. . 5778
— 1639. 4°. 5794
Cadell or Caddell (Peter). *See* Harris (P.). Excommunication. 1632. 4°.
Cademan (Sir Thomas), *M.D.* Verses in Hippocrates. 1633. . 5812
Caelius or Celius (Michael). *See* Jonas (J.). The true hystorye. [1546?] 8°.
Cænalis (Robertus), *bp. See* Cenalis.
Caesar. Cæsar's Dialogue. *See* N. (E.). Cæsars Dialogue. 1601.
Caesar (C. Julius). Cæsar. Commentarii. 1590. 16°. . . 2064
The eyght bookes. Trans. A. Golding. 1565. 8°. . . . 926
Observations upon Cæsars Commentaries. By C. Edmonds. Books I—V. For M. Lownes, 1604. F°. 2471
— Books I—VII. For W. Ponsonby, 1604. F°. . . 7853
— 1609. F°. 2493
Abridgment of Caesars Warres. *See* Rohan (H. duc de). The complete captain. 1640.
Caesar (Sir Julius). [Acts of the Court of Requests. Ab. 16– ?] 4°. 6802
See Exchequer Court. 1608.
Caesar (P.). General Discourse against...Vsurers. 1578. 4°. . . 1182
Caius (J.). De antiquitate Cantabrigiensis Academiæ. 1568. 8°. 1458
— 1574. 4°. 839
De canibus britannicis. 1570. 8°. 936
— Of Englishe Dogges. 1576. 4°. 1442
De pronunciatione Grecæ & Latinæ linguæ. 1574. 4°. . . 841
Historiæ Cantebrigiensis Academiæ liber. 1574. 4°. . . 840
See Castiglione (B.). De Curiali. 1571 *etc.*
Caius (T.). Assertio Antiquitatis Oxoniensis Academiæ. 1574. 4°. . 842
— *See* Caius (J.). De antiquitate. 1568.
Verses in Stanyhurst (R.). Harmonia. 1570. . . . 749
See Longland (J.). Tres conciones &c. [1527?] . . . 304

No.

Caius (T.) *cont.* Sermones. [1521?] 305
Calabria. *See* Dreadful news. 1638. 4°.
Calamy (Edmund). *See* Fenner (W.). The sovles Looking-glasse. 1640. 8°.
Calderwood (David). Parasynagma Perthense. 1620. 4°. . . . 7682
Solution of Doctor Resolutus...for kneeling. 1619. 4°. . 7806
Caledons complaint against infamous Libells. [Ab. 1640.] 4°. . 5994
Calendar (Xylographic). Ab. 1537. 7063
Calendar of Scripture. 1575. 4°. 968
Calendar of Shepherds. *See* Shepherds.
Calendar. Kalendar of the New Legend of England. 1516. *See* Capgrave (J.).
Calendar of years. 1547. *See* The just reckenyng. 8°.
Calepinus (Ambrosius). Dictionarium [Polyglot]. Lyons, 1585. F°. 6409
Dictionarium octolingue. Rec. J. Passeratius. Genevae, 1620. F°. 6323
Dictionarium undecim linguarum. Ed. 7. Basileae, 1627. F°. 6313
See Elyot (Sir T.). Bibliotheca Eliote. 1548. F°.
Calfhill (Jas.). An answere to the treatise of the crosse. 1565. 4°. 1398
Verses in Wilson (Sir T.). Vita, 1551. 631
Calligraphy. 1636. Davies (J.). The Writing Schoolmaster.
Callimachus. [Gr. Lat.] *See* Poetae minores. 1635.
Calmeteus (Antonius). *See* Chalmeteus.
Calphilus (Jacobus). *See* Calfhill.
Calthorpe (Charles). The relation between the lord of a mannor and the coppyholder. 1635. 4°. 5122
Calverley (Geo.), *Pet.* Verses in Cam. Univ. Voces. 1640. . 5836
Calvert (George). *See* King (H.), *bp.* A Sermon. 1621.
Calvin (J.). Admonicion against astrology. [1560?] 8°. . . . 1306
Aphorismes of christian religion. 1596. 8°. 2238
Catechisme. [1565?] 8°. 1187
Certaine homilies. 'Rome, Castle of S. angel,' 1553. 8°. . 1047
Commentarie...upon...Genesis. Trans. T. Tymme. 1578. 4°. . 7283
— Actes...Trans. C. Fetherstone. 1585. 4°. 7305
— Romanes. Trans. C. Rosdell. 1583. 4°. 7304
— Colossians. Trans. R. V. [1581?] 4°. 7246
— Hebrewes. 1605. 4°. 7466
— I John and Jude. [158-?] 8°. 1188
Faythful and most godly treatyse conc. the sacrament. Trans. Lacius...Church of Denmark. [1546?] 8°. . . . 6704–5
Fovr Godlye Sermons. 1561. 8°. 1295
Harmonie upon the three Euangelistes... Comm. vpon S. John. 1610. 4°. 7309
Institution of christian religion. Trans. T. Norton. 1561. May 6. F°. 7106
— 1574. 4°. 7108
— 1582. 4°. 7285
— 1587. 4°. 1653
— 1599. 4°. 2072
— 1611. F°. 2371
Institucion de la religion christiana (Spanish). 1597. 4°. . 2245
— Abridgement by W. Lawne. Trans. C. Fetherstone. Edinburgh, 1585. 8°. 5921
Mynde of.. Caluyne, what a Faithfull man ..ought to do. J. Owen, Ipswich [1548]. 8°. 5882
Psalms of David, with Calvin's Commentaries. 1571. 4°. . 1569
Sermons...vpon the x Commandementes. 1579. 4°. . . . 1800
— Job. 1580. F°. 1807
— Ephesians. Trans. A. Golding. 1577. 4°. . . . 7281
Short instruction...agaynst...Anabaptistes. 1549. 8°. . . 903
Thirteene sermons...of the Free Election of God. 1579. 4°. . 1799
[Treatise conc. offences.] 1567. 8°. 7141

No.
Calvin (J.) *cont.* Two godly and learned sermons. [Ps. xvi. 3, Heb. xiii. 13.] (1584.) 8°. 1881
Two godly and notable sermons. [II Tim. i.] 1555. [1576.] 8°. 943
Very profitable treatise...of all Sainctes bodies. [1561?] 8°. . 1307
Consensio mvtva in re Sacramentaria Ministrorum Tigurinæ Ecclesiæ, & D. I. C. *See* Lasco (J. à). Brevis...tractatio. 1552. 1100
[Epistle.] *See* Bullinger (H.). Two Epystles. [1549?] 8°.
— — Spottiswood (J.). The execvtion. 1616.
[Life.] *See* Beza (T.). A discourse. [156–?]
See Anderton (J.). Luthers Life. 1624. 4°.
— Bridges (J.), *bp.* A defence. 1587.
— Carlile (C.). A discovrse. 1582.
— Liturgies. Geneva. The forme of common prayer and the catechism. 1550 *etc.* . . . . 669 *etc.*
— — Scotland. The book of common order. 1584 *etc.*
— Yates (J.). Gods arraignment. 1615. 4°.
Camber (Th.). *See* Comber.
Cambridge Town. *See* Cambridge University and Town.
Cambridge University. 1478. *See* Gulielmus (Laurentius) *de Saona.* 1480. 4°.
Cambridge, *Student of.* *See* Bernard (St.). The meditations... 1496 *etc.*
Cambridge University. 1510. [*Ad usum.*] *See* Libellus sophistarum. 4°.
1524. [Letter.] *See* Wakefield (R.). Oratio. [1524.] 4°.
1551. *See* Wilson (Sir T.). Vita et obitvs...H. et C. Brandoni... [1551.]
1564. *See* Hartwell (A.). Regina Litterata. 1565.
1568. *See* Caius (J.). De antiquitate. 1568 *etc.*
1584. *See* Copy of a letter. 1584.
1585. [*In usum.*] Willet (A.). De animæ natura. 8°.
Act Verses. Melior est. H. Denham, 1580. F°. . . . 7250
— Simplex cibus. 1580. F°. 7251
— Intellectus est 7252
— Ordinaria Daemonum 7253
— Omnes passiones 7254
— Opinio major 7255
— Vir prudens 7256
— Furem, a quo 7257
— Ingenui adolescentes 7258
— [Ab. 1577–1581.] F°. 7252
— Renati fide. [Ab. 1584.] F°. 5512
— Interpretatio. [Ab. 1584.] 5513
— Ab ecclesiastico iudice. 5 Julij 1585. Cantabrigiæ, F°. . 5514
— Ne sit magistratus. 5 Julij 1585. Cantabrigiæ, F°. . . 5519
— Carmina et characteres. [Ab. 1585.] F°. 5521
— Virtuti magis. [Ab. 1585.] F°. 5522
— Scholasticos. [Ab. 1585.] F°. 5523
— Coniuncta febrium. Julij 3. 1586. F°. 5524
— Salutis. Julij 3. 1586. F°. 5525
— Galeni. Julij 4. 1586. F°. 5526
— Verae notae. [Ab. 1586.] F°. 5529
— Doctrina ecclesiae. [Ab. 1587.] F°. 5531
— Minima vis. [Ab. 1587?] F°. 5532
— Is qui de se. [Ab. 1588.] F°. 5536
— Ecclesia visibilis. [Ab. 1588.] F°. 5537
— Si crimini. [Ab. 1588.] F°. 5538
— Mulier, est ingeniosior. [Ab. 1588.] F°. 5539
Academiae...Lacrymae tumulo P. Sidneij sacratae. 1587. 4°. 2123, 7356
1590? *See* Greenwood (J.). M. Some.
[Printed label recording the gift of a casket, presented by John Banister. 1591.] 8°. 7772

No.

Cambridge University *cont.* 1598. Carmina Funebria... *See* Barlow (W.). Vita et obitvs...Richardi Cosin. 1598.
Threno-thriambeuticon. Cantabrigiae, 1603. 4°. 5616
1603–4. *See* Oxford. The Ansvvere of the vicechancelovr...to... the Ministers of the Church of England... 1603 *etc.*
1606. *See* Lewkenor (Sir E.). Threnodia... 1606.
Epicedium Cantabrigiense, in obitum...Henrici...Principis Walliae. 1612. 4°. 5665, 5666
1616. (Play.) Stubbe (E.). Fravs honesta. 1632.
1618–9. *See* Angelos (C.). Christopher Angell... 1618.
— — Ἐγκώμιον... 1619.
Lacrymae Cantabrigienses: in obitum...Reginae Annae. 1619. 4°. 5689
Gratulatio...de...Principis reditu ex Hispaniis. 1623. 4°. . . 5695
1622. True copies of all the Latine Orations...in the entertainment of Don Charles de Coloma etc. 1623. 4°. . . 3145
1623. *See* Herbert (G.). Oratio. 4°.
[1625 March 27.] Cantabrigiensium dolor et solamen. 1625. 4°. 5701
1625 April 1. Charles I. [Printing of Latin Books.] *See* Proclamations. 7453
1625 May. Epithalamium...Caroli...et H. Mariae. 1625. 4°. 5702
1626. (Plays.) *See* Stubbe (E.). Fraus honesta. 1632.
1629. *See* Rivers (P.). A new almanack. 8°.
1630. Proceedings...of the Vniversity Heads...against Mr. Barret... *See* Prynne (W.). Anti-arminianisme... 1630.
See Clare (J.). The Converted Iew. 1630.
Genethliacum...Caroli & Mariae. 1631. 4°. 5731
Anthologia in regis exanthemata. 1632. 4°. 5741
Ducis Eboracensis Fasciae. 1633. 4°. 5808
Rex redux. 1633. 4°. 5748
Carmen natalitium...Principis Elisabethae. 1635. 4°. . 5770
Συνῳδία, sive Musarum...congratulatio. 1637. 4°. . . 5790
1638. *See* Cowley (A.). Navfragium iocvlare. 1638.
Voces votivae. 1640. 4°. 5836
Cambridge University and Town. [Maps.] Lyne (R.). *See* Caius (J.). 1574. 839
— — Braun (G.). 1575.
— — Fuller (T.). 1634.
Corpus Christi College. Library. *See* Wiclif (J.). Two short treatises. 1608.
Caius College. *See* Deloney.
King's College. *See* Fletcher (P.). Sicelides. 1631. 4°.
Pembroke Hall. Verses in Cam. Univ. Epithalam. 1625. . 5702
Peterhouse. [Fragments from the library[1].] 96, 102
Queens' College. [NT.] 7704
— [16– ?]. 6912
— Play 1630, 1633. *See* Hausted (P.). Senile Odium. 1633.
Trinity College. 1590. (Play.) *See* Pedantius. 1631.
— 1602. (Play.) *See* Hawkesworth (W.). Labyrinthus. 1636.
— 1614. (Play.) *See* Albumazar. 1634.
— 1614. (Play.) *See* Ruggle (G.). Ignoramus. 1630.
— 1615. (Play.) *See* Tomkis (T.). Albumazar.
— 1631. *See* Randolph (T.). The iealovs lovers. 1634. 4°.
— Library. *See* Higden.
Selwyn College Hostel. *See* Verepaeus.
Cambridge Pilgrim, The. *See* Hall (J.). The discovery of a new world. 1620? 8°.
Camden (William). Annales rerum anglicarum et hibernicarum, ad ann. 1589. 1615. F°. 3106
— Tomus alter. 1627. F°. 3168

[1] See Dibdin *Ames* pp. 20—1.

No.

Camden (William) *cont.* Trans. A. Darcie. 1625. 4°. . . . 4756
— Trans. R. N. Ed. 3. 1635. F°. 4014
[Annales, Pt iv.] Tomus alter et idem: or The historie of... Elizabeth. 1629. 4°. 3980
— (The historie of Elizabeth.) 1630. F°. 4757
Britannia. Ed. 1. R. Newbery, 1586. 8°. 1324
— Ed. 2. R. Newbery, 1587. 8°. 1326
— Ed. 3. G. Bishop, 1590. 8°. 1723
— Ed. 4. G. Bishop, 1594. 4°. 1733
— Ed. 5. G. Bishop, 1600. 4°. 1743
— Ed. 6. (With maps.) G. Bishop and J. Norton, 1607. F°. 1758
— F. Kingston *etc.* 1637. F°. 3055, 3056
— Abridgment. 1626. Oblong 8°. 3530
Institutio graecae grammatices...in usum Scholae Westmonasteriensis. 1604. 8°. 7308
— 1608. 8°. 2363
— Rouen, 1633. 8°. 6258
Reges, reginæ, nobiles & alij in eccl. Westmon. 1600. 4°. . 2057
— Ed. 2. 1603. 4°. 3355
— Ed. 3. 1606. 4°. 3363
Remaines...concerning Britaine. Ed. 1. 1605. 4°. . . 3554
— Ed. 2. 1614. 4°. 3754
— Ed. 3. 1623. 4°. 3684
— Ed. 4. 1629. 4°. 2457
— Ed. 5. By J. Philipot. 1636. 4°. 4024
— 1637. 4°. 4026
Verses in Ascham (R.). Fam. epp. libri tres. 1576. . . 1654
Rogers (T.). A philosophicall discourse. 1576. . . . 1348
Rhys (J. D.). Cambrobrytannicæ linguæ. 1592. . . . 2215
[*Life &c.*] *See* Whear (D.)....Pietas erga Benefactores... 1628.
See Oxford University. Camdeni Insignia. 1624. 4°.
— Brooke (R.). A Discouerie of...errors... [1595?]
— Garnett (H.). Actio. 1607.
— Speed (J.). The Theatre. 1611.
Camerarius (Joachim). *See* Bible (Lat.). N.T. 1574 *etc.*
— — Eng. (Genevan). 1599 *etc.*
Camerarius (Phil.). The living librarie. 1621. F°. 2450
— Ed. 2. 1625. F°. 2454
Camers or Camertes (John). The excellent...worke of Julius Solinus. 1587. *See* Mela (P.). Worke. 1590. 4°.
Camilli (Camillo). *See* Huarte (Juan). Examen. 1594 *etc.*
Campanus (Jo. Ant.). *See* Æsop. Æsopi Phrygis Fabulæ... 1635.
Campaspe. 1591. *See* Lyly (J.).
Campbell (Ninian). Verses in Forbes (P.). Funerals. 1635. . . 6007
Campion (Edmund). Historie of Ireland. *See* Ware (Sir J.). The Historie of Ireland. 1633.
See Charke (W.). A replie to a censure... 1581.
— — A treatise against the defense. 1586.
— Hanmer (M.). The great bragge...of...Edmunde Campion... 1581.
— — The Iesuites Banner... 1581.
— Humphrey (L.). Iesvitismi pars...secunda. 1584.
— Nowell (A.). A true report of the Disputation... 1583.
— Parsons (R.). A defence of the censure. 1582.
— Stanyhurst (R.). Harmonia. 1570.
— Whitaker (W.). Ad rationes decem responsio. 1581.
— — Responsionis...Defensio. 1583.
— — An answere to the ten reasons. 1606. 4°.
Campion (Thomas). Songs of Mourning. *See* Coprario (J.). 1613.
Verses in Barnes (B.). Foure bookes. 1606. 2435

No.

Campion (Thomas) *cont.* Coryate (T.). Coryates crvdities. 1611. 3076
— Ravenscroft (T.). A briefe discourse. 1614. . . . 2029
See Daniel (S.). A panegyrike...With a defence of Ryme. 1603.
Camus (Jean Pierre). Admirable events. Trans. S. Du Verger. T. Harper for W. Brooks. 1639. 4°. 4036
— T. Harper for A. Roper. 1639. 4°. 4037
Discours hapned betwene...Nicephorus & Tristan. 1630. 8°. . 6622
Draught of eternitie. Trans. M. Car. Douai, 1632. 12°. . 6593
Spirituall director disinteressed. 'Roan,' 1633. 12°. . . 6270
Canaye (Philippe), Sieur de Fresnes. *See* La Noue (F. de). The politicke and militarie discourses. 1587(–8). 4°.
Cancellar (James). The pathe of Obedience. [1553?] 8°. . . 641
Candido (Il.). *See* Gwinne (M.).
Candish (Thomas). *See* Cavendish.
Canfield (Benedict). The rule of perfection. Rouen, 1609. 8°. . 6250
— Rouen [1609?]. 24°. 6256
Cangiserus or Canngiesser (Theophilus). *See* Lipsius (J.). Oratio... 1615.
Canini (Angelo). Ἑλληνισμός. 1624. 8°. 3150
Canisius (Petrus). Ane catechisme or schort instruction. Paris, 1588. 16°. 6200
Canne (John). A necessitie of separation. 1634. 4°. . . . 6404
See Bradshaw (W.). The unreasonablenes of separation. 1640.
Canngiesser (Theophilus). *See* Cangiserus.
Cannius. *See* Erasmus (D.). Two dyaloges. [Ab. 1550.] 8°.
Cannon (Thomas). Verses in Cam. Univ. Fasciae. 1633. *See also* Canon. 5808
Canon or Canonicus (John). Quæstiones super Aristotelis physica. St Alban's [1481]. F°. 85
Canon (Sir Thomas). Verses in Davies (J.). Antiquæ linguæ dictionarium. 1632. 4979
Canon of triangles. 1630. 4°. 4146
Canons. A booke of certaine Canons. 1571. (Liber quorundam &c.) [1571.] 4°. 873
— [1571.] 4°. 874
— (English part only.) [1571.] 4°. 875
— (Latin part only.) [1571.] 4°. 876
Canter (Gulielmus). *See* Dee (John). General & rare Memorials...1577.
Canterbury, Province. *See* England. Church.
See Articles (English Church).
— Convocation. (Canterbury Province.)
— Constitutions. 1603.
Canterbury Castle, *Prisoners in.* The copy of a letter. *See* Coverdale (M.). Certain...letters. 1564.
Canterbury (Map. 1588). *See* Braun (G.).
Canutus. Book of the Pestilence. Machlinia [1483]. 4°. . . . 96
Treatise agaynst pestelence. W. de Worde [1510]. 4°. . 7071
— — [Antwerp? 151– ? 4°.] 7856
Capel (Richard). Tentations. Ed. 2. 1635. 12°. 4363
— Ed. 3. 1636. 12°. 4371
— Part 3. 1636. 12°. 4987
See Pemble (W.). Workes. Ed. 3. 1635.
— — De sensibus. 1629.
— — Frvitfvll sermon. 1629.
— — Introdvction to the...Sacrament. 1629.
— — Salomons recantation. 1628.
— — Short and sweet exposition vpon...Zachary. 1629.
— — Vindiciæ fidei. 1629.
— — Vindiciæ gratiæ. 1629.
Capell (Moses). God's valuation of mans soule. 1632. 4°. . 5055

No.

Capelin (George). *See* Familiar & christian instruction. 1582.
Capgrave (J.). Nova Legenda Anglie. 1516. 4°. 174
The Kalendre of the Newe Legende of Englande. (The lyfe of Seynt Birgette.) 1516. 4°. 265
[Life of S. Bridgit.] *See* B. (B.), *Franciscan Friar*. The life. 1625. 4°.
Capitula seu Constitutiones. *See* Constitutions.
Capugnano (Giovanni). *See* Teixeira (J.). The strangest adventure. 1601. 4°. 7765
Car (Jac.). Verses in Skene (Sir J.) Regiam. 1609. . . 3458
Car (Miles). *See* Carre (T.).
Caracciolo (Galeazzo). *See* Balbani (N.). Newes from Italy. 1608. 4°.
— The Italian convert. 1635.
Caradoc. The historie of Cambria. [1584?] 4°. 1439
Cardinalium, archiepiscoporum, episcoporum...de anonymis quibusdam... libellis sententiæ. 'A. Stephanus, Lutetiæ Parisiorum.' 1625. 8°. 4962
Careles (John). Letters. *See* Coverdale (M.). Certain...letters. 1564.
Certeyne letters...*See* Ridley (N.). A pitvovs lamentation. (1566.)
Carew (Peter). Verses in Camdeni Insignia. 1624. . . . 5346
Carew (Richard). The survey of Cornwall. 1602. 4°. . . 2877
See Huarte (J.). Examen. 1594 *etc.*
Carew (Thomas). Cœlum Britannicum. 1634. 4°. . 4482, 4483, 7601
Foure godlie and profitable sermons. 1605. 8°. . . . 3609
Verses in May (T.). The heire. 1633. 4574
— Sandys (G.). A paraphrase. 1638. 4736
See Huarte (J.). Examen. 1594 *etc.*
Carew (Wymond), *K.C.C.* Verses in Cam. Univ. Epithalam. 1625. . 5702
— — Genethl. 1631. 5731
— Hippocrates. 1631 *etc.* . . . . 5736 *etc.*
Carey (Henry), baron Carey of Leppington. *See* Monmouth, Earl of.
Carey (John), Viscount Rochford. Verses in Cam. Univ. Dolor et Solamen. 1625. 5701
Carey (Valentine). *See* Cam. Univ. Epicedium. 1612. 4°.
Carier (Ben). A copy of a letter. 1615. 4°. 6901
See Hakewill (G.). An answere. 1616.
Carion (J.). The thre bokes of Chronicles...App. by J. Funcke. 1550. 4°. 780
Carlell (Ludovick). Arviragus and Philicia. Pts. i. & ii. 1639. 12°. 4907
Carleton (Dudley). Speech...in the Estates Generall...touching... Arminius. 6 Oct. 1617. 1618. 4°. 3324
Carleton (George). Examination of...the author of the late Appeale. 1626. 4°. 4918
— Ed. 2. 1626. 4°. 4919
Ivrisdiction regall, episcopall, papall. 1610. 4°. 2369
Thankfvll remembrance. 1624. 4°. 3860
— Ed. 3. 1627. 4°. 4237
— Ed. 4. 1630. 4°. 4538
Tithes Examined. 1606. 4°. 1615
— Ed. 2. 1611. 4°. 2506
Vita B. Gilpini. 1628. 4°. 5037
The life of B. Gilpin. 1629. 4°. 5039
— Ed. 4. 1636. 12°. 7642
Verses in Camden (W.). Britannia. 1637. 3055
See Dort Synod. A ioynt attestation. 1626. 4°. . . . 4234
— — Suffragium Collegiale... 1626, 1627.
Carliell (Robert). Britaines glorie. 1619. 8°. 3591
Carlile (Chr.). Discourse concerning two diuine positions. 1582. 8°. 1871
Discourse wherein is proved...that Peter was never at Rome. 1572. 4°. 1570
Verses in Cheke (Sir J.). De obitu M. Buceri. 1551. . . 734
— Jones (J.). Wilson (Sir T.). Vita, 1551. 631

No.

Carlile (Chr.) *cont.* — Jones (J.). A briefe discourse. 1574. . 1366
— Chaloner (Sir T.). De rep. angl. 1579. 7270
— Batman (S.). The doome. 1581. 1314
— Lloyd (L.). The pilgrimage. 1586. 1941
Carmelianus (Petrus), *Poeta*. Verses in Anwykyll (J.). Compendium. 1489. 4°. 143
— Brant (S.). Stultifera Nauis. 1570. 999
Carolostadius (Andreas) [or Bodenstein]. *See* Anderton (J.). Luthers Life. 1624. 4°.
Carpentarius (Jacobus). *See* Ross (A.). Commentum. 1634.
Carpenter (Ed.). Verses in Oxf. Univ. Magd. Coll. 1612. . . 5302
Carpenter (John). Plaine mans spirituall plough. 1607. 4°. . 2741
Preparatiue to contentation. 1597. 4°. 2722
Carpenter (Nath.). Achitophel. 1629. 4°. 7411
— 1633. 12°. 4625
— Oxford, 1640. 12°. 7666
Chorazin and Bethsaida's Woe. Oxford, 1640. 12°. . . 7667
Geography delineated. Oxford, 1625. 4°. 5348
— Ed. 2. Oxford, 1635. 4°. 5413
Philosophia libera. Ed. 2. Oxoniae, 1622. 8°. . . 5342
— Ed. 3. Oxoniae, 1636. 8°. 5468
Carpenter (Richard). A pastoral charge...at the triennial visitation. (Christs Larum: Bell of Love). 1616. 8°. . . 3907
Carr (J.). Alarume Bell for London. [1573.] 8°. . . . 1764
Ruinous fal of Prodigalitie. 1573. 8°. 1763
Carr (N.). De scriptorum Britannicorũ paucitate. 1576. 8°. . . 1227
Verses in Wilson (Sir T.). Vita. 1551. . . 631
See Cheke (Sir J.). De obitu M. Buceri. 1551.
— Demosthenes...Olynthiacæ Orationes...1571.
Carr (Ralph). *See* Turkey. The Mahumetane or Turkish Historie. 1600.
Carre (Thomas) *alias* Miles Pinkney. *See* Richelieu. The principall points. 1635. 8°.
See Camus (J. P.), *bp*. A dravght. 1632.
— Francis de Sales (S). A treatise. 1630.
Carronus (Jacobus). *See* Gesner (C.). Historiae animalium Lib. v. 1587. F°.
Carta Feodi. W. de Worde, [15– .] 4°. 214
— Parvus Libellus...Carta Feodi. Pynson, [15– .] 4°. . 308
— R. Redman, 1530. 8°. 373
Cartari (V.). *See* Linche (R.). The fovntaine of ancient fiction. [1599.] 4°.
Carter (George). Verses in Hawkins (W.). Corolla. 1634. . 5803
Carter (John). Plaine exposition of Christs sermon. 1627. 4°. . 3169
Carter (John). Vindiciae Decimarum. Of tithes. 1640. 4°. . 4673
Verses in Hippocrates. 1633. 5812
Carter (John), *of Bramford, Suffolk*. *See* Hildersam (A.). Lectvres. 1629.
Carter (O.). An Answere. 1579. 8°. 1801
Carter (Peter). *See* Seton (J.). Dialectica. 1611 *etc.*
Carter (Robert), *Joh.* Verses in Camb. Univ. Epithalam. 1625. . 5702
Carter (Walter), *K.C.C.* Verses in Cam. Univ. Epithalam. 1625. . 5702
Carter (William). Verses in Seton (J.). Dialectica. 1631. . 5739
Cartner (M.). Verses in Smith (J.). The true travels. 1630. . 4836
Cartwright (Christopher), *Pet.* Verses in Camb. Univ. Lacrymae. 1619. 5689
— — Epithalam. 1625. 5702
Cartwright (Fulke), *Pet.* Verses in Camb. Univ. Voces. 1640. . 5836
Cartwright (T.). Confutation of the Rhemists...new testament. [Leyden,] 1618. F°. 6505
In librum Salomonis. 1604. 4°. 2259

No.

Cartwright (T.) *cont.* Replye to an answere made of M. Doctor Whitgifte against an Admonition. [Ab. 1574.] 4°. 5899
— [Ed. 2. Ab. 1574.] 4°. 5900
Rest of the second replie. 1577. 4°. 6762
— [Another state of the errata.] 6762*
Second admonition to the parliament. [1572.] 8°. . . . 5897
Second replie...touching the Church Discipline. [Zurich,] 1575. 5°. 6300
Σὺν θέῳ ἐν χριστῷ. The answere to the preface of the rhemish testament. Edinburgh, 1602. 8°. 5942
See Bancroft (R.). A Svrvay of the...Discipline...1593.
— Collection of certain Letters. 1590.
— Defence. A defense of the Ecclesiasticall Regiment. 1574. 1748
— Whitgift (J.). An answer to a certen Libell. 1573. 4°.
— — Defence. 1574. F°.
— — Examination of M. Doctor Whytgiftes censvres...1575.
Verses in Cam. Univ. Rex redux. 1633. 5748
Chaucer (G.). Amorum Troili. 1635. 5414
Oxf. Univ. Horti. 1640. 5499
Cary (Elizabeth), viscountess Falkland. *See* Falkland.
Cary (Lucius), second viscount Falkland. *See* Falkland.
Cary (Thomas). *See* Puget de la Serre (J.). The mirrour. 1639. 8°.
Cary (Walter). Present state of England. 1627. 4°. . . . 4969
Casa (Giovanni della). Galateus...interpr. N. Chytraeo...de officiis. Oxoniae. 1630. 8°. 5382
Casaubon (Isaac). Answere...to the Epistle of...Cardinell Peron. 1612. 4°. 2976
Ad epistolam Cardinalis Perronij responsio. 1612. 4°. . . 2373
Ad Frontonem Ducæum. 1611. 4°. 2370
De rebus sacris et ecclesiasticis. 1614. F°. 3461
The originall of idolatries. Trans. A. Darcie. 1624. 4°. . 4082
The originall of popish idolatrie. 1630. 4°. 6998
Verses in Ussher (J.). Gravissimæ quæstionis. 1613. 4°. . 2798
See Bible. N.T. (Gr.). 1622, 1633.
— Casaubon (M.). M. Casauboni Pietas. 1621.
— — Vindicatio patris. 1624.
— — The vindication... 1624.
— Prideaux (J.). Castigatio. 1614.
Casaubon (Meric). Pietas. 1621. 8°. 3284
Treatise of vse and custome. 1638. 4°. 4738
Vindicatio patris. 1624. 4°. 2819
Vindication of I. Casaubon. 1624. 4°. 2820
See Antoninus (M. Aurelius). Meditations... 1635.
— Optatus. 1631.
Case (John). Ancilla philosophiae. Oxoniae, 1599. 4°. . . . 5251
Sphaera civitatis. Oxonie, 1588. 4°. 5231
Svmma vetervm interpretvm in vniuersam dialecticam Aristotelis. 1584. 4°. 1557
— Oxoniae, 1598. 8°. 5248
See Holyoake (F.). Dictionarium. 1640. 4°.
— Lomazzo (G. P.). A Tracte... 1598.
— Byrd (W.). A gratification. [1586?] F°. 1589
Caselius (Johannes). *See* Casa (G. della)...Galatevs. 1630.
Cashel, *Archbishopric.* *See* Ware (Sir J.). Archiepiscoporum. 1626.
Casimir (John), *Count Palatine.* *See* John Casimir.
Casmannus (O.). Vade mecum. 1606. 8°. 1862
Cassander (Georgius). Sententia. *See* Hall (J.). Polemices Sacræ pars prior. 1612.
Castalio (Sebastianus) or Ca telio. *See* Castellion.
Castanæus. *See* Chasteigne
Castellion (S.). Dialogorum sacrorum libri quatuor. 1619. 8°. . 7408

No.

Castellion (S.) *cont.* Cantabrigiae, 1631. 8°. 5732
— Cantabrigiæ, 1633. 8°. 5749
See Theologia Germanica. 1632.
Castelvetri or Castelvitrius (Jacobus). *See* Porta (J. B.). De furtivis literarum notis. 1591.
Castiglione (B.). De Curiali sive Aulico. 1571. 8°. 824
— 1585. 8°. 1824
— 1593. 8°. 2065
— 1612. 8°. 2267
The courtyer. 1561. 4°. 923
Castile, Kingdom of. *See* Conestaggio (G.). The historie... 1600.
— Philip II., King of Spain.
Castillionæus (Gaspar). *See* Coligny (G. de), *admiral of France.*
Castle. The castell of laboure. 1506. *See* Gringore (P.).
Castleton (William), *Pet.* Verses in Cam. Univ. Voces. 1640. . 5836
Castriot (George), *surnamed* Scanderbeg. *See* La Vardin (I. de). The historie. 1596.
Castrobello (Stephanus à). *See* Longinus (D.). Περὶ ὕψους. 1636.
Catalogue of the dukes, marquesses, earles, viscounts, bishops, barons, in the Parliament...3 Nov. 1640. 1640. 8°. . . 4487, 4489
Names of the knights...burgesses...barons...for the House of Commons...3 Nov. 1640. 1640. 8°. 4488
Catalogue of Books. 1595. *See* Maunsell (A.). 1595. F°. 1773, 2140, 7843–4
[London.] Catalogus Librorum...ex Roma, Venetiis...selegit R. Martine. J. Haviland, 16[ ]. 4°. 4877
— In diversis locis Italiae emptorum. J. Legate, 1628. 4°. . 4705
Catalogus Universalis pro nundinis Francofurtensibus. 1623. 4°. 7842
— 1628. 4°. 4341
Catalogus librorum quos...ex Italia selegit R. Martine. 1633. 4°. 4567
In diversis Italiae locis...1636...ad insigne Rosae. J. Legate, 1637. 4°. 4733
Ex præcipius Italiæ Emporiis selectorum per R. Martin. T. Harper, 1639. 4°. 4038
(Sale.) Middelburg. Catalogus miscellaneus...librorum...J. Radermacheri. Middelburg, 1634. 4°. 6484
Catalogue. [Roman Catholic Books. English printed, 1622–4.] *See* Gee (J.). The Foot out of the Snare... 1624.
Cambridge University and Colleges (Manuscripts). 1600. *See* James (T.). Ecloga Oxonio-Cantabrigiensis. 1600.
Oxford University and Colleges (Manuscripts). 1600. *See* James (T.). Ecloga Oxonio-Cantabrigiensis. 1600.
— — Bodleian Library. Catalogus universalis...T. James. Oxoniae, 1620. 4°. 5337
— — 1620. Appendix. Rouse (J.). 5467
— — *See* James (T.). Catalogus interpretum. 1635.
— — — Rouse (J.). Appendix ad catalogum. 1635. 4°.
Catalogus Protestantium. *See* Webbe (G.). Catalogus. 1624.
Roman Catholic Professors of Faith. *See* D. (A.), *Student in Divinity.* A treatise. 1614.
Catanæus (Joannes Maria). *See* Aphthonius. Progymnasmata. 1631, 1635. 8°.
Catechism. Allen (E.). A shorte Cathecisme. [Zurich,] 1550. 16°. 6286
— Catechisme that is to say a christen instruccion newlye corrected. E. Whitchurch, 8 May 1551. 8°. 670
A short Catechism...by the Kings...authoritie... 1552. J. Day, 1553. 8°. 787
— *See* Prynne (W.). Anti-arminianisme... 1630.
Catechismus brevis. R. Wolfe, 1553. 8°. . . . 737, 738
(Calvin.) *See* Calvin (J.). [1565?] 8°.
— — Liturgies. Geneva.

No.

Catechism *cont.* *See* Liturgies. Scotland. 1584 *etc.*
(Geneva.) Catechismus...per Calvinum. J. Kingston, 1565. 8°. . 1174
— — W. How. 1572. 8°. 1762
— *See* Liturgies. Geneva. The forme of common prayer. 1550, 1556, 1561.
(Heidelberg.) *See* Heidelberg Catechism. 1578 *etc.*
Irish. *See* O'Hussey (B.). An teagasg. [1609?] 16°.
(Scotland.) *See* Liturgies. Scotland. Church. The forme. 1584.
— — — Book of Common Order. 1596.
— — — — Psalter. 1615.
See Bernard (Ric.). A Double Catechisme. 1607.
— Cockburn (P.). 1561.
— Coote (E.). The English Schoole-master. 1637.
— Craig (J.). A short Summe. 1583.
— Cranmer (T.). Catechismvs. 1548.
— Dering (E.). A shorte Catechisme. 1614.
— Gataker (T.). The christian mans care. 1624.
— Leech (Jas.). A plaine...catechisme... 1605.
— Mayer (J.). Mayers Catechisme abridged. 1623.
— — The English Catechisme. 1630.
— Micron (M.). Den Kleynen Cathecismus. 1566. . . 1293
— Nowell (A.).
— Rogers (D.). A practicall catechisme. 1633.
— Sparke (T.). 1588.
Catellanus (Laurentius). *See* Bauderon (B.). Pharmacopoea. 1639.
Cater (Edward). Verses in Camb. Univ. Genethl. 1631. . . 5731
Caterinus Senensis, *Doctor*. *See* Catharinus (Ambrosius).
Catharine of Siena. The orcharde of Syon. W. de Worde, 21 Sept. 1519. F°. 180
[Life.] *See* Vineis (R. de). Here begynneth... [1493?]
— — *See* Catharinus (A.). The Life of... 1609.
Catharine de Medici, *Queen Consort of Henry II of France*. [Life.] *See* Estienne (H.). A mervaylovs discourse... 1575.
Catharine Parr, *Queen*. The lamentacion of a sinner. 5 Nov. 1547. 8°. 654
— 28 March 1548. 8°. 656
Prayers or Medytacions. 1545. 8°. 482
— 6 Nov. 1547. 8°. 492
— n.d. 8°. 509
See Bentley (T.). The monvment of Matrones. 1582.
Catharinus (Ambrosius). The life of...Catharine of Siena. Trans. J. Fen. 1609. 8°. 6578
'Catholics,' *i.e.* Roman Catholics. *See* Powel (G.). The Catholikes. 1603.
— The supplication of certaine Masse-Priests. 1604. 4°. . 3200
Catholic Admonition. *See* Salisbury (R. Cecil, earl of). An answer. 1606.
Catholike Apologie against the libels...of the League...of France... By E. D. L. I. C. [1590?] 8°. 1846
Catholicon. *See* Balbus (J.).
— Ortus Vocabulorum. 1528. 4°.
Catholique iudge...by John of the Crosse...Trans. by Sir A. A. 1623. 4°. 3851
Catholike Moderator. *See* Du Perron (J. D., cardinal). The Catholike &c. 1623.
Catholikes Supplication. *See.* Powel (G.). The Catholikes Svpplication. 1603.
Catlin (Zachary). *See* Ovid. De tristibus. 1639. 8°.
Cato (Dionysius). Catho cum commento. Caxton, 1483. F°. . 20
— Parvus Cato—Magnus Cato. Caxton [1477–8]. 4° . 4
— Preceptes (Publius). Trans. R. Burrant. 1560. 16°. 1256.

No.

Cato (Dionysius) *cont.* Cato variegatus. Trans. Sir R. Baker. 1636. 4°. 3958
Disticha moralia...cum annott. R. Taverneri. 1562. 8°. . 7146
Cats (Jacob). *See* Beverwijk (J. van). Schat der Gesontheyt. 1638. 8°. 7811
See Heywood (T.). Pleasant dialogues. 1637.
Cattan (C. de). The geomancie...Trans. F. Sparry. 1591. 4°. . 7327
Caudrey (Thomas). Verses in Hippocrates. 1633. . . . 5812
Cauliaco (G. de). Guydos qvestions. 1579. 4°. . . . 1578
See Braunschweig (H.). The noble experyence. 1525.
Cauls (Salomon de). *See* Caus.
Caundishe (Richard). *See* Cavendish.
Caus (Salomon de). La Perspective. Londres; Francfort, 1612. F°. 6636–7
Caussin (Nicholas). The holy court. Tom. 1. Paris, 1626. 4°. . 6220
— Tom. 2. Paris, 1631. 4°. 6225
— Tom. 4. Trans. Sir T. Hawkins. Rouen, 1638. F°. . 6262
The unfortunate politique. Trans. G. P. Oxford, 1639. 8°. . 5488
Cavan (C. Lambert, Baron). Verses in Camb. Univ. Lacrymæ. 1619. 5689
Cave (Brian). *See* Smith (H.). Ivrisprvdentiæ...dialogvs... 1592.
Cavellus (Hugo). *See* MacCaghwell (H.).
Cavendish (Hon. Gilbert). *See* Horæ Subsecivæ. 1620.
Cavendish (R.). The image of nature and grace. [1570.] 8°. . 877, 878
Cavendish (Thomas). *See* Hakluyt (R.). The Principal Navigations... 1589 *etc.*
Cavendish (Hon. William). *See* Horæ Subsecivæ. 1620.
Cavill (   ). *See* Higgins (J.). A mirrour. 1610.
Cawdray (Robert). A treasurie or store-house of similies. 1600. 4°. 2729
— 1609. 4°. 2743
Cawdrey (Daniel). Humilitie, the saint's liverie...two sermons. 1624. 4°. 4788
Cawdrey (Thomas). *See* Caudrey.
Caxton (William). *See* Cato (D.). [Catho Magnus.] 1483.
— Chartier (A.). The Curial. [1484?] F°.
— Chess. The Game and Play. 1475?
— Christine de Pisan. The Fayt of Armes. [1489.] . . 34
— Chronicles of England. 1480. 13
— Cicero. De Senectute. 1481.
— Dicta Philosophorum. 1477 *etc.*
— Doctrinal of Sapience. [1489–91.]
— Gower (J.). Confessio Amantis. 1493 [1483] *etc.*
— Hieronymus. [Vitas Patrum.] 1495.
— Higden (R.). The Description of Britain. 1480.
— — Polychronicon. 1482, 1495.
— Jerusalem. The last siege and conquest. 1481.
— La Tour Landry (G. de). The Knight. [1484.]
— Le Fevre (R.). [The Recuyell of the Histories of Troy.] [1475–6?] *etc.*
— Legrand (J.). The Book of Good Manners. 1487.
— Malory (Sir T.). The most ancient...history. 1634. 4°.
— Mirror of the World. [Ab. 1480] *etc.*
See Royal Book. [1486?]
See Vergilius [Æneid]. [1490–1.]
Cayer (Palma). *See* Du Moulin (P.). The waters of Siloe. 1612. 8°.
Cebes. Table. [*Eng.*] Trans. by J. Healey. *See* Epictetus. Manuall. 1616.
Cecil (Sir Edward), *Colonel.* *See* Wimbledon (Sir Edward Cecil, *afterwards* Viscount).
Cecil (John). A discoverye of the errors...by W. Criton. [1599?] 8°. 6824
Cecil (Mary). *See* Cicella.
Cecil (Hon. Robert). Verses in Cambridge University. Carmen. 1635. 5770
Cecil or Cecill (Th.). Verses *bis* in Cam. Univ. Thr-thr. 1603. . 5616
Cecil (William), Baron Burghley (†1598). *See* Burghley.

No.

Cecil (William), second Earl of Exeter and Baron Burghley (†1640). *See* Exeter.
Celius (Michael). *See* Caelius.
Cellarius (Daniel). Speculum orbis terrarum. Antverpiae [1578?]. F°. 7731
Celsus. The flowers. *See* Enchiridion medicum. 1612.
Celsus *Veronensis*. *See* Maffeus.
Cenalis (Robertus), *bp*. *See* Bridges (J.). A defence... 1587.
Censura ad panegyricum in Laudem...Gustavi Adolfi. a D. Krusio *alias* E. de Nukrois evulgatum. 1628. 4°. . . . 7764
Ceremonies. *See* Our Sauiour Jesus Christ... 1544.
Certaine arguments to perswade and provoke...parliament...advance the sincere Ministery of the gospell. 1606. 4°. . . . 6867
— *See* Mild. A myld and iust defence of certayne argvments. 1606.
Certaine artycles collected and taken...by the Byshops out of...An Admonition...wyth an Answere. [1572.] 8°. . . 5898
Certaine articles or forcible reasons. 1600. *See* T. (H.).
— Wotton (A.). An answere... 1605.
Certayne Causes gathered together, wherin is shewed the decay of Englād. [1548.] 8°. 1060
Certaine considerations drawne from the Canons of the last Sinod. 1605. 4°. 6469
Certaine considerations touching the...Church of England. *See* Bacon (F., Lord). Certaine Considerations... [1604] *etc.*
Certaine demandes with their grounds, drawne out of holy Writ. 1605. 4°. 6470
Certayne deuout & godlye petitions...Iesus Psalter. Douai. 16°. . 6605
Certaine godly prayers. *See* Common Prayer *ad fin.* [1578?] 4°. 1687=7288
— [1614?] 4°. 7421
— 1620. 4°. 2662–3
Certayne newes of...poore Christians in the Low Countries. [1574?] 8°. 1796
Certaine Prayers collected...in the present Visitation. 1603. 4°. . 2578
Certaine qværes propounded to the Bowers at the name of Iesvs. 1636. 4°. *See* Prynne (W.). 7026
Certaine reasons and arguments of policie. 1624. *See* Scott (T.).
Cervantes. The history of...Don Quixote. 1612. 4°. . . 3081
Cessolis (J. de). The game and play of Chess. W. Caxton, Bruges [1476]. F°. 118
Ch. (Ed.). Verses in Dod (J.). A plaine exposition of the Ten Commandements. Ed. 18. 1630. 1892
Ch. (Ez.). *See* Bayne (P.). Christian letters. 1628.
Ch. (Ro.). Verses in Whitaker (W.). Praelectiones. 1599. . . 5598
Ch. (T.). [Qu. T. Churchyard?] Verses in Gascoigne (G.). The Posies. 1575. 1482
Chace (G.). Verses in Cambridge Lachrymae. 1587. . . . 7356
Chaderton (Laurence). Verses in Baro (P.). In Jonam. 1579. . 850
Chaderton (Laurence). *See* Bible. Eng. (Royal). 1611.
See Fruitful Sermon [on Rom. xii. 3—8]. 1584.
See Widdrington (R.). Responsio... 1612.
[Licence.] *See* Du Praissac. The art of warre. 1639.
Chaderton (William). *See* Certaine demandes. 1605.
— Covell (W.). A briefe answer. 1606.
Chaldaic Language. *See* Wakefield (R.). Oratio. 1524. 4°.
— Rive (E.). An Heptaglottie. 1618.
Chaliner (T.). *See* Chaloner.
Challenge to the Protestants. *See* Rastell (J.).
Chalmateus (Antonius), *Vergesatus*. *See* Banister (J.). A needefvll... treatise of Chyrurgerie... 1575.
See Banister (J.). The Workes... 1633.

No.
Chaloner (Edward). Credo ecclesiam. 1625. 4°. 3156
— 1638. 12°. 5110
Sixe Sermons. [Set 1.] 1623(-2). 8°. 3144
Six Sermons. [Set 2.] Oxford, 1629. 4°. . . . 5426
See Bédé (J.). The masse displayed. 1619. 4°.
— Hieron (S.). The Spirituall Fishing. 1618.
Chaloner (Fr.). Verses in Camdeni Insignia. 1624. . . . 5346
Chaloner (Sir T.). De rep. anglorum etc. 1579. 4°. . . . 7270
Verses in Wilson (Sir T.). Vita. 1551. 631
See Chrysostom (S. John). An homilie... 1544.
— Erasmus. The praise of Folie. 1549.
Chamber ( ). *See* Hooper (J.). An apologye. 1562.
Chamber (C.), *Christ's*. Verses in Cam. Univ. Voces. 1640. . 5836
Chamber (John). Treatise against ivdicial astrologie. 1601. 4°. . 1267
See Heydon (Sir Chr.). A defence. 1603.
Chamberlaine (Ed.). Verses in Oxf. Univ. Horti. 1640. . . 5499
Chamberlinus (Robertus), *Roman Catholic*. [Licence.] *See* Staney (W.). A treatise. 1617. 8°. 6582
Chambers (Richard). Sarahs sepulture (Countess of Northumberland). 1620. 4°. 3596
Chambers (Robert). Palestina. Florence, 1600. 4°. 6828
See Numan (P.). Miracles. 1606.
Champney (Ant.). Ans. to a pamphlet...The Fisher catched. 1623. 4°. 6552
Treatise of the vocation of bishops. 1616. 4°. . . . 6581
See Copies of certaine discourses. 1601.
— Pilkington (R.). Parallela. 1618.
Chancery. *See* Powell (T.). Direction for Search. 1622.
— — The Repertorie of Records. 1631.
Chandos (Grey Brydges, *fifth lord*). *See* Horæ Subsecivæ. 1620.
Channel Islands. *See* Common Prayer. T. Gaultier, 1553. 4°.
Chapman (Alexander). Iesvitisme described. 1610. 4°. . . 3209
Chapman (Edward). Verses in Cambridge Lachrymae. 1587. . 7356
Chapman (George). The conspiracie...of Charles dvke of Byron. 1625. 4°. 3689
Epicede or Funerall Song: On...Henry Prince of Wales. 1613(-13). 4°. 3398
Memorable maske of the two...Inns of Court. [1614?] 4°. . 3582
Verses in Jonson (B.). Works. 1616. 3115
See Homer. [Iliad and Odyssey.] The whole works. [c. 1612.] F°.
— — [Batrachomyomachia and Hymns.] The Crowne... [1624?] F°. 3519
— Nenna (G. B.). Nennio... 1595.
Chapman (John). Verses in Coryate (T.). Coryates crvdities. 1611. 3076
Chapman (Richard). Hallelu-jah. 1635. 4°. 7717
Chappel ( ). *See* Brabourne (T.). A Defence. 1632.
Chapperlinus (J.). Verses in Horatius. Odes. 1635 etc. . . 4857
Chappuys (Jean). *See* Lyndwood (W.). Constitutiones. 1504.
Charactery. *See* (Smith (H.). The benefite of Contentation. 1590. 8°. 7355
— The examination of Vsurie. 1591. 8°. 7368
Chard (Thomas). *See* Ursinus (Z.). Explicationum. 1587.
Charenton, *Four Ministers of*. *See* Richelieu. The principall points. 1635. 8°.
Charinæus (Nicholas). *See* Knewstub (J.). A Confutation. 1597.
Charity mistaken. *See* Knott (E.). Charity mistaken. 1630.
Charke (William). A replie to a censure. 1581. 8°. 1667
— Treatise against the defense of the censure &c. Cambridge, 1586. 8°. 5527
See Collection of certain Letters. 1590.
— Hanmer (M.). The Iesuites Banner. 1581.
— Nowell (A.) & W. Day. A true report of...Ed. Campion... 1583.

No.

Charke (William) *cont.* Parsons (R.). A defence of the censure. 1582.
Charles I. True relation...of the...entertainment given to...Prince Charles...by the King of Spain. 1623. 4°. 4773
Declaration of the true causes which moued his Maiestie to assemble and...dissolue...Parliament. 1626. 4°. . . . 2830
— 1628. 4°. 2834
Proclamation in Scotland...of the...covenant. 1639. 4°. . 5006
Large declaration. 1639. F°. 5002–5004
Declaration...of the causes which moved him to dissolve the last Parliament. 1640. 4°. 2712, 2713
Declaration conc. his proceedings with his subjects in Scotland (March 1640). 1640. 4°. 5020
Demands and behaviour of the rebels in Scotland. 1640. 4°. 5013
[Life.] *See* Powell (R.). The life of... 1634.
[Pedigree.] *See* Slatyer (W.). Genethliacon... 1630.
[*Portrait.*] W. Peake. 4°. 7634.
See Augustine (St.). Saint Avstins religion... 1625.
— Barclay (J.)...Argenis. 1629.. 3039
— Camb. Univ. Gratulatio. 1623.
— — Cantabrigiensium Dolor & Solamen. 1625. 4°.
— — Epithalamium...1625.
— — Anthologia. 1632.
— — Rex redux. 1633. 4°.
— — Voces. 1640.
— Convocation (Canterbury Province). A Grant. 1640.. . 2710
— Edinburgh City. The Entertainment... 1633.
— Wotten (Sir H.). Ad regem. 1633.
Charles II. *See* Cambridge University. Genethliacum. 1631.
— Oxford University. Britanniae Natalis. 1630.
Charles I, *Emperor* [Charlemagne]. *See* Ubaldino (P.). La vita... 1581.
Charles V, *Emperor*. *See* Ascham (R.). A report... [1670–1?]
See Augsburg Confession. [1536?]
— Avila y Zuñiga (L. de). The comentaries... 1555.
— Justinianus. 1553.
— Salomon, *the Jew*. A wounderfull Prophecie... (1543).
— Zwingli (U.). The Rekening. 1543.
Charles IX, King of France. *See* France. An historicall collection. 1598.
Charles de Bourbon, Duc de Vendôme, *Cardinal*. Advertisement from a French Gentleman (Declaration). 1585. 8°. . . . 6781
Charles Louis, *Count Palatine*. The manifest...translated. 1637. 4°. 3969
Protestatio. 1637. F°. 7560
Protestation. Translated. 1637. 4°. 4597
Charlet (Fr.). Verses in Butler (C.). The Feminin' Monarchi'. 1634. 5439
Charlier de Gerson (Jean). *See* Gerson.
Charron (P.). Of wisdome. Trans. S. Lennard. [1615?] 4°. . 2756
— — 1630. 4°. 4431
Charter Warren. A treatise...collected by Sir H. Yelverton. 1617. 4°. 2658
Charterhouse with the last will...of T. Sutton. 1614. 4°. . . 3583
Charteris (Henry). Verses in J. Adamson. Εἰσόδια. 1618. . . 5960
— Buchanan (G.). Ecphrasis. 1620. 3595
See Rollock (R.). Analysis. 1602.
— — Lectvres vpon...Thessalonians. 1606.
Chartier (Alain). The Curial. Caxton [1484?]. F°. 25
Chartresius (Vidamus). *See* Ferrières (Jean de). 1495
Chase (Stephen). Verses in Oxf. Univ. Horti. 1640. . . . 5499
Chassanion (J.). The merchandises of popish Priests. 1604. 4°. 1787
Chasteigner (Henri Louis). Celebriorum distinctionum...synopsis. 1617. 4°. 3268

No.
Chastillon (Gaspard de), *admiral of France.* *See* Coligny (Gaspard de).
Chastising of Gods Children. W. de Worde [1493?]. F°. . . 61
Châteillon (Sebastien). *See* Castellion.
Chaterton (G.). Verses in Palingenius (M.). The Zodiake. 1576. . 1622
Châtillon (Gaspard Coligny, de). *See* Coligny.
Chaucer (G.). Workes. T. Godfray, 1532. F°. 554
— J. Reynes, 1542. F°. 415
— R. Kele [1552?]. F°. 1004
— A. Islip for B. Norton, 1598. F°. 2423
— G. Bishop, 1602. F°. 1749
Anelida and Arcite. Caxton [1477]. 4°. 5
Book of Fame. Caxton [1483]. F°. 21
Canterbury Tales. W. de Worde, 1498. F°. 50
[Minor Poems. Fortune; and Truth.] *See* Lydgate (J.). The prouerbes of Lydgate. 1519. 233
Parliament of Fowls etc. Caxton [1477–8]. 4°. 6
Story of Constance. [Ab. 154– .] 4°. 6688
Temple of Brass etc. Caxton [1477–8]. 4°. 6
[Troilus and Cressida (Lat.).] Amorum. Oxoniae, 1635. 4°. . 5414
See Beverwijk (J. van). Schat der Gesontheyt. 1638. 8°. . 7811
— Boethius. Boecius de consolacione philosophie.
Chauncy (Charles). Verses (*bis*) in Camb. Univ. Lacrymae. 1619. . 5689
— — Dolor. 1625. 5701
— — Epithalam. 1625. 5702
Chaundler (Daniel), *Queens' College.* Verses in Camb. Univ. Genethliacum. 1631. 5731
— — Rex redux. 1633. 5748
Cheaste (Thomas). The Christian Pathway... 1611. 1613. 4°. . 3648
Chedsey (William). *See* Redman (J.). A reporte... 1551.
Cheisholmus. *See* Chisholm.
Cheke (Sir J.). De obitu...M. Buceri... 1551. 4°. 734
Hurt of sedicion. 1549. 8°. 904
— 1569. 8°. 932
— 1576. 8°. 939
[Letter to T. Hoby, 16 July 1557.] *See* Castiglione (B.). The covrtyer. 1561. 923
Verses in Carlile (C.). A discourse. 1582. 1871
Seton (J.). Dialectica. 1611 etc. . . . . . 3249 etc.
Wilson (Sir T.). Vita. 1551. 631
See Bible. Polyglot. N.T. (Lat. and Eng.). 1550.
— Chrysostom (J.). Ὁμιλίαι δύο. 1543.
— — An homilie. . 1544.
— Cranmer (T.). Reformatio legvm. 1571 *etc.*
— Remedy. A remedy for sedition... 1536.
Chelidonius. A most excellent Hystorie...of Christian Princes. 1571. 4°. 1470
Chemnitius (M.). A discouerie...of...the Councell of Trent. (A Confutation of vnwritten verities.) 1582. 4°. . . . 1374
A substantial...exposition of...the Lords praier. Cambridge, 1598. 8°. 5592
Cherpontius (Johannes). *See* Bible, New Test. (Lat.). 1587. 8°. . 7272
Chertsey (Andrew). *See* Ars moriendi. 1505.
— Flower. Jhesus, The floure. 1510 *etc.*
— Passion of our Lord. 1521.
Chess. *See* Cessolis.
— Damiano da Odemira. The pleasant play. 1562. 8°.
— Saul (A.). 1640.
Chester, *Earldom of.* *See* Doddridge (Sir J.). The History... 1630.
Chester (Map, 1588). *See* Braun (G.).

No.
Chester (G.). Verses in Camb. Univ. Dolor. 1625. . . . 5701
Chester (John), *Captain.* Gilbert (Sir H.). A true reporte. 1583. . 1354
Chetham (Tho.). *See* Chitham.
Cheus (Thomas). Verses in Stanyhurst (R.). Harmonia. 1570. . 749
Chevallier (Guillaume de). The ghosts of...de Villemor, and de Fontaines. Ed. 3. Cambridge. 1624. 8°. 5699
Chibald (Will.). A tryall of faith. 1622. 8°. . . . 7573
Chichele (Henry), *abp.* *See* Duck (A.). Vita... 1617.
Chichester Cathedral. Synod. 3 Oct. 1632. *See* Johnson (R.). The gospell. 1633. 4°.
Children of the Revels. Lyly (J.). Alexander Campaspe and Diogenes. 2213
Chillester (James). *See* Chelidonius. A most excellent Hystorie. 1571. 4°.
Chillingworth (William). Motives maintained. 1638. 4°. . . . 6560
Religion of protestants. Oxford, 1638. F°. 5481
— Ed. 2. 1638. F°. 4495
See Floyd (J.), *jesuit.* The Chvrch Conquerant. 1638–9.
— Knott (E.). Christianity maintained... 1638.
— — A direction to be observed... 1636.
— — The ivdgment of an vniversity-man. 1639.
Chilmead (Edmund). *See* Ferrand (J.). Ἐρωτομανία. 1640. 8°.
Chilmead (John). *See* Hues (R.). A learned treatise. 1639. 8°.
China. *See* Barri (C.). Cochin-China... 1633.
— Baudier (M.). The History...of the Grand Seigneur. 1635.
— Gonzalez de Mendoza (J.). The historie. 1588.
Chisholm (William). Examen confessionis. Avignon. 1601. 8°. . 6514
Chitham (Thomas). Verses in Hill (W.). The Infancie of the Soule. 1605. 2303
Chitting (H.). Verses in Brooke (R.). A discovery. 1622. . 2793
Cholmley (Hugh). The state of the now-Romane Chvrch... 1629. 8°. 4253
See Burton (H.). Babel no Bethel. 1629.
— Spencer (T.). Maschil Vnmasked... [1629.]
Chorl. *See* Churl.
Chorlton (Jeffrey). *See* Garey (Samuel). Two Treatises. 1605.
Chouneus (Thomas). *See* Chowne.
Chowne (Thomas). Collectiones theologicarum quarundam conclusionum. 1635. 12°. 4594
Christian II, *king of Denmark.* *See* North (G.). The Description of Swedland... 1561.
Christian IV, *king of Denmark.* *See* Tricorones. 1607. 4°. . 7807
Christian and modest offer of a...conference...about the...Prelats and... deprived Ministers. 1606. 4°. 6868
Christian and wholesom Admonition, directed to the Frenchmen. 1587. 8°. 1945
Christian Directory. *See* Parsons (R.). 1607.
Christian Exhortation. *See* Coverdale (M.). A christē exhortacion. [154– .] 16°.
Christian Letter of certaine English Protestants...unto Mr R. Hoo[ker]. 1599. 4°. 6454
Christian Prayers. *See* Bull (H.). 1584.
Christian Religion. *See* A summary. 16°. 6602
— A briefe summary. 16°. 6602
Christian Renunciation. *See* Treatise of Christian Renunciation...
Christina, *queen of Sweden.* *See* Poland. Vladislaus IV. 1635. The forme.
Christine de Pisan. The Fayttes of Armes and of Chyualrie. Caxton, 1489. F°. 34
— The body of Polycye. J. Skot, 1521. 4°. 355
Christlicke Ordinanciē der Nederlātscher Ghemeynten Christi...te Londen. 'C. Volckwinner, Londen,' 1554. 8°. 6290

No.

Christmas (John). *See* Heywood (T.). The Hierarchie. 1635.
Christmas (Matthew). *See* Heywood (T.). The hierarchie. 1635.
Christopherson (J.). An exhortation. 1554. 8°. 990
Christopherson (M.). A treatise conc. Antichrist. 1614. 4°. . . 6893
Chronicles of England. Ed. 1. Caxton, 10 June 1480. F°. . 13
Ed. 2. Caxton, 1482. F°. 18
— with the Fruit of Times. St Albans [1483]. F°. . 86
— Machlinia [1484?]. F°. 97
— G. Leeu, Antwerp, 1493. F°. 127
— with the Fruit of Times. W. de Worde, 1498. F°. . . 51
— — J. Notary, 1504. F°. 328
— — Pynson, 1510. F°. 260
— — Notary, 1515. F°. 332
Chronicles of England. W. de Worde, 25 June 1530. 4°. . . 202
Chrymes (G.), *S.J.C.* Verses in Cam. Univ. Voces. 1640. . . 5836
Chrysostom (John). Opera graece. 8 Voll. Etonae, 1613–2. F°. . 5903
Exposition vpon...the Ephesians. 1581. 4°. 1507
Homilie...with also a discourse vpon Job. Trans. Cheke, & T. Chaloner. 1544. 8°. 473
Sermon...that No man is hurted but of hym selfe. Trans. T. Lupset. 1542. 8°. 463
Sermo...of pacience. N. Hill for J. Shefelde, 1550. 8°. . . 1022
Ὁμιλίαι δύο...Latinæ factæ, a. J. Cheko. R. Wolfe, 1543. 4°. 721
[Hom. iii.] *See* Whitford (R.). Instructions. 1541. 4°.
[Of praying unto God.] *See* Treatise of Justification. 1569.
Theorremωn. Trans. J. Willoughbie. Oxford, 1602. 8°. . 5257
See Lupset (T.). Workes. 1546.
Church Conquerant. *See* Floyd (J.), *Jesuit.* The Church Conquerant. 1638.
Church (Henry). Divine and christian letters. 1636. 12°. . 7644
Good mans treasury. 1636. 12°. 5092
Miscellanea philotheologica. 1637. 4°. 5094
Churche (Rooke). *See* Fumée (M.). The historie of...Hvngarie. 1600.
Churchyard (Thomas). The fortunate farewel to the earle of Essex. 1596. 4°. 2054
Verses in Jones (J.). A briefe discourse. 1574. . . . 1366
Lloyd (L.). The pilgrimage. 1586. 1491
See also Ch. (T.).
— Grassi (G. di). Arte of Defence. 1594. 4°.
— Higgins (J.). A mirrour. 1610.
— Meteren (E. van). A true discourse. 1602.
— Whetstone (G.). The Censure of a loyall Subject. 1587.
Churl and the Bird. Caxton [1477–8]. 4°. 7
— W. de Worde [1520]. 4°. 215
Chytræus (David). A postil or orderly disposing of certaine Epistles. 1570. 4°. 1468
Chytræus (Nathan). *See* Buchanan (G.). Psalmorum Davidis. 1640. 12°.
— Casa (G. della)...Galatevs. 1630.
Ciacconius (Petrus), *Toletanus.* *See* Sallustius. Opera. 1615. 8°.
Cicella (Maria). Verses in Cheke (Sir J.). De obitu M. Buceri. 1551. 734
Cicero. De officiis...De amicitia...De senectute: Paradoxa, et De somno. Cantabrigiae, 1630. 8°. 5727, 5728
— Cantabrigiae [1633?]. 12°. 5831
— Cantabrigiae, 1639. 8°. 5795
De Amicitia. Trans. J. Tiptoft. Caxton, 1481. F°. . . . 16
— (Eng. Trans. J. Tiptoft.) [W. Rastell? 1530?] F°. . . 7703
— Trans. J. Harrington. Berthelet, 1550. 16°. . . . 501
[De consolatione.] Consolatio...de filiae morte. 1583. 8°. . 7286

No.
Cicero *cont.* [De officiis (Lat. & Eng.)] The thre bookes. Trans. R. Whytinton. W. de Worde, 30 Sept. 1534. 8°. . 208
— Trans. N. Grimald. R. Tottell, 1558. 8°. 1111
— 1568. 8°. 1117
— 1574(5). 8°. 1128
— 1583. 8°. 1143
— T. East, 1596. 8°. 1606
— (English only) Book 1. Trans. J. Brinsley. 1616. 8°. . 2525
— 1631. 8°. 1893
[De Senectute.] Tully of Old Age. Caxton, 1481. F°. . 16
— (Latin and English.) Trans. R. Whitinton. J. Byddell, n.d. 8°. 573
Epistolae ad familiares. 1585. 8°. 2095
Epistolarum libri quatuor...a J. Sturmio. Cantabrigiae, 1631. 8°. 5733
Epistolarum familiarium...Epitome. Cantabrigiae, 1602. 8°. . 5608
The familiar epistles. Ed. J. Webbe. n.d. 12°. . . . 3951
An Epistle...to...Quintus. Trans. G. Gilby. 1561. 8°. . 1296
— *See* Fleming (A.). A Panoplie of Epistles. 1576. 4°.
Orationes Philippicae. Pynson, 1521. 8°. 274
Orationum volumen primum, a J. M. Bruto emendatum. 1601. 16°. 7379
— [Pro M. Marcello (*Eng.*).] *See* Sherry (R.). A Treatise. 1555.
[Rhetoric.] *See* Datus (A.). Super Tullianis elegancijs. 1479.
Quaestiones Tusculanæ per Erasmum. 1577. 8°. . . 1181
Tusculanarum Quaestionum...libri quinque. 1628. 8°. . . 3809
— Trans. J. Dolman. 1561. 8°. 1207
[Appendix.] *See* Greene (R.). Ciceronis Amor. 1605.
See Draxe (T.). Calliepeia. 1625.
Cistercians in Ireland. *See* Ware (Sir J.). Archiepiscoporum etc. 1626.
City. Cities Advocate. 1629. *See* Philipot (J.).
Citye match. *See* Mayne (J.).
Cl. (Ja.). Verses in Beaumont (Sir J.). Bosworth-field. 1629. . 3040
Clain (Joh. Theodor). *See* S. (E.). Historia. 1640. 12°. . . 5501
Clapham (Henoch). Antidoton or a soveraigne remedie. 1600. 4°. . 1986
Bibliotheca Theologica. Amsterdam, 1597. 4°. . . . 6374
Briefe of the bibles history. Ed. 3. 1608. 12°. 7335
— Ed. 4. 1639. 8°. 4039
Errovr on the right hand. 1608. 8°. 2304
Manuell of the bibles doctrine. 1606. 12°. 7334
Song of Songs. 1602. 8°. 2851
Theological axioms. 1597. 4°. 6818
Historie of England. 1602. 4°. 2852
— 1606. 4°. 2862
Clare, *Saint*. *See* Wadding (L.). The history of...S. Clare. 1635.
Clare (John). *See* The Converted Jew. 1630. 4°.
Clares. *See* Poor Clares.
Clarke (H.). Verses in Oxf. Univ. Horti. 1640. 5499
Clarke (John). Dux grammaticus. 1633. 12°. 4568
Holy Oyle for the Lampes of the Sanctuarie. 1630. 4°. . . 4539
Parœmiologia Anglo-Latina. 1639. 8°. 3057
Clarke (Josias). Verses in Coryate (T.). Coryates Crudities. 1611. . 3076
Clarke (R.). *See* Bible. Eng. (Royal Version). 1611.
Clarke (Thomas). The Popes deadly wound. 1621. 4°. . . 3427
Claudianus. Selection. (Trans.) *See* Beaumont (Sir J.), Bart. Bosworth-field. 1629.
Claudus (Dauid). Verses in Beza (T.). Psalmorum libri quinque. 1580. 1539
Clavel (William). Verses in Coryate (T.). Coryats Crudities. 1611 . 3076
Clavell (John). Verses in Massinger (P.). The emperor. 1632. . 3998
Clavering (James), *Magd. Coll.* Verses in Camb. Univ. Συνῳδία. 1637. 5790
Clavering (Ro.), *K.C.C.* Verses in Cam. Univ. Epicedium. 1612. 5665

No.
Clavering (Tho.). Verses in Camb. Univ. Lacrymæ. 1619. . . . 5689
— — Epithalamium. 1625. 5702
Clavis Apocalyptica. *See* Mede (J.). 1627.
Clavius (Christophorus). *See* Lydiat (T.). Tractatus. 1605. 8°.
Clay (H.). Verses in Oxf. Univ. Horti. 1640. 5499
Clay (Mat.). [Licence.] *See* Horatius. [De arte poetica.] 1640.
Clayton (Giles). Approoued order of Martiall discipline. 1591. 4°. 1362
Clayton (Th.), *M.D.*, *Prof. Reg.* Verses in Camdeni Insignia. 1624. 5346
— Hippocrates. 1633. 5812
— Holyoake (F.). Dictionarium. 1640. 3058
— Oxf. Univ. Horti. 1640. 5499
See Hakewill (G.). An apologie. 1630.
— Parkinson (J.). Theatrum. 1640. F°.
Cleaver (Robert). Declaration of the christian sabbath. 1625. 12°. . 4529
Godly forme of household gouernment...augmented by J. Dod and R. C. 1630. 8°. 7320
— *See* Dod (J.) and R. Cleaver *passim*.
Cleland (Ben), *Emman.* Verses in Cam. Univ. Epithalam. 1625. . 5702
Cleland (James). Ἡρωπαιδεία. Oxford, 1607. 4°. . . . 5278
Clemangiis (Nic. de). Speculum Ecclesiæ Pontificiæ. 1606. 8°. . 1756
See Bullinger (H.). A hundred Sermons. 1561.
Clement I. Πρὸς Κορινθίους ἐπιστόλη. (Gr. Lat.) P. Junius. Oxonii, 1633. 4°. 5398
Clement VII. *See* Henry VIII. Divino implorato. [1530?]
Clement (William), *M.D.* Verses in Hippocrates. 1633. . . 5812
[Licence.] *See* London. College of Physicians. 1633.
Clerimond (B. D. de). Proclamation...under the name of James. '1511' [1611]. 4°. 6523
Clerk (Bartholomew). *See* Chaloner (Sir T.). De rep. angl. 1577. 4°.
Clerk (John), *bp. of Bath & Wells.* († 1541.) *See* Henry VIII. Libello huic regio insunt. 1521. 277
Clerk (John), *Roman Catholic writer.* († 1552.) De mortuorum resurrectione et extremo iudicio. 1545. 4°. 758
— 1547. 4°. 767
Clerk (Richard). Verses in Hippocrates. 1633. 5812
Clerk (Rob.). Verses in Cam. Univ. Anthologia. 1632. . . 5741
— Carmen. 1635. 5770
Clerk (William). Epitome of certaine late aspersions. Dublin, 1631. 4°. 6035
See Withals (J.). Dictionary. (Eng.-Lat.) 1634. . . . 4152
Clerke (B.). Fidelis servi, subdito infideli responsio. 1573. 4°. . 835
See Castiglione (B.). Balthasaris Castilionis...De Curiali... 1571 etc.
— Harvey (G.). Rhetor. 1577.
Clerke (John). *See* Ramus (P.). Via Regia ad Geometriam... 1636.
Clerke (Richard). Sermons...published...by C. White. 1637. F°. . 4549
Clerke (William), *Chorister.* *See* Directorium Sacerdotum. [1499.] 4°. 62
Clerke (William). The Triall of Bastardie. 1594. 4°. . . 2415
See C. (W.). Polimanteia. 1595.
Cleveland (John). Verses in King (E.). Ivsta. 1638. . . . 5829
— Horatius. De arte poetica. 1640. 3728
Cleves, *Duchy of.* *See* Briefe discourse. 1599.
— Briefe relation. 1599.
Cleybrooke (Paul). [Funeral.] *See* Stone (W.). A Curse. 1623. 4°.
Clifford (Phil.). Verses in Camb. Univ. Epicedium. 1612. . . 5665
Clifton or Clyfton (Richard). *See* Ainsworth (H.). An animadversion... 1613.
Clinton (Robert Fynes, *alias*). Verses in Cam. Univ. Voces. 1640. 5836
Clitherow (John). Verses in Oxf. Univ. Horti. 1640. . . . 5499
Clive. *See* Clyve.
Closet for Ladies and Gentlewomen, or, The Art of preseruing. 1608. 8°. 3383
Clotterbook (Will.), *T.C.C.* Verses in Camb. Univ. Carmen. 1635. . 5770

No.
Clotterbook (Will.), *T.C.C. cont.* Verses in *Συνωδία*. 1637. . . 5790
— — Voces. 1640. 5836
Clowes (William). A profitable and necessarie booke. Ed. 3. 1637. 4°. 3895
A right frutefull...Treatise for...Struma. 1602. 4°. . . 2013
Verses in Baker (G.). The composition of Oil. [1574.] . . 1286
— Dodonæus (R.). A niewe herball. 1578 etc. . . 6130
See Banister (J.). The Workes... 1633.
Clusius (Carolus). *See* L'Escluse (C. de).
Clutterbuck. *See* Clotterbook.
Clyfton (Richard). *See* Clifton.
Clyue (St.). Verses in Brooke (R.). A discovery. 1622. . . 2793
Coakes (Tom). *See* Marprelate (M.). Hay any worke. [1589.] 4°.
Coal. A Coale from the altar... *See* Heylyn (P.)... 1636.
Coal (D.). *See* Cole (H.).
Coale (John), *Christ's*. Verses in Cam. Univ. Voces. 1640. . 5836
Cobham (Henry Brooke, *Lord*). *See* S. (C.). The copie. 1603.
Cocburnus (Patricius), Scotus. *See* Cockburn (P.).
Coccius (Jodocus). *See* Perkins (W.). Problema. 1604.
Cochlæus (Joannes). *See* Morison (Sir R.). Apomaxis. 1537.
Cockburn (P.). In secundæ partis catechismi...enarrationem...præfatio. 1561. 4°. 796
Cocke (I.). Verses in Stephens (J.). New essayes. 1631. . 7823
Cockeram (Henry). English dictionarie. Ed. 2. 1626. 8°. . . 3975
— Ed. 6. [After 1637.] 8°. 4671
Cocks (Roger), *T.C.C.* Verses in Cam. Univ. Epicedium. 1612. . 5665
Cocus (Johannes). *See* Cook.
Cocus (Robertus). *See* Cooke.
Codrinton (I.). Verses in Smith (J.). The generall historie. 1624. 3864
Codrington (Robert). *See* Seneca...Consolation to Marcia. 1635. 4°.
Coëffeteau (Nicolas). *See* Du Moulin (P.). The accomplishment. 1613.
— — De Monarchia Temporali Pontificis Romani... 1614.
Coelum Britannicum. 1634. *See* Carew (T.).
Coeuure (Marquis de). *See* France. Louis XIII. 1617.
Cogan (T.). The haven of health. 1584. 4°. 1646
— 1605. 4°. 3361
— 'Ed. 4.' 1636. 4°. 3959
See Cicero. *Appendix*. 1602.
Cogitosus. [Life of S. Bridgit.] *See* B. (B.), *Irish Franciscan*. The life. 1625. 4°.
Cognet (Sir Martin). *See* Matthieu Coignet.
Coignet (Matthieu). Politiqve discourses. 1586. 4°. . . 1325
Coignet (Michiel). *See* Ortelius (A.). His Epitome. 1603. 8°.
Coimbra. *See* Paiva (H. de). Brevissimum Logicæ Compendium. 1627.
Coin of the Realm. Proclamation. [Ab. 1507.] Single sheet. . 7072
— — 1619. 7446
Cokayne (Sir Aston). Verses in Massinger (P.). The emperovr. 1632. 3998
— — The Maid of honovr. 1632. 3819
Coke ( ) [qu. J. Coke?]. Verses in King (E.). Ivsta. 1638. . 5829
Coke (Antony). *See* Cooke (Sir Antony).
Coke (Sir Edward). A booke of entries. 1614. F°. . . . 3258
The first part of the Institutes of the Lawes of England. Or a commentarie vpon Littleton. 1628. F°. . . . 3298
— 1629. F°. 7855
— Ed. 4. 1639. F°. 4326
Les reports. 1609. F°. 3236
— — Le second part. (Le tierce part.—Le qvart part.) 1610. F°. 3240
Quinta pars relationum. The fift part. 1606. F°. . . . 3225
— — 1607. F°. 3226
Quinta pars...of the Reports. 1612. F°. 3252
La size part. 1607. F°. 3227, 3228

No.

Coke (Sir E.) *cont.* La sept part des Reports. 1608. F°. . 3231, 3233
La huict part des Reports. 1611. F°. 3246
— [Stationers. 1611 ?] F°. 3247
Le neuf^me^ part des Reports. 1613. F°. 3255
La dix^me^ part des Reports. 1614. F°. 3259
La unz^me^ part. 1615. F°. 3260
Epitome undecim librorum relationum... E. Trotman. 1640. 8°. 5084
Fasciculus Florum. Per T. Ashe. 1618. 8°. 7536
Little treatise of baile and maineprize. 1635. 4°. . . . 5123
— Ed. 2. 1637. 4°. 5125
Speech and Charge. 1607. 4°. 3539
See Ashe (T.). Table a tovts les......livers del Reportes de Sir E. Coke... 1606.
— Parsons (R.). An answere to the fifth part of Reports... 1606.
— — A quiet and sober reckoning. 1609.

Coke (J.). Debate betwene the heraldes of Englande and Fraunce. 1550. 8°. 1077

Coke (Sir John). [Licence.] *See* May (T.). The Victorious. 1635.
— — Monro (R.). Expedition. 1637.

Coke (John), *T.C.* Verses in Camb. Univ. *Συνωδία.* 1637. . 5790
— — *quater* in Voces. 1640. 5836
See also Coke.

Coke (Roger), *Regal.* Verses in Cam. Univ. Voces. 1640. . 5836

Coker (William). A letter. *See* Coverdale (M.). Certain...letters. 1564.

Colby (D.), *C.C.C.* Verses in Cam. Univ. Epithalam. 1625. . 5702

Coldewel (George). *See* Colvile.

Cole (Gil.). Verses in Camb. Univ. Lacrymae. 1619. . . . 5689

Cole (Henry). *See* Jewel (J.). The copie of a Sermon. [1560.]
See Williams (J.), *abp.* The holy table. 1637.

Cole (Nathanael). The godly man's assurance. 1615. 4°. . . 3408
— Ed. 4. 1633. 4°. 7549

Cole (Richard). Verses *bis* in Camb. Univ. Lacrymae. 1619. . 5689

Cole (Thomas). A godly and learned sermon. 1 March 1564. 1564. 8°. 1397
See Bible. Eng. (Bishops'). 1568. F°. 963

Cole (William). Verses in Humphrey (L.). I. Ivelli vita. 1573. . 837
— Parkhurst (J.). Ludicra. 1573. 838
See Bible. Eng. (Genevan.) 1560.

Colebrand (Richard). Verses in Camb. Univ. *Συνωδία.* 1637. . 5790

Coles (Edm.). Verses *bis* in Oxf. Univ. Horti. 1640. . . . 5499

Coles (Gilb.). Verses *bis* in Oxf. Univ. Horti. 1640. . . . 5499

Colet (John). [Fragment. The .vii. Petycions of the Paternoster. Antwerp 153– ?] 8°. 6096
See Lily (W.). De octo orationis partium constructione. 1540. 455
— — A shorte introduction...

Colfe (Richard), *D.D.* [Funeral Sermon.] *See* Wilson (T.). Christs farewell. 1614.

Coligny (Gaspard de). [Life.] *See* Serres (J. de). The lyfe of... Shatilion. 1576. 8°.
See Varamundus (E.). De furoribus. 1573.
— — A true and plaine... 1573.

Collection of certain letters and conferences. [Dort,] 1590. 4°. . 6508

Collection of certaine sclaunderous Articles. [Dort,] 1590. 4°. . 6506

Collection of private devotions...called the Houres of Prayer. (By J. Cosin.) 1639. 12°. 5001

Collection of sundry matters. 1616. 8°. 6480

Colleton (John). A iust defence of the slandered priestes. 1602. 4°. 7394

Collins (James), *K.C.C.* Verses in Camb. Univ. Carmen. 1635. . 5770
— — Voces. 1640. 5836

Collins (John), *St John's College, M.D., Prof. Reg.* Verses in Hippocrates. 1633. 5812

No.
Collins (John), *Regal.* Verses in Cam. Univ. Voces. 1640. . . 5836
Collins (Samuel). Epphata to F. T. Cambridge, 1617. 4º. . 5681
Increpatio Andreæ Eudæmo-Johannis etc. Cantabrigiae, 1612. 4º. 5664
Sermon. 1 Nov. 1607. 1608. 4º. 2485
Collins (Sa.). Verses *bis* in Camb. Univ. Epicedium. 1612. . 5665
— Lacrymae. 1619. 5689
— Gratulatio. 1623. 5695
— Dolor. 1625. . . . . 5701, 5701 A
— Epithalam. 1625. 5702
— Genethl. 1631. 5731
— Anthologia. 1632. 5741
— Fasciæ. 1633. 5808
— *sexies.* Rex redux. 1633. 5748
— Carmen. 1635. 5770
— *bis.* Συνῳδία. 1637. 5790
— Voces. 1640. 5836
Fletcher (P.). Locvstæ. 1627. 5706
See Fitzherbert (T.). The Obmvtesce. 1621.
[Licence.] *See* Du Praissac. The art of warre. 1639.
Colloquia et dictionariolum. *See* Barlement (N.). 1631.
Colman (Tho.), *T.C.C.* Verses in Camb. Univ. Epithalam. 1625. . 5702
Cologne. The thre kynges. W. de Worde, 1511. 4º. . . 165
Cologne, *Abp of.* *See* Briefe discourse. 1599.
Coloma (Carlos), marquis of Espinar. The Attestation...by the lay catholikes...concerning the...Bishop of Chalcedon. Brussels, 1631. 8º. . . . . 7694+
See Cambridge University. True Copies... 1623.
Columba, Saint. *See* B. (B.), *Irish Franciscan.* The life. 1625. 4º.
— Villegas (A. de). The lives of saints. 1628.
Colvenerius (Georgius). [Censor of Books.] *See* Villegas. Lives of Saints. 1628. 4º. 6621
— T. (T.). The Whetstone. 1632. 8º. 7817
Colvile or Coldewel (George). *See* Boethius. Boetivs de consolationae philosophiæ... 1556.
Colville (John). The Palinod of John Colvill. Edinburgh, 1600. 8º. 5944
Colvius (Petrus). Verses in Whitney (G.). A choice. 1586. . 6496
Colynet (Anth.). True history of the ciuill warres of France. 1591. 4º. 2210
Combats. An edict or statute...by the French King concerning... Combats. 1609. 4º. 3205
See Duels.
— Espagne (J. d'). 1632.
Comber (Th.). Verses in Barlow (W.). Vita R. Cosin. 1598. . 1707
— Whitaker (W.). Praelectiones. 1599. 5598
— Camb. Univ. Genethl. 1631. 5731
— — Anthologia. 1632. 5741
— — Fasciæ. 1633. 5808
— — Carmen. 1635. 5770
— — Συνῳδία. 1637. 5790
— — Voces. 1640. 5836
— — Hippocrates. 1633. 5812
Comedy. A pleasant conceited comedy...how a man may choose a good wife. 1634. 4º. 4897
Comenius (Jan Amos). Conatuum...præludia. (Porta Sapientiæ.) Oxoniae, 1637. 4º. 5456
Janua linguarum. 1634. Cf. no. 4981.
Janua linguarum reserata. Ed. 4. Trans. T. Horne. 1638. 8º. 4998
Pansophiæ prodromus. Præfatio S. H(artlib). 1639. 12º. . 4327
Porta linguarum trilinguis. (The gate of tongues...by J. Anchoran.) 1631. 8º. 4434, 4435
— Ed. 2. 1633. 8º. 7613

No.

Comes (Natalis). *See* Ovid. Metamorphoses. 1584.
— Polemon (J.). All the famous Battels... [1577?]
Comines (P. de). Historie. 1596. F°. 2066
— 1614. F°. 3376
[History. Continuation.] *See* Danett (T.). A Continuation... 1600.
Commandino (Federigo). *See* Euclid. Στοιχείων βιβλία. 1620. F°.
Commission of Grace. 1630. *See* Proclamation. . . . 7424
Common Prayer. Grafton. Mense Martij (–Junij). 1549. F°. . 613
E. Whitchurch. Mense Maii (May 4). 1549. F°. . . 661
,, Mense Junii (June 16). 1549. F°. . . 662
,, [Mense Junii? 1549?] F°. 663
J. Oswen, Worcester. 1549. 4°. 5888
Grafton. (Noted). 1550. 4°. 619
,, 1552. F°. 624
E. Whitchurch. 1552. F°. 671
,, 1552. F°. 672
,, [1552?] 4°. 673
,, [1553?] 4°. 674
See Bible (Cranmer's). 1552. 4°.
(Morning and Evening Prayer.) *See* Bible, English [Coverdale's]. 1553.
Grafton. 1559. F°. 630
'Jugge & Cawood.' 1559. F°. 630, 958
— — *See* Bible. Eng. (Cranmer.) 1566.
(Morning and Evening Prayer.) *See* Bible (Bishops'). [1574?]
(Certaine godly prayers.) C. Barker. [1578?] 4°. . . 1687=7288
— — *See* Bible. Eng. (Geneva.) 1578.
The Booke of...with the Psalter. R. Barker. 1600. 4°. . 7414+
P. Short. 1600. 32°. 2337
[R. Barker. Between 1603 and 1612.] 24°. 7804
R. Barker. 1607. F°. 2603
,, 1611. F°. 2639
(Certaine godlie prayers.) Ab. 1614? 4°. 7421
[Ab. 1615?] 8°. 7422
[R. Barker. Not after 1619.] F°. 7775
(Certaine godly prayers.) R. Barker and J. Bill. 1620. 4°. 2662, 2663
('Godly Prayers'.) [2 cols. Ab. 1620.] 4°. 7450
Dublin. 1621. 4°. 6021
B. Norton and J. Bill. 1622. F°. 2814
Cambridge. 1629. F°. 5711
R. Barker and J. Bill. 1630. F°. 2667
[T. and J. Buck, Cambridge. 1630.] 4°. 7672
R. Barker and Ass. of J. Bill. 1631. 4°. 2675
[1632?] 12°. 7839
1633. F°. 2680
[1633?] 8°. 2681
1634. F°. 2688
— 1634. 8°. 2689
Cambridge. 1635. 4°. 5771
R. Barker and ass. of J. Bill. 1636. F°. 2690
— 1636. 4°. 2691
(Psalter [ed. 1].) R. Young. Edinburgh. 1637 (6). F°. . . 5979
(The psalter [ed. 2].) ,, ,, 1637–6. F°. . 7768
Cambridge. 1637. 4°. 5819
Dublin. 1637. 4°. 6060
R. Barker and Ass. of J. Bill. 1638. F°. 2698
— 1638. 4°. 2699
— 1638. 8°. 2700
Cambridge. 1638. F°. 5823
,, 1638. 4°. 5792

No.

Common Prayer, *cont.* R. Barker and Ass. of J. Bill. 1638. 12°. 2701
1638(-9). F°. 2703
— 1639. 4°. 2705
— 1639. 8°. 2706
— 1639. 16°. 7435
Cambridge, 1640. 4°. 7876
[1640?] 8°. 7863
'Morning & Evening Prayer.' 1566. F°. . . . . *See* 6249
Common Prayer. Selections. *See* Psalter. 1615. 4°. . . . 2524
See Advertisements. 1584. 1822
— Survey of the Book of Common Prayer.
(French). Le Livre des Prières. T. Gaultier, 1553. 4°. . . 1096
— La Liturgie Angloise. Nouv. traduit. 1616. 4°. . . 3473
(Greek and Latin). *Λειτουργία Βρεττανική*...Liber precum...studio E. Petil I....(*Ψαλτήριον*). 1638. 8°. 4664
(Irish). leabhar. J. Frankton, Dublin, 1608. F°. . . . 6014
(Latin). *See* Doctrina et Politia. 1617.
(Spanish). [1615?] 4°. 2652
Common Prayer (Frankfurt). *See* Brief discours.
(Geneva). By J. Calvin. Trans. by W. Huycke. E. Whitchurch, 7 June, 1550. 8°. 699
Communion, Order of the. 1548. 4°. 1604
Compendium questionum de luce et lumine. Oxonie, 1518. 4°. . 5218
Complete Justice. 1638. 8°. 7799
Compotus. *See* Computus.
Compton (James, baron). Verses in Camb. Univ. *Συνωδία*. 1637.. 5790
Computus. Compotus manualis. C. Kyrfoth, Oxonie, 1519. 4°. . 5222
Conam (Abraham). Verses in Baro (P.). In Ionam. 1579. . 850
Concordance. *See* Bible (Eng.). Concordance.
Condell (Henry). *See* Shakespeare (W.). Works. 1623 *etc.*
Conestaggio (G.). Historie of the vniting of Portugall to Castill. 1600. F°. 2073
Confession. A general confession...for all Men. [1550.] 8°. . . 879
Confession. The humble and unfained confession of...certaine poore banished men. 'Wittonburghe, N. Dorcaster,' 1554. 8°. . 6720
Confession, Form of. *See* Primer. 1555. 8°. 636
A breef (brefe) forme of confession. [Ab. 1600.] 16°. . . 6603
Prayers before and after confession. 16°. . . . 6604
Confession of Faith. [1568?] 8°. 1254
[Collection of translations.] *See* Bullinger (H.). Fiftie godlie sermons. 1577, etc.
An harmonie of the confessions... Cambridge, 1586. 8°. . 5528
Confession of Faith of the Garmaynes. *See* Augsburg Confession.
Confession of Faith. (Scotland.) 1580. *See* Chisholm (W.). Examen. 1601.
See Scotland, Kirk of.
See Adamson (P.). Poemata Sacra. 1619–8.
Confession of Faith. The Confession of faith of certayne English people living in exile, in the Low countreys...*See* Amsterdam, *English Church in.* An apologie... 1604.
Glastonbury (Church of Foreign Protestants). *See* Liturgies. London. 1552.
See Luther (M.). The chiefe...Articles. 1548.
...1638. *See* Proclamations. R. Young, Edinburgh, 1638. 4°.
Confession. A Confession and Protestation...[By H. Jacob.] 1616.
Conformity. *See* Dispute. 1608.
Confutation of the Popish Transubstantiation. *See* L'Espine (J. de).
Conham (Abraham). Address to the Reader. *See* Babington (G.). Works. (Certain profitable questions.) 1637. F°.
Coningsby (Rodolph). Verses in Camb. Univ. Lacrymæ. 1619. . 5689

No.
Coningsby (T.). Verses in Camb. Univ. Fasciae. 1633. . . 5808
Connestable (Henri), *pseud.* *See* Du Perron (J. D.). The Catholike Moderator. 1623.
Conradis (Michael de). *See* Henry VIII. Divino implorato. [1530?]
Conradus (Sigismund). Verses in Comenius. Porta Linguarum. 1631. 4435
Conroy (Florence). *See* Desiderius. 6427
Consilium delectorum cardinalium...de emendanda Ecclæsia...ex bibl. W. Crashaui. 1609. 4°. 2959
— 1609. 12°. 3631
Conspiracie for Pretended Reformation. *See* Cosin (R.). 1592.
Constable (Francis). *See* Pathomachia. 1630. 4°.
Constable (R.). Verses in Camb. Univ. Lacrymæ. 1619. . . 5689
Constantinus I. Treatise of the donation...of possessyons. T. Godfray [1532?]. F°. 557
[Life, & Oration to the Clergy.] *See* Eusebius. The ancient ecclesiasticall histories. Ed. 4. 1636 (1637). F°.
Constantinus, *Africanus.* *See* Herbal. 1561.
Constitutiones legitime seu legatine. 1504, 1506. F°. . . 6147, 6149
Constitutiones provinciales. *See* Lyndwood.
Constitutions. Capitula seu Constitutiones. 1597. 4°. . 1705, 1706
Constitutions and Canons Ecclesiasticall...Prouince of Canterbury. 1603. R. Barker, 1604. 4°. 2583–2585
1603. B. Norton and J. Bill, 1628. 4°. 2833
[R. Barker? 16–?] 4°. 2659
J. Norton, 1633. 4°. 4889
R. Barker and Ass. of J. Bill, 1640. 4°. 2709
See Treatise concernynge... [Ab. 1535.]
Consultorie for all Christians. 1549. *See* H. (H.).
Contarini (Gasparo). Commonwealth & gouernment of Venice. 1599. 4°. 2153
Contarini (Giovanni Pietro). *See* Polemon (J.). All the famous Battels... 1587
Contemplation of Sinners. W. de Worde [1499]. 4°. . . . 53
Continuation of our forraine avisoes. Nos. 18, 19, 20, 46 (April, September 1632). 1632. 4°. 3548
Continuation of our Weekely Avisoes. Nos. 32 and 35. 1632. 4°. . 3882
Continuation of our Weekly Newes. No. 23. (14 March 1631.) 1631(–2). 4°. 3547
Continuation of the German History. *See* Swedish Intelligencer. Part v.
Contre-Guyse. J. Wolfe, 1589. 4°. 1953
Converted Jew. 1630. 4°. 6999
Convocation. The Trew report of...conuocacyō... *See* Philpot (J.). [1554?]
— *See* James I. To the Reverend Fathers. 1604. F°. . . 7416
(Canterbury Province.) A grant of the benevolence or contribution to his Majestie. 1640. 4°. 2710
Conway (Sir J.). Meditations and Praiers. [Before 1571.] 8°. . 7230
Poesie of floured prayers. 1611. 12°. 2863
Coocus (Ant.). *See* Cooke.
Cook or Coocus (John). Verses in Demosthenes. Thre orations. 1570. 1409
— Baret (J.). An alvearie. 1573. 7249
— Wilson (Sir T.). A discourse. 1584. 1872
Cook or Cocus (John), Master of S. Paul's School. Verses in Lloyd (L.). The pilgrimage of princes. 1586. 1941
Cook (Joh.). Verses in Camb. Univ. Fasciae, *ter*. 1633. . . 5808
— — Rex Redux. 1633. 5748
Cooke (Alexander). More worke for a masse-priest. 1621. 4°. 3337, 3338
Worke, more worke...for a masse-priest. Ed. 3. 1630. 4°. . 5046
Pope Joane. 1610. 4°. 2264
— 1625. 4°. 4798
Weather-cocke of romes religion. 1625. 4°. 4087
See Augustine (St.). Saint Avstins religion... 1625.

No.
Cooke (Anne). *See* Bacon (Anne).
Cooke (Sir Antony). Verses in Cheke (Sir J.). De obitu M. Buceri. 1551. 734
— Wilson (Sir T.). Vita. 1551. 631
Cooke (Ed.). Verses in Leighton (Sir W.). The teares. 1613. . 2868
Cooke (Ed.), *T.C.C.* Camb. Univ. Genethl. 1631. . . . 5731
Cooke (Edm.). Verses in Camb. Univ. Thr-thr. 1603. . . 5616
Cooke (Edward). The character of warre. 1626. 4°. 4142
Cooke (F.). Principles of Geometrie. [1591.] 8°. . . . 2131
Cooke (John). Verses *bis* in Camb. Univ. Genethl. 1631. . . 5731
— — Anthologia. 1632. 5741
Cooke (Joshua). *See* Pleasant conceited Comedy. 1634.
Cooke (Robert). Censura quorundam scriptorum. 1614. 4°. . . 3737
— 1623. 4°. 2293
Verses in Oxf. Univ. Magd. Coll. 1612. 5302
Cooke (Thomas). Verses in Hoby (Sir E.). A curry combe. 1615. 3111
Cooke (Thomas), *B.N.C.* Verses in Hippocrates. 1633. . . 5812
Cookson (Tim.). Verses in Camb. Univ. Carmen. 1635. . . 5770
Cooper (Dru.). Verses in Shirley (J.). The royall master. 1638. . 4665
Cooper or Cowper (Edward). Verses *ter* in Wilson (Sir T.). Vita. 1551. 631
Cooper (Isaac), *Pemb.* Verses *bis* in Camb. Univ. Συνῳδία. 1637. 5790
— — Voces. 1640. 5836
Cooper (John). *See also* Cowper. Verses in Camb. Univ. Fasciae. 1633. 5808
Cooper (Mary). *See* Harsnett (S.). A discovery... 1599.
Cooper (Thomas), *Bishop.* Thesavrvs Linguae Romanæ & Britannicæ. Ed. 1. 1565. F°. 1249
— Ed. 2. 1573. F°. 6757
— Ed. 4. 1584. F°. 1517
Briefe exposition of...the olde testament. 1573. 4°. . . . 1413
See Elyot (Sir T.). Bibliotheca Eliote. 1548 *etc.* F°.
— Jewel (J.). An Apologie of private Masse. 1562.
— Lanquet (T.). The Cronicles. 1549 *etc.*
— Marprelate (M.). Hay any worke for Cooper. 1589. 4°.
Cooper (Thomas), *Divine.* The Churches deliverance. 1609. 4°. . 3569
Wonderfull mysterie of spirituall growth. 1622. 8°. . . 7584
Cooper (Will.). Verses in Oxf. Univ. Horti. 1640. . . . 5499
Coote (Edward). English Schoole-Maister. 1638.... 4°. . . . 3309
Coote (William). Verse in Camb. Univ. Epicedium. 1612. . 5665
Cooth (John). *See* Lake (A.). Sermons. 1629.
Cope (Alan), *D.D.* *See* Humphrey (L.). J. Jvelli vita. 1573.
Cope (Sir Antony). *See* Livivs. The historie of Anniball and Scipio. 1548 *etc.*
[Funeral.] *See* Harris (R.). Samuels Funeral. 1618 etc. 4°.
Copenhagen. 1554. *See* Lindsay (Sir D.). No. 5995.
Coperus. *See* Cooper.
Copie, Copies. *See* Copy.
Copland (Robert). *See* Aristotle. [Supposititious Works. Secreta Secretorum. Lat.] 1528.
See Edmond Rich, 1521.
— Elias, Knight of the Swan. 1512. 4°.
— Passion of our Lorde. 1521.
— Primer. 1531 *etc.*
— Ravennas (P.). The Art of Memory... [154–?]
Copley (Ant.). Answere to a letter. 1601. 4°. 6838
See James I. Placcaet. 1603.
Copley (John). Doctrinall and morall observations. 1612. 4°. . 3082
Copley (Sir Thomas). *See* Treatise of Justification. 1569. 4°.
Coppinger (Edmund). *See* Cosin (R.). Conspiracie for Pretended Reformation... 1592.
Coprario (John). Songs of mourning...of Prince Henry. 1613. F°. . 3203

No.

Copus (Alanus). *See* Cope.
Copy. Copie of an Aunswere, made vnto a certaine letter...from Pelagius errors. *See* Crowley (R.). An apologie... 1566.
Copie of a certaine letter...to a prelate of Brabant. 1599. 4°. . 1981
Copie of a letter written by one in London...conc....the Lady Marie of Scotland. [1572?] 8°. 6756
Copie of a letter written out of Scotland...of the Quene of Scotland. [Antwerp, 157- .] 12°. 6124
Copie of a letter wryten by a master of arts of Cambridge. 1594. *See* Parsons (R.). 6810
Copie of the letter of the Nationall Synod of the Reformed Churches of France. 1631. 4°. 3545
Copies of certaine discourses. 'Roane, heires of Ia. Walker,' 1601. 4°. 7360
Corbet (John). The epistle congratulatorie of Lysimachus Nicanor. 1640. 4°. 7637, 7638
Ungirding of the Scottish Armour. Dublin, 1639. 4°. . 6064–6067
Verses in Chaucer (G.). Amorum. 1635. 5414
See Baillie (R.). Ladensium Αὐτοκατάκρισις. 1640.
Corbet (Richard). Verses in Coryate (T.). Coryates Crvdities. 1611. 3076
Corbet (Rob.). Verses in Vaughan (R.). Waterworkes. 1610. . 3576
Corderius (Mat.) *See* Cordier.
Corderoy (Jeremy). A short dialogue. Ed. 2. Oxford. 1604. 12°. 5265
Warning for Worldlings. 1608. 12°. 1387
Cordiale. (The Four Last Things.) Caxton, 1479. F°. . . 12
Cordier (Mathurin). Colloquiorum scholasticorum libri IIII. Cantabrigiæ, 1633. 8°. 5750
Dialogues. Trans. J. Brinsley. 1614. 8°. 7845
— 1625. 8°. 3865
Corinthus, *Smyrnæus*. De Dialectis. *See* Crespin (J.). Lexicon. 1581.
Cornaro (Lud.). [Treatise of temperance and sobrietie. Trans. G. Herbert.] *See* Lessius (L.). Hygiasticon. 1634. 12°.
Corneliszen (J.). *See* Neck (J. van). The Journal. 1601. 4°.
Cornelius (Andreas). *See* Polemon (J.). All the famous Battels. 1587.
Cornelius (J.). Verses in Camb. Univ. Anthologia. 1632. . . 5741
— Fasciae. 1633.. 5808
Cornucopia. *See* Perottus.
Cornvallus (John). Verses in Adamson (J.). Εἰσόδια. 1618. . . 5960
Cornwaleys (Bevercotes), *C.C.C.* Verses in Camb. Univ. Συνωδία. 1637. 5790
Cornwall. *See* Carew (R.). The svrvey of... 1602.
— Doddridge (Sir J.). The History... 1630.
Cornwall, *Ministers of*. *See* Devon and Cornwall, *Ministers of*.
Cornwallis (John). *See* Cornvallus.
Cornwallis (Sir W.). First (second) part of Essayes. 1601 ('1606'). 8°. 7231
Essayes. (Discourses vpon Seneca.) 1606. 8°. 1273
— Newlie corrected. 1632(1). 8°. 3992
Essayes of certaine paradoxes. 1616. 4°. 4054
Corranus (Antonius). *See* Corro (A. de).
Corro (A. de). Dialogvs Theologicvs. 1574. 8°. 1369
A theological dialogue. 1575. 8°. 1370
Diuinorum operum tabula. [Ab. 157–.] Broadside . . 6751
Epistle or godlie admonition of a learned Minister. 1569. 8°. 1467
Tableau de l'œuvre de Dieu. 1569. Broadside. . . 5893
See Bible (Lat.), O.T. Ecclesiastes. 1579.
Corte (Cl.). The Art of Riding. 1584. 4°. 1427
Coryate (George), *B.D.* Posthuma... *See* Coryate (T.). Coryats Crudities. 1611.
Coryate (Thomas). Coryats Crudities. 1611. 4°. 3076
Cosin (John). Collection of private devotions. 1639. 12°. . . 5001
Verses in Camb. Univ. Epicedium. 1612. . . 5665, 5666
— Carmen. 1635. 5770

No.
Cosin (John), *cont.* Verses in Camb. Univ. Voces. 1640. . . 5836
Prynne (W.). A briefe svrvey... 1628.
[Licence.] *See* Rohan (H. duc de). The Complete Captain. 1640.
Cosin (Ric.). An abstract, of certaine acts of parlement. 1584. 4°. 1428–1430
Answer to the two first and principall Treatises *etc.* [Part II. 'An abstract,' *ut ante.*]
Apologie for sundrie proceedings. 1593. 4°. 1696
Conspiracie for pretended reformation. 1592. 4°. 1693
Ecclesiæ Anglicanae Politeia. 1604. F°. 2349
— Oxoniae, 1634. F°. 5408
[Life.] *See* Barlow (W.). Vita. 1598.
Coster (Francis). Meditations of the...Passion of Christ. Trans. R. W. Douai, 1616. 12°. 6610
Cosworth (Michael). Verses in Lok (H.). Ecclesiastes. 1597. . 2246
Cotgrave (R.). Dictionarie of the French and English tongves. 1611. F°. 2441
Coton (Pierre). The interiour occupation of the soule. Douai. 1618. 12°. 6611
Anti-coton. 1611. 4°. 3390–2
Declaratorie Letter... *See* Hellish and horrible Councell. 1610. 4°.
See Du Moulin (P.). Father Cotton... 1615.
See Prosopopeia... 1606.
Cotsford (Thomas). *See* Zwingli (U.). The accompt. 1555.
Cotta (John). Cotta contra Antonium. Oxford, 1623. 4°. . 5344
Short discoverie of the vnobserved dangers of ignorant Practisers of Physicke. 1612. 4°. 2268
The triall of Witch-craft. 1616. 4°. 4055
Cotton (Clement). The christians concordance. 1622. F°. . . 2290
Converts catechisme. 1616. 12°. 7473
Large concordance to the bible. Ed. 2. 1635. F°. . . 3748
Mirror of martyrs. 1615. 12°. 4139
— Ed. 5. 1639. 12°. 4667
See Calvin (J.). A Commentarie on...Hebrewes. 1605. 4°.
Assigns of. *See* Bible (Eng.). Concordance. 1632.
Cotton (Sir Dodmore). *See* Herbert (Sir T.). A relation. 1634.
Cotton (Henry). Verses in Humphrey (L.). I. Ivelli vita. 1573. . 837
Cotton (John). Gods promise to his plantation. [1630.] 4°. . 5050
See Pocklington (J.). Altare. 1637.
Cotton (John), *Magd.* Verses in Camb. Univ. Carmen. 1635. . 5770
— Συνῳδία. 1637. 5790
Cotton (Pierre), *jesuit.* *See* Coton.
Cotton (Sir R. B.). The danger wherein the Kingdome now standeth. 1628. 4°. 6978, 6979
Short view of the...raigne of Henry the third. 1627. 4°. . 6973
See More (Sir T.). Epistola... 1633.
— Speed (J.). The theatre. 1611.
[*Ex bibliotheca.*] *See* Eadmer. 1623.
Cotton (Roger). Direction to the waters of lyfe. 1590. 4°. . . 2193
Cotton (Rowland). Verses in Coryat (T.). Coryats Crudities. 1611. 3076
Cotton (Steven). The copy of a letter. *See* Coverdale (M.). Certain ...letters. 1564.
Cotton (William), *Bp.* [Visitation, 1599.] *See* Godwin (F.). Concio... 2058
[Triennial Visitation, 1616.] *See* Carpenter (R.). A pastoral charge. 1616.
See Certaine demandes. 1605.
Councils, General. *See* Augustine (St.). Two bokes... [1556?]
See Becanus (M.). Svpplicatio. 1613. 4°.
— Bullinger (H.). Fiftie godlie sermons. 1577 etc.
— Trent.
Fifth General Council. *See* Crakanthorp (R.). Vigilius. 1631.
Counsellor of Estate. *See* Bethune (P. de). 1634.
Counter-Poyson. 1584. *See* Fenner (D.).

No.

Couper (Mary). *See* Cooper.
Court Baron. *See* Modus. [15 .]
Court Leete. *See* Modus observandi. [1529] *etc.*
Court of Record. *See* Modus tenendi. [1516?] *etc.*
Court of Requests. *See* Caesar (Sir J.). In nomine domini. [1592.]
Court (Andrew). The true way to vertue and happinesse. 1623. 4°. 4754
See Du Vair (G.). A Bvckler against adversitie.. 1622.
Courthop (Richard). *See* Gascoigne (G.). The Posies. 1575.
Courtisanes. *See* Miroir.
Covell (William). Briefe answer vnto certaine reasons. 1606. 4°. . 3610
Modest and reasonable examination. 1604. 4°. . . 2469
See Defence of the ministers reasons... 1607.
— Dispute. 1608.
Coventry, *Charterhouse of St Anne*. *See* Thomas, Prior of St Anne's. 1501.
Coverdale (Miles). Certain most godly...letters. 1564. 4°. . . 802
Christen exhortation unto customable swearers. [Ab. 154-.] 8°. 6706
— N. Hill for R. Kele, [1550?] 8°. 1027
— N. Hill for J. Wyghte, [1550?] 8°. 1028
Confutacion of ... John Standish ... agaynst ... Barnes. [Zurich.] 1540. 8°. 6281
Fruitfull lessons upon the passion. 1593. 4°. 2382
Worke entytled of ye olde god & the newe. 1534. 8°. . . 567
See Bible (Eng.). 1535 *etc.*
— — [Matthew's.] 1537, 1549.
— — [Taverner's.] 1539.
— — (Cranmer's.) 1540 *etc.*
— — (Eng. & Lat.) N.T. 1538. 4°.
— Bullinger (H.). The Christian state of Matrimony. 1575.
— Calvin (J.). A faythfvl...treatyse concernynge the sacrament... [1550?]
— Erasmus (D). Paraphrase. 1548 *etc.*
— Exhortation. An Exhortacion to the carienge. [1554?]
— Wermueller (O.). The hope of the faythful. [1554?]
— — A Spyrytuall...Pearle. 1550.
— Wyclif (John). Wicklieffes Wicket... [1548?]
Covert (Robert). A true...Report of an Englishman. 1631. 4°. . 4886
Cowell (John). Institutiones iuris anglicani. Cantabrigiae, 1605. 8°. 5629
The interpreter. Cambridge, 1607. 4°. 5641, 7851
— 1637. 4°. 4955, 4956
Verses in Cambridge Univ. Lachrymae. 1587. . . . 7356
See Antisanderus. 1593. 4°.
Cowley (A.). Loves riddle. A pastorall comedie. 1638. 8°. . . 7647
Naufragium joculare. 1638. 8°. 4595
Poeticall blossomes. Ed. 3. 1637. 8°. 7576
Verses in Fletcher (P.). The Purple Island. 1633. . . 5752
— Camb. Univ. Συνῳδία. 1637. 5790
— — Voces *bis*. 1640. 5836
Cowley (W.). *See* C. (W.). A briefe discourse... 1578.
Cowper (Edward). *See* Cooper.
Cowper (John). *See also* Cooper. Verses in Cam. Univ. Genethl. 1631. 5731
Cowper (Mary). *See* Cooper.
Cowper (William). 'Workes.' 1623. F°. 3435
— Ed. 2. 1629. F°. 3810
Anatomie of a christian Man. 1611. 4°. 3393
— Ed. 2. 1613. 4°. 7827
Pathmos: or a commentary on the Revelation...iv...vii. 1619. 4°. 4066
Seven dayes conference, between a Catholicke Christian and... Romane. 1613. 8°. 3093
Three heavenly treatises vpon the eight chapter to the Romanes. 1609 (1613). 4°. . . . . . . 3386 (corrected)

No.
Cowper (William), *cont.* [Life and death.] 1619. 4°. . . . 4067
Cox (Leonard). Arte or crafte of Rhethoryke. R. Redman, n.d. 8°. 389
Verses in Palsgrave (J.). Les claircissement de la Langue Francoyse. 1530. 527
See Lily (W.). De octo orationis partium constructione. 1540.
Cox (Richard), *Bishop*. *See* Advertisements. 1584.
See Bible, English (Bishops'). 1568.
— Catechism. The Catechism. 1578(9?). 8°.
— Wilkinson (W.). A Confutation. 1579.
Cox (Ro.). Verses in Davies (J.). Humours Heau'n on earth. 1609. 2438
Cox (W.). Verses in Oxf. Univ. Horti. 1640. 5499
Cox (William), *B.A.*, *T.C.* Verses in Camb. Univ. Συνῳδία. 1637. 5790
Coxall ( ). Verses in Camb. Univ. Epicedium. 1612. . . 5665
Coxe (F.). Prognostication... 1566. 16°. 1285
Short treatise...of magicall sciences. [1560?] 8°. . . . 1288
Cozen or Cozens (John). *See* Cosin.
Cr. (Sa.). *See* Crooke (S.). 1632.
Cradocke (E.). The shippe of assured safetie. 1572. 8°. . . . 7264
Verses in Humphrey (L.). I. Ivelli vita. 1573. . . 837
Crafordius. *See* Crawford.
Craft to live and die well. *See* Ars moriendi.
Cragius (Thomas). *See* Craig.
Craig (Alexander). Verses in Adamson (J.). Εἰσόδια. 1618. . . 5960
Craig (J.). Short summe of the whole catechisme. 1583. 8°. . 1928
Verses in Gwinne (M.). Vertumnus. 1607. . . . 3621
Craig (Thomas). Verses in Skene (Sir J.). Regiam. 1613. . 3458
Crakanthorpe (George). *See* Crakanthorpe (R.). Vigilius. 1631.
Crakanthorpe (Richard). De providentia dei. Cantabrigiae, 1623. 4°. 5696
Defence of Constantine. 1621. 4°. 4164
Defensio ecclesiae anglicanae. 1625. 4°. 3294
Iustinian the Emperor. 1616. 4°. 3585
Sermon of predestination. 1620. 4°. 4753
Vigilius Dormitans. 1631. F°. 4263
Cranborne (Charles, viscount). Verses in Camb. Univ. Carmen. 1635. 5770
Crane (Francis), *T.C.* Verses in Cam. Univ. Voces. 1640. . 5836
Crane (Robert). Verses in Holyoake (F.). Dictionarium. 1640. . 3058
Cranfield (Lionel). Verses in Coryate (T.). Coryats Crudities. 1611. 3076
Cranmer (Samuel). Verses in Humphrey (L.). I. Ivelli vita. 1573. 837
Cranmer (T.). Answer...vnto a cauillation deuised by S. Gardiner... also...R. Smyth. 1551. F°. 733
— 1580. F°. 860
Catechismus...a shorte Instruction. 1548. 8°. . . 1019, 1020
Confutation of vnwrittē verities. [Ab. 1557.] 8°. . . 6740
— *See* Chemnitius (M.). A discourse. 1582.
Copy of certain lettres. 1556. 8°. 6724
Defence of the true and catholike doctrine of the sacrament. 1550. 4°. 731, 732
— *See* Smith (R.), *D.D.*, *Reg. Prof.* A Confutation. [1550.]
Reformatio legvm ecclesiasticarum. 1571. 4°. 825
— 1640. 4°. 4047
[Letter.] *See* Briefe examination. [1564.] 4°.
[Letters.] *See* Coverdale (M.). Certain...letters. 1564.
See A. (J.), *of Ailward*. An historicall narration... 1631.
— Bible, Eng. 1539 *etc.*
— Gardiner (S.). An explicatiō̃. 1551.
— Homilies. 1547.
— Philpot (J.). Vera expositio... 1554.
Crashaun (William). *See* Crashaw (W.).
Crashaw (Ralegh). Verses in Smith (J.). The generall historie. 1624. 3864

No.

Crashaw (Richard). Epigrammatum sacrorum liber. Cantabrigiae, 1634. 8°. 5759
Verses in Camb. Univ. Anthologia. 1632. 5741
— Fasciae. 1633. 5808
— Rex redux, *bis*. 1633. 5748
— Carmen. 1635. 5770
— Συνωδία. 1637. 5790
— Voces. 1640. 5836
— Lessius (L.). Hygiasticon. 1634 etc. 5833
— Shelford (R.). Five pious...discourses. 1635. 4°. . . 5774
Crashaw (W.). Ad Severinum Binnium...epistola commonitoria super conciliorum generalium editione. 1624. 4°. 7574
Complaint or Dialogue. *See below*, Querela. 1631.
Falsificationum romanarum. 1606. 4°. 2262
— *See* Mayhew (E.). A Treatise of the grounds. 1608.
Fatall vesper. 1623. 4°. 4772
Jesvites gospel. 1610. 4°. 2025
— Ed. 2. 1621. 4°. 4165
Mittimus to the ivbile at Rome. 1625. 4°. 4088
Querela sive Dialogus. 1632(1). 12°. 3815–6
Romish Forgeries. *See above*, Falsificationum &c.
Sermon. 14 Feb. 1607. 1608. 4°. 2486
See Augustine (S.). ...of the citie of God... 1620.
— Balbani (N.). Newes from Italy. 1608. 4°.
— — Italian convert. 1635.
— C. (W.). The fatall vesper... 1623.
— C. (W.), *Preacher of the word.* The Embassador. 1613.
— Consilium delectorvm... 1609. . . . . . 2959 etc.
— Consilivm... 1613. 2313
— Fiscus Papalis. 1617 *etc.*
— Floyd (J.). Overthrow of the protestants pulpit-babels. 1612.
— Henry IV. of France. A discovrse to the Lords... 1611.
— New Man. 1622.
— Pasquale (C.). False complaints. 1605. 4°.
— Perkins (W.). Works. Vol. 3. ('A clowd of faithfull witnesses,' 'Zephaniah,' and 'Of the Ministerie' etc.) 1609. F°. . 5656
— — Vol. 2. ('Επιείκεια.) 1617. F°. 3760
— Texeda (F. de). Texeda Retextus. 1623.
Cratford (Edward). *See* Redman (J.). A reporte... 1551.
Crawford (Thomas). Verses in Person (D.). Varieties. 1635. . . 4365
Crede mihi. *See* Directorium.
Creeds. [Collection of translations of text of various.] *See* Bullinger (H.). Fiftie godlie sermons. 1577, 1584.
See Luther (M.). The chiefe...articles. 1548.
Creed, *Apostles*. [Ab. 1538.] *See* Lords Prayer. . . . 6681
— Byfield (N.). The Rvle of Faith. 1626.
— Crompe (J.). Collections. [1638–9.]
— Perkins (W.). An exposition. 1595.
Creed, *Nicene*. [A.S. and Eng.] *See* Ælfric, *Abp*. A Testimonie of Antiqvitie... [1566.]
Creed, *Pius IV*. (Lat. and Eng.) *See* Lynde (Sir H.). Via Tuta. 1630.
— Sharpe (L.). Novvm fidei symbolvm. 1612.
Creed (William). Verses in A. (G.). Pallas armata. 1639. . . 5170
— Oxf. Univ. Horti. 1640. 5499
— Snelling (T.). Thibaldvs. 1640. 5502
Creighton or Creyghton (Robert). Verses in Camb. Univ. Dolor. 1625. 5701
See Francklin (R.). 'Ορθοτονία. 1630 *etc.*
Creighton (William). *See* Crichton.
Creitton (Rob.). *See* Creighton.
Crespin (Jean). Estate of the Church. Trans. S. Patricke. 1602. 4°. 2731

No.
Crespin (Jean), *cont.* Lexicon græcolatinum. 1581. 4°. . . . 1506
Creswell (G.). Harmonie of the Lawe and the Gospel. 1607. 8°. . 2484
Creswell (Ro.). Verses in Camb. Univ. Fasciae. 1633. . . 5808
— Rex redux. 1633. 5748
— Carmen. 1635. 5770
— *Συνωδία*. 1637. 5790
Creyghton (Robert). *See* Creighton.
Crichton, Creighton, or Criton (William), *jesuit*. *See* Cecil (J.), *D.D.* A discoverye. [1599?]
Crinitus (Petrus). *See* Æsop. Fabulæ. 1635.
Crisp (Mrs Rebecca). [Funeral.] *See* Gataker (T.). Two funeral sermons. 1620.
Crispinus (Joannes). *See* Crespin.
Criton (William), *jesuit*. *See* Crichton.
Critopulus (Metrophanes). Verses in Shaw (J.). Bibliorum summvla. 1623. 7381
Croce (Giov.). Musica Sacra. (Quintus.) 1608. 4°. . . . 1617
— (Sextus.) 1611. 4°. 2507
Crocus (Samuel). *See* Crooke.
Croftes (Antho.). Verses in Stephens (J.). New essayes. 1631. . 7823
Croke (J.). *See* Keilwey (R.). Relationes. 1602. F°.
Croket (Thomas). Verses in Paris and Vienna. 1628. . . 7552
Crole (Robert). *See* Crowley (R.).
Cromer (Martin). *See* Arsanes. [1560?]
Crompe (John). Collections...upon the first part of the Apostles Creed. 1638–9. 4°. 4875
Crompton (Richard). L'authoritie et ivrisdiction des courts. 1594. 4°. 2865
— 1637. 4°. 5081
Mansion of Magnanimitie. 1599. 4°. 1866
Star-chamber cases. 1630. 4°. 5072
Crompton (Thomas). *See* Cosin (R.). Ecclesiæ Anglicanæ Politeia. 1604 etc.
Crompton (William). *See* Augustine. Saint Austins religion... 1625.
— James I. Cygnea Cantio... 1629.
Cromwell (James). Verses in Camb. Univ. *Συνωδία*. 1637. . . 5790
Cromwell (Thomas, *lord*). *See* Augsburg Confession. [1536?]
— Primer (Hilsey). 1539. 4°.
Crooke (Helkiah). *Μικροκοσμογραφία*. Ed. 2. 1631. F°. . . 4687
Crooke (Samuel). Briefe direction to true happinesse. 1614. 8°. . 3898
Guide vnto true blessednesse. Ed. 2. 1614. 8°. . . 3899
Three sermons. 1615. 8°. 3107
Verses in Horne (C.). In obitum Whitakeri. 1596. . . 7332
— Whitaker (W.). Praelectiones. 1599. 5598
See Sweden. The Swedish Discipline. 1632.
Cropley (John). Verses in Barlow (W.). Vita R. Cosin. 1598. . 1707
Crosfield (Thomas). *See* Gregorius. A letter. 1633. 4°.
— Oxford University. Statuta. 1638.
Crosse (Henry). Schoole of Pollicie. 1605. 4°. 2859
Crosse (Richard). *See* Ursinus (Z.). The summe of christian religion. 1611 *etc.*
Crosse (William). *See* Grimstone (E.). Generall historie of the netherlands. Ed. 2. 1627. F°.
Crowch (J.), *Sen.*, *K.C.C.* Verses in Camb. Univ. Epithalam, *bis*. 1625. 5702
Crowch (Jo.), *Jun.*, *K.C.C.* Verses in Camb. Univ. Epithalam, 1625. 5702
Crowch (Thomas). Verses in Hippocrates. 1631, 1633. . 5736, 5812
— Camb. Univ. Rex redux. 1633. 5748
Crowley (Robert). Apologie or Defence of...Predestination. 1566. 4°. 1456
Briefe discourse against the outwarde apparell and ministring garmentes. (A declaration.) 1566. 8°. 6412
— 1578. 8°. 6764

No.

Crowley (Robert), *cont.* Confutation of the mishapen Aunswer to...the Abuse of yᵉ blessed sacrament... 1548. 8°. 899
Confutation of XIII Articles, wherunto N. Shaxton...subscribed. [1548.] 8°. 912, 913
Deliberat answere. 1588. 4°. 1358
Information and Peticyon agaynst the oppressours of the pore Commons. [1548?] 8°. 880
One and thyrtye Epigrammes. 1550. 8°. 1091
Sermon, 29 Sept. 1574. 1575. 8°. 1279
Setting open of...T. Watson. 1569. 4°. 1408
Way to wealth. [1549?] 8°. 1090
See Piers, the Ploughman. The vision. 1550.
— Rice (R.). An invective. 1579.
— Supper of the Lorde. 1533.
— Wyclif (J.). The true copye. 1550.
Crowne (W.). True relation of...travels. 1637. 4°. 7482
Crowther (Joseph). Chaucer (G.). Amorum. 1635. . . . 5414
Croyden (T.). Verses in Cam. Univ. Fasciae. 1633. 5808
Cruceius (Annibal). *See* Achilles Tatius. De Clitophontis amoribus. [1588.]
Cruell subtilty... *See* Sarpi (P.).
Cruso (A.). Verses in Camb. Univ. Lacrymæ. 1619. . . . 5689
Cruso (John). Militarie instructions for the cavallrie. Cambridge, 1632. F°. 5742
See Du Praissac. Art of warre. 1639.
— Rohan (Henri, duc de). The Complete Captain. 1640.
Cudworth (Ralph). Verses in Horne (C.). In obitum Whitakeri. 1596. 7332
— Whitaker (W.). Praelectiones. 1599. 5598
— Camb. Univ. Carmen. 1635. 5770
See Perkins (W.). A commentarie. 1604.
Cuff (H.). Differences of the ages of man's life. 1607. 8°. . . 2085
— 1633. 8°. 4205
Verses in Camden (W.). Britannia. 1637. 3055
Cuffetellus (Nicolas). *See* Coeffeteau.
Cuffius (H.). *See* Cuff.
Cuique suum. 'Αντωδη. Cantabrigiae, 1635. 4°. 5772
Culmer (Richard). Verses in Camb. Univ. Lacrymæ. 1619. . . 5689
Culpeper (John). Verses in Cheke (Sir J.). De obitu M. Buceri. 1551. 734
Culpepper (Martin). Verses in Humphrey (L.). I. Ivelli vita. . 837
Culpepper (Sir T.). Tract against vsurie. 1621. 4°. . . . 2791
Culverwell (Ezekiel). *See* Dent (A.). The Rvine of Rome. 1607.
— Rogers (R.). Seaven Treatises. 1605 etc.
— Sibbes (R.). Divine Meditations. 1638. 12°.
Culverwell (N.), *B.A.* Verses in Camb. Univ. Συνωδία. 1637. . 5790
Cummin (Sir Alexander). Verses in Forbes (P.). Funerals. 1637. . 6007
Cunæus (Petrus). Verses in Burgersdicius (F.)...Institutionum... 1637. 5789
Cunningham (W.). Cosmographical Glasse. 1559. F°. . . 791
Verses in Gale (T.). Certaine Workes. 1563. 1303
See Fulke (W.). Antiprognosticon. 1560.
— Gale (T.). Certaine Workes. 1563.
— Hall (J.). A most excellent...woorke. 1565.
— Vigo (J. de). The whole worke. 1586.
Cura Clericalis. 1542. 8°. 581
Curio (Cœlius Secundus). *See* Valdes (S. de). The hundred and ten considerations. 1638.
Curll (Walter). A sermon. 1622. 4°. 3505
Curranto. No. 84. The Norimberg Curranto. 1639. 4°. . . 7724
— No. 86. The Curranto...from Holland. 1639. 4°. . . 7725
— An Extraordinary Curranto. Century 2. Num. 41. 1639. 4°. 7726
Curry Combe for a coxe-combe. 1615. *See* Hoby, Sir (E.).

No.
Curtius (Q.). The historie...Trans. J. Brend. 1553. 4°. . . 1103
— 1602. 8°. 2732
Cusa (Nicholas de), *Cardinal.* *See* Constantine I. A treatyse. [c. 1525.]
Cyllenius *pseud.* *See* Roscarrock (N.).
Cyprianus. De Vnitate Ecclesiae, cum annott. I. Stephani. 1632. 8°. 3994
Sermon...on the Lordes prayer. Trans. T. Paynell. 1539. 8°. 447
Swete and devovte sermon...of mortalitie of men. Trans. by Sir T. Elyot. 1539. 8°. 448
[Of Alms-deeds.] *See* Treatise of Iustification. 1569.
See Lupset (T.). Workes. 1546.
Cyprus. Brief discourse of the warres of Cyprus. *See* Turkey. The Mahumetane or Turkish Historie. 1600.
Cyrillus, *Thessalonicus.* Dictionum collectio. *See* Crespin (J.). Lexicon. 1581.
Cyrus, *king of Persia.* *See* Xenophon. Cyrupædia. 1632.

Δ. Treatise of ecclesiasticall and politike power. 1612. 4°. . . 3083
D. (A.). Verses in Stubbes (P.). The anatomie of abuses. 1585. 1446
D. (A.). Briefe discourse concerning faith... *See* White (J.) *of Eccles.* The way to the true church. 1608 *etc.*
D. (A.), *Student in Divinity.* Reply made unto A. Wotton & J. White. Pt. 1. 1612. 4°. 6525
See Fisher (John). 1614.
D. (A.), B. *See* James I. The court. 1619. 4°.
D. (C.), *Christ's Coll.* Verses in Camb. Univ. Lacrymae. 1619. . 5689
D. (E.). Copy of a letter...for the preservation of health...of Tabacco. 1606. 4°. 3364
D. (E.), *Pemb.* Verses in Camb. Univ. Epithalam. 1625. . . 5702
D. (G.). Briefe discoverie of Doctor Allens seditious drifts. 1588. 4°. 1946
Verses in Horatius. Odes. 1635 etc. 4857
D. (G.), *Cantab.* Verses in Abernethy (J.). A christian...treatise. 1630. 4342
D. (H.). Godlie and fruitfull Treatise of Faith and workes. 1583. 8°. 1869
See D. (I.). Salomons Pest-House. 1630. 4°.
— Dod (H.). Certaine Psalmes... 1603.
— Wilkinson (R.). The stripping of Ioseph... 1625.
D. (I.). Salomons Pest-House...Mr Hollands Admonition etc. 1630. 4°. 3988
Newes. *See* Overbury (Sir T.). His Wife. 1638.
Verses in Gascoigne (G.). The Posies. 1575. . . . 1482
Jonson (B.). Workes. 1616. 3115
See Aristotle. Politiqves. 1598.
— Dade (J.). A triple Almanack. 1591. 4°.
— Davies (J.), *of Hereford.* The Scourge of Folly. 1611. 8°.
— Doddridge (Sir John). The Lawyers Light.
D. (I.), *Scoto-Britannus.* Verses in Crashaw (W.). Falsificationum. 1606. 2262
Holland (H.). Herωologia. 1620. 6642
D. (Sir I.), *Kt.* A New Post. 1620. 8°. 7342
See also Davies (Sir John).
D. (I.), *of the church of Scotland.* *See* Davidson (J.).
D. (Is.), *C.C.C.* Verses in Camb. Univ. Genethl. 1631. . . 5731
D. (J.). The Knave in graine. 1640. 4°. 3725
D. (J.), *G. and C. C.* [probably James Danyell]. Verses in Wadsworth (J.). Further Obss. 1630. 7788
D. (J.), *T.C.* [qu. Duport?] Verses in Camb. Univ. Voces. 1640. 5836
D. (M. E.). Verses in Hay (P.). A vision. 1614. . . . 3463
D. (N.). *See* Cooke (A.). Pope Joane. 1610 *etc.*
D. (N.) [=R. Parsons]. *See* E. (O.). A briefe replie. 1600.
See Parsons (R.). A treatise of three conversions of England. 1603 (1604).
D. (N.), *author of the Warn word.* *See* Parsons (R.).

No.

D. (R.). Booke of Christian Prayers. *See* Day (R.).
D. (R.). *See* Becon (T.). Demaundes of Holy Scripture. 1577. 8°.
D. (R.), *Coll. Pet.* Verses in Camb. Univ. Epicedium. 1612. . 5665
D. (R.), *Regal.* Verses in Camb. Univ. Gratulatio. 1623. . 5695
D. (R. H.). *See* Hacket (R.), *D.* A sermon. 1606.
D. (T.). The bloody banquet. 1620. 4°. 4601
Verses in Holland (H.). Herωologia. 1620. 6642
See Deloney (T.). Proper newe Sonet...of Beckles. 1586. F°.
— Linaker (R.). A comfortable Treatise. 1625. 12°.
D. (W.). Verses in Breton (N.). Characters. 1615. . . . 3902
See Audiguier (V. d'). Lisander & Calista. 1635. F°.
— Davenant (Sir W.).
— Phalaris. Epistles. 1634.
D. (W.), *Exoniæ.* Verses in Mercator (G.). Historia. 1635. . 4637
Dabitot (Giles). Verses in Hoby (Sir E.). A curry combe. 1615. . 3111
Daborn (Robert). Christian turn'd Turke. 1612. 4°. . . 3643
Dacres (Edward). *See* Macchiavelli (N.). Discourses. 1636.
Dade (J.). Almanacke and Prognostication. 1591. 8°. . . 1338
Triple Almanacke. (Prognostication.) 1591. 4°. . . 1339
New Almanacke. (A briefe Prognostication.) 1592. 8°. . . 1340
Almanacke & Prognostication. 1604. 8°. 1788
Dafforne (Richard). The apprentices time-entertainer. 3 Parts. 1640. 4°. 5010
Dakins (William). *See* Bible, English (Royal). 1611. . . 2635
Dalechamp (Caleb). Christian hospitalitie. (Harrisonus honoratus.) Cambridge, 1632. 4°. 5801
Exercitationes duae. 1624. 4°. 3346
Hæreseologia tripartita. Cantabrigiae, 1631. 4°. . . . 5779
Vindiciae Salomonis. 1622. 4°. 3339
Votum Davidis. 1624. 4°. 3347
Dallington (Sir Robert). Method for Trauell... 1598. [1605?] 4°. 2753
Survey of the great dukes state of Tuscany. 1605. 4°. . 3556–7
See Guicciardini (F.). Aphorismes Civill...out of the first Quarterne. 1629. F°.
Dalston (Will.). Verses in Camb. Univ. Genethl. 1631. . . 5731
Dalton (Michael). The Countrey Justice. Ed. 3. 1622. F°. . . 3288
— Ed. 5. 1635. F°. 5078
Officium Vicecomitum. The Office and avthoritie of Sherifs. 1623. F°. 3293
Daman (W.). Psalmes of David. (Bassus.) 1579. 8°. . . 857
Damascen (Nicholas). *See* Nicholas, of Damascus.
Damiano da Odemira. Pleasavnt and wittie Playe of the Cheasts. 1562. 8°. 1301
Damman (Adrian). Schediasmata. Edinburgh, 1590. 4°. . . 5922
Damon (William). *See* Daman.
Damport (R.). Verses in Camb. Univ. Lacrymæ. 1618. . . 5689
Danæus (Lambert). *See* Daneau.
Dand (O.). Verses in Camb. Univ. Genethl. 1631. . . 5731
Daneau (Lambert). Fruitfull commentarie upon the twelve small Prophets. Cambridge, 1594. 4°. 5565
Treatise touching antichrist. 1589. 4°. 2201
True and Christian Friendshippe. 1586. 8°. . . . 1072
Wonderfvll woorkmanship of the world. 1578. 4°. . . 1857
See Bridges (J.). A defence of the government. 1587.
Danes (John). Paralipomena Orthographiae. 1638 (1639). 4°. 4741–2
Danett (Tho.). Continuation of the Historie of France. 1600. 4°. 1609
See Comines (P. de). The historie. 1596 etc.
— Guicciardini (L.). Description of the Low Countreys. Epitome. 1593. 8°.
Danford (R.), *Sid.* Verses in Camb. Univ. Epicedium. 1612. . 5665
— Epithalam. 1625. 5702

No.
Danger wherein the Kingdome now standeth. 1628. *See* Cotton (Sir R. B.).
Dangerous Positions. *See* Bancroft (R.). Davngerous Positions. 1593.
Daniel (John). Verses in Philibert *de Vienne*. 1575. . . . 1485
See Daniel (S.). Whole Workes. 1623. 4°.
Daniel (John Jerome), *alias* Pickford, O. S. F. *See* Pickford.
Daniel (Samuel). Whole workes. 1623. 4°. 3685
Certaine small poems...with...Philotas. 1605. 8°. . . . 3555
Civile Wares. 1608. 4°. 2494
Collection of the historie of England. [1618.] F°. . . 3671
— 1621. F°. 3677
— 1634. F°. 4629
— (Continuation.) *See* Trussell (J.). A continuation. 1636. F°.
Panegyrike. 1603. 8°. 2754
Tethys Festival: or the Queenes Wake. [Masque.] *See* Henry Prince of Wales. The order and Solemnitie. 1610. 4°. . 3071
Verses in Du Bartas. Weekes. 1605–6 *etc.* 2476
— Florio (G.). Queen Anna's New World. 1611. . . 3374
— Guarini (G. B.). Il Pastor Fido. 1602. . . . 2109
— Montaigne (M. de). Essayes. 1613 *etc.* . . . 3375
See Jovius (P.). The worthy tract. 1585.
— Nenna (G. B.). Nennio. 1595
Daniel or O'Domhnuill (William), *abp.* *See* Bible (Irish), N.T. 1602.
See Common Prayer, (Irish). 1608. F°.
Danskin (Henry). Verses *ter* and Address in Adamson (J.). Εἰσόδια. 1618. 5960
— Baron (R.). Philosophia. 1621. *Qu. see also* Dantiscanus? 5997
Danter (John). *See* Middleton (C.). Famous Historie of Chinon of England... 1597. 4°.
Dantiscanus (Henricus). *Qu.* Danskin? Verses in Abernethy (J.). A christian treatise. 1630. 4342
Dantzig *Gymnasium*. *See* Keckerman (B.). Systema ethicæ. 1607.
Danvers (Sir Charles). *See* Bacon (F.). Declaration... 1601.
Danyell (James). *See* D. (J.), *G. and C.C.*
Darby (I.). Verses in Oxf. Univ. Magd. Coll. 1612. . . 5302
Darcie (Abraham). *See* Camden (W.). Annales. 1625.
— Casaubon (I.). The Original of Idolatries. 1624.
Darcy (B.). Verses in Oxf. Univ. Magd. Coll. 1612. . . . 5302
Dariot (C.). Briefe...Introduction to the Astrologicall Judgement of the Starres. (Treatise of Mathematicall Phisicke.) 1598. 4°. 1380
Darling (Thomas). *See* Darrell (John). A detection of that sinnfvl. 1600.
— Harsnett (S.). A discovery. 1599.
Darrell (John). Detection of...Harshnet. 1600. 4°. . . 6829
Treatise of the church. 1617. 4°. 3323
See Deacon (J.) and J. Walker. Summarie Answere.
— Harsnett (S.). Discovery of the Fravdvlent practises. 1599. 4°.
Datus (Augustinus). Super Tullianis elegancijs & verbis exoticis. St Albans. [1479.] 4°. 82
Daungerous Positions. *See* Dangerous.
Dauntsey (John). Verses in Jorden (E.). A discourse. 1633. . 4003
Daus (John). *See* Sleidanus (J.). A famovse Cronicle. 1560.
Davenant (Edward). *See* Letters Patent to Sir A. Aston, I. Auchmoty, R. Harding, and E. D. 1606. 4°. 2595
Davenant (John). Ad fraternam communionem...adhortatio. Cantabrigiae, 1640. 12°. 5837
Determinationes quæstionum. Cantabrigiae, 1634. F°. . 5718
— Ed. 2. Cantabrigiae, 1639. F°. 5804
Expositio...ad Colossenses. Cantabrigiae, 1627. F°. . . 5705
— Ed. 2. Cantabrigiae, 1630. F°. 5715, 7673

No.

Davenant (John), *cont.* Expositio...ad Colossenses. Ed. 3. Cantabrigiae, 1639. F°. 5805
One of the sermons...before Parliament. 1628. 4°. . . 4422
Praelectiones. Cantabrigiae, 1631. F°. 5734
See Carleton (G.). Examination. Ed. 2. 1626.
— Dort Synod. A ioynt attestation. 1626. 4°.
— — Suffragium Collegiale... 1626 etc.
— Durie (J.). De Pace. 1638.
— Hall (Jos.). The Reconciler. 1629.
Davenant (Sir W.). The triumphs of the Prince d'Amour. 1635. 4°. 5147
See Jones (I.). Britannia trivmphans. 1637. 4°.
— — The temple of love. 1634.
Davenport (J.). Apologeticall reply. Rotterdam, 1636. 4°. . . 6659
Royall edict for military exercises. 1629. 4°. 2036
See Paget (J.). An Answer. 1635.
— Preston (J.). The Breastplate. 1630(-1) *etc.*
— — New covenant. 1629 etc. 4°.
— — Saints daily exercise. 1629 *etc.*
— — Saints qvalification. 1634.
Davenport (R.). *See* D. (T.). The bloody banquet. 1620.
Davers (Sir Charles). *See* Danvers.
David Kimchi. Nomina Legis varia ex Chimhio in psal. 119. *See* Ferdinand (P.). Haec sunt. 1597. 4°. 5586
Davidson (John). D. Bancrofts rashnes in rayling. Edinburgh, 1590. 8°. 5924
Davies (David), *M.A.* Verses in Davies (J.). Antiquæ linguæ dictionarium. 1632. 4979
Davies (Edward). Art of war. 1619. 4°. 3931
Davies (John), *poet.* Humours heau'n on earth. 1609. 8°. . 2438
The Scourge of Folly. [1611?] 8°. 2026
The writing schoolemaster. Ed. 16. 1636. Oblong 8°. . 4340
[Eclogues.] *See* Browne (W.). The Shepherds Pipe. 1614. 8°.
— — Wither (G.). The Workes. 1620. 8°.
Verses in Du Bartas. Weekes. 1605–6 *etc.* 2476
— Vaughan (R.). Waterworkes. 1610 *bis.* 3576
— Coryate (T.). Coryates Crvdities. 1611. 3076
— Guillim (J.). A display. 1611 *etc.* . . . . . 3211 *etc.*
— Speed (J.). The theatre. 1611. 3215
— Ravenscroft (T.). A briefe discourse. 1614. . . . 2029
— Napier (J.). A description. 1618. 2112
— Smith (J.). The generall historie. 1624. 3864
— Mercator (G.). Historia. [Portrait of J. Smith.] 1635. . 4637
— Camden (W.). Britannia. 1637. 3055
Davies (Sir John), *attorney-general.* Discoverie...why Ireland was neuer ...subdued. 1612. 4°. 2777
New post. n.d. 8°. 4138
Le primer report des Cases...en Ireland. Dublin, 1615. F°. . 6016
— Stationers. 1628. F°. 3299
See Bacon (F.). A declaration... 1601.
— D. (Sir I.), Kt.
Davies (John), *lexicographer.* Antiquae linguae britannicae...Latinae, dictionarium... 1632. F°. 4979
See Bible (Welsh). 1620. F°.
Davies (Ric.), *Bp.* Funerall sermon...Walter Erle of Essex. 1577. 4°. 1416
See Bible, English (Bishops'). 1568. 964
— — Welsh. 1620. F°.
— — — (N.T.). 1567.
Davies (Robert), *of Flintshire.* *See* Gerard (J.). The Herball. 1633.
Davies (Silvanus). Verses in Vaughan (R.). Waterworkes. 1610. . 3576
Davis (John), *Captain.* *See* Fox (L.). North-west Fox. 1635.
Davison (Francis). Poetical Rapsodie. Ed. 3. 1611. 8°. . 3077

No.
Davity (Pierre). *See* Avity (P. d').
Davy Du Perron (Jacques), *Cardinal.* *See* Du Perron.
Davyes (Robert). *See* Davies.
Dawling (Ric.), *M.A.*, *Christ's.* Verses in Camb. Univ. Voces. 1640. 5836
Dawson (I.). Verses in Oxf. Univ. Horti. 1640. 5499
Day (Angel). *See* Nenna (G. B.). Nennio... 1595.
Day (James). New spring of divine poetrie. 1637. 4°. . . 4650
Day (John). Verses in Wilson (Sir T.). Vita. 1551. . . . 631
Day (John), *printer.* *See* Bullinger (H.). A hundred Sermons. 1561.
— Hutchinson (R.). A faithful declaration. 1560.
Day (John), *divine.* Day's Dyall. Oxford, 1614. 4°. . . 5319
Day's Festivalls. Oxford, 1615. 4°. 5323
Day's descant on Davids Psalmes. Oxford, 1620. 4°. . 5338
Day (Martin). Doomes-day. 1636. 4°. 4021
See W. (H.). Θρηνοικός. 1640.
Day (Matt.), *King's.* Verses in Camb. Univ. Genethl. 1631. . 5731
— — Anthologia. 1632. 5741
— — Fasciae. 1633. 5808
— — Rex redux. 1633. 5748
— — Carmen. 1635. 5770
— — Voces. 1640. 5836
Day (Ric.). Booke of Christian Prayers. J. Day, 1578. 4°. . 852
— Yardly and Short, 1590. 4°. 7383
— [Stationers? 1608.] 4°. 3233
See Testaments of the twelve Patriarchs. 1576. 8°.
Day (Richard), *K.C.C.* Verses in Hippocrates. 1631, 1633. . 5736, 5812
Day (Valentine). Comfortable and heavenly Inquisition. (Funerall of Mrs Neale.) 1618. 8°. 3924
Day (William), *Bp.* Verses in Wilson (Sir T.). Vita. 1551. . 631
— Hippocrates. 1631 *etc.* . . . . 5736 *etc.*
— Camb. Univ. Anthologia. 1632. 5741
— — Carmen. 1635. 5770
See Nowell (A.) and W. Day. True report of...Ed. Campion... 1583.
Dayrel (John). *See* Darrell.
De disciplina ecclesiastica. *See* Tilenus (D.). 1622.
De legato et absoluto principe. Oxonie, 1587. 8°. 5227
De vera differentia regiæ potestatis... *See* Fox (E.), *bp.* 1538.
De vera et genuina I. C....religione. [W. Brewster, Leyden,] 1618. 8°. 6505 A
Deacon (J.). Very godlie...sermon...at Ridlington. 1586. 8°. . 7287
Deacon (J.) and J. Walker. Summarie answere to...Darel. 1601. 4°. 1747
Deane (Drugo), *Jes.* Verses in Dolor. 1625. 5701
— — Epithalam. 1625. 5702
Deane (Edmund). Spadacrene Anglica...Forest of Knaresborow. 1626. 4°. 4232
Deane (Henry). Verses in Camb. Univ. Fasciae. 1633. . . 5808
Deane (Sir Richard). *See* Sictor (J.). Lacrymæ... 1637.
Death of usury. Cambridge, 1594. 4°. 5566
Debt, Imprisonment for. A petition. 1622. 4°. 6932
Decachordon. *See* Watson (W.). A decacordon of ten qvodlibeticall qvestions. 1602.
Decker (John). *See* Deckherr.
Deckherr (Johann). *See* Lydiat (T.). Emendatio. 1609.
Declaration. *See* Knel (T.), *junior.* Declaration of such tempestious, and outragious Fluddes. 1570. 8°.
Declaration 1585–1596. *See* Elizabeth.
1603–1625. *See* James I.
1626–1640. *See* Charles I.
Declaration of the Fathers of the Councell of Trent. *See* Treatise of Christian Renunciation.
Declaration of the ten Commandements. *See* Hooper (J.), *Bp.*

No.

Declinatour and protestation of the...Bishops...Refuted. Edinburgh, 1639. 4°. 5990
Dedicus (Joannes). Questiones moralissime super libros Ethicorum. Oxonie, 1518. 4°. 5217
Dee (J.). General and rare memorials pertayning to...Navigation. 1577. F°. 847
Letter. 1599. 4°. 2335
Parallaticae Commentationis Praxeosq; Nucleus. 1573. 4°. . 836
Προπαιδεύματα Ἀφοριστικὰ...de Præstantibus quibusdam Naturæ virtutibus... *See* Leowitz (C. von). Brevis...ratio ivdicandi genitvras. 1558. 4°.
See Euclid. Elements, trans. H. Billingsley. [1570?]
— Recorde (R.). The Grounde of Artes. 1582 *etc.*
Dee (Tho.). Verses in Camb. Univ. Fasciae. 1633. . . . 5808
— Rex redux. 1633. 5748
Defence of catholikes persecuted in England. Douai, 1630. 8°. . 6588
Defence of contraries. 1593. 4°. 2134
Defence of priestes marriages...agaynst...T. Martin. [1566?] 4°. . 975
Defence of Tabacco. 1602. 4° 2255
Defence of the ecclesiastical discipline ordayned of god...against...Maister Bridges. 1588. 4°. 7324
Defence. Defense of the Ecclesiasticall Regiment in Englande. 1574. 8°. 1478
Defence of the godlie Ministers. 1587. 4°. *See* Fenner (D.). . 6787
Defence of the Ministers' Reasons (Parts i, ii). 1607–8. 4°. . . 6385
— (Part iii.) A dispute. 1608. 4°. 6386
Defensorium. *See* Directorium.
Dekker (Tho.). Villainies discouered. 1616. 4°. 2343
Verses in Taylor (J.). Workes. 1630. 3812
Delafay (M.). Verses in Humphrey (L.). J. Jvelli vita. 1573. . 837
Delaine (Walter). *See* Bible (Lat.). Novum Testamentum. 1540.
Delamain (Richard). Gramelogia or the Mathematicall Ring. 1630. 8°. 4832
Making...of a...Horizontall Quadrant. 1637. 8°. . . 5146
See Oughtred (W.). To the english gentrie. [1632?] 4°.
Delaune (Pierre). *See* Common Prayer (French). 1616. 4°.
Delamothe (G.). The french alphabet. 1639. 8°. . . . 4474
Delawarr (Henry, Lord). *See* Markham (G.). Honour. 1624.
Delft, *English Company of Merchant Adventurers*. *See* Forbes (J.). A Frvitfvll Sermon... 1626.
Deloenus (Galterus). *See* Delaine.
Deloney (Thomas). Proper newe sonet...of Beckles. 1586. F°. . 7364
Demands Joyous. W. de Worde, 1511. 4°. 166
Democritus Junior, *pseud*. *See* Burton (Robert). 1632.
Demonology. 1605. Le Loyer (P.).
Demonstration of...Discipline. *See* Udall (J.). A Demonstration of the trueth... [Anon.] [1588] *etc.*
Demosthenes. Λόγοι ἐκλεκτοί. Cantabrigiae [1640?]. 12°. . 5854
[Orations, Olynthiac & Philippic (Lat.).] Interpr. N. Carr. 1571. 4°. 1411
[Olynthiac Orations (Eng.).] Three orations. Trans. T. Wilson. 1570. 4°. 1409
De Corona. *See* Æschines, Contra Ctesiphontem et D. Pro corona... 1624. 12°.
De pace. (Gr. Lat.) Prælectiones A. Dounæi. 1621. 8°. . 3502
Denakol, *pseud*. *See* Sack met die stucken. 1568. 8°. . . 1459
Deneius (Antonius). *Qu.* Denny? Verses in Cheke (Sir J.). De obitu M. Buceri. 1551. 734
Denham (N.). *See* Hemmingsen (N.). The way of lyfe... 1578.
Denison (John). Christian petitioner. 1611. 4°. 3078
Heavenly banquet. Ed. 2. 1631. 8°. 2038
Sinners acquaintance &c. 1624. 8°. 7622
Denison (Stephen). Doctrine of both the sacraments. 1634. 12°. 4582

No.
Denison (Stephen) *cont.* Exposition vpon II Peter i. 1622. 4°. . 2291
White wolfe. 1627. 4°. 4418
See Bible (Eng.). Concordance. (Cotton.) 1622.
Denmark. 1626. *See* B. (S.). An excellent...discourse.
Denmark, *Church of.* *See* Calvin (J.). A faythfull treatise. [1550?]
Denny (Antony). *See* Deneius.
Denny (Charles), *K.C.C.* Verses in Camb. Univ. Dolor. 1625. . 5701
— Epithalamium. 1625. 5702
Denny (W.), *Esq. Serg. Ma.* Verses in Du Praissac. The art of warre. 1639. 5834
Dent (Arthur). Learned...exposition vpon the Lords Prayer. 1613. 12°. 3742
Plaine mans Pathway to Heauen. 1605. 8°. 1384
— Ed. 25. 1640. 12°. 5011
Ruine of Rome. 1607. 4°. 2762
Sermon of repentance. 1588. 8°. 2046
— 1613. 8°. 3649
Dent (Dan.), *Regal.* Verses in Camb. Univ. Lacrymæ. 1619. . 5689
— Dolor. 1625. 5701
— Hippocrates. 1631, 1633. . . . . . 5736, 5812
Deodatus (Charles). Verses in Camdeni Insignia. 1624. . . 5346
Depup (Jo.). Verses in Baret (J.). An alvearie. 1573. . . 7249
Depup (T.), *B.A.*, *S.J.C.* Verses in Camb. Univ. Voces. 1640. . 5836
Derby Almanack. *See* Allestree (R.). Allestree. 1640.
Derby (Margaret, countess of Richmond and). *See* Richmond (Margaret, countess of).
Derendel (Pet.). True and lyuely historyke purtreatures of the woll bible. J. de Tournes, Lyons, 1553. 8°. 6407
Derham (Rob.). Verses in Camb. Univ. Genethliacon. 1631. . 5731
— Anthologia. 1632. 5741
Dering (E.). Certaine godly and verie comfortable letters. [159–?] 8°. 6819
Sermon...before the Quenes maiestie. 25 Feb. 1569. 8°. 7233, 7723
Sermon...11 Dec. 1569. 158[4]. 8°. 1357
Short catechisme for housholders. 1614. 8°. . . . 2781
XXVII Lectures...to the Hebrues. 1576. 4°. 1573
— 1577. 4°. 7282
Derricke (J.). Image of Irelande. 1581. 4°. 863
Desainliens (C.). De pronuntiatione linguæ gallicæ. 1580. 8°. 1541, 1542
French Littelton. 1566. 16°. . . . . . See p. 1733
Italian Schoolemaister...Arnald and Lucenda. Ed. 2. 1597. 8°. 1379
Description and Confutation of Antichrist the Familist. [1606?] 4°. 6866
Description of Britain. 1480. *See* Higden (R.).
Description. Discription of what God hath predestinated. 1620. *See* Murton (J.).
Desiderius. [Speculum religiosorum (*hibernicé*).] Ed. F. Conroy. Louvain, 1616. 8°. 6427
Desmarets de Saint Sorlin (Jean). *See* Ariane. Ariana. Translated out of the French. 1636. F°.
Destruction of Jherusalem. Pynson [15–]. 4°. 296
Dethick (Gilb.). Verses in Oxf. Univ. Horti. 1640. . . . 5499
Dethick (Henry). Verses in Stanyhurst (R.). Harmonia. 1570. . 749
— Castiglione (B.). De Curiali. 1571. 824
See Hill (T.). The Gardeners Labyrinth. 1608.
Dethyccus (H.). *See* Dethick.
Deus. Deus et Rex. 1615. *See* James I.
Devereux (Leicester), *T.C.C.* Verses in Camb. Univ. Συνωδία. 1637. 5790
Devereux (Robert), second earl of Essex. *See* Essex (Robert Devereux, earl of).
Devon and Cornwall, *Ministers of.* Remoouall of certaine imputations laid upon the ministers of Devon & Cornwall. 1606. 4°. . 6472
See Defence of the Ministers... 1607.

No.

Devon and Cornwall *cont.* *See* Hutton (T.). Reasons. 1605.
— — The second and last part. 1606.
Devout Psalms. *See* Psalms.
Dewhurst (Robert). Verses in Stanyhurst (R.). Harmonia. 1570. 749
Dialect, *Somerset.* *See* Ravenscroft (T.). A brief discourse... [ad fin.]. 1614.
Dialling. *See* Fale (T.). 1593.
Dialogue or familiar talke betwene two neighbours. 'Roane,' 20 Feb. 1554. 8°. 6243
Dialogue betwene a knighte and a clerke. *See* Ockham (W.).
Dialogue wherein is plainly laide open, the tyrannicall dealing of L. Bishopps. [1589.] 8°. 1917
— — 1640. 7054
Dialogue. *See* Saint Germain (C.). The fyrste dyaloge... 1531.
— — The Dialoges... 1569 etc.
— — Dialogus de fundamentis... 1528.
— Menewe (G.). A confutation. [1555?] 16°.
— — A plaine subversion. [1555?] 16°.
— New Dialoge. 1548.
— Watson (W.). Dialogve betwixt a secvlar priest, and a lay gentleman... 1601.
Dialogues. Here be .vij. Dialogues. The fyrst is of the Sōne and of the Moone. R. Wyer, n.d. 8°. 547
Dialogues in English. *See* Saint Germain (C.). The Dyaloges. 1569.
Dialogues. Dialoges of creatures moralysed. Pawlys Churche yarde. [Antwerp, ab. 1534.] 4°. 6093
Dialogus. Dialogus de fundamentis legum Anglie. 1528. *See* Saint Germain (C.).
Dice Play. *See* Walker (G.). A manifest detection. [15– .]
Dicher (George). [Latin verses translated.] *See* Du Bartas. Divine Weekes etc. 1633. F°. p. 647. 7847
Dickinson (Edmund). Verses in Camb. Univ. Lacrymæ. 1619. . 5689
Dickson (Alex.). De vmbra rationis & iudicij...Prosopopœia. 1583. 8°. 1552
See P. (G.), *Cantabrigiensis.* Antidicsonus. 1584. 8°. . . 1649
Dickson (David). A short explanation of...the Hebrewes. Aberdeen, 1635. 8°. 6006
Verses in Adamson (J.). Εἰσόδια. 1618. 5960
— Sempill (Sir J.). Sacrilege. 1619. 3331
Dictes or sayings of the philosophers. Caxton, 1477. F°. . . . 1
— Ed. 3. Caxton, '1477' [1490]. F°. 36
— W. de Worde, 1528. 4°. 196
Dictionary. Polyglot. (Lat.-Eng.-French.) *See* Estienne (R.). Dictionariolum. 1552. 736
See Baret (J.). An Alvearie. 1580.
— Calepinus (A.). Dictionarium. Lugd., 1585. F°.
— — Geneva, 1620. F°.
— — Basileae, 1627. F°.
— Junius (A.). The Nomenclator. 1585.
— Minsheu (J.). Ἡγεμων. 1617 *etc.*
— Barlement (N.). Colloquia. 1631.
— Alabaster (W.). Spiraculum. 1633.
— Thorndike (H.). Epitome Lexici. 1635.
Arabick-English. *See* Perceval (Richard). A Dictionarie in Spanish and English etc. 1599, 1623.
— Muhammad. Mohammedis Imposturæ. 1615.
— Thorndike (H.). Epitome. 1635.
Dutch-English. *See* Vocabulary. Den grooten vocabulaer. 1639.
English. *See* Cockeram (H.). The english dictionarie. 1626 *etc.*
English-Latin. *See* Promptorius. 1499 *etc.* F°. 108
Eng.-French-Lat. *See* Estienne (R.). Dictionariolum. 1552. 736

No.
Dictionary. English-Latin *cont.* *See* Withals (J.). A shorte dictionarie. 1586 *etc.*
See Thomas (T.). Dictionarium. 1620.
Dictionarie. 1623. 12°. 4774
See Holyoake (F.). 1640.
English-Spanish. *See* Perceval (P.). 1599, 1623.
French-Eng.-Lat. Estienne (R.). Dictionariolum. 1552. . 736
French-English. *See* Cotgrave (R.). A dictionarie. 1611.
Greek-Latin. *See* Crespin (J.). Lexicon. 1581.
— Camden (W.). Institutio. 1604.
— Scapula (J.). Lexicon. 1619. 7836
— — 1637.
Hebrew-English. *See* Martinius (P.). 1593.
— Thorndike (H.). Epitome. 1635.
Italian-English. *See* Florio (J.). A Worlde. 1598 *etc.*
Latin-English. *See* Ortus vocabulorum. 1528.
— Lily (W.). A shorte introdvction...
— Elyot (Sir T.). Bibliotheca. 1548 *etc.*
See Cooper (T.), *bp.* Thesaurus. 1565 *etc.*
— Thomas (T.). Dictionarium. 1587(8) *etc.*
— J. (W.). Dictionariolum. 1638.
— Holyoake (F.). 1640.
(*Abridgment*). *See* H. (J.). An abridgement. 1634.
Latin-English-French. Estienne (R.). Dictionariolum. 1552. 736
Latin-Greek-English. *See* Morelius (Gul.). 1583.
— Thomas (T.). Dictionarium. 1596.
Latin (Mediæval). *See* Spelman (Sir H.). Archæologvs. 1626.
Latin Synonyms. *See* Garlandia (J. de). Synonyma. 1494.
— Pelegromius (S.). Synonymorum sylva. 1603 etc.
Law. *See* Rastell (J.). Expositiones. 1527.
— — Exposition of certaine...words. 1592 *etc.*
— Cowell (J.). The Interpreter. 1607 *etc.*
— Les Termes. 1629, 1636.
Moorish-English. *See* Perceval (Richard). A Dictionarie in Spanish and English *etc.* 1599, 1623.
Mystical. *See* Alabaster (W.). Spiraculum Tubarum. [1633?]
Rabbinic. *See* Thorndike (H.). Epitome. 1635.
Spanish-English. Perceval (R.). A dictionarie. 1599, 1623.
Syriac. Thorndike (H.). Epitome. 1635.
Welsh-Latin. Davies (J.). Antiquæ linguæ britannicæ...dictionarium. 1632.
Dietary of ghostly helthe. W. de Worde, 20 Nov. 1520. 4°. . . 181
Dietrich (Veit) or Vitus Theodorus, *of Nürnberg*. *See* Eobanus (H.). Psalterivm. 1581.
Dietrich von Nieheim. *See* Clemangiis (N. de). Specvlvm... 1606.
Digby (Everard). His dissuasive. [Before 1597.] 4°. . . . 2190
Theoria Analytica. 1579. 4°. 1500, 1501
See Temple (W.). F. Mildapetti. 1580.
— — Pro Mildapetti de vnica methodo. 1581.
Digby (George), earl of Bristol. *See* Bristol (George Digby, earl of).
Digby (Kellam). [Name inserted in title.] *See* Digby (Everard). Theoria Analytica. 1579. 4°.
Digby (Sir Kenelm). *See* Hakewill (G.). An apologie. 1635.
— Jonson (B.). Workes. Vol. 2. 1640. F°.
Digestum. *See* Justinianus.
Digges (Sir Dudley). Defence of trade. 1615. 4°. 3108
Verses in Horne (C.). In obitum Whitakeri. 1596. . . . 7332
— Coryat (T.). Coryats Crudities. 1611. 3076
See Digges (T.). Foure Paradoxes. 1604.
Digges (Dudley), M.A. Verses in Chaucer (G.). Amorvm. 1635. 5414

No.

Digges (Dudley), M.A. *cont.* Verses *bis* in Sandys (G.). A paraphrase. 1638. 4736
See Digges (T.). Nova Corpora. 1634.
Digges (L.). Arithmeticall Militare Treatise, named Stratioticos. 1579. 4°. 1502
— 1590. 4°. 2225
Boke named Tectonicon. 1562. 4°. 1238
— 1605. 4°. 2936
— 1614. 4°. 2986
— 1634. 4°. 3050
Geometrical Practise, named Pantometria. 1571. 4°. . . 1471
— 1591. F°. 2105
Prognostication. 1555. 4°. 1236
— 1564. 4°. 1212
Verses in Aleman (M.). The Rogve. 1623, 1630. . . 4079, 5427
— Shakspeare (W.). Comedies, &c. 1623. 3972
— Poems. 1640. 4681
Digges (T.). Alæ sev Scalæ Mathematicæ. 1573. 4°. . . 1222
Foure Paradoxes. 1604. 4°. 2472
Nova corpora regularia... 1634. 4°. 4009
See Bradshaw (W.). Humble motives... 1601.
— Coignet (Sir M.). Politique discourses. 1586.
— Dee (J.). Parallaticae Commentationis. 1573.
— Digges (L.). An Arithmeticall Militare Treatise. 1579. 4°.
Dike (Daniel). *See* Dyke.
Dikson (David). *See* Dickson.
Dillingham (Francis). Disputatio brevis...de duabus quæstionibus. Cantabrigiæ, 1602. 8°. 5609
Disputatio de natura poenitentiae. Cantabrigiæ, 1606. 8°. . 5635
Godly...sermon conc. the magistrates dutie. Cambridge, 1605. 8°. 5630
Golden Keye. 1609. 8°. 3318
Progresse in pietie. Cambridge, 1606. 8°. 5636
Quartron of reasons. Cambridge, 1603. 4°. 5614
Tractatus brevis. Cantabrigiae, 1603. 8°. 5613
See Bible, English (Royal). 1611.
Dingley (R.). Verses in Oxf. Univ. Horti. 1640. . . . 5499
Dinham (William). *See* Dynham.
Dinoth (Richard). *See* Polemon (J.). All the famous Battels... 1587.
Diocles, *Carystius.* Epystle of Diocles vnto king Antigonus. *See* Petrus *Hispanus.* The treasury. [1550.]
Diogenes Laertius. [Lives and Answers.] *See* Baldwin (W.). A Treatise of Morall Philosophy.
Diomedes, *Grammarian.* *See* Whittington (R.). Editio. 1516.
Dionysius Carthusianus, *otherwise* de Leewis, or Rikel. [De quattuor novissimis rebus]. *See* Cordiale. 1479.
Mirroure of golde for the synfull soule. W. de Worde, 1522. 4°. 185
— J. Skot, 1522. 4°. 356
Dionysius *Periegetes.* Περιήγησις. Etonae [ab. 1615]. 8°. . . 5906
— In usum Eton. Cantabrigiae, 1633. 8°. 5809
Diotrephes. The state of the Church of England. 1588? *See* Udall (J.).
Diplodophilus, *pseud.* *See* Digby (E.).
Direction to be observed. 1636. *See* Knott (E.).
Directorium Sacerdotum (C. Maidstone). W. de Worde, 1495. 4°. . 43
(W. Clerke's revision). [1499.] 4°. 62
Directorium or Pica. 1530. 8°. 6157
Discipline. *See* Defence of the ecclesiastical Discipline. 1588. 4°. 7324
The first and second booke of Discipline. 1621. 4°. . . 6503
Svrvay of the pretended Holy Discipline. 1593. 4°. *See* Bancroft (R.).
See Tilenus (D.). Paraenesis. 1620.
— — De disciplina. 1622.
Disclosing of the Canon of the Popysh Mass, with a Sermon of Luther. 'Hans hitpricke' [1549?]. 8°. 6702

No.

Discourse upon...France. 1588. *See* Hurault (M.).
See Valtellina... 1628.
Discourses. *See* Copies of Certaine discourses. . . . 7360
Discourses of War. *See* Logue (B. de). Discourses. 1631.
Discoverie of a gaping gulf. *See* Stubbs (J.).
Discovery of a World in the Moone. 1638. *See* Wilkins (J.).
Displaying. *See* Huggard (M.). The displaying of the Protestantes. 1556.
Disputation of the Church. 1640. *See* Stratford (E.).
Dispute against the english-popish ceremonies. 1637. 4°. *See* Gillespie (G.).
Dispute upon the question of kneeling. *See* Defence of the Ministers Reasons [Pt iii.]. 1608.
Dissertatio brevis,...periculum...Angliae, Galliae, & reliquis. 1626. 4°. 6970
Ditchfield ( ). Considerations touching...Tobacco. 1625. 4°. . 6967
Divers frutful gatherynges of scripture and declarynge of fayth. R. Redman, n.d. 8°. 390
Divers Ghostly Matters. *See* Horologium Sapientie. [1490?]
Diversité de courtz. *See* Fitzherbert (Sir A.).
Diversities of Courtes. 1561. 8°. *See* Narrationes, Novae narrationes.
Dives and Pauper. *See* Parker (H.).
Divine and politike observations newly translated. (By Theophilus.) 1638. 4°. 6368
Dobree (P. P.). [ms. Notes in] Bible N.T. (Greek). 1632. 8°. . 5798
Dochen (Tho.). Verses in Oxf. Univ. Magd. Coll. 1612. . . 5302
— Holyoake (F.). Dictionarium. 1640. 3058
Doctor and Student. *See* Saint Germain (C.). The dialoges.
Doctrina et Politia Ecclesiae. 1617. *See* Mocket (R.).
Doctrinal of Sapience. Caxton [1489–91]. F°. 35
Doctrine of the Bible. 1616. 12°. 3415
— *See also* Way to true happiness.
Dod (H.). Certaine Psalmes of David. 1603. 8°. 1902
See D. (H.). A Godlie and fruitfull treatise. 1583.
Dod (John). Remedy against privat contentions. 1610. 4°. . . 2964
Verses in Camb. Univ. Lacrymæ. 1619. 5689
— Dolor. 1625. 5701
See Sibbs (R.). Bowels opened. 1639. 4°. 7824
Dod (J.) and R. Cleaver. Plaine and familiar exposition of Prov. ix, x. 1606. 4°. 1616
— Proverbs xv–xvii. 1611. 4°. 2968
— Ten Commandments. 1630. 4°. 1892
— — Ed. 18. 1632. 4°. 4844
Ten sermons. 1610. 4°. 3210
See Cleaver (R.). Godly forme of houshold gouernment. 1630. 8°.
Doddridge (Sir John). Compleat parson. 1630. 4°. 4194
English Lawyer. 1631. 4°. 5074
History of...Wales...Cornewall, and...Chester. 1630. 4°. . 3985
Lawyers Light. 1629. 4°. 4958
Dodington (Bart.). Verses in Jewel (J.). Adv. Thomam Hardingum. 1578. 1535
— Baro (P.). ...in Jonam. 1579. 850
— Digby (E.). Theoria. 1579. 1500
— Camden (W.). Britannia. 1586 *etc.* . . . . 1324 *etc.*
See Demosthenes...Olynthiacæ Orationes... 1571.
— Crespin (J.). Lexicon. 1581.
Dodoens (Rembert). A niewe herball. Trans. H. Lyte. Antwerp, 1578. F°. 6130
A new herball. N. Newton, 1586. 4°. 2107
— E. Bollifant. 1595. 4°. 2051
— E. Griffin. 1619. F°. 3932
Rams little Dodeon. Trans. H. Lyte. 1606. 4°. . . . 2886
Dodonæus. *See* Dodoens (Rembert).

No.
Doetecum (Jan van). *See* Most strange and wonderfull Herring. 1598.
D'oiley (Ol.), *K.C.* Verses in Camb. Univ. Συνωδία. 1637. . . 5790
Dolce (Lodovico). *See* Mexia (P.). The historie. 1604.
Doleman (Robert), *pseud.* *See* R. Parsons.
Dolman (John). *See* Cicero. [Tusculanæ Disputationes.] 1561. 8°.
— Higgins (J.). A mirrour. 1610.
Dominici (Dominicus). De cardinalium legitima creatione. *See* Dominis (M. A. de). De republica ecclesiastica, lib. iv., appendix. 1617. F°.
Dominis (Marco Antonio de). De republica ecclesiastica. 1617. F°. [*See Corrigenda*, p. 1738.] 3476
— Pars 2. 1620. F°. 3498
Alter Ecebolius. Ed. R. Neyle. 1624. 4°. 3517
His shiftings in religion. 1624. 4°. 3518
Manifestation of the motiues. (Decretum.) 1616. 4°. . . 3469
Papatus romanus. 1617. 4°. 3477
Rockes of christian shipwracke. 1618. 4°. 3487
Second manifesto. Trans. M. G. K. Liége, 1623. 4°. . 6431
Sermon...in the Mercers Chappel. 1617. 4°. . . . 3475
Suae profectionis consilium exponit. (Decretum.) 1616. 4°. 3468
— Edinburgh, 1617. 4°. 5958
See A. (C.). Monsig^r. fate voi. 1617. 4°.
— Crakanthorp (R.). Defensio. 1625.
— Lohetus (D.). Sorex Primvs. De Republica Ecclesiastica. 1618.
— Montagu (R.). Immediate addresse. 1624.
— Sarpi (P.). Historia del Concilio Tridentino. 1619.
— — (Lat.). 1620.
Dominus que pars. [Ab. 15– .] 4°. *See* 6074.
Donatists. *See* Brownists.
Donatus cum Remigio. *See* no. 7696.
Donatus devotionis. J. Rastell. [15– .] 8°. 348
Dondolus (Sigismondus), *de Pistorio.* *See* Henry VIII. Divino implorato. [1530.]
Done (John). Polydoron. 1631. 12°. 4609
See Aristeas. The Auncient History of the Septuagint... 1633. 8°.
Dones (John). Verses in Coryate (T.). Coryates Crvdities. 1611. . 3076
Donne (George). Verses in Massinger (P.). The great dvke. 1636. 4137
Donne (John), *dean.* Devotions vpon emergent occasions. 1624. 12°. 4523
LXXX Sermons. 1640. F°. 4331
Encænia. 1623. 4°. 4517
Ignatius his Conclave...Apology for Jesuites. 1611. 12°. . 3637
— 1621. 12°. 4233
— 1634. 12°. 4136
Juvenilia. 1633. 4°. 4103
Poems. 1633. 4°. 4267
— 1635. 8°. 4284
Psevdo-martyr. 1610. 4°. 3068
— *See* Fitzherbert (T.). A supplement. 1613.
Sermon...at Whitehall, 24 Febr. 1625. 1626. 4°. . . . 7513
Sermon of...Lady Danvers...with other commemorations...by G. Herbert. 1627. 12°. 4807
Sermon vpon Judges xx. 15. 1622. 4°. 3141
Sermon vpon Acts i. 8...to the...Virginian Plantation. 1622. 4°. 4505
Six sermons. Cambridge, 1634. 4°. 5760
Verses in Coryat (T.). Coryats crudities. 1611. . . 3076
— Camdeni Insignia. 1624. 5346
Donne (John), *the younger.* *See* Donne (J.), *dean.* LXXX Sermons.
Donters (C.). *See* Donthers.
Donthers (Cornelis). [Prayer.] *See* Manual of Prayers, p. 25. 1589. 16°.
Dorcaster (Nicholas). *See* Confession. 1553. 8°. 6720
Dorchester (Dudley Carlton, viscount). *See* Carleton.

No.
Dorington (Jo.), *K.C.C.* Verses in Camb. Univ. Epithalam. 1625. . 5702
Dorislaus (Isaac). Prœlium Nuportanum. 1640. 4°. . . 4396
Dorman (Thomas). Disproufe of M. Nowelles reproufe. Antwerp, 3 Dec. 1565. 4°.. 6114
— *See* Jewel (J.). A Confutation. [With text.] 1567.
See Nowell (A.). A reprovfe. 1568.
Dormont. *See* Briefe discourse. 1599.
Dornavius (Caspar). Verses in Camden (W.). Britannia. 1637. . 3055
Dorotheus, *Bp of Tyre.* [Eccl. Hist.] *See* Eusebius Pamphili. The avncient...histories. 1577 *etc.*
Dorpius (Martinus). *See* Æsop. Fabulæ. 1635.
Dorset (Thomas Sackville, earl of). Verses in Castiglione (B.). The covrtyer. 1561. 923
See Castiglione (B.). B. Castilionis Comitis De Curiali. 1571 *etc.*
— Higgins (J.). A mirrour. 1610.
— Wake (I.). Rex Platonicvs... 1607.
[Funeral.] *See* Abbot (G.). A sermon. 1608. 4°.
Dort, Synod of. A ioynt attestation...that the church of England was not impeached. 1626. 4°. 4234
Judgement of the synode holden at Dort. 1619. 4°. . . 3494
Suffragium Collegiale theologorum Magnae Britanniae. 1626. 4°. 4964
— (Gratia discriminans.) 1627. 4°. 4238
— 1633. 8°. 4268
See Carleton (G.). An examination...Wherevnto...is annexed a Joynt Attestation. 1626.
— Robinson (J.). A defence... 1624.
Douai, *English College.* *See* Bible (Eng.) O.T. 1609–10 *etc.*
— N.T. (Rhemes version). 1600.
Douai, *College of S. Gregory.* *See* Benedict, Saint, Order of. (Douai.) 1625?
Doughty (John). A discourse. Oxford, 1628. 4°. . . . 7813
Douglas, *monk of Glastonbury.* *See* Chronicles of England. . 1480 *etc.*
Douglas (Alexander). Verses in Adamson (J.). Εἰσόδια. 1618. . 5960
Douglas (Gawin). The palis of Honoure. [1553?] 4°. . . 1086
See Vergilius. Æneid. 1553. 4°.
Douglas (George). Verses in Adamson (J.). Εἰσόδια. 1618. . . 5960
Douglas (N.). *See* Rapta Tatio. 1604.
Dounaeus (Andreas). *See* Downes.
Dounaeus (Robert). *See* R. Downy.
Dousa (Jan), *the elder.* Verses in Harvey (G.). Gratulationum. 1578. 1495
— Lipsius (J.). De constantia. 1586. 7295
— Whetstone (G.). The honovrable. 1586. 6495
— Whitney (G.). A choice. 1586. 6496
Dousa (Jan), *the younger.* Verses in Whetstone (G.). The honovrable. 1586. 6495
Douza (Jan). *See* Dousa.
Dove and the Serpent. 1614. 4°. *See* T. (D.).
Dove (John). Advertisement to the English seminaries. 1610. 4°. 3633
Confutation of atheisme. 1605. 4°. 2016
Conversion of Salomon. 1613. 4°. 3094
Defence of church government. 1606. 4°. 2740
Of Divorcement. A sermon. 10 May 1601. 1601. 8°. . 2730
Sermon at Paules Crosse. 6 Feb. 1596. 1597. 8°. . . 2723
Verses in Holyoake (F.). Dictionarium. 1640. . . 3058
Dove (Thomas). *See* Certaine demandes. 1605.
Dow (Christopher). Discourse of the sabbath and the lords day. 1636. 4°. 4295
— Ed. 2. 1636. 4°. 4296
Innovations unjustly charged. 1637. 4°. 4307
Dowland (John). Verses in Ravenscroft (T.). A briefe discourse. 1614. 2029
Down and Connor, *Diocese of.* [Visitation 1638.] *See* Leslie (H.). Examen. 1639.

No.

Down and Connor, *Diocese of*, *cont.* *See* Leslie (H.). A speech. 1638.
Downame. *See* Downham.
Downe (John). Certaine treatises. Oxford, 1633. 4°. . . . 5399
Treatise of...iustifying faith. Oxford, 1635. 4°. 5415
See Hakewill (G.). An apologie. 1630.
Downes (Andrew). Verses in Cambridge Lachrymae. 1587. . 7356
— Horne (C.). In obitum Whitakeri. 1596. 7332
— Barlow (W.). Vita R. Cosin *bis.* 1598. 1707
— Greenham (R.). Workes. 1599 *etc.* . . . . 2912 *etc.*
— Whitaker (W.). Praelectiones. 1599. 5598
— Camb. Univ. Thr-thr. *bis.* 1603. 5616
— — Epicedium *bis.* 1612. 5665
— — Lacrymæ. 1619. 5689
— — Dolor. 1625. 5701
— — Epithalamium *bis.* 1625. 5702
See Bible, English (Royal). 1611.
— Chrysostom...opera... 1613.
— Demosthenes. Prælectiones. 1621. 12°.
— Lysias. Eratosthenes. 1593.
Downham (George). Abstract of the duties...and sinnes. 1635. 8°. 3051
Answere to a Sermon. 1609. 4°. 6878
Apostolicall Injunction. 1639. 4°. 3722
Christian arte of thriving. 1620. 4°. 3008
Christians sanctuarie. 1604. 4°. 2434
Covenant of grace. Dublin, 1631. 4°. 6036
Defence of the sermon...at the consecration of the Bishop of Bath and Welles. 1611. 4°. 2747
Funerall sermon...of...Sir P. Boteler. 1607. 8°. . . . 2947
Godlie and learned treatise of prayer. (The doctrine of prayer.) Cambridge, 1640. 4°. 5838
Papa antichristus. 1620. 4°. 3499
Replye answering a defence. 1613–4. 4°. 6501
Sermon defending...Bishops. 1608. 4°. 2487
— *See below.* Two Sermons. 1608.
Treatise concerning Antichrist. 1603. 4°. 2468
Treatise vpon Iohn 8. 36. 1609. 4°. 2953
Two sermons. 1608. 4°. 2951
See Baynes (P.). The Diocesans Tryall. 1621. 4°.
— Christopherson (M.). A treatise. 1614.
— Jacob (H.). An Attestation. 1613. 8°.
Downham (John). Briefe concordance to the Bible. 1630. 8°. . 2563
Christian Warfare. Ed. 3. 1612. 4°. 2977
— Ed. 4. 1634(–3). F°. 7496
Summe of sacred divinitie. [1630?] 4°. 3174
See Bible (Eng.). Concordance. 1632.
— Downham (G.). A godly...treatise... 1640.
— Sutton (T.). Lectures. 1632.
Downinge (Calybute). Discourse of the state ecclesiasticall. Oxford, 1633. 4°. 7662
— Ed. 2. Oxford, 1634. 4°. 5440
Downy (Alexander). Verses in Forbes (P.). Funerals. 1635. . 6007
Downy (Robert). Verses in Forbes (P.). Funerals. 1635. . . 6007
Dowsing (William). MS notes. *See* nos. 3338, 7101.
Draconites (Johan). *See* Joye (G.). The exposicion of Daniel. 1545.
Drake (Sir Francis). Verses in Gilbert (Sir H.). A true reporte. 1583. 1354
See Hakluyt (R.). The Principall Navigations... 1589 *etc.*
Drake (Ric.). Verses in Camb. Univ. Genethliacon. 1631. . 5731
— — Anthologia. 1632. 5741
— — Fasciæ. 1633. 5808
— — Rex redux. 1633. 5748

No.

Drake (Ric.) *cont.* Verses in Camb. Univ. Carmen. 1635. . 5770
— — Shelford (R.). Five...discourses. 1635. 5774
Dralymont (J. D.), *pseud.* *See* Montlyard (J. de).
Drant (Nevill). *See* Granger (T.). The tree of good and evill. 1616.
Drant (Tho.). Fruitfull and necessary Sermon...concernyng Almes geuing. 1572. [1572?] 8°. 881
The royall guest...Sarum... 1637. 4°. 4466
Three godly and learned sermons. 1584. 8°. 6776
Verses in Neville (A.). Kettvs. 1582. 1318–9
— Lloyd (L.). The pilgrimage. 1586. 1941
— Seton (J.). Dialectica. 1611 *etc.* . . . . 3249 *etc.*
See Horatius. Sermones. 1566. 4°.
Draper (Thomas). Verses in Hodson (W.). The holy Sinner. 1639. 5796
Draxe (Thomas). Calliepeia. Ed. 2. 1613. 8°. 2796
— 1618. 8°. 3488
— 1625. 4°. 3524
— 1631. 8°. 7834
Worldes resurrection. [Ab. 1610.] 4°. 7533
Drayton (Michael). Battaile of Agincourt...The miseries of Queene Margarite...Nimphidia...The Quest of Cinthia &c. Small F°. 4688
Englands heroicall epistles. 1630. 8°. 3175
Muses Elizium. 1630. 4°. 3986
Poems. [1619?] F°. 3128
Polyolbion. 1613. F°. 2518
— Part II. 1622. F°. 4506
Verses in Coryate (T.). Coryates Crvdities. 1611. . . . 3076
— Beaumont (Sir J.). Bosworth-field. 1629. 3040
See Higgins (J.). A mirrour. 1610.
Drayton (Nath.). Verses in Camb. Univ. Epicedium. 1612. . . 5665
Dreadfull Newes: or a true relation of the...Earthquake...at Callabria. 1638. 4°. 3719
Drekin ( ). Almanack & Prognostication. 1619. 8°. . . . 6914
Drelincourt (C.). The roote of romish rites. 1630. 4°. . . 7000
Drenton [*i.e.* Trondhjem]. *See* Most strange and wonderfull Herring. 1598.
Drexelius (Hieremias). Angel-guardian's clock. Rouen, 12°. . . 6263
Considerations...upon Eternitie. Trans. R. Winterton. 1632. 12°. 7789
— Cambridge, 1636. 12°. 5780
Nicetas. Trans. R. S. 1633. 8°. 7016
School of patience. Cambridge, 1640. 12°. 5839
Drontheim. *See* Trondhjem.
Drope (Joh.). Verses in Oxf. Univ. Magd. Coll. 1612. . . . 5302
Drope (Tho.). Verses in Oxf. Univ. Magd. Coll. 1612. . . 5302
Drue (T.). *See* D. (T.). The bloody banquet.
Drummond (William), *of Hawthornden.* Verses in Adamson (J.). Εἰσόδια. 1618. 5960
— Cowper (W.). Pathmos. 1619. 4066
— — Workes. 1629. 3810
— Person (D.). Varieties. 1635. 4365
Drury (Robert), *Jesuit.* *See* C. (W.). The fatall vesper. 1623.
— Goad (T.). The Dolefvll Euen-Song... 1623.
Drywood (George). Verses in Cambridge Lachrymae. 1587. . . 7356
Du (D.), *Tr. Med.* Verses in Owen (J.). Epigrammatum. 1634. 4583
Duarenus (F.). De sacris ecclesiae ministeriis. 1585. 8°. . 2096
Du Bartas (Guillaume de Saluste). Learned summary. Trans. T. L. D. M. P. 1621. F°. 7572
— 1637. F°. 4592
Divine Weekes & Workes. Trans. J. Sylvester. 1605–6. 4°. . 2476
— Ed. 2. 1608. 4°. 2488, 2489
— 1613. 4°. 2519

No.

Du Bartas (Guillaume de Saluste) *cont.* Divine Weekes...with...other workes... 1621. F°. 2535
— 1633. F°. 7847
Bethulians Rescue (Little Bartas). *See* Sylvester (J.). The parliament of vertues royal. [Ab. 1614.] 8°.
Du Bellay (G.). Instructions for the warres. 1589. 4°. . . 2202
Dublin, *Convocation at.* *See* Articles (Ireland, Church). 1615 *etc.*
Diocese. *See* Harris (P.). Excommunication. 1632. 4°.
Du Bosc (Jacques). The secretary of ladies. 1638. 12°. . . 7800
Compleat woman. Trans. N. N. 1639. 4°. 4040
Du Bourg (Adrian). Seauen Articles. *See* Oldenbarneveld (J. van). The true description. 1619.
Du Boys (Jean). *See* Bauderon (B.). Pharmacopoea. 1639.
Ducæus (Fronton). *See* Du Duc.
Du Castel (Christine). *See* Christine de Pisan.
Du Chesne (Joseph). A Breefe Aunswere... Pt 2. *See below.* The true and perfect spagerike *etc.* 1591.
The practise of chymicall, and hermeticall physicke. Trans. T. Timme. 1605. 4°. 2738
True and perfect spagerike preparation of minerals etc. J. Hester, 1591. 8°. 6798
Duck (Arthur). Vita H. Chichele. Oxoniae, 1617. 4°. . . 5328
Ducket (John). Verses in Camb. Univ. Lachrymae. 1587. . 7356
Du Coignet (Pierre). *See* Cotton (P.). Anti-coton. 1611.
Duditius (Andreas). Verses in Canini (A.). Ἑλληνισμος. 1624. . 3150
Dudley (Lady Jane). *See* Bentley (T.). The monvment of Matrones. 1582.
Dudley (Robert), earl of Leicester. *See* Leicester (R. Dudley, earl of).
Dudley (Robert), duke of Northumberland & Earl of Warwick. *See* Northumberland (Robert Dudley, Duke of) & Earl of Warwick.
Du Duc (Fronton) *or* Ducæus. *See* Casaubon (I.). I. Casavboni ad Frontonem Ducæum... 1611.
See Prideaux (J.). Castigatio. 1614.
Duello. *See* S. (J.). The Dvello Or Single Combat. 1610. 4°.
Duels. *See* Bacon (F.).
— Chevalier (G. de). The ghosts. 1624.
— France. Henry IV. An edict... 1609.
— Pvblication... 1613. 4°. 2648
Dufflæus (Cornelius Kilianus). *See* Kilianus.
Dugard (G.), *Sid.* *See* Dugard (W.).
Dugard (Richard). Verses in Camb. Univ. Lacrymae. 1619. . 5689
— — Dolor. 1625. 5701
— — Epithalam. 1625. 5702
— — Genethl. 1631. 5731
— — Carmen. 1635. 5770
Dugard (Thomas). Verses in Camb. Univ. Genethl. 1631. . . 5731
— Anthologia. 1632. 5741
Dugard (Will). Verses in Dolor. 1625. 5701
— Epithalam. 1625. 5702
Dugres (Gabriel). Breve...grammaticæ gallicæ compendium. Cantabrigiae. 1636. 8°. 5781
Du Jon (François). [The apocalypse.] 1594. 4°. 7376
— Cambridge, 1596. 4°. 5581
Sacrorum Parallelorum libri tres. [1588?] 8°. 1715
See Bible. Lat. 1580 etc.
— — Psalms. 1580.
— Bible, Eng. (Genevan, Tonson's Revision). 1602 etc. . 7782 etc.
Du Jon (François), *the younger.* The painting of the ancients. 1638. 4°. 4928

No.

Duke (Gilbert), *Cantabrigiensis*. Verses in Palingenius (M.). Zodyake of Lyfe. 1560 etc. . . . . . . 1257 etc.
Dulce (Lodovico). *See* Dolce.
Dulichius (Hartmann). *See* Coverdale (M.). A worke.
Du Moulin (Pierre). Accomplishment of the prophecies...of...James I. Oxford, 1613. 8°. 5311
Anatomy of Arminianisme. 1620. 4°. 3425
— 1626. 4°. 4965
— 1635. 8°. 4225
Antibarbarian. 1630. 12°. 4432
Boldnesse and confidence of a christian. *See below*, Coales from the altar. 1623. 8°.
Bvckler of the faith. 1620. 4°. 2289
Coales from the altar. Trans. N. M. 1623. 8°. . . . 7526
Comfort of a communicant. *See above*, Coales from the altar. 1623. 8°.
Comfortable instructions. *See above*, Coales from the altar. 1623. 8°.
Conference held at Paris. 1615. 4°. 3378
De monarchia temporali Pontificis Romani. 1614. 8°. . . 3462
Father Cotton...his two and thirtie demands. 1615. 4°. . 3903
Heavenly alarvm. 1622. 8°. 4764
Heraclitus. Trans. R. S(tafford). Oxford, 1609. 12°. . 5291
— — *See* Smith (R.). Munition against mans miserie. 1634. 12°.
Learned treatise of traditions...English by G. C. 1632. 8°. . 4557
Letter. 1621. 8°. 2536
Oppositions of the word of God. Trans. A. S. 1610. 4°. . 7485
Theophilus, or love divine. Trans. R. Goring. 1610. 12°. . 3607
— Newly corr. 1612. 12°. 2512
Waters of Siloe. Trans. I. B. 1612. 8°. 7656
Wittie encounter betweene M. du Moulin and M. de Balzac. 1636. 8°. 4758
See Cotton (P.). Anti-coton. 1611.
— Pattenson (M.). The image. 1623.
Du Moulin (Pierre) *the younger*. Letter of a French Protestant to a Scotishman of the Covenant. 1640. 4°. . . 5022, 5023
Dunæus (Andreas). *See* Downes.
Dunæus (Johannes). *See* Downe.
Dunbar (John). Epigrammaton centuriae sex, decades totidem. 1616. 8°. 4140
Duncombe (Fran.). Verses in Camb. Univ. Fasciae. 1633. . . 5808
Duncon (El.). Verses in Dolor. 1625. 5701
— Epithalam. 1625. 5702
— Anthologia. 1632. 5741
Duns, Joannes, *Scotus*. *See* Lugo (Peregrinus de). Principia. [1506?]
Dunton (John). True journall of the Sally Fleet. 1637. 4°. . . 5165
Du Perron (J. D.). Catholike Moderator. Ed. 2. 1623. 4°. . 3513
— Ed. 3. 1623. 4°. 3514
Discourse of the conference holden before the French king.
— 1600. 4°. 2012
— 1601. 4°. 2253
Reply...to the answeare of the...king. Tom. 1. Douai, 1630. F°. 6608
See Casaubon (I.). Responsio. 1612.
— — The answere. 1612. 4°.
— Dominis (M. A. de). De republica.. 1617- .
— E. (O.). A briefe replie. 1600.
— James I. Declaration dv Serenissime Roy... 1615.
— — [Latin.] Declaratio. 1616.
— — [English.] A remonstrance... 1619.
— O. (E.). A detection. 1602.
— Parsons (Robert). A treatise of three conversions.
— Widdrington (R.). Last reioynder. 1619 *etc.* 4°.

No.

Du Plessis, *French Protestant*. *See* Champney (A.). A treatise. 1616. 4°. 6581
Du Plessis (Armand Jean). *See* Richelieu (Armand Jean Du Plessis, duc de).
Du Plessis (Scipion). The Resoluer. 1635. 12°. 3700
Duport (James). Θρηνοθρίαμβος...Job graeco carmine redditus. Cantabrigiae, 1637. 8°. 5817
 Verses in Cam. Univ. Epithalam. 1625. 5702
 — Genethl. 1631. 5731
 — Anthologia, *bis*. 1632. 5741
 — Fasciae. 1633.. 5808
 — Rex redux, *quater*. 1633. 5748
 — Hippocrates. 1633. 5812
 — Camb. Univ. Συνωδία, *sexies*. 1637. 5790
 — Fuller (T.). Historie of the holy warre. 1639 *etc.* . 5806 etc.
 — Cam. Univ. Voces *ter*. 1640. 5836
 — Randolph (T.). The Jealous Lovers. 1640. . . . 5852
 See Bible, English (Royal). 1611. 2635
Duport (John). Verses in Cam. Univ. Epicedium. 1612. 4°. . 5665
 — Whitaker (W.). Answere to the ten reasons. 1606. 4°.
 — — Responsionis...Edmundus Campianus...Defensio contra Confutationem. 1583.
Du Praissac. Art of warre. Trans. J. Cruso. Cambridge, 1639. 8°. 5834
Du Premier Fait (Laurence). *See* Cicero. De Senectute. 1481.
Duræus (Johannes). *See* Durie (J.).
Durandus. *See* Gataker (T.). Iacobs Thankfvlnesse. 1624.
Durantinus. Conspiracie of Catiline...with...Jugurth. 1557. 4°. . 1005
D'Urfé (Honoré). *See* Urfé.
Durham (Map of). M. Patteson. C. Schuytzer, 1595. F°. . 7736
Durham (Thomas), *cartographer*. *See* Speed (J.). The theatre. 1611.
Durie (John). De pace inter evangelicos procuranda. 1638. 12°. . 4469
 See Davenant (J.). Ad fraternam communionem. 1640.
 — Humphrey (L.). Iesvitismi pars secunda. 1584.
Du Rosier (H.). *See* Vigor (S.). Acts... 1602.
Durward (John). Verses in Adamson (J.). Εἰσόδια. 1618. . . 5960
Dutifull and respective considerations vpon foure severall heads. 1609. 4°. 6519, 6520
Du Vair (Guillaume). Bvckler against adversitie...done into English by A. Court. 1622. 4°. 4169
 Moral philosophie of the Stoicks. Englished by T. James. 1598. 8°. 2907
Duval (A.). *See* Du Moulin (P.). The waters of Siloe. 1612. 8°.
Du Val (M.). Rosa hispani-anglica. 4°.. 6937
Du Verdier (Antoine). *See* Milles (T.). The treasvrie. 1613.
Du Verger (S.). *See* Camus (J. P.). Admirable events. 1639.
Du Voisin (Lancelot), *Sieur de la Popelinière*.
 See Polemon (J.). All the famous Battels... [1577?—]
Duza (Jan). *See* Dousa.
Dwelling Houses. *See* Briefe Declaration... 1636 etc.
Dyer (Sir Jas.). Vn abridgement de touts les cases. 1602. 8°. . 2390
 Nouel cases. 1585. F°. 1145
 Table allieur des Reports. 1588. 8°. 1149
Dyer (James), *the younger*. *See* Dyer (Sir James).
Dyetary. *See* Dietary.
Dygbæius (Everardus). *See* Digby (E.).
Dying. The deyenge creature. W. de Worde, 1514. 4°. . 171
Dyke (Daniel). Workes. Part 1. [1635.] 4°. 7550
 Certaine comfortable sermons. 1616. 4°. 3416
 Comfortable sermons upon the 124 Psalme. 1635. 4°. . . 3831
 Mystery of selfe-deceiving. 1616. 4°. 3908
 — 1633. 4°.. 3191

No.
Dyke (Daniel) *cont.* Two treatises. 1616. 4°. 3909
See Dyke (J.). Divers select Sermons. 1640.
Dyke (Jer.). Divers select sermons. 1640. 8°. 5097
Good conscience. Ed. 6. 1635. 8°. 4586
Mischiefe and miserie of Sandals (*sic*). 1632. 8°. . . . 3187
Righteous mans tower &c. 1639. 8°. 5202
Sermon...at the consecration of the chappell of Epping... 1623. 4°. 3852
Sermon...to the...Parliament. 5 April 1628. 1628. 4°. . . 4337
Sermon...to the Commons... 5 April 1628. 1629. 4°. . 5040
Worthy communicant. 1638. 8°. 5111
— 1640. 8°. 5138
See Dyke (D.). Two Treatises. 1616.
— — The Mystery... 1616 *etc.*
— — Works. 1635. 4°.
Dynham (William). Verses in Powell (E.). Propugnaculum. 1523. 283
See Owein (William). Le Bregement. 1521 *etc.*
Dyos (J.). Sermon... 19 July 1579. 1579. 8°. 858
Dyson ('Henry'). *See* Dyson (Humphry).
Dyson (Humphry). 'Humfridus Dyson Notarius publicus me possidet. 1611.' [Bookmark.] 7234
See Stow (J.). The Survey of London... 1633. 4106

E. (C.), *Jesuit.* *See* Art how to dye well. (A true relation of...Cardinall Bellarmine.) [1623.] 8°.
E. (C.), *Masse-Priest* or *Pseudo-Catholike Priest.* *See* Hall (Jos.), *Bp.* The honor of the Married Clergie. 1620.
E. (D.). Verses in Heywood (T.). Pleasant dialogues. 1637. . 5128
E. (F.). *See* Stratford (E.). A dispvtation. 1629, 1632.
E. (G.), *Practitioner.* *See* Vicary (T.). The Englishmans Treasure. 1626.
E. (I.). The right & iurisdiction of the prelate & the prince. Ed. 2. 1621. 8°. 6584
E. (I.), *Emm. Coll.* Verses in Camb. Univ. Lacrymæ. 1619. . 5689
E. (J.) [*qu.* Earle?]. Verses in Horatius. De arte poetica. 1640. 3728
E. (K.) [=E. Kinsman]. *See* Villegas (A. de). Flos sanctorum. [16– .] 4°.
E. (M.). Verses in Roberts (L.). The merchants mappe. 1638. . 5133
See Prynne (W.). XVI. New Qværes... 1637.
E. (O.). A briefe replie to a libel. 1600. 4°. 2074
E. (O.), *Minister* [*i.e.* M. Sutcliffe]. *See* Parsons (R.). A brief...confvtation. 1603.
— — Treatise of three conversions... 1603 (1604).
E. (R.). Verses in Cambridge Lachrymae. 1587. . . . 7356
E. (S.) [*qu.* Stephen Egerton?]. *See* Rogers (R.). The practice of christianitie. 1618 *etc.*
E. (S.), *chaplain to Richard Smith, bp of Chalcedon.* *See* Featley (D.). Transubstantiation. 1638.
E. (T.). *See* Lawes resolvtion. 1632. 4°.
E. (T.), *Armiger.* Verses in An excellent...discourse. 1626. . 6971
E. (V. M. C. F.). *See* Stratford (E.). A dispvtation. 1632.
Eadmer. Historia novorum. Ed. J. Selden. 1623. F°. . . 3146
Earle (John). Micro-cosmographie. Ed. 5. 1629. 12°. . . 5025
Earls (Jo.). Verses in Hippocrates. 1633. 5812
Earthly (Edward). Verses in Wilson (Sir T.). Vita. 1551. . 631
Earthquake in Calabria. 1638. *See* Dreadful news.
Ease for overseers of the poore. Cambridge, 1601. 4°. . . 5603
East India Company. Petition and remonstrance...exhibited to the... House of Commons. 1628. 4°. 3876
True relation of...Amboyna. 1624. 4°. 2547
See Wilkinson (R.). The stripping of Ioseph... 1625.

No.
East India Company *cont.* *See* East Indies. Netherlands East India Company. Remonstrance. 1632. 3880
East Indies. True relation of that sea fight which two of the East India Shipps had with 4. Portingals. 1622. 4°. 3846
See Acosta (J.). 1604.
— Anglerius (P. M.).
— Conestaggio (G.). The historie of...Portugall... 1600.
— Linschoten (J. H. van). Voyages. 1598.
— Neck (J. van). The Journal. 1601.
— Mun (T.). A discovrse of Trade... 1621.
— Hollanders Declaration. 1622. 4°. 6400
Netherlands East India Company. *See* Netherlands. More excellent observations. 1622. 2034
— Remonstrance. 1632. 4°. 3880
East (Michael). Fourth set of bookes. 1618. 4°. 3420
Sixt set of bookes. 1624. 4°. 3441
Eburne (Richard). Maintenance of the Ministery. 1609. 4°. . 3313
[Sig. E 1.] A sermon. 1613. 4°. 2984
Ecclesiastical Commissioners. *See* Fuller (N.). The argument. 1607.
Ecclesiastical protestant historie of...Rome, ouer...Britanie. 1624. 8°. 6951
Eden (Philip). *See* Proclamation. 1619. Broadside. . . 2806
Eden (Richard). *See* Anglerius (P. M.). The History. 1577.
— Gemini (T.). Compendiosa...Anatomie delineatio. 1559.
Edict. 1609. *See* Combats. 3205
Edinburgh City (Map, 1588). *See* Braun (G.).
The entertainment of...Charles... 15 June 1633. Edinburgh, 1633. 4°. 5972
Edinburgh University. Verses in Adamson (J.). *Εἰσόδια*. 1618. . 5960
Edlin (Phil.). Verses in Camb. Univ. Lacrymæ. 1619. . . 5689
Edmondes (Sir Clement). *See* Cæsar (C. J.). [De bello Gallico.] Observations. 1604. . . . . . . 2471, 7853
— [De bello civili.] Observations. 1609.
Edmondes (T.). *See* King (H.), *bp.* A Sermon. 1621.
Edmonds, *Father, Jesuit, pseud.* *See* Watson (W.).
Edmonds (Henry), *K.C.C.* Verses in Cam. Univ. Genethl. 1631. . 5731
— Hippocrates. 1631, 1633. . . . . . 5736, 5812
Edmund Rich. Myrrour of the chyrche. W. de Worde, 1521. 4°. . 184
Edmundus Vrsulanus, *pseud.* *See* Matthews (F.).
Edrych (G.). In libros aliquot Pauli Aeginetæ. 1588. 8°. . . 1593
Edward, *King*, and Robin Hood. *See* Hood.
Edward II., *King of England.* [Life & death.] *See* Hubert (Sir F.). 1628.
Edward III. [Metrical life.] *See* May (T.). The Victorious Reigne. 1635.
Edward IV. *See* Gulielmus (Laurentius), *de Saona.* 1480. 4°.
Edward VI. Epistola exhortatoria ad pacem... 1548. 4°. . . 728
O Lord...save the Kyng. (Single leaf.) 1549. F°. . . . 778
Genethliacon. *See* Leland (J.). 1543.
[Life.] *See* Hayward (Sir J.). 1630.
[Death.] *See* Knox (J.). A confession. 1554.
See Bellopoelius (P.). De Pace... 1552.
— Official Publications.
— Olde (J.). Acquital or purgation of...Edwarde VI. 1555.
— Philpot (J.). Vera expositio... 1554.
[Privilege.] Thucydides. History. 1550.
— [18 April 1552.] Justinianus. Digestorum. 1553. F°.
Edwards (R.), *Christ's.* Verses in Camb. Univ. *Συνωδία*. 1637. . 5790
Edwards (William). Verses in Camdeni Insignia. 1624. . . 5346
Effigies regum Anglorum. R. Peake. [Ab. 1640.] 8°. . . 3838
Egenolphus (Christianus). Verses in Buchanan (G.). Psalmorum Davidis. 1640. 5209

No.

Egerton (J.). *See* Collection of certain Letters... 1590.
Egerton (Stephen). Briefe methode of catechising. 1615. 8°. . 2278
See Baynes (P.). Helpe to true Happinesse. 1635.
— Greenham (R.). Workes. 1612 (1611). F°.
— Negus (W.). Mans active obedience. 1619. 4°.
— Rogers (R.). Practice of christianitie. 1618 *etc.*
— — Seaven treatises. 1605 *etc.*
— Virel (M.). Learned...Treatise... 1594 *etc.*
Egerton (Sir Thomas). Speech of the Lord Chancellor...in the Eschequer ...touching the Post-nati. 1609. 4°. . . . 3237, 3238
Eglestone ( ). *See* Featley (D.). The Romish Fisher. 1624.
Eglisemmius (Georgius). *See* Eglisham.
Eglisham (George), *M.D.* *See* Barclay (W.). Judicium, De Certamine... pro dignitate Paraphraseos Psalmi CIIII.... 1620.
Egypt. *See* Sandys (G.). A relation. 1627.
Eight learned personages lately converted...from papistrie. 1601. 4°. 1848
Eland (George). *See* Adams (T.). Heaven and earth. 1613. 4°.
Elder (J.). Copie of a letter sent in to Scotlande of the...marryage of... Philippe...to...Marye. [1555.] 8°. 642
Eles (John). Verses in Oxf. Univ. Magd. Coll. 1612. . . 5302
Elias, *Germanus.* *See* Elijah, ben Asher, *the Levite.*
Elijah, ben Asher, *the Levite.* *See* Ferdinand (P.). Hæc sunt verba. 1597.
Eliot (John). Svrvay or topographical description of France. 1592. 4°. 1964
See Loque (B. de). Discourses. 1631.
Elizabeth of Hungary, *Saint.* [Revelations.] *See* Vineis (R. de). [1493?]
Elizabeth, *Queen of England.* Declaration of the fauourable dealing... for...Traitours. 1583. 4°. 1673
Declaration of the causes mooving the qveene...in the lowe Countries. 1585. 4°. 1679, 1680
Declaration of the causes...to prepare a navy. 1596. 4°. . 1704
True report of the...message...where Thomas Appletree should have suffered. 1579. 4°. 1505
[Annales.] *See* Camden (W.). Annales. 1625.
[Prayer Book.] *See* Book of Christian Prayers. 1578.
[Prayers of the Household.] *See* Prayer Book. 1600. 32°.
[Progress.] *See* Somerset (Edward Seymour, duke of). The honorable Entertainment... 1591.
[Succession.] *See* Wentworth (P.). A pithie. 1598.
[Death.] *See* Camb. Univ. Threno-thriambeuticon. 1603. 4°.
— *See* Wright (T.). The passions. 1604.
See Bentley (T.). The monvment of Matrones. 1582.
— Broughton (H.). Letters... [1591?]
— Burghley (W. Cecil, Lord). Carmen Gratulatorium... [1571.]
— C. (R.). The copie of a letter. 1586.
— Hartwell (A.). Regina Litterata. 1565.
— Harvey (G.). Gratvlationvm Valdinensium. 1578.
— Humble Petition of the Communaltie. [158–.]
— Humphrey (L.). Ad Illustrissimam... 1572.
— Stubbs (J.). Discoverie of a gaping gvlf. 1579. 8°.
— Sutcliffe (M.). A True Relation. 1629. 4°.
— Renniger (M.). De Pii qvinti furoribus. 1582.
— Treatise of Treasons. 1572.
Elizabeth, *Princess,* afterwards *Queen of Bohemia.* [Marriage.] *See* Chapman (G.). The memorable maske. [1614?]
See King (J.). Vitis Palatina. 1614.
— Oxford University. Epithalamia. 1613.
— Willet (A.). A treatise. 1612.
— Withers (G.). Epithalamia. 1612.
— Aretius (J.). Primvla Veris... 1613.

No.

Elizabeth, *Princess, cont.* *See* Aurelius (A.). In nuptias. 1613.
— I. (S. R. N.). 1624.
Elizabeth, *Princess; daughter of Charles I.* *See* Camb. Univ. Carmen. 1635. 4°.
Elkin (John). *See* Biddulph (W.). The travels. 1609 *etc.*
Ellenberger (Henry). Verses in L'Obel (M. de). Balsami. 1598. . 2071
Ellesmere (Sir Thomas Egerton, Baron). *See* Egerton (Sir T.), &c.
Ellis (William), *M.A.* Verses in Camb. Univ. *Συνωδία.* 1637. . 5790
Ellithorne (Richard). *See* Redman (J.). A reporte. 1551.
Elmes (Henry). Verses in Contarini (G.). The Commonwealth. 1599. 2153
Elsynge (Henr.). Verses in Camdeni Insignia. 1624. . . 5346
Elton (Edward). Complaint of a sanctified sinner. 1618. 4°. . 3123
Exposition of the...Colossians. Ed. 2. 1620. F°. . . 3009
— Ed. 3. 1637. F°. 3964
Gods holy mind. 1625 (1624). 4°. 4528
Triumph of a true christian. 1623. 4°. 2294
See Brinsley (J.). The Third part of the true watch. 1622(–3). 4°.
— James I. Cygnea Cantio... 1629.
Elvetham, *co.* Hants. *See* Somerset (E. Seymour, duke of). 1591.
Elwes (Sir J.). *See* Niccols (R.). Sir T. Overbvries Vision. 1616.
Ely (Humphrey). Certaine briefe notes upon...the Archpriest. Paris [1603]. 8°. 6199
Elyot (Or.). *See* Elyott.
Elyot (Sir T.). Bibliotheca Eliotae. 1548. Aug. 8. F°. . . . 7086
— By T. Cooper. 1552. F°. 502
— 1559. F°. 505
Boke named the Gouernour. 1531. 8°. 423
— 1544. 8°. 478
— 1546. 8°. 483
— 1553. 8°. 503
— 1557. 8°. . . . . . . 1069 (and Vol. I, p. 240)
Castel of helth. Berthelet, 1541. 4°. 1541. 8°. . . 459, 460
— T. Marshe. 1561. 8°. 1208
Image of Governance. 1541 (1540). 4°. 458
— 1549. 8°. 496
— 1556. 8°. 7140
Of the Knowledg whiche maketh a wise man. 1533. 8°. . 426
Pasquill the playne. 1540. 8°. 454
See Cyprian (St). Swete and devovte Sermon. 1539. 8°.
Elyott (Or.). Verses in Yorke (J.). Union of Honour. 1640. . 5216
Emblems. Fraunce (A.). 1588.
Veen (O. van). Amorum Emblemata. 1608. 4°.
Montenay (G. de). A Booke of armes. Frankfort, 1619. 8°.
Wither (G.). A Collection. 1634–5. F°.
Farley (R.). Lychnocausia. 1638. 8°.
Emley (Laurence), *Magd. Coll. Oxon.* Verses in Coryate (T.). Coryates Crudities. 1611. 3076
En Priscianus. *See* Hawkins (W.). 1632.
Enchiridion. *See* Primer.
Enchiridion Medicum. 16[08]. 8°. 2897
— 1612. 4°. 3644
Enclosures. Proclamation. 1548. F°. 7094
Enderby (Percy). Verses in Yorke (J.). The Union of Honour. 1640. . 5216
Enghelram (Jan). Psevdographia G. Gossenii. 1587. 8°. 2098 and Corrigenda
ENGLAND. Chronicles. *See* Chronicles. 1480. F°. 13
See Fabyan (R.). 1516 *etc.*
— Lanquet (T.). 1549.
— Stow (J.). A Summarie. 1604.
Historie of England. 1602. *See* Clapham (J.).
See Godwin (F.). Annales. 1616.

No.

ENGLAND *cont.* *See* Exchequer.
— Official Publications.
— Privy Council.
Edward III. 'Regis pie memoriæ.' *See* Year Books.
[Henry VIII. Protestation for the Council of Mantua.] *See* Henry VIII. An epistle. 1538.
See Edward VI. 1552.
[Elizabeth.] *See* Humble Petition of the Communaltie. [158- .]
1630. Commission of Grace. *See* Proclamation. . . 7424
ARMY. 1635. *See* Tooke (G.). Legend of Britamart. 1635. 3835
CHURCH. *See* Advertisements. 1584. 4°. 1822
— *See* Articles.
— — Catechism. A short Catechism... 1553.
— — Rogers (T.). The English Creed. 1585–7.
— — The faith... 1607 etc.
Articles (Lat.). *See* Catechism. Catechismus brevis... 1553.
[Bishops' Book.] *See* Institution of a Christian Man. 1537.
Bishops. *See* England. Parliament. Certaine articles... 1572.
— *See* Exhortation to the Byshops... [1572.]
See Very lively Portrayture... 1640.
— Canons. (Eng. and Lat.)
Canterbury Province. *See* Constitutions. 1597.
— — Articles.
— — Certaine considerations...ad informandum animum... Episc. Wigorn. [G. Babington.] 1605.
— — Constitutions... 1604 etc.
Catechism. *See* Catechism.
— — Mayer (I.). The English Catechisme. 1623 *etc.*
— — Reeve (Edm.). The Communion Book Catechisme... 1636.
Constitutiones. *See* Lyndwood (W.). Provinciale. 1501 *etc.*
Constitutions. *See* Constitutions.
Convocation. *See* Convocation. 1604.
See Dort, Synod of. Suffragium. 1626.
— Ecclesiastical Commissioners. 1607.
Homilies. *See* Homilies. Certayne Sermons. 1547 etc. 597, 653 etc.
— *See* Bonner (E.). Homilies. 1555.
Letters Patent. (Collection for ministers in the Palatinate.) Broadside. 1627.
— — 1630.
Lincoln Diocese. *See* Lincoln Diocese.
Liturgy. *See* Trial. 1637.
London Diocese. License ab. 1640. 7061
[London Ministers.] *See* A briefe examination. [1564.] 4°.
Ministers. *See* Oxford University. The ansvvere...to the humble Petition of the Ministers of the Church of England, desiring Reformation of certaine Ceremonies... 1603 etc.
Ministers, Deprived. *See* Ames (W.).
— — Bradshaw (W.). A Protestation. 1605.
— — Certaine Arguments. 1606.
— — Powel (G.). A Consideration of the Depriued...Ministers... 1606.
— — Christian and modest offer. 1606. 4°. . . 6868
— — Defence of the Ministers reasons. 1607.
— — Devon and Cornwall, *Ministers of.*
— — London. *Ministers Deprived.*
— — Mild. A myld and iust defence. 1606. . . . 6869
— — Short dialogue. 1605.
Norwich Diocese. *See* Articles. 1638.
Provinciale. *See* Lyndwood (W.). 1501 *etc.*
Synod (1553). *See* Philpot (J.). Vera expositio. 1554.

No.

ENGLAND *cont.* Synod (1621). *See* Nicholas y Sacharles (J. de). 1621.
Visitation Articles. *See* Articles (Visitation).
Winchester Diocese. *See* Winchester.
See also Dialogue. [1589?]
— Englands Complaint... 1640.
The State of the Church of England. 1588. *See* Udall (J.).
See Volusianus. Epistolæ duæ... 1569.
KINGS. The most happy unions. F°. 7714
— A true chronologi. F°. 7715
— *See* Martyn (W.). The historie. 1638. F°.
PARLIAMENT.
— 1555. [Supplication to Philip II. and Mary.] *See* Elder (J.). The Copy of a Letter... [1555.]
— 1572. *See* Certain Articles. 1572.
— 1572. *See* Admonition.
— *See* England. Bishops. An exhortation... [Answer to An Admonition.] 1572.
— 1575. *See* Whitgift (J.). Examination of M. Doctor Whytgiftes censvres...
— 1584. [Prayer.] *See* Parry (W.). A true... [1584.]
— 1587. *See* Penry (J.). A treatise...of...Wales.
— 1589. — Penry (J.). Th'appellation. 1589.
— 1606. — Certaine arguments. 1606.
— 1606. — Philopatris. An humble petition.
— 1609. — James I. [Speeches.]
— (Commons.) 1624. *See* Cecil (Sir E.). A Speech. 1624.
— 1628, May 22. *See* Glanvill (Sir J.). The copies *etc.*
— 1628. *See* Leighton (A.). An appeal.
— *See* Rudyard (Sir B.). Speech. 1628.
— — Articles exhibited...against...W. Laud. 1640. 4°. . 7640
— 1640. *See* Selden (J.). A brief discourse. 1640.
— *See* Hall (Jos.). An humble remonstrance. 1640.
— — Shipmoney.
— (Commons.) Order made...to receive petitions for ministers. 1640. 4°. 7872
— — *See* Strafford (Thomas Wentworth, earl of). Depositions and Articles. 1640.
Star-chamber. *See* Bacon (F.). The Charge...touching Duells... 1614.
Statutes. *See* Statutes.
Year Books. *See* Year Books.
Englands complaint to Jesus Christ, against the bishops canons of the late sinfull synod. 1640. 4°. 7047
English Fugitives. *See* Lewkenor (Sir L.). The estate... 1596.
English, Latine, French, Dutch, Scholemaster. Ed. 1. 1637. 8°. 3965
English Protestants Recantation. 1617. 8°. 6908
English Puritanisme. *See* Bradshaw (W.). 1605.
English (Io.). Verses in Camdeni Insignia. 1624. . . . 5346
Épernon (J. L. de Nogaret, duc d'). *See* Nogaret.
Ephemerides of the Celestiall Motions for...1633–1636...Lansberg... Vlacq...Kepler. 1635. 4°. 5059
Ephemerides. *See* Almanack, Prognostication.
Ephraem Syrus. *See* Fitzherbert (T.). The Obmutesce. 1621.
Epictetus Manuall. Cebes Table. Theophrastus Characters. Trans. by Jo. Healey. 1616. 12°. 4056
Epigrams. *See* Farnaby (T.). 1629.
— Leech (J.).
— Owen (J.).
Epistle. An epistell, exhortatorye...of the false...god of the aulter. [Ab. 1549.] 8°. 6716

No.
Epistle, *cont.* *See* A moste pythye and excellent Epistell. Trans. R. Pownoll. 1556. 8°. 6730
Epistle of Comfort. *See* Southwell (R.).
Epistles and Gospels. Paris, 1538. 4°. 6179
R. Redman. 1538. 4°. 381–
[Paris], 1538. 8°. 6215
(...of every Sonday and holy daye in the yere). [Ab. 1540.] 4°. 6684–5
(Winter Part.) R. Bankes for T. Petit [1540?]. 4°. . . 366–
(Winter Part.) R. Bankes [1540?]. 4°. 367, 368
(Summer part.) R. Bankes, 1540. 4°. 362, 7859
— — R. Bankes for A. Clarke [1540]. 4° 369
R. Grafton, 1540. 16°. 588
W. Powell [1557?]. 4°. 1016
(Holy days.) [R. Bankes, ab. 1540.] 4°. 7077
Epistres et Evangiles. M. Crom, Antwerp, 1540. 8°. *See* p. 1743 (note on 6102).
Epseley (William). Verses in Hoby (Sir E.). A Curry-combe. 1615. 3111
Equivoca. *See* Æquivoca.
Erasmus (Des.). Apophthegmes. Trans. N. Udall. R. Grafton, 1542, Sept. 8°. 7093
De immensa dei misericordia. Trans. G. Hervet. 1533. 8°. . 427
— 1547. 8°. 493
[De pueris...instituendis.] That chyldren...should be well...broughte vp... *See* Sherry (R.). A treatise. [1550.]
Enchiridion militis christiani. W. de Worde for J. Byddell, 1534. 8°. 207
— J. Byddell, 1541. 8°. 571
— ,, 19 Nov. 1544. 8°. 572
— W. Powell, 1548. 8°. 1010
— A. Veale [155–?]. 8°. 1074
— W. How for A. Veale, 1576. 8°. 1768
Exhortation to the diligent studye of scripture. An exposition of 1 Cor. vii. 'H. Luft, Malborowe,' 20 June 1529. 8°. . 6271
Exposicyon of the .xv. psalme. 1537. 8°. 633
Familiarium Colloquiorum opus. H. Bynneman, 1571. 8°. . 7705
— Epitome colloquiorum. Cantabrigiae, 1634. 8°. . . 5832
Paraphrase upon the newe testamente. E. Whitchurch, 1548–9. F°. 658–660, 7097
— 1551. F°. 7099
Playne and godly exposytion of the cōmune Crede and of the .x. cōmaundmentes. [1533.] 8°. 391
Praise of Folie. Trans. Sir T. Chaloner. Berthelet, 1549, '1569.' 4°. 497, 7854
Preparation to deathe. 1543. 8°. 469
Two dyaloges...Polyphemus...of thynges and names. Trans. E. Becke. Canterbury. 8°. 5874
See Æsop. Fabulæ... 1635.
— Bible. N.T. (Lat. and Eng.) 1550.
— Cato. Preceptes. 1560. 16°.
— — Moralia. 1562. 8°.
— Cicero. De officiis &c. 1633.
— — Quæstiones tuscvlanæ. 1577.
— Clarke (J.). Parœmiologia. 1639.
— Hall (Jos.). The honor. 1620.
— Heywood (T.). Pleasant dialogues. 1637.
— Lily (W.). De octo orationis partium constructione. 1540.
— Lucianus. Dialogi. 1531.
— Plutarch. The gouernaũce of good helthe. [153–?] 8°.

No.

Erastus (Tho.). Explicatio grauissimae quaestionis. 'Pesclavii.' 1589. 4°. 1954
See Beza (T.). Tractatvs pivs. 1590. 8°.
Eratosthenes. [Gr. Lat.] *See* Poetae minores. 1635.
Erondelle (P.). Declaration and Catholick exhortation. 1586. 8°. 1842
Erpenius (Thomas). *See* Purchas (S.). Pilgrimage. 1626.
Erra Pater. Prognostycacyon. n.d. 8°. 548
Errol (Francis Hay, earl of). *See* Hay (P.). A vision. 1614.
Errol (William Hay, earl of). [Marriage.] *See* Wilkinson (R.). The merchant royal... 1607.
Erskine (William). Verses in Adamson (J.). Εἰσόδια. 1618. . 5960–
Escurial. *See* Wadsworth (J.). Further observations. 1633. 4°. . 7788
Espagne (Jean d'). Antidvello. 1632. 4°. 3995
Espernon. *See* Épernon.
Essays. 1632. Henshaw (J.). Horæ Succisivæ. 12°.
Essex Archdeaconry. *See* Articles. 1635.
Essex (R. Devereux, earl of). Apologie of the earle. 1603. 4°. . 1998
[Lawes and Orders of Warre...in Ireland. Ab. 1599.] 4°. . 6825
Declaration of the Practises and Treasons... *See* Bacon (Francis). 1601.
See Bacon (F.). Sir F. Bacon his apologie. 1604.
— Barlow (W.). A Sermon... 1601.
— Churchyard (T.). The fortunate Farewell... 1599.
— Elizabeth. Declaration. 1596, 1704.
— Markham (G.). Honour. 1624.
— Scott (T.). Robert earle of Essex his ghost. 1624.
— Tacitus. The ende of Nero &c. 1591 *etc.*
Essex (Walter Devereux, first earl of). *See* Davies (R.). A Funerall Sermon... 1577.
Estate of English Fugitives. *See* Lewkenor (Sir L.). The estate. 1595 *etc.*
Estella (D. de). Methode vnto mortification. 1586. 12°. . . 2118
Estey (George). *See* Estye.
Estie (George). *See* Estye.
Estienne (C.). Maison rustique. 1616. F°. 2447
Estienne (Henri). Mervaylous discourse upon. .K. de Medicis. 'Heydelberge,' 1575. 8°. 7280
World of wonders. 1607. F°. 2360
[Anthologia selecta.] *See* Stockwood (J.). Progymnasma. 1597.
Verses in Buchanan (G.). Psalmorum Davidis. 1640. . 5209
See Cicero. [Epistles.] 1631.
— Horatius. Poemata. 1607.
Estienne (Rob.). Dictionariolum puerorum. 1552. 4°. . . . 736
See Bible, Greek. N.T. 1622 etc.
Estmond (John). Verses in Holyoake (F.). Dictionarium. 1640. . 3058
Estoutevile (George). Verses in Heywood (T.). The exemplary lives. 1640. 4675
Estwick (Nicholas). Learned and godly sermon...funerall of R. Bolton. 1633. 4°. 4444
See Bolton (R.). Mr Boltons last...Things. 1635.
Estye (G.). Certaine godly...expositions. 1603. 4°. . . . 7300
Most sweete...exposition vpon the tenne commandements, and Psalm li. 1602. 8°. 1784
Ethelwerd. [Chronicles.] *See* Savile (Sir H.). Rervm Anglicarvm scriptores... 1596.
Etherege (George). *See* Edrych.
Eton College. *See* Dionysius... [1615?] *etc.*
Etten (Henry van). Mathematicall Recreations. Trans. W. Oughtred. 1633. 8°. 7614
Euchaitensis (Johannes). *See* John, metropolitan of Euchaita.

No.

Euclid. Elementorum libri 'tredecim.' (Gr. Lat.) Ex vers. F. Commandini. [Six books only.] 1620. F°. 3332
Elements of geometric. 1570. F°. 815
See Savile (Sir H.). Prælectiones. 1621.
Eucolpius [*pseud.*]. *See* Elyot (Sir Thomas).
Eudæmon-Joannes (Andreas), *Cydonius*. *See* Abbot (R.). Antilogia adversus Apologiam. 1613.
— Burhill (R.). De potestate regia.
— Collins (S.). Increpatio. 1612.
— Prideaux (J.). Castigatio. 1614.
Eudes (Morton). Catholique traditions...by Th. A. I. C. Trans. by L. O. 1609. 4°. 3062
— 1610. 4°. 3069
Eunapius. Lyves of Philosophers. R. Jones, 1579. 4°. . . 1444
Euonymus, *pseud.* *See* Gesner (C.).
Euripides. [Jocasta (Eng.).] *See* Gascoigne (G.). A Hundreth sundrie Flowers. [1572.] 4°.
[Phoenissae.] *See* Gascoigne (G.). The Posies. 1576.
Europe. *See* New Svrvey of...Evrope... 1623.
Eusebius Pamphili. Auncient ecclesiastical histories of...Eusebius...Socrates...Evagrius. Trans. M. Hanmer. 1577(-6). F°. . 1532
— 1585. F°. 1560
— 1619. F°. 2287
— 1636. F°. 4461
Life of Constantine. 1637. F°. 4651
Eusebius Pamphilus, *pseud.* *See* Pamphilus.
Eusebius Philadelphus, *pseud.* Dialogi. 'Edimburgi, J. Jamaeus,' 1574. 8°. 6760
Eustachius à Sancto Paulo. Summa philosophiae quadripartita. Cantabrigiae, 1640. 8°. 5840
Eutheo (Anglo-phile), *pseud.* *See* Salvianus, *Massiliensis*, *Presbyter*. A second and third blast. 1580.
Eutropius (F.). Briefe Chronicle...of the City of Rome. 1564. 8°. 1213
Evagrius Scholasticus. [Eccl. Hist.] *See* Eusebius Pamphili. The avncient...histories. 1577 *etc.*
Evan (Enoch ap). *See* Studley (P.). The looking glasse. 1634. 12°.
Evance (Dan). Verses in Camb. Univ. Rex redux. 1633. . . 5748
Evans (Edw.), *B.A.*, *Jes.* Verses in Camb. Univ. Fasciae. 1633. . 5808
Evans (Lewis). Castle of Christianitie. 1568. 8°. . . 1404
See Withals (J.). Shorte dictionarie. 1586 *etc.*
Evans (Samuel), *LL.B.* Verses in Chaucer (G.). Amorvm. 1635. . 5414
— Butler (C.). The principles of musik. 1636. . . 4860
— Oxf. Univ. Horti. 1640. 5499
Evelyn (Thomas), *Cath.* Verses in Camb. Univ. Συνωδία. 1637. . 5790
Evenus. [*Gr. Lat.*] *See* Poetae minores. 1635.
Everard (John). Britanno-romanus. 1611. 8°. . . . 3213
Everard (Sam.). Verses in Ferrard (J.). Ἐρωτομανία. 1640. . 5498
— Oxf. Univ. Horti. 1640. 5499
Everton (Francis). Verses in Oxf. Univ. Magd. Coll. 1612. . 5302
Evreux (Monsieur d'). *See* Du Perron (J. D.), *bp of Evreux*.
Excellent and materiall discourse...if...Germanie...be subdued. Trans. S. B. 1626. 4°. 6971
Exchequer. True copy of the ordynaũce...Henry the vi. R. Redman. N.D. 8°. 392
Directions for Commissioners. May 1608. 1608. 4°. . . 2611
See Powell (T.). Direction for Search. 1622.
— — The Repertorie of Records. 1631.
Execution of Justice. 1583. *See* Burghley (W. Cecil, Lord).
Exeter, *City and See.* 1575, 1584. *See* Hooker (J.), *alias* Vowell.

No.

Exeter (Henry Courtenay, marquis of). *See* Morison (Sir R.). An invective... 1539.
Exeter (William Cecil, second earl of). [Funeral.] *See* W. (H.). Θρηνοικος. 1640.
Exhortacion. *See* Exhortation.
Exhortation to the Byshops to deale brotherly... (An exhortation...to aunswer a little Booke.) [J. S., 1572.] 8°. . . . 5896
Exhortacion to the carienge of Chrystes crosse. 16°. 6307
Exhortation to the sycke. 1548. 8°. *See* A new boke. . . 5880
Exhortation vnto prayer...also a Letanie. Berthelet, 1544. 8°. 476, 477
Exhortations for the sicke. [Ab. 154–.] 6699
Exonoratorium Curatorum. T. Godfray [1532?]. 8°. . . 558
Experimentall discoverie of Spanish practises. 1624. *See* Scott (T.). 6944, 6957, 6959
Expositio hymnorum & sequentiarum (Sarum). [H. Quentell, Cologne, 1496.] 4°. 120
— Notary. 1510. 4°. 331
— Pynson, 1515. 4°. 263
Exposicion. *See* Exposition.
Exposition of certaine difficult and obscure words and Termes of the Law. *See* Rastell (J.).
Exposicion vppon the v. vi. vii. chapters of Mathew. *See* Tindale (W.). 1530.
Expositiones terminorum. 1527. *See* Rastell (John).
Extenta manerii. *See* Book of Surveying. 1525.
Exton (John, Lord Harington, baron of). *See* Harington.
Extraordinary Curranto. 18 Oct. 1639. *See* no. 7726.
Extravagants. *See* Boorde (A.). The Breuiary... 1557 *etc.* 4°.

F. (A.). Verses in Ferne (Sir J.). The blazon of gentrie. 1586. 2119
— Camb. Univ. Thr-thr. 1603. 5616
F. (A.). *See* Hooper (J.). Certaine comfortable expositions. 1580.
F. (A.) [=A. Fleming]. *See* Virgil. Bvcoliks. 1589. 4°.
F. (E.), *C.C.* Verses in Camb. Univ. Lacrymæ. 1619. . . 5689
F. (E. S.). *See* Stratford (E.). A disputation... 1640.
F. (G.). Verses in Gray (T. de). The compleat horseman. 1639. 4042
F. (G.), *T.C.* Camb. Univ. Epicedium *bis*. 1612. . . . 5666
F. (H.). *See* Pelegromius (S.). Synonymorvm sylva. 1603.
— Plinius. The historie of the world. 1601.
F. (I.). Differences...of urine. Cambridge, 1598. 8°. . . . 5593
F. (I.). A sermon preached at Ashby de la Zouch...Funerall of...Lady Elizabeth Stanley. 1635. 4°. 5060
F. (I.). Tuba academica. 1603. 12°. 2881
F. (I.). Verses in Stubbes (P.). The anatomie of abuses. 1585. 1446
— Aleman (M.). The Rogve. 1623 etc. . . . 4079 etc.
— Camdeni (Insignia). 1624. 5346
— Overbury (Sir T.). His wife. Ed. 11. 1622. . . 3380
See Beautiful Baybush. No. 6767.
F. (I.). [Prayer made for the Church...] *See* Bible. Psalms. Metrical Version. [Sternhold.] 1638.
F. (I.) [=J. Foxe]. *See* Cranmer (T.). Reformatio legvm. 1571 *etc.*
F. (I.), *T.C.* Verses in Camb. Univ. Gratulatio. 1623. . . 5695
F. (J.). *See* Bullinger (H.). A treatise. 1549. 8°.
— Frith (J.). A myrroure...of baptisme. [15 .] 8°.
F. (J.), *Coll. Pet.* Verses in Camb. Univ. Carmen. 1635. . 5770
F. (L.). Speedy remedie against spirituall incontinencie. 1640–1. 4°. 7053
F. (L. B. I. B.) [*qu.* L. Barlement?]. Verses. 1631. . . 6482
F. (N.) [=Field (N.)]. *See* Massinger (P.). The fatall dowry. 1632.
F. (R.), *of Gray's Inn.* Verses in Ferne (Sir J.). The blazon. 1586. 2119
F. (T.). *See* Fitzherbert (T.). A defence... 1602.

No.
F. (T.) [*qu.* Fitzherbert?]. *See* Torsellino (O.). The...life of S. Francis Xavier. 1632.
F. (T.) [=Fitzherbert (T.)]. *See* Widdrington (R.). A copy... 1614.
F. (T.). *See* Fuller (T.). Ioseph's party-colovred coat... 1640.
F. (T.), *Student. See* Thynne (F.). Newes from the North. 1585. 4°. 2002
F. (T.), *C.T.* Verses in Camb. Univ. Gratulatio. 1623. . . 5695
F. (T.), *Regal.* Verses in Camb. Univ. Gratulatio. 1623. . . 5695
Faber (Lodovicus). *See* Ravisius (J.). Dialogi. 1581. 16°.
Fabricius (Georgius). Verses in Buchanan (G.). Psalmorum Davidis. 1640. 5209
See Horatius. Poemata. 1607.
Fabricius (Philippus). Verses in Beurhusius (F.). De P. Rami dialecticæ capitibus. 1582 etc. . . . . . . 7268 etc.
Fabricius (Wilhelm). Lithotomia Vesicæ. Trans. H. Schobinger. Ed. N. C. 1640. 8°. 4912
Fabyan (R.). Chronicle. Pynson, 1516. F°. 264
— W. Rastell, 1533. F°. 533
— W. Bonham, 1542. F°. 719
— J. Kingston, 1559. F°. 1168
Fage (John). Speculum Ægrotorum. The Sicke Mens Glasse. 1606. 4°. 3385
Faier (Thomas). *See* Phaer.
Fairclough (Richard). *See* Bible, Eng. (Royal). 1611.
Fairebrother (Will.). Verses in Camb. Univ. Anthologia. 1632. . 5741
— Rex redux. 1633.. 5748
Fairfax (Edward). *See* Tasso (T.). Godfrey of Bulloigne. 1600 *etc.*
Fairfax (G.). Verses in Cambridge Lachrymae. 1587. . . 7356
Fairlæus (R.). *See* Fairly.
Fairlie (James). Theses and Verses in Adamson (J.). Εἰσόδια. 1618. . 5960
Fairly (Robert). Verses in Person (D.). Varieties. 1635. . . 4365
Faithful Admonition. *See* Luther (M.). A faythfull admonycion. 1554.
Faithfull and wise preventer or counseller. The Hague, 1621. 4°. . 6641
Faius (Anthony). *See* La Faye (A. de).
Faldo (C.), *K.C.C.* Verses in Camb. Univ. Epithalam. 1625. . 5702
Fale (T.). Horologiographia. The Art of Dialling. 1593. 4°. . 2220
Falkland (Elizabeth Cary, viscountess). *See* Du Perron (J. D.). The reply of the...cardinall of Perron... translated. 1630.
Falkland (Lucius Cary, second viscount). Verses in Sandys (G.). A paraphrase. 1636. 4943
— Grotius (H.). Christ's Passion. 1640. 4744
Fall of the Romish Church. [Ab. 1549.] 8°. 6715
False Complaints. *See* Pasquale. 1605. 7399
Familiar and christian instruction. Trans. G. C. 1582. . . 1551
Familist. *See* Antichrist.
Family of Love, Familists. *See* Antichrist. Description and Confutation of mysticall Antichrist. 1606? 4°.
See Knewstub (J.). A Confutation. 1579.
— Niclas (H.), *passim.*
— Rogers (J.). Displaying of an horrible Secte... 1578 *etc.*
— Supplication. 1606. 4°.
Fancoats (T.). Verses in Camb. Univ. Genethl. 1631. . . 5731
Fane (Antony). Verses in Camb. Univ. Fasciae. 1633. . . 5808
Fane (George). Verses in Camb. Univ. Fasciæ. 1633. . . . 5808
Fane (Hon. Mildmay). Verses in Camb. Univ. Lacrymæ. 1619. . 5689
Fane (Hon. Robert). Verses in Camb. Univ. Voces. 1640. . . 5836
Fane (Hon. William). Verses in Camb. Univ. Συνῳδία. 1637. . 5790
— Voces. 1640. 5836
Fantasy of the Passyon of the Fox. W. de Worde, 1530. 4°. . 200
Fancan. *See* Langlois.
Farar (David), *Rabbi. See* Broughton (H.). Ovr Lordes Famile... 1608.

No.

Farewell (R.). *See* Dyer (Sir J.). Ascuns nouel cases... 1585.
Fargarus (Martin). Verses in Cheke (Sir J.). De obitu M. Buceri. 1551. 734
See Perussellus (F.). Svmma. 1551.
Farley (Henry). Complaint of Paules. Cambridge, 1616. 4°. . 5677
Farley (Robert). Kalendarium humanae vitae. The Kalendar of mans life. 1638. 8°. 4659
Lychnocausia...Lights morall emblems. 1638. 8°. . . 4660
Farley (Samuel), *Regal.* Verses in Camb. Univ. Voces. 1640. . 5836
Farmer (James), *S.J.C.* Verses in Camb. Univ. Συνωδία. 1637. . 5790
Farmer (Richard). A sermon at Pauls crosse, 28 June 1629. 1629. 4°. 4959
Farmer (William). Verses in Camb. Univ. Epicedium. 1612. 5665, 5666
Farnaby (Thomas). Verses in Coryate (T.). Coryates Crvdities. 1611. 3076
— Camden (W.). Tomus alter. 1627. 3168
— Comenius. Porta linguarum. 1631 etc. . . . 4434
— Xenophon. Cyrupædia. 1632. 4714
— Hippocrates. 1633. 5812
— King (E.). Ivsta. 1638. 5829
See Juvenalis et Persius. Satyræ. 1615 etc.
— Lucanus. 1618.
— Martialis. 1615 *etc.*
— Seneca (L. A.). Tragoediæ. 1613 etc.
Farnace (P. de). *See* La Place (P. de). A treatise. 1576. 8°.
Faron (Jean). *See* Cessolis (Jacobus de). The Game and Play. 1475? 118
Farr (H.). Verses in Camb. Univ. Lachrymae. 1587. . . 7356
Farrand (William). *See* Blackwell (G.). A large examination... 1607.
Fasciculus florum: or a nosegay of flowers translated. 1636. 8°. 4590
Fastolf (Sir John). *See* Cicero, De Senectute. 1481.
Faukland. *See* Falkland.
Faustinus, *Diestensis.* [Life of F. Archangel.] *See* Joyeuse (H. de). The life. 1623. 8°.
Favour (John). Antiqvitie trivmphing over noveltie. 1619. 4°. . 2288
Favourites Chronicle. 1621. *See* Langlois.
Favyn (André). Theatre of honour and knighthood. 1623. F°. . 2794
Fawcet (Tho.). Verses in Camb. Univ. Genethl. 1631. . . 5731
See Lefèvre (R.). The ancient historie. 1636. 4°.
Fawkener (Antony). Comfort to the afflicted. 1626. 4°. . . 4966
Fawkes (Guy). *See* In homines nefarios. 5631
Faythfull admonycion... 1554. *See* Luther (M.).
Fayus (Antonius). *See* La Faye.
Feargussone (David). *See* Ferguson.
Featley (Daniel). Ancilla Pietatis. 1626. 12°. 4415
— Ed. 5. 1633. 12°. 4447
Clavis mystica. 1636. F°. 4988
Cygnea Cantio. 1629. 4°. 4254
Parallel. 1626. 4°. 4335
Parallelismus. 1626. 4°. 4336
Pelagius redivivus. 1626. 4°. 7592
Romish Fisher. 1624. 4°. 2548
Second parallel. 1626. 4°. 3529
Sermon...at Cobham. *See* Lynde (Sir H.). A Case. 1638.
Stricturæ in Lyndomastigem. *See* Lynde (Sir H). A Case. 1639.
Summe of saving Knowledge. 1626. 12°. 4416
Transubstantiation exploded. 1638. 12°. 4470
Verses in Shaw (J.). Bibliorum svmmvla. 1623. . . . 7381
— Mason (H.). The new art. 1624. 4083
See Bible (Eng.) Concordance. Cotton. 1635.
— C. (A.). An Answer to...The Fisher catched. 1623. 4°.
— Fletcher (P.). The purple island. 1633. 4°.
— Gataker (T.). A ivst defence. 1623.

No.

Featley (Daniel), *cont.* *See* Hayne (T.). Pax. 1639.
— James I. Cygnea Cantio... 1629.
— Jewel (J.). Works. 1609 *etc.*
— Mason (H.). The new art. 1624.
— Reply to D. White and D. Featly. 1625. 4°. . . 6554
— Texeda (F. de). Texeda Retextus. 1623.
— W. (H.). *Θρηνοικος.* 1640.
Featley (John). Obedience and submission. 1636. 4°. . . 4372
Feckenham (John de). *See* Stapleton (T.). A counterblast. 1567.
— Tomson (L.). Answere. [1570.] 8°.
Fecknam (John), *Abbot.* *See* Feckenham (J. de).
Fee Simple. *See* Carta Feodi.
Feild (Richard). *See* Field (Richard).
Feilde (Francis). Verses in Budden (J.). Gvl. Patteni vita. 1602. 5256
Feilde (John). *See* Field.
Fekenham (John). *See* Feckenham.
Felicius (Constantius), *Durantinus.* *See* Durantinus (C. F.).
Felinus (Aretius), *pseud.*, *i.e.* Bucer (M.). Incorrect ascription of no. 6091: see next entry.
Felix, *Friar of the Order of the Eremites of St Austin.* *See* Felix, *Pratensis.*
Felix, *Pratensis.* *See* Bible, Eng. Psalms. Davids Psalter. 1534. . 6091
Fell (Jo.). Verses in Oxf. Univ. Horti. 1640. 5499
Fell (Samuel). Primitiae. Oxoniae, 1627. 4°. 7812
Verses in Camdeni Insignia. 1624. 5346
See Hakewill (G.). An apologie. 1630.
Fell (Ow.), *qu.* Felltham? Verses in Barclay (J.). Argenis. 1625 *etc.* 4086 etc.
Felltham (O.). Resolues, A Duple Century. Ed. 3. 1628–9. 4°. . 7481
— Ed. 4. 1631. 4°. 7580
— Ed. 6. 1636. 4°. 4118
Verses in Randolph (T.). Poems. 1640. 5500
See also Fell. (Ow.).
Felton (N.). Verses in King (E.). Ivsta. 1638. 5829
Fen (John). *See* Fenn (J.).
Fenn (John). *See* Catharinus (A.). The Life of...Catharine of Siena. 1609.
Fenner (Dudley). Answere vnto the confutation of J. Nichols. 1583. 4°. 1929
Artes of logicke and rethorique. 1584. 4°. . . . 6444–5
— [1588?] 8°. 6448
Brief treatise vpon the first table of the Lawe. [1590?] 8°. . 6449
Certain godly and learned treatises. Edinburgh, 1592. 8°. . 5927
Counter-Poyson. [1584?] 8°. 1903
— *See* A parte of a register. [1593?].
Defence of the godlie ministers against...Bridges. 1587. 4°. . 6787
Short and profitable Treatise of...Recreations. Middelburg. 1590. 8°. 6450
Song of Songs. Middelburg, 1587. 8°. 6447
— Middelburg, 1594. 8°. 6451
See Antiqvodlibet. 1602.
Fenner (William). Compters Common-wealth. 1617. 4°. . . 3917
Soules looking glasse. Cambridge, 1640. 8°. 5841
Fens. *See* Bedford Level.
Fenton (Ed.). Certaine Secrete wonders of Nature. 1569. 4°. . 1462
See Beautiful Baybush. 6767
Fenton (Geoffrey). Forme of Christian pollicie. 1574. 4°. . 1619
See Corro (A. de). An epistle. 1570 (1569).
See Guicciardini (F.). The historie. 1579 etc.
Fenton (Roger). Treatise against the necessary dependance vpon that one head. 1617. 4°. 3918

No.

Fenton (Roger), *cont.* Treatise of vsurie. 1611. 4°. 2969
See Bible, English (Royal). 1611. 2635
Fenton (William), *of Knockfergus.* Verses in Coryate (T.). Coryates crvdities. 1611. 3076
Ferdinand I, *Emperor of Germany.* [Funeral.] *See* Grindal (E.). Concio. 1564.
— — Sermon. 1564.
Ferdinand II, *Emperor of Germany.* Plaine demonstration of the unlawful succession. Hage, 1620. 4°. 7860
See N. (N.). De conventv... 1631.
— Prague. A true relation of the bloudy execution... 1621. 4°.
— Sweden. Gustavus II Adolphus. 1631.
Ferdinand I, de' Medici, *Grand Duke of Tuscany.* *See* Medici (Ferdinand I, de') Grand Duke of Tuscany.
Ferdinand, *Infanta of Spain* (fl. 1523). [Letter.] *See* Wakefield (R.). Oratio. [1524.] 4°.
Ferdinand II, *Arch-Duke of Austria.* *See* Hungary. The Instrvments of the Pactions... 1620.
Ferdinand (Philip). Hæc sunt verba Dei. Cantabrigiae, 1597. 4°. . 5586
Fereby (Anthony). Verses in Smith (J.). The true travels. 1630. 4836
Ferguson (David). Ane answer to ane epistle. Edinburgh, 1563. 8°. 5911
Fermius (Carolus). Verses in Rollock (R). Analysis. 1594 . 5933
Ferne (Henry). Verses in Camb. Univ. Genethl. 1631. . . 5731
— Anthologia. 1632. 5741
— Fasciae. 1633. 5808
— Συνῳδία. 1637. 5790
Ferne (Sir J.). Blazon of gentrie. 1586. 4°. 2119
Fernelius. Treatise...of the Eyes. *See* Vaughan (Sir W.). Directions for health. Ed. 6. 1626 etc. 4°.
Ferrand (Jacques). Ἐρωτομανία. Oxford, 1640. 8°. . . . 5498
Ferrar (Nicolas). *See* Lessius (L.). Hygiasticon. 1634.
— Valdés (J. de). The hundred and ten considerations. 1638.
Ferrarius (Anger). *See* Ferrer.
Ferrarius (J.). Woorke...touchynge the good orderynge of a common weale. 1559. 4°. 1169
Ferrer, Ferrerius, Ferrarius, or Ferrier (Angerius). A generall diet...in the curatiõ of Vlcers. *See* Banister (J.). A needefvll... treatise. 1575.
See Banister (J.). Workes. 1633.
Ferrers (George). *See* Higgins (J.). A mirrour. 1610.
— Statutes. The boke of Magna Carta. 1534. 8°.
— — The great Charter. [Ab. 1541.] 8°.
Ferrier (Angerius). *See* Ferrer.
Ferrières (Jean de), *vidame de Chartres.* Verses in G. Harvey. Gratulationum. 1578. 1495
Ferris (Richard). *See* Gale (T.). Certaine Workes. 1563.
Ferrour (John). *See* Office of Generall Remembrance. 1617. . . 3588
Ferus (Johannes). *See* Wild.
Festial. *See* Mirk (J.).
Fetherstone (Christopher). *See* Bible, English. O.T. Lamentations. 1587.
— Calvin (J.). Abridgement. 1585.
— — Commentaries...vpon the Actes. 1585. 4°.
— Christian and wholsom Admonition. 1587.
— Grynæus (J. J.). Haggeus. 1586.
— Sixtus V. The brvtish thunderbolt. 1586. 8°.
Fetherstone (Henry). Catalogus Librorum. 1628. 4°. . . . 4705
Fetiplace (Charles). Verses in Roberts (L.). The merchants mappe. 1638. 5133
See also Phettiplace.

No.

Feugueræus (Gulielmus). *See* Bible (Lat.). N.T. 1587.
Few plaine and forcible reasons for the Catholike Faith. *See* Woodcoke (R.). Godly and learned answer. 1608. 4°.
Fewterer (John), *confessor of Sion Monastery*. *See* Mirror of Our Lady. 1530.
Feyerabend (Sigmund). *See* Livius. Libri omnes. 1589. 8°.
Field (James). Verses in Coryate (T.). Coryates Crudities. 1611. . 3076
Field (John), *chirurgeon*. Verses in Gale (T.). Certaine Workes. 1563. 1303
— Vigo (J. de). Works. 1586. 1588
Field (John), *Puritan*. Caveat for Parsons Howlet. [1581.] 8°. . 1904
Godly exhortation. 1583. 8°. 1894
See An admonition... 1572. 5895
— Beza (Th.). The Ivdgement... 1580.
— Calvin (J.). Thirteene sermons. 1579. 4°.
— Mornay (P. de). A notable treatise. 1580.
— — Treatise of the church. 1581. 8°.
— Norris (S). An antidote. 1615 etc. 4°.
— — The Guide. 1621. 4°.
— Nowell (A.) and W. Day. A true report of...Ed. Campion... 1583.
— Viret (P.). A faithfull...exposition. 1582. 1639
Field (Nathaniel), *Actor*. *See* Massinger (P.). The fatall dowry. 1632.
Verses in Jonson (B.). Catiline. 1611. 2902
Field (Nathaniel), *Rector of Stourton*. *See* Field (R.), *D.D.* Of the Church. 1628 etc.
Field (Richard). Of the Church. 1606. 4°. 2477
— Ed. 2. Oxford, 1628. F°. 5419
— Ed. 3. Oxford, 1635. F°. 5446
Fifth booke of the church. 1610. 4°. 3634
See Champney (A.). A treatise. 1616. 4°.
— Higgons (T.). The first motive. 1609. 6521
— Norris (S.). An Antidote... 1619.
Field (Theophilus). Christians preparation to the...Lords supper. 1622. 8°. 4507
Verses in Stradling (Sir J.). Divine poems. 1625. . . . 3159
Fielde (John). *See* Field.
Fiennes (Robert), *alias* Clinton. *See* Clinton.
Fiennes (Will.). Verses in Camb. Univ. Fasciæ. 1633. . . 5808
— Rex redux. 1633. 5748
Fifteen Oes. 1558. *See* Becon (T.). The Pomāder of Prayers.
Filding (Ferdinando). *See* Tossanus (D.). The exercise of the faithfull soule. 1583. 8°.
Filippi (Marco Antonio). Confessio fidei. 1631. 4°. 4610
Fills (Robert). *See* Geneva. Lawes and Statutes. 1562. . . . 1299
— Treatise conteining certaine meditations. [1563.]
Finch (Sir Henry). Law, or a discourse. 1627. 8°. 3295
Νομοτεχνία. 1613. F°. 3256
See Gouge (W.). The Calling of the Iewes. 1621.
Finet (John). *See* Lucinge (R. de). The beginning...of estates. 1606. 4°.
Finland. *See* North (G.). The Description of Swedland. 1561.
Fioravanti (L.). Compendium. 1582. 8°. 1186
Joyfull Jewell. [1579 ?] 4°. 1989
Firsbæus (Philippus Vincentius). *See* Vincent (P.).
First blast of the trumpet. 1558. *See* Knox (J.).
Fiscus Papalis sive Catalogus Indulgentiarum ex reliquiarum. Trans. W. Crashaw. 1617. 4°. 3669
— 1621. 4°. 4166
Fish (Simon). The supplication. *See* Supplication of the poore Commons. [1546.]

No.

Fish (Simon), *cont.* *See* Sum. The summe of the holy scripture. 1529 etc.
Fishburne (Richard). *See* Shute (Nat.). Corona. 1626.
Fisher (Ambrose). Defence of the liturgie of the Church of England. 1630. 4°. 3176
Verses in Crooke (Helk.) Μικροκοσμογραφία. 1631. . . 4687
Fisher (John), *Bishop of Rochester.* A mornynge remembraūce. W. de Worde [15–]. 4°. 216
Sermon agayn Luther. [152– .] 4°. 217
Seven penitential psalms. W. de Worde, 1508. 4°. . . 155
— W. de Worde, 12 June 1509. 4°. 159
Psalmi seu precationes. H. Wykes. 1568. 16°. . . . 1253
Psalms. [Ab. 154– ?] 8°. 6687
— *See* Preces Privatæ. 1573. 16°. . . . . . 937 etc.
Treatise concernynge...the seuen pentytencyall psalmes. 1555. 8°. 1203
Treatise of prayer. Trans. R. A. B. Paris, 1640. 12°. . . 6205
See Frith (J.). A disputaciō... [1535 ?].
Fisher (John), *Jesuit.* Answere unto the nine points of Controversy. 1626. 4°. 6556
Fisher catched in his own net. 1623. 4°. 6939
Treatise of faith. (A catalogue.) 1614. 8°. . . . 6531
See C. (A.). Answer to...The Fisher catched. 1623. 4°.
— — True relations of svndry Conferences. 1626. 4°.
— Featley (D.). The Romish Fisher. 1624.
— Laud (W.). Relation of the Conference. 1639.
— — Replie to a relation. 1640.
— Reply to D. White and D. Featley. 1625. 4°. . . . 6554
— Rogers (H.). An answer... 1623.
— White (Francis). A replie. 1624.
Fisher (Tho.), *K.C.C.* Verses in Camb. Univ. Epithalam. 1625. 5702
Fisher (William). Godly sermon. 31 Oct. 1591. 1592. 8°. . . 1592
Fiston (William). *See* Phiston.
Fitch (William). *See* Canfield (B.).
Fitzer (William). *See* Bry (J. T. de). Caracters... 1628.
Fitz-Geffrey (Charles). Affaniae. Oxoniæ, 1601. 8°. . . 5254
Verses in Du Bartas. Weekes. 1605–6 *etc.* 2476
Fitzgerald (Lord Gerald), *Baron of Offalye.* [Sonnet.] *See* Virgil. Æneis i–iv (Eng.). 1583.
Fitzherbert (Sir A.). Diuersite de courtz. R. Redman, '1523.' 16°. 371
— 1530. 8°. 418
Grand Abridgment. J. Rastell, 1516. F°. 343
Tabula. J. Rastell, 1517. F°. 344
— *See* Stanford (Sir W.). An exposition of the Kinges prerogative. 1567, *etc.*
La nouvelle natura brevium. 1553. 8°. 1104
— 1598. 8°. 2385
[New book of Justices of Peace. 1538?] 8°. 6683
— T. Petit, 1541. 8°. 580
Office of Shyriffes etc. R. Kele, 1552. 8°. 1003
See Book of Surveying. 1525 *etc.* . . . . . 287 etc.
— Year Book. Edward III. 1–10. 1596. F°.
Fitzherbert (John). [The booke of Husbandrye.] A newe tracte...for all husbāde men. Southwark [1525?]. 4°. . . . 5864
The boke of husbandry. Berthelet, n.d. 8°. 510
Fitzherbert (Tho.). Adioynder to the supplement of...Persons his discussion. 1613. 4°. 6529
Defence of the catholyke cause. 1602. 4°. 6515
First part of a treatise concerning policy and religion. Douai, 1606. 4°. 6571
Obmutesce of F. T. 1621. 8°. 6544

No.

Fitzherbert (Tho.), *cont.* Supplement to the discussion of M. D. Barlowes answere. 1613. 4°. 6528
Treatise conc. policy and religion. Pt. 1. Ed. 2. 1615. 4°. 6580
— Pt. 2. 1610. 4°. 6579
— — 1615. 4°. 6579
See Parsons (R.). A discussion. 1612.
— Torsellino (O.). The...life of S. Francis Xavier. 1632.
— Widdrington (R.). A cleare...confutation. 1616. 4°.
— — Copy of the Decree... 1614
— — R. W's last reioynder. 1611 *etc.* 4°.
Fitz-James (Richard). Sermo die lune. W. de Worde [1495]. 4°. 63
See Fruit of Redemption. 1514 *etc.*
Fitzrandolph (Th.). Verses in Camb. Univ. Epicedium. 1612. . 5665
Fitz-simon (Henry). Catholike confutation of M. John Riders clayme. 'Roan,' 1608. 4°. 6268
Justification and exposition of...the masse. 1611. 4°. . 6574
Fitzstephen (William). Libellus de situ & nobilitate Londini. *See* Stow (J.). A svrvay... 1603 *etc.* . . . . 2162 *etc.*
Fitzwaters (Bridget Ratcliffe, Lady). *See* Greene (R.). Philomela. 1631.
Fl. (T.). Verses in Vaughan (W.). The Golden Grove. 1608. . 2888
Flaccus (Verrius). Chronologie. *See* Livius. The Roman historie. 1600.
Flamel (Nicolas). Exposition of the hieroglyphical figures...in St. Innocents...Paris. 1624. 12°. 3442
Flammel (Nicholas). *See* Flamel.
Flanders. *See* Theophile, *D.L.* A Tragicall Historie. [1583.]
Flemish Language. *See* Barlement (N.). Colloquia. 1631.
Flathers (Tho.). Verses in Camb. Univ. Genethl. 1631. . . 5731
See also Fl. (T.).
Flathers (Will.). Verses in Camb. Univ. Epithalam. 1625. . 5702
— — Genethl. 1631. 5731
— — Fasciae. 1633. 5808
— — Rex redux. 1633. 5748
— Hippocrates. 1633. 5812
Flavel (John). Tractatus de demonstratione. Oxoniae, 1619. 8°. . 5335
Fleetwood (James). *See* Fletewood.
Fleetwood (W.). Annalium...Elenchus. 1579. 8°. 7883
— 1597. 12°. 2867
Verses in Chaloner (Sir T.). De rep. angl. 1579. . . 7270
Lambarde (W.). A perambulation. 1576. 1621
See Plowden (E.). Les commentaires. 1588, 1599.
Fleming (Abraham). The Diamond of Deuotion. *See below* The Footpath to Felicitie...
Footepath to Felicitie. 1586. 12°. 1433
Panoplie of epistles. 1576. 4°. 1620
Treatise of blazing starres. 1618. 4°. 4155
Verses in Palingenius. The Zodiake. 1576. 1622
— Baret (J.). An alvearie. 1580. 1418
See Caius (J.). Of Englishe Dogges. 1576.
— Foxe (J.). Eicasmi. 1587. F°.
— Hemmingsen (N.). The epistle...to the Ephesians. 1581 (1580). 4°.
— Holinshed (R.). Chronicles. 1587– .
— Junius (A.). The Nomenclator. 1585.
— Marnix (P. van). The Beehive. 1580 *etc.* 8°.
— Morelius (G.). Verborum...Comm. 1583. 1515
— Vergilius. Bvcoliks. 1589. 4°.
— Withals (J.). A shorte dictionarie. 1586 *etc.*
Fleming (Giles). Magnificence exemplified. 1634. 4°. . . . 4358
Fleming (Thomas), *alias* Barnwell, *Roman Catholic Archbishop.* *See* Harris (P.). Excommunication. 1632. 4°.

No.

Flemish Language. *See* Flanders.
Flemming (Thomas), *Abp.* *See* Fleming.
Fletcher (Ed.), *Pemb.* Verses in Camb. Univ. Fasciæ. 1633. . . 5808
Fletcher (Giles), *the elder.* De literis antiquæ Britanniæ etc. Cantabrigiae, 1633. 8°. 5751
Of the russe common wealth. 1591. 8°. 1827
Verses in Baro (P.). In Jonam. 1579. 850
— Cambridge Lachrymae. 1587. 7356
Fletcher (Giles), *the younger.* Christs victorie and triumph. Cambridge, 1610. 4°. 5659
— Ed. 2. Cambridge, 1632. 4°. 5743
— Cambridge, 1640. 4°. 5842
The reward of the faithfull etc. Cambridge, 1623. 12°. . 5703
Fletcher (Henry). Verses in Vaughan (R.). Waterworkes. 1610. . 3576
Fletcher (I.). *See* F. (I.). The differences. 1598.
Fletcher (John). Monsievr Thomas. 1639. 4°. 4041
Verses in Jonson (B.). Catiline. 1611. 2902
Aleman (M.). The Rogve. 1623. 4079
For plays by Beaumont and Fletcher see under Beaumont (F.).
Fletcher (Nath.). Verses in Barlow (W.). Vita Cosin. 1598. . 1707
Fletcher (Phineas). Locustae. Cambridge, 1627. 4°. . . 5706
The purple island. Cambridge, 1633. 4°. 5752
Sicelides. 1631. 4°. 4887
Sylva... *See* Fletcher (G.), *the elder.* De literis. 1633.
Way to blessednes. 1632. 4°. 3881
Verses in Camb. Univ. Thr. thr. *bis.* 1603. 5616
— Fletcher (G.), *the younger.* Christs victorie. 1610 etc. 5659 etc.
See Fletcher (G.), *the elder.* De literis. 1633.
Fletcher (Richard), *Bp.* *See* Lambeth Articles. [1629?] *etc.*
Fletcher (William). Verses in Holyoake (F.). Dictionarium. 1640. . 3058
Fletewood (James), *K.C.C.* Verses in Camb. Univ. Epithalam. 1625. 5702
Fletewood (William). *See* Fleetwood.
Flint (Robert), *twice mayor of Queenborough.* Verses in Hoby (Sir E.). A curry-combe. 1615. 3111
Flood (John). *See* Sheldon (R). A survey. 1616. 4°.
Floods. 1570. *See* Knel (T.), *junior.* A Declaration of such...Fluddes. 1571.
Florence & Siena (Francesco, *prince of*). *Qu.* Francesco Maria de' Medici? *See* Ubaldino (P.). Militia. 1597.
Florence *of Worcester.* Chronicon ex Chronicis. 1592. 4°. . . 1828
Florenius (Paulus). *See* Freake (W.). The doctrines... 1630.
Flores (Juan de). [Hist. de Aurelio et Isabelle] Anvers. 1556. 8°. . 7803
— Brussels, 1608. 8°. 6635
Florio (G.). Florios second frutes. 1591. 4°. 2211
Worlde of wordes. 1598. 4°. 2069
Queen Anna's New World of Words. 1611. F°. . . . 3374
See Montaigne (M. de). Essayes. 1613 *etc.*
Florus (Lucius Annæus). The Roman Histories. [1618.] 12°. . 3124
— 1636. 12°. 7798
Breviaries. *See* Livius. The Roman Historie. 1600. . . 2428
Florus (Lucius Julius). *See* Florus (Lucius Annaeus).
Flower of the Commandments. W. de Worde, 1510. F°. . . 163
— 8 Oct. 1521. F°. 183
Floyd (John). The church conquerant. 1638. 4°. 6563
Overthrow of the protestants pulpit-babels. 1612. 4°. . 6526
Paire of spectacles for sir H. Linde. 1631. 8°. . . . 6625
Purgatories triumph over hell. 1613. 4°. 6530
Totall summe. 1639. 4°. 6564
Word of comfort ..concerning...the Blackfriars at London. 1623. 4°. 7766
See Lynde (Sir H.). A Case. 1638.

No.
Floyd (Thomas). Picture of a perfit commonwealth. 1600. 12°. . 2874
Floyde ( ). *See* Collection of certain letters. 1590.
Flud (Roger). Verses in Horne (C.). In obitum G. Whitakeri. 1596. 4°. 7332
Fludd (Robert). Answer unto M. Foster...of the Weapon-salve. 1631. 4°. 3546
Fo. (Jo.). Verses in Overbury (Sir T.), his Wife. Ed. 11. 1622. 3380
Foglietta (Uberto). Causes of the greatness of the Turkish Empire. *See* Turkey. The Mahumetane or Turkish Historie. 1600.
Folieta (Hubert). *See* Foglietta.
Foliot (Gilbert). Expositio in Canticum Canticorum. 1638. 4°. . 2702
Folkingham (William). Feudigraphia...for Ireland or Virginia. 1610. 4°. 3070
Folkys (Thomas), *of Lincoln's Inn*. Verses in Clowes (W.). A right... Treatise. 1602. 2013
Fons Vitæ. *See* Fountain. The Foũtayne or well of lyfe. [153- .] 8°.
Fonseca (C. de). Devout contemplations. 1629. F°. . . . 2458
Fontaines (Sieur de). *See* Chevalier (G. de). The Ghosts. 1624.
Foord (J.). Synopsis Politica. 1582. 8°. 1510
See also Forde.
Foorth (John). *See* Foord.
Forbes (John). Fruitfull sermon. Amsterdam, 1626. 8°. . 6354
Gemitus eccl. scoticanæ. Aberdoniæ, 1631. 4°. 6004
Irenicum... Aberdoniae, 1629. 4°. 6002
— Ed. 2. Aberdoniae, 1636. 4°. 6008
Treatise...of justification. Middelburg, 1616. 4°. . . 6479
Verses in Forbes (P.). An exquisite commentarie. 1613. . 3218
Forbes (Patrick). Defence of the lawful calling. Middelburg, 1614. 4°. 6478
Eubulus. Aberdeen, 1627. 4°. 6001
Exquisite commentarie vpon the revelation of Saint Iohn. 1613. 4°. 3218
Funerals. Aberdeen, 1635. 4°. 6007
Forcett (Edward). *See* Jewel (J.). Adversus Thomam Hardingum volumen alterum. 1578.
See also Forset.
Ford (John), *Dramatist*. Verses in Massinger (P.). The great dvke. 1636. 4137
Forde (John), *Encomiastes*. Verses in Barnes (B.). Foure bookes. 1606. 2435
See also Foorde.
Forde (William). Sermon...at Constantinople...at the funerals of... Lady Anne Glover. 1616. 4°. 3910
Fore-rvnner. [1605?] *See* C. (B.).
Foreign Avisoes. *See* Continuation.
Forestry. *See* Manwood (J.). A treatise. 1598 *etc.*
— Standish (A.). New directions. 1615.
Forestus (I.). Verses in Schloer (F.). The death of the two...kings. 1633. 3890
Forestus (Petrus). Arraignment of vrines. Trans. I. Hart. 1623. 4°. 3601
Forgius (Yvo). Verses in Bellehachius (O.). Sacrosancta bvcolica. 1583. 1640
Form and Manner of making Bishops. *See* Ordination Service.
Form of agreement. (Water-company.) [Ab. 1640?]. 7060
Form of Confession. *See* Primer. Eng. 1555. 8°. . . . 636
Form of prayer.
Form of prayer twice a week. Jugge & Cawood, 1563. 4°. . 961
Fourme of prayer necessary for the present time and state. Deputies of C. Barker, 1588. 4°. 7294
Certaine Prayers...to be vsed in the present Visitation...with the order of a Fast...euery Wednesday. R. Barker, 1603. 4°. 2578
Fourme of Prayer with Thankesgiuing...the 24. of March. R. Barker [1603-4?] 4°. 2579
Form of Common Prayer...with an order of Fasting. Norton & Bill, 1625. 4°. 2823

No.

Form of prayer *cont.* Form of Thanksgiving, A short forme of thankesgiving for staying the...Plague. Norton & Bill, 1625. 4°. . 2824
Forme of Prayer necessary to bee vsed in these dangerous times of Warre. Norton & Bill, 1626. 4°. 2828
Forme of Prayer with Thankesgiuing. 27 March. Norton & Bill, 1626. 4°. 2829
Forme of prayer...Warre. Norton & Bill, 1628. 4°. . . 2835
Forme of common prayer, together with an order of fasting...to be read euery Wednesday. Barker & Ass. of J. Bill, 1636. 4°. 2692, 2693
Forme of Common Prayer (July 8) for the averting of the plague. R. Barker & Ass. of J. Bill, 1640. 4°. 2711
Forset (Edward). Comparative discourse of the bodies. 1606. 4°. 7350
See also Forcet.
Forster (Humph.). Verses in Oxf. Univ. Magd. Coll. 1612. . 5302
Forster (William). *See* Oughtred (W.). The circle. 1632.
See also Foster.
Fortescue (George). Verses in Beaumont (Sir J.). Bosworth field. 1629. 3040
— Horatius. Odes. 1635 *etc.* . . . . . 4857 *etc.*
Fortescue (Sir John). De politica administratione, et legibus ciuilibus. [1546?] 8°. 675
De Laudibus legum Angliæ etc. 1616. 8°. 3264
Learned commendation of the politique lawes of England. Trans. R. Mulcaster. R. Tottell, 1573. 8°. 1126
Fortresse of Fathers. Trans. I. B. 1566. 8°. 7698
Foster (Walter), *fellow of Emmanuel College.* Verses in Hippocrates. 1633. 5812
Foster (William). Hoplocrisma-spongus. 1631. 4°. 4611
Verses in Oxf. Univ. Magd. Coll. 1612. . . . 5302
See Fludd (R.). Doctor Flvdds Answer vnto M. Foster. 1631.
See also Forster (W.).
Fotherby (Car.). Verses in Camb. Univ. Genethl. 1631. . . 5731
— Rex redux. 1633. 5748
— Randolph (T.). The jealous Lovers. 1640. 5852
Fotherby (Martin). Atheomastix. 1622. F°. 3682
Foure sermons. 1608. 4°. 2898
Fougasses (Thomas de). Generall historie of...Venice. Trans. W. Shute. 1612. F°. 3579
Fouler (John), *Roman Catholic printer. See* Fowler.
Foulis (Edward). Verses in Chaucer (G.). Amorum. 1635. . . 5414
Fountain or well of lyfe. T. Godfray. [1532?] 8°. . . . 559
Fourguevaux (Raimond de Beccarie de Pavie, baron de). *See* Du Bellay (G.). Instructions for the warres... 1589.
Fowler (Abraham). Verses in Rogers (T.). A philosophicall discourse. 1576. 1348
Fowler (J.). Verses in Camb. Univ. Lacrymæ. 1619. . . 5689
Fowler (John), *Rom. Cath. Printer.* Verses in More (Sir T.). A dialogve. 1573. 6123
See Frarin (P.). An oration. 1566.
— More (Sir T.). A dialogve. 1573. 8°.
— Sampson (T.). A Warning to take heed. 1578.
Fowler (John). A shield of defence. Amsterdam, 1612. 4°. . 6351
Fowns (Richard). Trisagion. 1619 (1618). 4°. 2534
Fox. *See* Fantasy of the passyon of the fox. 1530.
Fox (E.). De vera differentia regiæ potestatis et ecclesiasticæ. 1534. 4°. 429
— — 1538. 8°. 442
True differẽs betwen yᵉ regall power and the Ecclesiasticall. [Ab. 1549.] 8°. 1087
Fox (Luke). North-west Fox, or Fox of the North-west passage. 1635. 4°. 4209

No.
Fox (Richard), *bp.* *See* Contemplation of Sinners. W. de Worde, 1499. 4°.
Fox (Simeon). *See* Foxe.
Fox (Tho.). Verses in Oxf. Univ. Magd. Coll. 1612. 5302
Foxe (J.). Actes and Monuments. J. Day, 1563. F°. . . . 800
— Ed. 2. J. Day, 1570. F°. 816
— Ed. 4. J. Day, 1583. F°. 865
— Ed. 5. P. Short by the ass. of R. Day, 1596. F°. . . 2330
— Ed. 6. Stationers, 1610. F°. 3241
— Ed. 7. Vol. 1. 1632. F°. 7780
— — Vol. 3. 1631. F°. 4975
Abridgement of the...actes & monumentes. 1589. 4°. . . 2126
Continuation of the histories of the forrein martyrs. 1632. F°. 2463
De christo crucifixo concio. 1571. 4°. 826
De Christo gratis iustificante. 1583. 8°. 1375
De non plectendis adulteris. 1548. 8°. 1046
De oliva evangelica concio... 1578. 8°. 7290
Eicasmi seu meditationes in sacram Apocalypsim. 1587. F°. 1711
Papa Confutatus. 1580. 4°. 1808
The Pope Confuted. 1580. 4°. 1809
Sermon of Christ crucified. 1570. 4°. 817
— 1575. 8°. 7122
— 1585. 8°. 1884
Sermon...at the christening of a certaine Jew. Trans. J. Bell. 1578. 8°. 7290
Syllogisticon...De re...Sacramenti Eucharistici. [1563.] 8°. . 882
Of God his Election. *See* Beza (T.). The Treasure of Trueth. [1576?] etc.
Verses in Humphrey (L.). J. Jvelli vita. 1573. . . . 837
See Bible. Anglo-Saxon (N.T.) Gospels. 1571.
— Cranmer (T.). Reformatio legvm. 1571 *etc.*
— Grindal (E.). Concio Funebris. 1564.
— Haddon (W.). Contra H. Osorium. 1577.
— — Against Ierome Osorius. 1581.
— Luther (M.). Comm. upon the xv. psalmes. 1637. 4°.
— — Special...sermons. 1578 *etc.*
— Œcolampadius (J.). Sarmon. [154 .]
— Parsons (R.). Treatise of three conversions of England. 1603 (1604).
— Regius (U.). An instruccyon. [1548?] 8°.
— — A Necessary instruction. 1579.
— — The sermon. 1578. 4°.
— Tindale (W.). The whole workes... 1573–2.
Foxe (Roger). Verses in Laurentius (A.). Discourse. 1599. . . 2913
Foxe (Samuel). *See* Foxe (J.). Eicasmi. 1587.
Foxe (Simeon), *M.D.* Verses in Hippocrates. 1633. . . 5812
[*Licence.*] *See* Primrose (J.). De vulgi in medicina erroribus. 1638.
Foxley (George). Groanes of the spirit. Oxford, 1639. 12°. . 5489, 5490
Foy (John). Verses in Isaacon (H.). Saturni Ephemerides. 1633. . 4206
Foyle (James). Verses in Aslachus (C.). Description of heaven. 1623. 4516
Fr. (Ed.), *Col. Chr.* Verses in Camb. Univ. Epicedium. 1612. . 5665
Fr. (N.). Verses in Camb. Univ. Thr-thr. 1603. 5616
Fragment. [C mery tales? Ab. 153- .] 4°. 6676
(Verse.) For J. Gough. [Ab. 1536?] 4°. 578
Te Deum. For W. Seres & R. Kele. [1552?] 8°. . . . 946
[The Cōmandements of God. Ab. 1549.] 8°. 6717
[Exhortations for the Sicke. Ab. 154- .] 16°. . . . 6699
'Loke in thy myrrour.' [Ab. 152- ?] 4°. 6666
[Preparation to death. Ab. 1540.] 8°. 6689

No.

Fragment *cont.* [Ready Reckoner.] R. Wolfe. [Before 1573.] 8°. . 7107
[Sacrament of the Altar. Ab. 153- .] 8°. 6677
[Sacrament of the Altar. Ab. 154- .] 8°.. 6686
Frampton (John). *See* Monardes (N.). Joyfvll nevves. 1577 *etc.*
Fran (E.), *Ch.* Verses in Camb. Univ. Epicedium. 1612. . . 5665
France. *See* Bellopoelius (P.). De pace. 1552.
— Serres (J. de). The three parts of Commentaries. 1574. 4°.
1585–1591. *See* Colynet (A.). 1591.
1586. *See* Henry IV., *king of France.* Three Letters. 8°.
— *See* Necessary Doctrine. 1586.
1588. *See* Hurault (M.). A Discourse. 4°.
1592. Excellent discourse vpon the now present estate of France. 1592. 4°. 1965
See Eliot (J.). The svrvay or topographical Description. 1592.
Mutable and wauering estate of France from 1460 to 1595. 1597. F°. 2724
Historicall collection...vnder the Raignes of Henry 2. Francis 2. Charles 9. Henry 3. Henry 4. 1598. F°. . . 2726
1607. *See* Serres (J. de). A generall inventorie. 1607.
1609. Edict. *See* Combats. 3205
French Herald. 1611. 4°. 2027
French King's Declaration against the Duke of Vendosme etc. 1617. 4°. 3739
See News from France. 1618.
Late newes from France. 1620. 4°. 6919
French Heraud. 1622. 4°. 6931
See Nantes, Edict of 1622. 4°. 2292
— Serres (J. de). A generall historie. 1624.
Articles of peace...betwixt...Great Brittaine and France. 1629. 4°. 3743
Epitome of all the Lives of the Kings. Trans. R. B. Esq. 1639. 8°. 7754
See Schomberg (H. de). A relation. 1632. 4°.
Manifesto...for a Warre with Spaine. *See* Modern History. 1635. 4°.
Church. *See* Duarenus (F.). De sacris ecclesiæ. 1585.
Jesuits. *See* Prosopopeia. 1606.
Ligue. *See* Catholicke Apologie. [1590?] 1846
— *See* Masque of the League. 1592. 8°.
Parliament. 1590. *See* Henry IV of France. The true discourse... 1590.
— 1594. July 12 & 13. *See* Arnauld (A.). The arrainement. 1594.
— 1610. June 8. *See* Paris. Sorbonne. The copye. 1610.
— 1614. [Decree.] *See* Widdrington (R.). A copy. 1614.
— 1618. (Injunction.) *See* Newes from France.
Reformed Churches. *See* Apology or defence. 1579.
— Declaration...conc....persecution. 1621. 4°. 6927
— *See* Rochelle, *Assembly in.* A letter. 1621.
— The Apologie. 1628. 4°. 7815
— Copie of the letter of the Nationall Synod. 1631. 4°.
— 1632. *See* Bible, English. Psalms (Metrical). 12°.
Universities. *See* Henry VIII. [Marriage.] Gravissimæ. 1530.
— — — The determinations.
Grammar. 1635. *See* Dugres (G.).
Franciosini (Lorenzo). *See* Cervantes. Don Quixote. 1612.
Francis of Assisi. Alcaron of the Barefote Friers. 1550. 8°. . 617
— 1603. 8°. 2299
See also Franciscans, Order of.
Francis de Sales. Introduction to a deuout life. Trans. I. Y. 1616. 12°. 3665
— Ed. 2. J. Heigham. 1617. 12°. 6583
— Paris, 1637. 16°. 6203
Treatise of the love of god. Trans. M. Car. Ed. 18. Douai, 1630. 8°. 6589
See Camus (J. P.). The spiritvall director. 1633. 12°.

No.

Francis Xavier, (S.). [Life.] *See* Torsellino (O.). 1632.
Francis II, *King of France*. *See* France. An historicall collection. 1598.
Francis (Richard). *See* Promptorium puerorum. 1499 *etc.*
Franciscans, *Order of*. *See* Francis of Assisi. The Alcaron. 1550 *etc.*
[Catalogue (Biographical).] *See* Staney (W.). A treatise of Penance. 1617.
Third Order. *See* Staney (W.). A treatise of Penance. 1617.
Francius (J.), '*Silesius*,' *Pet*. Verses in Camb. Univ. Anthologia. 1632. 5741
— — — Voces. 1640. 5836
Franck (M.), *B.A.*, *Pemb*. Verses in Camb. Univ. Fasciae. 1633. . 5808
Francke or Francken (Christianus). *See* Freake (W.). The doctrines. 1630.
Francklin (Richard), *Pet*. Verses in Whitaker (W.). Praelectt. 1599. 5598
Francklin (Richard), *S.T.B.* 'Ορθοτονία. 1630. 8°. 3987
— Ed. 2. 1633. 8°. 4569
Frankfurt-on-Main. Catalogus universalis pro nundinis. 1623. 4°. . 7842
— *See* Brief discours. 1628. 4°. 4341
Franklin ( ). *See* Niccols (R.). Sir T. Overbvries Vision. 1616.
Franklin (Ed.). Verses *bis* in Camb. Univ. Lacrymæ. 1619. . 5689
Franklin (Richard), *of Peterhouse*. *See* Francklin.
Frankpledge. *See* Modus observandi [1529] *etc.* 1530.
Frarinus (Petrus). Oration against the vnlawfull insurrections of the Protestantes. Antwerp, 1566. 8°. 6120
— Another edition. n. d. 6121
See Charke (W.). A Treatise. 1586.
Fraunce (Abraham). Insignium explicatio. 1588. 4°. . . . 2200
Lawiers logike. 1588. 4°. 1769
Fraunces (Edward). Verses in Randolph (T.). The jealous Lovers. 1640. 5852
Frauncis (Richard). *See* Francis (R.).
Freake (William). The doctrine and practises of the...Iesuites. 1630. 4°. 4195
Frear (Thomas), *M.D.* Verses in Gwinne (M.). Vertumnus. 1607. 3621
See also Frere.
Frederick I, Barbarossa, *Emperor*. Copie of a Letter. *See* Evans (L.). The Castle. 1568.
Frederick I, *King of Bohemia*. Declaration...of the crowne of Bohemia. Middelburg, 1620. 4°. 6485
[Marriage.] *See* Chapman (G.). A memorable maske. [1614?]
— — Willet (A.). A treatise. 1612.
— — Oxford University. Epithalamia. 1613.
See Wither (G.). Epithalamia. 1612.
[Death.] *See* Schloer (J.). The death... 1633. 4°.
See Alting (H.). A Votiue Oration... 1615.
— Aretius (Jac.). Primvla. 1613.
— Aurelius (A.). In nuptias. 1613.
— Bohemia. Articles. 1620. 6918
— I. (S. R. N.). 1624.
— Palatinate. A fvll declaration. 1614 etc. . . . 2988 *etc.*
— — Declaration. 1637.
— Three severall treatises. 1630.
Frederick III, *Count Palatine*. *See* Catechism. The Catechisme. 1578(9?). 8°.
Frederick IV, *Count Palatine*. *See* Ursinus (Z.). The summe. 1587.
Frederick V, *Count Palatine*, afterwards *King of Bohemia*.
See Frederick I, King of Bohemia.
Frederick Henry, *Prince of Orange*. *See* Hertogenbosch, 's. A Iornall. 1629.
[Siege of Hertogenbosch.] *See* France. Articles. 1629. . . 3743
Free Schoole of Warre. Trans. W. B. 1625. 4°. 3525
Frégeville (J. de). Palma Christiana. 1593. 4°. 1969
Freige (John Thomas). *See* Polemon (J.). All the famous Battels... 1587.

No.

Freind (Gabriel). Prognostication. 1596. 8°. 1343
Freman (Martin). Verses in Camb. Univ. Lacrymæ. 1619. . . 5689
— Dolor. 1625. 5701
French Herald svmmoning all true christian Princes. 1611. 4°. . 2027
French Herauld. 1622. 4°. 6931
French (Marie). *See* Hueber (C.). A riche storehouse. 1578. 8°.
French (Thom.). Verses in Bodleiomnema. 1613. . . . 7756
Frende (Gabriel). *See* Freind.
Frere (John). Verses in Cheke (Sir J.). De obitu M. Buceri. 1551. 734
Frere (John), *M.D.* Verses in Haddon (W.). Lucubrationes. 1567. 928
Frere (Thomas), *M.A.* Verses in Gill (A.). Πάρεργα. 1632. . . 4558
See also Frear.
Fresh Suit against hvmane ceremonies. 1633. *See* Ames (W.).
Fresnes (P. Canaye, Sieur de). *See* Canaye.
Freston (Robert), *M.D.* Verses in Hippocrates. 1633. . . 5812
Frewen (Accepted). Oratio Funebris and Verses. *See* Oxford Univ. Magd. Coll. 1612. 4°. 5302
— Oxf. Univ. Horti. *bis*. 1640. 5499
Frewen (John). Certaine sermons upon (Rom. xi. 2–8). 1612. 8°. 2778
Friar and the Boy. A mery geste. W. de Worde [1509?]. 4°. . 218
Friars. *See* Wiclif (J.). Two short treatises. 1608.
Friedland, Duke of. *See* Waldstein.
Friend (Gabriel). *See* Freind.
Friend (John). *See* Office of General Remembrance. 1617. . 3588
Friesland or Frisia, West. [*In usum scholarum.*] *See* Vossius (G. J.). Rhetorices libri v. 1631.
Frigevillæus Gautius. *See* Frégeville (J. de).
Frisia. *See* Friesland.
Frisney (G.), *Magd.* Verses in Camb. Univ. Epithalam. 1625. . 5702
Frith (John). [*Works.*] *See* Tindale (W.). The whole workes... 1573–2.
Boke...answerynge vnto M. Mores letter. [R. Jugge], 1546. 8°. 948
— R. Jugge, 1548. 8°. 949
— A. Scoloker & W. Seres, 1548. 8°. 1037
Disputaciō of purgatorye. [Ab. 153–.] 8°. 6680
Myrroure or lokynge glasse...of baptisme. 1533. [1548?] 8°. . 883
Mirrovr or glasse to know thy selfe... *See* Vox Piscis. 1627.
Pistle to the Christen reder. The revelation of Antichrist. Antithesis. 'H. Luft, Marlborowe,' 12 July 1529. 8°. . 6272
[The Preparation to the Crosse.] *See* Vox Piscis. 1627.
See Gwynneth (J.). The cōfutacyon of...Frythes boke. 1536.
— Tindale (W.). Supper of the Lorde... 1533.
— Tracy (W.). The Testament. 1535. 8°.
— Wyclif (J.). Uvicklieffes Wicket. [1548?]
Frith (Thomas). Verses in Hippocrates. 1633. . . . 5812
Frobisher (Sir Martin). Verses in Gilbert (Sir H.). True reporte. 1583. 1354
See Fox (L.). North-west Fox. 1635.
Froissart (J.). [Chronicle.] The first volum. Trans. J. Bourchier. Pynson, 1523–5. F°. 281
— Third & fourthe boke. Pynson, 1525. F°. 286
The firste volum. W. Middleton [1548?]. F°. . . . 714
Epitome...by J. Sleydane. 1608. 4°. 1388, 1389
Frontinus. Stratagemes, sleyghtes, and policies of warre. Trans. R. Morysine. 1539. 8°. 450
Frubach (Volradus a). Pomi Palæstini evaporatio. 1636. 4°. . 3960
Fructus Temporum. *See* Chronicles of England.
Fruit of redempcyon. W. de Worde, 1514. 4°. 172
W. de Worde, 1517. 4°. 177
Fruit of Times. *See* Chronicles of England.
Fruitfull Sermon vpon the 3–8 verses of the 12...Romanes. 1584. 8°. 1897

No.
Fulbeck (W.). Direction or preparatiue to the study of the Lawe. 1600. 8°. 2388
— 1620. 8°. 3283
Historicall collection. 1601. 4°. 1867
Pandectes of the Law of Nations. 1602. 4°. 2392
Parallele or conference of the Civil...Canon...Common Law. 1618. 4°. 3271
— The second part. 1602. 4°. 2393, 2394
Fulford (John), *B.A.*, *Magd.* Verses in Camb. Univ. Συνωδία. 1637. 5790
Fulke (W.). Antiprognosticon. 1560. 8°. 1158
Briefe Confutation of a Popish Discourse. 1581. 4°. . . . 1813
Comfortable Sermon of Faith. 15 Feb. 1573. [1574?] 8°. . 1280
Confutation of a treatise made by William Allen... *See* Charke (W.). A treatise. 1586.
D. Heskins, D. Sanders, and M. Rastel...overthrowne. 1579. 8°. 1626
De successione ecclesiastica. 1584. 8°. 1647
Defense of the...translations of the holie scriptures. 1583. 8°. . 1511
Godly and learned sermon 26 Feb. 1580. [1580?] 8°. . 1658
Goodly Gallerye... *See below*, A most pleasant Prospect... 1602 *etc.*
In...Apocalypsim prælectiones. 1573. 4°. 1368
Most pleasant prospect into the garden of naturall contemplation, to behold...Meteors. 1602. 8°. 2878
— Ed. 2. 1634. 8°. 4852
— Ed. 3. 1639. 8°. 5203
— Ed. '3.' 1640. 8°. 5210
Sermon...at Hampton Court...12 Nov. 1570. 1579. 8°. . . 1349
T. Stapleton and Martiall...confuted. 1580. 8°. . . . 7284
Text of the new testament...at Rhemes. 1601. F°. . . . 2571
— 1617. F°. 3478
— Ed. 4. 1633. . . . . 4570, 4571
[*Sermon on Gal. iv.*] *See* Foxe (J.). De Christo gratis iustificante. 1583.
Two Treatises written against the Papistes. 1577. 8°. . 1533
Two treatises...against Allens booke...against...P. Frarine. *See* Charke (W.). A treatise. 1586. 5527
Woman of Canaan. 1611. 4°. 3577
See Bible, Eng. N. T. (Rhemes). 1601 *etc.*
— Norris (S.). An antidote. 1615 etc. 4°.
— The Guide. 1621. 4°.
— Nowell (A.) & W. Day. A true report...of Ed. Campion... 1583.
— P. (G.). Cantabrigiensis.
— Serres (J. de). A godlie...Commentarie. 1585. 8°.
Full and Plaine declaration. 1574 *etc.* *See* Travers (W.).
Fuller (Nic.). Argument...in the case of T. Lad, and R. Maunsell. 1607. 4°. 6872
Miscellaneorum...libri tres. Oxoniae, 1616. 4°. 5326
Fuller (Thomas). Historie of the holy warre. Cambridge, 1639. F°. 5806: engraved title inserted in 5842.
— Ed. 2. Cambridge, 1640. F°. 5843
Joseph's party-coloured coat. 1640. 4°. 5181
Verses in Camb. Univ. Genethl. 1631. 5731
— — Rex redux. 1633. 5748
Fuller (William). Sermon 7 June 1625. 1625. 4°. . . . 2035
Fulsius (Gulielmus). *See* Fulke (W.).
Fulwood (W.). Enemie of idlenesse. 1571. 8°. 1568
— 1593. 8°. 2186
Fumée (Martin). Historie of the troubles of Hungarie. Trans. by R. C. 1600. F°. 2915
Funck (Johann). *See* Carion (J.). Thre bokes of Cronicles. 1550.
Furio Ceriol (F.). Very briefe...Treatise...howe many counsells...a Prince...ought to have. [1570.] 8°. 944

Furnace ( ). *See* Brabourne (T.). A Defence. 1632.
Furth or Furtho (John), *M.D.* Verses in Camb. Univ. Epicedium. 1612. 5665
— Hippocrates. 1633. 5812
Fynes (Robert) *alias* Clinton. *See* Clinton.

G. (A.). *See* Gilby (A.). An answer. 1547.
— Testaments of the twelve Patriarchs. 1576. 8°.
Verses in Fletcher (G.). De literis. 1633. 5751
See Bible, Eng. N. T. (Rhemes). 1633.
G. (B.). *See* Gilpin (B.). Godly sermon. 1581.
G. (B.), *Citizen of London.* Newyeares Gifte. 1579. 4°. . . 1503
G. (B.), *of the Inner Temple.* Verses in Overbury (Sir T.). His Wife. Ed. 11. 1622. 3380
G. (C.). *See* Gibbon (C.). Watch-worde for Warre. 1596.
See Knight (W.). A concordance. 1610. F°.
G. (C. H.). *See* Hugo (H.). The siege of Breda. [1627?]
G. (E.). Verses in Du Bartas. Weekes. 1605–6 *etc.* . . 2476
— Overbury (Sir T.), His wife. Ed. 11. 1622. . . . 3380
— Oxf. Univ. Horti. 1640. 5499
G. (E.) [*i.e.* Grimstone (E.)]. *See* Acosta (J.). The Naturall...East and West Indies.
See Baudier (M.). The History of the Grand Seigneur. 1635.
G. (G.). Briefe treatise against the priesthood...of Rome. 1635. 4°. 5061
Creatures praysing god. 1622. 4°. 3017
Verses in Boethius. Of philosophicall comfort. 1609. . . 2176
G. (G.). [=Gilby (G.).] *See* Calvin (J.). An admonition. [1560?] 8°.
G. (G.). *See* Harper (J.). The Iewel of Arithmetic. 1616–7.
G. (G.), *of King's Coll. Camb.* Verses in Whitaker (W.). Praelectiones. 1599. 5598
— Camb. Univ. Gratulatio. 1623. 5695
G. (H.). Verses in Day (J.). A new spring. 1637. . . . 4650
See Hugo (H.). The siege of Breda. [1627?]
G. (I.). Verses in Camb. Univ. Thr-thr. 1603. . . . 5616
— Wadsworth (J.). Further Observations. 1630. . . 7788
— Mercator (G.). Historia. 1635. 4637
See Greene (John). A refvtation... 1615.
[=I. Gregory.] *See* Ridley (Sir T.). A view... 1634.
See Shakspeare (W.). Poems. 1640. 8°.
G. (I.), *Ar.* Verses in Biondi (G. F.). Eromena. 1632. . . 7753
See Gough (I.). Strange discovery. 1640.
G. (I.), *gentleman.* *See* Grassi (G. di). Arte of Defence. 1594. 4°.
G. (J.). [Myrrour or lokyng glasse of lyfe.] R. Wyer. [1532.] 8°. . 538
G. (L.). Verses in Comenius (J. A.). Porta linguarum. 1633. . 7613
G. (L.), *Cantab.* Verses in Barthlet (J.). The Pedegrewe of Heretiques. 1566. 1400
G. (M.). Verses in Gostwyke (R.). Deo &c. 1616. . . . 5678
G. (M.), K. *See* K. (M. G.).
G. (N.) [*i.e.* N. Grimald]. *See* Sohn (G.). A brief...treatise. 1592.
G. (N.). Verses in Comenius. Porta linguarum. 1631 *etc.* . 4435 *etc.*
G. (R.). Salutem in christo. [Ab. 1571.] 8°. 7135
Verses in Parkhurst (J.). Ludicra. 1573. 838
See Calvin (J.). The Mynde of the Godly. [1548.] 8°.
— — Treatise of Treasons. 1572.
G. (R.), *C.C. or C.C.S.* Verses *ter* in Camb. Univ. Gratulatio. 1623. 5695
— — Anthologia. 1632. 5741
G. (R.), *C.C.C.* Verses in Wadsworth (J.). Further Observations. 1630. 7788
G. (T.). Friers chronicle. 1623. 4°. 4077
G. (T.), *Collegii Regalis Cantabrig. Socius* [T. Goad or T. Griffin]. Proditoris proditor. 1606. 4°. 3615

No.
G. (T.) *cont.* Verses in Humphrey (L.). J. Jvelli vita. 1573. . 837
— Taylor (J.). Workes. 1630. 3812
See Sibbs (R.). Christ's exaltation. 1639.
G. (T.). *See* Goad (T.). The Dolefull evensong. 1623. . . 4781
G. (T.). [=Goodwin (T.).] *See* Preston (J.), *D.D.* Sermons. 1630 *etc.*
G. (T.), *T.C.* Verses in Camb. Univ. Gratulatio. 1623. . . 5695
G. (W.). Discovery of certaine notorious shifts...by M. John White. Ed. 2. 1619. 4°. 7690
See Bolton (R.). Mr Boltons last...Things. 1635.
— Nantes, Edict of. 1622. 4°.
Ga (G.). Verses in Camden (W.). Britannia. 1637. . . . 3055
Gábor (Bethlen). *See* Gabriel.
Gabriel (Bethlen), *Prince of Transylvania.* *See* Bohemia. Articles. 1620. 6918
Gace (W.). *See* Hemmingsen (N.). Learned...Commentarie vpon the Epistle of Iames. 1577.
— Luther (M.). Special and chosen sermons. 1578 *etc.*
Gager (William). *See* Rainolds (J.). Th'overthrow of stage-playes. 1599 *etc.*
Gagge for the pope, and the iesvits: or the arraignement...of Antichrist. 1624. 4°. 3861
Gagge of the reformed Gospell. *See* Kellison (M.). 1623.
Gainsford (Tho.), *Captain.* Glory of England. [1619?] 4°. . 7559
Secretaries studie. 1616. 4°. 2752
True...history of Perkin Warbeck. 1618. 4°. 7558
Verses in Overbury (Sir T.), His Wife. Ed. 11. 1622. . . 3380
Gale (Charles). Verses in Camb. Univ. Carmen. 1635. . . 5770
— — *Συνωδία.* 1637. 5790
Gale (T.). Certaine Workes of Chirurgerie. 1563. 8°. . . 1303
— — *See* Vigo (J. de). The whole worke. 1586.
See Galen (C.). Certaine Workes. 1586. 4°. . . . 7770
— Hall (J.). A most excellent...woorke. 1565.
Galen (Claudius). Τῶν σωζομένων τινα...a...T. Goulstono...recensita. 1640. 4°. 4397
[De compositione medicamentorum, Lib. III.] *See* Baker (G.). The Composition or making of...Oil. 1574.
De naturalibus facultatibus. Pynson, 1523. 4°. . . . 282
De temperamentis et de inaequali intemperie. T. Linacro interpr. Cantabrigiae, 1521. 4°. 5504
Certaine Workes. Trans. T. Gale. 1586. 4°. 7770
[Third and Fourth Books. (*Eng.*).] *See* Cauliaco (G. de). Gvydos Questions. 1579.
Galens Bookes of Elementes. *See* Jones (J.). Briefe discourse. 1574.
See Braunschweig (H.). The noble experyence. 1525.
— Petrus *Hispanus.* The treasury. [1550.]
Galfridus [Starkey?], *Anglicus.* *See* Garlandia (J. de). Synonyma. 1494 *etc.*
Gall (St). *See* Belijdenisse. 1568. 8°. 7879
Gallard ( ). *See* Brabourne (T.). Defence. 1632.
Galloway (Patrick). *See* James I. Fruitfull Meditation... [1603?]
Gamaches (Ph. de). [Licence.] *See* Richeome (L.). Holy Pictures. 1619.
Game and Play of Chess. *See* Cessolis. 118
Game at Chess. 1625. *See* Middleton (T.).
Ganning (Ni.), *C.C.* Verses in Camb. Univ. Epithalam. 1625. . 5702
— Genethl. 1631. 5731
Gararde, *Friar Minor of the Order of the Observants.* *See* Gherit van der Goude.
Garbrand (J.). Verses in Wilson (Sir T.). Discourse. 1584. . 1872
— Blaxton (J.). The english usurer. 1634. 4895
See Jewel (J.). Certaine sermons. 1583. 8°.
— — Exposition. 1583.

No.

Garbrand (J.) *cont.* Viewe. 1582.
Garbrand (T.). Verses in Oxf. Univ. Magd. Coll. 1612. . . 5302
Gard (Ric.), qu. Gardiner? Verses in Baret (J.). An Alvearie. 1573. . 7249
Garden of flowers. Utrecht, 1615. Oblong F°. 6643
Garden. *See* Godlie garden. 1629. 7759
Garden (Al.). Verses in Forbes (P.). Funerals. 1637. . . 6007
Gardiner (Daniel). Verses in Hill (T.). The arte of vulgar arithmeticke... 1600. 2197
Gardiner (Edm.). Phisicall and approved Medicines. 1611. 4°. . 2508
Triall of Tabacco. 1610. 4°. 2505
Gardiner (Richard). Profitable Instructions for...Kitchin Gardens. 1603. 4°. 2014
Sermon preached...in Oxford. [John i. 14.] Oxford, 1638. 4°. 5482
Sermon conc. the Epiphany. [Matt ii. 2.] Oxford, 1639. 4°. . 5491
See also Gard.
Gardiner (Robert), *K.C.C.* Verses in Camb. Univ. Epithalam. 1625. 5702
— — Rex redux. 1633. 5748
Gardiner (Sam.). Dialogue or conference betweene Irenæus and Antimachus. 1605. 4°. 1999
Domes Day Booke. 1606. 4°. 2019
Foundation of the faithfull. 1611. 8°. 2306
Scourge of sacriledge. 1611. 8°. 2307
Way to heaven. 1611. 8°. 2308
Gardiner (Stephen). Communication betwene my Lord Chancelor and iudge Hales. 6 Oct. 1553, 'Rouen.' 8°. . . . 6241
De vera obediencia. 'M. Wood, Roane,' 26 Oct. 1553. 8°. 6239, 6240
De vera obedientia. 'Rome, Castle of S. Angel,' 1553. 8°. . 1048
Declaration of such true articles as G. Joye hath gone about to confute. 1546. 4°. 759
— 1546. 8°. 760
Detection of the Deuils Sophistrie...in the...Sacrament of the aulter. 1546. 8°. 761
Explicatiō and assertion of the true Catholique fayth. 1551. 8°. 6718
See Admonition to the bishoppes. 1553.
— Cranmer (T.). An answer. 1551 *etc.*
— Gilby (A.). An answer. 1547.
— Hooper (J.). Answer vnto my lord of wynchesters booke... 1547.
— Joye (George)....confuteth Uvinchesters Articles... 1543.
— — Refutation. 1546.
— Martin (T.). A traictyse. 1554.
— Poynet (J.). An apologie. 1556.
— Turner (W.). Rescvynge of the romishe fox. 1545. . 6282
Gardiner (Thomas). Verses in Cheke (Sir J.). De obitu M. Buceri. 1551. 734
Garey (Samuel). Cæsaris hostes. 1618. 4°. 3797
Jentaculum Iudicum. 1619. (A manuall for Magistrates. 1619.) B. Alsop, 1623. 4°. 4177
New yeares gift for the svole. 1615. 4°. 3109
Two Treatises. 1605. 8°. 1791
Garlandia (J. de). Synonyma. Paris, 1494. 4°. 133
— Pynson [1502]. 4°. 254
— (+Aequivoca.) W. de Worde, 1505. 4°. . . . 149+150
Garnett (Henry). Actio in H. Garnetum. 1607. 4°. . . . 2361
True and perfect relation of the whole proceedings against the late... Traitors. 1606. 4°. 2593, 2594
See Abbot (R.). Antilogia adversvs Apologiam. 1613.
— Sutcliffe (M.). A challenge. 1602.
— Wisbech. True relation of the faction. 1601.
Garnons (John), *D.D.* Verses in Camb. Univ. Lacrymae. 1619. . 5689
— Oldmayne (T.). Life's brevitie. 1636. 4°.

No.
Garrard (Edmond). Countrie gentleman moderator. 1624. 4°. . 7344
Garrard (John). Verses in Camb. Univ. Rex redux. 1633. . 5748
Garter, *Order of the*. *See* Heylyn (P.). History of S. George. 1633.
Garter (Bernard). *See* G. (B.). *Citizen*. New Yeares Gifte. 1579. . 1503
Garthwait (Henry). Μονοτέσσαρον. Evangelicall harmonie. Cambridge, 1634. 4°. 5813
Garthwaite (Henry). Verses in Roberts (L.). The merchants mappe. 1638. 5133
Garway (P.). Verses in Camb. Univ. Epicedium. 1612. . . 5665
Garway (William). Verses in Camb. Univ. Fasciae. 1633. . 5808
Gascoigne (G.). Hundreth sundrie Flowers. [1572?] 4°. . . 1519
Posies. 1575. 4°. 1482
Steele Glas. 1576. 4°. 1486
Verses in Turberville (G.). The noble arte. 1575 *etc*. 1525 *etc*.
Gascoigne (Nic.). Verses in Horne (C.). In obitum Whitakeri. 1596. 7332
Gascoigne (T.). *See* Mirror of Our Lady. 1530.
Gatacre (T.). *See* Gataker.
Gataker (Charles). Verses in Camb. Univ. Rex redux. 1633. . . 5748
Gataker (Mrs Dorothy). [Funeral.] *See* W. (H.). Θρηνοικος. 1640.
Gataker (Tho). Abrahams decease...funerall of...R. Stock. 1627. 4°. 4808
Anniversarie memoriall of...the Spanish Inuasion. 1626. 4°. 5800
Benefit of a good name. *See below*, Two funeral sermons. 1620.
Christian constancy... Sermon...buriall of W. Winter. 1624. 4°. 4789
Christian mans care... Sermon... Catechisme. 1624. 4°. . 4790
משכיל לדוד Davids Instructor. 1620. 4°. 3940
Decease of Lazarus. 1640. 4°. 5211
Discussion of the popish doctrine of Transsubstantiation. 1624. 4°. 4699
Gods parley with princes. 1620. 4°. 3941
Good wife gods gift: and a wife indeed. 1623. 4°. . . . 4776
Jacobs thankfulnesse. 1624. 4°. 4791
Joy of the just. 1623. 4°. 4777
Just defence...concerning...Lots. 1623. 4°. 4778
Of the nature and use of lots. 1619. 4°. 3928
Pauls desire of dissolution. *See below*, Two funeral sermons. 1620.
Spirituall watch. 1619. 4°. 3933
— Ed. 2. 1622. 4°. 4765
True contentment. 1620. 4°. 3942
Two funeral sermons. 1620. 4°. 3943
Two marriage sermons. 1620. 4°. 3944
Two sermons. 1623. 4°. 4779
Verses in Whitaker (W.). Praelectiones. 1599. 5598
See Bradshaw (W.). Plaine...exposition of II Thessalonians... 1620.
— Elton (E.). Gods holy mind.
— Galen. Τῶν σωζομένων τινα. 1640. 4397
— Ward (Sam). Balme from Gilead. 1622.
Gates (G.). Defence of Militarie profession. 1579. 4°. . . . 1627
Gatford (Lionel). Verses in Hippocrates. 1633. 5812
Gaudanus (Gul.). *See* Æsop. Fabulæ. 1635.
Gaudy (Will.). Verses in Camb. Univ. Genethl. 1631. . . . 5731
— — Fasciae. 1633. 5808
Gaule (John). Distractions or the holy madnesse. 1629. 12°. . 4825
Practique theories. 1628–9. 12°. 4922
Gautius (Frigevillæus). *See* Frégeville (J. de).
Gawen (John). *See* Trelcatius (L.). A briefe institution. 1610.
Gayton (Edward), *M.A. Joan*. Verses in Randolph (T.). Poems. 1640. 5500
Gaywood (G.). Verses in Du Bartas. Weekes. 1605–6 *etc*. . . 2476
Geale (Ric.). Verses in Oxf. Univ. Horti. 1640. 5499

No.
Gearing (Thom.). Verses in Camb. Univ. Anthologia. 1632. . 5741
Gedde (Walter). Booke of sundrie draughtes. 1615(-16). 4°. . 2346
Gee (Edward). Two sermons. 1620. 4°. 3130
Gee (George). *See* Gee (E.). Two sermons. 1620.
Gee (John). Foot out of the snare. 1624. 4°. 2549
New shreds of the old snare. 1624. 4°. 3862
See Gee (E.). Two sermons. 1620.
— Webbe (G.). Catalogus Protestantium. 1624.
Geers (John). Verses in Oxf. Univ. Horti. 1640. . . . 5499
Geffe (Nicholas). *See* Serres (O. de). The perfect vse of silk-wormes. 1607. 4°.
Gell (Robert), *B.D. Christ's.* Verses in Camb. Univ. Dolor. 1625. . 5701
— Hippocrates. 1633. 5812
— Camb. Univ. Carmen. 1635. 5770
— — *Συνῳδία.* 1637. 5790
— — Voces. 1640. 5836
Gelli (G. B.). Circes. Trans. H. Iden. 1557. 8°. 997
Fearefull Fansies of the Florentine Cooper. 1599. 8°. . . 1382
Gellibrand (Henry). Discourse...of the magneticall needle. 1635. 4°. 5062
See James (T.), *Captain.* The strange...voyage. 1633.
— Wells (J.). Sciographia. 1635.
Gellius (Aulus). *See* Æsop. Fabulæ. 1635.
Gellius (John). Verses in Adamson (J.). *Εἰσόδια.* 1618. . . 5960
Gello (John Baptista). *See* Gelli.
Gemini (T.). Compendiosa totius Anatomiæ. 1559. F°. . . 1237
Geminus (Papyrius). Hermathena. Cantabrigiae, 1522. 4°. . 5505
See Powell (E.). Propugnaculum. 1523.
Gemistus Pletho (Georgius). *See* Pletho (Georgius Gemistus). 1577.
Gemma Fabri. *See* Smyth (W.), *D.D.* Gemma Fabri. 1598.
Gemma vocabulorum. *See* Ortus vocabulorum. 1528. No. 195 and p. 1729.
Generall Demands conc. the late Covenant... Also the replyes. 1638. 4°. 4997
— R. Young, Edinburgh, 1638. 4°. 5980, 5981
General Pardon...by our Almightie Father. [Before 1590.] 8°. . 1771
Geneva. Lawes and Statutes. Trans. R. Filles. 1562. 8°. . 1299
Church. Catechism. *See* Liturgies. Geneva. English Church. The forme... 1550 *etc.*
City. [Further Relief.] *See* James I. To the...Convocation. 1604. F°. 7416
Discipline. *See* Tilenus (D.). Parænesis. 1620.
Pastors and Professors. *See* Bèze (T. de). Epistola. 1598.
University. *See* Bèze (T. de). Propositions and principles. 1595. 8°.
Gentili (Alb.). De Iuris interpretibus. 1582. 4°. . . . 1925
De Legationibus. 1585. 4°. 1561
Lectionum & Epistolarum...liber 1(-4). 1583(-4). 8°. . . 1931
Regales disputationes tres. 1605. 4°. 3604
Verses in Budden (J.). Gvl. Patteni vita. 1602. . . . 5256
— Florio (G.). Queen Anna's New world. 1611. . . 3374
See Howson (J.). Uxore dimissa... 1606.
— Rainolds (J.). Th' overthrow of stage-playes. 1599 *etc.*
Gentili (Scipione). Paraphrasis aliquot Psalmorum Davidis. 1581. 4°. 1544
In xxv. Davidis psalmos epicæ paraphrases. 1584. 4°. . 1933
See Tasso (T.). Solymeidos libri dvo. 1584.
— — Plvtonis Concilium. 1584.
Gentilis (Robert). *See* Gentili (A.). Regales Disputationes. 1605.
See Sarpi (P.). History of the inqvisition. 1639.
Gentillet (Inn.). Discourse upon...wel governiug. 1602. F°. . . 2430
— 1608. F°. 2437
Gentleman (Tobias). Englands way to win wealth. 1614. 4°. . 3541
Gentleness. *See* Heywood (John). Of Gentylnes & Nobylyte. [153–.]

No.

Geoffrey of Monmouth. *See* Chronicles of England. 1480 *etc.*
George, *saint, of Cappadocia.* *See* Heylyn (P.). The history. 1633.
George, *abp. of Alexandria.* *See* Chrysostom (John): opera. 1613.
George (David). *See* Joriszoon.
Geranius (Cephas). *See* Marcort (A.). Declaration. 1547.
Gerard (Fras.). Verses in Camb. Univ. Fasciae. 1633. . . . 5808
Gerard (John). The herball. 1597. F°. 2348
— 1633. F°. 2464
Gerard (John), *D.D.* *See* Gerhard.
Gerardus, *Abp of York.* *See* Volusianus. Epistolæ duæ. 1569.
Gerardus (Andreas), *Hyperius.* Foundation of the Christian Religion. Trans. I. H. [1583?] 12°. . . . . . 1895=7322+
Practise of preaching. Eng. J. Ludham. 1577. 4°. . . 7275
Gerbellius (Nicolas). *See* Æsop. Fabulæ. 1635.
Geree (John). *See* Pemble (W.). Vindiciæ fidei. 1629.
— — Works. 1635.
Gerhard (Johann). Conquest of Temptations. Trans. R. Bruch. Ed. 2. 1623. 12°. 4780
Gerards Prayers. Trans. R. Winterton. 1625. 12°. . . 3321
See below, Meditations and Prayers.
Golden chaine of divine aphorismes. Trans. R. Winterton. Cambridge, 1632. 12°. 5744
Meditationes sacrae. Cantabrigiae, 1634. 12°. 5761
Meditations. Trans. R. Winterton. Cambridge, 1627. 12°. . 5707
Meditations and Prayers. (Meditations. Ed. 2. Prayers. Ed. 3.) Cambridge, 1631. 12°. 5735
Meditations. Ed. 3. (Prayers. Ed. 4.) Cambridge, 1632. 12°. 5800
Meditations. Ed. 4. (Prayers. Ed. 5.) Cambridge, 1635. 12°. 5773
Meditations. Ed. 5. (Prayers. Ed. 6.) Cambridge, 1638. 12°. 5824
Meditations. Ed. 6. (Prayers. Ed. 7.) Cambridge, 1640. 12°.. 5844
Summe of christian doctrine. Cambridge, 1640. 24°. . . 5845
Soules Watch. 1621. 12°. 4075
German (Sam.). Verses in Oxf. Univ. Magd. Coll. 1612. . . 5302
Germany. Actes of the Ambassage...of the Lords...of Germany at Naumburg...conc....Pius the iiii. 1561. 8°. 7133
See Phiston (W.). The estate. 4° 1595.
[Letter from Paul V.] *See* Bohemia. Two letters. 1620.
Excellent and materiall discourse...if...Germanie...be subdued. Trans. S. B. 1626. 4°. 6971
See Three severall treatises. 1630.
Ferdinand II. 1630. *See* Sweden. Gustavus II, Adolphus. 1631.
Reformed Church. 1632. *See* Bible, Eng. Psalms (Metr.). 12°.
Lamentations of. *See* Vincent (P.). 1638. 7760
Gerrard (P.). Godly Inuectiue in the defence of the Gospell. 1547. 8°. 603
Gerson (John). *See* Betson (T.). Ryght profytable treatyse. [1499.] 4°. 59
— Clemangiis (N. de). Specvlvm... 1606.
[Imitatio Christi.] *See* Imitatio Christi.
See Sarpi (P.). An apology. 1607.
Gesner (Conrad). Hist. Animalium. Lib. 1-4. Tiguri, 1551-(1558). F°. 7745-6
— Lib. 5. Tiguri, 1587. F°. 7750
Icones animalium. Ed. 2. Tiguri, 1560. 7748-9
Nomenclator aquatilium animantium. Tiguri, 1560. F°. . . 7747
Mithridates. De differentiis linguarum. Tiguri, 1555. 8°. . 6292
— Ed. alt. Typis Wolfianis, Tiguri, 1610. 8°. 6305
New booke of destillatyon...called the Treasure of Evonymvs. Trans. P. Morwyng. 1565. 4°. 807
Newe Iewell of Health. Trans. G. Baker. 1576. 4°. . . . 1415
Onomasticon. *See* Calepinus (A.). Dictionarium. 1627. F°.
See Lord's Prayer (Polyglot). 6293

No.

Gesner (Conrad) *cont.* *See* Moffett (T.). Insectorum. 1634.
Geste (Edmund). *See* Guest.
Geveren (Sheltro à). Of the ende of the World[1]. Ed. 1. 1577. 4°. 7315
— Ed. 2. 1577. 4°. 1836
Geyn (J. de). Maniement d'armes. Amsterdam (Hague), 1608. F°. 6639
— Zutphen. 4°. 6647
Gheast (Edmund). *See* Guest.
Ghent. *See* Salomon, *the Jew*. Wounderfull Prophecie. (1543.) 8°. 6107
Gheijn (J. de). *See* Geyn.
Gherit van der Goude. Interpretacyon and sygnyfycacyon of the Masse...by Gararde. 8 Oct. 1532. 8°. 587
Ghostly Father. A boke of a Ghoostly fader. W. de Worde [15]. 4°. 219
Ghostly Matters. *See* Horologium Sapientiae.
Gibbens (Nicolas). Questions and disputations. T. i. Part 1. 1601. 4°. 2919
— 1602. 4°. 7465
Gibbon (Charles). Order of equalitie. Cambridge, 1604. 4°. . . 5623
Watch-word for warre. Cambridge, 1596. 4°. . . . 5582
Gibbons (Richard), *S.J.* *See* Puente (L. de la). Meditations. 1610.
Gibbons (William), *Captain.* *See* Fox (L.). Northwest Fox. 1635.
Gibbs (Charles). Verses in Camdeni Insignia. 1624. . . . 5346
Gibson (Abraham). Lands Mourning for vaine swearing. 1613. 8°. 3399
Gibson (Anthony). Verses in Guillim (J.). A display. 1611 *etc.* 3211 *etc.*
Gibson (C.). Verses in Camb. Univ. Fasciae. 1633. . . 5808
Gibson (Ed.). Verses in Camb. Univ. Epicedium. 1612. . . 5666
Gibson (Sam.). Sermon...at Oundle. 1620. 4°. 7477
Gibson (T.). Breue Cronycle of the Bysshope of Romes blessynge. [1548?] 8°. 884
Frvitful sermon. [1584?] 8°. 1905
Giessen School. *See* Scheibler (C.). Philosophia. 1628.
Giffard ( ). Verses in Barlow (W.). Vita R. Cosin. 1598. . 1707
Gifford (G.). Dialogue concerning witches. 1593. 4°. . . 2135
Discourse of the subtill Practises of Deuilles by Witches and Sorcerers. 1587. 4°. 1235
Plaine declaration that our Brownists be full Donatists. 1590. 4°. 2207
Sermons upon Revelation. 1596. 4°. 2067
— 1599. 4°. 2249
Short reply unto the...Donatists. 1591. 4°. 2212
Two sermons. 1597. 8°. 2904
See Greenwood (J.). Answere to George Giffords Pretended Defence... 1590.
— — More work for priests. 1640.
Gifford (John). Verses in Coryate (T.). Coryates Crvdities. 1611. 3076
[Licence.] *See* Jorden (E.). Discourse. 1633.
Gifford (William). *See* Sutcliffe (M.). De tvrcopapismo. 1599.
Gil (Alexander). *See* Gill.
Gilbert (Sir H.). True reporte...of the New-found Landes. 1583. 4°. 1354
Gilbert (Will.). De magnete. 1600. F°. 2338
See Barlow (W.), *archdeacon of Salisbury.* Magneticall Aduertisements. 1616 *etc.*
Gilby (Antony). An admonition... *See* Knox (J.). The appellation. 1558. 8°.
Answer to the deuillish detection of S. Gardiner. 1547. 8°. . 775
Commentarye vpon...Mycha. 1551. 8°. 784, 785
Of God his election and reprobation. *See* Beza (T.). Treasure of Truth. 1581. 8°.
To my louynge brethren...about the popish aparell. [1566?] 8°. 6413
See Bible, Eng. Psalmes. 1581 *etc.*
— Carter (O.). An Answere. 1579.

[1] These two editions do not 'agree textually' as stated in the catalogue.

No.
Gilby (Godred). *See* Calvin (J.). An admonition. [1560?] 8°.
— Cicero. An Epistle...to...Quintus. 1561.
Gildas. De excidio Britanniæ. 1568. 8°. 808
Epistle of Gildas. 1638. 12°. 4661
Giles (Nat.), *Mus.B.* Verses in Oxf. Univ. Magd. Coll. 1612. . . 5302
— Ravenscroft (T.). Briefe discourse. 1614. . . . 2029
Gill (Alexander), *the elder*. Logonomia Anglica. Ed. 2. 1621. 4°. 3803
Sacred philosophie of the holy scripture. 1635. F°. . . 3954
Verses in Speed (J.). The theatre. 1611. 3215
[Letter to M. Maier.] *See* Anthony (F.). Apologia. 1616. . 3759
Gill (Alexander), *the younger*. Πάρεργα. 1632. 12°. . . . 4558
Verses in Hawkins (W.). En Priscianus. 1632. . . 4562
— — Corolla. 1634. 5803
— Hodson (W.). The holy sinner. 1639. 5796
— Glapthorne (H.). Tragedy of Albertus Wallenstein. 1640. . 5098
See Gustavus II, Adolphus. The new starr... 1632.
Gill (George), *M.A.* Verses in Gill (A.). Πάρεργα. 1632. . . 4558
Gill (John) or Gyll. Verses in Dod (J.). Plaine...exposition of the Ten Commandements. Ed. 18. 1630. 1892
Gill (Nath.), *M.A.* Verses in Gill (A.). Πάρεργα. 1632. . . 4558
Gillespie (G.). Dispute...Church of Scotland. 1637. 4°. . . 7036
Gilpin (Bernard). Godly sermon. 1552. 1581. 8°. . . 1636
— 1636. 12°. 7642
[Life.] *See* Carleton (G.). Vita. 1628.
— — The life. 1629. 4°. 5039
— — Life and sermon. 1636. 12° 7642
Gilpin (George), *the elder*. *See* Marnix (P. van). Bee Hive. 1579 *etc.*
Gilpin (Rand.). Verses in Camb. Univ. Epicedium. 1612. . . 5665
— — Lacrymæ. 1619. 5689
Giovio (Paolo). *See* Polemon (J.). All the famous Battels... [1577?]
Giraldus Cambrensis. Itinerarivm *etc.* *See* Ponticus (L.). Pontici libri sex. 1585.
See Holinshed (R.). Chronicles. 1587- .
Girardus, *Abp of York*. *See* Gerardus.
Girodus (Johannes). Verses in Buridanus. Quæstiones. 1640. . 5463
Gittins (Rodolph). Verses in Juvenalis (J.)... Satyræ. 1615. . 2279
Glanfield (Ri.), *Pemb.* Verses in Camb. Univ. Carmen. 1635. . 5770
See also Glanvile.
Glanvile (Rich.), *Pemb.* Verses in Camb. Univ. Genethl. 1631. . 5731
See also Glanfield.
Glanville (Bartholomew de). *See* Bartholomæus, *Anglicus*.
Glanville (Sir John), *the younger*. Copies of two speeches in parliament. 1628. 4°. 6988
Glanville (R. de). Tractatus de legibus et consuetudinibus. [1555?] 8°. 1154
— 1604. 8°. 2400
Glanville (Ric.). *See* Glanvile.
Glapthorne (Henry). The Hollander. 1640. 4°. 3726
Tragedy of Albertus Wallenstein. 1640. 4°. . . . 5098
Wit in a constable. 1640. 4°. 3727
Glascock (Chr.). Verses in Camb. Univ. Carmen. 1635. . . 5770
Glascoke (Henry). Verses in Cambridge Lachrymae. 1587. . 7356
Glaser (Philip). Verses in Aristotle. [Ethics.] 1634. . . . 5717
Glasgow City. Verses in Adamson (J.). Εἰσόδια. 1618. . . 5960
Glass of life. *See* G. (J.). Myrrour or lokyng glasse of lyfe. [15 .] 8°.
Glastonbury. Church of Foreign Protestants. *See* Liturgies. London, 1552. 6719
Glegius (Jacobus). Verses *bis* in Adamson (J.). Εἰσόδια. 1618. . 5960
— Baron (R.). Philosophia. 1621. 5997
Glemham (Charles), *G.* *See* Vermigli (P.). Most Godly Prayers. 1569. 8°. 934
Glisson (Francis). Verses in Hippocrates. 1633. 5812

No.

Glory of their times. 1640. *See* Lupton (D.).
Glossary. English. *See* Wyclif (J.). Two short treatises... 1608. . 5290
Welsh-English. *See* Llwyd (H.). The Breviary of Britayne. 1573.
Gloucester (Prince Henry, Duke of). (1640–1660.) *See* Henry, Duke of Gloucester, Prince.
Glover (Lady Anne). [Funeral.] *See* Forde (W.). A sermon. 1616. 4°.
Glover (Edward). *See* Bredwell (S.). Detection of Ed. Glouer. [1586?]
Glover (George), *Engraver*. *See* Heywood (T.). The hierarchie. 1635. 2466
See also Index of Engravers.
Glover (Robert), *Protestant Martyr*. Letters. *See* Coverdale (M.). Certain...letters. 1564.
Glover (Robert), *Somerset Herald*. *See* Milles (T.). Nobilitas. 1608.
Go. (Tho.). *See* Goad (T.).
Goad (George), *K.C.C.* Verses in Camb. Univ. Epithalam. 1625. . 5702
— — Genethl. 1631. 5731
— — Anthologia. 1632. 5741
— — Fasciae. 1633. 5808
— — Rex redux. 1633. 5748
— Hawkins (W.). Corolla. 1634. 5803
— Camb. Univ. Voces. 1640. 5836
Goad (I.) Verses in Oxf. Univ. Horti. 1640. 5499
— Snelling (T.). Thibaldus. 1640. 5502
Goad (Roger). Verses in Whitaker (W.). Praelectiones. 1559. . 5598
See Nowell (A.) and W. Day. True report of...Ed. Campion... 1583.
Goad (T.), *Rector of Hadleigh*. Dolefull euen-song...which befell... Mʳ Drury a Jesuite. 1623. 4°. 4781
Verses in Whitaker (W.). Praelectiones. 1599. . . . 5598
— Camb. Univ. Thr. thr. 1603. . . . . . 5616 *bis*.
— — Epicedium. 1612. 5665
— — Gratulatio. 1623. 5695
— Shaw (J.). Bibliorum summula. 1623. 8°. . . . 7381
— Ward (S.). Gratia discriminans. 1627. 4245
— Camb. Univ. Carmen. 1635. . . . . . 5770 *ter*.
— — Συνῳδία. 1637. 5790
See Carleton (G.). An examination... Ed. 2. 1626.
— Dort Synod. A ioynt attestation. 1626. 4°.
— — Suffragium. 1626 *etc.*
— G. (T.). The Friers Chronicle. 1623. 4°. 4077
— G. (T.), *Collegii Regalis Cantabrig. Socius*. Proditoris Proditor. 1606. 3615
— Ward (S.). Gratia discriminaus... 1627.
Goad (Thomas), *Professor of Civil Law*. Verses in Camb. Univ. Epicedium. 1612. 5666
— — Lacrymæ. 1619. 5689
— Mason (H.). The new art. 1624. 4083
— Camb. Univ. Genethl. 1631. 5731
— — Anthologia. 1632. 5741
— — Fasciæ. 1633. 5808
— — Rex redux. 1633. . . . . . . 5748 *ter*.
— — Συνῳδία. 1637. 5790
— — Voces. 1640. 5836
Goade (Christ.). Verses in Camb. Univ. Lacrymae. 1619. . . 5689
Goade (G.). Verses in Camb. Univ. Dolor 1625. . . . 5701
Goche (Henry), *D.D.* *See* Hippocrates. 1633.
God. Gods Love to Mankind. 1633. *See* Hoard (S.).
Goddard (Vin.). Verses in Oxf. Univ. Magd. Coll. 1612. . . 5302
Goddard (William). Verses in Hippocrates. 1633. . . . 5812
Godelevæus (Wilhelmus). *See* Livius. Libri omnes. 1589. 8°.
Godfray (Thomas). *See* Godfrie.
Godfrey de Bouillon. Godfrey of Boulogne. Caxton, 1481. F°. . 17

No.
Godfrey de Bouillon *cont.* *See* Tasso (T.). Godfrey of Bulloigne. 1600.
Godfrey of Boulogne. *See* Godfrey de Bouillon.
Godfrey (Joh.). Verses in Oxf. Univ. Horti. 1640. . . 5499
Godfrey (Ric.). Verses in Oxf. Univ. Horti. 1640. . . . 5499
Godfrie (Thomas). [*qu.* T. Godfray?] *See* Hueber (C.). A riche Storehouse. 1578. 8°.
Godly and learned Sermon. *See* Fulke (W.). [1580?]
Godlie garden...of the wounded conscience. 1629. 16°. . . 7759
Godly Sermon: Preached at Detford. 1586. 8°. . . . 1886
Godly Treatise of the Blessed Sacrament. *See* Primer. 1555. 8°.
Godolphin (John). Verses in A. (G.). Pallas armata. 1639. . 5170
Godolphin (Sidney). Verses in Camdeni Insignia. 1624. . . 5346
— Sandys (G.). Paraphrase. 1638. 4736
Godorus (William). Verses in Clowes (W.). A profitable...booke. 1637. 3895
Godwin (Fras.). Annales of England. 1630. F°. 2461
Catalogve of the Bishops of England. 1601. 4°. . . . 1748
— 1615. 4°. 2799
Concio habita in domo Capitulari...Exon. 1601. 4°. . . 2058
De præsulibus Anglie. 1616. 4°. 3470
Ad comm. de praesulibus Angliæ... Appendix. [1621?] 4°. . 7529
Rerum anglicarum Annales. 1616. F°. 3471
— 1628. 4°. 3533
See Hakewill (G.). Apologie. 1630.
Godwin (Morgan). *See* Godwin (F.). Annales of England. 1630.
Godwin (Tho.). Moses and Aaron. Ed. 2. 1626. 4°. . . 4801
— Ed. 4. 1631. 4°. 4839
— Ed. 5. 1634. 4°. 4853
Rom. Hist. Anthologia. Oxford, 1614. 4°. . . . 5320
— Oxford, 1625. 4°. 7609
— Oxford, 1628. 4°. 5371
— Oxford, 1631. 4°. 5387
— Oxford, 1633. 4°. 5400
Synopsis antiquitatum hebraicarum. Oxoniae, 1616. 4°. . 5327
Goelerus (Frederichs). Letter. *See* Vincent (P.). Lamentations of Germany. 1638. 7760
Goffe (Thomas). Deliverance from the grave. A Sermon. 28 March, 1627. 1627. 4°. 2894
Golbourne or Golburne (John). *See* Valera (C. de). Two treatises. 1600. 4°.
— Vigor (S.). Acts of the Dispute. 1602.
— Voyon (S. de). A Discourse. 1598. 8°.
Golden Cabinet of True Treasure. Trans. W. Jewell. 1612. 8°. . 2514
Golden Legend. *See* Voragine.
Golden meane. 1638. 12°. 4865
Goldfinch (T.). Verses in Camb. Univ. Epicedium. 1612. . . 5665
— — Dolor. 1625. 5701
— — Epithalam. 1625. 5702
Golding (Arthur). Verses in Baret (J.). An alvearie. 1573. . 7249
See Bruni (L.). The historie. 1563.
— Cæsar (C. J.). The eyght bookes. 1565.
— Calvin (J.). The Psalmes. 1571.
— — Sermons...vpon...Job. 1579(–80).
— — Treatise concerning offences. 1567. 8°.
— Chytraeus (D.). Postil. 1570.
— Hemmingsen (N.). Postill. 1569.
— Hurault (J.). Politicke...discourses. 1595.
— Mela (P.). The Rare and Singuler worke. 1590.
— Mornay (P. de). Woorke. 1587 *etc.*
— Ovid. [Metamorphoses.] 1567. 4°.
— Serres (J. de). Lyfe of...Colignie. 1576. 8°.

No.

Golding (Arthur) *cont.* Solinus. The excellent...worke. 1587. 4°.
— Trogus Pompeius. Thabridgment. 1564. 4°.
Golding (Per.). *See* Froissart (J.). Epitome of Frossard. 1608.
Goldman (Peter). Verses in Adamson (J.). Εἰσόδια. 1618. . . 5960
Goldsmith (Edward). Verses in Oxf. Univ. Magd. Coll. 1612. . 5302
Golius (Theophilus). *See* Aristotle. [Ethics. Appendix.] Epitome. 1634.
Gomersall (Robert). Poems. 1633. 8°. 4270
Sermons on St Peter. 1634. 4°. 4279
Gomersall (Robert). Verses in Fuller (T.). The historie of the holy warre. 1639 *etc.* 5806
Gondomar (Diego de), *Count.* *See* Scott (T.). Second part of Vox Popvli. 1624.
See Scott (T.). Sir W. Raleighs ghost. 1626.
Gonsalvius Montanus (R.). Discovery of...the holy inquisition of Spayne. 1568. 4°. 809
Der heyligher Hispanischer Inquisitie. 1569. 8°. . . . 7880
Full...discovery of...the Spanish Inquisition. 1625. 4°. . 4598
Gontery (Jean). *See* Du Moulin (P.). Conference. 1615.
Gontier, *Jesuit.* *See* Gontery (J.).
Gonville (Henry). Verses in Wilson (Sir T.). Vita. 1551. . . 631
Gonzalez de Mendoza (Juan). Historie of...China. 1588. 4°. . 1947
Gonzalez de Mendoza (Pedro). *See* Staney (W.). Treatise of Penance. 1617.
Good lesson for young men. R. Faques [1525]. 4°. 337
Goodall (Baptist). Tryall of travell. 1630. 4°. 4881
Verses in Aslachus (C.). Description of heaven. 1623. . . 4516
Gooddin (John), *T.C.C.* Verses in Camb. Univ. Epicedium. 1612. 5665
Goodier (Henry). Verses in Coryat (T.). Coryats Crudities. 1611. . 3076
Goodly treatise of faith hope and charite...translated. Southwark, 1537. 8°. 5867
Goodman (Cardell). Verses in Camb. Univ. Fasciae. 1633. . . 5808
— — Rex redux. 1633. 5748
Goodman (Christopher), *preacher of Westchester.* *See* Bulkeley (E.). An apologie. 1608.
Goodman (Gabriel). Verses in Dyer (Sir James). Nouel Cases. 1585. 1145
See Bible. Eng. (Bishops'). 1568.
— Bible (Welsh). 1620. F°.
Goodman (Godfrey). Fall of man. 1616. 4°. 2995
See Hakewill (G.). Apologie. 1630 *etc.*
Goodrick (John). Verses in Camb. Univ. Rex redux. 1633. . 5748
Goodricus (John). Verses in Cheke (Sir J.). De obitu M. Buceri. 1551. 734
Goodridge (Richard). Verses in Ferrand (J.). Ἐρωτομανία. 1640. 5498
Goodrus (William). *See* Banister (J.). The Workes. 1633. . 4000
Goodwin (Ar.). Verses in Oxf. Univ. Magd. Coll. 1612. . . 5302
Goodwin (George). Melissa religionis pontificiæ. 1620. 4°. . 3945
Automachia. *See* Du Bartas. Divine Weekes. 1621 *etc.* 2535 *etc.*
Goodwin (John). Saints interest in god. 1640. 12°. . . 7590
Verses in Camb. Univ. Epicedium. 1612. 5665
— — Lacrymæ. 1619. 5689
Goodwin (Thomas). Aggravation of sinne. 1637. 4°. . . . 4308
Childe of light. 1636. 4°. 4297
— 1638. 4°. 4316
Happinesse of the saints. 1638. 12°. 5191
Returne of prayers. 1636. 4°. 4373
— 1636. 12°. 5030
Vanity of thoughts. 1638. 4°. 4317
See Preston (J.). Doctrine of the Saints Infirmities. 1636 *etc.* 12°.
— — Golden scepter *etc.* 1638. 4°.

No.
Goodwin (Thomas) *cont.* *See* Preston (J.). Life eternall. 1631 *etc.* 4°.
— — Sermons. 1630 *etc.*
— Sibbes (R.). Fountain Sealed. 1637 *etc.* 12°.
— — Christs exaltation. 1639. 12°. 7820
— — Bowels opened. 1639. 4°. 7824
Googe (Barnaby). *See* G. (B.), *Citizen.* New Yeares Gifte. 1579.
— Heresbach (C.). Whole art...of husbandry. 1614 *etc.* 4°.
— Naogeorgus (T.). The Popish Kingdome. 1570.
— Palingenius (M.). Zodyake of lyfe. Books i–iii. 1560 *etc.*
Goossenius (G.). Newe Almanacke and Prognostication. 1571. 8°. . 7263
Goossenius (Gerardus). *See* Enghelram (J.). Psevdographia. 1587.
Gord. (Ar.). *See* Gordon.
Gordon (Arthur). Verses in Ross (T.). Idæa. 1608. . . 2364
Gordon (James). Verses *bis* in Forbes (P.). Funerals. 1637. . 6007
See also Gordon-Huntley (J.).
Gordon (John). Antitortobellarminus. 1610. 4°. 6885
Εἰρηνηκοινωνία. 1612. 4°. 3395
England & Scotlands Happinesse. 1604. 4°. 2856
Orthodoxo-iacobvs et papapostaticus. 1611. 4°. . . . 2970
Panegyrique of Congratulation... Trans. E. G[rimstone]. *See below,* Vnion of Great Brittaine. 1604.
Vnion of Great Brittaine. 1604. 4°. 3551
Gordon (Robert), *Somerset Herald.* *See* Milles (T.). The Catalogve. 1610.
Gordon (Robert). Verses in Forbes (P.). Funerals. 1637. . 6007
Gordon-Huntley (Jas.). Treatise of the Unwritten Word. Cont. i. Pt. 2. 1614. 8°. 6894
Treatise conc. the properties...of the true Church. Cont. ii. Pt. 1. 1614. 8°. 6895
Treatise conc. the ground of faith. Cont. ii. Pt. 2. 1614. 8°. . 6896
Treatise conc. the church. Cont. ii. Pt. 3. 8°. . . . 6897
Gore (John). Summer sermon. 1635. 4°. 7616
Winter sermon. 1634. 1635. 4°. 7615
Gore (Sir John). *See* Sictor (J.). Lacrymæ. 1637.
Gore (T.). Verses in Gerhard (J.). The meditations. 1627 *etc.* 5707 *etc.*
— Camb. Univ. Genethl. 1631. 5731
Gorecius (L.). Oratio...de matrimonio. 1554. 4°. 1013
Gorges (Sir Arthur). *See* Bacon (F.). Wisedome of the ancients. 1622.
— Lucanus. Pharsalia. 1614.
— Letters Patent. A trve transcript... 1611.. . . . 3079
Gorges (Carew). *See* Lucanus. Pharsalia. 1614.
Gorges (Fr.). Verses in Camb. Univ. Carmen. 1635. . . . 5770
Goring (Hon. Charles). Verses in Camb. Univ. *Συνωδία.* 1637. . 5790
Goring (Richard). *See* Du Moulin (P.). Theophilus. 1610. 12°.
— — A letter. 1621.
— — Theophilus. 1612.
Gospels of the fower Euangelistes translated...into...Saxons. 1571. 4°. 822
Gospels and Epistles. *See* Epistles and Gospels.
Gosselin (Guillaume). *See* Tapp (J.). The Pathway. 1613.
Gosselin (Peter). *See* State-mysteries of the Iesvites. 1623.
Gossenius (Gerardus). *See* Goossenius.
Gosson (Stephen). Plays confuted. [1582.] 8°. 1921
School of Abuse. 1579. 8°. 1838
— [*Sequel.*] *See* Salvianus Massiliensis, *Presbyter.* Second and third blast. 1580.
Trumpet of Warre. Sermon at Paules Crosse. 7 May 1598. 8°. 2848
Gostelow (R.), *M.A.* Verses in Randolph (T.). Poems. 1640. . 5500
Gostlin (Joh.). Verses in Camb. Univ. Thr-thr. 1603. . . 5616
— — Lacrymæ. 1619. 4°. 5689
Gostwyke (Roger). Deo et Ecclesiae... The anatomie of Ananias. Cambridge, 1616. 4°.. 5678

No.

Gostwyke (Roger) *cont.* Verses in Camb. Univ. Lachrymae. 1587. . 7356
— Whitaker (W.). Praelectiones. 1599. 5598
Gotteschalcus. *See* Ussher (J.). Gotteschalci etc. 1631.
Gouge (Thomas). Verses in Hippocrates. 1631. 5736
— — 1633. 5812
— Drexelius (H.). Considerations. 1632 *etc.* 7789 *etc.*
— Camb. Univ. Rex redux. 1633. 5748
Gouge (William). Calling of the Jewes. 1621. 4°. 3949
Exposition on Iohn v. 1630. 4°. 7412
Gods three arrowes. 1631. 4°. 4436
Gvide to goe to god. Ed. 2. 1636. 4°. 4462
Of domesticall duties. 1622. 4°. 4766
— Ed. 3. 1634. 4°. 4450
Πανοπλία τοῦ Θεοῦ. The whole-armor of God. 1616. 4°. 3789
— Ed. 2. 1619. 4°. 3801
Recovery from apostacy. 1639. 4°. 4476
Whole armor of God. *See above*, Πανοπλία.
See Bible. Eng. Concordance. Cotton. 1635.
— Byfield (N.). Commentary. 1637.
— Hayne (T.). Pax. 1639.
— Rogers (R.). Practice of christianitie. 1623.
— Sym (J.). Lifes preservative. 1637.
— Woodward (E.). Childes patrimony. 1640.
Gough (John), *Divine.* *See* Tomson (L.). An Answere. [1570.] 8°.
Gough (John), *Dramatist.* The strange discovery. 1640. 4°. 5212
Gough (R.), *fl.* 1746. [Book in his possession], p. 953, note 1.
Goulart (Simon). *See* Du Bartas. Learned svmmary. 1637.
See Plutarch. [Parallel lives]... 1603 *etc.*
Goulston (Theodore). *See* Aristotle. [Poetica (Lat.).] 1623.
— — [Rhetorica.] 1619.
— Galen. Τῶν σωζομένων τινα. 1640.
Goulstone (Ger.). Verses in Camb. Univ. Lachrymae, 1587. 7356
Governal of Health. A lytell treatyse, with ye Medecyne of ye stomacke. W. de Worde [15—]. 4°. 220
Gowen (T.). Verses in Chaucer (G.). Amorum. 1635. 5414
Gower (Evers.). Verses in Camb. Univ. Genethl. 1631. 5731
— Shelford (R.). Five...discourses. 1635. 5774
— Camb. Univ. Συνῳδία. 1637. 5790
Gower (John). Confessio Amantis. Caxton, '1493' [1483]. F°. 22
— Berthelet, 1532. F°. 425
— Berthelet, 1554. F°. 504
See Chaucer (G.). Workes. 1532 *etc.*
Gower (John), *Jesus Coll. Camb.* Verses in Camb. Univ. Carmen. 1635. 5770
See Ovid. Fasti. 1640.
Gowrie (Earls of). *See* Ruthven.
Gr. (Vicar of). *See* Grantham.
Gr. (W.). [=Greenhill (W.).] *See* Burroughes (J.). The excellency. 1638.
Graces. The maner of saying grace. *See* Coverdale (M.). A christen exhortacion. [154–.] 16°.
See Primer. 1580. 16°.
Graduale (Sarum). N. Prevost, Paris, imp. F. Byrckman. 6 Kal. Jul. 1528. F°. 6192
Gradus comparationis. (De patronymicorum declinatione.—De grecorum nominum declinatione.) Pynson [1513?]. 4°. 297
Grafton (Ric.). Brief treatise containing many proper tables. 1611. 8°. 2405
Chronicle at large. 1569 (1568). F°. 1406
Abridgement of the Chronicles of England. 1562. 8°. 1113
See Holinshed (R.). Chronicles. 1587– .
— Harding (J.). Chronicle. 1543.
— G. (R.). Salutem. 1571.

No.
Grain. *See* Official Publications. Orders devised. 1586. . . 1682
Grain and Victual. *See* Official Publications. Orders appointed. 1608 (1622). 2816
— 1630. 4°. 2671, 2672
Grammar. Dutch-English. *See* Vocabulary. Den grooten Vocabulaer. 1639.
— — Whetstone (G.). The honourable reputation. 1586.
English. *See* Greaves (Paul).
— Butler (C.). The English Grammar (Phonetic). 1633. . 5435
French-English. *See* Palsgrave (J.). Lesclaircissement. 1530.
French-Italian-Latin. *See* Clerke (J.). De mortvorvm resvrrectione. 1547.
French-Latin. *See* Desainliens (C.). De pronvntiatione. 1580.
French-Eng. *See* Wodroephe (J.). The spared houres. F°. 1623.
French-English-Latin. *See* Graue (J. de). 1633. . . . 7663
French-Latin. *See* Dugres (G.). Breve compendium. 1636. . 5781
French-Italian-Spanish. *See* Bense (P.). 1637.
French-English. *See* Delamothe (G.). 1639.
Greek-Latin. *See* Camden (W.). Institutio. 1604 *etc.*
— — Canini (A.). 1624.
— — *See* Martinius (M.). 1629. 4828
— — Francklin (R.). 'Ορθοτονία. 1630 *etc.* . . . 3987 *etc.*
Hebrew-English. *See* Martinius (P.). 1593.
Italian-French-English. *See* Clerke (J.). De mortvorvm resvrrectione. 1547.
Italian-English. 1575. *See* Lentulo (S.). 7758
— *See* Desainliens (C.). The Italian Schoole-maister. 1597. 8°.
— — Torriano (G.). The Italian tutor. 4°.
Latin. *See* Albertus. De modis significandi. [1497?] 4°. . 116
— — Sulpitius (J.). Opus grammatices. 4°. 1499. . 54
— — Declensons of nownes by Joh... W. de Worde [15]. 4°. 221
— — Stanbridge (J.). Accidentia. 4°. (Title only.) [1515?] 312
— — Garlandia (J. de). Synonyma. 1502. 4°. . . 254
— — Garlandia (J. de). Synonima. 4°. 1505. (Æquivoca.) 149–150
— 1516. *See* Barchby. 7751
— *See* Whittington (R.).
— — Linacre (T.). De emendata structura. 1524.
— — Lily (W.). De octo orationis partium constructione. 1540. 4°. 455
— — Greenwood (J.). Syntaxis. 1590. 5549
— — Hume (A.). Prima elementa. 1612.
Latin-English. *See* Anwykyll (J.). Compendium. 1483. . 76–7
— — 1489. 143
— — Terentius. Vulgaria quedam. [1483.]
— — Perottus (N.). Institutio. [1486?] 4°.
— — Holt (J.). Lac puerorum. Ab. 1500. 6072
— — Qu. Donatus cum Remigio? (one leaf). Ab. 1510. 4°. 7696
— [Verse. Fragment.] Pynson [1512?]. 4°. 298
— *See* Stanbridge (J.). Accidence. [1521] *etc.*
— — Vulgaria quædam. 1529. 4°.
— Fragment (Prose). [Qu. A. van Berghen, Antwerp? Ab. 15—.] 4°. 6074
— *See* Aequivoca.
— [Conversation-book.] *See* Horman (W.). Vulgaria. 1519.
— *See* Lily (W.). Rudimenta. 8°.
— — Sherry (R.). A Treatise of Schemes. 1555.
— — Treatise of the Figures.
— — Terentius. Floures. 1560.
— — Ramus (P.). Latine Grammar (and Rudiments). 1585. 8°. 1899
— — — and Tullie. Cambridge, 1585. 8°. . . 5515
— — Stockwood (J.). A plaine... Accidence. 1590. 4°.

No.

Grammar *cont.* Latin-English. [The Royal Grammar.] *See* Lily (W.). A shorte introduction. 1607 *etc.*
— *See* Welde (W.). Janua linguarum. 16[1–]. 4°. . . . 7711
— — Brinsley (J.). The posing. 1615.
— — Gill (A.). Logonomia. [1619.] 1621.
— — Janua Linguarum. 1627.
— — Clarke (J.). Dux Grammaticus. 1633.
Latin-English. *See* Janua Linguarum. 1634 etc.
— — Bird (J.). 1639.
— — Hermes Anglo-latinus. 1639.
— — Hayne (T.). Grammatices Latinae compendium. 1637. 1640. 7819
Latin-English-French. 1633. *See* Comenius.
Spanish-English. *See* Perceval (R.). 1599 etc.
— — Luna (J. de). Arte breve. 1623.
— — Sanford (J.). Προπύλαιον... 1611.
— [Minsheu.] *See* Perceval (R.). 1623.
Welsh. *See* Rhys (J. D.). Cambrobrytannicae linguæ institutiones. 1592.

Granger (Thomas). Syntagma logicum. 1620. 4°. 3334
Tree of good and evill. 1616. 8°. 3666

Grant (Ed.). Verses in Baret (J.). Alvearie. 1573. . . . 7249
— Llwyd (H.). The breviary of Britayne. 1573. . . 1440
— Price (Jo.). Historia. 1573. 1473
— Serres (J. de). Three partes of Commentaries. 1574. . 7279
— Harvey (G.). Gratulationum. 1578. 1495
— Jewel (J.). Adv. T. Hardingum. 1578. . . . 1535
— Camden (W.). Britannia. 1586 *etc.* . . . 1324 *etc.*
— Lloyd (L.). The pilgrimage. 1586. 1941
See Ascham (R.). Familiarium epistolarum libri tres... [1576] *etc.*
— Crespin (J.). Lexicon. 1581.

Grant (John). *See* Fisher (A.). Defence of the liturgie. 1630.

Grantham, *Vicar of. See* Heylyn (P.). Coale from the Altar.
— Pocklington (J.). Altare Christianum. 1637.

Granthan (Henry). *See* Lentulo (S.). An italian grammar. 1575. 8°. 7758

Grashop (T.). *See* Bible. Eng. (Genevan). Tomson's Revision. 1611. F°.

Grassi (Giacomo di). True arte of defence. 1594. 4°. . . . 2758

Grave (J. de). Pathway to the gate of tongues. Oxford, 1633. 8°. 7663

Gravesend. *See* Hexham (H.). A tongue-combat. 1623. 4°.

Gravet (W.). Sermon. 1587. 8°. 2062

Gray (Ed.). Verses in Oxf. Univ. Horti *bis.* 1640. . . . 5499

Gray (Lady Jane). Letter. *See* Coverdale (M.). Certain letters. 1564.

Gray (Patrick), Lord of Fermiling. Verses in Camb. Univ. Lacrymæ. 1587. 7356

Gray (Robert). Alarum to England. 1609. 8°. 2889

Gray (Thomas de). Compleat horseman and expert ferrier. 1639. F°. 4042

Gray (Thomas, Lord). *See* Grey (Thomas), Baron Grey de Wilton.

Gray (Walter). Almanacke and Prognostication. 1593. 8°. . 1341

Great Britain and Ireland. *See* Official Publications.
Historie of Great Britannie. *See* Clapham (J.). 1606.
— Speed (J.).

Greaves (Nic.). Verses in Oxf. Univ. Horti. 1640. . . . 5499

Greaves (Paul). Grammatica Anglicana. Cantabrigiae, 1594. 8°. 5567

Greaves (Thomas). De linguae arabicae vtilitate. Oxonii, 1639. 4°. 5492, 5493

Green or Grene (Bartelet). Letters. *See* Coverdale (M.). Certain... letters. 1564.

Green (John). Verses in Camb. Univ. Anthologia. 1632. . . 5741
— — Rex redux. 1633. 5748

No.
Green or Greene (William). Verses in Camb. Univ. Genethl. 1631. 5731
— Hippocrates. 1633. 5812
— Camb. Univ. Συνωδία. 1637.. 5790
Greene (George). Verses in Stephens (J.). New essayes. 1631. . 7823
Greene (John). Refutation of the apology for actors. 1615. 4°. 2315
Greene (R.). Ciceronis Amor. 1605. 4°. 1792
Greenes farewell to follie. 1617. 4°. 2318
Greenes ghost havnting conie catchers. 1602. 4°. . . 3320
Greenes mourning garment. 1590. 4°. 1957
Philomela. The Lady Fitz-walter nightingale. 1631. 4°. . 4098
Quip for an vpstart courtier. 1620. 4°. 4071
Greene (William). *See* Green.
Greenham (Richard). Works. 1599. 4°. 2912
— Ed. 4. 1605. F°. 7467
— Ed. 5. Revised by H. Holland. 1612 (1611). F°. . 2749
— [Text-title] Godly instructions. 1600? 4°. . . . 2916
— Παραμύθιον. 1598. 8°. 1994
See Rogers (Ric.). Garden. 1625.
Greenhill (William). Verses in Camb. Univ. Lacrymae. 1619. . 5689
See Burroughes (Jer.). The excellency. 1638.
Greenland. *See* Pellham (E.). Gods power. 1631. 4°.
Greenwood (Henry). Workes. 1616. 8°. 4057
— Ed. 9. 1620. 8°. 4072
The blessed'st birth that ever was. 25 Dec. 1627. 1628. 8°. 4814
The jaylers jayl-delivery. 1620. 4°. 4073
The prisoners prayers. 1628. 12°. 4815
Greenwood (John). Answere to G. Giffords pretended defence. 1590. 4°. 6507
M. Some laid open in his coulers. [1590?] 8°. . . 1918
More worke for priests. 1640. 8°. 7048
See Barrow (H.). The examinations. [1593?]
— Brabourne (T.). Defence. 1632.
— Collection of certain Letters. 1590.
— Collection of certaine sclavnderous Articles. 1590.
— Gifford (G.). Plaine Declaration. 1590.
— — Short reply. 1591.
— Some (R.). Godly treatise. 1589.
Greenwood (John), *schoolmaster*. Syntaxis et prosodia. 1590. 8°. 5549
Gregorius I. De cura pastorali. Ed. a J. Stephano. 1629. 8°. . 3981
See Vulcanius (B.). De Literis. 1597. 8°.
— [Preface.] *See* Asser. Ælfredi regis gestae. 1574.
Dialogues. (A shorte relation.) Paris, 1608. 12°. . . 6218
Gregory XIII. *See* Renniger (M.). De Pii qvinti furoribus. 1582.
Gregorius, *Monk*. Letter relating the martyrdome of Ketaban. Oxford, 1633. 4°. 5401
Gregorius *Nazianzenus*. In Iulianum invectivae duae. Cum scholiis H. Savilii. Etonae, 1610. 4°. 5901
Λόγος εἰς τὰ θεοφάνια. Etonae, 1615. 8°. 5905
Gregorius *de Valentia*. *See* Valentia (G. de).
Gregory (Alex.). Verses in Oxf. Univ. Magd. Coll. 1612. . . 5302
Gregory (John), *M.A.* *See* Ridley (Sir T.). A view. 1634.
Grellius (Joachim). *See* Livius. Libri omnes. 1589. 8°.
Grene (Bartelet). *See* Green.
Greneacres. Verses in Boccaccio (G.). The Boke calledde John Bochas. 1496. 106
Greneway (A.). Verses in Verstegan (R.). A restitution. 1605 *etc.* 6140 *etc.*
Grenewey (Richard). *See* Tacitus. Annales. 1604 *etc.*
Grent (William). New and accurate map of the world. Ab. 1625. Wall map. 7857
Grenvile (R.). Verses *bis* in Oxf. Univ. Horti. 1640. . . . 5499
Gresley (H.). Verses in Oxf. Univ. Horti. 1640. . . . 5499

No.

Gressop (Thomas). *See* Nilus, *abp.* A briefe treatise. 1560. 8º.
Gretser (Jacob). *See* James (T.). A treatise. 1612.
Greville (Fulke), first Lord Brooke. *See* Brooke.
Grey (Arthur, Lord), de Wilton. [Funeral.] *See* Sparke (T.). A Sermon. 1593. 8º. 5238
Grey (John), *M.A.* Verses in Hawkins (W.). Corolla. 1634. . 5803
Grey (Thomas), Baron Grey de Wilton. *See* S. (C.). The copie of a letter. 1603. 4º.
Grey (Thomas de). *See* Gray.
Greys (Anth.). Verses in Davies (J.). Humours Heau'n on earth. 1609. 2438
Grievances. 1622. *See* Proclamation. 1622.
Griffin (George). Verses in Coryate (T.). Coryates Crvdities. 1611. 3076
Griffith (Geo.). Verses in Camdeni Insignia. 1624. . . 5346
— Davies (J.). Antiquæ linguæ dictionarium. 1632.
Griffith (Josias). Verses in Camb. Univ. Lacrymæ. 1619. . . 5689
Griffith (Matthew). Bethel. 1633(4). 4º. 4352, 4353
Griffith (William), *LL.D.* Verses in Davies (J.). Antiquæ linguæ dictionarium. 1632. 4979
Grilli. *See* Estienne (C.). Maison Rustique. 1616.
Grimald (N.). Oratio ad pontifices. 1553. 1583. 8º. . . . 1512
Verses in Turner (W.). A preseruatiue. 1551. 955
— Elyot (Sir T.). Bibliotheca *bis.* 1552. 502
See Cicero. [De officiis.] 1558 *etc.*
— Sohn (G.). A brief...treatise. 1592.
— Vergilius. [*Georgics.*] 1591.
Grimaldus (L.). The Covnsellor. 1598. Fº. 1995
Grimoaldus. *See* Grimald.
Grimstone (E.). Generall historie of the netherlands. 1609. Fº. 2439
— till 1627, by W. Crosse. 1627. Fº. 7397
See Acosta (J.). 1604.
— Avity (P. d'). The estates, Empires...of the world. 1615.
— Bethune (P. de). The Covnsellor of estate. 1634.
— Gordon (J.). The Vnion of Great Brittaine... 1604.
— Knolles (R.). The generall historie. 1621 etc.
— Matthieu (P.). The heroyk life. 1612.
— Mayerne Turquet (L. de). Generall historie of Spaine. 1612. Fº.
— Mexia (P.). The imperiall historie. 1623.
— Petit (J. F.). The low-country Commonwealth. 1609. 4º.
— Polybius. History. 1634.
— Serres (J. de). General inventorie. 1607.
— — Generall historie. 1624.
Grimstone (Harbottel). *See* Heywood (T.). The hierarchie. 1635.
Grindal (E.). Concio Funebris in obitum...Ferdinandi Caesaris. 1564. 4º. 804
Sermon, at the Funeral solemnitie of...Ferdinandus. 1564. 4º. 805
See Admonition. 1572.
— Advertisements. 1584.
— Articles (Canterbury Province). [1575 ?]
— Bible. Eng. (Bishops'). 1568.
— Jewel (J.). Apologie of priuate Masse. 1562.
Gringoire (P.). The castell of Laboure. W. de Worde, 1506. 4º. . 152
Grisons. Proceedings of the Grisons in...1618. 1619. 4º. . 4068
Grosseteste (Robert). *See* Henley (W. de). Boke of Husbandry.
— Testaments of the twelve Patriarchs. 1576. 8º.
Grotius (Guilielmus) *See* Grotius (H.). Poemata. 1639.
Grotius (Hugo). Christs passion. 1640. 8º. 4744
De veritate religionis. Ed. 5. Oxoniae, 1639. 8º. . . . 5494
Defensio fidei catholicae de satisfactione. Oxoniæ, 1636. 12º. 5448
Poemata. 1639. 8º 4929, 4930
True Religion explained. 1632. 12º. 4845
Verses in Veen (O. van). Amorum emblemata. 1608. . . 6138

No.

Groto (Lodovico). *See* Alabaster (W.). Roxana. 1632.
Gruget (Claudius). *See* Milles (T.). The treasvrie.
Gruter (Jan). Florilegium. Pars altera. Francofurti, 1611. 4°. . 6629
Verses in Camden (W.). Britannia. 1590. 1723
See Velleius Paterculus. 1632. 12°.
Gruzar (C.). *See* Damiano, da Odemira. 1562.
Grymestone (Edward). *See* Grimstone.
Grynæus (J. J.). Haggeus the prophet. 1586. 8°. . . 1940
Grynæus (Simon). *See* Aristotle [Ethics. App.]. Epitome... 1634.
Gryphius (Antonius). *See* Lucanus. De bello civili. 1589.
Gualtherus (Rodolphus). Antichrist. 'C. Trutheall, Sothwarke,' 1556. 8°. 6725
Hundred, threescore and fifteene Homelyes. Trans. J. Bridges. 1572. F°. 1412
Verses in Humphrey (L.). J. Jvelli vita. 1573. 837
See Admonition. 1572.
— Vermigli (P.). Loci communes. 1583.
— Whether it be mortall sinne. [1571 ?]
Guarini (G. B.). Il pastor fido. 1602. 4°. 2109
Guarna (A.). Bellum grammaticale. 1574. 8°. 1179
— 1635. 8°. 4210
Guazzo (S.). The ciuile conuersation. 1586. 4°. 1587
Guerdain (Aaron). Verses in Hippocrates. 1633. . . . 5812
Guest (Edmond). Treatise againste the preuee Masse. 1548. 8°. . 695
See Bible. Eng. (Bishops'). 1568.
— Advertisements. 1584.
Guevara (A. de). Chronicle...of tenne Emperours of Rome. 1577. 4°. 1310
Diall of Princes. Trans. T. North. 1557. F°. 638
— 1568. F°. 1118
— 1582. 4°. 1142
Dispraise of the life of a Courtier. Trans. Sir F. Bryan. 1548. 8°. 605
Familiar Epistles. 1584. 4°. 1322
Golden boke of Marcus Aurelius. Trans. J. Bourchier, Lord Berners. 1546. 8°. 484
— 1557. 8°. 1205
Mount of Calvarie. 1595. 4°. 2417
Guez (Jean Louis), *Sieur de Balzac*. See Balzac.
Guiana. *See* Ralegh (Sir W.). The discoverie. 1596.
Guibert (Philibert). The charitable physitian(-apothecarie). Trans. I. W. 1639. 4°. 4043
Guicciardini (Francesco). Aphorismes civill and militarie. Ed. 2. 1629. F°. 4255
Briefe inference upon Guicciardines digression, in...his Historie i. 4. 1629. F°. 4826
Historie of Italie. Trans. Fenton. 1578. F°. 1538
— Ed. 2. 1599. F°. 2250
— Ed. 3. 1618. F°. 2285
Two Discourses. 1595. 4°. 1864
See Polemon (J.). All the famous Battels. [1577 ?]
Guicciardini (L.). Description of the low countreys. 1593. 8°. . 2325
See Polemon (J.). All the famous Battels. [1577 ?]
Guido. *See* Cauliaco (Guido de).
Guido de Monte Rocherii. Manipulus curatorum. [Pynson, 1500.] 16°. 112
— Pynson, 1508. 8°. 255
Guild (William). Antidote against poperie. Aberdene, 1639. 12°. . 6010
Ignis fatuus. 1625. 4°. 4530
Moses Unvailed. 1620. 8°. 4074
— 1626. 8°. 4417

No.
Guillemeau (Jacques). Worthy treatise of the eyes. [159–?] 12°. . 1906
Treatise of...the Eyes... Ed. 2. 1622. 12°. . . . 3018
Guillim (John). Display of Heraldrie. 1611 (1610). F°. . 3211, 3212
— Ed. 2. 1632. F°. 7593
— Ed. 3. 1638. F°. 4662
Guillim (Thomas). Verses in Guillim (J.). A display. 1611 etc. . 3211 etc.
Guin (L.). Verses in Davies (R.). Funerall Sermon. 1577. . . 1416
Guinnus. *See* Gwinne.
Guise, *House of*. Advertisement from a French Gentleman. 1585. 8°. 6781
See Contre-Guyse. 1589.
— Necessary Doctrine. 1586.
— Regnier de la Planche (L.). Legendarie. 1577. 8°.
Guise (Henri de Lorraine, 3rd duke of). *See* France. A discourse. 1588.
Gulich, *Duchy of*. *See* Briefe discourse. 1599.
Gulielmus (Laurentius), *de Saona*. Rhetorica nova. St Albans, 1480. 4° and 8°. 83
Gulielmus Parisiensis. Postilla siue expositio. Notary, 1509. 4°. 330
Gulielmus de Saliceto. *See* Braunschweig (H.). Noble experyence. 1525.
See Wilhelmus.
Gulston (Jos.). Verses in Camb. Univ. Genethl. 1631. . . . 5731
Gulston (Theodore). [Licence.] *See* London. College of Physicians. 1633.
Gumbleden (John). Gods great mercy. Oxford, 1628. 4°.. . 7814
Gunning (Peter). Verses in Lessius (L.). Hygiasticon. 1634 etc. 5833 etc.
— Dugres (G.). Breve...compendium. 1636. . . . 5781
— Cam. Univ. Voces. 1640. 5836
Gunpowder Plot. [Sermon, Nov. 10, 1606.] *See* Barlow (W.). Sermon. 1606.
See Goad (T.). Proditoris Proditor. 1606.
— Garnett (H.). Actio. 1607.
— In homines nefarios. 1605.
Gunter (Edm.). Canon triangulorum. 1623. 4°. 7516
De sectore et radio. 1623. 4°. 3342, 7517
Description and use of the Sector. 1624. *See above*, De sectore et radio. 1623.
— Ed. 2. 1636. 4°. 5065
Gunter (P.). Sermon. 1615. 4°. 3110
Gunvillus, *see* Gonville.
Gurnay (Edmund). Demonstration of Antichrist. 1631. 12°. . 3813
Towards the vindication of the second commandment. Cambridge, 1639. 12°. 5807
Gustavus Vasa, *King of Sweden*. *See* North (G.). The Description of Swedland. 1561.
Gustavus II, Adolphus. Firme aliance and agreement...betweene...the King of Swethland...and...the Duke of Statin. (A Letter.) Delft, 1631. 4°. 6442
New starr of the north...('Επινίκιον). 1632. 4°. . . . 4559, 4560
[Death.] *See* Russell (J.). Two famovs pitcht battels. 1634. 4°.
— — Schloer (J.). The death. 1633. 4°.
[Funeral.] *See* Germany. The continvation. 1633. 4°.
See Censura ad panegyricum. 1628. 4°. 7764
— Sweden. Gustavus II, Adolphus. 1631.
— — Swedish Discipline. 1631.
— — Swedish Intelligencer. 1632.
Guy (George). Verses in Camb. Univ. Lacrymæ. 1619. . . 5689
Guy (John). Verses in Vaughan (W.). Golden fleece. 1626. . . 5029
Guyon (Loys). *See* Milles (T.). The treasvrie. 1613.
Guzman (John). Verses in Aretius (J.). Primula Veris. 1613. . 3090

No.
Gwin (N.). Verses in Slatyer (W.). History. 1621. 3137
Gwinne (John). Verses in Wilson (Sir T.). Vita. 1551. . . . 631
Gwinne (Matthew). Nero, Tragoedia Nova. 1639. 12°. . . . 4328
Vertumnus. 1607. 4°. 3621
Montaigne (M. de). Essayes. 1632. 4265
Vaughan (Sir W.). Golden Grove. 1608. 2888
See Florio (G.). A worlde of Wordes. 1598 etc. . . 2069 etc.
Gwynneth (John). Confutacyon of the fyrst parte of Frythes booke. St Albans, 1536. 8°. 5878
Gy (Na.). *See* Giles (N.).
Gybson. *See* Gibson.
Gyffard (George). *See* Gifford.
Gyfford. *See* Gifford.
Gylby (Goddred). *See* Gilby.
Gyles (Nat). *See* Giles.
Gyll (John). *See* Gill.
Gylpen (George). *See* Gilpin.

H. (A.). *See* Banister (J.). A compendiovs chirurgerie. 1585. 12°.
H. (A.). Verses in Hart (A.). The tragicomicall history. 1640. . 4220
See Banister (J.). Workes. 1633.
— Guillemeau (J.). Worthy treatise of the eyes. [159- .] 12°.
— Hildersam (A.). Doctrine of Communicating. 1634. 12°.
— — Treatise. [1603?]
H. (A.), *S.* Verses in Lok (H.). Ecclesiastes. 1597. . . . 2246
H. (A.), *Trinity Colledge, Cambridge.* *See* Holland (A.). London Looke-backe. 1630. 4°.
H. (C.). *See* Ursinus (J.). The romane conclave. 1609.
H. (E.). Verses in Gascoigne (G.). The Posies. 1575. . . 1482
H. (E.). *See* Cambridge University. Act verses. [Ab. 1581.] F°.
H. (E.). De fide. 1592. 8°. 2005
H. (E.). Verses in Horatius. Odes. 1635 *etc.* . . . 4857 *etc.*
H. (F.). Verses in Camb. Univ. Carmen. 1635. . . . 5770
— Overbury (Sir T.). His Wife. Ed. 11. 1622. . . . 3380
— Roberts (L.). The merchants mappe. 1638. . . 5133
See Godwin (F.). Rervm Anglicarvm. 1628.
H. (G.). Verses in Imitation of Christ. 1568. 1405
— Gascoigne (G.). The Posies. 1575. 1482
— Camb. Univ. Lacrymae. 1587 *bis.* 7356
— Camdeni Insignia. 1624. 5346
See Cotton (P.). Anti-coton. 1611.
De discenda Græca lingva orationes duæ. 1581. *See* Crespin (J.).
H. (G.), *C.P.* Verses in Camb. Univ. Gratulatio. 1623. . . 5695
H. (G.), *D.D.* *See* Hakewill (G.). An apologie. 1627.
— — Sermon. 1632. 4°.
H. (H.). Consultorie for all christians. Worcester, 1549. 8°. . 5887
Verses in Batman (S.). The doome. 1581. 1314
— Wright (T.). The passions. 1604. 2858
— Herbert (Sir T.). A relation. 1634. 3194
— Helpe to discourse. 1635. 3833
— Jewel (J.). Apologia. 1639. 5461
See Blague (T.). A sermon. 1603.
— H. (P.). Gutta Podagrica. 1633.
H. (H.) [=Henry Hawkins]. *See* Maffei (G. P.). Fuga Saeculi. 1632. 4°.
— Holland (H.). Ecclesia Sancti Pavli. 1633.
— — Monvmenta Sepvlchralia. [1614.]
— Rohan (H., duc de). A treatise. 1640.
H. (H.), *Anglo-britannus.* *See* Holland (H.). Herωologia. 1620. F°.
H. (I.). Christianity maintained. 1638. *See* Knott (E.).
H. (I.). Description of the church of Christ. 1610. 4°. . . 3605

No.

H. (I.). Verses in Camb. Univ. Thr-thr. 1603. 5616
— Guillim (J.). A display. 1611. 3211
H. (I.) [*qu.* Harrison (I.)?]. *See* Bohemia. Bohemica Ivra Defensa... 1620. 7515
H. (I.). *See* Bruce (R.). The way to true peace. 1617. 4°.
— Cotton (J.). Gods promise. 1630.
H. (I.) [*qu.* Hind (I.)?]. *See* Defence of Tabacco. 1602.
H. (I.). *See* Gerardus (A.). Foundation of the Christian religion. 1583? 12°.
H. (I.) [=J. Healey]. *See* Hall (J.). The discovery of a new world. 1620? 8°.
H. (I.). *See* Hayward (Sir J.). Treatise of vnion. 1604.
H. (I.), *Cantab. Col. Ioh.* Verses in Crashaw (W.). Falsification. 1606. 2262
H. (I.), *C.T.* Verses in Camb. Univ. Epicedium. 1612. . . 5665
H. (I.), *D.M.* 1639. *See* M. (I. H. D.).
H. (I.), *Gent.* The house of correction. (Certaine characters.) 1619. 4°. 4160
H. (J.) [=Healey (J.)]. *See* Augustine (S.). Of the Citie of God. 1610 *etc.*
H. (J.). Abridgement of Latine dictionary. 1634. 8°. . . . 4896
H. (J.) [=J. Hill]. *See* Sibbs (R.). The returning backslider. 1639.
H. (J.). Verses in King (E.). Ivsta. 1638. 5829
— Roberts (L.). The merchants mappe. 1638. . . 5133
H. (J.), *Chester Herald.* *See* Hart (J.).
H. (L.), *C.C.C.* Verses in Whitaker (W.). Praelectiones. 1599. . 5598
H. (L.), *Vicecan. Oxon.* 1572. *See* Humphrey (L.).
H. (M.). *See* S. (E.). [De Rebus Gestis...] 1640.
H. (M.), *C.C.* Verses in Camb. Univ. Gratulatio. 1623. . . 5695
H. (M.), *Emm.* Verses in Camb. Univ. Συνῳδία. 1637. . . 5790
H. (M. T.) [=Hutton (T.)]. *See* Devon and Cornwall, *Ministers of.* The Remoovall... 1606.
H. (N.). *See* Carpenter (N.). Chorazin. 1640. 12°.
H. (N.), *Regal.* Verses in Camb. Univ. Gratulatio. 1623. . . 5695
H. (P.). Gutta podagrica: a treatise of the Gout. 1633. 4°. . 4001
H. (P.). Verses in Helpe to discourse. 1635. 3833
H. (P.), *C.T.* Verses in Camb. Univ. Gratulatio. 1623. . . 5695
H. (R.). Arraignement of the whole creature. 1631(-2). 4°. . . 4202
H. (R.). Verses in Du Bartas. Weekes. 1605-6. *etc.* . . 2476 *etc.*
— Camdeni Insignia. 1624. 5346
— Taylor (J.). Workes. 1630. 3812
See Arcandam. The most excellent... [156-]
— Bullinger (H.). Comm. vpon the...Thessalonians. 1538.
— Chambers (Ric.). Sarahs sepvltvre. 1620.
[*qu.* R. Hole?] *See* Croce (G.). Mvsica... 1608 *etc.*
[=Hodgkinson (R.)]. *See* Grotius (H.). Poemata. 1639.
H. (R.). *See* Lavater (L.). Of Ghostes. 1596.
H. (R.), *D.* Sermon...of the crosse in baptisme. 1606. 8°. . . 2941
H. (R.), *Iohan.* Verses in Camb. Univ. Gratulatio. 1623. . . 5695
H. (S.). *See* Harsnett (S.). Declaration of...impostures.
— — Discovery... 1599.
H. (S.). Examination of a chirurgion. *See* Enchiridion Medicum. 16[ ] *etc.*
H. (S.). Verses in Withals (J.). Shorte dictionarie. 1586. . . 1376
— Sym (J.). Lifes preservative. 1637. 4313
H. (S.), *Coll. Jesu.* Verses in Camb. Univ. Anthologia. 1632. . 5741
H. (S. T.). Verses in Gray (T. de). Compleat horseman. 1639. . 4042
H. (T.). Sermon...at the funerall of...Sir R. Boteler. 1623. 4°. . 3686
Three godly sermons. 1638. 12°. 4944
[=Hawkins (Sir T.)]. *See* Caussin (N.). 1631. 4°.
See Hayne (T.). Equall wayes of God. 1632.
— Hooker (T.). Fovre learned...treatises. 1638.
— — Sovles effectual calling. 1637.

No.
H. (T.) *cont.* *See* Hooker (T.). Soules possession of christ etc. 1638. 12°. 4318
— — Sovles vocation. 1638?(–7).
Verses in Camb. Univ. Thr-thr. 1603. 5616
— Ravenscroft (T.). Briefe discourse. 1614. 2029
H. (T.) [*qu.* Hatcher?]. Verses in Seton (J.). Dialectica. 1631. . 5739
H. (T.), *A.B.*, *C.C.C.* Verses in Wadsworth (J.). Further Obss. 1630. 7788
H. (T.), *C.C.* Verses in Camb. Univ. Rex redux. 1633. . . 5748
H. (T.), *Gen.* Verses in Camden (W.). Britannia. 1637. . . 3055
— Bauderon (B.). Pharmacopoea. 1639. 5200
H. (T.), *M.A.*, *Trin. Coll.* Verses in Camb. Univ. Rex redux. 1633. 5748
H. (Sir T.) [=Hawkins (Sir T.)]. Horatius. [Odes and Epodes.] 1638.
See Matthieu (P.). Remarkeable considerations. 1638.
[*qu.* Sir T. Hawkins?]. [Trans. of Botero's Observations.] *See* Cause of the Greatnesse of Cities. 1635. 12°.
H. (T.), *Maister of Arts, and lately Minister.* *See* Higgons (T.). 1609.
H. (T. E.). *See* Drexelius (H.). Angel-gvardian's clock... [1621.]
H. (W.). *See* Calvin (J.). Comentaries. [156– ?]
See Hodson (W.). The holy sinner. 1639. 12°.
[i.e. Harrison (W.)]. *See* Holinshed (R.). Chronicles. 1577 *etc.*
H. (W.), *of Ex. in Ox.* *See* Heale (W.).
Ha. (Jo.), *T.C.C.* Verses in Barlow (W.). Vita R. Cosin. 1598. . 1707
Habermann (J.). *See* Avenar (John).
Habington (J.). *See* Gildas. The Epistle. 1638.
Habington (William). Queene of Arragon. 1640. F°. 4674
Hacket (John). Verses in Camb. Univ. Lacrymæ. 1619. . . 5689
Hacket (Roger). Learned Sermon. 1605. 8°. 2937
Hacket (Thomas). *See* Lobeira (V.). [Amadis of Gaul. 1567.]
Hacket (William). *See* Cosin (R.). Conspiracie for Pretended Reformation. 1592.
Haddon (W.). Contra H. Osorium...responsio...per J. Foxum. 1577. 4°. 848
Against I. Osorius...by J. Foxe. Trans. J. Bell. 1581. 4°. . 864
Liber precum publicarum. [1560.] 4°. 755
Lucubrationes. 1567. 4°. 928
[Letters.] *See* Fleming (A.). Panoplie. 1576. 4°.
Verses in Cheke (Sir J.). De obitu M. Buceri. 1551. . . 734
— Wilson (Sir T.). The rule of reason. 1552. . . 625
— Arte of Rhetorique. 1553. 626
— Demosthenes. Thre Orations. 1570. 1409
— Ascham (R.). Toxophilus. 1571. 1220
— Harvey (G.). Gratulationum. 1578. 1495
See Cranmer (T.). Reformatio legvm. 1571 *etc.*
See Wilson (Sir T.). Vita et obitvs... [1551.]
Hadington (John, Lord Ramsey, viscount). [Marriage.] *See* Jonson (B.). The description. [1608.]
Hadock (Richard). *See* Haydock.
Hagthorpe (John). Englands Exchequer. 1625. 4°. . . . 4227
Visiones rerum. [1623.] 8°. 7585
Hainhofer (Ierome), *Patritius Augustanus.* *See* Du Bosc (J.). The secretary of Ladies. 1638. 12°. 7800
Haius (Augustinus Aggeus). *See* Aggeus.
Hake (Edward). *See* Imitation of Christ. 1568. 8°.
See Daman (W.). Psalmes of David. 1579. Long 8°.
Hake (William). Verses in Camb. Univ. Lacrymæ. 1619. . . 5689
Hakewill (George). Answere to a treatise by Dr Carier. 1616. 4°. . 3472
Apologie of the power...of god. Oxford, 1627. F°. . . 5366
— Ed. 2. Oxford, 1630. F°. 5428
— Ed. 3. Oxford, 1635. F°. 5447
King David's Vow. 1621. 8°. 2537
— 1622. 8°. 2542

No.
Hakewill (George) *cont.* Scutum Regium. 1612. 8°. 3084
— 1613. 12°. 2376
Sermon preached at Barstaple. 1632. 4°. 7594
Vanitie of the eye. Ed. 2. Oxford, 1633. 12°. . . 5436
See Downe (J.). Certaine treatises... 1633.
Hakluyt (R.). Principall voyages. 1589. F°. 1716
— 1599 (1600). F°. 1739
Halberstadt (Henry Julius, bp of), *duke of Brunswick.* *See* Briefe discourse. 1599.
Hales (H.). Verses in Carlile (C.). A discourse. 1582. . . . 1871
Hales (Sir James). *See* Gardiner (S.), *bp.* The commvnication. [1553.] 8°.
Hales (John), *Marprelatist.* *See* Marprelate. Hay any worke for Cooper. [1589.] 4°.
Hales (John), *Canon.* Sermon...at St Maries. Oxford, 1617. 4°. . 5330
Haliburton (Antony). Verses in Camb. Univ. Carmen. 1635. . 5770
— — Συνῳδία. 1637. 5790
Halkerston (James). Verses in Cambridge Lacrymae. 1587. . 7356
Hall (E.). Vnion of the two...families of York and Lancaster. Berthelet [1542]. F°. 464
— Grafton, 1548. F°. 607
— „ 1550. F°. 618
Hall (George). Verses in Camb. Univ. Genethl. 1631. . . 5731
— Hippocrates. 1631, 1633. . . . . . 5736, 5812
— Camb. Univ. Fasciae *bis.* 1633. 5808
— — Rex redux. 1633. 5748
Hall (I.). Verses in Greenham (R.). Workes. 1599 *etc.* . . 2912
Hall (James). *See* Fox (L.). Northwest Fox. 1635.
Hall (John). Prouerbes of Salamon...Ecclesiastes...Sapientia...Ecclesiasticus...Psalmes. [1549?] 8°. 676
Certayn chapters...Prouerbes...Psalmes...of T. Sternholde. 1550. 8°. 700
Most excellent...woorke of chirurgerie. T. Marshe, 1565. 4°. . 1215
Verses in Gale (T.). Certaine Workes. 1563. 1303
Hall (Jo.), *of Gray's Inn.* Verses in Xenophon. Cyrupædia. 1632. . 4714
Hall (Joseph). Works. 1628. F°. 4248
— — The second tome. 1634. F°. 4280
Recollection of...treatises. 1615(-4). F°. 7405
— 1617. F°. 3919
— 1621 (1620). F°. 3746
Answer to Pope Urban. Trans. B. S. 1629. 4°. 5041
Arte of divine meditation. 1605. 12°. 2474
— 1607. 12°. 7400
— 1621. 12°. 7793
Αὐτοσχεδιάσματα. Vel meditationes subitaneae. (Henochismus.) 1635. 12°. 4287, 7718
Best bargaine. 1623. 8°. 7626
Certaine irrefragable propositions. 1639. 4°. 4329
Character of man. 1635. 8°. 4285
Characters of vertues and vices. 1608. 8°. 3370
— 1621. 12°. 7793
Christian moderation. 1640. 8°. 4332
Columba Noae. 1624. 4°. 3151
Contemplations upon the principall passages... Vol. I. 1612. 8°. 7522
— 1617. F°. 3120
Contemplations, the fifth Volume. 1620. 8°. 7846
Discovery of a new world. [1609?] 8°. 2755
Episcopacie by divine right. 1640. 4°. 4398
Epistles. Vol. 1. 1608. 8°. 2087
— Vol. 2. 1608. 8°. 2088
— Vol. 3. 1610. 8°. 2089
Heaven upon earth. 1606. 12°. 2170, 2478

No.
Hall (Joseph) *cont.* Heaven upon earth. Ed. 3. 1607. 12°. . 7401
— 1621. 12°. 7793
Henochismus. 1635. 12°. 4286, 7718
Holy Observations...Psalms. 1607. 12°. 7402
— 1621. 12°. 7793
Holy panegyrick. 8°. 3842
Honor of the married Clergie. 1620. 8°. 3131
Humble remonstrance to the...Parliament. 1640. 4°. . 4333, 7591
Meditations and Vowes. 1606. 12°. 2479
— 1616. 12°. 2526
— Newly enlarged &c. 1621. 12°. 7793
Mundus alter et idem. Francofurti [1605]. 8°. . . . 6628
Occasionall Meditations. Ed. 2. 1631. 12°. 3180
— Ed. 3. 1633. 12°. 4275
Olde religion. 1628. 8°. 3170
— Ed. 3. 1630. 8°. 3177
One of the sermons (April 5. 1628)...to...Parliament. (A sermon. March 30.) 1628. 8°. 7589
Passion Sermon, 1609. 1609. 8°. 3063
Peace of Rome. 1609. 4°. 3064
Pharisaisme and christianity. 1608. 8°. 3371
— 1609. 8°. 2495
Plaine and familiar explication...of...Scripture. 1633(2). F°. . 4269
Polemices sacræ pars prior. Roma Irreconciliabilis. 1612. 8°. 2091
Reconciler. 1629. 8°. 4256
Remedy of Prophanenesse. 1637. 8°. 4027
Righteous mammon. 1618. 8°. 7556
Salomons diuine arts. 1609. 8°. 2496
Some few of Davids Psalmes. 1621. 12°. 7793
Verses in Horne (C.). In obitum Whitakeri. 1596. . . 7332
— Du Bartas. Weekes. 1621. 2535
See Bedell (W.). The copies of...letters. 1624.
— Brinsley (J.). Lvdvs literarivs. 1612 *etc.*
— Burton (H.). Babel.
— Butterfield (R.). Maschil. 1629.
— Cholmley (H.). State of the now-Romane Chvrch. 1629.
— Downe (J.). Certaine treatises. 1633.
— Durie (J.). De Pace. 1638.
— Hakewill (G.). An apologie. 1635.
Hall (Robert). *See* Hall (Jos.). Occasionall Meditations. 1631.
— — 1633.
Hall (S.). Verses in Camb. Univ. Rex redux. 1633. . . 5748
Hall (Thomas). Verses in Hall (J.). A most excellent...woorke. 1565. 1215
Hall (Thos.), *Reginal.* Verses in Barlow (W.). Vita R. Cosin. 1598. 1707
Hall (William), *Christ's Coll.* Verses in Camb. Univ. Rex redux. 1633. 5748
— Camb. Univ. Carmen. 1635. 5770
— King (E.). Ivsta. 1638, 5829
Halle (Edward). *See* Hall.
Halse (Jo.). Verses in Camb. Univ. Thr-thr. 1603. . . 5616
Halswell (Nic.). Verses in Oxf. Univ. Magd. Coll. 1612. . . 5302
Halswell (Robert). Verses in Coryate (T.). Coryates Crvdities. 1611. 3076
Haly abbas. *See* 'Ali aben Rudwán.
Halyday (James). Speech in Adamson (J.). Εἰσόδια. 1618. . . 5960
Hamilton (Archibald). *See* Smeton (T.). Ad virvlentvm... 1579.
Hamilton (James), *first duke of Hamilton.* 'It will, no doubt, seeme strange.' *See* Aberdeen University. Generall Demands. 1638.
'Whereas some have given out.' Edinburgh, 1638. 4°. . 5943
See Charles I. Proclamation in Scotland... 1639. . . 5006
— Scotland. General Assembly. An answer. 1639. 4°. . 5989

No.

Hamilton (James). *See* Rollock (R.). Lectures...vpon Colossians. 1603. 4°.
Hamilton (James). Verses in Oxf. Univ. Horti. 1640. . . 5499
Hamilton (John). A facile traictise. Louvain, 1600. 12°. . 6426
See Hume (A.). A didvction. 1602. 5943
Hamilton (John). Verses in Forbes (P.). Funerals. 1635. . 6007
Hamlin (Giles). *See* Ramus (P.). Logike. 1581.
Hammersley (Sir Hugh). *See* Sictor (J.). Lacrymæ. 1637.
Hammilton. *See* Hamilton.
Hammon (Thomas). *See* Heywood (T.). Hierarchie. 1635.
Hammond (H.). Verses in Barlow (W.). Vita R. Cosin. 1598. . 1707
Hammond (John). Verses in Butler (C.). The Feminin' Monarchi'. 1634. 5439
Hammond (William). Verses in Camb. Univ. Fasciae. 1633. . 5808
Hamond (John). Verses in Jewel (J.). Adv. T. Hardingum. 1578. 1535
Hamond (Thomas). The late commotion of certaine papists in Herefordshire. 1605. 8°. 2884
Hampden (John). Verses in Oxf. Univ. Magd. Coll. 1612. . 5302
Hampole (Richard Rolle de). *See* Rolle.
Hampshire. *See* Bale (J.). An expostulation. [Ab. 1551.] 8°.
See Elvetham.
Hampton (William). Proclamation of Warre. 1627. 4°. . . 4879
Hampton Court Conference. *See* Barlow (W.). 1604 *etc.*
Hamus Charitatis. *See* Mirk (J.). The festial.
Hanapus (N.). Ensamples of Vertue and vice. Trans. T. Paynell. 1561. 8°. 1259
Hanbury (Edward), *Sid. Coll. Camb.* Verses in Camb. Univ. Fasciae. 1633. 5808
— Hippocrates. 1633. 5812
Hanburie (John). Verses in Hippocrates. 1633. . . . 5812
Hancock (Will.). Verses in Camb. Univ. Thr-thr. 1603. . . 5616
Handson (Ra.). *See* Pitiscus (B.). Trigonometry. [1630.]
Hanley (Robert). Verses in Hill (T.). Arte of vulgar arithmeticke. 1600. 2197
Hanmer (M.). Baptizing of a Turke. [1586.] 8°. . . . 1907
Great bragge and challenge of M. Champion. 1581. 4°. . . 1232
Chronicle of Ireland. *See* Ware (Sir J.). Historie of Ireland. 1633.
Iesuites Banner. 1581. 4°. 1814
See Charke (W.). Replie to a Censure. 1581.
— — Treatise against the defense. 1586.
— Eusebius Pamphili. The avncient...histories. 1577 *etc.*
— Parsons (R.). Defence of the censure. 1582.
Hans (Olve). *See* Swedish Discipline. 1632.
Hansley (John) [Licenses]. Gataker (T.). The decease of Lazarus. 1640. 4°.
Jackson (J.). Key of Knowledge. 1640.
Sedgwick (O.). Christs Counsell. 1640.
Hanson (Ralph). Verses in Roberts (L.). The merchants mappe. 1638. 5133
Harborowe for faithfvll...subiectes. 1559. *See* Aylmer (J.).
Harding (John) (fl. 1543). *See* Hardyng.
Harding (John). Verses in Dodonæus (R.). A newe herball. 1578 *etc.* 6130 *etc.*
Harding (John), *President of Magdalen College.* *See* Bible. Eng. (Royal). 1611.
Harding (Richard). *See* Letters patent to Sir A. Aston &c. 1606. . 2595
Harding (Thomas). Answere to maister ivelles chalenge. Antwerp, 1565. 8°. 6125
Reioindre to m. jewels replie. Antwerp, 1566. 4°. . . . 6119
— 1567. 4°. 6419
See Humphrey (L.). J. Jvelli vita. 1573.
— Jewel (J.). A replie. 1565. F°.
— — Defence of the Apologie. 1567 *etc.* F°.

No.
Harding (Thomas) *cont.* *See* Jewel (J.). Adversus Thomam Hardingum volumen alterum. 1578.
Hardyng (J.). Chronicle...of Englande. R. Grafton. 1543. 8° and 4°. 591
Hare (Rob.). Verses in Oxf. Univ. Horti. 1640. . . . 549J
Haren (John). Repentance. 1610. 4°. 2305
Harington (Francis) *See* Ariosto (L.). Orlando Fvrioso. 1591.
Harington (John), *of Kelston* (fl. 1549). *See* Harrington.
Harington (Sir John). Most elegant and witty epigrams. 1618. 8°. . 4065
— — 1633. *See* Ariosto. Orlando Furioso. 1634. . . 4448
Verses in Contarini (G.). Commonwealth. 1599. . . . 2153
— Coryat (T.). Coryats Crudities. 1611. . . . 3076
See Ariosto (L.). Orlando Fvrioso. 1591 etc. . . 2228 etc.
Harington (John), *first baron Harington of Exton.* *See* Stock (R.). The chvrches lamentation. 1614. 8°.
Harisius (Paulus). *See* Harris.
Harison. *See* Harrison.
Harlakenden (Katharine). [Funeral.] *See* Williamson (T.). Comfortable meditation. 1630. 4°.
Harleston (Tho.), *Pemb.* Verses in Swan (J.). Speculum. 1635. . 5777
Harley (Richard). Verses in Holyoake (F.). Dictionarium. 1640. 3058
Harmanus (Gul.). *See* Æsop. Fabulæ. 1635.
Harmar (Ch). *See* Teelinck (W.). Pavls complaint. 1621.
Harmar (John), *Warden of Winchester* (†1613). *See* Calvin (J.). Sermons...vpon the .x. Commandementes. 1570.
— Bible. Eng. (Royal). 1611. 2635
Harmar (John), *the younger.* Lexicon etymologicum. 1637. F°. . 3966
Verses in Oxf. Univ. Magd. Coll. 1612. 5302
— Camdeni Insignia. 1624. 5346
See H. (J.). 4896
— Parkinson (J.). Theatrum. 1640. 4680
— Janua Linguarum. 1627.
— Scapula (J.). 1637.
Harmer. *See* Harmar.
Harper (Jo.). Jewel of Arithmetic. [1616–7?] 4°. 2997
Harper (Thomas), *printer.* *See* Tunstal (C.). Sermon. 1633.
See Banister (J.). Workes (Storehouse). 1633. 4°. . . 4000
Harpsfield (John). *See* England. Church. Homilies. 1547.
See Bonner (E.). A profitable...doctryne. 1555.
Harpur (John). *See* Harper.
Harrice (Robert). *See* Harris.
Harries (George). *See* Harryes.
Harries (Richard). Verses in Vaughan (R.). Waterworkes. 1610. . 3576
Harries (Walter). [MS. notes.] *See* Davies of Hereford (J.). Writing Schoolmaster. 1636. 8°.
Harrington (John). *See* Wyat (Sir T.). Certayne psalmes. (1549.)
See Cicero. [De amicitia.] 1550. 16°.
Harrington (Villiers), *Clare Coll.* Verses in Camb. Univ. Voces. 1640. 5836
— Ovid Fasti. 1640. 5849
Harriot (Tho.). Artis analyticae praxis. 1631. F°. 2674
Harris (John), *of Westminster & Ch. Ch., Oxford.* Verses in Fisher (A.). Defence. 1630. 3176
Harris (Paul). Ἀρκτομάστιξ sine E. Vrsulanus. 1633. 4°. . . . 6045
Excommunication published by...T. Flemming...against...Peter Caddell. Dublin, 1632. 4°. 6038
Fratres sobrii estote. 1634. 4°. 6053
Harris (Richard). Concordia Anglicana de primatu ecclesiæ regio. 1612. 8°. 3216
English concord. 1614. 4°. 2522
Harris (Robert). Workes. 1635. 12°. 4986
Absaloms funerall: preached at Banbvrie. 1610. 4°. . . 3208
— 1617. 4°. 7474

No.

Harris (Robert), *cont.* Absaloms funerall: preached at Banbvrie. 1622. 4°. 4170
Blessednesse of a sound spirit. 1628. 4°. 4816
Davids comfort at Ziklag. 1628. 4°. 4970
Drunkards cvp. 1619. 4°. 3004
— 1626. 4°. 7575
Gods goodnes & mercie. Ed. 3. 1626. 4°. 2553
Hezekiahs recovery. Ed. 2. 1626. 4°. 4967
Peters enlargement. Ed. 3. 1625. 4°. 4799, 4761
— Ed. 6. 1629. 4°. 4096
Samuels funerall...funeral of Sir A. Cope. 1618. 4°. . . 7476
— 1622. 4°. 4171
— 1626. 4°. 4091
Sixe sermons of conscience. Ed. 2. 1630. 4°. 7413
Way to true happinesse. 1632. 4°. 4348
See H. (R.). The arraignement. 1631(–2).
Harrison (E.). Verses in Horne (C.). In obit. Whitakeri. 1596. . 7332
Harrison (G.). Verses in Cambridge Lachrymae. 1587. . . 7356
See also W. Harrison.
Harrison (Hen.). Verses in Cam. Univ. Fasciae. 1633. . . 5808
— Camb. Univ. Συνωδία. 1637. 5790
Harrison (I.). *See* Bohemia. Bohemica Ivra Defensa. 1620.
Harrison (John). Verses in Jewel (J.). Adv. T. Hardingum. 1578. . 1535
Harrison (John), *M.A.*, *T.C.* Verses in Camb. Univ. Συνωδία *bis*. 1637. 5790
Harrison (John). *See* Bale (J.).
Harrison (Thomas). Verses in Cambridge Lachrymae. 1587. . . 7356
— Whitaker (W.). Praelectiones. 1599. 5598
— Camb. Univ. Epicedium. 1612. 5665
— — Dolor. 1625. 5701
See Bible. Eng. (Royal). 1611. 2635
— Dalechamp (C.). 1632.
Harrison (William). Verses in Wilson (Sir T.). Vita. 1551. . 631
Harrison (William), *topographer* († 1593). *See* Holinshed (R.). Chronicles. 1577 *etc.*
Harrison (William), *His Majesty's Preacher in Lancashire.* Difference of hearers. 1614. 8°. 2750
Harrison (William), *Cath.* Verses in Camb. Univ. Συνωδία. 1637. 5790
Harry *the Portar.* Verses in Hoby (Sir E.). A curry combe. 1615. 3111
Harry (George Owen). Genealogy of...James. 1604. 4°. . . 2882
Harryes (George). Verses in Camb. Univ. Genethl. 1631. . . 5731
— — Rex redux. 1633. 5748
Harryson (John). *See* Bale (J.).
Harsnett (Adam). Touchstone of Grace. 1635. 12°. . . . 3955
Harsnett (S.). Declaration of...Popish Impostures. 160[3?]. 4°. . 1786
— 1604. 4°. 1789
Discovery of the fravdvlent practices of J. Darrel. 1599. 4°. 1982
Hart (Alexander). Tragi-comicall history of Alexto & Angelica. 1640. 12°. 4220
Hart (H.). Godly Newe short treatyse...in yᵉ Imytacyon of Vertu. 1548. 8°. 1062
See H. (H.). A Consultorie. 1549.
Hart (I.). *See* Smith (J.). Essex dove. 1629. 4°.
Hart (J.). Orthographie. 1569. 8°. 933
Hart (James). Anatomie of vrines. 1625. 4°. 2298
Κλινική or the diet of the diseased. 1633. F°. 3822
See Forestus (P.). Arraignment of vrines. 1623.
Hart (John), *Jesuit.* *See* Rainolds (J.). Svmme of the conference. 1584 *etc.*
— — Svmma colloqvii. 1610.
Hart (Sir William). Examinations, arraignment and conviction of George Sprot. 1609. 4°. 3373

No.
Hartlib (Samuel). *See* Comenius (J. A.). Conatvvm Comenianorvm Praelvdia. 1637.
— — Pansophiæ Prodromus. 1639.
Harttun (James). 1567. [Book-owner. His name printed in.] 1397, 6414
Hartwell (Abr.). Regina litterata. 1565. 8°. 927
Verses in Haddon (W.). Lucubrationes. 1567. 928
— Foxe (J.). Actes. 1570. 816
— Harvey (G.). Gratulationum. 1578. 1495
See Lopes (D.). Report. 1597.
— Minadoi (G. T.). The history. 1595.
Hartwell (Robert). *See* Blundeville (T.). Exercises. 1636.
See Record (R.). Grovnd of arts. 1618 *etc.*
Harvet (Gentian). *See* Hervet.
Harvey (Christopher). The synagogue. 1640. 12°. . . . 4745
Harvey (Gabriel). Ciceronianus. 1577. 4°. 1488
Gratulationum Valdinensium libri quatuor. 1578. 4°. . 1495
Rhetor. 1577. 4°. 1489
Smithus vel Musarum Lacrymæ. 1578 (1577). 4°. . . 1494
Verses in Spenser (E.). Faerie Queen. 1590 *etc.* . . 1960 *etc.*
Harvey (J.). Astrologicall Addition. 1583. 8°. 1337
Discovrsive probleme. 1588. 4°. 2100
Harvey (John). Verses in Camb. Univ. Fasciae. 1633. . . 5808
Harvey (Richard). Astrological discourse. 1583. 8°. . . . 1513
— [158– ?] 8°. 1514
Mercurius. *See* Harvey (G.). Smithus. 1578.
See Harvey (J.). Astrologicall Addition. 1583.
Harvey (William), *M.D.* *See* Primrose (J.). Exercitationes. 1630.
Harward (A.). Verses in Camb. Univ. Anthologia. 1632. . . 5741
See also Harwood.
Harward (Simon). Enchiridion morale. 1596. 8°. . . . 2052
Most profitable new Treatise ... of the Art of propagating Plants. *See* Lawson (W.). New orchard and Garden. [1623.] 4°.
— — *See* Markham (G.). Way to get wealth. 1638. 4°.
Two godlie and learned sermons. 1582. 8°. 1353
Harward (William). Verses in Cheke (Sir J.). De obitu M. Buceri. 1551. 734
Harwood (Andrew), *K.C.C.* Verses in Hippocrates. 1631, 1633. 5736, 5812
See also Harward.
Hasan ibn Muhammad al Wazzan. *See* Leo (J.).
Hasill (Robert). Verses in Barnes (B.). Foure bookes. 1606. . 2435
Hassia (Henricus de). *See* Cordiale.
Hastings (Sir Francis). Apologie...against...N.D. 1600. 4°. . . 2917
Watchword to all religious. 1598. 8°. 2908
See E. (O.) A briefe replie. 1600.
— Parsons (R.). The Warn-word. 1602. 8°.
Hastings (William, de Hastings, baron). *See* Mirror of the World. [1480?]
Hatcher ( ), *M.D.* Verses in Wilson (Sir T.). Vita. 1551. . 631
Hatcher (I.). Verses in Cambridge Lachrymae. 1587. . . 7356
Hatcher (Thomas). *See* Carr (N.). De scriptorum Britannicorum paucitate. 1576.
See Haddon (W.). Lucubrationes. 1567.
Hatton (Sir Christopher). *See* Elizabeth, *Queen.* Trve report. 1579. 1505
Hatton (Ric.), *Sid.* Verses in Camb. Univ. Epithalam. 1625. . 5702
Haubœsius (Carolus). *See* Canini (A.). Ἑλληνισμός. 1624.
Haughton (William). Englishmen for my money. *See below* A pleasant comedie called, A Woman will have her will. 1631. 4°.
Pleasant comedie called, A Woman will have her will. 1631. 4°. 4549
Haukins (William). *See* Hawkins.
Hausted (Peter). Rivall friends. 1632. 4°. 4561

No.

Hausted (Peter), *cont.* Senile odium. Cantabrigiae, 1633. 8°. . 5753
Ten sermons...with a Sermon...at Huntington. 1636. 4°. . 4298
Hauwenreuter (Joh. Ludwig). Σύνοψις τῆς φυσικῆς τοῦ Ἀριστοτέλους. Cantabrigiae, 1594. 8°. 5568
Haviland (John), *printer.* *See* Butler (C.). The principles of musik. 1636.
Haward (Nicholas). *See* Eutropius (F.). Briefe Chronicle. 1564.
Hawarden (Sa.). Verses *bis* in Camb. Univ. Thr-thr. 1603. . 5616
Hawenreuther (Johann Ludwig). *See* Hauwenreuter.
Hawes (S.). Example of virtue. W. de Worde [15—]. 4°. . . 222
Joyfull medytacyon to all Englonde of the coronacyon of...Henry the eyght. W. de Worde [1509]. 4°. 223
Hawfeld (H.). *See* Justinianus. Digestorum... 1553.
Hawgh (Walter). Verses in Parkhurst (J.). Ludicra. 1573. . . 838
Hawkesworth (Walter). Labyrinthus. 1636. 12°. . . . 5148
Hawkins (Arthur). Verses in Gilbert (Sir H.). A true reporte. 1583. 1354
Hawkins (Francis). Verses in Gray (T. de). Compleat horseman. 1639. 4042
Hawkins (H.). *See* Cambridge University. Act verses. [Ab. 1577.] F°.
Hawkins (Henry). Partheneia Sacra. Rouen, 1633. 8°. . . 6259
See Hieronymus. Certaine selected epistles. 1630. 4°.
— Maffei (G. P.). Fuga Saeculi. 1632. 4°.
Hawkins (Henry), *Petrensis.* Verses in Baro (P.). In Jonam. 1579. 850
Hawkins (J.). *See* H. (J.). Abridgement. 1634.
Hawkins (Sir John). Verses in Gilbert (Sir H.). A true reporte. 1583. 1354
Hawkins (John), *M.D.* *See* Soto (A. de). The Ransome of Time. 1634.
Hawkins (Ma.). Verses in Smith (J.). True travels. 1630. . 4836
Hawkins (Sir Richard). Observations of...the South Sea. 1593. 1622. F°. 3847
Hawkins (Sir Thomas). [Trans. of Botero's Observations.] *See* Cause of the Greatnesse of Cities. 1635. 12°.
See Caussin (N.). Holy covrt. 1626 *etc.*
— Horatius. Odes and Epodes. 1635 *etc.*
— Matthieu (P.). Remarkeable considerations. 1638.
— — Vnhappie Prosperitie. 1632 *etc.*
Verses in Beaumont (Sir J.). Bosworth field. 1629. . . 3040
Hawkins (William). Corolla varia. Cantabrigiae, 1634. 8°. . . 5803
Eclogae tres virgilianae. [1633.] 4°. 7497
En Priscianus. 1632. 4°. 4562
Verses in Gill (A.). Πάρεργα. 1632. 4558
— Camb. Univ. Rex redux. 1633.. 5748
— — Carmen. 1635. 5770
— — Συνῳδία. 1637. 5790
Hawkridge (William), *Captain.* *See* Fox (L.). North-west Fox. 1635.
Hawley (Richard). Verses in Hippocrates. 1633. . . . 5812
Hawtrey (Ed.), *K.C.C.* Verses in Camb. Univ. Epithalam. 1625. . 5702
— — Rex redux. 1633. 5748
Haxby (Stephen). Verses *bis* in Camb. Univ. Epicedium. 1612. 5665, 5666
— — Dolor. 1625. 5701
Hay any worke for Cooper. [1589?] 4°. 7779
Hay (Alexander). [Licence 1608.] Skene (Sir J.). Regiam. 1609.
— — 1613.
Hay (Peter). Vision of Balaams asse...for...Francis earl of Errol. 1614. 4°. 3463
Hay (Theodore). Theses in Adamson (J.). Εἰσόδια. 1618. . 5960
Hay (William). Speech in Adamson (J.). Εἰσόδια. 1618. . . 5960
Hay (William), *Earl of Erroll.* *See* Erroll (W. Hay, earl of).
Haydock (Richard), *Student in Physic.* *See* Lomazzo (G. P.). A Tracte. 1598.
Haydock (Richard), *D.D., Roman Catholick.* *See* Bellarmino (R.). An ample declaration of the christian doctrine... 1604.

No.
Haydon (Sir William). *See* Proclamation. 1630. 7424
Hayne (Thomas). Equall wayes of God. 1632. 4°. . . . 4204
Grammatices latinæ compendium. 1637. 1640. 8°. . . 7819
Linguarum Cognatio. 1639. 8°. 4908
Pax in terra. 1639. 8°. 4909
Hayward (James). *See* Haywarde.
Hayward (Sir John). Answer to the first part of a conference. 1603. 4°. 2110
Davids teares. 1623. 4°. 7530
First part of the life of King Henry IV. 1599. 4°. . . 1983
Life and raigne of Edward the sixt. 1630. 4°. . . 4951
— with Elizabeth. Ed. 2. 1636. 12°. 4989
Lives of the III. Normans, William I, II, Henry I. 1613. 4°. 2646
Of supremacie in...religion. 1624. 4°. 3520
Reporte of a discourse. 1606. 4°. 2942
Sanctvarie of a troubled soule. 1604. 4°. 2473
— 1623. 4°. 4080
— 1631. 12°. 4099
— 1636. 12°. 4119
Treatise of union of...England and Scotland. 1604. 4°. . 2931
See Williams (Sir R.). Actions of the Lowe Countries. 1618.
Hayward (John). Verses in King (E.). Ivsta. 1638. . . . 5829
Hayward (William). *See* General Pardon. [156–?] 8°.
Haywarde (James). *See* Biondi (G. F.). Eromena. 1632.
— — Donzella Desterrada. 1635. F°.
Haywood (Thomas). *See* Heywood.
Haywood (William), *Chaplain to Abp Laud.* [Licence. 31 Dec. 1632.]
Herbert (E.) 1633. 4572
[— 19 Dec. 1633.] Mercator. 1635. F°. 4637
[— 26 Aug. 1634.] Chowne (T.). Collectiones. 1635. . 4594
— — Gill (A.). Sacred philosophie. 1635.
— — Reynolds (E.). The shieldes. 1636.
Heale (William). Apologie for women. Oxford, 1609. 4°. . . 5292
Healey (John). *See* Augustine (S.). Of the Citie of God. 1610 *etc.*
See Epictetus Manuall *etc.* 1616.
— Hall (J.). Discovery of a new world. 1620? 8°.
Hearding (T.). Verses in Camb. Univ. Thr-thr. 1603. . . 5616
Heath (Francis). Verses in Camb. Univ. Rex redux. 1633. . . 5748
— — *Συνωδία.* 1637. 5790
Heath (George). Verses in Camb. Univ. Fasciae. 1633. . . 5808
— — Rex redux. 1633. 5748
— — *Συνωδία.* 1637. 5790
Heath (John). *See* Du Moulin (P.). Accomplishment. 1613.
See H. (J.), *Gent.* House of Correction. 1619.
Heath (Nicholas), *bp.* *See* Bible. Eng. (Cranmer's). 1541.
Heath (R.). Verses in Dugres (G.). Breve compendium. 1636. . 5781
Heath (Robert), *C.C.C.* Verses in Camb. Univ. *Συνωδία.* 1637. . 5790
Heavenly acte...how man shal lyue. Amsterdam [1547?]. 8°. . . 6338
Hedrington (Robert). 1577. Name stamped in [AB. 10. 33.] . 17
Heidelberg Catechism. Catechisme or manner how to instruct. 1578. 8°. 1625
[Text.] *See* Ursinus (Z.). Explicationum. 1587 *etc.*
Exposition. By I. Bastingius. Cambridge [1589?]. 8°. . . 5541
— — Cambridge, 1589. 4°. 5548
— — Cambridge, 1595. 8°. 7359
See Book of Common Order. Edinburgh, 1615. 8°. . 5953, (corrected, p. 1743).
Heigham (Francis). Verses in Camb. Univ. Voces. 1640. . . 5836
Heigham (J.). Devout exposition of the holie masse. Ed. 2. St Omer, 1622. 12°. 6545
Life of our blessed lord. Ed. 2. 1622. 6585

No.

Heigham (J.), *cont.* *See* Catharinus (A.). Life of...Catharine of Siena. 1609.
See Puente (L. de la). Meditations. 1619. 4°.
Heigham (Thomas). *See* Chevalier (G. de). Ghosts. 1624.
Heiland (Sam). Aristotelis ethicorum ad Nicomachum libri decem. 1581. 8°. 7267
Heinsius (Daniel). Sacrarum exercitationum ad novum testamentum libri xx. Ed. 2. Cantabrigiae, 1640. 4°. 5846
Verses in Veen (O. van). Amorum Emblemata. 1608. . . 6138
— Seneca. Tragœdiæ. 1624. 3444
— Vossius (G. J.). Rhetorices libri v. 1631. 5433
— Burgersdicius (F.). Institutionum. 1637. 5789
— Tesauro (E.). Cæsares. 1637. 5476
Helias, Knight of the Swan. *See* Helyas.
Heliodorus. Famous historie...in verse...by W. Lisle. 1638. 4°. . 5166
Hellish and horrible Councell, practised...by the Iesuites...to murther a King. 1610. 4°. 3749
Hellowes (Edward). *See* Guevara (A. de). Chronicle. 1577. 4°.
— — Familiar Epistles. 1584. 4°.
Helpe to discovrse. Ed. 11. 1635. 12°. 3833
Ed. 12. 1636. 12°. 3703
Helsom (R.). Verses in Camdeni Insignia. 1624. 5346
Helvetia. *See* Switzerland.
Helwisse (Thomas). *See* Helwys.
Helwys (Thomas). *See* Robinson (J.). Of Religious Communion. 1614.
Helyas, Knight of the Swan. W. de Worde, 1512. 4°. . . 169
Heming (John). *See* Shakspeare (W.). Works. 1623, *etc.*
Heming (Nicholas). *See* Hemmingsen.
Hemming (Nicholas). *See* Hemmingsen.
Hemmingsen (N.). Epistle...to the Ephesians. 1581(–80). 4°. . 1581
Learned...Commentarie vpon the Epistle of Iames. 1577. 4°. 1837
Postill or Exposition of the Gospels. 1569. 4°. . . . 1463
— [1569?] 4°. 7269
Way of Lyfe. [1578.] 4°. 1454
[Commentaries.] *See* Cæsar (P.). General Discovrse. 1578.
Henderson (Robert). *See* H. (R.). The arraignement. 1631(–32).
Hendricq (Francis). *See* Wadding (L.). History of...S. Clare.
Hengham (Ralph de). [Summæ.] *See* Fortescue (Sir John). De Laudibus Legum Angliæ. 1616.
Henisch (George). *See* Cooke (F.). Principles of Geometrie. 1591.
Henley (W. de). Boke of husbandry. W. de Worde [15]. 4°. . 224
Henricpetri (Adam). Chronyc. Historie der Nederlandtscher Oorlogen. Norwich, 1579. 8°. 5894
Henrietta Maria. *See* Cambridge University Epithalamium. 1625.
Henry I, *of England.* [Life.] *See* Hayward (Sir J.). 1613.
Henry II, *of England.* *See* May (T.). The reigne. 1633.
Henry III, *of England.* *See* Cotton (Sir R. B.). A shorte vievv. 1627.
Henry IV, *of England.* [Life.] *See* Hayward (Sir J.). 1599.
Henry V, *of England.* *See* Lydgate (J.). The life of our Lady. [1484?] F°.
Henry VII, *of England.* *See* Bacon (F.). Historie of the raigne of Henry the Seuenth. 1622 *etc.*
Henry VIII, *of England.* Assertio septem sacramentorum. Pynson, 1521. 4°. 276
— (Oratio J. Clerk etc.) Pynson, 1521. 4°. 277
Sigismondus Dondolus de Pistorio...et M. de Conradis de Tuderto...Conclusiones. n.d. 8°. 511
Epistle to the Emperours maiestie. 1538. 8°. 443
Libello huic regio insunt... 1521. 4°. 277
Literarum...ad epistolam M. Lutheri. 1526. 8°. 288

No.
Henry VIII, *of England, cont.* [Life. Coronation.] *See* Hawes (S.). Joyfull medytacyon. [1509.]
— [Marriage.] Gravissimae...Italiæ et Galliæ Academiarũ censuræ. 1530. 4°. 416
— Determinations of the vniuersities. [1531.] 8°. . . . 421
— — 1531. 8°. 422
— *See* Cowell (J.). Antisanderus. 1593.
[Death.] Lamentation of the death of...Henry the eyght. [1547.] F°. 1018
[The King's Book.] *See* Necessary doctrine. 1543.
['The King's Psalms' (Lat.).] *See* Psalmi. 1544 *etc.* . . . 479 *etc.*
See More (Sir T.). Eruditissimi viri G. Rossei opus. 1523.
— Necessary Doctrine. 1543 *etc.*
— Proclamation. 1509. Broadside.
— Supplication. A supplycacion. 1544.
[Translation of Froissart.] *See* Froissart (J.). Chronicles. 1523 *etc.*
'Biblioscopus' to. *See* Delaine (W.). 1540.
Henry II, *of France.* *See* Bellopoelius (P.). De Pace. 1552.
See France. An historicall collection. 1598.
— Justinianus. 1553. F°.
Henry III, *of France.* [Letters patent.] *See* France. A discourse. 1588.
See France. An historicall collection. 1598.
— John Casimir, *Count Palatine.* Certaine Orations. 1579.
— Hurault (M.). Antisixtvs. 1590.
— Discoverie of a gaping gulf. 1579.
— Warmington (W.). A moderate defence. 1612.
— Sixtus V. The brvtish thunderbolt. 1586. 8°.
— W. (R.). Martine Mar-Sixtus. 1591.
Henry IV, *of France.* Three letters...to the States. 1586. 8°. . 1843
True discourse of the wonderfull victorie. 1590. 4°. . . . 2208
Order of Ceremonies. [1594.] 4°. 2139
Discourse to the...Parliament. 1611. 4°. 1392
[Murder.] *See* Brisset (G.). The apologie. 1610. 4°.
— Colynet (A.). True History of...France. 1591.
— Cotton (P.). The Hellish...Councell. 1610.
— French Herald. 1611. 4°.
— Pelletier (P.). Lamentable discovrse... 1610.
See Cotton (P.). Anti-coton. 1611.
— Du Perron (J. D.). Discovrse. 1600 *etc.*
— France. An historicall collection. 1598.
— Matthieu (P.). The heroyk life. 1612.
— Prosopopeia. 1606.
— Skory (E.). Extract ovt of the Historie. 1610. 4°.
[Official Documents &c.] *See* France. Henry IV.
Henry, *Prince of Wales.* Order and solemnitie of the Creation of... Henrie...with the ceremonies of the Knights of the Bath. 1610. 4°. 3071
[Visit of Christian IV.] *See* Tricorones. 1607. 4°. . . . 7807
See Cambridge University Epicedivm. 1612.
— Chapman (G.). Epicede or Funerall Song. 1612–3.
— Nethersole (Sir F.). Memoriæ Sacra. 1612.
— Nixon (A.). Oxfords Triumph. 1605.
— Oxford University Ivsta. 1612.
— — Magdalen College. Luctus Posthumus. 1612.
— Sharpe (L.). Oratio. 1612.
— Sylvester (J.). Lachrimæ Lachrimarvm. [1612?] 4°. . 2516
— — Parliament of Vertues Royal. [Ab. 1614.] 8°. . 6898
— Ward (J.). The First Set. 1613.
— Wither (G.). Abuses stript. 1617.
Henry, *Prince, Duke of Gloucester* (1640–1660). *See* Cambridge University Voces. 1640. 4°. 5836

No.
Henry de Bourbon, *Prince de Condé*. *See* Sixtus V. The brvtish thunderbolt. 1586. 8°.
Henry Frederick, *Prince of Orange*. [Portrait.] '1631.' F°. . 7650
Henry, *of Huntingdon*. [Histories.] *See* Savile (Sir H.). Rervm Anglicarvm scriptores. 1596.
Henry, *of Marlborough*. Chronicle of Ireland. *See* Ware (Sir J.). Historie of Ireland. 1633.
Henry, *the Minstrel*. The life and acts of...Sir William Wallace. Edinburgh, 1611. 4°. 5947
Henryson (Edward). *See* Scotland. Parliament. 1566.
Henshaw (Joseph). Horæ succisivæ. Ed. 3. 1632. 12°. . . 3817
— Ed. 4. 1640. 12°. 4048
— Ed. 5. 1640. 12°. 5099
Henton (William). Verses in Jewel (J.). Adv. T. Hardingum. 1578. 1535
Hepinus (Joannes). *See* Æpinus.
Heraclius. *See* Godfrey of Boulogne. 1481. F°.
Herbal. The grete herball. Southwarke, 1526. F°. . . 5858
— — 1529. F°. 5860
A newe marer. R. Bankes, 1526. 4°. 361
See C. (W.). A boke of...Herbes. 1549. 8°. . . . 1085
The greate Herball. J. King, 1561. F°. 1242
Herberay (Nicholas de), *Seigneur des Essars*. *See* Lobeira (Vasco). Amadis de Gaule. 1619(–18).
Herbert (Edward, lord). De veritate. 1633. 4°. 4578
Herbert (Sir Edward), *Kt*. Verses in Horatius. De arte poetica. 1640. 3722
Herbert (George). Oratio qua...Caroli reditum...celebrauit. Cantabrigiae, 1623. 4°. 5697
The Temple. Ed. 1. Cambridge, 1633. 12°. 5810
— Ed. 2. Cambridge, 1633. 12°. 5811
— Ed. 3. ,, 1634. 12°. 5814
— Ed. 4. ,, 1635. 12°. 5816
— Ed. 5. ,, 1638. 12°. 5827
Verses in Camb. Univ. Epicedium. 1612. 5665
— — Lacrymae. 1619. 5689
— Tesauro (E.). Cæsares. 1637. 5476
See Donne (J.). Sermon of Commemoration. 1627.
— Lessius (L.). Hygiasticon. 1634. 12°.
— Valdés (Juan de). Hundred and ten considerations. 1638.
Herbert (Henry). [Licence.] Sadler (J.). Masquerade. 1640.
Herbert (James). Verses in Oxf. Univ. Horti. 1640. . . 5499
Herbert (Joh.). Verses in Oxf. Univ. Horti. 1640. . . . 5499
Herbert (Mary), *Countess of Pembroke*. *See* Pembroke.
Herbert (Sir Thomas). Relation of some yeares travaile. 1634. F°. 3194
Herbert (William). Verses in Camb. Univ. Fasciae. 1633. . . 5808
Herd (John). Verses in Cheke (Sir J.). De obitu M. Buceri. 1551. 734
Hereford, County of. *See* Hamond (T.). The Late Commotion. 1605.
— Vaughan (R.). Waterworkes. 1610.
Heresbach (Conrad). Whole art...of husbandry. Trans. B. Googe. 1614. 4°. 7524
— Enlarged by G. Markham. 1631. 4°. 4612
Heretical Churches. *See* Treatise of Christian Renunciation.
Hering (Francis). Verses in Gerard (J.). Herball. 1597. . . 2348
— L'Obel (M. de). Balsami. 1598. 2071
— Greenham (R.). Workes, *bis* 1599 *etc.* . . . . 2912 *etc.*
— Laurentius (A.). Discourse. 1599. 2913
— L'Obel (M. de). G. Rondelletii animadversiones. 1605. . 7247
— Stock (R.). The chvrches lamentation. 1614. . . . 3784
Herle (Charles). Contemplations and devotions. 1631. 12°. . . 4550
Hermannus, *Abp*. Simple and religious consultation of...a Christian reformation. 1547. 8°. 776

No.
Hermannus, *Abp., cont.* 1548. 8°. 900
Hermes Anglo-latinus. 1639. 12°. 4931
Hermes Trismegistus. Intromathematica. *See* Harvey (J.). Astrologicall Addition. 1583. 1337
Hernia, *Duke of. See* Boccaline (T.). New-found Politicke. 1626. 4°.
Herodian of Alexandria. History of twenty roman caesars. Interpreted. Ed. I. M. 1629. 4°. 4827
— 1635. 12°. 5137
Herodotus. *See* Estienne (H.). World of wonders. 1607.
Heron (Ed.). Verses in Camb. Univ. Epicedium. 1612. . . . 5665
Heron (Haly). Newe discourse of Morall Philosophie...The Kayes of Counsaile. 1579. 8°. 1311
Heronus, *Ludimagister Roffensis.* Verses in Elyot (Sir T.). Bibliotheca. 1552. 502
Herrey (R. F.). Two right profitable and fruitfull concordances. Deputies of C. Barker [1587?]. 4°. 1690
R. Barker, [Not after 1603]. 4°. 2577
B. Norton and J. Bill, 1622(-1). 4°. 2813
Herring. *See* Most strange and wonderfull Herring. 1598.
Hertford, *County of. See* Norden (J.). 1598.
Hertford (Edward Seymour, earl of). *See* Somerset.
Hertogenbosch ('s.). Iornall of certaine...passages. 1629. 4°. . . 3744
[Siege, 1629.] *See* France. Articles. 1629. 3743
Hervet (Gentian). *See* Erasmus. De immensa dei misericordia. 1533 *etc.*
See Marnix (P. van). The Bee-hiue. 1579 *etc.*
See Xenophon. [Œconomica.] 1537.
Hervey (Fr.). Verses in Oxf. Univ. Horti. 1640. 5499
Hervey (T.). Verses in Oxf. Univ. Horti. 1640. 5499
Hesiodus. [Opera (Gr. Lat.).] *See* Poetæ minores. 1635.
Heskyns (Thomas). Parliament of chryste. Antwerp, 1566. F°. . 6126
See Fulke (W.). D. Heskins...ouerthrowne. 1579.
Hesse (Philip, Landgrave of). *See* Philip, *Landgrave* etc.
Hester (John). *See* Du Chesne (J.). True and perfect spagerike. 1591.
— Fioravanti (L.). Compendium. 1582.
— — Joyfull Jewell. 1579.
Hetherington (John). *See* Denison (S.). White Wolfe. 1627.
Heurnius (Johannes). *See* Hippocrates. Aphorismorum... 1631.
Hewes (Lewes). *See* Hughes.
Hexham (Henry). Tongue-combat. 1623. 4°. 6938
See Mercator (G.). Atlas. 1633 (1636). F°.
— Polyander (J.). Dispvtation. 1611.
Heydon (Sir Christopher). Defence of iudiciall astrologie. Cambridge, 1603. 4°. 5615
Heydon (Marmaduke). Verses in Camb. Univ. Lacrymae. 1619. . 5689
Heygate (Tho.). Verses in Oxf. Univ. Magd. Coll. 1612. . . 5302
Heylyn (Edward). Verses in Heylyn (P.). Microcosmus. 1621 *etc.* 5339 *etc.*
Heylyn (Peter). Antidotum Lincolniense: or an answer to...The holy table. 1637. 4°. 4214
Brief...answer to...H. Burton. 1637. 4°. 4926
Coale from the altar. 1636. 4°. 4591
— Ed. 3. 1637. 4°. 4593
— *See* Prynne (W.). A quench-coale. 1637.
History of the sabbath. Ed. 2. 1636. 4°. 4642
Historie of...St George of Cappadocia. Ed. 2. 1633. 4°. . . 4002
Microcosmus. Oxford, 1621. 4°. 5339
— Ed. 2. Oxford, 1625. 4°. 5349
— Ed. 3. Oxford, 1627. 4°. 7658
— Ed. 7. Oxford, 1636. 4°. 5449
See Williams (J.). The holy table. 1637.
Heyne (Io.). Verses in Camb. Univ. Lacrymæ. 1619. . . . 5689

No.

Heyward (Ed.). Verses in Selden (J.). Jani Anglici... 1610. 3389
— Verses in Jonson (B.). Workes. 1616. 3115
Heywood (Jasper). *See* Seneca. Hercules Furens. 1561. 8°.
— — Thyestes. 1560. 8°.
Heywood (John). Workes, newlie imprinted. 1598. 4°. 2909
Dialogve...of...prouerbs. 1556. 8°. 1243
Fourth hundred of Epygrams. 1560. 8°. 6744
Of Gentylnes and Nobylyte. J. Rastell [15—]. F°. 349
Play of the wether. W. Rastell, 1533. 4°. 534
Spider and the flie. 1556. 4°. 1244
Heywood (Thomas). Apology for actors. 1612. 4°. 3645
Englands Elizabeth. Cambridge, 1632. 12°. 5745
Exemplary lives and memorable acts of nine the most worthy women of the world. 1640. 4°. 4675
Γυναικεῖον. 1624. F°. 7396
Hierarchie of the blessed angells. 1635. F°. 2466
Loves Mistresse. Ed. 2. 1640. 4°. 5157
Pleasant dialogues and dramma's. 1637. 8°. 5128
Royall King. 1637. 4°. 3710
Troia Britannica. 1609. F°. 2769
Verses in Paris and Vienna. 1628. 7552
— Welby (H.). Phœnix. 1637. 3713
— Xenophon. Cyrupædia *bis*. 1632. 4714
— Yorke (J.). Union of Honour. 1640. 5216
See Barckley (Sir R.). Felicitie of man. 1631.
— Greene (I.). Refvtation. 1615.
— Lydgate (J.). Life and Death of Hector. 1614. F°.
— Sallust. The two...Histories. 1608–9.
Hickes (Francis). *See* Lucian. Certaine select dialogves. 1634. 4°.
Hickes (Th.). Verses in Camdeni Insignia. 1624. 5346
See Lucian. Certaine select dialogues. 1634. 4°.
Hide (Edward). Verses in Camb. Univ. Carmen. 1635. 5770
— Randolph (T.). The Jealous Lovers. 1640. 5852
Hide (Tho.). Consolatorie Epistle to the afflicted Catholikes. Louvain, 1580. 8°. 6424
Hierome of Ferrara. *See* Savonarola.
Hieron (Samuel). Workes. 2 vols. W. Stansby (J. Legate, etc.) for I. Parker [ab. 1620]. F°. 3132, 4700
— (title only). W. Stansby and I. Beale [ab. 1620]. F°. 7805
— 1624(5). F°. 4700
— [Vol. 1.] The sermons. 1620. F°. 4692
— 1635 (1632, 1634). F°. 4726
— Vol. 2. 1629. F°. 3172
Aarons bells a-sounding. 1623. 4°. 6486
Christians iournall. 1609. 8°. 2744
Davids penitentiall psalme. Cambridge, 1617. 4°. 5682
Helpe vnto deuotion. Ed. 10. 1618. 12°. 3798
Spirituall Fishing. 1618. 4°. 3799
Three sermons. Cambridge, 1609. 4°. 5655
Truths purchase. Cambridge, 1606. 4°. 5637
See Defence of the Ministers. 1607.
Hieronymus. Vitas patrum. W. de Worde, 1495. F°. 44
Expositio in simbolum apostolorum. *See* Rufinus (T.). '1468.'
Certaine selected epistles. [Paris,] 1630. 4°. 6223
See Betson (T.). A ryght profytable treatyse. [1499.] 59
Higden (Ralph). Description of Britain. Caxton, 1480. F°. 14
— *See* Chronicles of England. 1497 etc.
Polychronicon. Caxton [1482]. F°. 19
— W. de Worde, 1495. F°. 45
Polychronycon. P. Treveris, Southwark, 1527. F°. 5859

No.

Higden (Ralph), *cont.* 'Policcronicon.' Southwark, 1527. F°. . 7676
Higgins (Antony). Verses in Digby (E.). Theoria. 1579. . . 1500
Higgins (J.). Mirour of Magistrates. 1575. 4°. 1225
— 1610 (1609). 4°. 2961
See Junius (A.). The Nomenclator. 1585.
Higginson (Francis). New-Englands Plantation. 1630. 4°. . . 4684
Higgons (Robert). *See* Hoby (Sir E.). Letter. 1609.
Higgons (Theophilus). First motive. 1609. 8°. 6521
Sermon. 3 March 1610. 3214
— 1611. 4°. 3619
— *See* Sheldon (R.). Certain general reasons. 1611.
See Hoby (Sir E.). A letter. 1609.
— Morton (T.). A direct answer. 1609.
Hilarion, *Saint.* *See* Hieronymus. Certaine selected epistles. 1630. 4°.
Hildericus (Edo). *See* Æschines. Contra Ctesiphontem. 1624.
Hildersam (Arthur). The Doctrine of Communicating. Ed. 8. *See* Bradshaw (W.). A preparation. 1634. 12°.
Doctrine of fasting and prayer, 1625 (1629). 1633. 4°. . . 4445
— 1636. 12°. 4990
Lectures vpon the fourth of John. 1629. F°. 4427
Treatise of the ministery. [1595?] 4°. 6814
Hildersam (Samuel). *See* Hildersam (A.). Doctrine of fasting. 1633 etc.
Hilermius (Robertus). Verses in Wilson (Sir T.). The Arte of Rhetorique. 1553. 626
Hill (Adam). Defence of the Article: Christ descended. 1592. 4°. 7358
Hill (Edmund Thomas), *D.D.* *See* Hill (Thomas), *D.D.*
Hill (John). Penitent sinners entertainment. 1614. 8°. . . 3783
See Elton (E.). God's holy mind. 1625.
— Sibbs (R.). Returning backslider. 1639.
Hill (R.). Verses in Roberts (L.). The merchants mappe. 1638. . 5133
Hill (Robert). Life everlasting. Cambridge, 1601. 4°. . . 5604
Pathway to prayer and pietie. 1613. 8°. 3095
Verses in Robartes (F.). The Revenve. 1613. . . . 5670
See Bucanus (Gugl.). Institutions. 1606.
— Greenham (R.). Workes. 1612.
— Hieron (S.). Workes. 1624–5.
— Newhouse (.). Learned and fruitfull sermon. 1612. 8°.
— Perkins (W.). Golden chaine. Ed. 2. 1592 etc.
— — Works. Vol. 3. (Revelation.) 1609. F°. . . . 5656
— Seller (J.). Sermon. 1611.
Hill (Tho.), '*Londoner.*' Arte of gardening. 1608. 4°. . . . 2023
Arte of vulgar arithmeticke. 1600. 4°. 2197
Contemplation of mankinde. 1571. 8°. 6753
Gardeners Labyrinth. 1608. 4°. 2899
Pleasaunt instruction of the parfit ordering of Bees. 1568. 8°. . 1218
Proffitable Arte of Gardening. [Parts 2 and 3 only, consisting of 'A pleasaunt instruction' &c. *ut ante.*] 1568. 8°.
See Fioravanti (L.). A Joyfull Jewell. 1579.
— Fulke (W.). Antiprognosticon. 1560.
Hill (Tho.), *alias* Buckland. Plaine path-way to heaven. Pt. 2. 1637. 12°. 7037
See Dillingham (F.). Quartron of Reasons. 1603.
Hill (W.). Verses in Oxf. Univ. Horti. 1640. 5499
Hill (William). Infancie of the Soule. 1605. 4°. 2303
Hillenius (Michael). *See* Lucianus. Lvciani dialogi. 1531.
Hilsey (John), *bp.* *See* Primer. 1539. 4°.
Hilton (W.), *Schoolmaster of S. Anthony's.* *See* Regius (U.). The sermon. 1578 etc.
Hilton (Walter). Scala perfectionis. W. de Worde, 1494. F°. . 42
— J. Notary, 1507. 4°. 329

No.

Hilton (Walter), *cont.* W. de Worde, 27 May, 1533. 4°. . . 206
— Hereafter foloweth a deuoute Boke...to a deuoute man... *See* Capgrave (J.). The Kalendre. 1516.
Hind (J.). *See* Defence of Tabacco. 1602.
Hinde (William). Office and use of the morall Law of God. 1623. 4°. 4782
Hipolito. True history of the tragicke loves of Hipolito and Isabella. Ed. 2. 1633. 8°.. 7566
Hippocrates. 'Αφορισμοί (Gr. Lat.). Interpr. J. Heurnio. Cantabrigiae, 1633. 8°. 5812
— — Liber primus. Cantabrigiae, 1631. 4°. 5736
See Braunschweig (H.). Noble experyence. 1525.
— Petrus *Hispanus.* Treasury. [1550.]
— Prognostication. 153–.
Historia Britannica. *See* S. (E.). [De Rebus Gestis.] 1640. . 5501
History of Astræa. *See* Urfé (H. d'). 1620.
Historie of England. *See* Clapham (J.). 1602.
— Historie of Great Britannie. *See* Clapham (J.). 1606.
History of the World. *See* Plinius.
— — Ralegh (Sir W.). 1614 etc.
Hitchcock (Francis). *See* Hitchcock (R.). Pollitique Platt. 1580. . 1185
Hitchcocke (Ric.). Verses in Oxf. Univ. Horti. 1640. . . 5499
Hitchcock (Robert). Pollitique Platt. 1580. 4°. 1185
See Sansovino (F.). Quintessence of Wit. 1590.
Hitchcock (Rob.), *M.A.* Verses in Oxf. Univ. Magd. Coll. 1612. . 5302
Hitchcockes (William). Verses in Philibert *de Vienne.* 1575. . . 1485
Hiud (Johan). Storie of stories. 1632. 8°. 4264
Hoard (Samuel). Churches authority. 1637. 4°. 4309
Gods love to mankind. 1633. 4°. 7017
Soules miserie and recoverie. 1636. 8°. 4299
Hobart (Edward). Verses in Camb. Univ. Dolor. 1625. . . 5701A
Hobart (Henry). Verses in Camb. Univ. Συνωδία. 1637. . . 5790
Hobart (Nic.). Verses in Camb. Univ. Dolor. 1625. . . 5701
— — Epithalam. 1625. 5702
— — Genethl. 1631. 5731
— — Rex redux. 1633. 5748
— Hawkins (W.). Corolla. 1634. 5803
— Camb. Univ. Carmen. 1635. 5770
— — Voces. 1640. 5836
Hobart (Robert). Verses in Camb. Univ. Dolor. 1625. . . 5701A
Hobbes (Thomas). *See* Thucydides. Peloponnesian Warre. 1634.
Hobbes (William), *M.A. Magd.* Verses in Oxf. Univ. Horti. 1640. . 5499
Hobbs (G.), *M.A. Magd.* *See* Hobbes (W.).
Hobbynoll, *pseud.* *See* Harvey (G.).
Hobman (Francis). Verses in Francklin (R.). 'Ορθοτονία. 1630 etc. 3987 etc.
Hobson (William). Pleasant conceits. *See* Johnson (R.). 1634 etc.
Hoby (Sir Edward). Counter-snarle. 1613. 4°. 3540
Cvrry-combe for a coxe-combe. 1615. 4°. 3111
Letter to Mr T. H. 1609. 4°. 2954, 2955
See Coignet (Sir M.). Politique discourses. 1586.
— R. (I.). Purgatories triumph...maugre...Sir Edward Hobyes Counter-snarle. 1613. 4°.
Hoby (Peregrine), *Ætonensis.* Verses in Hoby (Sir E.). Curry combe. 1615. 3111
Hoby (Thomas). *See* Castiglione (B.). The covrtyer. 1561.
Hoccleve (Thomas). *See* Chaucer (G.). Workes. 1532 *etc.*
Hodge (Ant.). Verses in Oxf. Univ. Horti. 1640. . . . 5499
Hodgeson (Samuel). Verses in Digby (E.). Theoria. 1579. . . 1500
Hodgkinson (Richard), *printer.* *See* Grotius (H.). Poemata. 1639.
Hodgson (William). *See* Hodson.
Hodson (Phineas). The kings request. 1628. 4°. 3979

No.
Hodson (Phineas), *cont.* The last sermon preached before His Maiesties Funerals. 1625. 4°. 4228
Hodson (William). Credo resurrectionem carnis. Cambridge [1636]. 12°. 5787
Divine cosmographer. Cambridge, 1640. 12°. 5847
Holy sinner. 1639. 12°. 5796
Verses in Camb. Univ. Lacrymæ. 1619.. 5689
— Jonson (B.). Workes. 1640. 5115
Hogarde (Miles). *See* Huggarde.
Hogenbergius (F.). *See* Hohenberg.
Hoggarde (Miles). *See* Huggarde.
Hohenberg (Franz). *See* Braun (G.) and F. Hohenberg. Civitates. 1588. F°.
Holbech (Thomas). Verses in Hippocrates. 1633. 5812
Holborne (Ant.). Cittharn schoole. 1597. 4°. 2331
Holbrooke (William). Sermon. 1609. 8°. 2956
See Randall (J.). Great mysterie of godlinesse. Ed. 2. 1630. 4°.
— — Twenty nine lectures. 1631.
Holder (H.), *Peterhouse.* Verses in Camb. Univ. Voces. 1640. . 5836
Holder (William), *Pemb.* Verses in Camb. Univ. Fasciae. 1633. . 5808
— — Carmen. 1635. 5770
Hole (Robert). *See* H. (R.). 1608 etc.
Holiday (Barten). *See* Holyday.
Holinshed (R.). Chronicles. Vol. 1. For G. Bishop, 1577. F°. . 1490
— For L. Harrison, 1577. F°. 1491
— Vol. 2. For L. Harrison, 1577. F°. 1492
— 3 vols. 1587. F°. 1435, 1436, 7259, 7260
Holland. *See* Netherlands.
Holland (Abraham). London Looke-backe. *See* D. (I.), *Preacher.* Salomons Pest-Hovse. 1630. 4°.
Baziliωlogia. 1618. *See* p. 1744 note.
Naumachia...Lepanto. *See* Xenophon. Cyrupædia. 1632.
Holland (Elizabeth). *See* Greenham (R.). Workes. 1612.
Holland (Henry). An admonition concerning...Physick. *See* D. (I.), *Preacher.* Salomons Pest-House. 1630. 4°.
Christian exercise of fasting. 1596. 4°. 7376
Ecclesia S. Pauli illustrata. 1633. 4°. 4891
Herωologia anglica. Arnhem [ab. 1620]. F°. . . . 6642
Historie of Adam. 1606. 4°. 7277
Monumenta sepulchralia S. Pauli. [1614.] 4°. . . . 3377
— — *See above* Ecclesia Sancti Pavli illustrata. 1633.
Treatise against witchcraft. Cambridge, 1590. 4°. . . . 5550
See Bauderon (B.). Pharmacopoea. 1639. 5200
— Calvin (J.). Aphorismes. 1596. 8°.
— Greenham (R.). Workes. 1599 *etc.*
— Rollock (R.). Lectures vpon...Colossians. 1603. 4°.
— Verheiden (J.). History of the Moderne Protestant Divines. 1637.
— Xenophon. Cyrupædia. 1632.
Holland (Hugh). Verses in Coryat (T.). Coryats Crudities. 1611. . 3076
— Jonson (B.). Workes. 1616. 3115
— Shakspeare (W.). Comedies etc. 1623. 3972
— Seneca. Tragoediæ. 1624. 3444
— Horatius. Odes. 1635 etc. . . . . . 4857 etc.
Holland (Philemon), *M.D.* Verses in Hippocrates. 1633. . . 5812
See Bauderon (B.). Pharmacopoea. 1639. 5200
— Camden (W.). Britain. 1637.
— Livius. Roman Historie. 1600.
— Marcellinus (A.). Roman historie. 1609.
— Plinius. Historie of the world. 1601 *etc.*
— Suetonius. Historie of the twelve Caesars. 1606.

No.

Holland (Philemon), *M.D.*, *cont.* *See* Thomas (T.). Dictionarium. 1620.
— Xenophon. Cyrupædia. 1632.
Holland (Robert). *See* Harry (G. O.). Genealogy. 1604.
Holland (Tho.), *Cantab.* Verses in Camb. Univ. Lachrymae. 1587. 2123 =7356
Holland (Tho.), *Oxon.* *See* Bible. Eng. (Royal). 1611.
Verses in Holyoake (F.). Dictionarium. 1640. . . . 3058
[Funeral.] *See* Kilby (R.). Sermon. 1613.
Hollanders Declaration of the affaires of the East Indies. Amsterdam, 1622. 4°. 6400
See Answere to the Hollanders Declaration. 1622. . . . 3681
Holles (Dens), *Chr.* Verses in Camb. Univ. Epicedium. 1612. . 5665
Holliman (Leonel). Verses in Camb. Univ. Lachrymae. 1587. . 7356
Holloway (William). *See* Zarain Aga. A relation. 1639.
Hollyband (Claude). *See* Desainliens (C.).
Hollybush (John). [i.e. H. van Ruremonde.][1] *See* Bible. Polyglot. N.T. The new testament. 1538. 4°.
See Braunschweig (H.). Most excellent...apothecarye. 1561.
Holman (John). Verses in Camb. Univ. Lacrymæ. 1619. . . 5689
Holme (John). Burthen of the ministerie. 1592. 8°. . . 2412
Holsome Exercise. 16°. 6598
Holt (James). Verses in Camdeni Insignia. 1624. . . . 5346
Holt (John). Lac puerorum. Antwerp [15—]. 4°. . . . 6072
See Grammar (Lat.). [15—.] 4°. Declensiones. . . 221
Holt (Th.). Verses in Camdeni Insignia. 1624. . . . 5346
Holway (W.). Verses in Ferrand (J.). Ἐρωτομανία. 1640. . 5498
Holy Bull, and Crusado of Rome. 1588. 4°. 1949
Holy Table. *See* Williams (J.), *abp.* The holy table. 1637.
Holyday (Barten). Philosophiae politobarbarae specimen. Oxoniae, 1633. 4°. 5437
Τεχνογαμία. 1618. 4°. 7710
— 1630. 4°. 4833
Three sermons. 1626. 4°. 3161
Verses in Horatius. Art of poetry. 1640. 3728
Holyoake (Francis). Dictionarium etymologicum (Rider's Dictionarie.) 1640. 4°. 3058
Homer. Iliad (Gr.). 1591. 8°. 1729
Works. Trans. G. Chapman. [1612?] F°. 2892
Batrachomyomachia (Latin). 1580. 4°. 1372
— (English) Hymns and Epigrams. Trans. G. Chapman. [1624?] F°. 3519
Homes (Nathanael). *See* Schickard (W.). Horologium. 1638–9. 8°.
Homilies. Certain Sermons or Homilies. Grafton, 1547. 4°. . 597
Certayne Sermons. Whitchurch, 20 Aug. 1547. 4°. . . 653
Certaine Sermons. 2 tom. Jugge and Cawood, 1563. 4°. . 960
Certaine Sermons. 1587. 4°. 7293
— J. Bill, 1623. F°. 3515
— J. Norton *etc.* 1633. F°. 4890
— J. Norton *etc.* 1635 (1633). F°. 4900
— R. H. and J. N. *etc.* 1640. F°. 7633
Homilie against Disobedience and wylfull Rebellion. [1571?] 4°. 976
Hommius (Festus). LXX. disputationes theologicae. Ed. 2. Oxoniae, 1630. 8°. 5429
— Ed. 3. Oxonii, 1639. 8°. 5460
Verses in Ames (W.). Coronis. 1632. 4711
Hondius (Jodocus). *See* Mercator (G.). Atlas. 1633(6). F°.
— — Historia mvndi. 1635.

[1] See p. 1742 (note on no. 5870).

No.

Hondius (Jacobus), *cont.* Atlas minor. 1630. 4°.
Hongar (Thomas). The Suplication of Thomas Hongar. *See* Mary Queen of England. Sc. F. Delaram. F°. 7713 (and note p. 1744)
Honywood (M.), *C.C.* Verses in Camb. Univ. Epithalam. 1625. . 5702
— — Rex redux. 1633. 5748
— Hippocrates. 1633. 5812
— King (E.). Ivsta. 1638. 5829
[Monogram.] 6265
Hood (Robin). A lytell geste. W. de Worde [before 1529]. 4°. . 225
Hood (T.). Making and use of a sector. [1598?] 4°. 2151
Vse of both the Globes. 1592. 8°. 1829
See Cooke (F.). Principles of Geometrie. 1591.
Hooker (J.), *alias* Vowell. Catalog of the Bishops of Excester. 1584. 4°. 1431
Discription of the cittie of Excester. [Ab. 1580.] 4°. . . 7234
Orders enacted for Orphans. [1575?] 4°. 1289
Pamphlet of the Offices...of the Citie of Excester. 1584. 4°. 1432
See Holinshed (R.). Chronicles. 1587– .
Hooker (Ric.). Answere...to a supplication...by...W. Travers. Oxford, 1612. 4°. 5297
Certayne divine tractates and other godly sermons. 1618. F°. 3125
— 1622. F°. 3142
— 1632. F°. 3188
— 1639. F°. 3199
Learned and comfortable...sermon of...faith. Oxford, 1612. 4°. 5298
Learned sermon...of pride. Oxford, 1612. 4°. 5299
Of the lawes of eccl. politie. Book v. Ed. 1. 1597. F°. . 2143
— Books i–iv. Ed. 2. 1604. F°. 2165
— Books i–v. Ed. 4. 1617–6. F°. 3119
— Ed. 5. (Certayne tractates.) 1622. F°. 3142
— Ed. 6. (Certaine tractates. 1632–6.) F°. 3188
— Ed. 7. 1638. (Certaine tractates. 1639–6.) F°. . . 3199
Remedie against sorrow. Oxford, 1612. 4°. 5300
See Christian letter of certaine English Protestants. 1599.
Hooker (Thomas). Foure learned and godly treatises. 1638. 12°. . 4663
Soules vocation. 1638. 4°. 4866
See H. (T.). Three godly sermons. 1638. 12°.
— Rogers (J.). Doctrine. Ed. 5. 1633. 7892
Hooper (John). Answer unto my lord of Wynchesters booke. Zurich, 1547. 4°. 6302
Apologye...againste the vntrue...report. 1562. 8°. . . . 1261
Briefe and Cleare Confession. *See* Baker (J.). Lectures. 1613. 8°.
Certaine comfortable expositions...vpon the xxiii, lxii, lxxiii, and lxxxvii psalmes. 1580. 4°. 1631
Declaracion of Christe and of his offyce. Zurich, 1547. 8°. . 6303
Declaration of the ten holy commaundementes. [Zurich,] 1548. 8°. 6283
— R. Jugge [1549?]. 8°. 953
— R. Jugge, 1550. 8°. 954
Declaration of the . x . holye commaundements. N. Hill, 1550. 8°. 1023
Funerall oratyon...14 January 1549. 1549. 8°. 666
Godly...Annotations in y^e^. xiij...Romaynes. Worcester, 1551. 8°. 5891
Godly Confession and Protestacion of the christian fayth. 1550. 4°. 779
Homelye...in the tyme of pestylence. Worcester [1553?]. 8°. . 5892
Ouersight, and deliberacion vpon...Jonas. Day and Seres, 1550. 8°. 909
Ouersighte and deliberation vpon...Jonas. 1550. J. Tysdale [ab. 1558]. 8°. 1262
[Letter.] *See* Briefe examination. [1564.] 4°.
[Letters.] *See* Coverdale (M.). Certain...letters. 1564.
See A. (J.), *of Ailward.* An historicall narration. 1631.
— Whether Christian faith. [1553?]
Hope of the Faithful. *See* Wermueller (O.). The hope etc. [1554?] 16°.

No.
Hope (Thomas). Verses in Adamson (J.). Εἰσόδια. 1618. . . 5960
Hoper (D.), *Pet.* Verses in Camb. Univ. Fasciae. 1633. . . 5808
Verses in Camb. Univ. Rex redux. 1633. 5748
Hoper (Jo.). Verses in King (E.). Ivsta. 1638. . . . 5829
Hopkins (I.), *Chaplain to James I.* A sermon. 1604. 8°. . . 2301
Hopkins (John). *See* Bible. Eng. O. T. Psalms (Metrical).
Hopkins (John). Verses in Stanyhurst (R.). Harmonia. 1570. . 749
— Foxe (J.). Actes and monumentes. Ed. 5. 1596. . 2330
Hopkins (Richard). *See* Luis de Granada. A memorial. 1586 etc.
Hopkins (Thomas). Two sermons. 1609. 4°. 2957
Hopton (Arthur). Concordancy of yeares...augmented... 1615. 8°. . 3659
— 1616. 8°. 3265
— Enlarged by J. Penkethman. 1635. 8°. 3956
Speculum Topographicum. 1611. 4°. 3638
Verses in Leighton (Sir W.). The teares. 1613. . . . 2868
Horae. *See* Primer.
Horae subseciuae. Observations and discourses. 1620. 8°. . 2893
Horarium. *See* Breviarium. 6184
Horatius. Poemata omnia...scholiis illustrata (Juvenalis et Persii Satyrae). 1578(-9). 8°. 1332
— 1592. 8°. 1334
— Scholiis et argymentis ab H. Stephano illustrata. Juvenalis et Persii Satyrae. 1607. 8°. 3366
Poemata. 1614. 8°. 2274, 2275
Odes of Horace. Trans. Sir T. Hawkins. Ed. 3. 1635. 12°. . 4857
— Ed. 4. 1638. 12°. 4867
Odes and Epodes. Trans. H. Rider. 1638. 12°. . . . 4868
Art of Poetry. Eng. by B. Jonson. 1640. 12°. . . 3728
Medicinable Morall. T. Drant. 1566. 4°. 1217
Selection. (Trans.) *See* Beaumont (Sir J.). Bosworth field. 1629.
Hord (Richard). Verses in Whitaker (W.). Praelectiones. 1599. . 5598
Verses *bis* in Camb. Univ. Thr-thr. 1603. . . . 5616
— — Epicedium. 1612. 5665
Horman (W.). Antibossicon. 1521. 4°. 279
Vulgaria (Lat. and Eng.). Pynson, 1519. 4°. . . . 267
Horn. *See* Horne.
Horne (Charles). In obitum...G. Whitakeri. 1596. 4°. . . 7332
— Verses in Camb. Univ. Lachrymae. 1587. . . 7356
Horne (Robert), *bishop.* *See* Advertisements. 1584.
— Bible. Eng. (Bishops'). 1568.
— Calvin (J.). Certaine homilies. 1553.
— — Two godly...Sermons. (1584.)
— Stapleton (T.). A counterblast. 1567.
Horne (Robert), †1640. Certaine sermons. 1619. 4°. . . 4161
History of the woman of great faith. 1632. 12°. . . . 3996
Shield of the righteous. 1625. 4°. 7382
Horne (Sam). Verses in Camb. Univ. Anthologia. 1632. . . 5741
— Hippocrates. 1633. 5812
Horne (Thomas). *See* Janua Linguarum. Ed. 8. 1634. 8°.
— Comenius (J. A.). Janua linguarum. 1638.
Horologium Sapientiæ. Caxton [1490]. 4°. 37
Horse, the Sheep, and the Goose. *See* Lydgate (J.).
Horsey (Sir Jerome). *See* Purchas (S.). Pilgrimage. 1626.
Horton (Thomas). Verses in Camb. Univ. Συνωδία. 1637. . . 5790
Hortulus animae secundum usum Sarum. Paris, 1531. 18°. . 7838
Hortus vocabulorum. *See* Ortus.
Hosius (Stanislas). Moste excellent treatise of...heresyes. Trans. R. Shacklock. The hatchet of heresyes. Antwerp, 10 Aug. 1565. 8°. 6129
See Foxe (J.). De Christo gratis iustificante. 1583.
Hoskins (Ant.). Briefe and cleare declaration.. 1611. 4°. . . 6524

No.
Hoskins (John). Sermons. 1615. 4°. 3112
Verses in Vaughan (R.). Waterworkes. 1610. 3576
— Coryate (T.). Coryats Crudities. 1611. 3076
— Davies (J.). Antiquæ linguæ...dictionarium. 1632. . . 4979
— Owen (J.). Epigrammatum. 1634. 4583
Hotham (Charles). Verses in Camb. Univ. Carmen. 1635. . . 5770
— — Voces. 1640. 5836
Hotham (Durand). Verses in Camb. Univ. Carmen. 1635. . . 5770
Hotman (François). *See* Sixtus V. The brvtish thvnderbolt. 1586. 8°.
— Varamundus (E.). 1573.
House of Commons. *See* England. Parliament.
Hovæus (Robertus). Theses in Adamson (J.). *Εἰσόδια*. 1618. . 5960
Houel (T.). *See* Howell (T.).
Hoveden or Howden (Roger). [Annals.] *See* Savile (Sir H.). Rervm Anglicarvm scriptores. 1596.
Howard (Charles), Lord Howard of Effingham, Earl of Nottingham. *See* Nottingham (Charles Howard, earl of).
Howard (Ed.), *B.A. Trin.* Verses in Camb. Univ. Voces. 1640. . 5836
Howard (Henry), earl of Northampton. *See* Northampton (Henry Howard, earl of).
Howard (Henry), earl of Surrey. *See* Surrey.
Howard (Thomas), duke of Norfolk. *See* Norfolk.
Howard (Hon. Thomas), *heir of Lord Escreick.* Verses in Camb. Univ. Voces. 1640. 5836
Howard (Lord William), *of Naworth.* *See* Florence of Worcester. Chronicon. 1592. 4°. 1828
Howard (William). A patterne of christian loyaltie. 1634. 4°. . 4359
Howe (Jos.). Verses in Oxf. Univ. Horti. 1640. 5499
— Randolph (T.). Poems. 1640. 5500
Howell (James). *Δενδρολογία*. 1640. F°. 5139
Verses in Biondi (G. F.). Eromena. 1632. 7753
Howell (Thomas). *See* Daneau (L.). Treatise. 1589.
Howes (Edmond). *See* Stow (J.). Annales. 1615 etc.
— — Abridgement of the English Chronicle. 1618.
Howgrave (Henry). Verses in Camb. Univ. Thr-thr. 1603. . . 5616
— — Epicedium. 1612. 5665
— — Lacrymae. 1619. 5689
Howlet (John), *pseud.* [i.e. R. Parsons]. *See* Fulke (W.). A briefe Confutation. 1581.
Howlet (Laur.). Verses in Camb. Univ. Epicedium *bis.* 1612. 5665, 5666
Howlett (Ric.), *Sid.* Verses in Camb. Univ. Epicedium. 1612. . 5665
— — Epithalam. 1625. 5702
Howorth (John), *Magd.* Verses in Camb. Univ. Epithalam. 1625. . 5702
— — Genethl. 1631. 5731
— — Carmen. 1635. 5770
Howson (John). Certaine sermons, 1616. 1622. 4°. . . . 3429
Sermon. 4 Dec. 1597. 1597. 4°. 2068
Second sermon. 21 May 1598. 1598. 4°. 2070
Sermon...at St Maries...17 Nov. 1602 in defence. Oxford, 1602. 4°. 5258
— Ed. 2. Oxford, 1603. 4°. 5262
Uxore dimissa...tertia thesis. Oxoniae, 1606. 4°. . . . 5273
— Ed. alt. 1606. 4°. 5274
See Pie (T.). Epistola. 1603.
Hu (St), 1632. *See* Hurius (S.).
Huarte Navarro (J. de Dios). Examen de Ingenios. 1594. 4°. . 2416
— 1596. 4°. 7393
— 1616. 4°. 2448
Hubbocke (Will.). Oration gratulatory. Oxford, 1604. 4°. . 5266
Huberine (Caspar). *See* Hueber.
Hubert (Sir Francis). Deplorable life and death of Edward the Second... Gavestone and Spencer, 1628. 8°. 5068

No.

Hubert (Sir Francis), *cont.* Egypts favorite. 1631. 8°. . . 4551
Huchenson (William). *See* Hutchinson.
Huddleston (John). Verses in Whitaker (W.). Praelectiones. 1599. . 5598
Hudson (Henry). *See* Fox (L.). North-west Fox. 1635.
Hudson (J.). *See* Microphilus. New-yeeres Gift. 1636. 12°.
Hudson (Thomas). *See* Du Bartas. Divine Weekes. 1608 *etc.*
Hueber (Caspar). Riche storehouse or treasurie for the sicke. Trans. T. Godfrie. 1578. 8°. 7235
Hues (R.). Tractatus de globis. 1594. 8°. 1830
Learned treatise of globes. 1639. 8°. 5091
Huet (Thomas). *See* Bible (Welsh). 1620. F°.
Huetus (Robertus). Verses in Braunschweig (H.). The vertuose boke. 1527. 412
Huggard (M.). Displaying of the Protestantes. June, 1556. 8°. . 1198
— July, 1556. 8°. 1199
Mirroure of loue. 1555. 4°. 1195
New treatyse...Dialoge...of mannes nature. [1550?] 4°. . . 549
See Crowley (R.). Confutation of...the Abuse of yᵉ blessed sacrament. 1548.
Hughes (Edward), *Archdeacon.* Verses in Davies (J.). Antiquæ linguæ ...dictionarium. 1632. 4979
Hughes (John). Sᵗ Pauls exercise. 1622. 4°. 3430
Hughes (Lewis). Certaine greevances. 1640. 4°. . . . 7049
— 1640. 4°. 7050
Hughes (Richard). Verses in Coryate (T.). Coryates crvdities. 1611. 3076
Hugo, *of Caumpeden.* *See* Boccus. History of Kyng Boccus. [15 .]
Hugo (Hermann). Seige of Breda (G. Barry). Louanii, 1627–8. F°. 6423
Siege of Breda. Trans. C. H. G. J. Dooms, Ghent. F°. 6657 (corr.)
Huguenots. *See* C. (H.). Catholike Moderator. 1623.
Huish (Alexander). Lectures upon the Lords prayer. 1626. 4°. . 4968
Verses in Adamson (J.). Εἰσόδια. 1617. 5960
— Camdeni Insignia. 1624. 5346
See Flavel (J.). Tractatvs de demonstratione. 1619.
Huit (Ephraim). Anatomy of conscience. 1626. 12°. . . . 3868
Hull (John). Exposition vpon a part of the Lamentations. 1618. 4°. 7582
Saint Peters prophesie. 1611. 4°. 7487
Vnmasking of the politike atheist. Ed. 2. 1602. 8°. . 2921
Verses in Oxf. Univ. Magd. Coll. 1612. 5302
Hull (Will.). Repentance. 1612. 8°. 2092
Hullier (John). *See* Hullyer.
Hullyer or Hullier (John). Letters. *See* Coverdale (M.). Certain... letters. 1564.
Humble and unfained confession. . . . . . . *See* 6720
Humble motion with submission, 1590. *See* Penry (J.).
Humble motives for association. 1601. *See* Bradshaw (W.).
Humble petition of the communaltie to...the ladie Elizabeth. [Ab. 158–.] 8°. 6793
Humble remonstrance to the high court of Parliament. *See* Hall (Jos.). 1640.
Humble supplicacion. *See* Becon (T.). Humble supplicacion. 1554.
Hume (Alexander). Diduction of...This is my bodie. Edinburgh, 1602. 8°. 5943
Prima elementa grammaticae. Edinburgi, 1612. 8°. . . 5968
Hume (Alexander), *of Bath.* *See* Hill (A.). The defence. 1592. 4°. 7358
Hume (David). Verses *ter* in Adamson (J.). Εἰσόδια. 1618. . . 5960
Hume (I.), *Jes.* Verses in Camb. Univ. Epithalam. 1625. . 5702
Hume (John). Iewes deliverance. 1628. 4°. 7494
Hume (L.). Verses in Oxf. Univ. Magd. Coll. 1612. . . 5302
Hume (Sir Patrick), *Kt.* Promine...of...King James. Edinburgh, 1580. 4°. 7678

No.
Hume (Sir Patrick), *cont.* Verses in Adamson (J.). Εἰσόδια. 1618. . 5960
Humes (Alexander). *See* Hume. 7358
Humfredus (Laurentius). *See* Humphrey.
Humfrey (Richard). *See* Ambrosius. Christian offices. 1637. 4°.
Humphrey (L.). Ad Ill. R. Elizabetham...oratio Woodstochiae. 1572. 4°. 830
Jesuitismi pars prima. 1582. 8°. 1637
— Ed. 2. 1582. 8°. 1638
Jesuitismi pars secunda. 1584. 8°. 1648
J. Jvelli...vita et mors. 1573. 4°. 837
Nobles or of Nobilitye. 1563. 8°. 1210
Verses in Wilson (Sir T.). Vita. 1551. 631
— Bernard (J.). Oratio. 1568. 930
— Foxe (J.). Actes. 1570. 816
— Stanyhurst (R.). Harmonia. 1570. 749
— Parkhurst (J.). Ludicra. 1573. 838
— Chaloner (Sir T.). De rep. anglorum. 1579. . . 7270
— Godwin (T.). Romanæ Historiæ Anthologia. 1614. . . 5320
See Gemma Fabri. 1598.
— Higgons (T.). The first motive. 1609.
— Shaw (J.). Bibliorum summula. 1623. 8°.
Hun (Maurice van), earl of Valkenstein and Brooke. *See* Broeck.
Hundred Merry Tales. . . . . . . *See* 6676 note.
Hundreds. *See* Modus tenendi. [1516 ?] *etc.*
Hungaria (Michael de). Sermones tredecim. [J. de Westfalia, Louvain. Not after 1483.] 4°. 7066
— Louvain [1484]. 4°. 128
— s. l. [1485]. 4°. 130
— Argentine, 1487. 4°. 7067
— „ 1490. 4°. 7068
— Daventriae, 1491. 8°. 7070
— [Argentine,] 1494. 4°. 7069
Hungary. *See* Fumée (M.). History of...Hvngarie. 1600.
Hungary, *Kingdom of.* 1617. *See* Bohemica Jura defensa. 1620. . 7515
See Bohemia. Articles. 1620. 6918
Hungerford (Anthony). Verses in Camdeni Insignia. 1624. . 5346
Hunlok (Hen.). Verses in Camb. Univ. Fasciae. 1633. . . 5808
— — Rex redux. 1633. 5748
Hunnis (W.). Certayne psalmes. 1550. 8°. 773
Hyve full of honye. 1578. 4°. 1229
Seven Sobs of a Sorrowfull Soule. 1589. 12°. . . . 1437
Hunt (G.). *See* Hunt (W.).
Hunt (Jo.). Verses in Oxf. Univ. Magd. Coll. 1612. . . 5302
Hunt (Matthias). *See* S. (E.). [De Rebus Gestis.] 1640.
Hunt (Nicholas). Hand-maid to arithmetick. 1633–32. 8°. . . 3821
New-borne christian. 1631. 4°. 4552
Hunt (Tho.). Verses in Horne (C.). In ob. Whitakeri. 1596. . 7332
Hunt (William), *K.C.C.* Verses in Camb. Univ. Voces. 1640. . 5836
Hunting of the Fox. *See* Turner (W.).
Huntingdon (Elizabeth, Countess of). [Funeral sermon.] *See* F. (I.). A sermon. 1635.
Huntingdon (Henry, Earl of). *See* Hutton (M.). A sermon. 1579. 8°.
Huntingdon, Henry of. *See* Henry.
Huntingdon (John). A mysterye. The Genealogye of heresye...by Ponce Pantolabus. *See* Bale (J.). Mysterye of inyquyte. 1545.
Huntley (James Gordon). *See* Gordon Huntley (J.).
Huntley (W.), *Esquire*, pseud. *See* Prynne (W.).
Hunton (Antony). Verses in Gerard (J.). The herball. 1597. . 2348
Hurault (Jaq.). Politicke, moral, and martial discourses. 1595. 4°. 2418
Hurault (Michel), *Sieur du Fay.* Antisixtus. 1590. 4°. . . . 1958
— (Translated.) 1590. 4°. 1959

No.

Hurault (Michel), *cont.* Discourse upon the present state of France. 1588. 4°. 1948
Discourse upon the present estate of France...two letters...by the Duke of Guize. Trans. E. Aggas. 1588. 4°. . . . 6789
Hurius (Stephen), *M.A.* Verses in Hawkins (W.). En Priscianus. 1632. 4562
— — Corolla. 1634. 5803
Hurleston (Randolph). Verses in Turner (W.). Preseruatiue *bis*. 1551. 955
See Newes From Rome. [c. 1550.]
Hurt of sedicion. *See* Cheke (Sir J.). 1549.
Hurtado (Luis). *See* Palmerin of England. 1639. 4°.
Husbandman. [What the husbandman should practise. Ab. 1549.] 8°. 6701
Husbandry. *See* Book of Husbandry. [1525?] 4°.
Hussey (Barthol.). Verses in Camdeni Insignia. 1624. . . 5346
Hutchinson ( ). *See* Brabourne (T.). A Defence. 1632.
Hutchinson (Ralph). *See* Bible. Eng. (Royal). 1611.
Hutchinson (Roger). Faithfvl declaration of Christes holy supper... 1552. 1560. 8°. 793
Image of God, or laie mans boke. 1560. 8°. 794
— 1580. 8°. 861
Hutchinson (William). Verses in Barlow (W.). Vita R. Cosin. 1598. 1707
Hutten (Joshua). Verses in Rogers (T.). Philosophicall discourse. 1576. 1348
Hutten (Leonard). *See* Bible. Eng. (Royal). 1611. . . . 2635
Hutten (Robert). *See* Hutton.
Hutten (Ulrich von). De morbo gallico. Trans. T. Paynel. Berthelet, n.d. 8°. 512
See Castiglione (B.). De Curiali. 1612.
See Constantine I. A treatyse. [c. 1525.]
Hutter (Elias). *See* Bible. New Testament (Polyglot). 1599. F°.
— — St. Matthew. 1599. 4°.
— — St. Mark. 1600. 4°.
Hutton (Hen.), *Coll. Jesu. Cantab.* Verses in Camb. Univ. Carmen. 1635. 5770
— — *Συνῳδία.* 1637. 5790
— Fuller (T.). Holy Warre. 1639 *etc.* . . . . 5806 *etc.*
Hutton (Matt.). A sermon. 1579. 8°. 1802
Hutton (Ric.). Verses in Camb. Univ. Genethl. 1631. . . 5731
Hutton (Samuel), *T.C.C.* Verses in Barlow (W.). Vita R. Cosin. 1598. 1707
Hutton (Thomas). Reasons for refusal of...the booke of Common praier...with an answere. Oxford, 1605. 4°. . . . 5271
Second and last part of reasons for refusall of subscription. 1606. 4°. 2171
See Defence of the Ministers reasons. 1607.
See Devon and Cornwall, *Ministers of.* The Remoouall. 1606.
Huycke (William). *See* Liturgies. Geneva. The forme of common praiers. 1550.
Hylles (Thomas). *See* Hill.
Hylton (Walter). *See* Hilton.
Hymns (Sarum). Hymnorum cum notis opusculum. Paris, 1518. 4°. 6612
— Antwerp, 1524. 4°. 6082
Hymns (Sarum and York). *See* Expositio.
See Psalter. 147
Hynde (Ed.). Verses in Camb. Univ. Thr-thr. 1603. . . . 5616
Hyperius (Andreas). *See* Gerardus (A.).
Hyrde (Richard). *See* Vives (L.). Instruction of a christen woman. 1557 *etc.*

I. (A.). Verses in Lucanus. Pharsalia. 1614. 3655
I. (A.), *Regal.* Verses in Camb. Univ. Epicedium. 1612. . . 5665
I. (B.). *See* Jonson (B.). 1604.
Verses in Seneca. Tragoediae. 1613. 7781

No.
I. (B.). Verses in Warre (James). The touchstone. 1630. . 4546
— Stafford (A.). Femall glory. 1635. 4018
I. (C.). *See* Stow (J.). Survey of London. 1633.
I. (F.), *Master*. The adventures. *See* Gascoigne (G.). Hundreth sundrie Flowers. [Ab. 1572.] 4°.
I. (G.). *See* La Primaudaye (P. de). The french academie. 1589 *etc.*
I. (G.). Verses in Camb. Univ. Thr-thr. 1603. . . . 5616
I. (G.), *Coll. Reg.* Verses in Camb. Univ. Epicedium. 1612. . 5665
I. (G. W.). *See* W. (G.) I[unior?].
I. (H.). Jacobs ladder. 1638. 12°. 4596
See Hoskins (A.). A briefe and cleare declaration. 1611.
— Jacob (H.). A Treatise... 1598.
I. (H.), *student in Divinity*. *See* Bullinger (H.). Fiftie godlie sermons. 1577 *etc.*
I. (I.), *King's Coll.* Verses in Camb. Univ. Epicedium. 1612. . 5665
— — Lacrymae. 1619. 5689
I. (P. A. S.) = Anderson (P.), *S.J.* q.v.
I. (R.). Nova Britannia...Virginia. 1609. 4°. 3606
I. (R.). [= Iohnson (R.).] *See* Botero (G.). Relations. 1608 *etc.*
I. (R.), *Regal.* Verses in Camb. Univ. Gratulatio. 1623. . . 5695
I. (R.), *Trin. Coll.* Verses in Barlow (W.). Vita R. Cosin. 1598. 1707
I. (S.). Verses in Drexelius (H.). Considerations. 1632 etc. . 7789 etc.
I. (S. R. N). *See* Scott (T.). Votivae Angliae. 1624.
— — Vox Coeli. 1622.
I. (T.). Verses in Day (J.). A new spring. 1637. . . . 4650
— Shirley (J.). The royall master. 1638. . . . 4665
I. (W.). *See* C. (A.). True relations of svndry Conferences. 1626. 4°.
— Guicciardini (F.). Two Discourses. 1595.
— Lessius (L.). A consvltation. 1621.
Icones stirpium, seu plantarum. Antwerp, 1591. 4°. . . . 6118
Iden (Henry). *See* Gelli (G. B.). Circes. 1557.
Ignatius his Conclaue. *See* Donne (J.). 1611 *etc.*
Ignatius Loyola. *See* Loyola.
Ignoramus Comœdia. *See* Ruggle (G.). 1630.
'Ignoto.' Verses in Spenser (E.). Faerie queen. 1590 *etc.*. . 1960 *etc.*
Iles (Th.). Verses in Oxf. Univ. Horti. 1640. . . . 5499
Image of both Churches. *See* Pattenson (M.). 1623.
Image of Pity. *See* Indulgence. Image of Pity.
Imitatio Christi. [Books i—iv.] By W. Atkinson. Pynson, 7 Oct. 1517. 4°. 266
— — Pynson, n.d. 4°. 299
[Books i—iii.] W. de Worde [1510?]. 4°. 226
— W. de Worde [1520?]. 4°. 227
[Book iv.] W. de Worde [1519?]. 4°. 228
[i—iv.] R. Redman, n.d. 8°. 393
The followyng of Christ... Also...the Spirituall Glasse. T. Godfray [1532?]. 8°. 560
[J. Cawood? 1556?] 8°. 1000
Trans. E. Hake. Ed. 2. H. Denham, 1568. 8°. . . . 1405
Trans. T. Rogers. 1616. 12°. 2528
Trans. F. B. 1620. 12°. 6540
See Catharine Parr. Prayers. 1545.
Immerito, *pseud.* *See* Spenser (E.). Shepheardes Calender. 1586. 1942
Important Considerations. 1601. *See* Watson (W.).
In homines nefarios. Cantabrigiae, 1605. 4°. 5631
Ince (Randulph). *See* Ince (W.). Lot's little one. 1640. 12°.
Ince (William). Lot's little one. Dublin, 1640. 12°. . . 5158
Indagine (J. ab). Brefe Introductions...vnto...Chiromancy...and Phisiognomy. 1558. 8°. 790
Indentures. *See* Introduction to the knowledge of *etc.* [154-?] 8°.

No.

Index Expurgatorius. *See* James (T.). Index. 1627.
Indictment against Mother Masse. *See* A New Dialogue.
Indulgence. Image of Pity. Caxton [1490]. 4°. 38
[Leo X.] Pynson [1515]. Broadside. 300
[Leo X to St Thomas of Acres, London.] Pynson [1517?] . 301
Information to all good Christians...from the...Kingdome of Scotland. Edinburgh, 1639. 4°. 5991, 5992
Informations from the Estaits of the Kingdome of Scotland. 1640. 4°. 7679
Informations, or a protestation, and a treatise from Scotland. 1608. 8°. 6388
Ingelram. *See* Enghelram.
Ingham (Edward). Verses in Smith (J.). The true travels. 1630. . 4836
Inglefield (Sir F.). *See* Parsons (R.). Conference. 1594.
Ingmethorp (Thomas). Verses in Shaw (J.). Bibliorum summula. 1623. 7381
Ingpen (W.). Secrets of numbers. 1624. 4°. 2550
Ingram (John). Verses in Camb. Univ. Lacrymæ. 1619. . . 5689
Ingulph. [Histories.] *See* Savile (Sir H.). Rervm Anglicarvm scriptores. 1596.
Injunctions exhibited. Berthelet, 1538. F°. 444
Injunctions gyven...to the clergie. Berthelet, 1536. F°. . . 432
Injunctions geven by the Kynges Maiestie. Grafton, 1547. 4°. . 598
Edward VI. Grafton [1547]. 4°. 599
— Grafton, 1547. 4°. 600–602
Injunctions geven by the Quenes Maiestie. Jugge and Cawood. 1559. [1559?] 4°. 977–979
[C. Barker, 1580?] 4°. 1686
[J. Kingston for C. Barker? 1584?] 4°. 1190
Innocent VIII, *Pope*. Proclamation. [Ab. 1496.] . . 7064–5
Inquisition of Spain. *See* Gonsalvius. A discovery. 1568 *etc.*
Institutio graecae grammatices. *See* Camden (W.). 1604.
Institution of a Christian Man. Berthelet, 1537. 4°. . . . 439
Institutions in the lawes of Englande. [J. Byddell] n.d. 8°. . 574
Institutions or principall grounds of the lawes and statutes of England. '1574.' 8°. 364
Instructions and Prayers. 16°. 6598–6601
Instructions for Mvsters. *See* Privy Council. 1623. Instrvctions.
Instructions for the Rosary. 1613. 12°. *See* Rosary.
Instructions when it ringeth to Evensong. 16°. 6601
Instrument Makers. *See* Allen (E.). 1623.
— — (J.). 1637.
— Thompson (J.). 1623.
Instruments, The book of sundry. *See* Book of Presidents [162–?] 8°. 7410
Insula (Gulielmus de). *See* Lisle.
Insulanus Menapius (Gulielmus). Aula Dialogus. *See* Castiglione (B.)... De Curiali. 1612. 8°. 2267
Interest. *See* Tables of Leases and Interest. 1628.
Intrationum excellentissimus liber. Pynson, 1510. F°. . . . 258
Intrationum liber. H. Smyth (W. Middleton), 1546 (1545). F°. . 774
Introduction to the knowledge and vnderstanding. [Ab. 1550.] 8°. 1008
Inuectyue against dronkennes. J. Oswen, Ipswich [1548]. 16°. . 5881
Io. (F.). *See* Hildersam (A.). Treatise of the Ministery. [1603?]
Irby (Sir Anthony). *See* Fletcher (P.). The Purple Island. 1633.
Ireland. Statutes. *See* Statutes. 10 Henry VI—14 Elizabeth. 1572. F°.
[Lawes and Orders of Warre...for...Ireland.] *See* Essex (Robert Devereux, earl of). 1599.
Proclamations (Tobacco). 1619. 2806
Church of. Act for the granting of eight entire subsidies. Dublin, 1634. F°. 6051
— Articles. *See* Articles. Ireland.
— Constitutions and Canons. 1634. Dublin, 1635. 4°. . 6056
— Visitation Articles. *See* Down and Connor, Diocese.

No.

Ireland, *cont.* *See* Ware (Sir J.). Archiepiscoporum. 1626.
Cistercian Houses. *See* Ware (Sir J.). Archiepiscoporum. 1626.
Courts of Justice. His Majesties directions. 1622. 4°. . . 6023
See Birchensha (R.). A discourse. 1602. 4°.
— Davies (Sir J.). Discoverie of the trve cavses. 1612.
— Folkingham (W.). Feudigraphia. 1610.
— M. (A.). True reporte of the...successe...against...our Romaine enemies. [1580?]
— Rich (B.). A New Description. 1610. 4°.
— — Short svrvey. 1609. 4°.
— Ryves (Sir T.). Regiminis anglicani in hibernia defensio. 1624.
— S. (E. C.). The government etc. 1626.
— Sibthorp (Sir C.). A friendly advertisement. 1622.
Ireland (Thomas). Oath of allegeance. 1610. 4°. 3635
Irenæus Rodoginus, *pseud.* Differences in matters of religion, betweene the easterne and westerne churches. 1625. 4°. . . 4531
Ironside (Gilbert). Seven questions of the sabbath. Oxford, 1637. 4°. 5473
Isaacson (Henry). Saturni Ephemerides. 1633. F°. . . 4206
Verses in Camb. Univ. Epicedium. 1612. 5665
Isaacson (William), *D.D.* Verses in Isaacson (H.). Ephemerides. 1633. 4206
Isabella Clara Eugenia, *Infanta of Spain.* *See* Netherlands, *Southern Provinces.* 1599.
Isackson ( ), *Pemb.* *See* Isaacson (H.).
Isidore, *Saint, Bishop of Seville.* Monita de verbis beati ysidori. *See* Speculum Christiani. [148-.] 4°. 99
[To eschewe vices &c.] *See* Whitford (R.). Holy Instructions. 1541. 4°. 711
[Gathered Counsayles.] *See* Lupset (T.). Workes. 1546. . 485
Isidore, *of Pelusium.* *See* Chrysostom...opera. 1613.
Isocrates. Λόγοι καὶ ἐπιστόλαι. (Gr.). 1615. 8°. 2377
Orationes tres...Plutarchi...de liberis. (Gr.) Cantabrigiae, 1638. 8°. 5828
Archidamus (Eng.). Trans. T. Barnes. 1624. 4°. . . 3348
[Letters.] *See* Fleming (A.). A panoplie. 1576. 4°.
Italicus (P.) de Lugo. *See* Lugo (Peregrinus de). 302
Italy. *See* Guicciardini (F.). 1579 *etc.*
— Sandys (G.). A relation. 1627.
— Thomas (W.). The historie. 1549 *etc.*
Universities. *See* Henry VIII. [Marriage.] Gravissimæ. 1530.
— — Determinations. 1530.
Itzuertus (Jacobus). *See* Yetsweirt.
Ive (Paul). Practise of Fortification. *See* Du Bellay (G.). Instructions for the warres. 1589.
Iveson (William). Verses in Camb. Univ. Carmen. 1635. . . 5770
— King (E.). Ivsta. 1638. 5829
Ivry, *Battle of.* *See* Henry IV of France. A true discourse. 1590.

J. (G.). *See* L'Espine (J. de). A very excellent discourse. 1592.
J. (W.). Dictionariolum quadruplex: or a fourefold dictionarie. 1638. 4°. 4186
See Doddridge (Sir J.). Compleat Parson. 1630.
J. (S.) [*qu.* Jackman?]. Verses in Lessius (L.). Hygiasticon. 1634. 5762
Jackman (Simon). Verses in Hodson (W.). The holy sinner. 1639. 5796
See also J. (S.).
Jackson (Arthur). *See* Sibbes (R.). Beames of divine light. 1639.
— — Evangelicall Sacrifices. 1640.
— — Light from heaven. 1638.
Jackson (Henry). *See* Hooker (R.). Certayne divine tractates. 1618 *etc.* F°.
— Wyclif (J.). Wickliffes wicket. 1612.
Jackson (J.). Verses in Lessius (L.). Hygiasticon. 1634. . . 5762
Jackson (J.), *Pemb.* Verses in Camb. Univ. Fasciae. 1633. . 5808
Jackson (James), *M.A.*, *Clar.* Verses in Camb. Univ. Genethl. 1631. 5731

No.
Jackson (James), *cont.* Verses in Camb. Univ. Voces. 1640. . . 5836
Jackson (John). Key of Knowledge. 1640. 12°. 3059
Verses in Coryate (T.). Coryates Crvdities. 1611. . . 3076
— Shirley (J.). The royall master. 1638. 4665
Jackson (R.), *printer.* *See* Gerhard (J.). Prayers. 1625.
Jackson (Thomas). Christs answer vnto Johns qvestion. 1625. 4°. 4089
Converts happines. 1609. 4°. 7362
Eternall truth of scriptures. 1613. 4°. 3096
Judah must into captivitie. 1622. 4°. 4767
Ivstifying faith. 1615. 4°. 3787
Raging tempest stilled. 1623. 4°. 4783
Third booke of commentaries vpon The Apostles creede. 1614. 4°. 3100
Treatise containg the originall of Vnbeliefe. 1625. 4°. . . 3866
Treatise of the divine essence. Part 1. 1628. 4°. . . 4249
— Part 2. 1629. 4°. 4257
Treatise of the consecration of the sonne of god. Oxford, 1638. 4°. 5483
Treatise of the holy catholike faith and Church. 1627. 4°. . 4239
Verses in Fuller (T.). Holy warre. 1639 *etc.* . . . 5806 *etc.*
See Twisse (W.). A discovery. 1631. 4°. 7012
Jackson (Tho.), *C.C.C.* Verses in Holyoake (F.). Dictionarium. 1640. 3058
Jackson (William). Celestiall husbandrie. 1616. 4°. . . . 2321
Jacob. Thystorye of Jacob and his twelue sones. W. de Worde [before 1519]. 4°. 229
Jacob, ben Asher, *of Toledo.* Nugæ Rabbini Jacob Bagual ha Turim supra primum caput Geneseos. *See* Bible (Latin). Pentateuch. 1597. 5586
Jacob, *Ship.* *See* A relation. 1622. 4°. 3506
Jacob (H.). Attestation of many learned. 1613. 8°. . . . 6477
Confession and protestation of the faith. 1616. 8°. . . . 6481
Declaration and plainer opening. 1612. 8°. 6500
Defence of a treatise touching the sufferings...of christ. 1600. 4°. 6459
Defence of the churches and ministery of England. Middelburg, 1599. 4°. 6455–7
Divine beginning and institution. Leyden, 1610. 8°. . . 6493
Plaine and clear exposition of the Second Commandement. 1610. 8°. 6494
Reasons taken out of gods word. 1604. 4°. 6467
Treatise of the sufferings and victory of Christ. 1598. 8°. . 6821
Verses in Puget de la Serre (J.). The mirrour. 1639. . . 4125
See Collection of sundry matters. 1616.
— Treatise of the nature. 1605.
Jacob (Henry), *Mert. Coll.* Verses in Hippocrates, 1633. . . 5812
Jacobus *ad Portum.* *See* Portusius.
Jacomotus (Theodore), *Geneuensis.* Verses in Camb. Univ. Lacrymæ. 1619. 5689
Jacson (John). *See* Jackson.
Jaggard (William). *See* Favyn (A.). Theater of Honour. 1623.
Jamerius or Jamericus. *See* Braunschweig (H.). The noble experyence. 1525.
James I. Workes. 1616. F°. 2653
Opera. 1619 (1620). F°. 2807
Apologia pro ivramento fidelitatis. 1609. 4°. 2366
— 1609. 12°. 2367
Apologie for the oath of allegiance. (Triplici nodo &c.) 1609. 4°. 2615
— April 8, 1609. 4°. 2616, 2617
— *See* Andrewes (L.). Tortvra Torti. 1609.
— — Barlow (W.). Answer to a catholike Englishman. 1609.
— — Du Moulin (P.). Accomplishment. 1613.
— — Parsons (R.). Ivdgment of a catholicke Englishman. 1608.
— — Tooker (W.). Duellum. 1611.
ΒΑΣΙΛΙΚΟΝ ΔΩΡΟΝ. 1603. 8°. 2926, 2927

No.
James I., *cont.* ΒΑΣΙΛΙΚΟΝ ΔΩΡΟΝ. 1604. 8°. 2350
— Princes looking glasse...from...Βασιλικὸν Δῶρον...by W. Willymat. Cambridge, 1603. 4°. 5617
Britannia triumphans. 1607. 8°. 7388
De execrabili et nefanda fratrum Ruvenorum...conjuratione. Edinburgh, 1601. 4°. 5945
[Declaration 16 July 1604.] *See* Wilkes (W.). Obedience. 1605.
Declaration...in matter of Bountie. 1610. 4°. 2627
Declaration concerning...C. Vorstius. 1612. 4°. . . . 2644
Declaration...sur ses actions devers les Estats Generaux. 1612. 4°. 2374
Declaration...pour le droit des rois. 1615. 4°. 3466
Declaratio pro jure regio. 1616. 4°. 7757
— (English). *See below* Remonstrance.
Declaration touching his proceedings in the late...Parliament. 1621. 4°. 2812
Deus & rex: sive dialogus. 1615. 4°. 6902
Directions for...the Courts...of Ireland. Dublin, 1622. 4°. . 6023
Fruitfull Meditation...of 7–10 verses of Revelation xx. [1603?]. 8°. 2854
Instructions and directions. 9 Jan. 1610. To...the Court of Wards and Liueries. 1610. 4°. 2628
Meditation vpon the lords prayer. 1619. 8°. 2803
Meditatio in orationem dominicam. 1619. 8°. . . . 2804
Naupactiados, s. Lepantiados Metaphrasis. 1604. 4°. . . 2351
Peace Maker. 1619. 4°. 4141
Placcaet des Coninex. 'Londen, R. Barker,' 1603. 8°. . . 6850
[Premonition to Christian Princes.] *See* Dutifull and respective considerations. 1609.
Publication...against priuate combats. 1613. 4°. . 2648, 2649
Remonstrance...against an oration of...Perron. Cambridge, 1616. 4°. 5679
— Cambridge, 1619. 4°. 5687, 5688
Speech...in the upper house of the Parliament. 19 March 1603. 1604. 4°. 2586
Speach in this last Session. 1605. 4°. 2589
Speech to both the Houses. 31 March 1607. 1607. 4°. . 2606
Speach. 21 March 1609. 4°. 2618
Speach. 20 June 1616. [1616?] 4°. 2654
Speach in the Vpper House. 26 March 1621. 1621. 4°. . 2810
To the reuerend Fathers in God...at the Conuocation. [Relief of Geneva.] 1604. Single leaf. F°. 7416
Triplici nodo triplex cuneus (Latin). 1607. 4°. 2604
— (English). 1607. 4°. 2605
— *See above* Apologia.
True lawe of free Monarchies. Edinburgh, 1598. 8°. . . 5938
Verses in Camb. Univ. Lacrymae. 1587. 7356
The court of...James the first. 1619. 4°. 3929
[Succession.] *See* Leslie (J.). A treatise. 1584.
[Entry to Tower 12 Feb. 1604.] *See* Hubbocke (W.). An oration. 1604.
[Genealogy.] *See* Harry (G. O.). Genealogy. 1604.
— *See* Slatyer (W.). Genethliacon. 1630.
[Gunpowder plot.] *See* In homines nefarios. 1605.
[Letters.] *See* Lindsay (D.). Trve narration. 1621.
[Marriage.] *See* Damman (Sir A.). Schediasmata. 1590.
Triumphs. *See* Marcelline (G.). 1610. 4°.
[Visit to Oxford 1605 Aug. 27.] *See* Wake (I.). Rex Platonicus. 1607 etc. 12°. . . . . 5281 *etc.*
[Visit of Christian IV.] *See* Tricorones. 1607. 4°. . . 7807
[Death.] *See* Camb. Univ. Dolor et solamen. 1625. 4°.
— *See* Wedderburn (D.). Abredonia. 1625.
[Funeral.] *See* Williams (J.). Great Britains Salomon. 1625.
[Portrait.] [1619?]. F°. 7551

No.

James I., *cont.* *See* Andrewes (L.). Responsio. 1610. . . . 2622
— Aretius (Jac.). Primvla Veris. 1613.
— B. (A. D.). The Court of James I. 1619.
— Barlow (W.). Summe...of the conference...at Hampton Court. 1604 *etc.*
— Bible. English Psalms (Metrical). 1631 etc. . . 5430 *etc.*
— Cambridge University. True Copies. 1623.
— Casaubon (M.). Vindication. 1624.
— — Vindicatio. 1624.
— Cecil (J.). Discoverye. [1599?]
— Du Moulin (P.). De Monarchia Temporali Pontificis Romani. 1614.
— Du Perron (J. D.). Reply...to the answeare of the...King. 1630.
— I. (S. R. N.). Votivæ Angliæ. 1624.
— Nixon (A.). Oxfords Triumph. 1605.
— Official Publications.
— Oxford University. Oxoniensis Academiae Parentalia. 1625.
— Palatinate. 1624.
— Peace-maker. 1619. 4°.
— Ross (T.). Idæa. 1608.
— Supplication of certaine Masse-Priests. 1604.
— Supplication to the Kings most excellent Maiestie. 1604.
— Thomson (G.). Ἀνακεφαλαίωσις. 1604.
— Wake (I.). Rex Platonicvs. 1607 etc. . . . . 5281 etc.
James II, *King of England.* *See* Camb. Univ. Fasciæ. 1633. 4°.
James (Dane). *See* Catharine of Siena. Orcharde of Syon. 1519. F°. 180
James (Francis), *B.A.* Verses in Chaucer (G.). Amorvm. 1635. . 5414
James (Richard). Concio habita ad clerum Oxoniensem. Oxoniae, 1633. 4°. 5402
Sermon concerning...the sacrament. 1632. 4°. . . . 3818
Sermon delivered in Oxford. (A sermon.) 1630. 4°. . . 7495
Verses in Smith (J.). The true travels. 1630. . . . 4836
See More (Sir T.). Epistola. 1633.
James (Stephen). *See* verses in Lessius (L.). Hygiasticon. 1634. 5833
James (Tho.). Apologie for J. Wickliffe. Oxford, 1608. 4°. . 5282
Bellum papale. 1600. 4°. 1744
Catalogus interpretum s. scripturae. Oxoniae, 1635. 4°. . 5416
Concordantiæ...libri canticorum...expositio. Oxoniae, 1607. 4°. 5279
Ecloga Oxonio-Cantabrigiensis. 1600. 4°. 2075
Explanation...of the ten Articles. Oxford, 1625. 4°. . . 5350
Index generalis librorum prohibitorum. Oxoniae, 1627. 12°. . 5417
Index generalis sanctorum patrum ad v. Matt. 1624. 8°. . 7628
Jesuits Downefall. Oxford, 1612. 4°. 5301
Manuduction...vnto divinitie. Oxford, 1625. 4°. . . 7610
Treatise of the corruption of scripture. 1612. 4°. . . . 2513
Verses in Holyoake (F.). Dictionarium. 1640. . . . 3058
— Vaughan (W.). The Golden Grove. 1608. 2888
See Brucioli (A.). Commentary. 1598.
— Bury (R. de). Philobiblon. 1599.
— Catalogue. Oxford. Bodleian Library. 1620.
— Du Vair (G.). The morall philosophie of the Stoicks. 1598. 8°.
— Wicelius (G.). Methodus. 1625.
— Wyclif (J.). Two short treatises. 1608.
James (Thomas), *Captain.* Strange and dangerous voyage...of the Northwest Passage. 1633. 4°. 4716
James (W.). Sermon...19. of Feb. 1578. 8°. 1496
Sermon...at Paules crosse, 9 Nov. 1589. 1590. 4°. . . 7296
Verses in Camb. Univ. Lachrymae. 1587.
James (William). Verses in Owen (J.). Epigrammatum. 1634. . 4583
Jametsz. *See* La Nove (F. de). The declaration. 1589.

No.

Jamison (Patrick). Verses in Forbes (P.). Funerals. 1637. . 6007
Janua linguarum. Ed. 6. Opera J. Harmar. 1627. 4°. . . 2555
Ed. 8. Studio T. Horne. 1634. 8°. 4981
Trans. W. Welde. [.] 4°. 7711
See Comenius.
Japan. [Jesuits.] *See* Neville (E.). The palme. 1630.
Jason. *See* Le Fèvre (R.). The veray trew history. 1492.
Jay (Sir Thomas). Verses in Massinger (P.). The Picture. 1630. . 4882
— A new way. 1633. 4104
Jeamsius (Will.). *See* James. 2123
Jeanes (Henry). Treatise concerning evil. Oxford, 1640. 12°. . 5464
Jeanisius (William). Verses in Camb. Univ. Lachrymae. 1587. . 2123
Jefferie, Little [*i.e.* J. Hudson]. *See* Microphilus. The new-yeeres Gift. 1636. 12°.
Jemmat (William). *See* Taylor (T.). Christ revealed. 1635.
— — Parable of the Sower. 1634. 4°.
— — Principles of christian practice. 1635. 12°.
Jena University. *See* Wittenberg University. The Considerations. 1620.
Jeninges (E.). A briefe discouery of...diet. 1593. 4°. . . 1875
Jenison (Robert). The Cities Safety. 1630. 8°. . . . 4834
The height of Israels heathenish idolatrie. 1621. 4°. . 3597
See R. (I.). Purgatories triumph. 1613. 4°.
Jenison (Thomas). Verses in Camb. Univ. Lachrymae. 1587. . 2123
Jenkinson (Anne). Meditations upon the Lamentations of Jeremie, translated. 1609. 12°. 3206
Jennings (Ralph). *See* Aslachus (C.). The description of heaven. 1623.
Jennison (Robert). *See* Floyd (J.). A paire of spectacles. 1631. 8°.
Jermin (Michael). Comm. upon...Ecclesiastes. 1639. F°. . . 4932
Paraphrasticall Meditations...upon...the Proverbs of Solomon. 1638. F°. 4385
Jerome, *Saint*. *See* Hieronymus.
Jerome of Brunswick. *See* Braunschweig (H.).
Jerome, of Ferrara. *See* Savonarola.
Jerome (Stephen). Englands iubilee. Dublin, 1625. 4°. . . 6029
Seaven helpes to heaven. Ed. 3. 1620. 8°. 4498
See H. (R.). The arraignement. 1631(-2).
Jerusalem. Last siege and conquest. *See* Godfrey of Boulogne. 1481. F°.
See Destruction. Dystruccyon of Jherusalem. [15—.] 4°. . 296
Jervis (Edmund). Verses in Camb. Univ. Lachrymae. 1587. . 2123
Jessop (Edmond). Discovery of the errors of the English Anabaptists. 1623. 4°. 3343
Jesuits. The Iesuites catechisme. 1602. 4°. 6845
Legend of the Jesuites. Or...the reasons, for which the citizens of Troyes...refuse to receive the Societie. 1623. 4°. . . 4518
See Aphorismes...selected. (A short treatise.) 1609.
— Arnauld (A.). The arrainement. 1594.
— Beza (T.). Epistola. 1598.
— Neville (E.). The palme...in Iaponia. 1630.
— Nîmes University. Academiae...responsio. 1584.
— Paris. Sorbonne. The copie. 1610.
— Prosopopeia. 1606.
— State-mysteries of the Iesvites. 1623.
Jesus Christ. Our saviour Jesus Christ hath not overcharged his chirche with many ceremonies. 'Zijrik, Feb. 1543.' 8°. . . 6105
[Genealogy.] *See* Sympson (W.). A fvll...genealogie. 1619. . 5690
Life. *See* Heigham (J.). 1622.
[Life. (Engravings.) Ab. 1640.] F°. 7059
See Passion of our Lord. 1521.
— Rosary of our Saviour.

No.

Jesus Christ, *cont.* *See* Seven sheddings. 1509.
[Seven last words.] *See* Bellarmino (R.). Of the seaven words. 1638. 12°.
Jesus, Name of. *See* Prynne (W.). Certaine quaeres. 1636. 4°.
Jesus Psalter. *See* Manual of prayers. 1589. 16°.
— Douai. 16°. 6605
Jew. The Converted Jew. 1630. 4°. 6999
Jewel (John). Works. 1609. F°. 2368
— 1611. F°. 2372
Adv. T. Hardingum, volumen alterum. 1578. 4°. . . . 1535
Apologia Ecclesiæ Anglicanæ. 1562. 8°. 743
— 1584. 8°. 2060
— 1591. 12°. 1861
— 1626. 12°. 2554
— 1637. 12°. 4993
— Cum versione graeca. Oxonii, 1639. 8°. 5461
Apologie or aunswer in defence of the Church of England. 1562. 4°. 744
— 1564. 8°. 745
Apologie of private Masse. 1562. 8°. 1245, 1246
Certaine sermons. 1583. 8°. 1674
Confutation, as wel of M. Dormans...Disproufe...as also of D. Sander. 1567. 4°. 1457
Copie of a Sermon. *See below* True copies. 1560.
Defence of the apologie of the Ch. of Eng. 1567 Oct. 27. F°. . 7228
— 1570 Junij 16. F°. 7229
Exposition vpon...Thessalonians. 1583. 8°. 1320
Replie vnto m. hardinges answeare. 1565. F°. . . . 1252
Sermon made in latine in Oxenforde. [1580?] 8°. . . . 1373
True copies of the letters betwene John Bisshop of Sarum and D. Cole. [1560.] 8°. 885, 886
Viewe of a seditious Bul. 1582. 8°. 1316
[Life.] *See* Humphrey (L.). I. Ivelli vita. 1573.
See Doctrina et Politia. 1617.
— Harding (T.). Answere to maister ivelles *etc.* 1565.
— — Reioindre. [No. 1.] 1566. 4°.
— — — [No. 2.] 1567. 4°.
— Heskyns (T.). The parliament of chryste. 1566.
— Homilies. Certaine Sermons. 1563.
— Nowell (A.). A reprovfe. 1565.
— Rastell (J.). Confutation of a sermon. 1564.
— Rudyerd (Sir B.). His speech. 1628. 4°.
Jewell (W.). The golden cabinet. 1612. 8°. 2514
Jhones (Richard). *See* Jones.
Jhonston (A.), *Clerk.* *See* Scotland. General Assembly. An answer. 1639. 4°.
— Warriston (Archibald Johnston, lord). 1640.
Jo. (F.). *See* Io. (F.).
Joan, *Pope.* *See* Cooke (A.). Pope Joane. 1610 *etc.*
See Dillingham (F.). Tractatus... 1603.
Joannes Canonicus. *See* Canon (John).
Joannes, *Grammaticus.* De Græcarum linguarum proprietate. *See* Crespin (J.). 1581.
Joannes de Mediolano. *See* Regimen.
Joannes Sarisburiensis. *See* John of Salisbury.
Jobson (Richard). The golden trade. 1623. 4°. 3687
Jocelinus, *monk of Furness.* The life of S. Patricke. *See* B. (B.), *Irish Franciscan.* 1625. 4°. 6553
John XXI, *Pope.* Medical works. *See* Petrus *Hispanus.*
John de Bordeaux. *See* Governal of Health.
John Chrysostom, *Saint.* *See* Chrysostom.

No.
John, *Abp of Euchaita.* Versus Iambici, cura M. Busti. Etonae, 1610. 4°. 5902
John of Salisbury, *Bp of Chartres.* *See* Clemangiis (N. de). Specvlvm. 1606.
John of the Cross. *See* Catholick Iudge. 1623.
John of Tynemouth. *See* Capgrave (J.). Nova Legenda. 1516.
John Casimir, *Count Palatine.* Certaine orations...vnto the French King. 1579. 8°. 7128
John Frederick, *elector of Saxony.* *See* Avila y Zuniga (L. de). Comentaries. 1555.
John, *Little.* *See* Little John.
Johnes (Richard). *See* Jones.
Johnson or Jonson (Christopher). [Carmina.] *See* Willes (R.). Poematvm liber. 1573.
See Homer. Batrachomyomachia. 1580.
— White (Ric.). Orationes. 1566.
Johnson (Fras.). Brief treatise. 1609. 8°. 6879
Christian plea. Amsterdam, 1617. 4°. 6394
See Ainsworth (H.). An animadversion. 1613.
— Amsterdam, *English Church in.* Apologie or defence. 1604.
— Brabourne (T.). A Defence. Ed. 2. 1632. . . . 6403
— Bradshaw (W.). Unreasonablenes of the separation. 1640.
— Hildersam (A.). Treatise of the Ministery. [1603?]
— Jacob (H.). Defence. 1599.
Johnson (John). Johnsons Arithmatick. (1622.) 8°. . . . 4514
Johnson (John), *fellow of Pemb. Hall.* Verses in Hippocrates. 1633. 5812
Johnson (Richard). Pleasant conceits of old Hobson. (Fragment.) [1634?] 8°. 3614
— 1640. 8°. . . . . 5216* (p. 1168)
Johnson (Richard), *K.C.C.* Verses in Camb. Univ. Epithalam. 1625. 5702
Johnson (Robert), *Gent.* *See* Botero (G.). Relations. 1608 *etc.*
Johnson (Robert), *Preacher.* Gospell and his maintenance. 1633. 4°. 4626
Johnson (S.). Verses in Camb. Univ. Lachrymae. 1587. . . 2123
Johnson (Thomas). Mercurius Botanicus. 1634. 8°. . . . 4630
Verses in Parkinson (J.). Paradisus terrestris. 1629. . . 2561
See Bauderon (B.). Pharmacopœa. 1639.
— Gerard (J.). The Herball. 1633.
— Paré (A.). The workes. 1634. F°.
Johnson (William), *Queens' Coll., Cambridge.* Verses in Fuller (T.). Holy warre. 1639 *etc.* . . . . . . 5806 *etc.*
Johnston (Archibald), *Clerk to the General Assembly, Scotland.* *See* Warriston (A. Johnston, Lord.)
Johnston (Arthur), *M.D.* Paraphrasis poetica psalmorum Davidis etc. Aberdoniae, 1637. 8°. 6009
Verses in Chaucer (G.). Amorvm. 1635. 5414
— Person (D.). Varieties. 1635. 4365
— Forbes (P.). Funerals. 1637. 6007
Johnston (James). Verses in Gerard (J.). The herball. 1597. . 2348
See Sidney (Sir P.). Countesse of Pembrokes Arcadia. 1638.
Johnston (John). Verses in Forbes (P.). Funerals. 1635. . . 6007
Johnston (Patrick). Verses in Adamson (J.). *Εἰσόδια.* 1618. . 5960
Johnstoun (James). *See* Johnston.
Jonathan ben Usiel. *See* Bible. Chaldaic. Song of Solomon. 1614.
Jonas (Justus). *See* Cranmer (T.). Catechismvs. 1548.
Jonas (Richard). *See* Roesslin (E.). Birthe of Mankynde. 1540.
Jones (Hugh), *bishop of Llandaff.* [Qu. translator of I Peter v. etc.?] *See* Bible (Bishops'). 1568. F°. 964
Jones (Inigo). Verses in Coryate (T.). Coryats Crudities. 1611. 3076
See Chapman (G.). The memorable maske. [1614?]

No.

Jones (Inigo), *cont.* *See* Daniel (S.). Tethys. 1610.
— Shirley (J.). The trivmph of peace. 1633.
— and W. Davenant. Britannia Triumphans. 1637. 4°. . . 4862
Temple of love. A masque. 1634. 4°. 4484
Jones (J.). Arte and science of preseruing bodie and soule in healthe. 1579. 4°. 1504
Bathes of Bathes Ayde. 1572. 4°. 1572
Benefit of Buckstones. 1572. 4°. 1571
Briefe...discourse...of Phisicke. Parts 1–3. 1574(–2). 4°. . 1366
— Part 4. 1572. 4°.
Jones (John). Verses in Camb. Univ. Geneth. 1631. . . . 5731
— Hippocrates. 1631. 5736
— Camb. Univ. Anthologia. 1632. 5741
— — Rex redux. 1633. 5748
Jones (John) *otherwise* Leander de St Martin, *Vicar General.* [Licence.] *See* Staney (W.). A treatise. 1617.
— — *See* Benedict, St. Order of. (Douai) 1625? . . 6612
Jones (Luke). Verses in Leighton (Sir W.). The teares. 1613. . 2868
Jones (P.). Certaine sermons. 1588. 8°. 1826
Jones (R.). Verses in Oxf. Univ. Horti. 1640. 5499
Jones, Jhones, or Johnes (Richard). *See* Booke of Honor. 1590.
Jones (Stephen). Verses in Camb. Univ. Fasciae. 1633. . . 5808
— — Rex redux. 1633. 5748
Jones (Stephen). Verses in Russell (J.). The two famous pitcht battles. 1634. 5767
— Camb. Univ. Carmen. *bis.* 1635. 5770
— Dugres (G.). Breve compendium. 1636. . . . 5781
— Saltmarsh (J.). Poemata sacra. 1636. 5785
Jones (William). Briefe exhortation to all men. 1631. 4°. . . 5052
Commentary vpon...Philemon...Hebrewes...II and III John. 1635. F°. 4364
Treatise of patience...Teares of the Isle of Wight. 1625. 4°. 3351
See Guicciardini (F.). Two Discourses. 1595.
— Lipsius (J.). Sixe bookes. 1594.
— Nenna (G. B.). Nennio. 1595.
Jones (William), *Printer.* *See* Sutton (T.). Iethroes covnsell. 1631.
Jones (Zachary). *See* Le Loyer (P.). A treatise of specters. 1605. 4°.
Jonson (.). *See* Gagge for the pope. 1624.
Jonson (Ben). Workes. 1616. F°. 3115
Works. Vol. 1. 1640. F°. 5115
— Vol. 2. 1640. F°. 4221
Bartholomew Fayre etc. 1631. F°. 3814
Catiline his conspiracy. 1611. 4°. 2902
Characters of Two royall Masques. [1609.] 4°. . . . 3450
Description of the masque...marriage of John, Visct. Hadington. [1608?] 4°. 6876
His part of King James his...entertainment. 15 March. 1603. 4°. 2857
[Masque of the Gypsies (Epigrams).] 1640. 12°. 3728
Verses in Wright (T.). The passions. 1604. 2858
— Coryat (T.). Coryats Crudities. 1611. 3076
— Du Bartas. Weekes. 1621. 2535
— Shakespeare (W.). Works. 1623. 3972
— Aleman (M.). The Rogve. 1623 *etc.* . . . . . 4079 *etc.*
— Lucanus. Pharsalia. 1627 *etc.* . . . . . . 3532 *etc.*
— Beaumont (Sir J.). Bosworth field. 1629. 3040
See Horatius. [De arte poetica] (—Masque—Epigrams). 1640. . 3728
— Shakespeare (W.). Poems. 1640. 8°.
Jonson (Christopher). *See* Johnson.
Jonston (Arthur). *See* Johnston.
Jordan (Agnes), *Abbess of Sion Monastery.* *See* Mirror of Our Lady. 1530.
Jordanus. Meditationes de vita et passione iesu christi. Pynson, 1513. 16°. 262

No.
Jorden (E.). Briefe discourse of the Suffocation of the Mother. 1603. 4°. 2160
Discourse of naturall Bathes. Ed. 3. 1633. 4°. 4003
Verses in Smith (J.). The true travels. 1630. 4836
Joriszoon (David). *See* Knewstub (J.). A Confutation. 1579.
See Rogers (J.). The displaying of an horrible Secte. 1579.
Joscelyn or Josselin (John). *See* Ælfric, *abp.* Testimonie of Antiqvitie. [1566?]
See Gildas. Gildæ...de excidio. 1568.
— Parker (M.). De antiqvitate. 1572.
— — Life of the 70. Archbishopp. 1574.
Joseph ben Gorion. Compendious...Historie of...the Jewes. Trans. P. Morwen. 1575. 8°. 969
— 1579. 8°. 941
— 1602. 8°. 7392
Joseph of Arimathea. A treatise. W. de Worde [1519]. 4°. . . . 230
Joseph Coecus (Sagi-Nahor). *See* Bible. Chaldaic. Song of Solomon. 1614.
Josephus (Flavius). Εἰς Μακκαβαίους (Gr. Lat.). Oxonie, 1590. 8°. . 5234
Workes. Trans. T. Lodge. 1609. F°. 2497
— 1632. F°. 4712
— 1640. F°. 4746
Josiah. *See* Reformation of religion.
Josselin (John). *See* Joscelyn.
Jovius (P.). Imprese. 1585. 8°. 2108
See Lanquet (T.). Coopers Chronicle. 1560 *etc.*
— Polemon (J.). All the famous Battels. [1577?] . . . 1522
Joye (G.). Apologye...to satisfye...W. Tindale...of hys new Testament. Nov. 1534 (1535). 8°. 568
Exposicion of Daniel the Prophete. 'Geneva' 1545 August. 8°. . 6695
Exposycion of Daniel. 1550. 8°. 701
Exposiciõ of Daniell. 1550. 8°. 908
George Joye confuteth Winchester's false articles. 'Wesill,' June 1543. 8°. 6109
Jeremy the Prophete. 1534. 8°. 6098
Letters which Johan Ashwel...sente...to the Bishope of Lyncolne. [Antwerp, ab. 153–?] 8°. 6092
— 'Strassburge 10 June.' 8°. 6668
Prophete Isaye. 'Straszburg 1531 x Maye.' 8°. . . . 6094
Refutation of the byshop of Winchesters derke declaration of his false articles. 1546. 8°. 762
Vnite and schisme of the olde Chirche. [Antwerp?] June 1543. 8°. 6108
See Bible (Eng.) Psalms. Dauids Psalter. 1534.
— Gardiner (S.). A declaration of svche...articles. 1546.
— Primer. A goodly prymer. [1536?] 4°.
— Osiander (A.). The coniectures. 1548.
— Supper of the lorde. 1533.
Joyeuse (Henri de). Life of...Fa. Angel...Bennet...Archangell. Douai, 1623. 8°. 6586
Joyner (Will.). Verses in Oxf. Univ. Horti. 1640. 5499
Juan de Santa Maria. Christian Policie. Trans. E. Blount. 1632. 4°. 3997
Policie unveiled. Trans. I. M. 1632. 4°. 7564
— — 1634. 4°. 7567
Policie Vnveiled, or Maximes and Reasons of State. Written by I. M. 1637. 4°. 4652
Juda (Leo). *See* Bullinger (H.). An holsome Antidotus. 1548.
See Erasmus (D.). Paraphrase. 1548 etc.
Judgment of a most reverend...Man. *See* Beza (Th.). The Ivdgement. [1580.] 1910
— Bridges (J.), *bp.* A defence. 1587.
Judgment of a Catholike English-man. *See* Parsons (R.). The ivdgment... 1608.

No.

Judicial of Urines. [Ab. 1530.] F°. 6667
— [Headline.] *See* Recorde (R.). The Urinall of Physick. 1547. 8°.
Jukes (Vincent). *See* Gouge (W.). Recovery from apostacy. 1639.
Julius II., *Pope*. *See* Constantine I. A Treatyse. [c. 1525.]
Julius III., *Pope*. *See* Justinianus. Digestorum. 1553.
— Rome, *Church of*. Julius III. Consilium. 1613.
Julius (Alexander). *See* Buchanan (G.). Ecphrasis Paraphraseos...in Psalmos. 1620.
Junius (Adrianus), *Hornanus*. The Nomenclator. 1585. 8°. . . 1323
See Eunapius. Lyves Of Philosophers. 1579.
— Ravisius (J.). Epithetorum epitome. [1588?] 16°. . 7354
Junius (Andreas). *See* Young.
Junius (Franciscus). *See* Du Jon (F.).
Junius (Patricius). *See* Young (P.).
Junius (R.). *See* Younge (Richard).
Just reckonyng or accompt of...yeares. 6 June, 1547. 8°. . . 7149
Justice of the Peace. *See* Fitzherbert (Sir A.). New boke of Justices of Peace. 1541 *etc.*
See Lambarde (W.). Eirenarcha.
— Complete Justice. 1638. 8°. 7799
Justices of the Peace. *See* Book of Justices.
Justinianus. Digestorum seu pandectorum libri quinquaginta. Florentiae, 1553. F°. 6406
See Crakanthorp (R.). Iustinian. 1616.
— Ryves (Sir T.). Imperatoris. 1626.
Justinus. *See* Trogus Pompeius. Thabridgment. 1564. 4°.
Jvstitia Britannica. *See* Burghley (W. Cecil, lord). [Execution of Justice.] 1584.
Juvenalis. Satyræ. *See* Horatius. Poemata. 1578(-9).
— — 1592.
— — 1607.
Juvenalis et Persii Satyrae. Cum Annott. Ed. 2. 1615. 8°. . 2279
— Ed. 4. 1633. 8°. 7716
[Selection (Trans.).] *See* Beaumont (Sir J.). Bosworth field. 1629.
Juvenalis (Guido). *See* Terentius. Comedie. 1504.
Juxon (William), *bp*. *See* Articles. London Diocese. 1637.
— — 1640.

K. (E.). [Qu. E. Kirke?] *See* Spenser (E.). The Faerie queen. 1611.
— — Shepheardes Calender. 1586 *etc.*
K. (G.), *Trin. Coll.* Verses in Barlow (W.). Vita R. Cosin. 1598 . 1707
K. (I.). Verses in Camb. Univ. Thr.-thr. 1603. . . . 5616
K. (J.). [= J. Kepers.] *See* Romei (A.). The Courtiers Academie. [Ab. 1598.] 4°.
K. (M. G.). *See* Dominis (M. A. de). Second manifestation. 1623.
K. (R.), *Lincoln Coll., Oxford*. *See* Kilbye (R.).
K. (s W. M.), *Gentleman*. [Qu. Sir William Mure, Knight?] *See* Caledon's Complaints. [Ab. 1640.] 4°.. . . . 5994
Kalendar. *See* Calendar.
Kamintus, episcopus. *See* Canutus, *bp. of Aarhuus.*
Kamitus, episcopus. *See* Canutus, *bp. of Aarhuus.*
Karne (Edward), *LL.D.* *See* Henry VIII. Sigismondus. [1530?] . 511
Karuill (Nicolas). Verses in Cheke (Sir J.). De obitu M. Buceri. 1551. 734
Katharine. *See* Catharine.
Ke. (Le.), *King's College*. *See* Kempe.
Keckerman (B.). Systema ethicæ. 1607. 8°. 2362
Keene (J.). New almanack and prognostication. 1617. 8°. . . 7507
Keightley (Thomas), *Pet.* Verses in Camb. Univ. Συνωδία. 1637. 5790
Keightley (William), *Pet.* Verses in Camb. Univ. Συνωδία. 1637. . 5790

No.
Keilwey (Robert). Relationes quorundam casuum. 1602. F°. . 2395
Kellet (Edward). Miscellanies of divinitie. Cambridge, 1633. F°. . 5757
Verses in Camb. Univ. Thr.-thr. 1603. 5616
Kellison (Mat.). Gagge of the reformed gospell. 1623. 12°. . . 6619
Survey of the new religion. Douai, 1605. 4°. . . . 6570
— *See* Sutcliffe (M.). An abridgement. 1606.
— — Montagu (R.). A Gagg. 1624.
— — Sutcliffe (M.). Examination and Confutation of...The Suruey of the newe Religion. 1606.
— — Wilson (M.). Reply to M. Nicholas Smith. 1630.
Kello (Samuel). Verses in Adamson (J.). Εἰσόδια. 1618. . . 5960
Kelly (John). Verses in Meara (D.). Pathologia. 1619. . . 6017
Kemeis (G. Owen D.). *See* Camden (W.). Britannia. 1637.
Kemes, Lord. *See* Owen (G.), lord Kemes.
Kemp. *See also* Kempe.
Kemp (Ar.), *Clar.* Verses in Camb. Univ. Dolor. 1625. . . 5701
— — Epithalam. *bis.* 1625. 5702
Kemp (Ed.), *Queens' Coll., Cantab.* Verses in Hausted (P.). The Rivall Friends. 1632. 4561
— Camb. Univ. Fasciae. 1633. 5808
— Hausted (P.). Senile Odium. 1633. 5753
— Isaacson (H.). Ephemerides. 1633. 4206
Kempe (John). Verses in Forbes (P.). Funerals. 1637. . . 6007
Kempe (Leonard), *King's Coll.* Verses in Camb. Univ. Lacrymæ. 1619. 5689
Kempe (Margaret). Short treatyse of contemplacyon. W. de Worde [1501]. 4°. 231
Kempe (W.). Dvtifvll invective against... Ballard and Babington. 1587. 4°. 1448
Kempis (Thomas à). [For editions of the 'De Imitatione Christi.'] *See* Imitatio Christi.
Ken (George). Verses in Wilson (Sir T.). Vita. 1551. . . 631
Kent, *County of.* *See* Lambard (W.). A perambulation. 1576 *etc.*
Kent (Henry, earl of). [Funeral.] *See* B. (I.), *D.D.* A sermon. 1615.
Kent (Henry), *K.C.C.* Verses in Camb. Univ. Genethl. 1631. . 5731
— Hippocrates. 1631, 1633. . . . . 5736, 5812
Kent (T.). Verses in Camb. Univ. Lacrymæ. 1619. . . . 5689
Kenyngham (William). *See* Cuningham (W.).
Kepers (John). *See* Romei (A.). Courtiers Academie. [Ab. 1598.] 4°.
Kepler (John). *See* Keppler.
Keppler (John). *See* Ephemerides. 1635.
Kethe (W.). Sermon made at Blanford Forum. 1571. 8° . . 827
[Ps. xciv.] *See* Knox (J.). The appellation. 1558. 8°.
Ketlewell (Seth). Verses in Camb. Univ. Genethl. 1631. . . 5731
Kett (Robert). *See* Neville (A.). De furoribus. 1575.
Keuchenius (Gualtherus). Rasche Theboth. *See* Alablaster (W.). Spiraculum. [1633?] 5057
— — Thorndike (H.). Epitome lexici. 1635.
Kevinus (Matt. Scaricaeus). *See* Scaricæus.
Key to vnknowne knowledge. 1599. 4°. 2425
Key (Thomas). *See* Erasmus (D.). Paraphrase. 1548 *etc.*
Keythe (James). Verses *bis* in Forbes (P.). Funerals. 1635. . 6007
Kidson (Robert). *See* Francklin (R.). Ὀρθοτονία. 1633.
Kiel (Cornelis van). *See* Kilianus.
Kiffen (Maurice). Verses in Contarini (G.). Commonwealth. 1599. . 2153
Kil. (R.), *Coll. Regal.* *See* Killigrew (R.).
Kilby (Richard). Burthen of a loaden conscience. Ed. 5. Cambridge, 1614. 8°. 5671
Sermon...at the funerall of T. Holland. Oxford, 1613. 4°. . 5312
See Bible. Eng. (Royal). 1611. 2635
— Sutton (C.). Disce Mori. 1600.

No.

Kilianus (Cornelius), *Dufflaeus* [i.e. C. van Kiel.] Verses in Verstegan (R.). A restitution. 1605 *etc.* . . . . . . 6140 *etc.*
Killigrew (R.), *Coll. Regal.* Verses in Camb. Univ. Lacrymæ. 1619. 5689
Kimchi (David). *See* David Kimchi.
Kin. (Ph.). Verses in Beaumont (Sir J.). Bosworth field. 1629. . 3040
King (Adam). Verses in Adamson (J.). Εἰσόδια. 1618. . . 5960
See Canisius (P.). Ane Cathechisme. Paris, 1588. 16°.
King (Edward). Justa...ab amicis moerentibus. (Obsequies.) Cantabrigiae, 1638. 4°. 5829, 5830
Verses in Camb. Univ. Genethl. 1631. 5731
— — Anthologia. 1632. 5741
— — Fasciæ. 1633. 5808
— — Rex redux. 1633. 5748
— — Carmen. 1635. 5770
— — Συνωδία. 1637. 5790
— Hausted (P.). Senile Odium. 1633. 5753
King (Geoffrey), *Bp.* *See* Bible, English (Royal). 1611. . . 2635
King (Henry). Exposition vpon the Lords Prayer. Ed. 2. 1634. 4°. 3952
Sermon of deliverance. [Ps. xci. 3.] 1626. 4°. 4802
Sermon preached [John xv. 20] 25 November 1621 upon...John King...Thomas Preston. 1621. 4°. 3011
Sermon...at St Paul's March 27, 1640. 1640. 4°. . . . 5213
Two sermons upon the act sunday. Oxford, 1625. 4°. . 5351
Verses in Sandys (G.). A paraphrase. 1638. . . . 4736
King (Henry), *Cantab.*? Verses in Camb. Univ. Rex redux. 1633. 5748
— King (E.). Ivsta. 1638. 5829
King (John). Fourth sermon...at Hampton Court. Sept. 1606. Oxford, 1606. 4°. 5275
— Oxford, 1607. 4°. 5280
Lectures vpon Ionas. Oxford, 1597. 4°. 5244
— Oxford, 1600. 4°. 5253
— 1618. 4°. 7407
Sermon...at Oxford, 24 March. Oxford, 1608. 4°. . . 5283
Sermon...at Whitehall, 5 November, 1608. Oxford, 1608. 4°. 5284, 7655
Sermon at Paules Crosse on behalfe of Paules Churche. 1620. 4°. 3946
Sermon of pvblicke thankesgiuing for...his Majesty. 1619. 4°. . 3934
Vitis palatina. 1614. 4°. 3464, 3465
See Blackwell (G.). Large examination. 1607.
— King (H.), *Bp.* A sermon. 1621.
— Musket (G.). The Bishop of London. 1623.
King (John), *the younger.* *See* King (H.), *Bp.* Two sermons. 1625.
King (William). Theses and Verses in Adamson (J.). Εἰσόδια. 1618. 5960
King (William), *C.C.C.* Verses in Camb. Univ. Carmen. 1635. . 5770
Kingsmill (A.). Most excellent...treatise. 1577. 8°. . . . 1662
Kingsmill (Thomas). Classicum Poenitentiale. Oxoniae, 1605. 4°. 5272
Kinloch (David). Verses in Adamson (J.). Εἰσόδια. 1618. . . 5960
Kinloch (Patrick). Verses in Adamson (J.). Εἰσόδια. 1618. . 5960
Kinschot (Ludovicus a). *See* Thorius (R.). Hymnus. 1626.
Kinsman (Edward). *See* Villegas (A. de). Flos sanctorum. [16–] *etc.* 4°.
Kinwelmarsh (Antony). *See* Gascoigne (G.). The Posies. 1575.
Kinwelmarsh (Francis). *See* Gascoigne (G.). The Posies. 1575.
Kirbie (Jeffrey). *See* Biddulph (W.). Travels. 1609 etc.
Kirchner (Hermann). *See* Coryate (T.). Coryats Crudities. 1611.
Kirke (E.). *See* Spenser (E.). Shepheardes Calendar. 1586.
— — The faerie queen. 1611.
Kirke (John). Seven champions of Christendome. 1638. 4°. . . 3720
Kis (Stephanus) *Szegedinus.* Tabulae analyticae. 1593. 4°. . 7785
Kitchin (J.). Court leete and Court Baron. 1587. 8°. . . 1147
Kitchin (R.). *See* Kytchin.
Knaresborough. *See* Deane (E.). Spadacrene Anglica. 1626.

No.
Knatchbull (No.). Verses in Camb. Univ. Lacrymæ. 1619. . . 5689
Kneeling at the Lord's Supper. *See* Dispute. A Dispvte. 1608.
— Calderwood (D.). Solution. 1619. 4°.. 7806
Knel (Tho.), *junior*. Declaration of...Fluddes. 1571. 8°. . . 1761
See Northbrooke (J.). Poore mans garden. 1573.
Knewstub (J.). Confutation of monstrous and horrible heresies. 1579. 4°. 1803
Lectures...vpon Exodus xx. 1577. 4°. 1575
Sermon preached. 1579. 8°. 1804
Knight of the Tower. *See* La Tour Landry. [1484.]
Knight (Francis). Relation of seaven yeares slaverie under the Turkes of Argeire. 1640. 4°. 4676
Knight (John), *Captain*. *See* Fox (L.). North-west Fox. 1635.
Knight (William). Concordance axiomaticall. 1610. F°. . . 3453
See Hall (J.). Mundus alter et idem. [1605.] 8°.
Knivett. *See* Knyvett.
Knole (Henry). Verses *bis* in Wilson (Sir T.). Vita *bis*. 1551. . 631
Knolles (Ric.). Generall historie of the Turkes. Ed. 3. 1621. F°. . 2451
— Ed. 4. 1631. F°. 2462
— Ed. 5. 1638. F°. 2467
See Bodin (I.). Sixe bookes of a commonweale. 1606.
Knollys (Sir Francis). Speaches vsed in the Parleament... *See* Assertion for true and Christian Church-Policie. 1604.
See Informations. 1608.
Knott (E.). Charity mistaken. 1630. 8°. 7001
Christianity maintained. 1638. 4°. 6561
Direction to be observed by N. N. 1636. 8°. 7023
[Mercy and Truth.] *See* Chillingworth (W.). The Religion of Protestants. 1638.
Reply to M. Nicholas Smith. Douai, 1630. 8°. . . 6592
See Potter (C.). Want of Charitie. 1633 *etc.*
Knowles (James). Verses in Camb. Univ. Anthologia. 1632. . 5741
Knox (John). Answer to...an Anabaptist. Geneva, 1560. 8°. . 6319
Appellation (An admonition...Ps. xciiii). Geneva, 1558. 8°. . 6324
Confession...vpon the death of...Edward VI. 'Rome,' 1554. 8°. 1050
Copie of a letter sent to...Mary dowagire. 1556. (Sermon.) 16°. 6308
Copie of an epistle...vnto...Newcastle, and Barwike. Geneva, 1559. 16°. 6325
Fayth-full admonition. Kalykow, 20 Julij 1554. 8°. . . 6289
First blast of the trumpet against the monstrous regiment of women. 1558. 8°. 6318
[First booke of the history of the Reformation of Religion...of Scotland. 1587.] 8°. 7271
Godly letter sent to the fayethfull. 'Rome, S. Aungel,' 1554. 8°. 1051
[Letter to the Assembly at Stirling.] *See* Forbes (J.). Gemitus. 1631.
Sermon [on Isaiah xxvi. 13–20]. 1566. 8°. 7248
[Life.] *See* Smeton (T.). Ad virvlentvm A. Hamiltonii...dialogvm. 1579.
See Aylmer (J.). An harborowe. 1559.
— Ferguson (D.). Answer to ane Epistle...by R. Benedict. 1563.
— Turner (W.). Hunting of the Fox. [1561?]
Knyvett (Henry). Verses in Humphrey (L.). J. Juelli vita. 1573. . 837
Koenigsberg, *University*. *See* Ovid. Metamorphoses. 1584.
Koninck (Jan de). *See* Regius.
Koran. *See* Muhammad. Mohammedis Imposture. 1615.
Korydaleus (Theophilus). Ἔκθεσις περὶ Ῥητορικῆς. 1625. 8°. . . 3157
Krusius (Daniel), *pseud.* *See* Nukrois (E. de).
Kyffin (Maurice). *See* Kiffen. *See also* no. 7920.
Kynaston (Sir Francis). *See* Chaucer (G.). Amorvm. 1635.
Kynaston (Samuel), *M.A.* Verses in Chaucer (G.). Amorum. 1635. . 5414

No.

Kynder ( ), *Medicus*. Verses in Jones (J.). A briefe discourse. 1574. 1366
Kytchin (Richard). Verses in Cheke (Sir J.). De obitu M. Buceri. 1551. 734

L. (A.). Antimartinus. 1589. 4°. 1717
See Cowell (J.). Antisanderus. 1593.
— Leighton (A.). Speculum Belli sacri. 1624. 4°.
L. (C.), *I.C.* Gomersall (R.). Poems. 1633. 4270
L. (D.). *See* Drexelius (H.). School of Patience. 1640. 12°.
L. (Donaldus). Verses in Bauderon (B.). Pharmacopoea. 1639. . 5200
L. (E.), *M.D.* Verses in Holyoake (F.). Dictionarium. 1640. . 3058
L. (E.), *Oxon.* Verses in Du Bartas. Weekes. 1605–6 *etc.* . 2476 *etc.*
L. (Sir F.), *Kt.* Verses in Horatius. Odes. 1635 *etc.* . . 4857 *etc.*
L. (G.). Verses in Comenius. Porta linguarum. 1631. . . 4434
L. (H.). [Translator of I Peter v, *etc.* Qu. Hugh Jones, bishop of Llandaff?] *See* Bible, English (Bishops'). 1568. F°. . 964
L. (H. C.). *See* Monmouth, Earl of.
L. (H. N.). *See* N. (H.) L.
L. (I.), *Jesuit.* *See* Gordon Huntley (J.). Treatise. Controversy I, Pt. 2. 1614. 8°. 6894
— — Cont. II, Pt 3. 1614. 8°. 6895
L. (I.). *See* Lawes resolvtion. 1632. 4°.
L. (Jo.), *Merton.* Verses in Oxf. Univ. Horti. 1640. . . . 5499
L. (M. I.). *See* Anderson (P.). The ground. 1623.
L. (P.). *See* Musculus (W.). Of the lawful and vnlawful usurie. 1556.
L. (T.). Exposition of the xi–xiii. Revellation. 1623. 8° . . 6940
Verses in Camb. Univ. Gratulatio. 1623. . . . 5695
L. (T.) [*Anabaptist*]. *See* Some (R.). A godly treatise. 1589.
L. (T.), *D.M.P.* *See* Du Bartas. A learned summary. 1621. F°.
L. (W.). Verses in Spenser (E.). The faerie queen. 1590 *etc.* 1960 *etc.*
Helpe to discourse. 1635. 3833
Roberts (L.). The merchants mappe. 1638. . . . 5133
L. (W.), *of the Inner Temple.* Verses in Ferne (Sir J.). The blazon. 1586 2119
La. (Ed.). Verses in Oxf. Univ. Magd. Coll. 1612, . . . 5302
Laberius (Henricus). Verses in Ravisius (J.). Dialogi. 1581. . 1508
Labyrinthus Comoedia. 1636. *See* Hawkesworth (W.).
Lacey (Will.). Ivdgment of an university-man. 1639. 4°. . 6565
Lacius. *See* Calvin (J.). A faythfvl...treatyse. [1546?] . 6704–5
La Croix (Jean de). *See* Catholick Judge (The). 1623.
Lacy *Family*. *See* Ferne (Sir J.). The blazon. 1586.
Lad (Thomas). *See* Fuller (N.). Argument. 1607. 4°.
Ladensium Αὐτοκατάκρισις. 1640. *See* Baillie (R.).
Ladies Cabinet opened. 1639. 4°. 4949
Laet (Jaspar). Prenosticatio. Oxonie [1518]. Broadside. . . 5221
— Pynson. 1520. 4°. 271
Almanack and Prognostication. 1544. 12°. 6692
La Faye (A. de). Verses in Beza (T.). Psalmorum libri quinque. 1580. 1539
See Bèze (T. de). Propositions and principles. 1595. 8°.
La Grey (Thomas de). *See* Gray (T. de).
Laiton (Alexander). *See* Leighton.
Lake (Arthur). Sermons. 1629. F°. 3173
Ten sermons. 1640. 4°. 5140, 7801
Lake (Osmund). Probe theologicall. 1612. 4°. 2978
See Baro (P.). In Jonam. 1579.
— — De fide. 1580.
Lake (Stephen). Verses in Baro (P.). In Jonam. 1579. . . 850
Lake (Tho.). Verses in Camb. Univ. Epicedium. 1612. . . 5665
Lakyn (Daniel). Verses in Massinger (P.). The Renegado. 1630. . 4543
L'Allouette (Edmond de). *See* Catholicke Apologie. [1590?] 8°.

No.
L'Allouette (Edmond de), *cont.* *See* Du Perron (J. D., Cardinal). The Catholike Moderator. 1623.
La Marche (O. de). Resolved Gentleman. 1594. 4°. . . 7239, 7920
Lambarde (W.). Ἀρχαιονομία, s. de priscis anglorum legibus. 1568. 4°. 810
Archion. 1635. 8°. 5144
Dueties of constables. 1602. 8°. 2396
— 1610. 8°. 3242
— 1619. 8°. 3275
Eirenarcha. 1581. 8°. 1315
— 1602. 8°. 2397
— 1610. 8°. 3243
— 1619. 8°. 3276
Perambulation of Kent. 1576. 4°. 1621
— Ed. 2. 1596. 4°. 2053
— Ed. 3. [1640?] 8°. 4941
— — [With fresh title dated 1656.] 8°. 4942
Lambert (Hon. Carew). Verses in Camb. Univ. Lacrymæ. 1619.. 5689
Lambert (John). †1538. Treatyse. [1547?] 8°. 7905
Lambert (John), *Minister of Elham.* Of predestination and election. Canterbury, 1550. 8°. 5873
Lambeth Articles. Nine Assertions...20. day of Nouember...1595. *See* Prynne (W.). Antiarminianisme. [1629?] *etc.*
Lambinus (Dionysius). *See* Cicero. Epistolæ. 1585 *etc.*
Lambton (William), *S.J.C.* Verses in Camb. Univ. Voces. 1640. . 5836
Lamentable complaint of the Commonalty... For a Learned Ministery. [R. Waldegrave.] 1585. 8°. 1898
Lamentacion of England. 1558. 8°. 6741
Lamentacion of our Lady. W. de Worde. [1519.] 4°. . . . 232
La Motte Aigron (Jacques de). *See* Balzac. Letters. 1634. 4°.
Lamphire (Jo.). Verses in Oxf. Univ. Horti. 1640. . . . 5499
Lan (T.), *Coll. Reg. Soc.* [qu. Lancaster or Langley?]. Verses in Holyoake (F.). Dictionarium. 1640. 3058
Lancashire. *See* White (J.). The way. 1608.
Lancaster (Ric.). Verses in Camb. Univ. Epicedium. 1612. . . 5665
Lancaster (T.). *See* Lan.
Laney (Ben.). Verses in Camb. Univ. Anthologia. 1632. . . 5741
— — Fasciæ. 1633. 5808
— — Rex redux. 1633. 5748
Lanfrancus, *Mediolanensis.* *See* Braunschweig (H.). The noble experyence. 1525.
— Hall (J.). A most excellent...worke. 1565.
Langbaine (Gerard). Verses in Holyoake (F.). Dictionarium. 1640.. 3058
See Longinus (D.). Περὶ ὕψους. 1636.
— Ranchin (G.). A review. 1638.
Langdale (Alban). Verses in Seton (J.). Dialectica. 1631. . 5739
Langford (George). Manassehs miraculous metamorphosis. 1621. 4°. 3598
Search the scriptures. 1623. 4°. 4081
Langford (T.), *Camb. Brittan.* Verses in Yorke (J.). Union of Honour. 1640. 5216
Langham (William). Garden of health. Ed. 2. 1633. 4°. . 4004
Langhorne (Lancelot). Mary sitting at Christs feet. (Mris Mary Swaine.) 1630. 8°. 4260
— 1633. 8°. 4271
Verses in Camb. Univ. Lacrymae. 1619. 5689
Langius (Joseph). Verses in Aristotle. [Ethics.] 1634. . . 5717
Langland (William). *See* Piers the Ploughman. The vision. 1550.
Langley (Thomas). *See* Vergil (P.). An abridgement. 1546 *etc.*
See Lan.
Langlois ( ). Favorites chronicle. 1621. 4°. . . . 6928
Langston (Edmund). Verses in Hoby (Sir E.). Curry-combe. 1615. 3111

No.
Langton (Christopher). Introduction into phisycke. [1549?] 8°. . 677
Langton (G.). *See* Langton (William).
Langton (Will.). Verses in Oxford Univ. Magd. Coll. Luct. posth. 1612. 5302
— Camdeni Insignia. 1624. 5346
Langworth (Thomas), *T.C.C.* Verses in Camb. Univ. Epicedium. 1612. 5665
La Noue (F. de). Declaration...for Sedan and Iametz. 1589. 4°. 1955
Politicke and militarie discourses. 1588. 4°. . . . 2198
La Noue (Odet de), *sieur de Teligny*. Profit of Imprisonment etc. *See* Du Bartas. Weekes. 1605.
Lanquet (T.). Coopers Chronicle...with...Iovius and Sleidane. 1560. 4°. 506
— 1565. 4°. 6750
Epitome of Cronicles...of England...continued by T. Cooper. '1569.' 1549. 4°. 498
Lansbergen (Philip von). *See* Ephemerides. 1635.
— Ross (A.). Commentum. 1634.
Lant (Tho.), *Coll. Jesu.* Verses in Camb. Univ. Genethl. 1631. . 5731
— — Fasciæ. 1633. 5808
— — Rex redux. 1633. 5748
— — Hippocrates. 1633. 5812
— — Συνῳδία. 1637. 5790
Lany (Benjamin). *See* Laney.
La Perriere (G. de). Mirrour of policie. 1598. 4°. . . . 2424
— 1599. 4°. 2426
La Place (P. de). Treatise of the excellencie of a christian man. 1576. 8°. 1660
— 1577. 8°. 1661
La Planche (L. Regnier de). *See* Regnier de la Planche.
La Popelinière (Le Sieur). *See* Mercator (G.). Atlas minor. 1630. 4°.
La Popelinière (Henri Lancelot Du Voisin, sieur de). *See* Du Voisin.
La Primaudaye (P. de). French academie. 1589. 4°. . . . 1718
— 1618. F°. 3766
Lapworth (Ed.), *M.D.* Verses in Oxf. Univ. Magd. Coll. 1612. . 5302
— Camdeni Insignia. 1624. 5346
— Hippocrates. 1633. 5812
— Jorden (E.). A discourse. 1633. 4003
See Hakewill (G.). An apologie. 1630.
La Ramée (Pierre de). *See* Ramus.
Larke (John). *See* Book of Nobleness. [153–.] 545
La Roche de Chandieu (Antoine). *See* Sadeel.
Las Casas (B. de). Spanish Colonie. 1583. 4°. 1819
Lasco (J. a). Brevis et dilucida de sacramentis Eccl. Christi tractatio. 1552. 8°. 1100
Toute la forme et maniere du Ministere Ecclesiastique...a Londres. G. Ctematius, Emden, 1556. 8°. 6410
See Ames (W.). A fresh svit... 1633.
— Liturgies. London (Reformed Churches). L'ordre des prieres. 1552. 6719
— — Dutch Church. 1554. 8°. 3290
— Micron (M.). Den Kleynen Cathecismus. 1566.
— Whether Christian faith...[1553?]
La Serre (J. Puget de). *See* Puget de la Serre (J.).
Lassels (John). *See* Wyclif (J.). Uvicklieffes Wicket. [1548?]
Late newes from France. 1620. 4°. 6919
Lathbury (John). Liber moralium super trenis Iheremiae. Oxford, 1482. F°. 75
Lathom (W.). Verses in Xenophon. Cyrupædia. 1632. . . . 4714
Latimer (H.). Concio...28 Henrici octavi. Southwarke, 1537. 8°. 7818
Certayne godly sermons. 1562. 4°. 797
Fyrste Sermon. (The seconde Sermon.) [1549.] 8°. . . 914, 915
Frutefull sermons. 1571. 4°. 828
— 1584. 4°. 867

No.

Latimer (H.), *cont.* Frutefull sermons. 1596. 4°. 2846
— 1635. 4°. 4636
Sermon to the clergie. Berthelet, 1537. 8°. 438
27 Sermons preached. (The seven sermons.) 1562. 4°. . 798
Certayne...conferences. *See* Ridley (N.). 1556 *etc.*
See A. (J.), *of Ailward.* An historicall narration. 1631.
La Tour Landry (Geoffrey de). Knight of the Tower. Caxton [1484]. F°. 24
La Trimouille (Gratiana). Conuersion of a most Noble Lady. 1608. 4°. 1390
Latteburius (Johannes). *See* Lathbury.
Laud (Will.). Articles exhibited against. 1640. 4°. 7640
Relation of the conference betweene W. Lawd...and Mr Fisher. 1639. F°. 4393
Replie to a relation of the conference. 1640. 4°. 7051
Sermon at White Hall. 24 March. 1621. 1622. 4°. . . 2815
Sermon Feb. 6. at Westminster. 1625. 4°. 2822
Speech...in the starr-chamber. 14 June 1637. at the censure of J. Bastwick etc. 1637. 4°. . . . 4378, 4379, 7596, 7719
Answer To Mr Fishers Relation. *See* White (F.). Replie. 1624. 2453
[Visitation at Canterbury 14 April 1635.] *See* Boughen (E.). Two sermons. 1635. 4362
[Metropolitical Visitation. June 3. 1635.] *See* Wall (G.). Sermon. 1635.
[Visitation. March 1. 1636.] *See* Hoard (S.). Churches avthority. 1637. 4641
See Andrewes (L.). xcvi. sermons... 1629 *etc.*
— Articles. (London Diocese.) 1628 *etc.*
— Augustine. Saint Avstins religion. 1625.
— Baillie (R.). Ladensium Αὐτοκατάκρισις. 1640.
— Divine and politike observations. 1638.
— Prynne (W.). Lord Bishops not Lords Bishops. 1640.
— Scotland, Church of. Common Prayer. 1637. F°. 5979, 7768
Lauder (Will.). Verses in Forbes (P.). Funerals. 1637. . 6007 *bis*
Lauderdale (J. Maitland, duke of). [Autograph.] 5797
Laudinius, *Knight of Jerusalem.* *See* Laudivius.
Laudivius, *Knight of Jerusalem.* *See* Muhammad II. The Turkes Secretorie. 1607. 4°.
Launay. *See* Boiaistuau.
Launæus (G.). *See* Lawne (Will.).
Laurens (Bartholomaeus). *See* Mantuanus (B.). Adolescentia. 1569 *etc.*
Laurent (Frere). *See* Royal Book.
Laurentius, *grammarian.* *See* Valla (L.).
Laurentius (Ægidius). *See* Lawrence (Giles).
Laurentius (Andreas). Discourse of the preservative of the sight &c. Trans. R. Surphlet. 1599. 4°. 2913
See Crooke (H.). Μικροκοσμολογία. 1631.
Laurentius (Bartholomeus). *See* Laurens.
Laurentius Gulielmi, *de Saona.* *See* Gulielmus (Laurentius). . . 83
Laval (Antoine de), *sieur de Belair.* *See* Tilenus (D.). True Copy. 1605.
La Vardin (J. de). Historie of G. Castriot, surnamed Scanderbeg. 1596. F°. 2239
Lavater (Ludwig). Of ghostes and spirites. Trans. R. H. 1596. 4°. 2719
Lavender (Theophilus). *See* Biddulph (W.). Trauels of certaine Englishmen. 1609 *etc.*
Lavinius (Lucius). *See* Du Val (M.). Rosa Hispani-Anglica. [1623?]
Law. *See* Lawes resolution.
Lawe (Robert). Effigiatio veri sabbathismi. 1605. 4°. . . . 2352
Lawne (Christopher). *See* Ainsworth (H.). Animadversion. 1613.
Lawne (Will.). Verses in Gerard (J.). Herball. 1597. . . 2348
See Calvin (J.). An abridgement. 1585.

No.

Lawrence (Giles), *Prof. of Greek*. Verses in Bernard (J.). Oratio. 1568. 930
— Demosthenes. Thre orations. 1570. 1409
— Humphrey (L.). J. Jvelli vita. 1573. 837
See Bible, English (Bishops'). 1568. 964
Lawrence (John). Golden trumpet...11 April 1624. 1624. 4°. . 4792
Lawrence (Thomas). Sermon...at White-Hall. 7 Feb. 1636. 1637. 4°. 4377, 7720
Laws and Statutes. *See* Statutes.
Lawes and Ordinances of Warre for...his Maiesties army royall...for the northern parts...under...Thomas earl of Arundel. Newcastle, 1639. 4°. 5907
Lawes resolution of womens rights. 1632. 4°. 5075
Lawson (Charles). Verses in Camb. Univ. Thr.-thr. 1603. . . 5616
— — Epicedium. 1612. 5665
Lawson (William). New orchard and garden...with the Country Housewifes garden...as also the husbandry of bees. Ed. 2. 1623. 4°. 4784
— *See* Markham (G.). Way to get wealth. 1631. 4°.
— Ed. 3. 1638. 4°. 5192
Layfield (Edward), *M.A.* *See* Articles. Essex Archdeaconry. 1635 *etc.*
Layfield (John). Verses in Leighton (Sir W.). Teares. 1613. . 2868
See Bible, English (Royal). 1611.
Lea (Roger). *See* Ley.
League. *See* Masque of the League. 7243
Leak (William). Sermon...by the Cape of Good Hope...1614. 1617. 4°. 4059
Leake (Jaspar). *See* Proclamation. 1619. Broadside. . . 2806
Leander à Sto. Martino. *See* John Jones.
Leander de S. Martin. *See* John Jones.
Leases. *See* Tables of Leases. 1628.
Leaver (Thomas). *See* Lever.
Leche (William). Verses in Cheke (Sir J.). De obitu M. Buceri. 1551. 734
Leche (William). Verses in Camb. Univ. Genethl. 1631. . . 5731
Lechmere (Edmund). *See* Stratford.
L'Écluse (Charles de). *See* Plutarchus. [Parallel Lives.] 1603 *etc.*
L'Écluse (Jean de). *See* Fowler (J.). Shield of defence. 1612.
Ledenbergh (Gilles van). *See* Proclamation. 1618. 4°. . . 7914
Lee (Edward), *M.A.* Verses in Bodleiomnema. 1613. . . . 7756
Lee (Richard). Spirituall spring. 1625. 4°. 3445
Leech (David). *See* Leochaeus.
Leech (Humphry). *See* Benefield (S.). Doctrinæ christianæ. 1610.
Leech (James). Plaine...catechisme. Cambridge, 1605. 8°. . . 5632
Leech (John). Verses in Baret (J.). Alvearie. 1573. . . 7249
Leech (John). Musae priores. 1620. 8°. 7548
Verses *ter* in Adamson (J.). Εἰσόδια. 1618. . . . 5960
Leech (William). *See* Leche.
Leek (*Hon.* Edward). Verses in Camb. Univ. Συνῳδία. 1637. . 5790
Leek (James), *Pet.* Verses *bis* in Camb. Univ. Fasciae. 1633. . 5808
— — Συνῳδία. 1637. 5790
Leet, Courts. *See* Modus observandi. 1530.
Leet (J. D.). Verses in Parkinson (J.). Theatrum. 1640. . 4680
Leeuwis (Dionysius de). *See* Dionysius Carthusianus.
Lefèvre (R.). Recuyell of the Histories of Troy. W. Caxton, Bruges [1475]. F°. 117
Recuile of the Histories of Troie. 1553. F°. 1078
Ancient historie of the destruction of Troy. Ed. 5. 1617. 4°. . 4153
— Ed. 6. 1636. 4°. 4211
History of Jason. Antwerp, 1492. F°. 126
Lefrancus. *See* Bullinger (H.). A hundred Sermons. 1561.
Legard (Chr.). Verses in Camb. Univ. Lacrymae. 1619. . . 5689
Legard (Ric.). Verses in Camb. Univ. Genethl. 1631. . . 5731
Legate (John). *See* Thomas (T.). Dictionarium. 1592 etc.

No.
Legenda (Sarum). Higman and Hopyl, Paris [1490]. F°. . . 132
W. Hopyl, Paris, imp. F. Byrckman, 1518. F°. . . . 6154
Legenda Aurea. *See* Voragine (J. de).
Legh (Edward). *See* Leigh.
Legh (G.). Accedens of Armory. 1562. 8°. 1114
— 1576. 4°. 1133
Legrand (Jacques). Book of good manners. Caxton, 11 May, 1487. F°. 31
— W. de Worde [1499]. 4°. 64
— — 1507. 4°. 154
Legraunt (Jacques). *See* Legrand.
Le Grys (Sir Robert). *See* Barclay (J.). Argenis. 1628 *etc.*
See Velleius Paterculus. 1632. 12°.
Legthus (Henry). Verses in Cambridge Lachrymae. 1587 (fol. 43). . 2123
Leicester (Robert Dudley, earl of). *See* C. (R.). Copie of a letter to the Earl of Leicester. 1586. 1681
See Parsons (R.). Copie of a letter. 1594. . . . 6810
Leicestershire. *See* Burton (W.). The Description. [1622.]
Leigh (Dorothy). Mothers blessing. 1618. 12°. 7917
— 1640. 12°. 4677
Leigh (Edward). Critica Sacra. 1639. 4°. 5005
Treatise of the divine promises. 1633. 4°. . . . 4446
Leigh (Nicolas). Verses in Baret (J.). Alvearie. 1573. . . 7249
Leigh (Olliphant). Verses in Camb. Univ. Lacrymae. 1619. . 5689
Leigh (Richard). *See* Mendoza (B.). The copie of a letter. 1588.
Leigh (Richard). Verses in Taylor (John). Workes. 1630. . . 3812
Leigh (Val.). Moste profitable...science, of Surueying. 1577. 4°. 1856
Leighton (Alex.). Appeal to the parliament. [1628.] 4°. . . 6980
Speculum belli sacri. 1624. 4°. 6952
See Canne (J.). A necessitie of separation. 1634.
Leighton (Sir William). Teares or lamentations of a sorrowfull soule. 1613. 4°. 2868
Leipzig, Battle of. *See* Russell (J.). The two...battels. 1634.
See Sweden. The Swedish Discipline. 1632.
— — The Swedish Intelligencer.
Leitrim (Bened. Sherard, baron of). Verses in Oxf. Univ. Horti. 1640. 5499
Leius (Matthias). De triumphata barbarie. 1621. 4°. . . 7491
Le Jay (President). *See* France. Louis XIII. 1617.
Le Jeune ( ), *Surgeon to Louis XIII.* *See* Guillemeau (J.). A worthy treatise. [159-] *etc.*
Leland (J.). Assertio inclytissimi Arturij. 1544. 4°. . . . 757
Ἐγκώμιον τῆς εἰρήνης. 1546. 4°. 724
Genethliacon...Eaduerdi principis. 1543. 4°. . . . 722
Κύκνειον ᾆσμα. Cygnea cantio. [1545.] 4°. . . . 723
Laboryouse Journey...for Englandes Antiquitees...enlarged by J. Bale. 1549. 8° 952
Learned and true assertion of Prince Arthure. 1582. 4°. . 1926
Naeniae in mortem T. Viati equitis. 1542. 4°. . . 720
Principum ac illustrium encomia. 1589. 4°. . . . 2203
[New Yeares Gyft and Leland's Ghost.] *See* Brooke (R.). Discouerie of...errors. [1595?]
Le Loyer (P.). Treatise of specters. 1605. 4°. . . . 2860
Le Macon (R.). Funerailles de Sodome. 1610. 8°. . . 2265
Le Maire (Jaques). Verses in Caus (S. de). La Perspective. 1612. . 6636
Lemnius (L.). Herbal for the bible. 1587. 8°. . . . 2044
Touchstone of Complexions. 1633. 4°. 2040
See Linius.
Lemoine (G.). *See* Monachus.
Lennard (Samson). Verses in Brooke (R.). A discovery. 1622. . 2793
See Charron (P.). Of Wisedome. [1615?] *etc.*
— Mornay (P. de). The mysterie of iniquitie. 1612. F°.

No.

Lennard (Samson), *cont.* *See* Perrin (J. P.). The bloody rage. 1624.
Lennox (James, duke of). Verses in Camb. Univ. Dolor. 1625. . 5701
— — Epithalamium. 1625. 5702
Lenton (Francis). The Young Gallants Whirligigg. 1629. 4°. . 7802
Lentulus (Scipio). Italian grammer. Trans. H. Granthan. 1575. 8°. 7758
Leo, *Emperor.* [Λόγος ἐγκωμιαστικὸς εἰς...Ιωάννην τὸν Χρυσόστομον.] *See* Chrysostom...opera... Tom. 8. 1613. 5903
Leo I, *the Great.* [Certain Sermons.] *See* Treatise of Iustification. 1569.
Leo X, *Pope.* *See* Henry VIII. Libello huic insunt. 1521.
— Indulgence. 1515, 1517.
Leo (Johannes). Geographical historie of Africa. 1600. F°. . 1745
Leochaeus (David). Verses in Adamson (J.). Εἰσόδια. 1618. . . 5960
— Forbes (P.). Funerals. 1635. 6007
Leochæus (Joannes). *See* Leech.
Leonard (Samson). *See* Lennard.
Leone (Giovanni). *See* Leo (J.).
Leopold, *Duke of Austria.* Euerlasting Prognostication. *See* Hill (T.). Arte of Gardening. 1608. 4°.
Leowitz (C. von). Brevis et perspicua ratio ivdicandi genituras. 1558. 4°. 1155
Le Petit (Jean François). Low-country Commonwealth. Trans. E. Grimeston. 1609. 4°. 3571
See Grimstone (E.). Generall historie. 1609, 1627.
Leppington (Henry Carey, baron Carey of). *See* Monmouth, Earl of.
Lepton (John). Verses in Leighton (Sir W.). Teares. 1613. . 2868
Lepus (Constantinus). *See* Breviarium. Sarum. 1524. 8°.
— — Ab. 1525? 16°.
Le Roy (Guillaume). *See* Eneydos. [1490.] F°.
Le Roy or Regius (L.). Of the interchangeable course. Trans. R. Ashley. 1594. F°. 7460
See Aristotle. Politiques. 1598.
Lery (Jean de). *See* Boemus (J.). Manners...of all nations. 1611. 4°.
L'Escluse (De). *See* L'Écluse.
Lesdiguiéres (François de Bonne, duc de). *See* Rochelle, *Assembly in.* A letter. 1621.
Leslæus (Will.). Verses in Forbes (P.). Funerals. 1635. . . 6007
Leslie (Henry). Examen conjurationis scoticae. Dublini, 1639. 4°. 6068
Sermon...before his Majesty. 19 July 1625. Oxford, 1625. 4°. 5352
Sermon. 28 Aug. 1627. 1627. 4°. 2556
Speech...visitation...1638. 1639. 4°. 5152
Treatise of...the church. Dublin, 1637. 4°. 6061
Leslie (John). [Part 2] A treatise touching...Marie Queene of Scotland. [Part 3]...the Regiment of Women. Liége, 1571. 8°. . 6430
Treatise touching...Marie queene of Scotland. 1584. 8°. . 6253
Lesly (John). Epithrene. 1631. 8°. 4553
L'Espine (J. de). Confutation of Popish Transubstantiation. 1592. 8°. 2379
Very excellent...discourse touching the Tranquilitie. Cambridge, 1592. 4°. 5552
See Rouspeau (Y.). Two treatises. 1584. 8°.
— Vigor (S.). Acts. 1602.
Lesse (Nicholas). *See* Augustine. Worke of the predestination of saints. 1550.
Lessius (L.). Consultation what faith and religion is best. (Appendix.) 1621. 8°. 6542
Hygiasticon etc. Trans. Ed. 1. Cambridge, 1634. 12°. . 5833
— Ed. 2. Cambridge, 1634. 12°. 5762
— Ed. 3. Cambridge, 1636. 12°. 5782
Rawleigh his ghost. Trans. A. B. 1631. 8°. . . . 7008
See Widdrington (R.). Last reioynder. 1619 etc. 4°.

No.
Letters Patent. (Sir A. Aston etc.) 20 Nov. 1606. [1606?] 4°. . 2595
True transcript and publication...for...the Publicke Register for generall Commerce. By Sir A. Gorges. 1611. 4°. . . 3079
See Office of Generall Remembrance. 1617. 4°.
29 Jan. 1627. (Ministers of the Palatinate.) 1627. Broadside. . 2831
6 Aug. 1630. (Exiled ministers of the Palatinate.) 1630. Broadside. 2673
Lettow, Grand Dukedom of. *See* Poland. Vladislaus IV. 1635.
Leucus (I.), Ὁμότεχνος. *qu.* White? Verses in Hawkins (W.). En Priscianus. 1632. 4562
— — Corolla. 1634. 5803
Leurechon (Jean). *See* Etten (Hendrik van).
Leus (Edwardus), *M.A. Merton College. See* Lee.
Lever (Christopher). Heaven and Earth, Religion and Policy. 1608. 8°. 2900
Historie of the defendors of the catholiqve faith. 1627. 4°. . . 4419
Holy pilgrime. 1631. 8°. 5117
Lever (Ri.). Verses in Napier (J.). A description. 1618. . . 2112
Lever (Thomas). Letter... *See* Coverdale (M.). Certain...letters. 1564.
Sermon...14 Dec. 1550. [1550?] 8°. 887
Three faithful sermons. [1572?] 8°. 1178
Levin (William). *See* Harvey (W.). Ciceronianus. 1577.
Levingston (Alexander). Verses in Camb. Univ. Anthologia. 1632. . 5741
Lewis (William). *See* Lodovicus.
Lewkenor (Edmund). Verses in Stanyhurst (R.). Harmonia. 1570. . 749
Lewkenor (Sir Edward). Threnodia. 1606. 4°. 2082
Lewkenor (Edward). [Funeral.] *See* Oldmayne (T.). Lifes brevitie. 1636. 4°.
Lewkenor (Sir L.). Estate of English fugitives. 1595. 4°. . . 2383
— Newly corrected. 1596. 4°. 2384
Verses in Coryate (T.). Coryats Crudities. 1611. . . . 3076
See Contarini (G.). The Commonwealth. 1599.
— La Marche (O. de). The Resolved Gentleman. 1594. 4°. 7920
Lewkenor (S.). Discourse of forraine cities. 1600. 4°. . . 2154
Lewsus (Thomas). Verses in Cheke (Sir J.). De obitu M. Buceri. 1551. 734
Ley (John). Patterne of pietie... Mrs Jane Ratcliffe. 1640. 8°. . 3060
Ley (Roger). Bruising of the serpents head. 1622. 4°. . . 3848
Two sermons...by R. L. and J. Squire. 1619. 4°. . . 3329
Ley (Will.). Verses in Oxf. Univ. Horti. 1640. . . . 5499
Leyden University. *See* Hommius (F.). LXX. disputationes. 1630 *etc.*
— Vossius (G. J.). Theses theologicæ. 1628.
Leyden, *Church at. See* Ainsworth (H.). An animadversion. 1613.
Leydenberg (Gilles van). *See* Ledenbergh.
Lhoyd, Lhuyd, or Lhwyd. *See* Lloyd, Llwyd.
Libanius Sophista. *See* Chrysostom...opera. 1613.
Libellus sophistarum. W. de Worde, 1510. 4°. 162
Libellus supplex imperatoriæ maiestati...nomine Belgarum ex inferiori Germania. 1571. 8°. 829
Liber assisarum et placitorum corone. J. Rastell [1516?]. F°. . 342
Liber festivalis. *See* Mirk (J.). Festyall. [149–] *etc.*
Liber precum publicarum. [1560.] 4°. 755
— 1574. 8°. 1527
— 1594. 8°. 2101
— 1638. 8°. 4664
Liber precum. *See* Preces.
Liber soliloquiorum. *See* Psalter. Sarum and York. 1504.
Licence of Books. *See* Alsop (J.). 1639.
— Arundel and Surrey. 1639.
— Austine (Robert). 1633.
— Baker (S.). 1635–1638.
— Bray (W.).
— Brown (Tho.). 1640.

No.

Licence of Books, *cont.*:
See Coke (Sir J.). 1634-1637.
— Fox (Simon).
— Hansley (J.). 1640.
— Hansley (J.). 1639.
— Hay (Alex.). 1608.
— Haywood (W.). 1633 (1635).
— Herbert (H.). 1640.
— Martin (Edward). 1629-1631.
— Oliver (J.). 1637-1638.
— Reade (R.). 1639.
— Saravia (H.). 1605.
— Weekes (T.). 1637-1640.
— Windebank (F.). 1639.

Cambridge. [5 Feb. 1638.] *See* Davenant (J.). 1639. . . 5805
— — Du Praisac. Art of Warre. 1639.
— — Rohan (H. duc de). Complete Captain. 1640.
London. *College of Physicians.* [Licence signed by W. Clement, T. Gulston, I. Argent.] *See* Hart (Jas.). Κλινική. 1633.
— — *See* Jorden (E.). A discourse. 1633.
Ireland. Parry (E.). 1639.
[Bancroft's licensing of Jesuit books.] *See* Hughes (L.). Certain grievances. Pp. 14, 15. 1640. 4°.
Roman Catholic. *See* Bergaigne (Joseph). 1625 6553
— Bondot (P.), *Bp.* 1625. 6553
— Chamberlinus (R.). 1617.
— Colvenerius (G). 1635. 7894
— Gamaches (P. de). 1619.
— Jones (J.). 1617.
— Mulet (I.). 1619.
— Redman (J.). 1617.
— Soto (A. de). 1617.
— St (Ed.), *S.T.D.* 1635 7894
Licence (Ecclesiastical). London Diocese. Ab. 1640. 7061
Lichefield (Nicholas). *See* Lopes de Castanheda (F.). 1582.
Lichfield, *Cathedral Chapter.* (Visitation.) *See* Overton (W.). Oratio. 1601.
Lichfield (Ed.). Verses in Barlow (W.). Vita R. Cosin. 1598. . 1707
Lichfield (Leonard), *printer.* Verses in Oxf. Univ. Horti. 1640. . 5499
Lidley. Praiers. *See* Bull (H.). Christian Praiers. 1578. 16°.
Liebault (Jean). *See* Estienne (C.). Maison Rustique. 1616.
Liebler. *See* Temple (W.). Pro Mildapetti. 1581.
Light for the ignorant. 1638. 4°. 6369
Lightfoot (Ant.). [Engraved metal plate.] 1636. 8°. . . . 7024
Lightfoot (John). Erubhin or miscellanies. 1629. 8°. . . . 4428
Lilburne (John). Worke of the beast. 1638. 4°. 6370
Lilly (John), *the Euphuist.* *See* Lyly.
Lily (Dorothy). *See* Lily (Peter). Two Sermons. 1619.
Lily (John). Verses in Lok (H.). Ecclesiastes. 1597. . . . 2246
Lily (Maria). Verses in Lily (P.). Two Sermons. 1619. . . . 3424
Lily (Peter). Two sermons. 1619. 4°. 3424
Lily (W.). De octo orationis partium constructione libellus...emendatus ab Eras. Roter. et scholiis H. Primæi, L. Coxi. 1540. 4°. . 455
Rudimenta. J. Byddell. n.d. 8°. 575
Short introduction of grammar...Latine...(Brevissima institutio). [Geneva.] 1557. 8°. 6316
— [1560?] 4°. 756
[Introduction to the eight parts of speech.] Assignes of J. Batersbie. 160- ? 8°. 6794

No.
Lily (W.), *cont.* Brevissima institutio ... grammatices cognoscendae. Assign. J. Battersbij. 1602. 8°. 7307
Short introduction to grammar. J. Norton. 1606. 8°. . . 7387
Short introduction. (Brevissima institutio.) J. Norton, 1607 (-6). 8°. 2359
Shorte introduction. (Brevissima institutio.) Cambridge, 1634. 8°. 5763
Verses in Horman (W.). Vulgaria. 1519. 267
See Horman (W.). Antibossicon. 1521.
Limbert (Stephen). Verses in Parkhurst (J.). Ludicra. 1573. . 838
— Whitney (G.). A choice. 1586. 6496
Limbo-mastix. 1604. 4°. 1889
Linacre (Robert. *See* Linaker.
Linacre (T.). De emendata structura latini sermonis. 1524. 4°. . 285
See Galen. De naturalibus facultatibus. 1523. 4°.
— — De temperamentis. 1521.
Linaker (Rob.). Comfortable treatise. 1590. 8°. 2226
— Ed. 2. 1601. 8°. 1781
— Ed. 5. 1625. 12°. 3446
Linche (Ric.). Fountaine of ancient fiction. 1599. 4°. . . . 2427
Lincoln, County of. Answere to the petitions of the Traytours and rebelles. 1536. 4°. 434
Lincoln Diocese. Form of Thanksgiving. Lincoln and Westminster. 1603. 4°. 6854
Abridgement of that booke which the ministers of Lincoln delivered to his Maiestie. 1605. 4°. 6378-9
— 1617. 8°. 6909
See Heylyn (P.). Antidotvm Lincolniense. 1637.
— Form of Thanksgiving. *See* Williams (J.). The holy table. 1637. 4°. 7040
Lincoln (Edm.), *Magd. Coll.* Verses in Camb. Univ. Fasciae. 1633. . 5808
— Carmen. 1635. 5770
— *Συνωδία.* 1637. 5790
Lindesius or Lindesay (Joannes). Verses in Buchanan (G.). Rerum scoticarum historia. 1582. 5920
Lindsay (Sir David). Ane Dialog betuix Experience and ane Courteour. St Andrews. [Ab. 1554.] 4°. . . . - . . . 5995
Dialogue betweene Experience and a Courtier. T. Purfoot and W. Pickering. 1566. 4°. 1367
— T. Purfoot. 1581. 4°. 7245
Lindsay (David), *bishop of Edinburgh.* True narration of...the generall assembly of the Church of Scotland. 1621. 4°. . . . 3136
Theses in Adamson (J.). Εἰσόδια. 1618. 5960
Verses in Person (D.). Varieties. 1635. 4365
Forbes (P.). Funerals. 1637. 6007
See Calderwood (D.). Solution. 1619. 4°. 7806
Lindsay (John). *See* Lindesay.
Lindsell (Augustine), *Bp.* *See* Theophylactus. Commentarii. 1636. F°.
Linford. *See* Lynford.
Ling (N.). *See* Lynge.
Lingelsheim (G.). *See* Dominis (M. A. de). A manifestation. 1606.
Linius (Livinus) [*qu.* Lemnius?]. Verses in Lucianus. Lvciani dialogi. 1531. 376
Linschoten (J. H. van). Discours of voyages. 1598. F°. . . 1975
Linus. [*Gr. Lat.*] *See* Poetae minores. 1635.
Lipsius (Justus). De constantia. Ed. auctior. 1586. 8°. . . 7295
Two Bookes of Constancie. Trans. J. Stradling. 1595. 4°. 1453
De militia Romana. *See* Xenophon. Historie. Trans. J. Bingham. 1623. F°. 7627
Sixe bookes of politickes. 1594. 4°. 2232
Oratio in calumniam. 1615. 4°. 2991
Oration against calumnie. *See* Stafford (A.). Meditations. 1612. 12°. 2515

No.
Lipsius (Justus), *cont.* Tractatus ad historiam romanam cognoscendam. Cantabrigiae, 1592. 8°.
See Seneca (L. A.). The workes. 1614 *etc.*
— Thomson (G.). Vindex Veritatis. 1606.
Lisbon. [English Nunnery.] *See* Robinson (T.). Anatomy. 1622.
L'isle (Francis de), *pseud.* *See* Regnier de La Planche (L.).
L'Isle (Gul. de). *See* Insulanus.
Lisle (Lau.). *See* Overbury (Sir T.). His Wife. 1638.
Lisle (William). Divers ancient monuments. 1638. 4°. 5193, 7652, 7653
Saxon treatise concerning the old and new testament...with...a Testimonie of Antiquitie. 1623. 4°. 4785
Verses in Camb. Univ. Lacrymæ. 1619. 5689
— — Dolor. 1625. 5701
— — Epithalam. 1625 *bis.* 5702
— — Genethl. 1631. 5731
— — Anthologia. 1632. 5741
— — Fasciae. 1633. 5808
— — Rex redux. 1633. 5748
— — Hippocrates. 1633. 5812
See Heliodorus. 1638. 4°.
Lister (Lawrence), *K.C.* Verses in Camb. Univ. Συνῳδία. 1637. . 5790
Lister (Sir Matthew), *M.D.* Verses in Hippocrates. 1633. . . 5812
— Parkinson (J.). Theatrum. 1640. 4680
Litany. [London? 1558?] 8°. 6743
See Becon (T.). The Pomāder of Prayer. 1558.
Litany of B.V.M. *See* Scupoli (L.). The Spiritual Conflict. 1613.
Litchfield. *See* Lichefield.
Lithgow (William). Totall discourse of...nineteene yeares. 1640. 4°. 3729
True...discourse upon the...last siege of Breda. 1637. 4°. . 3715
Lithodius (Joannes). Verses in Bale (J.). Illustrium scriptorum. 1548. 6314
Little John. *See* Book of Courtesy.
Little (Francis). *See* Sutton (T.). The Good Fight of Faith. 1624. 4°.
Littleton (A.). Verses in Hopton (A.). Speculum. 1611. . . 3638
Littleton (Sir T.). Tenores Novelli (French). Lettou and Machlinia, 1482. F°. 90
— Rouen [1490]. F°. 139
Teners newe correcte. Pynson [1510]. F°. 303
— [Ab. 1510.] F°. 7074
— R. Redman [1530?]. 394
— Berthelet, 1530. 8°. 419
— 1579. 8°. 1138
— R. Tottell, 1591. 8°. 1151
— Stationers, 1612. 12°. 3253
— Ass. of J. More, 1639. 16°. 7643
Tenures (English). W. Powell, 1548. 8°. . . 713 (Corr. p. 1594)
— T. Wight, 1600. 8°. 2389
— Stationers, 1621. 8°. 7794
See Coke (Sir Ed.). The first part. 1628 etc.
— Rastell (J.). Exposiciones Terminorum. . . . 352, 414
Liturgia Inglesa. [R. Barker, 1615?] 4°. 2652
Liturgies. Denmark. *See* Calvin (J.).
Dutch Church in London. *See below* Holland. 3290
England. Bidding Prayer. *See* Bidding Prayer.
Common Prayer. *See* Common Prayer.
— *See* Triall of the English Liturgie. . . . 7039
— (Latin). *See* Liber precum publicarum.
Form of Prayer. *See* Form of Prayer.
Form of Thanksgiving. *See* Form of Prayer.
Litany. *See* Litany.
Orarium. 1546. 596
Order for Prayer. 1594. 1699

No.

Liturgies. England, *cont.*
Order of Communion. *See* Communion (Order of the). 604
Order of Matrimony. *See* Order of Matrimony. . 7151
Order of Prayer. 1580. 1666
Order of the Communion. 1548. . . . 604
Ordination Service. *See* Ordination Service.
Primer. *See* Primer. *See also* Orarium.
Psalter. *See* Psalter.
Glastonbury. *See below* London.
London (Reformed Churches). L'ordre des prieres...de Londres et...de Glastonbury. 1552. 16°. . . 6719
Dutch Church. 1554. 3290
Sarum. Antiphoner. *See* Antiphoner.
Breviary. *See* Breviarium.
Directorium. *See* Directorium.
Epistles and Gospels. *See* Epistles.
Expositio hymnorum et sequentiarum. *See* Expositio.
Horae. *See* Primer.
Hymni. *See* Expositio hymnorum.
— Hymns.
— Psalterium cum hymnis.
Legenda. *See* Legenda.
Manual. *See* Manuale.
Missal. *See* Missale.
Ordinale. *See* Directorium.
Pica. *See* Directorium.
Portiforium. *See* Breviarium.
Primer. *See* Primer.
Psalter. *See* Psalterium.
Rituale. *See* Manuale.
Sequences. *See* Expositio.
York. Breviary. *See* Breviarium (York).
Hymns. *See* Psalterium cum hymnis.
Missal. *See* Missale (York).
France. Reformed Church. *See* Bible, English. Psalms (Metr.). 1632. 12°. 3993
French Church, Glastonbury. *See above* London (Reformed Churches). 6719
— London. *See above* London (Reformed Churches). 1552. 16°. 6719
— — Lasco (J. a). Toute la forme. 1556. 8°.
Geneva. Forme of common praiers, and the Catechism, by J. Caluyne. 1550. 8°. 669
(English Congregation.) Forme of prayers...(One and fiftie psalmes.) Geneva, 1556. 8°. 6317
— Forme of prayer. 1561. 8°. 6326
— Forme of prayers...in the Eng. Church at Geneua, approued... by the Church of Scotland. 1584. 16°. 6777
Germany. Reformed Church. *See* Bible, English. Psalms. Metr. 1632. 12°. 3993
Holland. *See above* London. Dutch Church. 1554. . . 3290
Ireland. *See* Common Prayer. 1621, 1637.
— — (Irish). 1608.
Rome. Manual. *See* Ritual.
Missal. *See* Missae aliquot. 1615. 4°. 6615-6
— Missale parvum. 1626. 4°. 6620
— Disclosing. The dysclosing of the Canon of the Masse. [1549.]
See Viret (P.). De Cautelen. 1568 etc.
Scotland. *See* Book of Common Order. 1584, 1596, 1615 etc.
Order of Excommunication. 1569. *See* Book of Common Order. 1596.

No.

Liturgies. Scotland, *cont.* Order of Fasting. 1565. *See* Book of Common Order. 1596.
Forme of prayers. *See above* Geneva. (English Congregation.) 1584. 6777
Psalter. *See* Bible O.T. Psalms (Metrical) (S. and H.) Dort, 1601. 8°. 6509
Scotland, *Episcopal Church.* Common Prayer. 1637. F°. 5979, 7768
Strassburg. Liturgia sacra seu ritus ministerii in ecclesia peregrinorum...Argentinæ...per V. Pollanum. 1551. 8°. . . 1097
[History.] *See* Vergil (P.). Abridgement. 1551. . . 622
Lively (E.). Annotationes in quinque priores ex minoribus Prophetis. 1587. 8°. 1712
True chronologie of the times of the Persian Monarchy...against M. Beroald. 1597. 8°. 2905
Verses in Baro (P.). In Jonam. 1579. 850
See Bible, English. (Royal.) 1611.
Lives and Answers. *See* Baldwin (W.). Treatise of morall philosophy.
Livius. Libri omnes. 1589. 8°. 2048
Romane historie. 1600. F°. 2428
Historie of...Anniball and Scipio...by Antonie Cope. '1568.' 1548. 4°. 495
Hystory of...Annibal and Scipio. 1590. 8°. 1770
[Decade I.] *See* Macchiavelli (N.). Discourses. 1636.
Ll. (D.), *Dr J. C.* [*qu.* David Lloyd?] Verses in Salisbury (Sir T.). History of Ioseph. 1636. 4023
LL. (R.), *Theo-muso-philus.* Verses in Ravenscroft (T.). Briefe discourse. 1614. 2029
LL. (T.), *artium Magister.* [*qu.* Lloyd?] Verses in Salisbury (Sir T.). History of Ioseph. 1636. 4023
Lloyd (David). *See* Ll. (D.).
Lloyd (H.), *Jesus College, Cambridge.* Verses in Davies (J.). Antiquæ linguæ dictionarium. 1632. 4979
Lloyd (John). *See* Josephus. De Maccabaeis. 1590.
Lloyd (Lodowick). Briefe conference of diuers Lawes. 1602. 4°. 2733
Consent of time. 1590. 4°. 1724
First part of the Diall of Daies. 1590. 4°. 1874
Linceus Spectacles. 1607. 4°. 3622
Pilgrimage of princes. 1586. 4°. 1941
Stratagems of Ierusalem. 1602. 4°. 2734
Verses in Llwyd (H.). The breviary of Britayne. 1573. . 1440
Lloyd (Thomas), *LL.B.* Verses in Chaucer (G.). Amorvm. 1635. . 5414
See also LL. (T.).
Lluellin (Martin). Verses in Ferrand (J.). 'Ερωτομανία. 1640. . 5498
— Oxf. Univ. Horti. 1640. 5499
Llwyd (Humphrey). Breuiary of Britayne. 1573. 8°. . . . 1440
De Mona Drvidvm Insvla...Epistola. *See* Price (Sir J.). Historiae Brytannicae. 1573.
Epistle of...the iland of Mona. *See* Ortelius (A.). Theatrum. 1606.
See Caradoc. Historie of Cambria. 1584.
— Petrus *Hispanus.* Treasury of healthe.
Llwyd (Lodowick). *See* Lloyd.
Llyn (H.). Verses in Davies (R.). Funeral sermon. 1577. . . 1416
Lo (Ro.). *See* Hall (J.). Works (Table). 1625. F°. . . 7909
Loarte (Gaspare). Exercise of a christian life. Trans. J. Sancer. 1584. 12°. 6440
Lobeira (Vasco de). Amadis of France. Trans. T. Paynell. [1567?] 4°. 1520
Amadis de Gaule. Trans. A. Munday. 1619 (1618). F°. . 3674
L'Obel (M. de). Balsami, opobalsami etc. explanatio. 1598. 4°. . 2071
In G. Rondelettii...officinam animadversiones. 1605. F°. . . 7247
Plantarum seu stirpium historia. Antwerp, 1576. F°. . . 6117
See Gerard (J.). Herball. 1597. F°.
— Parkinson (J.). Theatrum. 1640.
Locher (Jacob). *See* Brant (S.) Stultifera Nauis. 1570. F°.
Locke (Henry). *See* Lok.
Locke (Tho.), *Trin. Hall.* Verses in Camb. Univ. Dolor. 1625. . 5701

No.
Locke (Tho.), *Trin. Hall, cont.* Verses in Camb. Univ. Epithalam. 1625. 5702
Lockyer (Nicholas). Christs communion. 1640. 8°. 5214
Divine discovery. 1640. 8°. 5215
Lodge (Th.). Treatise of the Plague. 1603. 4°. 1879
Verses in Bales (P.). The writing Schoolemaster. 1590. . 2205
See Gosson (S.). Playes confuted. [1582.]
— Josephus (F.). Workes. 1609 *etc.*
— Seneca (L. A.). Workes. 1614.
Lodovicus (Gulielmus) [*qu.* Lewis?]. Verses in Cheke (Sir J.). De obitu M. Buceri. 1551. 734
Loe (William). The Kings shoe. 1623. 4°. 4697
The merchant reall. Hamburg, 1620. 4°. 6652
Vox clamantis. 1621. 4°. 3428
Loe (William), *T.C.* Verses in Camb. Univ. Carmen. 1635. . . 5770
— Συνωδία. 1637. 5790
Loeus (Robert). *See* Lawe.
Loft (Tho.). Verses in Oxf. Univ. Magd. Coll. Luctus posth. 1612. 5302
Logan (James). Verses in Adamson (J.). Εἰσόδια. 1618. . . . 5960
Logic. [Nineteen Latin Treatises. Oxford, 1483.] 4°. . . . 78
See Fenner (D.). Artes of Logike. 1584.
Logie (Andrew). Cum bono deo. Raine from the clouds. Aberdene, 1624. 4°. 5999
Lohetus (Daniel). Sorex primus. 1618. 8°. 3489
Loiseau de Tourval (Jean). Verses in Coryate (T.). Coryates Crvdities. 1611. 3076
Lok (Henry). Ecclesiastes. 1597. 4°. 2246
Lomas (Ellis). *See* Redman (J.). Reporte. 1551.
Lomazzo (Giov. Paolo). Tracte...of curious painting... Oxford, 1598. F°. 5249
Lon (Henry). Almanack and Prognosticacion. 1554. 16°. . 1161
Prognostication in Salisbury. 1569. 8°. 7225
London, City of. Baylifs, Custos maiers and sherefs. Antwerp [ab. 1503]. F°. 6073
— Ed. 2. [Southwark, ab. 1521.] F°. 5865
Alarume Bell for London. *See* Carr (J.). [157-?]
Map. 1576. *See* Braun (G.).

Apprentices. *See* Philipot (J.). The Cities Advocate. 1629.
Blackfriars. *See* Goad (T.). 1623. 4781
— Sermon. 1623. *See* R. (I.), *P.*. 7766
— Something written by occasion. 1623. 4°. . . . 6947
Chapel Royal. Children. *See* Lyly (J.). Sixe covrt comedies. 1632.
Charterhouse. *See* Burrell (P.). Sutton's Synagogue. 1629.
College of Physicians. 1618 *etc.* *See* Pharmacopeia Londinensis.
— Certain necessary directions...for...the plague. 1636. 4°. . 2694
— *See* License. London. College &c.
Companies. Carpenters. *See* More (Ric.). Carpenters Rvle. 1602.
— East India Merchants. 1614. *See* Lesk (W.). A sermon. 1617.
— — *See* Woodall (J.). The surgions mate. 1617. 4°.
— Grocers. Profitable...discourse. [1593?] 4°. . . 2567
— Merchant Adventurers, Society of. *See* Wheeler (J.) Treatise of commerce. 1601.
— [New River?] Form of agreement. [1640?] 7060
— Pewterers. Statutes. [Before 1590.] 4°. 1772
— Shipwrights. Charter. Ab. 1612? 4°.. 6888
— Virginian Plantation. *See* Donne (J.). Sermon. 1622. 4°.
Diocese. Articles of Visitation. *See* Articles. (London.)
— — (Essex Archdeaconry.)
Homilies. *See* Bonner (E.). Profitable...doctryne. 1555.
— License. Ab. 1640. 7061
Dutch Community. *See* Micron (M.). Den kleynen Cathechismus. 1566.

No.

London, City of, *cont.* Dutch Community. *See* Texeda (F.). Texeda Retextus. 1623.
— — Letters Patent 29 Jan. 1627. Broadside.
— — — 6 Aug. 1630. Broadside.
Dutch Consistory. *See* Vincent (P.). Lamentations of Germany. 1638. 7760
Exchequer. True copy. *See* Book of Justice of the peace. 1544.
French Church. *See* Texeda (F. de). Texeda Retextus. 1623.
Inns of Court. *See* Shirley (J.). Trivmph of peace. 1633.
— Lincoln's Inn. 1613. *See* Chapman (G.). The memorable maske. [1614?]
— Middle Temple. 1613. *See* Chapman (G.). The memorable maske. [1614?]
Ministers. Briefe examination for the tyme. [1564.] 4°. . 7143
— *See* Answere for the tyme. 1566.
— — Crowley (R.). Briefe discourse against...apparell. 1566 *etc.*
— — Jacob (H.). Treatise of the svfferings...of Christ. 1598.
— — Survey of the Booke of Common Prayer...with a View of London Ministers exceptions... (Humble Petition of 22. Preachers, in London...) 1606.
St Bartholomew's Hospital. *See* Vicary (T.). Profitable Treatise. 1577.
St Martin's in the Fields. *See* Sermon...funerall of Lady Blount. 1620.
St Paul's Cathedral. 1561. *See* Pilkington (J.). Burnynge of Paules. 1563.
— *See* Farley (H.). Complaint of Paules. 1616. 4°.
— — Holland (H.). Ecclesia. 1633.
— — — Monumenta. [1614.]
— [Repairs of.] *See* Fleming (G.). Magnificence. 1634.
— The Children. *See* Lyly (J.). Most excellent Comedie. 1591.
— — — Lyly (J.). Sixe covrt Comedies. 1632.
St Thomas of Acres. *See* Indulgence. 1517.
Sion College. *See* Willan (R.). Eliahs wish. 1630. 4°.
Synod. *See* England. Church. Synod.
Theatre. The Fortune. *See* D. (J.), *Gent.* Knave in Graine. 1640.
Tower. (Conference.) *See* D. (H.). Godlie and fruitfull treatise. 1583.
— *See* Hubbocke (W.). An oration. 1604.
— — Powell (T.). Direction. 1622.
— — — Repertorie of Records. 1631.
University. *See* Stow (J.). Annales. 1615. F°.
[London's Complaint. 1636?] 4°. 7025
London (R.). Verses in Shelford (R.). Five...discourses. 1635. . 5774
Long (Kingsmill). *See* Barclay (J.). Argenis. 1625 *etc.*
Long (Walter). Verses in Oxf. Univ. Magd. Coll. 1612. . . 5302
Longinus (Dionysius). Περὶ ὕψους. (Gr. and Lat.) Curavit G. L. Oxonii. 1636. 8°. 5450–5452
— — Ed. postrema. Oxonii, 1638. 8°. 5458
Longland (J.). Sermones. Pynson [1521?]. F°. 305
Tres Conciones (Quinque sermones). Pynson [1527]. F°. . 304
See Joye (G.). Letters whyche Johan Ashwell. [1527?] *etc.*
Looking-glasse for all lordly prelates. 1636. 4°. *See* Prynne (W.).
Looking-glass of the fairest Courtiers. [Ab. 1635?] Obl. 8°. . 6405
Lopes (Duarte). Reporte of the Kingdome of Congo. 1597. 4°. . 1973
Lopes de Castanheda (F.). Discouerie of the East Indies. Book I. 1582. 4°. 1585
Lopez (Odoardo). *See* Lopes (Duarte).
Loque (B. de). Discourses of warre and single combat. Trans. J. Eliot. 1631. 4°. 7009

No.
Loque (B. de), *cont.* Treatise of the Church. 1581. 8°. . . 2001
Lord (Henry). Displaye of two forraigne sects in the East Indies. 1630. 4°. 4685
Lord Bishops none of the Lords Bishops. 1640. *See* Prynne (W.).
Lord's Day, the Sabbath Day. *See* Prynne (W.).
Lord's Prayer (Polyglot). Ed. C. Gesner. Tiguri, 1555. Single sheet. 6293
[Ang.-Sax. and Eng. (Ælfric.)] *See* Testimonie of Antiqvitie. [1566?] . . . . 895 *etc.*
[English.] Paternoster the Crede and the commandementes of God in Englysh. [Ab. 1538.] 8°. 6681
See Babington (G.). Profitable exposition. 1588. 8°.
— Broughton (H.). Exposition. [1613?]
— Burton (W.). Exposition. 1594.
— Colet (J.). vii. Petycions... 6096
— Gouge (W.). Guide. 1636. 4°.
— Huish (A.). Lectures. 1626. 4°.
— Perkins (W.). Exposition. 1593. 12°.
— S. (Tho.). Touchstone. 1602.
[Latin.] Expositio oracionis. *See* Speculum Christiani. 148-?
Preparatio ad orandum. Day and Seres [ab. 1549]. 8°. . . 7139
[Swedish.] *See* North (G.). The Description of Swedland. 1561.
Lord's Supper. *See* Dispute. A dispute. 1607.
See also Supper.
Loreto. *See* Richeome (L.). 1630.
— Torsellino (O.). History. 1608.
Lorichius (Reinhardus). *See* Aphthonius. Progymnasmata. 1631.
Lorkyn (Tho.). Recta regula and victus ratio. 1562. 8°. . . 6747
Lorraine (Charles, Cardinal of). *See* Regnier de la Planche (L.). Legendarie. 1577. 8°.
Loselerius Villerius. *See* Loyseleur.
Lost Lady. 1638. *See* Berkeley (Sir W.).
Λῶστος ('Αρκτουρ. ὁ). [qu. A. Best?] Verses in Selden (J.). Jani...1610. 3389
Lou (Henry). *See* Lon.
Louis XIII. The French Kings declaration against the Dukes of Vendosme and Mayenne. 1617. 4°. 3739
[Letter.] *See* Copie of a letter. 1631. 4°.
Louus. *See* Lowe (H.).
Love (N.). *See* Bonaventura (S.). Speculum vitæ Christi. [1485-6.]
Love (Ric.). Verses in Oxf. Univ. Magd. Coll. 1612. . . . 5302
— — Camb. Univ. Lacrymæ. 1619. 5689
— — Dolor. 1625. 5701
— — Epithalam. 1625. 5702
— — Anthologia. 1632. 5741
— — Fasciae. 1633. 5808
— — Rex redux. 1633. 5748
— — Carmen. 1635. 5770
— — Voces. 1640. 5836
[Licence 5 Feb. 1638.] Davenant (J.). 1639. 5805
Lovelace (Richard). Verses in A. (G.). Pallas armata. 1639. . 5170
Lovering (Thomas). Verses in Camb. Univ. Lacrymæ. 1619. . 5689
— — Dolor. 1625. 5701
— — Epithalam. 1625. 5702
— Hawkins (W.). En Priscianus. 1632. 4562
— — Corolla. 1634 *bis.* 5803
— Hippocrates. 1633.
Low Countries. *See* Netherlands.
Lowe (Henry). *See* Fulke (W.). Antiprognosticon. 1560.
Lowth (John). Verses in Jones (J.). Briefe discourse. 1574. . 1366
Loyola (I.). Manuall of devout meditations. 1618. 12°. . . 6536
Loyseleur (Pierre de), *Villerius.* Verses in Humphrey (L.). J. Jvelli vita. 1573. 837

No.

Loyseleur (Pierre de), *Villerius, cont.* *See* Bible. Lat. N.T. 1574 etc.
— — Eng. (Genevan). 1599 *etc.*
Lucanus. De bello civili. 1589. 16°. 1719
Pharsalia. R. Field. 1618. 8°. 2286
— Trans. Sir A. Gorges. 1614. F°. 3655
— Trans. T. May. 1627. 8°. 3532
— — Ed. 2. 1631. 8°. 4554
— — Ed. 3. 1635. 8°. 4587
See May (T.). Continuation. 1630.
Lucar (Cyprian). Treatise named Lucarsole. 1590. 4°. . . . 2227
Lucar (Adrian van). Verses in Lucianus dialogi. 1531. . . . 376
Lucianus. Dialogi. 1531. 8°. 376
See Heywood (T.). Pleasant dialogues. 1637.
Certaine select dialogves. Trans. F. Hickes. Oxford, 1634. 4°. . 5441
Lucinge (René de). Beginning, continuance and decay of estates. Trans. I. F. 1606. 4°. 7351
Lucy (George). Verses in Jonson (B.). Workes. 1640. . . . 5115
Ludham (John). *See* Baro (P.). Speciall Treatise. [1588?]
See Gerardus (A.). Practise of preaching. 1577. 4°.
Ludus (Johannes), *archdeacon of Nottingham.* *See* Lowth.
Lugo (Peregrinus Italicus de). *See* Italicus (Peregrinus).
Luidus (Joannes). *See* Lloyd.
Luis de Granada. Memoriall of a christian life. Rouen, 1586. 8°. . 6254
— 1599. 8°. 6255
Of prayer and meditation. 1602. 12°. 1785
Sinners guyde. 1598. 4°. 1775
— 1614. 4°. 2276
Lukyn (Rob.). Verses in Camb. Univ. Lacrymæ. 1619. . . 5689
Luna (Juan de). Arte breve...para aprender...la lengua espanola. 1623. 8°. 3344
Lundine (John). Verses in Forbes (P.). Funerals. 1637. . . 6007 *bis*
Lundorpius (Johannes). Verses in Buchanan (G.). Psalmorum Paraphrasis. 1640. 5209
Lunnæus (Rob.). Verses in Camb. Univ. Lacrymae. 1619. . 5689
Lupset (T.). Workes. 1546. 8°. 485
— 1560. 8°. 1241
Compendiovs...treatyse...of Dyenge well. 1541. 8°. . . . 461
Exhortation to yonge men. 1538. 8°. 445
See Chrysostom. Sermon. 1542. 8°.
Lupton (Donald). Emblems of rarities. 1636. 12°. 3704
Glory of their times. 1640. 4°. 3730
See Verheiden (J.). History of the Modern Protestant Divines. 1637.
Lupton (Thomas). Sivqila. Too good to be true. 1587. 4°. . . 7832
— The second part. 1581. 4°. 7833
Thousand notable things. 1601. 4°. 1782
— 1631. 8°. 4840
Verses in Jones (J.). Briefe discourse. 1574. 1366
Lusing (R. de). *See* Lucinge.
Lustier (Robert). Verses in Camb. Univ. Lachrymae. 1587. . 2123
Lute Music Book. [Ab. 1600.] F°. 7730
Lute (Rob.). Verses in Oxf. Univ. Horti. 1640. 5499
Luther (M.). Chiefe and pryncypall Articles of the Christen faythe. 1548. 8°. 950
Commentarie vpon the xv. psalmes. Trans. H. Bull. 1637. 4°. 4467
Commentarie of...Galathians. 1575. 4°. 1529
— 1588. 4°. 1563
— 1635. 4°. 4456
Every-dayes sacrifice. Trans. W. R. S. 1624. 12°. . . . 7409
Faythfull admonycion of a certen trewe pastor. 'C. Freeman, Grenewych,' May, 1554. 8°. 6288

No.

Luther (M.), *cont.* Frutefull and godly exposition...of Jeremye xxiii., with...viij. Psalme. 1548. 8°. 7767
Frvitfvll Predication...concerning Matrimony. *See* B. (R.). Watchword for Wilfull Women. 1581.
Luthers Predecessors. 1624. 4°. 3025
Prophesie out of the nienth chapter of Esaie. 1578. 8°. . . 1497
Special and chosen sermons. 1578. 4°. 1536
— 1581. 4°. 1545
Treatise touching the Libertie of a Christian. 1579. 8°. . 1312
[Letter to Henry VIII.] *See* Henry VIII. Literarum... 1526.
[Sermon.] *See* Disclosing. The dysclosing of the Canon. [1549?]
[Death.] *See* Jonas (J.). True hystorye. [Ab. 1546?] 8°.
See Anderton (J.). Luthers Life. 1624. 4°.
C. (T.). Spirituall purgation. [Ab. 1548.]
Fisher (J.). Sermon. [152–.] 4°.
— Henry VIII. Assertio. 1521.
— More (Sir T.). Dyalogue. 1531. F°.
— — Eruditissimi viri G. Rossei opus. 1523.
— Powell (E.). Propugnaculum summi sacerdotij. 1523.
Lutzen, Battle of. *See* Russell (J.). The two...battels. 1634.
Luynes (Charles d'Albert, duc de). *See* Langlois. Favorites Chronicle. 1621.
Lycophron. Ἀλεξάνδρα. Oxonie, 1592. 4°. 5237
— Cantabrigiae, 1595. 8°. 5572
Lydgate (John). Assembly of gods. W. de Worde [1499?]. 4°. . 65
Horse the ghoos and the sheep. Ed. 1. Caxton [1477–8]. 4°. 9
— — Ed. 2. Caxton [1477–8]. 4°. 10
Horse the sheep and the ghoos. W. de Worde [1500]. 4°. . 66
Life and Death of Hector. 1614. F°. 1396
Lyfe of our Lady. Caxton [1484]. F°. 26, 27
[Medicina stomachi.] *See* Governal of Health.
Prouerbes upon the fall of Princes. W. de Worde [1519]. 4°. . 233
Serpent of diuision. 1559. 8°. 1281
Temple of glas. Caxton [1477–8]. 4°. 8
— W. de Worde [1500]. 4°. 67
Testament. Pynson [1515?]. 4°. 306
See Boccaccio. Falle of Princys. 1494.
— — Tragedies. [1554.]
— — Treatise. 1554.
— Chaucer (G.). Workes. 1532 *etc.*
— Churl and the Bird.
— Sulpitius (J.). Stans puer ad mensam. [1477] *etc.*
Lydiat (Tho.). Ad clar. virum D. H. Savilium. 1621. 8°. . 2538
De variis annorum formis. 1605. 8°. 2353
Defensio tractatus de variis annorum formis. 1607. 8°. . 2948
Emendatio temporum. 1609. 8°. 2958
Prælectio astronomica etc. 1605. 8°. 3451
Lyford (William). *See* Pinke (W.). Tryall of...loue. 1631 *etc.*
Lyly (J.). Euphues. T. East for G. Cawood. 1580. 4°. . . 1579
— Ed. 8. G. Eld for W. Barrett and A. Johnson. 1617. 4°. 3587
— J. Beale for J. Parker. 1623. 4°. 3804
— J. Haviland. 1636. 4°. 7632
Most excellent comedy of Alexander, Campaspe, and Diogenes. 1591. 4°. 2213
Sixe Court Comedies. 1632. 12°. 3189
Lymmonerius Gallus. Verses in Barlow (W.). Vita R. Cosin. 1598. 1707
Lynch (Jo.), *Coll. Jes.* Verses in Camb. Univ. Epicedium. 1612. . 5665
Lynche (Richard). Historical treatise of the travels of Noah. 1601. 4°. 7395
Lynd (G.), *Andreapol.* Verses in Abernethy (J.). A christian...treatise. 1630. 4342

No.

Lynde (Sir Humphrey). Case for the Spectacles. 1638. 4°. . . 4945
Via devia. 1630. 12°. 4540
— Ed. 2. 1632. 12°. 7605
Via tuta. 1628. 12°. 4423. Ed. 3. 1629. 12°. . . 7890
— Ed. 4. 1630. 12°. 4541
— Another edition (frag). 12°. 4542
— *See* T. (T.). The Whetstone of Reproofe. 1632. 8°. . 7817
— — Floyd (J.). Paire of spectacles. 1631. 8°.
— — Ratramnus. Booke of Bertram. 1623.
Lyndesius (David). *See* Lindsay.
Lyndwood (William). Constitutiones provinciales. Ed. 1. Oxford, [1485?]. F°. 80
— W. de Worde, 1496. 8°. 47
Constitutiones legitime seu legatine. W. Hopyl, Paris, Id. Sept. 1504. F°. 6147
— W. Hopyl, Paris. (H. Jacobi and J. Pelgrim.) 1506. F°. . 6149
Constitutiones prouinciales et Othonis (Octoboni). W. de Worde, 1517. 8°. 176
— T. Marshe. 1557. 8°. 1206
Constitutions prouinciallés of Otho and Octhobone. R. Redman, 1534. 8°. 379
Prouinciale seu Constitutiones Angliae. A. Bocard, Paris, 28 Maij, 1501. F°. 6161, 7685
— W. Hopyl, Paris, imp. W. Bretton, apud bibliopolas, London. 23 Mart. 1505–6. F°. 6148
— F. Byrckman, cura C. Endouien. Antwerpie. 20 Dec. 1525. F°. 6084
Lyne (R.). Map of Cambridge. *See* Caius (J.). De antiquitate. 1574. 839
Lynford (Sam.). Verses in Camb. Univ. Fasciae. 1633. . . 5808
— — Carmen. 1635. 5770
— — Συνῳδία. 1637. 5790
Lynge (Nicholas). *See* Svm, or a brief collection. 1563.
See Six godlie treatises. 1608. 8°. 3627
Lynn (Edward). Verses in Whitaker (W.). Praelectiones. 1599. . 5598
Lynne (Walter). Beginning and endynge of all popery. [1548?] 4°. 769
See Bullinger (H.) A treatise. 1549. 8°.
— Carion (J.). Thre bokes of Cronicles. 1550.
— Regius (U.). Declaration. 1548.
Lysander and Calista. *See* Audiguier (V. d'). 1635. F°.
Lysias. Eratosthenes...A. Dunæi. Cantabrigiae, 1593. 8°. . 5562
Lysimachus Nicanor, *pseud.* *See* Corbet (J.).
Lyte (Henry). *See* Dodoens (R.). Nievve Herball. 1578 *etc.*
— — Rams little Dodeon. 1606.
Lyttleton (Hen.). Verses in Oxf. Univ. Horti. 1640. . . . 5499

M. (A.). True reporte of...successe...in Ireland. [1580?] 4°. 1877, 1878
See La Noue (F. de). Declaration. 1589. *See also* Primaleon. 1619.
[A. Munday.] *See* Lobeira (V.). Amadis de Gaule. 1619 (1618).
[qu. Munday?]. *See* The Masque of the League. 1592. 8°.
[A. Munday.] *See* Palmerin d'Oliva. 1637. 4°.
— — Teixeira (J.). The strangest adventure. 1601. . 7765
M. (C.). *See* Watson (T.). Amintæ gavdia. 1592.
M. (C.). [qu. C. Mason?] Verses in Ovid. Fasti. 1640. . . 5849
M. (Ch.). Meditations and devovt discourses. Douai. 1639. 8°. 6577
M. (E.). *See* Plowden (E.). Commentaries. 1578. F°.
M. (G.). Verses in Mary *Queen of Scots*. De Maria. [1572?] . 6754
— Camb. Univ. Gratulatio. 1623. 5695
See Marcelline (G.). Vox militis. 1625.
[G. Markham.] *See* Berners (Jul.). The Gentlemans Academie. 1595. 4°.
See Markham (G.). Honovr in his perfection. 1624.

No.
M. (H.). Verses in Gascoigne (G.). Posies. 1575. . . . 1482
— Camb. Univ. Thr-thr. 1603. 5616
— Henshaw (J.). Horæ Succisivæ. 1640. . . . 5099
See Fletcher (P.). Locvstæ. 1627. 5706
M. (I.). Spirituall food, and physick. Ed. 2. 1623. 8°. . . 2543
— [Ab. 1624?] 8°. 6941
Verses in Jewel (J.). Adv. T. Hardingum. 1578. . . 1535
— Shakspeare (W.). Comedies etc. 1623. . . . 3972
[Qu. James Mabbe?] *See* Butler (C.). Rhetorica. 1600.
See Monipenny (I.). Abridgement. 1633.
M. (I.), *C.C.C.* Verses in Camb. Univ. Gratulatio. 1623. . . 5695
M. (I.), *Londinensis.* Verses in Demosthenes. Thre orations. 1570. 1409
M. (I. H. D.). Verses in Gray (T. de). The compleat horseman. 1639. 4042
M. (I.). Verses in Overbury (Sir T.). His Wife. Ed. 11. 1622. . 3380
M. (I.), *Master of Arts.* Soules pilgrimage. 1634. 4°. . . 7607
M. (I.), *Magdalen College, Oxford* [I. Mabbe]. *See* Fonseca (C. de). Devout contemplations. 1629.
See Juan de Santa Maria. Christian Policie. 1632. (Policie Unveiled. 1637.) 4°.
M. (I.), *M.A. utriusque Academiæ.* [Qu. James Maxwell?] *See* Herodian. Historie of twenty roman Cæsars. 1626 etc.
M. (Jo.). Verses in Price (Sir J.). Historie. 1573. . . . 1473
M. (L.) [qu. Mascall (L.)?]. *See* Præpositus (N.). Prepositas his Practise. 1588.
M. (L.) [Mascall (L.)]. *See* Profitable booke. 1596. 4°.
M. (M.). *See* Rogers (Ric.). Garden. 1625.
M. (M.) [M. Mainwaring]. *See* Paris and Vienna. [1628?] 4°.
M. (M.), *C.P.M.D.E.E.P.C.* Verses in Anthony (F.). Apologia. 1616. 3759
M. (P.). Verses in Imitation of Christ. 1568. . . . 1405
M. (P.) [Massinger (P.)]. Verses in the Fatall dowry. 1632. . 4888
M. (P.). Verses in Holyoake (F.). Dictionarium. 1640. . . 3058
See Matthieu (P.). The powerful favorite. 1628.
— Muffet (P.). Commentarie vpon Proverbs. 1592.
M. (P. D.). *See* Pattenson (M.). The image. 1623.
M. (R.). Verses in Davies (R.). Funerall sermon. 1577. . . 1416
— Turkey. The Mahumetane...Historie. 1600. . . 1610
[Dedication to Robert Lord Willoughby Broke and Eresby.] *See* Cuff (H.). The differences. 1607 *etc.*
M. (R.), *Joh.* Verses in Camb. Univ. Epicedium. 1612. . . 5665
M. (R. G. S. D.). *See* Defence of Contraries. 1593.
M. (S. T.). [qu. Sir T. Matthew?] *See* Augustine. Confessions. Ed. 2. 1638. 12°.
M. (T.). Verses in Paris and Vienna. 1628. . . . 7552
— Stafford (A.). Femall glory. 1635. 4018
See Arias (F.). Treatise of patience. 1630. 12°.
— Morton (T.). Exact discoverie. 1605.
— Mun (T.). Discovrse. 1621.
— S. (C.). The copie of a letter. 1603. 4°.
M. (T.), *C.C.* Verses in Wadsworth (J.). Further Obss. 1630. 4°. 7788
M. (T.), *Esq.* *See* May (T.). Tragedy. 1639. 8°.
M. (Tho.). Verses in Baret (J.). Alvearie. 1580. . . . 1418
M. (W.). Verses in Thynne (F.). Newes from the north. 1585. . 2002
— Hart (A.). The tragi-comicall history. 1640. . . 4220
Mab or Mabbe (James). Verses in Florio (G.). Queen Anna's New World. 1611. 3374
See Aleman (M.). The Rogve. 1623 etc.
— Butler (C.). Rhetorica. 1600.
— Fonseca (C. de). Devovt contemplations. 1629.
— Juan de Santa Maria. Christian Policie. 1632. 4°.
— — Policie Unveiled. 1637. 4°.

No.

Mabb (Ralph). *See* Austin (W.). Haec homo. 1638. 12°.
— Guillim (J.). A display. 1638.
Macabre, Danse. *See* Boccaccio. A treatise. 1554.
Macalpine or Machabæus (Christianus), *Alpinas*. Verses in Lorkyn (T.). Recta regula. 1562. 6747
See Macalpine (J.). Enarratio. 1563.
Macalpine (J.). Enarratio in devteronomium. 1563. 8°. . . . 1304
See Lindsay (Sir D.). Ane Dialog. [1554?] 5995
Macarnesse (John). Verses in Camb. Univ. Lacrymae. 1619. . . . 5689
Macarnesse (Thomas). Verses in Camb. Univ. Epicedium. 1612. . 5665
MacCaghwell (Hugo). Scathan Shacramuinte. Louvain, 1618. 12°. . 6428
Macchiavelli (N.). Discourses upon Livius. Trans. E. Dacres. 1636. 12°. 5093
Florentine Historie. Trans. T. Bedingfield. 1595. F°. . . 2717
See Fitzherbert (T.). First part of a treatise. 1606. 4°.
— Gentillet (I.). Discovrse...against N. Machiavell. 1602 etc.
Machabæus, *Dr.* *See* Macalpine (J.).
Machabæus (Christianus). *See* Macalpine.
Machabæus (Johannes). *See* Macalpine.
Machin (Lewis). *See* Markham (G.). Dvmbe Knight. 1633.
Macilmaine, or Makylmenæus (Rollo). *See* Ramus (P.). Logike. 1581.
MacKey (Sir Donald), *lord Rhees*. *See* Rhees.
Mackwilliam (Henry). *See* Corte (C.). Art of Riding. 1584.
Marcollo (Joannes). Iatria chymica. 1622. 8°. . . . 3508
Macropedius (Georgius). Verses in Pelegromius (S.). Synonymorum sylva. 1603. 8°. 7881
Madd (I.). *See* W. (Ez.). Answere of a mother.
Maddison (Sir Ralph). Englands looking in and out. 1640. 4°. . 5141
Maden (Richard). Christs Love and affection. 1637. 4°. . . 4310
Verses in Camb. Univ. Lacrymae. 1619. 5689
Madox (John), *M.A., fellow of All Souls Oxon.* *See* Madoxe (R.).
Madoxe (R.). Learned and a godly sermon. 1581. 8°. . . 1350
Maetellanus (John), *Vice-chancellor of Scotland.* *See* Maitland (Sir John).
Maffei (Giovanni Pietro). Fuga seculi. Trans. H. H. Paris, 1632. 4°. 6226
Maffeus (Celsus), *Veronensis*. [Dissuasive to the Senate of Venice.] *See* Digby (E.) Dissuasive. [Ab. 1589.] 4°.
Magdalen Augustine, *Sister*. *See* Wadding (L.). History of...S. Clare. 1635.
Magirus (A.). Verses in Purchas (S.). Purchas his pilgrimage. 1614 *etc.* 3101 *etc.*
Magna Charta. *See* Statutes.
Magnomontanus (Banatusius). *See* Montemagno (B. da).
Magnus (Jacobus). *See* Legrand (Jacques).
Magnus (Robert). Verses in Forbes (P.). Funerals. 1635. . . 6007
Mahat (Philip). *See* Lake (A.). Sermons. 1629.
Mahomet. Life. *See* Ralegh (Sir W.). 1637.
Maidstone (Clement). Directorium Sacerdotum. G. Leer, Antwerp, 1488. 4°. 7808. 1495. 4°. 43
— (W. Clarke), 1499. 4°. 62
Maier (Michael), *M.D.* [Letter to him by A. Gill.] *See* Anthony (F.). Apologia. 3759
Maigret (Louis). *See* Polybius. History. 1634.
Maihew (Edw.). Treatise of the grounds of the old and newe religion. 1608. 4°. 6875
See Manuale (Sarum). 1604. 4°. 6569
Maimonides (Moses). *See* Moses, *ben Maimon.*
Mainardi (A.). Anatomi...of the mass. With a sermon. 1556. 8°. . 6732
Mainwaring (John). Verses in Paris and Vienna. [1628?] . 7552
Mainwaring (Matthew). *See* Paris and Vienna. [1628?] 4°. . . 7552
Mainwaring (Ralph). Verses in Paris and Vienna. [1628?] . 7552
Mainwaring (Roger). *See* Manwaring.

No.
Mainwaring (Thomas). Verses in Paris and Vienna. [1628?] . 7552
See Heywood (T.). Hierarchie. 1635.
Mainwaring (W.). Verses in Camb. Univ. Genethl. 1631. . . 5731
Maister (William). Verses in Parkhurst (J.). Ludicra. 1573. . 838
Maisterson (H.). Verses in Camb. Univ. Rex redux. 1633. . . 5748
Maitland (Sir John), Baron Maitland. Verses in Camb. Univ. Lachrymae. 1587. 2123
Maitland (Patrick). Verses in Forbes (P.). Funerals. 1637. . . 6007
Makylmenæus (Rollus). *See* Macilmaine (R.).
Malavici (Hermes). *See* Anthony (F.). Apologia. 1616.
Malchus, St. *See* Hieronymus. Certaine selected epistles. 1630. 4°.
Malcolm (I.). Verses in James I. Fruitful Meditation. [1603?] . 2854
Malestroict (De). *See* Malynes (G. de). Englands view. 1603.
Malga or Malgo, *King of England*. *See* Fox (L.). North-west Fox. 1635.
Malim (William). *See* Chaloner (Sir T.). De rep. anglorum. 1579. 4°.
Malines (G. de). *See* Malynes.
Malmesbury, William of. *See* William.
Malone (Will.). Reply to Mr J. Ussher. 1627. 4°. . . . 6974
See Synge (G.). Reioynder. 1632.
Malory (Sir T.). Story of...Kynge Arthur. W. Copland, 1557. F°. . 1081
— T. East [1581?] F°. 1583
Most ancient and famous history of...Arthur. 1634. 4°. . . 3195
Malta, History of. *See* Turkey. Mahumetane or Turkish Historie. 1600.
Maltsters. 1637. *See* Proclamations.
Malvezzi (Virgilio). Romulus and Tarquin...by H. C. L. 1637. 12°. 4863
Malynes (Gerard de). Consuetudo...ancient law-merchant. 1622. F°. 7712
Englands view. 1603. 8°. 2256
See Misselden (E.). Circle of Commerce. 1623.
Man, Isle of. *See* Price (Sir J.). Historiae Brytannicae. 1573.
Man (John). *See* Musculus (W.). Common Places. 1578. 4°.
Man (Abr.). Verses in Oxf. Univ. Magd. Coll. 1612. . . . 5302
Man (Bartholomew). Verses in Jorden (E.). Discourse. 1633. . 4003
Man (Richard). Verses in Hill (T.). Arte of vulgar arithmeticke. 1600. 2197
Man (Thomas). *See* Gifford (G.). Two sermons. 1597.
See Smith (H.). Thirteen sermons. 1592. 8°. 7791
Manardinus (Marsilius), *Patavinus*. *See* Menandrinus.
Manchester School. *See* no. 5608.
Manchester (Henry Montagu, earl of). Manchester al mondo. 1633. 12°. 2683
— 1635. 12°. 4858
Mancin (Dominic). Mirrour of good Maners. *See* Brant (S.). Stultifera Nauis. 1570. F°.
Mandeville (Sir John). Of the wages of the holy londe. W. de Worde, 1499. 4°. 55
Manelli (Giovanni Maria). *See* Tacitus. Vita di Givlio Agricola. 1585.
Manfredi (F). *See* Venice. Declaration. 1606.
Manifest Detection of Dice Play. *See* Walker (G.).
Manifold wisedome of God. 1640. 12°. 4934
Manipulus Curatorum. *See* Guido *de Monte Rocherii*.
Manner of subuention of poore people. Trans. W. Marshall. [1532?] 8°. 561
Manners (Roger). Verses in Camb. Univ. Dolor. 1625. . . 5701
Manor. Extenta manerii. *See* Book of Surveying. 1525.
See Exchequer, Court of. 1608.
Manor, Rights of. *See* Calthorpe (C.). 1635.
Mansfeld (Ernst von), *Count*. *See* Marcelline (G.). Vox militis. 1625.
See W. (S.). Appollogie. 1622. 4°.
Mansfield, *Count*. *See* Mansfeld.
Mantuanus (Baptista). Adolescentia seu bucolica. 1569. 8°. . . 7223
— Cantabrigiae, 1632. 8°. 5746

No.

Mantuanus (Baptista), *cont.* Adolescentia seu bucolica. Cantabrigiae, 1634. 8°. 5764
— — 1635. 8°. 5776
Manual of prayers. 1589. 16°. 6439
Manuale (Sarum). Paris, imp. F. Byrckman [ab. 1515]. F°. . 6208
J. Caillard, Rouen, 24 Dec. 1522. 4°. 6234
F. Regnault, Paris, 1529. 4°. 6166
[152-?] 4°. 6665
Vidua C. Ruremund, Antwerpie, Jan. 1543. 4°. . . . 6086
[Kingston and Sutton.] 1554. 4°. 1162
— 1555. 4°. 7221
Sacra institutio baptizandi. Ed. E. Maihew. 1604. 4°. . . 6569
Manuale Sacerdotum. Douai, 1610. 8°. 6573
Manutius (A.). Phrases linguae latinae. 1599. 8°. . . . 2251
— Cantabrigiae, 1636. 8°. 5783
Manutius (Paulus). [Letters.] *See* Fleming (A.). Panoplie. 1576. 4°.
See Cicero. Epistolæ. 1585.
— Virgil. Opera. 1572.
Manwaring (Roger). Religion and alegiance: in two sermons. 1627. 4°. 4809
Manwood ( ). *See* Briefe Declaration. 1636.
Manwood (John). Treatise and discourse of the lawes of the forrest. 1598. 4°. 2386
— 1615. 4°. 3262
Manwood (Sir Peter). *See* Williams (Sir Roger). Actions. 1618.
Manzolli (Pietro Angelo). *See* Palingenius (M.).
Mapes (Walter). Vae genti inutili. *See* Daneau (L.). Treatise. 1589. 4°. 2201
Maps.
Authors.
See Cellarius (D.). 1578. 7731
— Saxton (C.). England. 1579. . . . . . 6765 *etc.*
— Braun (G.) and F. Hohenberg. 1588. 7732-5
— Camden (W.). Britannia. 1607. F°. 1758
— Mercator. 1613-1638. . . . . 7738—7743
— — 1635[1]. 4637
— Roberts (L.). 1638[1]. 5133
— Grent (W.). 1625. 7857
Places.
See Bergen op Zoom. 1588.
— Bristol. 1588.
— Cambridge. 1574 etc.
— Canterbury. 1588.
— Chester. 1588.
— Durham. 1595.
— Edinburgh. 1588.
— England. Saxton's Maps. 1579. . . . . . 6765 *etc.*
— Greenland. 1625. 7635
— London. 1576.
— Newfoundland. 1626. 5029
— Norwich. 1588.
— Oxford. 1575.
— Windsor. 1572.
Maraffi (B.). [Arnalt and Lucenda.] *See* Desainliens (C.). Italian Schoole-Maister. 1597. 8°.
Marandé (Léonard de). Iudgment of humane actions...englished by J. Reynolds. 1629. 8°. 4536
Marbeck (J.). Booke of Notes and Common Places. 1581. 4°. . 1582
Concordance...the whole Bible. 1550. F°. 616
Lyues of holy Sainctes. 1574. 4°. 1414

[1] Several maps in these two volumes are identical.

No.

Marbeck (J.), *cont.* *See* Common Prayer. 1550.
Marbeck (Robert). Verses in Bentley (T.). Monument of Matrones.1582. 1425
Marbeck (Roger). *See* Defence of Tabacco. 1602.
Marblestone (Marmaduke). Verses in Gascoigne (G.). Posies. 1575. 1482
Marbury (Ed.). Verses in Barlow (W.). Vita R. Cosin. 1598. . 1707
Marbury (Fras.). Fruitful sermon. 1602. 8°. 2340
Sermon. 1602. 8°. 2341
Marcelline (George). Triumphs of K. James I. 1610. 4°. . . 2774
Vox militis. 1625. 4°. 4184
Marcellinus (Ammianus). Roman historie. 1609. F°. . . 2440
Marcort (Antony). Declaration of the Masse. 'H. Lufft, Wittenberg.' 1547. 8°. 6707–8
Mardeley (J.). Declaration of thee power of Gods worde. [1548?] 8°. 706
Necessarie instruction for all Couetous ryche men. (The Daungerous...Mammon.) [1548?] 8°. 707
Shorte Resytal...that the naturall body of christ is not...in the Sacrament. [1548?] 8°. 708
Marforius. *See* Nash (T.). 7242
Margaret d'Angoulême, *Queen of Navarre.* Godly Medytacyon of the christen sowle. Trans. Elizabeth. 1548. 8°. . . 7689
See Bentley (T.). The monvment of Matrones. 1582.
Margaret Beaufort, *countess of Richmond and Derby.* *See* Richmond and Derby (Margaret, countess of).
Maria (Juan de Santa). *See* Juan, *de Santa Maria.*
Mariana (Joannes), *S.J.* *See* Paris. Sorbonne. The copie. 1610.
Marie de Medicis, *wife of Henry IV.* *See* Mary.
Marius (Leonardus), *Coloniensis.* *See* Lohetus (D.). Sorex. 1618.
Marius (Nathaniel). *See* Texeda (F. de). Texeda Retextus. 1623.
Markham (Francis). Booke of honour. 1625. F°. 4532
Five decades of epistles of warre. 1622. F°. 4508
Markham (Gervase). Cavelrice. [160–.] 4°. 7338
— 1617(–6). 4°. 2032
Complete farriar. 1639. 8°. 5171
Country Contentments. Ed. 5. 1633. 4°. 4005
Dumbe Knight. 1633. 4°. 4573
English house-wife. Ed. 5. 1637. 4°. 3967
Honour in his perfection. 1624. 4°. 4182
Hungers prevention. 1621. 8°. 4499
Inrichment of the weald of Kent. 1636. 4°. 3961
Markham's faithfull farrier. 1640. 8°. 4678
Markhams farwell to hvsbandry. Newly reuiewed. 1625. 4°. . 4229
— Ed. 4. 1638. 4°. 5194
Markhams Maister-Piece. 1631. 4°. 3691
Way to get Wealth. Ed. 5. 1631. 4°. 3692
— Ed. 6. 1638. 4°. 5195
See Berners (J.). Gentlemans Academie. 1595. 4°.
— Heresbach (C.). Whole art. 1631.
Markham (Sir Griffin). *See* S. (C.). Copie of a letter. 1603. 4°.
Markham (W.). Verses in Shirley (J.). Royall master. 1638 . 4665
Marlborough or Marleburgh (Henry of). *See* Henry.
Marlianus (J. B.). Topographie of Rome. *See* Livius. Romane historie. 1600.
Marlorat (A.). Catholike and Ecclesiasticall Exposition of...Marke and Luke. 1583. 4°. 1234
Propheticæ et apostolicæ....Scripturæ Thesaurus. 1574. F°. . 1528
Treatise of the sin against the holy ghost. [157– ?] 8°. . . 1290
See Willet (A.). Hexapla in Genesin. 1605.
Marlowe (Christopher). *See* Watson (T.). Amintæ gavdia. 1592.
Marmion (Shackerly). Verses in Heywood (T.). Pleasant Dialogues. 1637. 5128

No.
Marmion (Shackerly), *cont.* Verses in Welby (H.). The Phoenix. 1637. 3713
Marnix (P. de). Bee hiue of the Romishe Churche. Trans. G. Gilpin. 1579. 8°. 7303, 1805
— — 1580. 8°. 1810
— — 1623. 8°. 3853
Marow (Ed.). Verses in Oxf. Univ. Horti. 1640. 5499
Marow (Fra.), *M.A. New Coll.* Verses in Oxf. Univ. Horti. 1640. 5499
Marprelate (Martin), *pseud.* [i.e. J. Penry?] Dialogve. [1589?] 8°. . 1917
— 1640. 4°. 7054
Hay any worke for Cooper. [1589?] 4°. 7779
Protestacyon. *See* Penry (J.). [1589.] 8°.
See L. (A.). Antimartinus. 1589.
Marrande (Leonard). *See* Marandé.
Marriot (John), *printer.* *See* Gomersall (R.). Poems. 1633. 8°.
Marrow. *See* Marow.
Marsh (George). Letters. *See* Coverdale (M). Certain...letters. 1564.
Marshall (John), *Roman Catholic Divine.* *See* Martiall.
Marshall (William). *See* Manner. [The maner of subvention.] [153-?] 8°.
See Menandrinus (M.). Defence of peace. 1535.
— Primer. Goodly prymer. 1534? 4°. 576
Marshe (George). *See* Marsh.
Marsilius Paduanus *s.* Patavinus. *See* Menandrinus.
Marten (Anthony). *See* Martin.
Martialis (M. Val.). Epigrammaton libri...comm. T. Farnabii. 1615. 8°. 2992
— Ed. 2. 1633. 8°. 4980
Martiall (John). Treatyse of the crosse. Antwerp, 1564. 8°. . 6112
See Calfhill (J.). Avnswere...of the Crosse. 1565.
— Fulke (W.). T. Stapleton and Martiall. 1580. 8°.
— Harding (T.). Answere to Mr iewel. 1565.
Martin (Anthony). Exhortation. 1588. 4°. 2125
Reconciliation of all the pastors and cleargy of...England. 1590. 4°. 2129
Second sound or warning. 1589. 4°. 7366
Verses in Ussher (J.). Gravissimæ quæstiones. 1613. . . 2798
See Vermigli (P. M.). Common Places. 1583. . . 1426
Martin (Edward), *D.D.* *See* Hippocrates. 1633.
[Licence.] *See* Francklin (R.). Ὀρθοτονία. 1630 *etc.* . 3987 *etc.*
— Isaacson (H.). 1633.
Martin (Gregory). Discoverie of the manifold corruptions of the h. scriptures. Rheims, 1582. 8°. 6433
Treatyse of christian peregrination. 1583. 8°. . . . 6438
See Bible. New Testament. Rhemes, 1582. 4°.
— Fulke (W.). Defense. 1583.
— Rainolds (J.). Svmme. 1584 *etc.*
— Bible, O.T. Douai, 1609–10 *etc.*
Martin (Sir Henry), *Kt.* *See* Glanvill (Sir J.). Copies of two Speeches. 1628.
Martin (James). De prima...generatione disputatio. Cantabrigiae, 1584. 8°. 5508
Verses in Aretius (J.). Primula Veris. 1613. 3090
Martin (Richard). Verses in Coryat (T.). Coryats Crudities. 1611. . 3076
Martin (Thomas). *See* Martyn.
Martin (William). *See* Martyn.
Martinez (Marcos). *See* Mirror of Knighthood. Pt iii. 1598–1601.
Martinius (Matthias). Graecae linguae fundamenta. 1629. 8°. . 4828
Martinius (P.). Key of the holy tongue. Leyden, 1593. 8°. . 6497
Martinus (Jacobus). *See* Martin.
Martius (Laurentius), *Palatinus.* Index latinus in J. Scapulæ lexicon graeco-latinum. 1637. F°. 4654
Martyn (Edward). Verses in Martyn (W.). Historie. 1615. . 7489

No.
Martyn (Nicholas). Verses in Martyn (W.). Historie. 1615. . 7489
Martyn (Tho.). Treatise declaryng...the pretended marriage of Priestes ...forbidden. 1554. 4°. 1193, 7224
See Cranmer (T.). Copy of certain lettres...[ab. 1556]. 8°.
— Defence of priestes marriages. [1566?]
— Madox (R.). Learned...Sermon. [1581.]
— Poynet (J.). Apologie. 1556.
Martyn (William). Historie...of twentie kings of England. 1615. F°. 7489
Historie and lives of the Kings of England (title only). 1638. F°. . . . . 4999 and p. 1744
Martyn (William). Theses and Verses in Adamson (J.). Εἰσόδια. 1618. 5960
Martyn (William) *the son.* Verses in Martyn (Will.). Historie. 1615. 7489
Martyr (Petrus), Anglerius. *See* Anglerius.
Vermylius. *See* Vermigli.
Martyrology. *See* Wilson (J.). The English Martyrologe. 1608.
Marvell (Andrew), *T. C.* Verses in Camb. Univ. Συνῳδία. 1637. . 5790
Mary, *The Blessed Virgin.* *See* Lamentation.
See Mirror of Our Lady. 1530.
— Numan (P.). Miracles wrought. 1606.
— Stafford (A.). Femall glory. 1635. 8°.
Order of the Immaculate Conception. *See* Wadsworth (J.). Further Observations. 1630. 4°. 7788
Mary I., Queen of England. [Coronation.] *See* Seton (J.). Panegyrici. 1553.
[Marriage.] *See* Elder (J.). The Copie of a letter. [1555.]
— — Gorecius (L.). Oratio. 1554.
[Portrait with the 'Suplicatiõ of T. Hongar. 22.'] F°. . . 7713
See Erasmus (D.). Paraphrase. 1548.
— Philip II., of Spain. [Genealogical Table. Ab. 1554.]
— Philpot (J.). Vera expositio. 1554.
Mary, Queen of Scots. De Maria scotorum regina. (Actio.) [1571?] 8°. 6754
[*Life.*] *See* Udall (W.). 1624 *etc.*
[Succession.] *See* Leslie (J.). Treatise. 1584.
See Adamson (P.). Poëmata sacra. 1619–18.
— Blackwood (A.). Martyre de la royne. 1587.
— Buchanan (G.). Ane detectioun. [1572?] 8°.
— C. (R.). Copie of a letter. 1586.
— Copy of a letter written by one in London. [1572?]
— Copy of a letter written out of Scotland. [157–?] 12°.
— Kempe (W.). A dvtifvll invective. 1587. 4°.
— Knox (J.). The copie of a letter.
— Kyffin (M.). Apologie or defense. 1588.
— Leslie (J.). Treatise. 1571.
— Norfolk (Thomas Howard, duke of). Discourse. [1571?]
Mary de' Medici, *Wife of Henry IV. of France.* *See* France. Mary de' Medici. 1638.
Declaration de la Reyne Mere du Roy...de la sortie des pais bas. 1638. 4°. 5070
Declaration...of her departure out of the Low-Countreys. 1639. 4°. 5153
See Puget de la Serre (J.). Histoire de l'entreè. 1639. F°.
Mary, *Princess, daughter of Charles I.* *See* Camb. Univ. Genethliacum. 1631.
Mas. (Nic.), *Christ's Coll.* Verses in Camb. Univ. Lacrymae. 1619. 5689
Mascall (L.). Booke of the Arte...to plant and graffe...Trees. 1590. 4°. 1598
Gouernment of cattell. 1627. 4°. 4143
See Præpositus (N.). Prepositas his Practise. 1588.
— Profitable booke. 1596. 4°.
Mason (Charles). Verses in Camb. Univ. Anthologia. 1632. . . 5741
— — Fasciae. 1633. 5808
— — Rex redux. 1633. 5748

No.

Mason (Charles), *cont.* Verses in Camb. Univ. Carmen. 1635. . 5770
— — Συνῳδία. 1637. 5790
— King (E.). Ivsta. 1638. 5829
— Camb. Univ. Voces. 1640. 5836
See also M. (C.).
Mason (Edmund). Sermon. 28 July 1622. 4°. . . . 3509
Mason (Francis). Authoritie of the Church in making Canons. 1605. 1607. 4°. 7353
— Oxford, 1634. 4°. 5409
Of the consecration of the bishops. 1613. F°. . . . 2647
Vindiciæ ecclesiæ anglicanæ. Ed. 2. 1625. F°. . . 3029
See Champney (A.). Treatise. 1616. 4°.
Verses in Bodleiomnema. 1613. 7756
See Fitzherbert (T.). Adioynder to the supplement. 1613.
— Norris (S.). The Guide. 1621. 4°.
Mason (Henry). Christian humiliation. 1625. 4°. . . . 4090
— Ed. 2. 1627. 4°. 4240
Cure of cares. 1627. 4°. 4241
— 1628. 4°. 4250
— Ed. 3. (Tribunall of the conscience. Ed. 4.) 1634. 12°. 4493
Epicures Fast. 1626. 4°. 4092, 4240
Hearing and doing. 1635. 12°. 4288
New art of lying. 1624. 4°. 4083
— 1634. 12°. 4494
Tribunall of the conscience. 1626. 4°. 4093
— Ed. 2. 1626. 4°. 4094
— Ed. 4. 1634. 12°. . . . . . . cf. 4493
See Jackson (T.). Jvstifying faith. 1615.
Mason (James). Anatomie of sorcerie. 1612. 4°. . . . 3752
Mason (John). Excellent tragedy of Mulleasses the Turke. 1632. 4°. 4148
Mason (John), *Captain.* [Map of Newfoundland.] *See* Vaughan (W.). Golden fleece. 1626. 5029
Mason (Richard), *Jesus Coll.* Verses in Camb. Univ. Carmen. 1635. 5770
— — Συνῳδία. 1637. 5790
— King (E.). Jvsta. 1638. 5829
Mason (Robert). Reasons Academie. *See* D. (Sir J.), *Kt.* A New Post. 7342
Reasons Moane. *See* Davies (Sir J.). A New Post. [16 .] . 4138
Reasons Monarchie. 1602. 8°. 2853
See Sictor (J.). Lacrymæ. 1637.
Mason (Thomas). Christs victorie. 1615. F°. 3584
Revelation of the revelation. 1619. 8°. 3592
Masque of the League and the Spanyard discouered. 1592. 8°. . 7243
Masques. *See* Carew (T.). Cœlum Britannicum. 1634.
— Chapman (G.). Memorable Maske. [1614?] . . 3582
— Daniel (S.). Works.
— — Tethys. 1610.
— Heywood (T.). Loves mistresse. 1640.
— Jones (I.). Britannia Trivmphans. 1637.
— — Temple of love. 1634.
— Jonson (B.). Characters. [1609.]
— — Description. [1608.]
— — Masque of the Gypsies. *See* Horatius. De arte poetica. 1640.
— Shirley (J.). Trivmph of peace. 1633.
Mass. *See* Disclosing.
— Of the Masse. [Headline.] *See* Svm or a brief collection. 1563.
Massie (William). Sermon...at Trafford. Oxford, 1586. 8°. . . 5225
Massinger (Philip). Bond-man. Ed. 2. 1638. 4°. . . . 5150
Duke of Millain. Ed. 2. 1638. 4°. 5151
Emperour of the east. 1632. 4°. 3998

No.
Massinger (Philip), *cont.* Fatall dowry (with N. Field). 1632. 4°. . 4888
Great duke of Florence. 1636. 4°. 4137
Maid of honour. 1632. 4°. 3819
New way to pay old debts. 1633. 4°. 4104
Picture. 1630. 4°. 4882
Renegado. 1630. 4°. 4543
Unnatural combat. 1639. 4°. 5204
Massonius (Robertus). *See* Vermigli (P.). Loci Commvnes. 1576 *etc.*
Master (Ben). Verses in Ferrand (J.). Ἐρωτομανία. 1640. . 5498
Master (Thomas). Verses in Hippocrates. 1633. 5812
— Oxf. Univ. Horti. 1640. 5499
Masterson (T.). First booke of arithmeticke. 1592. 4°. . . . 2229
Addition to his first booke. 1594. 4°. 2233
Third booke of arithmetick. 1595. 4°. 2236
Arithmetick. Ed. H. Waynman. 1634. 8°. 7797
Materen (E. van). [Grimstone's General Historie. 1609.] *See* Meteren.
Mathew or Mathieu (Peter). *See* Matthieu.
Matrimony. *See* Order of Matrimony.
Matthew of Westminster. De rebus Britannicis. 1570. F°. . . 1219
Flores Historiarum. 1567 Oct. 20. F°. 7142
— 1570. F°. 7226
Matthew (Roger). Flight of time. 1634. 4°. 4451
Matthew (Thomas), *pseud.* *See* Rogers (J.).
Matthew (Tobias), *abp.* Verses in Humphrey (L.). J. Jvelli vita. 1573. 837
Matthew (Sir Tobias). *See* Augustine. Confessions. Ed. 2. 1638. 12°.
See Bacon (Francis). Saggi. 1618.
— Savelli (T.). Relation. 1620. 8°.
Matthews (Francis), *alias* Edmundus Ursulanus. *See* Harris (P.). Ἀρκτόμαστιξ. 1633.
Matthews or Matthew (Thomas), *pseud.* *See* Rogers (J.).
Matthias II., *Emperor of Rome.* *See* Hungary. Instrvments of the Pactions. 1620.
Matthieu (Pierre). Heroyck life...of...Henry the fourth. Trans. E. Grimstone. 1612. 4°. 3580
Powerful favorite. Paris, 1628. 4°. 6221-2
Remarkeable considerations...of M. Villeroy...Sejanus. 1638. 4°. 5196
Vnhappy Prosperitie...Ælius Sejanus and Philippe. Trans. Sir T. Hawkins. 1632. 4°. 4846
— Ed. 2. 1639. 12°. 4044
See Serres (J. de). General inventorie. 1607.
— — Generall historie. 1624.
Mauldæus (Jo.), *Germanus.* Verses in Du Bartas. Weekes. 1621. . 2535
Maunsell (A.). First part of the catalogue. 1595. F°. . 7843, 2140
— Part 2. 1595. F°. 7844, 1773
Maunsell (Richard). *See* Fuller (N.). Argument. 1607. 4°.
See Staresmore (S.). Vnlawfvlnes of reading in prayer. 1619.
Maunsell (T.). *See* Davenant (Sir W.). Triumphs. 1635. . . . 5147
Maurice, *Prince of Orange.* Triumphs of Nassau. Trans. W. Shute. 1613. F°. 2445
True report of...Bercke. 1601. 4°. 2320
See Ælianus, *Tacticus.* Tactiks. 1616.
— Briefe discourse. 1599.
— Faithfvll and wise preventer. 1621.
— Marcelline (G.). Vox militis. 1625.
— Steenwyk. True declaration. 1592. 4°.
Mauritius (Joh.). *See* Morris.
Maurus, a Sancta Maria. *See* Benedict, Order of. Douai. 1625? . 6612
Maxey (Ant.). Certaine sermons. Ed. 7. 1634. 8°. . . . 7568
Copie of a sermon. 2 March, 1610. 1610. 8°. 7470
Five sermons. Ed. 5. 1614. 4°. 3402

No.
Maxey (Ant.), *cont.* Goulden chaine of mans saluation. Ed. 3. 1607. 8°. 7278
Maxey (Will.). Verses in Camdeni Insignia. 1624. . . 5346
Maximus Tyrius. Disputationes tres (Lat.). I. Rainoldo Interprete. 1614. *See* Rainolds (J.). Orationes 5. 1613.
Maxwell (James). Admirable and notable prophecies. 1615. 4°. . 2031
New eight-fold probation. 1617. 4°. 3763
See Herodian. Historie of twenty roman Cæsars. 1635. 12°.
— Richelieu. Emblema Animæ. 1635.
— Treasure of Tranquillity. 1611.
Maxwell (Rob.). Verses in Leslie (H.). Examen. 1639. . . . 6068
May (Edward), *Chaplain to Lincoln's Inn.* Sermon of...saints. 1621. 4°. 3844
May (Edward). Most certaine...relation of a strange monster. 1639. 4°. 4477
May (Henry), *Pemb.* Verses in Camb. Univ. Voces. 1640. . 5836
May (Thomas). Continuation of Lucans historicall poem. 1630. 8°. 4923
— Ed. 2. 1633. 8°. 4924
The heire. 1633. 4°. 4574
Reigne of King Henry the second. 1633. 8°. 4575
Tragedy of Julia Agrippina. 1639. 8°. 4933
Victorious reigne of King Edward the third. 1635. 8°. . . 4485
Verses in Camb. Univ. Epicedium. 1612. . . 5665, 5666
— Gill (A.). Πάρεργα. 1632. 4558
— Hodson (W.). Divine Cosmographer. 1640. . . 5847
See Barclay (I.). Argenis. 1628 *etc.*
— — Mirrour of Mindes... 1631.
— Lucanus. Pharsalia. 1627 *etc.*
Maydestone (Clement). *See* Maidstone.
Mayenne (Henri de Lorraine, duc de). *See* France. Louis XIII. 1617.
Mayer (John). Antidote against popery. 1625. 4°. 4230
Commentarie vpon the new testament. Vol. 1. 1631. F°. . 4613
— Vol. 2. 1631. F°. 4841
Ecclesiastica Interpretatio.. of the seven epistles...Catholic, and the Revelation. 1627. 4°. 4810
English catechisme explained. Ed. 3. 1623. 4°. 4519
— Ed. 4. 1630. 4°. 4544
Mayer's catechisme abridged, or the A. B. C. inlarged. Ed. 2. 1623. 8°. 4520
Praxis Theologica. 1629. 4°. 3811
Treasury of ecclesiasticall expositions. 1622. 4°. 3849
Mayerne (L. Turquet de). Generall historie of spaine. 1612. F°. 2443
Mayerne (Sir Theodore Turquet de). *See* Moffett (T.). Insectorum... 1634.
See Parkinson (J.). Paradisus terrestris. 1629. F°.
— — Theatrum. 1640. F°.
Mayhew (Edward), *O.S.B.* *See* Maihew.
Mayne (Jasper). Citye match. Oxford, 1639. F°. 5495
Maynson (Oliver). Verses in Vaughan (R.). Waterworkes. 1610. 3576
Maynwaring (Roger). *See* Manwaring.
Meade (Richard). Verses in Smith (J.). True travels. 1630. . 4836
Meara (Dermod or Dermitius de). Ormonius. 1615. 8°. . . 3409
Pathologia hereditaria generalis. Dublin, 1619. 12°. . . 6017
Meares (Fr.). Verses in Randolph (T.). Jealous Lovers. 1640. . 5852
Measius (P.). Verses in Isaacson (H.). Ephemerides. 1633. . 4206
Meckleburg, Duke of. *See* Waldstein (A. W. E. von).
Medcalf (O.). *See* Metcalfe.
Mede (Joseph). Churches. 1638. 4°. 4319
Clavis apocalyptica. Cantabrigiae, 1627. 4°. 5708
— Ed. 2. 1632. 4°. 5802
Name Altar, or Θυσιαστήριον. 1637. 4°. 4311
Reverence of gods house. 1638. 4°. 4320

No.
Medici (Cosimo de'), *Grand Duke of Tuscany.* *See* Ubaldini (P.). Militia. 1597.
Medici (Ferdinand I., de'), *Grand Duke of Tuscany.* *See* Dallington (Sir R.). Svrvey. 1605.
Medici (Francesco Maria, de'), *Grand Duke of Tuscany.* *See* Ubaldini (P.) Militia. 1597.
Mediolano (Johannes de). *See* Johannes, *de Mediolano.*
Meditations and Prayers. 16°. 6597
Medulla Grammatices. *See* Promptorium puerorum. 1499.
— Ortus Vocabulorum. 1528. 4°. . . 195 and p. 1729
Medwall (H.). Nature. W. Rastell, n.d. F°. (351 corr.=) 535 cf. p. 1730
Meetkerkius (Edw.). Verses in Camdeni Insignia. 1624. . . 5346
Μέγας (Ῥόβερτος ὁ). Verses in Oxf. Univ. Horti. 1640. . . 5499
Mela (P.). Rare and singular worke. Trans. A. Golding. 1590. 4°. 1361
Melampus. Treatise on moles. *See* Hill (T.). Contemplation of Mankinde. 1571. 8°. 6753
Melanchton (Andreas) [i.e. Ph. Melanchthon]. *See* Anderton (J.). Luthers Life. 1624. 4°.
Melanchthon (P.). Apologie...defense of the confessyon of the Germaynes. Trans. R. Taverner. 1536. 8°. 380
— [Another edition.] *See* Augsburg Confession. [1536?]
Epistle...vnto...Henry the eyght, for the reuokynge...of the six Artycles. 'Weesell, 18 May 1547' n.d. 8°. . . 550
Godlye treatyse of Prayer. Trans. J. Bradford. [1551.] 8°. . 1102
Newe work cõcerning...the sacrament. 1543. 8°. . . 7688
Newe worck concernyng...the Sacrament. [1548?] 8°. . . 980
Very godly defense...the mariage of Preistes. Trans. L. Beuchame. 'U. Hoff, Lipse, 1541.' 8°. 5883
Waying and considering of the Interim. Trans. J. Rogers. 1548. 8°. 657
De officiis concionatoris. *See* Reuchlin (J.). De arte concionandi. 1570. 8°.
[Epitome of Moral Philosophy.] *See* Whether it be mortall sinne. [1570?]
[Oracyon at the buryall of Luther.] *See* Jonas (J.). True hystorye. [1546?] 8°.
Verses in Macalpine (J.). Enarratio. 1563. . . . 1304
See Anderton (J.). Luthers Life. 1624. 4°.
— Joye (G.). Exposicion of Daniel. 1545.
— Luther (M.). A faythfull admonycion. 1554.
— Palladius (P.). Introduction. 1598.
Melissus (Paulus), *Francus.* *See* Melissus (P.), *Schedius.*
Melissus (Paulus), *Schedius* [i.e. Paul Schede]. Verses in Beza (T.). Psalmorum libri quinque. 1580. 1539
— Buchanan (G.). Psalmorum Davidis. 1640. . . . 5209
Mellis (John). *See* Recorde (R.). Grounde of Artes. 1582 *etc.*
Melton (John). Astrologaster. 1620. 4°. 7583
Melvill (Andrew). Antitamicamicategoria. *See* Calderwood (D.). Parasynagma. 1620. 4°. 7682
Musae et P. Adamsoni vita. 1620. 4°. 7681
Verses in Buchanan (G.). Rervm scoticarum... 1582. . . 5920
— Sempill (Sir J.). Sacrilege. 1619. 3331
Melville (James). *See* Short relation of the State of the Kirk. . 1638
Memnon. *See* Agatharchides. Agatharcidis et Memnonis historicorum omnia. 1597.
Menandrinus (Marsilius), *Patavinus.* Defence of peace. Trans. W. Marshall. 1535. F°. 539
See Clemangiis (N. de). Specvlvm. 1606.
Menapius (Gulielmus Insulanus). *See* Insulanus.
Mendoza (Bernardino de). Copie of a letter. 1588. 4°. . 1564, 1565
See True Discourse. 1588.

No.

Mendoza (Francesco de). *See* Briefe relation. 1599.
Mendoza (Juan Gonzalez de). *See* Gonzalez.
Menecrates [*Gr. Lat.*]. *See* Poetae minores. 1635.
Menewe (Gracious). Confutacion of...the sacrament vnder one kind. 16°. 6309
Plaine subuersyon...of auricular confession. 16°. . . . 6310
Merbury (C.). Briefe discourse of royall monarchie. 1581. 4°. . 1546
Merbury (Francis). *See* Rogers (R.) Seaven Treatises. 1605 *etc.*
Mercator (Gerard). Atlas (latiné). Ed. 4. Hondius, Amsterodami. 1613. F°. 7738
— 'Ed. 4.' 1616. F°. 7739
— (gallicé.) Ed. 10. H. Hondius, Amsterodami. 1628. F°. 7740
— (latiné.) 'Ed. 10.' 1630. F°. . . . 7741
— (latiné.) 'Ed. 10.' 1631. F°. 7742
— 'Ed. 10.' 1633, '1636,' 1641. F°. 6355–6
Atlas Novus. H. Hondius et J. Janssonius, Amsterodami. 1638. F°. 7743
Atlas Minor...trad. en François par La Popeliniere. J. Jansson, Amsterdam. 1630. Obl. 4°. 7744
Historia mundi: or Mercators Atlas...rectified by J. Hondy. Englished by W. Saltonstall. 1635. F°. 4637
Mercerus (J.). *See* Willet (A.). Hexapla in Genesin. 1605. . . 5634
Merchants Adventurers. *See* Wheeler (J.). Treatise. 1601.
Mercurius Britannicus. *See* Hall (Joseph). Mundus alter et idem. 1605. 8°.
Mere, Town of, co. Wilts. *See* Fantasy of the Fox. W. de Worde. 1530. 4°.
Meredeth (Richard). Two sermons. 1606. 4°. 3560
Meredith (John). Judge of heresies. 1624. 4°. 4524
Sinne of blasphemie. 1622. 4°. 4133
Meredith (Richard). *See* Meredeth.
Meres (Francis). *See* Luis de Granada. Sinners guyde. 1598 *etc.* 4°.
Merideth (John). *See* Meredith.
Meriell (Thomas), *M.A.* Verses in Camden (W.). Britannia. 1637. 3055
Merike (Ed.). Verses in Dolor. 1625. 5701
Meriton (George). Sermon of nobilitie. 1606, 1607. 4°. . . 3565
Sermon of Repentance. 1607. 4°. 3566
Merry Devise. Mery devise calld the Troublesome travell. 1589. 4°. 6791
Mervyn (James). Verses *bis* in Shirley (J.). The royall master. 1638. 4665
Mery devise. *See* Merry devise.
Meslier (Hugo). *See* Lugo (P. de), Italicus. Principia. R. Pynson (1506?] 4°. 302
Mesne (Johannes). *See* Mesue.
Mesue (Johannes). *See* Herbal. 1561.
Metamorphosis of Tabacco. 1602. 4°. 2922
Metaxas (Nicodemus). *See* Korydaleos (Th.). Ἔκθεσις περὶ Ῥητορικῆς. 1625. 8°.
Metcalfe (Nicholas). *See* Du Moulin (P.). Coales from the altar. 1623. 8°.
Metcalfe (Oswald). Verses in Cheke (Sir J.). De obitu M. Buceri. 1551. 734
— Wilson (Sir T.). Vita. 1551. 631
Metcalfe (Robert). Censura. *See* Hippocrates. 1633. . . 5812
Meteren (Demetrius van). *See* Grimstone (E.). Generall historie of the Netherlands. 1627. F°.
Meteren (Emanuel van). True discourse...of the...governors in the Netherlands. Trans. T. Churchyard. 1602. 4°. . . 2873
See Grimstone (E.). Generall historie. 1609.
Methold (William). *See* Purchas (S.). Pilgrimage. 1626.
Metrodorus [*Gr. Lat.*]. *See* Poetae minores. 1635.
Meverell (Ottwell), *M.D.* Verses in Parkinson (J.). Paradisus terrestris. 1629. 2561
— Hippocrates, 1633. 5812

No.
Mews (Peter). Verses in Oxf. Univ. Horti. 1640. 5499
— Snelling (T.). Thibaldus. 1640. 5502
— Buchler (J.). Sacrarum...phrasinm...thesaurus. 16[4 ?]. . 4878
Mexia (Pedro). Historie of all the romane emperors. 1604. F°. . 2932
Imperiall historie. 1623. F°. 2544
See Milles (T.). Treasvrie. 1613.
Meyvius (Petrus). *See* Mews.
Michaell (Edward). Verses in Gardiner (E.). The triall. 1610 *etc.* 2505 etc.
Michaeas. The Converted Jew. 1630. 4°. 6999
Michaelis (Seb.). Admirable historie of the...penitent woman. Trans. W. B. 1613. 4°. 7472
Michaelsone (J.). Verses in Narne (W.). The pearle of prayer. 1630. . 5971
Michelborn (Edward). Verses in Fitzgeffrey (C.). Affaniae. 1601. 5254
— Budden (J.). Gvl. Patteni vita. 1602. 5256
— Camdeni Insignia. 1624. 5346
Michelborne (Laurence). Verses in Holyoake (F.). Dictionarium. 1640. 3058
Michelborne (Thomas). Verses in Barnes (B.). Foure bookes. 1606. . 2435
Michell (Sir Francis). View of France. 1604. 4°. . . . 2883
Michell (Henry). Verses in Camb. Univ. Lachrymae. 1587. . . 2123
Michell (Thomas). Verses in Forbes (P.). Funerals. 1637. . 6007
Micklethwait (Paul). Verses in Camb. Univ. Dolor. 1625. . . 5701
Micro-cosmography. *See* Earle (J.).
Microen (Marten). *See* Micron.
Micron (Marten). Den kleynen Cathecismus. 1566. 8°. . . 1293
See Knewstub (J.). A Confutation. 1579.
— Liturgies. London. Dutch Church. 1554. 8°. . . 3290
Micronius (M.). *See* Micron.
Microphilus. New-yeeres gift...to the Lord Minimus. 1636. 12°. . 3705
Middelburg. Middleborow. Briefe Rehersall of...Middleborow and Armevv. 1574. 8°. 1455
[Middelburg Prayer Book.] Book of Form of Prayers. . . 6446
Middelton (T.). *See* Middleton.
Middelton (Tho.). Verses in Oxf. Univ. Horti. 1640. . . . 5499
Middlesex, *County of.* *See* Norden (J.). 1593.
Middleton (T.). Game at chesse. 1625. 4°. 6968
Middleton (W.). Papisto-mastix. 1606. 4°. 1386
Mielot (Jean). *See* Cordiale. 1479.
Miggrode (Jacques de). *See* Las Casas (B. de). Spanish Colonie. 1583. 4°. 1819
Mignotius (Cardanus), *Rothomagensis.* Verses in Humphrey (L.). I. Ivelli vita. 1573. 837
Mikron (Marten). *See* Micron.
Milbourne (R.). Verses in Camb. Univ. Lachrymae. 1587. . 2123
Milbourne (Robert). *See* James I. Cygnea Cantio. 1629.
Milbourne (William). Sapientia Clamitans. 1638. 8°. . . 4869
Wisdome crying out. 1639. 8°. 4950
Mild. A myld and iust defence...in behalfe of the Ministers suspended...against...M. Gabril Powel. 1606. 4°. 6869
Mildapettus (Franciscus), Navarrenus, *pseud.* *See* Temple (W.).
Miles et Clericus. *See* Ockham (W.). A Dialogue. [1540?] 8°. . 513
Miles (Henry). *See* Office of General Remembrance. 1617. 4°. . 3588
Mill (Humphrey). Poems occasioned by a...vision. 1639. 8°. . 5172
Miller (George), *Printer.* *See* Bentham (J.). Saints societie. 1636. 4°.
Milles (Robert). Abrahams suite for Sodome. 1612. 8°. . . 3085
Milles (Tho.). Ἀρχαιόπλουτος. 1619. F°. 2788
Catalogve of honor. 1610. F°. 2770
Nobilitas politica. 1608. F°. 2765
Treasurie of auncient and moderne times. 1613. F°. . . 2780
Milles (Tho.), *Clar.* Verses in Camb. Univ. Thr-thr. 1603. . 5616
Milles (Tho.), *K.C.C.* Verses in Camb. Univ. Epithalam. 1625. . 5702

No.
Milton (John). Verses in King (E.). Ivsta. 1638. . . . 5829
— Shakspeare (W.). Poems. 1640. 4681
See Ralegh (Sir W.). Tubus Historicus. [A second copy of no. 4022 with MS. dedication.] Cf. pp. 1739, 1740.
Mimi Publiani. *See* Publilius.
Mimnermus [*Gr. Lat.*]. *See* Poetæ minores. 1635.
Minadoi (G. T.). History of the warres between the Turkes and the persians. Tr. A. Hartwell. 1595. 4°. 1971
Ministers, Deprived. *See* England, Church. *Ministers, Deprived.*
Ministry of the Gospel. *See* Certaine arguments. 1606.
Minne (Franc.). Verses in Camdeni Insignia. 1624. . . . 5346
Minsheu (John). *See* Percivall (R.). Dictionarie in Spanish and English. 1599.
— — Spanish grammar. 1599.
Ἡγεμὼν εἰς τὰς γλώσσας. Ductor in Linguas. 1617. F°. . 3204
— [List of subscribers.] F°. 7850
Minshaei emendatio. Ed. 2. 1626. F°. 4803
— 'Ed. 2.' 1627. F°. 4811
Children of. *See* Stafford (T.). Pacata Hibernia. [Ed. 2.] 1633.
Minshull. *See* Mynshul.
Minucius Felix. Octavius. Oxonii, 1636. 12°. 5453
Mirk (John). Festial. Oxford, 1486. F°. 81
— (Quatuor Sermones.) Caxton [1491?]. F°. . . . 41
— Pynson [1493]. F°. 113
— M. Morin, Rouen, 1499. 4°. 141
— W. de Worde, 11 May 1508. 4°. 157
Miroir des plus belles Courtisanes. [Ab. 1635.] Obl. 8°. . . 6405
Mirror and dyscrypcyon of the worlde. [1527?] F°. . . . 413
Mirror for Magistrates. *See* Higgins (I.).
Mirror of Gold. *See* Dionysius Carthusianus. The mirror. 1522.
Mirror of Health. *See* Mirror or Glass of Health.
Mirror of Knighthood. (Part i.) T. East. [1578?] 4°. . 1576, 1577
Book VI. (Part iii, Book 1.) E. Allde for C. Burby. 1598. 4°. 2011
Book VII. (Part iii, Book 2.) T. Purfoot for C. Burby. 1598. 4°. 1381
Book VIII. (Part iii, Book 3.) T. Creede for C. Burbey. 1599. 4°. 2728
'Part' IX. (Part iii, Book 4.) For C. Burbie. 1601. 4°. . 2876
Mirrour of New Reformation. Ed. 2. Rouen, 1634. 8°. . . 6260
Mirror of Our Lady. R. Faques. 1530. F°. 336
Mirrour of Policie. *See* La Perriere (G. de). 1598 *etc.* 4°.
Mirror of Princely Deeds. *See* Mirror of Knighthood.
Mirror of the Chirch. *See* Edmond Rich.
Mirror of the World. Caxton [1480]. F°. 15
Ed. 2. Caxton [1490?]. F°. 39
Myrrour or glasse for them that be syke. Translated. Southwark [1536?]. 8°. 5866
Mirror or Glass of Health. *See* Moulton (T.).
Mirrour or Looking glasse of lyfe. *See* G. (J.). [15 .] 8°.
Missale (Sarum). M. Wenssler, Basle [ab. 1488]. F°. . . . 142
Venice. 1 Sept. 1494. F°. 123
Venice. 1 Dec. 1494. 8°. 124
J. Notary, 20 Dec. 1498. F°. 71
Pynson, 10 Jan. 1500. F°. 110
A. Vérard, Paris, 29 Jun. 1504. F°. 6144
M. Morin, Rouen, 12 Maij 1506. 4°. 6230
W. Hopyl, Paris, imp. F. Byrckman, 10 Kal. April, 1510 (7 Feb. 1511). 6152
Pynson, 22 Feb. 1512. F°. 261
B. Rembolt, Paris, 21 Jan. 1513. F°. 6158
W. Hopyl, Paris, imp. F. Byrckman. 28 Nov. 1514. F°. . 6153
Kerbriand al. Huguelin et Adam, imp. Petit et Bienayse. 21 Aug. 1516. 8°. 6185

No.
Missale (Sarum), *cont.* E. Hardy, imp. J. Caillard, Rouen, 5 Jun. 1518. 4°. . . . . 6235+
N. Higman, imp. F. Regnault and F. Byrckman, 29 Oct. 1519. 4°. 6160
P. Olivier, exp. J. Cousin, Rothomagi. 24 Dec. 1519. F°. . 7702
Pynson, 9 Kal. Jan. 1520. F°. 270
F. Regnault, Paris, 29 Oct. 1526. F°. 6162
N. Prevost, imp. F. Byrckman, 3 Kal. Mart. 1527. F°. . . 6191
M. Morin, Rouen, imp. J. Richardi, 27 Maij 1528. F°. . 6231
F. Regnault, Paris, 31 May 1532. F°. 6170
F. Regnault, Paris, 27 May 1533. 4°. 6173
R. Hamillon, in edibus R. Valentini. 1554. 4°. . . . 6244
J. Amazeur, pro G. Merlin, Paris, 1555. F°. 6194
Kingston and Sutton. 1555. 4°. 1165
J. Day, 1557. F°. 788
Missale (York). P. Olivier, Rouen, sumpt. J. Gachet, 5 Feb. 1516. F°. 6233
F. Regnault, Paris, 1533. 4°. 6174
Missae aliquot pro sacerdotibus itinerantibus in Anglia. 1615. 4°. 6615-6
Missale parvum pro sacerdotibus...itinerantibus. 1626. 4°. . . 6620
Misselden (Edward). Circle of commerce. 1623. 4°. . . . 3854
Free Trade. 1622. 8°. 4695
— Ed. 2. 1622. 8°. 4696
Mithridatium. A discourse. 1585. 8°. 6782
Mocket (Richard). Doctrina et politia ecclesiae anglicanae. 1617. 4°. 3479, 3480
See James I. Deus et Rex.
Modern History of the World. *See* Swedish Intelligencer, Part VIII.
Modus obseruandi curiam cum leta. J. Skot [1529?]. 4°. . . 357
R. Redman, 1530. 8°. 372
Modus tenendi curiam Baronum. H. Pepwell [1521]. 4°. . . 335
Modus tenendi curiam Baronum cum visu franci plegij. R. Copland [15—]. 4°. 341
See Book of Justice of the Peace. 1544.
Modus tenendi vnum Hundredum siue curiam de Recordo. [1516?] 4°. 307
R. Redman, n.d. 8°. 395
Moffet (Thomas). Insectorum sive minimorum animalium theatrum. 1634. F°. 4631
Moffet (Will.). Verses in Hodson (W.). Holy sinner. 1639. . 5796
— Divine cosmographer. 1640. 5847
Mogul, The Great. *See* Covert (R.). A trve...Report. 1631.
See Herbert (Sir T.). A relation. 1634.
Molinier (Étienne). Mirrour for christian states. Trans. W. Tyrwhit. 1635. 4°. 4015
Molle (Henry). Verses in Camb. Univ. Epicedium. 1612. . . 5665
— — Lacrymæ. 1619. 5689
— — Dolor. 1625. 5701
— — Epithalam. 1625. 5702
— — Genethl. 1631. 5731
— — Anthologia. 1632. 5741
— — Fasciae. 1633. 5808
— Hawkins (W.). Corolla. 1634. 5803
— Camb. Univ. Voces. 1640. 5836
See Camerarius (P.). Living librarie. 1625. F°. . . . 2454
Molle (John). *See* Camerarius (P.). Living Librarie. 1621 *etc.* . 2450 *etc.*
See Mornay (P. de). A treatise of the chvrch. 1606. 4°.
Momford (Thomas). Verses in Coryate (T.). Coryates crvdities. 1611. 3076
Monachus (Guido), *Gallus*. [*qu.* Lemoine?] Verses in Comenius. Porta linguarum. 1631 *etc.* 8°. . . . . . 4434 *etc.*
Monardes (N.). Ioyfvll newes out of the newe founde worlde. Trans. J. Frampton. 1577. 4°. 1331
— — 1580. 4°. 1811

No.

Monardes (J.), *cont.* Ioyfvll newes out of the newe founde worlde. Trans. J. Frampton. 1596. 4°. 200
Moncaster (Richard) [*qu.* Mulcaster?]. Verses in Baret (J.). Alveare. 1573. 7249
Monger ( ). *See* Hooper (J.). Apologye. 1562.
Monginot (François de). Resolution of doubts. 1618. 4°. . . 4156
Monipennie (John). Abridgement or summarie of the Scots Chronicles. Edinburgh, 1633. 8°. 5973
Certaine matters composed...of Scotland. Edinburgh [1594?]. 4°. 5934
Certeine matters concerning the realme of Scotland. 1603. 4°. 2078, 2757
Monmouth (Henry Carey, Earl of). *See* Malvezzi (V.). Romulus and Tarquin. 1637. 12°.
Monro (David). Theses in Adamson (J.). Εἰσόδια. 1618. . . . 5960
Monro (Robert). Monro his expedition. 1637. F°. . . . 5067
Montacutius (Richardus). *See* Montagu.
Montagu (Christopher). Verses in Camb. Univ. Rex Redux. 1633. . 5748
Montagu (Edward). Verses in Camb. Univ. Lacrymæ. 1619. . 5689
— — Genethliacum. 1631. 5731
— — Anthologia. 1632. 5741
Montagu (George). Verses in Camb. Univ. Voces. 1640. . . . 5836
Montagu (Henry Pole, baron). *See* Morison (Sir R.). Invective. 1539.
Montagu (Henry), earl of Manchester. *See* Manchester.
Montagu or Mountague (James), Bp. *See* Blackwell (G.). A Large examination. 1607.
See Downham (G.). Two sermons. 1608.
— James I. Workes. 1616.
— — Opera. 1619.
Montagu (James), *Sid.* Verses in Camb. Univ. Dolor. 1625. . . 5701
— — Epithalam. 1625. 5702
Montagu (Richard). Analecta ecclesiasticarum exercitationum. 1622. F°. 3289
Apparatus ad origines ecclesiasticas. Oxoniae, 1635. F°. . . 5466
Appello Caesarem. 1625. 4°. 2825
— — *See* Mocket (R.). Doctrina. 1617 [this copy]. . . 3480
De originibus ecclesiasticis comm. tomus 1. 1636. F°. . 4300
Diatribae vpon the first part of the late History of Tithes. 1621. 4°. 3013
Gagg for the new gospel? 1624. 4°. 3442
Immediate addresse vnto God alone. 1624. 4°. 3154
Θεανθρωπικόν. 1640. F°. 4332
— Pars posterior. 1640. F°. 5134
See Carleton (G.). Examination. 1626.
— Featley (D.). Parallel. 1626. 4335
— — Second parallel. 1626.
— Gregory *Nazianzene*. Invectivæ. 1610.
— Johnson (R.). The gospell. 1633. 4°.
— Articles of Enquiry. (Norwich Diocese.) [1638.]
— Pelagius. Parallel. 1626.
— — Parallelismus. 1626.
— Wotton (A.). Dangerovs plot. 1626.
— Yates (J.). Ibis ad Caesarem. 1626. 4°.
Montagu (Tho.) ['Ορος-ὀξύ]. Verses in Coryate (T.). Coryates crvdities. 1611. 3076
Montagu (Tho.), *King's.* Verses in Camb. Univ. Fasciae. 1633. . 5808
— — Rex redux. 1633. 5748
— — Carmen. 1635. 5770
— — Voces. 1640. 5836
Montagu (Walter). Verses in Camb. Univ. Lacrymæ. 1619. . 5689
Montagu (William). Verses in Camb. Univ. Anthologia. 1632. . 5741
— — Rex redux. 1633. 5748
Montaigne (Michael de). Essayes. Trans. J. Florio. Ed. 2. 1613. F°. 3375
— Ed. 3. 1632. F°. 4265

No.
Montanus. *See* Arias Montanus (Benedictus).
Montanus (Gul.). Verses in Castiglione (B.). De Curiali. 1571. . 824
Montanus (Jacobus), *de Spira*. *See* Vineis (R. de). Lyf of S. Katherine of Senis. [1493?]
Montanus (Philippus). *See* Theophylactus. Commentarii. 1636. F°.
Monteigne (George), *bp*. *See* Sibthorpe (R.). Apostolike Obedience. 1627.
Montemagno (Buonaccorso da). *See* Cicero. De Senectute. 1481.
Montemayor (Jorge de). [Diana. Selection.] *See* p. 499 of Sidney (Sir P.). Arcadia. 1621. F°.
Diana. Trans. B. Yong. 1598. F°. 7924
Montenay (G. de). Booke of armes. Frankfurt, 1619. 8°. . . 6631
Montford (John), *T.C.C.* Verses in Barlow (W.). Vita R. Cosin. 1598. 1707
Montford (Thomas). *See* Barlow (W.). Sermon. 1601.
Montjoy (Montjoy Blount, Lord). *See* Markham (G.). Honour. 1624.
Montlyard (Jean de). *See* Ol. (P.), *Spanish Pilgrim*. Treatise parænetical. 1598.
— Spanish Pilgrime. 1625.
Montpellier University. *See* Primrose (J.). Academia. 1631.
Moody (Sir Henry). Verses in Camdeni Insignia. 1624. . . 5346
— Massinger (P.). New way. 1633. 4104
Moone (Peter). Short treatyse of certayne thynges. [Ab. 1548.] 4°. . 5879
Moore (Horatio). Verses in Oxf. Univ. Horti. 1640. . . 5499
Moore (John). A mappe of mans mortalitie. 1617. 4°. . 7709(=3418)
Target for tillage. 1613. 8°. 2273
Moore (P.). Hope of health. 1565. 8°. 1173
Moore (Robert). Diarium historicopoeticum. Oxonii, 1595. 4°. . 5241
Moore (William), *Gonville and Caius*. Verses in Hippocrates. 1633. . 5812
— Camb. Univ. Carmen. 1635. 5770
Moors. *See* Conestaggio (G.). Historie. 1600.
Moraes (Francisco de). *See* Palmerin of England. 1639. 4°.
Moral philosophie of the Stoicks. 1598. 8°. *See* Du Vair.
Moravius (Thomas), *Scotus*. *See* Murray (T.).
Morbred (Antony). Verses in Oxf. Univ. Magd. Coll. 1612. . . 5302
Mordaunt (Joh.). Verses in Oxf. Univ. Horti. 1640. . . 5499
More work for a masse-priest. 1621. *See* Cooke (A.).
More (Christopher). *See* More (Cresacre).
More (Cresacre *alias* Christopher). *See* M. (Ch.). Meditations. 1639.
More (Sir George). Demonstration of God. 1597. 4°. . . 1774
— 1598. 4°. 1776
More (George), *Esquire*. Principles for young princes. 1611. 12°. . 7537
More (Henry), *Jesuit*. *See* Platus (H.). Happines of a religious state. 1632.
More (Hen.), *Platonist*. Verses in Camb. Univ. Anthologia. 1632. 5741
— — Rex redux. 1633 *bis*. 5748
— King (E.). Ivsta. 1638. 5829
— Camb. Univ. Carmen. 1635 *bis*. 5770
— — Συνῳδία. 1637. 5790
— — Voces *ter*. 1640. 5836
More (John). Table from the beginning of the world. Cambridge, 1593. 8°. 5561
More (Nic.), *K.C.* Verses in Camb. Univ. Fasciae. 1633. . . 5808
— — Συνῳδία. 1637. 5790
More (Richard). Carpenters Rule. 1602. 4°. 2923
More (Sir T.). Workes. 1557. F°. 996
Commonwealth. 1639. 12°. 4218
Confutacyon of Tyndales answer. 1532(-3). F°. . . . 532
Debellacyon of Salem and Bizance. 1533. 8°. . . . 535
Dialogue of cumfort. Antwerp, 1573. 8°. 6123
Dyaloge...of the veneracyon and worship of ymagys. 1531. F°. . 528
Epistola...ad Acad. Oxon...Poemata...R. Cotton etc. Oxon, 1633. 4°. 5403
Epistola ad Germanum Brixium. 1520. 4°. 272

No.

More (Sir T.), *cont.* G. Rossei opus. 1523. 4°. 284
Supplycacyon of soulys. [Ab. 1529.] F°. 7930
Utopia. Trans. R. Robinson. Ed. 2. [1556.] 8°. . . 1075
— — 1624. 4°. 4183
[Poetry.] *See* Virgil Æneis i–iv. 1583.
Prayers. *See* Manual. 1589. 16°.
Verses in Holt (J.). Lac Puerorum. Antwerp, 15—. . . 6072
See Frith (J.). Boke...answerynge vnto M. Mores letter. 1546 etc.
— — Disputacion. [1535?]
— Tindale (W.). An answere. [1530.]
— — Supper of the Lorde. 1533 [155–?].
More (W.). Verses in King (E.). Ivsta. 1638. 5829
See also Moore.
Morecock (T.), *T.C.* Verses in Camb. Univ. Συνωδία. 1637. . 5790
Morel (Guillaume). *See* Morelius.
Morelius (Gul.). Verborum Latinorum cum graecis anglicisque coniunctorum Commentarii. 1583. F°. 1515
Morella (Camilla). Verses in Harvey (G.). Gratulationum. 1578. 1495
Moresinus (Thomas). *See* Morison.
Morgan (R.), *M.A.*, *S.J.C.* Verses in Camb. Univ. Συνωδία. 1637. . 5790
Morgan (William), *bp.* *See* Bible. Welsh. 1620. F°.
Morgan (William), *S.J.C.* Verses in Camb. Univ. Συνωδία. 1637. 5790
Morice (James). Briefe treatise of Oathes. [Ab. 1590.] 4°. . . 6796
Morillon (Guido). *See* Ovid. Heroidum Epistolæ. 1583. 16°.
Morisius (Gulielmus). Verses in Stanyhurst (R.). Harmonia. 1570. 749
Morison (Sir R.). Apomaxis calumniarum. 1537. 4°. . . . 440
Invective ayenst...treason. 1539. 8°. 451
See Defence of priestes marriages. [1566?]
— Frontinus (S. J.). Stratagemes. 1539.
— Sturmius (J.). Epistle. 1538. 8°.
— Vives (J. L.). Introduction to vvysedom. 1540.
Morison (Thomas). Papatus. Edinburgh, 1594. 8°. . . 5928, 5929
Morisot (Claude Barthélemy). *See* Barclay (J.). Euphormionis Lusinini... partes quinque. 1634. 12°.
Morley (Tho.). Canzonets. 1597. 4°. 2332
— 1602. 4°. 1612
Madrigalls to fovre voyces. Book 1. 1594. 4°. . . . 1602
Madrigals. The Triumphes of Oriana. 1601. 4°. . . . 1611
Plaine and easie introduction to practicall musicke. 1608. F°. 2490
Mornay (P. de), *Seigneur du Plessis-Marly.* Christian and godly view of death and life. 1593. 8°. 2231
Fowre bookes of the eucharist. Ed. 2. 1600. F°. . . . 2155
Homily. Trans. I. V. Oxford, 1615. 12°. 5324
Mysterie of iniqvitie. 1612. F°. 2444
Notable treatise of the church. 1580. 8°. 1665
Three homilies. Ed. A. R. 1626. 12°. 3869
Treatise of the church. 1581. 8°. 1670
— 1606. 4°. 3612
Woorke conc. the trewnesse of Christian religion. Trans. Sidney and Golding. 1587. 4°. 2183
— Ed. 4. 1617. 4°. 4060
See Du Perron (J. D.). Discourse of the Conference. 1600 etc.
— E. (O.). Briefe replie. 1600.
— Parsons (R.). Treatise of three conversions of England.
Morrell (Roger). Verses in Cambridge Lachrymae. 1587. . . 2123
— Whitaker (W.). Praelectiones. 1599. 5598
Μοῤῥῆνος (Ἰοάννης). Verses in Wilson (Sir T.). Vita. 1551. . . 631
Morris (John), *Regius Professor.* *See* Hakewill (G.). Apologie. 1630.
Morris (John) or Mauritius. Verses in Parkinson (J.). Theatrum. 1640. 4680
Mors (Roderick), *pseud.* *See* Brinkelow (H.).
Morse (Philip), *C.C.C.* Verses in Camb. Univ. Συνωδία. 1637. . 5790

No.

Morton (Alb.). Verses in Camb. Univ. Thr-thr. 1603. . . 5616
Morton (Ed.), *K.C.C.* Verses in Camb. Univ. Epithalam. 1625. . 5702
Morton (Hoby). Verses in Hoby (Sir E.). Currycombe. 1615. . 3111
Morton (John), *cardinal.* *See* Missale (Sarum). 1500. F°.
Morton (Thomas). Antidotum adv. eccl. Rom. de merito. Cantabrigiae, 1637. 4°. 5791
Apologia catholica. 1605. 4°. 2354, 2355
— Pars secunda. 1606. 4°. 1757
Catholike appeale. 1610. F°. 1760
Defence of the innocencie of the three ceremonies of the church of England. 1619. 4°. 3740
Direct answer unto...Higgons. 1609. 4°. 7380
Discharge of five imputations. 1633. 8°. 4272
Exact discoverie of romish doctrine. 1605. 4°. 2938, 2939, 7468
Full satisfaction concerning a double romish iniquitie. 1606. 4°. 2263
Grand imposture of the (now) church of Rome. [1628?] 4°.. 4424
— Ed. 2. 1628. 4°.. 4425
Of the institution of the sacrament. 1631. F°. . . . 3181
— Ed. 2. 1635. F°. 4588
Preamble vnto an incovnter with P. R. 1608. 4°. . . . 3372
Replica seu...brevis velitatio. 1638. 4°. 4386
Sermon...in...Durham, 5 May 1639. Newcastle, 1639. 4°. . 5909
Totius doctrinalis controversiae de eucharistia decisio. Cantabrigiae, 1640. 4°. 5848
Treatise of the nature of God. 1599. 8°. 7707
See Ames (W.). Fresh svit... 1633.
— — Reply to Dr Mortons generall defence. 1622.
— Anderton (J.). Protestants apologie. 1608.
— Anderton (L.). Progenie of Catholicks. 1633. . . 6264
— Booke intitvled: the english Protestants Recantation. 1617.
— Burgess (J.). Answer...to...a reply to Dr Mortons Generall Defence. 1631.
— Durie (J.). De Pace. 1638.
— Hall (Jos.). Reconciler. 1629.
— Higgons (T.). First motive. 1609.
— Parsons (R.). Quiet and sober reckoning. 1609.
Morwen or Morwyng (Peter). *See* Gesner (C.). Treasure. 1559.
— Gesner (C.). New booke. 1565.
— Joseph ben Gorion. Compendious...Historie. 1575 etc.
Morwyng. *See* Morwen.
Moryson (Fynes). Itinerary. 1617. F°.. . . . . 3794, 3795
Mosan (Jacob). *See* Wirsung (C.). General practise of physicke. 1617. F°.
Moschus [*Gr. Lat.*]. *See* Poetæ minores. 1635.
Moseley (John). Verses in Oxf. Univ. Magd. Coll. 1612. . . 5302
Moses, *Rabbi.* *See* Moses *ben Maimon.*
Moses ben Maimon. הלכות תשובה Canones poenitentiæ. Cantabrigiae, 1631. 4°. 5737
Mishneh-Torah [Extract. (Text and Eng. Trans.).] *See* Broughton (H.). Comment upon Coheleth. 1605.
See Ferdinand (P.). Haec sunt verba. 1597.
— Herbal. 1561. 1242
Moses Sephardi, *Rabbi.* *See* Alfunsi (P.).
Mosley (Humphry), *printer.* *See* Bacon (F.). Historie of Life and Death. 1638.
Mosse (Miles). Arraignment and conviction of vsvrie. 1595. 4°.. 2223
Justifying and saving faith. Cambridge, 1614. 4°. . . 5672
Scotlands welcome. 1603. 8°. 7520
Most happy unions contracted...from the Norman conquest to...James I. Single sheet. F°.. 7714
Most pythye and excellent Epistell. Trans. R. Pownoll. 1556. 8°. 6730

No.
Most strange and wonderfull Herring. 1598. 4°. 1976
Moston (S.). Verses in Camb. Univ. Thr-thr. 1603. 5616
Motives maintained. *See* Chillingworth (W.). 1638.
Moufet (Thomas). *See* Moffett.
Mouleine (Peter). *See* Du Moulin (P.).
Moulson (John), *of Hargrave.* [Funeral at Banbury.] *See* W. (H.). Θρηνοικός. 1640.
Moulton (T.). Myrrour or Glasse of Helth. E. Redman [1540?]. 8°. 407
— [ab. 1540]. 8°. 6691
— W. Middleton [1545?]. 8°. 715
— R. Toye [ab. 1546]. 8°. 7144
— R. Kele. 8°. 7145
— H. Jackson [bef. 1616]. 8°. 1855
Moundeford (Richard). Verses in Camb. Univ. Epicedium. 1612. 5665
Moundeford (Thomas). Vir bonus. 1622. 8°. 3019
Mounslowe (Alex.). Almanacke and prognostication. 1561. 8°. 6745
Mounson ( ). *See* Briefe Declaration. 1636.
Mount (William). Verses in L'Obel (M. de). Balsami. 1598. 2071
Mountagu, Mountague. *See* Montagu or Mountague.
Mountain (Didymus), *pseud.* *See* Hill (T.).
Mountjoy (Charles, Lord). *See* Birchensha (R.). Discourse. 1602. 4°.
Mowtlowe (Hen.). Verses in Camb. Univ. Dolor. 1625. 5701
— — Rex redux. 1633. 5748
Muenster (Sebastian). Liber Psalmorum. *See* Common Prayer (Lat.). 1574.
— — Liber precum. 1594. 8°.
— North (G.). Description of Swedland. 1561.
Muffet (Peter). Comm. upon Proverbes. 1592. 8°. 2230
Muhammad, *Prophet.* Mohammedis Imposturae. 1615. 4°. 2280
Muhammad II. The Turkes Secretorie. 1607. 4°. 3367
Muirhead (Arthur). Verses in Adamson (J.). Εἰσόδια. 1618. 5960
Mulcaster (Ric.). Positions...for the training vp of children. 1581. 4°. 1547
Mulcaster (Ric.). Verses in Baret (J.). Alvearie. 1580. 1418 (cf. 7249)
— Ockland (C.). Anglorum praelia (Εἰρηναρχία). 1582. 1317
See Strigelius (V.). Third proceeding. 1595. 4°. 2844
Mulcaster (Robert). *See* Fortescue (Sir John). De Laudibus Legum Angliæ. 1616.
— — Learned commendation. 1573.
Mulet (I.). [Licence.] *See* Richeome (L.). Holy Pictures. 1619.
Mullins (John). Verses in Wilson (Sir T.). Vita. 1551. 631
Multibibus (Blasius). *See* Brathwaite.
Mun (Thomas). Discourse of trade. 1621. 4°. 3678
Munday (Anthony). Briefe chronicle. 1611. 8°. 2775
Verses in Thynne (F.). Newes from the north. 1585. 2002
See Calvin (J.). Two godly...Sermons. (1584.)
— Defence of Contraries. 1593.
— Masque of the league. 1592. 8°.
— Palmerin d'Oliva. 1637. 4°.
— Palmerin of England. 1639. 4°.
— Primaleon. 1619. 7895
— Stow (J.). Survey of London... 1633.
— Teixeira (J.). Strangest adventure. 1601. 4°. 7765
Mundey (John), *C.C.C.* Verses in Camb. Univ. Lacrymæ. 1619. 5689
— — Epithalam. 1625. 5702
Mundy (J.). Songs and Psalmes. 1594. 4°. 1603
Munster (S.). *See* Muenster.
Mure (Sir William), *Kt.* *See* Caledon's Complaints. [1640.] 4°. 5994
Mure (Sir William), *the younger.* Verses in Adamson (J.). Εἰσόδια. 1618. 5960
Muretus (M. Antonius). [Institution for Children. (Trans.).] *See* Downe (J.). Certaine treatises. 1633 *etc.*

No.
Murgatrod (Michael). Verses in Barlow (W.). Vita R. Cosin. 1598. 1707
Murmelius (Joannes). *See* Mantuanus (B.). Adolescentia. 1569 *etc.*
Murray (John). Sermon. *See* Informations or a protestation. 1608. 8°.
Murray (John), *K.C.C.* Verses in Camb. Univ. Genethl. 1631. . 5731
— — Anthologia. 1632. 5741
— — Fasciae. 1633. 5808
— — Rex redux. 1633. 5748
Murray (Thomas). *See* James I. [Lepanto.] Naupactiados. 1604.
Murray (Will.). Verses in Camb. Univ. Genethl. 1631. . . 5731
— — Anthologia. 1632. 5741
— — Fasciae. 1633. 5808
— — Rex redux. 1633. 5748
Mursæus (Joannes). Verses in Bale (J.). Scriptores. 1548. . . 6314
Murton (John). Discription of what God hath predestinated. 1620. 8°. 6920
— *See* Robinson (J.). Defence. 1624.
Musculus (Wolf.). Common Places. 1578. 4°. 1498
Of the Lawful and vnlawful usurie amongest Christians. 16°. 6311
Musaeus [*Gr. Lat.*]. *See* Poetae minores. 1635.
Musgrave (Christopher). Musgraves motives. 1621. 4°. . . . 3013
Music-Book for the Lute. F°. 7730
Musket (G.). Bishop of London his Legacy. 1623. 4°. . . . 6549
'Musophil. (Anonym).' *See* Tuvil (D.). Vade mecum. 1629. 12°.
Mussemius (J.). Prognosticon. 1544. 8°. 689
Mussendine (William). Verses in Camb. Univ. Συνῳδία. 1637. . 5790
Mustapha I., *Sultan.* *See* Osman I., *Sultan.* True and faithfull relation. 1622
Mychelborn. *See* Michelborne.
Mychell (Francis). *See* Michell (Sir F.).
Mylbourne (Robert). *See* Milbourne.
Mylles (F.). *See* Kingsmill (A.). Most Excellent...Treatise. 1577. 8°.
Mylles (Jo.). Verses in Camdeni Insignia. 1624. 5346
Mylles (Ric.). Verses in Camdeni Insignia. 1624. 5346
Mynshull (Richard). Verses in Paris and Vienna. 1628. . . 7552
Myre, town. *See* Mere.
Myrepsius (Nicolas). *See* Nicolaus, *Præpositus.* Prepositas. 1588.
Myreus (Ludovicus). *See* L'Obel (M. de). In G. Rondelletii...officinam. 1605.
Myriell (Thomas). Devout soules search. 1610. 8°. 2746
See Wilkinson (R.). Stripping of Ioseph. 1625.
Mystic sweet Rosary. *See* Rosary.

N., *Regal.* Verses in Camb. Univ. Gratulatio. 1623. . . 5695
N. (A.). *See* Nowell (A.). Catechismus.
N. (C.). Verses in Breton (N.). Characters. 1615. . . . 3902
N. (C.). Unfortunate politique. 1639. *See* Caussin (N.).
N. (E.). Caesars Diologve. 1601. 8°. 1383
N. (E.), *Regal.* Verses in Camb. Univ. Gratulatio. 1623. . . 5695
N. (G.) [*of Trin. Coll. Camb.?*]. *See* Moses *ben Maimon.* הלכות תשובה 1631. 5737
N. (H.). *See* Nicholas (H.). Dicta HN. [1574?] 8°. . . . 6346
— — Evangelium Regni. [1574?] 8°. 6339
— — Epistola XI. [1574?] 8°. 6342
— — Exhortatio I. [Ab. 1574.] 8°. 6340
— — First Epistle. [1574?] 8°. 6341
— — Prophetie. 1574. 8°. 6343
— — Proverbia HN. [1575?] 8°. 6345
— — Publishing of the Peace. 1574. 8°. 6344
— — Revelatio Dei. [1574?] 8°. 6347
N. (H.), *Father of the Family of Love.* See under Nicholas (H.).
N. (H.), *L.* Verses in Camden (W.). Britannia. 1586 *etc.* . 1324 *etc.*
N. (I.), *C.C.C.* Verses in Wadsworth (J.). Further Obss. 1630. . 7788

No.
N. (I.), *Syd.* Verses in Camb. Univ. Gratulatio. 1623. . . 5695
N. (M.). *See* Camden (W.). Remaines. 1605 etc.
N. (N.). De conventu cæsaris Ferdinandi cum quibusdam Imperii Electoribus Ratisbonae celebrato, 1630. 1631. 4°. . . 4199
N. (N.). [Qu. L. Anderton?] *See* Society of Twelve. 1626.
See Anderton (L.). The progenie of catholicks. 1633.
— Downe (J.). Certaine treatises. 1633.
— Du Bosc (J.). The compleat woman. 1639. 4°.
N. (N.) [=W. Chillingworth]. *See* Knott (E.). Direction. 1636.
N. (P.) [=P. Nye]. *See* Sibbs (R.). Christs exaltation. 1639. 12°. 7820
N. (R.). Verses in Du Bartas. Weekes. 1605–6. *etc.* . . 2476 *etc.*
N. (R.) [qu. Norton?]. *See* Camden (W.). The historie. 1630. F°.
N. (R.), *Gent.* [Qu. R. Norton?] *See* Camden (W.). Annales. 1635.
[=Norton (R.).] *See* Record (R.). Ground of arts. 1618.
N. (R.), *Oxon.* *See* Niccols (R.). 1616.
N. (S.). Verses in Heywood (T.). Pleasant dialogues. 1637. . 5128
N. (S.), *Doctour of Diuinity.* *See* Norris (S.).
N. (T.). Verses in Dering (E.). xxvii. Lectures. 1576. . . 1573
— Powell (T.). Attovrney's academy. 1630. . . 7625, 7873
See Bracton (H. de). Henrici...de Legibus. 1569.
[=T. Norton.] *See* Calvin (J.). The institution. 1561. F°.
[Qu. T. Newton?] *See* Mexia (P.). Plessaunt dialogue. 1580.
N. (T.). '*Petit ardua virtus.*' [Qu. T. Newton?] Verses in Dodonæus (R.). A niewe herball. 1578 etc. . . . . 6130 *etc.*
N. (Thomas). *See* Grafton (R.). Chronicle. 1569.
Nabbs (Tho.). Verses in Welby (H.). The Phoenix. 1637. . . 3713
Nantes. True originall edict of Nantes. 1622. 4°. . . . 2292
Nanton (R.). Verses in Camb. Univ. Lachrymae. 1587. . . 2123
Naogeorgus (T.). Popish Kingdome. Trans. B. Googe. 1570. 4°. 1410
Naophilus (Theophilus). Verses in Hawkins (W.). Corolla. 1634. 5803
Napier (John). Arithmetica Logarithmica. Ill. H. Briggs. 1624. F°. 3349
Description of...Logarithms. 1618. 12°. 2112
Logarithmaticall arithmetike...by H. Briggs. 1631. F°. . . 4437
Mirifici logarithmorum canonis descriptio. Edinburgh, 1614. 4°. 5952
— (constructio). Edinburgh, 1619. 4°. 5961
Plaine discovery of the...Revelation of Saint Iohn. Edinburgh, 1593. 4°. 5930
— Edinburgh, 1611. 4°. 5948.
— 'London, 1611.' 4°. 5949
Rabdologiae...libri duo. Edinburgi, 1617. 12°. 5959
See Barton (W.). Arithmeticke Abreviated. 1634.
— Speidell (J.). New Logarithmes. 1619.
Napier (Robert). *See* Napier (J.). Mirifici logarithmorum canonis descriptio. 1619.
Narne (Will.). Christ's Starre. 1625. 4°. 4702
Pearle of prayer. Edinburgh, 1630. 8°. 5971
Narrationes. Nove narrationes. Pynson [1490]. 4°. . . . 114
Novae Narrationes...Articuli...booke of diuersites of courtes. R. Tottell, 1561, April 1. 8°. 7169
See Articuli ad narrationes novas.
Narssius (Joan), *M.D.* Verses in Munro (R.). Monro his expedition. 1637. 5067
Nash (Gaguin.). Verses in Camb. Univ. Genethl. 1631. . . 5731
— — Anthologia. 1632. 5741
— Hawkins (W.). En Priscianus. 1632. 4562
— — Corolla. *bis* 1634. 5803
Nash (Thomas). Pierce Penniless his supplication to the Diuell. 1595. 4°. 2718
Qvaternio. 1633. 4°. 3889
— 1636. 4°. 3706

No.

Nash (Thomas), *cont.* Returne of the renowned Caualliero Pasquill with Marforius. 1589. 4°. 7242
See Curryknave (C.), *pseud.* An Almond. [159–.]
Nassau. The Triumphs of Nassau. *See* Maurice of Nassau.
Nathanael, *converted Jew.* Confession of Faith. 1577. *See* Foxe (J.). Sermon. 1578. 8°.
Natura Brevium (French). Pynson [1500?]. F°. 115
— Pynson, 1528. 8°. 290
— Newly corrected. [Ab. 1516?] F°. 7075
In Englyshe, with dyuers addicions. T. Petit, n.d. 8°. . 584
Nouvelle natura brevium. (Sir A. Fitzherbert.) R. Tottell, 1553. 8°. 1104
Natura Brevium in English. R. Tottell, 1576. 8°. . . . 1130
Novel natura brevium. (Sir A. Fitzherbert.) T. Wight, 1598. 8°. 2385
Naugerius (Andreas). *See* Navagero (A.).
Naumachius [*Gr. Lat.*]. *See* Poetae minores. 1635.
Naumburg. *See* Germany. Actes of the Ambassage. [1561.] 8°. . 7133
Navagero (Andreas). *See* Ovid. Heroidum Epistolae. 1583. 16°.
Navarre, *King of.* 1586. *See* Henry IV., *King of France.*
Navarre (Casuist). *See* M. de Azpilcueta.
Nayler (Jos.). Verses in Camb. Univ. Lacrymae. 1619. . . 5689
Naylor (Daniel). Verses in Cambridge Lachrymae. 1587. . . 2123
Neal (J.). Verses in Camb. Univ. Anthologia. 1632. . . 5741
Neal (T.). *See* Windsor (M.). Academiarum quæ aliquando. 1590.
Neale ( ) M^ris^. 1618. *See* Day (V.).
Neale (Richard), *Bp.* *See* Neile (R.).
Necessary Discourse concerning...the house of Guyze. 1586. 8°. . 1844
Necessary Doctrine and erudition for any christen man. Berthelet, 1543. 4°. 466
Berthelet, 1543. 8°. 467, 468
J. Mayler, 1543. 8°. 688
Pia et Catholica...Institutio. 1544. 4°. 472
Neck (Jacob van). [Journal...to the East Indies. 1601.] 4°. . 7398
Negus (Jonathan). *See* Negus (W.). Mans active obedience. 1619. 4°.
Negus (William). Mans active obedience. 1619. 4°. . . . 3005
Neile (Richard), *Abp.* *See* Blackwell (G.). Large examination. 1607.
— Dominis (M. A. de). Alter Ecebolius. 1624.
Nemesius. Nature of man...englished...by Geo. Wither. 1636. 12°. . 4301
Nemius (Johannes). Verses in Pelegromius (S.). 1603. . . 7881
Nenna (G. B.). Nennio. 1595. 4°. 2329
Nepair or Neper (John). *See* Napier.
Nepenthiacus (Eucapnus). *See* Brathwaite.
Nepos (Cornelius). Lives of Epaminondas...and...other. *See* Plutarch [Parallel Lives]. 1603 *etc.*
Nero, *Emperor.* *See* Bolton (E.). Nero Cæsar. 1624(–7). F°.
Nesbit (E.). *See* N. (E.). Cæsars Dialogve. 1601.
Netherlands [General History]. *See* Grimstone (E.). Generall historie. 1609.
See Meteren (E. van). True discourse. 1602. 2873
Subdivisions: I. Down to 1581. II. Southern Provinces (Spanish). III. United Provinces.
I. *See* Certain News. 1574?
— Apologeticon. [1580?]
— Henricpetri (A.). Chronyc. 1579. 8°.
— Libellvs svpplex. 1571.
II. *English Church in.* *See* Amsterdam, *English Congregation.* 1597.
Second Admonition, sent by the subdued Prouinces. 1598. 4°. 1977
[Proclamation.] *See* Copie of a certaine letter. 1599. . 1981
Coppie of the proclamation made by the...Infanta. 1599. 4°. 1985
Proclamation or Edict. Touching...Traffique. 1603. 4°. . 2300

No.

Netherlands, *cont.* III. United Provinces. *See* Elizabeth, *Queen.* Declaration of the cavses mooving the queene...in the lowe Countries. 1585.
Proclamation of the Lords the generall states of the United Provinces. 1599. 4°. 1984
See Oration or speech... 1608. 1624
— Overbury (Sir T.). Sir T. Overbury.. 1609. . . 1626
— James I. Declaration dv...Roy. 1612.
— — Declaration...in the cause of D. Conradvs Vorstius. 1612.
See Maurice of Nassau. The Triumphs. 1613.
[Proclamation against exportation.] *See* Gentleman (T.). Englands Way. 1614.
— — S. (E.). Britaines Busse. 1615.
[6 Oct. 1617.] *See* Carleton (D.). Speech. 1618. 4°.
See Oldenbarneveld (J. van). The trve description. 1619.
Observations concerning the present affaires of Holland. 1621. 8°. 7691
See Faithfvll and wise preventer. 1621.
Observations concerning the present affayres of Holland. Ed. 2. 1622. 8°. 6547
More excellent observations. 1622. 4°. 2034
See Hexham (H.). Tongue combat. 1623. 4°.
— Hertogenbosch. Iornall. 1629.
[Treatises on the Truce, 1630.] *See* Three Severall Treatises. 1630.
See France. Mary de Medici. Declaration. 1638.
[*In usum scholarum.*] *See* Vossius (G. I.). Rhetorices libri v. 1631.
East India Company. Remonstrance...presented to the Lords States Generall...touching...Amboyna. 1632. 4°. . . 3880
Nethersole (Sir Francis). Memoriae sacra...Henrici Walliae Principis. Cantebrigiae, 1612. 4°. 5667
Verses in Fletcher (G.). Christs victorie. 1610 *etc.* . 5659 *etc.*
Netley (James). Verses in Hart (A.). Tragicomicall history. 1640. 4220
Nettles (Stephen). Answer to...Selden's history of tithes. Oxford, 1625. 4°. 5353
Neufville (Nicolas de), *seigneur de Villeroi.* *See* Matthieu (P.). Remarkable considerations. 1638.
Considerations upon...Villeroy. *See* Matthieu (P.). Unhappy Prosperity. 1639. 12°.
Nevill. *See* Neville.
Neville (Alexander). De furoribus Norfolciensium. 1575. 4°. . 1483, 1484
Kettus. *See* Ockland (C.). Anglorum praelia. 1582.
— Gascoigne (G.). The Posies. 1575.
Neville (Charles), earl of Westmoreland. *See* Westmoreland.
Neville (Charles), *K.C.C.* Verses in Hippocrates. 1631. . . 5736
Neville (Edm.). Palme of christian fortitude. 1630. 8°. . . 6623
Neville (Sir Edward). *See* Morison (Sir R.). Invective. 1539.
Neville (Henry) [*afterwards* Lord Abergavenny?]. Verses in Coryat (T.). Coryats Crudities. 1611. 3076
Neville (Lady Mary). *See* Owen (J.). Epigrammatum. 1612, *etc.*
Neville (Thomas). Verses in Beaumont (Sir J.). Bosworth field. 1629. 3040
New and accurate map of the world. [1625.] *See* W. Grent. . 7857
New and easy method. '1617.' [1667.] *Error in date.*
Newe Boke, contayinge An exhortation to the sycke etc. Ipswich, 1548. 8°. 5880
New dialoge called the enditement agaynst mother messe. 1548. 8°. 1031
New England. Humble request of his maiesties loyall Subjects, the Governor and the company late gone for New-England. 1630. 4°. 4599
See Smith (J.). Generall history. 1624.
— Higginson (F.). New-Englands Plantation. 1630.

No.

New England, *cont.* *See* Wood (W.). New Englands prospects. 1634.
New Irish Prognostication. 1624. *See* Rich (B.).
New man...of a generall Councell...of Paul V. [By M. Becanus[1].] Trans. W. Crashaw. 1622. 4°. 4172, 4173
New survey of the affaires of Europe. 1623. 4°. 3542
Newbery (Nathanael). *See* Du Moulin (P.). Anatomie of Arminianisme. 1635.
Newce (Thomas), *C.C.C.* Verses in Camb. Univ. Συνῳδία. 1637. . 5790
Newes. *See* News.
Newfoundland. *See* Vaughan (W.). Golden fleece. (Map.) 1626. 5029
— Whitbourne (R.). Discourse. 1622.
Newhouse (Thomas?). Learned and frvitfull sermon...in Norwich, ed. R. Hill. 1612. 8°. 3396
Nevvlus (Laurentius). Verses in More (Sir T.). G. Rossei opus. 1523. 284
Newman (John). Looking-glasse for petitioners. 1619. 8°. . 3936
Newman (Rich.). Verses in Oxf. Univ. Horti. 1640. . . . 5499
Newman (Rob.). Verses in Camb. Univ. Genethl. 1631 *bis* . 5731
— Hippocrates. 1631, 1633. . . . . . 5736, 5812
— Camb. Univ. Anthologia. 1632. 5741
— Gerhard (J.). Golden chaine. 1632. 5744
— Camb. Univ. Fasciae. 1633. 5808
— — Rex redux. 1633. 5748
Newport (Andr.). Verses in Oxf. Univ. Horti. 1640. . . 5499
News. Newes from France[2]. Or a relation of a...disaster. 1618. 4°. . 7514
News from Pernassvs. 1622. *See* Scott (T.).
Newes from Rome conc. the...Masse. Canterbury [1550]. 8°. . 5875
Newes of certaine commands...by the french king. 1629. 4°. . 3745
Newton (Francis). Verses in Cheke (Sir J.). De obitu M. Buceri. 1551. 734
Newton (Sir Henry). Verses in Camb. Univ. Rex redux. 1633. . 5748
Newton (Humphry), *Magd. Coll. Oxon.* Verses in Butler (C.). The principles of musik. 1636. 4860
Newton (Theodore). Verses in Wilson (Sir T.). Vita. 1551. . 631
Newton (Thomas). Illvstrivm aliquot Anglorvm Encomia. *See* Leland (J.). Principum etc. 1589.
Verses in Patrizi (F.). Moral methode. 1576. 1228
— Dodonæus (R.). Niewe herball. 1578 etc. . . . . 6130 etc.
— Bullein (W.). Bulwark. 1579. 1230
— Ockland (C.). Anglorum prælia. 1580 *etc.* . . . 1313 *etc.*
— Carlisle (C.). Discovrse. 1582. 1871
— Du Bellay (G.). Instructions. 1589. 2202
— Bales (P.). Writing Schoolemaster. 1590. 2205
— Adrichomius (C.). Hierusalem. 1595. 2328
— Gerard (J.). Herball. 1597. 2348
— Heywood (J.). Workes. 1598. 2909
— Higgins (J.). A mirrour. 1610. 2961
— Seton (J.). Dialectica. 1611 etc. . . . . . 3249 etc.
— Slatyer (W.). History. 1621. 3137
See Daneau (L.). Trve and Christian Friendshippe. 1586.
— Lemnius (L.). Herbal for the bible. 1587.
— Mexia (P.). Pleasaunt dialogue. 1580.
— Stanbridge (John). Vocabula. 1577.
Neyle (Richard), *Bp.* *See* Neile (R.), *Abp.*
Nicanor (Lysimachus), *pseud.* *See* Corbet (J.).
Niccols (Richard). Sir Thomas Overburies Vision. 1616. 4°. . 4222
See Higgins (J.). Mirrour. 1610.
Nicetas. Catena graecorum patrum in beatum Iob. Studio P. Junii. 1637. F°. 2696
Nicholas of Damascus. *See* Boemus (J.). Manners. 1611. 4°.

[1] Cf. nos. 2795, 7443. [2] Cf. Herb. 1165.

No.

Nicholas (Henry). Dicta H. N. Documentall Sentences. [Ab. 1574.] 8º. 6346
Epistle sent vnto two daughters of Warwick. *See* Ainsworth (H.). Epistle &c. 1608. 4º.
First epistle of H. N. A crying-voyce. [Ab. 1574.] 8º. . 6341
Epistola XI. H. N. Correttion. [Ab. 1574.] 8º. . . . 6342
Evangelium Regni. A joyfull message. [Ab. 1574.] 8º. . 6339
Exhortatio. I. The first exhortation. [Ab. 1574.] 8º. . . 6340
Proverbia H. N. [Ab. 1575.] 8º. 6345
Prophetie of the Spirit of Loue. 1574. 8º. . . . 6343
Publishing of the peace upon earth. 1574. 8º. . . 6344
Revelatio Dei. [Ab. 1574.] 8º. 6347
See Knewstub (J.). Confutation. 1579.
— Rogers (J.). Displaying of an horrible Secte. 1579.
— Wilkinson (W.). Confutation. 1579.
Nicholas (T.). *See* Zarate (A. de). History of Peru. 1581.
Nicholas y Sacharles (Juan de). Hispanus Reformatus. 1621. 12º. 2903
Nicholay (Nicholas). *See* Nicolay.
Nicholls (J.). Declaration of the recantation. 1581. 8º. . 1668, 1669
Oration and Sermon made at Rome. 27 May 1578. 1581. 8º. 1351
— (1581 April 25). 8º. 1352
Pilgrimage. 1581. 8º. 1815
See Fenner (D.). Answere vnto the confvtation of Iohn Nichols. 1583.
Nichols (Francis). *See* Proclamation. 1619. Broadside. . . 2806
Nichols (John). True report. Rhemes, 1583. 8º. . . . 6435
Nichols (Josias). Plea of the innocent. 1602. 8º. . . . 6462
See Covell (W.). A Modest...examination. 1604.
Nicholson (Samuel). Acolastus his afterwitte. 1600. 4º. . . 3312
Niclas (Hendrik). *See* Nicholas (Henry).
Nicodemus Gospel. W. de Worde, 1509. 4º. 158
— 12 April, 1532. 4º. 205
J. Skot [1537?]. 4º. 358
Nicolaus, *Buscoducensis*. *See* Lucianus. Lvciani dialogi. 1531.
Nicolaus, *Præpositus*. Præpositas his practise. 1588. 4º. . . 1950
Nicolay (N. de). Nauigations...into Turkie. 1585. 4º. . . 1825
Nicoll (Basil). *See* Downham (G.). Abstract. 1635.
Nicolls (Sir Augustine). *See* Bolton (R.). Last...Things. 1635.
Nicolls (Fr.). Verses in Oxf. Univ. Horti. 1640. . . . 5499
Nicolls (R.). Verses in Oxf. Univ. Horti. 1640. . . . 5499
Nicolls (P.). Godly newe story of XII men...sent to spy...Canaan. 1548. 8º. 1029
Nicolls (Thomas). *See* Thucydides. History. 1550.
Nicols (John), *M.D.* Verses in Hippocrates. 1633. . . 5812
Nicolson (James). Prognostication. 1563. 16º. . . . 7763
Nicolson (Robert). Verses in Norden (J.). Speculum Britanniae Pars 1. 1593. 6804
Nicolson (Thomas). Verses in Adamson (J.). Εἰσόδια. 1618. . 5960
Nicolson (William). Verses in Oxf. Univ. Magd. Coll. 1612. . 5302
Nieuwport. Prælium Nuportanum. 1640. *See* Dorislaus (Is.).
Niger (Franciscus). *See* Whittington (R.). [Grammar Pt. II.] Whittyntoni Editio. 1516.
Nilus. Briefe treatise...of the Popes vsurped Primacye. 1560. 8º. . 1156
Nîmes University. Brevis et modesta responsio. 1584. 8º. . 1558
Nimmo (John). Verses *bis* in Adamson (J.). Εἰσόδια. 1618. . . 5960
Nisbet (E.). *See* N. (E.). Cæsars Dialogve. 1601.
Nisbet (Patrick). Verses in Adamson (J.). Εἰσόδια. 1618. . 5960
Nismes. *See* Nîmes.
Nisus, *pseud.* *See* Hawkins (W.). En Priscianus. 1632.
Nixon (Ant.). Dignitie of man. 1612. 4º. 2028
Oxfords Triumph. 1605. 4º. 2017

No.
Nixon (Ant.), *cont.* Warres of Swethland. 1609. 4°. . . . 3065
Nixon (James). *See* Roe (W.). Epilogvs. 1615.
Noare (John). Verses in Gerhard (J.). Prayers. 1625 *etc.* . 3321 *etc.*
— — Meditations. 1638. 5824
Noble Arte of Venerie. [1611?] *See* Turberville (G.).
Noel (Baptista). Verses in Gill (A.). Πάρεργα. 1632. . . 4558
Noel (Sir Edward). *See* Owen (J.). Epigrammatum. 1618.
Noel (Henry). Verses in Camb. Univ. Genethl. 1631. . . 5731
— — Anthologia. 1632. 5741
Nogaret (Jean Louis de), duc d'Epernon. *See* Oldenbarnevelt (J. van). Trve description. 1619.
Nogdi-beg. *See* Herbert (Sir T.). Relation. 1634.
Noot (J. van der). Theatre. 1568. 8°. 812
Norden (John). Godlie mans guide to happinesse. 1624. 12°. . 4525
Load-starre to spirituall life. 1614. 12°. 7488
Mirror for the Multitude. 1586. 8°. 2120
Pensiue mans practise. 1584. 8°. 1057
— 1600. 12°. 7349
— 1615–(16). 12°. 3788
— Parts 2 and 3. 1616. 12°. 3911
Sinfull mans solace. 1585. 8°. 1447
Speculum Britanniae. Pars i. Middlesex. 1593. 4°. . . 6804–6
Speculi Britanniae pars (Description of Hertfordshire). 1598. 4°. 6823
Svrveiors dialogue. 1610. 4°. 3072
— Ed. 3. 1618. 4°. 3421
See Camden (W.). Britannia. (Maps drawn by him.) F°. 1607 etc. 1758 etc.
— Speed (J.). The theatre. 1611.
Norfolk (Tho. Howard, duke of). Discourse touching the pretended match...the quene of Scotes. [Ab. 1571.] 8°. . . . 6755
See G. (R.). Salutem. [1571.]
Norice (Sir John). *See* Norris.
Norimberg Curranto. See no. 7724.
Norman (Robert). *See* Safeguard of saylers. 1612. 4°.
Norrice, *popish Priest.* *See* Norris (S.).
Norrice (Will.), *K.C.C.* *See* Norris.
Norris (Sir John). *See* Meteren (E. van). Trve discovrse. 1602.
Norris (Sylv.). Antidote or soveraigne remedie. Part 1. 1615. 4°. . 6533
— 1622. 4°. 6546
— Part 2. 1619. 4°. 6537
— — 1622. 4°. 6546
Part 3. Guide of faith. 1621. 4°. 6543
See Walker (G.). Svmme of a dispvtation. 1624.
Norris (Will.), *K.C.C.* Verses in Camb. Univ. Epithalam. 1625. . 5702
— Gerhard (J.). Meditations. 1627 *etc.* . . . . 5707 *etc.*
— Hippocrates. 1631 *etc.* . . . . 5736 *etc.*
North (Sir Dudley). Verses in Camb. Univ. Lacrymæ. 1619. . . 5689
North (George). Description of Swedland, Gotland, and Finland. 1561. 4°. 1274
See Philibert, *de Vienne.* Philosopher of the Court. 1575.
North (John). Verses in Camb. Univ. Thr-thr. 1603. . . . 5616
North (Sir Thomas). *See* Guevara (A. de). Diall of Princes. 1557 *etc.*
See Plutarch. [Parallel Lives.] 1603 *etc.*
Northampton, County of. 1607. *See* Wilkinson (R.).
Northampton (William Parr, marquis of). *See* Catharine [Parr], Queen. The lamentacion. 1547 *etc.*
Northampton (H. Howard, earl of). Defensatiue against...Prophesies. 1583. 4°. 1355, 1356
— Newly reuised. 1620. F°. 2790
See Defence of the Ecclesiasticall Regiment. 1574.
— Garnet (H.). Trve and perfect relation of the...late...Traitors. 1606.

No.

Northbrooke (J.). Breefe and pithie summe of the Christian fayth. [1582.] 8°. 1365
Poore mans garden. [Ab. 1569.] 8°. 7301
— [1571?] 8°. 1795
Treatise wherein Dicing, Dauncing, Vaine plaies...are reprooued. 1579. 4°. 1806
— [158-?] 4°. 1521
Northumberland (Dorothy, countess of). [Funeral Sermon.] *See* Chambers (Ric.). Sarahs sepulture. 1620.
Northumberland (Thomas Percy, first earl of). *See* Harriot (T.). Artis Analyticae. 1631.
See Norton (T.). To the Quenes...Subiectes. 1569.
— S. (W.). Aunswere. 1569.
Northumberland (Henry Percy, third earl of). *See* Golden Mean. Ed. 3. 1638. 12°. 4865
Norton ( ). *See* Norfolk (Thomas Howard, duke of). A discourse. [1569-1570?]
Norton (John), *printer*. *See* Ortelius (A.). Theatrum. 1606.
Norton (John). *See* Fabricius (W.). Lithotomia. 1640.
Norton (Robert). Gunner. 1628. F°. 4535
See Camden (W.). Historie. 1630. 4757
— — Annales. 1635. F°.
— Record (R.). Grovnd of arts. 1618.
— Stevin (S.). Disme. 1608.
— Vigo (J. de). Whole worke. 1586.
Norton (T.). To the Quenes Maiesties poore deceyued Subiectes. 1569. 8°. 1464–1466
Warning agaynst the dangerous practises of Papistes. [1570?] 8°. 888
Verses in Turner (W.). Preseruatiue. 1551. 955
— Humphrey (L.). J. Jvelli vita. 1573. 837
See Calvin (J.). Institvtion of Christian Religion. 1561 *etc.*
— Merbury (C.). Briefe discovrse. 1581.
— Nowell (A.). Catechisme. 1570.
Norton (Thomas), *B.A.*, *C.C.C.* Verses in Camb. Univ. Συνωδία. 1637. 5790
— King (E.). Ivsta. 1638. 5829
Norwich, City. *See* Neville (A.). De furoribus. 1575.
Map. 1588. *See* Braun (G.).
[Autograph Inscription. 1632.] *See* no. 5742.
Diocese. *See* Articles. 1638.
Norwich (Will.), *Pet.* Verses in Camb. Univ. Anthologia. 1632. . 5741
— — Rex redux. 1633. 5748
— — Carmen. 1635. 5770
— Shelford (R.). Five...discourses. 1635. 5774
— Camb. Univ. Voces. 1640. 5836
Nostradamus. *See* Fulke (W.). Antiprognosticon. 1560.
Nottingham (Charles Howard, earl of). [Embassy to Spain.] *See* Treswell (R.). Relation of...the Journey... 1605.
See Elizabeth, Queen. Declaration. 1596. 4°.
— Shipwrights Company [Charter. 1612?]. 4°.
Nova Britannia. *See* I. (R.).
Nova Legenda Anglie. 1516. *See* Capgrave (J.).
Nove narrationes. *See* Narrationes.
Novus Homo, *pseud.* *See* Becanus (M.). Svpplicatio. 1613. 2795 *etc.*
— [English.] 1622. 4°. *See* 4172–3.
Nowell (A.). Catechisme, Eng. by T. Norton. [No. 1. 'Quum præceptorem.'] J. Day, 1570. 4°. 818
Catechismus. (Lat.) [No. 1.] R. Wolfe, 16 Cal. Jul. 1570. 4°. 750
— [,,] ,, 3 Cal. Jun. 1571. 4°. 752
— [,,] ,, 1572. 4°. 753
Κατηχισμός. (Gr. Lat.) [No. 1.] R. Wolfe, 1573. 8°. . . 754

No.

Nowell (A.), *cont.* Catechismus parvus (Lat. Gr.). [No. 2. 'Quo nomine.'] J. Day, 1574. 8°. 843
Χριστιανίσμου στοιχείωσις...institutio. (Gr. and Lat.) [No. 3. 'Narra mihi.'] J. Day, 1577. 8°. 849
— J. Day, 1578. 8°.. 853
Christianae pietatis prima institutio. [No. 3.] Cantabrigiæ, 1633. 8°. 5754
— Cantabrigiæ, 1636. 8°. 5784
— [163-?] 8°. 7608
Reprovfe...of...A provfe of certayne articles. H. Wykes, 30 May 1565. 4°. 1250
— H. Wykes, 13 July 1565. 4°. 1251
True report of...Campion. 1583. 4°. 1676
Verses in Cheke (Sir J.). De obitu M. Buceri. 1551. . . 734
— Humphrey (L.). J. Jvelli vita. 1573. 837
— Parkhurst (J.). Ludicra. 1573. 838
See Dorman (T.). Disprovfe of M. Nowelles reprovfe. 1565.
See Redman (J.). Reporte. 1551.
Nowell (H.), *T.C.C.* Verses in Camb. Univ. Συνωδία. 1637. . 5790
Nowell (Robert). [Bookplate.] 1587. 8°. 6788
Nürnberg. *See* Norimberg Curranto. 7724
Nukrois (E. de). *See* Censura ad panegyricum. 1628. 4°. . . 7764
Numan (Philips). Miracles lately wrought by the Virgin Marie, at Montaigu. Trans. R. Chambers. Antwerp, 1606. 8°. . 6133
Nummi Britannici Historia. '1626' [1726]. *Erroneous date.*
Nunc Dimittis. *See* Anderson (A.). Shield of our Safetie. 1581.
Nuthall (John). Verses in Laurentius (A.). Discourse. 1599. . 2913
Nychodemus. *See* Nicodemus.
Nycolls (Philip). *See* Nicolls.
Nye (Philip). *See* Sibbes (R.). Fountain Sealed. 1637 *etc.*
— — Christs exaltation. 1639. 12°. 7820
— — Bowels opened. 1639. 4°. 7824
— — Two sermons. 1637 *etc.* 12°.

O. (E.). Detection of divers notable vntruthes. 1602. 8°. . 6846
See Sutcliffe (M.). Challenge. 1602.
O. (G.), *King's Coll. Camb.* [qu. W. Oughtred?] Verses in Whitaker (W.). Praelectiones. 1599. 5598
O. (H.). Verses in Norden (J.). Speculum Britanniæ. Pt 1. 1593. 6804-6
O. (H.). [=H. Olney.]. *See* Cornwallis (Sir W.). Essayes. 1606 *etc.*
O. (I.). [=Olde (J.).] *See* Confession of Fayth. [1568?]
See Gualtherus (R.). Antichrist. 1556.
— Ridley (N.). Certayne...conferences. 1556.
O. (I.). Verses in Camb. Univ. Thr-thr. 1603. 5616
O. (L.). Enchiridion Controversiarum. 1633. 8°. 3823
O. (L.). [=Owen (L.)] *See* Eudes (M.). Catholiqve traditions. 1609.
See Owen (L.). Speculum Jesuiticum. 1629. 4°.
O. (S.). *See* Casaubon (I.). Originall of popish idolatrie. 1630.
O. (S.). [qu. T. Scott B.D.?] *See* Experimentall discoverie. 1623-4.
O. (T.), *C.C.C.* Verses in Camb. Univ. Epicedium. 1612. . . 5665
O. (Mr W.). *See* Oughtred (W.). Circles. 1632.
Oath of Allegiance. *See* Ireland (T.). Oath. 1610.
— Hoskins (A.). Briefe and cleare declaration. 1611.
Observations concerning...Holland. 1621. 8°. *See* Netherlands III. 7691 *etc.*
Ochino (Bernardino). Sermons. Trans. R. Argentine. 1548. 8°. . 5884
Certaine godly...sermons. 1580. 4°. 1580
Certayne Sermons. [1550?] 8°. 889
Tragoedie or Dialoge of the Bishop of Rome. 1549. 4°. . . 1021
See Anderton (J.). Luthers Life. 1624. 4°. 7692
Ockham (W.). Dialogue betwene a knyght and a clerke, concerning the power spiritual and temporal. n.d. 8°. 513

No.
Ocland (C.). Anglorum prælia. 1580. 4°. 1313
— 1582. 8°. 1317–1319
Octher or Octhur. *See* Fox (L.). North-west Fox. 1635.
O'Domhnuill (William). *See* Daniel.
O'Donnell (Rory), earl of Tyrconnel. *See* Tyrconnel.
Oecolampadius (J.). Sarmon...to yong men, and maydens. [1548?] 8°. 1035
See Joye (G.). Exposicion of Daniel. 1545.
Oes, The Fifteen. *See* Fifteen Oes.
Of the Old God and the New. *See* Coverdale (M.). Worke entytled of yᵉ olde god & the newe. 1534. 8°.
Of unwrytten verities. *See* Smith (Richard). Of vnwrytten verities. 1548.
Offa, *King of Mercia*. *See* Paris (M.). Historia major. 1640.
Offaly (Gerald Fitzgerald, baron of). *See* Fitzgerald.
Offenbecius (Dietrichus). Verses in Buchlerus (J.). Sacrarum...phrasium ...Thesaurus. 16– 4878
Office of christian parents. Cambridge, 1616. 4°. 5680
Office of Generall Remembrance. (J. Ferrour, J. Friend, H. Miles). 1617. 4°. 3588
Official Publications:
1536. *See* Lincoln, County of. Answer to the petitions. 4°.
1536. — Yorkshire. Answere made. 4°.
1551 July 18. — A Proclamation. R. Grafton. Broadside. . 621
1583. — Elizabeth. Declaration.
1585. — Elizabeth. Declaration.
1586. — Orders devised. 1586. 1682
1591 Nov. 29. — Parsons (R.). Elizabethae. 1592.
1596. — Elizabeth. Declaration of...a navy. . . 1704
1601. — London. College of Physicians. 1636.
1603 Dec. 9. — S. (C.). The copie.
1604 March 25, May 2. [City of Geneva.] F°. 7416
1604 July 16. [Proclamation.] *See* Wilkes (W.). Second memento. 1608.
1604. [Petition of the Brownists.] *See* Amsterdam, *English Church in*. Apologie or defence.
1606 Nov. 20. Letters patent for the dying and colouring of wools etc. (Sir A. Aston etc). 4°. . . . 2595
1608 June 1. Orders. Dearth of Grain. 1622. 4°. . . . 2816
1608. *See* Articles of...Alehouses. 1609. 4°.
1608. — Exchequer Court.
1608. *See ante* 1604 Wilkes.
1609 July 28. (Rates of Merchandize.) [1609?] 4°. . . 2620
1609. *See* London. College of Physicians. 1636. . 2694
1610. Instructions. Wards and Liveries. . . 2628
1611. Letters Patent for Office of Publick Register. . 3079
1611. Baronets. 2638
1611. Proclamation... against Catholikes. *See* Clerimond (B. D. de).
1612 Aug. 1. [Patent.] *See* Standish (A.). New directions. 1615.
1612 Sept. 10. London Shipwrights Company (Charter). 4°. 6888
1612. Declaration concerning C. Voritius. . . 2644
— — *See* Precedence. 2374
1613. James I. Publication. Private combats. . 2648
1614 Oct. 10. *See* Proclamations.
1615 July 16. — Proclamations.
1617. Baronets. 2657
1617. *See* Charter Warren. Treatise containing divers Benefits and Priviledges. 4°.
1618. Commission. Wards, Ideots etc. . . . 2800

No.

Official Publications, *cont.*:
1618. Declaration...concerning lawful sports. *See below* 1633.
1618–9 March 12. *See* Proclamation.
1619. Declaration...of bountie. 4°. 2805
1619 July 31. *See* Proclamation.
1619 Nov. 10. Proclamation (Tobacco). Broadside. . . 2806
1620 May 5. *See* Proclamation (Starch). 1620. F°.
1620 June 22. — Virginia. Declaration.
1621. Proclamation (Dissolving of parliament). 4°. . 2811
1621. James I. Declaration touching...the late...Parliament.
1621. *See* Ossolinski (Jerzy). Trve copy.
1622. *See above* 1608 June 1.
1622. Directions for...Courts...of Justice, within...Ireland. 4°. 6023
1622. Petition. .for debt. 6932
1622–3 Feb. 14. *See* Proclamation.
1623 Sept. 25. *See* Proclamation.
1623. *See* Charles I. A true Relation.
1623. Army. *See* Privy Council Instructions.
1623? [Not before Feb. 14.] *See* Spain. Philip IV. 4°.
1624–5 March 3. *See* Proclamation.
1625 March 28. — Proclamation.
1625 April 1. — Proclamation.
1625 April 1. — Proclamation (Oxford University Latin Books).
1625 July 3. — Proclamation.
1625 July 12. — Proclamation.
1626. Declaration. 2830
1627 Jan. 29. Letters Patent (Ministers of the Palatinate). . 2831
1627 July 21. *See* Buckingham (G. duke of). Manifestation.
1627 Aug. 4. — Proclamation (Ireland). 6054
1628. Declaration. 2834
1628. Proclamations. *See* Mocket (R.). Doctrina... 3480
1629. Articles of Peace. *See* France. Louis XIII. . 3743
1630. After Jan. 23. *See* Proclamation. Abstract. . 7424
1630. Orders and directions. (Poor Law.) . . 2670
Grain and Victual. 2671–2
1630 Aug. 6. Letters Patent. (Dutch Church.) . . . 2673
1632 Feb. 18 } 1633 Oct. 13 }. *See* Proclamation.
1633. Book of Sports. 4°. 2682
1633 Dec. 14. [Confirmation.] *See* Star Chamber. . . 2685
1636. *See* London. College of Physicians.
1636. Declaration (Private dwelling houses). . 5124
1637 April 30. *See* Proclamation.
1637 July 9. — ,,
1638 Sept. 9. — ,,
1638 Dec. 21. — ,, (Wines).
1638. *See* Hamilton (James, duke of).
1639. Briefe declaration concerning private dwelling houses. 4666
1639. *See* Charles I. Proclamation. 4°.
1639. — Charles I. Large declaration. F°.
1639. Lawes and ordinances of Warre. 4°. . . 5907
Ogle (Thomas), *Jes.* Verses in Camb. Univ. Συνωδία. 1637. . . 5790
Oglebye (John). Verses in Shirley (J.). Royall master. 1638. . 4665
Oh read over D. John Bridges. [1588?] 4°. 1915, 1916
O'Hussey (Maelbrighde). An teagasg criosdaidhe. [Ab. 1619.] 16°. . 6429
Ol. (P.). Spanish pilgrime. 1625. 4°. 4185

No.

Ol. (P.), *cont.* Treatise parænetical. 1598. 4°. 1865
Old Catholick Church. *See* Luther (M.). Chiefe...Articles. 1548.
Olde (John). Acquital or purgation of...Edward the VI. 'Waterford.' [Ab. 1555.] 8°. 6723
Confession of the...olde belefe. 'Sothewarke.' 1556. 8°. . 6726
See Confession of Fayth. [1568?] 8°. 1254
Short description of Antichrist. [155-?] 8°. . . . 6291
See Erasmus (D.). Paraphrase. 1548 etc.
— Gualtherus (R.). Antichrist. 1556.
— Ridley (N.). Certayne...conferences. 1556.
Oldenbarneveld (Joan van). Arraignment. 1619. 4°. . . 3935
Newes out of Holland. *See below* Trve description. 1619.
See Netherlands. States General. The arraignment. 1619.
True description of the execution. 1619. 4°. . . . 3006
Oldis (Will.). Verses in Camdeni Insignia. 1624. . . . 5346
Oldisworth (Michael). Verses in Oxf. Univ. Magd. Coll. 1612. . 5302
Oldmayne (Timothy). Life's brevitie...sermon...funerall of...E. Lewkenor. 1636. 4°. 3707
Oley (Barnabas). Verses in Camb. Univ. Genethl. 1631. . . 5731
— — Rex redux. 1633. 5748
— Hippocrates. 1633. 5812
— Lessius (L.). Hygiasticon. 1634. . . . . 5762, 5833
— Camb. Univ. Carmen. 1635. 5770
Oliver (John). [Licence] Goodwin (T.). 1638(7). . . . 4317
[Licence] Boughen (E). 1638.
Verses in Hippocrates. 1633. 5812
Oliver (Thomas). De sophismatum praestigiis etc. Cantabrigiae, 1604. 4°. 5624
New handling of the planisphere. 1601. 4°. 2920
Olivier (Isaac). *See* Ollivier.
Ollivier (Isaac). Verses in Camb. Univ. Anthologia. 1632. . . 5741
— — Fasciae. 1633. 5808
— — Rex redux. 1633. 5748
— — Συνῳδία. 1637. 5790
— King (E.). Ivsta. 1639. 5829
Oln. (Ar.). Verses in Norden (J.). Speculum Britanniæ. Pt. 1. 1593. 6804-6
Olney (H.). *See* Cornwallis (Sir W.). Essayes. 1606. 8°.
O'Maelconaire (Finghin). *See* Desiderius. 6427
O'More (Rory). *See* Derricke (J.). Image of Irelande. 1581.
O'Neale (Thyrlaghe Leonaghe). *See* O'Neill.
O'Neill (Hugh), earl of Tyrone. *See* Tyrone.
O'Neill (Turlough Luineach). *See* Derricke (J.). Image of Irelande. 1581.
Onkelos. *See* Bible, Chaldaic. Song of Solomon. 1614.
Onslow (Robert). Verses in Humphrey (L.). J. Jvelli vita. 1573. . 837
Ophovius or Ophovens (Michael van), *bp of 'sHertogenbosch.* Sermon. *See* Hertogenbosch ('s). Iornall. 1629.
Optatus. De schismate Donatistarum...notae...M. Casauboni. 1631. 8°. 4708
Opus eximivm. 1534. *See* Fox (E.).
Orandus (Eirenæus), *pseud.* *See* Flamel (N.). 1624.
Orange (Maurice, Prince of). *See* Maurice.
Orange (William, Prince of). *See* William I. 1575.
Orarium sev libellus precationum. 1546. Grafton (5 Sept. 1545). 8°. 596
Oration or speech...of the netherlandish warre (1608). Trans. T. Wood. 1624. 4°. 6953
Orbicius. De exercitus ordinibus. 1581. *See* Crespin (J.).
Orchard and the garden. 1602. 4°. 2431
Orchard of repentance. *See* Whetstone (G.). Rocke of Regard.
Orchard of Sion. *See* Catharine of Siena.
Order for Prayer and Thanksgiuing...for...safetie. Deputies of C. Barker, 1594. 4°. 1699

No.
Order of Matrimonye. A. Scoloker. 8°. 7151
Order of Prayer vpon Wednesdayes and Frydayes. C. Barker, 1580. 4°. 1666
Order of the Communion. Grafton, 1548. 4°. 604
Orders and directions...tending to the reliefe of the Poore. 1630. 4°. 2670
Orders appointed by his Maiestie...of the dearth of Graine. 1 June 1608. 1622. 4°. 2816
Orders deuised...for the...dearth of Graine. C. Barker, 1586. 4°. . 1682
Ordinal. *See* Directorium *and* Ordination Service.
Ordinal or statutes concernynge Artyfycers. [1542?] 8°. . . . 551
Ordinary of Christian Men. W. de Worde, 1502. 4°. 145
W. de Worde, 1506. 4°. 153
Ordination Service. Forme and maner of making...Archebishoppes... Deacons. Grafton, 1549. 4°. 612
— R. Barker, 1607. F°. 2607
— B. Norton and J. Bill, 1629. F°. 2837
— R. Barker and J. Bill. [1630?] 4°. 2668
— 1638. F°. 2698
Ordre des prieres. 1552. 16°. 6719
Original and sprynge of all sectes and orders...translated. Southwark, 1537. 8°. 5868
Ormerod (Oliver). Picture of a papist...Pagano-papismus. 1606. 8°. 3616
Picture of a Puritane. 1605. 4°. 2018
Ormonde (Thomas Butler, tenth Earl of). *See* Meara (D.). Ormonius. 1615. 8°.
Ornithoparcus (Andreas). Micrologus. Trans. J. Douland. 1609. F°. 3387
Orologium Sapientiæ. *See* Horologium.
'Ορος-ὀξύ (Τὸ). *See* Montagu (Tho.).
O'Rourke (Brian). Verses in Smith (J.). True travels. 1630. . 4836
Orphans. *See* Hooker (J.). Orders. [1575?] 4°.
Orpheus. [*Gr. Lat.*] *See* Poetae minores. 1635.
Orpheus. Animalium...avium, florum... Booke of Beast. [Ab. 1628?] Oblong 4°. 4917
Orpheus Junior, *pseud.* *See* Vaughan (W.).
Ortelius (Abr.). Theatrum orbis terrarum. 1606. F°. . . . 2356
Epitome of the theatre of the worlde. By M. Coignet. 1603. 8°. 3354
Orthius (Wigandus). [Oration.] *See* Gerardus (A.). Practise. 1577. 4°.
Ortuñez de Calahorra (Diego). *See* Mirror of Knighthood. Pt i. 1579.
Ortus vocabulorum. W. de Worde. 1 April, 1528. 4°. . . . 195
Os facies mentum. *Erroneous entry of* Stanbridge (J.). Vocabula. W. de Worde. [1508.] 4°. 234
Osborne (Charles), *King's*. Verses in Camb. Univ. Voces. 1640. . 5836
Osburne (Peter). Verses in Bernard (J.). Oratio. 1568. . . 930
Osiander (And.). Coniectures of the ende of the worlde. Trans. G. Joye. 1548. 8°. 986
See Anderton (J.). Luther's Life. 1624. 4°.
Osman I. True and faithful relation...concerning the death of Sultan Osman. 1622. 4°. 4755
Osorio da Fonseca (Jeronimo). [Epistolæ.] *See* Ascham (R.). Libri tres. 1590.
See Haddon (W.). Against Ierome. 1581.
— Humphrey (L.). J. Jvelli vita. 1573.
Osorius (Hieronymus). *See* Osorio.
Ossolínsky (Jerzy). True copy of the latine oration...with the translation. 1621. 4°. 3950
Ostler (Fran.). Verses in Camb. Univ. Dolor. 1625. 5701
— — Genethl. 1631. 5731
Otes (Th.). Verses in Oxf. Univ. Magd. Coll. 1612. . . . 5302
Othen (Ed.). Verses in Oxf. Univ. Magd. Coll. 1612. . . . 5302
Otho, *Cardinal*. *See* Constitutiones.
See Lyndewood (W.). Constitutions. 1504 *etc.*

No.

Ottobone, *Papal Legate.* *See* Adrian V, *Pope.* [Ottobone Fieschi.]
Oughtred (William). Circles of proportion and the horizontall instrument. Trans. W. Forster. 1632. 4°. . . . 4563, 4564
Addition unto...the circles of Proportion. 1633. 4°. . . 4576
To the english gentrie...against...R. Delamain...Grammelogia. [1632?] 4°. 7606
See Etten (H. van). Mathematicall Recreations. 1633. 8°.
— O. (G.), *King's Coll. Camb.*
Overall (John), *Bp.* *See* Bible, English (Royal). 1611. . . 2635
[Consecration of Shrewsbury School Chapel.] *See* Price (S.). Beavty of holines. 1618. 4°.
Overbury (Sir Thomas). Bloody downfall of Adultery...for the murder. [1637?] 4°. 5183
Observations...upon the...xvii. provinces. 1609. 1626. 4°. . 7586
His wife. Ed. 11. 1622. 8°. 3380
— Ed. 12. Dublin, 1626. 8°. 6031
— 'Ed. 12.' 1627. 8°. 3976
— Ed. 14. 1630. 8°. 5026
— Ed. 15. 1632. 8°. 4349
— Ed. 16. 1638. 8°. 4870
See Niccols (R.). Sir Thomas Overbvries Vision. 1616.
Overton (John). Jacobs Troublesome iourney to Bethel. Oxford, 1586. 8°. 5226
Verses in Baro (P.). In Jonam. 1579. 850
Overton (William). Oratio. Oxoniæ, 1601. 4°. 5255
Verses in Wilson (Sir T.). Vita. 1551. 631
Ovid. Heroidum Epistolae etc. 1583. 16°. 1554
— Cantabrigiae, 1635. 8°. 5775
Heroicall epistles. Trans. W. Saltonstall. 1639. 8°. . . 5173
[Fasti (Eng.).] Festivalls. Trans. J. Gower. Cambridge, 1640. 8°. 5849
Metamorphoseωn libri xv. Cantabrigiae, 1631. 12°. . . 5738
— Fabularum...interpretatio...a G. Sabino...industria T. T. Cantabrigiae, 1584. 8°. 5509
Metamorphoses. Trans. A. Golding. 1567. 4°. . . . 929
— Trans. G. Sandys. Oxford, 1632. F°. 5396
— — Ed. 3. 1638. 12°. 4387
— — 1640. F°. 4747
De ponto. Trans. W. Saltonstall. Ed. 2. 1640. 8°. . . 4679
De tristibus. Trans. Z. Catlin. 1639. 8°. 4668
Ibis. Trans. T. Vnderdowne. 1577. 8°. 1493
See Gascoigne (G.). Hundreth sundrie Flowers. [Ab. 1572.] 4°.
— Heywood (T.). Pleasant dialogues. 1637.
Owen (A.). Verses in Camb. Univ. Rex redux. 1633. . . . 5748
Owen (David). Anti-Paraeus. Cantabrigiae, 1622. 8°. . . 5694
Herod and Pilate reconciled. Cambridge, 1610. 4°. . . 5660
Owen (George), 'D. Kemeis.' *See* Camden (W.). Britannia. 1637.
Owen (Jane). Verses in Owen (J.). Epigrammatum. 1634. . 4583
Owen (John). Epigrammatum...libri tres. Ed. 2. 1618. 12°. . 3672
— Ed. 4. (Epigrammatum. Ed. 2.) 1612. 12°. . . 3753
— Ed. 5. (Epigrammatum. Ed. 3.) 1622. 12°. . . 3683
— Ed. 6. 1634. 12°. 4583
Verses in Coryate (T.). Coryates crvdities. 1611. . . . 3076
— Seneca Tragoediae. 1613. 7781
Owen (John), *bp.* Verses in Davies (J.). Antiquæ linguæ britannicae dictionarium. 1632. 4979
Owen (Lewis). Running register...of the English Colledges...in forraine parts. 1626. 4°. 3032
Speculum Jesuiticum. 1629. 4°. 4606
Unmasking of all popish monks. 1628. 4°. 7629
See Eudes (M.). Catholiqve traditions. 1609 *etc.*
Owen (Rob.), *Jes.* Verses in Camb. Univ. Carmen. 1635. . . 5770

No.
Owen (Rob.), *Jes., cont.* Verses in Camb. Univ. Συνῳδία. 1637. . 5790
Owen (Sir Roger). *See* Owen (J.). Epigrammatum. 1618.
Owen (Will.). Verses in Camb. Univ. Dolor. 1625. 4°. . . . 5701
Owsolde (Walter). Varietie of memorable and worthy matters. 1605. 4°. 3550
Oxenbridge (Daniel), *M.D.* Verses in Hippocrates. 1633. . . 5812
Oxford University. [Ad usum.] *See* Compotus. 1519.
See Wilson (Sir T.). Vita et obitvs...H. and C. Brandoni. [1551.]
Assertio Antiquitatis. *See* Caius (T.). 1568 *etc.*
See Humphrey (L.). Ad Illustrissimam R. Elizabetham. 1572.
— Lycophron. 1592.
— Catalogue. Oxford University. 1600 *etc.*
Answer...to the...ministers of the Church of England, desiring reformation. Oxford, 1603. 4°. 5263
— — 1604. 4°. 5267
See Amsterdam, *English Church in.* An apologie. 1604.
— Nixon (A.). Oxfords Triumph. 1605.
— Wake (I.). Rex Platonicvs. 1607.
Justa Oxoniensium. 1612. 4°. 3086
Epithalamia, sive Lusus Palatini. Oxoniae, 1613. 4°. . . 5313
Justa funebria...T. Bodleii. Oxoniae, 1613. 4°. 5314
See Angelos (C.). Christopher Angell. 1618.
— — Ἐγκώμιον. 1619.
Ultima Linea Savilii. Oxonii, 1622. 4°. 5343
Camdeni Insignia. Oxoniae, 1624. 4°. 5346
Oxon. Acad. Parentalia. Oxoniæ, 1625. 4°. 5354
Britanniae Natalis. Oxoniae, 1630. 4°. 5383
See Clare (J.). The Converted Iew. 1630.
— More (Sir T.). Epistola. 1633.
Statuta selecta...Universitatis. Oxoniae, 1638. 8°. . 5458, 7867
[Arabic Lecture 1637.] *See* Greaves (T.). De linguæ. 1639.
Horti Carolini rosa altera. Oxoniae, 1640. 4°. . . 5499

Bodleian Library. *See* Catalogue. Oxford University. 1600 *etc.*
See Wiclif (J.). Two short treatises. 1608.
— James (T.). Index generalis librorum prohibitorum. 1627.
— Wright (A.). Delitiæ. 1637. 5479
Christchurch. *See* Holyday (B.). Τεχνογαμία. 1630. 4°.
Exeter College. Threni...in obitum...J. Petrei, Gul. Petrei. Oxoniae, 1613. 4°. 5315
See Prideaux (J.). A sermon. 1625. 4°.
Magdalen College. Luctus posthumus...erga...Henricum Walliæ principem. Oxoniae, 1612. 4°. 5302
Merton College. Bodleiomnema. 1613. 4°. 7756
St John's College. *See* Gwinne (M.). Vertumnus. 1607.
Wadham College. *See* Flavel (J.). Tractatvs. . 1619.
[Meridian.] Almanack (Mounslowe). 1561. 8°. . . . 6745
[View of Oxford 1575.] *See* Braun (G.).
Oxford (John de Vere, earl of). 1504. *See* Aymon. The right plesaunt historie. 1554.
Oxford (Edward de Vere, earl of). *See* Castiglione (B.). De Curiali. 1571 *etc.*
Oxford (Henry de Vere, 18th earl of). *See* Markham (G.). Honour. 1624.

P. (A.). *See* Hurault (M.). Antisixtvs. 1590.
P. (A.), *B.A., C.B.* Verses in Oxf. Univ. Horti. 1640. . . 5499
P. (C.). Verses in Smith (J.). True travels. 1630. . . 4836
P. (C.) [=C. Potter]. *See* Sarpi (P.). History of the quarrels. 1626.
P. (C.), *C. Regal.* Verses in Camb. Univ. Gratulatio. 1623. . . 5695
P. (D. B.). *See* W. Bishop, Bishop of Chalcedon.

P. (E.). *See* Ainsworth (J.). Trying ovt of the Trvth. 1615.
See Cranmer (T.). A Confutation. [Ab. 1557.]
P. (E.), *King's Coll. Camb.* Verses in Whitaker (W.). Praelectiones. 1599. 5598
P. (E.), *Philomathem.* Countrey-mans councellor. *See* Helpe to discourse. 1635 *etc.* 12°. . . . . . . 3833 *etc.*
P. (G.). Verses in Camb. Univ. Gratulatio *bis.* 1623. . . 5695
P. (G.) [=Sir G. Peckham]. *See* Gilbert (Sir H.). Trve reporte. 1583.
P. (G.). *See* Caussin (N.). Unfortunate politique. 1639. 8°.
P. (G.), *Cantab.* Antidicsonus. 1584. 8°. 1649
P. (H.). Duty of all true subiects. 1639. 4°. *See* Peacham (H.).
P. (I.), *Priest.* Safegarde from ship-wracke. Douai, 1618. 8°. . 6607
P. (I.), *Cant. Coll. Syd. Suss.* Verses in Stock (R.). The chvrches lamentation. 1614. 3784
P. (I.), *Clare Hall.* Verses in Camb. Univ. Epicedium *bis.* 1612. 5665, 5666
P. (I.), *King's Coll.* Verses in Camb. Univ. Genethl. 1631. . . 5731
P. (I.), *Oxon.* Verses in Abernethy (J.). Christian...treatise. 1630. 4342
P. (I. R.). *See* R. (I.), P. 1623. 7766
P. (J.). Christs confession and complaint. 1629. 4°. . . . 6991
Romes ruin. 1629. 4°. 6992
P. (L.). Verses in Lok (H.). Ecclesiastes. 1597. 2246
P. (M.). Verses in Camb. Univ. Lachrymae. 1587. . . . 2123
P. (N.). Verses in Davies (R.). A funeral sermon. 1577. . . 1416
P. (P. S.). *See* Camus (J. P.). Discovrs hapned betwene an hermite. 1630.
P. (R.) [=R. Parsons]. *See* Bunny (E.). A Briefe Answer. 1589.
See Bunny (E.). Of divorce. 1610 *etc.*
— Parsons (R.). Booke of christian exercise. 1585 *etc.*
— — Christian directorie. 1598.
P. (R.). *See* Coke (Sir E.). Speech. 1607.
See Mirror of Knighthood Part iii. 1598.
P. (R.). Verses in Holyoake (F.). Dictionarium. 1640. . . 3058
P. (R.), *C.C.C.* Verses in Camb. Univ. Epicedium. 1612. . 5665
P. (R.), *Ioan.* Verses in Oxf. Univ. Horti. 1640. . . . 5499
P. (*Mr* R. C.), *Bachelor of Diuinitie.* *See* Chambers (R.).
P. (S.). Verses in Slatyer (W.). History. 1621. 3137
P. (T.). Verses in Camb. Univ. Thr-thr. 1603. . . . 5616
See Procter (T.). Of the knowledge of warres. 1578.
P. (T.) [=T. Price]. *See* Torsellino (O.). History of...Loreto. 1608.
P. (T. L. D. M.). *See* Du Bartas. Learned Summary. 1621 *etc.*
P. (T. W.). *See* Worthington (T.). Whyte dyed black. 1615.
P. (Tho.). *See* Holy Bull. 1588. 4°.
P. (W.). *See* New Dialogue. 1548.
P. (W.) [=W. Phillip]. *See* Linschoten (J. H. van). Voyages. 1598.
P. (W.). Verses in Breton (N.). Characters. 1615. 3902
P. (W.), *Mr of Arts in Cambridge.* *See* Bernard (Saint). Meditations. 1631.
Pace (Richard), *Dean.* [Letter.] *See* Wakefield (R.). Kotser. 1528. 4°.
Pachet (Nicolas). Verses in More (Sir T.). Eruditissimi viri G. Rossei opus. 1523. 284
Pacius (Julius), a Beriga. Institutiones logicae. Cantabrigiae, 1597. 12°. 5587
Packer (Thomas). True catholike. 1632. 12°. 4439
Paddy (Sir William). Verses in Gwinne (M.). Vertumnus. 1607. . 3621
— Rawlins (T.). Admonitio. [1620?] 2033
Page (Samuel). Allegeance of the cleargie. 1616. 4° (fragment). . 3667
God be thanked. A sermon...East Indies. 1616. 4°. . . 7539
Nine Sermons. 1630. 4°. 7541
Verses in Coryate (T.). Coryates crvdities. 1611. . . . 3076
Page (Th.), *K.C.C.* Verses in Camb. Univ. Genethl. *bis.* 1631. . 5731
— Hippocrates. 1631 *etc.* . . . . 5736 *etc.*

No.
Page (Th.), *K.C.C., cont.* Verses in Camb. Univ. Anthologia. 1632. 5741
— Gerhard (J.). Golden chaine. 1632. 5744
— Camb. Univ. Fasciae. 1633. 5808
— — Carmen. 1635. 5770
— — Voces. 1640. 5836
Page (William). Treatise...of bowing at the name of Iesus. Oxford, 1631. 4°. 5388, 5889
See Stubbs (J.). Discoverie of a gaping gvlf. 1579. 8°.
Paget (Charles). *See* Ely (H.). Certaine briefe notes. [1603.]
Paget (John). Primer of christian religion. 1601. 8°. . . 1268
Answer to...W. Best. Amsterdam, 1635. 4°. 6360
See Best (W.). Chvrches Plea. 1635.
Paget (Thomas). Verses in Camb. Univ. Anthologia. 1632. . . 5741
— — Rex redux. 1633. 5748
Pagit or Pagitt (Ephraim). Christianographie. Ed. 2. 1636. 4°. . 5066
— Ed. 3. 1640. F°. 3731
Verses in Laurentius (A.). Discourse. 1599. . . . 2913
Pagit (Eusebius). Godlie and frvitefull sermon. 1583. 8°. . 1930
Historie of the bible...question and answer. Cambridge [1602?]. 12°. 5612
— 1627. 8°. 4704
See Calvin (J.). Harmonie vpon the...Euangelistes. 1610. 4°.
— Godly Sermon. 1586. 8°. 1886
Pagninus (Santes). *See* Willet (A.). Hexapla in Genesin. 1605.
— — Exodvm. 1608.
Painter (Richard). *See* Paynter.
Paiva (Hieronymus de). Brevissimum totius Conimbricensis Logicæ Compendium. 1627. 12°. 3872
Palatinate of the Rhine. [Catechism.] *See* Bastingius.
See Catechism. 1578(9?). 8°.
— Ursinus (Z.). The summe. 1587.
— Heidelberg Catechism. 1595. 8°.
— John Casimir, *Count Palatine.* Certaine Orations. 1579. . 7128
Fvll declaration of the faith...in the dominions of...Fredericke 5. Trans. J. Rolte. 1614. 4°. 2988
See W. (S.). Appollogie. 1622. 4°.
— Wells ( ), Dr. Trve and ample relation. 1622.
Briefe information of the affaires. 1624. 4°. 6954
See Scott (T.). Votivæ Angliæ. 1624.
— Letters Patent (Exiled Ministers). 29 Jan. 1627. Broadside.
— — 6 Aug. 1630. Broadside.
Declaration of the Pfaltzgraves: concerning the faith...in his Churches. Trans. I. R. 1637. 4°. 3314
See Charles Louis. The Manifest. 1637. 3969
— Protestatio. 1637. 4°. 7560
— — Trans. 1637. 4597
— Frubach (V. à). Pomi Palæstini. 1637.
Palfreyman (T.). Myrrour or cleare glasse. 1560. 8°. . . 1157
See Baldwin (W.). Treatise of morall philosophie. 1567 *etc.*
Palingenius (M.). Zodiacus vitæ. 1602. 8°. 2345
— 1615. 8°. 3266
— 1639. 8°. 3310
Zodyake of lyfe. Trans. B. Googe. 1560. 8°. 1257
— 1576. 4°. 1622
Palladius (A.). Introduction into the Bookes of the Prophets and Apostles. 1598. 8°. 2196
Palm of Christian Fortitude. 1630. *See* Neville (E.).
Palm. (Ed.). *See* Palmer.
Palmer (Ed.), *Trin. Coll.* Verses in Camb. Univ. Epicedium. 1612. . 5665
— — Lacrymæ. 1619. 5689
Palmer (F.). Verses in Ferrand (J.). Ἐρωτομανία. 1640. . . 5498

No.
Palmer (I.). Verses in Cambridge Lachrymae. 1587. . . 2123
Palmer (Sir Tho.). Essay of...trauailes. 1606. 4°. 2480
Palmerin d'Oliva. Trans. A. M. Parts 1 and 2. 1637. 4°. . 4215
Palmerin of England. Trans. by A. Munday. Parts 1 and 2. 1639. 4°. 4219
Palmistry. *See* Indagine (J. de). Briefe Introductions. 1558. 8°. 790
Palsgrave (J.). Lesclaircissement de la langue Francoyse. 1530. F°. 527
Pament (Robert). Verses in Ovid. De tristibus. 1639. . . 4668
Pamphilus (Eusebius), *pseud.* *See* Luther (M.). Faythfull admonycion. 1554.
Panaretus, *Prince* [i.e. Henry Prince of Wales]. *See* Sylvester (J.). Lachrimæ. 1612. 4°.
Pandectarius (Matthæus). *See* Sylvaticus.
Pandects. *See* Justinianus.
Panedonius (Philogenes), *pseud.* *See* Brathwait (R.).
Panke (John). Fal of Babel. Oxford, 1608. 4°. 5285
Pantaleon (Heinricus), *Basiliensis.* Verses in Palingenius. 1615 *etc.* 3266 *etc.*
Panter (Patrick). Verses in Forbes (P.). Funerals. 1637. . . 6007
Pantolabus (Ponce) [pseud. of J. Huntingdon]. Genealogye of heresye. *See* Bale (John). Mysterye of inyquyte. 1545. 8°. 6693, and pp. 109, 140
Panyasis. [*Gr. Lat.*] *See* Poetae minores. 1635.
Papa Confutatus. 1580. *See* Foxe (J.).
Papatus Romanus. 1617. *See* Dominis (M. A. de).
Paradise of the soul. *See* Primer. 1536. 8°.
Paradoxes. *See* Defence of Contraries. 1593.
Paræus (David). *See* Pareus.
Parallel, Parellelismus. 1626. *See* Featley (D.).
Parasynagma Perthense. *See* Calderwood (D.). 1620.
Paré (Ambroise). Workes. Trans. T. Johnson. 1634. F°. . . 4632
Explanation of...Instruments. *See* Crooke (H.). Μικροκοσμογραφία. 1631.
Pareus (David). *See* Owen (D.). Anti-Paræus. 1622.
See Ursinus (Z.). Summe. 1611 *etc.*
Paris. *See* Henry IV., *King of France.* Three letters. 1586. 8°.
— Philopatris. Humble petition. 1606.
Parliament. 1626, March. *See* Santarelli (A.). Articles. 1626. 4°.
Sorbonne. Copie of a late decree...for the condemning...the murthering of Princes. 1610. 4°. 2629
— (Licence). *See* Richeome (L.). Holy Pictures. 1619.
University. 1594, April 18. [Resolution.] *See* Arnauld (A.). Arrainement of...Jesuites. 1594.
— Summa actorvm facultatis Theologiae...contra librum...Controversia. 1513 [1613]. 4°. 2797
— *See* Becanus (M.). Svpplicatio...Svmma. 1613. . . 2795
— — Cotton (P.). Anti-coton. 1611.
— — Santarelli (A.). Articles. 1626. 4°.
Paris and Vienna. [Ab. 1628.] 4°. 7552
Paris (Matthew). Historia major. 1571 (1570). F°. . . 751, 7786
Historia major cum Rogeri Wendoveri, W. Rishangeri...MSS. Acc. vitae. Ed. W. Wats. 1640. F°. . . . 4935, 7862
Parke (R.). *See* Gonzalez de Mendoza (J.). Historie.
Parker (H.). Dives and Pauper. Pynson, 1493. F°. . . 105
— W. de Worde, 1496. F°. 48
See Shipmoney. Case. 1640.
Parker (M.). De antiquitate Britannicæ Ecclesiæ. 1572. F°. . 831, 832
— [1572–4.]. F°. 890
Life off the 70. Archbishopp off Canterbury. 1574. 8°. . 6298
See Admonition. 1620. F°. 3675
— Answere for the tyme. 1566. 8°.
— Asser. Ælfredi res gestæ. 1574.
— Bible (*A.S.*). Gospels. 1571.

No.

Parker (M.), *cont.* *See* Bible, English (Bishops'). 1568.
— Bible, English Psalms Metrical [1567?]. The whole Psalter. 892
— Briefe examination for the tyme. [1566?] 4°.
— Defence of priests marriages. [1566?]
— Advertisements. England. Church. (1565) 1584. . . 1822
— Godly and necessary admonition. 1564. 4°.
— Jewel (J.). Apologie. 1564.
— Paris (M.). Historia major. 1571.
— Testimonie of Antiqvitie. [1566?] 8°. 895
Parker (Richard). Verses in Camb. Univ. Epicedium. 1612. . . 5665
— Camden (W.). Britannia. 1637. 3055
Parker (Robert). Scholasticall discourse against symbolizing. 1607. F°. 6383
Parkes (Ric.). Briefe answere...of Christ into hell. Oxford, 1604. 4°. 5268
See Willet (A.). Loidoromastix. 1607.
Parkhurst (Anthony). Verses in Gilbert (Sir H.). A trve reporte. 1583. 1354
Parkhurst (John). Ludicra s. Epigrammata Juuenilia. 1573. 4°. 838
Verses in Wilson (Sir T.). Vita. 1551. 631
— Gesner (C.). Hist. Animalium libri IIII. 1558. . . 7746
— Gualther (R.). Hundred...homelyes. 1572. . . . 1412
— Becon (T.). Displaying. 1637. 3963
See Bible, English (Bishops'). 1568.
— Admonition. 1572. 5895
Parkhurst (Sir Robert). *See* Sictor (J.). Lacrymæ. 1637.
Parkin (Samuel). Verses in Digby (E.). Theoria. 1579. . . 1500
Parkin (Thomas), *professor of chirurgery*. Verses in Clowes (W.). Right...Treatise. 1602. 2013
Parkins (John). *See* Perkins.
Parkinson (John). Paradisus Terrestris. 1629. F°. . . 2561
Theatrum Botanicum. 1640. F°. 4680
Parks (William). Rose and lily. 1638. 4°. 4904
Parliament. *See* England. Parliament.
Parliament of Christ. *See* Heskyns (T.).
Parliament of devils. W. de Worde, 1509. 4°. 160
Parma (Prince of). *See* Berghen op Zoom. The besieging. [Ab. 1588.]
Parr (Catharine). *See* Catharine.
Parr (Elnathan). Workes. Ed. 3. 1632. F°. 7935
Grounds of Divinitie. 1614. 8°. 3656
— Ed. 3. 1619. 8°. 3937
Parr (Ric.), *Bp.* Concio ad clerum. Oxon, 1628. 8°. . . . 5420
Parre (R.). *See* Parry (Robert).
Parriett (Thomas). *See* note to no. 4196.
Parry (Ed.). [Licence.] *See* Corbet (I.). The vngirding. 1639.
Parry (Henry), *Bp.* De regno dei et victoria christiana. 1606. 4°. . 2943
See Rainolds (J.). Svmma colloqvii. 1610.
— Ursinus (Z.). Summe. 1587 *etc.*
Parry (Henry), *the younger*. *See* Parry (H.), *Bp.* De regno. 1606.
Parry (Richard), *Bp.* *See* Bible, Welsh. 1620. F°.
Parry (Robert). *See* Mirror of Knighthood. Part iii. 1598.
Parry (W.). True and plaine declaration of...Treasons. [1584.] 4°. . 1688
Parsees. *See* Lord (H.). Display. 1630.
Parsons (Bartholomew). Boaz and Ruth. Oxford, 1633. 4°. . 5404
Parsons (Iarcas). Verses in Hoby (Sir E.). Curry-combe. 1615. . 3111
Parsons (R.). Answere to the fifth part of reportes...by Sir E. Cooke. 1606. 4°. 6870
Booke of Christian Exercise... Perused...by E. Bunny. 1585. 8°. 7306
— Oxford, 1585. 12°. 5224
— 1585. 8°. 2106
— Part 2. 1592. 12°. 1363
— Part 1. 1594. 12°. 2050
— Parts 1 and 2. 1598. 12°. 1777

No.

Parsons (R.), *cont*. Booke of Christian Exercise...Perused...by E. Bunny. 1602. 12º. 2398
— Part 1. 1609. 12º. 2960
— Part 2. 1610. 12º. 2771
— 1615. 12º. 2993
— Part 2. 1615. 12º. 7442
— 1619. 12º. 2789
Brief, and cleere confutation of...O. E. 1603. 8º. . . . 6851
Briefe apologie. [1601?] 8º. 6839
Christian Directory. *See above* Booke of Christian exercise. Part 2. 1592.
Christian directorie. Louvain, 1598. 8º. 6425
— 1607. 12º. 6874
— Ed. 6. 1622. 12º. 6548
Conference about...the Crowne of Ingland. 1594. 8º. . . 6809
Copie of a letter...about...the Earle of Leicester. ['Father Parsons Green coat[1].'] 1594. 8º. 6810
Defence of the censure...of W. Charke and M. Hanmer. 1582. 8º. 6436
Discussion of the answere of M. W. Barlow. 1612. 4º. . 6527
First part of the Resolution of Religion. Antwerp, 1603. 4º. . 6141
— 1603. 8º. 6852
Ivdgment of a catholicke Englishman ... conc. ... Triplici nodo. 1608. 4º. 6517
Quiet and sober reckoning with T. Morton. 1609. 4º. . 6522
Relation of the triall. 1604. *See below* Third part of a treatise.
Review of ten publike disputations. 1604. *See below* Treatise. Part 3.
Resolution of Religion. *See above* First Part of the Resolution.
Treatise of three conversions of England. Parts 1 and 2. 1603. 8º. 6853
— Part 3. 1604. 8º. 6856, 6857
Treatise tending to mitigation...against...T. Morton. By P. R. 1607. 8º. 7701
Warn-word to Sir F. Hastinges wast-word. By N. D. 1602. 8º. 7700
[Life.] *See* James (T.). The Iesuits Downefall. 1612.
See Barlow (W.), *Bp*. Answer to a catholike Englishman. 1609.
— Bunny (E.). Briefe Answer. 1589.
— — Of divorce. 1610 *etc.*
— C. (B.). Fore-rvnner of Bels Downefall. [1605?]
— Charke (W.). Replie to a Censure. 1581.
— Copies of certaine discourses. 1601.
— E. (O.). Briefe replie. 1600.
— Ely (H.). Certaine briefe notes.
— Fitzherbert (T.). Adioynder to the supplement. 1613.
— Fulke (W.). Briefe Confutation. 1581.
— Hastings (Sir F.). Apologie. 1600.
— Hayward (Sir J.). Answer. 1603.
— James (T.). Apologie for John Wickliffe. 1608.
— Morton (T.). Preamble. 1608.
— Sutcliffe (M.). Challenge. 1602.
— — Ful and round answer. 1604.
— — Threefold answer. 1606.
— Watson (W.). Sparing discoverie. 1601.
— Wentworth (P.). Pithie exhortation. 1598.
— Wisbech. True relation. 1601.
Parte of a register. [Edinburgh, 1593.] 4º. 5931
Partibus (Jacobus de). *See* Petrus *Hispanus*. Treasury. [1550.]
Partridge (Jas.). Letters patent of the presbyterie. 1632. 4º. . 7013
Parvulorum institutio. 1534. *See* Stanbridge (J.).

[1] *See also* Notes and Queries, 17 May 1890, p. 383 *b*.

No.

Parvus libellus. *See* Carta Feodi. [15—], 1530 *etc.*
Pascalius (Carolus). *See* Pasquale.
Paschasius, *Saint.* *See* Hieronymus. Vitas patrum. 1495.
Pasor (Matthias). Oratio pro linguæ Arabicæ professione. Oxoniae, 1627. 8°. 5367
Pasquale (C.). False complaints. Trans. W. C. 1605. 4°. . 7399
Pasquier (E.). Jesuite displayed. 1594. 4°. 1845
See Jesuites Catechisme. 1602.
Pasquils. Palinodia. [Ab. 1634?] 4°. 4050
Passe (C. de). Garden of flowers. Utrecht, 1615. F°. . . 6643
Passeratius (Joannes). *See* Calepinus (A.). Dictionarium. Genevæ, 1620. F°. 6323
Passion of Our Lorde. W. de Worde, 1521. 4°. . . . 182
Passion of the fox. *See* Fantasy. 1530.
Passy (I.), *M.A.* Verses in Hopton (A.). Speculum. 1611. . 3638
Pastilew (Henr.). Verses in Camdeni Insignia. 1624. . . . 5346
Patericke (Simon). *See* Patrick.
Paternoster. *See* Lord's Prayer.
Pathomachia: or the battle of the affections. 1630. 4°. . . 7621
Pathose, or an inward passion of the pope. [1548?] 8°. . . 916
Patriarchs, Twelve. *See* Testaments. 1567. 8°. . . . 7124
Patricius (Franciscus), *Bp.* *See* Patrizi.
Patrick, *Saint.* [Life.] *See* B. (B.), *Irish Franciscan.* Life. 1625. 4°.
See Villegas (A. de). Lives of saints. 1628.
Patrick (Simon). *See* Crespin (J.). Estate of the Church. 1602.
See Gentillet (I.). Discourse. 1602 *etc.*
Patrizi (F.). Moral methode of ciuile Policie. 1576. 4°. . . 1228
Patten (William), *of Waynflete.* *See* Waynflete.
Patten (William). Expedicion into Scotlande of.. Edward, duke of Somerset. 1548. 8°. 606
See Calendar of Scripture. 1575.
— Polemon (J.). All the famous Battels. [1577?]
Pattenson (Matt.). Image of bothe churches. Tournai, 1623. 8°. 6655–6
Patteson (Matthew). [Map. 'Dunelmum, 1595.'] F°. . . . 7736
Paul III, *Pope.* *See* Rome, *Church of.* Paul III.
Paul V, *Pope.* [Letter to the Emperor.] *See* Bohemia. Two letters. 1620.
See Becanus (M.). Svpplicatio. 1613. 4°.
— Rome, *Church of.* Paul V, *Pope.*
— Sarpi (P.). The history. 1626.
— Widdrington (R.). Copy. 1614.
— — Supplicatio. 1616.
Paule (Sir George). Life of...John Whitgift. 1612. 4°. . . 3397
Paulfreyman (Thomas). *See* Palfreyman.
Pauli (Georgius). *See* Keckerman (B.). Systema ethicæ. 1607. . 2362
Paulus Ægineta. [De crisi.] *See* Galen. De naturalibus facultatibus. 1523. 4°.
See Edrych (G.). In libros. 1588.
Paulus Eremita. *See* Hieronymus. Certaine selected epistles. 1630. 4°.
Pavie (Raimond de Beccarie de). *See* Fourquevaux.
Pawlet (John), *of George Hinton.* Verses in Coryate (T.). Coryats Crudities. 1611. 3076
Paybody (Thomas). Iust apologie for...kneeling. 1629. 4°. . . 5042
Paynell (Thomas). *See* Bernard, *Saint.* Compendius...treatyse. [154–?]
— Cyprianus (S.). Sermon. 1539.
— Durantinus (C. F.). Conspiracie of Catiline. 1557.
— Hanapus (N.). Ensamples of Vertue. 1561. 8°.
— Hutten (U. von). [De morbo gallico. 1533.]
— Lobeira (V.). [Amadis of Gaul.] [1567.]
— Regimen. 1541 etc.
— Vives (J. L.). Office and duetie of a husband. [1550?] 8°.

No.
Paynter (Ric.). Verses in Oxf. Univ. Horti *bis*. 1640. . . . 5499
— Snelling (T.). Thibaldus. 1640. 5502
Payton (John), *junior*. Verses in Coryat (T.). Coryats crudities. 1611. 3076
Peacham (Henry). Compleat gentleman. 1622. 4°. . . . 4129
— 1626. *See* no. 4721.
— (The Gentlemans Exercise.) 1634. 4°. 4721
Duty of all true subjects. 1639. 4°. 4124
Valley of varietie. 1638. 12°. 4946
Verses in Coryate (T.). Coryates Crvdities. 1611. . . 3076
Pearce (George), *K.C.C.* Verses in Camb. Univ. Epithalam. 1625. . 5702
Pearson (Andrew). *See* Bible, English (Bishops'). 1568. . . 964
Pearson (Cuthbert), *K.C.C.* Verses in Camb. Univ. Epicedium. 1612. 5665
— — Lacrymæ. 1619. 5689
— — Dolor. 1625. 5701
— — Epithalam. 1625. 5702
— — Genethl. 1631. 5731
— — Anthologia. 1632. 5741
— — Fasciae. 1633. 5808
— — Rex redux. 1633. 5748
Pearson (Jo.). Verses in Camb. Univ. Anthologia. 1632. . . 5741
— — Rex redux. 1633. 5748
— — Συνῳδία. 1637. 5790
— King (E.). Ivsta. 1638. 5829
— Camb. Univ. Voces. 1640. 5836
Pecke (Richard). Christs Watchword...funerall of...L. Bodley. Exeter, 1635. 4°. 3957
Peckham (Sir George). *See* Gilbert (Sir H.). Trve reporte. 1583.
Pecock (Reginald), *Bp.* Verses in Carlile (C.). Discourse. 1582. 1871
Pedantius. Comoedia. 1631. 12°. 3182
Peerse (John). Verses in Camb. Univ. Carmen. 1635. . . 5770
Peerson (Martin). Verses in Ravenscroft (T.). Briefe discourse. 1614. 2029
Peeter or Peeters (Gerard). Verses in Cambridge Lachrymae. 1587. 2123
See P. (G.), *Cantabrigiensis*. Antidicsonus. 1584. 8°.
Peeterhouse (John). Verses in Thynne (F.). Newes from the north. 1585. 2002
Peirce (George), *K.C.C.* Verses in Hippocrates. 1631 *etc.* 5736 *etc.*
Peirce (Thomas). *See* Piers.
Peirson (John), *K.C.C.* Verses in Camb. Univ. Fasciae. 1633. . 5808
Peirsoun (Alexander). Verses in Adamson (J.). Εἰσοδία. 1618. . 5960
Pelagius. *See* Crowley (R.). Apologie. 1566.
— Turner (W.). Preseruatiue. 1551.
Pelagius redivivus. *See* Featley.
Pelagius (Alvarus). *See* Pelayo (Alvaro).
Pelayo (Alvaro), *Bp of Silves*. *See* Clemangiis (N. de). Specvlvm. 1606.
Pelegromius (Simon). Synonymorum sylva. 1603. 8°. . . 7881
— 1639. 8°. 5205
Pelham (Edward). *See* Pellham.
Pelham (Sir William). Verses in Gilbert (Sir H.). A true reporte. 1583. 1354
Pelletier (P.). Lamentable discourse. 1610. 4°. 2180
Pellham (Edward). Gods power and providence. 1631. 4°. . 7635
Pellham. *See also* Pelham.
Pellicanus (Conrad). *See* Joye (G.). Exposicion of Daniel. 1545.
Pelling (John). Sermon of the providence of God. 1607. 4°. . 3623
Pember (John). Verses in Camdeni Insignia. 1624. . . 5346
Pember (Robert). Verses in Cheke (Sir J.). De obitu M. Buceri. 1551. 734
Pemble (William). Workes. Ed. 3. 1635. F°. 4638
Briefe introduction to geography. (Summe of moral philosophy.) 1635. F°. 4289

No.
Pemble (William), *cont.* De sensibus internis. Oxoniae, 1629. 12°. . 5377
Five godly...sermons. Oxford, 1628. 4°. 5372
Fruitfull sermon on I Cor. xv. 18, 19. 1629. 4°. . . . 4972
Introduction to...the Lords supper. 1629. 4°. . . 2557
Salomons recantation...the Booke of Ecclesiastes. 1628. 4°. . 4817
Short and sweete exposition vpon...Zachary. 1629. 4°. . 4973
Vindiciae fidei. Ed. 2. Oxford, 1629. 4°. 5378
Vindiciae gratiae. Ed. 2. 1629. 4°. 2559
See Gouge (W.). Exposition. 1630. 4°.
Pembroke (Mary Herbert, countess of). *See* Sidney (Sir P.). Arcadia.
Pembroke (William, earl of). [Funeral.] *See* C. (T.). Ivst mans memoriall. 1630. 4°.
Pembroke and Montgomery (Philip, earl of). *See* Saulnier (G.). Love and armes of the greek princes. 1640. F°.
Pena (P.) and M. de L'Obel. Stirpium adversaria nova. 1571. F°. 7244
See L'Obel (M. de)...in G. Rondellettii...animadversiones. 1605.
Pendilton (H.). [Homilies.] *See* Bonner (E.). Profitable...doctryne. 1555.
Penitent Sinner. *See* Carr (J.). Alarume Bell for London. [157–?]
Penketh (Thomas). *See* Andreæ (A.). Quæstiones. 1480. F°.
Penkethman (John). Artachthos. 1638. 4°. 5197
See Hopton (A.). Hoptons Concordancy. 1635.
— Vergilius. (Appendix.) Epigrams. 1624.
Pennant (John). *See* May (E.). Relation of a...monster. 1639.
Penny (Thomas). *See* Moffett (T.). Insectorum. 1634.
Pennyman (W.). Verses in Camdeni Insignia. 1624. . . 5346
Penruddock (Ed.). Verses in Camb. Univ. Fasciae. 1633. . . 5808
— — Carmen. 1635. 5770
— — Συνωδία. 1637. 5790
Penry (John). Appellation of John Penri. 1589. 8°. . . 1919
Exhortation vnto the Gouernours and people of Wales. [1588?] 8°. 1912
Hay any worke for cooper. [1589.] 4°. 7779
Humble motion with submission vnto the...privie counsell. [Edinburgh,] 1590. 4°. 5923
Protestatyon of martin marprelay. [1589.] 8°. 7325
Treatise...in the behalfe of...Wales. Oxford, 1587. 8°. . 5228
See Bancroft (R.). Briefe discovery. [1590?]
— Barrow (H.). The examinations. [1593?]
— Bèze (T. de). Propositions and principles. 1595. 8°.
— Greenwood (J.). M. Some laid open. [1590?]
— Humble Motion. 1590.
— Marprelate (M.).
— Some (R.). Godly treatise...touching the Ministerie. 1588.
— — Godly treatise, wherein are examined...Henry Barrow and I. Greenewood. 1589.
Pepys (Edward), *T.C.* Verses in Camb. Univ. Συνωδία. 1637. . 5790
Per (R.), *B.D.*, *C.C.C.* *See* Pernham.
Perceval (Ric.). Dictionary in Spanish and English. 1599. F°. 2055, 7921
— Enlarged by J. Minsheu. (Grammar; Dialogues.) 1623. F°. 4775
Spanish grammar (Dialogues). 1599. F°. 2056, 7922
— 1623. F°. 4775
Percy (John), *jesuit.* *See* Fisher (J.), *jesuit* (*pseud.*).
Percy (Thomas), earl of Northumberland. *See* Northumberland.
Percy (W.). Verses in Barnes (B.). Foure bookes. 1606. . 2435
Percyvall (Richard). *See* Perceval.
Peregrin (James), *pseud.* *See* Partridge (James).
Peregrinus de Lugo, *Italicus.* *See* Lugo (Peregrinus de).
Pérez (Alonso). *See* Montemayor (J. de). Diana. Part 2. 1598. F°. 7924
Perez (Antonio de). *See* Ol. (P.), *Spanish Pilgrim.* Treatise parænetical. 1598.
Perier (H.). Verses in Oxf. Univ. Magd. Coll. 1612. . . . 5302

No.

Perin (John). *See* Perrinne.
Periodical Publications[1]. *See* Continuation of our forraine avisoes.
— — our weekly avisoes.
— — our weekly newes.
— — the German History.
— Curranto. No. 41. An extraordinary C. 1639.
— — No. 84. The Norimberg C. 1639.
— — No. 85. The C...from Holland. 1639.
— Extraordinary Cvrranto. 18 Oct. 1639. 4°.
— Modern History. 1635. 4°.
— Newes from France. 1618. 7514
— Norimberg Curranto. 21 June 1639. 4°.
— Swedish Intelligencer.
Perkins (J.). Explanatio quorundam capitulorum. Aug. 1541. 8°. 710
Profitable Booke...of the lawes of England. 1576. 8°. . . 1132
Perkins (Samuel). New almanacke and prognostication. 1637. 8°. 5129
Perkins (William). Works. Cambridge, 1603–2. F°. . . . 5618
— Vol. 1. Cambridge, 1608. F°. 5645
— 1612. F°. 3751
— 1616. F°. 3760
— 1635. F°. 4727
— Vol. 2. Cambridge, 1609. F°. 5646
— 1617. F°. 3760
— Vol. 3. Cambridge, 1609. F°. 5656
— Cambridge, 1613. F°. 7671
— Cambridge, 1618. F°. 5683
Armilla aurea. Ed. 2. Cantabrigiae [1590]. 8°. . . . 5542
— Ed. 3. [1592?] 8°. 5543
Case of conscience. 1595. 4°. 6815
The first part of the cases of conscience. Cambridge, 1604. 8°. . 5626
Whole treatise of the cases of Conscience. Ed. T. Pickering. Cambridge, 1606. 8°. 5638
— 1608. 8°. 7670
— 1635. 4°. 4728
Comm....vpon...Galatians...R. Cudworth. Cambridge, 1604. 4°. 5625
De praedestinationis modo. Cantabrigiae, 1598. 5595
Declaration of...Christ crucified. n.d. 12°. 3769
Direction for the government of the tongue. Cambridge, 1593. 8°. 5563
— Cambridge, 1603. 12°. 5619
— n.d. 12°. 3770
Discourse of...witchcraft. Cambridge, 1608. 8°. 5652
— Cambridge, 1610. 8°. 5661
Exposition of the lords praier. Edinburgh, 1593. 12°. . . 5932
— 1595. 4°. 6816
Exposition of the symbole or creed. Cambridge, 1595. 4°. . 5573
— Cambridge, 1596. 4°. 5583
— Cambridge, 1597. 8°. 5588
— 1631. 4°. 4709
Foundation of christian religion. [Ab. 1590.] 4°. . 6817 (corrected)
— Cambridge, '1061.' 8°. 5605
Godlie...exposition vpon...Iude. 1606. 4°. 7755
Godly...exposition of Christs sermon in the mount. Cambridge, 1608. 4°. 5653
Golden chaine. Trans. R. Hill. Ed. 2. Cambridge, 1592. 8°. 5555
— Ed. 2. Cambridge, 1595. 4°. 5574
— 'Ed. 2.' 1597. 4°. 7374–5

[1] See J. Nichols, *Literary Anecdotes*, Vol. IV. pp. 38—9.

No.

Perkins (William), *cont.* Golden chaine. Trans. R. Hill. Cambridge, 1600. 4°. 7669
— 1612. 8°. 7544
Graine of mustard-seede. 12°. 7545
How to live and that well. n.d. 12°. 3771
Of the calling of the ministerie. 1605. 8°. 1793
Problema de romanae fidei ementito catholicismo. Cantabrigiae, 1604. 4°. 5627
Prophetica. 1592. 8°. 5554
Reformed Catholike. Cambridge, 159[7 ?]. 8°. 5589
— 1598. 8° 5594
— 1611. 8°. 3750
— 1634. 8°. 4722
Salve for a sicke man. Cambridge, 1595. 8°. . . . 5575
Salve for a sicke man (declaration of...Christ crucified.—Discourse of conscience. Ed. 2). Cambridge, 1597, 4°. . . . 5590
Salve for a sicke man. 12°. n.d. 3772
Sixe principles of christian religion (=Foundation of Christian Religion). [Ab. 1590.] 4°. . . . . 6817 (corrected)
Treatise of gods free grace. Cambridge, 1602. 8°. . . . 5610
Treatise of mans imaginations. Cambridge, 1607. 12°. . . 5642
Treatise tending unto a declaration. [Ab. 1590 ?] 8°. . . 7365
— 1591. 8°. 7367
— 1595. 4°. 7371
— 1619. 12°. 3767
True gaine. Cambridge, 1601. 8°. 5606
Two treatises. Cambridge, 1593. 8°. 5564
— Ed. 2. Cambridge, 1595. 4°. 5576
— — Cambridge, 1595. 8°. 5577
— 'Ed. 2.' 'J. Legate.' 1597. 4°. 7377
— n.d. 12°. 3773
Warning against the idolatrie. Cambridge, 1601. 8°. . . . 5607
See Abbot (R.). Defence of the reformed catholicke. 1606. 4°.
— Bishop (W.). Disproofe. 1614.
— P. (D. B.) Second part of the reformation of a Catholike Deformed. 1607.
— Rogers (Ric.). Garden. 1625.
— Rudyerd (Sir B.). Speech. 1628. 4°.
— Wotton (A). Defence of M. Perkins booke. 1606.
— Yates (J.). God's arraignment. 1615. 4°.
Pernam (R.). *See* Pernham.
Perne (Andrew). *See* Bible, English (Bishops'). 1568.
Pernham (R.) *B.D., C.C.C.* Verses in Camb. Univ. Epicedium. 1612. 5665
— Robartes (F.). Revenue. 1613. 5670
Peron, *Cardinal.* *See* Du Perron.
Perottus (N.), *Sipontinus.* Cornucopia. *See* Ortus vocabulorum. 1528. 4°. . . . . 195 (and p. 1729)
Institutio Grammaticalis. Louvain [1486]. 4°. 129
See Anwykyll (J.). Cōpendium totius grāmatice. [1489.]
See Whittington (R.). Grammatica. Pt I. Lib. 2. . . . 199
Perpetual reioyce of the Godly. *See* Imitation of Christ. 1568. 8°.
Perret (Clement). Exercitatio alphabetica. 1569. obl. F°. . 7684
Perrin (Jean Paul). Bloudy rage of...Antechrist...in the...Waldenses and Albigenses. Trans. S. Lennard. 1624. 4°. . . . 4223
— Luthers fore-runners: or a cloud of witnesses. 1624. 4°. 4224
Perrinne or Perin (John). *See* Bible, English (Royal). 1611. . 2635
Perrot (Sir James). Verses in Vaughan (W.). Golden Grove. 1608. 2888
Perrot (Sir John), *Kt.* *See* S. (E. C.). Government of Ireland. 1626.
Perrot (Richard). Iacobs vowe...tithes. Cambridge, 1627. 4°. . 5709
Perse (St.). Verses in Camb. Univ. Thr-thr. 1603. 5616

No.

Persia. *See* Herbert (Sir T.). Relation. 1634.
See Minadoi (G. T.). The history. 1595.
Persius (Aulus). Satyrae sex. Cum comm. posth. J. Bond. 1614. 8°. 2987
Satyræ. *See* Horatius. Poemata. 1578(–9) *etc.*
Satyræ. *See* Juvenalis. Satyræ. 1615, 1633.
Selection. (English.) *See* Beaumont (Sir J.). Bosworth field. 1629.
Person (David). Varieties. 1635. 4°. 4365
Perth, General Assembly. *See* Cowper (W.). Life. 1619.
See Lindsay (D). True narration. 1621.
Parasynagma perthense. 1620. 4°. 7682
Perth, Bridge of. Verses in Adamson (J.) Εἰσόδια. 1618. . . 5960
Peru. *See* Zarate (A. de). Strange and delectable History. 1581.
Perugino (M. A.). Verses in Gascoigne (G.). Posies. 1575. . 1482
Perusinus (Petrus). Verses in Cheke (Sir J.). De obitu M. Buceri. 1551. 734
Perussellus (F.). Summa christianae religionis...per H. Bellopoelivm. 1551. 8°. 1098
Peryn (John). *See* Perrinne.
Peryn (W.). Thre godly and notable Sermons...of the Aulter. [1548?] 8°. 770
Pestilence, Book of. *See* Canutus. 96
Peterhouse (J.). *See* Peeterhouse.
Peters (I.). Verses in Camb. Univ. Thr-thr. 1603. . . 5616
Peterson (Robert). *See* Botero (G.). A treatise concerning...Cities. 1606. 4°.
Petilius (Elias). *See* Petley.
Petit (Jean François). *See* Le Petit (J. F.).
Petition directed to her most excellent Maiestie. [Ab. 1590]. 4°. 7916
Petition to the Kings...Maiestie for debt. 1622. 4°. . . . 6932
Petley (Elias). Royall receipt...sermon...1623. 4°. . . . 4178
See Common Prayer. (Greek.) 1638.
Petra (Gabriel de). *See* Longinus (D.). Περὶ ὕψους. 1636.
Petrarca (Franceso). Phisicke against Fortune. Trans. T. Twyne. 1579. 4°. 1336
[Verses Ital. and. Eng.] *See* Daneau (L.). Treatise. 1589. . 2201
See Gascoigne (G.). Hundreth sundrie Flowers. [Ab. 1572.] 4°.
— Plat (Sir Hugh). Manuale. 1594.
Petre (John) of Writtle, *first baron*. *See* Oxford University. Exeter College. Threni. 1613.
Petre (Sir William). *See* Oxford University. Exeter College. Threni. 1613.
Petrus Carmelianus. *See* Carmelianus.
Petrus Hispanus. Treasury of health. [Ab. 1550.] 8°. . . 1088
Petter (John). Verses in Camb. Univ. Lacrymæ. 1619. . . 5689
— — Genethl. 1631. 5731
Pettie (G.). Petite Pallace. [1576?] 4°. 1346
See Guazzo (S.). The ciuile Conuersation. 1586.
Pettie (W.). Verses in Jones (W.). Treatise. 1625. . . . 3351
Pewdæus (G.). Verses in Dent (A.). Sermon. 1588. . . 2046
Pewterers. *See* London. Pewterers Company.
Peyton (Ro.). Verses in Camb. Univ. Epicedium. 1612. . . 5665
Pflacher (M.). Analysis typica. 1587. 4°. 2045
Phaëton. Verses in Florio (F.). Florios second frvtes. 1591. . 2211
Phædrus. [Fables. Lat. and Eng.] *See* Æsop. Etymologist, 1602.
Phaer (T.). New boke of Presidentes. 1543. 4°. 651
Regiment of life. E. Whitchurch, 1550. 16°. 7098
— Kingston and Sutton, 1553. 16°. 1160
— East and Middleton, 1567. 16°. 1566
— E. Allde, 1596. 4°. 2008

No.

Phaer (T.), *cont.* [Prescription.] *See* D. (I.), *Preacher.* Salomons Pest House. 1630. 4°.
See Higgins (J.). Mirrour. 1610.
— Purlilia (James, earl of). Preceptes. 1544. . . . 652
— Vergilius. [Æneid.] 1596 etc.
Phaire (Thomas). *See* Phaer.
Phalaris. Epistles. Trans. W. D. 1634. 12°. 4356
Pharmacopoeia Londinensis. 1618. F°. 4130
Ed. 3. 1627. F°. 4812
Ed. 5. 1638 (9). F°. 4325
Phayer (Thomas). *See* Phaer.
Phesaunt (Steph.). Verses in Camb. Univ. Anthologia. 1632. . 5741
Phettiplace or Fettiplace (Michael). Verses in Smith (J.). Generall historie. 1624. 3864
Phettiplace (William). Verses in Smith (J.). Generall historie. 1624. 3864
Philadelphus (Eusebius), *pseud.* *See* Barnaud (N).
Philadelphus (Theophilus), *pseud.* *See* Theophilus.
Philalethes (Andreas), *pseud.* Answere made...to...G. Blackwels. 1602. 4°. 6847
Φιλαλεξανδρος, S. Verses in Camb. Univ. Epicedium. 1612. . 5665
Philanactophil, *pseud.* *See* Florus. Roman Histories. [1618] etc.
Philbert, *de Vienne.* *See* Philibert.
Philibert de Vienne. Philosopher of the Court. 1575. 8°. . . . 1485
Philip II, King of Spain. Relation of the...receiving in Valliodolid etc. 1592. 8°. 6801
[Marriage.] *See* Elder (J.). Copie of a letter. [1555.]
— — Gorecius (L.). Oratio. 1554.
[Genealogical Table. 1554?] Single Sheet. F°. 6721
See Lewkenor (Sir Lewis). Estate. 1596.
— Ol. (P.)., *Spanish Pilgrim.* Treatise Parænetical. 1598.
— — Spanish Pilgrime 1625.
— True Discourse. 1588.
Philip III, of Spain. [Proclamation 1599.] *See* Copie of a certaine letter... 1599.
See Bohemica Jura. 1620. 4°. 7515
— Oration or speech. 1608. 1624
— Spain.
Philip IV, *King of Spain.* *See* Barry (G.). Siege of Breda. 1627–8.
— Charles I. True Relation. 1623.
Philip, *Landgrave of Hesse.* *See* Avila y Zuñiga (L. de). The Comentaries. 1555.
Philip Lewis, Earl of Hanau etc. [Death.] *See* Appelius (J.). True relation. 1612. 4°.
Philipot (John), *Somerset Herald.* Catalogue of the Chancellors of England. 1636. 4°. 4643
Cities Advocate. [1629.] 4°. 4691
Verses in Brooke (R.). Discovery. 1622. 2793
See Camden (W.). Remaines. 1637.
Philippa, *the Catanian.* *See* Matthieu (P.). Vnhappy Prosperitie. 1632. 4°.
Philippe (François). *See* Common Prayer (French). 1553.
Philippes ( ). [Grants privilege for printing of a book.] 1574. 1528
Philippes (Morgan), *pseud.* *See* Leslie (J.), *Bp.*
Phillipus (Henricus). Theses in Adamson (J.). Εἰσόδια. 1618. . 5960
Philips (E.). Certain godly and learned sermons. 1605. 4°. . . 2261
Countrey-Mans Counsellor. *See* Helpe to discourse. Ed. 12. 1636. 12°. 3703
Philips (Robert). *See* Phillips.
Phillips or Philips (Robert). Verses in Coryat (T.). Coryats Crudities. 1611. 3076
Philippson (John), *Sleidanus.* *See* Sleidanus.

No.

Philips (Thomas). Booke of Lamentations. 1639. 12°. . . 5174
Phillip (William). *See* Linschoten (J. H. van). Voyages. 1598. F°.
Phillippes (W.). Caueat or warnyng to Englande. *See* Carr (J.). Alarume Bell for London. [157–?] 1764
Phillips (George). [Good sheepheardes dutie. 1597.] 8°. . 7386
Phillips (Jerome). Fisherman. 1623. 4°. 3345
Philo, *Judæus.* Lytle treatise concernynge Nobilitye. *See* Humphrey (L.). Nobles. 1563.
Philo-brittanicos [*pseud.* of Roe (Sir T.)]. *See* Sarpi (P.). Discourse. 1628.
— — Cruell Subtilty. 16—.
Philo-Kuriaces (Theophilus), Loncardiensis. *See* Young (T.).
Philomathes, *pseud.* *See* Clapham (J.). Historie of England. 1602.
Philomusus. *See* Locher (Jacob).
Philopater (Andreas), *pseud.* *See* Parsons (R.).
Philopatris. Humble petition offered to...Parliament. 1606. 4°. . 2480
Φιλοπατρις (C.), *pseud.* *See* James I., King.
Philophrastes. *See* Seneca. Consolation to Marcia. 1635. 4°.
Philostratus. *See* Æsop. Fabulæ. 1635.
Philpot (Jo.). Examination. (Apologie.) [Ab. 1556.] 8°. . . 6727
Trew report of the dysputacyon...in the conuocacyon hows. ‘Basill,’ Oct. 1544. 8°. 6111
Letters. *See* Coverdale (M.) Certain...letters. 1564.
Phioravanti (Leonardo). *See* Fioravanti.
Phiscerus (Joannes). *See* Fisher.
Phiston (William). Estate of the germaine empire. 1595. 4°. . 7337
See Ochino (B.). Certaine...Sermons. 1580.
— Voyon (S. de). Testimonie. [158–?]
Phlegon. [Περὶ τῶν Ὀλυμπίων. *Gr. and Eng.*] *See* Broughton (H.). Apologie. 1592.
Phocylides. [*Gr. and Lat.*] *See* Poetae minores. 1635.
Photius. *See* Chrysostom...opera. 1613.
Φρεαρριος. *See* Frear.
Physiognomy. *See* Hill (T.). Contemplation of Mankind. 1571. 8°. 6753
Pia et Catholica Christiani Hominis Institutio. *See* Necessary Doctrine. 1544.
Pibrac (Guy du Faur, sieur de). Τετραστικα. *See* Du Bartas. Weekes. 1605.
Pica or Directorium. Sarum. (Breviarium cum pica.) 1530. . . 6157
Picern (Bartholomew). *See* Pincernus.
Pickering (Thomas). *See* Perkins (W.). First part of the cases of conscience. 1604. 8°.
— — Whole treatise of the cases of conscience. 1606 etc.
— — Discourse of the damned art of witchcraft. 1608 etc.
— — Works. Vol. 3. (‘Christian Oeconomie.’) 1609. F°. . 1656
Pickering (William). Verses in Camdeni Insignia. 1624. . . 5346
Pickford (John Jerome), *alias* Daniel, *O.S.F.* *See* P. (I.), *Priest.* 1618. 6607
Pico della Mirandula (Giovanni Francesco). Rules of a christian life. *See* Cyprian. Swete and devovte sermon. 1539. 8°.
The lyfe. *See* More (Sir T.). Workes. 1557.
See Clemangiis (N. de). Specvlvm... 1606.
— Lupset (T.). Workes. 1546.
Pie (T.). Epistola. 1603. 4°. 2079
Houreglasse. 1597. 4°. 1974
Usuries Spright coniured. 1604. 4°. 3358
Piedmont (Victor Amadeus, prince of). *See* Victor Amadeus I, duke of Savoy.
Pierce (Robert). Verses in Camb. Univ. Genethl. 1631. . . . 5731
— Jorden (E.). Discourse. 1633. 4003

No.
Piers the Plowman. Vision. Ed. 1. R. Crowley. 1550. 4°. . 7762
— Ed. 2. R. Crowley. 1550. 4°. 1092
— [Another edition.] R. Crowley. 1550. 4°. . . . 7153
— O. Rogers. 1561. 4°. 1282
Crede. 1553. 4°. 739
Piers (Cad.), *B.A.*, *S.J.C.* Verses in Camb. Univ. Συνῳδία. 1637. . 5790
Piers (John), *abp. of York.* *See* Articles (York, Diocese). 1590.
[Funeral sermon.] *See* King (J.). Lectvres. 1597 *etc.*
Piers (Thomas). Verses in Ravenscroft (T.). Briefe discourse. 1614. 2029
See also Pierse.
Piers (William), *D.D.* Verses in Oxford University. Camdeni Insignia. 1624. 5346
Pierse (T.). Verses in Oxf. Univ. Horti. 1640. . . 5499 *bis*
See also Piers.
Pierson (Thomas). *See* Perkins (W.). Treatise of mans imagination. 1607. 12°.
— — Godly...exposition of Christs Sermon. 1608. 4°.
— — Works. Vol. 3. ('A clowd of faithful witnesses' and 'Revelation' and 'The Combate.') 1609. F°. . . 5656
Pigafetta (Philippo). *See* Lopes (D.). Report. 1597.
Piggot (Ralph). Verses in Camb. Univ. Genethl. 1631. . . 5731
Pighius (Albertus). *See* Poynet (J.). Apologie. 1556.
Pile of Troy Waightes. 1588. Broadside. 1691
Pilger (Andreas). Letter. *See* Vincent (P.). The lamentations of Germany. 1638. 7760
Pilgrimage of man. 1635. 4°. 3834
Pilgrimage of Perfection. (Rosary.) Pynson, 1526. 4°. . . 289
— W. de Worde. 23 Feb. 1531. F°. 203
Pilkington (Jas.). Aggeus the Prophete. 1560. 8°. . . . 922
— 1562. 8°. 924
Burnynge of Paules church. 1561. W. Seres. 1563. 8°. . 925
Godlie exposition...of Nehemiah. Cambridge, 1585. 4°. . 5520
Pilkington (Richard). Parallela. 1618. 4°. 3490
Pill to purge out Poperie. *See* M. (I.). Spirituall Food. 1600 *etc.*
Pincernus (Bartholomæus), *de Monte Arduo.* *See* Constantine I. Treatyse. [Ab. 1525.]
Pinck (Jo.), *M.A.*, *New College, Oxford.* Verses in Butler (C.). Principles of Musik. 1636. 4860
Pinck (Rob.). Verses in Oxf. Univ. Horti. 1640. - . . . 5499
Pinke (William). Tryall of a Christians syncere love. Oxford, 1631. 4°. 5390
— Ed. 2. Oxford, 1634. 12°. 7660
— Ed. 3. Oxford, 1636. 12°. 5470
Pinkney (Miles). *See* Carre (Thomas).
Piper (John). *See* Urfé (H. d'). History of Astræa. 1620.
Pirr (Thomas), *qu.* Pirry? Verses in Wilson (Sir T.). Vita. 1551. 631
Pirry (Thomas). Verses in Ridley (N.). Pitvovs lamentation. 1566. 1017
See also Pirr.
Piscator (J.). Analysis logica evang. sec. Lucam. 1596. 8°. . 2241
Analysis logica...S. Lucæ... Acta Apostolorum. 1597. 8°. . 2906
Analysis logica evangelii sec. Johannem. 1595. 8°. . . 7297
Analysis logica omnium epp. Pauli. Ed. 2. 1594. 8°. . . 1734
Analysis logica septem epp. apostolicarum. Ed. 2. 1597. 8°. 1738
See Calvin (J.). Aphorismes. 1596. 8°.
— Ramus (P.). Dialecticae libri duo. 1584.
— Temple (W.). Pro Mildapetti. 1581.
Pithie, and most earnest exhortation, conc. the estate of Christiandome. Antwerp, 1583. 8°. 6135
Pitiscus (Bartholomaeus). Trigonometry. [Ab. 1630?] 4°. . . 4145
Pits (J.). Poore mannes beneuolence. 1566. 8°. . . 1308
Pius II. Historie of Eurialus and Lucretia. Trans. C. Aleyn. 1639. 8°. 7913

No.
Pius II., *cont.* [De miserie Curialium.] Egloges of Alexander Barclay. [1548?] 4°. 1036
See Brant (S.). Stultifera Nauis. 1570. F°.
— Castiglione (B.). De Curiali. 1612.
Pius IV. *See* Actes of the ambassage. [1561.] 8°.
Pius IV. Bull 1564. *See* Lynde (Sir H.). Via Tuta. Ed. 3. 1629. 7890
[Bull Creed (Lat. and Eng.).] *See* Lynde (Sir H.). Via Tuta. 1629.
Pius V. *See* Renniger (M.). De Pii qvinti furoribus. 1582.
Placentinus. *See* Braunschweig (H.). Noble experyence. 1525.
Plague. Orders thought meet...in such Townes...as are...infected. 1625. 4°. 3526
Plague. *See* London. College of Physicians. 1636.
Plaine and godly treatise. *See* Primer. 1555. 8°. . . 636
Plaine explanation of the whole revelation of Saint John. 1622. 4°. . 3434
Plaix (César de). *See* Cotton (Pierre). Anti-coton. 1611.
Plancius (Petrus), *cartographer*. *See* Eliot (J.). Svrvay or topographical description of France. 1592.
Planters Plea. 1630. 4°. 5047
Plantin (Christopher). *See* Icones Stirpivm. 1591. 4°.
Planudes (Maximus). *See* Æsop. Fabulæ. 1635.
Plat (Sir H.). Delightes for Ladies. 1609. 12°. 2498
Jewell house of art and nature. 1594. 4°. 2327
Manuale. 1594. 16°. 2326
Platearius. *See* Herbal. 1561.
Platt (Sir Hugh). *See* Plat.
Platus (Hieronymus). Happines of a religious state. 1632. 4°. . 6269
Playfere (Tho.). [Sermons.] Cambridge, 1609. 4°. . 7708, 5657
Whole sermons. 1623. 8°. 3436
— Ed. 6. 1633. 8°. 4892
Caesaris superscriptio. 1606. 4°. 7352
Hearts delight. 1617. 8°. 3764
— 1633. 8°. 4717
Meane in mourning. 1595. 1616. 8°. 7538
Nine sermons preached. Cambridge, 1612. 8°. 5668
— Cambridge, 1621. 8°. 5693
— 1633. 8°. 3824
Sick-mans couch. Cambridge, 1605. 4°. 5633
Verses in Camb. Univ. Lachrymae *bis*. 1587. 2123
Playters (Thomas). Verses in Camb. Univ. Rex redux. 1633. . 5748
Pleasant comedie called, A Woman will have her Will. 1631. *See* Haughton (W.).
Pleasant conceited comedy...how a man may choose a good wife. 1634. 4°. 4897
Plees del Corone. *See* Stanford (Sir W.).
Plessis (Monsieur). *See* Mornay (P. de), *sieur du Plessis-Marly*.
Pletho (Georgius Gemistus). *See* Dee (J.). General and rare Memorials. 1577.
Plinius Secundus (C.). Historie of the world. 1601. F°. . . . 2429
— 1634. F°. 2465
[Letters.] *See* Fleming (A.). Panoplie. 1576. 4°.
See Æsop. Fabulæ. 1635.
Ploughman. Lytell geste how the plowman lerned his pater noster. W. de Worde. [15—.] 4°. 235
Plowden (E.). Comentaries. 1571. F°. 1123
Commentaries...Table...per W. Fletewode. (Cases Reportes.) 1578(-9). F°. 1136-7
— 1588. F°. 1150
— 1599. F°. 2387
— 1613. F°. 7504
Abridgement des touts les Cases...per T. A. 1607. 8°. . . 3229

No.

Plowden (E.), *cont.* *See* Briefe Declaration. 1636.
Plumme (S.) [*qu.* Plummer? *q.v.*]. Verses in Camb. Univ. Genethl. 1631. 5731
Plummer (Steph.). Verses in Camdeni Insignia. 1624. . . 5346
See also Plumme.
Plumptre (Huntingdon), *M.D.* Verses in Hippocrates. 1633. . 5812
Plutarchus. Lives. Trans. Sir T. North. 1603. F°. . . 2257
— 1612(-10). F°. 2269
— 1631. F°. 4438
Gouernaũce of good helthe...Trans. Erasmus. R. Wyer, n.d. 8°. 552
Περὶ τοῦ ἀκούειν. Cantabrigiae, 1595. 8°. 5578
De dialectis Homericis. *See* Crespin (J.)... 1581.
De liberis educandis. [Gr. only.] *See* Isocrates. Orationes tres. 1638.
De vtilitate ex hostibus capienda. 2. De morbis animi et corpore. I. Rainoldo Interprete. 1614. [Lat. only.] *See* Rainolds (J.). Orationes 5. 1613.
See Blundeville (T.). Three morall treatises. 1580.
'Plym (Adam).' [Owner's name stamped in. Acton Library copy.] 2927
Pocklington (John). Altare Christianum. 1637. 4°. . . 4381
Sunday no Sabbath. 1636. 4°. 4991
See Prynne (W.). A quench coale. 1637.
Poe (James), *K.C.C.* Verses in Camb. Univ. Epithalam. 1625. . 5702
Poe (Leonard). Verses in Camb. Univ. Lacrymæ. 1619. . . 5689
Poetae minores graeci. Cantabrigiae, 1635. 8°. . . . 5719
Poeton (Edward). *See* Bonham (T.). Chyrvrgeons closet. 1630.
Poggio (G. F.). Fables. *See* Æsop. Fables. 156-. . . . 1635
Poland. Forme of the agreement...betwixt...Poland...and...Sweden. 1635. 4°. 4016
Pole (Sir Geoffrey). *See* Morison (Sir R.). Invective. 1539.
[*Ad instantiam.*] *See* Xenophon. [Œconomica.] 1537.
Pole (Reg.). Seditious and blasphemous oration. Trans. F. Wythers. [Ab. 1588?] 8°. 1283
See Elder (J.). Copie of a letter. 1555.
— G. (B.), *Citizen.* New Yeares Gifte. 1579.
— Treatise of Iustification. 1569.
— Tunstall (C.). A letter. 1560.
Pole (Tim.). *See* Poole.
Polemon (J.). All the famous Battels. [1578[1]?] 4°. 1522
Second part of the booke of Battailes. 1587. 4°. . . . 1849
Poley (Edm.). Verses in Camb. Univ. Carmen. 1635. . . 5770
Poley (I.), *Pemb.* Verses in Camb. Univ. Epithalam. 1625. . 5702
Policy. Body of Policy. 1521. *See* Christine de Pisan.
Politi (Lancelot). *See* Catharinus (Ambrosius).
Politic Discourses. Trans. Æ. Ratcliffe. 1578. 4°. 1841
Poliziano (Angelo). *See* Æsop. Fabulæ... 1635.
Pollanus (Valerandus). *See* Poullain.
Pollard (J.), *Pemb.* Verses in Camb. Univ. Epicedium. 1612. . 5665
Polmon (John). *See* Polemon.
Polo (Gaspar Gil). *See* Gil Polo (G.).
Polyander (John). Disputation against the...reliques of Saints. Dort, 1611. 8°. 6512
Verses in Du Jon (F.). Sacrorum Parallelorum. [1588?] . 1715
Polybius. History. Trans. E. Grimstone. 1634. F°. . . 3696
Polyphemus. *See* Erasmus (D.). Two Dyaloges. [Ab. 1550.] 8°.
Pomander of Prayer. 1558. *See* Becon (T.).
Pomerane (John). *See* Bugenhagen (J.), *Pommer.*
Pomerania. Bogeslaus XIV, Duke. *See* Sweden. Gustavus II, Adolphus. 1631.

[1] Correction. Licence 1577, July 1.

No.

Ponce Pantolabus. *See* Pantolabus.
Pond (E.). New Almanacke for 1629. 8°. . . . . 3301=5724
Prognostication. 1603. 8°. 7933
Ponet (John). Apologie...aunsweringe...S. Gardiner, Smith, Pighius, and others. 1556. 8°. 6295
Defence for mariage of Priestes. 1549. 8°. 729
Notable sermon concerning the...Lordes supper. 1550. 8°. . 7116
Shorte treatise of politike power. 1556. 8°. 6731
— 1639. 4°. 7044
See Catechism. 1553.
— Defence of priestes marriages. [1566?]
— Martin (T.). Traietise. 1554.
— Ochino (B). Tragoedie. 1549.
Pont (Robert). De sabbaticorum annorum periodis. 1619. 4°. . 3330
Newe treatise of the right reckoning of years. Edinburgh, 1599. 4°. 5939
Pont (Timothy). New description of the Shyres of Lothian and Linlitquo. *See* Mercator (G.). Atlas. Ed. 10. 1630(-1). F°. 7741 etc.
Pontanus. Verses in Fleming (A.). Treatise. 1618. . . . 4155
Pontanus (Joannes Isaacius). *See* Hues (R.). Learned treatise of Globes. 1639. 8°.
Pontanus (Joannes Jovianus). Epistle. *See* Flamel (N.). 1624.
Pontanus (Robertus). *See* Pont.
Ponticus (L.), *Virunius*. Britannicæ historiæ libri sex. 1585. 8°. . 2043
Poole (Henry). Verses in Coryat (T.). Coryats Crudities. 1611. . 3076
Poole (Timothy). *See* Janua Linguarum. Ed. 8. 1634. 8°.
Poor Clares. *See* Aire. Poor Clares. 1635.
Poor Help. Pore helpe. The buklar and defence of mother holy kyrke. [1547?] 8°. 917
Poor Laws. *See* Orders and directions. 1630. 4°. 2670
Pope Confuted. 1580. *See* Foxe (J.).
Pore. *See* Poor.
Porphyrius. Isagoge ad Categorias Aristotelis. *See* Andreæ (Antonius). [1480.] 4°.
See Stanyhurst (R.). Harmonia. 1570.
Porta (Joan Baptista). De furtivis literarum notis. 1591. 4°. . 1961
Porter (Endymion). *See* Bolton (E.). Nero. 1624.
Porter (Jerome). Flowers of the lives of the saincts. Tom. 1. Douai, 1632. 4°. 6613–4
Porter (T.). Verses in Camb. Univ. Thr-thr. 1603. . . . 5616
Portia (Hierome, count of), *the elder*. *See* Scupoli (L.). Spiritual conflict. 1613.
Portius (P.). Pugna porcorum. 1586. 8°. 1840
Portman (Sir Henry). Verses in Oxf. Univ. Magd. Coll. 1612. . 5302
Portugal. *See* Conestaggio (G.). Historie. 1600.
— Lisbon. 1622.
Portus (Æmilius). Verses in Beza (T.). Psalmorum libri quinque. 1580. 1539
Portus (Francis), *Cretensis*. Verses in Beza (Th.). Psalmorvm libri qvinque. 1580. 1539
— Buchanan (G.). Psalmorum Davidis. 1640. 5209
Portusius or ad Portum (Jacobus). *See* Longinus (D.). Περὶ ὕψους. 1636. 8°.
— Leslie (H.). Examen. 1639. 4°.
Pory (Robert). Verses in Camb. Univ. Genethl. 1631. . . . 5731
— Hippocrates, 1633. 5812
Posidippus. [*Gr. Lat.*] *See* Poetæ minores. 1635.
Posselius (Joannes). Dialogues containing all the most vsefvll words of the Latine tongue. (Lat. Eng.) E. Rive. 1623. 4°. . 7343
Σύνταξις Græca...et Varennii. Cantabrigiae, 1640. 8°. . . 5850
Possevino (Antonio). *See* James (T.). Treatise. 1612.

No.

Posthius (Joh.). Verses in Buchanan (G.). Psalmorum Davidis. 1640. 5209
Postille. 1509. *See* Gulielmus Parisiensis.
Posy of Flowred Prayers. *See* Conway (Sir J.).
Pots or Potts (John). Verses in Camb. Univ. Carmen. 1635 . 5770
— — Συνωδία. 1637. 5790
— King (E.). Ivsta. 1638. 5829
Potter (Barnabas), *Bp.* *See* Potter (C.). Sermon. 1629.
Potter (Christopher). Sermon...at the consecration of B. Potter. 1629. 8º. 4258
Want of charitie justly charged. Oxford, 1633. 8º. . . 5438
— Ed. 2. 1634. 8º. 4281
See Sarpi (P.). History of the quarrels *etc.* 1626.
Potts. *See* Pots.
Poulett (Giles). Verses in Oxf. Univ. Magd. Coll. 1612. . . 5302
Poullain (Valerand). *See* Ordre des prieres. 1552. 16º. . . 6719
— Liturgia sacra. 1551. 1097
— Philpot (J.). Vera expositio. 1554.
Poundage. *See* Rates of merchandize. (1609, July 28.) . . 2620
Powel. *See* Powell.
Powell (Amb.). Verses in Oxf. Univ. Magd. Coll. 1612. . . 5302
Powell (Daniel). *See* Whitbourne (R.). Discourse. 1622.
Powell (David). *See* Bible, Welsh. 1620. Fº.
— Caradoc. Historie of Cambria. 1584.
— Ponticus (L.). Libri sex. 1585.
Powell (E.). Propugnaculum. Pynson, 1523. 4º. 283
Powell (Gabriel). Catholikes Supplication. 1603. 4º. 2928
Consideration of the depriued and silenced Ministers arguments. 1606. 4º. 3561
Consideration of the Papists...in England. Oxford, 1604. 4º. . 5269
De adiaphoris. 1606. 8º. 2596
Disputt. theologicarum libri ii. 1605. 8º. 2168
Prodromus. Oxford, 1602. 8º. 5259
Resolved Christian. 1607. 12º. 7521
— 1623. 8º. 3437
Theologicall...Positions concerning Usurie. Oxford, 1602. 8º. . 5260
— 1605. 8º. 2940
Verses in Greenham (R.). Workes. 1605. 7467
— Laurentius (A.). Discourse. 1599. 2913
See Mild. A myld and iust defence. 1606.
— Symonds (W.). Pisgah evangelica. 1606.
Powel (Griffin). *See* Aristoteles. Analysis analyticorvm posteriorvm. 1594. 8º. 5239
— Ed. 2. Oxoniæ, 1631. 8º. 5391
Powell (John). *See* Assize of Bread. 1601 *etc.*
Powel (Richard). Verses in Hippocrates. 1633. 5812
Powell (Robert). Depopulation arraigned. 1636. 8º. . . . 4374
Life of Alfred. 1634. 12º. 4357
Powell (Thomas). Attornies almanacke. 1627. 4º. 7875
Attourney's academy. Ed. 3. 1630. 4º. . 7625 (imperfect), 7873
Direction for search of records. 1622. 4º. 4174
Repertorie of records. 1631. 4º. 4200, 4201, 7874
Powell (Thomas), *C.T.* Verses in Camb. Univ. Gratulatio. 1623. 5695
Power (G.), *Christ's Coll.* *See* Power (W.).
Power (Henry), *Coll. Jesu.* Verses in Camb. Univ. Συνωδία. 1637. . 5790
Power (W.), *Christ's.* Verses in Camb. Univ. Dolor. 1625. . 5701
— — Epithalam. 1625. 5702
Pownall (Robert). *See* Moste pythye and excellent Epistell. 1556. 8º.
Pownoll (Robert). *See* Pownall.
Poynet (John). *See* Ponet.
Pr. (I.), *qu.* Price? Verses in Vaughan (W.). Golden Grove. 1608. . 2888

No.
Practical Catechism. 1633. *See* Rogers (D.), B.D.
Pradel (O. de Serres, lord of). *See* Serres.
Præpositus (Nicolas). *See* Nicolas, Præpositus. 1588. 4°. . . . 1950
Prague. True relation of the bloudy execution. 1621. 4°. . 6930
Praise. Prayse and commendacion of suche as sought comenwelthes. [1548?] 8°. 1041
Prakhurst. *See* Parkhurst.
Pratt (William). Arithmeticall Jewell. 1617. 8°. . . . 3796
Prayers. *See* Day (Richard). Book of Christian Prayers. 1578. . 852
— Booke of the forme of common prayers. 1586, etc. . 6446, etc.
Certaine Prayers. 1603. 2578
Deuoute Prayers to be sayde. 16°. 6600
Prayers and Thanksgiving...5 Nov. 1605. [1605?] 4°. . . 7417
Three Prayers. 1592. *See* Smith (H.).
Morning (Evening) Prayer to bee vsed in private families. (Prayer... by one alone.) *See* Worship (W.). Christians Mourning Garment. 1610 etc. . . . . 3317 etc.
Liber precum Publicarum. Ed. W. Whitaker. 1569. 8°. . . 748
See also Liber precum publicarum . . . . . 1560 etc.
Preces privatae. W. Seres, 1573. 16°. 937
— W. Seres, 1574 (1573). 16°. 938
Precedence. Decree...of Precedence betweene the yonger sonnes of Viscounts and Barons and the Baronets. 1612. 4°. 2642, 2643
Precedents. *See* Book of Presidents. 1586.
— Phaer (Tho.). New boke of Presidentes. 1543.
Preces. *See* Prayers.
Predestination. *See* Crowley (R.). Apologie. 1566.
Certaine Questions and Answers touching...Predestination. *See* Prynne (W.). Anti-arminianisme... 1630.
Premier Fait (Laurence de). *See* Cicero. De Senectute. 1481. F°.
Prempart (Jacques). Historicall relation of the...siege of...Busse. Amsterdam, 1630. F°. 6358
Prenner (Stephan.). Verses in Aristotle. [Ethics.] 1634. . . 5717
Preparation to the Crosse. *See* Vox Piscis. 1627.
Prepositas. *See* Nicolas Præpositus.
Presidents. *See* Precedents.
Preston (James). Verses in Camb. Univ. Fasciae. 1633. . . 5808
Preston (John). Breast-plate of faith and love. Ed. 2. 1630–1. 4°. 5051
— [1631?] 4°. 4100
— Ed. 5. 1634. 4°. 4994
Deformed forme of a formall profession. Edinburgh, 1634. 4°. 5975
Doctrine of selfe-deniall. 1632. 4°. 7587
Doctrine of the saints infirmities. 1636. 12°. . . . 3708
— 1637. 12°. 3711
— 1638. 4°. 3721
Foure godly and learned treatises. Ed. 3. 1633. 4°. . . 4627
— Ed. 4. 1636. 4°. 3962
Fulnesse of Christ. 1640. 4°. 3732
Golden scepter. 1638. 4°. 4388-4390
Heavenly treatise. 1640. 4°. 5100
Law out lavved. Edinburgh, 1633. 4°. 5974
Life eternall. 1631. 4°. 4345
— Ed. 3. 1632. 4°. 4350
— 1633. 4°. 4351
— Ed. 4. 1634. 4°. 4108
Liveles life. 1633. 4°. 3825, 4101
— Ed. 3. 1635. 4°. 3832
New Covenant. 1629. 4°. 7553
— Ed. 8. 1634. 4°. 3892
Onely love of the chiefest of ten thousand. 1640. 12°. . . 5185

No.

Preston (John), *cont.* Remaines. 1634. 4°. 3829
— Ed. 2. 1637. 4°. 4382
Saints daily exercise. 1629. 4°. 5043
— Ed. 3. 1629. 4°. 5044
— Ed. 5. 1631. 4°. 4346
— Ed. 8. 1633. 4°. 4105
— Ed. 8. 1634. 4°. 4109
— Ed. 9. 1635. 4°. 4113
Saints qualification. 1633. 4°. 4354
— Ed. 2. 1634. 4°. 4360
Sermons preached before his majestie. 1630. 4°. . . . 2564
— 1631. 4°. 7347
— Ed. 4. 1634. 4°. 3830
Sinnes overthrow. Ed. 3. 1635. 4°. 3052
Three sermons vpon...the Lords supper. Oxford, 1631. 4°. . 5431
— 1631. 4°. 4614
Preston (Thomas). *See* King (H.). Sermon. 1621.
Preston (Thomas), *Benedictine*. *See* Widdrington (R.).
Price (Ar.). Verses in Jones (W.). A treatise. 1625. . . . 3351
Price (Daniel). Creation of the prince. 1610. 4°. 3574
Marchant. Oxford, 1608. 4°. 5286
Maries memoriall. 1617. 4°. 3920
Prælium et præmium. Oxford, 1608. 4°. 5288
Recusants conversion. Oxford, 1608. 4°. 5287
Sauls prohibition staide. 1609. 4°. 2871
Spiritual Odours to...Prince Henry. Oxford, 1613. 4°. . . 5316
[Funeral discourse.] *See* C. (B.). Pvritanisme. 1633.
Price (Edward). Verses in Camdeni Insignia. 1624. . . . 5346
See Bible, Welsh. 1620. F°.
Price (I.). Verses in Oxf. Univ. Horti. 1640. 5499
See also Pr. (I.).
Price (Sir John). Historiae Brytannicae defensio. 1573. 4°. . 1473
Description of Cambria. *See* Caradoc. Historie of Cambria. 1584.
Price (Richard). *See* Price (Sir J.).
Price (Sampson). Beauty of holines. 1618. 4°. 4157
Clearing of the saints sight. 1617. 4°. 4061
Ephesus warning. 1616. 4°. 3586
Two twins of birth and death...5 Sept. Sir W. Byrde. 1624. 4°. 7345
Price (Th.). Verses in Oxf. Univ. Horti. 1640. 5499
Price (Thomas). *See* Torsellino (O.). History of...Loreto. 1608.
Price (William). Janitor Animae. 1638. 12°. 5167
Prich (W.). Verses in Camb. Univ. Threno-thriambeuticon. 1603. 5616
Prichard (Humphry). *See* Rhys (J. D.). Cambrobrytannicæ linguæ institutiones. 1592.
Prideaux (John). Castigatio cuiusdam circulatoris. Oxoniae, 1614. 8°. 5321
Certaine sermons. Oxford, 1637–6. 4°. 5476
Concio...ad Artium Baccalaureos, Feb. 22, 1626. Oxoniae, 1626. 4°. 5361
Doctrine of the Sabbath. 1634. 4°. 4110
— Ed. 2. 1634. 4°. 4111
— Ed. 3. 1635. 4°. 4114
Eight sermons. 1621. 4°. 3014
Lectiones decem. Oxoniae, 1626. 4°. 5362
Orationes novem. Oxoniae, 1626. 4°. 5363
Perez-uzzah. Oxford, 1625. 4°. 5355
Sermon...5 Oct. 1624...in Exceter colledge. Oxford, 1625. 4°. . 5356
See Hall (Jos.). Reconciler. 1629.
Priest (William). *See* Bacon (Francis). The Charge of Sir Francis Bacon. 1614.
Priests' Marriage. *See* Defence.

No.

Primæus (Henricus). *See* Lily (W.). De octo orationis partium constructione. 1540.
Primaleon of Greece. Trans. A. M. 1619. 4°. 7895
Prime (John). Exposition...vpon...Galatians. Oxford, 1587. 8°. . 5229
Treatise on the sacraments. [1582?] 8°. . . . 1689
Primer (Sarum)—

Lat.		Will. de Machlinia	[1484?]	8°	98
,,		W. de Worde	[1494]	4°	68
,,		G. Wolf and J. Philippi for J. Richard (and T. Kerver), Paris	1497	8°	135
,,		P. Pigouchet for S. Vostre, Paris	16 May, 1498	8°	134
,,		J. Jehannot for N. Lecomte, Paris	1498	8°	137
,,		s. t. n., Paris	1499	64°	138
,,		A. Vérard, Paris	[Ab. 1503]	4°	6145
,,		S. Vostre, Paris	[Ab. 1507]	8°	6146
,,		imp. F. Byrckman	12 Sept. 1511	4°	6207
,,		W. de Worde	24 July, 1514	12°	170
,,		Paris, imp. F. Byrckman	9 April, 1521	4°	6213
,,		C. Endovien., Antwerpie, imp. F. Byrckman	Maij, 1525	4°	6083
,,		J. Cousin, Rouen	28 Julij, 1525	12°	6236
,,		W. de Worde	[Ab. 1525]	4°	236
,,		F. Regnault, Paris	1527 (1 Martij, 1526)	4°	6164
,,		,,	17 March, 1527	4°	6165
,,		,,	1530	4°	6168
,,	Enchiridion	G. Hardouin, Paris	11 Maii, 1530	8°	6182
Eng. Lat.			[Ab. 153–]	8°	6670
Lat.		F. Regnault, Paris	1531	8°	6169
,,		,,	1531	18°	7838
,,		W. Rastell	30 April, 1532	8°	531
Eng.		T. Godfray	[1532?]	8°	562
Lat.	'This prymer'	imp. J. Growte, Y. Bonhomme, vid. T. Kerver	Aug. 1532	16°	6190
,,	,,	F. Regnault, Paris	4 Nov. 1533	16°	6175
Eng. Lat.		,,	[1533?]	16°	7686
Lat.	Hore	,,	1534	4°	6176
Eng.	A Goodly Prymer. Trans. G. Joye, ed. W. Marshall	J. Byddell	[1535?]	4°	576
,,			[Ab. 1535]	8°	6672
,,			[Ab. 1535]	16°	6673
Lat.	Hore	F. Regnault, Paris	1535 (25 May, 1536)	4°	6177
Eng. Lat.		Rouen	1536	8°	6265
Eng.	With the Paradyse of the soule	J. Gowhe	1536	8°	7092

Primer (Sarum)—*cont.*

					No.
Eng. Lat.		T. Petit	[After 1536]	4°	585
,,		Paris	1538	4°	6178
,,		R. Redman	1538	4°	381
Eng.		N. le Roux for F. Regnault, Rouen	1538	8°	6237
Eng. Lat.	Manual of Prayers (Hilsey)	Wayland	15 July, 1539	4°	635
,,			[Ab. 1540]	8°	6690
,,		W. Bonham	1542	4°	589
,,	and Exposition of li. Psalme	R. Toye	1542	4°	590
		R. Grafton	[1543 ?]	32°	592
,,		,,	6 Sept. 1545	4°	593
Eng.		Grafton	16 March, 1546	32°	595
,,		J. Day	[1546 ?]	8°	891
,,		R. Kele	[1546 ?]	16°	1002
,,			[Ab. 1548]	16°	6698
Eng. Lat.		R. Valentine, Rouen	1555	8°	6246
Lat.		J. Le Prest, imp. R. Valentini, Rouen	1555	8°	6248
Eng.		Wayland	1555	8°	636
Eng. Lat.		,,	1555	4°	637
Lat.			[Ab. 1556]	8°	6733
Eng.		J. King	1556	8°	1240
Eng. Lat.		Kingston and Sutton	1557	4°	1166
Lat.		Assignes of J. Wayland	1557	8°	644
Eng. Lat.		Wayland's Assigns	22 Aug. 1558	16°	645
		W. Seres	1568	8°	931
Eng.			[Ab. 1580?]	12°	6769
Lat. Eng.	According to the reformed Latin	A. Conings, Antwerp	1599	12°	6131
,,		,, ,,	1604	12°	6132
			1617	12°	6617
		J. Heigham, St Omer	1631	12°	6566-7
		,, ,,	1631	12°	6567

Primerose (Gilbert). *See* Primrose.
Primo Facto (Laurentius de). *See* Premier Fait.
Primrose (David). Treatise of the sabbath. Englished by G. P. 1636. 4°. 4375
Verses in Adamson (J.). Εἰσόδια. 1618. 5960
Primrose (Gilbert). Table of the lord. 1626. 12°. 3870
See Hall (J.). Answer to Pope Vrban. 1629.
— — Reconciler. 1629.
— Primrose (D.). Treatise. 1636.
Primrose (James). Academia Monspeliensis. Oxoniae, 1631. 4°. . 5392
De vulgi in medicina erroribus. 1638. 12°. 4216
Exercitationes... de motu cordis. 1630. 4°. 5048
[Privilege.] *See* James I. Deus and Rex. 1615. . . . 6902
Principall lawes and statutes of Englande. R. Bankes, 1542. 8°. 363, 364
Principall passages of Germany. *See* Swedish Intelligencer Part 8. . 4644
Priscianus. *See* Whittington (R.). Grammatica. Pt. 1. Lib. 2. De nominum declinatione. 199
See Hawkins (W.). En Priscianus. 1632.

No.

Prise (Sir John) *or* Prisevs. *See* Price (Sir J.).
Privas, *Siege of.* *See* France. Articles. 1629.
Privileges. *See* Indulgence. 1517.
[Granted.] *See* Justinianus. Digestorum. 1553. F°.
— — Primrose (J.).
Privy Council. *See* Humble Motion. 1590.
1612. *See* no. 5297.
Instructions for musters and Armes. 1623. 4°. 2818
See Off. Pub. Orders. 1630.
— London. College of Physicians. 1636.
Proast (Jonas). *See* Cruso (J.). 5742
Processionale (Sarum). [R. Pynson, ab. 1510?]. 4°. 7076
[Paris, ab. 1529?] 4°. 6167
N. Prevost, Paris, imp. F. Byrckman, 2 kal. Jan. 1530. 4°. . 6193
Vid. C. Ruremund, Antwerpie, 1544. 4°. 6087
R. Hamilton, imp. R. Valentini, 15 Oct. 1555. 4°. . . 6245
[T. Raynald or Marshe?] 1555. 4°. . . . 705 (see p. 240)
Proclamation.
1496. (Supplement.) W. de Worde. F°. . . 7064, 7065
1507? Proclamation of the Coyne. [R. Pynson] S. sh. . . 7072
1509. These be the articles. Pynson. F°. 256
1548. Proclamation ... against enclosures. 1 June. Grafton. Broadside. 7094
1550. All suche...as haue been sette furthe...from the last daie of Januarie. Grafton. 8°. 620
1551 July 18. Abasing the coin. Grafton, 1551. Bds. . . 621
1614 Oct. 10. Importation of Allome. R. Barker, 1614. F°. . 7420
1615 July 16. Buildings. R. Barker, 1615. F°. . . . 7423
1618–9 March 12. Matter of Buildings. Norton and Bill, 1618. F°. 7444, 7445
1619 July 31. Coynes of this Realme. Norton and Bill, 1619. F°. 7446
Tobacco in England and Ireland etc. Norton and Bill, 1619. Broadside. 2806
1620 May 5. (Manufacture of starch.) Barker and Bill, 1620. Single sheet. F°.
1621. Dissoluing of the present convention of Parliament. Norton and Bill. 4°. 2811
1622–3 Feb. 14. Publique grievances. Norton and Bill, 1622. F°. 7448
1623 Sept 25. Disorderly printing. Norton and Bill, 1623. F°. 7449
1624–5 March 3. Proroguing of Parliament. Norton and Bill, 1624. F°. 7451
1625 March 28. Office of Government. Norton and Bill, F°. . 7452
1625 April 1. Sale of Latine Bookes. Norton and Bill, 1625. F°. 7453
1625 July 3. Fast. Norton and Bill, 1625. F°. . . . 7454
1625 July 12. Adjournement of Parliament. Norton and Bill, 1625. F°. 7455
1625 Dec. 24. Dominions of the King of Spaine etc. Norton and Bill, 1625. F°. 7456
1625 Dec. 31. Ships carying corne. Norton and Bill, 1625. F°. 7457
1627 Aug. 4. (Ireland.) Stationers, Dublin, 1634. F°. . . 6054
[1630 after Jan. 23.] Abstract...power to compound. R. Barker, 1630. F°. 7424
1632 Feb. 18. For prizing of wines. Barker and Ass. of J. Bill, 1632. F°. 7428
1633 Oct. 13. Retailing of Tobacco. R. Barker and Ass. of J. Bill, 1633. 7429
1637 April 30. Against transporting...to...America. R. Barker and Ass. of J. Bill, 1637. F°. 7430
1637 July 9. Maulsters and Brewers. R. Barker and Ass. of J. Bill, 1637. F°. 7431

No.

Proclamation *cont.*
1638 Sept. 9. (The Confession.) R. Young, Edinburgh, 1638. 4°. 5982
1638 Dec. 21. Vent of Wines. Barker and Ass. of J. Bill, 1638. F°. 7432
Proclamation (Gelderlandt). 1618. 4°. 7914
Proclus. Σφαῖρα Πτολομαίου περὶ ὑποθέσεων πλανωμένων. (Gr. Lat.) Acc. Ptolomæi Canon Regnorum. Ill. J. Bainbridge. 1620. 4°. 3335
Procter (William). Watchman warning. 1625. 4°. . . . 4533
Proctor (John). Fal of the late Arrian. 1549. 8°. 1011
Historie of wyates rebellion. 1554. 8°. 1194
Proctor (Tho.). Of the knowledge and conducte of warres. 1578. 4°. 1135
Verses in Thynne (F.). Newes from the north. 1585. . . 2002
Profitable and necessarie discourse...of Spices. [1593.] 4°. . . 2567
Profitable booke...to take out spotts and staines. Ed. 3. 1596. 4°. 1378
Progeny of Catholics. 1633. *See* Anderton (L.).
Prognostication.
[15—]. W. de Worde. 8°. 237
1517–8. *See* Laet (J.). Prenostica.
1520. *See* Laet (J.).
1530. — Thibault (J.).
1531. Prognostication Drawen out of...Ipocras, Auicen, and other. [After 1531.] 8°. 553
1544. *See* Mussemius (J.).
1555. — Digger (L.).
1563. — Nicolson (Jas.).
1564. — Digges (L.).
1566. — Cox (F.).
1569. — Lon (H.).
1591. *See also* Almanack and Prognostication. 1591 *etc.*
159–? 8°. 7240
1603. *See* Pond (E.). 7933
Promptorius puerorum. Pynson, 1499. F°. 108
Promptuarium paruulorum. W. de Worde, 5 Sept. 1516. 4°. . 175
Promptuarium parvulorum clericorum. W. de Worde [1510?]. 4°. . 238
Proper new Ballad wherein are contayned Catholike questions. *See* Rhodes (J.). An Answere. 1602. 4°.
Prophesie that hath lyen hid...about...Rome. 1610. 4°. . . . 7339
Prophesie lyen hid...of Rome. 1614. 4°. 7341
Propositiones catholicae. 1633. 4°. 4273
Prosopopeia. Or the complaint of the Pyramis erected by the French King. 1606. 4°. 3562
Protestant Divines. *See* Verheiden (J.). History of the Moderne Protestant Divines. 1637.
Protestation. *See* Scotland, Church of.
Protestation of the King's Svpremacie. 1605. *See* Bradshaw (W.).
Prowse (Anne). *See* Taffin (J.). Of the markes of the Children... 1615.
Prowse (Roger). *See* Persius (A.). Satyræ. 1614.
Prudential ballance of religion. 1609. *See* Smith (Ric.).
Prudentius. [Selection, English.] *See* Beaumont (Sir J.). Bosworth-field, 1629.
Prugean (Jo.). Verses in Yorke (J.). Union of Honour. 1640. . 5216
Pruican (Francis), 'June M.D.' *See* Prujean.
Pruijs (Paul), *Amsterdamensis.* Verses in Camb. Univ. Lacrymae. 1619. 5689
Prujean (Sir Francis). Verses in Guillemeau (J.). Treatise. 1622. 3018
— Hippocrates. 1633 *bis.* 5812
Prynne (W.). Anti-arminianisme. Ed. 2 etc. 1630. 4°. . . . 7002
Breviate of the prelates. By W. Huntley. Ed. 3. 1637. 4°. 6362
Brief answer to a late treatise of the Sabbath day. [1635?] 4°. 7020
Briefe instructions for churchwardens. [Ab. 1637?] 4°. . 6363
Briefe survay...of Mr Cozens. 1628. 4°. 6981, 6982
Certaines quaeres propounded. Ed. 4. 1636. 4°. . . . 7026

No.

Prynne (W.), *cont.* Church of Englands old antithesis to new arminianisme. 1629. 4°. 6993
God no impostor nor deluder. 1629. 4°. 6994
— 1630. 4°. 7003
— [1630?] 4°. 4880
— *See above.* Anti-arminianisme. [1629?] etc. 7002
Healthes sicknesse. 1628. 4°. 6983
Histrio-mastix. 1633. 4°. 2041
Lame Giles his havltings. 1630. 4°. 5103
Looking-glasse for all lordly prelates. 1636. 4°. 7027
Lord bishops none of the Lords bishops. 1640. 4°. 7052
Lords day. Ed. 2. 1636. 4°. 7028
Perpetuitie of a regenerate mans estate. 1626. 4°. 7518
— Ed. 2. 1627. 4°. 5033
— Ed. 3. 1627. 4°. 5034
Quench-coale. 1637. 4°. 6365
XVI. new quaeres proposed. 1637. 4°. 7038
Vnbishoping of Timothy and Titus. 1636. 4°. 6361
Unlovelinesse of Lovelockes. 1628. 4°. 6984
See Bastwick (J.). Briefe relation. 1637. 4°.
— Laud (W.). Speech. 1637.
— Page (W.). Treatise. 1631.
— White (F.). Examination...of...A briefe Answer. 1637.
— White (M.). Newes from Ipswich. 1636. 4°.
— Widdowes (G.). The Lawlesse...Puritan. 1631.
Psalms. Devout Psalmes and Colletes. E. Whitchurch, 1547. 8°. 655
— E. Whitchurch, 1550. 16°. 668
Psalmes or prayers taken out of holye scriptures. 1545. 8°. 480
'1545.' 1548. 8°. 494
'1545' [Ab. 1549]. 16°. 481
n. d. 8°. 514
Psalmi seu precationes. 1544. 8°. 479
Deuout psalmes and colletes. '1567.' E. Whitchurch, 1547. 8°. 655
— E. Whitchurch, 12 April, 1550. 16°. 668
Psalms (Metre). Sternhold and Hopkins. *See under* Bible.
Psalter with Hymns (Sarum and York). W. de Worde, 1504. 16°. 147
— Paris, imp. F. Byrckman, 7 June, 1522. 4°. 6214
(Latin). [Paris? 152–?] 16°. 7687
(Latin). Sarum. Anthony Kitson [1555]. 8°. 1094
(Latin). (Ab. 155–.] 8°. 6734–6
(Jesu's). Douai. 16°. 6605
Ptolemæus. [Περὶ ὑποθέσεων πλανωμένων κ.τ.λ.] *See* Proclus. Σφαῖρα. 1620.
Publication of his Maties Edict...against private Combats. 1613. 4°. 2648
Publick Register Office. Letters Patent. 1611. 3079
Publilius Syrus. Sententiæ. Trans. R. Burrant. *See* Cato (D.). Preceptes. 1560. 16°. 1256
— (Lat. Eng.). *See* Cato (D.). Moralia. 1562.
Publius. *See* Publilius.
Puckering (Cicely). [Funeral.] *See* Bryan (J.). Vertvovs davghter. 1636 *etc.*
Puede-Ser (Diego), *pseud.* [J. Mabbe.] *See* Aleman (M.). The Rogve. 1623.
— *See* Fonseca (C. de). Devout Contemplations. 1629.
Puente (Luis de). Meditations uppon the mysteries. Trans. R. Gibbons. Part 1. 1610. 8°. 6251
— Parts 1, 2. Trans. J. Heigham. S. Omers, 1619. 4°. 6538
Puget de la Serre (J.). Histoire de l'entrée de la reyne mere...dans les provinces vnies. 1639. F°. 5154

No.
Puget de la Serre (J.), *cont.* Mirrour which flatters not. Trans. T. Cary. 1639. 8°. 4125
Pullein (Thomas). Jeremiahs Teares. 1608. 4°. 2766
Pullen (John). Verses in Camb. Fasciæ. 1633. 5808
— — Rex redux. 1633. 5748
— — Carmen. 1635. 5770
— King (E.). Ivsta. 1638. 5829
— Russell (J.). Two...battels. 1634. 5767
Pulton (Ferdinando). Collection of sundrie statutes. 1632. F°. . 5076
De pace regis et regni. 1610. F°. 3244
— 1623. F°. 7904
Kalendar or table...of all the Statutes. 1608. F°. . . . 7502
See Statutes. Abstract. 1581. 4°.
Purallee. *See* Manwood (J.). Treatise. 1598 *etc.*
Purchas (Samuel). His pilgrimage. Ed. 1. 1613. F°. . . 7848
— Ed. 2. 1614. F°. 3101
— Ed. 3. 1617. F°. 3121
— Ed. 4. 1626. F°. 3163
Pilgrim. Microcosmus. 1619. 8°. 3129
Pilgrimes. 4 parts. 1625. F°. 3158
Pilgrim. Microcosmus. 1627. 8°. 4191
Purefey (Edw,), *K.C.C.* Verses in Camb. Univ. Epicedium. 1612. . 5665
Purefey (Luke). Verses in Wilson (Sir T.). Vita. 1551. . . 631
Purlilia (James, earl of). Preceptes of warre. Trans. P. Betham. 1544. 8°. 652
Puteanus (Erycius). Amoenitatum humanarum diatribae duae. Oxoniae, 1640. 12°. 5465
Comus...Somnium. Oxonii, 1634. 12°. 5443
Historiæ insubricæ libri VI. Oxonii, 1634. 12°. . . . 5442
Puttenham (G.). Arte of English poesie. 1589. 4°. 2224
Puttock (Roger). Reioynder vnto W. Malone's reply. Dublin, 1632. 4°. 6039
Pyning (Henry). *See* Treatise of Justification. 1569.
Pyper (John). *See* Piper.
Pythagoras [Gr. Lat.]. *See* Poetæ minores. 1635.
Wheel. *See* Cattan (C. de). Geomancie. 1591. 4°.

Q. (T. M.). Verses in Turberville (G.). Noble arte. 1575. . 1525
Quæstio Qvodlibetica. 1630. *See* Sarpi (P.).
Quarles ( ), *B.A.*, *Pemb.* [qu. William?] Verses in Camb. Univ. Carmen. 1635. 5770
Quarles (Francis). Argalus and Parthenia. 1632. 4°. . . . 4134
— [1632?] 4°. 4135
Diuine poems. 1633. 8°. 4274
— 1634. 8°. 4282
Divine poems containing Jonah. 1638. 8°. 4321
Feast for wormes. 1620. 4°. 3010
Hadassa...Queene Ester. 1621. 4°. 3747
Hieroglyphikes. 1638. 8°. 4322
Job Militant. 1624. 4°. 3026
Verses in Fletcher (P.). Purple island. 1633. 5752
— Blaxton (J.). English usurer. 1634. 4895
— Sibbs (R.). Sovles Conflict. 1636 *etc.* . . . . 4304 *etc.*
Quarles (William), *Pemb.* *See above.*
Quattuor Sermones. *See* Mirk (J.). Festial.
Queen of Arragon. 1640. *See* Habington (W.).
Quelch (William). Church-customes vindicated: in two sermons. 1636. 4°. 4302
Quench-coale. 1637. *See* Prynne (W).
Quentin (Jean). Maner to lyue well. *See* Primer. Sarum. 1531 *etc.*
Quercetanus (Josephus). *See* Du Chesne.

No.
Querimonia Ecclesiae. 1592. 4°. 2132
Quersitanus (Josephus). *See* Du Chesne.
Quilibet. Let Quilibet beware of Quodlibet. [1602.] 8°. . . . 6849
Quin (Walter). Corona virtutum principe dignarum. 1613. 12°. . 3457
The Princes Epitaph. *See* Sylvester (J.). Lachrimæ. [1612?] 4°.
Verses in Coryate (T.). Coryats Crudities. 1611. . . 3076
Quir (Ferdinand de). *See* Quiros.
Quiros (Pedro Fernando de). Terra Australis incognita. [Frankfurt?] 1617. 4°. 3319

R. (A.). Verses in Lobeira (V.). Treasurie of Amadis. 1567. . 1520
— Greenham (R.). Workes. 1599 *etc.* . . . . 2912 *etc.*
— Lessius (L.). Hygiasticon. 1634. . . . . 5833, 5762
See Mornay (P. de). Three homilies. 1626.
R. (B.). Newes. *See* Overbury (Sir T.). His Wife. 1638.
Verses in Warre (James). Tovch-stone. 1621 etc. . . 4503 *etc.*
R. (C.), *Theologus.* *See* Morton (T.). Replica. 1638.
R. (D.), *B. of Divin.* *See* Rogers (Daniel).
R. (D.), B.D., *Minister.* *See* D. Rogers.
R. (E.). *See* Familiar and christian instruction. 1582.
R. (E.), *of Hereford.* *See* Hamond (T.). Late Commotion. 1605.
R. (E.), *Magd. Coll. Cant.* [Qu. E. Rainbowe?] Verses in Wadsworth (J.). Further Obss. 1630. 7788
R. (Ed.). Verses in De la Grey (T.). Compleat horseman. 1639. 4042
R. (F.). *See* Rous (F.). Meditations. 1616.
— Lilburne (J.). Worke of the beast. 1638. 4°.
R. (G.). Verses in Camb. Univ. Lachrymae. 1587. . . . 2123
— Overbury (Sir T.). His Wife. Ed. 11. 1622. . . 3380
R. (H.). Newes. *See* Overbury (Sir T.). His Wife. 1638.
Verses in Camb. Univ. Gratulatio. 1623. 5695
R. (I.). *See* Rhodes (J.). Answere to a Romish Rime. 1602. 4°.
R. (I.). Purgatories triumph. 1613. *See* J. Floyd.
The trades increase. 1615. 4°. 3660, 3661
The spy. 'Strasburgh.' 1628. 4°. 6985
[=Rolte (I.).] *See* Palatinate. Frederick V. A declaration. 1637.
Verses in Dyer (Sir James). Nouel Cases. 1585. . . . 1145
— Breton (N.). Characters. 1615. 3902
— Hausted (P.). Rivall Friends. 1632. 4561
See Floyd (J.). Paire of spectacles. 1631. 8°.
R. (I.), *Cantabrigiensis.* *See* Racster (J.).
R. (I.), *C. Regal.* Verses in Camb. Univ. Gratulatio. 1623. . . 5695
R. (I.), *fellow of the Inner Temple.* Verses in Crashaw (W.). Falsificationum etc. 1606.. 2262
R. (I.), *P.* Word of comfort. 1623. *See* Floyd (J.).
R. (I.), *Student in Diuinity.* 1612. *See* Floyd (J.).
R. (I.), *Trin. Coll. Camb.* [qu. J. Richardson?] Verses in Whitaker (W.). Praelectiones. 1599. 5598
R. (J.). *See* Rogers (J.). The displaying of an horrible Secte. 1578 *etc.*
R. (J.). [=J. Floyd.] *See* Lynde (Sir H.). A case. 1638.
R. (James), *Citizen.* [Perfect pathway to saluation. Ab. 158–.] 16°. 6768
R. (L.). *See* Roy (W.). Reade me frynde and be not wrothe. 1546.
R. (L.). *See* Rochfort (Luke). Antidot. 1624. 4°.
R. (M.). Verses in Mercator (G.). Historia. 1635. . . . 4637
R. (N.). Verses in Gascoigne (G.). The Steele Glas. 1576. . 1486
See Heywood (T.). Englands Elisabeth. 1632. 12°.
R. (P.). [=R. Parsons.] *See* Morton (T.). A Preamble. 1608.
— Parsons (R.). Treatise. 1607. 8°.
— — Quiet and sober reckoning. 1609.
R. (P.), *Scotus.* Verses in Mary, *Queen of Scots.* De Maria. [1572?] 6754
R. (R.). Verses in Davies (R.). Funeral sermon. 1577. . . 1416

No.
R. (R.), *cont.* Du Bartas. Weekes. 1621. 2535
Paris and Vienna. 1628. 7552
R. (R.), *Catholique Priest.* *See* Joyeuse (H. de). The life. 1623. 8°.
R. (R.), *King's Coll. Camb.* Verses in Whitaker (W.). Praelectiones. 1599. 5598
R. (Rob.). Verses in Foxe (J.). Actes. 1570. 816
R. (S.). Verses in Ortelius (A.). His epitome. 1603. . . . 3354
R. (S.). [=S. Rowlands.] *See* Greene (R.). Greenes ghost. 1602. 4°.
R. (S.). *See* Smith (R.), bp. 1608.
See Appelius (J.). True relation. 1612. 4°.
R. (S.). *See* Rowley (S.). The noble souldier. 1634.
R. (S.), *C.P.C.* Verses in Camb. Univ. Anthologia. 1632. . . 5741
R. (S.), *Gent. and Student in the Vniuersitie of Cambridge.* *See* Robson (S.). Choise of Change. 1585.
R. (S.), *V.M. Eccl. Belg. Lond.* *See* Ruydinck (S.).
R. (T.). Cornelianum Dolium. 1638. 8°. 4033
Verses in Williamson (T.). A comfortable meditation. 1630. . 4837
[Book-mark. Ab. 155–.] *See* Rogers (T.).
See James I. Meditatio. 1619.
— Robinson (T.). Anatomy. 1622. 4078
R. (Sir T.). Newes. *See* Overbury (Sir T.). His Wife. 1638.
R. (T.), *Gentleman.* Verses in Bale (J.). Pageant of Popes. 1574. . 1223
R. (T.), *S. John's Coll. Camb.* Verses in Whitaker (W.). Praelectiones. 1599. 5598
R. (Thom.), '*printer.*' *See* Maihew (E.). Treatise. 1608.
R. (W.). Treatise of...confirmation. Douai, 1629. 8°.. . . . 6587
Verses in Spenser (E.). The faerie queen. 1590 *etc.* . . 1960 *etc.*
— Lucanus. Pharsalia. 1614. 3655
See Parsons (W.). A brief...confvtation. 1603.
— Seneca. Workes. 1620.
R. (W.), *M.A., C.C.C.* Verses in Robartes (F.). The Revenve. 1613. 5670
R. (W.), *S.* *See* Luther (M.). Every-dayes sacrifice. 1624. 12°.
Raban (Edward), *Printer.* Verses in Forbes (P.). Funerals. 1637. . 6007
Rabbett (Michael). *See* Bible Eng. (Royal). 1611. 2635
Rabbotenu (Isaac), *pseud.* *See* Marnix (P. van).
Racster (John). Booke of the seven planets. 1598. 4°. . . . 2333
De hypocritis vitandis. Cantabrigiae, 1595. 4°. . . . 5579
Radcliffe (Jeremiah). Verses in Camb. Lachrymae. 1587. . . 2123
Radclyf (Ralph). Verses in Verstegan (R.). Restitution. 1605 *etc.* 6140 *etc.*
Radermacherus (Joannes). *See* Catalogus miscellaneus. 1634. 4°. 6484
Radermacherus (Stephanus). *See* Catalogus miscellaneus. 1634. 4°. 6484
Radford (John). Directorie teaching the way to the truth. 1605. 8°. 6863
Raemond (Florimond de). *See* Cooke (A.). Pope Joane. 1610 *etc.*
Rainbow (Edward). Labour forbidden and commanded. 1635. 4°. . 4916
Verses in Camb. Univ. Carmen. 1635. 5770
— — Συνῳδία. 1637. 5790
— *See* R. (E.), *Mag. Coll. Camb.*
Rainolde (Richard), *M.A.* *See* Reynolds (R.).
Rainolds (John). De rom. eccl. idolatria. Oxoniæ, 1596. 4°. . 5242
Defence of the judgment of the reformed churches. 1609. 4°. 6880
— Dort, 1610. 4°. 6511
Doctor Reignolds his letter to Sir Fravncis Knollis, concerning Doctor Bancrofts Sermon at Paules crosse. 9 Feb. 1588. *See* Informations. 1608.
Letter of Dr Reinolds to his friend. 1613. 12°. 7547
Orationes 5. Oxoniae, 1614. 12°. 5317
Overthrow of stage-playes. 1599. 4°. 6458
— Ed. 2. Oxford, 1629. 4°. 5379
Sex theses de sacra scriptura et ecclesia. 1580. 8°. . . 1632
— 1602. 8°. 1750

No.

Rainolds (John), *cont.* Summa colloquii...cum J. Harto. Oxoniae, 1610. F°. 5295
Svmme of the conference between I. R. and J. Hart. 1584. 4°. 1934
— 1598. 4°. 7706
— 1609. 4°. 3207
Verses in Humphrey (L.). I. Ivelli vita. 1573. . . . 837
See Bible, English (Royal). 1611. 2635
— Broughton (H.). Letters. [1591?]
— Downham (G.). A reply. 1613(4). 4°.
— Howson (J.). Uxore dimissa. 1606.
— Norris (S.). Antidote. 1615 etc. 4°.
— — Guide. 1621. 4°.
Rainolds (William). Verses in Stanyhurst (R.). Harmonia. 1570. 749
See Whitaker (W.). Answer to...A Refutation. 1585. 8°.
Rainsford (Edward). Verses in Greene (R.). Ciceronis Amor. 1605. 1792
Rainsford (H.). Verses in Barlow (W.). Vita Cosin. 1598. . 1707
— Camb. Univ. Thr-thr. 1603. 5616
Rainsford (Robert). Verses in Camdeni Insignia. 1624. . . 5346
Raitenau (Wolf. Dietrich von), *Bp of Salzburg. See* Briefe relation. 1599. 1979
Raius (John). *See* Ray.
Ralegh (Sir W.). Declaration. 1618. 4°. 2801
Discoverie of...Gviana. 1596. 4°. 2188
History of the World. 1614. F°. 3102
— (Title only.) 1614. F°. 4982
— 1614 (1617). F°. 2785
— 1614 (1621). F°. 2792
— 1634. F°. 4982
Instructions to his sonne... Ed. 5. (Dutifull advice.) 1636. 8°. 7543
Life and death of Mahomet. 1637. 12°. 4927
Prerogative of parliaments. Middelburg, 1628. 4°. . 6487–9
Perogative (*sic*) of Parliaments. 1640. 4°. 7619
Sir Walter Rawleighs ghost. 1626. *See* Scott (T.).
Rawleigh his ghost. *See* Lessius (L.). 1631. 8°.
Tvbvs historicus. 1636. 4°. 4022
Verses in Gascoigne (G.). Steele Glas. 1576. 1486
Ram (William). *See* Dodoens (R.). Rams little Dodeon. 1606.
Ramisæus (Johannes). *See* St Andrew's University. 1629. Decermina. 4°. 5970
Ramon (Master), *Minister of the Word, prisoner at Valencia. See* Two Letters. 1603. 4°.
Ramsay (Andrew). Poemata sacra. Edinburgi, 1633. 8°. . . . 5964
Warning to come out of Babylon. Edinburgh, 1638. 4°. . 5985
Ramsay (I.). Verses in Oxf. Univ. Horti. 1640. 5499
See also Ramisæus.
Ramsay (John, lord), viscount Hadington (1580–1626). *See* Hadington.
Ramsden (William), *Regal.* Verses in Camb. Univ. Voces. 1640. 5836
Ramsey (John). *See* Ramisæus (J.).
Ramus (Petrus). Dialecticae libri duo, scholiis G. Tempelli etc. Cantabrigiae, 1584. 8°. 5510
Dialecticae libri duo... Disq... auth. F. Beurhusio. 1589. 8°. . 1720
Dialecticae libri duo. Cantabrigiae, 1640. 12°. . . . 5851
— *See* Beurhusius (F.). De P. Rami dialecticae capitibus. 1582. 8°.
Latine Grammar. 1585. 8°. 1899
— Cambridge, 1585. 8°. 5515
Logike. 1581. 8°. 1548
— *See* Richardson (A.). Logicians schoolmaster. 1629. 4°.
Via regia ad geometriam. Trans. W. Bedwell. 1636. 4°. . 4645
See Greaves (P.). Grammatica Anglicana. 1594.
— S. (A. P.). Ode Natalitia. 1575
— Talæus (A.). Rhetorica. 1631 *etc.*
— Temple (W.). F. Mildapetti...admonitio. 1580.

No.
Ramus (Petrus), *cont.* *See* Temple (W.). Pro Mildapetti...defensione. 1581.
Ranchin (Guillaume). Review of the councell of Trent. Oxford, 1638. F°. 5459
Rand (Samuel), *M.D.* Verses in Hippocrates. 1633. 5812
Randall (John). Great mysterie of godlinesse. Ed. 2. 1630. 4°. 2565
Three and twentie sermons. 1630. 4°. 4261
Twenty nine lectures of the church. 1631. 4°. 3046
Verses in Camb. Univ. Genethl. 1631. 5731
Randall (Joshua). *See* Randall (John). Three and twentie sermons. 1630. 4°.
Randol (John), *B.D.* Noble Blastus. 1633. 4°. 5127
Randolph (Ro.), *Ch. Ch. Oxon.* Verses in Randolph (T.). The Jealous Lovers. 1640. 5852
— — Poems. 1640. 5500
Randolph (Tho.). Aristippus. 1630. 4°. 7563
Jealous lovers. Cambridge, 1634. 4°. 5766
— Cambridge, 1640. 8°. 5852
Poems. Ed. 2. Oxford, 1640. 8°. 5500
Verses in Camb. Univ. Epithalam. 1625. 5702
— Genethl. 1631. 5731
— Rex redux. 1633. 5808
See R. (T.). Cornelianum Dolium. 1638.
Rant (Thomas). Verses in Vaughan (R.). Waterworkes. 1610. . 3576
Raphelengius (Fr.). *See* Sallustius. Opera. 1615. 8°. . . 7406
Rapta Tatio. Mirrour of his Maiesties present Gouernment. 1604. 4°. 2302
Rastell (J.). Exposiciones terminorum legum...et natura brevium, n.d. F°. 352
— 1527. 16°. 414
Exposition of certaine difficult...words. R. Tottell, 1592. 8°. . 1152
— T. Wight, 1602. 8°. 2391
— 1607. 8°. 7501
— 1615. 8°. 3261
See Termes de la ley. 1629.
Pastime of People. [1529.] F°. 353
See Fitzherbert (Sir A.). [Grand Abridgment. Table.] 1517.
— — — 1565.
— Statutes. (Abridgment.) [1527.]
— Frith (J.). Disputacion of purgatorye. [1535?]
Rastell (John), *Jesuit.* Confutation of a sermon...by M. Juell. A. Diest, Antwerp, 1564. 8°. 6127
Replie against an answer. Antwerp, 1565. 8°. 6128
See Fulke (W.). D. Heskins, D. Sanders, and M. Rastel...ouerthrowne. 1579.
Rastell (William). Table collected of the yeares. 1639. 8°. . 4394
See Expositiones. 1527.
— Fitzherbert (Sir A.). La novvelle natvra brevium. 1553 *etc.*
— More (Sir T.). The workes. 1557.
— Rastell (J.). Exposition of certaine...words. 1592 *etc.*
— Statutes. Collection. 1559 *etc.*
— Table Collected of the yeres. 1571.
Ratcliffe (Ægremont). *See* Politique Discourses. 1578.
Ratcliffe (Lady Elizabeth). [Marriage.] *See* Jonson (B.). The description. [1608.]
Ratcliffe (Mrs Jane). [Life.] *See* Ley (J.). Patterne. 1640.
Rates of Merchandize. [1609?] 4°. 2620.
Rathborne (Aaron). Surveyor. 1616. F°. 3116
Ratisbon, Diet of. *See* N. (N.). De conventv. 1631.
Ratramnus, *Corbiensis.* Boke of Barthram...of the bodye and bloude of Christ. 1548. 8°. 696
— Ed. 3. 1623. 8°. 3855
Ravennas (Petrus). *See* Tommai (P.).
Ravenscroft (T.). Briefe discourse. 1614. 4°. 2029

No.

Ravensperger (Hermann). *See* Grotius (H.). Defensio. 1636.
Ravilliac (François). *See* Cotton (P.). Hellish...Councell. 1610.
Ravis (Thomas), *Bp.* *See* Bible, English (Royal). 1611. . . 2635
See Blackwell (G.). Large examination. 1607.
Ravisius (Joannes), *Textor.* Dialogi aliquot. 1581. 16°. . . 1508
Epithetorum...epitome...Acc. poëtica. 16°. 7354
See Heywood (T.). Pleasant dialogues. 1637.
Rawely (Walter). *See* Ralegh.
Rawley (William). *See* Bacon (F.). Opera...Tomvs primvs. 1623.
— — Certaine Miscellany Works. 1629.
— — History naturall and Experimentall. 1638.
— — Operum moralium et civilium tomus. 1631 (1620).
— — Sylva Sylvarum. 1627 *etc.*
Rawlins (Tho.). Admonitio pseudo-chymicis. [1620?] 4°. . . 2033
Rawlinson (John). Quadriga salutis. Oxford, 1625. 4°. . . 5357
Romish Iudas. 1611. 4°. 7500
Unmasking of the hypocrite. 1616. 4°. 7554
Vivat rex. A sermon. Oxford, 1619. 4°. 5336
Ray (John). Verses in Skene (Sir J.). Regiam. 1613. . . 3458
— Adamson (J.). Εἰσόδια. 1618. 5960
— Buchanan (G.). Ecphrasis. 1620. 3595
— Forbes (P.). Funerals. 1637. 6007
Raynald (Thomas). *See* Roesslin (E.). Byrth of Mankind. 1545 *etc.*
Raynsford (H.). *See* Rainsford.
Re (I.). Verses in Davies (R.). Funeral sermon. 1577. . . 1416
Read (Alexander), *D.D.* Sermon, April 8, 1635. 1636. 4°. . 4212
Read (Alexander), *M.D.* *See* Reid.
Read (John). Verses in Case (J.). Svmma. 1598. . . . 5248
See Arcæus (F.). Method of curing woundes. 1588.
Read, Reed, or Reid (Thomas). *See* Rhædus.
Reade (R.), *Licenser.* *See* Norimberg Curranto. No. 84. 1639. 4°.
— Curranto. No. 86. 1639. 4°.
Reade (Thomas), *LL.B.* Verses in Chaucer (G.). Amorvm. 1635. . 5414
Reading (John). Davids Soliloquie. 1627. 12°. 5024
Faire warning...sermons. 1621. 4°. 4167
Old mans staffe, Two sermons. 1621. 4°. 4168
Reasons Academy. *See* D. (Sir I.), Knight. New Post. No. 7342.
Reasons for a generall assemblie. June 29, 1638. 1638. 4°. . . 5986
Reasons for which the Service Booke urged upon Scotland ought to be refused. 1638. 4°. 5987
Rebuffi (Pierre). Tractatus de Decimis. *See* Duarenus (F.). De sacris ecclesiæ ministeriis. 1585.
Reckoner (Ready). [Fragment.] 7107
Record, Matters of. *See* Office. 1617. 3588
Records. *See* Powell (T.). Direction. 1622.
— — Repertorie of Records. 1631.
Recorde (R.). Castle of Knowledge. 1556. F°. 741
Grounde of Artes. 1582. 8°. . . . . 1264 *[*see* p. 1733]
— 1618. 8°. 3800
— Augmented by...Dee...Mellis...Hartwell. 1632. 8°. . . 3999
Pathway to knowledge. 1551. 4°. 735
Vrinal of Physick. 1547. 8°. 725
Whetstone of witte. 1557. 4°. 1167
See Fabyan (R.). Chronicle. 1559.
Records. *See* Record.
Recuyell of the Histories of Troy. *See* Lefèvre (R.).
Redman (John), † 1551. Compendious treatise called the complaint of Grace. [1556?] 8°. 1202
Reporte...answeres, to questions...Whereunto diuerse articles...by M. Chedsey. 1551. 8°. 703

No.

Redman (John), *D.D., of St Omer* (fl. 1617). [Licence.] *See* Staney (W.). Treatise.
Redshawe (George). Verses in Camb. Univ. Carmen. 1635. . . 5770
Reed (Sir Robert), † 1518. *See* Missale. Sarum. 1520.
Reeve (Edmond). Christian divinitie. 1631. 4°. 4960
Communion Book catechisme vindicated. 1636. 4°. . . 4303
See Prynne (W.). Quench-coale. 1637.
Reformatio legvm ecclesiasticarvm. 1571 *etc.* *See* Cranmer (T.).
Reformation of religion by Josiah. [Ab. 1600.] 8°. . . 6831
Regemorterus (Ambrose). *See* Texeda (F. de). Texeda Retextus. 1623.
Regimen sanitatis salerni. Trans. T. Paynel. T. Berthelet, 1541. 4°. 7984
— A. Veale, 1557. 8°. 1070
— W. How for A. Veale, 1575. 8°. 1766
— T. Creede, 1597. 4°. 2725
— B. Alsop for J. Barnes, 1617. 4°. 7581
Registrum omnium breuium. W. Rastell, 1531. F°. . . . 529
W. Rastell, 1531. (R. Tottel, 1553.) F°. 530
Regius (Adam). *See* King.
Regius (John), *or* De Koninck. *See* Texeda (F. de). Texeda Retextus. 1623.
Regius (Ludovicus). *See* Le Roy.
Regius (Urbanus). Comparison betwene the olde learnynge and the newe. Trans. W. Turner. Southwark, 1538. 8°. 5872
Declaration of the twelue articles of the christen faythe. 1548. 8°. 951
Homily upon Matthew ix. *See* Luther (M.). Frutefull and godly exposition. 1548. 8°. 7767
Instruccyon of Christen fayth. [1548?] 8°. 1061
Necessary instruction of Christian faith. 1579. 8°. . . 1055
Olde learnyng and the new...by W. Turner. 1548. 8°. . 1064
Sermon...on the way to Emaus. 1578. 4°. 854
— 1612. 4°. 2311
Solace of Sion. Trans. R. Robinson. 1591. 8°. 7261
Regnier de la Planche (L.). Legendarie...of the...Cardinal of Lorraine, etc. 1577. 8°. 6763
Reid or Rhead (Alexander), *M.D.* Chirurgicall Lectures of Tumours and Ulcers. 1632–4. 1635. 4°. 4859
Σωματογραφία ἀνθρωπίνη. 1634. 8°. 4633
Treatise of the first part of Chirurgerie. 1638. 4°. . . 4871
Verses in Hippocrates. 1633. 5812
Reid (James). Theses and Verses in Adamson (J.). Εἰσόδια. 1618. 5960
Reignoldes (John). *See* Rainolds.
Reinolds, Dr. *See* Rainolds (J.).
Relation of the state of Religion. 1605. *See* Sandys (Sir E.).
Relation strange and true of a ship of Bristol...the Jacob. 1622. 4°. 3506
Remedy ayenst the troubles of temptacyons. W. de Worde, 21 Jan. 1519. 4°. 178
Remedy for sedition. Berthelet, 1536. 4°. 435, 436
Remembrancers General, *Office of.* 1617. 4°. . . . 3588
Remicius. *See* Æsop. Fabulæ. 1635.
Remigius, Grammarian. *See* no. 7696.
Remington (Samuel). Verses in Hippocrates. 1633. . . . 5812
Remonstrance of the Nobility...of Scotland. Edinburgh, 1639. 4°. 5993 and p. 1435
Remonstrance or plaine detection of a Demonstration of Discipline. 1590. 4°. 1725
Remonstrants or Arminians. *See* Dort Synod. Suffragium Collegiale. 1626.
See Johnson (F.). A Christian Plea... 1617.
Remorse of conscience. W. de Worde [15–]. 4°. 239
Renaudot (Théophraste). Nos. 1–4. A question etc. 1640. 4°. . 4401–4

No.

Renecher (Herman). Golden chayne of saluation. Trans. 1604. 4°. 7458
Renniger (M.). De Pii quinti et Gregorii decimi tertii furoribus. 1582. 8°. 1817
Syntagma hortationum. 1604. 8°. 1831
Repertory of Records. 1631. *See* Powell (T.).
Reporte of a discovrse. 1606. *See* Hayward (Sir John).
Requests, Court of. *See* Caesar (Sir J.). In nomine. [Ab. 1592.] F°.
Rerum Anglicarum Henrico VIII. *etc.* 1616. *See* Godwin (F.).
Resolution of Religion. *See* Parsons (R.).
Resolutus (Dr) [*i.e.* D. Lindsay]. *See* Calderwood (D.). A solution. 1619. 7806
Responsa. *See* Returna Brevium. No. 309 etc.
Returna breuium. Pynson [15]. 4°. 309
[Ab. 153- .] 4°. 7697
R. Redman, 1532. 8°. 375
See Book of Justice of the Peace. 1544.
Returne of the renowned Caualiero. *See* Nash (T.). 1589. 4°.
Reuben (Abraham). *See* Ruben.
Reuchlin (J.). De arte concionandi. 1570. 8°. 7262
Reuter (Adam). De consilio tractatus. Oxoniae, 1626. 4°. . 5364
Libertatis Anglicanae defensio. 1613. 4°. 3780
Revell (Tho.). Verses in Biondi (G. F.). Eromena. 1632. . 7753
Revels, Children of his Majesty's. *See* Mason (J.). The Turke. 1632.
Revels, Children of the. *See* Davenant (Sir W.). The Triumphs. 1635.
Reynolde (W.). *See* Reynolds.
Reynolds (Edward). Explication of Ps. 110. Ed. 2. 1635. 4°. 3053, 7826
Meditations on the...Lords Supper. Ed. 2. 1639. 4°. . . 4910
Shieldes of the earth. 1636. 4°. 3054
Three treatises. Ed. 1. 1631. 4°. 3047
— Ed. 2. 1631. 4°. 3048
— Ed. 3. 1634. 4°.. 7825
Treatise of the passions and faculties. 1640. 4°. . . . 4936
Reynolds (John), *D.D.* *See* Rainolds.
Reynolds (John), *instrument maker.* 1582. *See* no. 7931.
Reynolds (John), *merchant.* Triumphs of gods revenge against...Murther. 1635(-4). F°. 7631
Reynolds (John), *translator.* *See* Apologie of the Reformed churches of France. 1628. 4°. 781ɔ
See Marandé (L. de). Ivdgment of Humane Actions. 1629.
Reynolds (Ric.). Booke...the Foundacion of Rhetorike. 1563. 7 Marcii. 4°. 7222
Chronicle of...Emperours of the Romaines. 1571. 4°. . 7227
Reynolds (William). *See* Hume (A.). Didvction. 1602.
Rhædus (Thomas). [Paraphrasis Psalmi civ.] *See* Barclay (W.), *M.D.* Judicium. 1620.
Rhæsus (Johannes David). *See* Rhys (J. D.).
Rhead (Alexander). *See* Reid.
Rhees (Sir D. Mackey, Lord). 1637. *See* Monro (R.).
Rheims. English College. *See* Bible, English. N.T. (Rheims.)
See Bernard (R.). Rhemes against Rome. 1626.
Rheinberg, Siege of. *See* Maurice, *Prince.* True Report. 1601. 4°.
Rhianus [*Gr. Lat.*]. *See* Poetae minores. 1635.
Rhodes (John). Answere to a romish rime...entituled A proper new Ballad. 1602. 4°. 2879
Rhodes (Matthew). Verses in Roberts (L.). Merchants mappe. 1638. 5133
Rhodes (T.). Verses in Camb. Univ. Lacrymae. 1619. . . 5689
Rhodes (Tim.). Verses in Camb. Univ. Anthologia. 1632. . . 5741
Rhys (John Dafydd). Cambrobrytannicae cymraecæve linguæ institutiones et rudimenta. 1592. F°. 2215
Ribadeneira (Pedro de). *See* Villegas (A. de). Lives of Saints. 1628 *etc.*
Riberius (Joannes). Verses in Aleman (M.). The Rogve. 1623. . 4079

No.
Riccomontanus (Robert). *See* Richmond.
Rice (R.). Invective against vices. 1579. 8°. 1183
Rich (B.). [Allarme to England.] *See* Marcelline (G.). Vox militis. 1625.
Catholicke conference. 1612. 4°. 2406
Honestie of this age. 1615. 4°. 3756
— 1616. 4°. 3758
Irish hubbub. 1617. 4°. 4062
— 1619. 4°. 4069
My ladies looking glasse. 1616. 4°. 2409
New description of Ireland. 1610. 4°. 2772
— *See below:* New Irish Prognostication. 1624.
New Irish Prognostication. 1624. 4°. 3973
Opinion diefied. 1613. 4°. 2408
Short survey of Ireland. 1609. 4°. 3630
True and kind excuse of A Newe Description of Irelande. 1612. 4°. 2407
Rich (Charles), *T.C.* Verses in Camb. Univ. Carmen. 1635. . 5770
— — Συνωδία. 1637. 5790
Rich (Hattonus), *son of Lord Warwick.* Verses in Camb. Univ. Voces. 1640. 5836
'Richard IV., *King of England.*' *See* Gainsford (T.). The true history. 1618. 4°.
Richardson (Alexander). Logicians school-master. 1629. 4°. . 4259
Richardson (Charles). The repentance of Peter and Iudas. 1612. 4°. 3087
Richardson (Gabriel). Of the state of Europe. Oxford, 1627. F°. 5368
Richardson (John). *See* Bible, English (Royal). 1611. . . 2635
See R. (I.), *of Trin. Coll. Camb.*
Richardson (Nic.). Verses in Oxf. Univ. Magd. Coll. 1612. . 5302
Richelieu, *Card.* Emblema Animae. Trs. J. Maxwell. 1635. 12°. 3701, 3702
Principall points of the faith of the catholike church. Paris, 1635. 8°. 6201
Richeome (Louis). Holy Pictures of the...Eucharist. Trans. C. A. 1619. 4°. 6618
Pilgrime of Loreto. Trans. E. W. Paris, 1630. 4°. . . 6224
Richer (Edmond). Treatise of ecclesiasticall and politike power. 1612. 4°. 3083
Richmond and Derby (Margaret, countess of). [Funeral.] *See* Fisher (J.). Mornynge remembrance. [15– .] 4°.
See Dionysius Carthusianus. The mirror. 1522.
— Fisher (J.). [Seven penitential psalms.] 1508 etc.
— Hilton (W.). Scala perfeccōnis. 1494.
— Imitatio Christi. [Ab. 1503?]
Richmond (Robert). Verses in Coryat (T.). Coryats Crudities. 1611. 3076
Richworth (William). *See* Rushworth (W.).
Rider (Henry). *See* Horatius. Odes and Epodes. 1638. 12°.
Rider (J.), *bp of Killaloe.* *See* Fitz-simon (H.). A catholike confutation. 1608.
Ridgeley (L.). Verses in Camb. Univ. Carmen. 1635. . . . 5770
Ridgeley (Thomas). [Licence.] *See* Jorden (E.). A discourse. 1633.
Ridley (L.). Commentary...upon the Ephesyans. 1540. 8°. . 383, 384
Exposition...vpon...Philippians. Canterbury [1550?] 8°. . . 5876
Exposition vpon...Jude. [1550?] 8°. 1089
Ridley (Mark). Magneticall Animadversions...from W. Barlow. 1617. 4°. 3670
Short treatise of magneticall bodies. 1613. 4°. 3650
See Barlow (W.), *archdeacon of Salisbury.* Magneticall Aduertisements. Ed. 2. 1618.
Ridley (Nic.). Breef declaration of the Lordes supper. 1586. 8°. 1073
Certayne godly...conferences. 1556. 8°. 6737
Certē godly...conferences. 1556. 8°. 6296
— 1574. 8°. 1277
Pituous lamentation of the miserable estate of the chvrche. [1566.] 8°. 1017

No.

Ridley (Nic.), *cont.* [Letters.] *See* Coverdale (M.). Certain...letters. 1564.
Ridley (Sir Thomas). View of the civile and ecclesiastical Law. 1607. 4°. 3230
— Ed. 2. Oxford, 1634. 4°. 5444
Verses in Foxe (J.). Actes. 1583. 865
Right fruitful Book of Examples. [Text-title. Ab. 1620.] 8°. . 7410
Rightwich (John). Verses in Horman (W.). Vulgaria. 1519. . 267
Rikel (Dionysius de). *See* Dionysius Carthusianus.
Riley or Ryley (Tho.). Verses in Camb. Univ. Genethl. 1631. . 5731
— — Fasciae. 1633. 5808
— — Rex redux. 1633. 5748
— Russell (J.). Two...battels. 1634. 5767
— Randolph (T.). Jealous Lovers. 1640. 5852
Rimicius. *See* Remicius.
Riolan (Jean). Treatise of the eyes. *See* Vaughan (Sir W.). Directions for health. Ed. 6. 1626 etc. 4°.
Rishanger (Willielmus). *See* Paris (M.). Historia major. 1640.
Rive (Edmund). Heptaglottie. 1618. 8°. 3325
See Posselius (J.). Dialogues. 1623. 4°.
— Targum. *Song of Solomon.* 1614.
Rivers (Anthony Woodvile, earl). *See* Cordiale. 1479.
See Dicta Philosophorum... 1477 etc.
Rivers (George). Heroinae. 1639. 12°. 7882
Rivers (Peregrine). New almanacke and prognostication. Cambridge, 1629. 8°. 5725
Rives (Joh.). Verses in Oxf. Univ. Horti. 1640. 5499
Rivius (Edmundus). *See* Rive (E.).
Rivius (J.), *of Attendorn.* Of the foolishnes of men. Trans. T. Rogers. 1583. 8°. 1820
Rivius (Thomas). *See* Ryves.
Robartes (Foulke). Gods holy house and service. 1639. 4°. . . 4669
Revenue of the gospel. Cambridge, 1613. 4°. . . . 5670
Robert the Devil. Lyf. W. de Worde. [1502?] 4°. . . . 240
Robertes (William). Verses in Camb. Univ. Epicedium. 1612. . 5665
Roberts (Gabriel). Verses in Roberts (L.). The merchants mappe. 1638. 5133
Roberts (John). Compleat cannoniere. 1639. 4°. 3723
Roberts (Lewis). Merchants mappe. 1638. F°. 5133
Warrefare epitomized. 1640. 4°. 5135
Verses in Fletcher (P.). Purple Island. 1633. 5752
Roberts (Robert), *of Llanvair.* Verses in Roberts (L.). Merchants mappe. 1638. 5133
Roberts (W.). *See* Robertes.
Robertson (Bartholomew). Crowne of life. 1618. 12°. . . . 7557
Robertson (George). Verses in Forbes (P.). Funerals. 1635. . 6007
Robertus Castellensis. [Advertisement of absolution.] Pynson. [1499.] 107
Robinson (John). Defence...against J. Murton. 1624. 4°. . 6955
Ivstification of separation. 1610. 4°. 6499
— 1639. 4°. 6372
New essayes. 1628. 4°. 6986
Of religious communion. 1614. 4°. 6142
Vox ducis. 1631. 8°. 3990
See Ainsworth (H.). An animadversion. 1613.
— Murton (J.). Discription of what God. 1620.
— R. (I.). No. 6985.
Robinson (John). Verses in Camb. Univ. Dolor. 1625. . . 5701 A
Robinson (Ralph). *See* More (Sir T.). Vtopia. 1556 *etc.*
Robinson (Richard). Verses in Norton (R.). Gunner. 1628. . 4535
See Leland (J.). Learned and true Assertion of Prince Arthur. 1582. 4°.
— Meteren (E. van). True discourse. 1602.

No.

Robinson (Richard), *cont.* *See* Patrizi (F.). Moral methode. 1576.
See Regius (U.). Solace of Sion. 1591. 8°.
— Strigelius (V.). Part of the harmony. 1582. 4°.
— Proceeding. [1593?] 4°.
— Second proceeding. 1593. 4°.
— Third proceeding. 1595. 4°.
Robinson (Thomas). Anatomy of the english nunnery at Lisbon. 1622. 4°. 4078
Schoole of mvsicke. 1603. F°. 1613
Robson (S.). Choise of Change. 1585. 4°. 1873
Rochelle. Letter...by...the Assembly. 1621. 4°. 6654
Rochfort (Luke). Antidot for laziuesse. 1624. 4°. . . . 6026
Rodeknight (John). [Bookplate.] *See* 6912 n.
Rodoginus (Irenaeus), *pseud.* *See* Irenaeus.
Rodolph II, *emperor of Germany*. *See* Rudolph.
Rodriguez (Alonso). Christian mans guide. 1630. 8°. . . . 7005
Christian Perfection. Part i. Treatises 1 and 2. 1631. 8°. . 7011
Short and sure way to heaven. 1630. 8°. 6624
Treatise of humility. 1632. 12°. 6626
Treatise of mentall prayer. 1627. 8°. 6557
Treatise of modesty and silence. 1632. 8°. 6627
Roe (Cheynie). Verses in Camb. Univ. Epicedium. 1612. . . . 5665
Roe (Nathaniel). Tabulæ Logarithmicæ...by E. Wingate. 1633. 8°. 4276
Roe (Sir Thomas). Verses in Stock (R.). The chvrches lamentation. 1614. 3784
See Sarpi (P.). Cruell subtilty. [16—.] 4°.
— — Discourse. 1628.
Roe or Rowe (Thomas), *B.D.*, *K.C.C.* Verses in Camb. Univ. Epicedium. 1612. 5665
— — Genethl. 1631. 5731
— — Anthologia. 1632. 5741
— — Rex redux. 1633. 5748
— Hawkins (W.). Corolla. 1634. 5803
— Hippocrates. 1631, 1633. . . . . . 5736, 5812
— Camb. Univ. Carmen. 1635. 5770
Roe (William). Epilogus ad quatuor colloqvia D. D. Wrighti. 1615. 4°. 3410-1
Roesslin (E.). Birthe of Mankynde. Trans. R. Jonas. 1540. 4°. . 692
— 1545. 4°. 693
— 1552. 4°. 704
— 1598. 4°. 1344
— 1613. 4°. 3651
Rogerius, *physician*. *See* Braunschweig (H.). The noble experyence. 1525.
Rogers (——). Glory and happines of a true Christian. 1618. 8°. 3326
Rogers (Daniel). Practicall catechisme. Ed. 2. 1633. 4°. . . 4628
Treatise of the two sacraments. Ed. 2. 1635. 4°. . . 4639
Verses *ter* in Humphrey (L.). J. Jvelli vita. 1573. . . 837
Rogers (G.), *Joh.* Verses in Camb. Univ. Rex redux. 1633. . 5748
Rogers (Henry). Ans. to Mr Fisher. 1623. 4°. 6942
Protestant Church existent. 1638. 4°. 4391
Rogers (John), *martyr*. (1500?—1555.) *See* Bible, English [Matthew's]. 1537 *etc.*
— — [Taverner's.] 1551.
— Melanchthon (P.). A waying. 1548.
Rogers (John) (fl. 1578). Displaying of...the Famile of Loue. 1578. 8°. 1710
— 1579. 8°. 1628
Rogers (John), *minister of Chacombe*. Discovrse of christian watchfvlnesse. 1620. 8°. 3336
Rogers (John), *minister of Dedham*. Treatise of Love. Ed. 2. 1632. 12°. 3883

No.

Rogers (John), *Queens' Coll. Camb.* Verses in Hausted (P.). Senile Odium. 1633. 5753
Rogers (Neh.). Christian Curtesie. 1621. 4°. 2539
Strange vineyard in Palaestina. 1623. 4°. 4786
True convert. 1632. 4°. 4441
Wild Vine. 1632. 4°. 7888
Rogers (Richard). Certaine sermons. ...S. Wright. 1612. 4°. . 2981
Garden of spirituall flowers. 1625. 8°. 3447
Practice of christianitie. 1618. 12°. 3002
— Ed. 3. 1623. 12°. 4179
Seaven treatises. 1603. F°. 7938
— Ed. 2. 1604. F°. 2470. 1605. F°. 2475
— Ed. 3. 1610. F°. 7471
— Ed. 5. 1630. 4°. 7822
Rogers (Thomas). [Book-mark. Ab. 155–.] 7771
English Creede. 1585. F°. 2115
— Part 2. 1587. F°. 1901
Faith, doctrine, and religion...in the realme of England. Cambridge, 1607. 4°. 5643
— 1621. 4°. 4694
— 1629. 4°. 4706
— 1633. 4°. 4718
Philosophicall discourse...Anatomie of the minde. 1576. 8°. . 1348
Two dialogues or conferences. 1608. 4°. 2901
See Augustinus. A pretiovs booke. 1581 *etc.*
— — A right Christian Treatise. 1591. 12°.
— Avenar (Jo.). Enimie of Securitie. 1580 *etc.*
— Cæsar (P.). General Discovrse. 1578.
— Dispute. 1608.
— Estella (D. de). Methode vnto Mortification. 1586.
— Geveren (S. à). Of the ende. 1577.
— Imitatio. Of the Imitation of Christ. 1617(–6). 12°.
— Rivius (J.). Of the Foolishnes etc. 1583. 8°.
Rogers (Timothy). Righteous mans evidences for heaven. 1627. 12°. 4420
Roman-Catharist. 1621. 4°. 2540
Rogers (William). Verses in Roberts (L.). Merchants mappe. 1638. 5133
Rogers (William), *M.A.*, *S.J.C.* Verses in Camb. Univ. Συνωδία. 1637. 5790
Rohan (Henri de Rohan, duc de). Complete captain, or an abridgement of Caesars warres. Trans. J. Cruso. Cambridge, 1640. 8°. 5863
Declaration...for the...Reformed Churches. Translated. 1628. 4°. 4251
Treatise of the interest of the princes...of Christendome. Paris, 1640. 4°. 6229
Rolewinck (Wernerus). *See* Clemangiis (N. de). Specvlvm. 1606.
Rolle (Richard). Contemplations. W. de Worde [15—]. 4°. . . 241
Rolle (Richard). De emendatione vita ac de regula bene vivendi. *See* Speculum spiritualium. 1510. F°.
Explanationes super Job. (Sermo.) [Oxford, 1483.] 4°. . 79
Rolle (Robert), *New Coll.* Verses in Holyoake (F.). Dictionarium. 1640. 3058
See also Rollus.
Rollenson (Fras.). Twelve prophetical legacies. 1612. 4°. . . 7438
Rollock (P.). Verses in Skene (Sir J.). Regiam. 1613. . . 3458
Rollock (Robert). Analysis dialectica...ad Romanos. Edinburgi, 1594. 8°. 5933
Analysis logica in epistolam...ad Galatas. 1602. 8°. . . 2924
In librum Danielis. Edinburgh, 1591. 4°. 5926
Lectures vpon...Colossians. 1603. 4°. 2929
Lectures vpon...Thessalonians. Edinburgh, 1606. 4°. . . 5946
Tractatus de vocatione efficaci. Edinburgi, 1597. 8°. . . 5937
Verses in Buchanan (G.). Rerum scoticarum historia. 1582. . 5920
Rollocus. *See* Rollock.
Rollus (Rob.). Verses in Humphrey (L.). I. Ivelli vita. 1573. . 837

No.
Rollus, (Rob.) *cont.* Serres (J. de). Three partes of Commentaries. 1574. 7279
See also Rolle.
Rolte (John). *See* Palatinate. Fvll declaration. 1614. 4°. . 2988
— — Frederick V. A declaration. 1637.
— R. (I.). The spy. 1628. 6985
Romani (Gaspar). Verses in Montemayor (J. de). Diana. 1598. F°. 7924
Rombouts (John). Verses in Verstegan (R.). Restitution. 1605 etc. 6140 *etc.*
Rome, History of. *See* Eutropius (F.). A briefe chronicle. 1564.
— *See* New and easy method. '1617.'
Emperors of. [Julius Caesar to Rodolph II.] *See* Mexia (P.). Historie. 1604.
— — Imperiall historie. 1623.
— [Trajan to Alexander Severus.] *See* Guevara (A. de). 1577. 4°.
See Prophecy. A prophesie. 1610.
Church of. Ecclesiastical protestant historie...over...Britanie. 1624. 8°. 6951
— Fall of the Romish Church. [Ab. 1549.] 8°. . . 6715
— Cancellaria Apostolica. *See* Crashaw (W.). A mittimus. 1625. 4°.
— [Silvester, *Pope.*] *See* Constantine I. A Treatyse. [c. 1525.]
— [Boniface IX, *Pope* (1389—1394).] [Pardon to Sir Gerard Braybroke.] *See* Holland (H.). Ecclesia Sancti Pavli. 1633.
— [Ab. 1496.] Proclamation. 7064-5
— [Julius II, Pope (1503—1513).] *See* Constantine I. A treatyse. [c. 1525.]
— [Clement VII (1523—1534).] *See* Henry VIII. Sigismondus. [1530?] 511
— [Paul III (1534—1550).] *See* Consilium delectorum. 1609. 4°.
— [Julius III (1550—1555).] Consilivm quorundam episcoporum Bononiæ congregatorum. 1613. 4°. 2313
— — *See* Justinianus.
— [Pius V (1566—1572).] [Bull.] *See* Jewel (J.). A viewe. 1582. 1316
— [Gregory XIII (1572—1585).] *See* Holy Bull. 1588. 4°.
— [Sixtus V (1585—1590).] *See* Holy Bull. 1588. 4°.
— — *See* James T.). Bellum Papale. 1600.
— [Clement VIII (1592—1605).] *See* James (T.). Bellvm papale. 1600.
— — *See* Parsons (R.). A briefe apologie. [1602?]
— [Paul V (1605—1621).] [17 April, 1606.] *See* Venice. Declaration. 1606.
— — *See* Vignier (N). Concerning. 1607.
— — [Brief.] *See* James I. Triplici nodo. 1607.
— — [Brief.] *See* James I. Apologie. 1609.
— — *See* Sarpi (P.). Fvll and satisfactorie answer. 1606.
— — — New Man. 1622.
— — — Sarpi (P.). Quarrels. 1626.
— [Gregory XV (1621—1623).] *See* Scott (T.). Aphorismes. 1624.
— [Urban VIII (1623—1644).] Bull, May 30, 1626. *See* Burton (H). Baiting. 1627.
— — [Brief. 20 Nov. 1628.] *See* Hall (J.). Answer to Pope Vrban. 1629.
— Congregation of the Index. [*Decree.*] *See* Widdrington (R.). A copy. 1614.
— — *See* Dominis (M. A. de). Manifestation. 1616.
— — — James (T.). Index generalis. 1627.
— Discourse. Briefe discourse against the outwarde apparel...1578.
— — Fiscus Papalis. 1617 *etc.*
— — Powel (G.) Catholikes Supplication. 1603.
— — Secular Priests.
— — Sixe Demands from an vnlearned Protestant. 1609.

No.

Rome, Church of, *cont.* *See* Solemne Contestation. [156–.]
— *See* Supplication of certaine Masse-Priests. 1604.
— — Svpplication to the Kings.. Maiestie. 1604.
— [Books. English printed, 1622–4.] *See* Gee (J.). The Foot. 1624.
English College. *See* Everard (J.). Britanno-romanvs. 1611.
Order of the Immaculate Conception. *See* Wadsworth (J.). Further Observations. 1630. 4°. 7788
Rome, *Empire of.* *See* Constantine I. Treatyse. [c. 1525.]
Romei (Annibale). Courtiers Academie. Trans. I. K. [1598?] 4°. . 2849
Rondeletius (Gulielmus). *See* Gesner (C.). Nomenclator. 1560. F°.
See L'Obel (M. de). In...Officinam. 1605.
Ronigerus (Michael). Verses in Wilson (Sir T.). Vita. 1551. . 631
Rooke (Laur.), *Regal.* Verses in Camb. Univ. Voces. 1640. . 5836
Roper (Henry). Verses in Camb. Univ. Fasciæ. 1633. . . 5808
Rorie Oge. *See* O'More (R.).
Rosa (Thomas). *See* Ross.
Rosarium Mysticum. Antwerp, 1534. 8°. . . . See p. 1743
Rosary of our Lady in Englysshe. [Ab. 1510.] 16°. . . . 6663
Rosary of Our Saviour. *See* Pilgrimage of Perfection. 1526. 4°.
Rosary. The Mystik sweet Rosary of the faythful soule. Antwerp, 1533. 8°. 6088
Roscarrock (Nicholas). Verses in Bossewell (J.). Workes. 1597. . 2895
Rosdell (Christopher). *See* Calvin (J.). Commentarie vpon...Romans. 1586. 4°.
Roseletto (Cosmo). Verses in Harvey (G.). Gratulationum. 1578. . 1495
Ross (Alexander). Christiados libri XIII. 1638. 8°. . 4739, 4740
Commentum de terræ motu circulari. 1634. 4°.
Exposition on Genesis i.–xiv. 1626. 8°. 4187
Κουρεὺς ἀπόξυρος. 1627. 8°. 4242
Virgilius Evangelisans. 1634. 8°. 4723
Ross (Thomas). Idæa. 1608. 8°. 2364
Rosse (Abraham). *See* Ross (Alexander).
Rosse (Gabriel), *T.C.C.* Verses in Barlow (W.). Vita R. Cosin. 1598. 1707
Rosseus (Gulielmus), *pseud.* *See* More (Sir T.).
Rote or myrroure of consolacyon and conforte. W. de Worde, 1511. 4°. 167
— 23 March 1530. 4°. 201
Roth or Rothe (Richard). Letter. *See* Coverdale (M.). Certain... letters. 1564.
Rothe (David), *bishop of Ossory.* *See* Ryves (Sir T.). Regiminis anglicani defensio. 1624. 4°.
Rough (John). Letter. *See* Coverdale (M.). Certain...letters. 1564.
Rous (Francis), *the elder.* Diseases of the time. 1622. 12°. . . 3143
Meditations of instruction. 1616. 12°. 3761
Mysticall marriage. 1635. 12°. 5063
Oile of Scorpions. 1624. 12°. 3153
Testis veritatis. The doctrine of King James. 1626. 4°. . 3353
— — *See below:* Trvth of three Things. 1633.
Truth of three things. 1633. 4°. 7018
Rous (Francis), *the younger.* Archæologiae Atticæ libri tres. Oxford, 1637. 4°. 5475
Rouse (John). Appendix ad catalogum librorum in bibl. Bodl. Ed. 2. Oxoniæ, 1635. 4°. 5467
Rouspeau (Yves). Two treatises of the lord his holie supper...John de l'Espine. Cambridge, 1584. 8°. 5511
Row (Brian). *See* Antiphoner Sarum. [1519–20.] . . . 6155-6
Rowbotham (James). *See* Damiano da Odemira. 1562.
Rowe (C.). Verses in Camb. Univ. Rex redux. 1633. . . . 5748
Rowe (Thomas). *See* Roe.

No.
Rowlands, *alias* Verstegan (Richard). Post for diuers partes of the world. 1576. 8°. 1574
Restitution of decayed intelligence. Antwerp, 1605. 4°. . . 6140
— Ed. 2. 1628. 4°. 3534
— 1634. 4°. 4898
Theatrum crudelitatum haereticorum. Ed. alt. Antwerp, 1604. 4°. 6134
Verses in Veen (O. van). 1608. 6138
See Primer. 1599 *etc.*
Rowlands (Samuel). *See* Greene (R.). Greenes ghost. 1602. 4°.
Rowley (R.). Verses in Cambridge Lachrymae. 1587. . . 2123, 7356
Roy (W.). Boke Reade me frynde and be not wrothe. 'Wesel, 1546. By H. Nycolson.' 8°. 983
Lytle treatous or dialoge. *See* True beliefe. 1550.
See Erasmus. Exhortation. 1529.
Royal Book. Caxton [1486?] F°. 30
Royal Slave. 1640. *See* Cartwright (W.).
Roydon (Matthew), *M.A.* Verses in Gilbert (Sir H.). Trve reporte. 1583. 1354
Ruben (Abraham), *Rabbi*. *See* Broughton (H.). Ovr Lordes Famile. 1608.
Rudd (Anth.). Sermon. 1604. 8°. 2260
Rudierde (Edmund). Thunderbolt of gods wrath. 1618. 4°. . 3327
Rudolph II, *emperor of Germany*. *See* Briefe relation. 1599.
Rudstone (John). Verses in Norton (R.). Gunner. 1628. . . . 4535
Rudyerd (Sir Benjamin). Speech in behalfe of the Clergie. Oxford, 1628. 4°. 5373
Rufinus (Tyrannius). Expositio Ieronimi in simbolum apostolorum. Oxford, '1468.' 4°. 72
Rugeley (Nich.). Verses in Ferne (Sir J.). The blazon. 1586. . 2119
Ruggle (George). Ignoramus. 1630. 12°. 5089
— Ed. 2. 1630. 12°. 3989
See Stephens (J.). New essayes etc. 1631. 8°. 7823
Rupipozæus. *See* Chasteigner de la Roche-pozai.
Ruremonde (Hans van), *i.e.* John Hollybush, q.v.[1]
Ruscelli (Girolamo). *See* Alessio *Piemontese*.
Rush or Rushe (Ant.). President for a Prince. 1566. 4°. . . 1401
Rushworth (William). Dialogues. Paris, 1640. 12°. 6206
Russell (John). Two famous...Battels of Lypsich, and Lutzen. Cambridge, 1634. 4°. 5767
Russell (John), *advocate*. Verses in Skene (Sir J.). Regiam. 1609. . 5967
Russell (William, first Lord). [Funeral.] *See* Walker (W.). A sermon. 1614.
Russhe (Antony). *See* Rush.
Russia. *See* Fletcher (G.). Of the russe commonwealth. 1591.
See Smith (Sir T.). Voyage. 1605.
Ruthven (Alexander). *See* Garey (S.). Caesaris Hostes. 1618.
— James VI. De execrabili conjuratione. 1601.
Ruthven (John, third earl Gowrie). *See* Garey (S.). Cæsaris Hostes. 1618.
See James VI, of Scotland. De execrabili...conjuratione. 1601.
Ruthven (William). *See* Ladies Cabinet. 1639. 4°. 4949
Ruydinck (Simon), *the younger*. Verses in Holland (H.). Heroologia. 1620. 6642
Ryley (Tho.). *See* Riley.
Ryvers (Antony Woodvile, earl). *See* Rivers.
Ryves (Sir Thomas). Historia navalis. 1629. 8°. 3982
— 1633. 8°. 2684
Historiae navalis mediae libri tres. 1640. 8°. 4937

[1] See p. 1742 (note on no. 5870).

No.

Ryves (Sir Thomas), *cont.* Imperatoris Iustiniani defensio adv. Alemannum. 1626. 12°. 3164
Poore vicars plea. 1620. 4°. 3500
Regiminis anglicani in hibernia defensio. 1624. 4°. . . 2551

S. (A.). Newes. *See* Overbury (Sir T.). His Wife. 1638.
Verses in Adamson (J.). Εἰσόδια. 1618. 5960
See Du Moulin (P.). Oppositions. 1610. 4°.
S. (A.), *Gent.* *See* Du Moulin (P.). Wittie Encounter. 1636.
See Tossanus (D.). Synopsis. 1635.
S. (A.), *Mr.* *See* Smyth (J.). Paralleles. 1609.
S. (A. C.) [=Champney (A.)]. *See* Pilkington (R.). Parallela. 1618.
S. (A. H.). *See* H. (A.), S.
S. (A. P.). Ode Natalitia. 1575. 8°. 1530
S. (B.). *See* Hall (J.). Answer to Pope Vrban. 1629.
S. (C.). Copie of a letter written...to Master H. A. 1603. 4°. . 7415
Verses in Turkey. The Mahumetane...Historie. 1600. . . 1610
S. (D. D.). *See* Tilenus (D.). True Copy. 1605.
S. (E.). Britaines Busse. 1615. 4°. 2784
S. (E.) [Qu. E. Spenser?]. De rebus gestis Britanniæ. [1582?] 12°. 1523
Historia Britannica. Oxoniæ, 1640. 12°. 5501
S. (E.), *C.G.* Verses in Camb. Univ. Gratulatio. 1623. . . 5695
S. (E.), *T.C.* Verses in Camb. Univ. Gratulatio. 1623. . . 5695
S. (E. C.). Government of Ireland under...Sir John Perrot. 1626. 4°. 4534
S. (G.). Sacrae heptades. 1625. 4°. 6504
Verses in Barclay (W.). Judicium. 1620. 3594
— Camdeni Insignia. 1624. 5346
S. (G.), *K.C.C.* Verses in Horne (C.). In ob. Whitakeri. 1596. 7332
S. (H.). *See* Sidney (Sir P.). Arcadia. 1593 *etc.*
S. (I.). Christian exhortation taken oute of the holy scriptures. 1579. 8°. 7266
Verses in Turkey. The Mahumetane...Historie. 1600. . 1610
— Doddridge (Sir J.). Lawyers Light. 1629. 4958
See Beza (T.). Discovrse. [156–?]
— Bolton (R.). Helpes to hvmiliation. 1633 etc.
S. (I.), *K.C.C.* Verses in Camb. Univ. Dolor. 1625. 4°. . . 5701
S. (J.). *See* Lydgate (J.). Serpent of diuision. 1559.
Dvello. 1610. *See* Selden (J.).
See Sadler (J.). Masquerade du Ciel. 1640.
— Speed (J.). Genealogies.
[=Spencer (J.)] *See* Hooker (R.). Of the laws. 1617 etc.
See S. (J. T. J.).
S. (J. T. J.). *See* England. Parliament. Certaine Articles. 1572.
S. (L.). Resurgendum. A notable sermon. 1593. 4°. . . 7331
Verses *bis* in Bentley (T.). Monument of Matrones. 1582. . 1425
See Church (H.). The good Mans Treasury. 1636. 12°.
S. (M.). *See* Bolton (R.). Short...Discourse. 1637.
S. (M.) [qu. M. Sparke, publisher?] *See* English, Latin, French, Dutch, Scholemaster. 1637. 8°.
S. (M. M.). *See* Las Casas (B. de). Spanish Colonie. 1583.
S. (N.), *Oxoniae.* Verses in Mercator (G.). Historia. 1635. . 4637
S. (R.). Iesuites play at Lyons in France. 1607. 4°. . 3060* (page 635)
Newes. *See* Overbury (Sir T.), His Wife. 1638.
Verses in Gascoigne (G.). Posies. 1575. 1482
— Cambridge Lachrymae. 1587. 2123
— Spenser (E.). Faerie queen. 1590 *etc.* . . . 1960 *etc.*
— Whitaker (W.). Praelectiones. 1599. 5598
See Drexelius (H.). Nicetas. 1633.
— Mornay (P. de). Fowre bookes. 1600.
— Southwell (R.). Moeoniae. 1595.
— — Triumphs ouer Death. 1596.

No.

S. (R.), *Gent.* *See* Stafford (R.). 1609.
S. (R.), *Priest.* *See* Sheldon (R.). Certain general reasons. 1611. 4°.
S. (S.). Verses in Lucanus. Pharsalia. 1614. 3655
— Rive (E.). Heptaglottie. 1618. 3325
— Sempill (Sir J.). Sacrilege. 1619. 3331
S. (S. G.). *See* Goulart (Simon), *Senlisien.*
See Ursinus (Z.). Doctrinae. 1585.
S. (T.). Verses in Camb. Univ. Threno-thriambenticon. 1603. . 5616
S. (T.) [=T. Stocker]. *See* Bèze (T. de). The Popes Canons. 1587. 8°.
S. (T.). *See* Lessius (L.). Hygiasticon. 1634 etc. . . 5833 *etc.*
S. (T.), *of U.* *See* Scott (T.), of Utrecht.
S. (T. M.). *See* Sutcliffe (M.). De Tvrco-papismo. 1604.
S. (Tho.). Touch-stone of Prayer. 1602. 8°. 3382
S. (W.). Aunswere to the Proclamation of the Rebels in the North. 1569. 8°. 935
Newes. *See* Overbury (Sir T.). His Wife. 1638.
Verses in Overbury (Sir T.). His Wife. Ed. 11. 1622. . 3380
[=W. Stansby?] *See* Hooker (R.). Certayne divine tractates. 1618. F°.
— — Of the lawes. (1622.)
See Intrationes. Intrationum liber. 1546. F°.
— Smith (H.). Sixe sermons. 1594. 4°.
— — Ten sermons. 1596. 4°.
— — Two (foure) sermons. 1605. 4°.
— — Two sermons. 1613(–2.) 4°.
S. (W.), *D.D., Chaplaine to his Majestie.* 1606. *See* Smyth (W.).
S. (W.), *Gentleman.* *See* Stafford (W.). Compendious...examination. 1581.
S. (W.), *Strict. Obser.* *See* Staney (W.). Treatise of Penance. 1617.
Sabbath-day. *See* Soveraigne Antidote. 1636.
S. (W. R.). *See* Luther (M.). Every-dayes sacrifice. 1624. 12°.
Sabinus (Angelus). *See* Ovid. [Selected Works.] 1635.
Three responsive epistles. *See* Ovid. Heroicall Epistles. 1639. 8°.
Sabinus (Georgius). *See* Ovid. Metamorphoses. 1584.
Sabunde (R. de). Theologia naturalis. Frankfurt, 1635. 8°. . 6633
Sack met die stucken voor den Paus van Roomen. '1578' [1568]. 8°. 1459
Sackville (Thomas), earl of Dorset and baron Buckhurst. *See* Dorset (T. Sackville, earl of).
Sacra institutio baptizandi. *See* Manuale.
Sacrament of the Altar. *See* Primer. 1555. 8°. 636
Sadeel (Antonius). Disputationes. Cantabrigiae, 1584. 4°. . . 5507
Sadelerus (Andreas), *Britannus.* [*qu.* Sadler?] Bale (J.). Ill. Maj. Brit. script. 1548. . . . . . . 6314, 6315
Sadler (Andrew). *See* Sadelerus.
Sadler (John). Masquerade du Ciel. 1640. F°. 4405
Praxis medicorum. 1637. 12°. 5130
Verses in Camb. Univ. Carmen. 1635. 5770
See Vegetius Renatus (F.). Fovre bookes. 1572.
Safegard of Saylers or great Rutter. Trans. R. Norman. Augm. E. W. 1612. 4°. 7340
Saffron Walden. *See* Harvey (G.)...Gratulationum Valdinensium. 1578.
Sainctes (C. de). *See* Vigor (S.). Acts of the Dispute. 1602.
Saint Albans Abbey. *See* Paris (M.). Historia major. 1640.
Chronicle. *See* England. Chronicles of England. 1498, 1504, 1515.
St Andrews University. Decermina quædam philosophica. J. Wreittoun, Edinburgi, 1629. 4°. 5970
St George (Henry). *See* Brooke (R.). Discovery. 1622. F°.
St George (John). Verses in Guillim (J.). A display. 1611 *etc.* 3211 *etc.*

No.

Saint George (Richard), *Norrey King at Arms.* Verses in Speed (J.). The theatre. 1611. 3215
See Brooke (R.). Discovery. 1622. F°.
Saint Germain (C.). Dialogus de fundamentis legum Anglie et de conscientia. 1528. 8°. 347
— 1604. 8°. 2401
Dyaloge in Englysshe betwyxt a Doctoure of Dyuynyte and a Student in the Lawes of Englande. [1531.] 8°. . . 540
Fyrst dialoge in Englysshe with new additions. [1531?] 8°. . 541
Dialogve in English. 1604. 8°. 2402
— 1613. 8°. 3257
Secunde dialoge in Englysshe. Southwarke, 1530. 8°. . 5861
— — with new addycyons. Southwarke, 1531. 8°. . . 5862
Newe addicions. Berthelet, 1531. 8°. 424
Dyaloges in Englishe. R. Tottell, 1569. 8°. 1121
— R. Tottell, 1580. 8°. 1141
— R. Tottell, 1593. 8°. 1153
Salem and Bizance. 1533. 8°. 428
See Treatise concernynge. [153– .]
St John (Oliver). Speech to the lords in…Parliament…concerning Ship-money. 1640. 4°. 7055
St John (R.), *Clarenceux.* *See* Guillim (J.). A display. 1638.
Saint Peters Complaint. 1615 *etc.* *See* Southwell (R.).
St Trond. Sendbrief. 1581. 8°. 1549
S. Truyden. *See* St Trond.
Sala (Angelus). Opiologia…by T. Bretnor. 1618. 8°. . . . 3673
Salem and Bizance. 1533. *See* Saint Germain (C.).
Salerno. Schola Salernitana. *See* Regimen.
Sales (Francis de). *See* Francis *de Sales.*
Salesbury (William). *See* Bible. Welsh. 1620. F°.
— — N.T. 1567.
Saliceto (Gulielmus de). *See* Gulielmus *de Saliceto.*
Salignac (Baronne de). *See* Du Moulin (P.). A conference. 1615.
Salisbury Almanack. 1554. 16°. *See* Lon (H.).
Prognostication. 1569. *See* Lon (H.).
Salisbury (Jo.), *sen.* Verses in Salisbury (Sir T.). History of Joseph. 1636. 4023
Salisbury (Jo.), *jun.* Verses in Salisbury (Sir T.). History of Joseph. 1636. 4023
Salisbury (Margaret, countess of). [*Ad instantiam.*] *See* Erasmus. De immensa dei misericordia. 1533.
Salisbury (Robert Cecil, earl of). Answere to certaine scandalous Papers. 1606. 4°. 2597
See Exchequer Court. 1608.
— Playfere (T.). Caesaris svperscriptio. 1606.
Salisbury (Sir Thomas). History of Ioseph. 1636. 4°. . . . 4023
Verses in Biondi (G. F.). Eromena. 1632. 7753
Salkeld (John). Treatise of angels. 1613. 8°. 3400
Treatise of paradise. 1617. 8°. 3921
Sallustius. Opera omnia…cum Petri Ciacconii…notis. 1615. 8°. 7406
Cronycle of the warre agaynst Iugurth. Trans. A. Barclay. [Pynson, 1520?] F°. 310, 311
Two…Histories…Cateline…and…Iugurthe. 1608(9). F°. . 2768
See Durantinus (C. F.). Conspiracie of Catiline. 1557.
Salomon, *Jew and Physician.* Wonderfull Prophecie or pronostication. 1531…within…Gandt. May, 1543. 8°. 6107
Salmon (Peter), *K.C.C.* Verses in Camb. Univ. Lacrymae. 1619. 5689
— — Epithalam. 1625. 5702
Salter (Edw.). Verses in Camb. Univ. Genethl. 1631. . . . 5731
Salt. Theological and philosophical treatise. 1612. 4°. . . 2982

No.
Salter (Robert). Wonderfull Prophecies. 1627. 4°. . . . 5035
Salter (William). Verses in Sharpe (L.). Oratio. 1612. . . 3217
Saltern (George). Of the antient lawes of great Britaine. 1605. 4°. 2759
Saltmarsh (John). Holy discoveries and flames. 1640. 12°. . . 5014
Poemata sacra. Cantabrigiae, 1636. 8°. 5785
Verses in Russell (J.). The two...battels. 1634. . . . 5767
— Camb. Univ. Carmen. 1635. 5770
— Dugres (G.). 1636. 5781
Saltonstall (Wye). Clavis ad portam. Oxford, 1634. 8°. . . 7664
Picturae Loquentes. Ed. 2. 1635. 12°. 4640
See Eusebius. Ancient ecclesiasticall histories. 1636(-7). F°.
— Mercator (G.). Historia mundi. 1635.
— Ovid. Heroicall Epistles. 1639. 8°.
— — De ponto. 1640. 8°.
Salusbury. *See* Salisbury.
Saluste (Guillaume de), sieur Du Bartas. *See* Du Bartas.
Salviani (Ippolito). *See* Gesner (C.). Nomenclator. 1560. F°.
Salvianus Massiliensis. De gubernatione dei, etc. Oxoniæ, 1633. 12°. 5405
Quis dives salvus. Eng. trans. N.T. 1618. 8°. . . 6910
Second and third blast of retrait from plaies and theatres. 1580. 8°. 1421
Salzburg, Bp of. *See* Raitenau. 1979.
Sampson ( ). *See* Norfolk (Thomas Howard, duke of). Discourse. [1571?]
Sampson (John). *See* Awdelay (Jo.).
See Antiphoner Sarum. [1519-20.] 6155-6
Sampson (Richard). In priores quinquaginta psalmos. 1539. F°. . 452
Explanationis psalmorum, secunda pars. 1548. F°. . . 768
In D. Pauli epistolam ad Romanos atque in I Cor. breuissima explanatio. 1546. 8°. 763
Sampson (T.). Letter to the trew professors of Christes Gospell. 'Strasburgh,' 1554. 8°. 1054
[Prayers and Meditations.] 1592. 16°. 6803
Warning to take heede of Fowlers psalter. 1578. 8°. . . 1537
See Chrysostom. Sermon. 1550. 8°.
Samuell (Robert). Letters. *See* Coverdale (M.). Certain...letters. 1564.
Samways (P.), *T.C.* Verses in Camb. Univ. Carmen. 1635. . . 5770
— — Συνωδία. 1637. 5790
— — Voces. 1640. 5836
Sancer (John) [*pseud.* of S. Brinkley]. *See* Loarte (G.). Exercise. 1584.
Sancta Maria (Maurus à). *See* Maurus.
Sancto Paulo (Eustachius à). *See* Eustachius.
Sancto Vinculo (Claudius à). *See* Desainliens (C.).
Sandæus (Patricius). *See* Sands.
Sandeland (Andrew), *C.C.C.C.* Verses in Hawkins (W.). Corolla. 1634. 5803
Sanders (Nicolas). Antisanderus. 1593. *See* Cowell (J.).
Briefe treatise of vsvrie. Louvain, 1568. 8°. 6421
Rocke of the church. S. Omers, 1624. 8°. 7693
Supper of our lord. Louvain, 1566, Januar. 4°. . . . 6417
See Abbot (R.). The Mirrour. 1594.
— Acworth (G.). De Visibili Romanarchia. 1573.
— Clerke (B.). Fidelis servi...responsio. 1573. . . . 835
— Fulke (W.). D. Heskins, D. Sanders...ouerthrowne. 1579.
— Humphrey (L.). J. Juelli vita. 1573.
— Jewel (J.). A Confutation. 1567.
— Rich (B.). New Irish Prognostication. 1624.
— Whitaker (W.). Ad N. S. responsio. 1583.
Sanderson (John). Institutionum...libri iv. Oxoniæ, 1602. 8°. . 5261
Verses in Speed (J.). The theatre. 1611. 3215
Sanderson (Robert). Logicæ artis compendium. Ed. 2. Oxoniæ, 1618. 8°. 5333

No.
Sanderson (Robert), *cont.* Twelve sermons preached. 1632. 4°. . 4565
Two sermons. 1635. 4°. 4290
Sanderson (Thomas). *See* Bible, English (Royal). 1611. . . 2635
Sanderson (William). *See* Hues (R.). Tractatus de globis. 1594.
Sandes (Milo). Verses in Cambridge Lachrymae. 1587. . . 2123
Sandeus. *See* Sands.
Sandford (James). *See* Agrippa (H. C.). Of the Vanitie and vncertaintie of Artes. 1575. 4°.
Sandilands (James). Verses in Adamson (J.). Εἰσόδια. 1618. . 5960
Sandisius. *See* Sands.
Sandius (Jac.). Verses in Forbes (P.). Funerals. 1637. . . 6007
Sands (Patrick). Verses in Skene (Sir J.). Regiam. 1613. . 3458
— Napier (J.). Logarithmorum descriptio. 1614. . . 5952
— — Rabdologia. 1617. 5959
Theses and Verses in Adamson (J.). Εἰσόδια. 1618. . . 5960
Verses in Buchanan (G.). Ecphrasis. 1620. . . . 3595
— Abernethy (J.). Christian...treatise. 1630. . . . 4342
Sandsbury (John). Verses in Gwinne (M.). Vertumnus. 1607. . 3621
— Gwinne (M.). Nero. 1639. 4328
Sandys (E.). Sermons. 1585. 4°. 1652
— 1616. 4°. 3790
See Bible, Eng. (Bishops'). 1568.
— Luther (M.). Commentarie...vpon...Galathians. 1575 *etc.*
Sandys (Sir E.). Europae speculum. Hague, 1629. 4°. . . 6640
— 1632. 4°. 4618
— 1637. 4°. 4653
Relation of the state of religion. 1605. 4°. . . 2111, 2861
Sandys (George). Paraphrase vpon the divine poems. 1638 (1637). F°. 4736
Paraphrase upon the Psalmes of David and hymnes. 1636. 8°. . 4943
Relation of a journey. 1615. F°. 2281
— Ed. 3. 1627. F°. 4603
— 1632. F°. 4442
Sacrae heptades. 1625. 4°. *See* S. (G.).
See Grotius (H.). Christ's passion. 1640.
— Ovid. [Metamorphosis (Eng.).] 1632 *etc.*
[Vergil Æn. I.] *See* Ovid. Metamorphoses. 1640. F°.
Sandys (Sir Miles). Prima pars parvi opusculi. 1634. 12°. . . 4954
Sandys (Will). Verses in Oxford Univ. Horti. 1640. . . 5499
Sanford (H.). Verses in Horatius. Poemata. 1614. . . 2274–5
Sanford (James). Verses in Batman (S.). Doome. 1581. . . 1314
Sanford (John). Gods arrowe of the pestilence. Oxford, 1604. 8°. . 5270
Προπύλαιον...to the Spanish tongue. 1611. 4°. . . 3620
Verses in Godwin (T.). Romanae Historiæ Anthologia. 1614. . 5320
Sansbery. *See* Sandsbury.
Sansovino (F.). Quintessence of Wit. 1590. 4°. 2003
See Milles (T.) Treasvrie. 1613.
Sant-Perez (Hieronymo). *See* Sempere (G.).
Santa Maria, Juan de. *See* Juan.
Santarelli (Antonio). Articles...propounded to the Jesuites to subscribe ...14 March 1626. 'Rouan,' 1626. 4°. 4188
Santry (J. Barry, baron). *See* Barry.
Saona (Gulielmus Laurentius de). *See* Laurentius (Gulielmus) *de Saona.*
Sarate (Augustine). *See* Zarate.
Saravia (Hadrian à). Diversi tractatvs theologici. 1611 (–10). F°. 2266
De diversis ministrorum evangelii gradibus. 1590. 4°. . . 1726
De imperandi avthoritate. 1593. 4°. 1698
Defensio tractationis de diversis ministrorum evangelii gradibus. 1594. 4°. 1700
See Bible, English (Royal). 1611. 2635

No.
Saravia (Hadrian à), *cont.* [Licence] L'Obel (M. de)...in G. Rondelletij. 1605.
Sarcerius (E.). Common places of scripture. Trans. R. Taverner. 1538 Aug. 12. 8°. 7091
Sarpi (Paolo). Apology. 1607. 4°. 3624
— *See* Vignier (N.). Concerning...the Venetians. 1607. . . 3368
Cruell subtilty of ambition...concerning...the Valteline...Trans. Sir. T. Roe. [16—.] 4°. 4690
Discourse upon the...Valteline against the...Grisons...1628. 4°. 4689
Full and satisfactorie answer to the Bull by Paul V. 1606. 4°. 2083
Historia del Concilio Tridentino. 1619. F°. 3495
Historiae Concilii Tridentini libri octo. 1620. F°. . . 7528
Historie of the Councel of Trent. Trans. N. Brent. 1620. F°. 2665
— Ed. 2. 1629. F°. 2838
— Ed. 3. 1640. F°. 5015, 5016
History of the inquisition. Trans. R. Gentilis. 1639. 4°. . . 3724
History of the quarrels of pope Paul V. with the state of Venice. Trans. C. Potter. 1626. 4°. 3531
Interdicti Veneti historia de motu Italiae. Cantabrigiae, 1626. 4°. 5704
Quaestio quodlibetica. An liceat stipendia ... Cantabrigiæ, 1630. 4°. 5729
See Potter (Ch.). Sermon. 1629.
— Valtellina. 1628.
Sassen (Francis). *See* Lessius (L.). Hygiasticon. 1634.
Satyræ seriæ or the secrets of things. 1640. 12°. 3733
Saul (Arthur). Famous game of Chesse-play. 1640. 8°. . . . 5136
Saulnier (Gilbert), *Sieur Du Verdier.* Love and armes of the greeke princes. Trans. Earle of Pembroke. 1640. F°. . . . 4049
Saunder (Nicolas). *See* Sanders.
Saunders (Clement). *See* Fowler (J.). Shield of defence. 1612.
Saunders (Laurence). Letters. *See* Coverdale (M.). Certain...letters. 1564.
Saunderson (Robert). *See* Sanderson.
Savelli (T.). Relation of the death. 1620. 8°. 6541
Savile (Sir Henry). Praelectiones tresdecim...elementorum Euclidis. Oxonii, 1621. 4°. 5340
Rerum Anglicarum scriptores. 1596. F°. 1736
See Bible. English (Royal). 1611. 2635
— Bradwardine (T.). De Cavsa Dei. 1618.
— Chrysostom. Opera. 1613–2. F°.
— Gregory *Nazianzene.* Invectivæ. 1610.
— Lydiat (T.). Ad clarissimum virum. 1621.
— Oxford University. Vltima Linea. 1622.
— Tacitus. End of Nero etc. 1591 *etc.*
— [Type used at Cambridge.] *See* Bible N.T. (Greek). 1632. 8°. 5797–9
Savile (Sam.), *King's Coll.* Verses in Camb. Univ. Epicedium. 1612. 5665
Saviolo (V.). His practise. 1595. 4°. 1972
Savonarola (G.). Exposition...vpon the li. psalme. [1535?] 8°. . 577
Goodly exposycyon...vpon the li. Psalme. [After 1536.] 8°. . 586
Exposition...vpon...Miserere. [1548?] 4°. 771
Exposycyon...vpon...Miserere mei Deus...In te domine. *See* Primer. 1538 *etc.* 4°.
Meditacyon of Jerom de fararia vpon the Psalme of In te Domine speraui. *See* Primer. 1536. 8°.
An other meditation...upon the lxxx. Psalme. [Ab. 155–.] 8°. . 6729

No.

Savoy (Victor Amadeus I., duke of). *See* Victor Amadeus.
Saxony. *See* John Frederick, elector.
Saxton (Chr.). [35 maps of England.] 1579. F°. 6765
See Burton (W.). Description of Leicester Shire. [1622.]
— Camden (W.). Britannia. 1607 *etc.* . . . 1758 *etc.*
— Speed (J.). Theatre. 1611.
England. The Kingdome of England. Augmented by J. Speed. 1632. F°. 7546
Sayre (John). Verses in Camb. Univ. Lacrymae. 1619. . . 5689
Sc. (Anton), *B.A. Trin.* *See* Scattergood.
Scala Perfectionis. 1494. *See* Hilton (W.). 42
Scaliger (Joseph). *See* Bible. N.T. Greek. 1622, 1633.
— Lydiat (T.). Tractatus. 1605. 8°.
— — Defensio. 1607.
— — Emendatio. 1609.
— Sempill (Sir J.). Sacrilege. 1619.
Scaliger (Julius Cæsar). Verses in Buchanan (G.). Psalmorum Davidis. 1640. 5209
Scamp (Tho.). Verses *bis* in Camb. Univ. Epicedium. 1612. . 5665, 5666
Scanderbeg. *See* Arsanes. [1560?]
— La Vardin (J. de). Historie of. 1596.
Scapula (Joannes). Lexicon Græco-Latinum Novum. Editio ultima. 1619. F°. 7836
— Editio novissima. 1637. F°. 4028
Scarborough (Charles), *M.A. Caius.* Verses in Camb. Univ. Voces. 1640. 5836
Scaricæus (Matthaeus), *Kevinus.* Verses in Kis (S.). Tabulae. 1593. 4°. 7785
Scattergood (Anton), *T.C.C.* Verses in Camb. Univ. Fasciae. 1633. 5808
— Carmen. 1635 *bis.* 5770
— Συνῳδία. 1637. 5790
Scauranus (Thomas). Verses in Palingenius. Zodiacus. 1615 *etc.* 3266 *etc.*
Schaffhausen. Reformed Church. *See* Belijdenisse. 1568. 8°. . 7879
Senatus. *See* Kis (S.). Tabulae Analyticae. 1593. 4°. . 7785
Scharpius (Patricius). *See* Sharp.
Schede (Paul). *See* Melissus (P.), *Schedius.*
Schegkius (Jacobus). *See* Heiland (S.). Aristotelis Ethicorum libri. 1581. 8°.
Scheibler (Christopher). Philosophia compendiosa. Oxoniae, 1628. 8°. 5421
Scheprevus, *Oxoniensis.* *See* Shepreve (W.).
Schickard (Wilh.). Horologium hebraeum. Ed. 7. (Rota hebraea. Ed. 3.) 1638 (9). 8°. 7645
Schloer (Friedrich). Death of the two renowned Kings of Sweden and Bohemia. 1633. 4°. 3890
Schobinger (Heinrich). *See* Fabricius (W.). Lithotomia. 1640.
Scholasticall discourse. 1607. *See* Parker (R.).
Schomberg (Henri de). Relation...of the fight...neare to Castelnau-d'Ary. 1632. 4°. 3884
Schonaeus (Cornelius). Terentius Christianus, sive Comœdiæ duæ. Tobæus. Juditha, etc. Cantab., 1632. 8°. . . . 5747
— 1635. 8°. 7674
Schonerus (L.). De numeris geometricis. 1614. 4°. . . . 2277
Schottus (Andreas). *See* Sallustius. Opera. 1615. 8°.
Schulckenius (Adolphus). *See* Widdrington (R.). Cleare...confutation. 1616.
— Last reioynder. 1619 *etc.*
— Supplicatio. 1616.
Sclater (John). Verses in Camb. Univ. Threnothr. 1603. . . 5616
— Hippocrates. 1633. 5812
Sclater (William), *the elder.* Exposition...upon I and II Thessalonians. 1627. 4°. 4244

No.

Sclater (William), *the elder*, *cont.* Exposition...upon I and II Thessalonians. 1630. 4°. 4835
Briefe exposition...upon II Thessalonians. 1627. 4°. . . . 4421
— Ed. 2. 1629. 4°. 4537
Christians strength. Oxford, 1612. 4°. 5303
Key to the key of scripture. 1611. 4°. 3394
Ministers portion. Oxford, 1612. 4°. 5304
Quæstion of tythes. 1623. 4°. 4698
Sermon...at Taunton. 1616. 4°. 3912
Sermons Experimentall. 1638. 4°. 7929
Sermons. 1638. 4° 7929
Sick souls salve. Oxford, 1612. 4°. 5305
Three sermons. 1629. 4°. 3983
Sclater (William), *the younger*. Worthy communicant rewarded. [1639.] 4°. 5018
Verses in Hippocrates. 1631, 1633. . . . . . 5736, 5812
See Sclater (W.), *the elder*. Sermons. 1638. 4°. . . . 7929
— — Three sermons. 1629. 4°.
Scogan (Henry). *See* Chaucer (G.). Workes. 1532 *etc.* . 554 *etc.*
Scogan (John). *See* Skogan.
Scoloker (Antony). *See* Brief Sum. Bryefe summe of the whole Bible. [154–] *etc.*
— Just reckenyng. 1547. 8°.
— Viret (P.). Notable collection. 1548.
Scorte. *See* Short.
Scory (Edmond), Kt. Verses in Drayton (M.). Poems. 1630. 8°. 7930
See also Skory.
Scory (John). Verses in Coryat (T). Coryats Crudities. 1611. . 3076
See Augustine. Two bokes. [1556?]
Scot (Patrick). Table-book for princes. 1622. 8°. 4175
Scot (Reginald). Discoverie of witchcraft. 1584. 4°. . . . 1847
Scot (Thomas). God and the king. Cambridge, 1633. 4°. . . 5756
Scot (Thomas), *B.D.* *See* Scott (Thomas), *B.D.*
Scotland. *See* Edward VI. Epistola. 1548.
— Monipenny (J.). Certaine matters composed together. [1597?]
— Cecil (J.), *D.D.* A discoverye. [1599?] 6824
— Monipenny (J.). Abridgement of the Scots Chronicles. 1633.
— Reasons. 1638. 5986–7
— Charles I. Large declaration. 1639. F°.
— — Proclamation. 1639.
— Remonstrance. 1639.
Army. Intentions of the armie of the Kindome of Scotland. 1640. 4°. 6348
— *See* Off. Publ. Demands. 1640.
Church. Confession of the true and christian Fayth. [1581.] 8°. 1908
— General Assembly. 1618. Perth. *See* Cowper (W.). Life. 1619.
— — *See* Lindsay (D.). True narration. 1621.
— *See* Gillespie. 1637.
— Principall acts of the solemne generall assemblie...21 Nov. 1638. Edinburgh, 1639. F°. 5965
— Protestation. 1638. 4°. 6011, 6012
— Declinator and Protestation of the Archbishops. 21 November 1638. 1639. 4°. 5155
— *See* Reasons for a General Assembly.
— Answer to the...Marques of Hammilton. Edinburgh, 1639. 4°. 5989
— *See below*. Episcopal Church. Declinator. 1639.
— Confession of the Faythe. 1561. 8°. 1297
— — 1580. 1638. 4°. 6367, 6662, 7041
Informations from the Estaits. 1640. 4°. 7679
True representation of the proceedings. 1640. 4°. . . . 7680

No.

Scotland. Church, *cont.* Reasons for which the Service Book...ought to be refused. 1638. 4°. 5987
— Short relation. 1638. 4°. 7042
— *See* Beast is wounded. 1638.
— — Burne (N.). Disputation. 1581.
— — Discipline. First and second booke of Discipline. 1621.
— History. *See* Knox (J.). 1587. 8°.
— *See* Informations. 1608.
— — Psalms. 1632. 4°.
— Gillespie (G.). Dispute against the english-popish ceremonies. 1637. 4°.
— *See* Short relation of the State. 1638.
Covenant. Answers of some brethren...to...the ministers...in Aberdene. 1638. 4°. 5000
— Protestation of the noblemen, barrons...of the Confession of Faith...the 4. of Julij. 1638. 4°. 5976
— — 22 Sept. 1638. 1638. 4°. 5988
— Protestation of the generall assemblie of...Scotland...Glasgow, 28, 29 November 1638. Glasgow, 1638. 4°. . 6011, 6012
— *See* Aberdeen University. Generall Demands. 1638.
— — Corbet (J.). Vngirding of the Scotish Armour. 1639.
— — — Epistle. 1640.
— — Leslie (H.). Speech. 1638. 4°.
— — — Examen. 1639.
Episcopal Church. *See* Declinator and protestation. 1639. 4°. 5155
Parliament. *See* Informations. 1608.
Statutes. *See* Statutes (Scotland).
Scott (James). Verses in Adamson (J.). *Εἰσόδια.* 1618. . . . 5960
Scott (Tho.). Aphorismes of state. Utrecht, 1624. 4°. . . . 6644
Belgicke Pismire. 1622. 4°. 6933, 6934
Belgicke Pismire...the Projector. 1623. 8°. 6943
Belgick Souldier. Dort, 1624. 4°. 6513
Certaine reasons and arguments of policie. 1624. 4°. . 6956
Christs politician and Salomons pvritan. 1616. 4°. . . . 3913
Digitus dei. [Ab. 1623.] 4°. 6949
Experimentall discoverie of Spanish practises. 1623. 4°. . . 6944
— 1624. 4°. 6957
Second part of the Spanish practises. 1624. 4°. . . . 6959
Highwaies of God and the King. 1623. 4°. 6945
— *See below* Vox populi. 1622–4.
Newes from Parnassus. 'Helicon.' 1622. 4°. 6935
Projector. 1623. 4°. 6946
Robert earle of Essex his ghost. 1624. 4°. 6958
Sir W. Rawleigh's ghost. Utrecht, 1626. 4°. 6646
Spaniards perpetuall designes. 1624. 4°. 6960
Speech made in...Parliament...by Sir E. Cecill. 1621. 4°. . 6926
— 1624. 4°. 6961
Votivae angliae. Utrecht, 1624. 4°. . . . . 6645, 6645 A
Vox coeli. 1624. 4°. 6963
Vox dei. [1624?] 4°. 6962
Vox populi vox dei etc. (11 tracts). 1622–3. 4°. 6948
Vox populi. 1620. 4°. 6648–9
— Part 2. 1624. 4°. 6650–1
Vox regis. [1624?] 4°. 6964
See Excellent...discourse. 1626. 6972
— Palatinate. A brief information. 1624.
Scott (William). Verses in Wilson (Sir T.). Vita. 1551. . . . 631–
— Adamson (J.). *Εἰσόδια.* 1618. 5960
Scotus (Joannes Duns). *See* Duns.
Scribonius (Gulielmus Adolphus). *See* Bright (T.). In physicam... Animaduersiones. 1584.

No.
Scroop (Lawrence). *See* Anderton (L.), *alias* Scroop.
Scruby (James). Verses in Baro (P.). In Jonam. 1579. . . 850
Scudamore (Jas.). Oxf. Univ. Horti. 1640. 5499
Scudder (Henry). The christians daily walke. Ed. 7. 1637. 12°. 7889
Scultetus (Abraham). Secular sermon. 1618. 4°. 3328
Verses in Ussher (J.). Gravissimæ quæstiones. 1613. . . 2798
Scupoli (Lorenzo). Spiritual conflict. Rouen, 1613. 12°. . . 6252
Seager (Francis). *See* Segar.
Seaman (J.). *See* Seman.
Seaman (L.). *See* Sibbs (R.). Glance of heaven. 1638. 8°.
Sebastian, King of Portugal. *See* Teixeira (J.). Strangest adventure. 1601. 4°. 7765
Second Parallel. 1612. *See* Featley (D.).
Secular Priests. *See* Antiquodlibet.
— Bell (T.). Anatomie of popish tyrannie. 1603.
— Bradshaw (W.). Humbler motives. 1601.
— Jesuites Catechisme. 1602.
— Watson (W.).
— Wisbech. True relation. 1601.
Sedan. *See* La Nove (F. de). The declaration. 1589.
Seddon (John). *See* Sparke (T.). Catechisme. 1588. 4°.
Sedgwick (J.). Bearing and burden of the spirit. 1639. 12°. . 7599
See Sibbes (R.). Beames of divine light. 1639.
— — Evangelicall Sacrifices. 1640.
— — Light from heaven. 1638.
Sedgwick (Obadiah). Christs counsell to...Sardis. 1640. 8°. . . 5142
Sedgwick (William), *G. and C.C.* Verses in Du Praissac. The art of warre. 1639. 5834
Sedley (Isaac), *Magd. Coll.* Verses in Camb. Univ. Carmen. 1635. 5770
— Συνῳδία. 1637. 5790
Sedley (John). Verses in Oxf. Univ. Magd. Coll. Luctus. 1612. . 5302
Seeing of Urines. R. Bankes. [1526?] 4°. 370
J. Walley. [1550?] 8°. 1009
Segar (Francis). Certayne Psalmes. 1553. 8°. 921
Segar (Sir W.). Honor Military and Civill. 1602. F°. . . 2575
Verses in Guillim (J.). Display. 1611 *etc.* . . . . 3211 *etc.*
— Brooke (R.). Discovery. 1622. 2793
See Booke of Honor. 1590.
— Philipot (J.). Cities Advocate. 1629.
Seile (Henry). *See* Augustus. 1632.
Seissell. *See* Seyssel.
Sejanus. *See* Matthieu (P.). Vnhappy Prosperitie. 1632. . . 1639
— — Remarkable considerations. 1638.
Selden (John). Brief discourse concerning...Parliament. 1640. 4°. 7056
De Dis Syris. 1617. 8°. 3122
De iure naturali et gentium. 1640. F°. 5116
De successionibus. 1631. 4°. 3183
— 1636. F°. 5106
Duells or single combat. 1610. 4°. 3575
Historie of tithes. 1618. 4°. 6911
Jani anglorum facies altera. 1610. 8°. 3389
Mare clausum. 1635. F°. 3198
— [Leyden,] 1636. 12°. 6492
Marmora arundelliana. 1628. 4°. 3171
Titles of honor. 1614. 4°. 3104
— Ed. 2. 1631. F°. 3184
Verses in Drayton (M.). Poems. 1630. 8°. 7926
— Purchas (S.). Pilgrimage. 1613 *etc.* . . . . 7848 *etc.*
— Jonson (B.). Workes. 1616. 3115
— Hopton (A.). Concordancy. 1635. 3956

No.

Selden (John), *cont.* *See* Brooke (R.). Discovery of errours. 1622. F°.
— Eadmer. Historiæ. 1623.
— Fortescue (Sir J.). De Laudibus Legum Angliæ. 1616.
— Montagu (R.). Diatribæ vpon the...History of Tithes. 1621.
— Nettles (S.). Answer to the...history of tithes. 1625.
— Sclater (W.). Quæstion of tythes. 1623.
— Sempill (Sir J.). Sacrilege. 1619.
— Tillesley (R.). Animadversions. 1619 *etc.*
Seller (John). Sermon against halting betweene two opinions. 1611. 4°. 2748
Seman (John). Verses in Cheke (Sir J.). De obitu M. Buceri. 1551. 734–
Samper (Geronimo). *See* Sempere (G.).
Sempere (Geronimo). Verses in Montemayor (J. de). Diana. 1598. F°. 7924
Sempill (Sir James). Sacrilege sacredly handled. 1619. 4°. . 3331
Semple (William). Speech in Adamson (J.). Εἰσόδια. 1618. . . 5960
Seneca. Tragoediae. 1589. 8°. 2185
L. et M. Annæi Senecae atque aliorum tragoediae. Animadversionibus (T. Farnabii). 1613. 8°. 7781
— 1624. 8°. 3444
Workes. Trans. T. Lodge. 1614. F°. 3103
— 1620. F°. 3133
Hercules Furens (Lat. Eng.). Trans. J. Heywood. 1561. 8°. . 7220
Thyestes. Trans. J. Heywood. 1560. Mart. 26. 8°. . . 7087
Booke of consolation to Marcia. 1635. 4°. 4115
Discourses upon Seneca. 1601 *etc.* *See* Cornwallis (Sir W.). Essayes. 1606 *etc.*
Separatists. *See* Proclamation. 1618. 4°. 7914
Sephardi (Moses), *Rabbi*. *See* Alfunsi (P.).
Seres (William), *printer*. *See* S. (W.). Aunswere. 1569.
Serle (Jo.). Verses in Gardiner (E.). Triall. 1610 *etc.* . 2505 *etc.*
Serlio (Seb.). First (—fift) book of Architecture. 1611. F°. . 2891
Sermon. [John iv. 22.] *See* Epistle. Epistell exhortatorye. [1560?]
[Rom. xii. 3–8.] *See* Fruitful Sermon.
Preached before the Queenes Maiestie. 1575. *See* Young (J.).
Serranus (Johannes). *See* Serres (J. de).
Serres (J. de). Commentaries of the Ciuill warres in Fraunce and... Flaunders. Part iv. 1576. 4°. 1487
General inventorie of the history of France...vnto...1598. Trans. E. Grimeston. 1607. F°. 3567
— Contynued by P. Mathew...unto 1622. By E. Grimstone. 1624. F°. 3603
Godlie...commentarie vpon...Ecclesiastes. 1585. 8°. . . 2114
Life of...J. Colignie Shatilion. 1576. 8°. 1531
Three partes of Commentaries...Trans. T. Timme. 1574. 4°. 7279
See Pelegromius (S.) Synonymorum sylva. 1603 *etc.*
Serres (Olivier de). Perfect vse of silk wormes. 1607. 4°. . . 2949
See Estienne (C.). Maison Rustique. 1616.
Servius (Honoratus), *grammarian*. *See* Anwykyll (J.). Compendium totius grammatice. [1489.]
Seton (Alexander). Verses in Cambridge Lachrymæ. 1587. . 2123
Seton (John). Dialectica. Annott. P. Carteri. Acc. G. Buclæi. Arithmetica. 1611. 8°. 3249
— Cantab., 1631. 8°. 5739
Panegyrici in Victoriam...Mariae...congratulatio. 1553. 4°. . 740
Seven points of true love. *See* Book of diuerse...matters... [1490.]
Seven Profits of Tribulation. *See* Book of diuerse...matters. [1490.]
Seven Sheddings of the blode of Ihesu cryste. W. de Worde, 1509. 4°. 161

No.

Seven Wise Men. Sage and Prudent Saynges. *See* Cato. Preceptes. 1560. 16°.
Severn (Tho.). Verses *bis* in Oxf. Univ. Horti. 1640. . . . 5499
Seyliard (Thom.). Verses in Camb. Univ. Anthologia. 1632. . 5741
— — Carmen. 1635. 5770
— — Voces. 1640. 5836
Seymour (Edward), earl of Hertford, *afterwards* duke of Somerset. *See* Somerset.
Seys (Evan). Verses in Camdeni Insignia. 1624. 5346
Seyssel (Claudius de), *abp.* *See* Thucydides. Hystory. 1550.
Sh. ( ). *See* Hooper (J.). Apologye. 1562.
Shacklock (Richard), *M.A.* *See* Hosius (J.). Moste excellent treatise. 1565.
Shakespeare (William). Comedies, histories and tragedies. Ed. 1. 1623. F°. 3972
— Ed. 2. 1632. F°. 4619
Troublesome Raigne of John King of England. 1622. 4°. 4509
Romeo and Juliet. 1637. 4°. 4996
Taming of the Shrew. 1631. 4°. 3185
Tragedy of Hamlet. 1637. 4°. 4995
Poems. 1640. 8°. 4681
Sharp (Patrick). Doctrinae christianae brevis explicatio. Edinburgh, 1599. 8°. 5940
Sharpe (Andrew), *M.A.*, *Procurator General.* Verses in Sharpe (L.). Oratio. 1612. 3217
Sharpe (Edward), *B.D.* Verses in Sharpe (L.). Oratio. 1612. . 3217
Sharpe (Leonell). Dialogus inter Angliam et Scotiam. Cantab., 1603. 8°. 5620
Novum fidei symbolum. 1612. 4°. 2270
Oratio funebris in honorem Henrici...Principis. 1612. 4°. . 3217
Sermon...at Cambridge. Cambridge, 1603. 8°. 5621
Sharpe (Rob.). Verses in Oxf. Univ. Horti. 1640. 5499
Sharpe (William), *B.D.* Verses in Sharpe (L.). Oratio. 1612. . 3217
Sharphell (Ed.). Verses in Davies (J.). Humours Heau'n on Earth. 1609. 2438
Shatilion (Iasper Colignie). *See* Coligny (G. de).
Shaw (John). Bibliorum summula. 1623. 8°. 7381
Shaxton (Nicolas), *bp.* *See* Bible (Coverdale) [Title]. 1535. F°. . 6280
[Six Articles.] *See* Crowley (R.). Confutation. 1548.
Sheafe (Edmund). Verses in Camb. Univ. Lacrymæ. 1619. . . 5689
Gerhard (J.). Prayers. 1625 *etc.* . . . . . 3321 *etc.*
— Meditations and Prayers. 1631 *etc.* . . . . . 5735 *etc.*
Sheafe (Grindal), *K.C.C.* Verses in Camb. Univ. Genethl. 1631. 5731
— Hippocrates. 1631 *etc.* . . . . 5736 *etc.*
— Camb. Univ. Anthologia. 1632. 5741
Sheff. (Phi.), *Em. Coll.* Verses in Camb. Univ. Epicedium. 1612. . 5665
Sheffield (James), *T.C.C.* Verses in Camb. Univ. Carmen. 1635. . 5770
— Συνῳδία. 1637. 5790
Sheffield (John). Verses in Cheke (Sir J.). De obitu M. Buceri. 1551. 734
Sheldon (Richard). Certain general reasons...of the Oath of Allegiance. 1611. 4°. 2971
First sermon...after his Conuersion. 1612. 4°. 3779
Motives...for...renouncing of Communion with...Rome. 1612. 4°. 3088
Survey of the miracles of the church of Rome. 1616. 4°. . 3914
Shelford (Richard). *See* Prynne (W.). Quench-coale. 1637.
Shelford (Robert). Five pious and learned discourses. Cambridge, 1635. 4°. 5774
Shelton (Tho.). Centurie of similies. 1640. 8°. 7648
Verses in Rowland (R.). Restitution. 1605 *etc.* . . 6140 *etc.*
See Cervantes. Don Quixote. 1612.
Shepherds Kalendar. W. Powell. 1556. F°. 1014

No.

Shepherds Kalendar, *cont.* [Ab. 1556.] F°. 6738
[Ab. 158–?] F°. 6770
Shepreve (John). Argumenta in nouum Testamentum. *See* Shaw (J.). Bibliorum svmmvla. 1623. 8°.
Shepreve or Shepery (William). *See* Gemma Fabri. 1598.
Sherard (Benedict). *See* Leitrim.
Sherard (Philip). Verses in Oxf. Univ. Horti. 1640. 5499
Sheriffs. Office of Sheriffs. 1552. 8°. 1003
Sherman (Abraham). *See* Chaloner (E.). Six sermons. 1629. 4°.
Sherman (John), *M.A.*, *T.C.C.* Verses in Camb. Univ. Συνωδία. 1637. 5790
Sherman (Mar.). Verses in Camb. Univ. Lacrymæ. 1619. 5689
Sherry (Richard). Treatise of Schemes and Tropes. [1550.] 8°. 893
Treatise of the Figures of Grammer and Rhetorike. 1555. 8°. 1107
See Brenz (J.). Verye fruitful Exposicion. (1550.)
'SHertogenbosch. *See* Hertogenbosch, 'S.
Sherwin (Ralph). *See* White (P.). Answeare. 1582. 8°.
Sherwood (Robert). *See* Bédé (Jean). Right...of Kings. 1612.
Shetterden (Nicholas). Letter. *See* Coverdale (M.). Certain...letters. 1564.
Shilling (Andrew). *See* East Indies. The true relation. 1622.
Shipmoney, Case of. 1640. 4°. 7057
Case of...briefly discoursed. 1640. 4°. 7058
Shipwrights Company. Charter. [Ab. 1612?]. 4°. 6888
Shirley (Sir Charles). Verses in Oxf. Univ. Horti. 1640. 5499
Shirley (James). Hide parke. 1637. 4°. 4655
Humorous courtier. 1640. 4°. 4682
Maides revenge. 1639. 4°. 4670
Royall master. 1638. 4°. 4665
St Patrick for Ireland. Part 1. 1640. 4°. 5159
Triumph of peace. 1633. 4°. 4893
Verses in Massinger (P.). Renegado. 1630. 4543
Shirley (Sir Robert). *See* Herbert (Sir T.). Relation. 1634.
Shirrye (Richard). *See* Sherry.
Short description of Antichrist. *See* Olde (J.).
Short dialogue proving that the ceremonyes...are defended. 1605. 4°. 6864
Short instruction. Scorte instrvction vpon the...vse of Calivers. *See* Geyn (J. de). Maniement d'Armes. [1619.] 4°. 6647
Short questions and answeares, contayning the Summe of Christian Religion. 1614. 8°. 1834
Short relation of the state of the Kirk of Scotland. 1638. 4°. 7042
Short treatise contayning all the Principall Grounds of Christian Religion. Ed. 9 (1633). Ed. 11 (1637). *See* Ball (J.).
Shorte treatise of politike pouuer. 1556 *etc.* *See* Ponet (J.).
Shotbolt (Jo.). Verses in Camb. Univ. Epicedium. 1612. 5665
Shoute (T.)? *See* Viret (P.). Christian Instruction. 1573.
Shrewsbury School. [Consecration of Chapel.] *See* Price (S.). Beauty of holines. 1618. 4°.
Shute (John). First and chief grovndes of architecture. 1563. F°. 1211
See Viret (P.). Christian Instruction. 1573.
Shute (Nathaniel). Corona charitatis. 1626. 4°. 3165
Shute (W.). *See* Fougasses (T. de). Generall historie of...Venice. 1612.
See Maurice of Nassau. Triumphs. 1613.
Sibbs (Richard). Beames of divine light. 1639. 4°. 4478
Bowels opened. 1639. 4°. 7824
— (frag.) [1641 or 1648?] 4°. 4479 (corr.)
Bruised reede. Ed. 5. 1635. 12°. 7835
— 1639. *See above:* Beames of divine light.
Christs exaltation. 1639. 12°. 7896
Divine meditations. 1638. 12°. 7617
Evangelicall Sacrifices. Tom. 3. 1640. 4°. 5143

No.
Sibbs (Richard), *cont.* Fountain sealed. 'Ed. 2.' 1637. 12°. . 4029
— 'Ed. 3.' 1638. 12°. 4034
Glance of heaven. 1638. 12°. 5198
Light from heaven. 1638. 4°. 4122
Returning backslider. 1639. 4°. 4480
Riches of mercie. 1638. 12°. 5168
Saints cordialls. 1637. F°. 4312
Soules conflict. 1635. 8°. 4291
— 1636. 8°. 4304
— Ed. 4. 1638. 8°. 4323
Two sermons. Ed. 3. 1637. 12°. 4030
— Ed. 4. 1638. 12°. 4035
Verses in Camb. Univ. Fasciæ. 1633. 5808
See Ball (J.). Treatise of faith. 1637.
— Baynes (P.). Commentarie upon Ephesians. 1618. 4°. . 7908
— Capel (R.). Tentations. 1635 *etc.* . . . . 4363 *etc.*
— Gataker (T.). Christian Constancy crowned. 1624. 4°.
— Preston (J.). Breastplate. 1630 (-1) *etc.*
— — New Covenant. 1629 *etc.* 4°.
— — Saints daily exercise. 1629 *etc.*
— — Saints qvalification. 1634.
— Texeda (F. de). Texeda Retentus. 1623.
— W. (H.). Θρηνοικος. 1640.
Siberch (John). *See* Baldwin. De altaris sacramento. 1521.
Sibthorp (Sir Christopher). Friendly advertisement. Dublin, 1622. 6024
— 1623. 4°. 6025
Reply to an answere. 1625. 4°. 6030
Surreplication to the reioynder. 1627. 4°. 6033
Apostolike Obedience. 1627. 4°. 4243
Counter-plea to an apostataes pardon. 1618. 4°. . . 4158, 4159
Sicelides. 1631. *See* Fletcher (P.).
Sictor (Johannes). Lacrymae reipublicae Londinensis. 1637. 4°. . 4656
Sidenham (George). *See* Sydenham.
Sidley (Sir William). Verses in Camden (W.). Britannia. 1637. . 3055
See Owen (J.). Epigrammatum. 1618.
Sidney (Lady Frances). Verses in Cambridge Lachrymae. 1587. . 2123
Sidney (Sir Philip). Countesse of Pembrokes Arcadia. Ed. 2. 1593. F°. 2715
— Ed. 3. 1598. F°. 7378
— Ed. 5. Dublin, 1621. F°. 6022
— Ed. 6. 1627. F°. 7493
— Ed. 7. 1629. F°. 2562
— Ed. 9. 1638. F°. 4920
See Brooke (F. Greville, first lord). Certaine...workes... 1633.
— Cambridge Lachrymae. 1587.
— Mornay (P. de). A Woorke. 1587 *etc.*
Sidney (Sir Robert). Verses in Cambridge Lachrymae. 1587. . 2123
Sidney (Thomas). Verses in Cambridge Lachrymae. 1587. . 2123
Sidney (Sir William). *See* Sylvester (J.). Parliament of vertues. [Ab. 1614.] 8°.
Siena. [1566.] *See* Ubaldino (P.). Militia. 1597.
Sigismund III. *of Poland.* *See* Nixon (A.). Warres of Swethland. 1609.
Sigiswicke (William). *See* Sedgwick.
Sigonius (C.). *See* p. 1744 note on no. 7286.
Silesio (Mariano). Arcadian Princesse. 1635. 8°. 4017
Silhon. *See* Balzac. Letters. 1634. 4°.
Silvester, *Pope.* *See* Sylvester.
Silvester (Edward). Verses in Hippocrates. 1633. 5812
— Verses in Oxf. Univ. Horti. 1640. 5499
Sim, *the Butler.* Verses in Hoby (Sir E.). Curry combe. 1615. . 3111

No.
Simeon, *Metaphrastes*. Vitæ sanctorum evangelist. Johannis et Lucæ. Oxoniæ, 1597. 8°. 5245
See Chrysostom...opera. 1613.
Simler (Josias). *See* Vermigli (P.). Common Places. 1583.
— — Loci Communes. 1583.
— — Most Godly Prayers. 1569. 8°.
Simmias. [*Gr. Lat.*] *See* Poetae minores. 1635.
Simon, *Anker of London Wall*. *See* Fruit of Redemption. 1514.
Simonides. [*Gr. Lat.*] *See* Poetae minores. 1635.
Simonides (A.). *See* Simson.
Simonides (Wilhelmus). *Qu.* Simonson or Sympson? Verses in Skene (Sir J.). Regiam. 1613. 3458
Simpson (William). *See* Sympson.
Sims (Valentine), *Printer*. *See* Conway (Sir J.). Poesie. 1611.
Simson (A.). Verses in Adamson (J.). Εἰσόδια. 1618. . . 5960
See Simson (P.). The historie of the church. 1624.
Simson (Archibald). Sacred septenarie. 1638. 4°. . . 5095
Simson (Cuthbert). *See* Symson.
Simson (Edward). Mosaica. Cantab., 1636. 4°. 5786
Simson (Patrick). Historie of the church. 1624. 4°. . . . 3863
— Ed. 3. 1634. F°. 3893
Short compend of the...III centuries. Edinburgh, 1613. 4°. . 5950
— IIII, V, and VI centuries. 1615. 4°. 5954
— VII, VIII, and IX centuries. 1616. 4°. 5955
Sinan (Sheikh). *See* Muhammad. Mohammedis Imposturæ. 1615.
Singleton (Hugh). *See* Regius (U.). Necessary instruction. 1579.
Singleton (Isaac). Downefall of Shebna. 1615. 4°. . . . 3467
Singleton (William). Verses in Massinger (P.). Emperovr. 1632. . 3998
Singleton (Wilhelm), *pseud.* *See* Lessius (L.). 1619 *etc.*
Sion Monastery [*ab.* 1530]. *See* Mirror of Our Lady. 1530.
Sipontinus. *See* Perottus (N.), *Sipontinus*.
Six godlie Treatises necessarie for Christian instruction. 1608. 8°. . 3627
Sixe Demands from an unlearned protestant. 1609. 4°. . . 2890
Sixesmith (Thomas). *See* Brerewood (E.). Tractatvs Ethici. 1640.
— — Tractatvs qvidam. 1628 *etc.*
Sixtus V. Brutish thunderbolt. 1586. 8°. 2061
[De Henrici tertii morte sermo. 1589.] *See* Hurault (M.). Antisixtus (Lat.). 1590. 4°.
— — (English). 1590. 4°.
— — *See* Warmington (W.). Moderate defence. 1612.
See W. (R.). Martine Mar-Sixtus. 1591.
Skelton (J.). Bowge of court. W. de Worde. [15—.] 4°. . 242
Magnyfycence. J. Rastell. [15—.] F°. 354
Skene (Sir John). De verborum significatione. Ed. 1. Edinburgh, 1597. F°. 5936
— Ed. 2. 1599. F°. 5941
Regiam majestatem: Scotiae veteres leges. Edinburgh, 1609. F°. 5966
— J. Bill. 1613. F°. 3458
Regiam majestatem. The auld lawes. Edinburgh, 1609. F°. . 5967
See Scotland. Statutes. 1597.
Skinner (Sir John). *See* Rapta Tatio. 1604.
Skinner (Mat). Verses in Oxf. Univ. Horti. 1640. . . . 5499
Skinner (Robert). Sermon...before the king. Dec. 3. 1634. 4°. . 4724
Skinner (Ste.). Verses in Oxf. Univ. Horti. 1640. . . . 5499
Skinner (Vincent). *See* Gonsalvius. Discovery. 1568 *etc.*
Skip (John). *See* Institution of a Christian Man. 1537. 4°. 439 and page 1730
Skippon (Lucas). Verses in Camb. Univ. Fasciae. 1633. . . 5808
— Hippocrates. 1633. 5812

No.

Skogan (Henry). *See* Scogan.
Skogan (John). *See* Chaucer (G.). Temple of Brass. [1477–8.]
Skory (Edmond). Extract out of the historie of the last French king Henry the fourth. 1610. 4°. 2630
See also Scory.
Slatyer (John). Verses in Slatyer (W.). The history. 1621. . 3137
Slatyer (William). Genethliacon...pedigree of King James, and King Charles. 1630. F°. 4433
History of Great Britanie. 1621. F°. 3137
Psalmes, or Songs of Sion...Christmas Carols. [Ab. 1634.] 12°. . 5017
Sleepe (Ant.). Verses in Camb. Univ. Epicedium. 1612. . . 5665
Sleidanus (J.). Famouse Cronicle. 1560. F°. 792
Key of History. Ed. 2. 1631. 12°. 4952
— Ed. 3. 1635. 12°. 7641
See Froissart (J.). Epitome. 1608.
— Languet (T.). Coopers Chronicle. 1560 *etc.*
Sloper (John), *K.C.C.* Verses in Hippocrates. 1631 *etc.* . . 5736 *etc.*
— Camb. Univ. Anthologia. 1632. 5741
Sm. (R.). Verses in Barlow (W.). Vita R. Cosin. 1598. . . 1707
Smallwood (A.). Verses in A. (G.). Pallas armata. 1639. . . 5170
Smarlet (Josua), *practitioner.* Verses in Clowes (W.). A right... Treatise. 1602. 2013
Smart (Ithiel). *See* Randall (J.). Twenty-nine lectvres. 1631.
Smart (Peter). Sermon...in...Durham. 1628. 4°. . . . 6987
— 1640. 4°. 7620
Smeton (Thomas). Ad virulentum A. Hamiltonii...dialogum...responsio. Edinburgi, 1579. 4°. 5915
Smiglecius (Martin). Logica. Oxonii, 1634. 4°. . . . 5410
Smith ( ), *a popish Priest.* [pseud.] *See* Norris (S.), D.D.
Smith (Ed.). Verses in Camb. Univ. Lacrymae. 1619. . . 5689
Smith (G.), qu. W. Smyth? Verses in Camb. Univ. Threnothr. 1603. 5616
Smith (Gervase). Verses in Parkhurst (J.). Ludicra. 1573. . 838
Smith (Henry). Benefite of contentation. 1590. 8°. . . . 7355
Christians sacrifice. 1591. 8°. 7318
Examination of Vsurie. 1591. 8°. 7368
Gods arrow against atheists. 1604. 4°. 2933
— 1611. 4°. 2972
— 1614. 4°. 2523
— 1631. 4°. 7830
— 1632. 4°. 4847
Jvrisprvdentiae medicinæ et theologiæ dialogus dulcis. 1592. 8°. 2413
Micro-cosmo-graphia. Transl. *See* Sylvester (J.). Parliament of vertues. [Ab. 1614.] 8°.
Preparative to marriage. [1591?] 8°. 7319
Satans encompassing the earth. 1592. 8°. . . . 7792 (=2380)
Sinfull mans search. (Maries choice.) 1592. 8°. . . . 2381
Three prayers. 1592. 8°. 1888
Treatise of the Lords supper. 1591. 8°. 7369
Wedding garment. 1591. 8°. 6799
Two or more Sermons, in chronological order.
Sermons. T. Orwin for T. Man, 1592. 8°. 2216
Thirteene sermons. 1592. 8°. 7791
Sixe sermons. R. Field for R. Dexter, 1594. 4°. . . . 2234
[Qu. sermons? 'Widow Orwin for T. Man, 1595.'] 4°. . 7372
Ten sermons. R. Field for R. Dexter, 1596. 8°. . . . 2242
Three sermons. F. Kingston for N. Ling, 1604. 4°. . . 2934
Two sermons (foure sermons). For W. Leake, 1605. 4°. . 7459
— T. Creede for C. Burby, 1605. 4°. 7436
Sermons. F. Kingston for T. Man, 1611. 4°. . . . 2973
Six sermons. T. Dawson for N. Bourne, 1612. 4°. . . 1832

No.

Smith (Henry), *cont.* *Two or more Sermons, in chronological order.*
Two sermons. (Foure sermons.) H. Lownes for W. Leake, 1613(2). 4°. 2517
Three sermons. For J. Smethwick, 1613. 4°. 3097
Sixe sermons. T. Dawson for N. Bourne, 1614. 4°. . . . 1833
— W. Stansby for W. Barret, 1615. 4°. 3113
Three sermons. H. Lownes for J. Smethwick, 1616. 4°. . 2527
— 1632. 4°. 7828
[Twelve sermons.] 1632. 4°. 7829
Verses in Camb. Univ. Lacrymæ. 1619. 5689
— — Carmen. 1635. 5770
Smith (John), *Captain*, 'Hungariensis.' Verses in Norton (R.). The Gunner. 1628. 4535
Smith (John), *M.A.*, *fellow of Magd. Coll. Camb.* Verses in Camb. Univ. Carmen. 1635. 5770
Smith (John), *fellow of Magd. Coll. Oxon.* Verses in Oxf. Univ. Magd. Coll. 1612. 5302
— Camdeni Insignia. 1624. 5346
See Jewel (J.). Apologia. 1639.
Smith (John), *Governor of Virginia.* Advertisements for the unexperienced planters of New England...Virginia. 1631. 4°. 4842
Generall historie of Virginia, New England and the Summer Isles. 1624. F°. 3864
True travels...together with a continuation of his generall history of Virginia...since 1624. 1630. F°. 4836
Smith (John), *Minister of Clavering.* Essex dove. 1629. 4°. . 2455
Smith (John), *Minister at Reading.* Doctrine of praier in generall. 1595. 4°. 2419
Smith *or* Smyth (John), *Sebaptist.* Paralleles, censures, observations. 1609. 4°. 6881
Smyth (John). *See* H. (I.). Description. 1610.
See Robinson (J.). Of Religious Communion. 1614.
Smith (Jonathan), *B.A.*, *Sid.* Verses in Camb. Univ. Συνωδία. 1637. 5790
Smith (Jude). Misticall deuise. 1575. 8°. 1794
Smith (Miles), *bp.* *See* Babington (G.). Works. 1637.
See Bible. English (Royal). 1611. 2635
Smith (Nicholas). Verses in Coryate (T.). Coryates Crudities. 1611. 3076
— Smith (J.). Generall historie. 1624. 3864
Smith (Nicholas), *pseud.* *See* Wilson (Mat.).
Smith (Peter), *D.D.* *See* Willet (A.). Hexapla in Leviticum. 1631.
— — Synopsis Papismi. 1634.
Smith (Richard) (1500–1563). Assertion and defence of the sacramente of the aulter. 1546. 8°. 764
Confutation of...a defence of...the sacrament. [R. Chaudière, ab. 1550.] 8°. 6196
Defence of the blessed masse. 1546. 8°. 765
Defence of the sacrifice of the masse. 1546. 8°. . . . 766
Godly and Faythfull Retractation. 1547. 8°. 727
Of vnwrytten verytyes. 1548. 8°. 697
Playne Declaration. 1547. 8°. 726
See Carlile (C.). Discovrse. 1582.
— Cranmer (T.). Answer. 1551 *etc.*
— Poynet (J.). Apologie. 1556.
Smith (Richard), *Bp of Chalcedon.* Munition against mans misery. Ed. 2. Oxford, 1612. 12°. 5306
Prudentiall ballance of religion. Part 1. 1609. 8°. . . . 6882
See Bulkeley (E.). Apologie. 1608.
— Featley (D.). Transubstantiation. 1638.
Smith (Richard), *Bookseller.* Verses in Gascoigne (G.). The Posies. 1575. 1482

No.
Smith (Richard), *Preacher in Barnstaple.* Munition against mans miserie. Ed. 3. Oxford, 1634. 12°. 5445
Smith (Richard), *Secondary of the Poultry Compter.* MS. notes to Cowell's Interpreter. 1607. 4°. 7851
Smith (Rob.). Verses in Camb. Univ. Lacrymæ. 1619. . . . 5689
— Oxf. Univ. Horti. 1640. 5499
See Smyth.
Smith (Roland). Verses in Camb. Univ. Fasciae. 1633. . . . 5808
Smith (Samuel), *Incumbent of Prittlewell.* Davids blessed man. 1614. 8°. 3657
Davids Repentance. 1625. 8°. 7540
Noahs dove. 1634. 8°. 3697
Smith (Sam.), *of Magd. Coll. Oxon.* Verses in Oxf. Univ. Magd. Coll. 1612. 5302
Smith (Sir T.). Common-welth of England. 1589. 4°. . . . 2127
— 1601. 4°. 1783
— 1609. 4°. 3066
— 1612. 4°. 3089
— 1621. 4°. 7492
— [1633? 1640?] 12°. 3193
— 1635. 12°. 7498
De republica Anglorum. The maner of government. 1583. 4°. 1642
— 1584. 4°. 1650
De repub. et administratione Anglorum. [1610?] 8°. . 2375
Voyage and entertainment in Rushia. 1605. 4°. 3538
[Death.] *See* Harvey (G.). Smithus. 1578.
See Mary, *Queen of Scots.* De Maria. [1572?]
Smith (Tho.). Verses in Oxf. Univ. Horti. 1640. 5499
Smith (W.). Verses in Shirley (J.). The royall master. 1638. . 4665
Smith (William), '*Treasurer.*' *See* Prempart (J.). Historicall relation. 1639. F°.
Smithson (I.), *K.C.C.* Verses in Camb. Univ. Epithalam. 1625. 5702
Smyth (Edward), *M.A., S.J.C.* *See* L'Espine (J. de). Very excellent... discourse. 1592.
Smyth (G.). *See* Smyth (William).
Smyth (John), *Sebaptist.* *See* Smith.
Smyth (Richard), *D.D.* *See* Smith (R.).
Smyth (Richard), *of Barnstaple.* *See* Smith.
Smyth (Robert), *of the Chapel at Windsor.* Letters. *See* Coverdale (M.). Certain...letters. 1564.
Smyth (Robert). Verses in Adamson (J.). Εἰσόδια. 1618. . 5960
Smyth (Seb.). Verses in Camdeni Insignia. 1624. 5346
Smyth (Thomas), *servant to Queen Mary.* *See* Redman (John). Compendious treatise. [1556?] 1202
Smyth (William), *D.D.* Blacksmith. 1606. 8°. . . . 2020, 2021
Gemma Fabri. 1598. 8°. 2910
Smyth (William). Verses in Cambridge Lachrymae. 1587. . 2123
See also Smythe.
Smyth (William), *D.D., Master of Clare Hall, and Provost of King's.* *See* Camb. Univ. Threno-thriambeuticon. 1603. 4°.
Verses in Camb. Univ. Epicedium. 1612. 5665
Smyth (William), *assistant to Speed.* *See* Speed (J.). The theatre... 1611–2 etc.
Smythe (Sir J.). Certain Discourses...of weapons...Archers. 1590. 4°. 1451
Snape (Jo.). Verses in Camdeni Insignia. 1624. 5346
Snawsell (Thomas), *Jesus.* Verses in Camb. Univ. Συνωδία. 1637. . 5790
Snelling (Laurence). Verses in Oxf. Univ. Magd. Coll. 1612. . 5302
Snelling (Thomas). Thibaldus. Oxoniae, 1640. 8°. 5502
Snow (William). Verses in Oxf. Univ. Horti. 1640. . . . 5499
Soame (Stephen). Verses in Camb. Univ. Rex redux. 1633. . . 5748
Society of Twelve. Book of the holy Societye. Douai, 1626. 24°. 6576

No.

Socinus (Faustus). *See* Grotius (H.). Defensio fidei. 1636.
Socrates Scholasticus. [Ecclesiastical History.] *See* Eusebius Pamphili. Avncient...histories. 1577 *etc.*
Sohn (Georg). Brief...treatise...of the Antichrist. Cambridge, 1592. 8°. 5556
Solemne Contestation of diuerse Popes. [1560?] 8°. . . . 894
Solinus (Caius Julius). Excellent and pleasant worke. Trans. A. Golding. 1587. 4°. 7241
See Mela (P.). The Rare and Singuler worke. 1590.
Solon. [*Gr. Lat.*] *See* Poetæ minores. 1635.
Solution of Doctor Resolutus. 1619. *See* Calderwood (D.). . 7806
Some (Ro.). Godly treatise. 1588. 4°. 1714
— 1589. 4°. 1721
Three questions. Cambridge, 1596. 8°. 5584
See Greenwood (J.). M. Some laid open. [1590?]
— Pilkington (J.). Godlie exposition. 1585. 4°.
Some or Somus (Thomas). Verses in Turner (W.). Preseruatiue. 1551. 955
See Latimer (H.). [27 Sermons.] 1562. 4°.
Somers (William). *See* Darrell (J.). Detection. 1600.
— Harsnett (S.). Discovery. 1599.
Somerset (E. Seymour, duke of). Honourable entertainment...to the Queenes Maiestie...at Elvetham. 1591. 4°. . . . 1962
See Edward VI. Epistola. 1548. 728
— Patten (W.). Expedicion. (1548.)
— Wermueller (O.). Spyrytuall...Pearle. 1550.
Something written by occasion of...Blackfriers. 1623. 4°. . 6947
Somme le roi. *See* Royal Book.
Somner (William). Antiquities of Canterbury. 1640. 4°. . . 4748
Somus (Tho.). *See* Some.
Sonnibank (C.). Eunuche's conversion. 1617. 8°. . . . 2529
Sorocold (Thomas). Supplication of saints. Ed. 25. 1639. 12°. . 5175
Sotheby (John). Verses in A. (G.). Pallas armata. 1639. . 5170
Sotheby (T.). Verses in Camb. Univ. Rex redux. 1633. . . 5748
Soto (A. de). Ransome of time. Trans. J. Hawkins. Douai, 1634. 8°. 6590
[Licence.] *See* Stańey (W.). A treatise. 1617.
Soto (Hernando de). Verses in Aleman (M.). The Rogve. 1623 *etc.* 3599 *etc.*
Soul's Desire and Hope of Heaven[1]. [Ab. 1610?] 8°. . . . 3073
Southampton (Elizabeth, countess of). *See* Jones (W.). Treatise of patience. 1625. 4°.
Southampton (Henry Wriothesley, third earl of). *See* Bacon (F.). Declaration of the Practises & Treasons... 1601.
See Markham (G.). Honour. 1624.
[Funeral.] *See* Jones (W.). Treatise. 1625. 4°.
Southampton (Thomas Wriothesley, fourth earl of). *See* Markham (G.). Honour. 1624.
Southwell (Robert). Epistle of comfort. Paris [1604?]. 8°. . . 6217
Mæoniæ. 1595. 4°. 2843
Marie Magdalens funerall Teares. 1609. 4°. 3388
St Peters complaint. Newly augmented. [Ab. 1609.] 4°. . 2501
— 1615. 4°. 3114
Triumphs over death. 1596. 4°. 2847
Southwell (Lady). *See* Overbury (Sir T.), His Wife. 1638.
Soveraigne Antidote against Sabbatarian errovrs. 1636. 4°. . . 4025
Sp. (Mr.), *of Queens' College, Cambridge.* *See* Sparrow (Antony.)
Sp. (Th.), *Ebor.* Verses in Fleming (A.). A Panoplie. 1576. . 1620
Spagnuoli (B.), *Mantuanus.* *See* Mantuanus (Baptista).
Spain. *See* Mayerne Turquet (L. de). Generall historie of Spaine. 1612. F°.
Philip III. *See* Netherlands II. Southern Provinces. 1603. Proclamation.

[1] Qu. by J. Hodges? *See* Offor Sale Catalogue, Lots 1956—7.

No.
Spain. Philip III. *cont.* *See* Articles. (James I.) 1605. . . . 2590
— — Oration or speech. 1608. 1624
Philip IV. Proclamation for reformation...translated. [1623.] 4°. 7513
— *See* Coloma (C. de). 1623.
See Hexham (H.). Tongue-combat. 1623. 4°.
— Scott (T.). Certaine reasons. 1624. 4°.
— Articles of Peace. (Charles I.) 1630.
[Truce.] *See* Three Severall treatises. 1630.
Manifesto...for a Warre with France. *See* Modern History. 1635. 4°.
[Inquisition.] *See* Gonsalvius. Discovery. 1568 *etc.*
[Armada.] Certaine Advertisements... *See* Mendoza (B.). The Copie of a letter. 1588.
See Fourme of Prayer. 7294
— True Discourse. 1588.
— Masque of the League. 1592.
— Bennett (E.). [Treatise...touching...the Importation of Tobacco out of Spaine. 1620?]
— Castile.
— Experimentall discoverie of Spanish practises. 1623.
— Proclamations. 24 Dec. 1625.
— — 31 Dec. 1625.
— Wimbledon (Sir E. C., viscount). A iovrnall. 1626.
Spaniards perpetvall designes. *See* Scott (T.). 1624.
Spanish Cruelties. *See* Las Casas (B. de). The Spanish Colonie. 1583. 4°.
Spanish Pilgrime. *See* Ol. (P.).
— Wadsworth (J.). 1629, 1630.
Spanish Practises. *See* Experimentall discouerie. 1623–4.
Spalding (Robert). *See* Bible. English (Royal). 1611. . . 2635
Spangenberg (J.). Margarita theologica. 1566. 8°. . . . 1294
Summe of Diuinitie. 1567. 8°. 1275
Sparing discoverie. 1601. *See* Watson (W.).
Spark (Archibald). Verses in Camb. Univ. Carmen. 1635. . 5770
Spark (W.). *See* Sparke.
Sparke (Thomas). Brotherly perswasion to vnitie. 1607. 4°. . 3625
— Ed. 2. 1607. 4°. 3626
Catechisme. Oxford. 1588. 4°. 5232
Sermon preached at...buriall of...the Earle of Bedford. 1585. 8°. 6783
Sermon...at...buriall of...Lord Grey. Oxford, 1593. 8°. . 5238
See Defence of the ministers reasons. 1607.
— Dispute. 1608.
— Norris (S.). Antidote. 1615 *etc.* 4°.
— — Guide. 1621. 4°.
Sparke (William). Mystery of Godlinesse. Oxford, 1628. 4°. . 5374
Verses in Oxf. Univ. Magd. Coll. 1612. 5302
Sparkes (Thomas). *See* Sparke.
Sparrow (Antony). Sermon concerning confession of sinnes. 1637. 4°. 5108
Sparry (Francis). *See* Cattan (C. de). Geomancie. 1591. 4°.
Speculum christiani. Machlinia [1484]. 4°. 99
Speculum spiritualium. W. Hopyl, Paris, imp. W. Bretton, 1510. 4°. 6151
Speculum vitae. [Irish.] *See* Desiderius. 1616.
Speed (John). Clowd of Witnesses. 1616. 8°. 3791
— 1628. 8°. 3036
Description of the ciuill warres of England. 1600. Broadsheet . 6830
Direction to find all those names...of Scripture. 4°. . . 6887
England Wales Scotland and Ireland described and abridged. 1627. Oblong 8°. 3774–5
Genealogies. [Ab. 1611.] F°. 7419, 7727–8
— [Ab. 1617–1611.] F°. 7729
— [162–.] 4°. 7561

No.

Speed (John). Genealogies, *cont.* [Ab. 1631.] 4°. 7425
— [Ab. 1633.] F°. 7426
— [Ab. 1633.] F°. 7427
— [1637–6?] 4°. 7433–4
— [Ab. 16—.] 4°. 7483
— [1620.] 12°. 6923
— 1640. 8°. 7864
History of great britaine. Ed. 1. *See below* Theatre of the empire. 1611.
— Ed. 2. 1627. F°. 3873
— Ed. 3. 1632. F°. 3885
Prospect of the most famous parts of the World. 1627. F°. 3874
— [1631?] F°. 3878
Theatre of the empire of great britaine. (The history.) 1611 (1610). F°. 3215
— 1627. F°. 3875
— 1631. F°. 3879
— [Map of Cambridgeshire. For H. Overton.] F°. . . . 5086
[Map of Munster. 1610 *etc.*] *See* Stafford (T.). Pacata Hibernia. 1633. F°. 4577–9
Verses in Guillim (J.). A display. 1611 *etc.* . . . . 3211 *etc.*
See Parkinson (J.). Theatrum. 1640. F°.
Speed (John), *M.D.* Verses in Hippocrates. 1633. 5812
Speght (Thomas). Verses in Baret (J.). Alvearie. 1580. . . 1418
— Rawlins (T.). Admonitio. [1620?] 2033
See Chaucer (G.). Workes. 1598 *etc.*
Speidell (John). New logarithmes. 1619. 4°. 6915
Spelman (Sir Henry). Archaeologus. 1626. F°. 3805
Concilia, decreta, leges, constitutiones, in re ecclesiarum orbis britannici. Tom. 1. 1639. F°. 4395
De non temerandis ecclesijs. 1613. 12°. 3781
— Ed. 2. 1616. 8°. 3792–3
Verses in Speed (J.). Theatre of the empire. 1611. . . . 3215
See Rudyerd (Sir B.). Speech. 1628. 4°.
— Speed (J.). Theatre. 1611.
— Bible. Polyglot. O.T. Psalms. 1640.
Spence (George), *M.D.* Verses in Spence (R.). Illustrissimi ducis διαγραφή. 1628. 6995
Spence (James). Verses in Spence (R.). Illustrissimi ducis διαγραφή. 1628. 6995
Spence (Joseph). Verses in Spence (R.). Illustrissimi ducis διαγραφή. 1628. 6995
Spence (Paul). *See* Abbot (R.). Mirrour of Popish Svbtilties. 1594.
Spence (Robert). Illustrissimi ducis διαγραφή. 4°. . . . 6995
Verses in Comenius (J. A.). Porta linguarum. 1633. . . 7613
Spencer (Broket), *Sid.* Verses in Camb. Univ. Epithalam. 1625. . 5702
Spencer (John), *divine.* *See* Spenser.
Spencer (John), *Sublibrarian of Sion College.* *See* Willan (R.). Eliah's wish. 1630. 4°.
Spencer (John), *Bookseller.* *See* Guarda (A). Bellum Grammaticale. 1635. 8°.
Spencer (Thomas). Maschil Vnmasked...against...Mr Cholmley. [1629.] 4°. 5045
Spens. *See* Spence.
Spenser (Benjamin). Vox civitatis. 1625. 4°. 3867
Spenser (E.). Faerie qveene, Part 1. 1590. 4°. 1960
— — Ed. 2. 1596. 4°. 2243
— Part 2. 1596. 4°. 2244
— 1609. F°. 2499
— Shepheards calendar etc. 1611. F°. 2510

No.
Spenser (E.). Faerie qveene *cont.* 1617 (1628?). F°. 2530
Shepheardes Calender. 1586. 4°. 1942
— 1611. F°. 2509
View of the state of Ireland. 1596. (Certaine Verses.) *See* Ware (Sir J.). Historie of Ireland. 1633.
Verses in La Vardin (J. de). Historie. 1596. 2239
— Contarini (G.). Commonwealth. 1599. 2153
See Nenna (G. B.). Nennio. 1595.
— S. (E.). De rebus gestis. [1582?] *etc.* . . 1523, 5501
Spenser (John). *See* Bible. English (Royal). 1611. 2635
See Hooker (R.). Of the lawes. 1617 *etc.*
Sperin (Thomas). *See* Collection of certain Letters. 1590.
Spicer (Richard), *M.D.* Verses in Hippocrates. 1633. . . 5812
Spices. Profitable discourse. [1593.] 4°. 2567
Spigel...der alderschoonste Courtisanen. [Ab. 1635.] Obl. 8°. . 6405
Spinelli (Vincenzo). Verses in Aleman (M.). The Rogve. 1623 *etc.* 3599 *etc.*
Spinola (Ambrosio de). *See* Barry (G.). Seige of Breda. 1627(-8).
Spires, City of. *See* Libellvs svpplex. 1571.
Spirit of detraction, conjured and convicted. 1611. 4°. . . 3080
Spiritual Conflict. 1613. *See* Scupoli (L.).
Spirituall purgation sent vnto al them that laboure of Luthers Errour. [Ab. 1548.] 8°. *See* C. (T.).
Spottiswood (James). Concio...ad Clerum. 25 Julij 1616. Edinburgi, 1616. 4°. 5956
Execution of Neschech. Edinburgh, 1616. 4°. . . . 5957
Saint Patrick's Purgatory. [Ab. 1632.] 4°. 6040
Spring (William). *See* Ovid. De tristibus. 1639. 8°.
Sprint (John). Cassander anglicanus. 1618. 4°. . . . 3491
Propositions...of the Christian Sabbath. 1635. 12°. . . 4412
Sprot (George). *See* Hart (Sir W.). Examinations. 1609.
Squire (Adam). Verses in Humphrey (L.). J. Jvelli vita. 1573. . 837
— Jones (J.). Briefe discourse. 1574. 1366
Squire (Edward). *See* Fitzherbert (T.). Defence. 1602.
Squire (Henry). Verses in Wilson (Sir T.). Vita. 1551. . . 631-
Squire (John). Plaine exposition upon...II Thess. i. 1630. 4°. . 5027
Sermon...on White-sunday, 1619. 1621. 4°. 3679
Sermon. [16 Dec. 1619.] *See* Ley (Roger). Two Sermons. 1619. 3329
Sermon on the second commandement. 1624. 4°. . . 3154
See Texeda (F. de). Texeda Retextus. 1623.
St. (Ed.), *S.T.D.* [Approbatio.] *See* M. (Ch.). Paraphrasticall... discourses. 1635. 8°. 7894
St. (I.). Verses in Gorden (E.). Discourse. 1633. . . . 4003
Stafford (Anthony). Femall glory...life...of our Blessed Lady. 1635. 8°. 4018
Meditations, and Resolutions. 1612. 12°. 2515
Stafford (Henry, baron). *See* Fox (E.). The true differens. [1548?]
Stafford (John), *Bookseller.* *See* Preston (J.). Fulnesse of Christ. 1640. 4°.
Stafford (R.). *See* Du Moulin (Pierre), *sen.* Heraclitvs. 1609.
Stafford (Thomas). Pacata Hibernia. 1633. F°. . . 4577-9
Stafford (W.). Compendious or briefe examination of...complaints. 1581. 4°. 1233, 7861
Stalbrydge (H.) *pseud.* Epistel Exhortatorye. [1544.] *See* Bale (J.).
Stamford (Sir William). *See* Stanford.
Stanbridge (John). Accidentia. [Ab. 1510?] 4°. 6664
— [Pynson 1515?] 4°. 312
— J. Skot [1529]. 4°. 359
— Ed. R. Whittington. Canterbury [1550?]. 4°. . . . 5877
Parvulorum institutio. W. de Worde, 1526. 4°. 192
Sum es fui. Pynson [1515?]. 4°. 313

No.

Stanbridge (John) *cont.* Vocabula. [W. de Worde, ab. 1508.] 4°. 234 (corrected)
— Pynson, 1516. 4°. 314
Vocabula...studio T. Newtoni. 1577. 4°. 1287
Vulgaria. J. Skot [1529]. 4°. 360
? Declension of nowns. *See* Grammar. Lat. (frag.). 15—. 4°. . 221
Verses in Whittington (R.). Syntaxis. 1522. 4°. . . 5863
Standish (A.). New directions...for the increase of timber. 1615. 4°. 6903
Standish (J.). Lytle treatise...agaist the protestacion of R. Barnes. 1540. 8°. 385
Triall of the supremacy. 1556. 8°. 1204
See Coverdale (M.). Confutacion. [154–.] 8°.
Standish (John), *Archdeacon.* *See* Justinianus. Digestorum. 1553. F°.
Staney (Will.). Treatise of the third order of S. Francis. Pt 1. Penance. Douai, 1617. 8°. 6582
Stanford (Henry), *M.A.* Verses in Camden (W.). Britannia. 1637. 3055
Stanford (Sir W.). Exposition of the kinges prerogatiue...out of... Fitzherbert. 1567. 4°. 1116
— 1568. 4°. 1119
— 1577. 4°. 1134
Les plees del coron. 1557. 4°. 7165
— 1583. 4°. 1144
See Glanville (R. de). Tractatus. [1555 ?]
— Pulton (F.). De pace. 1610. 3244
Stanhope (Edward). *See* Blackwell (G.). Large examination. 1607.
Stanhope (Ed.), *K.C.C.* Verses in Camb. Univ. Epithalam. 1625. . 5702
Stanihurst. *See* Stanyhurst.
Staninough (I.), *Q.C.C.* Verses in Camb. Univ. Dolor. 1625. . 5701
— — Epithalam. 1625. 5702
— — Fasciae. 1633. 5808
— — Rex redux. 1633. 5748
— Isaacson (H.). Saturni Ephemerides. 1633. . . . 4206
Stanley (William). *See* Roe (W.). Epilogvs. 1615.
Stans puer ad mensam. *See* Sulpitius (J.), *Verulanus.*
Stansby (William), *printer.* *See* Hieron (S.). Workes. [1624–5.] F°.
See Hooker (R.). Certayne divine tractates. 1618. F°.
— — Of the lawes. 1622. 3142
See Smith (H.). Sixe sermons. 1615. 4°.
Stanyhurst (Ric.). Harmonia seu catena dialectica, in Porphyrianas institutiones. 1570. F°. 749
See Vergilius [Æneis i–iv (*Eng.*)]. The first fovre. 1583.
Verses in Rowlands (R.). Restitution. 1605 *etc.* . . 6140 *etc.*
Staphylus (Fridericus). Apologie. Trans. T. Stapleton. Antwerp, 1565. 4°. 6115
Stapleton (Tho.). Counterblast to M. Hornes vayne blaste. Louvain, 1567. 4°. 6420
Fortresse of the faith. Antwerp, 1565. 4°. 6116
See Bede. History of the Church of Englande. 1565 etc.
— Fulke (W.). De svccessione. 1584.
— — T. Stapleton and T. Martiall. 1580. 8°.
— Rainolds (J.). Svmme. 1584 *etc.*
— Staphylus (F.). Apologie. 1565. 4°.
— Whitaker (W.). Adversvs Thomæ Stapletoni...Defensionem. 1594.
— — Dispvtatio. 1588.
— — Tractatus...de peccato originali. 1600. 8°.
Star-chamber. 1598. *See* London. College of Physicians. 1636.
— James I. Speach. 1616.
— Crompton (R.). Star-chamber cases. 1630.
Decree (16 Nov. 1633)...and...Confirmation (Chandlers, Bakers etc. 14 Dec. 1633). 1633. 4°. 2685

No.

Star-chamber *cont.* [1637 June 14.] *See* Bastwick (J.). Briefe relation. 1637. 4°.
Decree...concerning Printing (11 July 1637). 1637. 4°. . . 2695
See Laud (W.). Speech. 1637.
— Divine and Politike observations. 1638.
Starch. *See* Proclamation 5 May 1620.
Staresmore (S.). Vnlawfulnes of reading in prayer. 1619. 8°. . 6502
Starkey (Galfridus). *See* Galfridus [Starkey?], *Anglicus.*
State of the Church of England. 1588? *See* Udall (J.).
State-mysteries of the Iesvites. Trans. P. Gosselin. 1623. 4°. . 3602
States General. *See* Netherlands. States General.
Statham (N.). Abridgement des livres annales. Rouen [1490]. F°. 140
Statutes (French). Nova Statuta. 1 Edw. III.—22 Ed. IV. Machlinia [1483?]. F°. 100
— 1 Edw. III.—12 Henry VII. Pynson [1501]. F°. . . 315
Abbreviamentum. Lettou and Machlinia, 1482. F°. . . . 91
— Pynson, 1499. 8°. 109
Abridgement. Le Bregement. Pynson, 1521. 8°. . . . 275
— J. Rastell, 1528. 8°. 346
— Pynson, 1528. 8°. 291
Statutes (Latin). Statuta Antiqua. Pynson, 1519. 12°. . . 268
Magna Carta cum aliis antiquis statutis. Berthelet, Nov. 1531. 8°. 7081
Secunda pars veterum statutorum. Berthelet, Jan. 1532. 8°. . 7082
Magna charta, cum statutis. R. Tottell, 1556 (1555). 8°. . 1109
— R. Tottell, 1556 (1556). 8°. 1110
— R. Tottell, 1587. 8°. 1148
— T. Wight, 1602. 8°. 2399
— Stationers, 1608. 8°. 3235
— Stationers, 1618. 8°. 3272
Statutes (English). Boke of magna charta with diuers other statutes. Redman, 1534. 8°. 7079
Great charter...with diuers olde statutes. E. Redman [1540?]. 8°. 408
Second Volume (1–37 Henry VIII.). Berthelet, 1543. F°. . 470
— (1–48 Henry VIII.). Marshe, 1575. F°. 1226
Statutes at large. C. Barker, 1587. F°. 1683
— 1618. F°. 2802
Collection of all the Statutes...vnto 1557. Ed. W. Rastell. R. Tottell, 1559. 4°. 1112
Collection...vnto...1572. R. Tottell, 1572. F°. 1124
Collection in English. C. Barker, 1583. F°. 1677
— Stationers, 1615. F°. 7506
— until 35 Eliz. Deputies of C. Barker, 1594. F°. . . 1701
— Stationers, 1621. F°. 3285
See Pulton (F.). Collection of sundry statutes. 1632. F°. . 5076
Abridgement. J. Rastell, 1527. 8°. 345
— Great Abridgment. R. Redman [1539]. 8°. . . . 396
— With the abredgemētes of xxxiij Henry VIII. 1542. 8°. . 582
Abridgment untyl xxxiii. of Henry VIII. Middleton, 1542. 8°. 712
Abridgement. *See* Pulton (F.). Kalendar. 1608. F°.
See Principall lawes and statutes of England. 1542. 8°. . 363, 364
Kalendar of Statutes to 4 James I. *See* Pulton (F.). 1608. F°. 7502
Table to al the Statutes...from Edward the . vi .... Tottell [1570]. F°. 1122
1 Henry VIII. Berthelet [1543]. F°. 515
3–7 Henry VIII. Berthelet [1543]. F°. 516
6 Henry VIII. [Ab. 153–.] F°. 7090
14, 15 Henry VIII. Berthelet [1543]. F°. 517
21 Henry VIII. Berthelet [1543]. F°. 518
21 Henry VIII. (Abridgment.) R. Redman [after 1530]. 8°. 397–8
22 Henry VIII. Berthelet [1543]. F°. 519
— T. Powell [1556?]. F°. 1247

No.

Statutes (English) *cont.* 22 Hen. VIII. (Abridgment.) R. Redman [after 1531]. 8°. 399
23 Henry VIII. Berthelet [1543]. F°. 520–1
— Abridgment. E. Redman [1540?]. 8°. 409
24 Henry VIII. Berthelet 1538. F°. 446
— Berthelet, 1546. F°. 487
24, 25 Henry VIII. Abridgment. R. Redman, n.d. 8°. . . 400
— — W. Middleton [1548?]. 8°. 717
25 Henry VIII. Berthelet [1543]. F°. 522
26 Henry VIII. Berthelet [1543]. F°. 523
— Abridgment. R. Redman [after 1535]. 8°. 401
27, 28 Henry VIII. (Abridgment.) R. Redman, n.d. 8°. . . 402
28 Henry VIII. Berthelet [1543]. F°. 524
31 Henry VIII. Berthelet 1539. F°. 453
— Berthelet, '1539,' 1546. F°. 489
— Abridgment. E. Redman [1540?]. 8°. 410
32 Henry VIII. Berthelet, 1540. F°. 457
— Abridgment. E. Redman [1540?]. 8°. 411
33 Henry VIII. Berthelet, 1542. F°. 465
— Abridgment. W. Middleton [1542?]. 8°. 718
34, 35 Henry VIII. Berthelet, 1547. F°. 491
35 Henry VIII. Berthelet, 1544. F°. 474–5
37 Henry VIII. Berthelet, 1546. F°. 490
1 Edward VI. Grafton, 1548. F°. 608–10
2 and 3 Edward VI. Grafton, April 1549. F°. 614
— Grafton, June 1549. F°. 615
3 and 4 Edward VI. Grafton, 1549. F°. 611
5 and 6 Edward VI. Grafton, 1552. F°. 623
7 Edward VI. Grafton, April 1553. F°. 627
1 Mary I. Cawood, 1554. F°. 989
1 and 2 Philip and Mary. Cawood, 1555. F°. 993
2 and 3 Philip and Mary. Cawood, 1555. F°. . . . 994
4 and 5 Philip and Mary. Cawood, 1558. F°. 998
1 Elizabeth. Jugge and Cawood, 1559. F°. 957
5 Elizabeth. Jugge and Cawood, 1563. F°. 962
8 Elizabeth. Jugge, 1566. F° 963
1 James I. R. Barker, 1604. F°. 2588
3 James I. R. Barker, 1606. F°.. 2598
4 James I. R. Barker, 1607. F°. 2609
7 James I. R. Barker, 1610. F°. 2624
21 James I. Norton and Bill, 1624. F°. 2821
1 Car. I. Barker and Bill, 1630. F°. 2666
3–4 Car I. Norton and Bill, 1628. F°. 2836
16 Car. I. Barker and Ass. Bill, 1640. F°. 2714
See Institutions or principall groundes...Statutes.
Abstract of all penal statutes, by F. Pulton. 1581. 4°. . . 1671
Statutes (Ireland). 10 Henry VI.—Elizabeth. 1572. F°. . . 7194
Dublin, 1620, 1621. F°. 6018–6020
10, 11 Charles I. 1635. F°. 6057–6059
Act for...free pardon. 1635. F°. 6055
See Ireland, Church of. An act. 1634. 6051
Statutes (Scotland). Actis and constitutiounis. Edinburgh, 1566. F°. 5912
In the parliament...at Striuiling 28 Aug. 1571. St Andrews, 1573. F°. 5996
— Edinburgh, 1575. F°. 5914
Actes. Edinburgh, 1575, F°. 5913
In the parliament...at Striuiling 25 Julij...(Edinburgh 24 October). Edinburgh, 1579. F°. 5916
In the parliament...at Edinburgh 25 October. Edinburgh, 1582. F°. 5918
Lawes and actes...(De verborum significatione...be M. Iohn Skene). Edinburgh, 1597. F°. 5936

No.
Statutes (Scotland) *cont.* xxiii. Parliament...4 August 1621. Edinburgh, 1621. F°. 5969
Staunford (Sir William). *See* Stanford.
Stedman (R.), *Oxon.* Verses in Hopton (A.). Speculum. 1611. . 3638
Steenwyk. True declaration of the streight siedge. 1592. 4°. . 1966
Stell (John). *See* Marnix (P. van). The Bee hive. 1580 *etc.* 8°.
See Nicolay (N. de). Nauigations. 1585.
Stella Clericorum. W. de Worde, 20 Oct. 1531. 8°. . . . 204
Στέφανος (Ρίκαρδος). Verses in Palingenius. The Zodiake. 1576. . 1622
Stephanus (Henricus and Robertus). *See* Estienne.
Stephanus (Jeremias), *S.T.B.* *See* Stephens.
Stephen (Henry). *See* Estienne.
Stephen or Stephens (Robert). Verses in Adamson (J.). Εἰσοδια, 1618. 5960
Stephens (Jeremy), *B.D.*, *Oxon.* *See* Cyprianus. De Vnitate. 1632.
See Gregory (S.). De Cura Pastorali. 1629.
Stephens (John). New essayes and characters. 1631. 8°. . . 7823
Stephens (Richard). Verses in Seton (J.). Dialectica. 1611 *etc.* . 3249 *etc.*
Stephens (Thomas), *B.A.*, *Jes.* Verses in Camb. Univ. Συνωδία. 1637. 5790
Stephenson (Andrew). Verses in Adamson (J.). Εἰσόδια. 1618. . 5960
Sterne (Ric.), *B.D.* Verses in Camb. Univ. Genethl. 1631. . 5731
— — Anthologia. 1632. 5741
— — Fasciae. 1633. 5808
— — Rex redux. 1633. 5748
— Hippocrates, 1633. 5812
— Camb. Univ. Carmen. 1635. 5770
— — Voces. 1640. 5836
Sternhold (Thomas). Certayne chapters of the prouerbs of Salomon. *See* Hall (J.). Certayn chapters. 1550.
See Bible. English. Psalms. Metrical versions.
Stettin, Duchy of. *See* Pomerania.
Stevens (Charles). *See* Estienne.
Stevens (T.). Verses in Oxf. Univ. Horti. 1640. 5499
Stevin (Simon). Disme: the art of tenths. By R. Norton. 1608. 4°. 2887
Steward (Thomas). *See* Styward.
Stinnet ( ). *See* Brabourne (T.). A Defence. 1632.
Stinton (Georg). Verses in Camdeni Insignia. 1624. . . 5346
Stirkaeus (George). Verses in Adamson (J.). Εἰσόδια. 1618. . . 5960
Stirling School. Verses in Adamson (J.). Εἰσόδια. 1618. . . 5960
Stirling (William Alexander, earl of). Encouragement to colonies. 1624. 4°. 3155
— *See below* Mapp and description. 1630.
Mapp and description of New-england. 1630. 4°. . . . 3179
Monarchicke Tragedies. Ed. 3. 1618. 8°. 3117
Recreations with the muses. 1637. F°. 4031
Verses in Abernethy (J.). Christian...treatise. 1630. 4°. . 4342
— Drayton (M.). Poems. 1630. 8°. 7926
See Bible. English. Psalms. Metrical. 1631 *etc.* . . 5430 *etc.*
— Sidney (Sir P.). Arcadia. 1621 *etc.*
Stock (Richard). Churches lamentation for...John Lord Harington. 1614. 8°. 3784
Sermon preached at Paules crosse, 2 Nov. 1606. 1609. 8°. . 2745
See Whitaker (W.). An answere to the ten reasons. 1606. 4°.
[Funeral]. *See* Gataker (T.). Abrahams decease. 1627.
Stocker (Thomas). *See* Bèze (T. de). Popes Canons. 1587.
— Theophile, *D.L.* Tragicall Historie. [1583.]
— Viret (P.). Cavteles...of the...masse. 1584.
Stockwood (J.). Plaine and easie...English Accidence. 1590. 4°. . 1797
Progymnasma scholasticum. 1597. 8°. 2421
Sermon, 24 August 1578. 8°. 1499
See Bèze (T. de). Treasure of Trueth. [1576?], *etc.* 8°.

No.

Stockwood (J.) *cont.* *See* Brenz (J.). Right...discourse vpon...Ester. 1584.
— Daneau (L.). Frvitfvll commentarie vpon the twelue Small Prophets. 1594.
— James I. Fruitfull Meditation. [1603?]
— Serres (J. de). Godlie Commentarie vpon Ecclesiastes. 1585. 8°.
Stoics. *See* Du Vair (G.). Morall philosophy of the Stoicks.
Stokes (Robert). *See* DORT (printing). p. 1465.
Stokesley (John), *Bp.* *See* Alesius (A.). Of the auctorite of the word. [Ab. 1537.] 8°.
[Letter to Cardinal Pole.] *See* Tunstall (C.). Letter. 1560.
— — *See* G. (B.), *Citizen.* New Yeares Gifte. 1579.
Stone (William). Curse become a blessing. 1623. 4°. . . . 4787
Stonehouse (James), *T.C.C.* Verses in Camb. Univ. Συνωδία. 1637. . 5790
Stonhowse (Sir John). Verses in Gill (A.). Πάρεργα. 1632. . 4558
Stonhowse (Walter), *B.D.* Verses in Gill (A.). Πάρεργα. 1632. . 4558
Stories. Storys and prophesis out of the holy scriptur. Antwerp, 1535. 8°. 6078
Story (J.). Declaration of the lyfe and death of. 1571. 8°. . . 1329
See Cranmer (T.). Copy of certain lettres. [Ab. 1556.] 8°.
Stoughton (John). Arraignement of covetousnesse. 1640. 4°. . 4600
Baruch's sore. 1640. 4°. 4406
Choice sermons. 1640. 4°. 4938
Christians prayer. 1640. 4°. 5182
XI Choice sermons. 1640. 4°. 4407
XV Choice sermons. 1640. 4°. 4939
Forme of wholsome words. 1640. 4°. 5160
Learned treatise. 1640. 4°. 4940
Righteous mans plea to true happinesse. 1640. 4°. . . 4683
Seaven sermons. 1640. 4°. 5085
XIII Sermons. 1640. 4°. 5161
Stoughton (Nicholas). Verses in Jorden (E.). Discourse. 1633. . 4003
Stoughton (Thomas). Christians sacrifice. 1622. 4°. . . 7887
Generall treatise against poperie. Cambridge, 1598. 8°. . . 5596
Two profitable treatises. 1616. 4°. 3915
Stoughton (William). *See* Assertion. 1604.
Stow (J.). Annales of England. 1601. 4°. 1327
— 1605. 4°. 1754
— 1615. F°. 1835
— Continued by E. Howes. 1631(2). F°. 4556
Chronicles of England. 1580. 4°. 7944
Summarie of the Chronicles of England. 1598. 16°. . . 1996
— 1604. 16°. 1272
Abridgement of the English Chronicle. 1618. 8°. . . 3273
Survay of London. 1603. 4°. 2162
— 1633. F°. 4106
See Holinshed (R.). Chronicles. 1587.
Stra. (W.) *qu.* Strachey? Verses in Overbury (Sir T.). His Wife. Ed. 11. 1622. 3380
Strachey (Will.). Verses in Michell (Sir F.). View of France. 1604. 2883
See also Stra. (W.).
Stradling (Geo.). Verses in Oxf. Univ. Horti. 1640. . . . 5499
Stradling (Sir John). Divine poemes. 1625. 4°. . . . 3159
Verses in Rhys (J. D.). Cambrobrytannicæ linguæ. 1592. . 2215
— Camden (W.). Britannia. 1637. 3055
See Lipsius (J.). Two bookes. 1595.
Strafford (Thomas Wentworth, earl of). Depositions and articles. 16 Feb. 1640. 4°. 4126–8
Strang (John). Theses in Adamson (J.). Εἰσόδια. 1618. . . 5960
Verses in Abernethy (J.). Christian...treatise. 1630. . . 4342
Strangius. *See* Strang.

No.
Strangvage (William). *See* Udall (William), *alias* Strangvage.
Strangwage (John). Verses in Vaughan (R.). Waterworkes. 1610. 3576
Strangwayes (John). Verses in Coryat (T.). Coryats Crudities. 1611. 3076
Stransam (Edward). *See* page 159 of A Treatise. [1600?] 8°. . 6832
Strasburg Preachers. Treatise declaryng...that pyctures...are in no wise to be suffred. [1532?] 8°. 564
Reformed Church. 1551. *See* Liturgies.
University. *See* Aristotle. [Ethics.] Epitome... 1634.
— [*In usum.*] *See* Hauwenreuter (J. L.). 1594.
Stratford (Edmond). Disputation of the church. Douai, 1629. 8°. 6591
— 1632. 8°. 6594
— 1640. 8°. 6596
Stratham (N.). *See* Statham.
Stratius ( ). *See* Polemon (J.). All the famous Battels... 1587.
Strigelius (V.). Part of the harmony of king davids harp. 1582. 4°. 1924
Proceeding in the harmonie of King Davids harpe. Ps. 22–35. [1593?] 4° 1970
Second proceeding. 1592. 1593. 4°. 1364
Third proceeding...Ps. 45–61. 1595. 4°. 2844
Strode (Lady). [Funeral.] *See* Barlow (J.). Trve gvide. 1619. 4°.
Strode (Tho.). Verses in Camb. Univ. Fasciae. 1633. . . 5808
— — Rex redux. 1633. 5748
Strode (William). Verses in Camdeni Insignia. 1624. . . 5346
— Chaucer (G.). Amorum. 1635. 5414
— Oxf. Univ. Horti. 1640. 5499
Strozza (Pandolfo). Verses in Harvey (G.). Gratulationum. 1578. 1495
Strumsdorff. *See* Stumsdorf.
Struther (William). True happines. Edinburgh, 1633. 4°. . . 5977
Verses in Adamson (J.). Εἰσόδια. 1618. . . . 5960
Stuart, *House of*. Trewe description of the nobill race. Amsterdam, 1603. F°. 6375
Stuart (Lady Arabella). *See* Owen (J.). Epigrammatum. 1612.
Stuart (Bernard), *T.C.C.* Verses in Camb. Univ. Συνῳδία. 1637. 5790
Stuart (John). Verses in Adamson (J.). Εἰσόδια. 1618. . . 5960
Stuart (John), *T.C.C.* Verses in Camb. Univ. Συνῳδία. 1637. . 5790
Stubbe (Edmund). Fraus honesta. 1632. 12°. 4566
Verses in Camb. Univ. Epicedium. 1612. 5665
— — Lacrymæ. 1619. 5689
Stubbes (Katharine). *See* Stubbes (Ph.). Christal glasse. 1612.
Stubbs (J.). Discoverie of a gaping gvlf. 1579. 8°. . . 1056
Stubbs (Justinian). *See* Bayne (P.). Commentarie on Col. i. and ii. 1634. 4°.
Stubbs (Ph.). Anatomie of Abuses. Ed. 3. 1585. 8°. . . . 1446
Christall glasse. 1612. 4°. 1880
Verses in Foxe (J.). Actes. 1583. 865
See D. (H.). Godlie and fruitfull Treatise of Faith. 1583.
Stubs (J.), *of Lincoln's Inn.* *See* Parker (M.). Life off the 70. Archbishopp. 1574.
Stuckius (Joannes Guilielmus). *See* Beza (T.). Theodori Bezæ... Epistola. 1598.
Studley (John). *See* Bale (J.). Pageant of Popes. 1574.
Studley (Peter). Looking-glasse of schisme. 1634. 12°. . . . 7595
Stumsdorf, Treaty of. *See* Poland. Vladislaus IV. 1635.
Sturmius (J.). Epistle...sent to the Cardynalles. Trans. R. Morysine. 1537. 8°. 7083
[Epistolæ.] *See* Ascham (R.). Libri tres. 1590.
See Cicero. [Epistles.] 1631.
Sturtevant (Simon). *See* Æsop. The Etymologist. 1602. . . 2254
Styles (Matthias). *See* Hayne (T.). Pax. 1639.
Styward (T.). Pathwaie to martiall discipline. [1585.] 4°. . . 1586

No.
Suares (Jacques). *See* Du Moulin (P.). Waters of Siloe. 1612. 8°.
Suarez (Franciscus). *See* Abbot (R.). De svprema potestate regia. 1619.
See Dominis (M. A. de). De republica. 1617.
— Widdrington (R.). A copy. 1614.
Svbpaena from the high Imperiall Court of Heauen. 1618. 8°. . 3977
Subscription. *See* Dispute. 1608.
Suckling (Sir John). [Gift plate.] 1618. 8°. 6912
Suetonius. Historie of twelve Cæsars. 1606. F°. . . . 2483
See Horatius. Poemata. 1614.
Suffolk (Catharine, duchess of). *See* Catharine [Parr], *Queen*. Lamentacion. 1547 etc.
Suffolk (Charles Brandon, third duke of). Verses in Cheke (Sir J.). De obitu M. Buceri. 1551. 734
See Wilson (Sir T.). Vita et obitvs. [1551.]
Suffolk (Henry Brandon, second duke of). Verses in Cheke (Sir J.). De obitu M. Buceri. 1551. 734
See Wilson (Sir T.). Vita et obitvs. [1551.]
Suinglius. *See* Zwingli.
Suite (Timothy). *See* Texeda (F. de). Texeda Retextus. 1623.
Sulpicius (C.), *Apollinaris*. Verses in Terentius. Terence in English. 1607. 5644
Sulpicius (Joannes), *Verulanus*. Opus grammatices. W. de Worde, 1499. 4°. 54
Stans puer ad mensam. Caxton [1477–8]. 4°. 11
— (Lytell Johann). W. de Worde [15–]. 4°. . . . 243
See Lucanus. De bello civili. 1589.
— Whittington (R.). Grammatica. Pars I. Lib. 2. . . . 199
Sulpitius. *See* Sulpicius.
Sum of the holy scrypture. Redman, n.d. 8°. 403–4
Summe of the holye scripture. [Antwerp?] 1529. 16°. . . 6095
Sum of the holy scripture and ordynarye. [After 1537.] 8°. . 643
Summe of the holy Scripture. Hill, 1548. 8°. 1030
See Brief sum.
Sum or a brief collection of holy signes. 1563. 8°. . . . 1305
Summary of Christian Religion. 16°. 6602
Summer Isles [Bermudas]. *See* Smith (J.). Generall history. 1624. 3864
Supper. Souper of the Lord... 'Nornburg,' 5 April 1533. 8°. . 6709
— More against J. Fryth. 1533. [1549?] 8°. 918
Supplicatio ad Imperatorem. 1613. 4°. *See* Becanus (M.).
Supplication of beggars. *See* 6711.
Supplication of certaine Masse-Priests. 1604. 4°. 3200
Supplication of the family of love. 1606. 4°. 2482
Supplication of the poore Commons. [Ab. 1546.] 8°. . . . 6710-1
Supplication to the Kings most excellent Maiestie. *See* Supplication of certaine Masse-Priests. 1604.
Supplication to our most soueraigne lorde...Henry the eyght. Dec. 1544. 8°. *See* Tracy (R.).
Surflet or Surphlet (Richard). *See* Estienne (C.). Maison Rustique. 1616.
See Laurentius (A.). Discourse. 1599.
Surius (Laurentius). *See* Villegas (A. de). Lives of Saints. 1628.
Surphlet (Richard). *See* Surflet.
Sursinus (J.). *See* Camden (W.). Institutio. 1604.
Survay. *See* Survey.
Survey of the Booke of Common Prayer. 1606. 8°. 6473
— 1610. 8°. 6474
Survay of the pretended Holy Discipline. 1593. *See* Bancroft (R.).
Susenbrotus (J.). Epitome troporum ac schematum et grammaticorum et rhetorum. 1562. 8°. 1292
Suslyga (Laurentius). *See* Lydiat (T.). Emendatio. 1609.

No.

Suso (Henricus de). *See* Horologium Sapientie. [1490.]
Sutcliffe (Matthew). Abridgement or survey of Poperie. 1606. 4°. 3365
Adv. R. Bellarmini de Purgatorio. 1599. 4°. 1742
Answere vnto...Throkmorton. 1595. 4°. 1703
Challenge concerning the Romish Church. 1602. 4°. . . 2077
De catholica, orthodoxa, et vera christi ecclesia. 1592. 4°. . 1694
De missa papistica. 1603. 4°. 2432
De pontifice romano. 1599. 4°. 1740
De presbyterio. 1591. 4°. 1730
De recta studii theologici ratione. 1602. 8°. 7519
De turcopapismo. 1599. 4°. 1741
— 1604. 8°. 1751
Examination and confutation of The Survey of the newe Religion. 1606. 4°. 2022
Ful and round answer to...R. Parsons. 1604. 4°. . . . 1752
Petition apologeticall of Lay papists. 1606. 4°. . . . 7336
Practice, proceedings, and lawes of armes. 1593. 4°. . . 1697
Threefold answer vnto...Three supposed conversions of England. 1606. 4°. 2357
Treatise of ecclesiasticall discipline. 1591. 4°. 1731
True relation of Englands happinesse. 1629. 4°. . . . 6996
See Apologia pro Christiano Batavo. 1610. 8°. 6884
— E. (O.). Briefe replie. 1600.
— — Detection. 1602.
— Parsons (R.). Brief...confvtation. 1603.
— — Treatise of three conversions... 1603 (1604).
Sutclin (John). Verses in Coryate (T.). Coryats Crudities. 1611. 3076
Sutton (Christopher). Disce mori. 1600. 12°. 1987
Disce vivere. 1603. 12°. 2342
Godly Meditations vpon...the Lordes Supper. 1601. 12°. . 7333
— With Appendix. 1630. 12°. 7795
Sutton (Edward). Serpent anatomized. 1626. 4°. 4957
Sutton (Richard). *See* Catharine of Siena. Orcharde of Syon. 1519. F°.
Sutton (Thomas). Englands first and second summons. Ed. 3. 1633. 12°. 4894
Englands summons. 1613. 8°. 3219
Good fight of faith. 1624. 4°. 2552
Jethroes counsell to Moses. 1631. 4°. 5053
Lectures upon Romans xi. 1632. 4°. 4848
See Burrell (P.). Sutton's Synagogue. 1629.
— London. Charterhouse. 1614.
Swadon (William). [Upon the death of Q. Anne.] *See* Camden (W.). Remaines. 1623.
Swaine (M^ris^ Mary). [Funeral sermon.] 1630 etc. *See* Langhorne (L.).
Swale (Sir Richard). *See* Blackwell (G.). Large examination. 1607.
Swan (John). Speculum mundi. Cambridge, 1635. 4°. . . 5777
See Daneau (L.). Treatise tovching Antichrist. 1589.
Swayne (Arthur), *Regal.* Verses in Camb. Univ. Voces. 1640. . 5836
Sweden. *See* Nixon (A.). Warres of Swethland. 1609.
See North (G.). Description of Swedland. 1561.
Short svrvey of the kingdome of Sweden. 1632. 4°. . . 3820
See Poland. Vladislaus IV. 1635. The forme.
Swedish Intelligencer (by W. Watts)[1].
Part I. Ed. 1? 1632. 4°. 7612
Ed. 2. 1632. 4°. 4620
Ed. 3. 1632. 4°. 4621
II. Ed. 1. 1632. 4°. 4713
Ed. 2. 1632. 4°. 7918

[1] See J. Nichols, *Lit. Anec.* IV. 39 *n.*; Lowndes; J. Venn, *Biog. History*, s.v.

No.

Swedish Intelligencer *cont.*
III–IV. 1633. 4°. 4719
V. 'Continuation.' 1633. 4°. 4961
VIII. Modern History of the World. 1635. 4°. . . 3549
1. Principall passages. 'No. 1.' 1636. . . 4644
Swedish discipline. Ed. 2. 1632. 4°. 3886–7
Sweeper (Walter). Briefe treatise. 1622. 4°. 3340
Sweert (Francis). Life of Ortelius. *See* Ortelius (A.). Theatrum. 1606.
Sweet (J.), *Jesuit.* *See* Featley (D.). Romish Fisher. 1624.
Swinburne (Henry). Briefe treatise of testaments and last willes. 1590(–1). 4°. 7357
— Corrected. 1640. 4°. 4749
Swineshede (Roger). Insolubilia. *See* Logic. [19 Latin treatises. Oxford, 1483?] 4°. 78
Swinnerton (John). *See* Swynnerton.
Switzerland. Reformed Church. Belijdenisse. A. de Solemne, Nordwitz, 1568. 8°. 7879
See Confession. [1568?]
Swyburggen. *See* Zweibrücken.
Swynnerton (John). Christian love-letter. 1606. 4°. 2761
Sydenham (George). Verses in Coryate (T.). Coryates Crvdities. 1611. 3076
Verses in Camdeni Insignia. 1624. 5346
Sydenham (Hopton). Verses in Oxf. Univ. Magd. Coll. 1612. . 5302
Sydenham (Humphrey). Athenian Babler. 1627. 4°. . . . 4192
Jacob and Esau. 1626. 4°. 4602
Natures overthrow...funerall of Sir J. Sydenham. 1626. 4°. 4804
Sermons vpon Solemne occasions. 1637. 4°. 3836
Sydenham (Sir John), Kt. [Funeral.] *See* Sydenham (H.). Natvres overthrow. 1626.
Sydley (Sir William). *See* Sidley.
Sydrach. Certayne reasons. *See* Aristotle. Secreta secretorum. 1528. 4°.
Sydserf. *See* Synserfius.
Syl. (Jos.) [*i.e.* Sylvester]. *See* Matthieu (P.). The heroyk life. 1612.
Sylburgius (Frid). Verses in Buchanan (G.). Psalmorum Davidis. 1640. 5209
Sylvaticus (Matthæus). *See* Herbal. 1561.
Sylvester I, *Pope.* *See* Constantine I. Treatyse. [Ab. 1525.]
Sylvester (J.). Lachrimæ Lachrimarum. [1612.] 4°. 2516
Parliament of vertues royal. [1614.] 8°. 6898
— [Ab. 1614.] 8°. 7403
Verses in Blaxton (J.). English vsurer. 1634. . . . 4895
See Du Bartas (G., sieur). Devine Weekes. 1605–6 etc.
— Matthieu (P.). Heroyk life. 1612.
Sylvius (A.) [qu. And. Woode?]. Verses in Camb. Univ. Epicedium. 1612. 5665
See Sylvius (Andreas).
Sylvius (Æneas). *See* Pius II, *Pope.*
Sylvius (Andreas). Verses and Theses in Adamson (J.). Εἰσόδια. 1618. 5960
See Sylvius (A.).
Sylvius (Dominicus). Verses in Pelegromius (S.). 1603. . . 7881
Sym (John). Lifes preservative against self-killing. 1637. 4°. . 4313
Syme (John). *See* Negus (W.). Mans active obedience. 1619. 4°.
Symeon, *Metaphrastes.* *See* Simeon.
Symmachia. *See* Scott (T.). Vox populi. 1622–4.
Symonds (William). Pisgah evangelica. 1606. 4°. . . . 2944
Symonds (W.). Virginia. 1609. 4°. 2179
Sympson (Cuthbert). *See* Symson.
Sympson (William). Full...Genealogie of Iesus Christ. Cambridge, 1619. 4°. 5690
See Simonides.

No.

Syms (Christopher). Apology for...his...method of teaching. 1633. 4°. 6046
Symson (A.). *See* Simson.
Symson (Cuthbert). Letter. *See* Coverdale (M.). Certain...letters. 1564.
Symson (Patrick). *See* Simson.
Synagogue. 1640. 12°. *See* Harvey (C.).
Synge (George). Reioynder to the reply...of W. Malone. Part 1. Dublin, 1632. 4°. 6041
Synod. *See* Certaine considerations. 1605. 6469
Synods, General. *See* Bullinger (H.). Fifte godlie sermons. 1577 etc.
Synserfius (Georgius). Verses in Adamson (J.). Εἰσόδια. 1618. . 5960
Synserfius (Thomas). Verses in Adamson (J.). Εἰσόδια. Ibid. 1618. 5960
Szegedinus (Stephanus), *Pannonius*. *See* Kis.

T. (A.). *See* Broughton (H.). Letter to a friend. 1612. 4°.
T. (A.), *Practitioner in Physicke and Chyrurgery*. *See* W. (G.). Rich storehouse. 1630.
T. (B.). Verses in Jewel (J.). Adv. T. Hardingum. 1578. . . 1535
T. (C.), *I.C.F.A.* Verses in Crashaw (W.). Falsificationum. 1606. 2262
T. (D.). Dove and the Serpent. 1614. 4°. 2751
Verses in Overbury (Sir T.). His Wife. Ed. 11. 1622. . 3380
See Tuvill (D.). Vade Mecum. 1629 etc.
T. (D.), *Gent.* *See* Tuvill (D.). Essaies. 1608.
T. (F.). [=T. Fitzherbert.] *See* Collins (S.). Epphata. 1617.
See Fitzherbert (T.). Supplement. 1613.
— — Adioynder to the supplement. 1613.
T. (G.). Verses in Gostwyke (R.). Deo et ecclesiae. 1616. . . 5678
See Travers (W.). Answere to a Supplicatorie epistle. [158–]. 8°.
T. (H.). Certaine articles or forcible reasons. Antwerp, 1600. 8°. 6137
See Barlow (W.). Defence of the Articles of the Protestants Religion. 1601.
T. (H.). [qu. T. Heywood?] *See* Barckley (Sir R.). Felicitie of Man. 1631.
T. (H.). *See* Bulkeley (E.). Apologie. 1608.
T. (H.), *C.T.* Verses in Camb. Univ. Anthologia. 1632. . . 5741
T. (H.), *Minister.* *See* Casmannus (O.). Vade Mecum. 1606. 8°.
T. (I.). *See* Boethius. Five bookes of philosophicall Comfort. 1609.
T. (I.), *A.M.* Verses in Randolph (T.). Poems. 1640. . . 5500
T. (I.), *B.A. Ball. Coll.* Verses in Oxf. Univ. Horti. 1640. . . 5499
T. (I.), *C. Iohan.* Verses in Camb. Univ. Gratulatio. 1623. . 5695
T. (I.), *C.T.* Camb. Univ. Gratulatio. 1623. 5695
T. (J.). Verses in Welby (H.). Phœnix. 1637. . . . 3713
T. (J.), *C.C.* Verses in Camb. Univ. Fasciae. 1633. . . . 5808
T. (Katharine), *Catholic gentlewoman.* *See* Swynnerton (J.). Christian love-letter 1606.
T. (L.). Iudgement... *See* Knewstub (J.). Confutation. 1579.
See Avila. Avdi filia. 1620. 4°.
— Tomson (L.). Answere. [1570.] 8°.
T. (M.). *See* Drelincourt (C.). Roote of romish rites. 1630. 4°.
T. (N.). *See* Salvianus. Quis Diues Salvus. 1618. 8°.
T. (P.). Verses in Cambridge Lachrymae. 1587. . . . 2123
T. (R.). De Templis. 1638. 12°. 5112
See Carlile (C.). Discourse. 1572.
T. (R.), *B.D.* *See* Tyrer (R.).
T. (R.), *T.C. Gen.* Verses in Camb. Univ. Epicedium. 1612. . 5665
T. (S.). *See* W. (H.). Θρηνοικος. 1640.
T. (T.). Verses in Bate (J.). The mysteries. 1635. . . 4012
See Tuke (T.). Discovrs against Painting.
— Tymme (T.). Silver watch-bell. 1606.
T. (T.), *Sacristan and Catholike Romanist.* Whetstone of Reproofe. 'Catuapoli.' 1638. 8°. 7817

No.
T. (W.). Godlie and comfortable letter. 12°. 6785
Vindiciae Ecclesiae Anglicanae. 1630. 4° 4686
Verses in Doddridge (Sir J.). Lawyers Light. 1629. . . 4958
[=W. Tindale.] *See* Bible. English Pentateuch. 1534.
[=W. Traheron.] *See* Mexia (P.). The imperial historie. 1623.
See Tindal (W.). Exposicion. [1530?]
— — Practyse of Prelates. 1530.
T. (Z.), *C.T.* *See* Tuttesham (Z.).
Tables and Easie Rules. 1582. 8°. 1007
Table collected of the yeres. 1564 (1565). 8°. 1172
— 1571. 8°. 1006
Tables of leases and interest. 1628. 8°. 5038
See Brief Treatise. 1582. 8°.
Tacitus. Annales...Germanie. Trans. R. Grenewey. 1604. F°. . 2080
— 1612. F°. 2093
— 1622. F°. 7447
— 1640. F°. 4750
Vita di G. Agricola. 1585. 4°. 1937
Ende of Nero and beginning of Galba...Histories...Agricola. Trans. Savile. Oxford, 1591. F°. 5236
— Ed. 3. 1604–5. F°. 2081
— Ed. 4. 1612. F°. 2094
— Ed. 5. 1622. F°.
— Ed. 6. 1640. F°. 4751
Taffin (J.). Amendment of life. 1595. 4°. 1735
Of the markes of the Children of God. Trans. A. Prowse. 1615. 8°. 3412
Tagaultius (Joannes). *See* Banister (J.). Needefvll...treatise. 1575.
— — Workes... 1633.
Tailor (Robert). Sacred Hymns. 1615. 4°. 3413
Talæus (Audomarus). Rhetorica. Cantab., 1631. 8°. . . . 5740
— 1636. 8°. 4120
Tanfield (Sir Lawrence). *See* Exchequer Court. 1608.
Tanner (Salo). Verses in Smith (J.). True travels. 1630. . . 4836
Tapp (J.). Pathway to knowledge. 1613. 8°. 1395
Tapper (Ric.). Verses in Camdeni Insignia. 1624. . . . 5346
Tarlton[1] (Ric.). [Toyes of an Idle Head. 1576?] 4°. . . 1443
Tartaglia (Niccolo). *See* Tapp (J.). Pathway. 1613.
Tasso (T.). Godfrey of Bulloigne. Trans. E. Fairefax. 1600. F°. . 2076
— Ed. 2. 1624. F°. 3521
Plutonis concilium...Solymeidos. 1584. 4°. 1935
Solymeidos libri duo. 1584. 4°. 1936
Tasss [*qu.* brother of L. Roberts?]. Verses in Roberts (L.). Merchants mappe. 1638. 5133
Tatius. *See* Achilles Tatius.
Tauler (John). Commvnication of Doctor Thaulervs. *See* Francis de Sales. Introduction. 1616.
Taurinus (Jacobus). *See* Proclamation. 1618. 4°. . . . 7914
Taverner (Richard). *See* Augsburg Confession. The confession. [1536?]
— *See* Melanchthon (P.). Apologie. 1536.
See Bible. English. 1539 etc.
— Cato (D.). Moralia. Mimi Publiani. 1562. 8°.
— Epistles and Gospels. 1540. 4°. . . . . 362, 366 etc.
— Erasmus. Proverbes. 1552.
— Sarcerius (E.). Common places of scripture. London. 1538. 8°.
Taylor (Jeremy). Sermon preached in Saint Maries. Gunpowder Treason. Oxford, 1638. 4°. 5484
Taylor (John). All the workes. 1630. F°. 3812

[1] Wrong ascription. *See* Breton (N.). The Flourish.

No.

Taylor (John), *cont.* The great O Toole. 1622. 8°. . . . 3384
The needles excellency. Ed. 12. 1640. Oblong 8°. . . . 4925
Verses in Forbes (P.). Funerals. 1637. 6007
— Welby (H.). Phoenix. 1637. 3713
Taylor (Rowland). [Letters.] *See* Coverdale (M.). Certain...letters. 1564.
Taylor (Theophilus). Mappe of Moses. 1629. 4°. 3984
Taylor (Tho.). Christs combate and conquest. Cambridge, 1618. 4°. 5684
Christ revealed. 1635. 4°. 4292
Christs victorie over the dragon. 1633. 4°. 4277
Circumspect walking. 1631. 12°. 7891
Commentarie vpon...Titus. Cambridge, 1619. 4°. . . . 5691
Japhets first public perswasion. 1612. 4°. 5669
Man in Christ. 1628. 12°. 7602
— Ed. 3. 1632. 12°. 4490
Mappe of Rome. 1620. 4°. 7478
— 1634. 4°. 4150
Meditations from the creatures. Ed. 3. 1632. 12°. . . . 4491
Parable of the sower. 1621. 4°. 3015
— Ed. 3. 1634. 4°. 4150
Practice of repentance. 1628. 12°. 7603
— Ed. 3. 1632. 12°. 4492
Regula Vita. 1635. 12°. 4293
Three Treatises. 1633. 12°. 3826
Two Sermons. 1624. 4°. 7778
See Perkins (W.). Godlie exposition upon Jude. 1606. 4°.
— — Works. Vol. 3. (Jude.) 1606. F°. 5656
— W. (H.). Θρηνοικος. 1640.
Te Deum. (Metrical version.) Fragment of book not identified. [Ab. 1550.] *See* no. 946.
Tedder (Richard). Sermon preached at Wimondham...Visitation. 1637. 4°. 4032
Tedder (W.). Recantations. 1588. 4°. 1359
Teelinck (Willem). Pauls complaint. 1621. 4°. 3845
Teigh (Robert). *See* Tighe.
Teixeira (José). Strangest adventure...concerning...the King of Portugal Dom Sebastian. 1601. 4°. 7765
See Ol. (P.), *Spanish Pilgrim.* Treatise Paræneticall. 1598.
Tejedas (Fernando de). *See* Liturgia Inglesa. [1613?] 4°.
Temple, Temples. *See* T. (R.). De Templis. 1638.
Temple of Glass. [1500?] 4°. *See* Lydgate (J.).
Temple (W.). Fran. Mildapetti Navarreni ad Everardum Digbeium... admonitio de unica P. Rami methodo. 1580. 8°. . . . 1633
Logical analysis of twentie select psalmes. 1605. 4°. . . 7469
Pro Mildapetti de vnica methodo defensione. 1581. 8°. . . 1885
Verses *quater* in Cambridge Lachrymae. 1587. . . . 2123
— Cheke (Sir J.). De obitu M. Buceri. 1551. 734
— Wilson (Sir T.). Vita. 1551. 631
See Martinus (J.). De prima Generatione. 1584.
— Ramus (P.). Dialecticae libri dvo. 1584.
Temporis filia veritas. A mery devise. 1589. 4°. 6791
Ten Commandments. *See* Hooper (J.). Declaration. . 953, 954, 6283
[Ab. 1538.] *See* Lord's Prayer. 8°. 6681
[Ang.-Sax. and Eng.] *See* Ælfric. A Saxon treatise. 1623.
— — Testimonie of Antiquitie. [1567?]
See Dod (J.) and Cleaver (R.). 1630.
(Metrical.) *See* Smith (Jude). Misticall deuise. 1575.
Tenures (frag.). W. de Worde [15–]. 8°. 244
(Olde). J. Rastell [15–]. F°. 350
— R. Redman, 1532. 8°. 378

No.
Tenures (Olde), *cont.* Berthelet, 1530. 8°. 420
Tenores novelli. 1496? etc. *See* Littleton (Sir T.).
Teonville (Jean de). *See* Dicta Philosophorum. 1528.
Terceira, Island of. *See* Conestaggio (G.). Historie. 1600.
Terentius. Comedie a Guidone Juvenale ter explanate. Paris, 15 Julij 1504. F°. 6183
Terence in English. (Lat. Eng.) Ed. R. Bernard. Cantabrigiae, 1598. 4°. 5597
— Ed. 2. Cantabrigiae, 1607. 4°. 5644
— Ed. 4. 1614. 4°. 3755
— Ed. 5. 1629. 4°. 4707
Andria. (Lat. Eng.) Dr Webbe. 1629. 4°. 3042
Eunuchus. (Lat. Eng.) 1629. 4°. 2459
Vulgaria. Oxford [1483]. 4°. 76
— Machlinia [1483]. 4°. 101–2
— Antwerp, 1486. 4°. 125
— W. de Worde, 3 Aug. 1529. 8°. 198
— W. de Worde [15–]. 8°. 245
Flovres for Latine speaking...by N. Udall. 1560. 8°. . . 507
'Terinin.' Verses in Davies (R.). A funeral sermon. 1577. . . 1416–
Termes de la Ley. *For earlier entries see* Rastell (J.).
Stationers, 1629. 8°. 2460
Assignes of J. More, 1636. 8°. 5080
Terrent (Tho.), *M.A.*, *Ch. Ch. Oxon.* Verses in Randolph (T.). Poems. 1640. 5500
Terry (John). Reasonablenesse of wise...truth. Oxford, 1617. 4°. . 5331
Theologicall Logicke. Oxford, 1625. 4°. 5358
— Oxford, 1626. 4°. 5365
Tesauro (Emanuele). Cæsares; et...carmina. Ed. 2. Oxonii, 1637. 8°. 5476–7
Testament (New). *See* Bible.
Testaments of the twelve Patriarchs. 1576. 7124
Testimonie of Antiqvitie...in the Saxons tyme. [1567?] 8°. . . 895
Ed. 2. *See* Lisle (W.). Saxon treatise. 1623. 4°.
— Divers ancient monuments. 1638. 4°.
Texeda (Fernando de). Hispanus conversus. 1623. 4°. . . . 3438
Hispanus retextus. 1623. 4°. 3439
Miracles vnmasked. 1625. 4°. 3448
Scrutamini Scripturas: the exhortation of a spanish converted monke. 1624. 4°. 3978
Texeira. *See* Teixeira.
Textor (Benedictus). Of the nature...of Cancers. *See* Banister (R.). Treatise. 1622.
Textor (Ravisius). *See* Ravisius.
Th. (Jo.). *See* Parry (W.). True...declaration. [1584.]
Th. (T.). [=T. Thorpe, *bookseller*?] *See* Epictetus. 1616. 12°.
Th. (Th.). [T. Thorpe.] *See* Augustine. Of the Citie of God. 1610.
Theloall (S.). Digest des Briefes originals. 1579. 8°. . . . 1139
Theobalds. [22 Sept. 1571.] *See* Burghley (W. Cecil, lord). Carmen Gratulatorium... [1571.]
1606. *See* no. 7352.
Theocritus. [*Gr. Lat.*] *See* Poetae minores. 1635.
Theodolus. *See* Theodulus.
Theodoricus de Niem, Nyem. *See* Dietrich von Nieheim.
Theodorus, *bp. of Mopsuestia.* *See* Chrysostom...opera. 1613.
Theodorus (Vitus), *Norimbergensis.* *See* Dietrich.
Theodosius, *emperor.* *See* Nicodemus. Nychodemus Gospell. 1509 *etc.*
Theodulus. Liber Theodoli cum Commento. 1508. 4°. . . . 6075
— W. de Worde, 1515. 4°. 173
Theognis. [*Gr. Lat.*] *See* Poetae minores. 1635.
Theologia Germanica. Libellus aureus...I. Theophilo, interprete. 1632. 8°. 7565

No.

Theophile, D. L. Tragicall Historie of the troubles...of the lowe Countries. [1583.] 4°. 1191
Theophilus. *See* Henricpetri (A.). Chronyc. 1579. 8°.
See Wilkinson (W.), *M.A.* Confutation. 1579.
— Divine and politike observations. 1638.
Theophilus (Johannes), *pseud.* *See* Castalio (Seb.).
Theophilus Philadelphus. Ad reverendissimos patres...episcopos. 1625. 4°. 6969
Theophilus Philanthropus. *See* Lockyer (N.). Christs commvnion. 1640.
Theophrastus. Characters. [English] by J. Healey. *See* Epictetus Manuall. 1616.
Theophylactus. Ἐξήγησις τῶν ἐπιστολῶν Παύλου (Gr. Lat.). Studio A. Lindselli. 1636. F°. 7649
Thesaurus Amicorum. Lyons. 8°. 6408
Thesaurus Pauperum. *See* Book of Medicines. [1526.]
Thesaurus (Emanuel). *See* Tesauro.
Thibaldus Tragœdia. *See* Snelling (T.). 1640.
Thibault (J.). Prognosticacyon. 1530. 8°. 536
Thin (Francis). *See* Thynne.
Thomas à Kempis. *See* Imitation.
Thomas, *Prior of the Charterhouse of St Anne, near Coventry.* *See* Alcock (J.). Mons Perfectionis. 1497 *etc.*
Thomas (Thomas). Dictionarium linguae lat. et angl. Cantebrigiae [1588?]. 8°. 5535
— Ed. 3. Cantabrigiae, 1592. 4°. 5557
— Ed. 4. „ 1594. 8°. 5569
— Ed. 5. (Lat. Eng. Gr.) Cantabrigiae, 1596. 4°. . . 5585
— Ed. 6. (Lat. Eng.) „ 1600. 8°. . . 5600
— Ed. 7. „ „ 1606. 4°. . . 5639
— Ed. 8. „ „ 1610. 8°. . . 5647
— Ed. 11. (Lat. and Eng.) 1619. 8°. . . . 3768
— Ed. 12. (Lat. Eng. and Eng. Lat.) 1620. 4°. . . 4693
See Ovid. Metamorphoses. 1584.
Thomas (W.). Historie of Italie. 1549. 4°. 499
— 1561. 4°. 1209
Vanitee of this world. 1549. 8°. 500
Verses in Oxf. Univ. Horti. 1640. 5499
Thomitanus (Bernandinus). Verses in Harvey (G.). Gratulationum. 1578. 1495
Thomlynson (Robert). *See* Tomlinson.
Thompson (John), *instrument maker.* *See* Gunter (E.). De sectore. 1623.
Thompson (Marmaduke), *Jesus Coll.* Verses in Camb. Univ. Lacrymæ. 1619. 5689
— — Epithalam. 1625. 5702
Thompson (Richard), *M.A.* *See* Bible, English (Royal). 1611. . 2635
Thompson (Sam), *Windsor Herald.* Verses in Brooke (R.). A discovery. 1622. 2793
Thompson (Thomas). Friendly farewell. 1616. 4°. . . . 3417
Thomson (George). Ἀνακεφαλαίωσις s. de reductione regnorum britanniae. 1604. 8°. 3359
Vindex veritatis. 1606. 8°. 2358
Thomson (Richard). Elenchus refutationis Torturae Torti. 1611. 8°. 2640
Thorius (Raphael). Hymnus Tabaci. (Hiems.) 1626. 12°. . 4805
— Verses in Camden (W.). Annales. 1615(-27). . . 3106
— Fisher (A.). A defence. 1630. 3176
L'Obel (M. de). In G. Rondelletii...officinam. 1605. . . 7247
Thornburgh (John). Λιθοθεωρικός. Oxoniae, 1621. 4°. . . 5341
Thorndike (Herbert). Epitome Lexici hebraici, syriaci, rabinici, et arabici. 1635. F°. 5064

No.

Thorndike (Herbert), *cont.* Verses in Hippocrates. 1633. . . 5812
Thorne (Edward). Verses in Gardiner (R.). Profitable Instructions. 1603. 2014
Thorney (Thomas). Verses in Gerard (J.). Herball. 1597. . 2348
Thornton (Richard). Ægyptian Courtier. 1635. 4°. 4116
Thorold (Ed.). Verses in Camb. Univ. Carmen. 1635. . . 5770
Thorold (Timothy), *M.D.* Verses in Hippocrates. 1633. . . 5812
Thorold (William). Verses in Camb. Univ. Carmen. 1635. . 5770
Thorp (Edmund), *Christ's Coll.* Verses in Camb. Univ. *Συνωδία.* 1637. 5790
— — Voces. 1640. 5836
Thorpe (John), *Reginal.* Verses in Camb. Univ. Voces. 1640. . 5836
Thorpe (Thomas). *See* Augustine. Of the Citie of God. 1610.
See Th. (T.).
Thorys (J.). Verses in Florio (G.). Queen Anna's New World. 1611. 3374
Thou (Jacques Auguste de). *See* Apologia pro Christiano Batavo. 1610.
See Barksdale (C.). Monvmenta litteraria... 1640.
— Foxe (J.). Actes and Monuments. 1610 *etc.*
Three severall treatises concerning the truce. 1630. 4°. . . . 3544
Θρηνοικος. 1640. *See* W. (H.).
Throckmorton (Francis). Discoverie of the treasons. 1584. 4°. . 6779
Throckmorton (Job). *See* Penry (J.). Protestacyon of martin marprelay. [1589.] 8°.
[Defence.] *See* Sutcliffe (M.). Answere. 1595.
Thuanus (Jacobus Augustus). *See* Thou (J. A. de).
Thucydides. Hystory. Trans. T. Nicholls. 25 July 1550. F°. . 7154
— Trans. T. Hobbes. 1634. F°. 5069
Thulesius (Gulielmus). Verses in Cheke (Sir J.). De obitu M. Buceri. 1551. 734
Thurston (Joseph), *B.D.* Verses in Hippocrates. 1633. . . 5812
Thynne (Francis). Newes from the north. 1585. 4°. 2002
Verses in Chaucer (G.). Workes. 1602. 1749
See Holinshed (R.). Chronicles. 1587 etc.
Thynne (Sir Thomas), *Kt.* [Funeral.] *See* W. (H.). Θρηνοικος. 1640.
Tichborne (Sir Benjamin). *See* S. (C.). Copie of a letter. 1603. 4°.
Tighe or Teigh (Robert). *See* Bible, English (Royal). 1611. . . 2635
Tignonville (Guillaume de). *See* Dicta Philosophorum. 1528.
Tilenus (Daniel). De disciplina ecclesiastica. Abredoniae, 1622. 8°. 5998
Paræenesis ad Scotos. 1620. 8°. 3134
True copy of two letters. 1605. 4°. 2885
Tillesley (Richard). Animadversions vpon M. Seldens history of tithes. 1619. 4°. 3496
— Ed. 2. 1621. 4°. 3680
Tilly (Jean Tserclæs), *General.* *See* Sweden. The Swedish Intelligencer. 1632.
Timme (Thomas). *See* Tymme.
Timotheus. Ad ecclesiam Catholicam. *See* Salvianus. De gubernatione dei. 1633.
Tinckler (Isaac). *See* Tinkler.
Tindal (Fran.). Verses in Camb. Univ. Genethl. 1631. . . . 5731
Tindal (Humphry). Verses in Cambridge Lachrymae. 1587. . 2123
Tindale (W.). Whole workes of Tyndall, Frith and Barnes. 1573 (1572). F°. 833
Answere vnto Sir T. Mores dialoge. [Ab. 153- .] 8°. . . 6679
— *See* More (Sir T.). Confutacyon. 1532-3.
Briefe declaration of the sacraments. [1548?] 8°. . . . 1066
Exposicion vppon the v. vi. vii. chapters of Matthew. [Ab. 1539- ?] 8°. 6097
— [Ab. 153- .] 8°. 6682
— 1548. Day and Seres. 8°. 901

No.
Tindale (W.). Exposicion vppon the v. vi. vii. chapters of Matthew *cont.*
— W. Hill. [1550.] 8°. 1032
Obedience of a christen man. 'H. Luft, Marlborowe, 29 Oct. 1535.' 8°. 6100
— T. Ranalde and W. Hyll for R. Jugge. 8°. 7101
— T. Berthelet. [Ab. 1541?] 4°. 7088
— W. Copland. 1561. 8°. 1082
Parable of the wycked mammon. 'Malborowe, 8 May 1528.' 4°. 7089
— [1548?] 4°. 1033
Practyse of Prelates. 'Marborch,' 1530. 8°. 6274
See Bible, English (Matthew's). 1537 *etc.*
— — (Taverner's). 1539 *etc.*
— — Pentateuch. 1534.
— — Newe Testament. 1534 *etc.*
— Joye (G.). Apologye. 1535.
— More (Sir T.). Dyaloge. 1531. F°.
— Supper of the Lorde. 1533.
— Tracy (W.). Testament. 1535. 8°.
— Wiclif (J.). Wycklyffes wycket. 1546 *etc.*
Tinkler (Isaac), *Caius.* Verses in Camb. Univ. Voces. 1640. . 5836
— Ovid. Fasti. 1640. 5849
Tipper (Robert). *See* Broadside. 1630. 7424
Tireman (Joh.). Verses in Camdeni Insignia. 1624. . . . 5346
Tirwhyt (William). *See* Tyrwhitt.
Titus. *See* Destruction. Dystruccyon of Jherusalem.
To my faythfull Brethren now afflycted. [1566?] *See* Whittingham (W.).
To my louynge brethren. [1566?] *See* Gilby (A.).
To the Reader. To my faythfull Brethren... (An answere.) [1566?] 8°. 6416
To the Seminarye Priestes. 1592. 4°. 2006
Tobacco. *See* Metamorphosis of Tabacco. 1602.
See D. (E.). Copy of a Letter. 1606.
— Gardiner (E.). The triall. 1610.
— Brathwaite (R.). Disputation. 1617. 8°.
— Proclamations. 1619. Broadside.
— Bennett (E.). [1620?]
— Considerations tovching. 1625.
— Thorius (R.). Hymnus. 1626.
— Proclamations. 13 Oct. 1633.
— Venner (T.). Via recta. 1638.
Toledo (Pedro de). *See* France. Louis XIII. 1617.
Tolly (John). Verses in Camb. Univ. Anthologia. 1632. . . 5741
Tolwyn (William). *See* Bale (J.). Yet a course at the Romyshe foxe. 1543.
Tom tell troath. [1630?] 4°. 7006
Tombes (John). *See* Pemble (W.). Five godly sermons. 1628.
Tomkins (Na.). Verses in Seneca. Tragœdiæ. 1613 *etc.* . 7781 *etc.*
Tomkis (Thomas). Albumazar. 1615. 4°. 3662
— [1615?] 4°. 3663
— 1634. 4°. 3698
Tomkys (John). *See* Bullinger (H.). Most godly...Discourse. 1579. 8°.
Tomlinson (Robert). Verses in Turner (W.). Preseruatiue. 1551. . 955
[Book-label. Ab. 1590.] 8°. 6797
Tommai (Petrus), *Ravennas.* Art of Memory. Trans. R. Copland. [1548?] 8°. 716
Tomson (John). Verses in Cheke (Sir J.). De obitu M. Buceri. 1551. 734
Tomson (L.). Answere to...Fecknam. [1569?] 8°. . . 1524
See Bible, English N.T. (Genevan). 1583 *etc.*
— La Place (P. de). Treatise. 1576. 8°.
Tomson (William). In Canticum Canticorum...explanatio. 1583. 8°. 1896
Tongue-Combat. *See* Hexham (H.).

No.
Tonstall (Anthony). *See* Hoby (Sir E.). Curry-combe. 1615.
Tooke (George). Legend of Brita-mart. 1635. 8°. 3835
Tooker (Will.). Charisma. 1597. 4°. 2145
Duellum s. singulare certamen cum M. Becano. 1611. 8°. . 3578
Of the fabrique of the Church. 1604. 8°. 3360
Toomes (William). *See* Heywood (T.). Hierarchie. 1635.
Top (Alexander). *See* Bible, Eng. Psalms. Book of prayses. 1629.
Topham (Ant.). Verses in Cam. Univ. Dolor. 1625. . . . 5701
Topping (John). Verses in Cam. Univ. Rex redux. 1633. . . 5748
— — Carmen. 1635. 5770
— — Συνωδία. 1637. 5790
Topsell (Edward). Times lamentation...on...Joel. 1599. 4°. . . 7348
See Holland (Henry). Historie of Adam. 1606. 4°.
— Richardson (C.). The repentance of Peter. 1612. 4°.
Torporley (Nathaniel). Diclides coelometricae. 1602. 4°. . . 2925
Torquemada (A. de). Spanish Mandeuile. 1600. 4°. . . . 1779
Torriano (Giov.). Italian tutor. 1640. 4°. 5101
New and easie directions. Cambridge [1640?]. 4°. . . . 5855
Torsellino (Orazio). Admirable life of S. Francis Xavier. Trans. T. F. Paris, 1632. 4°. 6227
History of our B. Lady of Loreto. 1608. 8°. 6219
Torshel (Samuel). Saints humiliation. 1633. 4°. 3891
Tossanus (Daniel). Exercise of the faithfull soule. 1583. 8°. . 1643
Synopsis...of the fathers. Trans. A. S. [1635.] 8°. . . 5145
Total Summe. *See* Floyd (J.). Chvrch Conquerant. 1638–9.
Tottell (Richard). *See* Assizes. Abridgement. 1555.
See Statutes. England. Magna Charta. 1556.
Tounley (Zouch). *See* Townley.
Tournon, Jesuits at. *See* Nîmes University. Academiae...responsio. 1584.
Toussain (Daniel). *See* Tossanus.
Towers (W.), *Chr. Ch.* Verses in Ferrand (J.). Ἐρωτομανία. 1640. 5498
Townley (Zouch). Verses in Horatius. De arte poetica. 1640. . 3728
See Oxford University. Camdeni Insignia. 1624. 4°.
Townsend. *See* Townshend.
Townshend (Sir Roger). *See* Year Book. 2 Edward IV. . . 323
Tract against Vsvrie. 1621. *See* Culpepper (Sir T.).
Tracy (Richard). Brief and short declaracyon...what is a sacrament. 1548. 8°. 1063
[Preparation to the Crosse.] *See* Vox Piscis. 1627.
Profe and declaration of...Fayth. [Ab. 154–.] 8°. . . . 7096
Supplycacyon to our most soueraigne lorde...Henry the eyght. Dec. 1544. 8°. 6110
Supplication. [158–.] 8°. 7790
Tracy (William). Testament...expounded by W. Tindall and J. Frith. 1535. 8°. 6101
See Wiclif (J.). Wycklyffes wycket... 1546 etc.
Trades Increase. 1615. *See* R. (I.).
Trafford (Sir Edmond). *See* Massie (W.). Sermon. 1586.
Traheron (Barth.). Exposition of a parte of S. Johannes Gospel. 1557. 8°. 7152
— 1558. 8°. 6742
Exposition of the 4 chapter of S. Johns Revelation. 1573. 8°. 1474
— 1583. 8°. 1821
Verses in Cheke (Sir J.). De obitu M. Buceri. 1551. . . 734
— Parkhurst (J.). Ludicra. 1573. 838
See Vigo (J. de). Most excellent workes of chirurgerie. 1571. F°.
— — Whole worke. 1586.
Traheron (W.). *See* Mexia (P.). Historie. 1604.
— Imperiall historie. 1623. F°.
Transportation. *See* Proclamations. 30 April, 1637.

No.
Transylvania. Bethlen Gabriel. *See* Bohemia. 1620. Articles.
Travers (E.). Verses in Camb. Univ. Lacrymæ. 1619. . . 5689
— — Dolor. 1625. 5701
— — Epithalam. 1625. 5702
Travers (Walter). Answer to a svpplicatorie Epistle. [1583.] 8°. . 1991
Full and plaine declaration of Ecclesiasticall Discipline. 1574. 4°. 6299
— Geneva, 1580. 8°. 6330
Supplication made to the privy Counsel. Oxford, 1612. 4° . 5307
— *See* Hooker (R.). Certayne divine tractates. 1618 etc. 3125 etc.
See Collection of certain Letters. 1590.
— Hooker (R.). Answere. 1612.
Treasure of Knowledge. 1626. 12°. 3806
Treasure of Pore Men. [1526?] 4°. 365
— 1575. 8°. 1330
Treasure of Tranquillity. Trans. I. Maxwell. 1611. 12°. . . 3639
Treasurie of auncient and moderne times. 1613. *See* Milles (T.).
Treasurie of Hidden Secrets. 1633. 4°. 2042
— 1637. 4°. 5131
Treatise concernynge divers of the constitutions prouynciall and legantines. [1532?] 8°. 565
Treatise concernynge the diuision betwene the spirytualtie and temporaltie. [After 1523.] 8°. 405
[After 1528.] 8°. 525
Treatise concerninge the power of the clergye and the lawes of the Realme. [1532?] 8°. 566
Treatise conteining meditations of trew and perfect consolation. Trans. R. Filles. [1563?] 8°. 1291
Treatise. *See* Briefe Treatise containing...Tables. 1582. 8°. . 1007
Treatise how by the worde. [1557?] *See* Bucer (M.).
Treatise of blazing Starres. 1618. *See* Fleming (A.).
Treatise of Christian Renunciation. [Ab. 1600.] 8°. . . . 6832
Treatise of divine worship. 1604. 8°. 6468
Treatise of ecclesiastical and Politicall Power. 1612. *See* Δ.
Treatise of justification. Louvain, 1569. 4°. 6422
Treatise of love. W. de Worde [1493]. F°. 69
Treatise of Melchisedek. 1591. *See* Broughton (H.).
Treatise of the cohabitacyon of the faithfull. 1555. 8°. . . 6294
Treatise of the grounds of the old and newe Religion. 1608. *See* Mayhew (E.).
Treatise of the Ministery. [1595?] *See* Hildersam (A.).
Treatise of the nature and use of things indifferent. 1605. 8°. . 6862
Treatise of the nature of God. 1599. 8°. *See* Morton (T.).
Treatise of the perpetuall visibilitie. 1624. *See* Abbot (G.).
Treatise of ye seuen poyntes of true love. *See* Horologium.
Treatise of treasons against Q. Elizabeth. 1572. 8°. . . . 6122
Treatise of use and cvstome. 1638. *See* Casaubon (M.).
Tredwey (H.). Verses in Cambridge Lachrymae. 1587. . . 2123
Trelcatius (L.). Briefe institution...of Sacred Divinitie. 1610. 8°. . 1391
Scholastica, et methodica...institutio. Oxoniae, 1606. 8°. . 5276
Tremellius (Immanuel). *See* Bible. Latin. 1580 (1579) *etc.*
— — — Psalms. 1580.
— — English Psalms. 1581 *etc.*
— — — Jeremiah (Selection). 1587.
— Willet (A.). Hexapla in Genesin. 1605.
Trent, Council of. Declaration of the fathers. [Ab. 1600.] 8°. . 6833
Godly and necessary admonition. 1564. 4°. 803
[Sixth Session.] *See* Treatise of Justification. 1569.
See Actes of the Ambassage. [1561.] 8°.
— Chemnitius (M.). Discourse. 1582.
— Consilivm. 1609.

No.

Treswell (Robert). Relation of...the Journey of...Earle of Nottingham... to the King of Spaine. 1605. 4°. 3362
Trevisa (John). *See* Bartholomæus, *Anglicus*. De proprietatibvs rervm. [1495?] *etc.*
— Chronicles of England. 1498 *etc.*
— Higden (R.). Description of Britain. 1480. F°.
— — Polychronicon. [1482] *etc.*
Trew report. *See* True.
Triall of the English liturgie. 1637. 4°. 7039
Tribulation, Twelve profits of. *See* Horologium.
Tricorones, sive soles gemini in Britannia. Aug. Trinob. 1607. 4°. 7807
Trigge (Francis). Noctes sacrae. Oxonie, 1590. 4°. . . 5235
Touchstone. 1600. 4°. 2339
Trigge (Hen.). Verses in Camb. Univ. Carmen. 1635. . . 5770
Trion (Peter). Verses in Gill (A.). Πάρεργα. 1632. . . . 4558
Triplet (Th.). Verses in Camdeni Insignia. 1624. . . . 5346
Triplici nodo. *See* James I. [Apology.] 1607.
Trippus (Simon). Verses in Stanyhurst (R.). Harmonia. 1570. . 749
Triumph of Faith. *See* Du Bartas.
Trogus Pompeius. Abridgment of the Histories. 1563. 4°. . 1214
Trondhjem or Drontheim. *See* Most strange and wonderfull Herring. 1598.
Trott (D.). Verses in Camb. Univ. Rex redux. 1633. . . . 5748
Troublesome Travell of Tyme. 1589. 4°. 6791
Troyes, *City of*. *See* Jesuits. Legend. 1623.
True beliefe in Christ and his sacramentes. 1550. 8°. . . . 6287
True discourse of the armie of the King of Spaine. 1588. 8°. . 1951
True lawe of free Monarchies. 1598. *See* James I.
True relation of that worthy Sea Fight. 1622. *See* East Indies.
True report of the dysputacyon. [1554?] *See* Philpot (J.).
True reporte of the prosperous successe...in Ireland. [1580?] *See* M. (A.).
True representation of the proceedings of the Kingdome of Scotland. 1640. 4°. 7680
True sincere and modest defence. [1584.] *See* Allen (W.).
True transcript of letters patent. 1611. 3079
Trussell (John). Continuation of the collection of the history of England. 1636. F°. 3894
Verses in Southwell (R.). The Triumphs ouer Death. 1596. . 2847
Truth of three Things. 1633. *See* Rovs (F.).
Tryamour, Sir. W. de Worde [15—]. 4°. 246
Tryon (Pet.). Verses in Camdeni Insignia. 1624. . . . 5346
Trypho, *Alexandrinus*. De passionibus dictionum. *See* Crespin (J.). 1581.
Tuam, *Archbishopric*. *See* Ware (Sir J.). Archiepiscoporum. 1626.
Tuba Academica. 1603. *See* F. (I.).
Tubbing (John), *Pemb*. Verses in Camb. Univ. Carmen. 1635. . 5770
— — Συνωδία. 1637. 5790
Tübingen University. [Letter.] *See* Wakefield (R.). Oratio. [1524.] 4°.
Tuke (Thomas). Discovrs against painting and tincturing of Women. 1616. 4°. 3841
Discourse of death. 1613. 4°. 3098
Improbus foeneratorum spiritus. Francofurti, 1618. 4°. . . 6630
Index fidei. [1617.] 4°. 3481
See Perkins (W.). Works. Vol. 2. (Arte of prophecying). 1609. F°. 5646
— ('A Christian and plaine treatise...of predestination.') 1617. F°. 3760
Tunstall (C.). De arte supputandi. Pynson, 1522. 4°. . . . 280
Letter written...vnto Reginalde Pole. 1560. 8°. 742
— *See* G. (B.), *Citizen*. New Yeares Gifte. 1579.
Sermon...on palme sunday before King Henry VIII. 1633. 4°. 4006

No.

Tunstall (C.), *cont.* *See* Bible. English (Cranmer's). 1541.
— Gildas. Opus novum. [Ab. 153– ?]
Turberville (G.). Booke of Falconrie or Hawking. 1611. 4°. . . 1393
Epitaphes, Epigrams, Songs and Sonets. 1567? 8°. . . 1403
Noble arte of Venerie. [1575.] 4°. 1525
— 1611. 4°. 1394
Tragical Tales. 1587. 8°. 2102
Turberville or Turbervile (S.). Verses *bis* in Camb. Univ. Fasciae. 1633. 5808
Turcopapismus. De Turcopapismo. 1599. *See* Sutcliffe (M.).
Turkey. Mahumetane or Turkish Historie. 1600. 4°. . . . 1610
Policy of the Turkish empire. Book i. 1597. 4°. . . 2146
See Baudier (M.). History...of the Grand Seigneur. 1635.
— Knolles (R.). Generall historie. 1621 *etc.*
— Minadoi (G. T.). History. 1595.
— Sandys (G.). Relation. 1627.
Turk's Secretary. 1607. 4°. *See* Muhammad II.
Turler (Jerome). Traveiler...oversea. 1575. 8°. 1767
Turnbull (George). *See* Baron (R.). Ad G. Turnebulli Tetragonismvm Apodixis. 1631.
Turnbull (R.). Exposition vpon S. James etc. 1592. 8°. . . 2133
— 1606. 4°. 2172
Turnebus (Adrian). Verses in Buchanan (G.). Psalmorum Davidis. 1640. 5209
Turner (M^{ris}). *See* Niccols (R.). Sir T. Overbvries Vision. 1616.
See Overbury (Sir T.). Bloody downfall.
Turner (John). Verses in Camb. Univ. Lacrymæ. 1619. . . 5689
Turner (Math.). Verses in Camdeni Insignia. 1624. . . 5346
Turner (Thomas). Sermon...before the King...March 10. 1635. 4°. . 4366
Turner (William). Herball (Part 2). Cologne, 1562. F°. . . 6334
Herball (Parts 1–3). Cologne, 1568. F°. 6335
Names of herbes. Day and Seres [1548?]. 8°. . . . 919
New Herball. S. Mierdman, 1551. F°. 1099
Huntyng and fyndyng out of the Romyshe foxe. 'Basyll, 1543.' 8°. 984
Hunting of the fox and the wolfe. [1561?] 8°. . . . 6746
Huntyng of the Romyshe Vuolfe. [1554?] 8°. . . . 6297
New dialogue. [1548?] 8°. 6697
Preseruatiue, or triacle, agaynst...Pelagius. 1551. 8°. . . 955
Rescuynge of the romishe fox. Hans hit pirk, 1545. 8°. . 6282
[The English Bathes.] *See* Vicary (T.). Englishmans Treasure. 1626 etc.
See Catechism. 1578(9?). 8°.
— Hutton (R.). Summe of Diuinitie. 1567.
— Regius (Urbanus). Comparison. 1538.
— — Olde learnyng. 1548.
Turpinus, *bp.* *See* Nicodemus. Nychodemus gospell. 1509.
Tursellinus (Horatius). *See* Torsellino (O.).
Tuscany, Grand dukes of. [House of Medici.] *See* Ubaldino (P.). Militia... 1597.
Tuscany (Ferdinand I, de' Medici, Grand Duke of). *See* Medici (Ferdinand I, de').
Tusser (T.). Fiue hundred pointes of good Husbandrie. 1580. 4°. . 1422
— 1586. 4°. 1434
— 1604. 4°. . . . . 3222=7276
Tutt (Tho.). Verses in Oxf. Univ. Magd. Coll. 1612. . . 5302
Tuttesham (Zachariah), *T.C.C.* Verses in Camb. Univ. Lacrymæ. 1619. 5689
— — Gratulatio. 1623. 5695
— — Genethl. 1631. 5731
Tuvill (D.). Essaies politicke and morall. 1608. 8°. . . 2491

No.
Tuvill (D.), *cont.* Vade mecum. 1629. 12°. 7484
— Ed. 3. 1638. 12°. 4123
See T. (D.). The dove and the serpent.
Twelve generall Arguments. 1605. *See* Bradshaw (W.).
Twelve Patriarchs. Testaments. Trans. R. Grosthed. 1576. 8°. . 7124
Twine or Twinus. *See* Twyne.
Twisse (Will). Discoverie of D. Jacksons vanitie. 1631. 4°. . 7012
Two guides to a good life. Anathomy of sinne &c. 1608. 12°. . 2767
Two letters: one written by a Protestant to his brother. 1603. 4°. 1614
Twyne (Brian). Antiquitatis academiae Oxon. apologia. Oxoniæ, 1608. 4°. 5289
Verses in Camdeni Insignia. 1624. 5346
Twyne (J.). De rebus Albionicis. 1590. 8°. 2049
Verses in Llwyd (H.). Breviary of Britayne. 1573. . . 1441
See Boccus. History of Kyng Boccus. [1530?]
Twyne (Lawrence). Verses in Llwyd (H.). Breviary of Britayne. 1573. 1441
Twyne (Thomas). Verses in Stanyhurst (R.). Harmonia. 1570. . 749
See Bullinger (H.). Tragedies of Tyrantes. 1575.
— Daneau (L.). Wonderfvll woorkmanship. 1578.
— Llwyd (H.). Breuiary of Britayne. 1573.
— Petrarca. Phisicke against Fortune. 1579.
— Vergilius. [Æneid.] 1596.
Tye (C.). Actes of the Apostles. [1553?] 8°. 945
Tye (William). Matter of moment. 1608. 8°. 3734
Tyler (Margaret). *See* Mirror of Knighthood. Part i. 1579.
Tymme (T.). Plaine discouerie of ten English Lepers. 1592. 4°. . 2324
Siluer watch-bell. Ed. 3. 1606. 8°. 3381
— Ed. 10. 1614. 8°. 3403
— Ed. 11. 1616. 8°. 2869
— Ed. 16. 1630. 8°. 5073
— Ed. 18. 1638. 8°. 4873
See Adrichomius (C.). Briefe Description of Hierusalem. 1595.
— Calvin (J.). Commentarie of Genesis. 1578. 4°.
— Du Chesne (J.). Practise of...Physicke. 1605.
— France. Fourth parte of Commentaries. 1576.
— Marlorat (A.). Catholike...Exposition of...Marke and Luke. 1583. 4°.
— Serres (J. de). Commentaries. 1574. 4°.
Tyndale (William). *See* Tindale.
Tyndall (John), *C.C.C.* Verses in Camb. Univ. Genethl. 1631. . 5731
Tynemouth, John of. *See* John of Tynemouth.
Tynlie (Martin). Verses in Camdeni Insignia. 1624. . . 5346–
Tyon (Jasper). *See* Biddulph (W.). Travels. 1609 *etc.*
Tyrconnel (Rory O'Donnell, earl of). *See* Birchensha (R.). Discourse. 1602. 4°.
See Tyrone (H. O'Neill, earl of). Declaratio. 1607. 4°.
Tyrell (John). Verses in Wilson (Sir T.). Vita. 1551. . . . 631
Tyrer (R.). Five godlie and learned Sermons. 1602. 8°. . . . 1270
Tyrling (Robert). Verses in Fuller (T.). Historie of the holy warre. 1639 *etc.* . . . . 5806 *etc.*
Tyrone (Hugh O'Neill, earl of). *See* Birchensha (R.). Discourse. 1602. 4°.
Declaratio de Tyronensis et Tirconelii comitum...fuga. 1607. 4°. 2608
Tyrrell (Anthony). Fruitfull sermon 13 July 1589. 8°. . . 2128
See Tedder (W.). Recantations. 1588.
Tyrtaeus. [Gr. Lat.] *See* Poetæ minores. 1635.
Tyrwhit (William). *See* Balzac. Letters. 1634. 4°.
See Molinier (E.). A mirrour for christian states. 1635. 4°.
Tyrwhitt (Lady Elizabeth). *See* Bentley (T.). Monvment of Matrones. 1582.

No.
Ubaldino (Pet.). Militia del gran duca di Thoscana. 1597. 4°. . 6820
Scelta di alcune attioni. 1595. 4°. 6811
Vita di Carlo Magno. 1581. 4°. 1923
Vite delle donne illustri. 1591. 4°. 1963
Udal (Ephraim). *See* Hayne (T.). Pax. 1639.
Udall (John). Certaine sermons. 1596. 8°. 2420
Commentarie vpon the Lamentations. 1593. 4°. . . . 7370
— 1599. 4°. 7464
— 1637. 4°. 4760
Demonstration of the trueth of that Discipline. [1588.] 8°. . 1913
— [Ab. 1593?] 4°. 6807
State of the Church of Englande. [1588.] 8°. 1914
True remedie against Famine and warres. [1587?] 8°. . 1909
See Martinius (P.). Key of the holy tongue. 1593.
— Remonstrance...to the Demonstration of Discipline. 1590. 4°.
Udall (Nicholas). Verses in Cheke (Sir J.). De obitu M. Buceri. 1551. 734
— Wilson (Sir T.). Vita. 1551. 631
— — Arte of Rhetorique. 1553. 626
See Erasmus (D.). Apophthegmes. 1542. 8°.
— — Paraphrases. 1548 etc.
— Gemini (T.). Compendiosa...Anatomie delineatio. 1559.
— Terentius. Floures. 1560.
Udall (William). Historie of...Mary Stuart. 1624. F°. . . . 4793
— 1636. 12°. 4861
Uduardus (N.). *See* Udward.
Udward (Nicolas). Verses in Adamson (J.). Εἰσόδια. 1618 *bis*. . 5960
Ulloa (Alfonso d'). *See* Furio Ceriol (F.). Very briefe...Treatise. 1570.
Ulster. [Collections.] *See below* Conditions. 1610. 4°.
Conditions to be observed by the Brittish Vndertakers of the escheated lands. 1610. 4°. 2631
See Blenerhasset (T.). Direction. 1610. 4°.
Underdown (Thomas). *See* Ovid. Ibis. 1577.
Underhill (John). Verses in Holyoake (F.). Dictionarium. 1640. . 3058
Underwood (Edm.). Verses in Oxf. Univ. Horti. 1640. . . 5490
United Provinces. *See* Netherlands III.
Unlawfull practises of prelates. [1584?] 8°. 1911
Unton (Henry). *See* Merbury (C.). Briefe discovrse. 1581.
Upchering of the messe. [1548?] 8°. 920
Upton (Nicolas). [De studio militari.] *See* Berners (J.). [Boke of St Albans.] 1486.
Urban VIII. [Order of Immaculate Conception.] *See* Wadsworth (J.). Further Obss. 1630. 4°. 7788
See Rome, Church of. Urban VIII.
Urfé (Honoré d'). History of Astræa. Part 1. 1620. 4°. . . 3676
Ursinus (Joachimus). Romane conclave. 1609. 4°. 3067
Ursinus (Zacharias). Doctrinae christianae compendium. Cantabrigiae, 1585. 8°. 5516
Explicationum catecheticarum Ed. altera. 1587. 8°. . . . 5530
Summe of christian religion. Oxford, 1587. 8°. . . . 5230
— 1611. 4°. 2511
— 1617. 4°. 2531
Catechisme. *See* Book of Common Order. Edinburgh, 1615. 8°. 5953 and p. 1743
See Sparke (T.). Catechisme. 1588. 4°.
Urso. *See* Bacon (R.). Libellvs. 1590. 5233
Ursulanus (Edmundus), *pseud.* *See* Matthews (F.).
Ussher (James). Answer to a challenge...by a Iesuite. Dublin, 1624. 4°. 6027
— ...with other treatises. 1631. 4°. 4976
Briefe declaration of the universalitie of the church of Christ. [1625?]. 4°. 4963

No.
Ussher (James). Briefe declaration *cont.* Ed. 3. 1629. 4°. . . . 3877
— 1631. 4°. 4615
Britannicarum ecclesiarum antiquitates. Dublinii, 1639. 4°. 6069–6070
Discourse of the religion anciently professed. 1631. 4°. . . . 4977
— *See above.* Answer. 1631. 4976
Epistle. *See* Sibthorp (Sir C.). Friendly advertisement. 1622.
Gotteschalci, et praedestinationae controversiæ...historia. Dublin, 1631. 4°. 6037
Gravissimæ quæstionis de christianarum ecclesiarum ... partibus. 1613. 4°. 2798
Immanuel. 1638. 4°. 4874
— Dublin, 1638. 4°. 6063
Sermon...before the commons...18 Feb. 1620. Ed. 2. 1631. 4°. 4710=4976
Speech...at Dublin, 22 November 1622. 1631. 4°. . 4978=4976
Substance of...a sermon before the House of Commons. 18 Feb. 1620. 1621. 4°. 3016
Veterum epp. hibernicarum sylloge. Dublin, 1632. 4°. . 6042-4
See Hakewill (G.). Apologie. 1630.
— Malone (W.). Reply to Mr Iames Ussher. 1627.
— Synge (G.). Reioynder. 1632.
Usury. *See* Culpepper (Sir T.). Tract against Usurie. 1621.
— Death of Usury. 1594.
— Musculus (W.). Of the lawful...usurie. [1556?]
Utenhovius (Carolus). Verses in Harvey (G.). Gratulationum. 1578. 1495
— Buchanan (G.). Psalmorum Davidis. 1640. . . 5209
Uthalmus (Lerimos), *pseud.* [qu. T. Willmer?]. *See* Fasciculus Florum. 1636. 8°.
Utie (Emanuel). Mathew the publican. 1616. 4°. 3916
See Fenton (R.). Treatise. 1617.
Utrecht. *See* Proclamation. 1618. 4°. 7914

V. (A.) [=Adrian Vlacq.] *See* Ephemerides. 1635.
V. (D.). *See* Bible. English Concordance. Cotton. 1622.
V. (E.), *sometime Fellow of S. John's College, Cambridge.* *See* Utie (E.). Mathew the Publican. 1616. 4°.
V. (H.). Verses in Lucanus. Pharsalia. 1627 *etc.* . . 3532 *etc.*
V. (I.). [*Qu.* I. Vaughan?] Verses in James I. Court of James I. 1619. 3929
Verses in Mercator (G.). Historia. 1635. 4637
See Mornay (P. de). An homily. 1615.
V. (M.), *C.C.C.* Verses in Wadsworth (J.). Further Obss. 1630. 7788
V. (R.). Olde Fayth of great Brittaygne. [1548?] 8°. . . 1042
V. (R.) [=R. Vaux]. *See* Calvin (J.). Commentarie vpon Colossians. [1581?] 4°. 7246
V. (R.). *See* Chemnitius (M.). Discouerie. 1582.
— Jewel (J.). Sermon. [1586?]
— Primer. 1599 etc.
— Martin (G.). Treatyse. 1583.
— Rowlands (R.). Theatrum crudelitatum. 1604. 4°.
V. (S.). Verses in Rowlands (R.). Restitution. 1605 *etc.* . 6140 *etc.*
V. (T.), *C.T.* Verses in Camb. Univ. Gratulatio. 1623. . . 5695
V. (Th.), *C.T.* Verses in Camb. Univ. Gratulatio. 1623. . 5695
Va. (Ric.) [*qu.* Vaughan?]. Verses in Price (Sir J.). Historia. 1573. 1473
Vadianus (Glareanus). Verses in Coryate (T.). Coryates crvdities. 1611. 3076
Vænius (Otto). *See* Veen.
Vaghamus: *see* Vaughan (Lewis).
Valdes (Juan de). Hundred and ten considerations. Oxford, 1638. 4°. 5485
Valencia (Jacobus de). *See* Thomas de Walleis.
Valencius, Doctor. *See* Thomas de Walleis.

No.
Valentia (Gregorius de). *See* Rainolds (J.). De Romanæ Ecclesiæ idolatria. 1596.
Valentine: *see* Ballentinus.
Valentine (Henry). Foure sea-sermons. 1635. 4°. 4294
God save the King. A sermon. 1639. 4°. 4330
Noahs dove. 1627. 4°. 4813
Valera (Cypriano de). Two treatises. Trans. J. Golburne. 1600. 4°. 1266
See Bible. Spanish. N.T. 1596.
— Calvin (J.). Institucion. 1597.
Valerius (C.). In vniuersam benedicendi rationem tabula. 1580. 8°. 1634
Valerius Maximus. Little Epitomy...concerning dreames. *See* Artemidorus. Ivdgement. 1606.
Valkensteyn and Brooke. *See* Broeck.
Valla (Laurentius). Declamation. *See* Constantine I. Treatyse. [c. 1525.]
See Æsop. Fabulæ. 1635.
— Anwykyle (J.). Compendium totius grammatice. 1489.
— Thucydides. Hystory. 1550.
Valladolid, English College. *See* Philip II. Relation. 1592. . 6801
Valtellina. *See* Sarpi (P.). Cruell subtilty.
— — Discourse. 1628.
Vanderhaghen (Godefridus). Verses in Adamson (J.). Εἰσόδια. 1618. 5960
Vander Noot (J.). Theatre. 1568. 8°. 812
Varamundus (E.). De furoribus Gallicis. 1573. 8°. . . . 1475
— 'Edinburgi,' 1573. 4°. 6758
— True and plain report. Striveling. 1573. 8°. . . . 6759
Varchi (Benedict). Verses in Harvey (G.). Gratulationum. 1578. . 1495
Varennius. *See* Posselius (J.). Σύνταξις. 1640.
Varnet (Thomas). *See* Bernardin (St). The chirche. 1511.
Vastellabus (Hermannus). *See* Muhammad II. Turkes Secretorie. 1607. 4°.
Vatablus (Franciscus). *See* Willet (A.). Hexapla in Exodvm. 1608.
Vaughan (Edward). Method, or briefe instruction for...the old and new testament. 1590. 8°. 2209
Vaughan (Ed.), *M.A.* Verses in Camdeni Insignia. 1624. . . . 5346
— Gill (A.). Πάρεργα. 1632. 4558
See Palladius (P.). An introduction. 1598.
Vaughan (Herbert). Verses in Oxf. Univ. Horti. 1640. . . 5499
Vaughan (I.). Verses in Lucanus. Pharsalia. 1627 *etc.* . . 3532 *etc.*
Vaughan (John). *See* Gascoigne (G.). The Posies. 1575.
Vaughan (Lewis). *See* Fulke (W.). Antiprognosticon. 1560.
Vaughan (Richard). Verses in Price (Sir J.). Historia. 1573. . 1473
See Bible. Welsh. 1620. F°.
— Certaine demandes. 1605.
— Lambeth Articles. [1629?] etc.
Vaughan (Rowland). Most approved...Water-Workes. 1610. 4°. 3576
Vaughan (Th.). Verses in Oxf. Univ. Horti. 1640. . . . 5499
Vaughan (William). Church militant. 1640. 8°. 5102
Directions for health. Ed. 6. 1626. 4°. 3807
— Ed. 7. 1633. 4°. 4007
Golden fleece...Newfoundland. 1626. 4°. 5029
Golden-groue. Ed. 2. 1608. 8°. 2888
Vaughan (William). *See* Boccalini (T.). The New-found Politicke. 1626. 4°.
Vautrollier (Thomas). *See* Manutius (A.). Phrases. 1599 *etc.*
Vaux (Laurent). Catechism. See p. 1743 and no. 6439 n.
Vaux (Robert). *See* Calvin (J.). Comm. upon Colossians. [1581?] 4°. 7246
Vavasour (Nicholas), *bookseller.* Verses in Helpe to discourse. 1635. 3833
Vavasour (Thomas). Verses in Seton (J.). Dialectica. 1631. . 5739
Vedel (Anders Sørensen). *See* Hemmingius (N.). Way of lyfe. 1578.

No.
Veen (Otto van). Amorum emblemata. Antwerp, 1608. 4°. . . . 6138
Vegetius (F.). [De re militari.] *See* Christine de Pisan. The Fayttes of Armes. 1489. F°.
Fovre bookes of...Martiall policye. 1572. 4°. 1221
Vegius (Mapheus). *See* Vergilius. Æneid. 1553 etc.
Velleius (Andreas Severini). *See* Vedel (Anders Sørensen).
Velleius Paterculus (Caius). Romane Historie. Trans. R. Le Grys. 1632. 12°. 4266
Vendôme (César, duc de). *See* France. Louis XIII. 1617.
Venice. Declaration of the Variance betweene the Pope and the Segniory. 1606. 4°. 2599
See Contarini (G.). Commonwealth. 1599.
— Fougasses (T. de). Generall historie. 1612.
— Sarpi (P.). Full and satisfactorie answer. 1606.
— — History of the quarrels. 1626.
— Vignier (N.). Concerning...the Venetians. 1607.
[Ambassadors.] *See* Arsanes. [1560?]
Vennar (Richard). Apology...called Englands Joy. 1614. 8°. . 3658
Venner (Tobias). Via recta ad vitam longam. Ed. 1. 1620. 4°. 3947
— Ed. 2. 1622. 4°. 3431
— 1628. 4°. 3037
— 1638–7. 4°. 5109
Vera expositio disputationis. 1554. *See* Philpot (J.).
Verdere (Monsieur). *See* Saulnier (G.), Sieur de Verdier.
Vere (Edward), earl of Oxford. *See* Oxford (Edward Vere, earl of).
Vere (Hilary)? *See* Verus.
Verepæus (Simon). Enchiridion. *See* Manual. 1589. 16°. . 6439 *n.*
Vergerius (P. P.). *See* Valdes (J. de). Hundred and ten considerations. 1638. 5485
Vergesatus (Antonius Chalmeteus). *See* Chalmeteus.
Vergil (Polydore). Abridgement...by T. Langley. Grafton, 1546. 8°. 594
— Grafton, 1551. 8°. 622
— J. Tysdale [ab. 1558]. 8°. 1263
See Gildas. De excidio Britanniae. 1568. 808
Vergilius. Opera. H. Bynneman, 1572. 8°. 1472
Eneydos. Caxton, 22 June, 1490. F°. 40
XIII Bukes of Eneados. Trans. G. Douglas. [W. Copland,] 1553. 4°. 1079
Æneid. Trans. T. Phaer and T. Twyne. 1596. 4°. . . 2720
— — 1607. 4°. 2742
[Æneid. I–IV.] Trans. R. Stanyhurst. 1583. 8°. . . . 1516
Æneid. Trans. J. Vicars. 1632. 8°. 5121
[Æneid. Bk I.] Trans. G. Sandys. *See* Ovid. Metamorphosis. 1632 etc.
Bucolicks. 1589. 4°. 2204
Eclogues with...de apibus. Translated. 1633. 4°. . . . 7321
[Georgics.] N. Grimoaldi...Paraphrasis. 1591. 8°. . . . 1732
[Selection. Translation.] *See* Beaumont (Sir J.). Bosworth-field. 1629.
Epigrams of Virgilius Maro and others. Trans. J. Penkethman. 1624. 8°. 4084
[Appendix.] *See* Ross (A.). Virgilius Evangelisans. 1634. . 4723
— — Christiados. 1638. 4739–40
Lyfe of Virgilius. Antwerp [ab. 1518]. 4°. 6076
Verheiden (Jacobus). History of the moderne protestant divines. Trans. D. Lupton. 1637. 8°. 3712
Verius Flaccus. *See* Verrius.
Verlensis (Hieronymus). Verses in S. Pelegromius. 1603. . . . 7881
Vermigli (Pietro Martire). Loci communes. 1576. F°. . . . 1180
— 1583. F°. 1553

No.
Vermigli (Pietro Martire). Loci communes, *cont.* Common Places. 1583. F°. 1426
Most Godly prayers. 1569. 8°. 934
Most learned...Commentaries...vpon the Epistle...to the Romanes. 1581. F°. 811
Tractatio de sacramento evcharistiæ. 1549. 4°. 730
[Letter.] *See* Briefe examination. [1564.] 4°.
See Jewell (J.). Apologia ecclesiæ anglicanæ. 1591 *etc.*
— Treatise of the Cohabitacyon of the faithfull. 1555.
— Whether it be mortall sinne. [1571?]
— White (J.). Diacosiomartyrion. 1553.
Verneuil (John). *See* James (T.). Catalogus interpretum. 1635. 4°.
— Mornay (P. de). An Homily. 1615.
Verney (Grevill). Verses in Camb. Univ. Thr-thr. 1603. . . . 5616
Vernon (Dorothy). [Off-set of book label.] 6777
Veron (J.). Fruteful treatise of Predestination. [1561?] 8°. . . 1264
Godly saiyngs of the...fathers vpon the Sacrament of...Chryste. Worcester, 1550. 8°. 5889
Hvntynge of Purgatorye to death. 1561. 8°. 1260
See Bullinger (H.). Holsome Antidotus. 1548.
— Estienne (R.). Dictionariolum. 1552.
— Zwingli (U.). Short pathwaye. 1550.
— — Ymage. 1550.
Verrius Flaccus. *See* Livius. Libri omnes. 1589. 8°.
Verro (S.). Physicorum libri x. 1581. 8°. 1509
Verstegan (Richard). *See* Rowlands.
Vertomannus (Ludovicus), *otherwise* Barthema. Navigations etc. *See* Anglerius (P. M.). History of Trauayle.
Vertue (Henry). Plea for peace. 1637. 4°. 4314
Verus (Hilarius). Verses in Fitzgeffrey (C.). Affaniae. 1601. . 5254
Very lively portrayture of the...archbishops. 1640. 4°. . . . 7579
Vespasian. *See* Destruction. Dystruccyon of Jherusalem.
'Via-porta.' Verses in Sheldon (R.). A svrvey. 1616. . . 3914
Vicars (John). Decapla in Psalmos. 1639. F°. 5007
Verses in Sylvester (J.). Parliament. [Ab. 1614.] . . 6898
— Du Bartas. Weekes. 1621. 2535
— Comenius (J. A.). Porta. 1633. 7613
See Vergilius. Aeneid. 1632.
Vicars (Thomas à). Verses in Mercator (G.). Historia. 1635. . 4637
Vicary (Thomas). English-mans Treasure. Ed. 7. 1626. 4°. . 4189
— Ed. 8. 1633. 4°. 4207
Profitable Treatise. 1577. 8°. 1860
Victor Amadeus I., *duke of Savoy*. *See* France. Louis XIII. 1617.
Victorinus (Georgius). Siren Coelestis. Ed. alt. 1638-9. 4°. . 4905
Victual. *See* Grain and Victual.
Vidam Chartresius. *See* Ferrières (J. de).
Viell (Abraham). Verses in Taylor (J.). All the workes. 1630. . 3812
Vienna. *See* Paris and Vienna. By M. Mainwaring. 1628. 4°.
Vigilius, *Pope*. *See* Crackanthorp (R.). Vigilius. 1631.
Vignay (Jehan de). *See* Cessolis (J. de). Game and Play. [1475?] F°.
Vignier (Nicholas). Concerning the excommunication of the Venetians. 1607. 4°. 3368
Vigo (J. de). Workes of chirurgerie. Trans. B. Traheron. 1571. F°. 7274
Whole worke. 1586. 4°. 1588
Vigor (S.). Acts of the dispute and conference at Paris. 1566. Trans. J. Golbourne. 1602. 4°. 2735
Vilars (— de). *See* Copie of the letter. 1631. 4°.
Vileers (Gerard de). *See* Lessius (L.). Hygiasticon. 1634 etc. 5762 etc.
Villa Nova (Arnaldus de). *See* Arnaldus, *de Villa Nova.*
Villacastin (Thomas de). *See* Loyola (I.). Manuall. 1618. 12°.

No.
Villainies Discovered. 1616. *See* Dekker (T.).
Villegas (Alf. de). Flos sanctorum. Trans. W. and E. K. B. Tom. 1. [1609.] 4°. 6883
Lives of Saints. 1628. 4°. 6621
— Ed. 4. Paris, 1638. 4°. 6228
Villemor, Sieur de. *See* Chevalier (G. de). The ghosts. 1624.
Villerius (Petrus). *See* Loyseleur (P. de), *Villerius.*
Villeroi (N. de Neufville, sieur de). *See* Neufville.
Villeroy. *See* Villeroi.
Villiers (George), duke of Buckingham. *See* Buckingham.
Villiers (George). Verses in Camb. Univ. Fasciae. 1633. . . 5808
— — Rex redux. 1633. 5748
Villiers (John). Verses in Camb. Univ. Fasciae. 1633. . . 5808
— — Rex redux. 1633. 5748
Vincent (Augustine), *Rouge-Croix.* *See* Brooke (R.). Discoverie. 1622, 2793
Vincent (Nat.). Verses in Camb. Univ. Lacrymæ. 1619. . . 5689
— — Dolor. 1625. 5701
— — Epithalam. 1625. 5702
— — Rex redux. 1633. 5748
Vincent (Philip), *Firsbaeus.* Lamentations of Germany. 1638. 8°. . 7760
Verses in Mercator (G.). Atlas. 1633, '1636.' 6355
Vincent (Tho.), *Trin. Coll.* Verses in Dolor. 1625. . . . 5701
— — Epithalamium *bis.* 1625. 5702
— Camb. Univ. Genethl. 1631 *bis.*. 5731
— Randolph (T.). The Jealous Lovers. 1640. . . . 5852
Vincentius Lirinensis. Peregrini adv. prophanas hæreses. Oxoniae, 1631. 12°. 5432
Pro catholicæ fidei antiquitate. 1591. 12°. 6800
Vineis (Raimundus de). Lyf of saint katherin of senis. [1493.] F°. 70
Vinet (Elie). *See* Estienne (C.). Maison Rustique. 1616.
Vintener (Henry), *K.C.C.* Verses in Camb. Univ. Epithalam. 1625. 5702
— — Genethl. 1631. 5731
— — Anthologia. 1632. 5741
— — Fasciae. 1633. 5808
— — Rex redux. 1633. 5748
— — Carmen. 1635. 5770
— — *Συνῳδία.* 1637. 5790
— Fuller (T.). Holy Warre. 1639 *etc.* . . . . 5806 *etc.*
— Hippocrates. 1631. 5736
— Camb. Univ. Voces. 1640. 5836
Virel (Matthieu). Learned and excellent treatise. Ed. 2. . . 2235
— Ed. 4. 1597. 8°.. 2189
— Ed. 7. 1607. 8°. 3537
Viret (P.). Cautelen...vander Misse. 1568. 8°. 1460
Cauteles, canons...of the...Masse. 1584. 8°. 1559
Christian Instruction. 1573. 8°. 1071
Faithfull...exposition vpon the prayer of our Lorde. 1582. 4°. 1639
Notable collection of...places of the sacred scriptures. 1548. 8°. 1043
Virgilius. *See* Vergilius.
Virginia. Declaration of the state of...Virginia. 22 June, 1620. 1620. 4°. 3426
See Donne (J.). A sermon. 1622, Nov. 13. 1622. 4°.
— Folkingham (W.). Fevdigraphia. 1610.
— I. (R:). Nova Britannia. 1609.
— Price (D.). Savls prohibition. 1609.
— Smith (J.). The generall history. 1624.
— Symonds (W.). Virginia. 1609.
Virginity, Sixt Lamp of. 1582. *See* Bentley (T.).
Viringus (Johann Walter). *See* Lessius (L.). Hygiasticon. 1634. . 5762
Virtue of yᵉ masse. W. de Worde [15—]. 4°. 247
Virunnius (Ponticus). *See* Ponticus (L.), *Virunius.*

No.
Visitation Articles. *See* Articles.
Vitallus (Johannes). *See* Withals (J.). 1523. 284
Vitas patrum. 1495. *See* Hieronymus.
Vitell (Christopher). *See* Nicholas (H.). Dicta H. N. [1574?] 8°.
— — Epistola XI. [1574?] 8°.
— — Evangelium Regni. [1574?] 8°.
— — Prophetie. 1574. 8°.
— — Proverbia H. N. [1575?] 8°.
— — Publishing of the Peace. 1574. 8°.
— — Terra Pacis. 1574.
Vitellius (Regnerus). *See* Camden (W.). Britannia. 1639. 12°.
Introduction to wysedome. Trans. R. Morysine. 1540. 8°. . 456
Linguae latinae exercitatio. Cantabrigiæ, 1633. 8°. . . 5755
Office and duetie of an husband. Trans. T. Paynell. [1550?] 8°. 1001
Very fruteful...instruction of a Christen women. Trans. by R. Hyrde. 1541. 4°. 462
— 1557. 4°. 1248
— 1592. 8°. 2414
See Augustine. Of the citie of God. 1610 *etc.*
Vivian (D.). Verses in A. (G.). Pallas armata. 1639. . . 5170
Vlacq (Adrian). *See* Ephemerides of the Celestiall Motions. 1635. 4°.
Vladislaus IV., *King of Poland.* *See* Poland. Vladislaus IV. 1635.
Vocabulary. Den grooten Vocabulaer Engels ende Duyts. Rotterdam, 1639. 8°. 6660
Volunteers. *See* Prempart (J.). A historicall relation. 1630.
Volusanus (Florentius). [Ode.] *See* Imitation of Christ. 1568. 8°. 1405
Volusenus (Sylvester). *See* Wilson.
Volusenus (Thomas). *See* Adamson (P.). De Sacro Pastoris Munere. 1619.
— — Poëmata Sacra. 1619–18.
Volusianus. Epistolæ duæ...de Celibatu Cleri. 1569. 8°. . . 1461
Voragine (J. de). The Golden Legend. Ed. 1. Caxton, 1483. F°. 23
— 'Ed. 2.' Caxton [1489]. F°. 33
— W. de Worde [1498]. F°. 52
— J. Notary, 1503. F°. 327
— W. de Worde, 1512. F°. 168
— ,, 27 Aug. 1527. F°. 194
Vorstius (Conrad). Enchiridion controversiarum ex 4 tomis R. Bellarmini. Oxoniae, 1606. 8°. 5277
See James I. Declaration. 1612. 2644
— — (French.) 1612. 2374
— Dort. Iudgement of the synode. 1619. 4°.
Vossius (Ger. J.). Rhetorices...libri V. Ed. alt. Oxoniae, 1631. 12°. 5433
Theses theologicae et historicae. Bellositi Dobunorum, 1628. 4°. 5422
Responsio ad Judicium Hermanni Ravenspergeri. *See* Grotius (H.). Defensio. 1636.
Verses in Burgersdicius (F.). Institutionum. 1637. . . 5789
Vowell *aliàs* Hooker (John). *See* Hooker (J.).
Vowell (Peter). Verses in Guarna (A.). Bellum Grammaticale. 1635. 4210
— Mercator (G.). Historia. 1635. 4637
Vox Dei. *See* Scott (T.). Vox populi. 1622–4.
Vox Piscis. 1627. 12°. 3808
Vox Populi. *See* Scott (T.). 1620.
Vox Regis. *See* Scott (T.). 1620.
Voyon (S. de). Discourse upon the Catalogue of Doctors of Gods Church. 1598. 8°. 1997
Testimonie of the trve church of God. [158–?] 4°. . . 1659
Voysin, *qu.* L. Du Voisin? *See* Newes from France. 1618. 4°.
Vraye (.). *See* Briefe Declaration. 1636.
Vrientius (Max). Verses in Veen (O.). Amorum Emblemata. 1608. 6138

No.

Vulcanius (B.). De literis and lingua getarum. Leyden, 1597. 8°. 6498
Verses in Lipsius (J.). De constantia. 1586. 7295
Whitney (G.). A choice. 1586. 6496
Vulgaria. *See* Terentius. Vulgaria quedam. 1483 etc.
See Horman (W.). 1519.
Vulpianus *Veronensis*. Verses in Harvey (G.). Gratulationum. 1578. 1495

W. (A.). Fruitfull and godly Sermon. 1592. 8°. 1992
Verses in Gascoigne (G.). Posies. 1575. . . . 1482
See Mornay (P. de). Christian and godly view. 1593.
W. (B.). Verses in Hart (A.). Tragicomicall history. 1640. . . 4220
W. (D.), *Arch.* Certaine necessary instructions...of the holy Communion.
See Rice (R.). Invective. 1579.
W. (D.), *M.A.C.T.S.* Verses in Dugres (G.). Breve...Compendium.
1636. 5781
W. (D. I. P. B. R.). *See* Ponet (J.), *Bp.*
W. (E.). Verses in Cooke (A.). More worke for a masse priest. 1621. 3337–8
See Cooke (A.). Worke, more worke. 1630.
— Richeome (L.). Pilgrime of Loreto. 1630.
— Safegard of saylers. 1612. 4°.
— Passe (Crispin de). Garden of flowers. 1615. . . . 6643
— Waterhouse (E.). 1577.
W. (Ez.). Ans. of a mother vnto hir seduced sonnes letter. 1627. 8°. 6975
W. (F.). Treatise of Warm Beer. Cambridge [1640?]. 12°. . 5856
W. (G.). Rich storehouse, or treasurie for the diseased. Ed. 7.
1630. 4°. 4343
Censure of a loyall Subiect. 1587. *See* Whetstone (G.).
Verses in Gascoigne (G.). Posies. 1575. 1482
— Stafford (T.). Pacata Hibernia. 1633. 4577
— Mercator (G.). Historia. 1635. 4637
See Baynes (P.). The Christians Garment. 1618.
— Wateson (G.). Cvres of the diseased. 1598.
W. (G.), *Coll. Emm.* Verses in Camb. Univ. Lacrymæ. 1619. . 5689
W. (G.), *Gent.* *See* Whetstone (G.). Aurelia. 1593.
W. (G.), *I[unior?]*. Verses in Spenser (E.). Faerie queen. 1611. . 2510
W. (G.), *Ioan.* Verses in Randolph (T.). Poems. 1640. . . 5500
W. (G.), *Neaberdeanus.* Verses in Barclay (W.). Iudicium. 1620. 8°. 3594
W. (G.), *senior.* Verses in Spenser (E.). The faerie queen. 1611. 2510
W. (H.). Θρηνοικος. 1640 (1639). F°. 5178
See Gascoigne (G.). Hundreth sundrie Flowres. [Ab. 1572.] 4°.
— Netherlands, *Southern Provinces.* Second Admonition. 1598.
W. (Sir H.). *See* Overbury (Sir T.). His Wife. 1638.
W. (I.) [*i.e.* T. W.=T. Wotton]. *See* Lambard (W.) A perambulation.
1596.
See Loyola (I.). Manuall. 1618. 12°.
— Rodriguez (A.). Treatise. 1627. 8°.
W. (I.), *Catholicke Priest.* *See* Wilson (J.). English Martyrologe. 1608.
W. (I.), *Esquire* [=Wells (J.)]. Sciographia. 1635.
W. (I.), *Gen.* Verses in Camden (W.). Britannia. 1586 *etc.* . 1324 *etc.*
W. (I.), *Printer.* *See* Treasury. Treasvrie of Hidden Secrets. 1633.
W. (I.), *Regal.* Verses in Camb. Univ. Gratulatio. 1623. . . 5695
W. (I.), *Theol.* Verses in Purchas (S.). Purchas his pilgrimages.
1613 *etc.* . . . . 7848 *etc.*
W. (J.). *See* Guibert (P.). Charitable physitian. 1639. 4°.
See Paris. Sorbonne. Copie of a late decree. 1610.
W (Jo.), *Gent.* Verses in Saul (A.). Famous game of chesse play. 1640. 5136
W. (M.). Verses in Isaacson (H.). Ephemerides. 1633. . . 4206
See Windsor (M.). Academiarum. 1590.
W. (N.). *See* Dyke (D.). Comfortable Sermons. 1635.
See Jovius (P.). Worthy tract. 1585.

No.
W. (P.). Verses in Gascoigne (G.). The Posies. 1575. . . 1482
See Gregorius I. Dialogues (shorte relation). 1608. 12°.
W. (R.). Martine Mar-Sixtus. A second replie. 1591. 4°. . 2214
Verses in Cambridge Lachrymae. 1587. 2123
— Allestree (R.). Allestree. 1640. 4672
W. (R.), *Esq.* *See* Coster (F.). Meditations. 1616. 12°.
W. (R.), *T.C.* Verses in Camb. Univ. Gratulatio. 1623. . . 5695
W. (S.). Apollogie of the...Earle of Mansfield. 'Heidelbergh,' 1622. 4°. 6936
Verses in Whitaker (W.). Praelectiones. 1599. . . 5598
— Butler (C.). The Feminin' Monarchi, 1634. . . . 5439
See Southwell (R.). Marie Magdalens funerall Teares.
W. (S.), *Emmanuel Coll. Camb.* Verses in Whitaker (W.). Praelectiones. 1599. 5598
W. (T.). Catalogue of the dukes, marqvesses, earles...With...the Knights. 1639. 8°. 4045
Verses in L'Espine (J. de). Very excellent discourse. 1592. . 5552
— Camb. Univ. Epicedium. 1612. 5665
— Comenius (J. A.). Porta linguarum. 1631 etc. . . 4434 etc.
— Lucanus Pharsalia. 1614. 3655
See Bible. Eng. N.T. Concordance. 1579.
[=H. T.] *See* Bulkeley (E.). Apologie. 1608. . . 3568
[=T. Wotton.] *See* Lambarde (W.). A perambulation. 1576 *etc.*
[=T. Wilcox.] *See* Loque (B. de). Treatise. 1581.
See Rudd (Ant.). Sermon. 1604.
— Wilcox (T.). Right godly...Exposition. 1586.
— Wright (T.). Succinct Philosophicall declaration. 1604. 4°.
W. (T.), *LL.B. Ioan.* Verses in Oxf. Univ. Horti. 1640 . . 5499
W. (T.), *M.A.* *See* Walkington (T.). Optick glasse of hvmors. [1631?]
W. (T.), *P.* *See* Worthington (T.). White died black. 1618 etc. 6904 etc.
— *See* White (F.). The orthodox faith. 1617. 4°.
W. (T.), *Preacher of the Word.* See Wilson (T.), *Preacher at Canterbury.* Theologicall Rules. 1615.
W. (Th.). *See* Worthington (T.). Anker. 1618.
W. (W.). *See* C. (H.). The Catholike Moderator. 1623.
[Qu. W. Watson?] *See* Lessius (L.). A consvltation. 1621.
See Watson (W.). A dialogve. 1601.
— — Important considerations. 1601.
— — Sparing discoverie. 1601.
[=Watts (W.).] *See* James (T.), *Captain.* Strange...voyage. 1633.
See Willymat (W.). Anchor of faith. 1628. 8°. 4252
W. (W.), *C.C.C. Socius.* Verses in Camb. Univ. Voces. 1640. . 5836
W. (W.), *Oxoniensis.* Verses in A. (G.). Pallas armata. 1639. . 5170
Wa. (Iz.). *See* Walton (Is.).
Wadding (Luke). History of...S. Clare. Ed. F. Hendricq. Douai, 1635. 8°. 6609
Waddington (Ralph). Verses in Baret (J.). Alvearie. 1573. . . 7249
Wade (Armigil). Verses in Wilson (Sir T.). Vita. 1551. . . 631
Wadsworth (James). English Spanish Pilgrime. 1629. 4. . . 4607
— Ed. 2. 1630. 4°. 7787
— Further observations. 1630. 4°. 7788
Present estate of Spayne. 1630. 4°. 4545, 7604
See Bedell (W.). Copies of...letters. 1624.
Waideson (Rob.), *S.J.C.* Verses in Camb. Univ. Rex redux. 1633. . 5748
— — Voces. 1640. 5836
Waite (John). Verses in Camb. Univ. Epicedium. 1612. . . 5665
Wake (Sir Isaac). Rex platonicus. Oxoniae, 1607. 4°. . . 5281
— Ed. 4. Oxoniae, 1627. 12°. 5369
See Oxford University. Jvsta fvnebria...T. Bodleii. 1613.
Wake (William). Verses in Camb. Univ. Lacrymæ. 1619. . 5689

No.

Wakefield (R.). Kotser codicis...coniugium cum fratria. [n.b. 1533.] 4°. 526
Oratio de laudibus et vtilitate trium linguarum Arab. Chald. et Hebr. W. de Worde [1524]. 4°. 249
Syntagma de hebreorum codicum incorruptione. (Oratio.) W. de Worde [1530?]. 4°. 248
Wakeman (R.). Poore mans preacher. 1607. 8°. 2086
Wal (Io.). Verses in Davies (R.). Funeral sermon. 1577. . . 1416
Walcot (Ber.), *Clar.* Verses in Camb. Univ. Epithalam. 1625. . 5702
Waldegrave (Robert), *printer.* *See* Fenner (D.). Certain godly and learned treatises. 1592.
Waldenses. *See* Perrin (J. P.). Bloudy rage. 1624.
Waldstein (Alb. W. E. von), *duke of Friedland.* Relation of the death of...the duke of Meckleburg. 1634. 4°. 7569
Wales. Historie of Cambria. *See* Caradoc. 1584.
See Doddridge (Sir John). 1630.
— Penry (J.). Exhortation. [1588?]
— — Treatise. 1587.
— Ponticus (L.). 1585.
Waleys (Thomas de). *See* Wallensis.
Walker (Ferdinand). *See* Torquemada (A. de). Spanish Mandeuile. 1600.
Walker (George), *fl.* 1550. Manifest detection of Dice Play. [1550?] 8°. 1076
Walker (Geo.), 1581—1651. Doctrine of the sabbath. Amsterdam, 1638. 4°. 6371
Summe of a disputation. 1624. 4°. 6965
See Featley (D.). Romish Fisher. 1624.
— Pemble (W.). Vindiciæ Gratiæ. 1629.
Walker (John), *Preacher.* *See* Deacon (J.) and J. Walker. 1601.
Walker (John), *D.D.* *See* Nowell (A.) and W. Day. True report of... Ed. Campion. 1583.
Walker (Tho.). Verses in Oxf. Univ. Horti. 1640. 5499
Walker (William). Sermon...at the funerals of...William Lord Russell. 1614. 4°. 3404
Sermon. 28 Nov. 1628. [1629.] 4°. 4193
See Alting (H.). Votiue Oration. 1615.
Walkington (Thomas). Optick glasse of humors. [Ab. 1631.] 8°. 7886
— 1639. 8°. 5176
Salomons sweet harpe. Cambridge, 1608. 8°. 5654
Verses in Camb. Univ. Thr-thr. 1603. 5616
— Camb. Univ. Epicedium *ter.* 1612. . . . 5665, 5666
Walkley (T.). *See* W. (T.). Catalogve. 1639. 8°.
Wall (George). Sermon (Visitation Metropoliticall). 1635. 4°. . 4641
Wall (Jo.), *D.D.* Verses in Holyoake (F.). Dictionarium. 1640. . 3058
Wallace (Sir William). *See* Henry the Minstrel. Life and acts etc. 1611.
Wallas (Michael). Verses in Adamson (J.). Εἰσόδια. 1618. . . 5960
Wallas (Thomas). Verses in Forbes (P.). Funerals. 1637. . 6007
Wallas (William). Verses in Adamson (J.). Εἰσόδια. 1618. . . 5960
— Forbes (P.). Funerals. 1637. 6007
Wallensis (Thomas). Expositiones Psalmorum xl. J. Lettou, 1481. F°. 89
Wallenstein. *See* Waldstein.
Waller (Ed.). Verses in Camb. Univ. Rex redux. 1633. . . 5748
Waller (Henry). Verses in Camb. Univ. Lacrymæ. 1619. . . 5689
Waller (Walter). Verses in Camb. Univ. Epicedium. 1612. . . 5665
Wallett (Thomas), *B.A.*, *S.J.C.* Verses in Camb. Univ. Συνῳδία. 1637. 5790
— — Voces. 1640. 5836
Walley (Henry), *pseud.* *See* Garnet (H.).
Walleys (Thomas). *See* Wallensis.
Wallis (John), *B.A.*, *Emm.* Verses in Camb. Univ. Συνῳδία. 1637. . 5790
Wallstein. *See* Waldstein.
Walpole (John). Verses in Guarna (A.). Bellum Grammaticale. 1635. 4210

No.
Walraven (Iacob). *See* Whetstone (G.). Honovrable repvtation of a sovldier. 1586.
Walsall (Fras.), *C.C.C.* Verses in Camb. Univ. Genethl. *bis.* 1631. 5731
— Camb. Univ. Carmen. 1635. 5770
Walsall (Godwin). Verses in Camb. Univ. Thr-thr. 1603. . 5616
Walsall (Sam.). Life and death of Iesvs Christ. 1607. 4°. . . 7532
— 1622. 8°. 3613
Verses in Butts (H.). Dyets dry dinner. 1599. . . . 2727
— Camb. Univ. Thr-thr. *bis.* 1603. 5616
— — Dolor. 1625 *bis.* 5701
— — Epithalam. 1625. 5702
Walsingham (Sir Francis). [Dedication.] *See* Pelegromius (S.). Synonymorum. 1603.
Walsingham (Fras.), *Priest.* Search made into matters of religion. Ed. 2. 1615. 4°. 6532
Walsingham (T.). Historia breuis. 1574. F°. 1479
Ypodigma Neustriæ vel Normanniæ. 1574. F°. . . . 844
Walstein. *See* Waldstein.
Walter (I.). Verses in Cambridge Lachrymae. 1587. . . 2123
Walther (Rudolph). *See* Gualtherus (Rodolphus).
Walton (Izaak). Verses in Roberts (L.). Merchants mappe. 1638. . 5133
See Donne (J.). LXXX Sermons. 1640.
Walwyn (William), *S.J.O.* Verses in Snelling (T.). Thibaldus. 1640. 5502
Wapull (G.). [Tyde taryeth no Man. 1576.] 4°. 1852
Warbeck (Perkin). *See* Gainsford (T.). True history. 1618. 4°.
Ward (John). First set of English Madrigals. 1613. 4°. . . 3401
Ward (Nathaniel). *See* Ward (Sam.). Jethro's Jvstice. 1618 etc.
Ward (Richard). Theologicall questions. 1640. F°. . . . 5162
Ward (Robert). Animadversions of warre. 1639. F°. . . 5177
Verses in Camdeni Insignia. 1624. 5346
Ward (Samuel), *of Cambridge.* Gratia discriminans. 1626. 4°. . 4235
— — emendatior. 1627. 4°. 4245
— *See* Dort Synod. Suffragium.
Magnetis reductorium theologicum. 1639. 12°. . . . 4743
Verses in Camb. Univ. Epicedium *bis.* 1612. 5665
— — Gratulatio. 1623. 5695
— — Dolor. 1625. 5701
— — Fasciae. 1633. 5808
— — Rex redux. 1633. 5748
See Bible. English (Royal). 1611. 2635
— Carleton (G.). Examination. 1626.
— Dort Synod. Joynt attestation. 1626. 4°.
— — Suffragium Collegiale. 1626 *etc.*
[Licence.] Davenant (J.). Determinationes. 1639.
Ward (Samuel), *of Ipswich.* Collection of...sermons and treatises. 1636. 8°. 4589
All in all. 1622. 8°. 4510
Balme from Gilead. 1618. 8°. 3422
— Ed. 2. 1622. 8°. 4768
Coal from the altar. 1616. 8°. 7404
— Ed. 3. 1618. 8°. 3925
— Ed. 4. 1622. 8°. 4511
Happinesse of practice. 1621. 8°. 4076
Jethro's Jvstice of peace. 1618. 8°. 3926
— 1621. 8°. 4501
Life of faith. 1621. 8°. 4502
— 1625. 8°. 4231
— 1627. 8°. 4246
Life of faith in death. 1622. 8°. 4512
— 1627. 8°. 4247

No.
Ward (Samuel), *of Ipswich, cont.* Peace-offering to god. 1624. 8°. 4526
Woe to drunkards. 1622. 8°. 4513
— 1624. 8°. 4527
See Montagu (R.). Appello Cæsarem. 1625. 4°.
— Perkins (W.). Problema. 1604.
Ward (William). Gods arrowes, or two sermons. 1607. 8°. . . 2896
Ward or Warde (William). Verses in Damiano da Odemira. Pleasavnt ..Cheasts. 1562. 1301
See Alessio *Piemontese.* [Secrets. Parts i–iii.] 1560 *etc.*
— Arcandam. Most excellent...booke. [1562?] . . . 1284
Ward (William) (fl. 1615). Sinners inditement. 1615. 8°. . 2316
Warde ( ). *See* Brabourne (T.). Defence. 1632.
Wards and Liveries, *Court of. See* James I. Instructions. 1610. . 2628
Commission with instructions...for Wards, Ideots, and Lunaticks. 11 Dec. 1618. 1618. 4°. 2800
Ware (Sir James). Archiepiscoporum Casseliensium et Tuamensium vitae. Dublin, 1626. 4°. 6032
De praesulibus Lageniae. Dublin, 1628. 4°. 6034
De scriptoribus Hiberniae. Dublin, 1639. 4°. 6071
Historie of Ireland...Hanmer...Campion...Spenser. Dublin, 1633. 6049–6050
Two histories of Ireland...Campion...Hanmer...(Spenser). Dublin, 1633. F°. 6047–8
Warham (William), *abp. See* Indulgence. Leo X, Pope. 1515.
Warmington (W.). Moderate defence of the oath of allegiance. 1612. 4°. 6889
Warmstrey (Gervase). Verses in Camdeni Insignia. 1624. . 5346
Warner (W.). Albions England. Ed. 3. 1592. 4°. 2217
— 1602. 4°. 2059
Warning agaynst...Papistes. [1570?] *See* Norton (T.).
Warre (James). Touchstone of truth. 1621. 8°. 4503
— Ed. 3. 1630. 8°. 4546
Warre (William). Verses in Camb. Univ. Epicedium. 1612. . . 5665
Warriston (Archibald Johnston, Lord). *See* Information to all good Christians. 1639. 4°.
See Baillie (R.). Ladensium Αὐτοκατάκρισις. 1640.
Warters (A.). Verses in Oxf. Univ. Magd. Coll. 1612. . . . 5302
Warwell (James). Verses in Ovid. De tristibus. 1639. . . . 4668
Warwick, City of. *See* Ainsworth (H.). Epistle. 1608. 4°.
Warwick (Wybrandt van). *See* Neck (J. van). Journal. 1601. 4°.
Waser (Casper). *See* Gesner (C.). Mithridates. 1610. 8°.
Washington (T.), *the younger. See* Nicolay (N. de). The Navigations. 1585.
Watchword for Wilfull Women. 1581. *See* B. (R.).
Waterhouse (Edward). *See* Davies (R.). Funerall Sermon. 1577.
Waterhouse (Tobias). Verses in Barlow (W.). Vita R. Cosin. 1598. 1707
Waterman (William). Verses in Wilson (Sir T.). Vita *ter.* 1551. 631
See Boemus (J.). Fardle of facions. 1555.
Waterson (Simon), *Printer. See* Guarini (G. B.). Pastor Fido. 1602.
Wateson (George). Cures of the diseased. 1598. 4°. . . . 2911
Watreman (William). *See* Waterman.
Wats. *See* Watts.
Watson (Anth.). Verses in Camb. Univ. Thr-thr. 1603. . . . 5616
Watson (George). *See* Wateson.
Watson (Henry). *See* Bernardinus. The Chirche. 1511. . . 164
Watson (John). English Martyrology. *See* Wilson (J.).
Watson (R.). Doble Almanacke or Kalender (Prognostication). 1600. 8°. 1345
Watson (Ric.), *Caius.* Verses in Camb. Univ. Fasciae. 1633. . 5808
— — Rex redux. 1633 *bis.* 5748
— — Carmen. 1635. 5770
— Shelford (R.). Five...discourses. 1635. 5774

No.
Watson (Ric.), *Caius*, *cont.* Verses in Camb. Univ. Συνωδία. 1637. . 5790
— — Voces. 1640. 5836
— Du Praissac. Art of warre. 1639. 5834
Watson (Robert). Verses in Forbes (P.). Funerals. 1637. . 6007
Watson (T.), *Bp.* Holsome and Catholyke doctryne concerninge the Seuen Sacramentes. 10 Feb. 1558. 4°. 1200
— 7 June 1558. 4°. 1201
Twoo notable sermons. 1554. 8°. 988
See Crowley (R.). A setting open of the subtyle Sophistrie. 1569.
Watson (T.), *Poet.* Amintæ gavdia. 1592. 4°. 1863
Compendium memoriae localis. [Ab. 1584–5.] 8°. . . . 6780
Verses in Ocland (C.). Anglorum praelia. (Εἰρηναρχία.) 1582. 1317
— Seton (J.). Dialectica. 1631. 5739
See Coluthus. Raptus Helenæ. 1586.
— Byrd (W.). Gratification. [1586?]
— Sophocles. Antigone. 1581.
Watson (Tho.), *Oxon.* Verses in Greene (R.). Ciceronis Amor. 1605. 1792
Watson (Will.). Decachordon. 1602. 4°. 6848
Dialogue. 'Rhemes.' 1601. 4°. 6840, 6841
Important considerations. 1601. 4°. 6842
Sparing discoverie of our English Jesuits. 1601. 4°. . . 6844
See Antiqvodlibet. 1602.
— Harsnet (S.). Declaration of egregious...Impostures.
— Jesuites Catechisme. 1602.
— Lessius (L.). Consultation. 1621. 6542
— Let Qvilibet beware. [1601?]
— Wisbech. True relation. 1601.
Watton (John). *See* Speculum Christiani. [148–?]
Watts (Gilbert). *See* Bacon (F.). Instauratio Magna. Pars 1. 1640.
[Lends J. Cowell's Interpreter (1607) to Richard Smith.] . 7851
Watts (J.). Verses in Camb. Univ. Epicedium. 1612. . . 5665
Watts (William). *See* Augustine. Confessions. 1631.
— James (T.), *Capt.* Strange...voyage. 1633.
Mortification apostolicall...sermon...May 21. 1637. 4°. . 4735
See Paris (M.). Historia major. 1640.
— Swedish Intelligencer.
Way to commende ourselves. 16°. 6599
Way to true happines. 1610. 8°. 7441
— 1615. 8°. 7525
— n.d. 8°. 5019, 7639
See also Doctrine of the Bible. 1616.
Waymouth (George), *Captain.* *See* Weymouth.
Waynflete (William), or Patten of Waynflete. *See* Budden (J.). Gvlielmi Patteni vita. 1602.
Waynman (Humfrey). *See* Masterson (T.). Arithmetick. 1634. 8°. 7797
Weale (Sam.). Verses in Camb. Univ. Lacrymæ. 1619. . . 5689
— Dolor. 1625. 5701
Weather-cock of romes religion. 1625. *See* Cooke (A.).
Web (Richard). Christs Kingdome. 1610. 4°. 3636
— Ed. 2. 1611. 4°. 3640
Webb or Webbe (Edward), *Roffensis.* Verses in Chaloner (Sir T.). De rep. angl. 1579. 7270
Catalogus Protestantium. 1624. 4°. 4226
Posie of spirituall flowers. 1610. 8°. 2965
Practice of quietnes. 1615. 8°. 3904
— Ed. 7. 1638. 12°. 4324
See Rogers (Ric.). Garden. 1625.
— Terentius. Andria. 1629.
— Eunuchus. 1629.
Webbe (I.). *See* Cicero. Familiar Epistles. [1620?] 12°.

No.
Webster (John). Devil's Law-case. 1623. 4°. 4521
Wechel (Andreas). *See* Talæus (A.). Rhetorica. 1631 *etc.*
Wecker (Hans Jacob). *See* Banister (J.). Compendiovs chirurgerie. 1585. 12°.
— — Workes. 1633.
Wedderburne (David). Abredonia atrata. Abredoniae. 1625. 4°. . 6000
Verses in Adamson (J.). Εἰσόδια. 1618 *bis*. 5960
— Forbes (P.). Funerals. 1637. 6007
Wedderburn (James). Verses in Adamson (J.). Εἰσόδια. 1618. . 5960
Weekes or Wykes (Tho.). [Licence.] Goodwin (T.). Aggravation. 1637.
— Du Bosc (J.). 1638. 12°. 7800
— Goodwin (T.). Childe. 1638.
— Du Bosc. 1639. 4°. 4040
— Sclater (W.). Sermons. 1638. 7929
— Stoughton (J.). XIII Sermons. 1640.
Weemes (John). Workes. Vol. I–III. 1633(2). 4°. . . . 4622
— Vol. IV. 1636. 4646
Christian Synagogue. 1623. 4°. 3856
Explication of the ivdiciall lawes of Moses. 1632. 4°. . . 3888
Pourtraiture of the image. 1627. 4°. 7893
Weever (John). Ancient Funerall Monuments. 1631. F°. . . 3991
Verses in Butts (H.). Dyets dry dinner. 1599. . . . 2727
Welby (Henry). Phœnix of these late times. 1637. 4°. . . . 3713
Welby (John). Verses in Hippocrates. 1633. 5812
Weld (Humfrey). Verses in Camb. Univ. Genethl. 1631. . . 5731
Weld or Welde (John). Verses in Cambridge Lachrymae. 1587. . 2123
— — Rex redux. 1633. 5748
Welde (William). *See* Janua Linguarum. 16[ ]. 4°. . . . 7711
Welles (John). Soules progresse. 1639. 4°. 7654
Wellington (Alice). *See* Hamond (T.). Late Commotion. 1605.
Wells ( ), *Dr.* True and ample relation of...occurrences...in the Palatinate. 1622. 4°. 3850
Wells (John). Sciographia. 1635. 8°. 4019
Welwod (Will.). De dominio maris. Cosmopoli, 1615. 4°. . 7535
Sea-law of Scotland. Edinburgh, 1590. 8°. 5925
Abridgement of all Sea-Lawes. 1613. 4°. 2520
— 1636. 8°. 4759
Wemesius, Wemesus, Wemysius. *See* Wemyss. *See also* Weemes.
Wemyss (John). Theses in Adamson (J.). Εἰσόδια. 1618. . 5960
Wemyss (Patrick). Theses in Adamson (J.). Εἰσόδια. 1618. . . 5960
Wendover (Roger). *See* Paris (M.). Historia major. 1640.
Wentworth (Michael), *S.J.C.* Verses in Camb. Univ. Voces. 1640. 5836
Wentworth (Peter). Pithie exhortation. (Treatise.) 1598. 8°. . 6822
Werdmueller (Otto). *See* Wermueller.
Wermueller (Otto). Hope of the faythful. 16°. 6312
Spyrytuall and most precyouse Pearle. 1550. 8°. . . . 782
Wescombe (Martin). Fabulae pontificiæ...dissipatae. Oxoniae, 1639. 8°. 5496
Wesel. *English Congregation.* *See* Traheron (B.). Exposition. 1557 *etc.*
West (John). Verses in Oxf. Univ. Magd. Coll. 1612. . . 5302
West (Richard), *B.A.*, *Ch. Ch.*, *Oxon.* Verses in Ferrand (J.). Ἐρωτομανία. 1640. 5498
— Oxf. Univ. Horti. 1640. 5499
— Randolph (T.). Poems. 1640. 5500
West (William). Symbolaeography. 1594. 4°. 2866
First part of symboleography. 1632. 4°. 5077
Second part of symboleography. 1627. 4°. 3297
West Indies. 1604. *See* Acosta (J.).
See Anglerius (P. M.).
— Linschoten (J. H. van). Voyages. 1598.

No.

West Indies, *cont.* *See* Monardes (N.). 1596.
Netherlands West Indian Company. *See* Holland. More excellent observations. 1622.
See Three several treatises. 1630.
Westerman (W.). Faithfull subiect. 1608. 8°. 1870
Jacobs Well. 1613. 8°. 3782
Two sermons of assise. 1600. 8°. 2570
Verses in Gerard (J.). Herball. 1597. 2348
Westfaling (Herbert). Treatise of reformation. 1582. 4°. . 1818
Verses in Humphrey (L.). J. Jvelli vita. 1573. . . . 837
Westley (Tho.). Verses in Oxf. Univ. Magd. Coll. 1612. . . 5302
Westminster [Abbey]. *See* Camden (W.). Reges, Reginæ. 1600 *etc.*
[Jurisdiction of]. *See* Lincoln Diocese. 6854
[School]. [*In usum.*] (Greek Grammar.) *See* Camden (W.). Institutio. 1604 etc.
[Treasury]. *See* Powell (T.). Repertorie of Records. 1631.
Westmorland (Charles Nevill, earl of). *See* Norton (T.). To the Quenes ...Subiectes. 1569.
See S. (W.). Aunswere. 1569.
Weston (Ben). Verses in Camb. Univ. Genethl. 1631. . . 5731
Weston (E.). *See* Richeome (L.). Pilgrime of Loreto. 1630.
Weston (Nic.). Verses in Camb. Univ. Genethliacum. 1631. . 5731
Weston (Richard). *See* Niccols (R.). Sir T. Overbvries Vision. 1616. 4222
— Overbury (Sir T.). Bloody downfall. [1616?]
Weston (William). *See* Watson (W.).
Westphalia. *See* Briefe discourse. 1599.
Wetenhall (Thomas). *See* Whetenhall.
Weymouth (George), *Captain.* *See* Fox (L.). North-west Fox. 1635.
Whalley (John). Gods plentie. 1616. 4°. 3118
Wharton (John). *See* Smith (Jude). Misticall deuise. 1575.
Whately (William). Bride bush. 1623. 4°. 4180–1
Charitable Teares. 1623. 4°. 3024
Gods husbandry. Part 1. Banbury, 1619. 4°. . . . 7932
— 1622. 4°. 4176
— Part 2. 1622. 4°. 7479
New birth. 1618. 4°. 3003
Sinne no more. 1628. 4°. 4818
Whear (Degory). Parentatio historica. *See* Oxford University. Camdeni Insignia. 1624. 4°.
Pietas erga benefactores. Oxon, 1628. 8°. 5423
Relectiones hyemales. Oxoniae, 1637. 8°. 5478
Verses in Seneca Tragoediae. 1613. 7781
See Hakewill (G.). An apologie. 1630.
Whear (William). Verses in Camdeni Insignia. 1624. . . 5346
Wheeler (Charles), *B.A.*, *T.C.* Verses in Camb. Univ. Voces. 1640. 5836
Wheeler (J.). Treatise of commerce...of the Societie of Merchants Aduenturers. 1601. 4°. 1269
Wheelocke (Abraham). Verses in Camb. Univ. Lacrymæ. 1619. . 5689
— — Epithalam. 1625. 5702
— — Genethl. 1631. 5731
— — Fasciae. 1633. 5808
— — Rex redux. 1633. 5748
Whetenhall (Thomas). Discourse of the abuses now in question. 1606. 4°. 6871
Whether Christian faith may be kepte secret. 'Roane,' 1553. 8°. 6242
Whether it be mortall sinne to transgresse ciuil lawes. [1570?] 8°. 985
Whetstone of Reproofe. 1632. 8°. 7817
Whetstone (G.). Censure of a loyall subiect. 1587. 4°. . . 1449
English Mirror. 1586. 4°. 2121
Heptameron of Civill Discourses. 1582. 4°. . . 7946 (=1452)

No.

Whetstone (G.), *cont.* Honourable reputation of a soldier. Leyden, 1586. 4°. 6495
Rocke of Regard. 1576. 4°. 7317
Whincop (Ioh.). Verses in Camb. Univ. Dolor. 1625. 5701
— — Genethl. 1631. 5731
Whincop (Tho.), *M.A.*, *Trin.* Verses in Camb. Univ. Epithalam. 1625. 5702
Whippey (George), *Book-collector?* *See* Baldwin (W.). Treatise. 1596. 8°.
Whistler (D.). Verses *bis* in Oxf. Univ. Horti. 1640. 5499
Whiston (Hen.), *K.C.C.* Verses in Camb. Univ. Genethl. 1631. 5731
— — Gerhard (J.). Golden chaine. 1632. 5744
— — Fasciae. 1633. 5808
— — Rex redux. 1633. 5748
— — Hippocrates. 1631 etc. 5736 etc.
Whitaker (Laurence). Verses in Seneca. Tragoediæ. 1624. 3444
See Coryate (T.). Coryates Crudities. 1611. 4°.
Whitaker (Richard), *printer.* *See* Bible. N.T. Greek. 1633.
Whitaker (Tobias). Tree of humane life. 1638. 8°. 5169
Whitaker (W.). Ad N. Sanderi demonstrationes responsio. 1583. 8°. 1555
Ad rationes decem E. Campiani responsio. 1581. 8°. 1550
Adversus T. Stapletoni...defensionem...duplicatio. Cantabrigiae, 1594. F°. 5570
Answere to a certeine booke...by William Rainolds. 1585. 8°. 6784
Aunswere to a certaine booke by William Rainoldes. Cambridge, 1585. 8°. 5517
Answere to the ten reasons of E. Campian. 1606. 4°. 2945
Disputatio de sacra scriptura. Cantabrigiae, 2 Maij, 1588. 4°. 5533-4
Praelectiones...cura J. Allenson. Cantabrigiae, 1599. 4°. 5598
— Cantabrigiae, 1600. 8°. 5601
Responsionis...defensio. 1583. 8°. 1644
Tractatus...de peccato originali. Cantabrigiae, 1600. 8°. 5602
See Jewel (J.). Adversus Thomam Hardingum volumen alterum. 1578.
— Common Prayer. (Gr. Lat.) 1569.
— Norris (S.). Antidote. 1615 etc. 4°.
— — Guide. 1621. 4°.
— Nowell (A.). Κατηχισμος. 1573.
— — Catechismus parvus. 1574.
Whitbourne (Richard). Discourse and discovery of New-found-land. 1622. 4°. 3022
White (Anthony). Truth and error discovered. Oxford, 1628. 4°. 5375
White (Charles). *See* Clerke (Ric.). Sermons. 1637.
White (Christopher). Of oathes. 1627. 4°. 4095
Sermon in Christchurch, Oxford. 12 May 1622. 1622. 4°. 2817
White (Francis). Examination and confutation of a lawlesse pamphlet. 1637. 4°. 4383, 7837
Londons warning. 1619. 4°. 4070
Orthodox faith. 1617. 4°. 2284
Replie to Jesuite Fishers answere. 1624. F°. 2453
Treatise of the sabbath-day. 1635. 4°. 4367
— Ed. 2. 1635. 4°. 4368
— Ed. 3. 1636. 4°. 4376
Verses in Camb. Univ. Epicedium. 1612. 5665
— Oxf. Univ. Magd. Coll. 1612. 5302
See Featley (D.). Romish Fisher. 1624.
— Fisher (J.). Answere vnto the nine points of Controuersy. 1626(5). 4°.
— Prynne (W.). Lords Day, the Sabbath Day. [1636?]
— Reply to D. White and D. Featly. Pt 1. 1625. 4°. 6554
— White (J.), *of Eccles.* Workes. 1624.
White (Harim). Ready way to true repentance. 1618. 8°. 3589

No.
White (Henry), *de Rougham*. Verses in Ovid. De tristibus. 1639. . 4668
White (John), *bishop of Winchester*. Diacosiomartyrion. 1553. 4°. 1192
White (John), *of Eccles*. Workes. 1624. F°. 2296-7
Way to the true church. 1608. 4°. 3452
— Ed. 2. 1610. 4°. 3454
— Ed. 3. 1612. 4°. 3456
Defence of the way to the true church. 1614. 4°. . . . 3738
— 1624. F°. 3027
— *See* G. (W.). Discovery. 1619. 4°.
See D. (A.), *student*. A reply. 1612. 4°.
— — Treatise. 1614.
— Leucus (I.).
— Worthington (T.). Whyte dyed black. 1615.
White (Matthew). Newes from Ipswich. Ipswich, 1636. 4°. . 5886
White (Nathanael). Verses in Camdeni Insignia. 1624. . . 5364
White (Peter). Answeare vnto certaine crabbed questions. 1582. 8°. 1927
White (Ph.). Verses in Holyoake (F.). Dictionarium. 1640. . 3058
White (Richard). Orationes duæ. 1566. 8°. 746
Verses in Verstegan (R.). A Restitution. 1605 *etc*. . . 6140 *etc*.
White (William), *cartographer*. *See* Speed (J.). Theatre. 1611.
White (William), *printer*. *See* Briefe Discourse of the Scriptures. 1614.
Whitehead (David). *See* Vermigli (P. M.). Commentaries...vpon Romanes. 1568.
Whitehorne (P.). Certain waies for the orderyng of Souldiers. 1562. 4°. 1171
Whiteway (Sam.). Verses in Camb. Univ. Anthologia. 1632. . 5741
— — Fasciae. 1633. 5808
— — Carmen. 1635. 5770
Whitfeld (Ralph), *C.C.C.* Verses in Camb. Univ. Συνωδία. 1637. 5790
Whitfield (H.). *See* Wilson (J.). Zacheus. 1631. 12°.
Whitford (Ric.). Holy instructions and teachynges for the helth of mannes soule. 1541. 4°. 711
Iesus Psalter. Douai. 16°. 6605
Pype or tonne of the lyfe of perfection. 1532. 4°. . . . 377
Werke for housholders. n.d. 4°. 406
Werke of preparation. 1531. 8°. 374
See Certayne Deuout and godly Petitions.
— Fruit of Redemption. 1514.
Whitgift (J.). Answer to a certen Libell...admonition to the Parliament. 1573. 4°. 1476
Defence of the Aunswere to the Admonition. 1574. F°. . 1480
Examination of...censures. 1575. 8°. 6761
Godlie sermon...26 of March. 1574. 8°. 1481
[Life.] *See* Paule (Sir G.). 1612.
See Broughton (H.). An epistle. 1597. 4°.
— — Letters. [1591?]
— — Two little workes. 1604.
— Cartwright (T.). Replye to an answere made of M. Doctor Whitegifte. [1574?]
— — Second replie...agaynst Maister Doctor Whitgiftes second answer. 1575.
— — Rest of the second replie...agaynst...Whitgiftes second answer. 1577.
— Defense of the Ecclesiasticall Regiment. 1574.
— Lambeth Articles. [1629?] etc.
— Penry (J.). Th'appellation. 1589.
— Vnlawfvll Practises of Prelates. [1584?]
Whiting (N.). *See* Whyting.
Whitney (Geoffrey). Choice of emblemes. Leyden. 1586. 4°. . 6496
Verses in Whetstone (G.). Honovrable reputation. 1586. . 6495
Whittel (Thomas). *See* Whyttel.

No.
Whittell (Robert). Way to the Celestiall Paradise. 1620. 4°. . 3948
Whittingham (W.). *See* Frankfort. Brieff discours. 1575.
Whittingham (William). To my faythfull Brethren now afflycted. [1566?] 8°. 6414
Whittington (Robert). [Grammar, Pt I. Bk 1.] De nominum generibus. W. de Worde, 3 Kal. Sept. 1526. 4°. 190
[— Pt I. Bk 2.] Grammaticæ Whitintonianae Liber secundus. De nominum declinatione. W. de Worde, 1529. 4°. . 199, 7752
[— Pt I. Bk 3.] De heteroclitis nominibus. Oxonie, 1518. 4°. 5220
[—] W. de Worde, Prid. Kal. Aug. 1525. 4°. 188
[—] De heteroclitis nominibus & gradibus comparationis. W. de Worde [1520]. 4°. 250
[Pt I. Bk 5, 6.] Verborum præterita et supina [Pt I. Bk 5], De verborum formis [Pt I. Bk 6]. W. de Worde, Id. Sept. 1526. 4°. 191
[De concinnitate grammatices.] *See post* Vulgaria. 1520. 4°.
De heteroclitis nominibus. *See* Pt I. Bk 3.
De nominum generibus. *See* Pt I. Bk 1.
De nominum declinatione. *See* Pt I. Bk 2.
De octo partibus orationis. J. Notary, 1516. 4°. . . . 334
— W. de Worde, 8 id. Apr. 1519. 4°. 179
De syllabarum quantitate. W. de Worde [1525?] 4°. . . 251–2
— J. Notary. [1516]. 333
Declinationes nominum. *See* Pt I. Bk 2.
[Pt II. §§ 1, 2.] Editio, cum interpretatione F. Nigri. Notary, 1516. 4°. 333
— Editio, cum interpretatione F. Nigri. Notary, 1516. 4°. . 251–2
Lucubrationes de synonymis. Pynson, 1520. 4°. . . . 273
Lucubrationes de synonymis, de epithetis, de variandi formulis, experientiæ, de veterum romanorum magistratibus. W. de Worde, Aug. 1523. 4°. 186
— W. de Worde, March 1529. 4°. 197
Syntaxis. 1522. P. Treveris, Southwarke. 4°. 5863
— W. de Worde, Id. Nov. 1524. 4°. 187
Vulgaria. Pynson, 1520. 4°. 269
Vulgaria, & de institutione grammaticulorum, libello de concinnitate grãmatices accomodatum. W. de Worde, 1526. 4°. . . 193
[Vulgaria. *Lat. Eng.*] Grammaticvlorvm institutio. *See* Clarke (J.). Dux grammaticvs. 1633.
See Cicero. De Senectute. 1540.
— Cicero. [De officiis.] 1534.
— Horman (W.). Antibossicon. 1521.
— Stanbridge (J.). Accidentia. [Ab. 1526?] etc. 4°.
Whittle (Thomas). *See* Whyttel.
Whitwell (C.). Verses in Camb. Univ. Fasciae. 1633. . . 5808
Whitwell (Charles), *instrument maker.* *See* Hood (T.). Making and use of a Sector. 1598.
Wholesome Exercise. [Ab. 1610.] 16°. 6598
Whyte (Alexander). Verses in Forbes (P.). Funerals. 1637. . 6007
Whyte (Peter). *See* White.
Whyte dyed black. 1615. *See* Worthington (T.).
Whyting (N.). Verses *bis* in Camb. Univ. Fasciae. 1633. . . 5808
Whyttel (Thomas). Certayne letters. *See* Coverdale (M.). Certain... letters. 1564.
Wiat (Francis). *See* Wyat.
Wicelius (Georgius). Methodus concordiae ecclesiasticae. Ed. T. James, 1625. 8°. 3527
Wicherley (Daniel). Verses in Camb. Univ. Genethl. 1631. . . 5731
— — Rex redux. 1633. 5748
Wickham (Hen.). Verses in Camb. Univ. Epicedium. 1612. . . 5665
Wickham (William). Verses in Wilson (Sir T.). Discourse. 1584. 1872
See Willes (R.). Poematum liber. 1573.

No.

Wiclif (John). *See* Wyclif.
Widdowes (Giles). Lawlesse kneelesse schismaticall puritan. 1631. 4°. 5393
Naturall Philosophy. Ed. 2. 1631. 4°. 4616
Schismaticall Puritan. Oxford, 1630. 4°. 5384
Schysmatical Puritan. Oxford, 1630. 4°. 7659
See Page (W.). Treatise. 1631.
— Prynne (W.). Lame Giles. 1630. 4°.
Widdrington (Ralph). Verses in Camb. Univ. Συνωδία. 1637. . 5790
— — Voces. 1640. 5836
— King (E.). Ivsta. 1638. 5829
Widdrington (Roger). Ad Paulum Quintum Supplicatio. 'Albionopoli,' 1616. 8°. 6907
Apologia card. Bellarmini. 'Cosmopoli,' 1611. 8°. . . . 6886
App. ad disp. theol. de juramento. 'Albionopoli,' 1616. 8°. . 6905
Cleare...confutation of the reply of T. F. 1616. 4°. . . . 6906
Copy of the decree. 1614. 8°. 6899
Discussio discussionis decreti magni concilii lateranensis. 'Augustae,' 1618. 8°. 6913
Disputatio theologica. 'Albionopoli,' 1613. 8°. . . . 6892
Last rejoynder to Mr T. Fitzherberts reply. 1619. 4°. . . 6916
— 1633. 4°. 7019
Responsio apologetica. 'Cosmopoli,' 1612. 8°. 6890
— *See ante* Disputatio.
Widley (George). Doctrine of the sabbath. 1604. 4°. . . . 2935
Wier (Johann). Observations. *See* Guillemeau (J.). A worthy treatise. [159-] etc. 12°.
Wiffing (Richard). Verses in Smith (J.). Generall historie. 1624. . 3864
Wight (Isle of). The Teares... *See* Jones (W.). Treatise. 1625. 4°.
Wigmore (Gilb.). Verses in Camb. Univ. Rex redux. 1633. . 5748
Wigmore (Michael). Holy citie. 1619. 4°. 4497
Meteors. 1633. 4°. 4008
Wilcock (William). *See* Andreæ (A.). Quaestiones. 1480. F°.
Wilcocks (Thomas). *See* Wilcox.
Wilcox (Thomas). Workes. 1624. F°. 4794
Right godly and learned Exposition vpon the whole Booke of Psalmes. 1586. 4°. 1887
See Admonition. 1572.
— Logue (B. de). Treatise. 1581.
— Mornay (P. de). Worke. 1617.
Wilcox (Tho.). Verses in Camdeni Insignia. 1624. 5346
Wild (Johann), *of Mainz*. *See* Crashaw (W.). Falsificationum. 1606.
Wilhelmus [*qu*. Gulielmus de Saliceto?]. *See* Herbal. Great Herbal. 1561. 1242
Wilkes (Richard). *See* Redman (J.). Reporte. 1551.
Wilkes (William). Obedience or ecclesiasticall vnion. 1605. 4°. . 3558
— *See below*, Second memento. 1608.
Second memento for Magistrates. 1608. 4°. 3570
Wilkie (Robert). Verses in Adamson (J.). Εἰσόδια. 1618. . . 5960
Wilkins (George). Miseries of inforst marriage. 1637. 4°. . 4902
Wilkins (John). Discovery of a world in the moone. 1638. 8°. . 5199
Discourse. (Discovery of a new world. Ed. 3.) 1640. 8°. (5184=) 4913
Wilkinson (John). *See* Avila y Zuñiga (L. de). Comentaries. 1555.
Wilkinson (John). Treatise collected out of the Statutes. 1628. 8°. 7510
Verses in Oxf. Univ. Magd. Coll. 1612. 5302
Wilkinson (Robert). Barwickbridge. 1617. 4°. 3922
Iewell for the eare. 1605. 8°. 3316
Merchant royall. 1607. 4°. 2950
Sermon June 21. 1607. 4°. 7439
Stripping of Joseph. 1625. 4°. 3160

No.
Wilkinson (W.). Confutation of certaine articles. 1579. 4°. . 859
Very godly...Treatise...of Fastyng. 1580. 8°. 862
Wilkinson (William). Verses in Camb. Univ. Carmen. 1635. . 5770
Willan (Robert). Conspiracie against Kings. 1622. 4°. . . 3512
Eliah's wish. 1630. 4°. 4608
Willeius (Ricardus). *See* Willes.
Willes (Richard). Poematum Liber. 1573. 8°. . . . 1127
See Anglerius (P. M.). History of Trauayle. 1577.
Willet (Andrew). Catholicon...of S. Ivde. Cambridge, 1602. 8°. 5611
De animae natura. Cantabrigiae, 1585. 8°. . . . 5518
De universali et novissima iudæorum vocatione. Cantabrigiae, 1590. 4°. 5551
Ecclesia triumphans... (Thesaurus ecclesiae.—Catholicon). Cambridge, 1614. F°. 5673
Harmonie vpon the first booke of Samuel. Cambridge, 1607. 4°. 5648–9
— 1614. F°. 5674
Harmonie vpon...II Samuel. Cambridge, 1614. F°. . . 5675
Hexapla in Genesin. Cambridge, 1605. F°. 5634
— Ed. 2. 1608. F°. 7437
— Ed. 3. 1632(3). F°. 4849
Hexapla in Genesim et Exodum. Ed. 4. 1633. F°. . . 4851
Hexapla in Exodum. 1608. F°. 2952
— 1633. F°. 4850
— *See above*, Hexapla in Genesim et Exodum. 1633.
Hexapla in Leviticum...Ed. P. Smith. 1631. F°. . . . 4555
Hexapla in Danielem. Cambridge, 1610. F°. . . . 5662
Hexapla...vpon the...Romans. Cambridge, 1611. F°. . . 5663
— 1620. F°. 5692
Loidoromastix. Cambridge, 1607. 4°. 5650
Retection, or discoverie...of...Synopsis Papismi, and Tetrastylon Papisticum. 1603. 8°. 2930
Sacrorum emblematum centuria una. [1596?] 4°. . . 5547
Synopsis Papismi. 1592. 4°. 2218
— Ed. 3. 1600. F°. 2918
— Ed. 4. 1614. F°. 2989
— 1634. F°. 4854
[Synopsis Papismi & Tetrastilon Papisticum.] *See* O. (E.). Detection. 1602.
Tetrastylon papismi. 1599. 4°. 2914
— *See above*, Synopsis.
Treatise of Salomons mariage. 1612. 4°. 2983
See W. (A.). Fruitfull and godly sermon. 1592. 8°.
Willet (James). Verses in Camb. Univ. Lacrymæ. 1619. . . 5689
William I, *King of England*. [Life.] *See* Hayward (Sir J.). 1613.
William II., *King of England*. [Life.] *See* Hayward (Sir J.). 1613.
William, *Prince of Orange*. Apologie or defence...against...the King of Spaine. Delft, 1582. 4°. 6441
Justification or cleering...agst. false Sclaunders. 24 Feb. 1575. 8°. 7121
See Middelburg. Middleborovv. [1574.]
William IV, *Landgrave of Hesse*. *See* Frederick III. Christian Confession. 1577.
William, *of Malmesbury*. [Works.] *See* Savile (Sir H.). Rervm Anglicarvm scriptores. 1596.
Williamot (Samuel). Verses in Roberts (L.). Merchants mappe. 1638. 5133
Williams (Griffith). Best religion. 1636. F°. 4464
True Church. 1629. F°. 4829
Williams (John). Great Britaines Salomon. 1625. 4°. . . 3528
Holy table. 1637. 4°. 7040, 7577
Perseuerantia sanctorum. Sermon. 18 Feb. 1628. 1628. 4°.
Sermon of apparell. 1620. 4°. 3501

No.
Williams (John), *cont.* Sermon preached in...Westminster, 6 April 1628. 1628. 4°. 3536
Verses in Camb. Univ. Thr-thr. 1603. 5616
Verses in Camb. Univ. Epicedium. 1612. 5665
See Heylyn (P.). Antidotvm Lincolniense. 1637.
— — Coale from the altar. 1636.
See Pocklington (J.). Altare. 1637.
[*Triennial Visitation.*] *See* Pocklington (J.). 1636.
Williams (John), *King's.* Verses in Camb. Univ. Fasciae. 1633. . 5808
— — Carmen. 1635. 5770
Williams (Johannes), *Oxoniensis.* *See* Bacon (R.). Libellvs. 1590.
Williams (Lewis). Verses in Camdeni Insignia. 1624. . . 5346
Williams (Ric.), *K.C.C.* Verses in Camb. Univ. Epithalam. 1625. . 5702
— — Genethl. 1631. 5731
— — Hippocrates. 1631, etc. . . . . . 5736 etc.
— — Anthologia. 1632. 5741
— Drexelius (H.). Considerations. 1632 etc. . . . 7789 etc.
Williams (Sir Roger). Actions of the Lowe Countries. 1618. 4°. 2533
Williams (Thomas). *See* Davies (J.), *D.D.* Antiquæ linguæ britannicæ ...dictionarium. 1632.
Williams (William). Verses in Camb. Univ. Anthologia. 1632. . 5741
Williamson (C. [Caesar or Columbus?]). Verses in Camb. Univ. Fasciae. 1633. 5808
Williamson (Cæsar), *T.C.C.* Verses in Camb. Univ. Anthologia. 1632. 5741
— — Rex redux. 1633. 5748
— Russell (J.). The two...battels. 1634. 5767
— Camb. Univ. Συνωδία. 1637. 5790
See Williamson (C.).
Williamson (Columbus). *See* Williamson (Dove).
Williamson (Dove), *K.C.C.* Verses in Camb. Univ. Epithalam. 1625. 5702
— — Genethl. 1631. 5731
— — Hippocrates. 1631. 5736
— Gerhard (J.). Golden chaine. 1632. 5744
— Hippocrates. 1633. 5812
Williamson (Thomas). Comfortable meditation of humane frailtie. 1630. 4°. 4837
Williamson (Thomas), *K.C.C.* Verses in Camb. Univ. Epicedium. 1612. 5665
Williatt (Andrew). *See* Willet (Andrew).
Willimat (William). *See* Willymat.
Willis (John). Schoolmaister to the art of stenographie. 1622. 12°. 3341
Willis (N.). *See* Willys.
Willis (Timothy), *M.D.* Propositiones tentationum. 1615. 8°. . 3757
Search of cavses...Alchemie. 1616. 8°. 3762
Verses in Anthony (F.). Apologia. 1616. . . . 3759
Willmer (Thomas). *See* Fasciculus Florum. 1636. 8°.
Willoughby (Charles). Verses in Wilson (Sir T.). Vita. 1551. . 631
Willoughby (John). *See* Chrysostom (John). Theorremων... 1602. 5257
Willoughby d'Eresby (Robert Bartue, Lord). *See* Markham (G.). Honour. 1624.
Willymat (W.). Anchor of faith. 1628. 8°. 4252
Loyal subiects looking-glasse. 1604. 4°. 3552–3
Physicke. 1605. 8°. 3201
— [Anchor of faith.] 1628. 8°. 4252
See James I. Princes looking glasse. 1603. 4°.
Willys (Nath.). Verses in Camb. Univ. Fasciae. 1633. . . 5808
— — Rex redux. 1633. 5748
Wilmot ( ), *minister of Clare, Suffolk.* [Funeral sermon.] *See* Hooker (T.). Sovles possession. 1638.
Wilmot (R.). Syrophænissa. 1601. 8°. 2850
Wilsford (Franc). Verses in Camb. Univ. Fasciae. 1633. . . . 5808

No.
Wilshaw ( ). Verses in Camb. Univ. Lacrymæ. 1619. 5689
Wilson (Christopher). Selfe Deniall. 1625. 4°. 3690
Wilson (Edmund), *M.D.* Verses in Hippocrates. 1633. 5812
Wilson (Henry). Verses in Jewel (J.). Adv. T. Hardingum. 1578. 1535
Wilson (John), *R.C. Priest.* English martyrologe. 1608. 8°. 6518
See Blackwell (G.). In Georgivm Blacvellvm quæstio bipartita. 1609. 4°.
Wilson (John), *Preacher.* Zacheus converted. 1631. 12°. 4617
Wilson (Jo.), *T.C.C.* Verses in Camb. Univ. Epicedium. 1612. 5666
Wilson (Matthew). *See* Knott (Edward).
Wilson (Miles). Verses in Cheke (Sir J.). De obitu M. Buceri. 1551. 734
Wilson (Sylvester). *See* Barclay (W.). Jvdicium. 1620.
Wilson (Thomas), *LL.D.* Arte of Rhetorique. 1553. 4°. 626
— 1567. 4°. 1177
— 1585. 4°. 2182
Discourse vpon vsvrie. 1584. 8°. 1872
Rule of reason. 1552. 8°. 625
— 1567. 4°. 1176
Vita et obitus...fratrum Suffolciensium, H. et C. Brandoni. [1551.] 4°. 631
Verses in Cheke (Sir J.). De obitu M. Buceri. 1551. 734
— Humphrey (L.). J. Jvelli vita. 1573. 837
— Parkhurst (J.). Ludicra. 1573. 838
— Ascham (R.). Fam. Epp. libri tres. 1576. 1654
See Demosthenes. Thre Orations. 1570. 4°.
— Haddon (W.). Lucubrationes. 1567. 4°.
— Mary, *Queen of Scots.* De Maria. [1572 ?]
Wilson (Thomas), *M.A.* Christs farewell to Jerusalem. 1614. 8°. 3405
Theologicall Rules. 1615. 8°. 3905
Wilton (Deliverance). Verses in Oxf. Univ. Magd. Coll. 1612. 5302
Wiltshire. *See* Mere.
Wiltshire (Thomas Boleyn, earl of). [*Ad instantiam.*] *See* Erasmus. Playne...exposytion. [1533–6.]
Wimbledon (E. Cecil, *Visct*). A journall and relation. 1626. 4°. 6972
Speech. *See* Scott (T.). Speech made. 1624.
See S. (E. C.). Government of Ireland. 1626. 4°.
Wimbledon (R.). Sermon at Paules Crosse. 1388. Ed. 11. 1617. 8°. 7858
— Ed. 12. 1617. 8°. 2786
Wimpen (Jo.). Verses in Hodson (W.). Holy sinner. 1639. 5796
Wimpew (Will.). Verses in Hodson (W.). Holy sinner. 1639. 5796
Winchcomb (Hen.). Verses in Oxf. Univ. Magd. Coll. 1612. 5302
Winchester College. *See* Willes (R.). Poematum liber. 1573.
Winchester Diocese. *See* James I. [Royal Letters.] 1604. 7416
Windebank (Francis). [Licence.] *See* Marie de' Medici. Declaration. 1639. 4°.
Windham (Hugo). Verses in Camdeni Insignia. 1624. 5346
Windsor, View of, 1572. *See* Braun (G.).
Windsor (Miles). Academiarum...catalogus. 1590. 4°. 1727
Wines. *See* Proclamations. 1632 (Feb. 18).
Wing (John). Abels offering. Flushing. 1621. 4°. 6653
Crowne coniugall. Middelburg, 1620. 4°. 6483
Wingate (Edmund). Arithmetique made easie. 1630. 8°. 4915
See Britton (J.). Britton. 1640.
— Roe (N.). Tabulæ Logarithmicæ. 1633. 8°.
Wingfield (Antony). Verses in Cambridge Lachrymae. 1587. 2123
See Pedantius. 1631.
Wingfield (H.). Compendious or shorte Treatise...of Phisycke. [1548 ?] 8°. 1067
Winston (John). *See* Dod (J.). Ten Sermons. 1610.
Winter (Thomas). *See* James I. Speach. 1605.
Winter (William). [Funeral.] *See* Gataker (T.). Christian Constancy crowned. 1624. 4°.

No.
Winterton (Francis). Verses in Gerhard (J.). Prayers. 1625 *etc.* 3321 etc.
— — Meditations. 1627 *etc.* . . . . . 5707 etc.
Winterton (Jo.), *M.B., Christ's Coll.* Verses in Camb. Univ. Fasciae. 1633. 5808
— — Rex redux. 1633. 5748
— — Carmen. 1635. 5770
— — *Συνωδία.* 1637. 5790
Winterton (Ralph). Verses in Camb. Univ. Lacrymae. 1619. . 5689
— — Dolor. 1625 *bis*. . . . . 5701, 5701 A
— — Epithalam, *ter*. 1625. 5702
— — Genethl. *bis* 1631. 5731
— — Anthologia. 1632. 5741
— — Fasciae. *bis* 1633. 5808
— — Rex redux. *bis* 1633. 5748
— — Carmen. 1635. 5770
— Seton (J.). Dialectica. 1631. 5739
See Drexelius (H.). Considerations...upon Eternitie. 1632 etc. 12°. 7789 etc.
— Gerhard (J.). Golden chaine. 1632. 12°.
— — Meditations. 1627 etc.
— — Prayers. 1625 *etc.*
— — Svmme of christian doctrine. 1640.
— Hippocrates. Aphorismorum. 1631.
— Ovid...Metamorphoseωn. 1631.
— Poetæ minores græci. 1635.
Wirsung (Christopher). General practise of physicke. Trans. J. Mosan. 1617. F°. 3765
Wirtzung (Christopher). *See* Wirsung.
Wisbech. True relation of the faction begun at Wisbech. 1601. 4°. 6843
Wischart (William). *See* Wishart.
Wisdome crying out. 1639 (1638). 8°. *See* Milbourne (W.).
Wisdom (Robert). Verses in Wilson (Sir T.). Vita. 1551. . 631
See Bible (Eng.). Psalms. (Sternhold and Hopkins).
Wiseman (Sir Richard). Verses in Isaacson (H.). Ephemerides. 1633. 4206
Wiseman (Sir Robert). Verses in Isaacson (H.). Ephemerides. 1633. 4206
Wishart (George). Verses in Forbes (P.). Funerals. 1637. . . 6007
Wishart (William). Exposition of the Lords Prayer. 1633. 12°. . 4278
Verses in Forbes (P.). Funerals. 1637. 6007
Withals (J.). Shorte dictionarie in Latine and English. 1586. 4°. 1376
Dictionary in english and latine. 1634. 8°. 4152
Withals (John). Verses in More (Sir T.). G. Rossei opus. 1523. . 284
Wither (Fabian). *See* Dariot (C.). Briefe...Introduction. 1598. 4°.
See Indagine (J. ab). Briefe Introductions. 1558. 8°.
— Pole (R.). Seditious...Oration of Cardinal Pole. [1560?]
Wither (George). Workes. 1620. 8°. 3802
A.B.C. for Layemen. 1585. 8°. 1900
Abuses stript, and whipt. 1614. 8°. 3406
— 1617. 8°. 2532
Britain's Remembrancer. 1628. 12°. 4410
Collection of emblemes. 1635(4). F°. 4584
Epithalamia...vpon...Prince Frederick V...and Princesse Elizabeth. 1612. 4°. 3840
Hymnes and songs of the Church. 1623. 8°. 4921
Schollers purgatory. n.d. 8°. 3311
View of the marginal notes of the Popish Testament. [1588.] 4°. 2047
Wither's motto. Nec habeo, nec careo, nec curo. [1621?] 8°. 4132
[Eclogues.] *See* Browne (W.). Shepherds Pipe. 1614. 8°.
Verses in Blaxton (J.). The English usurer. Ed. 2. 1634. . 4895
Butler (C.). Feminin 'Monarchi.' 1634. 5439
See Nemesius. The natvre of man. 1636.

No.

Withers (Steuen). *See* Calvin (J.). Very profitable treatise. 1561. 8°.
Withington (Oliver). Verses in Humphrey (L.). I. Ivelli vita. 1573. 837
Wits Theatre. 1599. *See* Bodenham (J.).
Witt (John). *See* Heywood (T.). Hierarchie. 1635.
Witt (Richard). Arithmeticall qvestions. 1613. 4°. 2521
Wittenberg University. Consideration...whether a state...be bound.. in the Warres of Bohemia. 1620. 4°. 6921
Witzel (Georg). *See* Wicelius.
Wodenoteus (Theoph), *K.C.C.* Verses in Camb. Univ. Epicedium. 1612. 5665
Wodford (Will.). *See* Woodeford.
Wodroephe (John). Spared houres of a souldier. Dort, 1623. F°. 6510
Wol (Io.), *K.C.C.* *See* Wolrich (J.).
Wolferstone ( ). Verses in Gray (T. de). 1639.. . . . 4042
Wolff (Caspar). *See* Gesner (C.). Historiae animalium Lib. v. 1587. F°.
Wolfius (Henricus). *See* Beroaldus (M.). Short view. 1590.
Wolfius (Hieronymus). Admonitio de vero & licito Astrologiæ usu. *See* Leowitz (C. de). Brevis et perspicva ratio. 1558.
See Isocrates. Orationes & Epistolæ. 1615. 8°.
Wollaeus (Joh.). Verses in Humphrey (L.). I. Ivelli vita. 1573. . 837
Wolphius (Caspar). *See* Wolff.
Wolrich (Jo.), *King's Coll.* Verses in Camb. Univ. Lacrymae. 1619. 5689
Wolsey (Thomas), *cardinal.* *See* Fisher (J.). The sermon. [152–.] 4°.
Womans Book. *See* Roesslin (E.). Byrth of mankynde. 1540 *etc.*
Women. *See* Lawes resolutions. 1632.
Wonderful shapes and natures of man. Trans. L. Andrewe. Antwerp, [1527?] F°. 6077
Wood (Ambrose). *See* Ward (Sam.). Coal from the altar. Ed. 2. 1616 etc.
Wood (Andr.). Verses in Camb. Univ. Epicedium. 1612. . . . 5665
— — Lacrymæ. 1619. 5689
— — Dolor. 1625. 5701
— — Epithalam. 1625. 5702
— — Genethl. 1631. 5731
— — *Συνωδία.* 1637 *bis.* 5790
Wood (Caleb). Verses in Camdeni Insignia. 1624. 5346
Wood (E.). Verses in Camb. Univ. Genethl. 1631. . . . 5731
See also Woodcock.
Wood (Michael). *See* Gardiner (S.). De vera obedientia. 1553.
Wood (Nic.), *Reginal.* Verses in Barlow (W.). Vita R. Cosin. 1598. 1707
Wood (Robert). *See* Artemidorus. Ivdgement. 1606.
Wood (Roger). Verses in Camb. Univ. Genethl. 1631. . . . 5731
Wood (Thomas). Verses in Passe (C. de). Garden of flowers. 1615. 6643
— Camb. Univ. Dolor. 1625. 5701
See Oration or speech. 1608. 1624
Wood (William). New Englands prospect. 1634. 4°. . . . 4634
Woodall (John). Surgions mate. 1617. 4°. 7555
— 1639. F°. 5008
Woodcock (Ed.). Verses in Camb. Univ. Fasciae. 1633. . . . 5808
See also Wood.
Woodcoke (Richard). Godly and learned answer. 1608. 4°. . 3628
Woodd or Woode (Andrew). *See* Wood.
Woodeford (William). Verses in Camb. Univ. Thr-thr. 1603.. . 5616
— — Epicedium. 1612. 5665
Woodes (Andrew). *See* Wood.
Woodes (Robert). Verses in Camb. Univ. Thr-thr. 1603 *bis.* . 5616
Woodford (W.). *See* Woodeford.
Woodhall (E.). Verses in Camb. Univ. Thr-thr. 1603. . . . 5616
Woodhall (John). Verses in Camb. Univ. Carmen. 1635. . 5770
Woodvile (Anthony), earl Rivers. *See* Rivers.
Woodward (Ezekias). Childes patrimony. 1640. 4°. 4752

No.

Woodyates (Thomas). *See* Lake (A.). Sermons. 1629.
Woolton (J.). Armoure of Proufe. 1576. 8°. 1858
Treatise of the Immortalitie of the Soule. 1576. 8°. . . 1371
Woorlich (T.). Verses in Camb. Univ. Fasciae. 1633. . . 5808
Worcester, Diocese of. *See* Certaine Considerations. 1605.
Worcester (John Tiptoft, earl of). *See* Cicero. De Senectute. 1481.
Worcester (Edward Somerset, earl of). [Players.] *See* Pleasant... Comedy. 1634.
Worde (Jan Wynkyn de). *See* Wynkyn.
Worke entytled of the olde god etc. 1534. 8°. *See* Coverdale (M.).
Worrall (Isaac), *B.A.*, *S.J.C.* Verses in Camb. Univ. Συνωδία. 1637. 5790
Worship (William). Christians mourning garment. 1610. 8°. . 3317
— 1630. 8°. 7900
Earth raining upon Heaven. 1614. 4°. 3407
Worsop (Ed.). Discoverie of sundrie errours. 1582. 4°. . . 7931
Worthington (Lawrence), *jesuit*. *See* Coster (F.). Meditations. 1616. 12°.
Worthington (Tho.). Anker of christian doctrine. Douai. 1618. 4°. 6606
— 1622. 4°. 6575
Whyte dyed black. 1615. 4°. 6904
— *See* White (F.). Orthodox faith. 1617 etc.
See Bible. Eng. New Testament. Rhemes, 1582. 4°.
— Bible. Eng. O.T. Douai. 1609-10.
— — 1635.
Wotton (Anthony). Answere to a popish Pamphlet. 1605. 4°. . 3559
Dangerous plot discovered. 1626. 4°. 3871
Defence of M. Perkins...reformed catholike. 1606. 4°. . . 2946
Rvnne from Rome. 1624. 4°. 3350
— 1636. 12°. 4647
Sermons upon John i. 1609. 4°. 2500
Verses in Whitaker (W.). Praelectiones. 1599. . . . 5598
See D. (A.), *Student in Divinity*. Reply. 1612. 4°.
— — Treatise. 1614.
Wotton (Edward). *See* Moffett (T.). Insectorum theatrum. 1634.
Wotton (Sir Henry). Ad regem è Scotia reducem. 1633. F°. . 4580
Elements of architecture. 1624. 4°. 3522
Wotton (Thomas). *See* Lambarde (W.). Perambulation. 1576 *etc.*
Wr (R.). [? Ro. Wright.] Verses in Davies (R.). Funeral sermon. 1577. 1416
Wragge (Christopher), *B.A.*, *S.J.C.* Verses in Camb. Univ. Συνωδία. 1637. 5790
Wraghton (William), *pseud.* *See* Turner (W.).
Wray (John). Verses in Camb. Univ. Carmen. 1635. . . 5770
Wrayford (Tho.). Verses in Camdeni Insignia. 1624. . . 5346
Wren (*qu.* Chr. or Mat?), *Pet.* Camb. Univ. Rex redux. 1633. . 5748
Wren (Matthew). Sermon...before the Kings Majestie...Feb. 17. Cambridge, 1627. 4°. 5710
Wrens Nest defil'd. 1640. 4°. 7651
Verses in Camb. Univ. Thr-thr. 1603. 5616
— — Epicedium. 1612. 5665
— — Dolor. 1625. 5701
— — Anthologia. 1632. 5741
— — Rex Redux. 1633. 5748
See Hippocrates. 1633.
Wrench (Richard), *MA.*, *S.J.C.* Verses in Camb. Univ. Carmen. 1635. 5770
— — Συνωδία. 1637. 5790
— — Voces. 1640. 5836
Wrench (Sa.), *S.J.C.* Verses in Camb. Univ. Voces. 1640. . 5836
Wright (Abraham). Delitiæ delitiarum. Oxoniae, 1637. 8°. . 7936, 5479
Wright (Ar.). Verses in Oxf. Univ. Horti. 1640. . . . 5499
Wright (Edward). Short treatise of dialling. 1614. 4°. . . 3785
See Gilbert (W.). De magnete. 1600.

No.

Wright (Edward) *cont.* *See* Napier (J.). Description. 1618.
Verses in Cheke (Sir J.). De obitu M. Buceri. 1551. . 734
— Wilson (T.). Vita. 1551. 631
Wright (Henry). First part of the disquisition of truth concerning political affaires. 1616. 4°. 3668
Verses in Rawlins (T.). Admonitio. [1620?] 2033
Wright (John). *See* Redman (J.). Reporte. 1551.
Wright (Katherine). *See* Harsnett (S.). Discovery. 1599.
Wright (Leonard). Display of dvty. 1616. 4°. 4058
Hunting of Antichrist. 1589. 4°. 1956
Summons for sleepers...newly corrected. 1615. 4°. . . 4052
Wright (Richard). Verses in Narne (W.). Pearle of prayer. 1630. 5971
See Bacon (Francis). Charge. 1614.
Wright (Robert). Verses in Baro (P.). In Jonam. 1579. . . 850
— Becon (Ric.). Solon. 1594. 5240
See also Wr. (R.).
Wright (Samuel), *B.D.* Sermons. *See* Rogers (R.). Certaine sermons. 1612.
Wright (Thomas). Passions of the minde. 1604. 4°. . . . 2858
— 1621. 4°. 4504
— 1630. 4°. 4262
Succinct philosophicall declaration. 1604. 4°. . . 2858=3449
See Roe (W.). Epilogvs. 1615.
Wright (William). *See* Cato. Preceptes. 1560. 16°.
See Darrell (J.). Detection. 1600.
Wright (William), *Sid.* Verses in Camb. Univ. *Συνῳδία*. 1637. . 5790
Wriothesley (Henry), earl of Southampton. *See* Southampton.
Wriothesley (Henry James, lord). [Funeral.] *See* Jones (W.). A treatise. 1625. 4°.
Wriothesley (Thomas, lord), *afterwards* 4th Earl of Southampton. *See* Southampton.
Writtle (John Peter, baron de). *See* Petre.
Würzburg, Bishop of. *See* Briefe relation. 1599.
Wyat (D.). Verses in Camb. Univ. Anthologia. 1632. . . 5741
— — Fasciae. 1633. 5808
— — Rex redux. 1633. 5748
Wyat (Francis). Verses in Sandys (G.). Paraphrase. 1638. . . 4736
Wyat (Sir T.), *the elder.* Certayne psalmes...penitentiall. 31 Dec. 1549. 8°. 699
See Leland (J.). Naeniæ. 1542.
Wyat (Sir Thomas), *the younger.* Historie of Wyates rebellion. 1554. 8°. *See* Proctor (J.).
Wyat (Thomas). Verses in Cambridge Lachrymae. 1587. . . 2123
Wybarne (Joseph). New age of old names. 1609. 4°. . . 3736
Wycherley (Daniel). *See* Wicherley.
Wyclif (John). Pathway to perfect knowledge. 1550. *See below.* True copy etc.
True copye of a Prolog...in an olde English Bible. 1550. 8°. . 1093
Two short treatises, against...the Begging Friars. Oxford, 1608. 4°. 5290
Wycklyffes wycket. (Testament of W. Tracie.) 'Norenburch, 1546.' 8°. 6712
Wicklieffes Wicket...Iohn Lassels...Tracie. [Ab. 1548.] 8°. . 6713
Wickliffes wicket. Oxford, 1612. 4°. 5308
See James (T.). Apologie. 1608.
Wydevile (Anthony), earl Rivers. *See* Rivers (Antony Wydevile, earl).
Wyer (Johann). *See* Wier.
Wykes (Aquila). *See* Bastwick (J.). The Letany. 1637. 4°.
Wykes (Thomas). *See* Weekes.
Wylshman (Walter). Sincere preacher. 1616. 8°. . . . 2996
Wynkyn de Worde (Jan). *See* Higden (R.). Polychronicon. 1495.

No.
Wynne (Edward). *See* Whitbourne (R.). Discourse. 1622.
Wynne (H.). Verses in Camb. Univ. Rex redux. 1633. . . 5748
Wynne (Rob.). Verses in Camb. Univ. Rex redux. 1633. . . 5748
Wyse (N.). Consolacyon for chrysten people. 1538. 8°. . . 634
Wythers (Fabian). *See* Wither.
Wythers (Stephen). *See* Withers.

Xavier (Francis). *See* Francis Xavier.
Xenophon. *Κύρου παιδείας βίβλια η.* (Gr.) Etonae, 1613. 4°. . 5904
Institution of Cyrus. 1567. 8°. 747
Cyrupædia. Trans. P. Holland. (Naumachia...by A. Holland) 1632. F°. 4714
[Oeconomicus.] Treatise of housholde. 1537. 8°. . . 441
Historie. Trans. J. Bingham. 1623. F°. 7627
Ximenez de Cisneros ( ), *cardinal.* *See* Calendar of Scripture. 1575.
Xylander (G.). Verses in Holland (H.). Herωologia. 1620. . 6642

Y. (I.). *See* Francis de Sales. Introduction. [161–] etc.
[*qu.* Awdelay (J.)?] *See* Fulke (W.). Comfortable Sermon. [1574?]
Y. (T.), *qu.* Yardley (T.)? Verses in Sym (J.). Lifes preservative. 1637. 4313
Yardley (T.), *T.C.* Verses in Camb. Univ. *Συνωδία.* 1637. . . 5790
— — Voces. 1640. 5836
See also Y. (T.).
Yate (George). Miraculous week. [Ab. 1640?] F°. . . 7059
Yates ( ). *See* Brabourre (T.). Defence. 1632.
Yates (John). Gods arraignment of hypocrites. Cambridge, 1615. 4°. 5676
— Cambridge, 1616. 4°. 7906
Ibis ad Caesarem. 1626. 4°. 7588
Treatise of the honour of gods house. 1637. 4°. . . 4657
See Montagu (R.). Appello Caesarem. 1625.
Yates (John), *surgeon.* Verses in Hall (J.). Most excellent...woorke. 1565. 1215
Yaxlee (Henry). Morbus et Antidotus. 1630. 4°. . . . 5049
Yaxley (Robert). Verses in Coryat (T.). Coryats Crudities. 1611. 3076
Year Books. Edward III. 1–10. 1596. Anni decem. In aed. I. Yetsweirt. F°. 7461
Edward III. 17, 18, 21–30, 38, 39. Le second part de les Reports. Stationers. 1619. F°. 3277
Edw. III. 40–50. R. Tottell, 15 Aug. 1565. F°. . . 7174
— R. Tottell, 1576. F°. 1131
— T. Wright, 1600. F°. 7390
Edward III. 40. R. Redman, 10 March 1534. F°. . . 7078
Henry IV.—Henry V. Omnes Casus. T. Wight, 1605. F°. . 7391
Henry V. 2, 5, 7–9. 1563 Jan. 2. R. Tottell, 1570. F°. . 7192
Henry VI. 1. H. Smyth [ab. 1546]. F°. . . . 7109
— R. Tottyll, 29 Jan. 1556. F°. 7155
— R. Tottyll, 1584. F°. 7207
Henry VI. 2. Pynson [15—]. F°. 316
— H. Smyth [1546?]. F°. 7110
— R. Tottyll, 29 Jan. 1556. F°. 7156
— R. Tottyll, 1584. F°. 7208
Henry VI. 3. Pynson, 1510. F°. 259
— H. Smyth [ab. 1546]. F°. 7111
— R. Tottil [1556?]. F°. 7212
— R. Tottell, 1582. F°. 7204
Henry VI. 4. H. Smyth [ab. 1546]. F°. 7112
— R. Tottel, 1556. F°. 7158
— R. Tottell, 1582. F°. 7205
Henry VI. 7, 8. W. Middleton [ab. 1546]. F°. . . . 7102

No.
Year Books *cont.* Henry VI. 7, 8. R. Tottyll, 12 Nov. 1559. F°. 7167
— R. Tottyl, 1584. F°. 7209
Henry VI. 9. Pynson [1513?]. F°. 317
— H. Smyth [ab. 1546]. F°. 7113
— R. Tottell, 22 Apryll 1562. F°. 7171
— R. Tottyll. 1570. F°. 7193
Henry VI. 10. H. Smyth [ab. 1546?]. F°. 7114
— R. Tottyll, 21 Feb. 1561. F°. 7168
— R. Tottyll, 1587. F°. 7211
Henry VI. 11. H. Smyth [ab. 1546]. F°. 7115
— R. Tottel, 12 June 1582. F°. 7206
— R. Tottil. F°. 7213
Henry VI. 12. W. Middleton [ab. 154–]. F°. 7103
— R. Tottell, 8 Apryll 1562. F°. 7170
— [1582?]. F°. 7214
Henry VI. 14. W. Middleton [ab. 1546]. F°. 7104
— R. Tottell, 22 Apryll 1562. F°. 7172
— [1582?]. F°. 7215
Henry VI. 18. R. Redman [154–]. F°. 7080
— R. Tottel. F°. 7216, 7217
Henry VI. 19. W. Middleton [ab. 1540]. F°. 7105
— R. Tottel [1562?]. F°. 7218
— R. Tottel, 1567. F°. 7184
Henry VI. 20. [Pynson, 1503?] F°. 318
— R. Tottyll, 29 Jan. 1556. F°. 7157
— [1582?]. F°. 7219
Henry VI. 21. R. Tottill, 1567. F°. 7185
Henry VI. 22. R. Tottill, 1567. F°. 7186
Henry VI. 27. Pynson [1512?]. F°. 319
— R. Tottell, 5 June 1562. F°. 7173
Henry VI. 28. Pynson [1512?]. F°. 320
— R. Tottel, '30 Feb.' 1567. F°. 7187
Henry VI. 30, 31. R. Tottel, 27 Feb. 1567. F°. 7188
Henry VI. 32. R. Tottel, 1566. F°. 7176
Henry VI. 33. Lettou and Machlinia, 1482. F°. 92
— Pynson [15—]. F°. 321
— R. Tottell, 6 March 1556. F°. 7159
Henry VI. 34. Machlinia, 1484. F°. 103
Henry VI. 35. Lettou and Machlinia, 1482. F°. 93
— Pynson [15—]. F°. 322
Henry VI. 36. Lettou and Machlinia, 1482. F°. 94
— R. Tottel, 10 Marche 1567. F°. 7189
Henry VI. 37. Machlinia [1484]. F°. 104
— R. Tottill, 1567. F°. 7190
Henry VI. 38. R. Tottel, 1566. F°. 7175
Henry VI. 39. R. Tottill, 17 May 1567. F°. 7191
Edward IV. Les ans. T. Wight and B. Norton, 1599. F°. 7389
Edward IV. 1. R. Tottill, 1556. F°. 7160
Edward IV. 2. Pynson [1512?]. F°. 323
— R. Tottell, 1566. F°. 7177
Edward IV. 3. R. Tottill, 1566. F°. 7178
Edward IV. 4. Pynson [15—]. F°. 324
— R. Tottill, 1558. F°. 7166
Edward IV. 5. [Pynson? 15—.] F°. 325
— R. Tottill, 1566. F°. 7179
— Assignes of J. More, 1638. F°. 5082
Edward IV. 6. R. Tottel, 1572. F°. 7195
Edward IV. 7. R. Pynson [ab. 1520]. F°. 7810
— R. Tottill, 30 Aprill 1567. F°. 7183
Edward IV. 8. R. Tottill, 1556. F°. 7161

No.
Year Books *cont* Edward IV. 9. R. Tottel, 24 July 1572. F°. . 7196
Edward IV. 10–12. R. Tottill, 1566. F°. 7180
Edward IV. 13. R. Tottel, 1572. F°. 7197
Edward IV. 14. R. Tottel, 1572. F°. 7198
Edward IV. 15. R. Tottell, 1572. F°. 7199
Edward IV. 16. R. Tottill, 1556. F°. 7162
Edward IV. 17. R. Tottel, 1572. F°. 7200
Edward IV. 18. R. Tottel, 1572. F°. 7201
Edward IV. 19. R. Tottill, 1556. F°. 7163
Edward IV. 20. R. Tottill, 1556. F°. 7164
Edward IV. 21. R. Tottill, 1566. F°. 7181
Edward IV. 22. R. Tottle, 1572. F°. 7202
Edward V.—Henry VIII. Anni regum...R. Brooki...annotatio. I. Yetsweirt, 1597. F°. 7462
Edward V.—Richard III. De termino trinitatis. [1619?] F°. 3278
Henry VII. In hoc volumine. Stationers, 1619. F°. . . 3279
Henry VIII. 12–14, 18, 19, 26, 27. De termino. [Stationers? Ab. 1619?] F°. 3280
Yeldard (Arthur). Verses in Humphrey (L.). I. Ivelli vita. 1573. 837
Yelverton (Sir Christopher). Verses in Gascoigne (G.). Hundreth sundrie Flowres. [1572?] 1519
See Gascoigne (G.). Posies. 1575.
Yelverton (Sir Henry). *See* Charter Warren. A Treatise. 1617. 4°.
See Philips (E.). Certain...sermons. 1605. 4°.
Yerburgh (Nic.). Verses in Camb. Univ. Genethl. 1631. . . 5731
Yetsweirt (James). Verses in Palingenius. Zodiake. 1576. . . 1622
Yong (Bartholomew). *See* Young.
Yonger (William). Sermon preached at great Yarmouth. 12 Sept. 1599. 1600. 8°. 2875
York, County of. Answere made by the kynges hyghnes to the Petitions of the rebelles. 1536. 4°. 437
Yorke (Ed.). Verses in Oxf. Univ. Horti. 1640. . . . 5499
Yorke (James). Union of honour. 1640. F°. 5216
Youll (H.). Canzonets. 1608. 4°. 1618
Young (Andrew). Verses in Napier (J.). Logarithmorum descriptio. 1614. 5952
— Rabdologia. 1617. 5959
Theses and Verses in Adamson (J.). Εἰσόδια. 1618. . . . 5960
Young (Bartholomew). *See* Guazzo (S.). Ciuile Conuersation. 1586.
See Montemayor (J. de). Diana. 1598. F°. 7924
Young (John). Sermon. 2 March 1575. 8°. 1347
See Redman (J.). Reporte. 1551.
— Wilkinson (W.). Confutation. 1579.
Young (John), *K.C.C.* Verses in Camb. Univ. Epicedium. 1612. 5665
— — Genethl. 1631. 5731
— — Hippocrates. 1631. 5736
— — Anthologia. 1632. 5741
— — Rex redux. 1633. 5748
— — Carmen. 1635. 5770
Young (Patrick). *See* Clement I. Ἐπιστόλη πρώτη. 1633. 4°.
See Foliot (G.). Expositio. 1638.
— Nicetas. Catena. 1637.
Young (Richard). Sinne stigmatizd. 1639. 8°. 4392
Young (Thomas). Verses in Camb. Univ. Epicedium. 1612. . 5665
Young (Will.). Verses in Oxf. Univ. Magd. Coll. 1612. . . 5302
Ypres. *See* Manner of subvention. [1532.] 8°. 561

Z. (R.), *I.C.P.R.* *See* Zouch (R.).
Z. (X.). Verses in Overbury (Sir T.). His Wife. Ed. 11. 1622. . 3380
[=Watts (W.).] *See* James (T.), *Capt.* Strange...voyage. 1633.

No.

Zanchius (H.). Miscellaneorum tomus alter. Neostadii. 1608. 4°. 7761
Briefe discourse. *See* Perkins (W.). Case of Conscience. 1595. 4°.
De religione christiana fides. 1605. 8°. 3608
Epistle to Queene Elizabeth. *See* Ames (W.). Fresh svit. 1633.
His confession. Cambridge, 1599. 8°. 5599
— *See* Hill (R.). Pathway. 1613.
See Ames (W.). Reply. 1622.
Zarain Aga. Relation of the late Seidge...of Babylon. Trans. W. Holloway. 1639. 4°. 5156
Zarate (A. de). Strange...History...of Peru. 1581. 4°. . . 1445
Zeland. *See* Netherlands, *Southern Provinces*. Coppie. 1599.
Zeni (Antonio and Nicolo). *See* Fox (L.). North-west Fox. 1635.
Zouch (Richard). Descriptio iuris et iudicii feudalis. Oxoniae, 1634. 8°. 5411
Elementa iurisprudentiae. Oxoniæ, 1636. 4°. 5471
Verses in Oxf. Univ. Horti. 1640. 5499
Zouche (Will.). Verses in Oxf. Univ. Horti. 1640. . . 5499
Zuinger (Jacob). *See* Zwinger (Jacob).
Zurich. *See* Stuckius (J. G.). 1598.
[Church.] *See* Bullinger (H.). Two Epistles. [1549?] 8°.
[— Ministers.] Consensio mvtva in re Sacramentaria Ministrorum et Caluini... *See* Lasco (J. a). Brevis...tractatio. 1552.
See Belijdenisse. 1568. 8°. 7879
Zweibrücken. *See* Vincent (P.). Lamentations of Germany. 1638. 7760
Zwinger (Jacob). *See* Scapula (J.). 1619. F°. 7836
— 1637. F°. 4028
Zwingli (Ulrich). Accompt rekenynge and confession...sent unto Charles V. Trans. T. Cotforde. Geneva, 1555. 8°. . 6722
Briefe rehersal of the death...of Christ. [1560?] 8°. . . 896
Certeyne preceptes. Trans. R. Argentine. Ipswich, 1548. 8°. 5885
Rekening and declaraciō of the faith...sent to Charles V. 'Zijrik Marche 1543.' 8°. 6106
Short pathwaye to the...scriptures. Worcester, 1550. 8°. . 5890
Ymage of bothe Pastoures. Trans. J. Veron. 1550. 8°. . 702
See Anderton (J.). Luthers Life. 1624. 4°.

INDEX II.

PRINTERS, STATIONERS, ETC.

PRINTERS, STATIONERS, ETC.

PAGE

A. (B.) and T. F. *See* Alsop (B.)
A. (E.). *See* Allde (Ed.). 1600—1628
—— *See* Allde (Eliz.). 1628—1638
A. (T.). *See* Archer. 1610
—— *See* Adams. 1615
—— *See* Alchorne. 1638
Adam (J.). Paris. 1516—1529 1382
Adams (Eliz.), widow. 1620—1625 502
—— (Tho.), bookseller. 1591—1620 . . . 499, 1646, and no. 7940
Adderton (W.), bookseller. 1629—1639 1115
Aelst (A. J. d'). Zutphen. 1619. *See* Janssen (A.) . . . 1499
Aggas (E.), bookseller. 1576 . . . . . 371, 1527, 1625
Albertus (Philippus). *See* Aubert
Alchorne (T.), bookseller. 1627—1639 . . . . . 1102, 1704
Alde (J.). *See* Allde
Allam (T.). Oxford. 1636—1639 1226
Allde (Ed.). 1584—1628 . . 417, 1632, 1734, 1738, and no. 7911
—— (Eliz.), widow. 1628—1640 . . . . . 423, 1634
—— (J.). 1560—1584 . . . . 258, 1608
Allen (B.), bookseller. 1632—1637 1134
—— (J.), bookseller. Leicester. 1639 1312
Allertson (Harmon). *See* no. 1978 409
Alley (W.), patentee. 1740
Allot (R.), bookseller. 1626—1636 . . . . 1098, 1703, 1723
Alsop (B.). 1616—1625 . . . . . 892, 1690, and no. 7885
—— and T. Fawcet. 1626—1640 . . . 898, 1723, and nos. 7873-5
Alsop (N.), bookseller. 1632—1640 . . . . 1134 and no. 7789
Amazeur (J.). Paris. 1544—1555 1385
Anderson (G.). Edinburgh. 1637-8 1331
—— Glasgow. 1638—1648? 1337, 1743
André (J.). Paris. 1535—1551 1731
Andrewe (L.). 1527 85
Arbuthnot (A.). Edinburgh. 1579—1582 1318
Archer (T.), bookseller. 1603—1634 . . . . . . 704, 1673
Ascensius (J. B.). *See* Bade.
Aspley (W.), bookseller. 1598—1640 . . . . . 660, 1667
Astley (H.), bookseller. 1588—1609 463
Atfend (A.), bookseller. Norwich. 1640 1307
Aubert (Philippe). Geneva. 1619 . . . . no. 7836
Aubri (D.). Hanau. 1607 1495
Awdeley (J.). 1559—1577 . . . . . . 255, 1607, 1724

B. (A.), bookseller. 1624 1072
B. (C.). *See* Barker. 1579—1584
—— bookseller. *See* Burby

PAGE

B. (E.). *See* Blackmore. 1635
B. (G.). *See* Bishop. 1587
B. (H.) *See* Ballard. 1608 602
B. (I.). 1496? 25
—— *See* Beale. 1618—1632
B. (I.) and R. M., stationers. 1626. *See* Boler (J.) and R. Milbourne
B. (L.). *See* Becket. 1608—1632
—— *See* Blaikelocke. 1639—1640
B. (M.). *See* Bradwood. 1607
B. (R.). *See* Bradock (414), Barker 534 etc. 1592—1613
—— *See* Badger. 1631—1640 938
B. (T.), with J. Beale. 1611
—— *See* Badger. 1635—1640
B. (T.), bookseller. *See* Bushell. 1610
—— *See* Barlow. 1618
B. (W.), bookseller. *See* Barret. 1617
—— 1618. *See* note on no. 5683 1742
Bach (Ellis), bookseller. 1610 809
Bache (John), bookseller. 1607—1614 790
Bade (Conrad). Geneva. 1550—1560 . . . . 1420, 1733
—— (Josse), Ascensius. Paris. 1503—1535 1382
Badger (R.). 1618—1640 . 938, 1692, 1723, 1735, and nos. 7795, 7825
—— (T.). 1635—1640 . . . . . 1141, 1706, and no. 7801
Badius (J.). *See* Bade
Bailey (J.). *See* Baylie
Baldwin (W.). 1549
Bale (J.). 1549—1551 214
Baligault (F.). Paris. 1488 30
Ball (Roger), bookseller. 1636 1149
Ballard (H.). 1597—1608 . . . . 602, 1661
Bamford (H.). 1577—1578 377
Bankes (R.). 1523—1546 . . . . 76, 1581, 1730 and no. 7859
Bankworth (R.), bookseller. 1594—1612 . . . . 566, 1655
Barbier (J.). Paris. 1497 . . . . 15, 25
—— Westminster. 1498 . . . . 15, 25
—— (N.). Lyons. 1552 . . . . 1421 n.
Barenger (W.). *See* Barrenger
Barker (C.). 1569—1588 . . . . 334, 1525, 1619
—— Deputies. 1588—1599 . . . . 339, 1620
—— (R.). 1593—1618, 1630 . . . . 534, 1651, and no. 7804
—— *Reprint.* 1603 1537
—— and J. Bill. 1616—1630 550
—— and J. Bill's assigns. 1630—1640 552, 1653, 1723, and nos. 7863, 7865
—— —— Newcastle. 1639 1312
Barley (W.). 1591—1614 . . . . 502, 1735
Barlow (T.), bookseller. 1616—1625 905
Barnes (John), bookseller. 1600—1621 683
Barnes (Joseph). Oxford. 1585 . . . . 1172, 1708
Barrenger (W.), bookseller. 1608—1622 . . . . . 803, 1680
Barret (H.), widow. 1624—1626 . . . . . 792 and no. 7909
—— (W.), bookseller. 1607—1624 . . . . 790, 1742
Barrevelt (G.), bookseller. 1494 24
Bartlet (J.), bookseller. 1619 . 970, 1694, and nos. 7778, 7896
Basset (T.), mapseller. 1659. *See* no. 4578
Basson (T.). Leyden. 1586. No. 6495 1461
Batersbie (J.), Patentee. 1597—1604 602
—— assignes. 1597—1604 . . . . . . 1527 and no. 6794
Baudois (R. de). Amsterdam. 1608 1429
Baudry (W.). Paris. 1640 1388
Baylie (J.), bookseller. 1600—1610 685

PAGE
Beale (J.). 1611—1640 . . . . . 814, 1682, and no. 7909
Bebel (J.). Basel . . . . 1290 n.
'Beckenth (B.). Strassburg.' 1531. (No. 6094) 1360
Becket (James), bookseller. 1636—1640 1149
—— (L.), bookseller. 1608—1628 795
Bee (C.), bookseller. 1639—1640 1142
Bell (H.), bookseller. 1606—1638 765
Bellamie (J.), bookseller. 1620—1640 . . 996 and no. 7893
—— with R. Smith. 1639—1640 7897
Benson (J.), bookseller. 1635 1142
Bentley (William). 1646. No. 5978 note 1330
Bercleus (T.). 1521. *See* no. 275 59
'Bercula (T.).' 1520 . . . . no. 269
Berghen (A. van). Antwerp. 1500—1534 1355
Berjon (M.). Geneva. 1620 1422
Berthelet (T.). 1528—1555 . 86, 1582, 1720, 1730, and no. 7854
—— In the house of late 100
Besonge (J.). Rouen. 1626 1404
Beys (Christoph). Paris and Lille. (No. 6229 note) . . . 1393
Beys (Gilles). Paris. 1577—1595. (No. 6229 note) . . . 1393
Bienayse (J.). Paris. 1511—1529 1382
Bill (John). 1604—1631 . . . . . . 721, 1550, 1675
—— Neustadt. 1608 . . . . no. 7761
—— Frankfurt. 1618 1493
—— Heirs. 1631—1633 739
—— Assignes. 1630—1640 . . . . 739, 1723
—— with B. Norton. *See* Norton
Birckman (Arnold), I. Cologne. †1542 1424
—— II. Cologne. 1561 1424
—— (F.), bookseller. 1510—1530 . . . . . . 71, 1729
Bird (R.), bookseller. 1623—1639 . . 1069 and nos. 7830, 7900
Bishop (E.), bookseller. 1604—1610 741
—— (G.), bookseller. 1569—1610 . 343, 1620, 1720 and no. 7924
—— (R.). 1631—1640 . 1128, 1740, and nos. 7798, 7837, 7882
Blackmore (E.), bookseller. 1618—1640 . . 950, 1693, and no. 7885
Bladen (W.), bookseller. 1611—1626 . . . . . . 826, 1742
Blaikelocke (L.), bookseller. 1638—1640 1158
Blangeart ( ). Paris. 1637 1388
Blome (J.), bookseller. 1619—1640 972
Blount (E.), bookseller. 1594—1632 567
Blower (R.). 1595—1618 591
Blunden (H.), bookseller. 1635—1640 1143
Blunt (E.). *See* Blount
Bocard (A.). Paris. 1496—1531 . . . . . . 1377, 1715
Boler (Anne), bookseller. 1635—1638. 1074
—— (James), bookseller. 1624—1634 . . . . 1072 and no. 7891
Bollifant (E.). 1584—1602 . 424, 1634, and nos. 7921-2, 7924
Bolton (R.). *See* Boulton
Bonham (W.). 1542 142
Bonhomme (Y.). Paris. 1532 *See* Kerver (T.), widow
Bonian (R.), bookseller. 1607 . . . . 793, 1739
'Bonifante (Radulphe). Basle.' 1542 . . . 1362, 1418 (no. 6104)
Bostock (Rob.), bookseller. 1628—1640 . . 1113 and nos. 7802, 7825
Bouckhout (Adriaen Kempe van), stationer. Antwerp. 1536. *See*
Kempe (A.) . . . . nos. 6078–9, 1356
Boulton (R.), bookseller. 1598—1610 662
Bourne (Nicolas), bookseller. 1608—1640 795, 1680, 1724, and nos. 7795, 7903
Boursette (M.). Paris. 1555. *See* Regnault (F.), widow
Bouvier (F.), bookseller. 1584-9 . . . . . . 427, 1734
Bouwenszoon (J.). Leyden. 1586 . . . . . 1461 (no. 6495)

PAGE

Bowler (J.). *See* Boler
Bowier (F.). *See* Bouvier
Bowman (F.), bookseller. Oxford. 1634–1639 . 1219 and no. 7798
Bowyer (F.). *See* Bouvier
Boyard (M.). Douai. 1630—1635 1488
Boyle (R.), bookseller. 1588?—1615 463
Boys (Daniel), bookbinder. Cambridge. 1626. (Mentioned at p. 10 in no. 3808)
—— (M.). Geneva. 1545 1420
Brachius (J.), bookseller. 1504 69
Bradock (R.). 1581—1615 . . . . . . 414, 1631
Bradwood (M.). 1602—1626 . . . . 697, 1672
Bramereau (J.). Avignon. 1601 1468
Bramridge (J.), bookseller. 1623 1069
Bretton (W.). 1505—1510. (Nos. 6148-6151) 69, 1373
Brewster (E.), bookseller. 1616—1640 . 906 and nos. 7830, 7888
—— (W.). Leyden. 1616—1619 1465
Bright (T.), patentee. 1589 481
Brinckley (S.). Rheims. 1584 . 1404 n, 1451, 1743, 1774 (no. 6440)
Britain's Burse. 1610 . . . . 809, 1681
Brome (Joane), widow. 1592—1601 373
—— (W.), bookseller. 1576—1591 372
Brooke (T.). Cambridge. 1608—1624? 1266
Brooks (W.), bookseller. 1636—1640 1150
Broome. *See* Brome
Browne (John), bookseller. 1598—1623 . . . . . 662, 1736
—— (Joseph). 1611—1621 1682
—— (N.), bookseller. 1617—1631 . . . . . 910, 1691
Bruneau or Bruney (R.). Antwerp. 1602—1608 1370
Bryson (J.). Edinburgh. 1638—1642 . . . . . 1332, 1714
—— (Robert). Edinburgh. 1640—1645 1714
Buck (G.), bookseller. 1562—1567 274
—— (J.). Cambridge. 1626 1266
—— (T.), alone. Cambridge. 1630—1669 1284
—— (T. and J.). Cambridge. 1626—1630 . . . . 1266, 1712
—— —— with L. Greene 1625—1630 1266
—— —— with R. Daniel. 1634—1640 . . . 1286 and nos. 7876-8
Budge (J.), bookseller. 1606—1626 765, 1678, 1736, and nos. 7827, 7917
Bull and Auvache, Messrs, referred to. (No. 7532 n) 1676
Burby (C.), bookseller. 1592—1607 . . . . 513, 1648
—— (E.), widow. 1607 . . . . 515, 1736
Burre (W.), bookseller. 1597—1621 . . . . 603, 1742
Burton (A.). *See* A. B. 1624 1072
Burton (F.), bookseller. 1603—1617 704
Busby (J.) I, bookseller. 1590—1619 487
—— II, bookseller. 1607—1631 487
Bushell (T.), bookseller. 1599—1617 667
Butler (J.). 1527 86
—— (W.), II. 1615—1619 883
Butter (N.), bookseller. 1604—1640 741, 1675, 1723, 1724, and nos. 7788, 7815, 7846, 7909
—— (T.), bookseller. 1576—1590 374
Byddell (J.). 1533—1544 . . . . 112, 1584, 1729
Byllet (A.). Dort. 1590 1465
Bynneman (H.). 1566—1583 . . . . 296, 1520, 1614, 1720
Byrckman. *See* Birckman

C. (F.), bookseller. *See* Constable (F.). 1640
C. (I.). *See* Charlewood. 1591
C. (S.). *See* Cartwright. 1626

PAGE
C. (T.). *See* Cadman. 1587 428
—— *See* Creede. 1593
—— *See* Cotes. 1620—1640 999
C. (W.). *See* Cotton
Cadman (T.), bookseller. 1584—1589 428
Caesar (M.). *See* Keyser (M. de)
Caillard (J.), bookseller. Rouen. 1518—1522 1395
Calderius (Reginaldus). *See* Chaudière
Caly (R.). 1553—1558 . . . . 237, 1606, (and no. 7899)
—— Rouen[1]
Campion (E.). Canterbury. 1550 1301
Canin (I. J.). Dort. 1598—1624 1466
Canne (John). Amsterdam. 1640 1433
Car (H.), bookseller. 1578—1604 384
Carmarden (R.). Rouen. 1566 1399
Cartwright (John), bookseller. Coventry. 1633 1311
—— (S.), bookseller. 1626—1640 1101
Casson (E.). Norwich. 1623 1307
Castellanus (G.), bookseller? Oxford. 1506 . . . . 64, 1171
Casus breves decretalium, printer *of the*. Strassburg. 1493 . . 1580
Cawood (G.), bookseller. 1576—1602 374
—— (J.). 1546—1572 192
Caxton (W.). Bruges. 1475 26
—— Westminster. 1477—1491 3
Cellius (Erhard). Tübingen. 1602 1718
Cervicornus (E.). Cologne. 1521 1410
Chambers (Ric.). 1618 . . . . (no. 7914)
Chapman (L.), bookseller. 1620—1640 998
Chard (T.), bookseller. 1577—1618 . . . . . . 377, 1625
Charlton (G.), bookseller. 1604—1614 748
Charlwood (J.). 1553[2]—1593 . . . . 275, 1521, 1610, 1613
Charteris (H.). Edinburgh. 1577—1599 1317
—— heirs of. 1601 1317
—— (R.). Edinburgh. 1599—1610 1322
Chaudiére (Regnault) I. Paris. 1546—1551 1385
Chevallon (C.). Paris. 1511—1537 1382
Chiswell (R.), mapseller. 1669 . . . . . (*See* no. 4578)
Chorlton. *See* Charlton
Claesz (Jan) van Dorpe. Leyden. 1616 1461
Clain (J. T.). Amberg. 1603 1225
Clarke (J.), bookseller. 1619 972
—— (M.), bookseller. 1606—1611 767
—— (T.), bookseller. 1604—1607 748
Clein (F.). *See* Cleyn
Clerke (A.), bookseller. 1540 136
Clifton (Fulke), bookseller. 1620—1640 998
Cloeting (J. A.). Delft. 1581 1451
Cloppenburg (Jan Evertsz). Amsterdam. 1589—1636 1428
Clotterbuck (R.). *See* Clutterbuck
Clouting (A.). Delft. 1631
Clutterbuck (R.), bookseller. 1633—1640 1136
Cnobbaert (J.). Antwerp. 1614—1637 1371
Coblentz (J. de). Paris. 1495—1509 . . . . . 1373, 1376
Cock (S. de). Antwerp. 1511—1562 1356
Cockyn (H.), bookseller. 1576—1578 374
Colby (J.), bookseller. 1638—1639 . . . . 1158 (and no. 7832)
Coldock (F.), bookseller. 1561—1602 . . . . . 270, 1608
—— (P.), bookseller. 1637—1640 1151

[1] See a copy of no. 6718 in the Bodleian Library.
[2] R. Lemon, *Cat. of Broadsides*, p. 11.

PAGE

Colin (Michael). Amsterdam. 1608 . . . . 1429, 1557 (no. 6953)
Collins (R.), bookseller. 1630—1635 . . . . . 1122, 1705
Collyne (Michael), bookseller. *See* Colin
Colman (N.), bookseller. Norwich. 1586 1307
Colwel (T.). 1561—1575 270
Combi (Giov. Bapt.). Venice, 1618—1627 . . . . . (no. 7934)
Confluentius (J.). *See* Coblentz
Conincx (A.). Antwerp. 1579—1608 1368
Constable (F.), bookseller. 1615—1640 . . . . . 883, 1689
Cooke (M.), bookseller. 1605-7 760
—— (T.), bookseller. 1578—1599 385
—— (W.), bookseller. 1632—1640 . . . . 1134 (and no. 7913)
Copland (R.). 1515—1533 72
—— (W.). 1549 214
Costerden (M.), bookseller. 1634—1640 1139
Cotes (R.). 1630—1631 1015
—— (T.), alone. 1620—1640 . . . . 999, 1562, 1573, 1696
(and nos. 7789, 7800, 7896, 7913)
—— (T. and R.). 1630—1631 . . . 1015, 1698 (and no. 7787)
—— (T.) and R. Young. 1634 1005
Cotton (C.), his assignes. 1632 1135
—— (W.), bookseller. 1602—1609 . . . . . . 702, 1738
Coules (F.). *See* Cowles
Courant (N.). Rouen. 1621—1633 1403
—— (P.). Rouen. 1610 1403
Cousin (J.). Rouen. 1519—1525 . . . . . . 1396, 1720
Cousturier (J.). Rouen. 1609—1638 1402
Cowke (S.). *See* Cock
Cowles (F.), bookseller. 1626—1640 1101
Cowper (J.), bookseller. 1637—1639 . . . . 1151 (and no. 7963)
Coxon (T.). *See* Cockson
Craffurt (T.). Amsterdam 1433
Cramoisy (S.). Paris. 1589—1653 1387
Creede (T.). 1593—1616 . . . . 559, 1534, 1655, 1721, 1736
Crespin (J.). Geneva. 1556 1421
Cripps (H.). Oxford. 1620—1628 1206
Crispin. *See* Crespin
Crom (M.). Antwerp. 1538 . . . . 1362, 1743
Crooke (A.), bookseller. 1630—1640 . . . 1123, 1705 (and no. 7837)
—— (J.) and R. Sergier. 1638 . . . . 1158, 1708
—— — — Dublin. 1640. 1351
Crossley (J.), bookseller. 1612 . . . . 828, 1736
Crouch (J.), bookseller. 1635—1640 1143
Crowley (R.). 1549—1550 . . . . . 217, 1596 (and no. 7762)
Ctematius (Giles). Emden. 1556—1566 1444
Curteyne (H.), bookseller. Oxford. 1625—1640 1216

D. (J.). *See* Danter (J.). 1592
—— *See* Dawson (J.). 1613—1640
D. (M.). *See* Dawson
D. (T.). *See* Dawson. 1612—1614
—— bookseller. With R. Young. 1638 804
Daniel (R.), bookseller. 1623—1628 . . . . . . 1070, 1701
—— — Cambridge. 1634—1650 1290
—— with T. Buck. 1634—1640 . . . . 1286 (and nos. 7876–8)
Danter (J.). 1591—1597 503
Davidson (T.). Edinburgh. 1528?—1542 1315
Davis (W.), bookseller. Oxford. 1638—1640. 1226
Dawlman (R.), bookseller. 1627 . . . . 1103, 1132
—— and L. Fawne. 1636 . . . . . . 1132 (and no. 7835)

PAGE

Dawson (E.), bookseller. 1609—1636 . . . 803, 1680
—— (J.), I. 1613—1634 . . . . 829, 1683 (and no. 7892)
—— II. 1637—1640 . . 1152, 1707 (and nos. 7872, 7889, 7897)
—— (Mary). 1635—1637 838
—— (T.). 1574—1617 . . . . 362, 1622 (and no. 7790)
Day (J.)[1]. 1546—1584 . . . 153, 1520, 1526, 1589, 1731
—— and W. Seres. 1546 . . . . . . 175, 1592
—— bookseller. 1629—1630 1116
—— (R.). 1578—1584 385
—— Assigns 386, 1626
Denham (H.). 1564—1589 . 284, 1521, 1611, 1733-4 (and no. 7958)
Dewe (T.), bookseller. 1621—1625 1030
Dewes (G.). 1560 260
Dexter (R.), bookseller. 1590—1603 . 487, 1645, 1721 (and no. 7938)
Diest (G. van). Antwerp. 1565—1573 1367
Dight (E.), bookseller. Exeter. 1635 1311
—— (W.). 1590—1627 488
Doesborch (J. van). Antwerp. 1505—1530 . . 1356 (and no. 7856)
Doeticum. *See* Dueticum
Dooms (Josse). Ghent. 1620—1636 1501
Dorcaster (N.). Wittenberg. 1554 1441
Dorp (J. Claessen van). *See* Claessen
Downes (B.), bookseller. 1621—1623 1031
—— (T.), bookseller. 1609—1635 . . . . . 804, 1680
—— and E. Dawson. 1620—1624
—— and R. Young. 1635 804
Drawater (J.). 1595—1597 591
Du Bois (Michael). Geneva. *See* Wood (M.).
—— (Simon). Alençon. 1530 . . . . . . 1397 n.
Dueticum (J. van). Rotterdam. . . . . . 409 (no. 1976)
Du Pré (J.). Paris. 1481 1729
Dunscombe (R.), bookseller. 1637—1640 1156
Durone (Francesco). 1562 . . . . 953 n.

E. (G.). *See* Eld. 1604—1625
—— bookseller. *See* Edmondson. 1628—1632
—— *See* Edwards. 1628—1640
E. (T.). *See* Este. 1607
Eaglesfield (F.). *See* Eglesfield
East (T.). *See* Este
Edgar (E.), bookseller. 1600—1613 685
'Edmonds (A.).' Basle. 1554 . . . . . 1364 (no. 6111)
Edmondson (G.), bookseller. *See* Emondson
Edwards (G.), bookseller. 1616—1640 . . 907 (and nos. 7824, 7829)
Eglesfield (F.), bookseller. 1635—1640 1143
Egmondt (F.), bookseller. 1493—1499 24
Eld (G.). 1604—1624 . . . . . 749, 1676 (and no. 7914)
Elsevier (B. and A.). Leyden. 1626—1653 1462
Emerson (G.), bookseller. 1637—1640 1156
Emery (J.), bookseller. 1629—1640 1116
Emondson (G.), bookseller. 1622—1634 1065
Empereur (M.). *See* Keyser
Endoviensis (C.). Antwerp. 1523. *See* Remunde
England (N.). 1558 . . . . 250, 1732-3
Erven (G. van der). *See* Ctematius
Esch (Hendrich van). Dordrecht. 1638 . . . . (no. 7811)
Este (T.). 1567—1609 . . . 317, 318, 1616, 1725 (and no. 7902)
Estienne (Antoine). Paris. 1625. (*See* no. 4962). 1084

[1] Verses to him in no. 816.

PAGE
Estienne (Charles) 1732
—— (Francois) . . . . 1269 n.
—— (Henri) 1734
—— (Robert): Insigne Olivae Rob. Stephani . . 1084 (no. 4962)
Eynhoven (C. van). *See* Remunde 1357

F. (L.), bookseller. *See* Fawne
F. (M.). *See* Flesher
F. (R.). *See* Field. 1594—1617
F. (T.). *See* Fawcett. 1625—1640
'Faber (T.). Albionopolis.' 1613 1546
Fairbeard (G.), bookseller. 1618—1629 951
Falkner (F.). *See* Faulkner
Faques (R.). 1509—1530 70
'Family of Love.' Amsterdam. 1574 1426
Faulkner (F.), bookseller. 1605—1636. 760
—— Southwark 1300
Fawcet (T.), with B. Alsop. 1616. *See* Alsop
Fawne (L.), bookseller. 1631 . . . . . 1131 (and no. 7823)
—— with R. Dawlman. 1635—1638 . . . . 1132 (and no. 7835)
—— with S. Gellibrand. 1639 1132
Ferberne (A.). Stralsund, 1630 . . . . . . (no. 7955)
Ferbrand (W.), bookseller. 1588—1609 463
Fetherstone (H.), bookseller. 1608—1627 801, 1680 (and nos. 7793, 7848)
Field (R.). 1588—1624 . . 464, 1530, 1531, 1535, 1537, 1642, 1735 (and nos. 7785, 7923)
Finlason (T.). Edinburgh. 1604—1627 1327
Firebrand (W.). *See* Ferbrand
Fisher (B.), bookseller. 1621—1637 . . . . . . 1032, 1699
—— with assignes of Joane Man. 1636-7 1033
Fitz (Hugo). Amsterdam 1433
Fitzer (W.). Frankfurt. 1628 1494
Flasket (J.), bookseller. 1594—1613 . . . . . . 569, 1655
Fleming (R.), bookseller. 1617—1619 910
Flesher (M.). 1617—1649 910, 1563, 1691 (and nos. 7802, 7835, 7909, 7915)
Flinton (G.). Rouen. 1583 1743
Flower (F.), patentee. 1573 362
Fogny (J. de). Rheims. 1561—1593 1449
Forrest (E.), bookseller. Oxford. 1628—1640 . 1216 (and no. 7813)
Fosbrooke (N.), bookseller. 1605—1629 761
Foster (R.), bookseller. York. 1626 1227
Fouler (J.). Antwerp. 1566—1582 1366
—— Louvain. 1566—1569 1445
Franciscus (Hercules). 1580 . . . . 412, 1734
Franckton (J.). Dublin. 1602 1338
—— Deputies. 1619 1339
'Freeman (C.). Greenwich. 1554' . . . . . . (no. 6283)
Frere (D.), bookseller. 1635—1640 1144
Fries (A.). Zurich. 1540—1547 1415
Froschauer (C.), I. Zurich, 1521—1564 . . . . . 1410, 1727
—— II. Zurich. 1563—1586 1414
Froschoviana, In officina. 1587 1728
Fuchs (H.). Cologne. 1521 1410
Fulke (Hester). *See* Ogden
Fussell (N.), bookseller. 1626—1639 . . . . . . 1101, 1703

G. (A.). *See* A. Griffin. 1621—1640
G. (E.). *See* E. Griffin. 1613—1621
G. (L.), bookseller. *See* Greene. 1618
Gachet J.). *See* Gatchet

PAGE
Gallaeus *or* Galle (P.). Antwerp. 1583 1725
Garbrand (A.), bookseller. 1610—1616 809
Gardiner (T.) and T. Dawson. 1574—1577 . . . . . 369, 1625
Garret (W.), bookseller. 1622—1640 1065
Gatchet (J.), bookseller. York. 1509—1535 1227
Gaultier (T.). 1550—1553 218
Gellibrand (S.), with L. Fawne. 1637 1132
Gemini (T.). 1555—1562 246
Gething (R.), master of the pen. 1635
Gibbs (G.), bookseller. 1613—1633 . . . . . 839, 1683, 1739
Gibkin (J.). *See* Gipkin
Gif (G.). *See* Gifford
Gilbertson (W.), bookseller. 1640—1672 1168
Giolito (G.) de Ferrari. Venice. Device 1716
Gipkin (J.), bookseller. 1551 220
Godfray (T.). 1532 . . . . 109, 1730
Godwin (J.), bookseller. Oxford. 1639 1226
Golding (Per.), bookseller. 1608 802
Gosson (H.), bookseller. 1603—1640 . . . . . . 705, 1738
—— (T.), bookseller. 1579—1600 397
Gough (John), bookseller. 1536—1543 . . 114, 1584 (and no. 7818)
Grafton (R.). 1537 . . . . .117, 1585, 1730 (and no. 6081)
Green (F.), bookseller. Cambridge. 1632—1634 1295
Greene (C.), bookseller. 1633—1640 1136
—— (Joane), widow. 1630—1637. 1265
—— (L.). Cambridge. 1607—1630 . . . . . . 1265, 1742
—— with T. and J. Buck. 1625—1630 1266
Griffin (A.), widow. 1621—1640 . . . . . 849, 1685
—— (E.). I. 1613—1621 . . . . 839, 1684 (and nos. 7846, 7925)
—— II. 1637—1640 . 1159, 1708, 1723 (and nos. 7760, 7777, 7818)
Grismand (J.), bookseller. 1618—1640 . . . 951 (and no. 7911)
Grove (J.), bookseller. 1629—1637 1116
Growte (J.), bookseller and bookbinder. 1532—1549 . . . 1584
Gryphius (S.). Lyons. *Device* 559
Gualtier (T.). *See* Gaultier.
Gubbin (T.), bookseller. 1587—1619 . . . . . . 456, 1639
Gueffier (J.). Paris. 1585 1737
Gwillim (J.), bookseller. 1615. 884
Gybken (J.). *See* Gipkin.

H. (A.). *See* Hatfield
H. (H.). *See* Hondius
H. (I.). 1496 25
—— Amsterdam. 1604 1428
—— *See* Haviland. 1622—1638
H. (R.). *See* Hodgkinson. 1637—1640 1074
—— *See* Harper. 1637—1640 1132
—— and J. N. *See* Hodgkinson (R.) . . . . 1702 (no. 7633)
—— bookseller. 1637 1156
H. (T.). *See* Harper. 1630—1640 856
Hacket (T.), bookseller. 1560—1590 . . . . . 260, 1608
Haestens (Hendrik van). Leyden. 1598—1629 1462
—— Louvain. 1628 1446
Haies (T.). *See* Hayes.
Hall (Rowland). 1560—1563 . . . . 261, 1518 (and no. 7763)
—— Geneva. 1560 1422
—— (W.). 1598—1614 . . . . 663, 1667
Hamillon (C.). Rouen. 1566—1613 . . . . . . 1400, 1544
—— (R.). Rouen. 1554—1557 1398

PAGE

Hamman de Landoia. *See* Hertzog
Hammond (W.), bookseller. 1632—1640 1136
Hamond (H.), bookseller. Salisbury. 1635 1311
'Hans Hit Prik.' 1545—1550 152
Hans (O.), cartographer. 1632
Hanse. Dort. 1590 1465
Hardouin (J.). Paris. 1500—1541? 1381
Hardy (E.). Rouen. 1518 1396
—— (J.), bookseller. 1594—1607 569
Harford (R.), bookseller. 1629—1639 . . . . . 1117, 1705
—— (W.). 1555—1559 246
Harper (R.), bookseller. 1631—1640 1132
—— (T.). 1614—1640 . . 856, 1685, 1737 (and nos. 7834, 7893)
—— (W.), bookseller. 1613—1614 853
Harrington (J.), bookseller. 1549—1550 218
Harris (W.), bookseller. 1640 1168
Harrison (J.). I. 1559—1616 . . . . 252, 1607
—— II, bookseller. 1579—1616 397
—— III. 1600—1604 252
—— IV, bookseller. 1603—1639 705
—— (L.), bookseller. 1559—1578 . . . . . . 256, 1608
—— (Richard). 1561—1562 1609
Hart (A.). Edinburgh. 1603—1621 . . . . 1323, 1433, 1726
—— heirs. 1622—1639 1326
—— (M.), bookseller. 1593 565
Hastenius. *See* Haestens
Hatfield (A.). 1584—1612 . . 428, 1543, 1635 (and no. 7956)
—— His device used at Eton 1310
Haukins (J.). 1530 104
—— (R.). *See* Hawkins
Hause. *See* Hanse
Haviland (J.). 1621—1640 1034, 1573, 1699 (and nos. 7829, 7909, 7952)
—— (T.). 1606—1611 767
Havius (Matthias), bookseller. Dordrecht. 1638 . . (no. 7811)
Hawkins (J.). *See* Haukins
—— (R.), bookseller. 1612 . . . . 828, 1683
Hayes (T.). 1600—1603 686
Hebb (A.), bookseller. 1625—1640 . . . 1079 (and no. 7818)
Heerstraten (Egidius van der). Louvain. 1486 29
Heigham (J.). Douay. 1609—1623 1482
—— St Omer. 1622—1631 . . . 1480, 1717 (and no. 7809)
Hellen (H.). Middleburg. 1618—1658 1459
Helme (Anne), widow. 1617—1627 793
—— (J.). 1607—1616 793
Hendricksen (A.). The Hague. *See* no. 1984
Henricpetri (S. and S.). Basel. 1564—1627 1418
Henson (Frances), bookseller. 1601 . . . . . (no. 7765)
Herford (J.). St Albans. 1534—1538 1302
—— London. 1544—1548 149
—— widow. 1550 152
Hertford (J.). *See* Herford
Hertzog (J.) *or* Hamman de Landoia. Venice. 1493 . . . 27
Hester (A.), bookseller. 1539—1564 133
—— (J.), bookseller. 1582—1591 . . . . . 416, 1528, 1632
Heyndricksen. *See* Hendricksen
Heyns (Z.). Amsterdam. 1605—1606 1428
Higman (J.) and W. Hopyl. Paris. 1490 29
—— (N.). Paris. 1495—1535 1376
Hill (N.). 1546—1554 . . . . 201, 1595

PAGE

Hill (W.). 1548—1549 203
Hillenius (M.). Antwerp. 1531 79
Hills (W.), bookseller. 1636—1640 1150
Hinde (J.), bookseller. 1579—1583 398
'Hitprik (Hans).' 1545—1550 152, 1411 (no. 6282), 1512 (no. 6702)
Hodges (G.), bookseller. 1621—1632 1056
Hodgets (J.), bookseller. 1601—1625 . . . . . 689, 1671
Hodgkinson (R.). 1624—1640 . . 1074, 1702, 1740 (and no. 7862)
Hoff (U.). Leipzig. 1541 . . . . . 1303, 1418 (no. 5883)
Hoffmann (W.). Frankfurt. 1635 1494
Holland (C.), bookseller. 1614—1620 . . . . . 868, 1687, 1744
—— (H.), bookseller. 1609—1633 . . . . 804, 1680, 1744
Hollybush (J.). *See* Remunde
Holme (W.), bookseller. 1590—1615 489
Hondius (H.). Amsterdam. 1629— after 1658 . . 1430, 1726, 1727
—— (J.). Amsterdam. 1604—1613 . . . . . 1428, 1726
—— *See* also H. (I.).
Honoratus (B.). Lyons. 1554—1587 1443
Hood (H.), bookseller. 1635—1638 1145
Hooper (H.), bookseller. 1596—1613 597
Hope (W.), bookseller. 1634—1640 . . . . 1139 (and no. 7800)
Hopyl (W.). Paris. 1489—1521 1372
Hovius (W.). Liége. 1621—1623 1448
How (W.). 1569—1590 354
Howell (R.), bookseller. 1600—1603 686
Huberti (Hadrianus). Antwerp. 1587—1604 1369
Huby (F.). II. Paris. 1602—1610 1387
Huggins (T.), bookseller. Oxford. 1625—1636 . . . . 1218, 1710
Huguelin (J.). *See* Kerbriant
Hulsius (Levinus), widow of. Frankfort. 1611—1612 . . . 1493
Humble (G.), printseller. 1610—1632 . . . . . 810, 1681
'Humpfridus (J.).' 1633 . . . . 1078, 1567
Hunt (M.), bookseller. Oxford. 1639—1640 . . . . 1226, 1711
Hunte (T.). Oxford. 1485-6 17
Hurlock (G.), bookseller. 1630—1640 1140
Hury (Pierre). I. Paris. 1585—1597 1387
Husner (G.). Strassburg. 1494 1580
Hutton (G.), bookseller. 1636—1640 . . . . . 1150, 1707
—— (R.), his assignes. 1583 417
Hyll (N.). *See* Hill
Hyry (P.). *See* Hury

I. (A.). *See* Islip
I. (I.). 1588. *See* Jackson (J.). 1584—1596
Jaggard (Is.). 1613
I. (W.). *See* Jaggard. 1607
—— *See* Jones (W.), III. 1618—1619 691
—— *See* Jaggard. 1621
—— 1623—1624. *See* Jones (W.), III. 1601—1626 . . . 691
—— and T. P. 1635. *See* Jones. . . . . 1110 (no. 5063)
Ireland (R.), bookseller. Cambridge. 1624—1640 . . . 1296, 1742
Irish College. Louvain. 1616. . . . . 1447 (nos. 6427 etc.)
Irish Stock, Partners of. (Stationers Company.) . . 1351, 1743
Isaac (G.), bookseller. 1581 416
Islip (A.). 1591—1640. . 503, 1536, 1647, 1722, 1733, 1735, 1738
(and nos. 7780, 7821, 7912)

J. (W.). 1632. *See* Jones (W.), IV
Jackson (H.). 1576—1616 374
—— (J.). 1584—1596 . . . . 435, 1636

PAGE
Jackson (J.), bookseller. 1634—1640 1140
—— (Ralph), bookseller. 1589—1602 . . . . . 481, 1644
—— (Roger), bookseller. 1601—1625 690
Jacobi (H.) and J. Pelgrim. 1505—1515 69
Jacobs (A.). Delft. 1633
Jacobszoon (J. P.). Leyden. 1586 1463
—— (O.). Zurich. 1543 1415
Jaggard (E.), widow. 1624 570
—— (Is.). 1613—1627 853
—— (John), bookseller. 1594—1624 569
—— (W.). 1594—1624 . . . . 571, 1656 (and no. 7858)
Jagger (J.). *See* Jaggard
'Jamaeus (J.).' Edinburgh. 1574 . . . . . 1333, 1521
Janss (Ash.). Gorcum. 1624 1499
Janssen (And.) d'Aelst. Zulphen. 1619 1499
Jansson (J.). Arnhem. 1604—1634 1497
—— Amsterdam. 1613—1636 . . . . . . 1430, 1727
Jehannot (J.). Paris. 1498 31
Jeffes (A.). 1584—1599 . . . . 436, 1636, 1741 (and no. 7832)
Jenings (M.). 1577—1585 379
Jenner (T.), printseller. 1619—1656 . . 1133, 1706 (and no. 7857)
Jode (G. de). Antwerp. 1578 1725
Johann of Paderborn (*or* de Westfalia). Ab. 1483 . . . 28, 1579
Johnes (R.). *See* Jones
Johnson (A.), bookseller. 1602—1630 . 702, 1673 (and no. 7906)
—— (John). Amsterdam. 1636. *See also* Jansson 1431
Jones (R.). 1565—1602 . . . . 293, 1613 (and no. 7946)
—— (T.), bookseller. 1600—1637 . . . . . . 686, 1670
—— (W.), I. 1562—1574 278
—— II, bookseller. 1589—1618 481
—— III. 1601—1626 . . . . . 691, 1671 (and no. 7887)
—— IV. 1627—1639 . . . . 1104, 1704
Jordanus de Quedlinburg, Printer of the. Strassburg. 1483 . 1579
Jove (M.). Lyons. Device . . . . . 1405 (no. 6269)
Jugge (R.). 1546—1577 . . . . 185, 1593 (and no. 7767)
—— and J. Cawood. 1559 187
Junius (R.). *See* Young
Junte (Jacques de). Lyons. 1587—1624 . . . . 1671 (no. 7514)

K. (A.) B. *See* Kempe (A.) van Bouckhout, stationer. 1536
K. (F.). 1621. *See* Kingston
Kaetz (Pieter). Antwerp and London. 1523—1526 . . . 85, 1357
Kearney (W.). 1590—1592 489
Kele (R.). 1546—1552? 196, 1587, 1594
—— with W. Seres 184
Kellam (L.). Louvain. 1598 1447
—— Douai. 1604—1614 1480
—— (T.). Douai. 1618 1488
Kembe (A.). Southwark. 1635—1639 1300
Kempe (Adriaen) van Bouckhout, stationer. Antwerp. 1536 1356 (and nos. 6078–9)
Kempen (J. and G. von). Cologne. 1546—1588 1424, 1716, 1725, 1737
Kerbriant (J.) alias Huguelin. Paris. 1516—1550 1383
Kerver (T.), bookseller. Paris. 1497 31
—— widow. Paris. 1522—1557 1383
Keyser (M. de). Antwerp. 1527—1536 1359, 1737, 1743 (and no. 6097 *n.*)
King (J.). 1555—1562 247
King's Printers, The. *See* Printers (Royal)
King's Printing House. 1636—1638 . . . . . 1157, 1707

PAGE

Kingston (A.). 1548 204
Kingston (F.). 1597—1640 604, 1528, 1535, 1661, 1736, 1742 (and nos. 7780–1, 7788, 7890, 7901, 7903, 7932, 7938)
—— (J.) and H. Sutton. 1553—1557 232
—— alone. 1557—1584 . . . . 233, 1605 (and no. 7943)
Kirkham (H). 1570—1593 360
—— (W.). 1593—1599 566
Kirton (J.) and T. Warren, booksellers. 1638 1165
Kitson (Abr.), bookseller. 1580—1593 . . . . 412, 1630
—— (Ant.). 1549—1579 218
Knight (C.), bookseller. 1595—1629 . . 591, 1660 (and no. 7961)
—— (T.), bookseller. 1629—1640 . . . . . 1117, 1705
Kyngston. *See* Kingston
Kyrfoth (C.). Oxford. 1519 1172

L. (H.). *See* Lownes
L. (I.). *See* Legate
L. (I. T.). *See* T. (I.) L
L. (M.). *See* Lownes. 1595
L. (N.). *See* Ling
La Coste (N. de). Paris. 1631 1387
Lacy (A.). 1560—1571 263
Laet (H. de). Antwerp. 1546—1566 1364
Lambert (T.), bookseller. 1633—1640 1136
Landoia (J. H. de). *See* Hertzog
Lang (Paul). Hamburg. 1620 1500
Langford (B.), bookseller. 1638—1639 1165
Langley (T.), bookseller. 1615 884
Langton (R.), bookseller. 1581 416
Lant (R.). 1542—1562 . . . . 142, 1416
Latham (G.), bookseller. 1620—1640 . . . 1016 (and no. 7952)
Laughton (A.). *See* Lawton
Laurensz (H.). Amsterdam. 1608—1648 1429
Law (M.), bookseller. 1595—1627 . . . . . 592, 1660
Lawton (A.), bookseller. 1570—1590 361
Layburne (——), barber chirurgeon. 1602 702
Leake (W.) I, bookseller. 1592—1634 . . . . . 515, 1648
—— II, bookseller. 1635—1640 1145
Le Blanc (J.). Paris. 1556—before 1602 1386
Leconte (N.), bookseller. 1493 24
Lee (——), partner of G. Wood. 1625—1634? 1083
Lee (R.), bookseller. 1615—1616 885
Lee (W.), bookseller 1017
Lee (G.). Antwerp . . . . 28 (and no. 7808)
Legate (J.), I. Cambridge. 1588—1609 1235, 1531, 1711 (and nos. 7949–7951)
—— London. 1609—1620 . . . . . . 805, 1685, 1735
—— II. 1620—1640 . . . . 1018, 1698
—— Newcastle. 1639 . . . . 1312 *n.*
Legge (C.). Cambridge. 1606—1629 1255, 1712, 1721, 1730 (and no. 7906)
Le Prest (J.). Rouen. 1555 1399
Le Preux (E.). Geneva. 1608—1613 . . . . 495, 1422, 1736
Lekpreuik (R.). Edinburgh. 1561—1582 1315
—— St Andrews. 1561—1581 1334
Lempereur (M.). *See* Keyser
Le Rouge (G.). Paris 1360
Le Roux (N.). Rouen. 1538 1396
Le Talleur (G.). Rouen. 1487 31
Lettersnyder (H.). Antwerp 1319, 1362, 1522, 1743
Lettou (J.). 1480—1481 19
—— and W. de Machlinia. 1482 19

PAGE

Levet (P.). Paris. 1485 . . . . 29, 1220
Ley (W.), bookseller. 1640 1168
'Liber (Joannes)'. 'Augustae.' 1618 1550
Lichfield (J.) and W. Wrench. Oxford. 1617 1190
—— and J. Short. Oxford. 1618 1191
—— and W. Turner. Oxford. 1624—1627 1194, 1709 (and no. 7812)
—— alone. 1627—1635 . . . 1197, 1709 (and nos. 7813–4)
—— (L.). Oxford. 1635—1640 . . 1220, 1710 (and nos. 7936, 7947)
Ling (N.), bookseller. 1580 . . . . 413, 1631
Linley (P.). 1595 594
'Lipsius (R.). Albionopolis.' 1616 1549
Lisle (L.), bookseller. 1607 . . . . 793, 1679
Lobley (M.), bookseller. 1539—1565 133
Loe (G. H. van der). Antwerp. 1578 1368
London, Printers to the City of:
Wolfe (J.). 1593 399
Windet (J.). 1603 441
'Long Shop in the Poultry.' *See* R. Bankes (1523—1539), 76; J. Mychell (ab. 1540), 196; R. Kele (1542), 196; J. Allde (1563—1584), 258; E. Allde (1584—9), 417; Eliz. Allde.
Low (G.), map-printer. 1624 1702
Lownes (H.), I. 1592—1629 . . 516, 1648, 1737, 1738 (and no. 7827)
—— and R. Young. 1629—1630 . . . . . . 532, 1651
—— (H.), II. 1612—1629 516
—— (M.), bookseller. 1595 . . . . . 594 (and no. 7923)
Loyselet (G.). Rouen. 1584—1599 1401
Luft (H.). Marburg. 1528 1406
—— Wittenberg. 1547 1513
Lugger (W.), bookseller. 1603—1638 706
Lyle (L.). *See* Lisle
Lynne (W.), bookseller. 1547—1550 . 198, 1732 (and no. 7767)
Lyon (J.). Louvain. 1580 1447

M. (A.). *See* Maunsell. 1576—1595
—— *See* Matthews. 1620—1634
M. (G.). *See* Miller
—— (J.), bookseller. 1632—1637. *See* Marriot?
M. (R.), bookseller. 1616 907
—— and I. B., booksellers. 1626 819
M. (S.), bookseller. 1634. *See* Macham
M. (T.), bookseller. 1600. *See* Man
M. (W.). *See* Middleton
Mabb (R.), bookseller. 1610—1640 . . . . . . 811, 1681
Macham (Joyce). 1615—1626. . . . . 763, 1677
—— (S.), I, bookseller. 1605—1615 . . . . . . 761, 1677
—— —— II, bookseller. 1632—1637 1136
Machlinia (W. de). 1482—1486 20
Man (Joane). Assignes. With B. Fisher. 1636—7 . . . 1033, 1150
—— (Jonas), bookseller. 1607—1635 . . . . . 794, 1679
—— (Paul). 1622—1635 1065
—— —— Assignes. 1631—1634 . . . . . . 1066, 1701
—— (Sam.), bookseller. 1613—1640 . . . . 854 (and no. 7935)
—— (Thomas), I, bookseller. 1578—1624 386, 1626 (and nos. 7791–2, 7938)
—— II, bookseller. 1604—1610 386
—— —— Assignes. 1629—1635 . . . 391, 1627 (and no. 7822)
Marchant (E.), bookseller. 1612—1616 828
Marcus (J.), bookseller. Leyden. 1609—1654 1462
Marprelate Press. 1588—1590 . . 395–7, 1628 (and no. 7779)
Marriot (J.), bookseller. 1615—1640 . . . . . . 885, 1689
—— (R.), bookseller. 1640 1168

PAGE
Marshall (W.). 1535—1542 114
Marshe (H.), bookseller. 1584—1589 437
—— (T.). 1554—1587 . . . . . 240, 1606 (and no. 7861)
Martens (Th.). Antwerp. 1502—1512 1355
Martin (E.). Paris. 1629 1106
Martine (Rob.), bookseller. 1633—1640 1137
—— (W.), bookseller. 1560 264
Mathewes (A.). 1619—1638 . . . . 974, 1695, 1741
Mattes (E.), bookseller. 1597—1613 . . . . . . 633, 1664
Maunsell (A.), bookseller. 1576—1596 375, 1625, 1734 (and nos. 7843–4)
Mayler (J.). 1539—1545 134
Maynard (J.), bookseller. 1637—1640 1157
Meighen (R.), bookseller. 1615—1640 . . . . . . 888, 1689
Melvill (D.), bookseller. Aberdeen. 1622 1337
Meredith (C.) with P. Stephens, booksellers. 1625?—1640 1066, 1701, 1722
Merlin (G.). Paris. 1538—1572 1385
Meslier (H.). 1506 . . . . 64 (and no. 302)
Mestais (J.). Paris. 1640 1388
Meteren (J. van). Antwerp. 1535 1410
Mettayer (Jamet). Tours . . . . . . 1610 (and no. 7243)
Meuris (A.). The Hague. 1621 1497
Michell (R.), bookseller. 1627—1631 1111
Middleton (H.). 1567—1587 . . . . 326, 1617 (and no. 7931)
—— (W.). 1541—1548 . . . . 140, 1587, 1594 (and no. 7954)
Mierdman (S.). 1550 . . . . 219, 1596, 1732
Milbourne (R.), bookseller. 1617—1640 . 930, 1692 (and nos. 7890, 7908)
Miller (G.). 1618—1640 953, 1693, 1735 (and nos. 7797, 7830, 7866, 7888, 7928)
'Molæus (Jacobus)'. Rouen. 1601 . . . . . . 1401, 1534
Mommart (Jean). Brussels. 1597—1608 1495
—— widow. Brussels. 1612—1634 1496
Moore (J.). *See* More
—— (R.). *See* More
Morberius (G.). Liége. 1560—1585 1448
More (A.). 1635—1636 1146
—— (J.), Assignes of. 1629—1640 . 1118, 1705 (and nos. 7855, 7948)
—— (Ric.), bookseller. 1608—1629 802, 1680 (and nos. 7855, 7909, 7953)
Morel (Claude). Paris. 1579—1626 1386
Moretus (J.). Antwerp. 1589—1591 1365
Morin (Martin). Rouen. 1491—1508 . . . . . . 32, 1394
—— (Michael), bookseller. 1504 69
Moseley (H.), bookseller. 1627—1640 . . . 1111, 1704 (and no. 7801)
Moulert (S.), widow and heirs of. Middelburg. 1631 . . . 1459
Moungwell (J.), bookseller. Exeter. 1635 1311
Mychell (J.). Canterbury. 1550 . . . . . . 1301, 1713
Mynne (R.), bookseller. 1627—1639 1112

N. (I.). 1603—1625. *See* Norton (John)
—— 1636—7. *See* Norton (Joyce) 851, 853, (nos. 3960, 3969) 1739
—— (W.). 1581. *See* Norton (W.)
Nafeild (J.). Edinburgh. 1587—9 . . . . 1333, 1526, 1527
Nealand (S.), bookseller. 1618—1632 967
Nevill (P.), bookseller. 1638—1640 1166
Newbery (N.), bookseller. 1616—1635 908
—— and H. Overton, booksellers. 1633 . . . . (no. 7892)
—— (R.), bookseller. 1560—1605 . 264, 1608 (and nos. 7919, 7958)
Newman (T.), bookseller. 1587—1593 456
Newton (N.). 1584—1586 437
Nicholes (T.), bookseller. 1637 1157
Nicholson (H.). Wesel. 1546
—— (James). Southwark. 1535 . . . . 1299 (and no. 7818)

PAGE
Nicholson (John), bookseller. 1639—1640 1167
Nicolai (Jacobus). *See* Nicholson (J.) . . . . (no. 7818)
Nivelle (S.). Paris. His device 1387
Nolck (M. A. van der). Flushing. 1621 1500
North (J.), bookseller. 1602 703
Norton (B.). 1594—1615 . . . . 577, 1656 (and nos. 7956–7)
—— with J. Bill. 1618—1630 . . . . 578, 1657
—— (F.), bookseller. 1600—1605 687
—— (G.), bookseller. 1610—1623 812
—— (John), I. 1590—1612 . . 489, 1645 (and nos. 7807, 7956–7)
—— —— Eton. 1610—1615 1310
—— —— Heirs of. 1615 495
—— —— II. 1621—1640 . . . . 1056, 1701 (and nos. 7900, 7935)
—— (Joyce), bookseller with R. Whitaker. 1632—1637 851, 853, 1739 *bis*
—— (W.), bookseller. 1561—1593 . . 271, 1609 (and no. 7785)
Nortoniana, Ex officina. 1606—1612. Apud J. Norton . . 495
—— 1614—1620. Apud J. Bill . 727, 728 (and nos. 3476, 3481)
Notary (J.). 1497—1520 . . . . 15, 25, 67

O. (H.). 1629. *See* Overton
—— (I.), bookseller. 1598? *See* Oxenbridge
—— (J.). *See* Okes
—— (N.). *See* Okes
—— (R.). *See* Oulton
Ockould (Ric.), bookseller. 1596—1639 597
Ogden (H.). Assigns. 1633 1137
Okes (J.). 1627—1640 . . . . 785 (and no. 7963)
—— (N.). 1606—1639 . . . . 768, 1548, 1678
—— (N. and J.). 1635—1637 783
Olivier (P.). Rouen. 1516 . . . . 1395, 1720
Olton (R.). 1633—1640 1137
Orwin (J.), widow. 1593—1597 . . . . . . 461, 1640
—— (T.). 1587—1593 . . . . 457, 1524, 1639
Oswen (J.). Ipswich. 1547—8 1302
—— Worcester. 1548—1553 1305
Oulton (R.). *See* Olton
Overton (H.), bookseller. 1629—1640 . 1120 (and nos. 7872, 7889)
—— with N. Newbery. 1633 . . . . (no. 7892)
—— (J.). Ipswich. 1548 . . . . 1303, 1743
Oxenbridge (J.), bookseller. 1591—1600 513

P. (E.). *See* Purslow
—— (G.). *See* Purslow
—— (M.). *See* Parsons
—— (T.). 1605. *See* Purfoot 278
—— —— bookseller. 1610. *See* Pavier 687
—— —— 1630?—1638 . . . . 891, 1124, 1705
—— —— Assignes. 1639 1125
—— and W. I. *See* Jones (W.)
—— (W.), bookseller. *See* Ponsonby
Paderborn (Johann of). *See* Johann
Paedts (J.), Jacobszoon. Leyden. 1586 1463
Paffroed (R.). Deventer. 1489 33
Paganus (Thibaldus). *See* Payen
Paine (T.). 1630 . . . . 1125, 1705
Painter (R.). Middelburg. *See also* Schilders 1452
Pakeman (D.), bookseller. 1635—1640 1146
Parker (J.), bookseller. 1617—1638 . . . . . . 934, 1721
Parsons (M.). 1625—1640 1079
Partridge (J.), bookseller. 1625—1636 . . . . . 1081, 1702

PAGE
Pavier (T.), bookseller. 1600—1625 . . 687, 1671, and no. 7909
Paxton (P.), bookseller. 1627 1112
Payen (Thibaud). Lyons. 1529—1570 . . . . . 1442, 1738
Payne (T.). *See* Paine
Peake (R.) I, printseller. 1611—1625? 827, 1739
—— II. 1625—1640 . . . . 1739, 1744
—— (W.), printseller. 1625? 1702
Peerse (E.), bookseller. Oxford. 1625—1635 1218
Pelgrim (J.), with H. Jacobi. 1504—1515 . . . . . 69, 1729
Pen (G.), bookseller. 1582 417
Pepwell (H.). 1518—1539 70
Perier (A.). Paris. 1584—1586 1393
Perrin (J.), bookseller. 1580—1592 1631
Perry (H.), bookseller. 1626—1637 1101
Peter Post Pascha. 1499 25
Peterz (J.). Amsterdam. 1546—1575 1426
Petit (J.), bookseller. Paris. 1492—1530? 1375
—— (T.). 1536—1554 . . . . . . 115, 1585, 1720
'Phigrius (R.). Albionopolis.' 1616 1549
Philippi (J.), with G. Wolf. Paris. 1494—1497 30
Pickering (W.). 1557—1572 248
Pigouchet (P.). Paris. 1498 30
Pinchon (G.). Douai. 1600—1634 . . . . 1484 (and no. 7894)
Pindley (J.). 1612—1613 828
Pinson (G.). *See* Pinchon
Piper (J.), bookseller. 1618—1624 967
'Pistus (Hieronymus). Basileia' . . . . . 772 (no. 3641)
Plantin (C.). Antwerp. 1555—1589 . . . . 1365, 1124 *n.*, 1715
—— Leyden. 1586 . . . . 1124 *n.*
—— (J.), widow, and J. Moretus. 1589—1591 1365
Plantiniana, Ex officina. (F. Rapheleng, Leyden) . . 1124 *n*, 1463
Plateanus (T.). Wesel. 1548 1419
Plater (R.). Amsterdam. 1626 1430
Ponsonby (W.), bookseller. 1577...1604 . 379, 1626 (and no. 7853)
Porter (J.), bookseller. Cambridge[1]. 1587—1607 462, 1641 (and no. 7949)
Post Pascha (P.). 1499 25
Potter (G.), bookseller. 1599—1616 . . . . . 667, 1668
Pounder (C.), bookseller. Norwich. 1616 1307
Powell (H.). 1548—1549 205
—— (T.). 1556—1562 247
—— (W.). 1547—1566 . . . . 199, 1594
'Pratus (T.). Cosmopolis.' 1611 1545
Prevost (N.). Paris. 1524—1532 1384
Printers (Royal)
Fakes (W.)
Pynson.
Berthelet. 1529
Grafton (R.)
Whitchurch }
Wolfe (R.). 1547. (Latin, Greek and Hebrew Books) . 143
Jugge (R.) and Cawood. 1558
Barker (C.). 1577—1599
(R.). 1599—1605 . . . . 534, 1651
Waldegrave (R.), at Edinburgh. 1590
—— 1603
Norton (J.). 1608. (Greek, Lat. and Hebrew and Foreign Languages) 489
B. Norton and J. Bill. 1618—1629

[1] See also R. Bowes, *University Printers* (Camb. Ant. Soc. v. 296).

PAGE

Printers (Royal) *cont.*
Barker (R.), and J. Bill. 1630
Ex Typographeo Regio. 1636—1638 . . . . 1157, 1707
Printer to the Prince's Highness:
—— R. Badger. 1639 938
Printers in Scotland:
—— Charteris (R.)
—— R. Waldegrave. 1602 1318
—— T. Finlason 1327
—— R. Young. 1639
Pullen (O.), with G. Thomason, booksellers. 1635—1639 . 1112, 1704
Purfoot (T.) I. 1562—1615 . . . . . . 278, 1610
—— II. 1615—1640 . . . . 889, 1689, 1744
Purset (C.), bookseller. 1604—1611 759
Purslowe (E.). 1633—1640 . . . . 878, 1688
—— (G.). 1614—1632 . . . . . 869, 1687 (and no. 7935)
Pynson (R.). 1493—1530 22, 54, 1580, 1729, 1730 (and nos. 7810, 7939)
Pyper (J.). 1618. *See* Piper

Quentell (H.). Cologne. 1496 27
Quinque (A.). Tournai. 1623 . . . . 1501, 1744

R. (H.). 1635—6 1146
—— (I.). 1597—1603. *See* Roberts
—— —— Douai. 1610 1486
—— —— 1640. *See* Raworth
—— (R.). 1589. *See* Robinson
—— —— 1610. *See* Redmer
—— (T.). 1540. *See* Raynalde
—— —— 1566. *See* T. Marshe
Raban (E.). St Andrews. 1621—2 . . . . . . 1334, 1714
—— Aberdeen. 1622—1649 . . . . . 1335 (and no. 7962)
Rademacher (S.). Middelburg. 1634 1460
Raimond (John). *See* Remunde (H. van) 1742
Rand (S.), bookseller. 1611—1634 827
Rapheleng (F.). Leyden. 1586—1597 . . . . 1463 (and no. 7406)
—— his Device . . . . 1124 *n.*
Rastell (J.). 1516—1533 . . . . 72, 1730
—— (W.). 1529—1534 . . 104, 1584, 1720, 1730 (and no. 7930)
Raworth (J.). 1635—1640 . . . . 1147, 1723
—— (R.). 1606—1608, 1633—1640 . . . . . 789, 1679
Raynald (T.). 1540—1551 . . . . 136, 1586
Raynes (J.). *See* Reynes
Redman (E.), widow of R. Redman. 1540 84
—— (J.). 1540—1542 . . . . . . 139, 1510 (no. 6693)
—— (R.). 1523—1540 . . . . 78, 1581
Redmer (R.), bookseller. 1610—1632 812
Reeve (J.), printseller. 1630 . . . . 1047, 1127
'Regio, Ex Typographeo.' 1637—8. *See* Printers (Royal)
Regnault (F.). London. 1496 . . . . 1377 *n.*
—— Paris. 1496—1541 . . . . 1377, 1715
—— widow. 1555 1381
Reinalme (A. de). *See* Rinialme
Rembolt (B.). *See* Renbolt
Remunde (C. van). Antwerp. 1524—1531? 1357
—— widow. 1531?—1546 1358
—— (H. van). Antwerp and London . . . . 1299, *corr.* 1742
Renbolt (B.). Paris. 1494—1518 1376
Reyne (John). Brussels. 1608 . . . . 1495 *n.*
Reynes (J.). 1527—1544 86

PAGE
Rhode (F.). Marburg. 1528—1534 1407
—— 'Hamburg.' 1536 1500
—— (Jonas). Frankfort. 1602—not after 1621 1493
Richard (J.), bookseller. Rouen. 1497—1508 . . . . 32, 1395
Richardson (W.), printseller 1279
'Richt Right' Press. Amsterdam. 1638—9 1433
Riddell (William). 1552—3 . . . . no. 7937
Rider (R.), bookseller. 1638 1166
Rime (J.), patentee. 1605 763
Rinialme (A. de), Heirs of. Frankfurt 1493, 1744
Ritherdon (A.), bookseller. 1630—1632 . . . . 1127, 1706
Roberts (J.) with R. Watkins. 1591—1600 . . . . 273, 1735
—— alone. 1595—1605 357, 1621, 1736, 1744 (and nos. 7299, 7300, 7844)
Robinson (G.). 1585—1587 453
—— (H.), bookseller. 1624—1649 . . . . . . 1077—8
—— (R.). 1585—1597 . . . . 453, 1639
—— (T.). Oxford. 1640
Rocket (H.), bookseller. 1602—1611 703
Rogers (O.). 1559—1566 257
Rood (T.). Oxford. 1481—1485 16
—— and T. Hunte 17
Roper (A.), bookseller. 1638—1640 1166
Ross (J.). Edinburgh. 1574—1580 . . . . . 1316, 1524, 1713
Rossius (J.). Bologna. 1583 1737
Rotherdon (A.), bookseller. 1630—1632 1127
Rothwell (J.), I, bookseller. 1628—1640 1114
—— II, bookseller. 1633—1640 . . 1114, 1704 (and no. 7760)
Rounthwaite (R.), bookseller, 1618—1626 967
Rowbotham (J.), bookseller. 1559—1580 . 258, 1518 (and no. 7763)
Rowlands (R.). *See* Verstegan
Roy (S. de). Utrecht. 1615 1498
Royal Printers. *See* Printers (Royal)
Royston (J.), bookseller. 1611—1612 827
—— (R.), bookseller. 1629—1640 1121
Ruremond (C. and H.). *See* Remunde

S. (G.). 1598—1600. *See* Simson
—— — 1605—1606. *See* Snowden
—— (I.), bookseller [qu. Spencer?] 1630 . . (nos. 3989, 5089)
—— (J.). Wandsworth. 1572—1575 1308
—— — bookseller. 1629. *See* Smethwick 633
—— — 1638 1166
—— (L.). 1606. *See* Snowden
—— (M.), bookseller. 1629—1631. *See* Sparke 935
—— (S.). *See* Stafford
—— (T.). 1611—1622. *See* Snodham
—— (V.). *See* Sims
—— (Val.). 1605. *See* Sims
—— (W.). 1597—1634. *See* Stansby
Sacon (Jacques). Lyons. 1498—1622. Device 1729
Sadler (L.), bookseller. 1631—1640 1133
Salisbury (J.). *See* Byddell
—— (T.), bookseller. 1593—1604 566
Salysbury (John). *See* Byddell
Saunders (T.), bookseller. 1612—1613 829
Scarlet (P.), bookseller. Cambridge. 1634—1640 1296
—— (T.). 1590—1596 . . . . . . 495 (and nos. 7791-2)
Schellem (J.). Utrecht. 1626 1498
Schilders (A.). Middelburg. 1620 1460
Schilders (R.). Middelburg. 1576—1617 . . . . 1452, 1726

PAGE

Schoeffer (J.). Mainz 1297
'Schoolmaster Printer. St Albans. 1480 18
Schramm (N.). Neustadt. 1608 . . . . . (no. 7761)
Scolar (J.). Oxford. 1517 1171
Scoloker (A.). 1548 . . . . 205, 1595
—— Ipswich. 1548 1303
Seaton (G.). *See* Seton
Seile (H.), bookseller. 1619—1640 . . . . . . 992, 1695
Seldeslach (J.). Antwerp. 1620—1621 1371
Selman (M.), bookseller. 1600—1612 688
Seres (W.), alone. 1548—1579 . . . . 180, 1593
—— with J. Day. 1548—1550 175
—— with R. Kele 184
—— Assignes of. 1580—1590 184
Sergier (R.), I, bookseller. 1579—1608 398
—— II, bookseller, with J. Crooke. 1638 . . . . 1158, 1708
—— Dublin. 1640 1351
Sermatelli (B.). Florence. 1574—1604 1442
Seton (G.), bookseller. 1577—1608 . . . . . 381 (and no. 7931)
Sevestre (Pierre). Paris. 1583—1612 1386
Seyle (H.). *See* Seile
Sharpe[1] (Henry). Banbury. 1619 . . . . (no. 7932)
Shawe (James), bookseller. 1601—1603 697
Sheares (W.), bookseller. 1625—1639 . . . . 1081, 1703
Shefelde (J.), bookseller. 1550 220
Sheffard (W.), bookseller. 1621—1630 1064
Shepherd (H.), bookseller. 1635—1640 . . . . . . 1149, 1706
Shepperd (J.), bookseller. 1576—1577 377
Short (E.), widow. 1603 486
—— (J.) with J. Lichfield. Oxford. 1618 1191
—— (P.) with R. Yardley. 1589 . . . 482, 1644, 1734, 1736
—— alone. 1592—1603 . . . . . . 483, 1644, 1734, 1736
Shorter (S.). 1594—1598 585
Siberch (J.). Cambridge. 1521 1228
Silvius (W.). *See* Sylvius
Sims (V.). 1594—1619 . . . . 586, 1659
Simson (G.). 1585—1600 . . . . 455, 1639 (and no. 7773)
Singleton (H.). 1548—1593 . . . . . . 207, 1443, 1595
Skot (J.). 1521—1537 74
—— St Andrews. 1552—1571 1334
Slater (T.), bookseller. 1629—1639 1122
Smethwick (J.), bookseller. 1597— . . . 633, 1664 (and no. 7828)
Smith (Ralph) with J. Bellamie, booksellers. 1639—1640 1167 (and no. 7897)
—— (Richard), bookseller. 1566—1595 . . . . 309, 1615, 1733
—— (Toby), bookseller. 1580—1583 413
Smits (Gerard). Antwerp. 1578 1725
Smyth (H.). 1545—1546 . . . . 153, 1588
—— (Richard). *See* Smith
Snodham (T.). 1603—1625 . 706, 1674 (and nos. 7895, 7908, 7953)
Snowden (G.). 1605 763
—— (L.). 1606 763
Solempne (A. de). Norwich. 1568—1569 1307 (and nos. 6751, 7879, 7880)
Sparke (M.), I, bookseller. 1617—1640 . 935, 1692 (and nos. 7787, 7886)
—— II, bookseller. 1638—1640 1166
Speed (D.), bookseller. 1616—1620 909
—— (J.), patentee 1744
Speidell (J.), author. 1619 1551

[1] See Arber, v. 264 (index).

PAGE
Spencer (J.), bookseller. 1624—1638 1078
Stafford (J.). 1631—1640 . . . . . 1157, 1707 (and no. 7965)
—— (S.). 1596—1632 . . . . . 597 (and no. 7917)
—— (T.). Amsterdam. 1640 . . . . 1433, 1743
Stallenge (W.), patentee. 1607 794
Stam (J. F.). Amsterdam. 1629—1657 1431
Stansby (W.). 1597—1639 . 634, 1665, 1721 (and nos. 7793, 7828, 7848)
Stationers Company. 1599--1640 667, 1668 1723 (and nos. 7794, 7836)
—— Dublin. 1620—1640 1339
—— Partners of the Irish Stock 1351, 1743
Steelsius (J.). Antwerp. 1556 . . . . . . (no. 7803)
Steinmann (T.). Jena. 1600 . . . . . . 1500 *n.*
Stell (J.), bookseller. 1569—1585 . . . . . 360, 1622
Stempe (J.), bookseller. 1628 955
'Stephanus (A.). Paris.' 1625. *See* Estienne 1084
—— (Robertus). *Ad insigne. See* Estienne. 1084
Stephens (P.), bookseller, alone. 1622 1066
—— and C. Meredith. 1625 . . . . . 1066, 1701, 1722
Stevenage (R.). St Albans. 1536 1302
Stolzenberger (J. N.). Frankfurt. 1628 1494
Stondo (B. von), bookseller with Vranckenbergh. 1482 . . 22
Stoughton (R.). 1548—1551 211
Sudbury (J.), printseller. 1610—1615 813
'Sultaceterum (Apud Baocium). Pesclavii.' 1589 405
Sutton (B.), bookseller. 1609 809
—— (H.) with J. Kingston. 1553—1557 . . . . 232, 1605
—— alone. 1558—1560 . . . . 231, 1605
Swayne (R.) I, bookseller. 1621—1632 1064
—— II, bookseller. 1629—1632 1064
Sweeting (J.), bookseller. 1639 1168
Sylvius (W.). Antwerp. 1561—1579 1367

Tailer (W.). 1596—1597 601
Tap (J.). 1600—1630 . . . . 689, 1671
Tate (John), papermaker 1729
Taunton (H.), bookseller. 1634—1638 1140
Teage (J.), bookseller. 1620—1623 . . . . . 1030, 1699
Telotson (W.). 1543—1544 149
Telu (P.). Douay. 1618 1488
Th. (Th.). *See* Thorpe. 1618
Theodoricus Plateanus. 1548 . . . . . . 1419, 1303
Thomas (John), bookseller. 1637—1640 1708
—— (T.). Cambridge. 1584—1588 . . . . 1229 (and no. 7772)
Thomason (G.) and O. Pullen, booksellers. 1627—1640 . 1112, 1704
Thompson (J.), instrument-maker. 1623 . . . . 1070, 1701
Thorney (Roger), papermaker 1729
Thorp (G.). Amsterdam. 1608—1613 1429
Thorpe (T.), bookseller. 1603—1625 . 718, 1676, 1738 (and no. 7914)
Thrale (R.), bookseller. 1628—1640 . . 1116, 1704 (and no. 7822)
Tillotson (W.). *See* Telotson
Timme (W.), bookseller. 1601—1615 697
Tisdale (J.). *See* Tysdale 250
Tomes (H.), bookseller. 1598—1607 666
Tomson. *See* Thompson
Torrentini (Lorenzo). Florence. 1553 1442
Tottell (R.). 1552—1594 . . . . 221, 1596
—— Assignes. 1581 230
Tournes (J. de). Lyons. 1540—1564 1443
Toy (H.), bookseller. 1560—1577 269
—— (J.), bookseller. 1531—1534 105

PAGE

Toy (R.), bookseller. 1542 . . . . 142, 1587
Treveris (P.). Southwark. 1522—1532 . . . . . 1297, 1713
'Trinity, Sign of the.' 1505—1539 . . . . . 69, 70
'Trutheall (C.).' Southwark. 1556 . . . 1300, 1515, 1516
Turcke (J.), bookseller. 1547—1561 201
Turner (D.), Heirs of. Frankfurt. 1601 . . . . 1492, 1534
—— (W.), bookseller. 1623—1635 1070
—— —— Oxford. 1624—1640 . . 1207, 1270, 1709 (and nos. 7796, 7867, 7886)
—— —— with T. Huggins. 1625 1218
—— —— with J. Lichfield. 1624—1627 . 1194, 1709 (and no. 7812)
Turona (Franciscus de). Savoy 1424
Tuthill (H.). Rotterdam. 1638 1503
Twonson (N.). Nürnberg. 1533 1409
Tylotson (W.). *See* Telotson
'Typographio Regio, Ex'. 1637—8 . . . . . 1157, 1707
Tysdale (J.). 1553[1]—1563 250

Unckels (J. K.), bookseller. Frankfurt. 1619 1494
University Printers. Cambridge. 1628—1637 1269
Upphill (A.), bookseller. 1623—1626 1070
Upton (J.), bookseller. 1630 1127

V. (R.). *See* Valentine
Vaenius. *See* Veen
Valentine (F.). Rouen. 1556 1399
—— (R.). Rouen. 1554—1557 1398
Van den Keere. *See* Kerius
Van der Erven (G.). *See* Ctematius
Van der Loe (G. H.). Antwerp. 1575—1578 1368
Van der Nolck. *See* Nolck
Vautrollier (J.), widow. 1588 . . . . . . 317, 1735
—— (T.) I. London. 1566—1588 . . 309, 1525, 1615, 1733
—— —— Edinburgh. 1584—1585 1318
—— —— II, bookseller. 1604—1605 759
Vavasour (N.), bookseller. 1622—1640 1068
Veale (A.), bookseller. 1548 212
Vele. *See* Veale
Venge (W.), bookseller. 1584—1585 437
Verard (A.). Paris. 1485—1513 1372
Vernon (R.), bookseller. 1581 416
Vervliet (D.). Antwerp. 1600 1370
Verstegan (R.). Antwerp. 1603 1371
Vincent (G.), bookseller. 1595—1629 597
Vincentsz ((N.). Dort. 1612—1632 1466
Violette (P.). Rouen. 1507 1395
Volmare (Anne Marie). Würzburg. 1628 1502
Vosterman (W.). Antwerp. 1528—1543 1357
Vostre (S.), bookseller. Paris. 1485—1520 . . . . . 30, 1372
Vrankenbergh (H.) and B. von Stondo, booksellers. 1482 . . . 22

W. (B.), bookseller. 1611 827
—— (E.), bookseller. 1605. *See* Weaver
—— (I.). 1584—1610. *See* Windet
—— —— 1620. *See* White or Wright
—— —— bookseller. 1605—1640. *See* Wright
—— (W.). 1588. *See* White
Waesberghe (Isaac van). Rotterdam. 1636 1502

[1] Cf. R. Lemon, *Cat. of Broadsides*, p. 11.

PAGE
Waesberghe (Jean van) . . . . 1502 n.
—— (Pieter van). Rotterdam. 1639 1502
Walbanke (M.). 1618—1639 . . . . . . (no. 7948)
Waldegrave (R.). 1578 . . . . . . 392, 1567, 1628
—— Edinburgh. 1589—1603 . . . . . . 1318, 1529
—— Marprelate . . . . . 396-7 (and no. 7779)
Waldkirch (Conrad). Schaffhausen. 1592 . . . (no. 7785)
Waley. *See* Walley
Walker (J.), Heirs of. Rouen. 1601 1402
Walkley (T.), bookseller. 1618—1640 . 968, 1694 (and nos. 7816 7925)
Walley (H.), bookseller. 1608—1637 803
—— (J.). 1546—1586 . . . . 197, 1594
—— (R.), bookseller. 1576—1591 . . . . . 377, 1625
Walters (G.). Dort. 1610. *See* Waters 1467
Ward (R.), bookseller. 1577—1598 382
Warren (T.), with J. Kirton, booksellers. 1638 1165
Washington (W.), bookseller. 1627—1629 1113
Waterhouse (P.), bookseller. 1629—1632 . . . . 1122, 1705
Waters (G.). Dort. 1610 1467
Waterson (J.), bookseller. 1623—1640 1071
—— (S.), bookseller. 1584—1634 . . . . . . 437, 1636
Watkins (R.). 1561—1598 . 272, 1523, 1609, 1735 (and no. 7920)
—— and J. Roberts. 1591—1600 . . . . . 273, 1610, 1735
Wayland (J.). 1537—1557 . . . . 125, 1515
—— Assignes. 1557—1558 127
Weaver (E.), bookseller. 1603—1638 . . . . . . 719, 1675
—— (T.), bookseller. 1631—1640 . . . . . . 1133, 1706
Webb (W.), bookseller. Oxford. 1628—1639 1218, 1710 (and nos. 7814, 7936)
—— bookseller. 1634 1141
Wechel (Device) 1495
Welby (W.), bookseller. 1604—1618 . 759, 1738 (and nos. 7781, 7901-2)
Wenssler (M.). Basel. [ab. 1488] 32
Westall (J.), bookseller. Oxford. 1638—1640 1226
Westfalia (J. de). *See* Johann
Whitaker (R.), bookseller. 1619—1640 994, 1696 (and nos. 7834, 7915)
—— with Joyce Norton. 1633—8 994
—— with G. Lathum. 1624 . . . . (no. 7952)
Whitchurch (E.). 1538—1560 128, 1586, 1730 (and nos. 6081, 7762)
White (E.) I, bookseller. 1577—1612 . 383, 1626 (and no. 7912)
—— —— II. 1605—1624 383
White (J.), bookseller. 1613—1625 855
—— (W.). 1588—1623 . . . . . 477, 1552, 1644, 1735
Widdowes (G.), bookseller. 1630 1128
Wight (J.), bookseller. 1551—1589 . . . . . . 220, 1732
—— (T.). 1590—1607 . . . . 497, 1646
—— and B. Norton, patentees. 1598—1599 . . . . 497, 1646
Wilcock (W.). 1481. *See* Lettou (J.)
Williams (F.), bookseller. 1626—1630 1102
—— (J.), bookseller. 1636—1640 . . . . . . 1150, 1707
Williamson (W.). 1571—1574 . . . . 361, 1502 *n*, 1622
Willis (R.), stenographer. 1617—1622 938
Wilmot (J.), bookseller. Oxford. 1637—1638 1226
Wilson (A.), widow. 1640 813
—— (R.), bookseller. 1610—1639 813
Winder (G.), bookseller. 1622—1628 1069
Windet (J.). 1584—1611 . . . 441, 1637, 1735 (and no. 7843)
Winnington (J.), bookseller. 1587—1595 463
Wise (A.), bookseller. 1593—1603 566
Wither (G.), Assigns of. 1623 1071
Wolf (G.) and J. Philippi. Paris. 1494—1497 30

PAGE

Wolfe (Joan), widow. 1574 1588
—— (John). 1579—1601 . . 399, 1523, 1629 (and no. 7765)
—— (R.). 1542—1573 . . . . 143, 1587 (and no. 7786)
Wolff (Johann). Zurich. 1590—1610 1416
Wolphianis, Typis. *See* Wolff. 1610 . . . . (no. 6305)
Wood (G.) and Lee. 1625—1634 1083
—— (J.). Edinburgh. 1629—1633 1329
—— (M.). Geneva. 1545 . . . 1420, 1510 (and no. 6693)
—— Rouen. 1553 1397
—— (W.), bookseller. 1598—1602 667
Woodcock (T.), bookseller. 1575—1594 . . . . 369, 1625, 1744
Woodroffe (R.), bookseller. 1614—1623 883
Worde (Wynkyn de). *See* Wynkyn (J.)
Wreittoun (J.). Edinburgh. 1624—1640 1328
Wrench (W.), with J. Lichfield. Oxford. 1617—1618 . . . 1190
Wright (E.), bookseller. 1615—1640 892
—— (J.) I, bookseller. 1605—1640 . . . . . 764, 1677
—— —— II. 1635—1640 764
—— (R.), bookseller. Oxford. 1591 1190
—— (W.), bookseller. 1579—1603 412
Wyer (J.). 1550 220
—— (Richard). 1548—1550 214
—— (Robert). 1531—1556 . . . . . . 106, 1510
Wyghte (J.), bookseller. *See* Wight
Wykes (H.). 1557—1568 . . . . 249, 1606
Wynkyn (Jan) de Worde. 1493—1535 . . . . 10, 37, 1579, 1580
Wyon (M.). Douai. 1609—1630 1485
—— widow. Douai. 1630—1640 . . . 1485 (and no. 7817)

Y. (R.). *See* Young
Yardley (R.) and P. Short. 1589—1593 . . . . . 482, 1644
Yetsweirt (C.), patentee. 1594 . . . . . . 590, 1659
—— (J.), widow. 1595—1597 . . . . . . 590, 1660
Young (R.), alone. 1625—1640 . . . . . 1084, 1702
—— [Edinburgh. 1632—1642] . . . 1329 (and no. 7927)
—— with H. Lownes. 1629—1630 532
—— with A. Islip and F. Kingston. 1632 . . . . (no. 7780)
—— with T. Cotes. 1634 1005
—— with M. Flesher 925
—— with T. D. 1638 804
—— with R. Badger. 1640 1098
—— (W.), bookseller. 1589—1600 . . . . . . 486, 1645

INDEX III.

ENGRAVERS, PAINTERS, ETC.

ENGRAVERS, PAINTERS.

A.
7811. Beverwijk. 1638.
A. (S.). *See* Sylvius (A.).
Abel (L.).
3090. Aretius (J.). Primula veris. 1613.

B. (A.). *See* Buchel (A.). [Ab. 1620.]
B. (A. K.). *See* Kempe, *printer*.
B. (G.).
2195. Broughton (H.). Daniel (end). 1597. 4°.
B. (I.). [qu. John Bettes?]
791. Cunningham (W.). The cosmographical. 1559. F°.
801. Becon (T.). Workes (Vol. II. fol. xlvi *b*). 1564. F°.
815. Euclid. 1570. F°.
831, 832. *See* Parker (M.). De antiq. 1572. F°.
B. (I.). F. *See* B. (I.).
B. (P.).
6130. Dodoens (R.). A Nievve Herball. 1578.
B. (R.).
2320. Maurice, Prince. A true report. 1601.
B. (R.).
967. Bible. 1572.
B. (R.). [qu. Sir R. Barckley?]
2247. Barckley (Sir R.). 1598.
1868. " " 1603.
B. (V.), or V. (B.).
6176. Primer. 1534. 4°.
Baes (M.).
6589. Francis de Sales (St). A treatise. 1630.
6226. Maffei (G. P.). Fuga Saeculi. 1632. 4°.
6613–4. Porter (J.) The Flowers of the Lives. 1632.
6227. Torsellino (O.). The...life of S. Francis Xavier. 1632.
6228. Villegas (A. de). The lives of Saints. 1638. 4°.
Bara *or* Barra (Jan.). 1624.
3864. Smith (J.). The generall historie. 1624.
Beckit (Robert).
1975. Linschoten (J. H. van). Voyages. 1598.
Bernard (Le petit). *See* Salomon (B.).
Bettes (J.), engraver. 1559. *See* B. (I.).
Blagrave (John).
1823. Blagrave (J.). The mathematical iewel. 1585.
Boel (Cornelius).
6138. Veen (O. van). Emblemata. 1608.

Boel (Cornelius), *cont.*
2635–6. Bible. (Royal Version.) 1611.
Brown (J.). Edinburgh. *Modern engraver.*
6980. Leighton (A.). Appeal. [1628.]
Bry (J. T. de).
6632. Caracters. 1628.
Bry (T. de).
4535. Norton (R.). The gunner. 1628.
Buchel (Arnold).
6642. Holland (H.). Herωologia. [1620?] F°.

C. (I.). [Nagler II. 80 (214).]
741. Recorde (R.). The castle of knowledge. 1556.
801. Becon (T.). Workes. 1564.
1498. Musculus (T.). Common Places. 1578.
6772. Almanack. 1581.
1612. Morley (T.). Canzonets. 1602.
3233. Day (R.). A book of Christian prayers. 1608.
3388. Southwell (R.). Marie Magdalens Teares. 1609.
2504. Byrd (W.). Gradualia. 1610.
Cecill (Thomas).
4806. Bacon (F.). Sylva Sylvarum. 1627.
7397. Grimstone (E.). A generall historie of the Netherlands. 1627.
2458. Fonseca (C. de). Devovt contemplations. 1629.
4536. Marandé (L. de). The ivdgment. 1629.
4539. Clarke (J.). Holy Oyle. 1630.
2461. Godwin (F.). Annales. 1630.
5428. Hakewill (G.). An apologie. 1630.
4836. Smith (J.). The true travels. 1630.
4099. Hayward (Sir J.). The Sanctuarie. 1631.
3991. Weever (J.). Ancient fvnerall monvments. 1631.
3992. Cornwallis (Sir W.). Essayes. 1632.
4845. Grotius (H.). True Religion. 1632.
4563–4. Oughtred (W.). The Circles. 1632.
4134–5. Quarles (F.). Argalvs and Parthenia. 1632.
4274. Quarles (F.). Divine poems. 1633 (1632).
4282. Quarles (F.). Divine poems. 1634 (1632).
5803. Hawkins (W.). Corolla. 1634.
4632. Paré (A.). Workes. 1634.
5069. Thucydides. Peloponnesian Warre. 1634.
5447. Hakewill (G.). An apologie. 1635.
2466. Heywood (T.). The hierarchie. 1635.
7570. Burghley (W. Cecil, lord). Precepts. 1637. 8°.
2467. Knolles (R.). The generall historie. 1638.
4321. Quarles (F.). Divine poems. 1638.
Clein (Francesco). *See* Cleyn.
Cleyn (Franz).
5396. Ovid. Metamorphoses. 1632.
4747. ,, 1640.
Cockson or Coxon (Thomas).
2223. Ariosto (L.). Orlando Fvrioso. 1591.
2453. White (F.). A replie. 1624.
4923. May (T.). A continuation. 1630.
3812. Taylor (J.). All the Workes. 1630.
4924. May (T.). A continuation (1630 reworked). 1633.
Cole (H.), engraver.
967. Bible. 1572.
Cornelius.
964. Bible. (Exodus xxvii.) 1568. (p. 1732.)
967. Bible. (,,) 1572. (,,)
Coxon. *See* Cockson.

D. (F.). *See* Delaram.
D. (H.). [=Henry Denham. Cf. Herb. 1211.]
 2066. Comines (P. de). Historie. 1596.
D. (I.). [qu. J. Day? Cf. Herb. 541.]
 791. Cunningham (W.). The Cosmographical Glasse. 1559.
 805. Grindall (E.). A sermon. 1564.
 4890. Homilies. 1633.
D. (M.). *See* Droeshout.
D. (Marten). *See* Droeshout.
D. (W.).
 2211. Florio (G.). Second fruites, Pt. 1 (ad fin). 1591.
Dalen (Cornelius van).
 7789. Drexelius (H.). 1632. 12°.
 3821. Hunt (N.). The Handmaid. 1633.
 5133. Roberts (L.). The merchants mappe. 1638.
Danckertsz (Cornelius).
 3874. Speed (J.). A prospect... (A briefe Description pp. 5–6.) 1627.
Darel.
 6203. Francis de Sales. An introduction. 1637.
 6243. A Dialogue. (Portrait of Q. Mary.) 1554.
Day (J.). *See* D. (I.).
Delaram (Fras.).
 2575. Segar (Sir W.). Honor Military. 1602.
 6117. Lobel (M. de). Plantarum historia. (Portrait.) 1615.
 2281. Sandys (G.). A relation. 1615.
 3116. Rathborne (A.). The Surveyor (Portrait of Charles I). 1616.
 7551. James I. (Portrait.) 1619.
 3971. Burton (W.). Description of Leicester Shire. [1622.]
 4514. Johnson (J.). Johnsons Arithmatick. 1622.
 4129. Peacham (H.). The compleat gentleman. 1622.
 3433. Bolton (E.). Nero Caesar. 1623.
 3440. „ „ 1627.
 4603. Sandys (G.). A relation. 1627.
Des Granges (D.).
 4352. Griffith (M.). Bethel. 1634.
Dr (Martin). *See* Droeshout.
Droeshout (Jo). 4011. Babington (J.). Pyrotechnia. 1635.
 2466. Heywood (T.). The hierarchie. 1635.
 3705. Microphilus. The new-yeeres Gift. 1636.
 4741(–2). Danes (J.). Paralipomena Orthographiae. 1638 (1639).
Droeshout (Martin).
 3972. Shakspeare (W.). Comedies. 1623.
 4836. Smith (J.). The true travels. 1630.
 4687. Crooke (H.) Μικροκοσμογραφία. 1631.
 4202. H. (R.). The arraignement. 1631.
 4560. Gustavus II, Adolphus. The new starr. 1632.
 5745. Heywood (T.). Englands Elizabeth. 1632.
 4265. Montaigne (M. de). Essayes. 1632.
 4619. Shakespeare (W.). Comedies. 1632.
Droeshout (Michael).
 3886. Swedish Discipline. 1632.
Dürer (Albert).
 3712. Verheiden (J.). History of Modern Protestant Divines. 1637.
Duetecum (Baptista a).
 1964. Eliot (J.). The svrvay or topographical description of France. 1592.
Du Monstier (D.), painter.
 4117. Barclay (J.). Argenis. 1636.
Du Tielt (Guillaume).
 6219. Torsellino (O.). The history of our B. Lady. 1608.

E. (H.). [HE].
964. Bible (Bishops'). 1568. (*See* p. 1732.)
6347. Nicholas (H.). Revelatio. [1574?] 1732.
E. (R.). *See* Elstracke.
Elstracke (Renald).
1975. Linschoten (J. H. van). Voyages. 1598.
2770. Milles (T.). The Catalogve of Honor. 1610.
3650. Ridley (M.). A short treatise. 1613.
3102. Ralegh (Sir W.). The History. 1614.
2785. ,, ,, (1617).
2792. ,, ,, (1621).
4982. ,, ,, (1634).
7405. Hall (J.). A Recollection. 1615.
3919. ,, ,, (1617).
3746. ,, ,, (1621).
2998. Bernard (R.). A Key. 1617.
3476. Dominis (M. A. de). De republica. 1617.
4130. Pharmocopeia Londinensis. 1618.
2807. James I. Opera. 1619.
3133. Seneca (L. A.). Workes. 1620.
2535. Du Bartas. Weekes and Workes. (1621.)
2537. Hakewill (G.). King Davids Vow. 1621.
3746. Hall (J.). A Recollection. 1621.
2542. Hakewill (G.). King David's vow. '1622.'
3603. Serres (J. de). A generall historie. 1624.
4793. Udall (W.). The historie. (Portrait of Mary Stuart.) 1624.
4700. Hieron (S.). The workes. ('J. Beale') [ab. 1620.]
7805. ,, ,, ('I. Parker') [1624–5.]
3158. Purchas (S.). His Pilgrims. Part 1. 1625.
4812. Pharmocopeia Londinensis. 1627.
3691. Markham (G.). Markhams Maisterpeece. 1631.
7847. Du Bartas. 1633. F°. (Altered from no. 2535.)
4306. Babington (G.). The Works. 1637.
3055. The most happy unions. (Before 1625.)

F. (I. B.). *See* B. (I.). F.
F. (I.).
6169. Primer (Sarum). 1531.
688. Henry VIII. A necessary doctrine. (Sig. B 8, D 8 *b*.) [1543?]
6097. Tindale (W.). An exposition. [1530.]
F. (S.).
964. Bible. (Cut of S. Matthew.) 1568. *See* p. 1732.
F. (S. H.). *See* H. (S.).
F. (Vo. J.). *See* J. (Vo.). F.
F. (W.) [qu. Faithorne?]
5014. Saltmarsh (J.). Holy discoveries. 1640.
3838. Effigies Regum Anglorum. 1640.
Faithorne (William). *See* F. (W.). 1640.

G. (D.).
265. Capgrave (J.). Kalendar. (Sig. X 1.) 1516.
697. Smith (R.). Of unwrytten verytyes. 1548.
G. (R.) [qu. R. Gethinge?]
6007. Forbes (P.). Funeralls. 1635.
G. (T.).
1369. Corro (A. à). Dialogus. 1574.
7580. Felltham (O.). Resolues. 1631.
Gabler (Jacob).
3886. Swedish Discipline. 1632.

Galle (Cor.), Junior.
4652. Juan a Santa Maria. Policie Vnveiled. '1637.'
Garrard (Mark). *See* Geeraerts.
Gaultier (Leonard).
5903. Chrysostom (John). Opera. 1613.
4117. Barclay (J.). Argenis. 1636.
Geeraerts (Mark).
812. Noot (J. van der). Le Theatre. 1568.
Gelius (Ægidius), of Wondrichem.
3379. Ælian. The Tactiks. 1616.
Gemini (Thomas).
1237. Gemini (T.). Compendiosa totius Anatomiae. 1559.
Gethinge (Richard), 'Master of the Pen.'
2466. Heywood (T.). The hierarchie. 1635.
See also G. (R.).
Geyn (Jacobus de).
6639. Geyn (J. de). Maniement d'Armes. 1608.
Gif (G.). *See* Gifford.
Gifford (George).
4012. Bate (J.). The mysteries. 1635.
7552. Paris and Vienna. 1628.
4636. Latimer (H.). Fruitful sermons. 1635.
Gleg (Silvanus).
6058. Statutes (Ireland). 10, 11 Charles I. 1635.
Glo (G.). *See* Glover (G.).
Glover (George).
4725. Austin (W.). Devotionis flamma. 1635.
4734. ,, ,, 1637.
2466. Heywood (T.). The hierarchie. 1635.
4637. Mercator (G.). Historia mundi. 1635.
4659. Farley (R.). Kalendarium. 1638.
4388. Preston (John). The golden scepter. 1638.
5133. Roberts (L.). The merchants mappe. 1638.
7617. Sibbes (R.). Divine meditations. 1638.
5173. Ovid. Heroicall Epistles. 1639.
4390. Preston (J.). The golden scepter. '1639.' See 1638.
4048 (5099). Henshaw (J.). Horæ Succisivæ. 1640.
3730. Lupton (D.). The Glory. 1640.
Goes (Abraham).
3874. Speed (J.). A prospect. 1627.
7546. Map. The Kingdom. 1632. F°.

H.
791. Cunningham (W.). The Cosmographical Glasse. 1559.
815. Euclid. The elements. (Letter 'T.') (1570.)
H. [D]
964. Bible (Bishops'). 1568.
H.
1406. Grafton (R.). A Chronicle. 1569.
H. (F.). *See* Hulseen (Frederick van), or Hulsius.
H. (G.). *See* Hardouyn (G.).
H. (H.). *See* Holbein.
Hh. *See* Hond (H.).
H. (N.).
1711. Foxe (J.). Eicasmi. 1587.
1335. Bible (Lat.). 1593.
1737. ,, 1597.
H. (S.).
964. Bible (Bishops'). 1568. (Gen. i. etc.) *See* p. 1732.
H. (W.). *See* Hole.

Hall (Ralph).
4637. Mercator (G.). Historia (p. 299). 1635.
Hardouyn (Germain).
6182. Primer (Sarum). 1530.
Haydock (Richard).
5249. Lomazzo (G. P.). A Tracte. 1598.
Hessels (J.), artist.
7811. Beverwijk (J. van). Schat der Gesontheyt. 1638. 8°.
Hoefnagel (Georg).
7733. Braun (G.). De praecipuis urbibus. 1588.
Hogenbergius (Remigius). *See* Hohenberg.
Hogius (Cornelius).
6765. Saxton (C.). Maps. 1574 (1579).
Hohenberg (F.), engraver. 1575.
—— (Remigius), engraver. [Herb. 1651–2.]
6765. Saxton (C.). Maps. 1578–9.
Holbein (Hans).
276. Henry VIII. Assertio. [Mutius and Porsenna woodblock.] 1521.
286. Froissart (J.). [Mutius and Porsenna woodblock.] 1525.
720. Leland (J.). Naeniae. (Portrait of Sir T. Wyat.) 1542.
1019. Cranmer (T.). Catechismus. 1548.
6407. Derendel (P.). The true and lyuely portreatvres. [Bible Cuts.] 1553. 8°.
Hole (William).
2601. Bible (Genevan). 1607.
1758. Camden (W.). Britannia. 1607. *See below* 1637.
2892. Homer. The whole workes. [Ab. 1612.]
2518. Drayton (M.). Polyolbian. 1613.
3375. Montaigne (M. de). Essayes. (Portrait.) 1613.
3111. Rathborne (A.). The surveyor. 1616.
3128. Drayton (M.). Poems. 1620.
3864. Smith (J.). The generall historie. 1624.
3158. Purchas (S.). Pilgrims. Part 4. 1625.
4431. Charron (P.). Of wisdom. 1630.
2677. Bible. 1633.
3055. Camden (W.). Britannia. 1637. *See above* 1607.
5115. Jonson (B.). Workes. 1640.
Hollar (Wencelas).
6937. Du Val (M.). Rosa Hispani-Anglica. [1623?]
5007. Vicars (J.). Decapla. 1639.
7801. Lake (A.), *bp.* Portrait. 1640.
4748. Somner (W.). The Antiquities of Canterbury (anon). 1640.
Hond (Hendrik), or Hondius.
4714. Xenophon. Cyrupædia. 1632.
3712. Verheiden (J.). History of Modern Protestant Divines. 1637.
3875. Speed (J.). The theatre. (1610.) [1627?]
Hondius (Jodocus).
3055. [The Kingdom of Irland. 1610].
3215, 3055. Speed (J.). The theatre. 1611 (1610).
4637. Mercator (G.). Historia Mundi, p. 535. [Map of Nassau.] 1635.
Hooghe (Corn. de).
7684. Perret (C.). Exercitatio. 1569.
Hulseen (Frederik van) or Hulsius.
4237. Carleton (G.). A thankful remembrance. 1627.
4419. Lever (C.). The historie. 1627.
4237. Carleton (G.). A thankfull remembrance. 1627.
4538. ,, ,, ,, 1630.
3532. Lucanus. Pharsalia. 1627.
4554. ,, ,, 1631.
4447. Featley (D.). Ancilla. 1633.

Hulsius (F.). *See* Hulseen.

I. (A. V.).
6819. Dering (E.). Certaine...sermons. [159 .]
I. (M.). *See* Mallart (J.).
I. (O.). [ϕ. Qu. O. J.? or Ph.]
7811. Beverwijk. 1638.
I. (S.). *See* S. (I.).
Ingheenram (Fran.).
4340. Davies (J.). The Writing Schoolemaster. 1636.
Isac (Jasper).
7776. Bible. 1629.

J. (Vo.) F.
277. Henry VIII. Assertio septem sacramentorum. 1521.
284. More (Sir T.). Eruditissimi viri G. Rossei opus. 1523.
Johnson (Laurence).
2451. Knolles (Richard). The generall historie. 1621.
2462. ,, ,, ,, 1631.
2467. ,, ,, ,, 1638.

'K' or 'R.'
1426. Vermigli (P.). Common Places. [Part 2. Letter W.] 1583.
K. (A.) B. *See* Kempe.
K. (H. S.). *See* Springinklee.
K. (I. V.). *See* Kempen.
K. (W.).
6333. Braunschweig (H.). A most excellent apothecarye. 1561.
6334. Turner (W.). Herbal, part II. 1562.
Kærius (P.). *See* Kerius.
Keere (Pieter van den). *See* Kerius.
Kempe (A.) [ ], printer. [Herb. 1545–6.]
6078. Stories. 1535 (1536).
6079. Bible. 1536.
Kempen (Johann van) [ ], with 'Amor vincit omnia.'
6331. Bale (J.). The first examinacyon. 1546.
Kerius or Keere (Pieter Vanden).
6804–6. Norden (J.). Specvlvm Britanniae. 1593.
3774–5. Speed (J.). England Wales *etc.* [Map. 46, 54, 55.] 1627.
4637. Mercator (G.). Historia (p. 271). 1635.
Kip (William).
6628. Hall (J.). Mundus alter et idem. [1605.]
3971. Burton (W.). The Description of Leicester Shire. [1622.]
1758. Camden (W.). Britannia. 1607.
3055. ,, ,, 1637.

L. (I. V.). *See* Langeren (Jacob van).
L. (P. v.). *See* Langeren.
L. (R.).
2574. Bible. (Bishops'.) [Title.] 1602.
2635. ,, (King James' Version.) 1611.
2655. ,, 1617 (1611).
Langeren (Jacob van).
4433. Slatyer (W.). Genethliacon. 1630.
6259. Hawkins (H.). Partheneia (*ad fin.*). 1633.
4637. Mercator (G.). Historia, p. 305. 1635.
Langeren (P. van).
6258. Camden (W.). Institutio. 1633.
6259. Hawkins (H.). Partheneia. 1633.

Le Blon (C.).
4922. Gaule (J.). Practique Theories. 1629.
5370. Burton (Robert). The Anatomy of Melancholy. 1628.
5395. ,, ,, ,, 1632.
Lightfoot (Antony).
7024. 'Iesus.' 1636.
Linsted ( ).
5057. Alabaster (W.). Spiraculum Tubarum. [1633?]
Lochom (Michel van).
6257. New Testament. 1633.
Lyne (Richard).
839. Caius (J.). De Antiqvitate. 1574.

M. (C.). *See* Mellan (C.).
M. (H.). (Henry Middleton, bookseller.)
1647. Fulke (W.). De successione. 1584.
M. (I.).
379. Lyndwood. 1534.
M. (I.). 1555. *See* Mallart (J.).
M. (R.).
6819. Dering (E.). Certaine...letters. [1591?]
M. (W.). *See* Marshall.
Mallart (Jean).
6246. Primer. 1555.
6249. Bible. 1566.
Marshall (William).
4685. Lord (H.). A display. 1630.
5831. Cicero. De officiis. [163– .]
4974. Barkley (Sir R.). The felicitie of man. 1631.
5430. Psalms. (Metrical.) Trans. James I. 1631.
4198. Brathwait (R.). The English gentlewoman. 1631.
5735. Gerhard (J.). Meditations and Prayers. 1631.
4714. Xenophon. Cyrupædia. 1632.
6257. Bible. N. T. (Rhemes). 1633.
4206. Isaacson (H.) Saturni Ephemerides. 1633.
3193. Smith (Sir T.). The commonwealth. [1633?]
4277. Taylor (T.). Christ's victorie. (Portrait.) 1633.
3194. Herbert (Sir T.). A relation. 1634.
4953. Abbot (G.). A briefe description. 1634.
4584. Wither (G.). A Collection of emblems. 1635(–4).
3700. Du Plessis (S.). The Resoluer. 1635.
2466. Heywood (T.). The hierarchie. 1635.
5719. Poetæ minores græci. 1635.
3701–2. Richelieu. Emblema animae. 1635.
4017. Silesio (M.). The Arcadian Princesse. 1635.
5777. Swan (J.). Speculum mundi. 1635.
4118. Felltham (O.). Resolues. 1636.
4989. Hayward (Sir J.). The life of Edward VI. 1636.
5450. Longinus (D.). Περὶ ὕψους. 1636.
5452. ,, ,, 1636.
5458. ,, ,, ('1638').
3708. Preston (J.). The doctrine. 1636.
4861. Udall (W.). The historie. 1636.
4029. Sibbes (R.). A Fountain Sealed. 1637.
4658. Balzac. New Epistles. 1638.
5821. Bible. 1638.
3718. Brathwait (R.). A survey of History. 1638.
5824. Gerhard (J.). Meditations. 1638.
4661. Gildas. Epistles. 1638.
4865. Golden Mean. 1638.

Marshall (William), *cont.*
4596. I. (H.). Iacobs Ladder. 1638.
4999. Martyn (W.). The historie. 1638.
5197. Penkethman (J.). Artachthos. 1638.
4033. R. (T.). Cornelianum Dolium. 1638.
4740. Ross (A.). Christiados libri XIII. 1638.
4034. Sibbes (R.). A fountaine sealed. 1638.
5806. Fuller (T.). The historie of the holy warre. 1639.
5843. ,, ,, 1640.
4042. Gray (T. de). The compleat horseman. 1639.
5796. Hodson (W.). The holy sinner. 1639.
4044. Matthieu (P.). Unhappy Prosperity. 1639.
5177. Ward (R.). Animadversions. 1639.
5008. Woodall (J.). The Surgeons Mate. 1639.
5497. Bacon (F.). Of the Advancement of learning. 1640.
5114. Brathwait (R.). Ar't a'sleepe Husband? 1640.
5839. Drexelius (H.). The school of patience. 1640.
5844. Gerhard (J.). Meditations and Prayers (altered plate). 1640.
3728. Horatius. Art of poetry. 1640.
5847. Hodson (W.). The divine cosmographer. 1640.
4680. Parkinson (J.). Theatrum Botanicum. 1640.
4681. Shakspeare (W.). Poems. 1640.
4913. Wilkins (J.). A Discourse (The discovery). 1640.

Mellan (C.).
4117. Barclay (J.). Argenis. 1636.

Merian (M.), Junior.
4331. Donne (J.). LXXX. Sermons. 1640.
5139. Howell (J.). *Δενδρολογία.* 1640.

Morton (Ri.).
6058. Statutes. 1635.

Mountain (Ge.).
4621. Swedish Intelligencer. Ed. 3. 1632.

N. (I.). *See* no. 1300 *note.*

379	(Title-compartment.)	1534	684	(Title-compartment.)	1543
650	,,	1541	685	,,	1543
679	,,	1542	686	,,	,,
680	,,	,,	687	,,	,,
681	,,	,,	690	,,	[ ]
682	,,	,,	691	,,	[ ]
683	,,	,,	7232	,,	1576

Oluf (Hans), Cartographer.
3886. Swedish Discipline. 1632.

P. (I). ab. 1630. *See* Payne (J.).
P. (P.). ['1612.' (Spanish?)] ['1612 (Spanish?).]
3472. Hakewill (G.). An answere (p. 133). 1616.
P. (R.). [ ], Paris.
6194. Missale Sarum. 1555.
6195. Breviarium Sarum. (Adventus Domini.) 1556.
P. (S.). *See* Simon van de Passe.
P. (W.). [ ]. *See* Pass (W. de).
Pass (Crispin van de). *See* p. 1744.
6643. Garden of flowers. 1614–5.
6948. Scott (T.). Vox populi. 1622(–1624).
3860. Carleton (G.). A thankfvll remembrance. 1624.
4237. Carleton (G.). A thankful remembrance. 1627.
6405. Miroir de plus belles Courtisanes. 1635.
6642. Holland (H.). Herωologia. 1620.

Passe (Magdalene van de).
6642. Holland (H.). Herωologia. 1620.
6590. Buckingham, Magdalena, duchess of. (Inserted.)
Passe (Simon van de). *See* p. 1744.
3864. [New England map. 1614. State I.] Smith (J.). Generall historie. 1624.
4637. [,, State II.] Mercator (G.). Historia mundi. 1635.
6643. *See* Passe (C. van de). Garden of flowers (pl. 15, 22, 33). 1614–5.
2792. Ralegh (Sir W.). History of the World. 1614 (1621).
2653. James I. Works. 1616.
3116. Rathborne (A.) the Svrveyor. (Portrait.) 1616.
2785. Ralegh (Sir W.). History of the World. 1617.
3124. Florus. The Roman Histories. [1618.] Cf. no. 7798.
3497. Bacon (F.). Instauratio magna. 1620.
4051. Butler (W.). Portrait. 1620.
7572. Du Bartas. A learned Summary. 1621.
4917. Orpheus. Animalium...delineationes. [Ab. 1628.]
4637. Mercator (G.). Historia. 1635.
7798. Florus. Roman Histories. 1636. Cf. no. 3124.
Passe (Willem van de). See p. 1744.
6643. Passe (C. van de). Garden of flowers (pl. 32). 1614–5.
6642. Holland (H.). Herωologia. 1620.
3603. Serres (J. de). A generall historie. 1624.
4951. Hayward (Sir J.). The life of Edward VI. (Portrait.) 1630.
Payne (John).
3139. Bacon (F.). Hist. of Henry VII. (Portrait.) 1622.
4762. Boys (J.). Workes. 1622.
4384. ,, ,, 1629.
4080. Hayward (Sir J.). The Sanctuarie. 1623.
5712. Bible. 1629.
4384 and 7871. Boys (J.). Workes. 1629(–1638).
3173. Lake (A.). Sermons. 1629.
5714. Bible. 1630.
4836. Smith (J.). The true travels. 1630.
4454. Bolton (R.). Four laste things (portrait dated 1632). 1635.
5121. Virgil. Aeneid. 1632.
5716. Bible. 1633.
5057. Alabaster (W.). Spiraculum Tubarum. [1633?]
2464. Gerard (J.). The Herball. 1633.
5815. Bible. 1635.
2466. Heywood (T.). The hierarchie. 1635.
5822. Bible. 1637–8.
7855. Coke (Sir E.). The first part. 1629.
4326. ,, ,, (1639.)
4125. Puget de la Serre (J.). The mirrour. 1639.
Picquet ( ).
6257. New Testament. 1633.
Porro (G.), engraver.
1735. Taffin (J.). Amendment. 1595.

Queboorn (C. van).
7811. Beverwijk (J. van). Schat. 1638.

R? *See* K.
R. (I.). *See* Reynes (J.).
R. (N.), Paris.
6194. Missale Sarum. (Assumption of the BVM.) 1555.
R. (P.). 1555. *See* P. (R.).

R. (R.).
7124. Testament of the twelve patriarchs. 1576.
R. (W.). [Qu. W. Rogers?]
1735. Taffin (J.). The amendment of life. 1597.
Reynold (Nicholas). [Herb. 1562.]
6765. Saxton (C.). Maps of England. 1575–9.
Reynes (John).
1164. Boemus (J.). The fardle (Initial A.). 1555 *et passim.*
Rogers (William).
2191–2. Broughton (H.). A concent of Scripture. [1588.]
2228. Ariosto (L.). Orlando Fvrioso. 1591.
2348. Gerard (J.). The herball. 1597.
1975. Linschoten (J. H. van). Voyages. 1598.
1743. Camden (W.). Britannia. 1600.
2575. Segar (Sir W.). Honor Military, and Ciuill. 1602.
See also R. (W.). 1597.
Rollos (Pieter).
6631. Montenay (G. de). A booke of armes. 1619.
Rucholle (P.)[1].
6974. Malone (W.). A reply. 1627.
6613–4. Porter (Jer.). The Flowers. 1632.
Ryther (Augustine). [Herb. 1652.]
6765. Saxton (C.). [Maps. No. 23 (York), 25 (Durham), 26 (Westmoreland).] 1575–9.

S. (C.). Qu. C. Swytzer?
2574. Bible. (Bishops'). 1602.
2635. ,, (Royal). 1611.
2655. ,, 1617 (1611).
S. (I.). 1526 *See* Schoeffer (J.).
S. (I.).
5745. Heywood (T.). England's Elizabeth. (Portrait.) 1632.
S. (J.).
4123. Tuvill (D.). Vade mecum. 1638.
S. (R.).
1522. Polemon (J.). All the famous Battels. [1587?]
S. (V.). *See* Solis (V.).
Saloman (Bernard).
6407. Derendel (P.). The true and lyuely portreatvres. 1553. 8°.
6408. Thesaurus Amicorum. [Before 1574.] 8°.
Sarret.
6514. Chisholm (W.). Examen. 1601.
Savery (Solomon).
3878. Speed (J.). A prospect. (Portrait of Speed.) 1629 [1631?].
5396. Ovid. Metamorphosis English. 1632.
4747. ,, ,, 1640.
3885. Speed (J.). The history. (Portrait of Speed.) 1632.
Scatter (Francis).
6765. Saxton (C.). Maps. (No. 22 Chester.) 1575–9.
Schoeffer (J.).
288. Henry VIII. Literarum. 1526.
Sichem (Christoffel von).
2439. Grimstone (E.). A generall historie. 1609.
Solis (Vergil).
964. Bible. (Cuts '1559' etc.) 1568. *See* p. 1732.
1406. Grafton (R.). A Chronicle at Large. 1569.
2706. Common Prayer. 1639.

[1] For a foreign book full of his illustrations, see H. Drexelius, *Opera.* Duaci, 1636, 4°, a copy of which is in the Library. [F. 10. 129.]

Springinklee (H.).
6195. Breviarium Sarum (Proprium Sanctorum). 1556.
Stent (P.).
5004. [Bust of Charles I.] A large declaration. 1639.
Surhon (Jean). [Zedler XLI. 405] p. 499.
4637. Mercator (G.). Historia Mundi (p. 499. Map of Namur). 1635.
Swytzer (Christopher). [Walpole *History* p. 185.]
7736. 'Dunelmum.' 1595.
2476. Du Bartas. Weekes. 1605–6.
2488. „ „ (1608).
2489. „ „ (Another state).
See also S. (C.).
Sylvius (Anton.). A.
964. Bible (Bishops'). 1568.
6130. Dodoens (R.). A niewe herball. 1578.

T. (C.). [Herb. 926.]
967. Bible (Bishops'). 1572.
1418. Baret (J.). Alvearie. (Initial A.) 1580.
1711. Foxe (J.). Eicasmi. 1587.
2210. Colynet (A.). The true history. 1591.
2211. Florio (G.). Second frutes. 1591.
1335. Bible (Latin). 1593.
1737. „ „ 1597.
2320. Maurice (Prince). A true report. 1601.
T. (I.).
Bibeus (S.). [Arms of the Colleges of Oxford and Cambridge.] 1602.
T. (S.), engraver. 1609.
2492. Blundeville (T.). The foure...offices. (Sig. A 2.) 1609.
Terwoordus or Terwoort (Leonard). [Herb. 1651–2.]
6765. Saxton (C.). Maps. (Leicester, 1576.) 1575–9.
Tory (Geoffrey), pp. 1645, 1730–33, 1735.
651. (p. 1730.)
742. (p. 1731.)
752. (p. 1731.)
1084. (p. 1732.)
1482. (p. 1733.)
1486. (p. 1733.)

V. (B.). [ ]
6176. Primer (Sarum). 1534.
V. (R.). *See* Valentine.
V. (T.). *See* Vic. (T.).
Vænius. *See* Veen.
Valentine (R.).
6248. Primer (Sarum). 1555.
Vanden Keere (P.). *See* Kerius.
Vandyck (Sir A.).
4577. Stafford (T.). Pacata Hibernia. (Portrait of Sir G. Carew.) 1633.
Vaughan (Robert).
3864. Smith (J.). The generall historie. 1624.
4756. Camden (W.). Annales. 1625.
7855. Coke (Sir E.). The first part of the Institutes, (Portrait of Sir T. Littleton.) 1629. F°.
4830. Botero (G.). Relations. 1630.
4951. Hayward (Sir J.). The life of Edward VI. 1630.
4831. Brathwait (R.). The English Gentleman. 1630.
4883. Augustine. Confessions. 1631.
4575. May (T.). The reigne of Henry II. (Portrait). 1633.
5001. Collection of private devotions. 1639.

Vaughan (Robert), *cont.*
4326. Coke (Sir E.). Institutes. (Portrait.) 1639. F°.
Veen (Gysbert van).
6138. Veen (O. van). Amorum emblemata. 1608.
Veen (Otto van).
6138. Veen (O. van). Amorum emblemata. 1608.
Vic. (T.). 'Pos. S.T.B.'
3860. Carleton (G.). A thankful remembrance. 1624.
4237. ,, ,, 1627.
4538. ,, ,, 1630.
Voerst (Robert van).
4577. Stafford (T.). Pacata Hibernia. (Portrait of Sir G. Carew.) 1633.
Vrints (Johannes Baptista).
2356. Ortelius (A.). Theatrum (Map of England, No. 12). 1606. F°.

W. (F.).
6227. Torsellino (O.). The...life of S. Francis Xavier. 1632.
W. (I.). *See* Windet.
Whitwell (Charles).
1971. Minadoi (G. T.). The history. (Map of Near Asia.) 1595.
Windet (John). 'I. W.'
2119. Ferne (Sir J.). The blazon. (Sig. Aij.) 1586.

Yate (George).
7059. Yate (G.). The Miraculous Week. [1640?]
Yo. (Ro.).
5001. Cosin (J.). A Collection. 1639.

INSTRUMENT MAKERS.

	No.
Bull (J.). 1582.	7931
Lockerson (J.). 1582.	7931
Reade (J.). 1582.	7931
Whitwell (C.). 1598.	2151
Allen (E.). 1623	3342, 7517, 4563 *etc.*, 5146
Thompson (J.). 1623.	Pages 1070, 1701 (3342, 7517)

INDEX IV.

TOWNS, ETC.

TOWNS, ETC.

	PAGE
Aberdeen	1335
Albionopolis . . .	1546, 1549
Alençon	1397 note
Amberg . . .	1225 (no. 5501)
Amsterdam	1426—1435, 1539, 1540, 1544, 1548, 1557, 1561
Antwerp. . . .	28, 1355—1371, 1506, 1715 (and nos. 7803, 7856)
Arnhem	1497
Augusta	1550
Augusta Trinobantum . .	549, 1675 (and nos. 7764, 7807)
Avignon	1468
Banbury	(no. 7932)
'Basileia' . . .	772 (no. 3641)
Basle	32, 1290 note, 1418, 1521
Bellositi Dobunorum . .	1208 (no. 5422)
Bologna	1737
Bruges	26
Brussels	1495, 1717
Cambridge . . .	1228—1296, 1711—2, 1721 (and nos. 7772, 7906)
Canterbury . . .	1301, 1713
'Catvapolis' . . .	(no. 7817)
Channel Islands . . .	1738 (no. 3473)
Cologne	26, 1424, 1716, 1725—6
'Comopolis'. . . .	1545
Copenhagen . . .	1334 (no. 5995)
Copmanhouin . . .	1545
Cosmopolis . . .	1545, 1677
Coventry	1311 (and no. 7779)
Daventry . .	396
Delft . . .	1451

	PAGE
DEVENTER	33, 1580
DORT	1465—1467
DOUAI	1480—1490, 1542, 1544, 1547, 1566, 1568 (and nos. 7817, 7894)
DUBLIN	1338, 1351, 1715
EAST MOLESEY	396 (no. 1915)
EDINBURGH	1315, 1562, 1572 (and no. 7927)
'ELISIUM'	1559 (no. 6963)
EMDEN	1444
ETON	1310
'EUROPE'	(no. 7779)
EXETER	1311
FAWSLEY	396 (no. 1916)
FLORENCE	1442, 1533
FLUSHING	1500
FRANKFURT AM MAIN	1492—1494 (and no. 7970)
GENEVA	1420, 1510, 1511, 1521, 1522 (and no. 7836)
GHENT	1501
GLASGOW	1337
GORCUM	1499
GREENWICH	1306, 1412 (no. 6288)
HAGUE	1496 (and no. 7860)
HAMBURG	1397, 1500
HANAU	1495 (and nos. 2361 corrected, 6884 corrected, 7807)
HEIDELBERG	1302, 1449, 1554
'HELICON'	1554 (no. 6936)
INGOLSTADT	1524 (no. 6771)
IPSWICH	1302
JENA	1500 note
KALYKOW	1412 (no. 6289)
LAMBETH	1308
LANCASHIRE PRESS	1550
LEICESTER	1311
LEIPZIG	1303 (no. 5883), 1418
LEYDEN	1461—1464, 1558
LIÉGE	1448, 1548 (no. 6901)

	PAGE
LONDON	19—25, 37—1168, 1580—1708, 1723 etc.
LOUVAIN	28, 1445—1447, 1579 (and no. 7941)
LYONS	1442—3, 1421 note
MAGDEBURG	1500 note
MARBURG	1406
MIDDELBURG	1452—1460, 1540—1, 1726
MONS	1449
'N'	1530 (no. 6809)
NEUSTADT	(nos. 3608 and 7761)
NEWCASTLE-ON-TYNE . .	1312
NORWICH	1307, 1520 (and nos. 7879, 7880)
NÜRNBERG	1409, 1513
OXFORD	16, 1171—1226, 1708—1711 (and nos. 7796, 7867, 7886, 7936)
'PARADISE'	1558 (no. 6958)
PARIS	29—31, 1372—1389, 1573 (and no. 7838)
PESCLAVII	405 (no. 1954)
RHEIMS	1449—1451, 1535 (no. 6840)
ROCHELLE	397, 1501, 1553
ROME	1443
ROTTERDAM	409, 1502, 1568
ROUEN	31, 1394—1404, 1534, 1544, 1568, 1743[1]
ST ALBANS	18, 1302
ST ANDREWS	1334
ST OMER	1468—1480, 1536, 1539, 1542, 1546, 1717 (and nos. 7766, 7809)
SALISBURY	1311
'SAVOY'	1424
SCHAFFHAUSEN	(no. 7785)
SHREWSBURY	1306, 1713
SOUTHWARK	1297, 1515, 1516, 1713 (and no. 7818)
STIRLING	1334, 1521
STRALSUND	(no. 7955)
STRASSBURG	1408, 1579
TOURNAI	1501, 1744

[1] See also a copy of no. 6718 in the Bodleian Library.

	PAGE
TOURS	1610 (no. 7243)
TÜBINGEN	1718
URSEL[1] (OBER)	1318 (no. 5920)
UTRECHT	1498, 1554
VENICE	27, 1716 (and no. 7934)
WANDSWORTH	1308
WATERFORD	1338
WESEL	1419, 1518
WESTMINSTER	3—15, 1579
WITTENBERG	1441, 1513 (no. 6708), 1515 (no. 6720)
WORCESTER	1305
WÜRZBURG	1502
YORK	1227
ZURICH	1410—1416, 1716, 1727
ZUTPHEN	1499

[1] Misprinted 'Oberwesel.'

INDEX V.

PORTRAITS.

PORTRAITS.

	No.
Abbot (George), Abp. A briefe description. *W. Marshall.* 1634. 12°.	4953
Abbot (Robert).	
Holland (H.). Heroologia (p. 185). *A. Buchel.* [1620.] F°. .	6642
Verheiden (J.). History (p. 311). 1637. 8°.	3712
Ambrosius, Saint. Christian offices. 1637. 4°.	5163
Anne of Denmark. A trewe description. 1603. F°. . . .	6375
Speed (J.). The theatre (p. 131). 1611 (1610). F°. . .	3215
Aretius (Benedictus).	
Verheiden (J.). History (p. 140). 1637. 8°.	3712
Ariosto (L.). Orlando. 1591. F°.	2228
Babington (Gervase).	
Holland (H.). Heroologia (p. 234). [1620.] F°. . . .	6642
Verheiden (J.). History (p. 299). 1637. 8°.	3712
Babington (John). Pyrotechnia. 1635. F°.	4011
Bacon (Francis). (aet. 66) 1626. Sylva. 1627. F°.	4806
Opera. 1638. F°.	5186, 5187
Advancement of learning. *W. Marshall.* 1640. F°. . .	5497
Bacon (Nicolas).	
Holland (H.). Heroologia (p. 60). [1620.] F°. . .	6642
Bale (John).	
Holland (H.). Heroologia (p. 165). *A. Buchel.* [1620.] F°. .	6642
Verheiden (J.). History (p. 197). 1637. 8°. . . .	3712
Barclay (John). Argenis. 1636. 4°.	4117
Bate (J.). The mysteries. 1635. 4°.	4012
Becon (T.). (aet. 41) 1553. The Pomaunder of Prayer. [1553?] 8°.	871
Reliques of Rome. 1563	799
The Sicke mans salve. 1577	846
The sicke mans salue. 1594. 8°.	7385
(aet. 49) 1560. Works. 1564. F°.	801
Holland (H.). Heroologia (p. 178). *A. Buchel.* [1620.] F°. .	6642
Verheiden (J.). History (p. 330). 1637. 8°.	3712
Berengarius.	
Verheiden (J.). History (p. 1). 1637. 8°.	3712
Beza (Theodorus).	
Verheiden (J.). History (p. 166). 1637. 8°.	3712
Bolton (Robert). 1632. Foure last Things. 1635. 4°. . . .	4454
Bradford (John).	
Holland (H.). Heroologia (p. 150). *A. Buchel.* [1620.] F°. .	6642
Verheiden (J.). History (p. 221). 1637. 8°.	3712
Brathwaite (Richard). (aet. 48.) A survey of history. 1638. 4°. .	3718
Bucer (Martin).	
Verheiden (J.). History (p. 68). 1637. 8°.	3712
Buckingham (Katharine, duchess of), ab. 1618–23.	
Magdalena van de Pass. . . . . Inserted in no.	6590.

No.
Bullein (W.). Bulwarke of defence. 1562. F°. 1170
Bullinger (Heinrich).
Verheiden (J.). History (p. 147). 1637. 8°. . . . 3712
Burghley (William Cecil, lord).
Bible (Bishops'). [Psalms.] 1572. F°. 967
Holland (H.). Heroologia (p. 111). *A. Buchel.* [1620.] F°. . 6642
Burton (Robert). Anatomy. 1628. F°. 5370
" " 1632. F°. 5395
Burton (William). Description of Leicestershire. 1622. F°. . 3971
Butler (William). *S. Pass.* 1620. 8°. 4051

Cæsar (Julius). Observations. 1604. F°. 2471
" " 1609. F°. 2493
Caius (John).
Holland (H.). Heroologia (p. 181). *A. Buchel.* [1620.] F°. . 6642
Calvin (Jean).
Verheiden (J.). History (p. 99). 1637. 8°. 3712
Camden (William). *For G. Humble.* [1627?] 3776
—— Another state 3777
Annales. 1615 (-1627). F°. 3106
[Another copy in]. Remaines. 1623. 4°. 3684
Candish (Thomas). *See* Cavendish.
Carew (George), earl of Totnes. *See* Totnes.
Carleill (Christopher).
Holland (H.). Heroologia (p. 93). [1620.] F°. . . 6642
Carleton (George), Bishop. A thankful remembrance. 1627. 4°. . 4237
" " " 1630. 4°. . 4538
Cavendish (Thomas).
Holland (H.). Heroologia (p. 89). *A. Buchel.* [1620.] F°. . 6642
Grent (W.). A new map. 1625 7857
Speed (J.). A prospect. 1627. F°. 3874
Chaloner (Sir T.).
De republica. 1579. 4°. 7270
Charles I. (as Duke of York).
Speed (J.). The theatre. (Vol. I. p. 131.) 1610. F°. . . 3215
Charles I. (as Prince of Wales). 1616. *S. Passe.*
James I. Works. 1616. F°. 2653
— 1616. *Delaram.*
Rathborne (A.). The svrveyor. 1616. F°. 3116
— 1619.
James I. Opera. 1619. F°. 2807
Smith (J.). The generall historie. 1624. F°. 3864
Charles I. (as King). *W. Peake.* [1625?] 4°. 7634
The large declaration. 1639. F°. 5002–3
" " *P. Stent.* 1639. F°. 5004
Gray (T. de). The compleat horseman. 1639. F°. . . 4042
Woodall (J.). The Surgeons Mate. 1639. F°. . . . 5008
Cheke (Sir J.)
Bale (J.). Illustrium scriptorum. 1548. 4°. . . . 6314–5
Holland (H.). Heroologia (p. 52). [1620.] F°. . . . 6642
Chemnitius (Martinus).
Verheiden (J.). History (p. 132). 1637. 8°. 3712
Coke (Sir Edward). First Part of the Institutes. *J. Payne.* 1629. F°. 7855
— — 1639. F°. 4326
Colet (John).
Holland (H.). Heroologia (p. 154). *A. Buchel.* [1620.] F°. . 6642
Verheiden (J.). History (p. 207). 1637. 8°. 3712
Coryate (Tho.).
Coryats Crvdities. 1611. 4°. 3076

No.

Cranmer (Thomas), abp.
Bible (Title of New Testament). 1540. F°. 587
" (" ") 1541. F°. 649
Holland (H.). Heroologia (p. 161). *A. Buchel.* [1620.] F°. 6642
Verheiden (J.). History (p. 227). 1637. 8°. 3712
Cumberland (George Clifford, earl of).
Holland (H.). Heroologia (p. 121). *A. Buchel.* [1620.] F°. 6642

Davies (J.) of Hereford. The writing Schoolmaster. 1636. 8°. 4340
Day (John). (aet. 40) 1562.
Becon (T.). Works. 1564. F°. 801
Dering (Edward).
Holland (H.). Heroologia (p. 194). *A. Buchel.* [1620.] F°. 6642
Dodonæus (R.). Niewe herball. 1578. F°. 6130
Passe (C. de). Garden of Flowers. 1615. 6643
Dominis (M. A. de). De republica. 1617. F°. 3476
Donne (John). LXXX. Sermons. *M. Merian, Jun.* 1640. F°. 4331
Drake (Sir F.).
Holland (H.). Heroologia (p. 106). [1620.] F°. 6642
Grent (W.). A new...map. 1625 7857
Speed (J.). A prospect. 1627. F°. 3874
Drayton (M.). Poems. [1620?] F°. 3128
Du Bartas (Verses by J. Vicars). [Not before 1618.] 8°. 6898
(Woodcut.) F°. 2535
Dudley (Lady Jane).
Holland (H.). Heroologia (p. 32). [1620.] F°. 6642
Du Jon (François).
Verheiden (J.). History (p. 178). 1637. 8°. 3712

Edward II.
Hubert (Sir F.). The deplorable life. 1628. 8°. 5068
Edward VI.
Bale (J.). Illustrium scriptorum. 1548. 4°. 6314–5
Latimer (H.). Sermons. 1571. 4°. 828
Holland (H.). Heroologia (p. 23). [1620.] F°. 6642
Godwin (F.). Annales. 1630. F°. 2461
Hayward (Sir J.). The life of Edward VI. 1630. 4°. 4951
— 1636. 12°. 4989
Elizabeth, Queen.
Gemini (T.). Compendiosa totius Anatomiae. 1559. F°. 1237
Bible. (Title of N.T.) Rouen. 1566. F°. 6249
Parker (M.). De antiquitate. 1572. F°. 831–2
Bible (Bishops'). [Copper.] 1572. F°. 967
Harvey (G.). Gratulationum. (Letter C.) 1578. 4°. 1495
Saxton (C.). Maps. 1575–9. F°. 6765
Puttenham (G.). The arte. 1589. 4°. 2224
Livius. The Roman Historie. 1600. F°. 2428
Holland (H.). Heroologia (p. 35). [1620.] F°. 6642
Smith (J.). The generall historie. 1624. F°. 3864
Camden (W.). Annales. 1625. 4°. 4756
Grimstone (E.). A generall historie. 1627. F°. 7397
Stafford (T.). Pacata Hibernia. 1633. F°. 4577–8
Hayward (Sir J.). The life. 1636. 12°. 4989
Heywood (T.). The exemplary lives. 1640. 4°. 4675
— [Tomb of Elizabeth.]
Holland (H.). Heroologia (p. 40). [1620.] F°. 6642
England, Kings of.
Speed (J.). The Theatre. 1610–2. F°. 3215
'A true chronologie of all the Kings of England, from Brute the first King vnto our most sacred King Charles Monarke of ye whol yles.' 7715

No.

England, Kings of, *cont.*
Effigies Regum Anglorum. [Ab. 1640.] 8°. 3838
Erasmus.
Verheiden (J.). History (p. 14). 1637. 8°. 3712
Essex (Robert Devereux, earl of).
Holland (H). Heroologia (p. 117). [1620.] F°. . . 6642
Essex (Walter Devereux, earl of).
Holland (H.). Heroologia (p. 58). [1620.] F 6642

Fagius (Paul).
Verheiden (J.). History (p. 60). 1637. 8°. 3712
Florio (Giovanni). *W. Hole.* 1611.
Montaigne (M. de). Essayes. 1613. F°. 3375
Forbes (Patrick), of Corse, Bp. Funeralls. 1635. 4°. . . 6007
Foxe (John).
Holland (H.). Heroologia (p. 201). *A. Buchel.* [1620.] F°. . 6642
Verheiden (J.). History (p. 276). 1637. 8°. 3712
Francis (S.) Xavier.
Torsellino (O.). Life. 1632. 4°. 6227
Frobisher (Sir Martin).
Holland (H.). Heroologia (p. 97). [1620.] F°. . . . 6642
Fulke (William), (aet. 50) A.D. 1589. *W. Marshall.*
The text of the New Testament. 1633. F°. 4570

Gale (Thomas), chirurgeon. Certaine Workes. 1563. 8°. . . 1303
Gerard (John). Herball. 1597. F°. 2348
— 1623. F°. 2464
Gerardus (Andreas), *Hyperius.*
Verheiden (J.). History (p. 81). 1637. 8°. 3712
Gilbert (Sir Humphrey).
Holland (H.). Heroologia (p. 64). *A Buchel.* [1620.] F°. . 6642
Gildas. Epistles. 1638. 12°. 4661
Gondomar (Diego de).
Scott (T.). The second part of Vox Popvli. 1624. 4°. . 6650–1
Grenville (Sir Richard).
Holland (H.). Heroologia (p. 84). [1620.] F°. 6642
Grey (Lady Jane). *See* Dudley (Lady Jane).
Grindal (Edmund).
Holland (H.). Heroologia (p. 198). *A Buchel.* [1620]. F°. . 6642
Verheiden (J.). History (p. 286). 1637. 8°. 3712
Gualter (Rodolph).
Verheiden (J.). History (p. 158). 1637. 8°. 3712
Gustavus II. Adolphus. The new starr. *M. Droeshout.* 1632. 4°. . 4560
Swedish Intelligencer. Ed. 3. 1632. 4°. 4621

Hall (John). 1564.
Most excellent treatise. 1565. 4°. 1215
Harington (Sir John). Ariosto (L.). Orlando. 1591. F°. . . 2228
Holland (H.). Heroologia (p. 135). [1620.] F°. 6642
Ariosto (L.). Another plate. 1634. F°. 4448
Harington (John), baron Harington of Exton.
Holland (H.). Heroologia (p. 132). *A. Buchel.* [1620.] F°. . 6642
Hawkins (Sir John).
Holland (H.). Heroologia (p. 101). [1620.] F°. 6642
Haydock (Ric.).
Lomazzo (J. P.). A tracte. 1598. F°. 5249
Hayward (Sir J.). The Sanctuarie. 1623. *J. Payne.* 4°. . . 4080
" " 1631. 12°. 4099
" " *T. Cecil.* 1636. 12°. . . 4119

No.

Hayward (Sir J.), *cont.*
Life of Edward VI. 1630. 4°. 4951
Henry II. of England.
May (T.). The reigne. 1633. 8°. 4575
Henry V.
Speed (J.). The theatre (p. 107). 1610. F°. 3215
Henry VII.
Bacon (F.). The historie of the reigne of Henry VII. *J. Payne.* 1622. F°. 3139
Henry VIII.
Bible. (Title of N.T.) 1540. F°. 587
Holland (H.). Heroologia (p. 1). *A. Buchel.* [1620.] F°. . 6642
Godwin (F.). Annales. 1630. F°. 2461
Henry, Prince of Wales. 1604.
Cæsar. Observations. 1604. F°. 2471
— 1609. F°. 2493
Speed (J.). The Theatre (p. 131). 1610. F°. 3215
Drayton (M.). Polyolbion. 1613. F°. 2518
Holland (H.). Heroologia (pp. 45, 48, 51). [1620.] F°. . 6642
Henry IV. of France.
Serres (J. de). A general inventorie. 1607. F°. . . . 3567
Matthieu (P.). The heroyk life. 1612. 4°. 3581
Henry Frederick, Prince of Orange. '1631.' F°. 7650
Heywood (John). The Spider and the Flie. 1556. 4°. . . 1244
Hieronymus Pragensis.
Verheiden (J.). History (p. 8). 1637. 8°. 3712
Holland, Earls of.
Grimstone (E.) A generall historie. 1609. F°. 2439
Holland (Philemon).
Xenophon. Cyrupædia. 1632. F°. 4714
Holland (Thomas).
Holland (H.). Heroologia (p. 237). *A. Buchel.* [1620.] F°. . 6642
Verheiden (J.). History (p. 304). 1637. 8°. 3712
Hudson (J.). 'Little Jefferie.'
Microphilus. The new yeeres Gift. 1636. 12°. 3705
Humphry (Laurence).
Holland (H.). Heroologia (p. 207). *A. Buchel.* [1620.] F°. . 6642
Verheiden (J.). History (p. 293). 1637. 8°. 3712
Hus (John).
Verheiden (J.). History (p. 1). 1637. 8°. 3712

James VI. of Scotland.
Leslie (J.). A treatise (aet 12). 1584. 8°. 6253
Stuart (House of). A true description. 1603, 1605. F°. . 6375
Speed (J.). The Theatre (p. 131). 1610. F°. 3215
F. Delaram sculp. J. Browne exc. 1619. F°. 7551
Opera. 1619. F°. 2807
Smith (J.). The generall historie. 1624. F°. 3864
Jefferie, Little. *See* Hudson (J.).
Jewel (John).
Holland (H.). Heroologia (p. 168). *A. Buchel.* [1620.] F°. . 6642
Verheiden (J.). History (p. 258). 1637. 8°. 3712
Junius (Franciscus). *See* Du Jon.

Lake (Arthur), bp. Sermons. 1629. *J. Payne.* F°. 3173
— 1640. *W. Hollar.* 4°. 7801
Latimer (Hugh).
Fruitfull Sermons. 1571. 4°. 828
Holland (H.). Heroologia (p. 153). [1620.] F°. . . . 6642
Fruitfull Sermons. 1635. 4°. 4636

No.

Latimer (Hugh), *cont.*
Verheiden (J.). History (p. 226). 1637. 8°. 3712
Leicester (R. Dudley, Earl of). Bible. 1568. F°. . . . 964
Bible. 1572. F°. 967
Holland (H.). Heroologia (p. 75). *W. Passe.* [1620.] F°. 6642
L'Escluse (C. de). 6643
Littleton (Sir Thomas).
Coke (Sir E.). Institutes. *R. Vaughan.* 1629. F°. . . 7855
— — 1639. F°. 4326
L'Obel (M. de.) Portrait. *F. Delaram.* 1615. F°. . . 6117
Lomazzo (J. P.). Tracte. 1598. F°. 5249
Louis XIII. Portrait. *W. Pass. sc. T. Jenner sc.* F°. . . 5118
Luther (Martin).
Verheiden (J.). History (p. 21). 1637. 8°. 3712

Magellanus (Ferd.). 1625. 7857
Speed (J.). A prospect. 1627. F°. 3874
Marlorat (Augustin).
Verheiden (J.). History (p. 108). 1637. 8°. . . . 3712
Mary, Queen of England. (With 'The Suplicatio of Tomas Hongar. Numbered '22.' *Fr. Delaram.*) F°. . . . 7713
Godwin (F.). Annales. 1630. F°. 2461
Mary Stuart, Queen of Scots.
Lesley (J.). A treatise. 1584. 8°. 6253
Udall (W.). The historie of Mary Stuart. 1624. F°. . 4793
— *W. Marshall.* 1636. 12°. 4861
Melanchthon (Philip).
Verheiden (J.). History (p. 30). 1637. 8°. . . . 3712
Montagu (James).
Holland (H.). Heroologia (p. 190). [1620.] F°. . . . 6642
Verheiden (J.). History (p. 339). 1637. 8°. . . . 3712
Montenny (Georgetta de). A booke of armes. 1619. 8°. . . 6631
More (John)
Holland (H.). Heroologia (p. 209). [1620.] F°. . . 6642
More (Sir T.). Dialogve of Cumfort. 1573. 8°. . . . 6123
Holland (H.). Heroologia. *A. Buchel.* [1620.] F°. . . 6642
Murad IV, Sultan. 1638. 4°. 7963
Musculus (Wolfgang).
Verheiden (J.). History (p. 90). 1637. 8°. 3712

Noort (Olivier van). 1625 etc. . . . . . 3874 etc., 7857
Norfolk (Thomas, duke of).
Sallustius. Jugurtha. [1520?] F°. 310, 311
Nowell (Alexander).
Holland (H.). Heroologia (p. 216). *A Buchel.* [1620.] F°. . 6642
Verheiden (J.). History (p. 251). 1637. 8°. . . . 3712

Oecolampadius (Johannes).
Verheiden (J.). History (p. 50). 1637. 8°. 3712
Ortelius (Abr.). Ortelius (A.). Theatrum. 1606. F°. . . . 2356
Owen (John). Epigrammata. 12°. 1634 4583

Paré (Ambroise). Workes. 1634. F°. 4632
Parker (Matthew)
Holland (H.). Heroologia (p. 174). *A. Buchel.* [1620.] F°. . 6642
Verheiden (J.). History (p. 269). 1637. 8°. . . . 3712
Parkinson (John). Paradisus terrestris. 1629. F°. . . . 2561
— 1640. F°. 4680
Pembroke (H. Herbert, earl of).
Holland (H.). Heroologia (p. 115). *A. Buchel.* [1620.] F°. . 6642

No.

Perkins (William).
Holland (H). Heroologia (p. 219). *A. Buchel.* [1620.] F°. . 6642
Verheiden (J.). History (p. 347). 1637. 8°. . . . 3712
Pole (Reginald).
Holland (H.). Heroologia (p. 17). *A. Buchel.* 1620.] F°. . 6642
Preston (John).
The doctrine. 1636. 12°. 3708
The onely love. 1640. 8°. 5185

Rainolds (John).
Holland (H.). Heroologia (p. 228). *A. Buchel.* [1620.] F°. . 6642
Ralegh (Sir Walter): History of the World. 1617. F°. . . 2785
— *S. Passe.* 1621. F°. 2792
Life of Mahomet. 1637. 12°. 4927
Rathborne (A.). The surveyor. *S. Passe.* 1616. F°. . . . 3116
Ridley (Mark). 1594. Short treatise. 1613. 4°. 3650
Ridley (Nicholas).
Holland (H). Heroologia (p. 155). *A. Buchel.* [1620.] F°. . 6642
Verheiden (J.). History (p. 231). 1637. 8°. 3712
Roberts (Lewis), merchant. 1596. The merchants mappe. 1638. F°. 5133
Rogers (John).
Holland (H.). Heroologia (p. 157). *A. Buchel.* [1620.] F°. . 6642
Rupert (Prince). *A. van Dyck pinxit. R. Peake.* [1640?] F°. . 3839

Salisbury (Robert Cecil, earl of).
Holland (H.). Heroologia. *A. Buchel.* [1620.] F°. . . 6642
Sandys (Edwin).
Holland (H.). Heroologia (p. 205). *A. Buchel.* [1620.] F°. . 6642
Verheiden (J.). History (p. 246). 1637. 8°. . . . 3712
Saunders (Laurence).
Holland (H.). Heroologia (p. 159). *A. Buchel.* [1620.] F°. . 6642
Scott (Thomas), of Utrecht.
Vox popvli. 1622-4. 4°. 6948
Segar (Sir W.). *F. Delaram sc. T. Jenner exc.* F°. 5119 (prefixed to 2575)
Shakespeare (W.). Comedies. *M. Droeshout.* 1623. F°. . . . 3972
,, ,, ,, 1632. F°. . . . 4619
Shakespeare (William). Poems. *W. Marshall.* 1640. 8°. . . . 4681
Sibbs (R.). The riches of mercie. 1638. 12°. 5168
(aet. 58) 1639. The returning backslider. 4°. 4480
Sidney (Sir Henry).
Holland (H.). Heroologia (p. 67) .*A. Buchel.* [1620.] F°. . 6642
Sidney (Sir Philip).
Holland (H.). Heroologia (p. 71). *A. Buchel.* [1620.] F°. . 6642
Smith (John), of New England.
Mercator (G.). Historia. 1635. F°. 4637
Somerset (Edward Seymour, Duke of).
Holland (H.). Heroologia (p. 28). *A. Buchel.* [1620.] F°. . 6642
Speed (John). A prospect. 1627. F°. 3874
[1629.] The historie. 1632. F°. 3885
Stuart (House of). The true description. 1603. F°. . . . 6375
Sutton (Thomas).
Holland (H.). Heroologia (p. 127). [1620.] F°. 6642

Taylor (John), water poet. Workes. 1630. F°. 3812
Taylor (Thomas), D.D. Christs victorie. *W. Marshall.* 1633. 4°. . 4277
Tindale (W.).
Holland (H.). Heroologia (p. 147). *A. Buchel.* [1620.] F°. . 6642
Verheiden (J.). History (p. 214). 1637. 8°. . . . 3712

No.

Totnes (George Carew, Earl). Stafford (T.). Pacata Hibernia. *After Vandyck by Voerst.* 1633. F°. 4577
Turkey, Sultans of.
Knolles (R.). The generall history. 1621. F°. 2451
" " 1631. F°. . . . 2462
" " 1638. F°. 2467

Van der Nort (Oliver). *See* Noort.
Vaughan (Richard).
Holland (H.). Heroologia (p. 231). *A. Buchel.* [1620.] F°. . 6642
Vermigli (Pietro Martire).
Verheiden (J.). History (p. 115). 1637. 8°. 3712

Walsingham (Sir Francis).
Holland (H.). Heroologia (p. 82). [1620.] F°. . . . 6642
Warwick (Ambrose Dudley, earl of).
Holland (H.). Heroologia (p. 79). [1620.] F°. 6642
Weever (John). Ancient Funerall Monuments. 1631. F°. . . 3991
Whitaker (William).
Holland (H.). Heroologia (p. 212). *A Buchel.* [1620.] F°. . 6642
Verheiden (J.). History (p. 356). 1637. 8°. 3712
White (Francis), bp. A replie. 1624. F°. 2453
Whitehead (David).
Holland (H.). Heroologia (p. 172). [1620.] F°. . . . 6642
Whitgift (J.), abp. Paule (Sir G.). The life. 1612. 4°. . . 3397
Holland (H.). Heroologia (p. 223). *A. Buchel.* [1620.] F°. . 6642
Verheiden (J.). History (p. 319). 1637. 8°. . . . 3712
Williams (John), Abp. (Portrait.) *For T. Jenner.* F°. . . 5120
Wolsey (T.).
Holland (H.). Heroologia (p. 15). [1620.] F°. 6642
Wyat (Sir T.).
Leland (J.). Næniæ. 1542. 4°. 720
Wyclif (John).
Bale (J.). Illustrium scriptorum. 1548. 4°. . . . 6314–5
Verheiden (J.). History (p. 190). 1637. 8°. 3712
The true copye. 1550. 8°. 1093

Zanchius (Hieronymus).
Verheiden (J.). History (p. 122). 1637. 8°. 3712
Zwingli (Ulrich).
Verheiden (J.). History (p. 40). 1637. 8°. 3712

INDEX VI.

MUSIC.

MUSIC.

No.

Amner (John). Sacred Hymnes. 1615. 4°. 2030
Anerio (Felice).
  Morley (T.). Canzonets. 1597. 4°. 2332

Bassano (Giovanni).
  Morley (T.). Canzonets. 1597. 4°. 2332
Bathe (W.). Briefe Introduction. [1596?] 8°. 1604
Bennett (John).
  Ravenscroft (T.). A briefe discourse. 1614. 4°. . . 2029
Bible. English. Psalms. Metrical.
  [For editions of Sternhold and Hopkins containing music *see* General Catalogue.]
  The whole Psalter. (By Abp Parker.) [1567?] 4°. . . 892
  Book of Common Order. 1596. 8°. 5919
  The CL. Psalmes. 1615. 5953
  Segar (F.). Certayne Psalmes. 1553. 8°. 921
  Slatyer (W.). Psalmes. 1634. 12°. 5017
  Daman (W.). The psalmes. 1579. Oblong 8°. 857
  (France & Germany.) All the French Psalm tunes. 1632. 12°. 3993
  [Ps. cxxvij, cxxx.] Whetstone (G.). The honourable reputation. 1586. 4°. 6495
  (Latin.) Buchanan (G.). Psalmorum paraphrasis. 1640. 12°. 5209
 Lamentations. The Lamentations. 1587. 8°. 1944
 Acts. Tye (C.). The actes. [1553?] 8°. 945
Braithwaite (William). His maiesties graciovs grant. 1636. 4°. . 7029
  Victorinus (G.). Siren Coelestis. 1638. 4°. 4905
Brathwaite (William). *See* Braithwaite.
Braythwaite (William). *See* Braithwaite.
Buchanan (G.). Psalmorum Davidis. 1640. 12°. 5209
Bull (John).
  Daman (W.). The psalmes of David. 1579. Long 8°. . . . 857
Butler (C.). The principles of musick. 1636. 4°. 4860
Byrd (W.). *See above*, Index I, p. 71.

Carols.
  Slatyer (W.). Psalmes or Songs. [1634.] 12°. . . . 5017
Caus (S de). Institution harmonique. 1615. F°. 7970
Common Prayer (noted). 1550. 4°. 619
Coprario (J.). Songs of Mourning. 1613. F°. 3203
Croce (Giovanni).
  Morley (T.). Canzonets. 1597. 4°. 2332

Daman (W.). The psalmes of David. 1579. Long 8°. . . . 857
Dowland (John).
  Ornithoparcus (Andreas). Micrologus. 1609. F°. . . . 3387

Fetherstone (Christopher). Lamentations. 1587. 8°. . . . 1944

Guido Aretinus. Dimension and perfect Vse of the Monochord. *See* Ornithoparcus (A.). Micrologus 1609. F°. 3387

No.

Holborne (William).
  Holborne (A.). The Cittharn Schoole. 1597. 4°. 2331
Hunnis (W.). Seven sobs. 1589. 12°. 1437

Ive (Simon).
  Shirley (J.). The trivmph of peace. 1633. 4°. 4893

'Labandalashot' (Tune).
  Rhodes (J.). An Answere. 1602. 4°. 2879
Lawes (Henry). [A paraphrase upon the Psalmes.]
  Sandys (G.). A paraphrase upon the divine poems. 1638. F°. . 4736
Lawes (William).
  Shirley (J.). The trivmph of peace. 1633. 4°. . . . 4893
Liturgies. Common Prayer (noted). 1550. 4°. 619
Lute Music, Book for. [Ab. 1600?] F°. . . . . . no. 7730

Marbeck (Jo.). Common Prayer. 1550. 4°. 619
Morley (Thomas). *See above*, Index I, p. 247.
Mundy (J.). Songs and Psalmes. 1594. 4°. 1603

Neapolitan tunes.
  (No no no no.) Sidney (Sir P.). Arcadia (p. 497). 1621. F°. 6022
  Villanelle ,, ,, (p. 498). 1621. F°. . . 6022
  Wilhelmus von Nassau ,, (p. 495). 1621. F°. . . 6022

Ornithoparcus (A.). Micrologus. 1609. F°. 3387

Peirs (Edward). *See* Piers.
Piers or Peirs (Edward).
  Ravenscroft (T.). A briefe discourse. 1614. 4°. 2029
Psalms. *See* Bible.

Ravenscroft (T.). A briefe discourse. 1614. 4°. 2029

Segar (Francis). Certayne Psalmes. 1553. 8°. 921
Slatyer (William). Psalmes or Songs of Sion intended for Christmas Carols. (With table of Tunes.) [1634.] 12°. . . . 5017
Solmization Letters.
  Psalms (Sternhold). [Ab. 1574.] 4°. 7120
  ,, ,, 1637. 4°. 3968
Syddael (W.). A Dial Song. *See* Butler (C.). The Principles of Musik (p. 43). 1636. 4°. 4860

Tailor (R.). Sacred Hymns. 1615. 4°. 3413
Tunes. *See* Labandalashot. 2879
  — Neapolitan Tunes. 6022
Tye (Christopher). The actes of the apostles. 1553. 8°. . . 945

Vecchi (Horatio).
  Morley (T.). Canzonets. 1597. 4°. 2332
Viadana (Ludovico).
  Morley (T.). Canzonets. 1597. 4°. 2332
Victorinus (G.). Siren Coelestis. 1638(–9). 4°. 5905
Vogelsang or Vogelgesang (Andreas). *See* Ornithoparcus (A.).

Ward (J.). Madrigals. 1613. 4°. 3401
Wilhelmus von Nassau (Tune). 1621. 6022
Wither (G.). The hymnes and songs of the Chvrch. 1623. 8°. . 4921

Youll (H.). Canzonets. 1608. 4°. 1618

INDEX VII.

BIBLIOGRAPHICA.

BIBLIOGRAPHICA.

No.
Ampersand. (Four kinds used on one page.) 7255

'Biblioscopus' to Henry VIII. Delaine (W.). 1540. . . . 678
Binders.
Gatchet (J.). 1509. p. 1227.
NS [=N. Spering?] 6159, 6160
W. (R.). *See* Wolfe (R.).
Wolfe (R.). 1547. . . . 682 and note on no. 725 (p. 1731).
Book-plate. *See* Marks of ownership.
Borders (Books printed within).
Primer (Sarum). 68
Ab. 1510. Canutus. 7071
1521. Primer (Sarum). 4°. 6213
1534. Primer (Sarum). 4°. 6176
[158–.] R. (J.). Pathway to Salvation. 16°. 6768
1584. Bull (H.). Christian Prayers. 1645
1594. Morley (T.). Madrigalls. 1602
1594. Mundy (J.). Songs. 1603
1609. Jenkinson (A.). Meditations. 12°. 3206
1613. C. (W.). The Ambassador. 3647
1618. Hieron (S.). Helpe unto devotion. 12°. . . . 3798
1601. Sutton (C.). Godly meditations. 12°. 7333
1613. C. (W.). The ambassador. 12°. 3647
1624. Luther (M.). Every dayes sacrifice. 12°. 7409
1624. Norden (J.). Imitation. 12°. 7952
Broadsides, single sheets, etc.
[ab. 1496.] Proclamation. F°. 7064–5
[ab. 1505.] Boston Parish Church. 294
[1507?] Proclamation. 7072
1509. Henry VIII. Articles. 256
[1515?] Indulgence of Leo X. 300
1517. Indulgence to St Thomas of Acres. 301
1547. Lamentation of the death of Henry VIII. . . . 1018
1548. Proclamation. 7094
1551. Proclamation. 621
1571. Burghley (W. Cecil Lord). Carmen Gratulatorium. . 6752
1580–1588. Cambridge Act Verses. F°. *See above*, Index I, p. 76.
1588. Pile of Troy Waightes. 1691
1619. Proclamation on Tobacco. 2806
1620. Manufacture of Starch. 2664
1625. Cambridge. Articles and Orders. 7868–9
[ab. 1625?] English Benedictines. 6612
1627. Jan. 29. Letters Patent. 2831
1630. Jan. 23. Proclamation. 7424
1630. Aug. 6. Letters Patent. 2673
1636. Almanack. 7675

Caligraphy.
1569. Perret. 7684
[ab. 159–?] 7959

No.

Caligraphy, *cont.*
1628. De Bry. 6632
1636. Davies (J.). The writing Schoolmaster. . . . 4340
Catalogus universalis pro nundinis Francofurtensibus. 1623. 4°. 7842
Chained Books. 1588. Case (J.). Sphaera. 5231
Chromotypography. *See* Colour-printing.
Colour-printing.
1597. Broughton (H.). 2195
1625. Wilkinson (R.). Stripping of Joseph. . . . 3160
1631. Reeve (W.). Christian divinitie. 4960
(Corrections of manuscripts.)
1633. Clement I. Ἐπιστόλη πρώτη. 4°. 5398
Coloured Books.
1508. Missale (Sarum). 6231
1570. Matthew of Westminster. 1219
1570. Foxe (J.). 816
1572–4. Parker (M.). De antiquitate. 890
1579. Saxton (C.). Maps. 6765
1588. Braun (G.). 7732–3
1607. Camden (W.). Britannia. 1758
1612. Maniement d'Armes. 4°. 6647
1622. Brooke (R.). Discoverie. F°. 2793
1629. Parkinson (J.). Paradisus. F°. 2561
1631. Mercator. Atlas. F°. 7742
'Corrector praeli.' 1619. 5689

Factotum Initials. *See* Initial Letters (Factotum).
French Pronunciation. *See* Phonetic.

Initial Letters.
Initial directors. 1574. 6760
(Factotum.) 1577. ['Gardiner and Dawson.'] . . . 7315
Initial P (Heraldic.) 1548. Bale (J.). 6314
Interlinear printing.
[Ab. 1508.] Stanbridge (J.). [W. de Worde. 1508?] 4°. . 234
[Ab. 15–.] Terentius. Vulgaria. ,, ... 245
1518. Whittington (R.). De heteroclitis nominibus. 4°. . . 5220
1525. ,, ,, ,, W. de Worde. 4°. 188
1525. ,, Grammatica. ,, 4°. 190
1525. ,, Verborum praeterita. ,, 4°. 191
1526. ,, ,, ,, ,, 4°. 193
1640. Psalterium. 4°. 4400

Map-printer.
3864. G. Low. 1624.
Marks of ownership.
Whippey (G.). [1596?] 1605
[Name printed in.] Harttun (James). 1567. . . 1397, 6414
— Dyson (Humphry). 1611. 7234
Plym (Adam). 2927
(Initials only.) Rogers (Tho.). 'TR.' [Ab. 155–.] . . 7771
— Book plate.
1574. Bacon (Nicholas). 7966
1587. Nowell (R.). 6788
Ab. 1590. Tomlinson (R.). 6797
Cambridge. Queens' College. [Ab. 1618.] 6912
1618. Suckling (Sir J.). 6912

Paper (Green).
Common Prayer [1578?]. 4°. . . . . . . 1687=7288

No.

Paper (Yellow).
Bible. N.T. (Tindale.) 1536. 4°. 6080
Primer. [1535?] 4°. 576
Bible. Eng. N.T. 1539. 8°. 6103
Epistles and Gospels. [1540?] 4°. 6684
Bible. The Great Bible. 1552. 4°. 1025
Psalms. (Sternhold.) 1579. 4°. 856
Littleton. Tenures. 1591. 8°. 1151
Fitzherbert (Sir A.). La novel Natura Brevium. 1598. 8°. . 2385
— (Cotton.) Selden (J.). Marmora. 1628. 4°. . . . 3171
Phonetic Spelling.
1569. Hart (J.). Orthographie. 933
1621. Gill (A.). Logonomia. 3803
1633. Butler (C.). English Grammar. 5435
(French) [two types]. *See* Desainliens (C). . 1541, 1542 (and note on p. 1733).

Phonetic type.
1636. Butler (C.). Principles. 4860
'Praeli Corrector.' *See* Camb. Univ. Lacrymae (p. 87). 1619. . 5689
Printing trade.
1623. Proclamations. 7449
1625. ,, ... 7453
1637. Star-chamber. Decree. 2695
Printsellers.
Jenner (Thomas). 1602—1631.
Holland (Compton). 1624
Low (George). 1624.
Peake (W.). Ab. 1625.
Reeve (J.). 1630.
Peake (Robert). 1636—1640.
Richardson (W.). 'Feb. 1 [17]96.' 5770
Privilege for books.
1574. Philippes. 1528
Pronunciation (French). *See* Phonetic Spelling.

Seals.
Benedict, St, Order of (Douai). 1625? 6612
Shorthand. 'Characterie.'
Bales (P.). The Writing Schoolemaster. 1590. 4°. . . 2205
Smith (H.). Benefite. 1590. 8°. 7355
Smith (H.). Examination. 1591. 8°. 7368
Willis (J.). Schoolmaister. 1622. 3341
Signature title 'm.' 6160
Solmization Letters.
Psalms (Sternhold). [Ab. 1574.] 4°. 7120
,, 1637. 4°. 3968
Stenography. *See* Shorthand.
Subscribers (List). 1617. Minsheu. 7850

Tachygraphy. *See* Shorthand.
'Trade' editions. . . . . . Cf. nos. 4406, 4600, 4683 *etc.*
Type, Anglo-Saxon.
[1567?] Testimonie. 8°. 895
1571. Gospels. 822
1574. Asser. 870
1593. Norden (J.). 6804
1598. [Types of J. Browne.] *See* p. 1737 (note on p. 662).
1600. Camden (W.). 2057
1607. Coke. 3227–8
1617. Minsheu (J.). 3204

No.

Type, Anglo-Saxon, *cont.*
1623. Lisle (W.). Saxon Treatises. 4785
1637. Camden (W.). Britannia. 3055
[1640?] Lambarde (W.). 4941
1640. Psalterium. . . . . . . 4400 (note on p. 1740)
— Arabic.
1639. Greaves (T.). De linguae Arabicae utilitate. . . 5492–3
1639. Vicars (J.). 5007
— Greek.
1521. Cambridge. 4°. 5503
1541. Whitford (R.). 711
1546. Gardiner (S.). [8 pages.] 761
1547. Gilby (A.). Answer (fol. VIII *b*). 775
1551. Gardiner (S.). [Rouen?] 6718
1554. Martin (T.). Traictise. 1193
1586. Act Verses. Cambridge. 5524
[1587?] ,, ,, ... 5531
1592. N.T. 1692
1598. Barlow. 1707
1592. L'Espine. 5552
1621. Savile (Sir H.). Oxford. 5340
1630. Slatyer (W.). 4433
1632. [Sir Henry Savile's type.] Testament. Cambridge. . 5797
1636. Selden (J.). De Successionibus. 5106
1638. Boughen (E.). Sermon. 5149
— Hebrew.
1568. [Preface to Psalms.] R. Jugge. 964
1579. Baron (B.). In Jonam. 850
1587. Cambridge. Lacrymae. J. Windet. . . . 2123
1592. Rhys (J. D.). . . . . . 2515 (note on p. 1735)
[1595?] Broughton. [G. Simson? 1595?] 4°. 7773
1596. Broughton (H.). Daniel. R. Field. 1596. 4°. . 2237
1597. ,, ,, G. Simson. 2195
1617. Minsheu. F°. 3204
1623. Shaw (J.). 7381
1625. Nettles (S.). Answer. Oxford. 5353
[1633?] Alabaster (W.). Spiraculum. W. Jones. . . . 5057
1636. Selden (J.). De successionibus. 5106
— Irish type (large Dublin). 1602. 6013
1608. 6014
1632. 6040
— — (small.) 1639. 6069
— Louvain. Desiderius. 1616. 6427
Mac Caghwell (H.). 1618. 6428
O'Hussey. [1619.] 6429
,, Poems. 7941
— Italic type.
Cicero. W. de Worde. 1534. 8°. 208
Liturgia. 1551. 8°. 1097
Perussellus. 1551. 8°. 1098
Lasco. 1552. 1100
[Abp. Parker's[1].] Parker (M.). De antiquitate. 1572. . . 831–2
— Saxon type. *See* Anglo-saxon type.
— Secretary type.
1620. Melvin (A.). Musae. 7681
Ab. 1640. Form of agreement. 7060
— Syriac type.
1618. Rive (E.). Heptaglottie. 3325

[1] See T. B. Reed, *History*.

No.

Type, Anglo-Saxon, *cont.*
1621. Heigham (J.). [St Omer?] 6545
1621. Fitzherbert (T.). 6544
1639. Vicars (J.). Decapla. 5007
— Type sideways, impression of. 1528. 6186

Vellum printing.
1482. Lathbury (J.). Liber moralium. F°. 75
1482. Horae (Sarum). 8°. 98
1494. ,, ,, 4°. 68
1498. ,, ,, 8°. 134
1498. ,, ,, 8°. 137
1499. Robertus Castellensis. 107
1504. Missale Sarum. 6144
1508. Fisher (J.). Treatise. 155
[1508.] Breviarium (Sarum). 7073
[1510?] Processionale. 7076
1511. Missale (Sarum). 6152
1514. ,, ,, ... 6153
1516. Missale (York). 6233
1520. Missale (Sarum). 270
1521. Christine de Pisan. Body of Policy. 355
1522. Tunstall (C.). De arte svppvtandi. 280
1526. Missale (Sarum). 6162
1532. ,, ,, ... 6170
1534. ,, ,, ... 6173
1537. Calendar (Xylographic). 7063
1555. Missale (Sarum). 6194
1572. Parker (M.). 831–2
1596. Broughton (H.). Concent. 2192
1640. Form of Agreement. 7060
1640? License. 7061
Virgil commas. Lord's Prayer. [1538.] 6681
[Half way through this volume only.] 1551. 6718

Xylography. 1538. Calendar. 7063

INDEX VIII.

SUPPLEMENT TO INDEX I.

SUPPLEMENT TO INDEX I.

No.
A. (R.). Verses in Simson (A.). Hieroglyphica. 1622. . . . 7992
A. (R.). Verses in Gaule (J.). Defiance. 1630. 8057
Abbot (Robert), *Bp.* *See* Petrucci (L.). Apologia. 1619. 4°. . 7983
Abecedarium. *See* Huloet (R.).
Acts. *See* Statutes.
Acuña (Hernando de). *See* La Marche (O. de). Resolved Gentleman. 1594. 4°. 7920
Adams (Francis). Writing Tables with a Kalender. 1594. 16°. . 8016
Æquivoca. 1514. 4°. 7942
Albert. *See* Godfridus. 7965
Alessio. Secretes. Part 1. 1558. 4°. 8067
Aleyn (Charles). *See* Pius II. Historie of Eurialus. 1639. 8°. . 7913
'Ali ibn Rudwan. *See* Godfridus. 7965
Alkindus (Jacobus). *See* Godfridus. 7965
Allen (Charles), Gent. *See* Aleyn.
Aloysius Gonzaga. *See* Gonzaga.
Angell (Christopher). [Letters testimonial. 1618?] F°. . . 8066
Aphthonius. Praeexercitamenta. [Ab. 1520.] 4°. . . . 8013
Apsley (Charles). *See* Richeome (L.). Holy Pictures. 1619. 4°. 6618
Arminians. *See* Proclamation. 1618. 4°. 7914
Arnhem. *See* Proclamation. 1618. 4°. 7914
Articles (Province of Canterbury) whereupon it was agreed. 157-. 4°. 8017
Arundel (Philip Howard, Earl of). 1583. *See* J. Charlwood, Printer. Page 275.
Ashe (T.). Ἐπιείκεια. 1609. 8°. 7984

B. (H.), *Rector of S. Matthew's, Friday Street.* *See* Burton (H.).
Bade (Jos.), Ascensius. *See* Sulpicius (J.). Grammatica. [Ab. 1505.] 4°. 7946
Bagshaw (Christopher). Relatio compendiosa. [1601?] 4°. . . 6836
Bagvley (H.). *See* Hall (J.). Works (p. 533). 1625. F°. . . 7909
Baker (Samuel). [Licence.] 1638. 7760
Baldwin (W.). Treatise of Morall Philosophie. 1600. 8°. . . 7975
Bale (J.) Christen Exhortation unto customable swearers. 154- etc., 6706, 1027, 1028.
Barbier (J.). Ianua linguarum quadrilinguis. 1617. 4°. . . . 7923
Barfeldus (L.). Verses in Rider (J.). Dictionarie. 1612. . . 8073
Barlement (N.). Colloquia et dictionariolum octo linguarum. Venetiis, 1627. 10°. 7934
Barlow (John). Exposition of Timothie etc. 1632. F°. . . 8004
Barneveld (J. van). *See* Oldenbarneveld.
Basterd (Thomas). Verses in Rider (J.). Dictionarie. 1612. . . 8073
Baynes (Paul). Commentarie upon...Ephesians. 1618. 4°. . . 7908
Beard (Thomas). Theatre of God's Judgment. (Abridgment by E. Rudierd.) 1618. 4°. 3327

No.
Beaumont (John). Verses in Drayton (M.). Poems. 1630. 8°. . 7926
Becanus (M.). The New man. 1622. 4°. 4172–3
Bell (Thomas). Speculation of Usurie. 1596. 4° 8078
Bendloes (William). Cases. *See* Ashe (T.). 'Επιείκεια. 1609. 8°. . 7984
Bene fundatum. [1527?] 4°. 8064
'Bercleus (Thomas).' *See* Statutes (Abridgment). 1521–8. 8°. . 8027
Bible (Polyglot). Daniel. [Ab. 1595.] 4°. 7773
Bible, English (Cranmer). Ed. 7. Grafton, 1540 (Dec. 1541). F°. . 7981
English (Royal). Edinburgh, 1634. 12°. 7927
Psalms (Sternhold). The whole booke. 1635. 12°. . . 7928
— — G. Miller. 1639. 8°. . . . . . . 4429 (corr.)
Song of Solomon. *See* Wilson (T.). Christian Dictionary. 1616. 4°. 7964
New Testament (Genevan). L. Tomson's revision. London, 1582. 8°. 7986
Ephesians. *See* Baynes (P.). Commentarie. 1618. . . 7908
Hebrews. *See* Wilson (T.). Christian Dictionary. 1616. 4°. 7964
Revelation. *See* Wilson (T.). Christian Dictionary. 1616. 4°. . 7964
Bible, Latin. Psalms. *See* Buchanan (G.). Paraphrasis. 1580. . 8054
Blandie or Blandy (William). *See* Osorio (J.). Five Bookes. 1576. 7972
Boanerges. Or...Supplication of...Scotland. 1624. 4°. . . 7960
Boetius (Joannes). *See* Boys (J.).
Bond (John). *See* Horatius. Poemata. 1608. 8°. 7968
Book. A boke of the propertyes of herbes. 1546. 8°. . . 7954
— Booke of Christian Questions and Answers. 1581. 8°. . 8052
Boraston (W.). *See* Vicary (T.). Englishman's Treasure. Ed. 8. 1633. 4°. 4207
Bouman (Maximilian). *See* Guillemeau (J.). French Chirurgerye. 1597. 8025
Bound (Nic.). [One entry in error under 'Bound'.] *See* Bownde.
Boys (John). The autumne part. 1612. 4°. 8022
Braithwait (Richard). *See* Brathwaite.
Brinsley (John). *See* Stanbridge (J.). Embryon. 1624. 4°. . 7961
Broke (Sir Robert). *See* Pulton (F.). De pace. 1610. . . . 3244
Brooks (James). A sermon...newly imprinted. 1554. 8°. . . 7899
Buchanan (George). Paraphrasis psalmorum et Jephthes. 1580. 16°. 8054
Budden (John). Verses in Rider (J.). Dictionarie. 1612. 4°. . 8073
Bull (John), *instrument maker*. 1582. *See* no. 7931.
Burton (Henry). Truth's Triumph over Trent. 1629. 4°. . 8002
Burton (Robert). *See* Rider (J.). Dictionarie. 1612. 4°. . . 8073
Butterwike (John). Verses in Osorio (J.). Five Bookes. 1576. . 7972

C. (E.). Verses in Dod and Cleaver. 1609. 8079
— *See* Baynes (P.). Commentarie upon...Ephesians. 1618. 4°. 7908
C. (W.), *B.C.L.* Decimarum et Oblationum Tabula. 1635. 4°. . 4151
C. (W.). *See* Covell (William). Polimanteia.
Caesar (C. J.). Commentarii. 1601. 16°. 7967
Cæsius. *See* Cesi.
Calligraphy. [Fragment. Ab. 1570?] 7959
Cambridge. Map. [Ab. 1596.] F°. 8070
Camden (Baptist, *Viscount*). *See* Campden.
Camden (W.). Institutio graecae grammatices. 1595. 8°. . . 8053
Campden (Baptist Hicks, *Viscount*). *See* Gaule (J.). Defiance. 1630. 8057
Casas. *See* Las Casas.
Case (John). Verses in Rider (J.). Dictionarie. 1612. 4°. . . 8073
Caus (S. de). Institution harmonique. 1615. F°. . . . 7970
Cepari (V.). Life of B. Aloysius Gonzaga. Paris, 1627. 8°. . . 8049
Cesi (Federico), *Cardinal*. *See* Lynde (Sir H.). Via Tuta. Ed. 3. 1629. 7890
Cespedes y Meneses (Gonzalo de). Gerardo the Unfortunate. Trans. L. Digges. 1622. 4°. 7973
Champney (Antony). Answer to a pamphlet. 1623. 4°. . . 6552
— — *See* C. (A.). True relations. 1626. 4°. . . . 6555
Chapman (Geo.). Verses in Holland (H.). Heroologia (p. 51). [1620.] F°. 6642

No.
Christen Exhortation. *See* Bale (J.).
Christian Questions. *See* Book of Christian Questions. 1581. 8°. 8052
Chrysostom (John). Homiliae sex. Oxonii, 1586. 8°. . . . 8041
Cicero. De officiis, etc. 1628. 8°. 8011
Cleaver (Robert). *See* Dod (J.) and R. Cleaver.
Clerke (William). *See* Directorium. 1503. 4°. 7939
Coke (Sir Edward). *See* Pulton (F.). De pace. 1610. . . 3244
Cole (Humphrey), *instrument maker*. 1582. *See* no. 7931.
Colloquia et dictionariolum octo linguarum. 1627 etc. *See* Barlement (N.). 7934 *etc.*
Colvenerius (G.). [Approbatio.] *See* M. (Ch.). Paraphrasticall...discourses. 1635. 8°. 7894
Common Prayer. [Ab. 1572?] 8°. 8037
Cornwallis (Sir William). Miraculous and happie Union. 1604. 4°. 7988
Corvinus (Antonius). Postill or collection. 1550. 4°. . . . 8014
Covell (William). Polimanteia. 1595. 4°. 5571
Crane (Robert). Verses in Rider (J.). Dictionarie. 1612. 4°. . 8073
Crosse (William). *See* Sallustius. Workes. 1629. 12°. . . 8034
Culverwel (Ezekiel). *See* Rogers (R.). Seven treatises. 1603. . 7938

D. (F.). Verses in Sallust. 1629. 12°. 8034
Dalison (William). Cases. *See* Ashe (T.). 'Επιείκεια. 1609. 8°. 7984
Darcie (A.). Honour of Ladies. 1622. 8°. 8012
Davenport (John). *See* Scudder (H.). The christians daily walke. 1637.
Davies (John). Antiquae linguae britannicae rudimenta. 1621. 8°. 8077
De Caus (S.). *See* Caus.
Declinator and Protestation. 1638. 1639. 4°. . . 5155 (and p. 1741)
De Gray (Thomas). *See* Gray (T. de).
De La Grey (T.). *See under* Gray (T. de).
Dering (E.). Sermon. 25 Feb. 1569. 1586. 8°. 7978
Des Gallars (N.). True report of...the assembly...at Poyssy. [1561?] 8°. 8035
Deseoso. *See* Desiderius.
Dictionary. Eng. Lat. By R. Huloet. 1552. F°. 7937
Dictionary (Lat. Eng.). Rider (J.). Ed. 3. By F. Holyoke. 1612. . 8073
— — — 1640. 4° 3058
— — — Dictionarium quadruplex. 1638. 4186
— — — *See* Veron (J.). Dictionarie. 1584. 4°. . . 7958
Diestemius (Cornelius). Verses in Pelegromius (S.). 1603. . . 7881
Digges (Leonard). *See* Cespedes (G. de). Gerardo. 1622. 4°. . 7973
Dillington (Rob.). Verses in La Marche (O. de). Resolved Gentleman. 1594. 4°. 7920
Direction for the English Traveller. 1635. 8°. 8082
Directorium Sacerdotum (C. Maidstone). Antwerp, 1488. 4°. . 7808
— 1495. 4°. . . . . 8081=43
— R. Pynson. 1503. 4°. 7939
Dochen (Tho.). Verses in Rider (J.). Dictionarie. 1612. . . 8073
Dod (John) and R. Cleaver. Ten Commandments. 1609. 4°. . 8079
Donato (L.), *Doge*. *See* Petrucci (L.). Apologia. 1619. 4°. . . 7983
Dove (John). Verses in Rider (J.). Dictionarie. 1612. 4°. . 8073
Downham (John). Foure treatises etc. 1609. 4°. 7901
Treatise against lying. 1636. 4°. 7903
Treatise of anger. 1609. 4°. 7902
Drant (Thomas). Verses in Foxe (J.). Actes. 1583. . . . 865
Draxe (T.). Bibliotheca scholastica. 1633. 8°. 7915
Drayton (M.). Poems. 1630. 8°. . . . . . . 7930=3175
Du Bartas (G.). Part of Du Bartas. [Fr. and Eng.]. 1625. 4°. 8083
Du Nesme (Jean). Sonnets upon the (late) miraculous peace in Fraunce. Trans. J. Sylvester. *See* Du Bartas (G.). Devine Weekes. 4°. 1605–6. 2476
Dunfermline (Alexander Seton, Earl of). *See* Statutes (Scotland). 1612. 7989

No.
Dunfermline (Alexander, Earl of). [Death.] Verses in Simson (A.). Hieroglyphica. 1622. 7992
Dyer (Sir James). *See* Pulton (F.). De pace. 1610. . . 3244

E. (G.). *See* Theodoretus. Ecclesiastical History. 1612. 4°. . 7982
Eburne (Richard). Twofold Tribute of Subjects. 1613. 4°. 2984 (corr.)
Edward IV. *See* Habington (W.). Historie. 1640. . . 8055
Egerton (Stephen). *See* Rogers (R.). Seven treatises. 1603. F°. . 7938
Elizabeth, Queen. *See* Petition directed. [Ab. 1590.] 4°. . . 7916
Engelen (E.). *See* Proclamation. 1618. 4°. 7914
England. Church. *See* Petition. [Ab. 1590.] 4°. . . . 7916
England. Miraculous and happie union. 1604. 4°. . . . 7988
English Traveller. By J. van Langeren. 1635. 8°. . . 8082
Epictetus. Manuell. Trans. by J. Sanford. 1567. 8°. . . 8038
Este (Thomas). Psalms. 1592. 8°. 1601
Estmond (John). Verses in Rider (J.). Dictionarie. 1612. . . 8073
Everard (John), *D.D.* The arriereban. 1618. 8°. . . . 7925
Exercise of a faithfull soule. [Text title.] [16—.] 8°. . . 7910
Exhortation. An exhortacyon to avoyde false doctryne. *See* Answere to a papystycall exhortacyon. [1548?] 6696

Farnaby (Thomas). *See* Juvenalis et Persius. Satyrae. 1612. 8°. 8039
Fennor (William). Compters Common Wealth. 1617. 4°. . 3917 (corr.)
Ferrarius (H.), *Badisleius*. *See* Ferrers (H.).
Ferrers (Henry). Verses in Osorio (J.). Five Bookes. 1576. . . 7972
Fiery Trial. Fierie Tryall of Gods saints. 1612. 4°. . . 8080
Fish (S.). *See* More (Sir T.). The supplycacyon of soulys. [1529.] F°. 7930
Fisher (John), *Jesuit*. *See* D. (A.).
Fitzherbert (Sir Antony). *See* Pulton (F.). De pace. 1610. F°. 3244
Fleming (Abraham). *See* Veron (J.). Dictionarie. 1584. 4°. . 7958
Fletcher (Giles), the elder. Verses in Foxe (J.). Actes. 1583. . 865
Fletcher (William). Verses in Rider (J.). Dictionarie. 1612. 4°. 8073
Florus (L.). Epitome. *See* Livius. 1589. 8°. . . 2048, 7976
Forbes (John), *of Corse*. A peaceable warning. Aberdene, 1638. 4°. 7962
Form of Prayers. *See* Book of Common Order. 1584. . . 6777–8
Foster (William). Verses in Osorio (J.). Five Bookes. 1576. . 7972
Foxe (John). Actes & Monumentes. Vol. II. (title). 1597. F°. 8031
France. Restorer of the French Estate. 1589. 4°. . . 8036

G. (R.), S.D.M. *See* Defence of Contraries. 1593.
Gallasius (Nicholas). *See* Des Gallars (N.).
Garey (S.). Great Britaines little Calendar. 1618. (Frag.) 3797 (corrected)
Garlandia (J. de). Synonyma et Equivoca. [1514.] 4°. . . 7942
Gataker (T.). Marriage duties. 1620. 4°. 3333
Gaule (J.). Defiance of Death. 1630. 12°. 8057
Gelderlandt, Council at. *See* Proclamation. 1618. 4°. . . 7914
Gifford (G.). A godlie zealous and profitable sermon. 1583. 8°. . 7977
Gildredge (Nicholas). Bookplate. 1633. 8028
Gil Polo (Gaspar). *See* Montemayor (J. de). Diana. Pt 3. 1598. F°. 7924
Glanville (John). Verses in Rider (J.). Dictionarie. 1612. 4°. . 8073
Glorierius (Cæs.). *See* Lynde (Sir H.). Via Tuta. 1629. . . 7890
Gobam, *ambassador*. *See* Murad IV. A Vaunting Letter. 1638. 4°. 7963
Godelevaeus (Wilhelmus). *See* Livius. 1589. 8°. . . 2048, 7976
Godfridus. The Knowledge of things unknown. 1640. 8°. . . 7965
Gonzaga (Aloysius). *See* Cepari (V.). Life. 1627. . . . 8049
Goulart (S). *See* Du Bartas. Part. 1625. 4°. 8083
Grafton (R.). Manuel of the Chronicles of Englande. 1565. 16°. 7943
Greek Grammar. *See* Camden (W.). Institutio. 1595 etc. . 8053 *etc.*
Greene (Thomas). Verses in Drayton (M.). Poems. 1630. 8°. . 7926

No.
Grellius (J.). *See* Livius. 1589. . . . . . 2048, 7976
Grenewey (Richard). *See* Tacitus. Annales &c. 1598. F°. . . 7956
Grimstone (E.). *See* Guillemard (I.). Combat. 1621. 12°. . 7979
Guevara (A. de). Familiar Epistles. Trans. E. Hellowes. 1577. 4°. 7919
Mount of Caluarie. Part 1. 1618. 4°. 7911
— — Part 2. 1597. 4°. 7912
Guil (John). Verses in Dod and Cleaver. 1609. 8079
Guillemard (I.). Combat betwixt Man and Death. 1621. 12°. . 7979
Guillemeau (Jacques). French Chirurgerye. 1597(-8). F°. . 8025
Gyer (N.). The English Phlebotomy. 1592. 8°. . . . 8003

H. (I.). *See* Harmer (J.). 7971
H. (R.)., *Coll. Nov.* Verses in Rider (J.). Dictionarie. 1612. . 8073
Habington (W.). Historie of Edward IV. 1640. F°. . . 8055
Hague. *See* Proclamation. 1618. 4°. 7914
Hakewill (G.). Scutum regium. J. Crosley. 1612. 8°. . . 8021
Hall (Joseph). Works. 1625(–4). F°. 7909
— Quo vadis? London, 1617. 8°. 8047
Hall (Robert). *See* Hall (J.). Works. 1625. F°. . . . 3909
Haly. *See* 'Ali ibn Rudwan. 7965
Hamond (John). *See* Cambridge. Map. Ab. 1596. . . . 8070
Harley (Richard). Verses in Rider (J.). Dictionarie. 1612. . 8073
Harmer (J.). *See* Lubin (E.). Clavis. 1640. 8°. . . . 7971
Harmer (John). *See* Chrysostom. Homiliae sex. 1586. 8°. . 8041
Hart (John). An orthographie. 1569. 8°. 8007
Hassel (Thomas). Verses in Drayton (M.). Poems. 1630. 8°. . 7926
Hellowes (Edward). *See* Guevara. Familiar Epistles. 1577. 4°. . 7919
Herbal. A boke of the propertyes. 1546. 8°. 7954
Hervet (Gentian). *See* Aphthonius. Praeexercitamenta. 4°. . . 8013
Heyward (E.). Verses in Drayton (M.). Poems. 1630. 8°. . 7926
Hieron (Samuel). Abridgement of the Gospell. 1609. 4°. . . 8029
Hieron (S.). Six sermons. 1608. 4°. 7997
— Three sermons. 1607. 4°. 7996
Hieron (S.). *See* Dispute upon the question of kneeling. 1608. 4°. 6386
Hieronymus Verlensis. *See* Verlensis.
Hodges (J.). *See above*, p. 323 note.
Holderus (Petrus). *See* Oldenbarneveld (J. van). 8076
Holland (H.). Baziliωlogia. . . . . Cf. no. 8055
Holland (Thomas). Verses in Rider (J.). Dictionarie. 1612. 4°. 8073
Holyoke (Francis). *See* Rider (J.). Dictionarie. 1612. 4°. . . 8073
Homelies. Tom. 1. 1569. 4°. 8018
— Tom. 2. 1567. 4°. 8019
Horatius. Poemata. Comm. J. Bond. Ed. 2. 1608. 8°. . . 7968
Houlderus (Robert). *See* Holderus (P.).
Howard (Philip), Earl of Arundel. 1583. *See* Arundel.
Howlet (Richard). *See* Huloet.
Huloet (R.). Abecedarium. 1552. F°. 7937
Hume (Alexander). Verses in Simson (A.). Hieroglyphica. 1622. 7992
Hurtado de Mendoza (Diego). Lazarillo de Tormes. 1634. 8°. . 8071
Husbandman's Practice. *See* Godfridus. 7965
Hutten (Robert). *See* Hutton.

Imprese. *See* Nos. 2108, 7983.
Insolubilia (ad usum shole paruisi, Oxon). [1527?] 4°. . . 8063
Institutio graecae grammatices. 1595 etc. *See* Camden (W.). 8053 *etc.*
Italicus (Peregrinus) de Lugo. Principia. [1506.] 4°. . . . 302

Jacob (Henry). Christian and modest offer. 1606. 4°. . . 6868
James I. Declaration...in matter of Bounty. 1619. 4°. . . 2805
James (Thomas). Verses in Rider (J.). Dictionarie. 1612. 4°. . 8073

No.
Janua linguarum quadrilinguis. 1617. *See* Barbier (J.).
Jonas (Justus). True hystorye of...M. Luther. [1546?] 8°. . 8040
Josephus. A Treatise. *See* Boetius (J.). The Fardle. 1555. . 1164
Jucundus (Joannes), *Veronensis*. *See* Caesar. Commentarii. 1601. 7967
Junius (Andreas). *See* Young.
Junius (R.). *See* Young (Ric.).
Juvenalis et Persius. Satyrae. 1612. 8°. 8039

Kellison (Matthew). Treatise of Eccl. Hierarchy. *See* Wilson (M.). Modest briefe discussion. 1630. 8°. 8050
Kiffen (Maur.). Verses in La Marche (O. de). Resolved Gentleman. 1594. 4°. 7920

L. (I.). *See* Saint Germain (C.). Exact Abridgement. 1630. . 7948
Langeren (Jacob van). Direction for the English Traveller. 1635. 8°. 8082
La Puente (Luis de). *See* Puente. Index I.
Lesk (W.). Sermon. 1617. 4°. 4059
Levens (P.). Right profitable...Pathway to Health. 1632. 4°. . 8046
Libellus Sophistarum. R. Pynson, London [about 1501–2]. 4°. . 8061
— [W. de Worde, ab. 1525?] 4°. 8062
Lisle (William). *See* Du Bartas. Part of Du Bartas. 1625. 4°. . 8083
Litany. *See* Exhortation unto prayer. 1544. 476–7
Livius. Libri omnes. 1589. 8°. 7976
— [Decas I.] *See* Macchiavelli (N.). I discorsi.
Lockerson (James), *instrument maker*. 1582. *See* no. 7931.
Logic. *See* Tractatus secundarum intentionum. 1527. 4°. . . 8064
London. Company of the Military Yard. *See* Everard (J.). Arriereban. 1618. 8°. 7925
Loper (C.). Laniena Paswalcensis. 1631. 4°. 7955
Lovelace (Leonard). Verses in Osorio (J.). Five Bookes. 1576. . 7972
Lubin (E.). Clavis graecae linguae. Ed. J. H. 1640. 8°. . . 7971
Lugo (Peregrinus de). Principia. [1506.] 4°. 302
Luna (Jean de). *See* Tormes (L. de). 1631. 8071

M. (A.). *See* Guillemeau (J.). French Chirurgerye. 1597 . . 8025
— *See* Primaleon. 1619. 7895
M. (Ch.). Paraphrasticall and devout discourses upon the psalme miserere. 1635. 8°. 7894
M. (P.). Verses in Rider (J.). Dictionarie. 1612. . . . 8073
M. (T.), *C.C.* *See* Mottershed (T.).
M. (T.), Q. *See* Q. (T. M.). 1488. 7808
Macchiavelli (N.). Il Prencipe. 'Palermo.' 1584. 8°. . . . 8023
I discorsi. 'Palermo.' 1584. 8°. 8024
Maidstone (Clement). Directorium Sacerdotum. 1495. 4°. . 8081
— — 1503. 4°. 7939
Makluire (John). Sanitatis semita. 1630. 8°. 7994
Manchester al Mondo. [Ed. 2? Fragment.] 1633. 12°. . . 8030
Maps. England and Wales. 1635. 8°. 8082
— Cambridge. Ab. 1596. F°. 8070
Markham (G.). Countryman's Recreation. [1640?] 4°. . . 8058
Maunsell (John). *See* Yarrow (R.). Soveraigne comforts. 1634. 12°. 8065
May (Thomas), *Esq.* Verses in Sallust. 1629. 12°. . . 8034
Maydeston (Clement). *See* Maidstone (C.).
Mendoza (Diego Hurtado de). *See* Hurtado.
Merbury (Francis). *See* Rogers (R.). Seven treatises. 1603. . 7938
Michelborne (Laur.). Verses in Rider (J.). Dictionarie. 1612. . 8073
Middleton (Chr.). The famous historie of Chinon. 1597. 4°. . 8005
Miraculous and happie union of England and Scotland. 1604. 4° . 7988
Mirk (J.). Festial. Oxford, 1486. F°. 81, 7969
Missale (Sarum). Rouen, 1508. F°. 6231

No.
Morton (Thomas). Prioris Corinth. epistolae expositio quaedam. 1596. 8°. 2343*
Mottershed (Thomas), *C.C.* Verses in Wadsworth (J.). English Spanish Pilgrime. 1629. . . . . . . 4607, 8020
Murad IV. A Vaunting...Letter. 1638. 4°. 7963
Mush (John). Declaratio motuum. 1601. 4°. 6835
Mychelborne. *See* Michelborne.

N. (I.). *See* Norden (J.), *M.A.* Imitation of David. 1624. . . 7952
Nausea (Fridericus). Treatise of blazing starres. Trans. A. Fleming. 1618. 4°. 4155
Newton (Thomas). *See* Stanbridge (J.). Embryon relimatum. 1624. 4°. 7961
Verses in Osorio (J.). Five Bookes. 1576. . . . 7972
Nisbet (George). Verses in Simson (A.). Hieroglyphica. 1622. . 7992
Noel (Baptist). Verses in Gaule (J.). Defiance. 1630. . . 8057
Noel (Henry). Verses in Gaule (J.). Defiance. 1630. . . . 8057
Norden (John), *M.A.* Imitation of David. 1624. 12°. . . 7952

O'Hussey[1] (Maelbrighde). [Three poems.] Louvain. [1616–9.] 16°. . 7941
Oldenbarneveld (J. van). Barnevels Apology. 1618. 4°. . . 8076
Oliver (Thomas). [De ponderibus etc.] *See* Thomas (T.). Dictionarium.
Ortus Vocabulorum. 15—. 4°. 8026
Osorio da Fonseca (Jeronimo). Five Bookes...of Civill, and Christian Nobilitie. 1576. 4°. 7972
Oxford University. [*Ad usum*—.] Insolubilia. [1527.] 4°. . . 8063
— The Answer of the Vice-chancelour etc. 1603. 4°. . 8008

Palfreyman (T.). *See* Baldwin (W.). Treatise. 1600. 8°. . . 7975
Parsons (R.). Christian Directory. 1633. 8°. 8072
— The doleful knell. 1607. 8°. 6267
Pasewalk. Laniena Paswalcensis. 1631. 4°. 7955
Peacham (H.). Minerva Britanna. 1612. 4°. 7945
Percy (John). Reply unto A. Wotton. 1612. 4°. . . . 6525
Peregrinus de Lugo. Principia. [1506.] 4°. 302
Perkins (William). Armilla aurea. Ed. 1. 1590. 8°. . . 8042
Direction for the government of the tongue. 1595. 4°. *See* below Two treatises. 7951
Exposition of the Lords Prayer. 1595. 4°. 7950
Foundation of the christian religion. 1595. 4°. . . 7949
Two treatises. Ed. 2. 1595. 4°. 7951
Persius Flaccus. Satyrae. *See* Juvenalis. 1612. 8°. . . . 8039
Persons (Robert). *See* Parsons.
Petition directed to her...Majestie. [1591?] 4°. . . . 7916
Petrucci (Lud). Apologia contra calumniatores. 1619. 4°. . 7983
Philipson (John). Verses in Rider (J.). Dictionarie. 1612. 4°. . 8073
Philpot (John). Vera expositio. 1554. 8°. *See* 1047 note.
Pierson (David). *See* Person.
Plancius (Peter). A plaine and full description of his Map. *See* Blundevile (T.). Exercises. 1594. 4°. 2136
Plutarchus. De utilitate ex hostibus capienda; et de morbis (Lat.). *See* Rainolds (J.). Orationes. 1628. 12°. 8033
Pond. Prognostication. 1603. 7933
Postill or collection of moste godly doctrine. 1550. 4°. . . 8014
Price (Edmund). Verses in Davies (J.). Rudimenta. 1621. 8°. . 8077
Prideaux (John). Certaine Sermons. Oxford. 1637–6. 4°. (Additional Parts.) 7947
Primer (Sarum). Latin. [Ab. 1508?] 4°. 8068
— — — [Ab. 1514?] 4°. 8069

[1] Bibliographical Register I. p. 4.

No.
Proclamation agaynst breakyng...Monumentes. Broadside. 19 Sept. 1560. 8056
Proclamation (Scotland). [2–18 Sept. 1629.] F°. 7993
Prognostication. *See* Pond. 1603. 7933
Ptolemaeus. *See* Godfridus. 7965
Purefey (John). Verses in Rider (J.). Dictionarie. 1612. 4°. . 8073

Quarles (F.). Divine Fancies. 1638. 4°. 8051

R. (I.). *See* Rhodes (John). 6985
Rainolds (John). Orationes duodecem etc. 1628. 12°. . . 8033
Ramus (P.). *See* Serres (J. de). Comentaries, Part iv. 1576. 4°.
Reade (John), *instrument maker*. 1582. *See* no. 7931.
Restorer of the French Estate. 1589. 4°. 8036
Rhodes (John), *Minister of Enborne*. The Spy. 1628. 4°. . . 6985
Rider (John), *Bp.* Dictionarie (Lat.-Eng.). Ed. 3. By F. Holyoke. 1612. 4°. 8073
— — 1640. 4°. 3058
Rituale. *See* Missale parvum. 6620
Robinson (John). *See* Hall (J.). Works (Apology for Brownists). 1615 *etc.* . . . . 7405 *etc.*
Robortellus (Franciscus). De convenientia supputationis Liuianae. *See* Livius. Libri omnes. 1589. 8°. 2048, 7976
Roesslin (E.). Birth of Mankinde. 1604. 4°. 7940
Rogers (Daniel). Practicall Catechisme. Ed. 3. 1640. 4°. . . 7897
Treatise. Ed. 3. 1636. 4°. 7898
Two Treatises. 1640. 4°. 7897
Rogers (John). Doctrine of Faith. Ed. 5. 1633. 12°. . . 7892
Rolle (Robert). Verses in Rider (J.). Dictionarie. 1612. 4°. . 8073
Rous (Francis). Book of Psalmes. Rotterdam, 1638. 12°. . 6661
Rowland (David). *See* Tormes (L. de). 1624 (1631). . . . 8071

S. (R.). *See* Cepari (V.). Life of Aloysius Gonzaga. 1627. . 8049
S. (S. G). *See* Goulart (S.). 8083
Saint Germain (C.). Exact Abridgement of ..Doctor and Student. 1630. 16°. 7948
Sallustius. Workes. Trans. W. Crosse. 1629. 12°. . . . 8034
Sanctarellus (A.). *See* Santarelli.
Sandys (G.). Relation of a Journey. Ed. 4. 1637. F°. . . 8032
Sanford (H.). Verses in Horatius. Poemata. 1608. . . . 7968
Sanford (Ja.). *See* Epictetus. Manuell. 1567. 8°. . . 8038
Saul (James). Verses in Sallust. 1629. 12°. 8034
Savile (Sir H.). *See* Tacitus. Ende of Nero etc. 1598. F°. . 7957
Scotland, *Ministers of*. Boanerges. 1624. 4°. 7960
Scotland. Miraculous and happie union. 1604. 4°. . . 7988
Scotland. Proclamation [2–18 Sept. 1629]. F°. . . . 7993
Scotland. The remonstrance of the nobility etc. 1639. 4°. . 7995
— *See* Statutes.
Sebastian, King of Portugal. A Continuation. 1603. 4°. . . 8059
Seneca. Tragoediae. Ed. 3. 1634. 8°. 8048
Seton (Alexander), Earl of Dunfermline. *See* Dunfermline.
Simson (Archibald). Christes testament. 1620. 8°. . . . 8006
Hieroglyphica animalium. Tom. 1. 1622(3). 4°. . . 7992
Sleidanus (J.). De quattuor summis imperiis. 1584. 8°. . . 7974
Smith (Sir T.). The Commonwealth of England. 1633. 12°. . 8074
— — 1640. 12°. 8075
Smyth (Nicholas). *See* Wilson (Matthew).
Sommaster (Henry). [Funeral.] *See* Hieron (S.). Three sermons. 1607. 4°. 7996
Spenser (E.) Complaints. (Part 4 only.) 1591 (1590). 4°. . . 7987

No.
Stanbridge (J.). Embryon relimatum. 1624. 4°. 7961
Statutes [England] (Abridgment). [Additional leaf. 1521–8. 8°.] . 8027
— (Scotland). The lawes and actes. [De verborum significatione only.] 1597. F°. 8010
— — xxi Parliament. 1612. F°. 7989
— — xxii Parliament. 1617. F°. 7990
— — Act anent the setling of Measures. 1618. F°. . . 7991
Suetonius. *See* Horatius. Poemata. 1608. 7968
Symson (Archibald). *See* Simson.

Tacitus. Annales...Germanie. Trans. R. Grenewey. 1598. F°. . 7956
Ende of Nero...Galba...Histories...Agricola. Trans. Savile Ed. 2. 1598. F°. 7957
Theodoretus. Ecclesiastical History. 1612. 4°. 7982
Tomson (L.). See Bible. N.T. (Geneva). 1582. 8°. 7986
Tormes (L. de). Pleasant History. 1624 (1631). 8°. . . . 8071
Tractatus secundarum intentionum logicalium. 1527. 4°. . . 8064
Turbevile (G.). Verses in Tormes (L. de). 1624. 8071
Turnetus (Patricius). Verses in Simson (A.). Hieroglyphica. 1622. 7992

Underhill (John). Verses in Rider (J.). Dictionarie. 1612. 4°. . 8073

Venner (Tobias). Via recta. 1622. 4°. 7953
Veron (Jean). Dictionarie (Lat.-Eng.). 1584. 4°. 7958
Vindiciae Ecclesiae Anglicanae. 1630. 4°. 4686
Vladislaus VII, *King of Poland*. *See* Murad IV. A Vaunting Letter. 1638. 4°. 7963

W. (W.). Verses in Dod and Cleaver. 1609. 8079
Waddington (Ralph). *See* Veron (J.). Dictionarie. 1584. 4°. . 7958
Wadsworth (James). The English Spanish Pilgrime. [Another state.] 1629. 4°. 8020
Wake (Isaac). Oratio funebris. *See* Rainolds (J.). Orationes. 1628. 12°. 8033
Wakeman (John). Verses in Osorio (J.). Five Bookes. 1576. . 7972
Walkley (Thomas). *See* Tormes (L. de). 1624 (1631). . . 8071
Ward (William). *See* Alessio. Secretes. 1558. 4°. . . . 8067
Warneford (Richard). Verses in Osorio (J.). Five Bookes. 1576. . 7972
Weemes (John). [Works, Vol. 3.] Exposition. (Partly J. Dawson.) 1632. 4°. 4622
— — M. Dawson (T. Cotes). 1636 (1634). 4°. 7985
Westminster School. [In usum—.] *See* Camden (W.). Institutio. 1595 etc. . . . . 8053 *etc.*
Wilson (John), *Priest*. *See* Fiery Trial. 1612. 4°. 8080
Wilson (Matthew). Modest briefe discussion. Rovan. 1630. 8°. 8050
Wilson (Tho.). A christian dictionary. Ed. 2. 1616. 4°. . . 7964
Wortley (Sir Francis), *Bart*. Verses in Sallust. 1629. 12°. . 8034
Wright (William). Discovery of certaine...shifts. 1619. 4°. . . 7690
Wright (William). *See* Gordon (J.). Treatise. 1614. 8°. . . 6894
Wright (Will.). *See* Lessius (L.). Consultation. 1621. 8°. . . 6542

Yarrow (Robert). Soveraigne comforts. 1634. 12°. . . . 8065
Year Books. 11 Henry IV. [Ab. 1530.] F°. 8044
[? 1—14] Henry IV. [Ab. 1549?] F°. 8043
1 Edward V. 1559. F°. 7998
1 Richard III. [Ab. 155–?] F°. 7999
2 Richard III. [Ab. 155–?] F°. 8000
1—21 Henry VII. 1555. F°. 8001
12—27 Henry VIII. 1591. F°. 8045
Young (Andrew). Verses in Simson (A.). Hieroglyphica. 1622. . 7992
Young (R.). The Drunkards Character. 1638. 8°. 7980

ADDENDA AND CORRIGENDA.

VOLUME I.

PAGE.	NUMBER.	
49.	219.	For a note on the author's name see sig. C5 *a*.
94.	464.	Hall (E.). *Dele* entry (*see* Lowndes).
165.	839.	Another copy of the map only, SSS. 12. 1.
188.	964.	Bible (Bishops'). The Tables in Leviticus are from the Italian Bible of 1562. (Note by Mr Aldis Wright.)
203.	1027, 1028.	By J. Bale not Coverdale. See MS. note by H. Bradshaw s. v. in Cooper's *Athenae*, Vol. I. p. 229 [MS. Add. 3098.]
487.	Line 3 from end.	*Before* Morton *read* 2343 A.
505.	2423.	With the copper-plate portrait of Chaucer signed by the unknown engraver 'I. S.' In this the Burwash arms display the chief purpure. The plate was afterwards reworked (for the 1602 edition?) with the chief gules. Cf. the copy in King's College, Cambridge [L. 2. 10].
517.	2476.	Note that J. Sylvester's translation of Jean Du Nesme's Sonnets is in this volume.
616.	2973.	*For* '2973' *read* '3097.' (1613.)
618.	2984.	This is Eburne's 'Twofold Tribute.' *See* Watt.

VOLUME II.

817.	Garey (S.). Caesaris hostes. *This is part of* Great Britans little Calendar. 1618. 3797	
837.	3888 = 4622.	
947.	4388.	Part 2 printed by E. Purslow.
637.	3076.	There is a third copy in the Sandars Collection with plates.
692.	3327.	This is an abridgment of T. Beard's Theatre of God's Judgment (no. 2442).
893.	4155.	This Treatise is by Fridericus Nausea, Bishop of Vienna. *See* Herb. 1106.
957.	4429.	*For* 1629 *read* 1639.
964.	4467.	Another copy. Adams 7. 63. 9^2.
1047.	4835.	Part 1 only. For part 2 see no. 4537.
1081.	4951.	In the first copy sig. L 3 is a cancel. In the second copy sig. L 2 is wanting.
1191.	5332.	Probably printed at Cambridge. The watermark agrees with *Encomium*, C. Legge, 1619.
1235.	5543.	The folding leaf at p. 300 of this is torn, and at p. 368 gone. For another copy with the leaf at p. 300 perfect, and a part remaining at p. 368 see Syn. 8. 59. 110^2.
1240.	5571.	This was by William Covell, of Christ's College and Queens' College, Cambridge. See a letter by Professor Edward Dowden in the *Athenæum*, 14 July 1906, p. 44, recording a copy in which the name is printed in full.
1263–4.	5695.	Sig. F 4 is retained in the first copy.

VOLUME III.

PAGE.	NUMBER.	
1342.	6030.	*For* Syn *read* Hib.
1343.	6033.	*For* Syn *read* Hib.
1357.	6081.	The woodcuts in this are copied from those in the Lübeck Low German Bible of 1533 (information kindly pointed out to me by Mr W. Aldis Wright). Those cuts are by Erhard Altdorfer (C. Dodgson *in litt.*, 12 Oct. 1906).
1404.	6267.	This was by Rob. Parsons.
1422.	6322.	Mr W. Aldis Wright points out that the type of this book is the same as that of the Italian Bible of 1562 described on p. 953. It may be questioned therefore if Hall was more than the publisher.
1458.	6475.	Line 4. *For* Heidelberg *read* Middelburg.
1470.	6521.	Line 7. *For* 6266 *read* 6267.
1470.	6525.	Contains Parts 1 and 2. (Part 2. A Challenge to Protestants.) By J. Percy. *See* Gillow (J.). Dictionary.
1474.	6542.	This was translated by W. Wright.
1476.	6552.	By A. Champney.
1477.	6554.	Two parts.
1477.	6555.	Qu. by A. Champney? Cf. no. 6552.
1483.	6582.	(Note, line 4.) *For* 6266 *read* 6267.
1490.	6618.	The translator was C. Apsley. *See* Gillow i. 54.
1512.	6706.	By J. Bale not Coverdale. See correction on no. 1027.
1527.	6795.	On p. 133 is pasted a marginal note of 22 lines.
1534.	6835.	By John Mush. *See* T. G. Law, *Jesuits and Seculars*, p. cxxviii.
1534.	6836.	By Christopher Bagshaw. *Ibid.* p. cxxxii.
1534.	6834.	(Note, line 2.) *For* 6837 *read* 6835, 6836.
	6835.	(Note.) *For* 6835 and 6837 *read* 6834 and 6836. The tract was by John Mush. See T. G. Law, *Jesuits*, p. cxxviii.
	6836.	By C. Bagshaw. See T. G. Law, *Jesuits*, p. cxxxii.
1540.	6864.	(Note.) *For* 6870 *read* 6869.
	6866.	(Note.) Wants also S 1, 2.
1541.	6867.	(Note.) *For* 6869, 6870, 6872 *read* 6868, 6869, 6871.
	6868.	(Note.) *For* 6868 etc., *read* 6864. Initial A of type of nos. 6453 and 6869. By H. Jacob. *See* Dexter and D.N.B.
1542.	6869.	(Note.) *For* 6869 *read* 6868.
	6872.	(Note.) *For* 6872 *read* 6871.
	6873.	(Note.) *For* 6876 *read* 6875.
1546–7.	6894.	Trans. by W. Wright.
1562.	6895.	By John Rhodes, minister of Enborne. *See* BM (Gen. Cat.).
1579.	7064.	The Bull of Alexander VI. was dated 21 Dec. 1498 (see MS. Cleopatra E. III in BM). The date of this Proclamation cannot therefore be before January 1499. (*In litt.* R. Steele).
1580.	7072.	Printed by W. Faques. See J. Gairdner, Letters and Papers of Richard III. and Henry VII. (Rolls Series), II. 379.
1589.	7117.	This copy has two leaves 'To the Reader.' Another copy without the two leaves. Syn . 7 . 61 . 100[9]
1632.	7338.	Date on sub-titles '1607 For E. White.'
1638.	7362.	Imperfect at end.
1676.	7533.	Printed in 1608. See BM (Supplement).
1677.	7534.	Pp. 388—455 are by the translator.
1717.	7690.	This is by William Wright.
1722.	7713.	Line 4. *Dele* from some...letter.

APPENDIX.

1756.	7811.	The engraver A was Adriaen van de Venne (E. W. Moes, *in litt.* 26 Jan. 1907).

VOLUME IV.

Index I. p. 30. Line 16. *Dele* Beaumont...cont.
37. 1549 (Matthew's). *For* Day *read* Day & Seres.
51. Bible (Latin), N.T. J. Mayler. Feb. *For* 1550 *read* 1540.
53. Line 43. Blundevile (T.) Exercises. *For* 1622–1 *read* 1594.
86. Ceremonies. *Dele* Our Saviour.
90. Chillingworth (W.). *For* Knott (E.). The Judgment, *read* Lacey (W.). The Judgment. 6565.
93. Clarke (R.). Sermons. 1637. *For* 4549 *read* 4649.
100. *Read* Cope (Sir Antony) †1614. [Funeral] etc.
144. Forde (W.). *For* funerals *read* funerall.
174. Hamilton (J.). Whereas. *For* 5943 *read* 5983.
256. Norden (John). *Before* nos. 6804 seq., *insert* Norden (John) *topographer*.
277. Philpot. *For* 1544 *read* 1554.
284. Prideaux (J.). Certaine Sermons. *For* 5476 *read* 5474.
319. Skene (Sir J.). De verborum significatione. *For* 5936 *read* '*see* 8010.'
325. Spelman (Henry). *For* Bible Polyglot, *read* Bible, Anglo-Saxon.
360. *Under* Webb (E.), *before* Catalogus Protestantium, *insert* Webb (George), *Bp.*
369. Wimbledon (E. C., *Viscount*). *See* Scott (T.). Speech. 1621 etc.
374. Year Books. *For* Henry V. 2 *etc. read* Henry V. 1–2 etc.
375. Year Books. Henry VI. 49. *See* Edward IV. 10–12. 7180.

Index II. p. 383. Bollifant. *Add* no. 7957.
395. *Add* Maylard (L.). 1566–1568. Cf. No. 8038.

Index III. p. 407. Altdorfer (Erhard). 6081. Bible (Matthew's). . 1537
409. Delaram (F.). *Add* 3864. Smith (J.). Virginia. [Portrait of Duchess of Richmond.] 1623.
413. Langeren (J. van). *Add* 8082. Direction. 1635.
417. S. (I.). 2423. Chaucer (G.). Portrait. . 1598
419. *Add* Venne (A. van de). 7811

Index IV. p. 424. Heidelberg. *Dele* 1302.
424. Ingolstadt : *for* no. 6771 *read* no. 6775

Index V. p. 430. Chaucer (G.). *J. S.* 1598. F°. . . . 2423
435. *Add* Richmond (Duchess of) 1623. . . . 3864

Index VI. p. 439. Allison (R.). *See* Psalms. 1592. . . 1601
Blancks (E.). *See* Psalms. 1592. . . . 1601
Cavendish (M.). *See* Psalms. 1592. . . 1601
Cobbold (W.). *See* Psalms. 1592. . . . 1601
Dowland (J.). *See* Psalms. 1592. . . 1601
Este (Thomas). Psalms. 1592. 8°. . . 1601
Farmer (John). *See* Psalms. 1592. . . 1601
Farnaby (G.). *See* Psalms. 1592. . . . 1601
Hooper (E.). *See* Psalms. 1592. . . 1601
Johnson (E.). *See* Psalms. 1592. . . . 1601
Kirby (G.). *See* Psalms. 1592. . . . 1601

Index VII. p. 444. Colour-printing. Corrections of manuscripts. *Add* 1628. Selden. 3171
445. *Add* Signatures to the sheet. 8061

CAMBRIDGE: PRINTED BY JOHN CLAY, M.A. AT THE UNIVERSITY PRESS.

LaVergne, TN USA
28 January 2010
171379LV00002B/41/P

9 781108 00780